EXPERIMENTAL METHODS AND INSTRUMENTATION IN PSYCHOLOGY

EXPERIMENTAL METHODS AND INSTRUMENTATION IN PSYCHOLOGY

Edited by JOSEPH B. SIDOWSKI   *Professor of Psychology*
San Diego State College

McGraw-Hill Book Company   *New York • St. Louis • San Francisco • Toronto • London • Sydney*

PREFACE

The unifying theme of this book is experimental methodology and instrumentation. Obviously the book does not presume to represent all areas of psychology, nor all methods within an area. A full and detailed treatise on this subject would require volumes and, by the very nature of scientific research, still be incomplete. Such areas as industrial and clinical psychology were considered and excluded by the editor because of their applied rather than basic research orientation, and their use of experimental techniques derived from other areas. Also, limitations of space would have made it difficult to cover the diverse methods used in these and other areas adequately; statistical methods and principles of formal experimental design are best discussed elsewhere. The result is a book containing eighteen chapters sectioned into six parts, with an editorial introduction to each. Fourteen chapters cover laboratory techniques in major areas of experimental psychology, and two emphasize the use of computers. The remaining chapters provide a general introduction to animal and human research and information on basic instrumentation. An Appendix gives a detailed list of names and addresses for various equipment firms and suppliers.

Writing for advanced level courses, each contributor to this volume has attempted to describe or reference a representative sample of basic research instruments and methods that he has deemed important in his particular area of experimental psychology. But not all chapters emphasize instrumentation (except Chapter 2); nor are all the same length, or of the same technical difficulty. This is due in part to author bias, methodological requirements or state of a particular field, and editorial request. In some cases techniques are detailed enough for a student or researcher to use in the laboratory; in others, reference is made to a more descriptive source. In either case, the emphasis throughout is upon methods and instrumentation, not results. For data are only as useful as laboratory procedures allow them to be, and neither formal experimental design, complex statistical analysis, nor theoretical bias can adequately compensate for unreliable equipment, careless experimentation, or lack of experience.

But any venture of this sort is beset with difficulties and delays; this book was no exception. Some drafts were submitted late, more than one revision of drafts was generally required, some early contributors were replaced, and final updating was requested before galley proof (1965). The subjection of all chapters to critical review by two specialists in each area added to completion time, as did the necessity for constant communication, with a minimum of unparliamentary language, between the editor and contributors, and the editor and publisher.

Of course it is the labors of the contributors that made this book possible, and it is to these individuals that I am most grateful. Their patience with an unruly, demanding, and obdurate editor knew few bounds.

Appreciation is also due to the many formal reviewers of individual chapters, especially the following persons whose comments in some way contributed to the final product:

N. H. ANDERSON, W. F. BATTIG, T. J. BANTA, L. E. BOURNE, C. S. BRIDGMAN, E. C. CARTERETTE, R. S. DANIEL, J. E. DEESE, D. A. GRANT, H. F. HARLOW, W. A. HILLIX, L. G. HUMPHREYS, H. H. KELLEY, H. H. KENDLER, M. LICHTENSTEIN, I. M. MALTZMAN, G. E. MOUNT, W. F. PROKASY, W. N. RUNQUIST, E. SACHS, R. W. SCHULZ, D. L. SKAAR, R. SROGES, M. J. WASKOW, AND J. C. WEBSTER. I also wish to thank W. W. Battersby, F. J. Clarke, H. D. Kimmel, W. T. Penrod, Jr., J. M. Wright, and others, too numerous to mention here, who commented on various drafts for individual authors. The editor, however, is solely responsible for the general orientation and direction of this book, and the selection of contributors and formal reviewers.

Acknowledgement is made to the following publishers and publications for permission to reproduce figures and tables: Academic Press, Inc., American Psychological Association, Addison-Wesley Publishing Company, Inc., American Journal of Psychology, Appleton-Century-Crofts, Inc., Holt, Rinehart and Winston, Inc., Journal of the Acoustical Society of America, The Journal Press, J. B. Lippincott Company, McGraw-Hill Book Company, Inc., New York Academy of Sciences, Psychometrika, The Ohio State Research Foundation, Southern Methodist University Press, U.C.L.A. Medical Center (Division of Biostatistics), John Wiley and Sons, Inc., the U.S. Navy, and the U.S. Air Force.

Joseph B. Sidowski

CONTENTS

CONTRIBUTORS

HARRY P. BAHRICK, Ph.D., Professor of Experimental Psychology, Ohio Wesleyan University, Delaware, Ohio.

WILLIAM F. BATTIG, Ph.D., Professor of Psychology, University of Maryland, College Park, Md.

M. E. BITTERMAN, Ph.D., Professor and Chairman, Department of Psychology, Bryn Mawr College, Bryn Mawr, Pa.

LYLE E. BOURNE, JR., Ph.D., Professor of Psychology, University of Colorado, Boulder, Colo.

ROBERT E. BOWMAN, Ph.D., Associate Professor of Psychology, University of Wisconsin, Madison, Wis.; Head, Psychochemistry Unit, Wisconsin Regional Primate Research Center, Madison, Wis.

ROBERT M. BOYNTON, Ph.D., Professor of Psychology and Optics and Director, Center for Visual Science, University of Rochester, Rochester, N.Y.

GEORGE E. BRIGGS, Ph.D., Professor of Psychology and Associate to the Vice President for Research, Ohio State University, Columbus, Ohio.

FRANK R. CLARKE, Ph.D., formerly Research Psychologist, Sensory Intelligence Laboratory, University of Michigan, Ann Arbor, Mich.; currently Senior Research Psychologist, Sensory Sciences Group, Stanford Research Institute, Menlo Park, Calif.

JAMES A. DINSMOOR, Ph.D., Professor of Psychology, Indiana University, Bloomington, Ind.

ROBERT G. EASON, Ph.D., Associate Professor of Psychology, San Diego State College, San Diego, Calif.

JAMES P. EGAN, Ph.D., Professor of Psychology and Director, Hearing and Communication Laboratory, Indiana University, Bloomington, Ind.

STEWART FLIEGE, Ph.D., Manager, Washington Division, Computer Sciences Corporation, Silver Spring, Md.

I. GORMEZANO, Ph.D., Associate Professor of Psychology, Indiana University, Bloomington, Ind.

HAROLD W. HAKE, Ph.D., Professor of Psychology, University of Illinois, Urbana, Ill.

IRA J. HIRSH, Ph.D., Director of Research, Central Institute for the Deaf, St. Louis, Mo.; Professor of Psychology, Washington University, St. Louis, Mo.

DONALD B. LINDSLEY, Ph.D., Professor of Psychology and Physiology, University of California at Los Angeles, Los Angeles, Calif.

ROBERT B. LOCKARD, Ph.D., Assistant Professor of Psychology, University of Washington, Seattle, Wash.

MERRILL E. NOBLE, Ph.D., Professor of Psychology, Kansas State University, Manhattan, Kans.

V. J. POLIDORA, Ph.D., Associate Professor of Psychology, University of Wisconsin, Madison, Wis.; Chief, Psychopharmacology Unit, Wisconsin Regional Primate Research Center, Madison, Wis.

ALBERT S. RODWAN, Ph.D., Assistant Professor of Psychology, Emory University, Atlanta, Ga.

WILLARD N. RUNQUIST, Ph.D., Associate Professor of Psychology, University of Alberta, Edmonton, Alberta, Canada.

MARVIN E. SHAW, Ph.D., Professor of Psychology, University of Florida, Gainesville, Fla.

JOSEPH B. SIDOWSKI, Ph.D., Professor of Psychology, San Diego State College, San Diego, Calif.

MANUEL J. SMITH, M.A., University of California at Los Angeles, Los Angeles, Calif.

HAROLD W. STEVENSON, Ph.D., Professor and Director, Institute of Child Development, University of Minnesota, Minneapolis, Minn.

RICHARD F. THOMPSON, Ph.D., Professor, Department of Medical Psychology, University of Oregon Medical School, Portland, Oreg.

JOHN C. WRIGHT, Ph.D., Associate Professor, Institute of Child Development and Center for Research in Human Learning, University of Minnesota, Minneapolis, Minn.

Part One

INTRODUCTION[1]

This volume covers a wide range of methods and instrumentation in the experimental study of human and animal behavior. This is not to imply that all techniques are represented here or that the secrets of good research lie hidden between these covers. Behavioral research consists of many little pieces, and the cumulative nature of knowledge depends upon how well the pieces can be fitted together. Only by working in the laboratory can one learn to recognize and appreciate the details of experimentation and gain the experience necessary for the proper choice and utilization of these or other research tools.

The 18 chapters included here are categorized into the following sections: Introduction (Part One), Psychobiology (Part Two), Sensation and Perception (Part Three), Learning and Conditioning (Part Four), Human Behavior (Part Five), and Computers (Part Six).

The two chapters of Part One cover some preliminary considerations in basic methodology and instrumentation that are applicable to the general areas of animal and human research. The material on subject and procedural variables in Chap. 1 supplements the information found in other chapters; recommendations for discarding subjects and data apply to all areas. An Addendum to this chapter provides a detailed discussion of variables influencing maintenance and research practices with monkeys.

[1] Bibliographical references for each Part introduction are cited on pages 735–736.

Basic Instrumentation (Chap. 2) provides an introduction to electricity and electronics before proceeding to more detailed information on circuitry. The emphasis throughout is upon solid state devices, although black-box descriptions are provided for equipment of the type discussed in Chap. 3, Physiological Psychology. Refer to Chap. 10, Operant Conditioning, and Chap. 11, Animal Learning, for additional circuitry and to Chap. 17, Analog Computers, for a discussion of the operational amplifier and analog networks. Citations of other apparatus with specific applications may be found in various chapters of this volume.

Advances in electronics, instrumentation, and computer technology (see Part Six) must not escape the constant scrutiny of the behavioral scientist for new developments in many areas of research are becoming more and more dependent upon the state of the technological art. Solid state devices are replacing most of the tube and relay equipment commonly used in behavioral research, and developments in biological telemetry offer the investigator a means of measuring psychophysiological responses that are free from the effects of restraint, connecting wires, and anesthesia. Techniques in semiconductor microcircuitry permit conventional circuit designs to be converted to new microcircuit format so that many different network functions may be fabricated on a single silicon wafer. The dimensions of these units are such that 20 transistors and 50 resistors may be fabricated into an area of

semiconductor chip measuring approximately 0.1 by 0.1 inch. Multiple-chip microcircuits are available for both linear and digital operations and include logic circuits of the functional type described in Chap. 2, as well as linear amplifiers. Since the individual components of these circuits generally do not have the tolerances of conventional parts, new logic circuits have been developed which have operations less dependent upon individual component values and which operate over a wide range of speeds and power levels. A completely integrated semiconductor network containing a flip-flop, gate, dual gate, and adder may be manufactured into a wafer the approximate size of a 5-cent piece. The IBM Computer System/360, for example, contains microminiaturized modules formed by printing on ceramic plates ($\frac{1}{2}$ inch square) with electroconductive ink. The transistors and diodes in these circuits are so small that several thousand fit into a thimble, yet computers of this type complete their operations in a few billionths of a second rather than the microseconds required in other machines.

Consult the Appendix for a list of major electronic instrument and computer manufacturers, many of whom (e.g., Texas Instruments) fabricate microminiature semiconductor networks according to designer specifications. The Appendix also lists names and addresses of suppliers for all types of laboratory equipment, supplies, and animals. Separate listings are provided for materials mentioned in individual chapters.

Chapter 1

SOME PRELIMINARY CONSIDERATIONS IN RESEARCH

JOSEPH B. SIDOWSKI *and* ROBERT B. LOCKARD

An experiment should make a lasting contribution to scientific knowledge. Yet achieving this aim is extremely difficult, for the long and intricate chain of events between hypothesis formulation and conclusion can be broken by a single impropriety. There is no single experimental procedure that is best for all investigations; each situation has its unique aspects. These unique elements, however, are mere problems to be surmounted in achieving conventional goals. The goals themselves do not change and might be summarized as follows: (1) An experiment should bear upon the problem or hypothesis stated. (2) The results should have a minimum ambiguity of interpretation. And (3) the experiment should provide empirical data of lasting value. This chapter will cover some basic considerations in research methodology that influence the attainment of these goals. Since many of the points touched upon here are treated elsewhere in this volume, our presentation is limited to a restricted range of information. Separate sections on animal and human research describe processes and variables of general importance in scientific methodology as well as those specific to the study of each population. An Ad-

dendum is provided for those interested in maintenance and methodological problems with monkeys.

ANIMAL RESEARCH

In some respects, an experiment can be thought of as a sequence of operations designed to allow a confirmation or disconfirmation of the hypothesis, where the hypothesis is considered a tentative statement about the way the world works. Thus, a close relationship between the hypothesis and the procedure of the experiment is essential. If the hypothesis is a statement about observable events, such as number of choices in a T maze, the obvious procedure requires use of a T maze and the counting of choices. On the other hand, if the hypothesis concerns unobservables, such as traits or internal states, the procedure of the experiment may not be relevant to the hypothesis. For example, the statement "Rats are altruistic" could lead to an experiment showing that a rat would bar-press to remove painful stimuli from a second rat. The experiment confirms one instance of altruistic behavior but it also supports the hypothesis "Squeals made in re-

3

sponse to painful stimuli are aversive to other rats." Thus the farther a hypothesis is removed from publicly verifiable physical events, the less any single experiment contributes to the confirmatory evidence.

Not all experiments involve testing hypotheses. An experimenter may simply wish to determine how some dependent measure varies with an independent one and set out, without a hypothesis, to obtain an estimate of the relationship. For example, in preparation for an experiment using electroconvulsive shock on rats, one might wish to discover that quantity of electric current through the ears which maximizes the probability of a resultant seizure but minimizes such side effects as bleeding from the eyes and paralysis. The procedure involves administering different amounts of current to different groups of subjects, measuring the proportion of seizures and side effects for each group, and plotting these dependent variables as a function of the number of milliamperes passed through the ears for a fixed duration of time. This type of experiment might be called *parameter estimation,* as opposed to hypothesis testing.

We can minimize the ambiguity of interpretation of an experiment by techniques that uniquely isolate the treatment applied to the experimental group. This would seem to be easily achieved with the classical experimental design in which an experimental group and a control group are given identical treatments differing in only one respect, the key treatment. In practice, however, groups receiving different treatments may inadvertently receive more than the intended experimental operation. For example, in an experiment comparing "visually deprived" animals with "normals," deprived subjects were kept in the dark in poorly ventilated chambers, while the normals were kept in open cages in the laboratory. Upon testing the deprived animals barpressed less than the controls, which was interpreted as reduced reactivity to stimulation caused by stimulus deprivation. Actually, the deprived animals weighed less, were less active, and showed less bar-pressing unrein-forced by stimulus change than did the controls. It is possible, therefore, that the results merely demonstrated that partially asphyxiated rats perform any activity less vigorously than healthy ones. Here, the two treatments, darkness and poor ventilation, were confounded and the result of the experiment could have been attributed to either treatment, or to some unknown combination of the two.

Since the confounding of treatments may be far from obvious, the careful experimenter might wish to make two lists showing the exact sequence of events for the experimental and control subjects, compare the lists, and adjust conditions until there is but one inequality. Detail is important here. It is not sufficient to list a test session as one item, for the test session can often be further subdivided. For example, to test the hypothesis that a tone delivered as the consequence of bar-pressing will have reinforcing properties, it might seem sufficient to compare response rate of an experimental group receiving contingent tone with that of a control group receiving no tone following bar-pressing. The two groups, however, differ in more ways than the contingent tone. In the experimental group, not only is the tone contingent, but the tone occurs. It might be that an animal in a test chamber is more active if a tone sometimes comes on and hence appears to bar-press frequently because the bar intercepts some of the activity. To eliminate this difficulty, Kling, Horowitz, and Delhagen (1956) introduced the yoked-control technique, in which an experimental animal and a control are tested simultaneously. When the experimental animal responds, the same consequence is delivered to both animals. Type and pattern of stimulation, duration, and testing time are the same for both subjects; only the contingency differs. But the yoked–control technique should not be applied uncritically, for yoked animals are often less of a control than they appear to be. As Church (1964) has pointed out, individual differences can lead to systematic effects differing between the experimental and control groups. For example, assume that mean daily water intake is constant within each subject of a group of animals but differs between subjects. When randomly assigned to experimental and control groups, each control subject is provided with whatever quantity of water the yoked subject drinks on an ad-lib schedule. All controls with daily intakes normally below those of experimental subjects will get enough water; some will remain uningested at the end of each day. Controls with normal daily intakes greater than those of experimental subjects will not get enough. In the long run, all experimental subjects receive just the "right amount" of water; half the controls are oversupplied, and about half are water-deprived. We might note, however, that in stimulus domains without clear satiation limits, methodological developments may show this kind of criticism to be less relevant.

But unintentional confounding of experimental treatments with other variables may be reduced by counterbalancing. For example, two treatments A and B are often applied in an $ABBA$ sequence. Of four groups of animals, the first might receive treatment A at 9 A.M.; group 2, treatment B at 11 A.M.; group 3, treatment B at 1 P.M.; and group 4, treatment A at 3 P.M. If some other variable C affects the behavior in question and if C changes at a linear rate throughout the day, the effects of C will contribute evenly to the effects of A and B. If, for example, C's contribution to the dependent variable at the four times of testing is 1, 2, 3, and 4 units, the mean contribution of C to the groups receiving treatments A and B is the same and equals $2\frac{1}{2}$. On the other hand, if the effects of C were not a linear function of time, the $ABBA$ order would be inappropriate. At worst, the effects of C might become maximum at noon and make contributions of 1, 4, 4, and 1 at the four testing times. In this case, the effects of C are confounded with the A and B treatments; B's apparent effect is an increase in the numerical value of the dependent variable, an increase due wholly or partly to C's nonlinear change in effectiveness.

Although our discussion so far has been limited to treatment variables, it is reasonable to assume that a large number of *effective* variables also influence the animal during the experiment. Many of these can be fixed or held at static levels; but those which cannot be held static, or are unsuspected, can be assumed to vary in a number of different ways with time. If the treatments the experimenter intended to impose were withheld and the dependent variables recorded as a function of time, the values of and fluctuations in the dependent variable would reflect the total effects of all other variables. Some animal behavior, such as running, shows this sort of fluctuation with time in the absence of, and prior to, treatments deliberately imposed by the experimenter. Other kinds of behavior, especially responses introduced into the animal's repertoire by shaping procedures, show no variation and zero frequency before the shaping treatment but fluctuate with time after the treatment. Thus each different dependent variable may have a different proportion of its variation associated with the total effects of all nontreatment variables, and that proportion may change after some imposed treatment. Because of the vast differences among research situations, no genuine panacea for the problem of confounding the effects of deliberate treatments with the effects of nontreatment variables can be offered.

Although this somewhat abstract discussion is intended to make the experimenter aware of certain kinds of problem, the quality of research is not aided by awareness alone. A translation into an appropriate procedure and experimental design must be made. Clever and efficient experimental designs are not difficult, but they do not necessarily solve the problems of creating a procedure relevant to the problem and generating unambiguous data. This is a matter for which the experimenter must devise his own best solutions.

It is possible to offer one guideline for minimizing the undesirable effects of nontreatment variables. In the model case of an n-group hypothesis-testing experiment, the experimenter provides positive information about a hypothesis if significant differences among means are found. Differences and their directions are relevant. The levels and possible effects of all nontreatment variables not specified by the hypothesis are irrelevant as long as their effects are but randomly contributing to the group means. In a model procedure, the researcher processes the n groups simultaneously so that each is treated exactly alike except for the deliberately introduced n treatments. Each group mean can then be thought of as having four components: (1) unique to the imposed treatment, (2) stemming from all pooled effects of all the nontreatment variables, (3) composed of the different ways the subjects responded to all variables, and (4) representing consistent differences between subjects. The first is the source of differences among means for the various treatment groups. The second is a constant for all groups, and the last two appear as random contributions to the n means. While an experiment of this type is impeccable if properly done, contributions of the second type may cause difficulties of interpretation and make replication by other experimenters a matter fraught with uncertainties. These matters are taken up later when the problems of static variables are discussed in detail for animal research.

In the model case of an n-group parameter-estimation experiment, the researcher provides positive information about a phenomenon and is not necessarily concerned with testing any hypotheses. For example, he might be interested in carefully estimating the amount of food consumed per day by rats as a function of age. In this type of investigation, unlike hypothesis-testing experiments, significant differences among the means for various age groups are not the main concern. The numbers that the dependent variable assumes are of prime importance, and an accurate estimate of the variability is needed. In addition, it is of value to manipulate other known effective variables, such as sex, room temperature, and strain, so that

separate functions for each may be plotted relating daily food intake to age. The ultimate result is a sort of handbook with sections, rows, and columns. To find the estimated daily food intake of a 90-day-old Long-Evans female rat living at 76°F and additional specifications representing levels of other relevant variables, one enters the tables within the appropriate section, row, and column and reads off the mean food intake tabulated within the cell. The mean is accompanied by an estimate of the error variance, representing the pooled effects of variations in all effective but untabulated variables. If the experimenter imagines himself attempting to provide the data for such a handbook, he can appreciate the difficulty of doing first-rate parameter-estimation research. At least three factors must be considered. (1) He must devise a means of ranking the effectiveness of variables affecting daily food intake. In all probability, he considers only those variables relevant to normal laboratory practice and does not include "amount of stomach removed" even though it is probably an effective variable, for normal laboratory practice holds this variable at the level of zero. (2) The experimenter must decide how many variables to include in his tables. The more he includes, the less the residual error variance, but the more time and effort is required. If he decides to build the tables around five variables, he must define the levels of certain other variables, e.g., type of food and cage size, which must be maintained for the tables to hold true. (3) The investigator must ensure that his estimate of residual error variance is not artificially reduced. Any practice during the collection of the data which constrains the fluctuating effects of all variables beyond the five selected for manipulation and those held static reduces the estimated error variance. In practice, the experimenter defines some small experimental unit consisting, perhaps, of one subject in one treatment combination on one measurement occasion. These units are then randomly assigned to experimental places and times, with the latter occupying, ideally, at least a year. By way of contrast, an entire parameter-estimation experiment carried out during one hour of a December evening constrains variation in numerous environmental factors such as barometric pressure and seasonal state of subjects. It samples neither adequately nor randomly from the population of possible environmental states.

In the introduction to this chapter we stated that experiments should provide empirical data of lasting value. This statement is pregnant with hidden complexities. Most experiments are situations in which measurements are taken at a few levels of one or more deliberately manipulated independent variables while all other variables are either fixed at static levels or allowed to vary in some way judged harmless to the experiment. The fixed values of the static variables define the combination of conditions unique to the experiment, e.g., a certain type of organism used in a certain size of experimental space at a certain temperature with specific levels of acoustical energy and visible light. The results are partly due to the combination of static variables. Different results are often obtained in a colder room, with a greater noise background, or in a different illumination. A subsequent experimenter attempting to replicate an earlier experiment can reproduce the earlier combinations of static variables only as well as they were measured and reported in the first place. Unreported or useless measures force the second experimenter to guess, and each guess increases the probability of selecting an entirely novel combination of conditions. In the context of this new combination of levels of static variables, the attempted replication is likely to produce results different from those of the first experiments, and when replication fails, doubt is cast upon both studies. The simple effects of a variable upon behavior become needlessly confused in a tangle of conflicting studies. The job of unconfusing, originally that of the experimentalist, but ill-done, is passed to the reviewer.

Although the list of static variables that affect animal behavior may be large, it is finite. One can view the aggregate of animal research as consisting of a list of variables that affect behavior differently at different levels. Since any experiment simply must be conducted at some combination of static variables, the experiment is inescapably located at two or more points in multidimensional space where the n dimensions of the space are the n variables affecting behavior. The "location" of the experiment can be determined and reported by the experimenter. If it is not, the experiment is lost somewhere in multidimensional space. Attempted replications are unknown approximations, located at some other region of multidimensional space.

The following paragraphs discuss some of the considerations relevant to the investigator using animals for research. While concessions to poverty may be required at present in most laboratories, the discussion assumes a striving toward optimal conditions and making compromises out of enlightened necessity, not from lack of consideration.

Subjects

There are over a million species of animals on this planet, and many are uniquely valuable to research because they can be conceived of as special preparations. If the experiment calls for a pure cone retina, a poikilotherm, or imprinting ability, species are available to fill the need. But if the experiment does not define the species, the experimenter must. Of course precedent is another rational guide in the selection of species, for results from a novel species would pose difficult problems of interpretation. Most of the common laboratory animals are mammals; man, several species of monkey, numerous rodents, a few carnivores, and one cetacean, the porpoise. Other than mammals, teleost fishes and one species of bird, the pigeon,[1] have mainly

---

[1] Appropriate methodology and maintenance techniques for the pigeon are covered in Bullock, Roberts, and Bitterman (1961); Ferster and Skinner (1957); and Reese (1964).

represented the other classes of chordates; amphibians and reptiles have been rare. The 21 phyla below the chordates have been underrepresented with a few cockroaches (arthropods), octopuses (mollusks), planarian worms (platyhelminths), and paramecia (protozoa). Precedent has, for better or for worse, established the albino variant of the brown rat (*Rattus norvegicus*) as the standard laboratory animal in behavioral research. Laws of behavior emerging from rat research will have unknown generality until the phenomena are explored at more phyletic levels.

When rats are used as subjects, the investigator must then consider choices among such variables as strain, sex, age, supplier, and prior treatments. The strains favored by precedent are the Long-Evans hooded (a pigmented strain), the Sprague-Dawley albino, and the Wistar albino. Because of the large gene pool and random breeding procedures used by the large animal-supply companies, these three strains will probably show little genetic change over the next few decades.[1] Consequently, studies of this decade using these strains will produce data applying to animals likely to be available in the future. Studies using locally developed variations of the above strains risk producing data relevant to a domestic animal during a period of rapid genetic change, or one likely to become extinct. Small or free-lance suppliers should be avoided for the additional reasons that higher mortality and importation of disease into the laboratory are more probable and that the animals in different shipments may have different histories, introducing unnecessary variability between replications of the experiment.

In selecting sex of subjects, the experimenter has a number of considerations. Males usually cost more and are more expensive to maintain, but produce more stable data across days because they lack the four-day estrous cycle and activity rhythm of the female. It would be informative to study sex as a two-level factor in many experiments, using half males and half females and producing data relevant to each. If this is done, the experimenter should take into account the possibility of olfactory traces left by estrous females when a common apparatus is used. Unless countermeasures are taken, subjects following estrous females might show a disruption of formerly stable behavior and engage in competing responses such as sniffing. This possible problem of competing responses applies equally well to the use of two different species in the same apparatus.

The most conventional age of rat subjects appears to be 90 days at the beginning of the experiment. There would seem to be little justification in arbitrary departures from this precedent unless the experimenter has a deliberate reason; and in that case, he would be well advised to run two groups, one of 90 days and the other of his choice. This would provide a control group of conventional age and would provide the opportunity to attribute uncommon results to the uncommon age of the other group if such should occur. Too few experiments include age as a variable; and until this practice becomes more common, we shall lack an estimate of the age range over which certain generalities apply.

Freshly received animals are not uniform products from an automatic production line, nor are they a random sample from the world's population of rats. Animal suppliers differ greatly in such environmental practices as the ambient temperature, light-dark cycle, type of food, cage size and animal density, and the physical arrangement of food and water devices. One well-known supplier of albino rats maintains a temperature of 78°F and continuous light, manufactures its own diet, heavily populates large cages, and feeds the animals from the well-lighted cage fronts while water is available in the much darker rear of the cage. Any such combination of conditions is likely to (1) have irreversible

---

[1] Behavioral differences between strains are important. For example, the effects of punishment differ not only for hooded and albinos but also between albino strains (Kleban, 1965; Nakamura and Anderson, 1962; Storms, Boroczi, and Broen, 1963).

early experience effects, (2) establish particular adaptation levels, and (3) promote the formation of particular habits regarding feeding, drinking, and social behavior. Since different animal suppliers employ different combinations of conditions, the same designated strain purchased from different suppliers is not a homogeneous population because of the different effects of the two environments. Although the two samples from the same strain might not show significant differences in all behavioral experiments, they would perform differently in those specific situations in which adaptation level or ingestion habits were effective variables. To further complicate the picture, two shipments from the same firm may not be equivalent. Most companies use tiers of cages, with some high and some almost on the floor. The high animals may be in as much as ten times the illumination as the low ones because of ceiling light fixtures. Vertical gradients of temperature are also common, with the high animals warmer. One might even conjecture that the low-housed animals could be adapted to human feet and the high animals to heads. In later test situations, a human head might be a novel stimulus to only the low animals.

Since shipments of animals tend to be drawn by the supplier from the same cage, a given shipment is not a random sample but rather an overly homogeneous subset not representative of the range of conditions within the colony. A truly random sample of one supplier's rats gives each animal in the colony an equal chance of inclusion in the sample. Actually, unusual constraints operate in that (1) the choice of the first rat by the shipper determines the lot and (2) only cage mates follow. It is obvious that a shipment of rats is also not a random sample of the United States domestic rat population; not all rats have an equal chance of being selected once the supplier is chosen. Contrary to some writers' generalizations, a shipment of rats is not a random sample of "animals" or "organisms."

Most experimenters may find such considerations distasteful and somewhat frustrating because of the inaccessibility and vagueness of the supplier's physical conditions, plus a large degree of ignorance about how past conditions may affect the experiment at hand. Nevertheless, it remains the task of the experimenter to render a solution appropriate to his own research. For example, many experimental situations using powerful treatments such as shock or food reinforcement have such a tremendous effect upon the animal's behavior that individual differences from previous treatments are entirely obscured. On the other hand, preference testing procedures for foodstuffs, temperature, or cage size tend to be affected by previous history. Even the most precise experiment, while yielding careful estimates of parameters, is still restricted in scope in that its functions apply to some specific sample of animals. The experimenter must decide to what population his results generalize in either parameter-estimation or hypothesis testing, and generalizations beyond the sample should be based upon samples beyond the one sample.

One practical and possibly partial solution to the problem of unknown effects of previous treatments is to purchase young animals or breed one's own and maintain them in a given describable maintenance environment for a lengthy period prior to testing. While this procedure solves no problems of random sampling, it (1) allows a description of the conditions unique to the sample, (2) allows independent replication, and (3) renders the experiment more complete by making it possible to know the maintenance-test relationships.

Maintenance environment

Once subjects are selected, ordered, and received, they are usually maintained in quarters for a period before testing and often maintained in these same quarters between test sessions. The state of the animal being tested is dependent mainly upon the maintenance environment, since the nontesting phase is usually quite long with respect to the testing phase; hence the maintenance practices can greatly affect the experiment. Animals that become diseased or are cold, underfed, or exposed to noxious stimuli for the 23 hours before testing are quite likely to perform differently than more optimally maintained subjects. Therefore, except for special treatments, e.g., drugs, food and water deprivation, and other procedures relevant to the experiment, experimenters should follow the best of recommended animal maintenance standards. References on care and maintenance are cited at the end of this chapter.

Animals are often maintained on a food-deprivation schedule intended to promote responding for food reward in a short daily test session. Three kinds of maintenance feeding schedule have been most commonly used: (1) animals are fed for a fixed interval of time (e.g., one-half hour) every day, (2) animals are given just enough food daily to keep them at a fixed percentage (e.g., 80 percent) of their predeprivation weight, and (3) subjects are given just enough food to maintain them at an adjusted percentage (e.g., 80 percent) of what their body weight would have been if normal growth had been maintained. When using any of these techniques, the experimenter usually hopes that changes or trends across days, on performance in the daily task, are the result of some aspect of the task and not of the food-deprivation schedule. But Davenport and Goulet (1964) showed that the kind of food-deprivation schedule used in maintenance affects the way response rates in a food-reinforced task change across days of testing. Lever-press rates under variable-interval reinforcement gradually increased across days under both the fixed-interval and the fixed-percentage deprivation schedules, whereas those animals maintained under the adjusted-percentage schedule maintained fairly constant response rates.

Transitional variables

There are numerous effective variables stemming from the fact that an animal is rarely tested continuously in its living environment, but is most commonly transported back and forth between two environments. Between tests, an animal is not stored; it is receiving treatments bearing some kind of relationship to those received in the test situation. For example, rats stored in a dimly illuminated laboratory but tested daily in a brightly illuminated apparatus might perform poorly because the entire test situation is aversive. If the laboratory had been illuminated more than the test situation, so that the situation was reversed, an extra preference for the test situation might have been added to the deliberate test treatments. In general, one might expect that the greater the difference in stimulation between the two environments, the greater the initial competing responses in the test situation and the slower the habituation. This general relationship should be suspected for all ambient physical variables such as temperature, light, odors, and noise level plus such other considerations as the transition from group housing to individual testing.

If the maintenance quarters are on a light-dark cycle, further considerations are in order. Rats and other nocturnal animals are most active in the dark phase of the lighting cycle and do most of their eating and drinking then. From the animal's point of view, the light portion of the day is for sleeping and inactivity but may be interrupted by an experimenter who requires him to run or bar-press for food. It is unfortunate that the amount of lighting and the timing of the cycle are usually arranged for the benefit of the caretaker and not for the animals or the experimenters. The light-dark cycle, in addition to its ability to produce quite different absolute levels of performance in different experiments, is an excellent candidate for sources of confounding. Suppose an experiment has two treatment groups, and the experimenter finds it convenient to run one before sundown and the other after. Without counterbalancing techniques, the second group is quite likely to show stronger performance measures in the test situation simply because it is tested during its active phase of the diurnal cycle.

The method of transport from home cage to test environment should also receive careful attention. Carrying by the tail or in the hand leaves open the possibilities of great individual differences in treatments, for one animal may be dropped while another is not. Carrying cages reduce such incidents, and the more elegant carrying cages are built to attach to the testing apparatus so that animals may gain access by direct locomotion, sometimes in serial fashion.

The careful investigator will not focus all his considerations upon the test environment. He will (1) consider what the animal can do, (2) perhaps measure what it does in the maintenance phase, and (3) work out a happy relationship between the two environments such that the best interests of the research are served. Most animal research, while appearing deceptively simple, must hide a multitude of complex effects, especially those operating across time. As trials in the experimental apparatus progress, the animal not only is learning what the experimenter knowingly arranged but is habituating to (1) the apparatus, (2) the transitions at test time, and (3) the handling procedures. The animal's ad-lib feeding schedule may undergo progressive shifts if he consumes any appreciable amount of food in the test situation. If either situation deprives the animal of a usual activity, e.g., chewing, sleeping, or exploration, the animal will compensate for the deficit in whichever situation allows it. These many temporal effects get lumped together in the final performance function across time. It is worth considering just what the subject should be habituated to and what should be a novel aspect of the environment on the first trial. At one end of the continuum is the common procedure of ensuring that all aspects of the test situation are novel. At the other end, one might habituate the animal to the test chamber by having it live there for a period, after which the only novel introduction is a contingency created by the experimenter.

Apparatus and procedural variables

Too much apparatus for the behavioral sciences is thrown together in haste by using unique dimensions, nonstandard materials, and less-than-elegant workmanship. The his-

tory of behavioral research no doubt contains a sprinkling of incidents in which the rat occupied himself with gnawing on exposed wood, sniffing screwheads, or chewing up the drinking tube's stopper instead of doing what the experimenter was prepared to measure. Unusual equipment coincides with the beginning of a research area, then gives way to standardized and commercially available hardware. A number of companies produce a variety of animal research apparatus at reasonable costs (see Appendix). The experimenter who wishes to produce empirical data of durable reference value should make every effort to anticipate which apparatus design is likely to persist. Otherwise, he runs the risk of producing results applicable to an antique apparatus not encountered in the future, and perhaps not found in other laboratories contemporaneously. In some cases, the apparatus established by precedent and that appearing likely to persist in time may differ. The experimenter must decide whether his results are better compared with past ones or his data might be classed with future research. In any case, a decision to make the results comparable to some substantial body of data is preferable to making them unique to a set of conditions unlikely to be recapitulated by other experimenters.

While the physical dimensions and materials adjacent to a subject are not likely to be the proper place for ingenious departures from convention, the functional properties of the apparatus, e.g., time delays, contingencies, and sequences, are entirely proper for innovation. To arrange these properly with a minimum cost and a maximum reliability sometimes requires considerable technological skill. Other chapters of this book aid in that development.

Once the hardware of the apparatus has been selected on rational grounds, one must consider a host of both transient and ambient physical variables beyond those constituting the treatments of the experiment. *Transient variables* are all those occurring briefly or in slow cycles, or having some connection with the experiment. The slamming of doors, traffic noise, radiator banging, and the like can introduce extra variability and mask subtle effects. The increasing use of sound-attenuating test chambers minimizes such intrusions and has the additional advantage of decreasing relay and timer clicks and other apparatus-produced noise that might negate the experiment by providing cues or response-contingent feedback. It is also probable that external stimuli invading the test chamber not only may disrupt behavior but may cause the animal to orient and approach in the direction of the stimuli. Animal noise is particularly effective in this way, and an animal may leave the instrumented end of the chamber and approach the sounds.

While many transient variables can be greatly reduced in effectiveness by sound insulation, masking noise, and enclosed chambers, others are beyond the control of experimenters. Thunder, sonic booms, low barometric pressure, and unusual odors sometimes intrude. Here, the researcher is faced with the problem of discarding any data he feels to be obviously contaminated with unwanted events versus including, with ethical rectitude, any and all data generated by his subjects within the experimental conditions. The problem is quite real, but no dilemma. The experimenter must decide, before the subjects are run, what environmental conditions are appropriate to the experiment. If he decides that his experimental environment is whatever happens, he must keep all data. If he decides that only data from healthy animals in a defined environment are to be gathered, he must discard data from environments whose properties exceed his established limits of tolerance. *The important thing is to define the rules and make decisions based upon the rules, not the data, and then to report the rules.* Discussions covering the elimination of data are given in the section on human research, (pages 21 to 22).

A number of environmental factors are cyclic with a wavelength of 24 hours: barometric pressure, temperature, building noises, and odors such as tobacco smoke. Measurement of the levels of these slowly changing variables often reveals a main daily cyclic component with smaller variations imposed upon it. The rumble of students' feet and the bells or buzzers for class periods have a subperiod within the daily cycle, and the tapping of typewriters may have a noon interruption coincident with the lunch hour, when food odors then make their daily intrusion into the ventilation system of the laboratory. In many ways, the experimenter is at the mercy of the architect, who probably designed the laboratory space for humans and for economy, not for animal research. Sometimes the cyclic and aperiodic environmental fluctuations can be reduced by modifications to the heating and ventilating system, by eliminating classrooms from the laboratory floor and disconnecting bells, and by moving out shop and cooking facilities. More often, the experimenter has administrative control over only a portion of the laboratory space and must do the best he can within only that space. Even then, much can be done. The door can be weatherstripped with rubber tape and acoustically insulated, and a "Quiet—Experiment in Progress" sign posted outside. Inside, an electric heater with self-contained thermostat can closely regulate temperature. Illumination can be fixed at a specified value. Airborne odors can be integrated into the daily routine by following a deliberate routine with respect to washing and use of odorous substances. Most important of all, the sequence of treatments within a day can be randomized or counterbalanced with the intent of unconfounding progressive environmental changes from treatments.

When the problems of transient and periodic variations in the levels of environmental variables have been minimized, there remains the problem of selecting a level for each of the static variables that must be present. The experimenter must select a noise level, a temperature, and an illumination. Various other static variables are difficult or impossible to control: the gravitational constant, radiation level, air composition and density, and magnetic field density. While these particular variables may often be assumed equal between laboratories and between replications of a given study, they may not be beyond consideration.

The three physical environmental variables most easily controlled and fixed at static levels are *temperature, noise level,* and *lighting.* The temperature most often encountered in buildings is 72°F, agreeable to humans but possibly low for many laboratory animals. Large animal suppliers often use 78°F, claiming less disease and mortality at that temperature. Noise level is seldom measured and reported, and practice varies between laboratories. Some use small blowers near the apparatus for a source of masking noise. Others use white noise piped around the laboratory rooms with a speaker system. A few use a radio or an FM receiver tuned to a 24-hour station not only to mask undesirable noise but to habituate the subjects to human speech and a wide variety of sounds. The researcher would be wise to report the type of background sound and to make a simple sound-level determination inside the test chambers, for this might protect the study against the embarrassment of subsequent research showing an interaction of various performance measures with sound pressure level. Intensity levels are measured in decibel units by a sound-level meter (SLM).

Shoddy measurement and reporting practice is especially evident for light, even when light intensity is an independent variable. Experimenters typically report irrelevant information. For example, the wattage of the test light is often reported; yet a 7½-watt long-life lamp is much dimmer than a household one, for the former has a cooler filament, is less efficient, and is redder in hue. Also, luminous intensity is different at different line voltages, varying approximately as the 3.6 power of the applied voltage. Statements about the source of light are irrelevant except to indicate spectral composition. Fluorescent lamps have more energy in the blue region of the spectrum than incandescents and both come in subtypes with different spectral properties. A recommended practice is to use long-life incandescent lamps, e.g., type 11S14/IF (3,000 hr) or the General Electric type 755 (50,000 hr) with a voltage-regulation transformer. The latter, though a miniature pilot lamp, will provide more than 1 foot-candle of illumination in most small animal chambers. For albino rats, 1 foot-candle is the lower end of the aversive range and should not be exceeded. Both types of lamp have long lives that fail to endanger most experiments, and the transformer prohibits intensity variations as the building line voltage fluctuates with the daily cycle of demand. Light intensity can be reduced by partial obscuration with opaque barriers. Reducing light intensity by voltage reduction shifts the spectral composition of the light toward the red and makes light measurements difficult, especially with instruments requiring an observer to make a heterochromatic match.

Some experimenters have reported careful measurements of the luminance of a translucent window through which light is admitted into the experimental space. This is akin to specifications about the source and tells nothing about the amount of light reaching subjects. The latter depends upon (1) the size of the luminous panel, (2) the distance to the subject, and (3) the albedo of the interior walls. Except for studies of the dark-adaptation type using a visual test patch, good general animal practice uses large low-luminance light sources. Diffuse lighting avoids the glare characteristic of small sources and helps promote a uniform distribution of light throughout the cage. Plastics and papers are unsuitable diffusers, for their spectral properties are difficult to specify and may change with age. Sandblasted window glass diffuses well, has known transmission properties, and is easy to clean. If the diffusing material forms the entire top of the test chamber, proper lamp placement can often result in such uniform illumination that a single reported value truthfully describes illumination throughout the cage.

Three measurements taken inside the experimental chamber will define the lighting conditions well enough to allow an independent investigator to re-create them: *source luminance, wall albedo,* and *illuminance at the subject.*

The luminance of the luminous panel serving as the source may show large variations from center to outside and may appear brighter at any point in line with the lamp and eye. Both conditions imply incomplete diffusion, remedied by additional translucent panels or indirect lighting. Luminance is measured with the Macbeth illuminometer and is reported in millilamberts.

The second desirable measurement is the luminance of the interior walls of the test chamber. Glossy surfaces reflect light from the source directionally, are difficult to measure, and may increase the light flux falling on the subject when it is near the walls. Flat gray would reduce these problems and allow the researcher to report the albedo of the gray.

The most essential measurement is the illuminance at the subject's eye level. Illuminance refers to the density of light flux falling on the subject's surface and eyes. All statements about the source of light and the mechanics of transmitting it to the subject are nearly irrelevant if the illuminance at the subject is specified, for any lighting arrangement achieving the same illuminance would closely replicate experimental conditions. Illuminance is commonly reported in foot-candles and can be measured either with the Macbeth illuminometer or with several photoelectric instruments. If a single value of illuminance is reported, the experimenter implies that it is uniform throughout the experimental space and constant over time. Area uniformity is greatly aided by the light-distributing procedures discussed above and should be confirmed by measurements throughout the cage. Temporal constancy of illuminance can be achieved by first aging the lamp for about a week, then making measurements at intervals and progressively deobscuring the lamp as its output declines across time. This assumes

that the voltage applied to the lamp is itself constant.

Luminance and illuminance should be sharply distinguished. A white surface and a black surface under equal illumination would have greatly different luminances. Chapter 7 provides an excellent discussion of these and other vision variables, lamps, and measuring instruments.

The question of just what illumination to use in the test chamber cannot be answered flatly, but some guidelines are becoming clear (Lockard, 1963). The prime consideration is that *the stimulation should not be aversive.* This usually means that the illumination should not exceed that of the maintenance quarters and should not exceed 1 foot-candle for albino subjects or 10 foot-candles for subjects with pigmented eyes. If behavioral research eventually adopts standards, the figure of 1 foot-candle may emerge as a standard. It is dimmer than most maintenance quarters, provides adequate visibility for humans, requires only small sources unlikely to overheat the test chamber, and is likely to be aversive only to those albino subjects with protracted experience in the dark or very dim light.

Although we have been emphasizing research with the rat, it is obvious that many of the variables and problems discussed in this section are pertinent to research with other animals, even though problems of experimental control can become more difficult as one ascends the phylogenetic scale. Refer to the Addendum of this chapter for a discussion of monkeys. Unlike rats, monkeys are generally housed in laboratories for long periods of time and are seldom used in only one experiment. The monkey section, therefore, stresses laboratory maintenance as well as method because of the expense and problems incurred when these animals are included in the laboratory colony.

The following section deals with several variables of importance in the study of human behavior. Supplementary information on human research may be found in Parts Three to Five.

HUMAN RESEARCH

The characteristics of the human being, plus the fact that both subject and experimenter are *Homo sapiens,* present methodological problems encountered in few other areas of experimental endeavor. The purpose of this section is to cover a few selected variables and problems of importance in the study of human behavior. These include subject sampling and assignment, instructions, experimenter effects, verbal reports, and a treatment of criteria for discarding data or subjects. The presentation is restricted in scope since other discussions of methodological problems in human research are presented or referenced elsewhere in this volume.

Subjects

In practice, human subjects are selected generally on the basis of convenience and availability. An investigator interested in adult learning settles for a population of introductory psychology students because they are in-house and available; a child researcher wishing to study the city school population of seven-year-olds settles for a school adjacent to the college because of lack of cooperation from other authorities. This means that the investigator often starts with a very select group from which to draw a working sample, a fact that generally restricts his ability to generalize to larger populations. The seven-year-olds at the campus lab school are seldom representative of the average city school group of the same age, and introductory psychology students at one college are not necessarily like those of any other institution, or of adult populations in general.

The sample is restricted further by problems of recruitment. Unlike the animal researcher, the investigator of human behavior must actively search out subjects and is often forced to find incentives which attract people to serve. Because of this, he is faced with the choice of selecting subjects from a population serving for the same reason or incentive, or obtaining a mixed sample consisting of those persons serving for a variety of motives. In practice, the former strategy is preferred. If class credit is offered, the sample, under most circumstances, consists exclusively of subjects selected from a school population offered class credit; but, if money is the lure, all subjects are paid.

But selection problems seldom end with the discovery of an enticement to serve. The method for obtaining subjects in many colleges and universities is a case in point for it can be replete with potential biasing factors, the effects of which are seldom known. For example, there is little way of knowing whether subjects who volunteer early in a semester differ in some respect from those who volunteer later, or whether experiments requiring short service, e.g., 10 minutes, draw a sample that is different from studies requiring an hour. This is especially true if the amount of total service time is advertised as an added inducement in one study but left unmentioned in another, or if the same amount of class credit is assigned to both. The fact that some subjects volunteer but fail to show up confuses the issue of random selection still further.

The solution to this problem is random assignment, a topic to be covered later in this section. At this point, it is sufficient to note that care must be taken in defining the specific population or group from which a sample is drawn, and generalizations made only to it, as limited as these may be. An adequate definition of the population and methods of selection is especially important in a coordinated series of studies where the investigator is interested in obtaining continuous samples from the same population. The reader is referred elsewhere for basic discussions covering sampling theories and procedures, parameter estimations, infinite and finite population definitions, and inferences based on extrastatistical considerations (Cox, 1958; Scott and Wertheimer, 1962; Hays, 1963; Kurtz, 1965).

Since random selection is difficult to guarantee in practice and can be very expensive in terms of time and effort, the experimenter's labor should be directed most often toward methods for assigning subjects to treatments. *Random assignment can ensure that each subject selected has an equal chance of being allocated to conditions and should be considered mandatory whenever subjects are assigned to different experimental treatments.* Unfortunately subjects are sometimes assigned to treatments in such a way as to increase the probability that the investigator's hypothesis will be supported. For example, subjects are occasionally allocated to conditions through personal judgment; i.e., the experimenter decides on the assignment subjectively as the person arrives for the session. The potential for bias here is obvious. Also, subjects are not usually assigned on a fill-one-treatment-at-a-time basis; e.g., in an experiment with two treatments, it would be wrong to assign and run subjects in one treatment first and then assign and run each subject in the second treatment. The potentially confounding influences of this technique are numerous. For example, with a college subject population, the better and/or more highly motivated students may volunteer early; or subjects run earlier might convey experimental information or complain of the task to potential subjects outside. In both instances, the effects may be reflected in some biased manner in the results. Similarly, the experimenter might alter his techniques in the course of the experiment or some unexpected change in equipment operation or reliability might bias effects in favor of one or another treatment.

Of course random assignment may be used with a restriction. For example, subjects can be randomly assigned to treatments with the restriction that an equal number of males and females appear in each treatment. This practice does not violate the assumption since balancing the sex variable represents no more than duplicating the experiment, once with males randomly assigned to treatments, and once with females.

In some experiments random assignment is not applicable, e.g., studies comparing clinical populations such as manic depressives and schizophrenics, but these are not without problems. Refer to Patterson (1956) for a discussion of some of the problems involved in trying to compare different groups by matching in studies of counseling. However even in the experimental work noted earlier the same sort of problem can arise when comparing the behavior of populations that are experimentally different (for example, when two groups receive different acquisition training). Anderson (1963) discusses this problem for comparisons of different populations in resistance to extinction and transfer; Underwood (1954) examines the measurement of retention after acquisition.

Whether restricted or otherwise, reporting the method of selection and assignment along with the characteristics of the subject supply helps other investigators determine the comparability of their results. Techniques of randomization should be mastered in any case since they have many applications in psychological research other than those cited above. Discussions governing the use of tables of random numbers may be found in Hays (1963, p. 65), Zimny (1961, p. 180), Cox (1958, p. 71), and numerous other sources covering experimental design and statistics; tables of random numbers may be found in the appendices of many of these same sources and in a publication by Rand Corporation (1955).

Apparatus and procedural variables

Plans for selecting and assigning subjects, administering stimuli, instructing or treating subjects, and observing and recording responses are set out in detail before the experiment begins. Here, the experience of the experimenter is essential in adequately defining the response of interest and in choosing a simple design that will allow him to answer the questions raised by the problem. Although the experimental design has an influence in determining the form of statistical evaluations, the two may be separated.

There is no rule specifying that one or another design method must be used, nor is there a rule forbidding the combination of several. There are, however, general rules and assumptions that accompany specific design methods. These should be respected once a commitment to a design has been made. On the other hand, there is no guarantee that different designs covering an investigation of the same problem will produce the same effects. For example, in two experiments investigating the effects of induced muscular tension and incentive on verbal learning, an independent-groups design failed to reproduce the effects resulting from a repeated-measurements design (Sidowski and Nuthmann, 1956). In the independent-groups design each of four treatments contained a different group of subjects; in the repeated-measurements design, each subject served in all four treatments with the order of treatments counterbalanced in a Latin square.[1] Grice and Hunter (1964) report the same type of difference for two experimental designs used to study stimulus intensity effects.

For detailed information covering various aspects of experimental design and data analysis, the reader is referred to Chapanis (1959), Cox (1958), Cochran and Cox (1957), Edwards (1960), Lindquist (1953), Underwood (1957), and Winer (1962). Sidman (1960) presents a description of the designs used in operant conditioning research.

But before running the experiment, it is generally advisable to carry out a *pilot study*. A pilot study might be considered a trial run. It is not a regular experiment executed in a sloppy manner, nor is it one in which the researcher is loath to use good equipment. It is the experimenter's attempt to identify or investigate any factor that may influence the design and procedure used in the experiment. He may, for example, attempt to determine the clarity of his instructions, length of the experimental session, adequacy of experimenter and equipment operations, or he may try to identify variables that might confound the results and/or require control. Well-controlled studies designed to estimate the probable success of an experiment might better be called *predictive research,* while any major experiment that is poorly designed or carried out improperly falls within the category of *slapdash research.* If a major experiment is well planned but an unforeseen difficulty in design or procedure is discovered at any stage of development, including the final write-up, the study is defined as *experiential research.* Regardless of the research category, some problems are common to the development of all. With human subjects, the formulation of a set of instructions is one of these.

Instructions define the subject's task, direct his attention, help to develop a preparatory set, and sometimes motivate. But if directions are unclear or ambiguous, subjects can be expected to formulate self-instructions which may be contradictory to the purpose of the study. Inexperienced subjects should not be expected to know as much as the experimenter and, when the procedure permits, should be told whether they are expected to maximize speed, minimize error, guess, or not rehearse, and generally should be informed of the rewards and/or penalties for certain actions.

---

[1] A Latin-square design consists of a square containing an equal number of rows and columns. Treatments are arranged so that each condition is coded in the form of a Latin letter that appears only once in each row and column. In the study cited above (a 4 × 4 Latin square), the four tension and incentive conditions were coded *ABCD,* with subject 1 receiving the *BCAD* order across row 1, subject 2 the *CADB* order across row 2, subject 3 *DBCA,* and subject 4 *ADBC,* the procedure being repeated for the remaining 20 subjects. The Latin square was chosen at random from many possible squares of this size and the rows and columns then randomized.

Although this design allows the experimenter to obtain independent estimates of treatment, row, and column effects, certain interactions are assumed to be zero. Latin squares of various sizes along with procedures for selection are presented in Fisher and Yates (1957). See the reference section of this chapter for sources covering other types of repeated measures or counterbalancing methods, and discussions of the problems involved.

The clarity of instructions may be tested by requesting comments from persons acquainted with the project, as well as those who are naive, and by running a pilot study. With long or complicated instructions, understanding is improved by concluding with a repetition of the task requirements.

Since the investigator is a stimulus object of major importance whose effect upon subject performance is often unknown, his influence and behavior should be as consistent and constant as possible for all subjects. The number of *experimenter variables* that can have a significant influence on the outcome of an investigation cover a wide range of behaviors. For example, Sidowski, *et al.* (1960), Archer, Cejka, and Thompson (1961), Hetherington and Ross (1963), and Stevenson and Allen (1964) report that male and female subjects perform differently with male or female experimenters in tasks ranging from learning in dyadic interactions to studies of verbal behavior. Sarason and Minard (1963) report that the degree of contact between subject and experimenter, and the investigator's prestige, contribute significantly to overall effects. Krasner (1958) cites a number of researcher characteristics including gender, appearance, and personality which influence verbal conditioning. It should not be surprising also to find that subjects perform differently for an experimenter who controls their rewards and punishments outside the experiment (e.g., professors, ward attendants, or military officers). Even the suggestion that the investigator may be an active participant in the experiment can influence the performance of male and female subjects differently (Sidowski and Smith, 1961). Thus, it is important that the experimenter develop an awareness of his potential influence as a stimulus object and attempt to control or balance across treatments any effects that he may have. General practice should also require that the assignment of male and female subjects to treatments be balanced, or that subjects of the same sex be used throughout.

A final point about the experimenter concerns his biases and expectations. Research indicates that the experimenter under some circumstances influences subjects to produce results which agree with his hypotheses (Orne, 1962; Rosenthal, 1964; Troffer and Tart, 1964; and Kintz, Delprato, Mettee, Persons, and Schappe, 1965). The conditions leading to this result are not yet clear, but it appears to occur more often when the interaction of subject and experimenter is an important part of the procedure, e.g., social, personality, verbal conditioning, clinical, hypnosis, or ESP studies. Opportunities for biased treatment of some subjects at the expense of others are generally high under such circumstances, as is the probability of providing cues, so the investigator should be especially aware of his potential influence.

When experimenter bias is combined with research naiveté, the problems become compounded. Brogden (1962), for example, reports that the rabbits of experienced investigators reached criterion faster than those of naive experimenters, and that as the naive researchers became more experienced, animal performance changed. An extreme but occasionally occurring example in human research is the use of inexperienced students in experimental or special study courses to collect data for class credit (sometimes from each other) in what is considered to be publishable research. Not only are the "experimenters" oriented toward class credit and teacher recognition, but many are told the type of data that is expected, and some obtain it by any means possible.

The problem here is one of professional competence, as well as ethics. But some control may be maintained by training experimenters thoroughly in the task of objectively handling subjects and collecting data, and/or, in some cases, automating the entire session.

Although individual experimenters are seldom selected from a larger population of researchers, it is not uncommon to use several investigators in the same study, a practice that should be encouraged. However when more than one experimenter is used, good design requires that each contribute equally to all conditions, i.e., subjects and treatments be balanced over experimenters. Even if this is done, the effects of multiple experimenters may vary to the extent that a significant interaction of experimenters and treatments results, or different investigators produce consistently high or low performance over all treatments. These effects are easily evaluated if one adheres to the suggestion for balancing and includes the experimenter effect as a variable in the analysis. [A more detailed discussion of experiments utilizing more than one experimenter and some coverage of problems concerning investigator generalization may be found in McGuigan (1963).]

Since the investigator is an added stimulus of some importance, a decision should be made as to the need for his immediate presence in the subject room. It is often advisable to arrange for the experimenter to be stationed elsewhere; but if his presence in the subject's room is required, an attempt must be made to eliminate any unnecessary cues that he may provide. Unfortunately subjects often look for feedback or encouragement and search for any type of verbal or facial response that might serve as an aid. Methodological controls include seating the investigator behind the subject, separating the subject and experimenter by a panel, and using an adjoining room with one-way-vision glass. Of course with one-way glass, some subjects will realize they are being observed and some will not; some will be affected and some will not. Since these may not be equally distributed over conditions, it may be desirable at the time of instructions to inform all subjects that they are being watched.

An alternative to one-way-vision glass is a closed-circuit television camera with a monitor placed elsewhere for observations. With video tape equipment, the televised material may be recorded and played back later. The same television system has tremendous potential for various other phases of laboratory research with all types of populations (e.g., see Gould and Smith, 1962, and Smith, 1962). See the Appendix for a list of equipment suppliers for closed-circuit television and communication systems.

Oftentimes subjects communicate experimental information to potential subjects outside of the experiment against the investigator's wishes. This problem has been handled by: (1) completely misinforming subjects of the purpose of the study, a technique applicable to very few experiments; (2) partially misdirecting by providing a plausible explanation without revealing the actual purpose; (3) asking the subject not to discuss the experiment; (4) requesting a pledge of secrecy (Turner and Solomon, 1962); (5) comparing the performance of those who had received such information against those who had not; and (6) running all subjects in a treatment at one time as a group with different treatments being run as close in time as possible.

Running a large group of subjects simultaneously in a single room instead of individually involves problems of stimulus presentation, response recording, etc., that are difficult and expensive to control. One solution is to automate by providing a visual display, earphones, and a response panel at each position, which is partially enclosed. A computer-controlled system is optimal but up to now expense has limited its use to automated classroom instruction.[1] In any case, a large automated system of any kind would generally appear worthy of consideration only in

[1] Whether subjects are run as a group or individually, it is often desirable to record responses in a manner that allows for easy translation to computer form for subsequent analyses. The Flexi-bit portable tape punch (Ohr-Tronics, Inc.) is a relatively inexpensive device that allows the subject to record his responses directly on Mylar or paper tape. The same punch may be used for manually generating program tapes, punching tape loops, or inserting corrections on existing tapes. A portable precision card punch (Wright) fulfills some of the same functions in 80-column card format. With slight alteration, both of these devices can be used in a wide variety of experiments.

those instances where the equipment will be used for a series of experiments. When only one study is planned, considerations of effort and economics are often much higher for the group method. In a rote serial learning study run with both the group (Sidowski, Kopstein, and Shillestad, 1961) and single subject methods, the operations necessary for adequately running subjects as a group took approximately 28 hours more total experiment plus preparation time than that required for running subjects individually. The results of both studies indicated the same relative differences between experimental treatments, but whether or not the two methods produce similar results in other situations is open to empirical investigation. Refer to Lindquist (1953) and Campbell and Stanley (1963) for discussions of experimental designs and statistics applied to group studies,[1] and to Anderson (1962) for an application of statistical techniques to individual subjects.

Although we continue to develop objective methods for understanding complex behavior from the experiments in which the behavior is recorded, introspective *verbal reports* often provide additional information. Occasionally these are unreliable (e.g., see Verplanck and Oskamp, 1956; Kendler and Kendler, 1962), but a subject's verbalizations are not necessarily invalid scientifically, and there is some information which is obtainable in no other way.

The study of verbal reports is in disrepute with many investigators because of its association with classical introspection in which the object of study was the subject's inner feelings, as reported in his verbal behavior. There is, however, another purpose; that is to obtain information about the experiment.

Although this information may occasionally be useless and misleading, it is often vital in illustrating defects in the experiment. It can also provide valuable information about the intuitive processes underlying behavior. But the use of verbal reports presents numerous technical problems, many of them minor, which must be solved. Here we can do little more than call attention to a few of them.

In some studies, investigators request reports covering thinking or strategy development to help understand a subject's behavior on the overt task. Here one must decide whether to request this information during the course of the experiment or after the session is completed. Interruption interferes with the chain of events as well as the subject's "set", and may provide indeterminable cues; but waiting until the end of the session may increase the probability that he will repeat his most recent thoughts and ignore or report unreliably the earlier ones.[2]

Formal interrogations are designed as an integral part of the experimental procedure before the study begins. These have been used for determining subject strategies, differentiating between incidental and intentional learners (Postman, 1964), and as a means of investigating the subject's awareness of certain experimental contingencies (Dulany, 1961). The formulation of a set of questions is important here and care should be taken to ensure that the subject's answers are not biased because of cues or suggestions arising from a poorly contrived questionnaire. Often, more general questions are asked first, and more specific and pointed inquiries later. Examples of formal questionnaires may be found in Dulany (1962), Spielberger and Levin (1962), and Eriksen

---

[1] Levonian (1963) presents a method of measuring and analyzing psychophysiological responses in groups that utilizes a portable 180 channel time-multiplexed FM tape recorder for collecting data and a computer for providing time (e.g., mean, variance, auto-correlation, and cross-correlation) and frequency (e.g., power spectrum and transfer

functions) domain analyses.

[2] In an investigation of strategy development during a two-choice discrimination task, Gregovich and Sidowski (1966) found no noticeable effect of interruption on learning or on reported strategies.

and Doroz (1963). Once the answers to the formal inquiry have been recorded, casual conversation often provides additional valuable information (Eriksen and Doroz, 1963; Sidowski and Naumoff, 1964). Informal questioning is desirable after most studies.

Of course the way in which the subject is interviewed and the responses evaluated can easily bias the results. Therefore, in some studies the experimenter may wish to use more than one interviewer and/or response evaluator and to keep these individuals uninformed of the subject's performance during the experimental session. However, complete agreement over the procedures involved is necessary whenever more than one person is used.

DeNike (1964) reports that the biasing effects introduced by post-session interviews are not large; but since biased interrogation can suggest strategies in retrospect which the subject would not normally state, Riecken (1958) cites a control condition in which one group of subjects fails to receive the experimental treatment but has it explained in detail. During post-session questioning these persons are requested to respond as though they had served in the experimental condition, and their verbal responses compared with those of subjects actually receiving the experimental treatment.

Discarding subjects or data

There are few valid justifications for eliminating either subjects or data.[1] The position presented here is one of extreme caution. *Subjects or data should be discarded only when absolutely necessary, and decisions or criteria for rejection should be made before the experiment begins.* Making this decision after an experiment has been completed produces results that could be suspect and increases the

probability that an experimenter will accept only those data which support his hypotheses. This section will consider some of the criteria that experimenters are sometimes tempted to use. Whether or not these are acceptable depends upon the experiment.

1. Unexpected *equipment malfunction* is a valid justification for eliminating subjects under most conditions. The problem here is identifying the time that the malfunction occurred. If this is difficult, all data collected before the problem was discovered are suspect since there is no way of knowing whether or not they were contaminated as a result of the equipment unreliability.

2. *Experimenter error* may result from setting a timer at an improper interval, throwing a switch to the wrong position, or any one of a hundred other things. Since the subject has received instructions and generally has proceeded through part of the session, there is often no alternative but to discard his data. Starting over with the same subject is improper under most circumstances unless the experimenter wishes to investigate the effects of his mistake.

3. *Misunderstood instructions* are often used as a legitimate reason for eliminating data, although they seldom are a justification for doing so. The development of a set of instructions should be such that this possibility is virtually eliminated. When the problem exists, it can be traced generally to an experimental series of events that is too difficult for the subject to understand or to an experimenter who did not take the time to instruct the subject properly.

4. *Deviant case* refers to a subject who understands and follows instructions but produces data extreme in their variation from those of other subjects in the group. Justifying the elimination of such data is extremely difficult. If the number of subjects is very small, the deviant case may not be so weird as one might think; if the sample is large, it will probably have little influence on the final evaluation. In some cases it might be preferable

---

[1] Sidman (1960) presents a thoughtful argument in support of the thesis that data should never be discarded.

to present the data with and without the deviant case. If the results are the same in both instances, few problems arise. On the other hand, several questions could be raised if the significance of a result depended on the presence or absence of the weird data.

5. *Unruly cases* include dishonest subjects as well as those who understand but refuse to follow instructions for some personal reason. An old adage among experimentalists is "Never trust a subject." Although there is some truth to the saying, the trust depends upon the amount of control that the experimenter has over the procedure. In practice, the investigator has no alternative but to accept the subject's performance in good faith. Besides, the adage of many subjects is "Never trust an experimenter," assuming that the behavioral scientist is searching for something other than the apparent. When they exist, these conditions of mutual distrust, plus such factors as the desire to do well in the study, may lead subjects to behavior that the experimenter considers dishonest. If the experimenter recognizes such an act, or the subject confesses that he "found a way to beat the game," the data collected from all other subjects are questionable. Under such conditions, identify and correct the conditions that afforded the opportunity for this type of behavior and *rerun the study*. Instructions are often a major source of such problems, since subjects sometimes assume that those matters not covered in the instructions are proper.

6. There are times when the *experimental problem* leads the researcher to specify a criterion for rejecting data before the experiment begins. For example, some studies include in the final analysis data only from those subjects who learn to a certain criterion or who cannot verbalize the purpose of the experiment. The problem here is to produce a valid justification for using such a criterion and to specify adequately the manner in which the discarded data will be handled. Postman (1964) discarded and replaced subjects who reported deliberate rehearsal or anticipation

of a test. Screening these subjects on the basis of post-experimental questions had the effect of sharpening the separation between experimental treatments.

Whatever the case, eliminate data with care and only when absolutely necessary. If a subject or his data must be excluded, report the exclusion and the reason in detail. For descriptions of methods for analyzing groups with unequal N's and for handling designs with incomplete cells, see Cochran and Cox (1957), Edwards (1960), Lindquist (1953), and Winer (1962).

Conclusions

Behavioral research is in transition, moving from the past of haphazard instrumentation and arbitrary selection of conditions toward refined procedures in carefully controlled and described environments. While we are still in the process of rough and casual exploration of the more powerful and obvious phenomena, we can continue to disregard the importance and effects of such factors as static variables, for their influences upon the experiment are in the shadow of the most powerful treatments. As we progress from the stage of simply demonstrating the existence of effects of treatments upon behavior and go on to systematic parametric exploration of them, we may find much of our past data of little use, for we may not know the precise conditions under which those results were gathered and therefore will not know under what conditions to expect the same functional relationship to recur. Of course earlier experiments will continue to contribute to the advancement of knowledge. They will also provide a foundation of experience from which we might advance in the design of future research.

In the above sections we were concerned only with certain selected methodological problems. The chapters to follow expand some of these and, in addition, cover a wide variety of other methods applicable to specific areas of psychology.

ADDENDUM

Monkeys[1,2]

The two most commonly used laboratory monkeys of the Old World Superfamily are the rhesus (*Macaca mulatta mulatta*) and the cynomolgus (*M. mulatta fascicularis*), although some researchers prefer the stump-tailed (*M. speciosa*) or pig-tailed (*M. nemestrina*) macaque because of their apparent docility. The squirrel (*Saimiri sciureus*) is the most common laboratory monkey of the New World Superfamily (Carmichael and MacLean, 1961; French, 1959; Miles, 1957, 1958). The popularity of this animal is due to its small size, ease of handling, and low purchase and upkeep costs. Squirrel-monkey performance on behavioral tasks is generally somewhat inferior to that of the macaque. Although lower in the primate order, the marmoset (Callithrix) has also been a popular animal for laboratory research (Miles, 1958; Miles and Meyer, 1956; Sandler and Stone, 1963; Stellar, 1960).

Regardless of family or superfamily, the first step in developing a standard primate facility is to purchase the stock. A sound animal is the prime prerequisite for developing an experimental colony, and the purchaser is advised to request opinions from experienced primate laboratory personnel before selecting a supplier. The problem of purchasing healthy animals is confounded by the fact that some monkey species and subspecies are very difficult to identify. A list of dealers in subhuman primates is presented in the Appendix.

Although purchasing practices vary, some labs prefer to buy *rhesus monkeys* weighing from 4 to 6 lb. The approximate relationship between age and weight in the rhesus is as follows: 18 oz at birth, 3 lb at 6 months, $4\frac{1}{4}$ lb at 1 year, $6\frac{1}{2}$ lb at 2 years, $7\frac{1}{2}$ lb at 3 years, and 9 lb at 4 years of age. In general, laboratory-reared monkeys will weigh more in early life than feral monkeys, and infants reared with their mothers will weigh less than laboratory-cared-for monkeys. A buyer interested in breeding can assume that the male rhesus reaches reproductive maturity at about 4 years and the female is most likely to conceive at $3\frac{1}{2}$ years. Menstruation begins at 30 to 36 months, and periods of pregnancy average about 165 days. Mature female monkeys often show periodic reddening of the anogenital region and swollen convoluted skin.

A recommended purchasing weight for young *squirrel monkeys* is 300 to 500 g. Older animals may weigh well over 1,000 g, but 650 to 750 g have been reported as average laboratory weights (Carmichael and MacLean, 1961; Kelleher, Gill, Riddle, and Cook, 1963). When breeding the *Saimiri sciureus* in the laboratory, the probability of live birth and subsequent nursing by the mother increases if the pregnant animals are secluded (Hafner and Woodburne, 1964). Mature *marmosets* weigh approximately 300 to 450 g.

Newly purchased animals generally require an isolation period before being introduced into the laboratory colony. This period ranges from two weeks reported for marmosets (Sandler and Stone, 1963) to 90 days or more reported by regional primate centers; 30 to 90 days is preferred. During the isolation period all animals are checked for tuberculosis (TB), intestinal parasites (common in newly purchased monkeys), and other illnesses.

When purchased and periodically thereafter, each animal is given a *tuberculin* test, most often by subcutaneous eyelid injection. The Mammalian Intradermic Tuberculin (U.S. Dept. of Agriculture, Bureau of Animal Husbandry) can be alternated with tests using Human P. P. D. (Purified Protein Deriva-

[1] Information covering the infant and adult rhesus monkey was gathered by the editor during visits to the Primate Laboratories at the University of Wisconsin. The editor wishes to thank Prof. Harry F. Harlow, Director of the Wisconsin Regional Primate Research Center, for permission to cite information from the Primate Center's *General Information and Testing Procedures* report. Thanks are also extended to Mr. Kenneth A.

Schiltz for contributing additional information during our conversations covering the care and maintenance of the rhesus monkey.

[2] Refer to the *Laboratory Primate Newsletter* edited by A. M. Schrier, Psychology Department, Brown University, for information of current interest.

tive) first strength (Parke, Davis) with the tests being administered every three months. If only one tuberculin is used, the Mammalian Intradermic is preferred. Animals showing a positive reaction to the tuberculin test are generally sacrificed.

Although a veterinarian should have primary responsibility for animal health, laboratory workers are usually the first to recognize unusual symptoms. A few of the more common symptoms are associated with the presence of intestinal parasites, respiratory ailments, dysentery, and cage paralysis. *Ringworm* can be identified by the appearance of bald spots and is diagnosed by a veterinarian from skin scrapings, whereas *tapeworms* appear in segments of the stool. Macaque monkeys showing evidence of parasites have been given Thibenzole (Merck & Co.) and Nemural (Winthrop Labs.) with success. Marmosets (Sandler and Stone, 1963) have been treated during the first week of isolation with three doses of an intramuscular injection [0.2 cubic centimeter (cc)] of 50 milligram (mg) per cc oxytetracycline (Terramycin, Pfizer) plus oral administrations of 0.5 cc of 125 mg per 5 cc syrup solution of chlortetracycline (Aureomycin, Lederle) and 0.1 cc of Dizan (7 mg) with piperazine citrate (8 mg) available from Corn States Laboratories.

Upper respiratory ailments have sometimes been a problem with marmosets. Stellar (1960) reports a marked reduction in fatalities with adequate maintenance of humidity (above 50 per cent), adaptation to the laboratory diet, Aureomycin treatment [oral doses of 5 mg per 100 grams (g) of body weight every day for a week], and the use of a glucose solution (5 to 10 per cent) in place of tap water in the home cage. The latter eliminates possible dehydration since the animal normally drinks much larger amounts of glucose solution than water.

Dysentery produces a loose stool often containing blood or mucus. This, with the resultant listless condition, inanition, and general dehydration, is common during the initial isolation period but may appear at any time. Dysentery is treated with antibiotics such as Chloromycetin succinate intramuscular (Chloramphenicol—Parke, Davis) and Terramycin; excellent results have been obtained with Chloromycetin. Since monkeys are often allergic to antibiotics, the animals should be kept under observation and a veterinarian consulted if allergic reactions occur.

Monkeys occasionally suffer from *cage paralysis,* which affects the hind limbs, although this condition is seldom found in animals reared on an adequate diet. In the rhesus such cases may be treated by intramuscular injections of thiamine hydrochloride 50 mg per day for 5 or 6 days. Vitamin B₁₂ (cyanocobalamin) may also be given.

Cuts and bites from other animals are treated with penicillin and streptomycin.

Since primates are expensive and often used in a number of experiments, it is advisable to keep and standardize health and experimental records for all animals from time of arrival until death or transfer elsewhere. *Arrival data sheets* should include date, supplier, cost, weight, species, sex, tattoo identification date, established age, and first TB test. *Subsequent health data sheets* cover TB test results and dentition, with the upper and lower teeth of the animal indicated on a dental chart. *Feces records* are often kept for infant monkeys or during periods of isolation or illness and indicate the daily state of feces (liquid, soft, and hard) over a monthly period. *Menstrual-cycle data* are recorded for each female. If *mating* is planned, an additional information sheet may indicate days menstruating, days mated, hours in mating, male, conceptions, and days pregnant. Individual *birth records* for laboratory births indicate the identification of father and mother, date of birth, time of delivery, disposition of cord and afterbirth, description of separation process, and time of separation. *Inspection of the infant* should reveal the following recordable data: defects, sex, open or closed eyes, weight, and teeth. Daily weight charts are kept on infant monkeys under 30 days. Weekly weights are then kept until two years of age, at which time the animals may be weighed biweekly.

A separate record is necessary for the *observed behavioral history* of the animal, e.g., sex, social, or motor behavior. *Experimental records* include the project, experimenter, subject, starting date, number of times used in the study, length of sessions, apparatus, date of completion, and a description of the experiment.

But it is diet, medication, housing, and handling procedures that determine the continuing good health of individual animals. The practices presented in this section are laboratory tested and generally representative of techniques used in many monkey laboratories. There is, however, no universal agreement on procedures for maintaining and running monkeys; methods other than these have been used very successfully.

Adult rhesus monkeys may be kept on a commercial monkey diet. This is supplemented in some laboratories with fresh fruit, vegetables, and a vitamin concentration. The diet utilized at the Wisconsin Regional Primate Center is as follows: (1) monkey chow, with the amount based on animal size; (2) one-fourth head of lettuce on Monday, one-half orange on Wednesday, and one-half apple on Friday; and (3) a vitamin concentration: 1 tablespoon of the vitamin mixture is placed on a half slice of bread and another half slice is placed on top of this to make a sandwich; this sandwich is given to adult and adolescent monkeys. Infant monkeys on solid foods receive one-half of the sandwich. The vitamin concentration is mixed in the laboratory and consists of the following: one $2\frac{3}{4}$-lb jar of Irradol-A (Parke, Davis), 50 cc Cecon (Abbott), 3.75 g isoniazid Panray Powder U.S.P. (Ormont Drug & Chemical Co., Englewood, New Jersey), 23 g Parvo, folic acid (American Cyanamid), and 4 cups Calf Supplement (any feed mill). Mix isoniazid powder in warm water. Blend the Calf Supplement and Parvo in a bowl and add Irradol-A Cecon, isoniazid, and water until the batter is of uniform color and consistency for spreading on bread. This mixture will yield about 120 servings and should be kept refrigerated. The vitamin sandwich contains about 30 mg of isoniazid. The infants on solids receive one-half of this dosage. Isoniazid dosage can safely be doubled or tripled in adult monkeys. In laboratories without adequate TB control isoniazid should be given in higher doses. A dose level of 5 mg per kilogram (kg) per day is recommended.[1] Adult animals are generally fed between 5 and 6 P.M. daily.

Infant rhesus procedures are covered by Mason and Harlow (1958; 1959) and Blomquist and Harlow (1961). Generally, infants are removed from their mothers about 12 hours after birth, weighed, checked, and marked for identification. On the first day, infant monkeys at the Wisconsin Primate Center are given one dose of vitamin K (Synkavite, Roche Laboratories), which helps to prevent brain hemorrhage. Dosage is based on 1 cc per 6-lb human infant, so an infant monkey weighing 419 to 445 g would be given 0.16 cc vitamin K.[2] Infants are placed on diapers warmed by a heating pad for the first 2 weeks, and given a liquid formula diet until approximately one year of age. The diet in Blomquist and Harlow (1961) cites one pitcher of a formula preparation combining $10\frac{1}{2}$ teaspoons dextrose, 630 cc water, 1,260 cc milk, and two drops of a vitamin preparation. This is presented in bottles for the first month starting with 2-hr feedings at birth and ending with five feedings per 24-hr period at the end of 30 days. Cup feeding is introduced at the beginning of the second month, and solids plus formula begin after $1\frac{1}{2}$ months. Recent changes in the above diet replace the milk formula with Similac with Iron (Ross Laboratories, Columbus, Ohio), which is available as a premixed liquid (13-oz cans) or in powdered form. The liquid form is diluted with equal parts of water. The powdered form is mixed by using 1 cup powdered Similac and 35 oz tap water. The formula is refrigerated after mixing and warmed before use. The early feeding procedure has also been changed. About 8 to 12 hr after birth, the infants are given 5 percent dextrose and water in a feeding bottle. This is repeated every 2 hr for 11 to 12 feedings. After these feedings the infants are given a mixture containing one-half Similac formula and one-half 5 percent dextrose and water for the next 36 hours at 2 hr intervals. The regular formula feeding schedule follows. Cow colostrum feeding has been eliminated.

Infants showing signs of dysentery are given Palmitate (Parke, Davis), an oral form of Chloramphenicol. This is added to the for-

---

[1] Although isoniazid is recommended here, not all primate researchers agree that it is a necessary part of the daily diet.

[2] A chart giving the dose levels for a wide range of infant weights may be obtained by writing the Wisconsin Primate Center, attention Mr. K. Schiltz.

mula and fed via feeding bottles or cup. If there is no improvement, or the animal fails to consume the formula, small intramuscular doses of Chloromycetin succinate are administered. If the infants show symptoms of constipation, Polyko Drops, a gentle stool softener (Upjohn & Co.), is used, 3 to 5 drops per day in the formula at one feeding.

Squirrel monkeys may also be maintained on monkey chow, although they are frequently given a supplemental diet consisting of lettuce, apple, banana, or orange daily; celery, carrots, and shelled egg may also be added. The food is left in the cage for about $1\frac{1}{2}$ hr and then removed. Small amounts of vitamin concentration are administered on a half slice of bread or monkey biscuit. Fresh water should be available at all times since dehydration can be a serious problem.

Although commercial monkey food is often used with marmosets, Stellar (1960) recommends a diet consisting of Beechnut Mixed Cereal (40 percent), whole powdered milk (40 percent), and wheat germ (20 percent by weight). Water is added to make up a dough that can be refrigerated or baked into biscuits. An added source of vitamins (Poly-Vi-Sol) is added to the above formula during mixing, or supplied in a sucrose solution, 1.0 to 80 to 100 cc of solution (Sandler and Stone, 1963; Stellar, 1960).

Laboratory temperatures reported for the rhesus and other macaques range from 68 to 80°F. For the squirrel and marmoset monkeys, about 75 to 85°F is recommended. Temperature may be maintained by a central heating unit with warm circulating air (intake and exhaust ventilation) and air conditioning included in the ventilation system. Humidity should be controlled.

Caging facilities vary, but an average cage size for the rhesus, cynomolgus, and other macaques is approximately 29 to 32 in. in length (L), 29 in. in height (H), and 29 in. in width (W). Cages are constructed of all gauge stainless steel expanded metal or, the preferred stainless steel woven wire mesh. The mesh for the sides of the cages is 1 in. square with 0.120 wire diameter. The floors are 1 in. square with 0.135 wire diameter. The 1-in.-square measurement is center to center, and the stainless steel covering the side is 16 gauge. An entrance door should

be sufficiently large for transfer of the animal to transport cages, e.g., 12 by 14 in. Since two animals are often housed in one cage, smaller facilities may be required for one large or two small animals. Smaller cages measure approximately 24 in. in each dimension. Transport cages are approximately 21 in. L by 14 in. H by 12 in. W with a sliding door covering both ends of the transport.

Infant rhesus monkeys may be housed in units measuring 24 in. L by 24 in. H by 18 in. W, with approximately 8 in. of the height allocated for the placement of a removable drop pan underneath. A sliding door covers one end.

Squirrel-monkey cages vary in size from 1 cu ft to 30 in. L by 30 in. H by 20 in. W. The size of the cage is governed somewhat by space available, length of occupation, and number of occupants. In most laboratories, two or three animals occupy the same unit: a reasonable cage size is 21 in. L by 21 in. H by 16 in. W, although the small rhesus cage, i.e., 24 in. each dimension, is fine. Cages are constructed of $\frac{3}{4}$-in. woven stainless steel. The insertion of a wooden dowel approximately 1 in. in diameter is recommended as a perch.

Caging recommendations for marmosets are approximately the same as those noted for squirrel monkeys, although Stellar (1960) cites cage measurements of 18 in. L by 18 in. W by 36 in. H, and the inclusion of a cage shelf as well as a dowel. Marmosets may be housed singly or in pairs.

Large walk-in cages are used in a number of laboratories for purposes of quarantine, breeding, and exercise. These vary in size but some are about 6 to 8 ft H, 4 to 6 ft W, and 6 to 10 ft L. Strength of construction depends on the size of the animal. A rigid frame covered with strong hardware cloth is sometimes sufficient for the squirrel or marmoset monkey. (A small room might be set aside for sick or implanted animals. Individual monkeys may be further isolated by being placed in living cages that are covered on all sides except the front and bottom.)

Methods for handling laboratory cleanliness and odor depend upon the particular installation. One procedure is to: (1) hose animal drop pans twice daily, in the morning and after the evening feeding; (2) apply deodorizer and detergent to floors and pans (coating the pans with Slipicone, a Dow Corning product, prevents waste products from adhering to and staining the pans); and (3) clean the entire cage block weekly. When cleaning the cage block, have an ample supply of transport cages and mark each transport with the cage number in order to avoid confusion in relocating animals. Each animal should have a personal identification mark or tag.

Weekly cleaning includes the following sequence: (1) remove monkeys with adequately marked transport cages, (2) hose the entire block unit, (3) apply a lye solution, (4) hose the block unit again, (5) apply disinfectant solution, (6) hose the block unit, (7) return cleaned water bottles, (8) return animals to correct home cages, and (9) thoroughly clean transport cages. Water bottles are filled at daily cleaning sessions and cleaned with a soap and disinfectant three times weekly. Portable cage cleaners, e.g., Kleen King, facilitate the above chore tremendously. When cages are being cleaned, *care should be taken not to wet the animals*. This is especially important with squirrel and marmoset monkeys.

The Appendix gives a list of commercial suppliers of deodorizers, detergents, feed, and cage equipment. Readers interested in caging should also contact local metal shops since they are often willing to bid competitively for the same or custom work.

A healthy and properly housed animal is not necessarily "ready" for research. Indeed, he may not be ready to enter the transport cage without some opposition. Adaptation, handling, or taming of some sort may be necessary. With rats, the problem is simple: the animal is taken out of the cage for a short time each day and fed by hand, stroked, or played with. The result, hopefully, is a more docile animal with one source of potential variability removed or controlled. With monkeys the problem is more difficult and includes adapting to the living cage, transport cage, and experimental cage.

Adaptation in the living cage often includes becoming familiar with the animal to the extent that he might be hand-fed. Attempts are sometimes made to stroke the animal and induce it to play with the hand but this can be dangerous with larger and older animals. As monkeys grow older and canine teeth develop, they present a potential source of injury and can easily bite through gloves. The young stump-tailed macaque (*Macaca speciosa*) has been reported as a docile experimental animal (Kling and Orbach, 1963), but the older animals have been more resistant to handling. Although this animal is more tractable than the rhesus, Bernstein and Guilloud (1965) report the pig-tailed macaque (*M. nemestrina*) to be more docile than either of the above animals, and the *Cebus albifrons* to be tractable to the point of allowing blood sampling without restraint. Even though the squirrel and marmoset monkeys are small and not so threatening as larger animals, they can also present a handling problem that requires gloves. The marmoset, for example, is highly emotional and may react rather violently to handling or restraint.

The following steps are helpful in adapting an animal to the transport cage: (1) open the door of the transport; (2) place food near the open door; (3) place food at the center, and then at the closed end, as the animal is lured inside; (4) close the doors when the monkey enters; (5) release the monkey after a brief restraining period; and (6) repeat procedure. After daily adaptation (sometimes 7 to 10 days is necessary), force the animal into the transport by (1) opening one door and (2) directing the animal into the cage with a stick or broom by a slight push (do not strike the animal). The above adaptation procedures should result in an animal who enters the transport cage readily on experimental days. If a monkey is uncooperative, wave a broom or stick over the living cage, or enlist the aid of another laboratory worker.

Infant monkeys are hand-fed in the home cage when they will readily take solid foods. Adaptation to the transport cage is usually accomplished by (1) picking up the animal with a cloth diaper, (2) placing the monkey in the transport cage, and (3) removing the diaper. After a few days an attempt is made to coax the animal into the transport cage. If the monkey does not respond by entering, it is picked up with the diaper again and placed in the transport cage. This training of infants is continued until the animal enters the transport cage readily.

Gentleness is necessary; *never frighten an infant monkey.* Transport-cage training with the infant monkey is carried on concurrently with adaptation to the experimental cage.

In some instances monkeys are adapted to and confined in restraining chairs. The chairs are convenient and easy to transport, especially when placed in a transport frame on wheels, but specifications cited for commercial chairs are sometimes inadequate for proper seating of larger adult macaques. With plastic chairs, spare parts are necessary since sections of the restrainers often break under the strain of an overly active animal. Handling the animal is facilitated by administering a tranquilizing drug. Once the monkey is adapted to a chair, it is relatively easy to insert the chair and animal into a structural support in the experimental chamber, which sometimes consists of little more than an old refrigerator fitted with a stimulus display, response panel, and an inexpensive ventilating system. Implanted animals may be kept in the chairs for long periods of time with little danger of disturbing surgical preparations. A list of chair manufacturers is cited in the Appendix.

Adaptation to the experimental chamber is generally necessary whether the apparatus is a Skinner box or a Wisconsin General Test Apparatus (WGTA). Shaping procedures for Skinner-box research are similar to those described for pigeons (Reese, 1964) and rats (Michael, 1963) and will not be discussed here. The following steps are used for macaque, squirrel, or marmoset monkeys in adapting to classical WGTA procedures. (The WGTA is shown in Fig. 11-8.) It is important to note that the animal must be adapted to the tray, the foodwell, and the two screens before any experimental work is done. The treatment and training of the animal during this phase of operation is important and can have unknown effects upon later behavior if not carried out properly. During training (1) place the test tray forward, (2) hand-feed the animal, (3) place food in the center of the test tray away from the foodwell, and (4) alternate hand and

tray feeding until 25 bits of food have been taken. After the above treatment shape the animal to take food from the foodwell by placing the food in the well until 25 pieces have been taken. Next, adapt to the back-and-forth movement of the test tray by (1) placing a bit of food in the tray while it is pulled back and away from the animal, (2) pushing the tray to the animal and allowing him to eat, and (3) alternate hand and tray feedings until the animal accepts 25 pieces of food. Adaptation to the one-way-vision screen involves (1) pulling back the tray and inserting food in the well, (2) pushing the tray forward, (3) lowering the screen, and (4) repeating until the animal eats 25 pieces of food, alternately feeding by hand. To adapt to the forward screen, (1) slowly lower the opaque screen after pulling the tray back; (2) place food in the foodwell, which is now out of sight of the animal; (3) lower the one-way screen; (4) slowly raise the opaque screen; and (5) push the tray to the animal. Repeat to the same criteria mentioned earlier. Although alternate hand feeding is suggested here, little data are available concerning the influence of this variable upon later performance. For that matter, little empirical information is available concerning the overall stimulus effect that the experimenter's presence has upon animal performance.

Classical WGTA procedures require the displacement of a fixed object from a foodwell, e.g., square, circular, or triangular blocks of various types, but the animal must first be adapted to the fixed object.[1] This involves (1) using a gray training board with one foodwell, (2) placing a gray block behind the foodwell, and (3) successively approximating the animal to the covering of the well by moving the object over the hole a little at a time from trial to trial (procedure is that cited for adaptation to the opaque screen) until (4) the object must be displaced to obtain food. In all phases of adaptation, it is necessary that the experimenter use slow, easy movements as opposed to fast, jerky movements since the latter tend to frighten the animals. It is obvious that the animal is re-

---

[1] Some modified WGTA procedures merely require that the animal touch the object of choice, which is held in position by a slot or magnet for easy removal by the tester; or touch an automatic visual display panel. The monkey is rewarded by an automatic pellet dispenser.

quired to "pay attention" to the proceedings. Paying attention is generally rigidly and automatically controlled in Skinner-box methodology but is seldom operationally defined or consistent in WGTA work. Thus, the experimenter should be trained to start a trial only when the animal is paying attention, since monkeys often jump around and turn away from the display. Variability among experimenters in techniques for obtaining attention is tremendous and may contribute an effect that confounds the results.

Animals frequently grasp and hold objects used in WGTA discrimination studies, or vigorously push them off the apparatus. Since this interferes with the formal procedure, it is often advisable to insert small screw eyes in the object to allow for the attachment of a retaining chain.

The incentives used with monkeys vary. Skinner-box research generally utilizes commercial food pellets. The use of other foods in this research is often precluded because of the habitual employment of automatic pellet-dispensing equipment. WGTA research utilizes peanuts, raisins, corn kernels, grapes, and cut apples, as well as pellets, although liquid nutrients are used prior to 40 to 60 days of age (Harlow, 1959). A single raisin, peanut, or pellet is placed under the correct object on each trial; sections of grapes or apple are sometimes used when these are refused. Since squirrel and marmoset monkeys satiate easily, raisins or other food are generally cut into sections, a piece being used on each trial.[1]

[1] With marmoset monkeys care should be taken in selecting and placing foodwells because of the clawlike paws which occasionally handicap grasping.

Experimenters in some laboratories determine the specific food preference of each animal during the adaptation and training sessions and utilize the preferred food during the experimental session. This practice is similar to the preexperimental selection of preferred incentives by children (see Chap. 14).

Although some experimenters prefer to keep experimental animals on a deprivation diet—e.g., 20 to 24 hr without food, water, or both—others keep animals at 80 percent of normal body weight. The latter practice is common with squirrel monkeys, especially in operant conditioning research. With the WGTA, animals are normally used as subjects prior to their daily feeding period (water is kept in the home cage at all times). Regardless of apparatus or experimental problem, monkeys become very thirsty in experiments utilizing pellets, peanuts, or raisins as incentives. Care should be taken to protect animals from dehydration.

Monkeys have been used successfully in research utilizing liquid incentives, e.g., milk or glucose solutions, and electric shock. Before selecting lever-press apparatus for avoidance conditioning studies, however, the researcher is advised to read a discussion of some of the problems involved (Meyer, Cho, and Wesemann, 1960). Further discussions of the above variables may be found in Chap. 10, Operant Conditioning, and Chap. 11, Animal Learning.

REFERENCES

ANDERSON, N. H. Application of an additive model to impression formation. *Science,* 1962, **138,** 817–818.

ANDERSON, N. H. Comparison of different populations: Resistance to extinction and transfer. *Psychol. Rev.,* 1963, **70,** 162–179.

ARCHER, E. J., CEJKA J. E., and THOMPSON, C. P. Serial-trigram learning as a function of differential meaningfulness and sex of subjects and experimenters. *Canad. J. Psychol.,* 1961, **15,** 148–153.

BERNSTEIN, I. S., and GUILLOUD, N. P. Reevaluation of *Macaca speciosa* as a laboratory primate. *Lab. primate Newsletter,* 1965, **4,** 5–6.

BLOMQUIST, A. J., and HARLOW, H. F. The infant rhesus monkey program at the University of Wisconsin Primate Laboratory. *Proc. Animal Care Panel,* 1961, **11,** 57–64.

BROGDEN, W. J. The experimenter as a factor in animal conditioning. *Psychol. Rep.,* 1962, **11,** 239–242.

BULLOCK, D. H., ROBERTS, W. A., and BITTERMAN, M. E. Techniques of housing and maintaining a large pigeon colony. *J. exp. Anal. Behav.,* 1961, **4,** 285–286.

CAMPBELL, D. T., and STANLEY, J. C. Experimental

and quasi-experimental designs for research on teaching. In N. L. Gage (Ed.), *Handbook on research on teaching*. Chicago: Rand McNally, 1963.

CARMICHAEL, M., and MACLEAN, P. D. Use of squirrel monkey for brain research with description of restraining chair. *EEG Clin. Neurophysiol.*, 1961, **13**, 128–129.

CHAPANIS, A. *Research techniques in human engineering*. Baltimore: Johns Hopkins, 1959.

CHURCH, R. M. Systematic effect of random error in the yoked control design. *Psychol. Bull.*, 1964, **62**, 122–131.

COCHRAN, W. G., and COX, G. M. *Experimental designs*. (2nd ed.) New York: Wiley, 1957.

COX, D. R. *Planning of experiments*. New York: Wiley, 1958.

DAVENPORT, D. G., and GOULET, L. R. Motivational artifact in standard food deprivation schedules. *J. comp. physiol. Psychol.*, 1964, **57**, 237–240.

DeNIKE, L. D. The temporal relationship between awareness and performance in verbal conditioning. *J. exp. Psychol.*, 1964, **68**, 521–529.

DULANY, D. E. Hypotheses and habits in verbal "operant conditioning." *J. abnorm. soc. Psychol.*, 1961, **63**, 251–263.

DULANY, D. E. The place of hypotheses and intentions: An analysis of verbal control in verbal conditioning. In C. W. Eriksen (Ed.), *Behavior and awareness—A symposium of research*. Durham, N.C.: Duke Univ. Press, 1962.

EDWARDS, A. L. *Experimental designs in psychological research*. New York: Rinehart, 1960.

ERIKSEN, C. W., and DOROZ, L. Role of awareness in learning and the use of correlated extraneous cues on perceptual tasks. *J. exp. Psychol.*, 1963, **66**, 601–608.

FERSTER, C. B., and SKINNER, B. F. *Schedules of reinforcement*. New York: Appleton-Century Crofts, 1957.

FISHER, R. A., and YATES, F. *Statistical tables for biological agricultural and medical research*. New York: Hafner, 1957.

FRENCH, G. M. Performance of squirrel monkeys in variants of delayed response. *J. comp. physiol. Psychol.*, 1959, **52**, 741–745.

GOULD, J., and SMITH, K. U. Angular displacement of the visual feedback of motion. *Science*, 1962, **137**, 619–620.

GREGOVICH, R. P., and SIDOWSKI, J. B. Verbal reports of strategies in a two-person interaction. *Psychol. Rep.*, 1966, **19**, 641–642.

GRICE, G. R., and HUNTER, J. J. Stimulus intensity effects depend upon the type of experimental design. *Psychol. Rev.*, 1964, **71**, 247–256.

HAFNER, E., and WOODBURNE, L. S. Breeding Saimiri sciureus. *Lab. primate Newsletter.*, 1964, **3**, 15–16.

HARLOW, H. F. The development of learning set in the rhesus monkey. *Amer. Scientist*, 1959, **47**, 459–479.

HAYS, W. L. *Statistics for psychologists*. New York: Holt, Rinehart, and Winston, 1963.

HETHERINGTON, M., and ROSS, L. E. Effect of sex of subjects, sex of experimenter, and reinforcement condition on serial verbal learning. *J. exp. Psychol.*, 1963, **65**, 572–575.

KELLEHER, R. T., GILL, C. A., RIDDLE, W. C., and COOK, L. On the use of the squirrel monkey in behavioral and pharmacological experiments. *J. exp. Anal. Behav.*, 1963, **6**, 249–252.

KENDLER, H. H., and KENDLER, T. S. Vertical and horizontal processes in problem solving. *Psychol. Rev.*, 1962, **69**, 1–16.

KINTZ, B. L., DELPRATO, D. J., METTEE, D. R., PERSONS, C. E., and SCHAPPE, R. H. The experimenter effect. *Psychol. Bull.*, 1965, **63**, 223–232.

KLEBAN, M. H. Strain differences in an experimental study of punishment. *Psychol. Rep.*, 1965, **16**, 531–536.

KLING, A., and ORBACH, J. The stump tailed macaque: A promising laboratory primate: *Science*, 1963, **139**, 45–46.

KLING, J. W., HOROWITZ, L., and DELHAGEN, J. E. Light as a positive reinforcer for rat responding. *Psychol. Rep.*, 1956, **2**, 337–340.

KRASNER, L. Studies of the conditioning of verbal behavior. *Psychol. Bull.*, 1958, **55**, 148–170.

KURTZ, K. H. *Foundations of psychological research*. Boston: Allyn & Bacon, 1965.

LEVONIAN, E. Analysis of physiological response to film. *Psychophys. Newsltr.*, 1963, **9**, 31–42.

LINDQUIST, E. F. *Design and analysis of experiments in psychology and education*. Boston: Houghton-Mifflin, 1953.

LOCKARD, R. B. Self-regulated exposure to light by albino rats as a function of rearing luminance and test luminance. *J. comp. physiol. Psychol.*, 1963, **56**, 558–564.

MCGUIGAN, F. J. Experimenter: A neglected stimulus object. *Psychol. Bull.*, 1963, **60**, 421–428.

MASON, W. A., and HARLOW, H. F. Learned approach by infant rhesus monkeys to the sucking situation. *Psychol. Rep.*, 1958, **4**, 78–82.

MASON, W. A., and HARLOW, H. K. Initial responses of rhesus monkeys to solid foods. *Psychol. Rep.*, 1959, **5**, 193–199.

MEYER, D. R., CHO, C., and WESEMANN, A. S. On problems of conditioning discriminated lever-press avoidance responses. *Psychol. Rev.*, 1960, **67**, 224–228.

MICHAEL, J. *Laboratory studies in operant behavior*. New York: McGraw-Hill, 1963.

MILES, R. C. Learning-set formation in the squirrel monkey. *J. comp. physiol. Psychol.*, 1957, **50**, 356–357.

MILES, R. C. Color vision in the squirrel monkey. *J. comp. physiol. Psychol.*, 1958, **51**, 328–331.

MILES, R. C., and MEYER, D. R. Learning sets in marmosets. *J. comp. physiol. Psychol.*, 1956, **49**, 219–222.

NAKAMURA, C. Y., and ANDERSON, N. H. Avoidance behavior differences within and between strains of rats. *J. comp. physiol. Psychol.*, 1962, **55**, 740–747.

ORNE, M. T. On the social psychology of the psychological experiment: With particular reference to demand characteristics and their implications. *Amer. Psychologist*, 1962, **17**, 776–783.

PATTERSON, C. H. Matching versus randomization in studies of counseling. *J. counsel. Psychol.*, 1956, **3**, 262–271.

POSTMAN, L. Short-term memory and incidental learning. In A. W. Melton (Ed.), *Categories of human learning*. New York: Academic Press, 1964.

THE RAND CORPORATION. *A million digits with 100,000 normal deviates*. Glencoe, Ill.: Free Press, 1955.

REESE, E. P. *Experiments in operant conditioning*. New York: Appleton-Century-Crofts, 1964.

RIECKEN, H. W. A program for research on experiments in social psychology. Paper presented at Univ. of New Mexico, 1958.

ROSENTHAL, R. Experimenter outcome-orientation and the results of the psychology experiment. *Psychol. Bull.*, 1964, **61**, 405–412.

SANDLER, J., and STONE, W. F. Laboratory observations of two subspecies of marmosets. *Psychol. Rep.*, 1963, **13**, 139–144.

SARASON, I. G., and MINARD, J. Interrelationships among subjects, experimenters, and situational variables. *J. abnorm. soc. Psychol.*, 1963, **67**, 87–91.

SCOTT, W. A., and WERTHEIMER, M. *Introduction to psychological research*. New York: Wiley, 1962.

SIDMAN, M. *Tactics of scientific research*. New York: Basic Books, 1960.

SIDOWSKI, J. B., KOSTANZER, A., NAUMOFF, H., and SMITH, M. Variables influencing learning in a minimal social situation. *Amer. Psychologist*, 1960, **15**, 490 (Abstract).

SIDOWSKI, J. B., and NAUMOFF, H. Pacing, problem-solving instructions, and hypothesis testing in verbal conditioning. *Psychol. Rep.*, 1964, **15**, 351–354.

SIDOWSKI, J. B., and NUTHMANN, C. Influence of induced tension and incentive upon performance and eyeblink rate in a verbal learning task. Paper presented at meetings of *Midwestern Psychol. Assoc.*, 1956.

SIDOWSKI, J. B., and SMITH, M. Sex and game instructions in a minimal social situation. *Psychol. Rep.*, 1961, **8**, 393–397.

SIDOWSKI, J. B., KOPSTEIN, F. F., and SHILLESTAD, I. J. Prompting and confirmation variables in verbal learning. *Psychol. Rep.*, 1961, **8**, 401–406.

SMITH, K. U. *Delayed sensory feedback and behavior*. Philadelphia: Saunders, 1962.

SPIELBERGER, C. D., and LEVIN, S. M. What is learned in verbal conditioning. *J. verb. learn. verb. behav.*, 1962, **1**, 125–132.

STELLAR, E. The marmoset as a laboratory animal: Maintenance, general observations of behavior, and simple learning. *J. comp. physiol. Psychol.*, 1960, **53**, 1–10.

STEVENSON, H. W., and ALLEN, S. Adult performance as a function of sex of experimenter and sex of subject. *J. abnorm. soc. Psychol.*, 1964, **68**, 214–216.

STORMS, L. H., BOROCZI, G., and BROEN, W. E., JR. Effects of punishment as a function of strain of rat and duration of shock. *J. comp. physiol. Psychol.*, 1963, **56**, 1022–1026.

TROFFER, S., and TART, C. T. Experimenter bias in hypnotist performance. *Science*, 1964, **145**, 1330–1331.

TURNER, L. H., and SOLOMON, R. L. Human traumatic avoidance learning: Theory and experiments on the operant-respondent distinction and failures to learn. *Psychol. Monogr.*, 1962, **76**, No. 40 (Whole No. 559).

UNDERWOOD, B. J. Speed of learning and amount retained: A consideration of methodology. *Psychol. Bull.*, 1954, **51**, 276–282.

UNDERWOOD, B. J. *Psychological research*. New York: Appleton-Century-Crofts, 1957.

VERPLANCK, W. S., and OSKAMP, E. Equivalent effects of reinforcing card placement and hypothesis statement in maintaining a concept under partial reinforcement. *Amer. Psychologist*, 1956, **11**, 421 (Abstract).

WINER, B. J. *Statistical principles in experimental design*. New York: McGraw-Hill, 1962.

ZIMNY, G. H. *Method in experimental psychology*. New York: Ronald Press, 1961.

The following publications are available to laboratories from the Institute of Laboratory Animal Resources, National Academy of Sciences–National Research Council, 2101 Constitution Ave., N.W., Washington 25, D.C.:

1. *Standards for breeding, care and management of laboratory mice* (ILAR).
2. *Standards for the breeding, care and management of laboratory rats* (ILAR).

3. *Guide for laboratory animal facilities and care* (ACP-ILAR).
4. *Principles of laboratory animal care* (ILAR).
5. *Laboratory facilities for small mammals,* Charles H. Southwick. Reprinted from *Turtox News,* 1959, **37,** 2–3.
6. *References on the design of animal quarters.* Reprinted from *Bull. med. Res.,* January–February, 1957.
7. *Optimum cage sizes for rats* (West Foundation).
8. *Thoughts concerning the design of animal quarters.* N. R. Brewer and T. W. Penfold. Reprinted from *Proc. Animal Care Panel,* December, 1961.

The following publication is available from the Printing and Publishing Office, National Academy of Sciences, 2101 Constitution Ave., N.W., Washington, D.C.:

1. *Laboratory Animals: Animals for research,* Publication No. 1413, revised 1966. (Catalog of commercial sources).

Chapter 2

BASIC INSTRUMENTATION

JOSEPH B. SIDOWSKI *and* MANUEL J. SMITH

This chapter presents a few of the fundamentals of electricity and electronics and emphasizes the utilization of solid state circuits. Black-box descriptions are provided for equipment that is purchased commercially and generally requires professional maintenance.

The chapter begins with a general discussion of analog and digital concepts, following which various sections cover d-c power supplies, active circuit control devices, schematic reading and module analysis, analog amplifiers and transducers, signal generators, digital stimulus displays, electronic test instruments and troubleshooting, and advanced transistor circuits.

Additional information on transistors may be found in Cleary (1962), Department of the Army TM 11-690 (1959), The Department of Defense Military Handbook 215 (1960), and Schure (1961); Conti (1958) discusses semiconductor diodes. Information on constructing etched-circuit boards and heat sinks is covered in Bailey (1963) and Gyorki (1963), respectively. Current developments in instrumentation are reported in the publications listed at the end of this chapter. A detailed list of equipment and parts suppliers is referenced in the Appendix.

ANALOG AND DIGITAL CONCEPTS

Analog information is continuous in form and is read out as an approximate position on a continuous scale; digital information is discrete and is read out as a digit or series of digits. We might think of digital information as analog information that is sampled often and quantified into discrete numbers. This means that numbers are assigned to range intervals of the analog data, and whenever the analog response value is within a particular interval, the number assigned to that interval is recorded. This number represents the analog value. The system is usually calibrated, and the number recorded has a direct mathematical relationship to the analog range interval that it represents. The amount of error introduced is a function of the width of the analog range interval or of the sensitivity of the quantifying instrument. Digitizing analog information also implies discontinuity since a time base is used to determine the time at which analog values are sampled.

It is obvious, of course, that data of some kind are being generated continuously by any organism. If respiration rate is being measured, the animal does not stop breathing simply because the experimenter stops meas-

33

uring it. Any discontinuity is due to the rate at which the data are being sampled. Even a simple button press outputs digital information that represents quantized analog data. In this instance, the basic response measure is the amount of force generated by the muscles of the arm and hand in pushing the button. A defined response occurs when the muscular force exceeds the analog range limit necessary to trip a spring lever inside the push-button switch. All partial responses are not recorded, e.g., resting the finger on the switch or pushing the switch lightly, although all these responses are part of a continuous physiological movement that eventually results in the operationally defined response and a digital value.

But when analog data are translated into digital, some information is lost. The experimenter, therefore, is faced with a choice between large amounts of detailed and unwieldy analog data that are difficult to process and analyze and incomplete digital data in easily manipulable numerical form. If the data are recorded in analog form, the experimenter still faces the problem of quantizing the information for processing, for much of the analog data will be of no practical interest. Thus, the choice is generally a compromise between complete records of continuous data and samples of the data containing, hopefully, most of the important information. The researcher's choice is determined by the problem and by the selection and limits of the apparatus at his disposal.

If the experimenter chooses the digital mode, he will deal generally with either a decimal or a binary number system. In the decimal system, data or stimuli are represented by 10 digits 0 to 9, with the higher numerical values, e.g, 20, 30, 40, . . . , 100, being expansions of the first 10 digits by decades. In the binary system, a datum or stimulus event occurs or it does not occur. When the event occurs, a binary logic 1 is recorded; if it does not occur, a binary logic 0 is recorded. This allows for simplicity, and the occurrence or nonoccurrence of the event may be represented electrically by a simple switch. Logic 1 is the

ON position, which supplies electrical energy to some item or apparatus subcircuit, while logic 0 represents OFF. Because of its simplicity, the binary system requires fewer switches or channels than the decimal system to handle the same amount of information. Thus, the electrical processing of data and stimulus events is usually done in binary form. In fact, the internal operations of digital computers are executed solely in the binary mode.

Because we generally deal with information of various kinds, we must often convert analog information to digital form, decimal information to binary form, and vice versa. A decimal-to-binary converter has an input of zero through nine electrical events and a binary electrical output. This is convenient since it allows us to think and use our common decimal numerical language at the input side and to utilize the more electrically expedient binary form at the output. The binary output consists of a coded combination of four signal channels in either an ON or an OFF condition. A binary coded decimal (BCD) system is useful since any of 10, or up to 16, events may be recorded or processed by using four channels (switches). An analog-to-digital converter (ADC) takes continuous analog inputs and outputs a signal in digital form, usually in BCD, at each time sample interval. The digital output corresponds to the range interval of the analog input. In a typical example, galvanic skin responses (GSRs) are recorded in analog form and converted to digital form on either punched paper tape, punched cards, or magnetic tape, which allows them to be fed into a computer with little or no preprocessing. Without the converter (ADC), the analog data are represented by the continuous sweep of an inked pen across calibrated moving chart paper. Refer to Part Six of this volume for additional information on analog and digital technology and to Brown and Thorne (1964) for a detailed discussion of the basic operations of digital logic. The remainder of this chapter will incorporate some of these concepts into our discussions of electronic equipment and circuitry. First, however, we shall present a brief review of basic electricity and electronics, including a discussion of series and parallel circuits as well as d-c power supplies.

ELECTRICITY AND ELECTRONICS

Electricity and electronics deal with the activity of electrical charges. The term *electronics* is limited to the actions of charges in vacuum tubes, gas tubes, and solid state devices, such as transistors and semiconductor diodes. Electrical items such as resistors, capacitors, coils, and transformers are used in circuits to control the activity of the electrons. *Circuit* is a term used to describe a connection of wires and electric components across a voltage source; i.e., a circuit forms a closed path through which current can flow. *Current* refers to the flow of positive or negative electric charges. These charges are repelled by a point that has an excess of electrons and are attracted to a point with less than the normal number of electrons. A point that repels electrons is considered to have a *negative potential,* and a point that attracts has a *positive potential. Voltage* refers to the difference in potential between these points. For example, an electrical wall outlet[1] or a battery has two terminals, one of which theoretically has an excess and the other a deficiency of electrons, resulting in a voltage difference between the two points. When an electric wire connects the two points, electrons flow through the conductor; i.e., a current flows. Normally, an electric wire is not the only item used to connect the points. Various electrical and/or electronic items are placed in the circuit and the pathway arranged so that electrons flow through these items. If the item is a light bulb and the correct voltage is used, it will light. If a switch is placed in the circuit, we can turn the item on or off, i.e., make or break

[1] With 60 cps a-c current the potential changes continuously with time.

the circuit. The circuit becomes more complicated as we add various items to control electron flow.

Before the advent of electron theory, current was presumed to flow from positive to negative, and many sources still cite current flow in this direction. Since *electron current flows from negative to positive*, the researcher should be certain of the notation used in any discussion. The direction of current flow is important since devices such as tubes, diodes, transistors, and certain types of capacitor are *polarized*. When these devices are *forward-biased*, i.e., have positive terminals connected to positive voltage and negative terminals to negative voltage, they operate properly. When they are *reverse-biased*, i.e., voltage connections are reversed, they operate differently or improperly.

Any circuit can have more than one point of potential difference. Therefore, most circuits have a *reference point of zero potential.* This common reference potential is called *ground,* and the most common ground is the earth.

To use electric energy in instrumentation work, material must be utilized that conducts this energy adequately. Conducting material also has some resistivity, i.e., it offers opposition to the flow of current. Indeed, most items that are part of a circuit offer some opposition to current flow, with the amount of opposition varying as a function of the item or material. *Resistance, capacitance,* and *inductance* are basic elements in circuits that supply opposition to current flow. Most items in a circuit have some of each type of opposition. Actual *resistors, capacitors,* and *inductors* are often inserted in circuits to control current flow, but the concept of opposition is an important consideration in the selection and use of most items, including light bulbs, amplifiers, and electric wire.

Current flow may be categorized as direct or alternating. *Direct current* refers to current flowing in one direction; i.e., the applied voltage does not alternate its polarity regularly. *Alternating current* changes direction periodically; i.e., the polarity regularly swings back and forth from positive to negative.

Either alternating current or direct current may be obtained from several types of voltage sources, with the battery serving as one simple type of direct-current (d-c) source. Batteries are polarized; i.e., one terminal is labeled or considered to be plus and one minus, with a voltage difference between the two electrical points. Typical output voltage ratings for batteries are 1.5, 6, 12, 48, and 110 volts. These voltage levels are usually described by referring to their polarity, positive or negative, with respect to the zero voltage point, ground. For example, the two terminals of a simple 1.5-volt flashlight battery are labeled + and −. In describing its use in a circuit, the experimenter could call one terminal +1.5 and the other −1.5, but this gives the impression that there is a 3 volts algebraic difference between them. This expression should be avoided. One of the terminals is arbitrarily called ground, or zero volts, and the other +1.5 volts or −1.5 volts with respect to ground. This arbitrary ground

need not have electrical continuity with the actual earth ground.

In some circuits, a battery supply is impractical since all batteries lose their charge with continued use and have to be replaced, if they are of the dry-cell type, or taken out of the circuit and recharged, if of the wet-cell type. An alternative source of electric energy is the regular alternating-current (a-c) house-line voltage. In this type of a-c power circuit, the current flow changes direction many times per second (sec). This is due to a change in voltage polarity occurring many times per sec and is obtained from the power source of the local electric company where the armature of a huge generator rotates once each $\frac{1}{60}$ sec. As the generator is rotated, i.e., its phase angle is shifted, its output voltage rises to a positive peak (see Fig. 2-1). As the generator is rotated still more, the voltage drops through zero or ground voltage to a negative peak. When the generator is rotated to the starting position, the voltage rises to ground again. This cycle takes $\frac{1}{60}$ sec. The number of cycles per second (cps) defines the *frequency* of a-c volt-

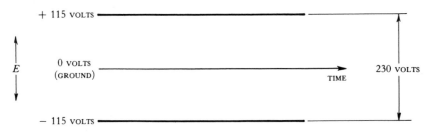

(a) D-C VOLTAGE STRAIGHT-LINE CHARACTERISTIC

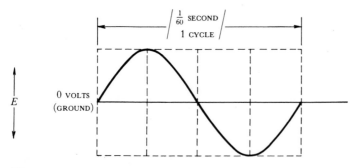

(b) A-C VOLTAGE SINE WAVE CHARACTERISTIC

Fig. 2-1   A comparison of d-c and a-c voltage characteristics.

age. A *sine wave* is the commonly occurring waveshape that results from this action. Unfortunately, many circuits require other types of waveshape which means that the naturally occurring sine wave obtained from the standard electrical wall outlet is purposely shaped, distorted, or manipulated in various ways to obtain the required signal. In fact, the most common source of d-c power in instrumentation work is a power supply with an a-c input.

The opposition of a resistor to d-c and a-c electron flow is defined as *resistance* and can be fabricated so that it is essentially independent of frequency. The opposition of a capacitor to a-c electron flow is *capacitive reactance,* which is different from resistor opposition because it has different phase relations, and it depends on frequency. The third type of opposition in a circuit is provided by inductors and is called *inductive reactance. Impedance* refers to the total opposition to alternating current, i.e., the combined opposition of resistance and reactance. Although the three oppositions to current flow are different, they are all measured in ohms.

Any conductors carrying current, including wires and resistors, induce an electromagnetic field. Changes in this field define *inductance,* which is a basic property of all circuits (resistance and capacitance are the other two). With wires and resistors the development of an electromagnetic field is unintentional, but with transformers it is used to increase or decrease an applied voltage. A basic *transformer* consists of two coils of wire, a primary (input) and secondary (output), wrapped around a core. If an a-c voltage is impressed upon the windings of the primary, a magnetic field is generated and a voltage is induced in the secondary coil which is coupled to the primary. A secondary coil containing more turns than the primary boosts the voltage. A secondary with fewer windings lowers the primary voltage.

There are only three basic electronic circuits: the *rectifier, oscillator,* and *amplifier.* All others are variations of these three. None of these circuits creates energy; i.e., each re-

quires a power source, generally d-c, for the operation of its tubes or semiconductor devices. In d-c power supplies, transformers are used to control the level of a-c input voltage to a rectifier. A rectifier converts alternating current to direct current by means of a tube or a semi-conductor device called a *diode.* An oscillator produces a required frequency in the form of either a sinusoidal or a non-sinusoidal output. Amplifiers enlarge or amplify signals in current, voltage, or power. Note that *impedance matching* is necessary for the maximum transfer of power from the amplifier to the load. Impedance matching refers to the equating of the two impedances.

Tubes used in electronic circuits are of two types: vacuum and gas. The *vacuum* tube is the most common and the diode tube the simplest. A diode contains a cathode and a plate, or anode, as its two basic elements, and a filament (heater) to heat the cathode. When the cathode is heated, it emits electrons which are attracted to the plate. Changing plate potential also controls current flow. When used as a rectifier, the diode plate is alternately made more positive and more negative than the cathode. A *triode* has a control grid as a third element placed between the plate and cathode. The third element controls the electron flow from cathode to plate. Triodes are used as amplifiers.

A vacuum-tube amplifier is similar in operation to a transistor. The three elements of the triode (cathode, grid, and anode, or plate) are analogous in function to the emitter, base, and collector of the NPN transistor respectively. Although the vacuum tube is a common item in most commercial analog amplifiers, it is rapidly being replaced by newer transistor circuits. The transistor has completely replaced the vacuum tube in digital circuits. The thyratron is a highly sensitive gas tube used in control switching circuits as a substitute for slower switching relays. A solid state control switching device, namely the silicon controlled rectifier (SCR), is replacing the tube in even this application. It is only a matter of time until the vacuum

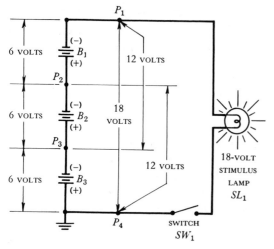

Fig. 2-2 Batteries in series: individual voltage ratings add to the voltage output of the series.

tube is relegated to exotic special-purpose applications. Readers interested in tube circuitry specific to research in the behavioral sciences are referred to Cornsweet (1963), Donaldson (1958), Grings (1954), and Stacy (1960).

We have noted that solid state electronics is represented by transistors and semiconductor diodes. *Solid state* refers to the fact that these items are solids, while *semiconductor* defines the material that has electrical resistance falling in a range between insulators and conductors. Two types of semiconductor material are germanium and silicon. This material is processed to a crystalline state (a poor conductor) and has to be modified to obtain current flow. The *N-type semiconductor* is obtained by adding pentavalent impurity atoms, such as arsenic, to the crystalline structure, resulting in a current flow consisting of an excess of negative electrons. The *P-type* modifies the crystalline material, e.g., with trivalent boron, so that it has spaces (holes) in the structure. Current flow is a function of these holes, which simulate positive charges.

Transistors have the following advantages over tubes: (1) they are small, (2) their circuitry is generally more simple and the number of circuit items fewer, (3) they permit subminiaturization and the use of printed cir-

cuits,[1] (4) their power consumption is lower, (5) they generally require lower voltages, (6) they deteriorate very little over indefinite periods of use, and (7) they require no "warm-up" periods to function properly. The sensitivity of transistor amplification parameters to temperature changes has required highly sophisticated circuit design to minimize this possible source of artifact and measurement error in transistorized analog amplifiers. Transistorized analog circuits have become still more complex to overcome difficulties arising from their typically low internal resistance, as compared with electron tubes. Solid state research in the space exploration fields is rapidly overcoming the few problems that semiconductors offer and is leading to the development of microminiaturization. The advantages of transistors over relays are cited in the section on transistors (pages 56 to 63)].

Detailed information covering the characteristics and utilization of solid state items is available throughout this chapter. Additional information is available from the sources cited earlier.

Series and parallel circuits

Three basic electrical concepts are *electromotive force* (emf), *resistance*, and *current flow*. The electrical unit of each is the volt, ohm, and ampere, respectively. If the voltage is increased or the resistance is decreased, more current will flow in the circuit. The relationship between voltage E, resistance R, and current I is described by Ohm's law, which states that $E/R = I$, $E/I = R$, or $E = IR$, where E is in volts, R in ohms, and I in amperes. A *volt* can be defined as that electromotive force which, when applied across 1 ohm of resistance, produces 1 ampere (amp) of current flow through the resistance. This formal statement, in a sense, also defines a circuit.

Resistive stimulus components such as a stimulus lamp, as well as other items in a cir-

[1] *Printed circuits* are electric circuits in which wiring is replaced by a conductive material. The conductive material is applied to sheets of glass, plastic, or ceramic.

cuit, have an *input voltage rating*. This means that they will not work properly or will work only marginally unless connected to a voltage source equal to their input voltage ratings. If an experimenter uses a 6-volt battery to light a stimulus lamp with an 18-volt rating, the lamp will glow dimly and not deliver the full illumination level produced by 18 volts. If the two terminals of the lamp are connected to a battery with a voltage rating higher than 18 volts, the lamp will illuminate brightly but have a shorter life expectancy.

If only 6-volt batteries are available, the power-source voltage may be raised to 18 volts by placing three 6-volt batteries in a series. The terms *series* and *parallel* describe two classes of circuit, a common third class being a combination of the two, i.e., *series-parallel*. Figure 2-2 shows a series battery circuit for lighting an 18-volt stimulus lamp with more than one battery. A series battery (⊸⊣⊢⊸) circuit refers to the way that the batteries are wired together, end to end, with the plus terminal of the first battery connected to the minus terminal of the second, the plus terminal of the second battery connected to the minus terminal of the third, and so on. When two or more batteries are placed in series, with the current equal in all parts, the individual battery voltages add to the total voltage across points P_1 and P_4. If a switch (⊸—⊶) SW_1 is wired between one side of the series battery and the stimulus lamp (⊗) SL_1, the

lamp will light at its full illumination when the switch is thrown to the ON, or closed, position (⊸—⊶), completing the electric circuit.

If an experimenter uses a single 18-volt battery to power more than one stimulus lamp at a time, e.g., to generate various light patterns, as shown in Fig. 2-3, the combined low resistance of the lamps that are lit will result in a large current flow. This will quickly deplete the battery and cause the lamps to dim, changing the stimulus environment. The experimenter can minimize this dimming effect by placing additional 18-volt batteries in *parallel* with the original battery shown in Fig. 2-3. When two or more batteries are placed in parallel, positive terminals are wired to positive, and negative terminals wired to negative. Under these conditions, the total current ratings of the batteries are additive. This results in a slower rate of depletion of their energy.

The concepts of series and parallel arrangements are important since all electronic components in circuits are arranged in series or parallel, or both. The experimenter can discern whether items are in series or parallel and determine their consequent voltage contributions to a circuit by examining the connections between terminals.

Regardless of circuit arrangements, the researcher's primary interest concerns the activity of the output component producing the

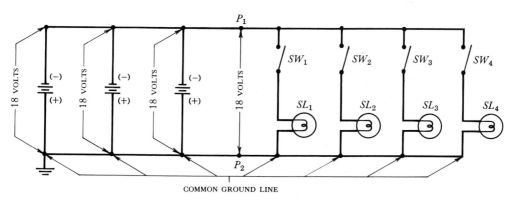

Fig. 2-3   Batteries in parallel: Current ratings add to the current output of the power source.

conditions necessary for the experiment, e.g., the operation of a shock generator, the appearance of a stimulus light at timed intervals, or the activity of a reinforcement dispenser. In many instances, it is not possible to connect these components *directly* to a power source and have them operate in the fashion that the experimental paradigm dictates. Other items, which may be thought of as controlling the operation of these components, must be placed between them and the power source. For this reason, it is necessary to examine the electrical operation of certain common control components that have no direct influence on a subject's performance but are necessary for the proper operation of the apparatus. The resistor and capacitor are the simplest and most common of these components.

Resistance

Unlike the stimulus components, which have some output function (light, sound) and

have some nominal resistance limiting current flow, the *resistor's primary function is to impede current flow in a circuit.* For example, if an experimenter wishes to use a 2-volt stimulus lamp and a 2-volt battery is unavailable, a resistor can be placed in series with the stimulus lamp, "dropping" the 6 volts of the battery and preventing the lamp from being overloaded and destroyed. A complete circuit to protect the stimulus lamp is shown in Fig. 2-4. This circuit has a battery ($\dashv\vdash$) as a power source, a 10-ohm (Ω) 2-volt stimulus lamp ($\bigotimes$) to provide the stimulus output, a resistor ($\dashv\!\!\wedge\!\!\wedge\!\!\wedge\!\!\dashv$) to limit current flow, an ammeter ($\textcircled{\scriptsize I}$) to indicate the amount of current flow, and an ON-OFF switch ($\dashv\!\!\frown\!\!\dashv$) to close and open the circuit. The ammeter has a negligible resistance, typically less than 1 ohm, and, for practical purposes, its resistance need not be considered.

When we say that 2 volts are needed across the terminals of the stimulus lamp to operate it properly, we mean that the stimulus lamp should have a *voltage drop* (VD) or difference of 2 volts from one terminal to the other. Since there is a VD of 6 volts across the two battery terminals, it is necessary to get rid of 4 volts. This is the purpose of resistor R_1. Resistor R_1 should be chosen so that it will have a 4-volt drop across its terminals. This can be done by specifying the amount of current it allows to flow in the circuit. From the stimulus-lamp specifications, i.e., two input volts across its terminals and 10 ohms internal resistance, and Ohm's law $E/R = I$, we see that the lamp operates at its nominal illumination with 0.2-amp current flowing through it. Since the nominal illumination of the stimulus lamp may be specified by saying that it has 2 volts across its terminals, or 0.2 amp flowing through it, we can specify the resistor needed in the 6-volt circuit to limit the illumination of the stimulus lamp. This is done by choosing a resistor that passes 0.2 amp when it is placed in the circuit. In a series circuit, an equal amount of current flows through each resistive component. Requiring that the resistor have a voltage drop of 4 volts across its termi-

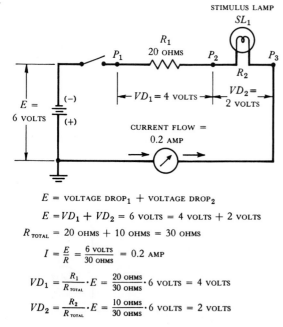

$E = \text{VOLTAGE DROP}_1 + \text{VOLTAGE DROP}_2$

$E = VD_1 + VD_2 = 6 \text{ VOLTS} = 4 \text{ VOLTS} + 2 \text{ VOLTS}$

$R_{\text{TOTAL}} = 20 \text{ OHMS} + 10 \text{ OHMS} = 30 \text{ OHMS}$

$I = \dfrac{E}{R} = \dfrac{6 \text{ VOLTS}}{30 \text{ OHMS}} = 0.2 \text{ AMP}$

$VD_1 = \dfrac{R_1}{R_{\text{TOTAL}}} \cdot E = \dfrac{20 \text{ OHMS}}{30 \text{ OHMS}} \cdot 6 \text{ VOLTS} = 4 \text{ VOLTS}$

$VD_2 = \dfrac{R_2}{R_{\text{TOTAL}}} \cdot E = \dfrac{10 \text{ OHMS}}{30 \text{ OHMS}} \cdot 6 \text{ VOLTS} = 2 \text{ VOLTS}$

Fig. 2-4   A simple voltage dividing network. This circuit uses a series resistor to drop the voltage supplied to a stimulus lamp from 6 to 2 volts.

,nals and that it pass 0.2 amp of current results in a desired resistance value of 20 ohms.

The resistor and the stimulus lamp in Fig. 2-4 form a *voltage divider* across the battery. This means that the VD across each resistance is proportional to its fractional value of the total circuit resistance. A general expression for the VD across any resistance R_i in a resistive series circuit is

$$VD_i = \frac{(E) \cdot R_i}{(R_1 + R_2 \cdots + R_i \cdots + R_n)}$$

where VD_i is the voltage drop across R_i; $R_i/(R_1 + R_2 \ldots + R_i \ldots + R_n)$ is the fractional value of R_i to the total resistance of the circuit, and E is the total circuit voltage (the battery voltage). It can be shown that

$$E = VD_1 + VD_2 \cdots + VD_i \cdots + VD_n$$

This means that the VD across each resistance add to the circuit voltage E. Since any series circuit has the same amount of current flowing through all the resistances, the VD across any of the resistances is determined from Ohm's law: $VD_i = R_i \cdot I$. The voltage-division technique is very useful in tracing through a circuit and should be fully understood.

If the 20-ohm resistor needed in Fig. 2-4 is not available, any two resistors whose values add to 20 ohms can be substituted in series to keep the same amount of current flow. If a 20-ohm resistor is not available, two 40-ohm resistors can be substituted in parallel and still pass the required amount of current. The general expression for the total resistance in a series circuit is

$$R_{\text{total}} = R_1 + R_2 \cdots + R_i \cdots + R_n$$

indicating that all resistances sum to the total resistance in the circuit. The expression for the total resistance in a parallel circuit is

$$\frac{1}{R_{\text{total}}} = \frac{1}{R_1} + \frac{1}{R_2} \cdots + \frac{1}{R_i} \cdots + \frac{1}{R_n}$$

that is, the sum of the reciprocals of the individual resistances in the circuit is equal to the reciprocal of the total resistance. This makes sense if you view the reciprocal of resistances as conductance (the mho). For example, at 1 volt the mho value and the ampere value are the same (Ohm's law). At any other voltage, the mho value and the amperage differ by a multiplicative factor. This multiplicative factor is the voltage, i.e., mho = $1/R$, $I = (E) \cdot 1/R$. The individual conductances in the parallel circuit add to the total conductance, which in turn is the reciprocal of the total resistance in the circuit.

Since a resistor can be overloaded and destroyed, resistors must be selected for their power ratings, in watts. The *watt* value indicates the amount of heat that the resistor can dissipate before it overheats and becomes inoperative. The higher the wattage rating, the more heat the resistor can dissipate. To determine the necessary watt value for a resistance, multiply the VD across the resistor by the current flowing through it (power rating in watts = $VD \cdot I$). The more voltage impressed across a fixed resistance, the greater the current flow; hence, the higher the resistor power rating has to be to avoid heat damage. The power rating of a resistor is usually indicated by its physical size. The larger the resistor, the greater its power rating. In the common carbon composition resistors, four power sizes are used typically: 0.25, 0.5, 1.0, and 2.0 watts. Higher power ratings are available with wire-wound resistors. Power ratings are often coded on resistors by manufacturers, so consult the manufacturer's technical data sheets.

Resistance values, in *ohms*, are printed on the resistor surface or given by a color-coded band of rings. Table 2-1 shows the resistor color codes. Note that the first significant digit of the resistance value is given by the first color band. This color band is the closest to one end of the resistor. The second color band indicates the second significant digit of the resistance value. With the two digits taken as a whole number between 1 and 99, the third color band provides the proper decimal multiplier to set the decimal place. For exam-

Table 2-1   Resistor color code

Color	First band, 1st digit	Second band, 2nd digit	Third band, multiply by	Fourth band, tolerance, %
Black	0	0	1	—
Brown	1	1	10	—
Red	2	2	100	—
Orange	3	3	1,000	—
Yellow	4	4	10,000	—
Green	5	5	100,000	—
Blue	6	6	1,000,000	—
Violet	7	7	—	—
Gray	8	8	—	—
White	9	9	—	—
Gold	—	—	0.1	5
Silver	—	—	0.01	10
No band	—	—	—	20

ple, a resistor with color bands of yellow, violet, and red, respectively, has two significant digits, 47, and a decimal multiplier of 10^{+2}, or 100. The resistance is 4,700 ohms ($47 \cdot 100 = 4,700$). For resistive values below 10 ohms, the first band might be black (zero); or a gold (0.1) or silver (0.01) color could be used in the third band as a decimal multiplier. The fourth color band is used to indicate the error tolerance (± 5 percent, ± 10 percent, or ± 20 percent).

A different coding system is used on resistors certified to meet certain Joint Army-Navy specifications (JAN SPEC), also known as United States military specifications (MIL SPEC). Since laboratories often use terminated inventories of military equipment as a source of circuit parts, a partial listing of the MIL SPEC resistor coding is presented in Table 2-2. Identical commercial resistors not intended for military use often have their resistance value coded with the same number system; however, the letter prefixes and suffixes are different. These letter codes are idiosyncratic to the manufacturer, and his technical data sheets must be consulted for meaning.

Adjustable (variable) resistors are (1) controlled by a sliding contact, which is difficult to adjust, or (2) easily adjusted by a shaft that projects from the circular resistance unit. The second type is called a *potentiometer* (*pot*). A *rheostat* is a potentiometer designed for higher power ratings. Potentiometers have connections at the two ends and at the tap, and rheostats usually have a center tap and one end terminal.

Capacitance

A capacitor (condenser) has the property of storing an electric charge after a voltage has been applied to its two terminals. Like a battery, it can store a charge; but, unlike a battery, it can be charged or discharged almost immediately. A capacitor consists of two metallic plates separated by a dielectric insulating material. Theoretically it should hold its charge indefinitely. However, leakage between the plates dissipates the charge over time.

The basic unit of capacitance is the *farad*. This value is too large for practical circuit application, so the common units are the microfarad (μf) and the micromicrofarad ($\mu\mu f$), also known as the picofarad (pf). Commonly used capacitors range from 20,000 microfarads (20 kμf) to 1 $\mu\mu f$. Larger-value capacitors, i.e., over 0.01 μf, are usually polarized and encased in a metal can since they may contain a wet dielectric. Smaller capacitors are nonpolarized and made of paper and tinfoil, ceramics, or mica. Irrespective of size and appearance, the choice of a capacitor is dictated by the farad value and the maximum voltage rating. The latter value is the maximum voltage for operating the capacitor continuously. A peak voltage value indicates the voltage above which the capacitor dielectric breaks down. Capacitance values are printed on the surface of the capacitor or indicated by color codes using three to six color dots or stripes. Capacitors with large values, i.e., the paper and tinfoil, mylar, tantalum, and electrolytic types, have values printed on the surface, typically 0.01 μf or larger. Some of the smaller-value capacitors are marked with a 10-digit coding

Table 2-2   MIL SPEC resistor code (a partial listing)

Sample 10-digit code word

RN	/	60B	/	3164	/	F
1		2		3		4

1. Two-letter prefix denotes type; RN for deposited carbon film. RW for wire-wound.
2. Two digits and letter denote power rating in watts at 70°C or 125°C and resistor temperature coefficient deviation in parts per million (PPM) per degree centigrade change (deg. C).

Code/	B 70°C 500 500 PPM/deg. C	C 125°C 50 50 PPM/deg. C	D 70°C 200 500 PPM/deg. C	E 125°C 25 25 PPM/deg. C	G 70°C 200 500 PPM/deg. C
55	0.100 watt	0.100 watt	0.125 watt	0.100 watt	0.100 watt
60	0.125 watt	0.125 watt	0.250 watt	0.125 watt	0.125 watt
65	0.250 watt	0.250 watt	0.500 watt	0.250 watt	0.250 watt
70	0.500 watt	0.500 watt	1.00 watt	0.500 watt	0.500 watt
75	1.00 watt	1.00 watt	2.00 watt	1.00 watt	1.00 watt
80	2.00 watt	2.00 watt	—	2.00 watt	2.00 watt

3. Four-digit number; first three digits denote first three significant digits of resistance value. Last digit denotes decimal multiplier:

Last digit:	0	1	2	3	4	5	6
Multiply by:	1	10	100	1,000	10,000	100,000	1,000,000

If the letter R is used in place of one of the first three digits of the resistance value, the position of the letter R sets the decimal place.

4. One letter suffix denotes percent error tolerance:

B	C	D	F	G	J	K	L	V	M
±0.1%	±0.25%	±0.5%	±1%	±2%	±5%	±10%	±15%	−10%, +20%	±20%

W	X	Y
−0%, +25%	−20%, +40%	−25%, +60%

system similar to the 10-digit MIL SPEC resistor code of Table 2-2. Although the full 10 digits are seldom used, the last four invariably are. A typical example is a 100M capacitor. The first two digits (10) denote the capacitance value in picofarads (10 pf). The third digit (0) denotes the decimal multiplier (1) as illustrated in Table 2-2. The letter suffix M denotes the error tolerance (0.2 pf) in a percent of the capacitance value for capacitors larger than 10 pf and in a fraction of 1 pf for capacitors 10 pf or smaller. Multiply the percent tolerance by 1 pf to obtain the fraction tolerance. The letter code used for capacitors is given in the MIL SPEC code for resistors in Table 2-2.

Although *ceramic capacitors* may have the capacitance printed on the surface in picofarads, they are more commonly color-coded with the system presented in Table 2-3. The starting point for reading values, i.e., the first dot, is clearly marked on one end and is typically much larger than the other dots. Interpretation of the color code is similar to that used for resistors.

The *mica capacitor* has two rows of three color dots, one row above and one below an arrow running the length of the ca-

Table 2-3   Ceramic capacitor color code

Color	End dot, temp coefficient, PPM/deg. C	2nd dot, 1st sig digit	3rd dot, 2nd sig digit	4th dot, decimal multiplier	5th dot, error tolerance,	
					C > 10 pf (in %)	C ≤ 10 pf (in pf)
Black	—	0	0	1	±20	2.0
Brown	−33	1	1	10	±1	0.1
Red	−75	2	2	100	±2	—
Orange	−150	3	3	1,000	±2.5	—
Yellow	−220	4	4	10,000	—	—
Green	−330	5	5	—	±5	0.5
Blue	−470	6	6	—	—	—
Violet	−750	7	7	—	—	—
Gray	30	8	8	0.01	—	0.25
White	General purpose	9	9	0.1	±10	1.0
Silver	Coupling	—	—	—	—	—
Gold	100	—	—	—	—	—

pacitor, as shown in Table 2-4. To read the six-dot code, hold the capacitor with one hand on each terminal lead. With the head of the arrow pointing toward the right hand, locate the first dot in the upper right-hand corner, the third dot in the upper left-hand corner, and the sixth dot in the lower left-hand corner. With this orientation, consult Table 2-4 for an interpretation of values using the six-dot color system.

Table 2-4   Mica capacitor code (pf)

	Mica capacitor dot diagram						
						6th dot	
Color	1st dot, 1st sig. digit	2nd dot, 2nd sig. digit	3rd dot, JAN* or EIA	4th dot, decimal multiplier	5th dot, error tolerance, %	Class	Temp coefficient, PPM/deg. C
Black	0	0	JAN	1	±20	A	±1,000
Brown	1	1	—	10	±1	B	±500
Red	2	2	—	100	±2	C	±200
Orange	3	3	—	1,000	±3	D	±100
Yellow	4	4	—	10,000	—	E	+100 −20
Green	5	5	—	—	±5(EIA)	—	—
Blue	6	6	—	—	—	—	—
Violet	7	7	—	—	—	—	—
Gray	8	8	—	—	—	I	+150 −50
White	9	9	EIA	—	—	J	+100 −50
Gold	—	—	—	0.1	±5(JAN)	—	—
Silver	—	—	—	0.01	±10	—	—

* *JAN* = Joint Army-Navy specifications

Paper dielectric and electrolytic capacitors are used in power supplies. Electrolytic capacitors are polarized; paper capacitors are not. The positive and negative terminals of the electrolytic type should be properly connected to a d-c input since failure to observe correct polarity leads to capacitor damage and possible damage to other parts. Electrolytic capacitor values range from 1 to 20,000 μf; these capacitors can be purchased in dry or wet electrolyte form. Generally, the dry type lasts longer. Compared with paper capacitors of the same size, electrolytics have higher capacitance.

DIRECT-CURRENT (d-c) POWER SUPPLIES

Circuits using tubes and transistors require a power supply. These electronic circuits change or convert the energy from the power supply into a usable signal of some kind. Generally, a d-c power supply is required for the emitter and collector bias of transistors and the plate voltage, screen-grid voltage, and control-grid bias of vacuum tubes.

The d-c power supply has an input of 115 volts a-c taken from a wall socket and an output d-c voltage level that is much lower or higher than the input. Most laboratory power supplies used for driving relays, solenoids, transistors, and stimulus components have low-voltage d-c outputs, typically 6, 12, 24, or 48 volts. Twenty-four volts is the most popular output level since (1) many relays used in research instrumentation have a 24-volt d-c rating and (2) higher voltage ratings can lead to severe electric shock for research personnel, although the 115-volt a-c relay is popular also because it can be operated very simply directly off an ordinary a-c wall receptacle.

The direct voltage output of a power supply often changes as the load varies; i.e., the voltage drops because of internal resistance. It should be noted that "load" and "current-drain" are used synonymously; i.e., if we increase the load we increase current-drain.

Since many circuit applications require that the voltage remain constant, power supplies for such applications must have good regulation characteristics. A voltage-regulator circuit is added to maintain constant terminal voltage in a *regulated power supply*. Many power supplies are unregulated.

The common 24-volt d-c power supply employs three units: (1) a voltage transformer, which steps down the input of 115 volts a-c to 24 volts a-c; (2) a rectifier unit, which converts 24 volts a-c to 24 volts d-c; and (3) a filter section, wherein the cyclic wave characteristic of the a-c voltage, which comes out of the rectifier along with d-c voltage, is eliminated or minimized.

Transformers

In most power-supply applications, the 105 to 125 power-line voltage is not the required input voltage of various stimulus components. Depending upon the particular components to be activated, the required input voltage is usually much higher or lower than the line voltage. A *transformer* is a device used to change one a-c voltage level to a higher or lower a-c voltage. Figure 2-5a presents a step-down voltage-transformer circuit used in changing 105 to 125 line voltage to 24 volts a-c. The 24-volt supply is cited as an example since it is a commonly used input voltage rating for psychological equipment. The two line-voltage wires leading from the wall outlet are wired to the external terminals a and b of the *primary coil winding* transformer input. The low voltage is taken off the terminals P_1 and P_2 of the *secondary coil winding* transformer output. An input and output terminal diagram, usually mounted on the transformer casing, describes the primary-input and secondary-output circuits. When wires are used as input and output connections instead of terminal boards, the wires will be color-coded to indicate their correct usage. The proper input and output voltage levels and the maximum current output flow that the transformer will handle are generally marked on the casing. The a-c transformer output voltage may

INPUT   OUTPUT

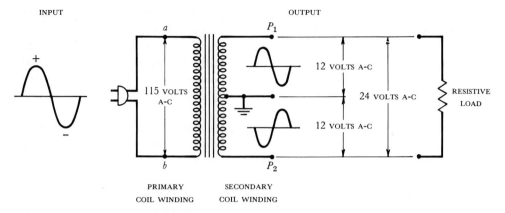

(a) 115 VOLT/12-24 VOLT TRANSFORMER CIRCUIT

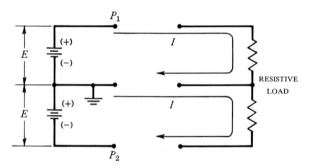

(b) BATTERY D-C EQUIVALENT ILLUSTRATING TRANSFORMER OUTPUT AT ONE PARTICULAR INSTANT IN TIME

Fig. 2-5 An a-c voltage step-down transformer and its battery equivalent at any one instant in time.

be connected directly to another equipment component if the voltage input rating of the component matches the output voltage of the transformer, provided that the component is one which is not restricted to use in d-c circuits only.

A *step-up transformer* has a low-voltage primary input and a high-voltage secondary output; a *step-down transformer* has a high-voltage primary input and a low-voltage secondary output. A step-up transformer may be used as a step-down device, but the practice is not recommended generally. For example, a 115-volt primary input, 230-volt secondary output step-up can be used as a step-down transformer by using the secondary as a primary with a 230-volt input and using the primary as a 115-volt output. Unless the experimenter is familiar with transformer characteristics, this practice may result in using the device beyond its power rating.

In simple a-c power applications, a transformer is not absolutely necessary. The voltage-division technique mentioned earlier for reducing d-c battery voltage may be used also for dropping 115 a-c voltage. Figure 2-6 shows a circuit that uses a series resistor to assume the major part of the 115-volt drop across the wall-socket terminals. From the voltage-division expression shown in Fig. 2-6, 2,275 ohms (Ω) is needed in series with the stimulus lamp to keep it from being over-driven by the 115-line voltage. This method of reducing the 115 nominal a-c line voltage is not recommended for use in large circuits with many components, but is ideally suited to power a single stimulus lamp or other component. A transformer step-down of line voltage is the preferred method since the transformer will decouple or isolate the low-output a-c voltage of the transformer secondary winding from the line voltage. This means that there will be zero voltage difference between any of the secondary coil terminals and any of the three receptacles in the modern laboratory wall plug. Since the D-shaped third receptacle of the wall outlet or receptacle and the wider of the other two receptacles are always at earth potential, the use of the *isolation transformer* will avoid the possibility of severe shock, especially if the experimenter is grounded with damp shoes and touches the bare lead running from the narrower of the wall receptacles. Isolation transformers that neither step up nor step down the input voltage are available commercially.

Naive researchers should investigate the features of a transformer before assuming that it is isolated. Connecting secondary terminals to other components indiscriminately may prove dangerous. An *autotransformer* provides transformer action with a single coil of wire. The total coil is considered to be the primary, and the secondary output is tapped off the coil at some fixed point. *Variac* is a commercial name for an adjustable voltage transformer with many uses. The input is standard 115 volts a-c, but the output is easily and continuously adjustable over a wide range of values. Autotransformers do not provide isolation of the secondary from the line voltage, although they may be used for either step-up or step-down action.

Now that we have completed a general discussion of transformers, refer back to Fig. 2-5a, which shows a transformer stepping down the line voltage. Note that the secondary winding has a center-tap terminal used as a ground or zero voltage reference. For purposes of analysis, at any one instant in the cycle, the output of the transformer can be considered static direct current and treated as two

batteries in series with their junction as ground, as shown in Fig. 2-5b. When the output of each secondary coil is treated as the output of a battery, the current in the top coil flows from P_1 to ground and the current in the bottom coil flows from ground to P_2. It follows that at any instant in time, the voltages at P_1 and P_2 are reversed in phase by 180° with respect to ground, generating the mirror-image transformer output voltage curves shown in Fig. 2-5a. At any time, there is a plus voltage and a negative voltage output with respect to the center-tap ground. At the same instant, the voltage developed between P_1 and P_2 is the absolute sum of the two smaller secondary series voltages developed with respect to the center tap.

Rectifiers

The rectifier section of the power supply changes alternating current to direct current. This conversion results when the output of the transformer is passed through a diode tube or a solid state device. Both of these devices are unilateral conductors, i.e., they allow the current to flow in one direction only, thus changing the applied a-c voltage to a pulsating d-c voltage. Although large numbers of rectifier tube circuits are still in operation, the

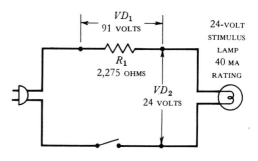

$VD_1 = 115$ volts $- 24$ volts $= 91$ volts

$$\frac{VD_1}{I} = R_1 = \frac{91 \text{ volts}}{0.04 \text{ a}} = 2{,}275 \text{ ohms}$$

Fig. 2-6 A simple a-c voltage dividing network. This circuit uses a series resistor to drop the a-c voltage supplied to a stimulus lamp from 115 to 24 volts.

balance of this section will cover the use of solid state diodes.

Semiconductor diodes (—▶—) used in low-voltage power supplies are typically germanium silicon (crystal) or selenium (metallic). The germanium and silicon types are cheaper and smaller than selenium. *Selenium is used because it (1) is rugged, (2) withstands high current surges, and (3) dissipates heat readily, requiring no heat sink.* Generally, the positive terminal of metal rectifiers is marked with a plus sign or colored red. The negative side is marked with a minus or colored black, and the a-c input is stamped a-c or coded yellow.

Silicon diodes (1) are able to maintain high power ratings at very high internal temperatures, up to 200°C, (2) are typically mounted on a copper or aluminum heat sink, and (3) are very susceptible to "turn on" current surges. Because of the last-named characteristic, the silicon diode should have a maximum current-limiting resistor, approximately 5 ohms or less, placed in series with its output. Even though it requires a heat sink, the overall volume of a silicon diode is much smaller than a comparably rated selenium unit.

Faulty in-circuit metallic rectifiers often may be identified by visual inspection, i.e., by the presence of discoloration and burned areas. Faulty crystal diodes must be identified by testing. Once a faulty rectifier has been identified it is simplest to use a direct replacement part. When replacing a selenium diode, (1) try not to touch the rectifier plates or terminals with the soldering iron, (2) replace everything in the original position unless the position does not allow adequate ventilation, and (3) inspect the load resistor for damage. When replacing silicon diodes, (1) do not cut the leads too short, if it is not a screw-type unit, since a little slack helps; and (2) use special care with the soldering iron. While soldering, a heat shunt may be provided by holding the diode between the terminal and body with a pair of long-nose pliers.

Half-wave rectification results from passing the output of the power-supply transformer through a single diode. The half-wave

rectification technique (1) is rarely used in a general-purpose d-c power supply that is designed for flexible multilaboratory use; (2) is often used where the power source is to be built into the apparatus to power a few relays, solenoids, or a reinforcement dispenser; and (3) is optimally used in applications requiring *minimal output power* to supply fixed work loads.

A diode will pass current only when it is forward-biased, or when the voltage presented to its anode is positive with respect to the voltage at the cathode. Note the arrow bar symbol of the diode in Fig. 2-7a. The tail of the arrow is the anode, and the bar the cathode. The arrow indicates the flow of current through a low resistance or low impedance path with the diode forward-biased. Thus, when the output of the upper terminal of the transformer is positive with respect to the center tap, the diode is forward-biased, if its negative terminal is connected through a resistive work load to the center tap. The resistive work load may be a relay or stimulus lamp. When the upper terminal of the transformer is negative with respect to the center tap, the diode is reverse-biased. It presents a high internal resistance to reverse current flow from the center tap, through the resistive work load and diode, to the upper output terminal of the transformer. Only the positive portion of the a-c wave is passed to the output of the power supply. The negative portion is blocked, with a resulting loss of half the power available in the a-c sine wave. Therefore, half-wave rectification is not the optimal technique for a general-purpose power supply.

Full-wave rectification utilizes both halves of the a-c wave and maximizes the output of the d-c power supply. There are two types of full-wave rectification: (1) the center tap, shown in Fig. 2-7b, and (2) the bridge, presented in Fig. 2-7c. The *full-wave bridge* gives twice the voltage output of the center-tap circuit. The full-wave bridge is a commonly used circuit in most multipurpose laboratory d-c power supplies since it utilizes the maximum power output of the transformer with a single output voltage and, in addition, does not re-

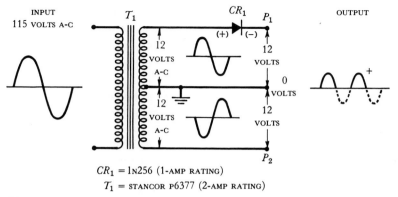

$CR_1 = 1\text{N}256$ (1-AMP RATING)

$T_1 = $ STANCOR P6377 (2-AMP RATING)

(a) HALF-WAVE RECTIFICATION CIRCUIT

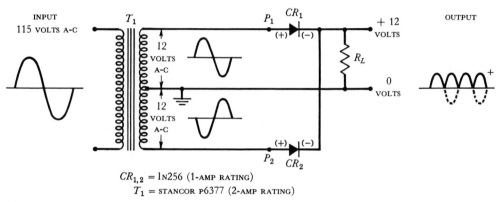

$CR_{1,2} = 1\text{N}256$ (1-AMP RATING)

$T_1 = $ STANCOR P6377 (2-AMP RATING)

(b) FULL-WAVE CENTER TAP RECTIFICATION CIRCUIT

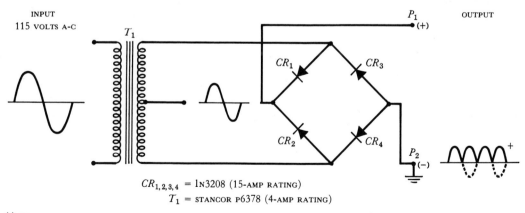

$CR_{1,2,3,4} = 1\text{N}3208$ (15-AMP RATING)

$T_1 = $ STANCOR P6378 (4-AMP RATING)

(c) FULL-WAVE BRIDGE RECTIFICATION CIRCUIT

Fig. 2-7 (a) A half-wave rectification circuit. This circuit uses a single diode to pass the positive portion and block the negative portion of a low-voltage a-c sine wave output of a step-down transformer. (b) A full-wave center-tap rectification circuit uses two diodes in parallel to pass alternate positive portions and block alternate negative portions of a low-voltage a-c sine wave output of a step-down transformer. (c) A full-wave bridge rectification circuit. This circuit uses two full-wave center-tap rectification circuits, each putting out a positive or negative d-c voltage with respect to center-tap ground. The doubled voltage may be taken off the positive and negative output terminals, ignoring center-tap ground.

quire the center-tapped transformer secondary. This is the circuit most commonly used to drive relays, solenoids, and other electromechanical devices which, in numbers, consume a large amount of power.

Full-wave center-tap rectification is accomplished by adding a second diode to the lower secondary output terminal of the transformer and joining the cathodes of both diodes, as shown in Fig. 2-7b. In this configuration each diode passes the positive half of the a-c wave in turn. In the first half of the wave, when P_1 is positive with respect to the center tap, CR_1 has a positive output and CR_2 blocks the negative half of the wave. In the second half of the wave, when P_2 is positive with respect to the center tap, CR_2 has a positive output and CR_1 blocks the negative half of the wave. The average or d-c output of the full-wave center-tap rectifier without a filter circuit is approximately $+12$ volts. Point P_1 is positive with respect to the center tap. To obtain a -12-volt output one of two methods may be utilized: (1) point P_2 may be ground reference rather than the center tap, or (2) diodes CR_1 and CR_2 may be reversed (both arrows pointed toward the transformer rather than the load), making point P_1 negative with respect to the center tap.

An average or d-c output voltage of approximately 24 volts, without filter circuitry, may be obtained by connecting the circuit as a full-wave bridge, as shown in Fig. 2-7c. The center-tap terminal is not used in this circuit, and the 24-volt output is taken off P_1 and P_2. Note that there is a slight drop in output voltage so that the values cited above, i.e., $+12$, -12, and 24 volts, are approximations. The actual values are closer to $+11$, -11, and nominal 22 volts d-c output.

Filters

The characteristics of rectifier circuits are such that their output voltage contains a combination of the desired d-c output and various unwanted a-c components. The a-c voltage variations called *ripple*, are reduced to tolerable limits by the following circuits: (1) *capaci-*tance filter*, (2) *resistance-capacitance* (RC) *filter*, (3) *inductance filter*, and (4) *inductance-capacitance filter*.

The simplest filter contains a capacitor across the load. Figure 2-8a shows a filter in which the capacitor is simply wired across the output of a diode section of the power supply. The use of the capacitor filter increases the d-c output voltage from the supply and reduces the a-c ripple. This characteristic of the capacitor is explained in some detail later in the chapter; for the present, suffice it to say that the capacitor is charged up quickly to essentially the peak value of the sinusoidal input voltage and discharges relatively slowly through the load. If no external work load such as a relay is drawing on the power supply, the voltage output of the power supply remains at the full charge level of the capacitor and assumes the straight-line d-c characteristic shown in Fig. 2-1a. If a resistive work load is drawing current from the power supply, the voltage level of the fully charged capacitor starts to fall when the rectified sine wave output voltage of the diode section falls. When this happens, the capacitor discharges current back into the circuit through the resistive work load and tends to keep the output voltage of the power supply up. The result of alternately charging and discharging the capacitor through the resistive work load is the smoothed output curve shown in Fig. 2-8a.

Some ripple is present even at light loads with a simple capacitor filter. The ripple can be reduced by placing a filter resistor in series with the load resistor and a capacitor in parallel with the load resistor. This circuit has the disadvantage that an appreciable d-c voltage is dropped across the filter resistor.

The charge-discharge action of a capacitor offers some drawbacks that an inductive filter overcomes. An inductance filter circuit is presented in Fig. 2-8b. This circuit smooths ripple because an inductor (1) impedes current change when building up a magnetic field because of rising voltage and (2) augments current flow when its magnetic field is dissipating

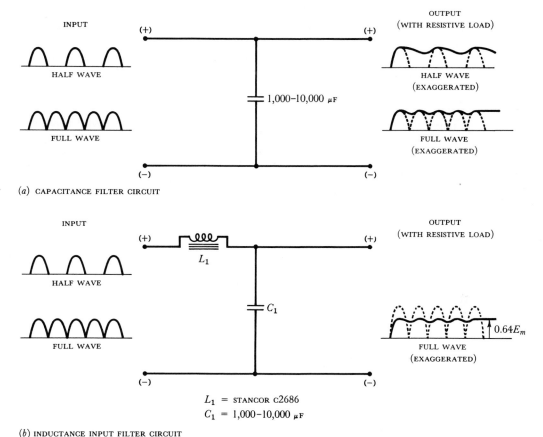

(*a*) CAPACITANCE FILTER CIRCUIT

(*b*) INDUCTANCE INPUT FILTER CIRCUIT

$$L_1 = \text{STANCOR } c2686$$
$$C_1 = 1,000\text{--}10,000 \ \mu\text{F}$$

Fig. 2-8 (*a*) **A capacitance filter circuit. A large-value capacitor is used to smooth out the output of any of the preceding rectifier circuits. (*b*) An inductance input filter circuit. This circuit uses a series inductor input and a parallel capacitor output to filter out the 60-cycle characteristic of the rectified a-c output of the preceding rectification circuits.**

because of the dropping rectified voltage. Stated simply, inductance impedes current flow; and the higher its inductive value, the more impedance the filter presents to current change. Resistance (d-c) measured in ohms is also associated with any inductance. Following Ohm's law, the d-c resistance in the inductive-filter section limits the maximum output current that the d-c power supply is capable of producing. The ideal inductive filter has a very low ratio of d-c resistance to inductance providing good filter characteristics and a high current rating. Inductors used in filter circuits are called *chokes* because they "choke out" a-c. Typical filter chokes are

rated for d-c resistance, maximum current flow, and inductance. Chokes are sometimes mistaken for transformers, so check the wire leads. Generally, two wires indicate a choke. More than two identify a transformer.

There are circuits that require a smoother output than that produced by a choke. More effective filters utilize inductance-capacitance circuits where the voltage input to the filter goes into a capacitor that bypasses the ripple to ground. The inductor offers high impedance to the a-c that is left. If a small amount of ripple is present in the output from the choke, it is shunted to ground by another capacitor.

The term *reactance* is used to refer to the effectiveness of a capacitor or inductor in impeding a change in current flow. When reactances are placed in a voltage dividing network and in series with a resistor or with each other, their reactances assume part of the total voltage drop across (1) the network and (2) the resistance. This is true whenever the input voltage to the dividing network is changing, e.g., the rectified a-c input voltage to the inductor-capacitor filter of the d-c power supply. When an unchanging d-c voltage is applied to the network, the capacitive reactance assumes practically the full voltage drop across the network as it charges up. With unchanging d-c voltage, (1) the reactance of the capacitor approaches infinity and the voltage drop across its terminals approaches the full voltage drop across the network, and (2) the voltage drop across the terminals of the resistor, in series with the capacitor, approaches zero. If an inductor is in series with the resistor, the inductive reactance of the inductor approaches zero as the input voltage to the network settles down and remains constant. The voltage drop across the terminals of the inductor is determined by its optimally low internal d-c resistance. Most of the total voltage drop of the network will appear across the terminals of the series resistor.

When a d-c voltage power supply is used for energizing external work loads, such as relays, solenoids, or stimulus lamps, the external work-load impedance is in series with the internal impedance, i.e., the inductor, diodes, etc., of the power supply. They both form a series voltage dividing network with the total voltage of the power supply appearing across the ends of the network. A portion of the total voltage appears across the internal impedance of the power supply, and the remaining portion appears at the output terminals, across the external work-load resistance. As the external work-load resistance goes down (more components are added in parallel across the output terminals), the voltage drop across the external resistance falls and the voltage drop across the internal impedance rises. If the internal impedance of the power supply is fairly high, typical of supplies with low output current ratings, it will assume a significant portion of the total voltage available as the current output of the supply approaches its current rating. This factor should be taken into account when using a power supply to energize components requiring a good deal of current. Power supplies with current ratings of 5 to 10 amp typically have very low internal impedances. With these units, the output voltage change as a function of current drain is minimized. The maintenance of output voltage as a function of current drain is known as *regulation*. Power supplies with high internal impedances have poor regulation, while those with low internal impedances have better regulation. Output voltage regulators are discussed in the section on advanced transistor circuits (pages 101 to 104).

Up to this point, we have briefly described resistance, capacitance, and d-c power supplies and have noted that one method of filtering unwanted alternating current is the use of a resistor-capacitor combination. Since the resistance-capacitance network has wide applicability in circuit designs, the following section will cover the operation of these networks in detail.

RESISTANCE-CAPACITANCE NETWORKS

A capacitor can be charged or discharged at various time rates by the use of resistors. This arrangement is called a *resistance-capacitance (RC) network*. The time rates are used to pace trials, set stimulus latencies, and generate other time intervals as needed. Figure 2-13 illustrates an RC network that presents a stimulus light for a brief period. In this circuit the ON-OFF switch (⌐ | ⌐) is slightly more complex than the simple switch used in Fig. 2-2. It has (1) a common or center-pole contact that moves, (2) a stationary normally open contact that the common presses against when the switch is thrown to the ON (⌐ / ⌐) position, and (3) a normally closed contact that the common presses against when the switch is thrown to the OFF ($\rightharpoonup\backslash\,\leftharpoonup$) position. This is a single-pole (common) double-throw (SPDT) switch. In the OFF position, the battery voltage is applied across the terminals of capacitor C_1 ($\dashv\vdash$). In practice a capacitor is usually charged through a resistance to minimize arcing across switch contacts since a fully discharged capacitor acts as a direct short circuit when placed across a voltage source. The time it takes for the capacitor to reach 63 percent of its full charge is given by the equation $T = RC$, where T is time in seconds, R is the series resistance in ohms, and C is the capacitance in farads. In other words, the larger the resistance and/or capacitance, the longer it takes to charge the capacitor. The value of 63 percent of full charge associated with the linear time constant expression $T = RC$ is used arbitrarily to simplify a more complex exponential time equation for quick practical use in circuits. From the time constant expression and the circuit in Fig. 2-9, it takes only 2 milliseconds (msec) for the capacitor to reach 63 percent of its full charge. When the experimenter wants to flash the stimulus lamp, he throws SW_1 to the ON position. When this happens, the common contact of the switch is pulled away from the normally closed contact, removing the negative terminal of the capacitor from the battery. As soon as the common presses against the normally open contact ($\leftharpoonup\,\rightharpoonup$), it completes the second subcircuit RC network of C_1 ($\dashv\vdash$) and the stimulus lamp SL_1. Since capacitor C_1 is now connected across the terminals of SL_1, C_1 discharges through SL_1 and the lamp lights. The time required for the capacitor to discharge 63 percent of its initial charge is also given by the expression $T = RC$. The larger the capacitor and/or the larger the internal impedance of the stimulus lamp, the longer the stimulus lamp will remain on. Since the charge on capacitor C_1 decays in an exponential fashion, it will cause the stimulus lamp to dim before cutting off. Because of the typical low internal resistance of stimulus lamps, it is diffi-

cult to obtain a reasonably long enough stimulus ON time to justify the use of the circuit in Fig. 2-13 without increasing the size of the capacitor to a very large value.

If a large capacitance is needed and only small capacitors are available, two or more capacitors can be placed in *parallel*. This increases the capacitance value in the RC network, thereby increasing the duration of the stimulus light. In parallel, the individual capacitances sum to the total capacitance: $C_{\text{total}} = C_1 + C_2 \cdots + C_i \cdots + C_n$. If, on the other hand, the smallest capacitor available keeps a stimulus light on too long, more than one capacitor can be placed in series to decrease the capacitance value in the RC network, thereby decreasing the duration of the stimulus light. When placed in *series*, the reciprocals of each capacitor sum to the reciprocal of the total capacitance in the RC network:

$$\frac{1}{C_{\text{total}}} = \frac{1}{C_1} + \frac{1}{C_2} \cdots + \frac{1}{C_i} \cdots + \frac{1}{C_n}$$

Since most capacitors with capacitances of over 1 μf are polarized, they should be connected together with respect to terminal polarity in the same manner as batteries placed in parallel with negative to negative and positive to positive and in

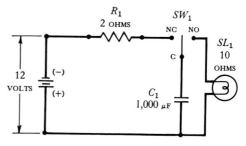

$T = RC$

T_1 = CHARGE TIME = 2 OHMS·0.0010 FARAD = 0.002 SEC

T_2 = DISCHARGE TIME = 10 OHMS·0.0010 FARAD = 10 MSEC

Fig. 2-9 A simple RC (resistance-capacitance) network. This circuit uses the discharge time of a series capacitance to set the ON latency of a stimulus lamp.

series with positive to negative and negative to positive.

RC circuits are important and should be understood. As a signal goes from point to point in a circuit, the RC values at the point determine the circuit effects. Simple RC circuits vary in effect as a function of the values of R and C. Couplers, integrators, and differentiators are similar RC circuits, one difference being their time constants. The *coupler* (i.e., the capacitor couples the signal to a resistor) outputs across a resistor and has a time constant longer than the period of the input signal. A *differentiator* outputs across the resistor as well, but it has a time constant that is short when compared with the input signal period. Differentiators are used to change the shape of input signals and deal with rate of change. The differentiators and integrators described here are used typically in amplifier feedback circuits, e.g., in analog computers. *Integrators* (1) output across the capacitor and (2) have a much longer time constant than the input signal period. Integrators add.

ACTIVE CIRCUIT CONTROL DEVICES

Typically when RC discharge networks are used to set latencies, an *active switching device* such as a *relay* or *transistor* is used as the discharge resistance. These switching devices have relatively high input resistance which the capacitor has to bleed through. The capacitor discharging through the relay or transistor input circuit activates the device, and the relay or transistor activates the stimulus lamp. This technique increases the discharge time constant of the RC network, keeping the stimulus light on much longer.

The relay is an active switch energized electrically by applying an input voltage across its two coil terminals. The simple switch, on the other hand, is a passive device that must be operated by hand. The purpose of both is to open or close a circuit.

Figure 2-10 shows a relay and a solenoid, both of which operate as a function of changes in magnetic fields. A *solenoid*, shown in Fig. 2-10a, consists of a long coil of wire wound around a spool with an iron armature shaft

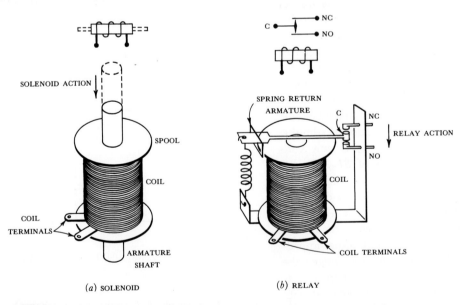

(a) SOLENOID   (b) RELAY

Fig. 2-10 Pictorial and schematic representations of a solenoid and a single-pole double-throw (SPDT) relay.

passed loosely through the spool. The coil of wire generates an electromagnetic field when its two terminals are connected across an input voltage source. The ability of the solenoid coil to generate this field is called *induction,* and the coil is called an inductor. With no field produced the iron armature shaft ordinarily moves freely through the coil spool. When the magnetic field generated by the coil builds up to full strength, the armature is drawn into and centered within the spool. The magnetic field breaks down and the shaft again moves freely through the spool when the voltage across the coil is withdrawn. Typically, one end of the iron shaft is mechanically connected to some other item so that activation of the solenoid results in vigorous movement of the shaft and subsequent action of the item. Although the operation of the solenoid and connected items is often very noisy, it is used for a number of purposes, e.g., to open liquid feeder valves, open and close runway gates, deliver reinforcements, or automatically withdraw manipulanda from Skinner boxes.

The *relay* has a permanently mounted iron core within the spool and a spring-return armature mounted over the core. The armature is pulled down against the iron core when the relay coil terminals are connected across a voltage source. When the input voltage is removed, the armature returns to the original position because of the action of the spring. When a set of SPDT contacts is mounted over the relay coil with the common contact mounted on the moving spring-return armature, as shown in Fig. 2-10b, the relay can be used to open and close various circuits wired through this set of contacts. Relay coils, like other electric components, should be connected to a voltage source equal to their operating input voltage rating. Typical coil ratings are 6, 12, 24, 48, and 110 volts a-c or d-c. The contacts are rated separately. This rating tells what the contacts can handle without getting too hot. When a set of contacts is used to turn on or turn off another relay

arcing occurs. Repeated arcing of contacts builds up deposits of carbon and metal weld. These deposits often cause the contacts to stick together and offer a high resistance to applied voltage. The arcing is due to the inductance of the relay coil. When a voltage is applied across the terminals of the coil by means of an external switch, an induced magnetic field builds up. The build-up of this field impedes current flow through the coil until the field reaches full strength. When the input voltage is removed from the coil, the magnetic field collapses, dissipating its stored energy back into the coil in the form of current flow. This current flow arcs across the external switch contacts that break the coil circuit. The arcing is reduced by placing a diode (——▸|——) in a reverse-biased position across the relay coil terminals. The diode is a polarized two-terminal semiconductor device that has a low internal resistance or impedance to current flow when it is forward-biased (anode connected to a voltage more positive than the voltage connected to the cathode). When reverse-biased, with the voltage polarities to the terminals reversed, it drastically limits current flow with a high internal impedance. When a diode is placed in a reverse-biased position across the relay coil, it provides a low resistance path for the induction current flow and a high resistance path for normal current flow. The diode, in effect, "shorts out" the relay coil when the collapsing field presents its reverse-polarity induced voltage to the relay coil.

The SPDT relay coil can be substituted for the stimulus lamp SL_1 as the discharge resistance of the capacitor C_1 in Fig. 2-9. The direct substitution of the relay coil for the lamp is indicated in Fig. 2-11. When the switch SW_1 is in the OFF (⌐\⌐) position, the capacitor charges from the battery (——|⊢——); when the switch is thrown to the ON position (⌐/), the capacitor discharges through the relay coil. From the time-constant expression of RC networks, that is, $T = RC$, it takes 200 msec for the capacitor to discharge 63 percent of its initial charge

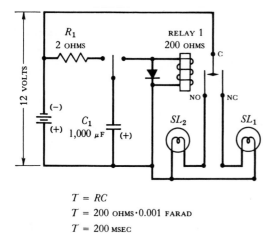

$$T = RC$$
$$T = 200 \text{ OHMS} \cdot 0.001 \text{ FARAD}$$
$$T = 200 \text{ MSEC}$$

Fig. 2-11   An RC circuit controlling the ON-OFF latency of a pair of stimulus lamps which uses a relay coil as the RC discharge impedance. The relay contact circuits switch the stimulus lamps on and off alternately.

through the relay coil. The relay may not open at exactly 63 percent of its coil voltage rating of 12 volts. The actual time-interval value has to be determined empirically.

When the relay is inactive, the SL_1 stimulus lamp subcircuit is closed through the common and normally closed contacts ( ) of the relay. When the relay is turned on by the capacitor discharge through its coil, it opens the SL_1 stimulus lamp subcircuit, turning SL_1 off. In the ON position, the common and normally open contacts of the relay close ( ), completing the SL_2 stimulus lamp subcircuit activating SL_2. The SL_2 stimulus lamp will remain on as long as the relay is energized. When the relay is de-energized, SL_2 goes off and SL_1 comes on again.

One of the more important aspects of this relay-circuit application is that neither of the output stimulus lights will grow dim prior to turning off, as is the case in the RC circuit in Fig. 2-13. The gross stimulus effect of manipulating the hand switch of this relay circuit is to turn off an existing stimulus, replacing it for approximately 200 msec with a second stimulus, then turning the original stimulus back on. The circuit under discussion also il-

lustrates a very common use of the SPDT switch or relay as a circuit control device. Typically when switched, the SPDT opens one circuit and closes another. It should be noted that a second SPDT relay could replace the SPDT switch in the circuit. The second relay would control the operation of the first. This notion of having one active device control the operation of another active device is the basis for complete or semiautomation of an experimental paradigm. The second relay would have to be controlled by an external relay or switch, typically from a trial-interval timing device, which will be discussed later in detail.

Transistors

The transistor is an active device that can be used either as a switch or as an analog amplifier. Its switching time is less than a microsecond when not deliberately slowed by RC networks; but the average relay requires 20 to 50 msec to perform the same operation. This feature of the transistor often enables the experimenter to utilize experimental parameters that relay apparatus is incapable of handling. In addition, (1) transistor life seems indefinite, (2) it is absolutely silent, (3) significantly less power is required for operation, and (4) the size is significantly smaller, resulting in more compact units.

A transistor is a polarized semiconductor device having three terminals, or regions: the *emitter*, the *base*, and the *collector*. The two basic types of transistor differ with respect to the polarities of voltages used at these terminals when they are in the ON condition. The *PNP* type has the emitter *positive*, base *negative*, and collector *more negative;* while the *NPN* type has the emitter *negative*, base *positive*, and collector *more positive*. The first two letters of either type indicate the voltage polarities normally applied to the emitter and collector. Since the voltage applied to the two types differs in polarity, the schematic symbols differ. Note the direction of the arrow on the emitter lead in Fig. 2-14 and remember that d-c electron flow is always opposite in direction to that of the arrow, as it is with semiconductor diodes. The remainder of this discussion will cover the PNP type. This choice is arbitrary since the NPN type could have been used.

The transistor can be thought of as having two internal subcircuits or current paths, one that controls the operation of the other crudely analogous to the way the coil of a relay controls the switching of the relay contacts. The *input* subcircuit is one in which current flows from the emitter terminal (positive) to the base terminal (negative). This controls the amount of current in the *output* or *work-load* subcircuit that flows from the emitter terminal (positive) to the collector terminal and through the work load (e.g., a relay coil, a solenoid, or a stimulus lamp) to a negative supply-voltage terminal of a battery or power supply. The amount of current flowing in the output or work-load emitter-collector circuit turns the work load (e.g., a stimulus lamp) on or off in the same manner as the resistor R_1 in Fig. 2-2 controlled the amount of current flowing in the stimulus lamp in that circuit.

The common emitter transistor is basically a current amplifier. With a small amount of current flowing in the input emitter-base subcircuit, a proportionally larger amount of current will flow in the emitter-collector output subcircuit. The amount of current flow in the output subcircuit is dependent upon the amount of current flow in the input circuit. If the amount of current flow in the emitter-base subcircuit is increased, the current in the emitter-collector subcircuit will increase proportionally. A small change in input means a large change in output current flow.

The amount of current flow in the input emitter-base subcircuit is a function of the difference in polarity of the voltage connected across the emitter-base subcircuit. The emitter-base subcircuit can be considered analogous to a diode. In a diode, internal impedance to current flow is a function of the degree of forward bias across its two terminals. If both terminals are approximately of the same

polarity, i.e., there is little difference in voltage, a high internal impedance to current flow exists. If the negative terminal is supplied with a voltage slightly more negative with respect to the positive voltage at the positive terminal, its internal resistance or impedance to current flow decreases. As the negative terminal is made more and more negative with respect to the positive terminal, i.e., a greater forward bias voltage difference between terminals, the diode's internal impedance drops sharply. Eventually, the diode's internal impedance reaches its lower limit and passes the maximum amount of current it is physically capable of. At this point, the diode is said to be in *saturation*, or saturated with current flow. In the case of the emitter-base "diode" path, the current is limited and kept out of saturation. This is done typically by means of a resistor placed in series with the base terminal and the negative input voltage. The reason for this is that the amount of current flowing in the emitter-base path is amplified greatly in the emitter-collector output path. The emitter-collector "diode" path will reach its lowest internal resistance or impedance to current flow, typically 1 to 80 ohms, and go into saturation, i.e., reach maximum current flow, long before the emitter-base path. The amount of current in the emitter-collector output circuit is a function of the internal resistance of the external work load that the transistor is turning on and off, since both are in series.

The operation of the transistor emitter-collector output path, which controls the voltage drop (VD) supplied to the external component it turns on and off, may be thought of in terms of the VD across the emitter-collector terminals. In any series resistance circuit, with one end connected to the positive power-supply terminal and the other connected to the negative power-supply terminal, the largest VD occurs across the terminals of the largest resistance in the circuit. If one resistor remains fixed and the resistance of the other drops, the voltage across the fixed resistance will increase and the voltage across the lowered resistance will decrease. The voltage supplied to the two terminals of the stimulus lamp is the power-supply voltage minus the VD across the internal impedance of the emitter-collector output circuit (VD power supply = VD transistor + VD stimulus lamp; VD power supply — VD transistor = VD stimulus lamp). With the internal impedance of the emitter-collector output circuit high, as determined by a minimum of current flowing in the emitter-base input circuit, there is a large VD across the emitter-collector output circuit terminals. This means that a minimal VD is supplied to the stimulus lamp, insufficient to light it. As the internal impedance of the emitter-collector circuit is decreased, passing more current, the voltage across the emitter-collector terminals decreases, allowing more of a VD to appear across the stimulus lamp terminals, lighting it dimly. As the internal impedance of the emitter-collector circuit drops to a minimum, the VD across it is reduced to a minimum, allowing a maximum VD to appear across the terminals of the stimulus lamp, lighting it brightly. The emitter-collector output circuit can be thought of as a variable resistor whose resistive value is changed as a function of the internal resistance existing in the emitter-base input circuit. In fact, the term transistor is a shortened form for *transfer-resistor*. Technically, the emitter-collector subcircuit is often referred to as a complex impedance.

In the transistor control circuit shown in Fig. 2-12a, the emitter-collector internal impedance determines the luminance level of the stimulus lamp ( ). The experimenter controls the amount of current flow in the emitter-collector path by varying the forward bias on the base with respect to the grounded positive emitter. He does this by turning the knob of a variable resistor ( ) placed across the terminals of the battery, forming a variable voltage divider network. The voltage divider shown in the circuit is called the *gain control* of the transistor amplifier. *Examine* Fig. 2-12b. As the experimenter turns the knob on the potentiometer clockwise, it

moves the slider point, which is connected directly to the base, toward the negative end of VR_1 ( ). The base of the transistor Q_1 is biased more negative with respect to the grounded positive emitter, and the stimulus lamp begins to glow. As the experimenter moves the knob all the way in a clockwise direction, the base is forward-biased to its maximum, and the stimulus lamp glows brightly. The fixed resistor R_2 is inserted between the negative end of VR_1 and the negative terminal of the battery so as not to overdrive the emitter-base input circuit.

Resistor R_2 is chosen also to set the upper limit of illumination of the stimulus lamp since it determines the maximum current flow in the input circuit. When the experimenter turns the knob on the potentiometer completely counterclockwise, the slider point moves to the positive end of the variable resistor ( ). This grounds the base and "shorts it out" to the emitter, turning the stimulus lamp off.

This may be classified as an analog circuit. The brightness of the stimulus lamp follows directly the continuous rotational movement of the experimenter's hand as he turns the potentiometer knob. The circuit may be used in the digital binary mode by replacing the potentiometer with a simple SPDT switch. The common contact can be wired to the base, and the normally closed contact wired to ground, positive. The normally open contact is wired to the fixed negative bias resistor R_2 leading to the negative terminal of the battery. In the OFF position, the common (base) is shorted to the positive ground, keeping the transistor off. When the switch is thrown to the ON position, the common is connected to a negative bias voltage through R_2, turning the transistor on.

It is important to note that the basic grounded-emitter circuit shown in Fig. 2-12 can be placed directly into larger circuits composed of many transistor subcircuits. The work load that the transistor turns on and off need not be a stimulus component. It may be another transistor or a relay. Likewise, a

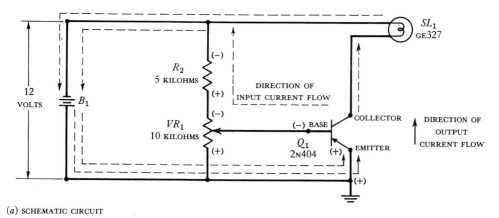

(*a*) SCHEMATIC CIRCUIT

(*b*) PICTORIAL REPRESENTATION

Fig. 2-12 **A simple grounded-emitter transistor amplifier circuit that controls the illumination level of a stimulus lamp. The transistor's input circuit is controlled by a variable resistor used as a voltage divider between positive and negative. The input current flow through the emitter-base subcircuit controls the output current flow through the emitter-collector subcircuit to the stimulus lamp.**

potentiometer need not be used to control the input to the transistor. The emitter-collector output impedance path of another transistor can be substituted directly for the potentiometer resistance. The new transistor must be controlled at its input also, so some other active subcircuit must be used to bias its emitter-base

input impedance. This type of active circuit network may be modified and used in the analog mode to amplify physiological response measures or in the digital binary mode, with the initial biasing input conditions of the network being a grounded input ("off") or a negative input ("on"), as illustrated in the

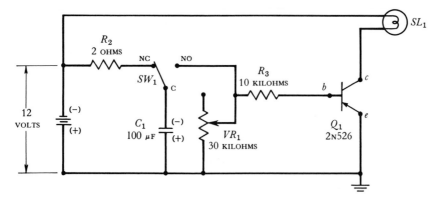

Fig. 2-13   A transistorized RC network controlling the ON latency of a stimulus lamp. The emitter-base input impedance of the transistor is used as the discharge impedance of the RC network. The input discharge current is amplified in the emitter-collector output subcircuit turning the stimulus lamp on.

previous paragraph. Both applications, analog and digital, will be discussed in later sections.

The use of the transistor need not be limited to turning other components on or off in either analog or digital fashion. Transistors can be used also in stimulus latency RC networks. Figure 2-13 shows a PNP transistor substituted in an RC network in place of the relay used in Fig. 2-11. The circuit is basically the same as the grounded-emitter configuration used in Fig. 2-12. Even though it is not the optimal transistor RC circuit, it can be used in apparatus if the stimulus light parameters are not important and the experimenter simply needs a fairly constant neutral light flash to signal the subject to respond or to indicate the start of a trial.

Trace the circuit operation. The experimenter throws the SPDT switch to the OFF position (⌐\ ⌐) between stimulus presentations, charging the capacitor (—⊣⊢—) through the arc-suppressing resistor R_2 from the negative terminal of the battery. When the experimenter wishes to present a stimulus light, or turn on some other circuit control component briefly, he closes the switch to the normally open contact (⌐ ⁄⌐). This discharges the capacitor through the current-limiting resistor R_3 and the emitter-base input circuit impedance ground (positive). The

transistor then turns on the stimulus lamp for a period of time until the current discharged through its emitter-base input subcircuit and amplified in the emitter-collector output subcircuit is insufficient to keep the lamp lit. Note that the variable resistor VR_1 provides an alternative current path from ground to the negative terminal of the capacitor. The variable resistor in parallel with the current-limiting resistor R_3 and the emitter-base impedance form the discharge resistance in the RC time-constant expression $T = RC$. This means that the experimenter can lengthen or shorten the ON time of the stimulus light flash by turning the knob of the variable resistor. In doing this, he either (1) decreases the time that the stimulus lamp is on by moving the slider point toward ground (⌐⌐⌐) (this reduces the discharge resistance between the negative terminal of the capacitor and ground, independent of the emitter-base discharge path, and discharges the capacitor faster) or (2) increases the time that the stimulus lamp is on by moving the slider point toward the base (⌐⌐⌐), increasing the resistance between the negative terminal of the capacitor and ground and discharging the capacitor slower.

Since the transistor is basically an analog amplifier and the relay is not (the relay is a digital amplifier), the transistor is superior in some aspects of RC operation. The transistor will amplify small amounts of RC discharge current into its emitter-base circuit, keeping its stimulus output component active longer than the relay. The relay would be insensitive to this tail of the exponential discharge curve of the capacitor and would open, turning its output component off much sooner. Irrespective of the fact that this particular circuit is given mainly for its simplicity in illustrating the use of the transistor in an RC network, the above paragraph points out a serious methodological problem of the circuit in specifying the duration of the stimulus light. The transistor output will approximately follow a form of the exponential discharge curve of the capacitor. It will always turn the stimulus lamp on very abruptly and turn it off gradually in an exponential fashion. This is serious in the longer time ranges and will be apparent to the eye as a soft reddish glow (when looking at the bare incandescent bulb) as the output current of the transistor gradually falls off. A problem of stimulus measurement and communication of the stimulus conditions is apparent since we commonly specify latency to mean onset to offset, with the intensity of the stimulus light implicit in the lamp's input voltage rating and the actual input voltage used. Experimental rigor requires that specifications for stimulus conditions be exact. In the case of the illustrated transistor RC circuit, the stimulus lamp goes on fast enough to measure its onset, but specifying the OFF condition is difficult. It goes off gradually rather than abruptly. This might appear in the experiment as a source of intra- and intersubject variability, since it is safe to assume that subjects would respond to it differentially. This transistorized RC timer should be used with caution, or not at all, if the stimulus is at all critical. Transistor timing circuits discussed later in this chapter avoid this problem by (1) placing a relay on the output of the transistor and using the relay to turn the stimulus on and off in a rapid all-or-none fashion or (2) using additional tran-

sistors to "square up" the exponential discharge curve of the capacitor.

The experimenter can control fairly precise stimulus latencies and illumination levels in an automatic or semiautomatic fashion by the use of circuit control components such as the resistor, capacitor, relay, and transistor. Illumination levels may be controlled by means of resistors and/or simple transistor amplifiers, while latencies may be controlled by manipulating resistance or capacitance values. Although variable capacitors are used in electronics, maximum capacitance values are so small that their use is impractical. Time constants of RC stimulus latency networks can be varied by switching various capacitors or resistors in and out of the circuit. There is an advantage in manipulating the time-constant value of an RC stimulus latency network by means of fixed capacitances or resistances instead of a variable resistor. The experimenter need only throw a digital switch to set a stimulus latency using this technique, while turning even a calibrated potentiometer knob will have some analog positioning error associated with it.

When transistors are used in control circuits, some general information concerning their operational limits should be obtained to avoid misuse and possible malfunction. Information concerning a number of parameters is available in most commercial transistor manuals, including the common-emitter forward-current transfer ratio and the maximum ratings of voltage, current, and transistor dissipation. The terms describing these parameters are often represented by abbreviated symbols; e.g., BV represents breakdown voltage, P_c is collector dissipation, and I_c refers to collector current.

The ratio of output current to input current is approximately linear over a wide middle range of current flow below saturation, and for most practical control purposes can be assumed to be a constant. This constant is given for most transistors and listed under the heading of h_{FE}, that is, "hybrid forward-current transfer ratio, grounded emitter."

This statement is meaningful enough except for the term "hybrid," which in this context refers to a matrix-theory procedure for measuring the current amplification ratio.

Transistors should never be operated above their maximum voltage ratings usually specified as a maximum permissible voltage difference between emitter and collector output circuit terminals. Even though the transistor output circuit impedance and the work load it drives are in series and form a voltage divider across the power-supply terminals, when the PNP transistor emitter-base input circuit is not forward-biased (base negative, emitter positive) the emitter-collector output impedance rises to a maximal value. When this occurs, the high emitter-collector output impedance assumes most of the VD across the power supply. A good rule is to use transistors that have an emitter-to-collector voltage rating above the output voltage rating of the power supply used in the circuit. Since most transistors can be operated at potentials as low as 3 volts, only the voltage rating of the stimulus component that the experimenter wishes to control determines the lower limit of the operating voltage. Transistors may be operated at any convenient voltage level as long as it does not exceed the maximum voltage rating of the emitter-collector output circuit.

Since transistors are primarily resistive impedances, they have a maximum power rating in watts. They also have maximum voltage and current ratings, which are independent of the maximum power rating. This means that the maximum power rating is usually much less than the product of the voltage and current rating, $E \cdot I >$ watt rating. These three independent ratings must be strictly observed in loading the output circuit of the transistor to avoid its destruction. The maximum rating in watts is a measure of the amount of heat the transistor can dissipate. As most transistors are small in size, their external casing aids very little in dissipating heat. The wattage rating of the transistor can be increased by placing its external casing in intimate contact with a large plate of aluminum or copper. This metal plate, called a *heat sink*, will draw off a considerable amount of the heat transmitted through the casing from the internal subcircuits and will allow the transistor to be operated above its rating in watts, given for ambient free air operation. The *ambient free air rating* should not be confused with a much larger watt rating measured when the transistor casing is mounted on an "infinite" heat sink, typically an aluminum plate 0.125 inch (in.) thick with a surface area on one side of 140 square inches (sq in.) or greater. The *infinite-heat-sink rating* in watts is often more than double the ambient free air rating and is used in commercial catalogs by some manufacturers to describe their products in a more attractive way.

The heat-sink procedure should be observed when constructing simple analog transistor amplifiers to be used in laboratories without air conditioning. Digital switching transistor amplifiers do not need heat sinks if they are used to control other transistors. If a transistor is used to control a relay or a solenoid drawing a large amount of current, its casing should be mounted on a heat sink. Additional information covering heat-dissipation techniques may be found in Gyorki (1963). Heat sinks may be purchased commercially for most transistors.

The maximum current flow through the emitter-collector output circuit occurs when its internal impedance is lowest (in saturation), i.e., when the transistor is turned on all the way. Transistors in the saturation state typically have internal output impedances as low as 1 to 80 ohms. This allows the transistor to pass more current flow than it is rated for unless the current flow through the transistor is limited externally. The external work-load resistance that the transistor turns on and off must be used to limit the maximum current flow through the transistor. This is done by assuming, in the worst case, an internal transistor impedance of zero ohms, with the full power-supply VD appearing across the external work-load resistance. To determine the minimum external resistance that will keep the transistor within its maximum current flow rating, simply divide the maximum current rating of the transistor into the power-supply voltage according to Ohm's law, that is, $E/I = R$. This resistance is the smallest resistive value that can be connected in series with the emitter-collector output terminals across the power-supply voltage and keep the transistor from burning out.

Since the power wattage generated by the transistor in the fully ON condition (i.e., highest output current times lowest output VD), and in the fully OFF condition (i.e., lowest output current times highest output VD) is at a minimum, somewhere in between these polar ON and OFF conditions the output impedance generates the maximum heat, medium output current times medium output VD. Maximum wattage can be shown to be generated when the transistor is halfway on, i.e., when the output VD across the emitter-collector terminals is equal to one-half the total voltage output of the power supply. The other half of the voltage appears across the terminals of the resistive work load that the transistor is driving on and off. The smallest resistive work load that will keep the transistor output subcircuit within its maximum watt rating in the half ON condition is given by

Minimum resistive load

$$= \frac{(\text{power-supply voltage})^2}{4 \times \text{maximum watt rating of transistor}}$$

Since the maximum current and the maximum power estimates of the smallest resistive work load may differ independently of each other, the largest of the two resistance values should be used as the smallest resistive work load permissible for the particular transistor at a particular power-supply voltage.

READING CIRCUITS (SCHEMATICS) AND ANALYZING MODULES

A schematic is a drawing of a circuit that contains a number of standard symbols used to indicate circuit components. Figure 2-14 shows a sample of the standard symbols cited in this chapter.

A schematic represents two-dimensional simplicity, and the drawing of interconnected electric components may not look like the completed circuit; e.g., a line drawn between two electric components may represent many wires in the actual apparatus. Flexibility is illustrated in Fig. 2-15, where circuits a and b are functionally identical although drawn differently, i.e., the electrical relationship is the same. The circuit illustrates an instrument for measuring simple reaction time; the experimenter measures the speed with which a subject removes his hand from a button switch when a stimulus light is activated. The procedure involves having the subject press the button when the experimenter says "Ready" and removing the hand as soon as possible when the light goes on. Reaction time is recorded and read off a clock timer incorporated into the circuit. Note that electrical points P_1 and P_4 do not refer to specific physical points. An electrical point refers to two or more physical points that for all practical purposes have zero ohms resistance and a zero-volt drop between them. For example, point P_4 in schematic a refers to the line connecting one side of buzzer B to the positive terminal of the battery, to one side of clock timer CT_1, and to one side of signal lamp SL_1.

Examine the operation of the circuit. The subject holds down push-button switch SW_1 upon command of the experimenter. This switch closes the buzzer B_1 subcircuit across the battery at points P_1 and P_4, presenting an auditory masking noise to minimize false starts from ambient auditory stimuli. The reaction stimulus is the lighting of stimulus lamp 1 (SL_1). When the experimenter wishes to start a trial, he holds down push-button switch 2 (SW_2). This closes the parallel SL_1 and clock timer CT_1 subcircuits through both switches across the battery at points P_1 and P_4. The latency clock timer starts simultaneously with the lighting of the reaction stimulus lamp. Switches 1 and 2 are an AND gate for

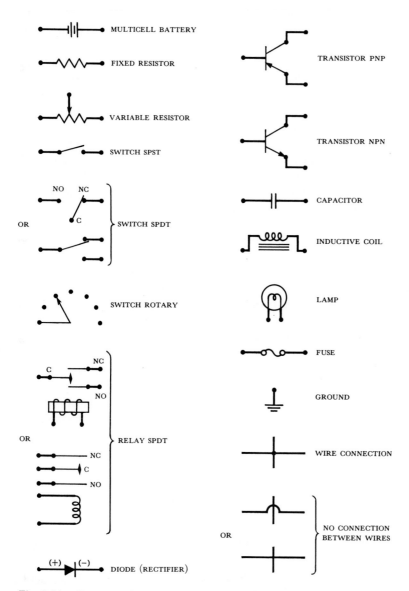

Fig. 2-14   Common schematic circuit component symbols.

turning on SL_1 and CT_1. This means that both SW_1 and SW_2 need to be closed to complete the SL_1 and CT_1 circuits. When the subject releases SW_1 upon reacting to the stimulus light, all subcircuits are broken from point P_1 through SW_1 to the negative terminal of the battery. Switches 1 and 2 are also an OR gate for turning off SL_1 and CT_1. This means that either SW_1 *or* SW_2 will turn off stimulus lamp 1 and clock timer 1 upon being opened.

When switch 1 breaks the subcircuits, the buzzer, the lamp, and the clock are shut off, ending the trial. The experimenter then throws SW_2 to its open position, reads the latency off the face of the clock, manually resets the clock, and then presents the "Ready" signal to the subject, who again closes the switch SW_1 and begins a new trial.

Figure 2-16 shows a pictorial representation of the completed reaction-time apparatus using the circuit presented in Fig. 2-15. The arrangement of wires and components in the circuit is left up to the technician who must build the apparatus. The important factor in reading the schematic is to follow the relationship between components, not the manner in which they are laid out in the drawing. In the example cited here, note that the subject's reaction-time switch turns on the buzzer and turns off the stimulus lamp and the clock, while the experimenter's switch turns on the stimulus lamp and the clock. The subject's and the experimenter's switches will turn on the components, but either of them will turn them off independently of the other switch.

The naive reader of schematics may gain some understanding of the operations of a system if the following steps are followed: (1) Look at the title of the circuit. This will usually give some indication of the gross function of the circuit, including the input and output elements. (2) Look for the power voltage source that supplies the entire circuit. Trace its common ground line to all components of the circuit. This is the common reference for determining the effect of operation of one component upon another. Look for the input lines and try to trace the input through to the output, taking into account the effect of various components on the input. (3) In looking at components in the system, try to recognize a standard subcircuit configuration of components and then tie its operation to other standard configurations that it controls. This may be difficult since there are many standard configurations that perform similar operations, but most of them have a similar basic configuration irrespective of individual details. These subcircuits, called *modules* since they perform a separate job from other subcircuits, are the key to the problem of circuit analysis. If one can recognize a modular or separate subcircuit and is familiar with its functional input requirements and its output characteristics, the circuit analysis becomes an integration of building blocks each of which performs a specific job in the apparatus, e.g., timing, switching, stimulus control, or response

amplification. A module is defined here as a physically separate subcircuit with its own input and output designed for a specific purpose. Most modular designs are optimally of the plug-in and pull-out type. This feature lends not only flexibility but also economy to an experimental instrumentation system. In most modular transistorized systems, one or several standard identical subcircuits are wired in a printed circuit on a glass epoxy card module. The printed card module typically has one to four independent timing circuits, digital amplifiers, binary data storage units, or an arrangement of small bimetallic diodes used in transistor switching circuits. These card modules typically plug into a larger multicard carriage unit. Cards are inserted from the rear of the carriage and mate with plug receptacles wired to a matrix board of banana jacks on the front of the unit. Various-length banana cables are used to patch together the electrical interconnections between various

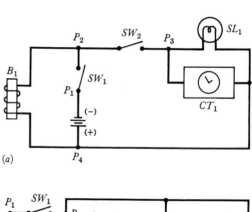

(a)

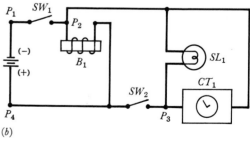

(b)

Fig. 2-15 Two schematics of a simple flexor response reaction-time circuit. Both circuits *a* and *b* are identical electronically, but drawn differently.

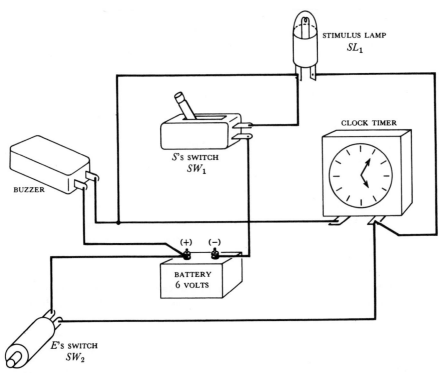

Fig. 2-16   Pictorial representation of completed flexor reaction-time apparatus from (b) in Fig. 2-15.

functional module cards in building up a complete apparatus for a specific experimental purpose. Various general-purpose card carriage programming units can be employed in the laboratory with a temporary circuit on the matrix patch board. Since only standard building block card modules are used, a module may be removed when not in use in one experimental situation and used in another carriage or laboratory. This procedure does not involve breaking down the original apparatus circuit since the matrix patch-board connections remain intact. The transfer operation takes a few minutes and can easily be completed between subject appointments. Another advantage is reduction of repair time. When a system becomes inoperative because of apparatus failure, a spare module card can be plugged in to keep the system operating while the original is repaired. Physical plug-in modules also speed and facilitate the detection of faulty subcircuits, as the experimenter need

only systematically replace each plug-in module until the system is again operative. See Bailey (1963) for construction details for custom and standard printed subcircuit module cards. Multipurpose cards with numerous terminal studs are available commercially.

Modular relay units of larger physical size often utilize intermodular connectors that snap onto the modules themselves. This prevents their removal from the apparatus without disrupting the circuit connections. Snap lead connectors have one spring surface that presses against the mating contact, while the banana coupling has four spring surfaces. Banana jack coupling takes less time and is easier to insert and remove.

A *flow chart* or *block diagram* is a very helpful device to use when designing a modular system. Figure 2-17 shows a flow chart instrumenting a simple two-choice discrimination problem in which the subject presses one of two buttons when presented with one of

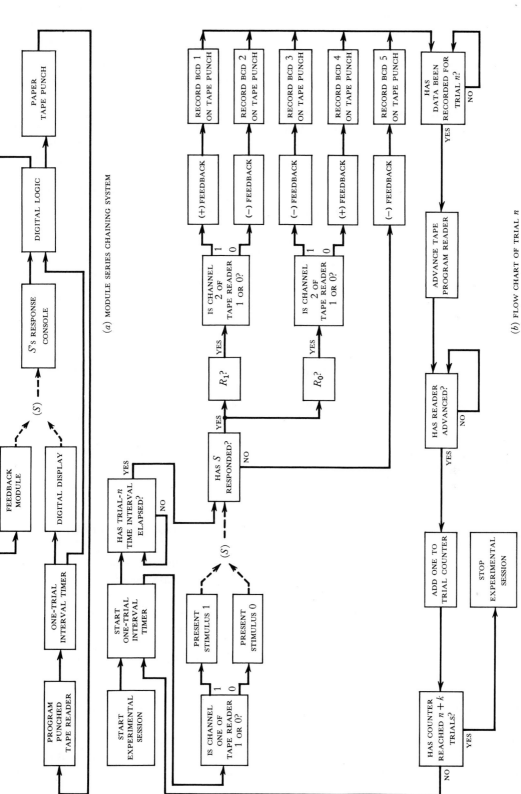

(a) MODULE SERIES CHAINING SYSTEM

(b) FLOW CHART OF TRIAL n

Fig. 2-17 A flow-chart diagram of a two-choice decision-learning paradigm illustrating the chaining sequence of each module's output function in time.

two stimuli. The arrangement is such that if the subject makes response R_1 to stimulus S_1 or response R_0 to stimulus S_0, positive feedback will be presented. R_1 and R_0 correspond to left and right push-button switches on the subject's response console. S_1 and S_0 correspond to colored symbols flashed on by a visual display module. Only the first response on trial n is accepted by the apparatus, and any subsequent responses on trial n are ignored.

The use of the flow chart in this paradigm illustrates the preferred experimental practice of chaining the functions of the various modules in a time sequence. Each module is similar to a link in a functional chain, electrically connecting the link preceding it to the one following. This means that each module is activated by the electrical output of the immediately preceding module in the chain. For example, in the series system flow chart of Fig. 2-17b, the punched paper tape reader module closes a switch that delivers an output signal to the one-trial interval timer. The timer then generates an output that turns on the stimulus lights. At the end of the trial, the timer activates a series of subcircuit modules in the digital logic section that deliver feedback and prepare the subject's responses for recording. When feedback has been delivered, the digital logic closes a switch that turns on the paper tape punch module. After the punch records the data and completes one trial operation, a switch is closed that turns the punched paper tape reader on. The reader module "reads in" the new stimulus conditions and then activates the one-trial interval timer. The functional time sequence automatically begins again. If one of the modules in the system fails to operate on a particular trial, it will not activate the next module in the sequence, and the whole system becomes idle and will not generate another trial. Modules placed in parallel without this chaining technique are independent of one another and may fail to operate on some trials and operate on others. This source of variability in the data may go unnoticed until a complete breakdown

of the module occurs and may obscure important effects of the experimental method.

The prime reason for requiring a *chaining* or *series dependence gate* technique is the assurance that if the control apparatus malfunctions and does not follow the experimental procedure *it does so only for one trial and has not contaminated the data collected on previous trials*. This may be the case with malfunctioning parallel modules. An adherence to this *fail-stop* chaining technique eliminates the possibility of marginal or sporadic operation over a whole series of subjects or trials, with the experimenter having no way of estimating how much of the variability in his data is due to intrasubject and intersubject variation and how much is due to apparatus variability.

Since modular analysis plays such an important part in the understanding and proper design of large experimental apparatus, the following section pays attention to some of the more common modular configurations. It is important to realize that the examples presented here are not the only subcircuit configurations that will perform the specific function. Even though these circuits are recommended for general-purpose use in psychological apparatus, many other configurations are just as adequate.

MODULES USED IN CONTROLLING LATENCIES AND TRIAL INTERVALS

Many experimenters require a reasonably accurate time-base generator. *Time bases*, known as *pulses*, are changes in voltage level for a specified time length. These are needed to generate trial interval times and stimulus latencies and to automate general apparatus control circuits. The *time-base-generator* module is designed to produce a change in voltage level at its output and is either (1) *nonrepeating*, i.e., needing a change in voltage level as an input to "trigger" it into operation each time an output voltage change pulse is needed, or (2) *repeating*, i.e., putting out voltage change pulses of T time length over and over until switched off. Nonrepeating time-base modules are called *pulse formers*. In digital connotation the nonrepeating pulse former is called a *"one-shot"* or *monostable multivibrator;* the repeating type is called an *"astable"* or *free-running multivibrator.* A pulse former typically accepts a pulse of indefinite time length and puts out a pulse of definite time length, either shorter or longer than the input pulse. Before a second output pulse can be generated, the input must return to its normal state, switched off. A one-shot circuit of this type is shown in Fig. 2-18. The characteristics of this pulse former are such that in the optimal mode of operation, the desired output pulse, a change in voltage level, has a shorter time latency than the input pulse. This means that the input pulse, called a *trigger pulse*, is of indefinite time length and the pulse former responds only to its onset or rise and its termination or fall. Before a second output pulse can be generated, the trigger pulse must first terminate and then be re-initiated. All pulse formers discussed in this chapter operate in this fashion.

The following discussion applies to the use of relay circuits for pulse-shaping functions. Later discussion will indicate how the functions may be performed in a more optimum manner with solid state devices.

The pulse former in Fig. 2-18 uses two relays and an RC discharge to deliver a high-voltage shock to a subject for a definite time length with each input trigger pulse. A pulse former is by no means limited to controlling stimulus latencies. It is often used in conjunction with other pulse formers and components in automating a complete experimental system. Typical uses of a pulse former as a circuit module in psychological apparatus include (1) controlling short intervals when a subject is to make a response, (2) reading out digital data collected on a trial to a digital event recorder, and (3) resetting memory circuit devices used to store data until it has been recorded. Each of these applications has a specific operating time associated with it. The circuit in Fig. 2-18 is used to generate time pulses

less than a second. These time pulse values are dependent upon the capacitance and relay coil resistance values. The experimenter may change the length of the output pulse by changing the farad value of the capacitor in the RC discharge network.

In tracing through any of these modular circuits, first look for the external switch or input that turns the circuit module on. Follow the connection leading into the circuit proper, and check the action of the component that the external switch affects directly. This is done as follows: when the external switch SW_e is closed (⊶⊷), a trigger pulse is presented through the common and normally closed contacts (⊶⊏⊐) of relay 2 to the coil of relay 1. This pulse charges capacitor C_1 and then energizes relay 1. When relay 1 closes, -24 volts is applied through the bottom normally open contact (⊶⊏⊐) to the

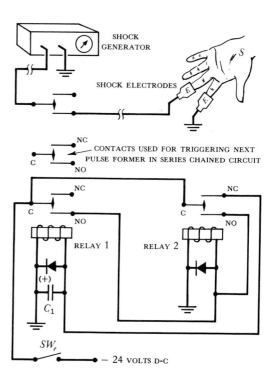

Fig. 2-18   A relay pulse former using the RC discharge technique. The switching latency of relay 1 is used to control the delivery of a high-voltage shock to finger electrodes attached to a subject's hand.

coil of relay 2, energizing it. When relay 2 closes, it (1) cuts off the —24 volts to relay coil 1 and (2) applies —24 volts through its own bottom normally open contact ( ) to its own coil. This locks relay 2 in the closed position. When the —24 volts is removed from relay coil 1, the capacitor ( ) C_1 discharges through relay coil 1, keeping relay 1 on, or closed, until the voltage across the capacitor falls below the minimal level necessary to keep relay 1 energized. When relay 1 opens, the cycle is completed and the input must be removed by opening the external switch SW_e ( ), unlocking ( ) relay 2. The input may then be reinstated, triggering a second output pulse. The output pulse in this case is controlled by the RC-determined opening and closing of the upper set of contacts of relay 1. When relay 1 closes, a high-voltage shock stimulus is passed through the normally open contact to the subject by means of electrodes taped to his fingers. One finger is grounded to the second terminal of the shock generator, completing the shock circuit. When the relay opens, the shock stimulus is terminated.

The time-constant expression $T = RC$ gives an approximation of the T value of the shock stimulus interval. Since relay 1 may not go off at exactly 63 percent of its coil voltage rating of 24 volts, the actual time interval must be determined empirically.

This circuit illustrates two common uses of relays. (1) A relay can be used as a digital "amplifier." Using a low-voltage input to a coil to control the switching of a high-voltage output at the contacts is often very useful. (2) A relay is often used to store a binary response. The subject's button-press switch is often used to turn the relay on, and a *locking subcircuit* identical to that of relay 2's common and normally open contacts ( ) is used to keep the memory relay on after the subject has completed his response. Typically the locking subcircuit is broken ( ) at the end of each trial after feedback is delivered and the response recorded.

This pulse-former circuit is ideally suited for use in the larger series functional time sequence module chain circuitry discussed earlier. In the flow chart presented in Fig. 2-17, one of the blocks is labeled "digital logic." This subcircuit block typically includes two storage relays with locking circuits, one for each push-button switch of the two-choice learning paradigm, and at least three of the pulse formers chained in sequence. The first pulse former briefly turns on a correct or incorrect feedback lamp at the end of each trial by wiring its output through the contacts of the two storage relays. The ON and OFF states of both relays determine whether the output pulse of the pulse former is routed to the positive or the negative feedback lamp. The trigger input for the first pulse former is taken off a normally closed contact of the trial interval timer that returns to the closed position at the end of the trial. The second pulse former is triggered by the middle normally closed contact on relay 1 of the first pulse former at the end of the first pulse former's output pulse. Pulse former 2 transfers the stored response information to the data solenoids of the tape punch by routing its output pulse through a second set of contacts on the storage relays. Pulse former 3, triggered by the middle normally closed contact of relay 1 of pulse former 2, has its output pulse directly connected to the clutch solenoid of the tape punch. The output activates the clutch solenoid, punching the data of the trial. Pulse former 3 breaks the locking circuits of the response storage relays and clears their memory. This is done by wiring the locking input of the relays through the middle normally closed contact of relay 1 in pulse former 3. A normally closed contact that closes at the end of the punch cycle of the tape punch is used to trigger another pulse former, which pulses the tape-advance coils of the tape reader and initiates the next trial.

The characteristics of the previous pulse former are such that the desired output pulse has a shorter time latency than the input pulse. A pulse former designed to output a

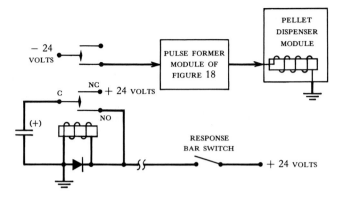

Fig. 2-19 A relay pulse-stretcher circuit module which uses a relay pulse stretcher to trigger the pulse-former module of Fig. 2-18. The pulse former circuit turns "on" a pellet dispenser for a brief interval.

pulse longer than the input trigger pulse is shown in Fig. 2-19. This circuit is known as a *pulse stretcher* and is used as one of a series of intermediary control modules between a response bar in a Skinner box and a reinforcement stimulus dispenser. An animal in a Skinner box often makes a response by gently leaning on the response bar. The electrical characteristics of this "weak" response are such that the response-bar switch is closed for only 10 to 30 msec, as compared with 400 to 500 msec for a normal response. A momentary closure is often not long enough to usefully activate a relay directly connected to the response bar. Even if the relay is activated, it may open immediately following the response, and its output is simply a reproduction of the response-bar output pulse. This is not long enough to energize a reinforcement dispenser. The pulse former presented in this circuit adds a standard-length pulse to a short irregular pulse generated by the action of the response bar.

Follow through the circuit at rest with no input from the response bar. Capacitor C_1 is charging through a normally closed contact of the relay. After a momentary pulse of sufficient duration to close the relay, typically 20 to 30 msec, one end of the capacitor is removed from +24 volts and switched to the relay coil through a normally open contact. When the

momentary trigger pulse is terminated, the capacitor discharges through the coil resistance, keeping the relay closed until the charge on the capacitor falls below the minimal activation voltage of the relay. Although this pulse former increases the sensitivity of the apparatus to a very short bar-press response, it will not generate separate output pulses for bar-press responses emitted while the relay is still closed. These rapid bar-press inputs recharge the capacitor and add the length of the standard RC output pulse to this series of bar presses. This module sets up a differential reinforcement schedule, low rate (DRL), for the animal and can be used to reinforce only the first response in a long, rapid series of bar presses. It should be noted that under this rapid series of bar presses, the pulse-stretcher output will possibly overdrive the coil of the pellet dispenser and create excessive noise. To avoid this, the output of the pulse stretcher is used as a trigger pulse input for the pulse former shown in Fig. 2-18. The fixed-length output of this intermediary pulse former is used to turn on the pellet dispenser.

A transistor-relay time-base generator is shown in Fig. 2-20. In this circuit the RC network below the transistor base generates the output time interval according to the time-constant function $T = RC$. The transistor turns relay 1 on and off, and relay 2 is

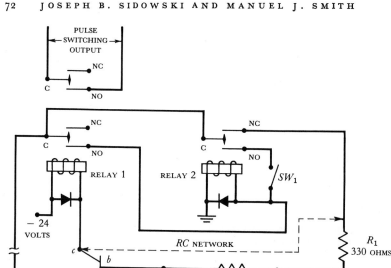

Fig. 2-20 A transistor-relay pulse-former circuit. This circuit can be used as either a pulse former or a recycling timer, depending upon the state of switch SW_1.

used as the switching output since its contacts can carry up to 5 amp or more without the experimenter's worrying about output voltage, current, and wattage ratings. This circuit is very flexible and recommended for applications such as trial-interval timing and control of black-box components that generate complex analog stimuli.

This circuit is similar to the 2-relay pulse former in Fig. 2-18 with a transistor RC network interposed between the relays to control the time interval. The transistor RC network serves the same purpose as the capacitor in the previous relay circuit. It determines the time interval that relay 1 remains closed and therefore the length of the output pulse.

Trace the circuit. When the external switch SW_e is closed, the -24 volts coming through the normally closed contacts of relay 2 charge the capacitor C_1 in the RC network through the resistor R_1. R_1 is used (1) to protect the contacts of relay 2 from charging arcs of the capacitor and (2) to reduce the 24 volts input presented to the RC network. When the capacitor is fully discharged, it acts as if it were a very-low-resistance conductor between the negative input voltage and the positive ground. When the capacitor is sufficiently charged, the negative input voltage triggers the transistor base through the 9.1-kilohm (9.1K) base current-limiting resistor R_2. The transistor, driven into conduction, turns relay

1 on. The output pulse is now initiated through the top contacts of relay 1. Relay 1 activates relay 2 through its bottom normally closed contact. When it closes, relay 2 "shuts off" the negative input voltage to the RC network. With switch SW_1 in the closed position, relay 2 remains locked in the ON position, providing its coil with −24 volts through its normally open contact and SW_1. After relay 2 cuts off the negative input to the RC network, the fully charged capacitor C_1 discharges through the 9.1K base resistor, keeping the transistor Q_1 in a conducting state, consequently keeping relay 1 on. Relay 1 opens when the current flow between the capacitor and ground, through the transistor-emitter input circuit, is insufficient to keep the relay on when amplified in the emitter-collector output circuit. Upon opening, the relay cuts off the switching output pulse at its upper contacts. Before a second output pulse can be generated, the external switch SW_e must open to break the locking circuit of relay 2 through its normally open contact and switch SW_1. When relay 2 opens, the external switch SW_e can again be closed to generate a second output pulse.

This circuit can be used as a *repeating time-interval generator*, putting out switching pulses over and over, if the switch SW_1 connecting the coil of relay 2 to its normally open contact is kept in the open position. This prevents relay 2 from locking in the closed position; it will open immediately after relay 1 opens and deliver the negative input voltage to the RC network, starting the time cycle again.

Time bases from 30 msec to 20 sec have been generated by using this circuit. The length of the output pulse delivered by the top set of contacts of relay 1 is varied by allowing the capacitor to bleed off its charge faster through the 50K and 3K variable-resistor bypass subcircuit. These resistors are used as coarse and fine time controls, respectively. Resistors R_3 and R_4 are used to stabilize the input circuit of the transistor. Since there is a very small leakage current between the base and collector that increases as the transistor heats up, R_3 provides an alternative resistive path between the base and ground, in addition to the emitter-base circuit. This alternative path tends to stabilize the emitter-base path when excess current flow due to heating takes place. Resistor R_4 removes the emitter terminal from ground and makes it slightly negative. This tends to equalize the polarities of the emitter-base input impedance when the capacitor C_1 is fully discharged, keeping the transistor off even with a slight leakage current from base to collector.

This transistor-relay time-base module has advantages over a time-base generator designed only with relays. (1) It can be used to generate a greater range of time intervals than a relay circuit because of the amplification of very low RC discharge currents that a relay would not respond to directly. (2) It can be used as a repeating time-base generator to pace trials, control stimulus components, or turn on other relays independently of other circuits in the apparatus, if this is desired. (3) It can be used as a pulse former to generate only one trial at a time. As a pulse former, it can be made dependent upon the operation of another apparatus module in a functional time-sequence chain. This module can be activated by a switch from the data recorder or some other module that performs the final operation on each trial. In both applications, the output latency can be varied simply by turning the knobs on the variable resistors. Extended time ranges are available by switching larger capacitances in parallel with the discharge capacitor C_1.

A *simple repeating time-base generator* that cannot be used compatibly with a series fail-stop chaining system is the *motorized cam-microswitch* arrangement shown in Fig. 2-21. This module is included in the discussion more for its widespread use in psychological laboratories than for its recommending characteristics. It is very gross in the accuracy and reliability of its output time intervals and requires frequent maintenance because of its mechanical construction. Its popularity is due

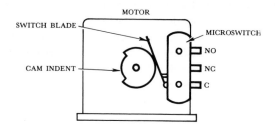

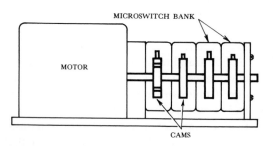

Fig. 2-21 An electromechanical timer using a motor, cam, and microswitch.

to simplicity of operation. In Fig. 2-21 the motor rotates the cam past the blade of the microswitch. When the indent of the cam allows the microswitch to drop, the common contact of the switch is brought in contact with the normally closed contact. When the indent has passed, the cam lifts the blade, switching the common contact back to the normally open position. This is the reverse of the normal switching procedure since the cam keeps the microswitch closed and allows it to open only when the indent passes by. The T time latency of the output pulse is set by the speed of the motor (rpm) and the cam indent. The arc width of the cam indent limits the ON and OFF pulses in the time cycle. Figure 2-21 also shows a typical microswitch bank for generating more than one output pulse in a serial time sequence. The output pulses are sequenced by staggering the cam indents from the first to the last cam.

This type of timing module has a defect inherent in its physical design. Since the phase of the output pulse sequence is determined by the angular position of the motor with respect to the blades of the microswitches, the

motor position must be reset to a zero position by hand prior to each experimental session. If this is not done, the experimental conditions on the first trial will not be presented properly or completely.

A better *time-interval generator* consists of a *motorized clutch, cam, and microswitch* arrangement. It has a clutch electromagnet similar to the relay, which is typically energized through the common and normally closed contacts of the microswitch. At the start of a trial cycle, the clutch engages the continuously rotating motor with a spring-return cam arm. This action rotates the cam arm toward the microswitch activation lever. When the cam arm presses on the microswitch lever and activates the switch, the electromagnetic clutch circuit through the normally closed contact of the microswitch is broken. At this point in the cycle, a short momentary output pulse can be taken from the normally open contact of the microswitch. The cam arm springs back to its starting position, deactivating the microswitch when the electromagnetic clutch disengages. As the common contact of the microswitch closes with the normally closed contact, the cycle begins again. An alternate switching output pulse that is "on" the length of the trial, except for a moment at the end of the trial, can be taken from the normally closed contact of the microswitch.

This simple motorized timer module is ideally suited to control trial time intervals using a series functional time sequence module chain circuit. In this arrangement the input voltage to the clutch coil through the common and normally closed contacts of the microswitch can first be routed through a common and normally closed contact of an external locking storage relay as discussed in the section on pulse formers. The locking relay is activated by the normally open contact of the microswitch when the timer completes its trial interval and prevents the timer from recycling a new trial cycle. As the locking relay and the microswitch break each other's circuits, the relay may tend to chatter or bounce while closing. This can be corrected by placing a capacitor, typically a few micro-farads or less, across the coil terminals of the relay. The locking subcircuit of the storage relay is broken by some other circuit module, typically by a switch on the data recorder. This permits the timer to generate a second trial interval.

AUTOMATIC CIRCUIT CONTROL WITH SWITCHING DEVICES

The concept of one switch controlling the operation of another is the basis for automatic circuit control. If an experimenter replaced the hand-operated switch in Figs. 2-11 and 2-13 with a relay, the circuits would become automatic and could then be controlled by another automatic module in the experimental circuit.

Any switching device may be classified according to its binary information storage capacity. The simplest switch can store a binary logical one or a logical zero; i.e., it is ON (1) or it is OFF (0). This simple switch can alternate between 1 and 0 (one *bit*, or binary digit of information) and is ideally used for the binary storage of data or stimulus events; i.e., a stimulus will or will not be presented on trial *n*—a response occurred on trial *n* or it did not. The simplest manually operated switch is the *single-pole single-throw* (SPST) toggle switch used in household lighting. When the switch toggle is thrown, the center pole or common contact of the switch closes with a normally open contact, completing a circuit; hence the designation SPST. Various types of SPST switch are used in psychological apparatus, e.g., toggle, push-button, and rotary switches. All these types may be either static or spring-loaded with an automatic return to the OFF position, and all may have a normally closed instead of a normally open contact. A switch having both the normally closed and normally open contact position is called a single-pole double-throw (SPDT) switch. Note that the SPDT switch has no OFF position but has two ON positions since the common contact is either resting against the normally closed contact, completing one circuit, or resting against the normally open contact, completing a second circuit. With the SPDT, binary 1 and 0 still refer to a response occurring or not occurring, respectively, but when the original response of interest does not occur and a logical zero state exists, a second response occurs. A more general definition of binary responses, therefore, is one in which logical 1 refers to the occurrence of a particular response of interest, and logical 0 refers to the occurrence of any of a class of responses not containing the response of interest. This seems reasonable if one is using an SPDT switch as a response bar in a shock escape paradigm, as shown in Fig. 2-22, and if one is attempting to establish the onset of stimulus lamp S_1 as a negative secondary reinforcer. In this experiment, the animal is presented with a high-voltage shock when he does not press the bar on any given trial. With a bar press defined as logical 1, any other class of responses that the animal emits when not pressing the bar is defined as logical 0. This means that if the animal makes any response not classified as logical 1 (bar press), he will be given a shock. The experimenter controls the trial interval by manipulating switch SW_2, which defines the time when either of the subcircuits can be active. The 6 volts available in the SW_2 circuit are not the shock voltage. The logical 0 circuit turns the output of the shock generator off or on. The relay is energized by the 6 volts of the SW_2 circuit and switches a high-voltage shock level into a polarity scrambler prior to routing it to a shock grid floor. The polarity of the shock voltage is switched rapidly from grid to grid of the floor by the scrambler to prevent the animal from standing on two grids with the same polarity and avoiding the shock.

The SPDT switch concept, in various forms, is the basic unit of the digital computer and of all switching control circuitry. If the experimenter wishes to activate more subcircuit modules independent of one another, it is necessary to add pole multiples of the SPDT switch. Two-, three-, four-, six-, eight-, and

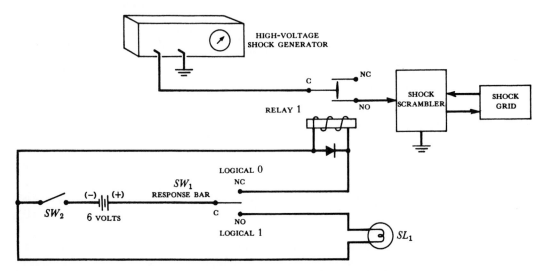

Fig. 2-22 A binary switching arrangement controlling the presentation of a light or a shock stimulus. This circuit can present a shock to an animal. When the animal presses the bar, the shock ceases and the stimulus lamp lights.

sixteen-pole double-throw arrangements are the most common. Though a number of poles may be added, the information capacity of the single switch remains at one bit, i.e., one binary digit. The multiple-pole arrangement adds electrically independent channels on which to transmit the same information.

To sequence more stimulus information than is needed on a single trial, the control circuit must add more bits of information capacity by having more than two contacts for the common center pole to switch to, one for each trial. For example, in a two-choice discrimination learning task, an experimenter may wish to present one or the other of two stimuli sequentially for sixteen trials. This may be done by using a single-pole sixteen-throw active *rotary stepping switch*. A circuit utilizing this switching arrangement is shown in Fig. 2-23. This stepping switch is typically activated at its coil by the output of a pulse former and may be preprogrammed so that the lights go on and off according to a random or specific sequence over the 16 trials. The output of the stepper is used to turn an SPDT relay on or off as the switch is stepped from position to position on each trial. The relay

controls the ON or OFF conditions of the lights. Thus, on any one trial, the lights are on or off, depending upon the specific electric connection between the contact point on the stepping switch and the relay. These connections may be made by means of *patch cords*, which are cables with banana plugs at either end. The patch cords can be plugged in and out of plug receptacles called *jacks*, which may be purchased singly or mounted on boards in multiple units. In this example, a jack is wired to each contact terminal of the 16-contact stepping switch. The relay coil terminal has a row of jacks wired to it, and the patch cords are used to connect the terminal jacks with the stepper contacts. These connections are plugged in or not according to the experimenter's program for presenting the lights on each of the 16 trials.

Commercial stepping switches vary in design and in number of contacts but, except for short trial sequences, seldom have enough stepping positions for most experimental requirements. Some steppers have automatic resets that make it possible to recycle and repeat the same sequence. Generally, rotating through the same sequence is not recommended when using a randomly selected sequence, since superstitious behavior artifacts may be repeated in each block of trials. The stepping switch is more suited for use in other types of circuits, e.g., to switch lights around a configuration in order to generate a stimulus movement effect. In this application, more than one lamp may be patched to each terminal of the switch.

The *punched tape reader* is a more suitable switching module for generating stimulus sequences from trial to trial. Since these modules were originally designed to transmit messages over Western Union telegraph lines, they are sometimes referred to as *tape transmitters*. The tape reader has two advantages over the simple stepping switch in programming stimulus sequences: (1) a practically unlimited program length and (2) a permanent record of the stimulus program in the form of a tape.

Electromechanical readers, such as the Western Union model 24 reader shown in Fig. 2-24, push a spring-loaded feeler against a paper tape. If the paper tape has a hole punched in one of the appropriate channels (logical 1), it allows the feeler to press through the hole. A contact coupled to the feeler is then pressed against a normally open contact. If the tape has no hole in it (logical 0), the feeler contact is held down against a normally closed contact. The reader typically has five independent feeler contacts and five normally open contacts that are wired in common. The five normally closed contacts are wired in common also. The reader is advanced by delivering the rated d-c voltage to its two coil terminals. Upon being energized, the armature of the coil rotates a feed sprocket that pulls the tape one position forward. The program tape, which determines the stimulus conditions, i.e., logical 1 or 0, on any trial is prepared in advance on a separate tape punch device similar to a typewriter. When purchased, the paper tape is in a roll containing no holes. The roll is placed in a tape punching unit, which punches a series of equally spaced center holes. These holes are

used in conjunction with the sprocket on the reader for advancing the tape. Additional holes may be punched in the channels to control various stimulus events. The number and channel location of the holes will be dependent upon the plans of the experimenter. If an experiment utilizes several schedules of reinforcement, e.g., 50/50, 60/40, 70/30 80/20, and 90/10, the researcher might enter a table of random numbers and record the specific series of reinforcements for each schedule over whatever number of trials he has chosen. After transcribing these on paper for each of the five reinforcement conditions, separate tapes are punched with appropriate logical 1 and 0 positions for each condi-

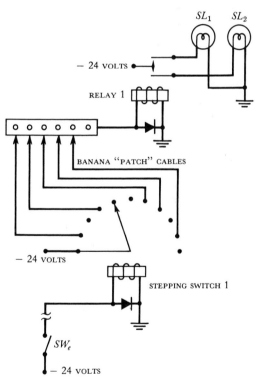

Fig. 2-23 Schematic representation of a rotary stepping switch used to program the occurrence of one or two stimulus lights from trial to trial over a series of trials. Banana jacks are used to make program connections between the "trial" contacts of the stepping switch and the common line to the relay coil. The relay contacts control the stimulus lamps.

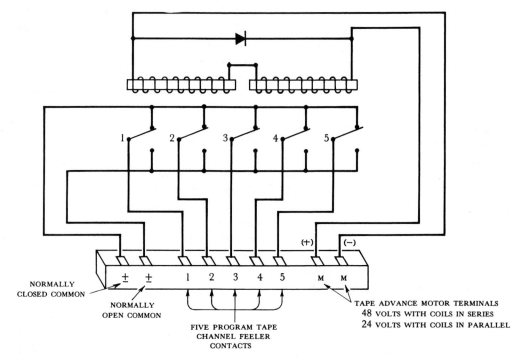

Fig. 2-24 A schematic representation of a Western Union five-channel tape transmitter (1A tape head) model 24, typically used to program stimulus schedules. This switching device has five electrically independent center-pole contacts that switch between an electrically common normally closed set of contacts and an electrically common normally open set of contacts. Although the tape stepping motors are shown wired in series, their input voltage rating may be cut in half, to 24 volts d-c, by rewiring them in parallel.

tion, duplicating the random series. Each of these tapes is then available for immediate insertion into the reader when needed for a particular subject or condition. Coupled with a timing device, the presentation of the sequence is automatic.

It is generally wise to make duplicate tapes to guard against holding up the experiment because of damage to the originals. These tapes may be stored for use in other experiments.

Some tape modules utilize motion-picture-type film upon which the experimenter cuts holes spaced according to the experimental requirements. A microswitch contact rides over the film and completes a circuit whenever the punched-hole portion of the film is encountered. Photoelectric cells are sometimes used

as hole sensors in place of mechanical feelers. The photoelectric cells are typically used as inputs to solid state amplifiers that produce a high enough output to operate control and stimulus circuits. Additional information on tape readers may be obtained from the manufacturers cited in the Appendix.

The use of the *IBM model 526 printing summary punch* is particularly attractive. The cards can be prepunched, the stimulus information read into the control circuitry, and the subjects' responses punched back onto the same card automatically. The 526 card reader senses holes punched in a standard IBM information card, which can store bits of stimulus information in each of 80 columns. The card reader senses the holes in each column sequentially from left to right. After the last column in a card is read, the reader automatically positions a new card in place and begins again in the first column. Much of the sequence of operations in reading the card can be programmed by banks of switches on the 526 module and an internal card programmer.

The rental fee for IBM equipment is low when it is used for educational research. Permission is necessary for minor rewiring of the printing summary punch for research adaptation. Additional information concerning the punch may be obtained from IBM publications, which are available through the local IBM distributor. Punched card programming and recording techniques specific to the behavioral sciences are covered by McConnell, Polidora, Friedman, and Meyer (1959), Polidora and Main (1963), and Uttal (1962).

The *magnetic tape recorder* is the most complex sequential programming device. Although magnetic tape recorders are commonly used as analog recording and playback devices, the tape recorder can feasibly be used as a sequential switch with practically unlimited storage capacity for bits of information. In a simple application, voltage pulses are recorded on the tape in known positions relative to one another. The tape is then played back and its output boosted by an amplifier prior to insertion in the control circuitry. When the recorded pulse passes by the tape head, the stimulus is presented by the control circuits. When no signal pulse passes by the head, no stimulus or an alternative stimulus is presented. Two- and four-channel tape recorders are available. One of the channels can be used to present verbal or auditory stimuli to the subject and another used to present digital pulses to the control circuits. The control circuits may be used to present visual stimuli such as lights, or slide projections in conjunction with the auditory stimuli prerecorded on the tape. If desired, the verbal responses of the subject to the auditory *or* visual stimuli can be recorded on the same tape. If this is done, only one channel should

be used for prerecorded stimulus control pulses or auditory stimuli. This leaves the other channel free for verbal response data.

Commercial tape transports are available that record and play back digital control and data information. *Digital transports* are radically different from the analog tape recorders. Although designed as data inputs and output recorders for digital computers, their speed and binary information capacity make them ideally suited for use in complex stimulus and response situations. They can be used not only for complex scheduling of stimulus presentations but also for recording more than one response measure on each trial, e.g., which response is emitted out of n possible responses, the latency of the response, or digitized GSR, EEG, and EMG. Their real worth in the psychological laboratory is the recording of many different digital response measures, physiological or otherwise, on each trial. The recorded information can then be forwarded to the computer center and fed directly into the computer for compilation and analysis.

Logic circuitry: gating circuits and truth tables

In automating an experiment, switch control circuits called *logic circuits* form a major part of the apparatus. In logic circuits, combinations of switches called *gates* are used to sort out data events and present the proper stimulus environment. The logic circuit description is used because the gates appear to make decisions. *Switching gates* and *switches* are also used to describe the same circuits. Two common gates used in logic circuits are the AND and the OR gates. The AND gate is exemplified by two switches placed in series to trigger a device, e.g., a pulse former, that activates a pellet dispenser. In this case, switch 1 AND switch 2 must be closed to trigger the pulse former. An OR gate can be set up by placing two switches in parallel, either of which will trigger the pulse former. This means if either switch 1 OR switch 2 is closed, the pulse former will activate the pellet dispenser. Pellet dispenser control circuitry is wired to work in the OR condition with a rotary switch on the unit turned to the position marked "parallel." It operates in the AND condition when the rotary switch is turned to the position marked "series." In the OR condition, either the animal pressing a bar OR the experimenter pressing a hand switch will dispense a reinforcement. The OR-gate condition is typically used in early shaping trials when training the animal to press the bar. In the AND-gate condition, the animal AND the experimenter must press their manipulanda simultaneously for reinforcement to occur. The AND gate is typically used in later training trials when the animal is put on a schedule of reinforcement other than the fixed ratio 1:1.

Consider the instrumentation of a simple two-choice discrimination paradigm, wherein a rat or monkey is given a food pellet for pressing one of two bars in a Skinner box. Each bar has a stimulus lamp over it, and the animal must press only the illuminated bar to receive a pellet. A noncorrection procedure is used, with the trial ending after each bar-press response, correct and incorrect. The programming of the discriminatory stimulus from left to right has been done by the experimenter, and the random sequence is read into the apparatus on each trial by a punched tape reader. A flow-chart diagram of the interrelations between circuit modules would be

similar to the one presented in Fig. 2-17, except for the one-trial timer. All control modules have serial time sequence chaining links between them. This means that the system will not operate unless each functional module is operating properly.

The number of OR and AND gates needed to instrument the paradigm is determined from a *truth table*. The truth table in Fig. 2-25 considers all possible response and stimulus conditions and defines all possible combinations of conditions under which reinforcement is delivered or withheld and the trial ended. The pertinent events in the paradigm are cited at the top of the table, and the result of the combination of events is presented on the side. Stimulus 2, the light over the right bar, is not in the table to avoid unnecessary redundancy, since stimulus 2 is never "on" when stimulus 1 is "on" and vice versa.

Each row of the truth table represents an AND gate for the reinforcement result at the side of the table. Note row 4. If the left stimulus lamp S_1 is off (logical 0) AND the right stimulus lamp S_2 is on (logical 1) AND the left response bar R_1 is not depressed (logical 0) AND the right response bar R_2 is depressed (logical 1), reinforcement will be delivered. If two or more rows represent the same reinforcement outcome, they represent jointly an OR gate for the reinforcement result. As the conditions in row 4 OR 5 both lead to reinforcement, reinforcement will occur if all the conditions in row 4 OR all the conditions in row 5 are satisfied. From the table, it takes two AND gates plus one OR gate to dispense reinforcement and end a trial. It takes four AND gates plus one OR gate to end a trial without reinforcement. The truth-table technique can be used to deduce the logic instrumentation for any experimental situation.

A series AND-gate circuit instrumenting the truth table is presented in Fig. 2-26. This series arrangement is called a *relay tree*. Relay S_1 is activated by channel 1 of the paper tape reader on trial n. Relay R_1 is activated through pulse former PF_1 by the left response bar R_1, and relay R_2 is activated through pulse

STIMULI AND RESPONSES

	S_1	R_1	R_2	REINFORCEMENT DELIVERED	TRIAL ENDED
COMBINATIONS OF BINARY LOGIC STATES	0	0	0	NO	NO
	1	0	0	NO	NO
	0	1	0	NO	YES
	0	0	1	YES	YES
	1	1	0	YES	YES
	1	0	1	NO	YES
	0	1	1	NO	YES
	1	1	1	NO	NO

Fig. 2-25   A truth table defining logic conditions under which a trial is ended with or without reinforcement in a two-choice learning paradigm.

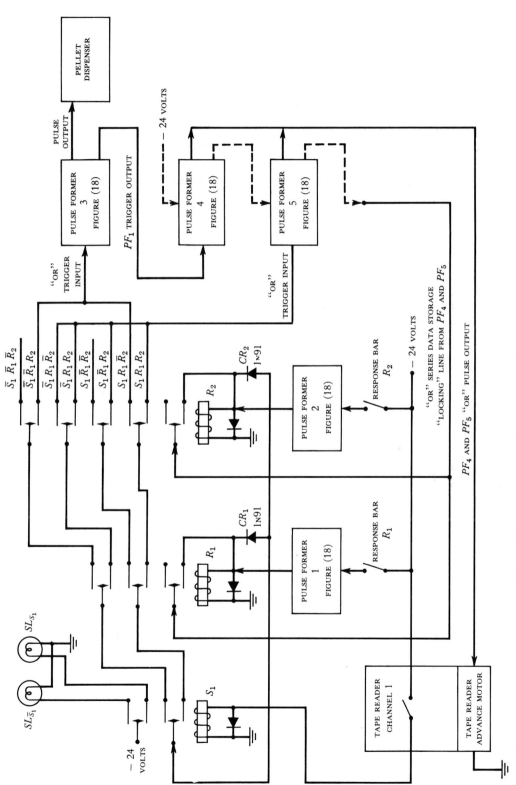

Fig. 2-26. A relay-tree circuit instrumenting the conditions presented in the truth table of Fig. 2-25.

former PF_2 by the right response bar R_2. The pulse formers PF_1 and PF_2 are placed between the response relays and the response bars to keep the apparatus from continuously recycling if the animal merely leans on the bar. Response relays R_1 and R_2 have data storage locking subcircuit features, which, in conjunction with PF_1 and PF_2, make the rest of the circuit independent of the latency of the bar-press response. Note that the contacts of relay R_2 terminate the branches of the relay tree. Only one of the branches of the tree is electrically complete when the subject presses one of the response bars. The contacts are labeled to indicate the conditions that are satisfied when their total branch is closed. The symbol $\bar{R}_i$ indicates the logical 0 state, and R_i the logical 1 state. The apparatus is idle when relays R_1 and R_2 are not activated, as shown in rows 1 and 2 of the truth table. The two contacts on relay R_2 representing these conditions are not used in ending the trial or dispensing reinforcement. The apparatus becomes active when either response bar is pressed. When this happens, the combination of the switched contacts of the three relays passes a trigger pulse to pulse former PF_3 or pulse former PF_5. The trigger pulse is taken from the latching subcircuit of the energized relay R_1 or R_2, passed through a diode CR_1 or CR_2, and presented to the tree at the lower common contact of relay S_1. The diodes CR_1 and CR_2 are arranged so that they are forward-biased for trigger pulses passing from the latching subcircuit to the bottom common of relay S_1 but are reverse-biased for any current flow between the latching subcircuits of relays R_1 and R_2. This prevents the two relays from turning each other on but allows either of them to pass a trigger pulse through the branches of the relay tree. Joining the outputs of the two reinforcement end-of-trial contacts of the tree and connecting them to the trigger input terminal of pulse former PF_3 makes up the OR gate needed to deliver reinforcement. Pulse former PF_3 energizes the pellet dispenser and, when it returns to the stable state, triggers pulse former PF_4 by means of one of its normally closed

contacts. Pulse former PF_4 advances the tape reader. Joining the outputs of the nonreinforcement end-of-trial contacts of the tree and connecting them to the trigger input terminal of pulse former PF_5, bypassing PF_3 and PF_4, makes up the OR gate needed to end a trial without reinforcement. Pulse former PF_5 parallels PF_4 and also advances the tape reader. The latching subcircuits of the data relays R_1 and R_2 are broken by means of a series connection running from -24 volts through the common and normally closed contacts of both PF_4 and PF_5, which are usually employed to trigger another pulse former (see Fig. 2-18). Activation of either PF_4 or PF_5 resets the data relays and advances the tape reader. These actions set up the circuit for trial $n + 1$.

This circuit makes no provision for recording the data. The data may be recorded on a tape punch by adding a few more pulse formers in the series chain before pulse formers PF_4 and PF_5. Data must be transferred to the tape punch by routing the output pulse of the first added pulse former to the data solenoids of the tape punch. This is done by wiring the PF in parallel through one set of common and normally open contacts on each of the three data relays. This circuit will transfer the stimulus and response information from the logic control circuit to the data solenoids of the tape punch and store it there in BCD form.

Note that the relay-tree configuration is a *binary-to-octal converter*. Its input is binary and its output is octal. If another set of relay contacts is added in series with the output of the tree, the number of outputs becomes 16, 10 of which are normally used in generating decimal outputs from binary relay systems.

With the completion of this section, the reader has been introduced to resistance, capacitance, d-c power supplies, RC networks, active circuit control devices, e.g., relays and transistors, schematic reading and module analysis, modular control of latencies and time intervals, logic circuitry, automatic circuit control with switching devices, truth tables, and gating circuits. The development of more complex solid state circuitry is covered in the last section of this chapter, Advanced Transistor Circuits (pages 101 to 114). An understanding of advanced solid state circuitry requires more knowledge of electronics than has been required heretofore, although it follows directly from the information covered up to this point. The sections immediately following are more descriptive and cover, in order, analog amplification, analog transducers, signal generators, recording devices, digital stimulus displays, and troubleshooting and electronic test instruments. More advanced laboratory workers may wish to skip these sections and proceed directly to the last section covering advanced transistor circuits.

ANALOG AMPLIFICATION

Most electrophysiological responses are measured as they are produced, i.e., in analog form. Typically, devices such as surface or implanted electrodes are used to pick up response changes, which are amplified and transmitted to continuous recording devices. The ability of the experimenter to measure and record these electrophysiological changes is directly dependent upon the input, transfer, and output characteristics of various electronic instruments used to amplify or transform these changes prior to recording. In fact, the electronic technology determines what is or can be measured, the error or artifacts introduced, and the interpretations that can be made from the recorded data. For this reason, much of our understanding of physiological experimentation revolves around the electronic instrumentation techniques used to process raw data generated by the organism. The conception of a response in modern neurophysiology is generally based upon the electronic techniques used to collect, process, and record the data. Each response measure is conceived of in terms of transducer, amplifier, and recorder characteristics.

Input to the amplifier

In neurophysiological instrumentation, the organism is often treated as a complex black box with stimulus inputs and various electrical responses as outputs. The outputs of this black box, like electronic black boxes, have various characteristics and electrical limitations. These characteristics determine how the organism's output must be connected to the input of the amplifier system. In other words, the input of the amplifier must be compatible with the output of the organism. For example, let us assume that the cortex is a complex network of resistive impedances that form complex voltage dividing networks across some internal voltage source or sources. In addition, assume that these voltage sources change the output impressed across these complex impedances as some function of the input stimuli applied to the organism. When we place pickup electrodes on or in the cortex, we tap across some portion of these impedances which, for simplicity of illustration, can be assumed to be a single impedance. When the two electrodes are connected to the two input terminals of a response amplifier system, the internal input impedance of the amplifier is placed in parallel with the cortex impedance between the electrodes. To measure the voltage difference between the two electrodes without interfering with it, the input impedance of the amplifier must be much higher than the cortex impedance between the electrodes. If the amplifier input impedance is very low, it tends to "short out" the cortex impedance. The reason for this is that the low input impedance replaces the high cortex impedance in the cortex voltage dividing network. If the amplifier internal input impedance is as high as possible, it reduces slightly the cortex voltage difference between the two electrodes. In the first of these two cases, the amplifier draws excessive current from the cortex and reduces the output voltage across that portion of the cortex impedance between the two electrodes. In the second case, the amplifier draws very little current from the cortex. A compromise input impedance may be found between these two extremes that provides the amplifier with a response signal with sufficient voltage and current for adequate and accurate amplification.

The *preamplifier* (preamp) is a very sensitive high-gain amplification unit and is generally used as the first module of an analog data collection system. A preamp contains a high input impedance designed to respond to minute voltage changes [approximately 50 microvolts (μv)] between the two pickup electrodes. Preamplifiers and amplifiers are classified as a-c and d-c devices. The a-c preamps amplify fast physiological responses e.g., EEG (electroencephalographic) and EMG (electromyographic), while the d-c types amplify slower changes, e.g., GSR (galvanic skin response) and VMR (vasomotor response).

In a simple a-c recording application, one of the pickup electrodes is connected to the ground input terminal of the preamp, and the other electrode to the second input terminal. In the typical a-c preamp, an internal capacitor is in series with the second pickup electrode terminal and the internal input of the first stage of amplification, i.e., the transistor or electron tube. The capacitor is used to block the resting voltage difference between the electrodes when the organism is idle and does not put out a response voltage change. When a response or change occurs in the voltage difference between the electrodes, the capacitor will pass it to the transistor or electron tube for amplification. What we have been saying here is that several cascaded stages of amplification are required in the typical a-c amplifier and that capacitors are usually used to couple, or connect, successive stages of voltage amplifiers. The capacitors block the d-c components of voltage but pass the a-c components with very small attenuation. So long as capacitive coupling is used, the bias voltages that keep each amplifier within approximately linear amplification range have no effect on the final output signal. Typically, an internal d-c voltage bias resistor is connected directly to the internal input of the transistor or tube to keep it halfway "on." This results in the input of the tube or transistor having a constant d-c input bias voltage that keeps the amplifier within approximately linear amplification range, irrespective of the

value of the electrical response input. The voltage characteristics of a combined a-c change in voltage response and a constant d-c input bias voltage are shown in Fig. 2-27a. The d-c bias level presented by the bias resistor is chosen to be greater than the total swing of the largest possible change in the response voltage input. When the response voltage change coming through the d-c blocking capacitor is combined with the fixed d-c bias input voltage, the latter voltage is added to or subtracted from by the rise and fall of the response voltage change. This means that the physiological response input will raise or lower the fixed d-c input bias voltage of the preamplifier, which appears at the output of the transistor or electron tube in amplified form. This is illustrated in the PNP transistor amplification characteristic curve of Fig. 2-27b showing the inverted output voltage as a function of the input voltage. The d-c bias at the input is chosen to turn the transistor halfway on. This keeps the resting output voltage level in the middle of the linear amplification range of the transistor. This middle range is not perfectly linear but will have a small distortion characteristic, with input signals on the upper portion of the curve being amplified slightly less than signals on the lower portion. The output voltage change is inverted with respect to the input voltage change. This is characteristic of the grounded-emitter configuration.

When peaks and fast voltage changes of the incoming physiological response signal are of no interest to the experimenter, the entire waveform of the response will be integrated over a certain time-interval base. This is done by passing the incoming signal through a set of diodes to rectify the a-c portions of the response, which are below the fixed d-c bias voltage at the preamp input shown in Fig. 2-27a. The rectified signal is then passed through a parallel capacitor, charging it with each input physiological response pulse. This method sums the voltage input changes over an integral time base, and the rising voltage on the capacitor is then amplified by the first stage. The capacitor is discharged periodically

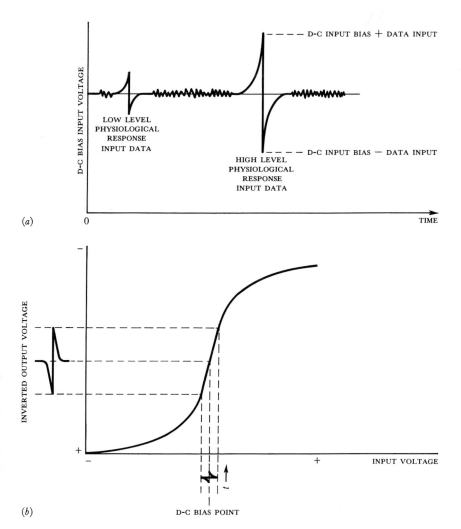

Fig. 2-27   A d-c input bias voltage with a high- and low-level physiological response voltage input change added.

at the end of each time interval to prevent it from being saturated and unable to integrate more input pulses.

A second transistor or tube amplification stage is used to amplify the output of the first stage even more for transmission over long-distance coupling cables to the main power amplifier for processing or recording. In this arrangement the output of the first stage is used as the input of the second stage. In a-c preamps, stages are usually coupled output-to-input with a capacitor in the same manner

that the pickup electrode is coupled to the first-stage input. Transformers may also be used since they will respond only to a change in input voltage and not to the d-c voltage input with respect to ground. This a-c coupling ensures that the subsequent stages will further amplify only the range of the physiological response output of the first stage and not the resting d-c output that does not change with respect to ground.

When an experimenter expects the input electrodes to pick up some noise, a *differential push-pull preamplifier* is often used to minimize it. With a differential preamp, each electrode is coupled to a hot terminal of two parallel amplification stages, and the common ground of both stages is often referenced to some indifferent portion of the body. This is in contrast to the previous procedure of using a single-ended amplification stage with one electrode grounded and the other connected to the hot input terminal. The differential-amplification technique is used when an organism is stimulated intracranially, e.g., with a 60-cps stimulus signal. One would expect the 60-cps noise common to both electrodes to appear at the input of the two parallel stages. The tubes or transistors operating in a *push-pull stage* complement each other, with one operating in the positive portion of the input response voltage change and the other in the negative portion of the response voltage change. By careful balancing of the biasing conditions of the parallel stages, any signal common to both their inputs, 60-cps noise, is nulled out. This technique is known as *common-mode rejection*. If the transistors or tubes used in the push-pull arrangement have similar or matched amplification characteristic curves, as in Fig. 2-27b, the problem of distortion, associated with the slight nonlinearity of the middle amplification range of the single-ended grounded emitter, can be minimized. For purposes of power and minimal distortion, a push-pull arrangement is often used as the last stage on a power amplifier having cascaded "single-ended" amplification stages. The nonlinear distortion involved in the middle range of the amplification characteristic curve is known as harmonic distortion, as it can be described mathematically by Fourier harmonic frequency analysis. It is often reduced in the single-stage amplifier by a technique known as *closed-loop feedback*, which is briefly discussed later in this section.

The output terminals of the preamp section typically have a low internal output impedance between them. This can result from using a different final amplification stage con-

figuration with a lower output impedance than the prior stages. The final stage reproduces the response voltage change of the prior stage output without amplifying it, but supplies a significantly higher output current than the previous stages. This output stage, called the *emitter follower* in the transistorized unit and the *cathode follower* in the electron-tube unit, consequently boosts the power output, in watts, of the preamp for transmission of the physiological response change to the main power amplifiers, usually located in a different section of the laboratory. The power input to the transmission-line coupling to the main amplifier is desirable, since the long cable will act as an antenna for low-frequency electrical noise and 60-cps artifacts generated by the a-c wall power and the heavy electric equipment in the building. The amplified response change put into these cables should be as powerful as possible to maximize the signal-to-noise ratio reaching the main amplifier.

The gain or response change "volume" controls are typically located on the preamp and used to vary the strength of the signal at the output terminals of the main power amplifier. To attach any absolute meaning to the output voltage levels read onto any of the recording devices used to transcribe the data collected, the output of the whole amplifier system must be calibrated by means of various standard input voltage signals inserted at the data pickup input of the preamp. Commercial preamps designed specifically for research purposes often have a push-button switch that inserts a standard 50-μv signal into the system. This signal is used to calibrate the system at the recording device by means of a preamp gain control knob. With laboratory-built systems, this procedure is simplified if the system uses linear amplifiers. This means that the input-output amplification ratio will be the same for any of a wide range of input voltages at the same gain control setting. Hence, a standard input voltage level can be inserted at the input terminals of the preamp and the system calibrated with the preamp gain control knob at the recorder.

Frequency response of the amplifier

The a-c amplification modules are sensitive to a change in input voltage and to the rate of change in voltage or frequency. The higher the frequency of the incoming response change, the faster will be its rise and fall times. Most amplifiers are designed to be frequency-sensitive over a range or a band of frequencies. This means that they will amplify certain bands of frequencies more than others. This is done deliberately in a physiological amplifier by choosing interstage coupling capacitors so that their farad value, in conjunction with the input impedance of the stage they feed into, determines the RC time constant of the amplifier. For example, the smaller the capacitance of the coupling capacitor, the smaller the time constant of the amplifier and hence the higher the input frequency must be for it to be amplified. The larger the capacitance of the coupling capacitor, the larger the time constant of the amplifier and the lower the frequency limit to which the amplifier is sensitive.

The transistor or electron-tube amplifiers in the circuit will introduce distortion into the signal being amplified. This distortion will be seen as a difference between the input and output signals that is not accountable to simple amplification alone. The distortion factor will also affect the frequency response of the amplifier. This means that various frequencies will not be amplified as much as other frequencies. To minimize this distortion artifact, negative feedback is employed by taking a portion of the output signal and feeding it back through a capacitor to the input. Although negative feedback will reduce the amplification factor of the amplifier for all frequencies, it will result in a flat frequency response over a wider frequency band. Feeding back a portion of an under-amplified output frequency would not reduce its amplification factor as much as feeding back a portion of a normally amplified frequency. This technique, known as *closed-loop gain*, is used in many preamplifier and most amplifier sections. *Open-loop gain* may be used in preamp sections to get as much amplification of the input physiological response change as possible, irrespective of distortion. The preamplifier is run wide open with no feedback compensation. Closed-loop gain is introduced in later amplification stages to compensate for distortion of the amplifier system.

Audio amplification

The output amplitude response curve of the amplifier system will approximate a straight line over its frequency band in a-c amplifier systems used primarily for amplification of audio-frequency stimuli. Common audio-frequency amplifiers are designed to operate in a usable frequency band from 0.1 to 10 kilocycles per second (kc). The more expensive a-c high-fidelity reproduction amplifiers have an extended usable frequency range from 0.03 to 30 kc. For this reason high-fidelity amplifiers are more sensitive to low-frequency noise and 60-cps artifacts and require more care in the arrangement and coupling of their transmission cables. In the electron-tube amplifiers, 60-cps hum is introduced since the tube filaments are heated by a low a-c voltage. To minimize this unwanted noise or hum, a built-in 60-cps negative feedback signal can be injected at the internal input by means of a potentiometer. The amplitude of the negative feedback voltage is varied by turning the potentiometer knob until the 60-cps hum at the amplifier output is minimized.

D-c amplification

The d-c amplifier, in contrast to the a-c amplifier, is used to amplify very slow-response voltage changes. The d-c amplifier is typically used in the frequency range from 0 to 100 cps. Internal capacitors, in parallel to the input impedance, are used to filter out any high-frequency noise or rapid changes in the slowly changing d-c input signal. This is done in the same way that d-c power supplies use filter circuits to eliminate rapid a-c changes in output voltage levels. Since d-c physiological amplifiers are concerned with absolute d-c levels of the voltage between two pickup electrodes as well as slow changes of these levels, successive amplification stages require resistive coupling or direct coupling of the amplifier. For this reason, d-c amplifiers are often called *direct-coupled amplifiers.*

In both transistorized and electron-tube amplifiers with direct-coupling features, the output voltage level over time will tend to drift or fall off toward ground when a resting d-c voltage level is used as an input. This is due to a thermal instability in both types of amplifier and is more pronounced in the transistor. Thermal instability is an inverse function of frequency, since more heat is generated at low-frequency than at high-frequency amplification. As the tube or transistor heats up, it will pass more current and the voltage impressed across the internal impedance will drop as the internal impedance begins to drop. This drift artifact in d-c amplification is minimized by using a d-c chopper input amplifier instead of a direct-coupled amplifier. A *chopper amplifier* converts d-c input into an a-c square pulse wave. It reverses polarity of the input terminals by means of a switching relay called a *multivibrator,* which alternates at a fast rate near 1 kc. This provides essentially an a-c input signal, the flat peaks of which are modified by the incoming physiological response. These slowly changing peaks contain most of the d-c voltage response information in a form more convenient for amplification. Of course, some of the information is lost since the chopper relay passes no input information while its common pole is in transit from one contact to another. After the data signal is amplified, the output of the last stage of the a-c coupled chopper amplifier is rectified again to direct current prior to recording the response data.

In spite of the disadvantages of thermal voltage drift and increased internal noise encountered when using transistors as low-frequency amplifiers, transistors are used because of their small size and low power and voltage requirements when compared with electron tubes. These two factors alone allow the experimenter to use transistors in miniature amplifiers that can be mounted on the organism, allowing free movement around the experimental environment without the use of encumbering and restrictive coupling cables. The amplified data are transmitted from the moving animal on a radio-frequency carrier wave generated by a miniature transistorized transmitter. The frequency of the carrier wave is modulated by the amplified physiological response signal data and demodulated at a radio receiver in another part of the laboratory. The data are then recorded. Although the data signal could be used for amplitude modulation (AM) of the carrier wave, frequency modulation (FM) provides better transmission for low-frequency data signals and maintains a better data signal to ambient noise ratio. More than one physiological response could be monitored by using such a system. Transistorized transmitters and amplifiers can be made to *time share* or alternately sample heart rate, GSR, and EEG from the same animal with only one data input and output channel. This technique of using radio signals to transmit the various data is known as *telemetering.*

External coupling

In most commercial physiological response amplification and recording systems, the separate modules are coupled together by cables provided by the manufacturer or by plug-in units that mount directly on the system chassis. Offner and Grass are two of the manufacturers who provide complete commercial units. The Grass polygraph model 5 has recording channels on a chart drive mechanism, each channel driven by a separate, identical power amplifier. The input to each power amplifier is taken from the output of a plug-in amplifier module. Various types of preamp may be used. Each is designed for a different purpose, e.g., galvanic skin recording, electroencephalography, cardiotachometry, and electromyography. Instructions in the proper coupling of these units and their various recording parameters, including calibration techniques, are given in the operations manual provided by the manufacturer.

In other recording applications, e.g., magnetic tape, the output of the pickup preamp bypasses the power-amplifier unit and is coupled to a pair of high- or low-impedance input terminals on the recording preamp of the tape transport. The output impedance of the physiological preamp, in this case, will determine which of the two sets of input recording terminals to use. For maximum power transfer between the two preamps, the output impedance of the first should match as closely as possible the input impedance of the recording preamp. This matching procedure should be used in any output-input coupling operation from unit to unit. Although an impedance mismatch ratio as large as 3:1 to 4:1 is not desirable, the power loss is usually not serious until a mismatch ratio of 5:1 is exceeded.

Commercial audio-frequency amplifier systems have numerous pairs of input terminals with different input impedances available. They are designed to match the output impedances of various units used as signal inputs, such as microphones, magnetic tape read heads, phonograph pickups, and other devices with different impedances. Typically the various inputs are located on the preamp unit and labeled. The preamp and power amplifier are often mounted on the same chassis and are permanently wired together. In other systems, the units are separate and a coupling cable between the preamp and the power amplifier is required. This usually consists of a simple coaxial shielded cable terminating in press-fit RCA pin jacks on either end that match the receptacles of the units.

The output of the power amplifier is taken off pairs of terminals of the secondary coil winding of the output transformer. Output components, such as speakers or earphones, can be wired directly to a set of these terminals. The output impedances of the sets of terminals are labeled, typically, 2, 4, 8, 16, or 32 ohms. Some laboratory amplifiers have higher output impedances of 50 to 600 ohms. The input impedance of the output component should match the output impedance of the set of terminals used. In addition, since the power amplifier delivers a significantly strong output signal in watts, the output component should have a power rating in watts equal to the output wattage rating of the amplifier. This will prevent the output component from being damaged if the amplifier gain is turned up all the way.

Unwanted noise and other artifacts are often introduced by loose junctions in the coupling cables, arrangement of the coupling cables and the a-c power-line cords, operation of the fluorescent lights in the laboratory, and the physical proximity of motors and other heavy electric equipment in the building. For these reasons, physiological amplification systems should employ only threaded or locking cable junctions and should be operated only in recording rooms with a double envelope of copper or galvanized sheet metal electrical shielding and with incandescent lighting. In all cases of amplification, each physical unit should have its chassis grounded to the rack or metal table supporting it, and the rack or table should be grounded to earth. Refer to Chap. 3 for a detailed discussion of physiological instrumentation techniques.

ANALOG TRANSDUCERS

A *transducer* converts one form of energy into another. The analog transducers considered here convert physical energy into a voltage and vice versa.

A number of sensing devices allow the researcher to continuously monitor a wide range of changes in behavior, e.g., microphones, strain gauges, and photocells. What-ever the *pickup* unit, the measured energy change is converted into an electric signal. This signal is then transmitted, amplified, and recorded or is used to control something else.

Audio transducers

Microphones and loudspeakers are famil-iar transducers used in the audio-frequency spectrum. Microphones are generally rated for frequency response (expensive models range from 30 to 20,000 cps), impedance, sensitiv-ity or output, and directional properties. Various types of microphone are available, but most operate under one of two princi-ples: (1) as a voltage generator or (2) as a varying impedance. The *dynamic (induc-tive) microphone* consists of an inductive coil that is moved through a magnetic field of a permanent magnet by sound pressure changes in the air. The induced output volt-age across its two terminals is usually coupled into preamp terminals labeled "mic." The dynamic microphone is rugged and widely used, its sensitivity is good, and a very fine frequency response can be obtained. Since it often contains an impedance-matching transformer, a wide range of output imped-ances is available. A *carbon microphone* pre-sents a variable resistance to a constant volt-age impressed across its two terminals. The change in sound pressure impinging on the microphone diaphragm compresses carbon granules in the mike cartridge, varying its internal impedance. Carbon microphones typically cannot be plugged in preamp inputs directly. They are usually wired from ground to the input of the first stage of the preamp. Carbon microphones are rugged, relatively inexpensive, and very sensitive. However, they have a high distortion level and their frequency response is not so good as that in other microphones.

Most audio-frequency *output transducers* are dynamic loudspeakers and earphones. *Dynamic speakers* are frequency-sensitive and typically constructed for use in low, mid-range, or high-frequency bands. These are commonly known as *woofer, midrange,* and *tweeter speakers,* respectively. When used outside their particular frequency band, speaker response falls off sharply. If a wide frequency range is needed, two speakers may be used, i.e., one designed for high-frequency responses and another for low fre-quencies. Speakers are often used as micro-phones by connecting their leads to the input of an amplifier, e.g., in intercom units. *Ear-phones* may be used as microphones also, but seldom are. Good earphones give a very flat response curve from 0.2 to 2 kc. Peaks and valleys can be expected from any ear-phone at values above 2 kc. For critical ex-perimental work, both earphones on a head-set should have matched amplitude response curves.

Pressure transducers: the strain gauge

The *resistive strain gauge* is essentially a resistor that changes its resistance as it is flexed or stretched. Its internal impedance varies directly with the stress angle applied across it. The resistance changes must be converted into a recordable signal, so the strain gauge is typically used as one leg of the *Wheatstone bridge* shown in Fig. 2-28. The resistances R_1 and R_2 are equal. Resistor R_3 is chosen to equal the resistance of the strain gauge, V_r, when it is at rest with no force applied. Resistor R_1 and V_r form a voltage divider for the input voltage to the bridge from the battery; R_2 and R_3 do the same. With the strain gauge at rest, the out-put voltage of the bridge from points P_3 and P_4 is zero, i.e., there is no voltage difference between them. When a force is applied to the strain gauge, its resistance V_r changes. This changes the voltage at P_3 in the divider network of V_r and R_1. The voltage at P_4 in the voltage divider of R_2 and R_3 remains constant. An output voltage difference ap-pears between P_3 and P_4, which is used as a preamp input. (This Wheatstone bridge arrangement can be used also as a GSR input to a d-c amplifier system. The palmar skin resistance of the subject is substituted for the strain-gauge impedance V_r in the bridge. Two electrodes, covered with electrolytic paste, are wired from points P_2 and P_3 in the bridge and clamped on the hands of the subject. As the subject's skin resistance changes, it acts in the same manner as the strain-gauge impedance in the bridge and produces a voltage difference output at points P_3 and P_4.)

Strain gauges may be used for a number of research activities, including the monitoring of animal cage activity and the measurement of muscular tension. In *monitoring cage activity*, a strain gauge may be mounted under each corner of the animal's cage. As the animal moves around the cage, the voltage outputs of the strain gauges will differ. The four voltage-difference outputs can be amplified and recorded and later transformed into a plot of the cage floor showing the animal's position as a function of time.

When *measuring muscle tension* in humans, strain gauges may be used in data recording systems as input transducers that substitute for the classical wrist or hand dynamometer. A small length of strain-gauge wire may be mounted on a piece of paper attached to a surface, the extension of which is measured. The surface may consist of a U-shaped piece of stiff, heavy metal with the strain gauge attached to the curved portion to measure bending, or to a plastic pistol or handgrip containing the strain gauge. (See Chap. 3 for a discussion of muscle tension.)

Light-sensitive pickup elements

The photocell and photomultiplier tubes are two types of light-sensitive transducer. The *photocell* is a two-terminal resistive device that changes its internal impedance as a function of the intensity of light falling upon it. A typical application of this element is in photoplethysmography (blood volume measurement). The photocell is encased in a black plastic or phenolic block with the light-sensitive element facing a small port

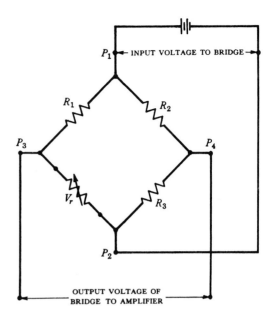

Fig. 2-28   Wheatstone resistive bridge. A resistive strain gauge or a subject's palmar skin resistance is used as one leg (V_r) of a voltage comparator network.

through which the incoming light passes. Opening in the same surface of the block, approximately 0.125 in. away, is a second port in which a grain-of-wheat lamp is deeply inserted. When the block is taped to the temple or the tip of the finger with the holes firmly pressed against the skin, the light from the lamp is reflected by the subdermal vascular tissue to the photocell. As the intensity of the reflected red light is modulated by the amount of blood in the tissue, the internal impedance of the photocell follows the vascular pulse and the vasoconstriction and vasodilation of the subdermal capillaries. The photocell impedance is typically placed in a resistive-bridge arrangement similar to the one presented in Fig. 2-28. The bridge outputs at points P_3 and P_4 are used as a preamp input. (Refer to Chap. 3 for further discussion covering blood volume measurement.)

The cathode *photomultiplier tube* is more sensitive than the photocell. It is an amplifier with photosensitive elements internally arranged so as to modify the internal impedance of the tube when stimulated by light. The photomultiplier is used as an external first stage of a preamp. This tube has been used for various purposes, including the detection of light and the measurement of light intensity.

Temperature transducers

The thermocouple and thermistor are two types of element that sense temperature change. *Thermocouples* consist of bimetallic junctions of two types: (1) the first can be used to detect temperature differences and act as a sensor analogous to an "electrical thermometer," while (2) the second can be used to effect a heat exchange, i.e., it can act as a heat or cold stimulator. *Thermistors* consist of a temperature-sensitive resistive element and can be purchased in a variety of forms. Some thermistors are so small that they can be inserted or implanted into tissue or small cavities. Refer to Chap. 3 for a more detailed discussion.

SIGNAL GENERATORS

Some instrumentation work may require a signal at a specific frequency. Electronic *oscillators* supply such energy by producing sinusoidal or nonsinusoidal output waveforms. The pure sine wave is the basic waveform, and nonsinusoidal waves are made up of pure sine waves of different amplitudes and frequencies. Laboratory audio signal generators or oscillators are capable of producing three common waveforms: (1) sine wave, (2) square wave, and (3) sawtooth wave. The *sine wave* is the most commonly used and, when delivered to an amplifier and then a loudspeaker, produces a pure audio tone. *Square waves* are used for timing and triggering and are developed by square wave generators or multivibrators (a form of relaxation oscillator). *Sawtooth waves* are frequently used in oscilloscope sweep circuits and can be obtained from sawtooth generators or relaxation oscillators. With the laboratory signal generator, sine, square, or saw-

tooth waves are selected by turning a rotary knob on the front of the generator. The signal generator operates from a 110 a-c line voltage. The output signal is taken off two terminals on the front of the generator and typically put into an amplifier before routing to a loudspeaker. This is done because most signal generators have low power output.

At the onset of an audio stimulus, the sharp rise or fall of the signal voltage often produces an audible click at the transducer that immediately precedes the stimulus. This transient response may be undesirable and may be lessened by controlling the rise time of the signal amplitude at the onset of the stimulus. An electronic switch is used to shape the signal envelope. The electronic switch consists of variable RC networks for exponential shaping of rise and fall slopes of the envelope and a time-base generator to control the total latency of the stimulus in a series of ON and OFF pulses. It draws its power from the 115-volt a-c wall socket and generally has (1) input terminals to which the output of a signal generator is connected and (2) output terminals that route the shaped signal to the main power amplifier.

With shaped pulses, e.g., a rectangular pulse, the first rising portion of the pulse is called the first or *leading edge*. The pulse later drops to zero and results in a *trailing edge*. *Pulse duration* is the difference in time between the two.

The *white-noise generator* is a device for producing noise of pseudo random frequency and amplitude. It is similar in operation to the signal generator in that (1) it operates off 115 a-c wall voltage and (2) the electrical noise output is taken off two terminals on the front of the instrument and routed through an amplifier prior to a loudspeaker. Cheaper commercial models, which generate white noise in a frequency band within the audio spectrum, have internal amplification circuits, and their output can be connected directly to a speaker. A good laboratory white-noise generator has (1) low power output and (2) frequency bands from zero to 20 kc, 500 kc, and 5 megacycles (Mc), allowing the experimenter to specify the frequency range used.

White-noise generators are used often in animal laboratories to mask extraneous stimuli. Since some animals have a greater sensitivity to high-frequency ambient noises than humans, it is recommended that the experimenter use a masking bandwidth of over 20 kc in conjunction with a high-quality tweeter that adequately reproduces frequencies over 20 kc. A second speaker capable of reproducing frequencies from 1 to 20 kc could be used in parallel with the high-frequency speaker.

RECORDING DEVICES

The designs of most experiments require the recording of data with respect to time in either a *sequential* or a *nonsequential* fashion. In general, sequential data gathering is preferred, but the amount of work involved in transcribing and analyzing such data often leads experimenters to the use of nonsequential methods. The optimal solution is a data-gathering system that allows for sequential recording in a form that is easily transformed for computer utilization.

Sequential data can be recorded in either digital or analog form. *Digital data* are usually recorded by (1) short pen excursions or (2) holes punched on tape or cards. *Continuous chart drive event recorders* (a chart moves at a constant speed) allow the experimenter to record the event and to time latencies. Various types of continuous chart drive recorder are available commercially. (1) The *pen and ink type* records binary events by the short excursion and recovery of an inked pen over a calibrated time-base chart record. The Esterline-Angus Event Recorder has as many as 20 separate pens riding over the moving chart paper, any one of which may be energized by a response. (2) A *scribe and waxed paper drive* records binary events by the short excursion and re-covery of a scribe over a blank waxed-paper record. (3) The *pen and ink cumulative chart drive,* used in operant conditioning research, records binary events by a stepwise excursion of a pen in staircase fashion over a blank paper record. The pen returns to the base after a fixed number of binary events have occurred and then "steps" again. Event latencies for the three recorders are read as the distance between binary events or as the distance between a binary event and a trial start marker on the side of the record. Typically, these recorders use 110 a-c line voltage to power the chart drive motors. Each pen marker, which is similar mechanically to a relay with a marker attached to its armature, is activated by switching a voltage to its two coil terminals. Various coil voltages are available, so in ordering, be certain to specify a voltage that fits into your apparatus inventory; and in utilizing, determine and input the proper voltage value.

Paper tape and card punch equipment use 110 volts a-c to drive the motors that advance the tape or card and cut the data holes. Trial data are transferred to the punch by activating a solenoid unit that locks in position after a proper input voltage has been connected across its two coil terminals. Solenoid coil voltages vary from 24 to 90 volts d-c. After the data solenoids have been energized and locked in position, a voltage is applied across the two terminals of the electromagnetic clutch mechanism that starts the punch cycle of the unit. When the punch cycle is finished and the data holes cut, the data solenoids are cleared automatically and the punch is ready for the next trial.

Simple *electromagnetic pulse-operated decade counters* are sufficient to record correct and incorrect sums of data in nonsequential digital recording situations. The counter is activated by pulsing the two coil terminals with the proper input voltage, which is cited on the unit. Input coil voltage ratings are available from 6 to 115 volts, a-c or d-c.

Print-out counters incorporate a counting

unit and a printing unit, which prints out cumulative data on a paper tape at times determined by the experimenter. The counting unit is pulsed in the same manner as a simple electromagnetic counter, while the printing unit utilizes a solenoid to imprint the numbers onto an inked ribbon and a roll of white paper. Print-out counters have a number of useful laboratory applications since they allow for an immediate numerical record of sequential operations, e.g., the number of bar presses per 10-sec period for a 30-min experiment, or the number of physiological responses of a certain amplitude range during each 30-sec interval of a 50-min session. Some commercial devices, e.g., those developed for work in radiation physics, count and print out at exceptionally high rates but are very expensive.

In biological work, recorders are categorized according to their *frequency response* as low (0 to 2 cps), intermediate (0 to 60 cps), and high (over 60 cps) frequency. These devices are used for the recording of *analog data*. In physiological research, the low and intermediate ranges are the most commonly used, with most analog data recorded on low-frequency continuous chart drive pen and ink recorders. High-frequency recorders often utilize optical writing devices that reflect light beams on photosensitive film or paper, requiring photographic development.

An *analog pen motor* is driven by a continuous changing voltage input to its coil. Since there is some friction between the pen and the chart paper and some mass inertia of the pen armature, the pen on some recorders will tend to lag behind the incoming voltage change and overshoot slightly when the incoming voltage changes direction. The pen motor also has a characteristic called *hysteresis*. Here, hysteresis describes an effect in which the pen motor tends to remain indifferent to small initial changes that begin and end a large response change. The above sources of error are magnified at the higher frequencies.

Analog recording systems are often influenced by the introduction of low-amplitude noise that tends to make the record fuzzy or wavy. If the noise amplitude is high, it will distort and possibly obscure low-level data. The ratio of data amplitude to noise amplitude is called the *signal-to-noise ratio* (S/N) and for most analog recording applications should be as high as possible; generally an S/N ratio of 100:1 is acceptable. If the S/N ratio is low and distorts the record, the amplifier system and coupling cables should be checked.

The problem of frequency limits, which is characteristic of the chart recorder, may be overcome by utilizing a magnetic tape transport unit. Developments in magnetic tape recording, e.g., the frequency-modulated (FM) systems, provide an expanded frequency response in the d-c recording ranges from 100 to 0 cps. The FM system introduces less noise and distortion than conventional amplitude-modulated (AM) tape recording systems, but is expensive.

DIGITAL STIMULUS DISPLAYS

In behavioral research most digital stimulus displays are visual. The reason for the emphasis on visual rather than auditory displays is simple: It is easier to add more bits of information to the stimulus complex by utilizing various colors, shapes, locations, brightnesses, and symbolic configurations.

Historically, the memory drum and motor-driven card display units have been used in experiments to present timed sequences of verbal material, or pictures and symbols of various sorts. Ordinary slide and strip film projectors fulfill the same functions, with the additional benefit of being easily connected to automatic control circuits of the total experimental system.

Slide projectors operate on 110 volts a-c and do not require a separate power supply. Long sequences of stimuli may be used, and most models accept rapidly changeable slide magazines. Random-access projectors allow the experimenter to present a series of stimuli in nonserial slide order by switching back and forth across a slide magazine and selecting the stimuli specified by the stimulus programming sequence. These projectors are expensive, so check operational reliability with other researchers before ordering.

Film-strip projectors are less noisy and more reliable than slide projectors. Stimuli are photographed one frame at a time on motion-picture film in the sequence directed by the experimental procedure. All conditions are photographed and, after developing, the film is cut into strips representing the stimulus presentation for each condition. These can be formed into a closed loop by splicing or can be kept in strip form and stored for other experiments. Before photographing, use care in (1) selecting and preparing the stimuli, (2) determining blank frames to represent interstimulus or response intervals, etc., (3) setting up adequate lighting, and (4) mounting the camera on a rigid frame. Strip projectors operate off 110 volts a-c and plug directly into the wall socket. If the municipal power supply is much lower than 110 a-c (as it is in some communities), some projectors, e.g., Dunning, may have a "mushy" advance; if it is much higher, the advance may strike exceptionally hard and present a noise problem. Both of these problems can be handled electrically. Strip and slide projectors can be advanced automatically by using a set of contacts off the timing devices cited earlier, or off commercial timers.

The *IBM 026 or 526 card punch console* is a sophisticated card display unit allowing for sequential presentation of stimuli and the recording of the subject's response on the same card. With this technique the data are recorded in a format compatible with the data processing system.

An excellent way of presenting complex visual stimuli is a commercial *single plane digital display* (Industrial Electronic Engineers, Inc.). A single display of this type will present up to 12 symbols, numbers, letters, colors, or written information on a small Lucite screen. The character sizes range from $\frac{5}{8}$ to $3\frac{3}{8}$ in., and a number of individual display units may be arranged in a parallel panel to form words, large numbers, or complex color and symbol arrangements. The single display unit has 12 lamps, each of which has one terminal wired to a common ground terminal line at the rear of the display. With this terminal connected to the ground of a battery or power supply, any or all the 12 stimuli may be projected by connecting the second lamp terminal to the other terminal of the power supply. The ON and OFF states of the various stimuli can be controlled automatically by a paper tape reader. The switching output of the tape reader can be used to control the operation of a relay tree similar to that in Fig. 2-26. The output of the tree would control the states of the stimuli. Lamps are available with input voltage ratings of 3 to 44 volts, with the average character brightness specified for each lamp number. The display (1) has no moving parts, (2) is completely silent, and (3) is very reliable. Also available are push-button viewing screens that activate external circuits when momentary contact is made with the screen, and quick-disconnect types for easy plug-in features. It is difficult to change the semipermanent transparencies within a single model to vary the original stimuli.

Some stimulus displays are best arranged through the utilization of *pilot lamps*. Pilot lamps have several advantages: (1) various colors are available; (2) an infinite number of stimulus-lamp configurations are possible; (3) they are small in size, varying from 0.25 to 1.0 in. in diameter; and (4) the input voltage may be used to vary brightness with incandescent-type lamps. Input voltage ratings range from 1.5 to over 50 volts. For critical stimulus applications use d-c voltages, since a-c voltages often produce a noticeable flicker. Filaments of all incandescent pilot lamps will have a reddish glow as the brightness is reduced by lowering the input voltage. Try not to use them below the rated voltage.

Neon lamps do not produce a color change since they light only when the rated input voltage is reached. This is of some advantage when using a transistor, to turn it "on" or "off," since it will not follow a slow rising or falling input. Neon pilot lamps provide a low current drain on the control circuit, typically less than a few milliamperes. Input voltage ratings are fairly high, typically over 50 volts. A resistance, typically 100K, is placed in series with the lamp to limit the current.

TROUBLESHOOTING AND ELECTRONIC TEST INSTRUMENTS

Since electronic apparatus is seldom perfect, some knowledge of simple troubleshooting procedures and test instruments is necessary for any researcher using complex equipment. Research is often brought to an abrupt halt or erroneous data collected because of an equipment malfunction that requires little more from the experimenter than the jiggling of a wire, turning of a switch, or replacement of a tube or fuse.

Troubleshooting

There are times when the identification of a malfunction requires little more than the use of one of the human senses. For example, (1) malfunctioning transformers or selenium rectifiers often result in an unpleasant odor that should alert the researcher to something wrong; (2) any part (e.g., a resistor) that feels hot to the touch or emits smoke should be checked; (3) melted or bubbling wax on a capacitor spells trouble (this could be due to a "hot" resistor); (4) a buzzing sound may indicate a "hanging" relay; and (5) a crackling sound may indicate a "short." An alert experimenter becomes familiar with the sounds associated with the proper operation of his equipment. This is especially true with apparatus containing relays and stepping switches. Any deviation from normal switching sounds should be checked immediately.

One of the easiest troubles to diagnose is *no output*. When the unit does not operate, (1) see whether the a-c voltage line is plugged into the wall socket; (2) be sure that the ON-OFF switch is on; (3) inspect the line fuse; (4) if tubes are used, see whether they are lighted; and (5) if a power supply is used, check the output with a meter. If the above steps fail to identify the problem, visually inspect the subcircuits for broken wires, loose connections, burned resistors, or general heat damage. This visual inspection is often accompanied by active manipulation of the wires. When jiggling wires or inserting a probe or clip lead, *keep one hand in your pocket*—under certain conditions, experimenters are easier to "burn out" than tubes and much more expensive to replace. If the above steps fail to locate the problem, relays or other switching devices may be activated independently with clip leads connected to the power supply. An oscilloscope or multimeter may be used to check relay or transistor switching characteristics.

It is routine to check the functional operation of various subcircuit modules and components of the module when equipment operates improperly. Check-out and repair are facilitated enormously if *plug-in modules* are designed into the system during the building of the apparatus. Spare modules may be kept on the shelf and used to replace suspected or defective modules rapidly. A defective unit may be located by substituting spare modules instead of using valuable research time for maintenance work. The defective module may be repaired at a later time. This results in a minimum of interference with the scheduled experimental operations.

Electronic test instruments

The three laboratory instruments that are basic to most electronic measurements are (1) the multimeter [volt-ohm-milliammeter

(VOM)], (2) the vacuum-tube voltmeter (VTVM), and (3) the cathode-ray oscilloscope (CRO).

The *multimeter* (VOM) is a battery-powered test instrument capable of measuring voltage, resistance, and current. A selector switch allows the user to choose the mode, i.e., volts, ohms, or amperes, and the range (kilohms, megohms, milliamperes) that he desires. Test leads, consisting of two probes or a clip lead and one probe, allow the experimenter to connect the meter into the circuit. Commercial VOMs provide a-c and d-c voltage ranges of 0 to 3, 12, 60, 300, 1,200, and 6,000 volts. Direct-current ranges are 0 to 60, 1.2, 12, and 120μa and 12 amp; and the resistance ranges cover 0 to 1,000 and 10,000 ohms and 0 to 1 and 100 megohms. Decibel (dB) ranges of -20 to $+77$ are accessory to the a-c voltage ranges.

The resistive mode of the multimeter is an excellent continuity checker for tracing out circuit leads suspected of being broken, e.g., to check out a switch that is malfunctioning. After first zeroing the meter, the multimeter is connected with the clip lead placed on the common contact of the switch. With the ohm range selector set to 1X, the probe is touched against the normally closed contact. If the switch is not faulty, the meter will read zero ohms. If more than 1 ohm is indicated between the two contacts, they are probably pitted and dirty and will shortly become inoperative, and the switch should be replaced. With the toggle in the same position, the probe is touched against the normally open contact. The meter should read infinity. If it reads some lower value, the common and normally open contacts are not operating properly, and the switch should be replaced. The procedure is repeated with the toggle of the switch thrown to the second position: the meter should read zero ohms for the normally open contact and infinity for the normally closed contact. If the readings deviate from these values, the switch will not operate properly and should be replaced. The range selector may be manipu-

lated, while following this procedure, if accurate resistive values are desired. When using the upper range intervals, the operator should not place himself in parallel with the switch by holding both the clip lead and the probe, since the meter will read the resistance between his hands and not indicate the actual resistance between the contacts. The resistive mode of the meter should be used only when the circuit under test is disconnected from the power supply.

The following operating instructions will aid in the proper use of the multimeter. (1) Set the selector switch to d-c or a-c, depending on the test. Switch to the output meter function if an a-c voltage is combined with a d-c component in a test. Some meters have no output function, so connect a 0.1 to 1-μf capacitor in series with one of the test leads. (2) The mechanical zero-set screw of the meter should be adjusted to keep the pointer over the zero line. This screw is generally found directly below the indicator dial. Do not apply current or voltage to the meter while adjusting. (3) When the VOM is idle, remove test leads and switch to the lowest d-c voltage range, or switch to the OFF position. If there is any possibility that the meter may be picked up and plugged into a high voltage through carelessness, you may wish to switch to the highest d-c voltage range. (4) Switch to a d-c range when transporting the instrument. (5) Be sure that the power is off when checking resistors in circuits. (6) When you switch to a new resistance range, reset the zero-ohms (Ω) adjustment on the front of the meter. This is done by touching the two test leads together. The result of this connection should be to swing the needle on the ohms scale to zero ohms. If it is not directly on zero while the test leads are touching, adjust the setting with the rheostat control. (7) Ohmmeter batteries should be renewed frequently to ensure resistance scale accuracy. In the zero-ohm adjustment mentioned above, experimenters are sometimes puzzled by the fact that the needle fails to swing all the way to the zero vicinity. This is caused by weak batteries. (8) Meters are often damaged if set on the wrong scale when connected to a circuit. Play it safe! *Start with the highest range of the instrument and switch down in range in steps.* (9) Be cautious when using the current mode. The meter can be severely damaged if it is not placed in series with the load resistance of the circuit under test. Parallel operation with the test circuit across the power supply simply shorts out the power supply through the meter. (10) Make the final voltage or current reading on the range that allows for the needle deflection to fall in the upper half of the meter scale. Try to read all resistances in the uncrowded portion of the meter.

The *vacuum-tube voltmeter* (VTVM) is equipped with an internal d-c power supply and requires 115 volts a-c to operate. It is typically used in the same manner as the multimeter but has a higher internal impedance than the typical multimeter, draws less current from the apparatus circuit, and interferes less with the operation of the apparatus circuit while tests are being made. The typical VTVM does not provide for measurement of current. General operating instructions are somewhat similar to those noted for the multimeter. Allow a suitable warm-up period before using.

Transistor and diode voltmeters are also available. Solid state meters have the advantage of instant operation, small size, long life, cool operation, freedom from microphonics, and simplified circuits.

The *cathode-ray oscilloscope* (CRO), or scope, is primarily a voltage and time measurement device that allows for the visual observation of the waveform of a signal. The CRO consists of a cathode-ray tube (CRT), a power supply, a sweep generator, and horizontal and vertical deflection amplifiers. The CRT displays the signal, which sweeps across the face of the tube from left to right. A phosphor is stimulated by the signal electrons and leaves a glow that persists on the face of the tube for a fraction of a second. The

inside face of a CRT may be covered with one of several types of phosphors, which vary in decay persistence and color. The characteristics of the phosphors are available from commercial suppliers and should be considered when purchasing the CRO unit.

The typical CRO is a rugged device that can withstand a great deal of abuse. It is used to observe waveforms and to measure the time, phase, voltage, or frequency of an input signal. Specifically, the researcher may determine a number of things, e.g., exponential decay times of RC networks, output pulse latencies, and switch contact bounce characteristics. The output of power supplies, power amplifiers, or high-voltage devices can be connected directly to the CRO input. The face of the display is calibrated in centimeters, with voltage on the ordinate and time on the abscissa. Internal vertical and horizontal deflection plates control the ranges of voltage and time along the axes. The operation characteristics of the deflection plates are changed by manipulating horizontal and vertical deflection control knobs on the front of the unit. These set the voltage and sweep time ranges of the scope. Since sweep is on a time base, which is linear, the duration of a signal and the time between signals can be measured. Other controls regulate intensity, focus, centering the signal vertically or horizontally on the scope face, and triggering.

The expensive scopes are generally more dependable, sensitive, and linear, and some have modular plug-in units. Some inexpensive scopes have a-c amplifiers only. Many research areas in psychology require scopes with d-c amplifiers. With proper attenuation probes, a well-designed laboratory CRO has a voltage range of 200 μv to 2,000 volts and a sweep rate of 5 sec to 1 microsecond per centimeter (1 μsec per cm). A feature found on most oscilloscopes is the *wave input trigger*. The trigger can be activated by the rise or fall of the input waveform and can be used to display asynchronous physiological waveforms in a synchronous manner by starting the display sweep from the left side of the scope at the initial rise or fall of the incoming waveform. This feature is especially useful in measuring the latency of a very short output pulse from a pulse former. The probe and clip leads are connected to the output terminal and the ground terminal of the pulse former, respectively. The horizontal sweep rate is set to a range interval that contains the expected latency value of the pulse, and the trigger knob is rotated until the rise of the incoming pulse appears on the face of the scope. The latency of the pulse is then read off the calibrated face from rise to fall.

Transistor operation and switching characteristics may also be determined with an oscilloscope. This application is pictured in Fig. 2-29. Since we are interested in this case in the d-c switching characteristics of the transistor, the mode selector knob is set to d-c. In this way absolute d-c voltage levels can be read off the scope face. In using the a-c mode, the trace on the scope face always returns to a center position after the transistor voltage output remains stable. The horizontal sweep range may be set to any position, since we are concerned at the moment with the voltage change at the collector, not particularly how quickly or slowly it changes. The probe and clip lead of the scope are connected to the collector and grounded emitter of the circuit, respectively. With the switch (a clip lead will do) between the base and emitter open, a line will appear on the face of the scope. It can be moved up or down by means of the vertical positioning knob to align it with any one of the vertical calibration markings on the

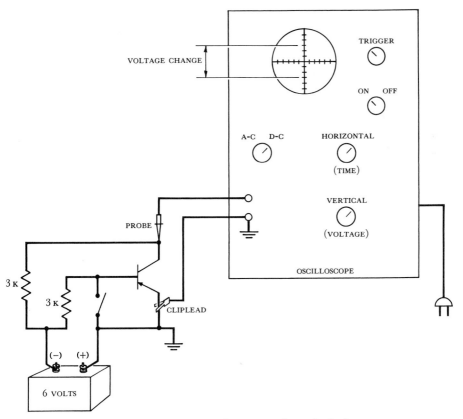

Fig. 2-29 A pictorial-schematic of an oscilloscope used to check the output voltage and switching operation of a PNP transistor.

scope face. The calibration mark is used as the positive ON collector output voltage level reference. When the switch is closed, the line should move to a lower position indicating that the collector has switched from a positive voltage level, ON, to a negative voltage level, OFF. The distance between the reference calibration mark and the lower position is the amount of voltage change at the collector output. It can be read directly off the scope face by referring to the volts-per-centimeter setting of the voltage range selector knob. If no collector voltage change is seen, the transistor is defective and usually has an internal circuit that is shorted between the emitter and the collector terminals. The transistor is switching properly if a voltage change is seen each time the switch is opened or closed. This testing arrangement can be used to check the switching operation and the time characteristics of the transistors in a completed circuit. To check out the timing operation of the transistor in Fig. 2-20, simply connect the clip lead to the ground and the probe to the collector. The external switch SW_e can be closed, and the amplified RC discharge curve will be displayed on the oscilloscope by setting the voltage range to at least 5 volts per c and the time sweep range to a value near the time length of the expected output pulse. If the circuit is operating properly, the output latency control knob can be calibrated by connecting the probe to the top normally open contact of relay 1 and running a clip lead from its common contact and −24 volts. When the external switch SW_e is again closed, the latency of the output pulse can be read off the face of the oscilloscope by means of the calibrated markings. The position of the control knob on the pulse former is now marked as to its latency and the knob moved to a different position and the procedure repeated. Several measures should be taken in each position.

The frequency and amplitude output of an a-c amplifier may also be checked by using the oscilloscope. The a-c mode selector is used, and the horizontal sweep setting is manipulated with the probe connected to an output terminal of the amplifier stage and with the clip lead connected to a ground terminal of the chassis. The input signal is not shorted, since varying the input signal (typically from a sine wave signal generator) is sufficient to vary the output signal to check amplification and frequency characteristics. To check the characteristics of the frequency, turn the horizontal sweep setting until less than 20 cycles of the input signal are displayed. The frequency of the signal can be determined by reading off the time markings on the scope between 10 peak-to-peak cycles of the signal. A defective a-c amplifier may be checked in this manner by tracing the input signal from stage to stage until the defective section is located. Typically, the defective section will have a distorted or weak output signal, or none at all.

There are times when an experimenter wishes to observe two or more phenomena simultaneously. This can be done by using (1) an electronic switch and a single-beam scope (the inexpensive way) or (2) a twin-beam oscilloscope. A commercial *electronic switch* contains controls for varying the switching rate between two amplifiers and the direct voltage output of two waveforms in order that they can be displayed and separated on the scope.

Twin-beam oscilloscopes are useful for a number of operations, including the comparison of lag and distortion from input signal to output signal of a response or stimulus processing device such as a transistor or electron-tube amplifier. The twin-beam scope has two sets of control knobs and input terminals, but both signals are displayed on the face of one CRT. Input and output signals can be visually compared and adjustments made to correct any processing defects in the output signal. When a separate electronic switch is used with the two vertical channels of a twin-beam scope, four signals may be displayed simultaneously; e.g., the characteristics of a transistor amplifier can be compared by displaying a-c collector voltage, collector current, base voltage, and base current.

Various other types of test equipment are available from the commercial suppliers cited in the Appendix. *Impedance-checking equipment* allows for quick measurement of impedances of coils, chokes, or transformers. *Capacitance meters* are available for checking capacitance directly. *Inductance-capacitance meters* give capacitance readings as well as direct values of inductance. *Sine* and *square wave generators,* used for testing audio-frequency equipment, cover various ranges, e.g., sine wave ranges from 20 to 20,000 cps and square wave frequencies from 60 to 30,000 cps. Often an experimenter may need to trace a signal through a circuit to see whether the signal is being distorted or reduced or is absent at any stage. Signal tracing requires a suitable test signal. Audio distortion may be measured with a *distortion meter,* which measures total harmonic distortion. *Wave analyzers* can measure each of a series of harmonics.

Relatively inexpensive *tube testers* are available in many styles. *Transistor testers* allow tests of shorts, leakage, and *beta* (base-collector current amplification). Some testers may be used for in-circuit tests, although more accuracy with all tests will generally be obtained with out-of-circuit measures.

ADVANCED TRANSISTOR CIRCUITS

The output voltage requirements of a power supply are more stringent for work with transistors than for work with relays. The output must be regulated to avoid transistors' being turned on and off because of voltage transients in the circuit. The output of any power supply varies with two factors: (1) the amount of current used by the working load at the output and (2) the input line variations. The output voltage in unregulated power supplies decreases as the current used by the working load increases. This is due to the internal impedance of the power

supply, diodes, filters, and so forth in series with the external work-load resistance forming a voltage divider. Assuming a relatively fixed internal impedance, the total resistance of the work-load circuits goes down as more and more parallel external work circuits are added to an apparatus. This increases the fixed internal impedance in proportion to the total circuit resistance and increases the voltage drop (VD) across the internal impedance of the power supply. The increased internal VD leaves less of the total voltage available for the external working resistance. Input a-c voltage variation of the power supply would be directly reflected at the power-supply output terminals. The regulated power supply should compensate for both sources of output voltage variation.

One solution to the problem is to have an initially high internal power-supply impedance that drops as the external working impedance begins to drop. Another is to have an initially low internal impedance in parallel with the external working resistance that increases as the external impedance begins to decrease, effectively keeping the voltage across the output terminals constant. Both techniques keep the VD across the local resistance fairly constant over a wide range of current output flow. Two types of transistor regulator use these techniques: (1) the series transistor regulated supply and (2) the shunt regulator. The *series transistor regulated supply* uses a transistor emitter-collector impedance in series with the external impedance load. As the external resistance is decreased, the emitter-collector impedance decreases, keeping the output voltage constant. Although the series regulator is the better of the two types, the transistor is easily overloaded with current flow and destroyed if the local resistance is shorted out or reduced to zero. While fuses are used to protect the series regulator against accidental short circuits, it is a race between the fuse and the transistor as to which blows out first. Most commercial transistorized power supplies have built-in short circuit protection; many also have adjustable current-limiting capability. The *shunt regulator* has a built-in safety against accidental short circuits and, because of this feature, is recommended over the series circuit for use in laboratories employing personnel who lack experience with electronic instrumentation. In these situations the probability of accidental short circuits is very high. The shunt regulator operates with the emitter-collector impedance in parallel with the external working resistance and shunts the full current flow rating past the output terminals when the external resistance is very high. As the external working resistance drops and more current is drawn from the power supply, the transistor shunt impedance increases, keeping the voltage across the output terminals constant. This, in effect, keeps the output voltage drop constant since whenever the external impedance draws more current the transistor internal impedance in parallel with it draws less. A drawback of the shunt supply is that the amount of current it uses is at a maximum with no external load. This means that the shunt transistor is run at its highest wattage when the load resistance is drawing the least current. With adequate heat-dissipation techniques the shunt-regulated power supply can be used quite effectively.

A nominal 12-volt output d-c shunt-regulated power supply is recommended for supplying power to general laboratory digital transistor circuits. Twelve volts is chosen since it is a commonly used voltage in many published transistor circuits. It is also a very convenient voltage level since (1) there are few transistors with a voltage rating of less than 12 volts; (2) most digital transistor circuits will operate quite adequately at 12 volts even though the circuit diagram calls for a higher voltage; and (3) the lower the voltage, the lower the current and hence the wattage consumed.

An output 12-volt *shunt-regulated supply circuit* is given in Fig. 2-30. The regulated supply typically has a voltage-control or reference section and a voltage-regulation section. The voltage-reference section uses a 12-volt Zener diode in series with resistor R_1 across the filter output section as the reference element. The characteristics of a 3Z12 Zener diode are such that when reverse-biased, it initially presents a high impedance to the current flow; but when the voltage drop across the diode equals the 12-volt reverse bias or Zener breakdown rating, the internal impedance of the diode falls off sharply and the diode begins to conduct current. The avalanche region of the reverse-bias portion of the curve indicates that a large change in current flow is correlated with a small change in voltage. R_1 limits the current through the Zener diode, and both form a series voltage divider across the 27-volt nominal output of the filter section. (With 29.8 volts RMS secondary voltage, the nominal d-c output will be about 27 v.) When the output of the filter section rises above 27 volts, the current flow through the diode increases. The excess voltage output of the filter section is assumed across the series resistor R_1. When the output of the filter section drops below 27 volts, the current flow through the Zener diode decreases. Series resistor R_1 has a fixed impedance and consequently a smaller VD. In either case the VD across the Zener diode remains at a nominal 12 volts, with the difference between 12 volts and the output voltage of the filter section appearing across the series resistor R_1.

In the regulator section, the power shunt transistor Q_1 and the series resistor R_2 form a dynamic voltage divider across the 27-volt output of the filter section also. The regulated voltage output is taken from the collector and emitter terminals of the shunt transistor. The difference in forward–bias voltage between the base and emitter determines the amount of current flowing in the emitter-collector impedance path. As the base of the transistor is connected to the 12-volt nominal junction of the Zener diode and the series resistor R_1, the operation of this base-emitter difference amplifier is such that the emitter-collector impedance VD is regulated to keep

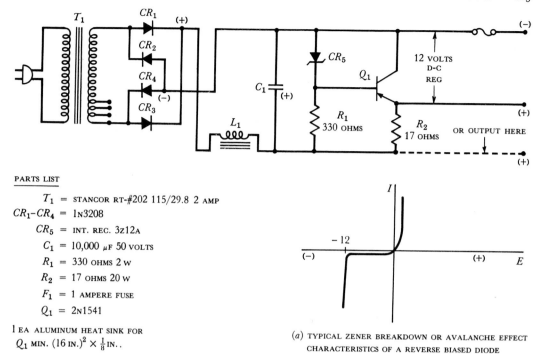

PARTS LIST

T_1 = STANCOR RT-#202 115/29.8 2 AMP
CR_1-CR_4 = 1N3208
CR_5 = INT. REC. 3z12A
C_1 = 10,000 μF 50 VOLTS
R_1 = 330 OHMS 2 W
R_2 = 17 OHMS 20 W
F_1 = 1 AMPERE FUSE
Q_1 = 2N1541

1 EA ALUMINUM HEAT SINK FOR
Q_1 MIN. $(16 \text{ IN.})^2 \times \frac{1}{8}$ IN..

(a) TYPICAL ZENER BREAKDOWN OR AVALANCHE EFFECT CHARACTERISTICS OF A REVERSE BIASED DIODE

Fig. 2-30   A shunt-transistor-regulated 12-volt 1-amp power supply.

the emitter a few tenths of a volt positive with respect to the base. The voltage level at the base terminal is fixed with respect to the fixed negative voltage at the collector by the referencing action of the 12-volt Zener diode. As the positive voltage level at the emitter terminal is the only one free to vary, the emitter-collector shunt impedance adjusts itself. This drops the voltage across it until there is only a minimal voltage difference between the emitter and base. This voltage difference provides just enough forward bias on the emitter-base input path to produce 1 amp of current flow through the emitter-collector's shunt impedance and the series resistor R_2. With 1 amp of current flow through the 15-ohm series resistor R_2, there is a 15-volt drop across its terminals. With 15 of the 27 volts output of the filter section across the series resistor, there is a 12-volt drop across a 12-ohm internal shunt resistance in the emitter-collector circuit. With the external working impedances drawing current from the circuit, the transistor shunt impedance increases, thus decreasing its cur-

rent flow by the amount of current the external load impedance is using. This keeps 1 amp total current flowing in the power-supply circuit at all times and preserves the 12-volt drop across the output terminals. If the output terminals are short-circuited, the shunt regulator is not damaged since the VD and current flow go to zero and the maximum output current is limited by the series resistor R_2.

If a higher-voltage shunt power supply is required, e.g., 24 volts, the following steps are required. (1) The transformer should be replaced with one that puts out a voltage at least 50 percent higher than the 24 volts regulated output. (2) The Zener diode should be replaced with one rated for 24 volts nominal. (3) Resistor R_1 should be adjusted to keep the new Zener within its wattage rating. (4) Resistor R_2 should be adjusted to assume the VD difference between the transformer output voltage and the regulated output voltage appearing across the emitter-collector shunt impedance. The new R_2 resistance is equal to the current flow

through the shunt emitter-collector impedance times the VD across R_2. (5) A larger
heat sink with a surface area of at least 40
sq in. on one side for cooling Q_1 is required.
Forced-air cooling can reduce this surface
area.

The shunt circuit of Fig. 2-30 can easily
be converted to series-regulated operation by
exchanging the position of R_1 and the Zener
diode, keeping the diode reverse-biased. The
series-regulated output is taken from the two
terminals of R_2. The resistive value of R_2
should be increased to at least 120 ohms
to limit the current flow through the transistor emitter-collector series impedance when
there is no external load. If 24-volt regulated
operation is required, the transformer, Zener
diode, and resistive value of R_1 should be
adjusted as noted in the previous shunt circuit instructions. Resistor R_2 should be increased to at least 240 ohms to limit no-load
current flow.

Standard transistor control circuit modules

The transistor equivalent of the storage
locking-relay circuit is the *flip-flop circuit*
presented in Fig. 2-31. The two transistors
are arranged so they form a *bistable multivibrator*. The flip-flop is designed so that
when one transistor turns "on" or is in the
conducting stage, it turns the other "off".
This is done by the cross-coupling network between the collector of each side to the base
of the other. Each transistor emitter-collector
impedance and the 6K collector resistor R_1
are a voltage divider between ground and
the 12 volts of the power supply. With its
base-emitter circuit forward-biased, the emitter-collector impedance is at its lowest value,
and the transistor conducts readily. In this
saturated condition, the VD across the emitter-collector impedance would be at a minimum compared with the VD across the 6K
resistor. This places the collector on the ON
transistor at very near ground potential.
With the base-emitter circuit reverse-biased
(emitter and base grounded), the emitter-
collector path would have a high internal
impedance. In this OFF or low-conduction
state, the VD across the 6K resistor would
be small in comparison with the VD across
the emitter-collector impedance. Consequently, in the OFF state the collector would
be very nearly at -12 volts.

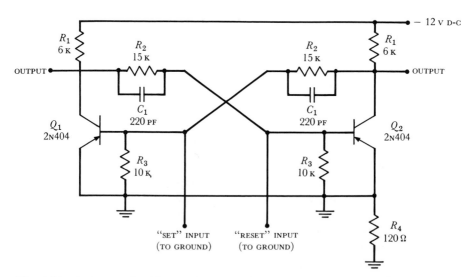

Fig. 2-31 A d-c coupled bistable transistor flip-flop circuit which serves as
a basic transistor memory device and is used as a building-block module in
transistor control circuits.

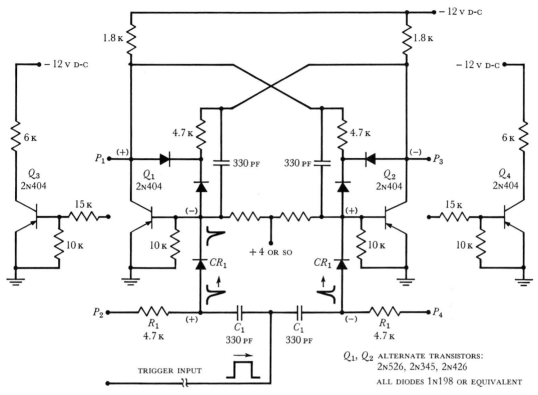

Fig. 2-32 A single-input flip-flop using a capacitor-diode-resistor steering network. This circuit steers the incoming positive pulse to shut off the ON transistor by biasing the steering diodes with collector feedback to the steering network.

In analyzing the operation of the flip-flop, the base of Q_2 would be biased nearly to ground through the 15K cross-coupling resistor R_2 from the collector of Q_1. If the base of Q_1 is grounded at the "set" input, Q_1 goes off, current flow drops, and its collector voltage goes to nearly -12 volts. The base of Q_2 is biased slightly negative through the 15K cross-coupling resistor from the collector of Q_1. Q_2, driven into conduction, turns on, and its collector approaches ground potential. Transistor Q_2's collector biases the base of Q_1 nearly to ground through the 15K cross-coupling resistor. This keeps Q_1 off even though the set input from ground is removed. If the reset input to the base of Q_2 is grounded, the reverse will occur, with Q_2 turned off, Q_2's negative collector turn-

ing Q_1 on, and Q_1's collector keeping Q_2 off.

The 10K base ground bias resistors R_3 are used to increase the switching stability of the transistors. The resistors parallel each emitter-base circuit impedance to form a more stable base bias voltage divider network in conjunction with the 15K cross-coupling resistor and the 6K collector resistor. The 10K resistor in parallel with the emitter-base impedance provides an alternative path for reverse leakage current between collector and base.

The flip-flop module is ideally suited for (1) long-term storage of data, i.e., for a trial interval or longer, and (2) conditional storage of logic events generated within the control circuits of the apparatus. In many circuit

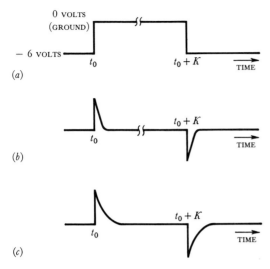

(a)

(b)

(c)

Fig. 2-33 The output of a series d-c blocking capacitor as a function of a square-wave input voltage change and the farad value of the capacitor. (a) The square-wave input voltage change rising from a negative voltage level to a positive level and then falling back to a negative level. (b) The waveform output of a low-value capacitance; rising to a positive peak when the square-wave input rises; decaying rapidly as the voltage at the input does not change; and dropping to a negative peak when the square-wave input falls, decaying rapidly as the voltage at the input does not change. (c) The waveform output of a larger-value capacitance, rising and decaying, dropping and decaying, slower than B with the same square-wave input.

applications, it is desirable to use a flip-flop with a single input that will switch the flip-flop on and off with alternate input trigger pulses. This input may be the output of one side of another flip-flop. This arrangement would have a change in voltage level, from negative to ground, at a collector of the first flip-flop as a trigger pulse for the input of the second flip-flop. A flip-flop circuit module that will switch on and off with alternate input trigger pulses is shown in Fig. 2-32. The basic cross-coupling configuration of the former flip-flop is used with capacitors and diodes added to aid in switching. The trigger input pulse used to switch the flip-flop is a voltage change from negative to ground. To switch the flip-flop a second time, the trigger pulse must first go negative and then

once again go to ground. Since there is only one input that branches to the bases of both Q_1 and Q_2, some means must be effected to steer the trigger "turn off" pulse to the base of the ON transistor and away from the base of the OFF transistor. This is accomplished by means of a *trigger pulse steering network* of d-c blocking capacitors C_1, collector feedback resistors R_1, and base input diodes CR_1. Examine the effect of the d-c blocking capacitors C_1 upon the input trigger pulse. Figure 2-33 shows the output of a series capacitance when presented with a changing voltage level at its input. The capacitor only passes the leading and trailing edge of the voltage change. After the voltage change from negative to positive has been completed, the charge on the capacitor varies exponentially. The size and wave shape of the output pip or pulse from the capacitor depends on how fast the voltage rises during its change and on the farad value of the capacitor. The output waveforms in Fig. 2-33a have a fast rise time and a fast decay latency. This is typical of a low-farad series capacitor. The waveforms in Fig. 2-33c decay slower with the same input wave. This waveform or pulse output is typical of a larger-farad-value series capacitor. More energy is transmitted in the output wave of the larger capacitor than in the smaller capacitor with the same input. The choice of input capacitors is determined, in part, by the frequency with which the single-input flip-flop is required to switch on and off. A low-value input capacitor is used with a high-frequency trigger repetition rate. The switching speed of the transistors sets an upper limit on this frequency. This switching speed, called *transient response time,* also determines the choice of input capacitors. If the transient response time of the ON transistor is relatively slow, a longer output wave from the input capacitor would be required to turn it off than a fast transistor would require. The choice of input capacitors must match the switching response of the flip-flop.

Note that the diodes CR_1 in the steering

network are placed between the output of the d-c blocking capacitors C_1 and the bases of the transistors. These diodes steer the positive input trigger pulse to the base of the ON transistor and block it from the base of the OFF transistor. If the diode leading to the base of the ON transistor is forward-biased and the diode leading to the base of the OFF transistor is reverse-biased, the forward-biased diode will pass the ground (positive) trigger pulse to the base of the ON transistor, while the reverse-biased diode will block the positive trigger pulse. This follows from the observation that a forward-biased diode presents a low impedance to current flow and a reverse-biased diode presents a high impedance to current flow. The biasing of the diodes is accomplished by use of the collector feedback resistors R_1. If Q_1 is on and Q_2 is off, the relative polarities of the various electrical points in the flip-flop are indicated in Fig. 2-32. (Note also that for this flip-flop, P_1 is connected to P_2, and P_3 to P_4.) The base of Q_1 is negative and its collector is positive with respect to its base. This means the anode of Q_1's steering diode will be biased positive through its feedback resistor, and the cathode of the diode will be biased negative by the polarity at Q_1's base. The base of Q_2 is positive with respect to the collector, and its collector is negative. This means that the anode of Q_2's steering diode will be biased negative through Q_2's collector feedback resistor, and the cathode of the steering diode will be biased positive by the positive polarity at Q_2's base. With this biasing condition, the positive (ground) trigger input pulse will be steered to the base of the ON transistor, turning it off, and blocked from the OFF transistor, allowing it to be turned on.

Adding capacitors to the cross-coupling arms increases the switching speed of the circuit. The cross-coupling capacitors transmit the full momentary changing voltage on the collector of one side to the base of the other side, while the 15K cross-coupling resistors have a VD associated with them. Diodes

are also added to the cross-coupling network. These are called *clamping diodes* since they limit the voltage swing possible at the collector of the ON transistor. This is done to keep the ON transistor out of saturation since it takes less trigger energy to turn off a partially conducting transistor than one in saturation.

Since the transistors used in this circuit were chosen primarily for their switching characteristics and low cost and not for a high current or wattage rating, it is recommended that they be used to turn other transistors on or off and not be used to control such items as relays, solenoids, or stimulus lamps that demand heavy current flow. If these components need to be activated, it is suggested that a grounded-emitter amplifier circuit, shown on either side of the flip-flop in Fig. 2-32, be used as an intermediate stage. This intermediate stage is often called a *buffer amplifier* or a *driver*. For turning on electromechanical devices that draw large amounts of current, it may be advisable to place a high-impedance relay between the output of the driver stage and the high-current device. This is recommended for turning on power solenoids or pellet dispensers.

The notion of having the output of one flip-flop switch another flip-flop on or off leads to some important logic applications utilizing two or more flip-flops connected in various arrangements. In Fig. 2-32, the physical points where the collectors are connected to the feedback resistors R_1 are labeled P_1, P_3, P_2, and P_4. These points are labeled specifically since in some arrangements P_1 is not connected to P_2, and P_3 is not connected to P_4. A transistor's base input steering diode may not be biased by its own collector feedback, but the biasing of the diode may be due to feedback from the collector on one side of another flip-flop. This is illustrated graphically by the block diagrams of Fig. 2-34. In Fig. 2-34a the interconnections between the flip-flop stages form a binary counter, or frequency divider,

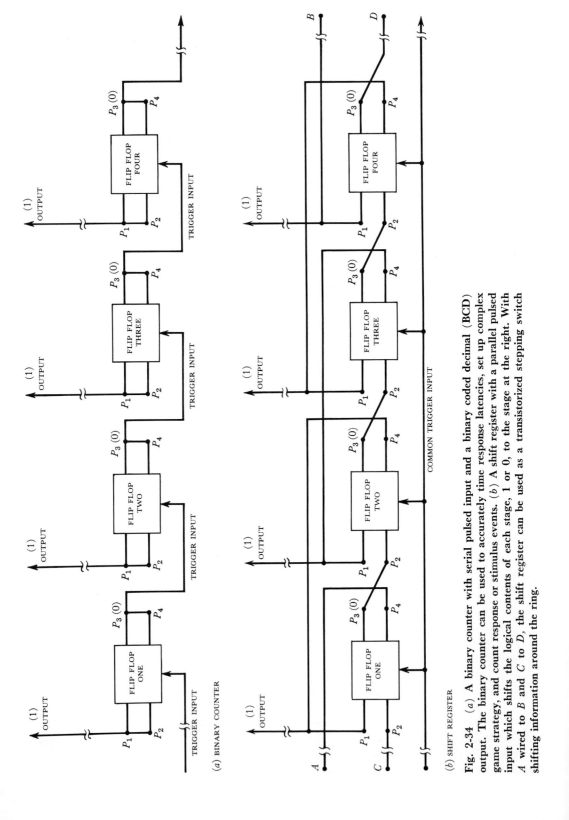

Fig. 2-34 (*a*) A binary counter with serial pulsed input and a binary coded decimal (BCD) output. The binary counter can be used to accurately time response latencies, set up complex game strategy, and count response or stimulus events. (*b*) A shift register with a parallel pulsed input which shifts the logical contents of each stage, 1 or 0, to the stage at the right. With *A* wired to *B* and *C* to *D*, the shift register can be used as a transistorized stepping switch shifting information around the ring.

with the P point connections the same as before. A *binary counter* takes in serial trigger pulses and has a binary coded decimal (BCD) output indicating the number of serial trigger pulses that it received. Analysis of this arrangement reveals that when transistor Q_1 is on or conducting and Q_2 is off and not conducting, Q_1 is said to be in a binary logical 1 state and Q_2 is in a binary logical 0 state. It is binary logic since whenever Q_1 is in a logical 1 state, Q_2 is in a logical 0 state, and whenever Q_1 is in logical 0, Q_2 is in logical 1. *Logical 1 means on, or a positive collector output, and logical 0 means off, or a negative collector output.* Note that the BCD output is taken from the Q_1 collectors of the four flip-flops, and the output voltage change from negative to positive (from off to on) of each Q_2 collector is used as the trigger input pulse of the next stage.

In examining the counter operation, the BCD outputs of all four stages are reset to logical 0 prior to receiving the first input pulse to be counted. Upon receiving the first pulse at its input, flip-flop 1 switches to the logical 1 state. The BCD output of all four serial stages is now 1000, BCD 1. At the second input pulse, flip-flop 1 BCD output switches back to the logical 0 state and the trigger output goes to logical 1, routing an input trigger pulse to flip-flop 2. The BCD output of flip-flop 2 now switches to logical 1. The BCD output of all four serial stages is now 0100, BCD 2. Upon the third input pulse to be counted, the BCD output of flip-flop 1 switches to logical 1 and the BCD output of flip-flop 2 remains in the logical 1 state. The BCD output of all four serial stages is now 1100, BCD 3. Following this same switching sequence, the BCD outputs of the four serial stages after the fourth through fifteenth input pulses are 0010, 1010, 0110, 1110, 0001, 1001, 0101, 1101, 0011, 1011, 0111, and 1111, respectively. After the sixteenth input pulse, the BCD outputs of the four stages switch back to BCD zero, 0000. Each series flip-flop switches half as

many times as does the flip-flop stage preceding it. For this reason the *binary counter is also called a frequency divider.* In BCD counting applications, the counter is usually wired by means of a diode AND gate of the BCD output so it will reset immediately to BCD zero (0000) when it reaches BCD ten (0101). Note that the BCD number can be converted into the decimal system by multiplying the logical state of the BCD output of each flip-flop stage, 0 or 1, by the number of the flip-flop stage it is taken from and summing the results.

The binary counter has numerous applications in psychological instrumentation. The most obvious is counting responses, stimuli, or control circuit events, and signaling in BCD form through a diode AND gate when a particular limit has been reached. A less obvious use of the counting technique is to set up complex game strategy schedules for use in decision paradigms. For example, a diode AND-gate output can be used to block reinforcement of a correct response after every third or fourth reinforced correct response. A pair of binary counters and diode gates can be used to control conditions to reinforce the response most reinforced or least reinforced in the past trials. Another application is to use the counter as a latency clock, counting regularly timed input trigger pulses. The accuracy of the time measures read off the BCD output of the counter would be limited only by the frequency error of the incoming trigger pulses.

Figure 2-34b shows a block diagram of the connections of the P points of the trigger steering network. This is called a shift register. A *shift register* arrangement of flip-flops can be used as the solid state equivalent of the *stepping switch.* Although only four stages are shown, any number can be used. Analysis of the arrangement of the P point connections of the steering network is straightforward and is similar to the analysis of the single flip-flop network, except that the blocking action is controlled by the voltage levels of the collectors of the preceding flip-flop. Upon being pulsed at the trigger input common to all stages, the register shifts the content of the first stage to the second stage, the second to the third, and the third to the fourth. Since the fourth stage is also the last stage, its prior content is lost upon each shift trigger pulse. The content of the last stage can be shifted into the first stage by biasing the first-stage steering network from the collectors of the last stage. This arrangement forms a *shift ring*, with the information of each stage stepping around the ring upon each shift trigger pulse. Without this ring connection from the last to the first stage, the content of the first stage is set by the user of the shift register according to the information he wants shifted to the successive stage following each trigger pulse. This is done by grounding the set or reset inputs of the first stage prior to each shift trigger pulse.

If the binary counter is to be used as a simple clock, a reasonably accurate clock pulse generator is needed to generate the trigger input pulses to the first stage of the counter. Such a circuit module is presented in Fig. 2-35. Although the output frequency of trigger pulses from this circuit is not highly accurate and will have frequency drift, its frequency error is tolerable for most psychological applications. The circuit is similar to the flip-flop arrangement, but the cross-coupling network uses only capacitors permitting only a-c coupling from collector to base.

Assume that Q_1 is turning on with its base forward-biased by resistor R_1. As the voltage level at the collector rises to ground potential, the cross-coupling capacitor C_1 passes a positive pulse to the base of Q_2, turning it off. The amount of time that Q_2 stays off depends upon the time constant of capacitor C_1 and the resistive value of R_2. The positive charge pulse coming through C_1 is bled through R_2, keeping the base of Q_2 positive. When the positive pulse output of C_1 is dissipated through R_2, allowing R_2 to slightly forward-bias Q_2's base, Q_2 begins to turn on. As Q_2's collector voltage rises to ground potential, a positive pulse is passed through C_2 to Q_1's base, turning Q_1 off. When the positive pulse output of C_2 dissipates through R_1, Q_1 begins to turn on again, completing the time cycle. The repetition rate of the circuit is determined by the farad value of C_1 and C_2, the resistances of R_1 and R_2, and the negative voltage level applied to R_1 and R_2. The more negative the voltage applied to R_1 and R_2, the faster the positive output pulse from C_1 and C_2 will dissipate. Variable resistors may be substituted for R_1 and R_2, allowing some variation in oscillation

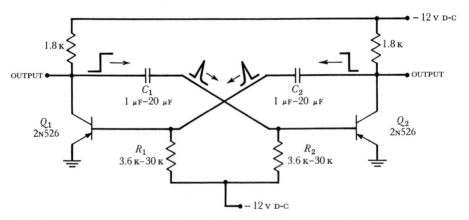

Fig. 2-35 A two-transistor astable multivibrator (recycling timer) typically used as a general-purpose clock pulse generator. The circuit is free-running, putting out strings of alternate positive pulses at both collectors.

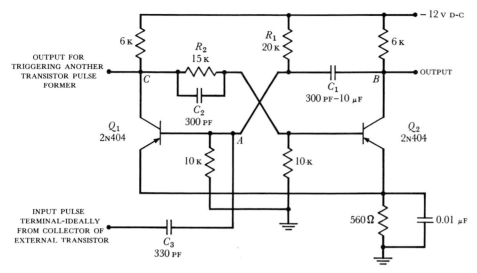

Fig. 2-36 A transistor monostable multivibrator (pulse former) which uses two transistor cross-coupled in flip-flop form, with one side permitting a-c coupling only.

rate without changing the capacitors or the voltage levels used in the circuit.

If a control circuit is fully transistorized, a transistorized pulse-former output is very useful as a capacitor-coupled set or reset input for flip-flops or as a trigger input for binary counters, shift registers, or to other pulse formers. A *transistor pulse former* of this type is shown in Fig. 2-36. The basic cross-coupling arrangement is used, but one side permits only a-c coupling through a timing capacitor C_1. With the circuit at reset, Q_1 is kept on by R_1, a 20K negative bias resistor that replaced the cross-coupling resistor to its base. R_1 also determines the sensitivity of the pulse former to its input trigger pulse. Q_2 is kept off by the 15K cross-coupling resistor R_2 from Q_1's positive collector. When a positive trigger pulse is applied to the base of Q_1 through input capacitor C_3, Q_1 is turned off and Q_2 is turned on by the negative voltage at Q_1's collector. When it goes on, Q_2's collector applies a positive voltage change to the cross-coupling capacitor C_1. The dissipation time of the output pulse of C_1 through R_1 and 10K emitter-base resistor determines how long Q_1

is kept off. Since the pulse-former output pulse is taken from Q_2's collector, the RC time constants of C_1 and R_1 determine the latency of the output pulse. When the output of C_1 has dissipated through R_1, the base of Q_1 is biased negative again, bringing the circuit to rest.

Two or more pulse formers may be chained, with the pulse termination of the first triggering the input of the second. For this sequence action, the input of the second pulse former is taken from the collector of Q_1 of the first pulse former, which goes positive at the finish of Q_2's output pulse. An indefinite number of pulse formers may be chained in this fashion, generating an indefinite length of chained output pulses.

To examine the control relationships between various transistor modules in an apparatus circuit, consider the circuit given in Fig. 2-37. This circuit is a transistor version of the two-choice learning paradigm circuit using relays shown in Fig. 2-26. The requirements are the same, and the truth table presented in Fig. 2-25 also describes the present circuit. Examine first the purpose of pulse former PF_1 which is the circuit presented

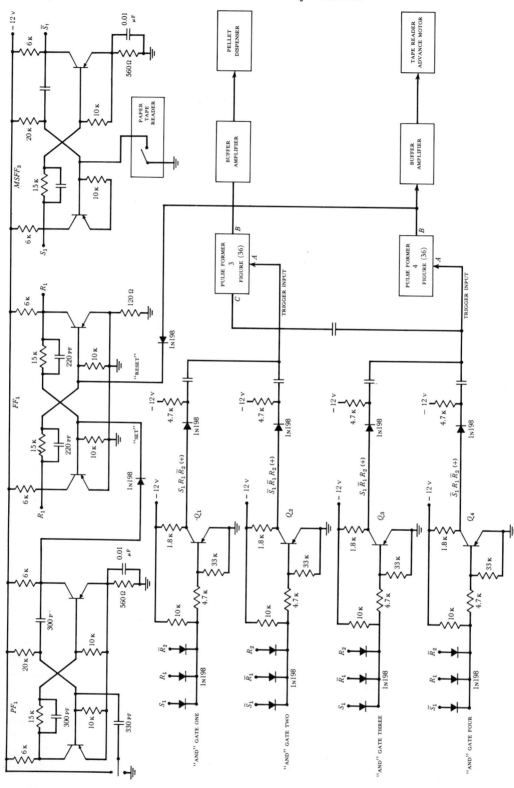

Fig. 2-37 A complex circuit instrumenting the two-choice learning paradigm truth table of Fig. 2-25. It consists of standard building-block transistor modules such as flip-flops, pulse formers, grounded-emitter amplifiers, and diode NAND gates.

in Fig. 2-36. This pulse former puts out a pulse of definite length that switches flip-flop FF_1 out of the $\bar{R}_1$ state into the R_1 state the first time a subject presses the left response bar RB_1 on each trial. FF_1 is used in the circuit as a response storage module and is identical to the circuit shown in Fig. 2-31. Pulse former PF_1 is placed between the response bar and the flip-flop to require the animal to release the response bar prior to the next bar-press response. This feature prevents the apparatus from continuously pumping out pellets if the animal leans on the bar. The pressing of the right response bar RB_2 is introduced into the AND/OR gate circuitry by duplicating PF_1 and FF_1 with pulse former PF_2 and flip-flop FF_2. Since the pulse-former module is designed for optimal sensitivity to trigger input pulses, it may sometimes trigger on the negative return of the trigger input at the response bar to the normally closed contact. If this occurs, it may be eliminated by placing a small diode, similar to the others used in the circuit, between the blocking-capacitor input and the input base of the pulse-former module.

The stimulus state S_1 or $\bar{S}_1$ is introduced to the circuit gates by having the paper tape program reader activate a monostable flip-flop $MSFF_3$ that switches from $\bar{S}_1$ to S_1 whenever a hole is present in any one of the information channels of the program tape. $MSFF_3$ is identical to the circuit in Fig. 2-36. Note that in all six flip-flop collector output cases, R_1 through $\bar{S}_1$, a negative output is arbitrarily defined as an output. These negative outputs are used as inputs to the diode-transistor amplifier AND gates 1 to 4. The first two AND gates are used to sort out conditions necessary to dispense reinforcement and to end a trial. The second two AND gates are used to end a trial without reinforcement. The operation of all the AND gates is the same. The output transistor Q_1, of AND gate 1, conducts only if all three collector inputs to the diodes are negative. If the three diodes were disconnected from the collectors, Q_1 would immediately turn

on since its base is biased negative by the 10K resistor leading to -12 volts. When the diodes are connected to their respective flip-flop collectors as indicated, and any one (or more) of the three collector outputs is positive, the input diode becomes forward-biased with a low VD across it. This consequently biases the base of Q_1 nearly to ground, effectively turning it off. All three input conditions S_1, R_1, $\bar{R}_2$ must be met before AND gate 1 delivers a positive output. All four AND gates have an inverted output; i.e., when all three inputs to the diodes are negative, the collector of the output transistor is positive. They are more correctly called inverted AND or NOT AND (NAND) gates. Conversely, as the input diodes are also a parallel inverted OR gate, with any positive input resulting in a negative output, they may be called a NOT OR (NOR) gate.

When either NAND gate 1 *or* NAND gate 2 has a positive output, pulse former PF_3 is triggered through an OR gate or two diodes and two capacitors. These diodes are used to prevent the trigger pulse output of one pulse former from appearing momentarily on the collector of the other. PF_3 is used to switch a monostable flip-flop identical to $MSFF_3$. The positive output of the monostable flip-flop is used to turn on a small 12-volt buffer relay with a coil impedance of not less than 300 ohms. The buffer-relay contacts are then used to activate the pellet dispenser. As the initial surge current of most pellet dispensers is approximately 10 to 15 amp, even though it is feasible to drive them directly with a power transistor, it is much simpler to substitute a relay to handle the large current flow required. Since pulse former PF_4 is chained to the resting output of PF_3, it is triggered when PF_3 goes into a stable state again. Upon being triggered, PF_4 ends the trial by advancing the tape reader. The same buffer conditions between the output of PF_4 and the tape reader are required as those between PF_3 and the pellet dispenser. If the nonreinforcement conditions are met at OR gate 2, PF_4 will end the trial without reinforcements being delivered. In addition to advancing the tape reader, PF_4 also triggers the reset diode inputs of the response storage flip-flops FF_1 and FF_2. This action sets the logic system for the next trial.

Note that the interconnections between the various modules in the circuit are set up in a *functional time sequence chain*. In all cases, *the circuit remains idle if one or any of the modules does not operate properly, with the exceptions of the pellet dispenser and the paper tape reader*. Flip-flops FF_1 and FF_2 are in the circuit because they lend themselves readily to storing the subject's bar-press response independent of the time length of the bar press. This frees the circuit from being concerned with performing its operations only during the time that the animal depresses the bar. In a more complex experimental situation with many more modules used in the circuit, this response storage technique greatly facilitates the design of the circuit.

The characteristics of various transistors may differ from one unit to another. This is true even for transistors of the same type, which means that circuit components may occasionally have to be varied slightly for normal operation. With lower-priced items it is quite possible that the experimenter may be forced to build a circuit around the characteristics of the transistor.

REFERENCES

BAILEY, R. W. Making etched circuit boards. *Electronics World*, 1963 (July), 38–39.

BROWN, C. C., and SAUCER, R. T. *Electronic instrumentation for the behavioral sciences*. Springfield, Ill.: Charles C Thomas, 1958.

BROWN, C. C., and THORNE, P. R. Basic operations of digital logic. *Psychophysiology*, 1964, **1**, 101–110.

CLEARY, J. F. (Ed.) *General electric transistor manual*. Syracuse: General Electric, 1962.

CONTI, T. *Metallic rectifiers and crystal diodes*. New York: Rider, 1958.

CORNSWEET, T. N. *The design of electrical circuits in the behavioral sciences*. New York: Wiley, 1963.

DEPT. OF THE ARMY. Basic theory and applications of transistors. TM 11-690. Washington: U.S. Government Printing Office, 1959.

DEPT. OF DEFENSE. Military standardization handbook selected semiconductor circuits. Mil. Hdbk.-215. Washington: U.S. Government Printing Office, 1960.

DONALDSON, P. E. K. *Electronic apparatus for biological research*. London: Butterworth, 1958.

GRINGS, W. W. *Laboratory instrumentation in psychology*. Palo Alto: National Press, 1954.

GYORKI, J. R. Selecting a suitable heat sink. *Electronics World*, 1963 (July), 46–48.

MCCONNELL, D. G., POLIDORA, V. J., FRIEDMAN, M., and MEYER, D. R. Automatic reading and recording of digital data in the analysis of primate behavior. *IRE Trans.*, 1959, **48**, 221–224.

POLIDORA, V. J., and MAIN, W. T. Punched card programming and recording techniques employed in the automation of the WGTA. *J. exp. Anal. Behav.*, 1963, **6**, 599–603.

SCHURE, A. *Basic transistors*. New York: Rider, 1961.

STACY, R. W. *Biological and medical electronics*. New York: McGraw-Hill, 1960.

TECHNICAL EDUCATION AND MANAGEMENT, INC. *Computer basics: Solid state computer circuits*. Indianapolis: Sams, 1962.

UTTAL, W. R. The use of a summary card-punch to generate stimuli and to collect data simultaneously *Amer. J. Psychol.*, 1962, **75**, 150–151.

Publications covering recent developments in instrumentation

American Journal of Medical Electronics, 466 Lexington Ave., New York, N.Y.

Instruments and Control Systems, 845 Ridge Ave., Pittsburgh 12, Pa.

Medical Electronics and Biological Engineering, Pergamon Press, 122 E. 55 St., New York, N.Y.

Medical Electronic News, Instruments Pub. Co., 845 Ridge Ave., Pittsburgh 12, Pa.

Science (Instrumentation issues), AAAS, 1515 Massachusetts Ave., N.W., Washington, D.C.

Instrumentation sections of *Amer. J. Psychol.*, *J. exp. Anal. Behav.*, and *Psychophysiology*.

Part Two

PSYCHOBIOLOGY

In this volume the area of psychobiology is represented by physiological psychology and psychochemistry. Chapter 3, Physiological Psychology, covers experimental procedures and instrumentation utilized in the study of neural, receptor, and effector processes, beginning with a consideration of the variables influencing electrophysiological recordings, i.e., electrodes and electrolytes, electrical shielding, electrical characteristics of tissue, and the distinctive features of amplifying-recording systems. Methods for recording nerve impulses and brain electrical activity are reported for acute and chronic preparations, with specific information provided on the use of the stereotaxic instrument, cortical recording electrodes, and electrode materials for chronic implants. Techniques for implantation and recording precede a description of microelectrodes, histological methodology, and procedures for producing lesions. The authors' coverage of receptor processes includes methods and instrumentation for the study of electrophysiological activity in the retina and optic nerve, inner ear and cochlea, and other senses. A section on effector processes emphasizes the measurement of peripheral physiological phenomena that reflect the activity of muscles and glands. Methods for preparing subjects, amplifying signals, and recording responses are cited for studies of electromyography, tremor and other types of muscular reaction. Thompson, Lindsley, and Eason also describe and reference methods for measuring voluntary eye movements, extraocular muscle activity, cardiovascular responses, respiration, and gastrointestinal activity.

A discussion of the galvanic skin response and glandular action concludes the chapter.

Additional information on measuring effector processes may be found in issues of *Psychophysiology*. Refer to Ellsworth (1963) for an animal preparation and polar stereotaxic system that combines many experimental advantages of the acute preparation with the physiological and behavioral advantages of the chronic preparation. Histological and histochemical techniques are described by Davenport (1960), and Geddes (1962) references a bibliography of biological telemetry. Detailed descriptions of telemetry techniques and applications may be found in Marko, McLennan, Correll, Potor and Gibson (1963) and Simons and Prather (1964). A short report by Fudim (1965) describes several types of display storage oscilloscopes and portable signal-averaging digital computers.

Although the basic electrophysiological laboratory instrument is still the multichannel polygraph, signal-averaging devices and electromagnetic tape recorders have extended the experimenter's ability to capture, retain, and store signals. Portable signal-averaging digital computers, such as Mnemotron computer of average transients (*CAT*) and the Enchancetron, have the ability to pull a small signal out of a noise background, retain it, and average recurring signals with time. With the *CAT*, outputs are provided for the digital and analog modes that allow the computer to continuously display its memory content on an oscilloscope, utilize analog *XY* plotters, or compute on-line auto and cross correlations. The use of a magnetic tape recorder allows the experimenter to store data, which may be played back at fast or slow speeds and simultaneously viewed on an oscilloscope, or to feed data into other instruments for subsequent analysis. Refer to Chap. 2 for additional information on digital and analog instrumentation and to Part 6 for data processing techniques.

Psychochemistry (*Chap. 4*) covers some of the experimental techniques used in psychopharmacology, psychoendocrinology, and psychoneurochemistry. Polidora and Bowman emphasize the conditions determining drug effects, drug administration, drug forms and preparation, and research methodology. The authors also discuss biochemical measurements, emphasizing the definition and description of assay techniques. Consult Barnes and Eltherington (1964) for additional information on drug dosage in laboratory animals, and the Psychopharmacology Service Center Bulletin (1963) for an extended list of drug compounds together with their respective structural formulas, symptoms, side effects, trade names, doses (sometimes by several routes and for several species), and manufacturers. Morris and Morris (1964) present a detailed treatment of separation methods in biochemistry, and Miller (1965) cites some of the variables and research methods involved in the study of chemical stimulation of the brain.

Chapter 3

PHYSIOLOGICAL PSYCHOLOGY

RICHARD F. THOMPSON, DONALD B. LINDSLEY, *and* ROBERT G. EASON

This chapter will cover the methodological aspects of physiological psychology, with the description of methods and instrumentation limited to *neural, receptor,* and *effector processes*. Although some space will be devoted to the measurement of respiratory, circulatory, metabolic, and secretory activities, it should be axiomatic that anyone contemplating the use of any of these functions as a behavioral indicator or as an index of homeostatic constancy or feedback control should consult standard physiology texts. Not only will they find more there on methods and instrumentation than can be given here, but they should also fully understand the significance of each of these systems and the potential influences upon, and interactions among, them. Unfortunately, psychologists often select heart rate or blood pressure as a simple indicator for correlation with other behavioral measures or as an index of behavioral change but have little understanding of the factors (other than a specific stimulus arrangement) that might account for the changes involved. Very often the results could have been predicted by a physiologist or psychologist who had taken the trouble to review carefully the system with which he contemplated working.

When using drugs or pharmacological agents as anesthetics or as facilitatory or inhibitory agents, the experimenter should understand (1) the recommended dosages, (2) the ways to evaluate the effects of the drug or anesthetic, and (3) the counteracting agents and auxiliary injections of other substances that may be necessary to maintain blood pressure or other physiological functions. Sometimes this information can be found in physiological or pharmacological texts, but often it can be found for a specific species and a specific type of experiment only in the research literature. Refer to Chap. 4 for specific information on psychochemistry.

NEURAL PROCESSES

Before taking up specific areas of electrical recording in the nervous system, it is necessary to consider some general principles applicable to all types of electrophysiological recording. These pertain to *electrodes and electrolytes,* to *electrical shielding against unwanted signals and extraneous electrical influences,* to *electrical characteristics of physiological tissues,* and to *electrical characteristics of amplifying-recording systems.*

Electrodes and electrolytes

In order to record the changes in electrical activity in a structure such as a nerve, a muscle, the brain, or a receptor organ, it is necessary to have two points of contact on the organism to complete the input circuit to the amplifying-recording system. Both points of contact may be *on* or *in* the specific part or tissue that is active; or one may be *on, in,* or *over* the specific part that is active and the other may be at some remote "inactive" or "indifferent" region. The former, involving two points of contact relative to active tissue, is referred to as a bipolar arrangement or pickup; the latter, as a monopolar pickup. In the case of the bipolar arrangement, changes in electrical activity may be going on in the region of both contacts, either successively or simultaneously. Any change of potential between the two contacts in this case is a function of the changes that may be going on under both. With the monopolar arrangement, changes in potential between the contact over an active region and that over the inactive region are thought to originate primarily under the former. The inactive region serves as a reference for changes going on in the active region. When the inactive region is also grounded, i.e., connected to earth, it provides a fixed reference level since it is at ground potential and any changes in the active region can be measured and stated with respect to ground. This latter procedure is sometimes referred to as a *single-ended input,* in contrast to two active connections which go to the input of a differential or push-pull amplifier and which are called a *push-pull input.*

Generally the points of contact are made by insulated wires bared at their tips or by metallic plates attached to the wires. Contact with the tissue may be made by a cotton wick attached to the wire and saturated with a conductive solution, or the wire may be in capillary tubing filled with an electrolyte solution that makes contact with the tissue at its constricted end. In any of these instances the wires lead from the contact source to the input circuit of the amplifier where the signal or difference of potential is increased markedly.

The points of contact with the tissues, whether by wires, plates, wicks, or fluids, are referred to as *electrodes,* although sometimes they are called *leads* since the electrodes and their wires lead off voltage fluctuations to the amplifiers. The electrodes or leads may come in direct contact with the tissue or make contact through an electrolyte. The *electrolyte* is usually a fluid, cream, or paste containing ionic salts that make the solution or substance conductive. Generally one attempts to find a salt, and to use a concentration of it in the solution, that will be nonreactive with the tissues and fluids with which it comes in contact. Typical creams or pastes used to make contact with the skin contain electrolytes such as sodium, potassium, or calcium chloride. When the electrolyte comes in direct contact with exposed tissue and body fluids, a physiological solution, such as Ringer's or Locke's, is used that matches, or is isotonic with, the body fluids. Ringer's solution, as modified by Locke for use with mammals, contains 0.9 percent anhydrous sodium chloride ($NaCl$), 0.042 percent potassium chloride (KCl), 0.18 percent calcium chloride ($CaCl_2$), 0.15 percent sodium bicarbonate ($NaHCO_3$), and 0.1 percent dextrose. Such solutions are made with distilled water and should be reasonably new or fresh when used.

If two electrodes are directly in or on an active structure or tissue and the electrodes are close together, within 1 to 2 millimeters (mm), it can be assumed that the electrical activity they pick up is locally generated. When the electrodes are further separated, there is a tendency to pick up activity from a wider field since electric currents generated in a conductive medium usually spread in some kind of patterned field. There are usually a *source* and a *sink* where electric currents originate and toward which they flow. This determines the direction and pattern of the field, whereas the magnitude of the current determines the extent of the electric field forces (see Fig. 3-1). The body is an excellent conductor of electric currents. When currents originate in and are locally conducted along the membranes of nerves and muscles, the rate of transmission is relatively slow, ranging from a few centi-

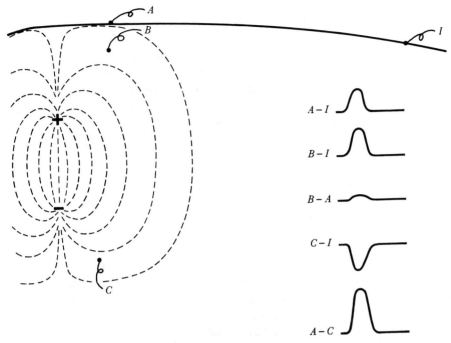

Fig. 3-1   A current "source-sink" where *I* is the distant indifferent electrode, *A* represents a cortical surface electrode, and *B* and *C* are recording electrodes in the depths of the cortex. Monopolar recording is measured by potential differences between *A-I*, *B-I*, or *C-I*; bipolar recording is measured across *A-B* and *A-C*. Potentials are compared on the right.

meters per second in the cortex and several meters per second in the smallest unmyelinated nerves, to 100 or more meters per second in the largest myelinated nerve fibers. When electrical activity originates in a local region and spreads by volume conduction through the tissues and fluids of the body (which together with their ionic salts constitute electrolytes), the speed of transmission to a distant source is almost instantaneous, as in the case of inorganic conducting materials. However, when currents are conducted or transmitted in nerves or muscles from a source of excitation to a point where the discharge is being recorded, one expects to find a measurable latency. If recording electrodes are over an area not expected to participate in a response elicited by stimulation, and a response having the same pattern or form occurs there as well as in the expected area and there is no difference in latency, it

might be that this electrical effect has been transmitted by volume conduction rather than by the process of nerve conduction. Usually one discovers that there is a gradient of electrical response diminishing in magnitude as a function of distance from the source of the origin of electrical activity. Because of the configuration of the body tissues, the distribution and direction of membranes, and the distribution and direction of nerve tracts and blood vessels, there can be some differential spread of electrical activity by volume conduction. Under these conditions one can have volume-conducted spread in one area and not in another. Mistakes can be made in interpreting responses recorded electrically unless one is aware of this and is aware of ways to detect the difference between electrical activity at the source of origin and volume-conducted spread of electric currents in the body.

When, instead of two electrodes in proximity on an active tissue, one uses the unipolar or monopolar system with the second electrode at a distance on an inactive or indifferent region as a reference electrode, any change of potential can be assumed to have occurred in or near the electrode in contact with the active tissue. Its form will be uncomplicated by electrical activities originating under two electrodes on the active tissue, as is the case in bipolar recording, which can result in algebraic summation or cancellation. Another obvious advantage is that any uniform simultaneous change in the electric potential of the active area, as in the case of a d-c shift relative to an indifferent or reference area, would be recorded. With two electrodes on the active tissue, as in the bipolar situation, if both shifted in a negative direction by the same amount and at the same time, there would be no difference in potential between the points of contact and therefore no indication of the d-c shift. If the electrical changes under the two electrodes on active tissue were exactly in phase and equal in magnitude but of opposite polarity, the push-pull or differential amplifier would cancel them out since it is supposed to reject in-phase signals at its two inputs. On the other hand, the uni- or monopolar system appears to pick up electrical changes from a greater area around the point of contact. This is due to the fact that its reference is at a distance, whereas with closely spaced electrodes in bipolar array the electrical activity seems to be picked up only from the local region of the pair of electrodes. This has certain analytic and localizing advantages, even though there may be complications about the form or pattern of the response recorded.

Another problem of importance concerns protection of electrodes against polarization. Although the use of nonpolarizable electrodes may not be critical in some electrical recording and stimulating situations, it is in others. The conditions under which it becomes critical are those in which direct, or unidirectional, currents may predominate, or where

the proportional current flow, in the case of alternating currents, is distinctly more negative than positive, or vice versa. This can be a problem where one is concerned with small quantitative differences in current flow or potential over appreciable periods of time, since the resistance of the electrodes to the flow of current will change as the ionic concentration of salts upon one or the other electrode increases differentially because of predominant flow of current in that direction. For a discussion of nonpolarizable electrodes and method of preparing them, see Hill and Parr (1950).

Briefly, it can be stated that when electrodes are in direct contact with tissues generating the currents to be measured or when some intervening electrode paste or gel containing an electrolyte connects them to the tissue, they should be nonpolarizable to protect against the difficulties mentioned above. They should be coated with a compound composed of the salt of the metal of which they are made and the acid radical which is plentiful in the electrolyte solution in which they are immersed. For example, if silver (Ag) wires or disks are used as the contacting points or surfaces, they should be made nonpolarizable by coating them with silver chloride (AgCl), resulting in silver–silver chloride (Ag-AgCl) electrodes. This can be done by immersing the electrodes in a 5 percent salt solution (NaCl) and connecting all of them to the positive or anodal pole of a $1\frac{1}{2}$- to 3-volt battery, with the cathodal or negative pole connected to a platinum electrode or to a piece of pure silver immersed in the solution. As the current flows in this solution, chloride ions will combine with silver salts to form a silver chloride coating on the silver electrodes constituting the anode. The electrodes will darken to a dull gray or olive color, indicating that a coating of silver chloride has been deposited. To check on the adequacy of this process, two of the electrodes immersed in the solution may be connected to the poles of a $1\frac{1}{2}$-volt battery and the current flow monitored by a meter for an hour or so. The experimenter may assume that the coating is adequate and stable and hence non-polarizable if the current flow remains steady and does not drop. Since the types of electrodes, their location, and manner of attachment will vary with the specific application, no further comment will be made on that here; it will be dealt with when particular types of recording are discussed subsequently.

Electrical shielding and grounding

The majority of electric potentials recordable from tissues or organs of the body range from a few microvolts (μv) to a few millivolts (mv). Nerve and brain potentials may be of the order of microvolts, whereas skeletal muscle, skin potential, and heart potentials may be of the order of millivolts or less. In the case of microvolt signals, amplification of at least a millionfold is required to boost the voltage to appropriate levels for recording; and even in the case of muscle, heart, and skin potentials, several hundred thousands of amplification may be required to see the smallest and weakest signals. With this amount of amplification, the electrodes, when dangled in air without physical contact between them, serve as an antenna and pick up electromagnetic radiations from electric power circuits in the floor or ceiling or about the room. When the electrodes are connected to a "dummy subject," i.e., a resistor of about 10,000 ohms, there will be a substantial reduction in the pickup of these radiated 60-cycle oscillations. As the input is moved about the room, some 60-cycle activity will be picked up, amplified, and recorded. This will be greater in some locations in the room. A flickering neon lamp, the make and break of a switch contact, the use of an elevator in the hall, and many other sources of electrostatic influence may also be reflected in the pickup by the electrodes when the amplification or gain of the amplifiers is high enough to record microvolt-level signals.

Proper electrical shielding and grounding may reduce or eliminate these extraneous sources of interference. Shielding the input to the amplifiers increases the signal-to-noise ratio, i.e., removes or reduces most of the 60-cycle and other extraneous electrical influences which otherwise, when amplified, exceed the size of the neural signals. The subject or the physiological preparation to which the electrodes are attached should be in an electrically shielded room or enclosure; the electrically screened room or enclosure should be grounded at one and only one point. Such shielding serves to reduce the effect of extraneous electrical fields and electrostatic influences, thus removing from the electrical recording unwanted signals and variations that are completely irrelevant to the physiological signals in which one is interested. Sometimes the outside influences can be so large as to completely mask or obliterate the wanted signals; at other times they may be a small but annoying intrusion which interferes with the measurements one wishes to make on the records; at still other times a minute amount of 60-cycle ripple in the record, or an occasional sporadic artifact from some extraneous source that is identifiable by its pattern, constitutes little interference with the objectives of studying some much larger electrophysiological response.

A room in which a subject sits or lies on a cot may be electrically shielded with copper-coated wallpaper. All walls, ceiling, floor, and door must be covered and in contact throughout. The metallic shielding must be connected to a suitable ground connection, preferably at only one point, to prevent ground loops. This ground connection might be a special heavy copper cable established and isolated from other ground or circuit connections throughout the building and embedded in a deep hole in the form of a coil under the building. Such systems have been installed in some recently constructed buildings where electrical shielding and grounding are required. On the other hand, one usually has to depend upon the use of some other ground source not specifically designed for the purpose, e.g., water pipes, steam or radiator pipes, or the grounded side of the house power supply. The last-named should be the larger of the two openings of a standard outlet for house current, but it is always well to determine in advance whether this is the grounded side of the line. Holding the insulated probes of a voltmeter set to measure a value above 220 volts a-c, one may insert the probes into the two receptacles of the outlet. If an a-c voltage of approximately 110 volts is obtained, one may withdraw one of the probes and contact the metal casing surrounding the outlet. If 110 volts is still indicated on the meter, one knows that the probe that is still in one receptacle of the outlet is on the "hot," or active, side of the line and has a voltage when measured to ground. The other receptacle of the outlet is probably the ground side. To test this, place one probe from the meter in this receptacle and the other one to the metal casing or conduit that encloses the house current line. If no potential difference is observed on the meter, the receptacle is at ground potential and is perfectly harmless to touch or make contact with, provided one does not simultaneously touch the hot side of the line or something connected to it. The ground connection on the outlet, if not identifiable by a larger opening than on the active side, should be marked as the ground side of the line. It may be used as a ground lead to the screened cage and to equipment that requires grounding, but care must be exercised so that no connection is unwittingly made to the other side of the line. The metal conduit often required around power lines would also be a suitable ground connection for an electrically shielded cage or for the electrical recording and accessory equipment that must be grounded.

If the electrical recording equipment can be outside the electrically shielded cage, it should be so placed. Recording equipment usually requires an a-c voltage supply, which if taken inside the subject's room will negate the effect of the shielding by bringing a-c electromagnetic fields into the neighborhood of the recording electrodes. If the equipment must be close to the subject or preparation to which the electrodes are attached, it can itself be shielded and grounded. Whether the equipment is inside or outside the shielded cage, the input leads should be shielded. This is done by stretching a mesh shielding material made for this purpose over the input wires. Commonly the input leads are made of electrically shielded cable, either uncovered or rubber- or plastic-covered. The shield of the shielded cable should be completely continuous and soldered at some point to ground, either at its connecting point with the apparatus or at some point enroute. The amplifiers are usually put up in metal-enclosing boxes, which, when grounded, constitute one shielding barrier. The power cords that supply power to amplifiers, if the latter are inside the shielded room, should also be electrically shielded with the wire mesh covering for that purpose and should be grounded. In other words, everything inside an electrically shielded room that involves an a-c power source in which current will flow should be shielded by some kind of electrical screening material and connected to ground. A piece of metal protruding through the screen of the room from the outside, or unused wires extending from outside to inside, may serve as an antenna to bring in unwanted 60-cycle influences, unless they too are connected to the screen or a ground connection. A screw or a nail intended to hold the screen of the shielded room to a frame of wood, if extending through the screen without touching it, may become a miniature antenna to carry into the room the very electrical influences one wishes to shield against. Care must be exercised in making a screened cage or box to be sure that all portions of it are soldered and that nails or other objects projecting through it are soldered to it or grounded at some point. The subject or preparation must be shielded electrically since the input connections will pick up physiological signals that will be amplified perhaps one millionfold. If any source of extraneous electrical effects is unwittingly provided with access to the interior of the electrically shielded enclosure, it too will be amplified by the same factor.

Of what material should electrically shielded rooms be made, and how should they be made? There are many different ways of accomplishing this. First, one must attempt to anticipate what size of room is needed. If a subject is to sit or recline on a cot, and it is anticipated that space must be available for some other apparatus or for an experimenter to move about the subject, it is almost axiomatic that at least a 6- by 9-ft room, about 7 ft high, will be needed. One convenient way to put up such a room is to make a series of panels much like an ordinary screen door, in this case about 3 ft wide and 7 ft high. Six of these would form the two sides of a 6- by 9-ft room, whereas four would form the two ends; six panels 3 by 6 ft would form the floor and ceiling. The floor could be covered additionally by $\frac{3}{4}$-in. plywood for a solid base to stand on and by linoleum if desired. The screening for the panels could be of copper screen-door type with fine mesh, or it could be of galvanized hardware cloth, that is, a hot-dipped galvanized $\frac{1}{4}$-in.-mesh screen. Either type of screening is effective when properly assembled on a frame with all sections in soldered contact with adjacent ones and the whole screened cage grounded by a suitable copper or galvanized wire to an appropriate grounding location. Structural metal such as Flex-angle or Uni-Strut is handy for making a metallic framework for a screened cage, either the 6- by 9-ft size or a small five-sided screened enclosure supported by ropes over pulleys on the ceiling or by upright rods at the four corners. This allows the cage to be raised or lowered over a table on which a small animal rests on a metal plate. The plate on the table serves as shielding from below, and the five-sided cage completes the electrically shielded enclosure.

The important point is that electrical shielding of the input to high-gain amplifiers is almost always needed and should therefore be provided. There are some locations and some commercial electrical recording instruments which, when combined under the proper conditions, do not seem to need additional shielding. However, such instances are rare, and sooner or later the electrical shielding will be necessary. The experimenter should be constantly on guard against possible intrusions into the recording situation that will introduce electrical artifacts. Often, careful tests may be made beforehand, e.g., at the time one calibrates instruments, to determine how well the shielding requirements have been met.

It is sometimes necessary to build double electrically shielded rooms when high-powered television or radio-transmitting stations are very near the laboratory. This amounts to having two screened rooms, one inside the other and independent of each other, with only the inner room grounded. A room built of $\frac{3}{4}$-in. plywood with zinc or galvanized metal sheeting on both sides would constitute another solution.

Electrical characteristics of physiologic tissues

Electrical changes in excitable tissues of the body range from very fast, as in the case of the spike potential of nerve or the motor unit response of skeletal muscle, to the slow potential changes of smooth muscle such as that of the gut, that of the uterus, or the arrector pili muscle attached to the base of the hair follicle. In a large mammalian A fiber the spike potential occupies less than 1 millisecond (msec) with a rise time of perhaps 0.2 msec and a fall time of possibly 0.7 msec, exclusive of the negative afterpotential and the positive afterpotential, which may together require another 10 msec or more. Spike potentials up to 1,075 per second have been elicited in the phrenic nerve of the cat, but with fairly rapidly decrementing response after a few seconds of repetitive stimulation. Motor unit responses in cat or human muscles give spikelike responses lasting several milliseconds and probably do not exceed a repetition rate of firing of more than 50 per second in a strong voluntary contraction, and possibly up to 100 per second in the fastest reflex contraction. In the case of either the nerve or the muscle the rise time of the spike is brief, and even the fall time is very short. To have a faithful record of the spike potential and to record repeated responses at a high repetition rate, it is necessary to have an amplifying-recording system capable of responding to high frequencies, perhaps up to 10,000 cycles per second (cps). This is necessary so that recovery from the response to one spike will be rapid enough that the amplifier will respond to a quickly recurring spike without blocking.

For the recording of potential waves, either positive, negative, or both, that persist for 1 sec or more, one must have either (1) resistance-capacitance coupled amplifiers of long time constant, perhaps 1 to 4 sec, or (2) direct-coupled amplifiers capable of responding to polarity shifts of even longer duration. For detecting and recording polarity differences of long-term d-c nature such as have been shown to exist on the pial surface of the cortex relative to the white matter on the undersurface of the cortex or the ventricular wall, one must use d-c amplifiers capable of maintaining a positive or negative potential as long as it exists. Changes in d-c potential at the surface of the cortex under conditions of spreading depression may last several minutes or more before returning to the original value.

The wavelike potentials that can be recorded from the brain, as in the electroencephalogram (EEG), may be as slow as one wave in 2 to 3 sec under some conditions of sleep and unconsciousness, or 1 to 3 per sec waves seen in sleep, in petit mal seizure discharges, or in brain tumors or other pathological conditions where pressure effects are imposed on the cortex. Waves from 3 to 7 per sec are seen in lighter stages of sleep, in normal waking states in infants and young children, and in some pathological conditions. Waves

of 8 to 12 per sec are common in states of relaxed wakefulness and are known as *alpha waves*. Alpha waves extend in frequency from 3 per sec in young infants to 8 to 12 per sec in older children and adults. Waves from 10 to 18 per sec are seen as spindles or spindle bursts in a light stage of sleep in humans and animals and are observed in some pathological conditions. Waves from 18 to 30 per sec are known as *beta waves,* are generally of considerably smaller amplitude than alpha waves, and are characteristically seen in the alert state. They may be superimposed on alpha waves or may be seen more clearly when alpha waves are blocked by stimulation. Waves from 30 to 50 per sec are sometimes known as *gamma waves* but are relatively little dealt with and are not a prominent part of most electroencephalographic records. This may be due to the fact that amplitude attenuation is frequently employed at higher frequencies or that other more prominent waves tend to mask the appearance of the faster and smaller waves. In any event, the usual frequencies encountered in the EEG, or for that matter from deeper subcortical structures, range from less than 1 cps to about 50 cps. The maximal range of voltages encountered in the EEG is from 1 to 500 μv, and most voltages are encompassed within the range of 1 to 100 μv.

Accordingly, amplifying-recording systems capable of responding faithfully to the low end of the frequency spectrum are required for the EEG in contrast to those required for recording the spike potentials of nerve and muscle. The latter extend to the higher end of the frequency spectrum, i.e., 5,000 to 10,000 cps, but also encompass some slower components and, therefore, require amplifiers that have the full range of frequencies from 1 to 5,000 or 10,000 cps. Nerve potentials are generally in the microvolt range, except when intracellular potentials are recorded with microelectrodes; resting or discharge potentials attain a magnitude in the millivolt range. Muscle potentials range from a few microvolts at the skin surface, when tension is low, to the millivolt level when tension is high, or when single unit responses are recorded with needle electrodes in the muscle substance. The electrocardiogram (EKG) or heart potentials are of the order of a millivolt and are relatively slow.

Electrical characteristics of amplifying-recording systems

The overall amplifying-recording system must have characteristics selected so that it is capable of responding faithfully to the range of durations of potentials, including the repetition rate of the responses. The overall amplification factor must also be appropriately selected and be capable of adjustment within the range of voltages encountered so as to provide records appropriate to analysis of the details desired. In the case of d-c potentials of prolonged duration, special direct-coupled amplifiers must be employed; these must have relative freedom from drift which might otherwise be interpreted as due to physiological changes. Their sensitivity must be great enough to accommodate the smallest d-c potentials it is desired to measure.

Let us consider the choice of an amplifier and its characteristics. The most common type is the a-c resistance-capacitance coupled amplifier. The first consideration is the time constant of the amplifier because that will determine the fidelity with which the amplifier can respond to and hold the duration of the electrical changes it receives for amplification. The time constant is measured by introducing a d-c potential as a calibration signal to the input of the amplifier. Because the coupling between stages of the voltage amplifier is a resistance-capacitance network, the capacitors involved will hold the charge imposed upon them by the amplified signals only a given length of time before the charge leaks off. The rate at which the charge leaks off is a function of the size of the capacitors and the grid-leak resistors. The d-c potential imposed will cause the amplified signal to deflect an inkwriting pen, an optical oscillograph

beam, or a cathode-ray oscilloscope beam to an amplitude determined by the amplification factor. In other words, a sudden d-c pulse or square wave will cause the recording instrument to peak quickly, but because the charge begins to leak off the capacitors immediately at a certain rate, the recording unit will gradually return to its base line, tracing out an exponential curve.

Roughly speaking, the time required for the amplitude to fall to half its initial deflection value is the time constant of the amplifier. If the d-c pulse is negative and by convention is indicated by an upward amplitude deflection of 20 mm, but falls to half of this deflection amplitude, or 10 mm, in 1 sec, the amplifier can be said to have a time constant of 1 sec. Something of this kind might be obtained with 2-microfarad (2-μf) capacitors and 1-megohm grid-leak resistors. The time constant would be increased if 4-μf capacitors and even larger grid-leak resistors were employed, perhaps to a value of 2 sec, but the likelihood is that the amplifiers would be subject to blocking when sudden signal surges occurred. The indicator would swing wide in a positive or negative direction and tend to stay there or to swing in a wide arc until it gradually recovered its base-line resting level. Incoming input signals would not be amplified and recorded during the swing and sway of the indicator because the grid potential would be heavily biased positively or negatively. To increase the time constant to a value consistent with recording very slow waves, in the hope of recording their true shape, tends to result in an unstable amplifying system subject to blocking unless potentials are uniform, small, and without sudden surges. A decrease in the size of the capacitors and the grid-leak resistors would cause the deflection of the indicator, after the first sudden surge, to return quickly to the base-line level and be ready for another pulse immediately after the recovery from the first one. Such a short time-constant coupling will accommodate high-frequency high-repetition-rate responses, and it should not be subject to blocking subsequent signals unless they are unduly large and sudden.

To control the time constant of an amplifier and the time characteristics of the physiological responses it will accommodate, some manufacturers provide a switch on their a-c preamplifiers and on electroencephalographs and polygraphs that permits changing the time constant in accordance with needs. One switch setting is labeled for the electromyogram (EMG) and throws into the amplifier coupling the necessary small capacitors and grid-leak resistors providing a short time constant and a stable high-frequency response. Another switch setting is for the EEG and introduces an intermediate set of capacitors and resistors providing an intermediate time constant. Still another switch setting couples the stages of the amplifier with the largest set of capacitors and resistors and provides the longest time constant of all for the EKG, as well as for other slower phenomena such as the galvanic skin response (GSR) potential measured by the Tarchanoff method. Although it may be that none of these couplings permits a completely faithful record of the durations (form and pattern) of the responses they are supposed to accommodate, they do so reasonably well. Commercial amplifiers have other flexibilities such as coarse and fine gain or amplification controls so that the amplification can be made appropriate to the level of the input signal and the size of indicator response required.

A nonblocking high-frequency amplifier of the resistance-capacitance coupled type may also be used to sample and record d-c potentials of long duration by utilizing a chopper circuit in its input. It samples momentarily and records the voltage by a deflection, as it would to a d-c pulse or square wave. The indicator returns to its base line rapidly and then, as the chopper switch closes, it samples again. It always remains within the limits of its own response characteristics and only samples the true voltage level of the slowly changing d-c potentials. A curve of the true d-c potential change over time is obtained by connecting these peaks representing the samplings. Various ways to record or photograph this curve lead to tracings not unlike those generated by a d-c amplifier.

The inkwriting oscillographs employed in the EEG and most polygraph recording devices will respond adequately only to relatively low frequencies. This is due in part to the friction of the pen on the recording paper but mainly to the mass that must be moved in an arc as pen deflections occur. The typical EEG inkwriting pen will have a flat frequency response, up to 70 or 100 cps for a constant voltage input at increasing frequencies. This is accomplished by correction networks that compensate for natural periodicities. The pens may respond to higher frequencies but with progressive amplitude decrement.

Optical oscillographs of the Duddell or galvanometer type will respond to a constant input voltage at frequencies ranging from 200 to 3,000 cps, depending upon their sensitivity to current changes. The advantages of such oscillographs are that they are adequate for most physiological frequencies, provide for multiple recording channels on the same photographic paper, and can record at speeds up to 3 or 4 ft per sec. The latter amply spreads out responses and makes it possible to measure brief latencies.

The ultimate in recording instruments is the cathode-ray oscilloscope (CRO). The focused electron beam that traces its path on the phosphorescent face of the tube is essentially inertialess and can be made to respond to frequencies far beyond any encountered in physiological recording. Its linear base-line sweep mechanism can readily be made to move the spot slowly or very rapidly, thus permitting the spreading out of responses for accurate measurement of various features such as short latencies between stimulus and response. Photographic cameras provide clear and sharp trace images on photographic paper or film by single-frame or continuous movement. Up to four traces can be recorded on a 5-in. scope face reasonably well. Its greatest deficiency occurs with regard to multiple-channel recording.

The researcher can record and measure just about any type of electrophysiological response given: (1) a broadband a-c preamplifier capable of flat frequency response from 1 to 10,000 cps, (2) a direct-coupled amplifier for d-c potentials, and (3) a flexible dual- or four-trace CRO and kymograph camera. When supplemented by an EEG or polygraph with more channels of recording and with variable time constants and recording speeds for monitoring ongoing electrical activity, greater efficiency and a greater range of data may be obtained. In some instances the optical oscillograph may still further enhance the recording and analyzing capacity.

Electrophysiological data may also be recorded on a multichannel frequency-modulated (FM) magnetic tape recorder. With 7 or 14 channels of input, such a tape recorder will accept and store simultaneously derived electrophysiological data in an analog form. Each channel of data may be played back individually to the input of a CRO and photographed on any time base found to be appropriate and with more or less amplification than was used to record it initially. If multichannel write-out is desired, it may be fed simultaneously into the input of an EEG or optical oscillograph. The taped data may also be fed into an on-line computer of average transients (CAT), provided that a series of stimulus-response sequences have been recorded. This procedure will bring out weak response signals, which otherwise would be masked by ongoing electrical activities of the brain, by a process of algebraic summation of responses time-locked to the oft-repeated stimulus and the cancellation of all activity not so time-locked and thus randomly distributed through the various stimulus-response sequences. Through conversion from analog to digital tape form, the data can be analyzed for auto- and cross-correlation, as well as variability analyses, by the use of large general-purpose digital computers. The taping of the data (1) supplements any of the recording systems since it preserves the data and permits recording of them on any of the systems available at any time and (2) permits simultaneous recording from several neural areas with opportunity to play back through one or more channels of a CRO for detailed analysis.

Recording nerve impulses

When a nerve is stimulated by mechanical, chemical, thermal, or electrical means, it can be made to generate an impulse that is conducted along the nerve from the point of stimulation to a more remote point on the nerve. The negative variation or action potential that accompanies the nerve impulse may be recorded from the nerve as the impulse is conducted from one region to another. Because of the instantaneous nature of electrical stimulation and the ability to control its strength, duration, and location of application, it is most commonly used as a means of stimulation. An electrical stimulus may be generated with (1) an inductorium, (2) a circuit that permits discharge of a previously charged capacitor, or (3) commercially available electronic physiological stimulators. The latter are easily controlled so as to produce square-wave pulses of varying duration, voltage, and frequency of repetition. They provide for single monophasic pulses of positive or negative polarity, for diphasic pulses that tend to prevent polarization changes that might be induced because of unidirectional current flow while stimulating, and for special isolation or grounding circuits that prevent the incorporation of interference or artifacts from stimulation into the electrical response of the tissue being recorded.

The process of recording nerve potentials can be simply explained and executed, although there are many complexities involved in highly precise measurement of nerve potentials and in details of the interpretation of the results. Briefly, if at some point along an exposed nerve there are placed two fine wire hook electrodes, insulated except for their region of contact with the nerve, the negative variation or potential associated with the passage of the nerve impulse can be led off to an amplifier and a CRO, and the electric potential observed or photographed from the CRO tube face. Since these electrodes are close together, perhaps 1 to 2 mm, and since the nerve impulse is exceedingly brief, there will be a rapid deflection of the spot of the CRO. The deflection will be in one direction as the impulse reaches the first electrode and in the other direction as the impulse passes the second electrode. If the spot is made to start at one edge of the 5-in. CRO screen and sweep to the opposite edge at a constant rate of speed regulated by a sweep circuit incorporated in the CRO, the two opposite deflections of the spot, as the nerve impulses pass the two electrodes, will trace a diphasic wave.

When one electrode is attached to the nerve and the other connection to the amplifier is made through a remote and inactive portion of the organism, e.g., the skin of the body or some exposed tissue, and this point is grounded, there will be only a single deflection of the CRO spot as the nerve impulse passes the electrode. Typically this is a negative potential and is usually displayed as an upward deflection of the spot on the screen. This is the negative spike potential accompanying the nerve impulse. It will be seen to be more complex than a simple, sharp spike if (1) it can be recorded from a single large nerve fiber and (2) the CRO sweep speed is fast enough to spread it out on the time base of the screen. Its rise time will be short, 0.5 to 1.0 msec, causing a sharp upward deflection to a peak. The descending phase of the spike will be slowed enroute, thus broadening slightly the base of the spike to accommodate the negative afterpotential. Finally the trace will dip slightly below the base line in a positive direction because of the positive afterpotential. The whole process may require only a few milliseconds, but the sharp negative spike will be complete in 2 or 3 msec. The magnitude of the voltage fluctuation may range from the order of microvolts to a few

millivolts, depending upon the type of nerve preparation and the size or diameter of the nerve.

In most instances when we refer to an exposed nerve of an organism we are talking about a nerve trunk, which may contain many nerve fibers, some sensory and some motor. Even a nerve trunk that is only sensory or only motor may be a compound nerve in that it has fibers of different diameter within it. These, in order of descending diameter and correspondingly slower conduction rates, are known as *A, B,* and *C* groups of fibers.

Perhaps the most straightforward type of electrophysiological experiment involves recording the *nerve action potential.* Although procedures are simple, the results of such an experiment appear rather complex and provide us with a great deal of information about the characteristics of nerves. The frog nerve is commonly used because of its durability; an excised piece placed in a moist chamber will conduct for hours. Mammalian peripheral nerve is more fragile and best studied by dissecting a section of nerve free from associated tissues and cutting the distal end, leaving it intact proximally. The nerve can then be placed on a pair of stimulating wires and a pair of recording wires. A *biphasic* response, i.e., deflections both above and below the base line, is recorded if the two recording electrodes are both in contact with intact nerve or if one is in contact with nerve and the other serving as a distant indifferent. Unfortunately, the amount of nerve activity cannot be directly related to biphasic response amplitude because of algebraic addition effects. If the nerve is crushed where it contacts the distal electrode, a *monophasic* response is recorded whose amplitude is exactly related to the amount of activity in the nerve.

An action potential develops and travels along the nerve to the recording electrodes if a single brief suprathreshold stimulus pulse is delivered to the nerve. As stimulus strength is increased, the amplitude of the response, which is the summed action potentials of all the nerve fibers activated, will also increase.

The "all-or-none" law of nerve fiber activity holds only for single fibers. If we could stimulate and record from only one fiber, the response would always have the same amplitude regardless of stimulus strength. A peripheral nerve is composed of many fibers of different sizes and thresholds; the larger the fiber, the lower the threshold. Consequently, the nerve response amplitude will grow with stimulus strength until all fibers are activated. Several bumps will be seen in the response if a fast oscilloscope sweep is used and a sufficiently long piece of nerve lies between the stimulating and recording electrodes. These reflect the differing conduction velocities of the various nerve fiber groups. Conduction velocity is directly proportional to fiber size. Fiber diameters do not have a single distribution in nerves; rather, there are several different groupings, with some overlap. If all fibers are stimulated, the largest-diameter group will conduct fastest and produce an initial (largest) deflection, the next group will yield a later smaller hump, and so on. Since these groups have different thresholds, it is possible to stimulate selectively, i.e., to stimulate only the largest-diameter group. The various groups have different types of origins and terminations.

The second response may be smaller than the first or entirely absent if a second stimulus is delivered close upon the first. During the sharp spikelike phase of the first response, which may persist only 0.5 to 1.0 msec, another impulse could not be set up since it is in a period of the *absolute refractory phase* of the nerve's excitability. During the next 2 to 3 msec a second pulse from the stimulator, if sufficiently brief, might give rise to a subnormal spike, particularly if the second pulse could be made stronger than the first. This indicates a period when the nerve is in a *relative refractory phase*. It can be excited in this phase if the stimulus is strong enough, since excitatability of the nerve is recovering rapidly. From about 3 to 15 msec during the negative after-potential, the second spike might be initiated with a second stimulus of lower intensity than

that required for the first spike, indicating a *supernormal phase* and increased excitability. Finally, during the period of the positive afterpotential, perhaps 15 to 50 msec or more, the excitability of the nerve seems to be slightly depressed and is in a *subnormal phase*.

In a relatively simple experiment, using an electronic stimulator capable of generating brief repetitive pulses, variable in frequency and in duration between pulse pairs, with suitable broadband frequency amplifiers coupled to a CRO capable of spreading out the electric potentials on a time base, one can determine a number of the characteristics of the action potential of nerve and in turn the excitability characteristics of the nerve itself. These may include (1) the conduction rate for different sizes of fibers, (2) the different components of the response for fibers of different size and the relation to these components of the excitability or sensitivity of the fibers of each class, and (3) the all-ornothing nature of the response, if dealing with a single fiber. Additionally, by placing electrodes on the sensory and motor roots and stretching the muscle so as to produce sensory impulses, one can determine that at low threshold of stimulation only the sensory roots give a response. If a reflex is set up, both sensory and motor nerve roots will respond with a measurable latency separating their potentials; such a latency difference between the roots would be of the order of a few milliseconds at most. Also, with stimulating electrodes on the motor or ventral root a stimulation can be detected by observing the twitch of the muscle or by placing electrodes on or in it in order to record the EMG, or action potential of the muscle. Indeed, the reflex time, from initiation of stretch in the muscle to the recording of the twitch or action potential in muscle, can be determined in this way. If this is done with fine wires insulated except for their tips inside the muscle, it may be possible to record only from that group of muscle fibers connected to a single nerve fiber and functioning as a unit, known as a *motor unit*.

The *Handbook of Physiology,* Vols. I, II, and III on *Neurophysiology* (1959–1960) covers a great range and volume of literature dealing with the most fundamental and basic electrophysiology of single-cell activity. It also encompasses the electrical activity of groups of sensory and motor fibers, pathways, and aggregates of neurones and their cell bodies as found in ganglia, nuclei, and the gray matter of the central neuraxis and brain. An elementary survey of electrophysiology has been provided by Brazier (1960); and Bureš, Petráň, and Zachar (1962) provide a detailed description of apparatus, techniques, and experiments in the broad field of electrophysiology. Morgan (1964), Teitlebaum (1966), and Thompson (1966) present a broad perspective of the general area of physiological psychology.

Recording brain electrical activity: acute preparations

Neurophysiological techniques employed by psychologists encompass essentially all available methods. Although it is not possible to describe all such procedures in detail, the following sections will discuss many of them and indicate further references for additional variations. Any particular experiment will probably differ in some details from others; it is hoped that the more generally useful procedures are covered here.

The reference experiment will utilize an acute preparation for the electrophysiological study of the visual system in the cat. It will be assumed that we wish to study the electrical activity of the visual cortex, especially the evoked potentials over those areas of the cortex known to give rise to discrete responses when a flash of light or repetitive flashes of light are directed into the cat's eye. Additionally, we shall assume that it is desirable to record simultaneously electrical responses at various stations along the visual pathways from the eye to the visual cortex, including the electroretinogram (ERG). The ERG is believed to be associated with the receptor processes of the eye and with some of the neural components of the retina. It provides an index of response of the receptor system and information about the temporal course of excitation of optic nerve fibers whose origin is the ganglion cells of the retina. The researcher might choose to record also from the optic nerves and/or the optic tracts, or from the optic chiasma, but probably not from all three since the fibers in any of these locations arise from the ganglion cells in the retina and would be expected to represent similar, but not necessarily the same, fibers of transit. Let us assume that we wish to place (1) the tips of paired needle electrodes in the optic tracts bilaterally and (2) three pairs of electrodes bilaterally in each lateral geniculate body, in order to have a representative sampling of activity in this visual relay nucleus of the thalamus. Electrodes might be arranged to record also from the optic radiations that leave the geniculate bodies and sweep around in a fan-shaped array on their way to the primary visual cortex. Because of the spreading out of the radiations, responses are not generally as clear-cut here as in the more condensed bundles of fibers in the optic nerve or optic tract.

At least two methods are available for recording the ERG (see below for an extended discussion). Plastic contact lenses may be shaped to fit the curvature of several representative cats' eyes, and a small silver disk may be embedded in it at the corneal margin and ground smooth with the inner surface, which is in contact with the cornea. A very fine insulated wire which is soldered to the disk and protrudes through a hole in the plastic may be made to connect with the lead-in wire to the input of the amplifying channel. The other electrode contact may be with the lobe of the ear or with a cut skin surface on the head which will have been reflected to approach the brain. A small alligator-type clip will generally suffice for this contact, which is grounded directly, or indirectly if the animal preparation is grounded elsewhere. In any case it is assumed that this electrode is on a relatively indifferent area so far as the ERG is concerned. The other type of electrode contact for the ERG is a wick electrode made of braided, soft cotton thread or other absorbent material. This wick is attached to a fine silver wire coil to prevent direct pressures or movement of the wick against the cornea. The wick is saturated with saline, and its contact to the chlorided silver wire is made by twisting the wire tightly around it. We have assumed that the lead-off method to be used here employs an active lead on the cornea and an indifferent, grounded lead elsewhere on the cat. It is sometimes necessary to record with the indifferent lead ungrounded in order to have the benefit of push-pull input in eliminating 60-cps or other interferences which reduce the signal-to-noise ratio.

For deep electrode recording in the optic tract and lateral geniculate body, we shall need some needle electrodes about 50 to 60 mm long in order that they may be held in the electrode carrier of the stereotaxic instrument and reach the desired structure in the brain. The appropriate dimensions can be calculated more precisely when the electrodes are placed in the stereotaxic instrument for preliminary calibration prior to the experiment. In an acute experiment it generally does not matter if the electrodes are a little long and protrude above the electrode carrier. It is important that they be long enough; otherwise they will not be able to reach the desired location in the brain. The next question is whether one wishes to have only a single needle electrode at each location, insulated except for about 0.5 to 1.0 mm at its tip, and the other connection made to some indifferent location such as the ear, the cut surface of the skin, or a metal probe inserted in the anus. The alternative is to have two fine stainless steel wires insulated and cemented together in a side-by-side arrangement with exposed surfaces only at the beveled tips sharpened to a point for insertion or to have one such insulated wire cemented into the lumen of a long hypodermic needle or tube in such a manner that its tip protrudes for 0.5 to 1.0 mm. In

this case the tip of the protruding wire is carefully scraped clean of insulation material, as is the bottom edge of the encasing tube, thus completing the input circuit by two exposed portions of the concentric electrode system within the structure recorded from. Other variations on the electrode design are possible, e.g., two fine wires within a hypodermic needle or stainless steel tube. The tube may be insulated or uninsulated on the outside; in the former case it could be connected to ground and serve as a kind of electrical shielding for the inner wires, which must protrude from the tube and be bared at their tips, though insulated from one another. The paired tips of electrodes connecting in push-pull arrangement to the amplifiers and immersed in the same structure tend to provide a good system for local recording; they probably do not sample electrical activity from neighboring structures as much as an individual electrode tip connected to a remote indifferent point on the animal. Let us assume that we are using either the concentric electrode system or the paired wires exposed only at the tips and that the interelectrode tip distance is only about 0.3 mm.

The experimenter is now faced with a choice of anesthesia or inactivation procedure. Typically, a long-lasting, even level of anesthesia has been sought in mapping the cortical potentials in response to stimulation of various sense modes. Much of our early, and even present, knowledge is based on electrocortical mapping under one or another form of barbiturate anesthesia, such as Pentothal, Amytal, or Nembutal. Dial-urethane, ether, chloralose, and chloralose-urethane are also used. The usual dosage of a barbiturate such as Nembutal or Pentothal is about 35 to 45 milligrams (mg) per kilogram (kg) of body weight if given intraperitoneally. Although a lone investigator can usually manage to hold a cat up by the nape of the neck and inject the anesthetic through the abdominal wall, it usually goes better when an assistant holds the cat thus and stretches the animal out by holding the hind legs with the other hand while the injector grasps the abdominal wall, inserts the hypodermic needle, and injects the anesthetic, making sure that the needle is clearly intraperitoneally placed. The animal may then be returned to its "cat-box" or container while the experimenter waits 15 or 20 min for it to show signs of deep anesthetization. The depth of anesthetization is determined from observing the slitlike pupils, the lack of ear twitching when the finger touches the hair of the ear, the failure to respond when the foot is pinched with the fingers or a tweezer, and by the animal's relaxed condition. If this fails to happen in 20 min or more, one should not be in too great haste to add more anesthetic; sometimes individual differences among cats, and even different batches of anesthetic, may cause them to react atypically. Additional amounts may be added cautiously, if in time it is clear that the animal is not anesthetized sufficiently. Ample time should be allowed for each new increment to take effect. It is often a good idea to clip the hair from the inner surface of the thigh and find a suitable leg vein, e.g., the femoral vein, and, after clearing it from surrounding tissues, nick or incise it so that a polyethylene tube may be inserted, tied in place, and connected to a small syringe. Additional small amounts of anesthetic may then be administered easily during later phases of the experiment when needed. A small indwelling needle may be left in the vein and connected by tubing to the syringe or may be directly connected with a small syringe taped to the leg. During a long experiment more Nembutal or Pentothal will have to be given periodically in fractions of the original amount.

The level of the anesthesia during the day may be judged by the above-mentioned signs or by any tendency of the animal to show signs of movement or restlessness; the electrical recordings from the cortex are also generally a good indicator of the state of the anesthesia since the barbiturate causes sleep spindles and slow waves when the anesthesia is at the required level. If the animal

is "too light," spindles tend to disappear and more irregular low-level activity appears; if the animal is too deep, the recording line tends to be devoid of slow waves and spindle bursts and appears "flat." One of the difficulties of experiments under anesthesia is to maintain approximately the same level and therefore the same state of excitability in the neural structures being investigated. If the anesthesia level should vary too widely, the electrocortical and subcortical responses will also vary.

Another difficulty with barbiturates is that reticular activation of the cortex is depressed. To test the cortex or other structures for their electrical responses is to test them for their anesthetized responses, not their normal waking ones. The only way to observe normal waking responses is with implanted electrodes in an otherwise awake and normal animal. There are some stratagems that may be employed with acute preparations, but these are not recommended to the inexperienced investigator and are even frowned upon in the hands of well-trained investigators. These must be used with great caution but, when used properly, can leave a brain in an essentially unanesthetized state. Caution must be exercised to ensure that the animal is properly protected against pain under these circumstances by injecting all cut surfaces and pressure points with procaine hydrochloride or other suitable local anesthesia frequently and to take every precaution to examine any source of sensitivity. One stratagem involves the use of curare-like substances such as D-tubocurarine or Syncurine, which may be injected intravenously. The injection is made only after the animal has been deeply anesthetized with a quick-acting anesthesia such as ether, which will blow off quickly, and has had its trachea cannulated for artificial respiration by means of a pump set appropriately for rate and depth of respiration. Such an immobilization technique does not permit an animal to struggle, and the experimenter is not apt to be so alert to lightening of anesthesia or to manifestations of pain. If all possible sources of pain due to the experiment are carefully assessed in advance and carefully monitored throughout by additional injections of local anesthetic, it is just possible to conduct electrical recording from brain structures which are unanesthetized and which when penetrated are not ordinarily painful. Another stratagem uses an operative procedure involving transection of the neuraxis, at either the first or the second cervical level of the cord, called an *encephale isolé* preparation, or at the intercollicular level of the midbrain, known as a *cerveau isolé* preparation (see below for procedure). Such animals are immobilized in body and limbs because of lack of control from higher centers and, at the same time, depending upon the level of transection, are immune to all the sensory input from those sensory sources innervated from below the transection. The higher transection, the *cerveau isolé,* cuts off all sensory input to the forebrain except that via the first and second cranial nerves, the olfactory and optic, if care is taken to be sure that all cranial nerve entries in the neighborhood of the transection level have been eliminated. If they have not been eliminated, local anasthetics must be applied to every possible source of pain input.

We shall assume that we are employing Nembutal anesthesia in this experiment and that every effort has been made to ensure an appropriate depth and maintained level throughout, including careful monitoring of the electrocortical activity. Under this form of anesthesia the trachea does not have to be cannulated, although it should be if it is anticipated that there may be need for artificial respiration. When the animal is ready for surgery, i.e., when it is deeply anesthetized, it may be placed in the stereotaxic instrument and properly positioned.

A *stereotaxic instrument* consists of a rigid metal framework within which the head of an animal may be fixed by means of ear bars inserted in the external ear canals (meatuses) and by other attachments that rest on the bony

infraorbital ridge under the eyes and push up against the teeth, holding the head in a fixed relation to the frame, which is exactly centered about the head. In addition to the head holder, there is usually a framework comprised of two parallel bars extending backward along the sides of the animal's body, either for support of the body in a hammock-like arrangement or for clamps that support the electrode carriers. The electrode carriers permit the clamping of electrodes in a vertical position. The electrodes may be lowered along a sliding calibrated scale, providing up-and-down movement in the vertical plane. The framework supporting the electrode carrier has two other adjustable dimensions, right and left and backward and forward, each with its calibrated scale.

The stereotaxic instrument usually employs rectangular coordinates to define the location of a point in space, but it could be made to employ spherical coordinates. The three dimensions or rectangular coordinates that locate a point in space in the brain must be relative to three planes, and these have been arbitrarily taken so as to intersect within the brain. One of these is a transverse-vertical plane cutting through the anterior-posterior (A-P) dimension at the level of the auditory meatuses and is known as the *interaural frontal plane.* Another is the longitudinal-vertical plane along the midline of the brain, known as the *midsagittal plane.* Still another is a horizontal plane at right angles to the two vertical planes and at a level 10 mm above the plane which is defined by the center of the ear bars in the meatuses and the infraorbital ridges of the eyes. This is known as the *zero-level horizontal plane,* or the *Horsley-Clarke plane,* arbitrarily chosen so that distances up and down from it, in a vertical dimension, can be measured as H values and thought of as horizontal levels or "heights" within the brain. To specify a point in space in the cat's brains as A6 L9 H+3 would be to say 6 mm anterior to the interaural frontal-vertical plane, 9 mm left of the midsagittal vertical plane, and 3 mm above the Horsley-

Clarke or zero-level horizontal plane. To lower a needle electrode to the point defined by these coordinates in the cat would be to place it in the approximate center of the left *lateral geniculate body*. This is one of the structures from which we wish to record electrical activity in studying the effect of flashes of light on the visual system of the cat. To place an electrode in the left *optic tract* between the geniculate body and the chiasma, we might choose the following set of coordinates: A11 L7 H—4, which would be translated 11 mm anterior to the interaural frontal plane, 7 mm to the left of the midline sagittal-vertical plane, and 4 mm below the zero horizontal plane.

The use of the stereotaxic instrument depends upon having maps or an atlas of the brain regions. These maps are usually arranged according to frontal plane sections at 0.5 or 1.0 mm intervals from the most anterior part to the most posterior part of the brain, although some atlases are limited to the region between the chiasma and the pons in an anterior-posterior direction, or to a more limited portion of the diencephalon. The atlases for the cat brain, such as Jimenez-Castellanos (1949), Jasper and Ajmone-Marsan (1954), and Snider and Niemer (1961), constitute enlarged coordinates laid out in cross section either over the histological picture of the structures encountered or over the outlined drawings of the structures, appropriately labeled for identification. Sometimes the histological picture is on one side of a double page and the outlined drawings of some of the structures on the other. Atlases for the monkey brain (*Macaca mulata*) have been prepared by Olszewski (1952) and Snider and Lee (1961); and for the squirrel monkey brain (*Saimiri sciureus*) by Gergen and MacLean (1962) and Emmers and Akert (1963). Atlases for the rat brain, especially diencephalic structures, are those of Kreig (1946) and de Groot (1959). Partial atlases may be found in Sheer (1961) for the rat, cat, and monkey; and in Bureš *et al.* (1962) for the cat, rabbit, and rat.

Most of the atlases agree fairly well, although there may be some divergences due to unspecified differences in the size of animals used to make them, slightly different skull configurations among various species, and variations in the fixation and staining techniques employed. Small errors can creep into the manipulations by the investigator making the atlas, such as his setting of the adjustments or the making of readings from the instrument, as well as slight inaccuracies of his stereotaxic instrument. The same applies to the investigator using the atlas and perhaps a different type of stereotaxic instrument, although for all practical purposes differences due to the use of various types of instrument are probably not the major source of error.

Other things being equal, that is, the instrument being a well-machined and accurate one, the visual stimulation experiment requires only that the instrument be free of protruding parts that interfere with the field of visual stimulation. Some instruments have been made with the location for the animal's head in such a position that light cannot be put directly into the eyes. The Johnson stereotaxic instrument for cats and monkeys was designed with freedom of access to the eyes and therefore has proved to be a boon for visual work of the type to be described here. Other American-made stereotaxic instruments for cats and monkeys are the Lab-Tronics, Baltimore Instrument Co., Trent Wells, and Kopf. The last two are of recent design and appear to incorporate a number of useful features. Each manufacturer's instrument seems to include some features that another does not have, but on the whole they are remarkably similar in terms of what can be accomplished with them. In this instance we shall assume that we are using the Johnson stereotaxic instrument.

Prior to the experiment, suitable paired bipolar electrodes should be made and tested for continuity of leads and tips by inserting the electrodes in saline and connecting the lead plugs to an ohmmeter. If the resistance reads 10,000 to 30,000 ohms and remains stable, the electrode may be judged to be good. If, on the other hand, a short circuit or infinite resistance occurs, the beveled surfaces of the electrodes should be rubbed lightly with a smoothly abrasive stone or cloth to make sure that the surfaces are clean and that small connecting metallic bridges are not responsible for the difficulty. Once the electrodes are in proper condition, each set in turn may be placed in its appropriate carrier, making sure that its depth is correctly located in the carrier to reach the structure required. In the carrier the tip of the pair of electrodes is adjusted to a calibration location, usually the center of the two ear bars when pushed close together (but leaving a small center space exactly equal on both sides). When the tips of the electrodes are lowered into this space so that the electrodes are properly centered in the anterior-posterior dimension, and similar adjustments are made for the up-down dimension and the right-left dimension, readings from each of the positioning scales may then be taken and recorded. This provides *zero calibration* coordinates for each pair of electrodes. It is important that these determinations be carefully made since all subsequent adjustments are made relative to these calibrations.

Next the coordinates must be determined for each point at which it is desired to place an electrode pair, as determined from the atlas. The difference between desired coordinates for any electrode pair and the coordinates for the zero location for that particular pair of electrodes should then be calculated. This requires care since it is easy to confuse the algebraic addition or difference between desired values and calibrated values that provide the Horsley-Clarke scale readings for the coordinates. If these are accurately set, the desired locations should be closely approximated, often with less than a millimeter of error. Greater discrepancies will occur if any reading or setting errors have been made.

When inserting a recording electrode, first center it over the exposed brain in the appropriate anterior-posterior and lateral planes. The dura is then cut away and a puncture hole made in the cortical surface where the electrode is to enter. If this is not done, the pressure of the electrode on the surface may distort the brain considerably before penetration occurs. The electrode is then lowered to the appropriate horizontal plane. It is best to stimulate and monitor as the electrode is being lowered into place. When short-latency responses to flash stimulation are first encountered, the border of the responsive region, e.g., lateral geniculate body, has been reached. This serves as a good check on the calculated stereotaxic coordinates.

Even with the most careful techniques, localization of the electrode tip in the depths of the brain can only be approximated by the procedures described. It is mandatory to determine the exact location of the electrode tip by subsequent histological methods. These are described in some detail below. They involve marking, fixing, sectioning, and staining the tissue for microscopic examination.

Cortical recording electrodes can be placed on the visual area by using the stereotaxic manipulator or any manipulator or microscope drive calibrated in rectangular coordinates. It is not possible to specify in advance the exact location on the visual cortex that will yield the largest visually evoked responses. Consequently a fairly wide region of visual cortex should be exposed, dura removed, and a map of the areal response distribution to light flash made. A convenient method is to draw a chart of the cortical surface on graph paper in terms of the manipulator coordinates and indicate relative response amplitudes at different locations. A rough map of this sort may be made in a few minutes. Fissures should be plotted on the map, or a brain photograph made. These are marked with the electrode position for future reference. Although some stereotaxic atlases have cortical fissures charted, there is too much interanimal variability for reliable localization of cortical fields.

If the cortical surface is simply exposed to air, it will rapidly dry and become unresponsive. Two techniques have been used for maintenance of moisture. A dam of clay or dental cement can be built up on the skull around the exposed cortex and filled with warm mineral oil. This keeps moisture in and, if kept warm, will maintain the cortex in normal physiological conditions. If cortical mapping is planned, a more convenient procedure is to construct a humidity chamber by building up walls of moist cotton felt or gauze around the exposed cortex. This can be partially covered with moist gauze and kept moist by repeated applications of physiological saline warmed to body temperature. Stable evoked responses can be obtained for periods up to one week in a barbiturate-anesthetized animal using this procedure.

Cortical evoked responses are commonly recorded monopolarly by placing a single electrode wire, ball, or wick on the surface of the cortex and measuring against a distant indifferent such as an alligator clip on the cut skin edge. Because of volume conduction, the response field may be wider than the region of electrically active cortex. Various maneuvers can be used to ascertain the extent of such effects. A bipolar electrode placed across the cortex, surface to depth, will give a more accurate indication of locally generated activity. Alternatively, a single small electrode can be pushed down through the cortex to measure monopolarly the field generated in the cortex. Microelectrode techniques can be used to determine whether cells are actually being discharged in the cortex.

Recording and stimulation
techniques: chronic preparations

As noted earlier, the majority of analytic studies measuring electrical acitvity of the brain have used some type of immobilization, either by anesthetics or by paralyzing agents. For the psychologist interested in relating brain activity to behavior, both procedures have obvious drawbacks. (1) Anesthetics by definition depress activity of the brain to the point where no behavior occurs, and (2) the use of paralyzing agents has both moral and practical difficulties. Although efforts are made to eliminate all sources of pain, it is unlikely that this is ever completely accom-

plished. Most local anesthetics do not last more than 1 to 2 hours. If the animal is in a sterotaxic machine, the intensely painful pressure of the ear bars on the ear canals cannot be repeatedly blocked by reapplication of locals without removing the sterotaxic holder. Further, the animal is unable to breathe and, if human reports are relevant, experiences a continuous sensation of suffocation. In addition to humane considerations, it is impossible to determine the behavioral state of a paralyzed animal. If the electrical responses being studied depend in any way upon the state of behavioral arousal or "attention," and recent evidence suggests that this may be the case for some types of activity, tne experimenter has no way to measure or control such variables. Finally, the problems of primary interest to psychologists, such as learning, motivation, or attention, *require* a behaving animal. For these reasons, permanently implanted chronic electrodes are widely used today.

The problem of *volume conduction* is fundamental when recording electrical activity from permanently implanted electrodes. In an anesthetized animal several simple procedures, such as shifting the position of the indifferent electrode or moving the active electrode through the potential field, can help determine the location of sources and sinks of current flow contributing to the measured voltage response. These methods are not practical with permanently fixed electrodes. A few of the various results that can be obtained from a current source-sink are illustrated in the simplified schematic of Fig. 3-1. Suppose the indifferent electrode (*I*) is some distance from the source-sink. A surface recording taken between *A* and *I* yields an evoked response, as indicated. The potential recorded between *B* and *I* is only slightly different if the electrode is moved to position *B*. If we compared the potential across *A* and *B*, only a small response would be seen since the potential change is almost the same at both. If we measured between *C* and *I*, the potential might be about as large as that between *A* and *I*, but of opposite sign.

Consequently, when a measure is taken across *A* and *C,* the algebraic sum of the difference will yield a larger potential than *A* to *I* or *C* to *I*. Monopolar recording (*A-I, B-I,* or *C-I*) gives the exact amplitude of the potential at a given point relative to the indifferent but may be influenced by potential gradients at the indifferent and gives only approximate location of the current source. Bipolar recording (*A-B, A-C*) gives better information about the location of a potential *gradient* but does not permit measurement of amplitude at either point alone. For these reasons, a combination of monopolar and bipolar recording will usually provide the greatest amount of information.

Many *electrode materials* have been tried as chronic implants, e.g., copper, silver, silver chloride, stainless steel, platinum, tungsten, and molybdenum (Sheatz, 1961). An even wider variety of insulating compounds has been employed.

Fischer, Sayre, and Bickford (1961) implanted the following materials in the cat's brain for periods up to 4 weeks: silver wire coated with silver chloride, bare copper wire, stainless steel wire, Tygon-insulated silver wire, Formvar-insulated copper wire, varnished silver wire, and stainless steel wire in a polyethylene tube. Subsequent histological analyses indicated extensive tissue reaction and degeneration when uninsulated copper or silver wire and silver chloride wire were in contact with brain tissue. Uninsulated stainless steel caused no such reaction. There was no tissue reaction to insulated portions of any of the insulated wires; but there were extensive reactions at the cut end, where no insulation was present, with the silver and copper wires. The lesson of this study is clear: stainless steel is the electrode material of choice. The particular type of insulation is relatively unimportant, as long as it is waterproof (a polyethylene tube might not be) so that recording or stimulation is localized to the uninsulated tip. Further, stainless steel wire with enamel insulation already baked on is available commercially in a variety of sizes. Two practical problems are

usually encountered with stainless steel wire: (1) it generally comes in spools, and cut sections tend to curl—the common method of straightening is to hang weights on various cut lengths for periods of several days; and (2) soldering—acid flux must be used to achieve a good solder joint with steel.

For monopolar recording from depth, the simplest electrode is a piece of straight enameled stainless steel wire. Several types of assemblies have been used for bipolar recording from depth. Perhaps the simplest is two enameled stainless steel wires stuck together, one being somewhat longer than the other. Stacked arrays of single-wire electrodes may also be used for multiple stimulation or recording at a graded series of depths. A slightly more elaborate version consists of stainless hypodermic-needle tubing with an enameled stainless steel wire slipped down the center and extending somewhat beyond the tubing. In cutting the tubing, care must be taken to ream out crimping, which might otherwise scrape off the insulation of the center wire. Both of these electrodes require the application of additional insulation. Several satisfactory types of enamel material are commercially available. They can be baked in an ordinary home electric oven. Beading of the enamel is a common problem but can be avoided by thinning the enamel sufficiently.

Testing insulation, or absence of insulation, on the recording tip, is a simple but important maneuver. The easiest method for a single-wire electrode is to place the wire in saline, connect it to one side of a battery ohmmeter, and connect the other side of the meter directly to the saline. If the electrode tip is free of insulation, the resistance will be from 5,000 to 35,000 ohms. To check for any leaks in the insulator, shine a bright light on the beaker of saline. Any point of leakage along the wire will produce a steady stream of small bubbles. Alternatively, a saline-soaked wick connected to one side of the ohmmeter can be run up and down the dry wire.

The use of a stereotaxic machine in acute experiments has been described above. There are only a few modifications of technique necessary for chronic implantation. First, sterile technique is advisable for the cat, dog, and monkey. It is disheartening to complete a long series of experiments with negative results only to find a large abscess surrounding the electrode. The experimenter may sterilize electrodes, wires, and plugs by soaking in Zephiran. A large supply of sterile hand towels is useful to permit manipulation of the stereotaxic machine without contaminating the field.

Particular caution must be used if animals are to be run in experiments involving auditory stimulation. The standard ear bar of the stereotaxic head holder breaks the ear drums when inserted. In fact, the slight "crunch" of the tympanic membrane is usually the best cue that the ear bar is properly seated. Ear-bar tips may be partially ground off to avoid this. Such ear bars are available from most manufacturers of stereotaxic machines. However, these ear bars increase the uncertainty of electrode placement.

Since most chronic implanted electrodes are rigidly fixed, electrode localization must be as precise as possible. In many instances the structure to be localized may be responsive to peripheral stimulation. Thus, if the experimenter is aiming for the lateral geniculate body, evoked responses to flash stimulation can be monitored while the electrode is being positioned. Alternatively, the structure may not itself respond but may be close to a known responsive system. For example, if the experimenter wishes to place the electrode 2 mm above the optic tract, the electrode can be inserted until an optic-tract response to flash is first encountered and can then be withdrawn 2 mm.

Many varied techniques have been devised for chronic implantation of depth and surface electrode arrays. Every investigator has altered details of the basic methods to his own particular requirements. Methods range in complexity from a phonograph needle pounded through the skull (Hoagland, 1940) to a 610 electrode array embedded in a plastic skull substitute casting (Lilly, 1958). The obvious common features are (1) rigid fixation of electrodes to the skull, (2) good contact of electrodes to tissue, and (3) a noise-free and convenient method of "plugging in" the electrodes to recording or stimulating equipment.

Miller, Coons, Lewis, and Jensen (1961) have developed a very simple method for use with the rat that exemplifies the basic requirements of an implanted electrode. Rats are anesthetized with Nembutal, 40 mg per kg, and placed in a stereotaxic instrument. The scalp is reflected, periosteum scraped away, and the skull surface thoroughly cleaned and dried. With the stereotaxic instrument, the point of entrance of the electrode is marked on the skull. Four holes are drilled in the skull, with a dental drill #75. Two of the holes are drilled in back and two in front of the electrode location, straddling the electrode locus. Stainless steel jewelers' screws (8AL No. 46 case) are screwed part-way down. These screws provide anchors for the dental cement. The hole for the electrode is then drilled and the electrode lowered into proper position stereotaxically. All bleeding is then stopped by applying pressure with cotton, using an air stream, or placing small amounts of bone wax on the drilled edge of skull. If the skull, electrode, and screws are not completely dry and clean, the dental cement will not adhere. Apply a layer of dental cement over the electrode and one or more of the anchor screws. Size 3/0 dress snaps, male element, are crimped over a tinned portion of the electrode wire about 2 mm above the skull. This may be done before implanting if the electrode is first measured and cut to proper length. The electrode is now bent slightly away from the angle of insertion and the dental cement is built up until it embeds the dress snap. An indifferent electrode may be added last by simply inserting a length of Surgaloy suture wire in the neck muscles and crimping on a dress snap, which is then embedded in the dental-cement cap. By using this method, up to four electrodes may be implanted in a single rat. There is not sufficient room for more dress snaps on the skull. To ensure firm connection a size 4/0 female dress snap is used. Flexible insulated lead wire is then soldered to the female snap.

A single multiple connector plug is preferred for larger animals such as the cat, dog, or monkey, and for the rat if more than four electrodes are required. The procedure described above can be modified by connecting the electrode leads to the terminals of a miniature socket. In Miller's technique, dental cement is built up over most of the skull surface, and the cut scalp is simply left open. Infection can develop rapidly in a cat or monkey with such a wide area of exposed cut scalp.

Sheatz (1961) uses a pedestal with a broad-flange base and narrow shaft that holds the connector plug away from the skull. Electrode wires are led up though the hollow shaft of the pedestal to the plug. Skin may then be sutured tightly around the shaft of the pedestal. Electrode wires are implanted stereotaxically as described above and fixed in position with individual blobs of dental cement. The wires are collected in a bundle and then drawn through the shaft of the pedestal. The pedestal base has three slot holes for screws. A "y" groove is drilled in the skull, three stainless steel screws are cemented head down in the grooves, and the pedestal base bolted to the screws. The electrode wires are then connected to the plug contacts by using dental amalgam. This is a useful way of avoiding the necessity of soldering during the implantation. Amalgam hardens to form a good conducting medium. The plug and connectors must be constructed and are rather complex (see Sheatz, 1961, for details).

A variety of ordinary small multiple connector plugs are commercially available and easily adapted for use as chronic implant plugs. They may be fastened to a Sheatz-type pedestal or simply embedded in the dental cement. If several enameled stainless steel wire electrodes are used, they may be brought to a central point on the skull and bent upward to the plug, which might be elevated above the skull by several millimeters. The electrode wires then can serve as a matrix for a dental-cement pedestal holding the plug above the skull. In this type of arrangement, a satisfactory indifferent electrode is a stainless steel machine screw screwed into the skull over the frontal-bone sinus. A connecting wire may then be led along the skull to the plug and covered with dental cement.

In general, plugs attached to the skull with dental cement are more fragile than plugs held in pedestal supports. A relatively simple and rigid framework can be made by drilling holes and slots in the skull, inserting stainless steel bolts with thinned heads in the slots, and bolting them to the skull so that the heads lie between skull and dura. Any kind of superstructure can then be attached to these rigid bolts. In fact, the bolts can be led out through the skin to provide connections for a rigid and painless head holder for use with the unanesthetized animal.

The techniques described above are primarily for use with *multiple implanted depth electrodes,* and require individual stereotaxic placement of the wires. This means that connections and final plug assembly must be made during the implantation. If only one depth electrode is used, it may be fastened to the plug and cut to approximate length ahead of time, saving considerable time in the actual implantation.

Electrode assemblies used for recording or stimulation of cerebral cortex are somewhat easier to implant, at least in principle. The simplest but perhaps the least satisfactory method is to pound small steel needles through the skull and run connecting wires to a central plug. The needles may not penetrate the dura or may penetrate partially or completely through the cortex. If the response to be recorded is generated within the layers of the cerebral cortex, the form and polarity of the recorded signal will be dependent upon the location of the electrode tip (see Fig. 3-1). A better method is to drill a small hole in the skull for each electrode, open the dura underlying the hole, and insert an insulated steel wire to touch the pial surface. The electrode wire can then be bent over the skull and cemented in place.

These methods also require connecting the electrode wires to the plug at the time of implantation. If the cortical area of interest lies on the surface, rather than in a fissure, the complete assembly can be constructed ahead of time, with the electrodes embedded in a "skull-substitute" plate of plastic or dental cement. If the electrodes are relatively close together, a flat plate may be used. The plate should cover a wider area than the region of skull removed and should be flanged, so that the section substituting for the skull extends downward beyond the flange for a distance equal to the thickness of the skull. The skull hole is drilled, trephined, or rongeured to the size of the extended portion of the plate, and the plate inserted. The flange portion of the plate then overlies skull and can be screwed to the skull and overlaid with dental cement. The easiest way of obtaining a good fit is to make the extended portion of the plate the exact size of the outer diameter of an appropriately sized trephine. This obviates the necessity for any further drilling or shaping of the skull opening.

The most satisfactory method of prefabricating such an electrode assembly is to use a cleaned skull from a previously sacrificed animal. There is relatively little interanimal variability in skull form and size within a species. The brain fissures can be seen on the inner surface of the skull and serve as guides. After the electrodes are soldered to the connector plug, the desired hole is drilled in the skull and the skull coated with bone wax or beeswax to prevent dental cement from adhering. The plug is then placed over the midline and the electrode wires molded along the skull, bent at right angles to pass through the hole in their approximate locations, and cut approximately 1 mm below the inner surface of skull. The entire assembly is then covered with dental cement.

A wax-coated plastic surface with holes for the electrode wires may be placed under the skull hole to form the brain surface mold. Dental cement is built up until a single rigid assembly is obtained. In the actual implantation, simply trephine a hole over the desired location, remove the dura, and seat the assembly on the skull with the electrodes fitted against the cortex. Additional dental cement is applied, and jewelers' screws attached in various locations to provide anchor points. If a large area of cortical surface must be covered, it is best to make a plastic "skull" containing the electrodes. Lilly (1958) has developed this method to the point where 610 electrodes were successfully implanted on the cortex overlying one hemisphere of a monkey.

Signal-to-noise ratio can be a troublesome problem when recording the surface-evoked response from the cerebral cortex. Reference to Fig. 3-1 illustrates the general situation. The potential difference is recorded between A and I. Many sources of activity from more distant regions, e.g., thalamus, ocular and temporal muscles, can contribute to the potential difference. Additionally, spontaneous cortical background activity unrelated to the stimulus-evoked response is present. A variety of high-powered computing devices are available commercially to pull out the average signal from background noise, but these are generally beyond the resources of the average investigator. Further, the investigator might well be interested in the effects of training conditions or other behavioral variables on brain activity over time. This requires measurement of individual responses.

The *bipolar electrode* provides a very simple method for minimizing effects of distant voltage sources and maximizing the locally generated cortical response. A bipolar recording electrode across the cortex gives the kind of measurement shown by A-C in Fig. 3-1 in contrast to the A-I response of the surface electrode.

Bipolar electrodes are most easily made by cutting short pieces of stainless steel hypodermic tubing, soldering connector wires to them, and inserting small enameled stainless steel wires to extend 2 to 3 mm beyond the tubing tip. These electrodes are then given several coats of insulation, the insulation is scraped off the bottom edge of the tubing, and they are soldered to the connector plug and placed in position for the assembly mold. In implantation, care must be taken to ensure that the center wires penetrate cortex rather than blood vessels and the tube edges rest on the cortical surface. Both bipolar and monopolar responses can be recorded if a bone sinus indifferent electrode is added.

Electrode resistance should be checked after the implant is completed. If a battery ohmmeter is used, make the measurements brief or the tissue at the electrode tip will electrolyze. The resistance will be about the same as it was in saline, if the electrodes are functional. High resistance suggests a break or failure to expose electrode tips, and low resistance indicates a short circuit, usually at the connector plug.

The characteristics of the cable connecting the animal to the recording or stimulating equipment are of some importance. A maximum flexibility is desirable, together with a minimum of electrical noise. Almost any insulated unshielded wires will do for stimulation purposes. When the experimenter is simultaneously stimulating and recording, it is best to twist the stimulating wires together throughout their length to reduce stimulus artifact. *Recording cables must be shielded.* Separate shielded and insulated wires are best. Some commercial wires, e.g., Microdot, combine good flexibility with negligible noise. Since the animal will be moving his head and/or other parts of the body during the experiment, the cables should be maintained above the animal in some type of elastic holder. Rubber bands, spring-loaded lever arms, and pulley arrangements have all proved satisfactory. The particular design depends upon the behavioral requirements of the experiment.

A variety of precautions and control proce-dures should be used when evaluating data from chronic recording electrodes. (1) Responses of the unanesthetized animal are always variable and must be analyzed statistically if changes related to manipulated variables are to be demonstrated. (2) A variety of nonrelevant factors may operate to change response amplitude over time. Tissue reactions, growth of scar tissue, regrowth of dura over cortex, deterioration of electrode tips, or loose connections, may result in progressive decreases of response amplitude. If such changes occur in studies of habituation or conditioning, for example, spontaneous recovery or extinction procedures should be used to show that the original response amplitude can still be obtained. A further check can be made by recording at the time of sacrifice from the anesthetized animal. This is less satisfactory since many responses cannot be obtained with anesthetics, and response amplitude is dependent upon anesthetic depth. Control animals implanted at the same time as the experimental groups but not given the training procedures may also be used. (3) A third source of error lies in alterations of effective stimulus intensities. Response amplitudes from primary sensory systems, in particular, are closely related to stimulus intensity. Head position in sound or light field, pupil diameter, and contractions of middle-ear muscles must be considered as possible sources of response amplitude change. Studies by Marsh, Worden, and Hicks (1962) and Worden and Marsh, (1963) discuss many of these problems and are models of "how to do" chronic recording experiments. They studied "habituation" of click-evoked responses in the cochlea nucleus of a cat, using both monopolar and bipolar electrodes. Statistical analyses demonstrated no consistent evidence of habituation. The most effective and reliable variable influencing evoked-response amplitude was head position in the sound field.

A good deal of caution is necessary in interpreting experiments comparing changes in neural activity with alterations of behavior. For example, shock avoidance conditioning is a very well described method, the necessary control procedures ruling out pseudoconditioning, sensitization, and other effects having been done many years ago. The fact that a change in brain activity occurs simultaneously with the development of the conditioned response does not demonstrate that it is necessarily related to the avoidance learning aspects of the experiment. A backward conditioning control group not developing the conditioned avoidance response might well exhibit precisely the same change in brain activity. Clearly, any change in neural activity correlated with behavioral alterations is of significance and interest; however, a number of control procedures are necessary to determine what aspects of the behavioral situation are most relevant to the neural changes.

Essentially everything that has been said about recording electrode systems holds for stimulation as well. It will be recalled that monopolar electrodes (Fig. 3-1, *A-I*) record activity over a much wider region than bipolar electrodes (*A-C*). In like manner, if *A* is now the active pole of a stimulating electrode and *I* the other pole, the potential field around electrode *A* will be diffuse. On the other hand, if *A* and *C* are the two poles of a bipolar stimulating electrode, the potential field will be much more localized to the region between the two electrodes. This becomes an important consideration when attempting to localize the anatomical structures stimulated. With monopolar stimulation a region 2 mm away from the active electrode may have a very much lower threshold than another structure only 1 mm away. Often this simply cannot be determined. The serious difficulties encountered in attempts to localize reward areas of the brain in self-stimulation experiments is a good example. Initially the septal area was believed to be a strong reward region, but more recent evidence indicates that it is in fact neutral (Olds, 1962).

There is much controversy over the parameters of the electrical stimulus to be preferred. The minimum requirement is a stimulus that elicits some kind of response, either behavioral or electrophysiological, and is not damaging to tissue. Lilly (1961) maintains that only one rather complex waveform is noninjurious when used over long periods of time. This waveform is produced by "quasi-differentiation" of a rectangular positive pulse of 120 microseconds (μsec), which results in a pulse pair of rounded waves: first a positive pulse lasting 34 μsec and then, after about 80 μsec, a negative pulse of 28 μsec. This pulse pair is then delivered at rates ranging from 50 to 200 per sec.

The 60-cps stimulator (Olds and Milner, 1954) is at the other extreme and is perhaps the ultimate in simplicity, consisting of a doorbell transformer and some resistance. Miller, Jensen, and Myers (1961) compared threshold changes by using the Lilly waveform and the simple 60-cps stimulus waveform. After periods of 120 min of continuous stimulation there were essentially no differences in threshold for the two types of stimulus. Lilly (1961) emphasizes that injurious effects of 60 cps will show up only over longer periods of stimulation, ranging from weeks to months. There seems to be agreement that 60 cps is noninjurious if used for a few sessions or a few days, but the Lilly waveform may be safer for experiments lasting for long periods of time. There is unanimous agreement on two extreme types of waveform to be avoided: (1) a simple d-c voltage and (2) radio frequencies (RF) above about 200 kc. Both cause considerable tissue damage, d-c voltage by electrolysis and RF by heat. In fact, these are traditional methods for producing lesions in the depths of the brain.

A simple recommendation for the proper frequency or repetition rate for a stimulus is not possible. A stimulus at one frequency may produce opposite effects to a stimulus of different frequency delivered to the same locus under otherwise identical conditions. Stimulation of the intralaminar thalamic nuclei is a dramatic example: at frequencies of 5 to 10 cps sleep is induced, but at higher frequencies arousal may occur (Jasper, 1960).

In many instances it is desirable to isolate

the animal and the stimulus pulse from the ground side of the stimulating equipment. If concomitant electrical recording is planned, this is mandatory to avoid the large shock artifact that will block the recording amplifier. The simplest isolation units are inexpensive commercial radio transformers. These are satisfactory if sine wave stimulus forms are used, but square-wave pulses are markedly distorted, appearing more like damped oscillations. A transformer has one further advantage in that the animal is protected against possible steady direct currents that could result from various junction potentials or from defects in stimulating equipment. An alternative solution is to utilize an RF isolation system. Such units transform the stimulus pulse to a radio frequency, then retransform it to the original pulse form, thus preserving the stimulus waveform. A variety of inexpensive RF isolation units are available commercially.

The measurement of stimulus characteristics is often unnecessary. If a behavioral response is to be elicited, the threshold stimulus intensity can be determined and the stimulus set in terms of threshold. Approximate measures of actual stimulus characteristics can be made by determining the resistance of the stimulating electrode, substituting such a resistance for the preparation, and measuring voltage and/or current. The ideal solution is a continuous monitoring system that measures current flow at the time of stimulation. This is straightforward if the stimulus is a square wave or is an alternating series of positive and negative square waves. A low resistance, e.g., 1 ohm, is placed in series on one side of the stimulus isolation unit output and the voltage drop across the resistor measured with an ordinary high input impedance differential amplifier and oscilloscope. Current flow in the resistor will be the same as in the animal, since they are in series, and the voltage drop across the resistor negligible in relation to that across the animal; e.g., if the animal resistance is 10,000 ohms, the voltage drop across the resistor will be one ten-thousandth of that across the animal. Current flow is calculated from the measured voltage by using Ohm's law: $I = E/R = E$ measured/1 ohm $= E$ measured. With a 1-ohm resistor, the conversion factor from measured voltage to calculated current is 1, e.g., a reading of 0.2 millivolt (mv) indicates a current flow of 0.2 milliamp (ma). The reader is urged to consult Becker, Peacock, Heath, and Mickle (1961) for detailed discussion of a variety of stimulus control and measurement problems.

Chemical stimulation of the brain by microinjection is a useful method for the study of possible chemoreceptor, endocrine, and other biochemical factors in brain function. Procedures do not differ from ordinary electrode implantation except that small hypodermic tubing is used and is connected through a stopcock to flexible plastic tubing. Substances are injected by a microsyringe, which may be made by fastening the syringe plunger to a microscope drive, although commercial units are available. Injection of comparable amounts of saline is a necessary procedure to control for the possibility that effects are due to the pressure of injected substances rather than to specific chemical characteristics.

Some knowledge of *histological methodology* is of the utmost importance in both acute and chronic experimentation. It is seldom possible to defend the position that electrode localization is irrelevant to the purposes of the experiment. Usually only the most general kinds of hypothesis can be tested without recourse to anatomical methods; viz., will an animal respond or become conditioned to brain stimulation? Most investigators wish to go beyond this to more detailed correlations of structure and function. When this is desired, histological control procedures must be used. The stereotaxic implantation procedure alone is never sufficiently precise. Several histological methods of increasing complexity. will be described here. There are standard texts on histological techniques giving complete details of the various sectioning and staining methods. Akert and Welker (1961) have published an excellent review of methods of anatomical localization.

The simplest methods are suitable only for very gross localization of large electrode placement. The first method permits determination only of general regions of the brain containing the electrode. When the animal is sacrificed, remove the skull and cut the brain with a sharp knife along the electrode tract. The cut surface with the electrode tract may be photographed, and thin sections can be cut to determine the width or depth of the tract.

Another procedure is to perfuse the brain with a 10 percent formalin solution at time of sacrifice, cut out a block containing the electrode tract, and section it [100 micron (μ) thickness] with a microtome by using the frozen-section method. The section showing the location of the electrode tip can be placed in an enlarger and prints made directly without further staining, fixing, or microphotography. This permits somewhat greater localization in terms of gross structures than the first method, but does not allow identification in terms of the usual histological characteristics of cell groups and nuclei.

This method and subsequent procedures to be described utilize perfusion and sectioning methods. The most convenient *perfusion apparatus* is simply a funnel or inverted container 1 to 3 ft above the animal with tubing and a perfusing pipette or needle. In perfusion through the heart, the animal is first deeply anesthetized, e.g., by injecting a lethal dose of Nembutal, the chest cavity opened, and the pericardial membrane opened. The descending aorta, lying ventral to the spinal column in the chest cavity, is clamped. The right auricle is cut open and the perfusion pipette inserted in the left ventrical. About 50 cubic centimeters (cc) (for cat) of saline should be placed in the perfusion funnel and tubing followed by 200 cc of 10 percent formalin. If the brain is not first perfused by saline, the formalin will fix blood in the brain tissues. Alternatively, the perfusing solution may be inserted directly into the carotid arteries with a hypodermic needle by using the funnel or a large syringe.

A variety of *microtomes* are available for slicing the tissue. Perhaps the most versatile are sliding microtomes, where the knife blade is pulled back and forth across the tissue block. Details of use depend upon the particular instrument and techniques, and are given in standard microtechnique and histology texts (Gatenby and Beams, 1950; McClung, 1929). Three general methods are used for *embedding tissues* for section. (1) The *frozen-section technique* is the easiest and fastest for electrode localization. Although commercial carbon dioxide (CO_2) gas freezing devices are available, a special tissue-block cup with a rim for holding dry ice is adequate. Tissue blocks as large as or larger than the rat brain can be handled this way, but a whole cat or monkey brain is too large to freeze evenly throughout. If physically separate tissues, e.g., cerebrum and cerebellum, are to be sectioned, gelatin may be added to the fixing solution to provide a temporary bond. (2) *Paraffin embedding* is particularly useful with a rotary microtome if a complete series of sections through a small brain or block are required. The sections remain attached end-to-end, simplifying labeling. (3) *Celloidin embedding* is the procedure of choice for large brains and analysis of cellular characteristics. The only drawback to this method is the 1- to 3-month period required for hardening.

If the electrodes are small, localization of the tip is often difficult. *Coagulation* is a common method of localizing electrode tips if detailed localization is not important. An electrolytic or RF lesion device, or any source of direct current that delivers 5 ma, is connected to the electrode for from 10 to 60 sec. This results in a cavity at the locus of the electrode tip and at any other portion of the electrode where insulation is not intact. This has the obvious disadvantage that cells in the vicinity of the tip are destroyed. A more precise method, applicable where steel electrodes have been used, involves depositing metal ions from the electrode tip (Marshall, 1940). The positive pole of a $1\frac{1}{2}$- to 6-volt battery is connected to the active electrode, and the negative pole to the indifferent, for a duration of 5 to 30 sec. The current flow will be of the order of 10 microamperes (μa), too low to cause coagulation. The simplest method of "developing" the deposited metal ions is to add a 5 percent solution of potassium ferrocyanide to the 10 percent formalin perfusion solution. This gives a greenish spot at the electrode tip locus without destroying cells. A better method is to perfuse first with 10 percent formalin and section, then immerse the sections in a 1 percent hydrogen peroxide solution for several minutes and then for 5 min in a 5 percent potassium ferrocyanide solution prior to staining (Akert and Welker, 1961).

The electrode tip is theoretically easy to locate with coagulation or ion-deposit marking procedures. In practice this is often difficult since the tissue sections will never be exactly parallel to the electrode tract. A method developed by Akert and Welker is very useful. (1) Two parallel series of marking needle tracts are made, each several millimeters away from the electrode tract. (2) The animal is perfused in the stereotaxic holder. (3) A knife blade is substituted for the needle electrode and the tissue block is cut 2 mm anterior and posterior to the marking tracts. (4) After the tissue block is placed on the microtome holder, sections are cut until the marking tracts are encountered. (5) The tissue block is tilted until the knife blade cuts parallel to them. It should then cut parallel to the electrode tract.

A variety of *staining methods* are commonly used. In frozen sections, cresyl violet is a simple and adequate procedure for electrode localization. If the Marshall ion-deposit method of marking is used, the green versus blue contrast is only moderate. A counterstaining procedure such as eosin is better here. Alternate sections may be prepared with Nissl stain to facilitate cellular analysis; or, if the structure in question is a fiber tract, alternate sections can be stained with the Weigert method (Gatenby and Beams, 1950; McClung, 1929).

In estimating the electrode position relative to brain structures, the marked tissue shrinkage resulting from histological procedures must be considered. Paraffin and celloidin methods result in up to 40 percent shrinkage of brain tissue. Shrinkage is considerably less with the frozen-section method. The degree of shrinkage can be measured by placing two electrode marks at different measured depths at the time of perfusion. It is important to note that localization of an electrode tip does not mean localization of the effective stimulation site. The activated structure producing a behavioral effect may be 2 mm or more away from the electrode tip, particularly when monopolar stimulating electrodes are used. *Only multiple replications of the experiment, threshold testing, and other control procedures will permit localization of the effective locus.*

Microelectrodes

Gross evoked responses recorded from depth or surface structures with large electrodes are now believed to represent primarily summated postsynaptic membrane potential shifts. The only exceptions to this are nerve or fiber tract recordings. Although such evoked responses provide a representative measure of the total population response, it is usually not possible to identify the cellular elements involved, or even to determine whether excitatory activity, inhibitory activity, or a combination of these is involved. The method is most useful for demonstrating functional connections and for interrelations of regional activity and stimulus or behavioral conditions. Analysis in terms of neural mechanisms is generally not possible. The development of microelectrode techniques for recording the activity of single nerve cells has added an important new dimension to the study of brain and behavior. These procedures permit analysis of the exact conditions that will excite or inhibit the activity of a given nerve cell and can provide information about synaptic processes involved. On the other hand, sampling is a very difficult problem in microelectrode studies, where the activity of 100 units might be studied in a population of many thousands of active cells.

Most complete information is obtained by a combination of gross and microelectrode methods.

There are two basically different types of microelectrode technique, *intracellular* and *extracellular recording*. The extracellular method provides more relevant kinds of information for the physiological psychologist at present and will be emphasized in this discussion. A number of methodological problems are common to both techniques.

Perhaps the first use of microelectrode recording was by Ling and Gerard (1949), although activity of single nerve fibers had been studied much earlier (e.g., Adrian and Bronk, 1929). The basic technique has not altered greatly since. A very small electrode is plunged blindly into the tissue and poked about until a single cell response is obtained.

To record the "isolated" *extracellular* response of a single cell, uncomplicated by activity of other cells, an electrode tip with outside diameter of 10 μ (0.01 mm) or less is usually required. A large variety of such electrodes have been used, none of which is particularly easy to make.

Perhaps the simplest type of metal microelectrode is electrolytically etched steel (Grundfest, Sengstaken, Oettinger, and Gurry, 1950). Stainless steel wire or needles of various diameters may be used. The electrode is pointed by dipping in an acid bath made up of 34 cc concentrate sulfuric acid, 42 cc orthophosphoric acid, and 24 cc distilled water. The positive pole of a 6-volt d-c source capable of delivering 30 ma is connected to the electrode, and the negative pole connected to the acid solution. The tip of the electrode is repeatedly dipped and raised to achieve the desired taper. Current should be reduced when the final tip is electrolyzed. After electrolysis, the tip is dipped in 10 percent hydrochloric acid (HCl) and washed in water and alcohol, and several coats of enamel are baked on.

Electrolyzed steel microelectrodes have the advantage of simplicity, but it is difficult to make small tips without pitting. An analogous procedure used with tungsten wire (Hubel, 1957) yields much smaller smooth tips. Commercially available 125-μ wire is electrolytically etched in a saturated solution of potassium nitrate, using a 2- to 6-volt alternating current from a filament transformer fed by a Variac. The wire may then be insulated as above or dipped in Insl-X or some other clear lacquer not requiring baking.

The most elaborate metal electrodes and the ones giving the best yield of cells are those developed by Dowben and Rose (1953). Glass pipettes are first drawn to tip diameters of 3 to 5 μ and then filled with molten indium on a hot plate. The indium tip is coated electrolytically with gold and then with platinum black. Of course metal microelectrodes have one major disadvantage—the tip easily becomes polarized and behaves somewhat like a capacitor, rejecting low-frequency signals. This effect can be partially compensated by using a special type of amplifier (see below).

The other general type of microelectrode is the glass micropipette. Glass tubing is heated, drawn to very small tip diameters, and filled with a salt solution to act as a conductor. The first micropipettes were hand-drawn, but commercial pullers are now available. Surprisingly, it is easier to draw fine tips than large tips. The fine tip can be "bumped" under a microscope to a diameter of 2 to 10 μ and the pipette filled with salt solution simply by squirting it in from a syringe. A 3-molar KCl solution may be satisfactory for large extracellular micropipettes. The glass microelectrode has good low-frequency response but tends to attenuate high frequencies.

Both metal and glass microelectrodes have resistance values ranging from about 100,000 ohms to several megohms. An ordinary high-gain differential amplifier does not have a much greater input impedance than this, nor a low enough input grid current to avoid polarization effects. Consequently, an additional amplifier must be inserted between the electrode and the regular amplifier. This negative capacitance amplifier must have (1) a very high input impedance, (2) a negligible grid current, and (3) a negligible effective capacitance between input and ground. Such amplifiers are often called *unity gain preamplifiers,* since they do not actually amplify the signal, but act as an impedance transformer isolating the signal source from the loading effects of the usual amplifier.

Mechanical control of the microelectrode movement must be precise; sudden advance or backlash of a few microns is enough to kill the cell being recorded. Ordinary electrode manipulators are not adequate; special commercial micromanipulators must be used. Movement of the animal and/or movement resulting from brain pulsations are a constant problem even in acute anesthetized preparations. Strategies for handling animal movement are the use of massive holders and microdrives with large mechanical impedance or the use of very light units attached to the animal. The latter type has obvious utility in chronic recording studies. An easy solution to the problem of brain pulsation is a plastic pressor foot such as a small lens with a center hole for the electrode, placed on the brain surface. If recording is from cortical cells, such a restraining device may interfere with blood supply. A more elaborate method is a saline-filled sealed chamber attached to the skull with a microdrive mounted on it (Davies, 1956). Another rapid method is to pour a warm solution of saline agar gel on the region of electrode entry. As it cools and gels, it tends to reduce pulsations. For chronic recording, the microdrive unit can be cemented to the skull to form an airtight seal.

The signal recorded by an extracellular microelectrode is a simple biphasic spike, often positive, then negative, lasting about 1 msec. With stable conditions, spike height remains constant and is a good criterion that activity from only one cell is being recorded. If the electrode is fairly close to the cell, spike amplitude will be 0.5 mv or more. Caution must be used in determining the origin of the spike response since it is not always certain that the response is from a cell body rather than an axon. Axon spikes are usually faster and of smaller amplitude. It is sometimes difficult to demonstrate that a given spike response is not from an injured cell, and hence abnormal. An excellent discussion of this problem can be found in Mountcastle, Davies, and Berman (1957). Perhaps the most operational criterion is that such cells usually cannot be held very long. A "good" cell can be held for periods up to several hours.

Chronic extracellular microelectrode recording is rather difficult. In addition to the usual problems of chronic implantation, the electrode is very fragile and must be moved *in situ* at the time of recording. A procedure developed by Hubel (1959) involves implanting a small microdrive in the skull and inserting microelectrodes when recordings are to be made. An alternative approach (Poggio and Mountcastle, 1963) is to section the fifth nerve and branches of the cervical plexus prior to the experiment. The animal's head is fixed in the stereotaxic holder under brief ether anesthesia, and recordings taken by using a paralyzing agent.

Extracellularly recorded single-cell response data may be transcribed in a variety of ways. The most common method is to photograph the oscilloscope tracing. Alternatively, the output of the high-gain differential amplifier can be fed into any ordinary tape recorder (a frequency response range of 20 to 5,000 cps is sufficient to record spike discharges) and subsequently fed into an oscilloscope for photography or an electronic counter set to count spikes. If large microelectrodes with tip diameters of 10 to 30 μ are used, single cell responses cannot be isolated, but spike responses from a number of cells will be recorded. This "hash" can be fed into an integrating circuit for a measure of overall population activity. Beidler (1953) and Pfaffmann (1955) have utilized this approach very successfully in recording peripheral nerve activity in response to gustatory stimulation. Many sensory stimuli, e.g., gustatory, olfactory, and ongoing auditory and visual stimulation, do not have synchronous onset times and will not yield gross evoked responses. Unit hash integration is a possible method under these conditions.

Intracellular microelectrode recording involves a number of specialized problems: (1) glass pipettes of less than 1 μ tip diameter must be used in conjunction with d-c recording systems, (2) the cell membrane must be penetrated without serious injury, and (3) the cell must be held impaled. This is usually not possible for more than an hour or two. Intracellular recording is simply not feasible at present in the normal behaving animal.

An electrode inside a nerve cell records the potential across the cell membrane relative to a distant indifferent electrode. In an inactive cell the membrane potential will be a d-c voltage of about −70 mv. The spike discharge changes the membrane potential by up to 100 mv ($\frac{1}{10}$ volt). The occurrence of a spike discharge can equally well be recorded extracellularly. The power of the intracellular method is that it permits recording of the synaptic events leading up to discharge, or failure to discharge. These postsynaptic potentials (PSPs) are brief shifts in the level of the resting membrane potential ranging in value from 1 to 15 mv or more. The spike discharge of a cell has a threshold level a few millivolts positive to the resting level. Excitatory synaptic activity causes a brief positive shift in membrane potential (EPSP), with a spike if discharge threshold is reached. Inhibitory synaptic activity causes a brief negative shift in the membrane potential (IPSP), thus moving the potential level further away from discharge threshold.

The analytic power of intracellular recording lies in the measurement of PSP shifts of the membrane. If an extracellular recording demonstrates that a given stimulus causes a cell to stop firing, this could be due to changes in cells prior to the cell in question or to synaptic inhibitory activity on the cell. Intracellular recording will demonstrate which possibility has occurred. If there is no membrane shift, the altered activity must be prior to synapses on the cell; but if there is an IPSP, decreased activity is due to synaptic inhibition of the

cell itself. The reader may consult Frank (1960) for technical information and further references on intracellular recording methods, and Eccles (1964) for an impressive demonstration of the analytic power of the technique.

Lesion methods

Lesions were the earliest method of studying brain function, and they have provided us with most of our information on the roles of various neural structures in behavior. The lesion method continues to be the *sine qua non* of the physiological psychologist.

As a general rule, chronic lesions in carnivores and primates require sterile technique. Although infections may be controlled with antibiotics, the effective lesion is often enlarged or altered is an uncontrolled manner if nonsterile technique is used. Semisterile techniques may be used with rodents and lower forms, although there is a positive correlation between extent of precaution and success of lesion.

Some of the more generally used methods of removing or inactivating brain tissue will be discussed here. In terms of technique, permanent lesions may be grouped under the general headings of transection, surface ablation, and depth destruction.

Transection of the spinal cord or brain stem is a widely used procedure. A rapidly dissipating anesthetic like ether is best for acute studies, but a blood pressure depressant drug such as Nembutal is preferable for chronic preparations. A variety of methods have been used to transect the spinal cord, including cutting, crushing, and tying. Extradural tying is perhaps the least traumatic. The dorsal vertebrae are removed over the locus of transection and the exposure widened laterally until the upper half of the cord is visualized. With dura intact, thread is passed under the cord by using a small curved needle inserted backward. The thread is then tied in a tight knot crushing the cord. If absolute certainty of transection is important, two ties may be made a few millimeters apart, and the cord and dura cut between them. Simple cutting of the cord without ties sometimes leads to uncontrollable bleeding. Oxycel, an oxidized cotton with powerful clotting properties, and thrombin, a clotting solution, are invaluable aids in this and all other surgical procedures.

Transection of the brain stem at the level of the upper mesencephalon yields the *cerveau isolé* preparation, first described by Bremer (1935). If the portion of the nervous system below the transection is to be studied, the following method can be used. (1) Ligate the carotid arteries in the neck, which lie just ventrolateral to the trachea. (2) Remove the skull over the lateral surface of one hemisphere and chop up the dura and cortex with sharp scissors. (3) Temporarily clamp the vertebral arteries by squeezing the sides of the neck at the juncture of the skull and vertebral column. (4) Remove the posterior portion of the hemisphere with a large (5-mm) pipette and strong suction. (5) Insert a smaller pipette (1 mm diameter) and transect the brain stem at the level of the superior colliculus. In carnivores the cerebrum and cerebellum are separated by a bony *tentorium,* which ends just above the superior colliculus and may be used as a guide. (6) After transection, remove the brain tissue several millimeters anterior to the section to prevent subsequent pressure on the brain stem from edema. If desired, all brain tissue anterior to the section may be removed. Bard and Macht (1958) were able to maintain chronic preparations of this type for periods up to 180 days by leaving the pituitary intact, surrounded by a neurally isolated island of hypothalamic tissue. The greatest difficulty lies in the fact that such animals have no temperature regulation and must be maintained in a constant-temperature environment.

If the nervous system above the section (i.e., the *cerveau isolé* portion) is to be studied, much greater care is required to avoid damage. One method is to use a spatula mounted in a stereotaxic machine and shaped and calibrated to section at the required level. The skull overlying the cerebellum is removed and the cerebellum aspirated. The spatula may then be inserted stereotaxically at an appropriate angle.

The *cerveau isolé* is by no means a normal animal, but a number of systems can be studied without anesthesia. All pain input to the cerebrum is eliminated, and it may be presumed that the brain stem below the level of section does not appreciate pain. Anterior to the section, the olfactory system and the retinocortical visual system are intact. The cortical EEG indicates a permanently "sleeping" cerebrum. All movement control is now posterior to the section, but such chronic animals are capable of a surprising range of behavior and may even be conditionable (Bard and Macht, 1958).

Ablation of cerebral cortex for acute and chronic preparations is best accomplished by subpial aspiration if adjacent structures are to remain intact. After exposure of the brain and reflection of dura, a small pipette (#18 to #22 rounded hypodermic tubing or drawn and polished glass tubing, with tip diameter less than 1 mm) is inserted under the pia and drawn along the undersurface of the pia. With proper pipette size and suction strength cerebral cortex will be aspirated but white matter and larger blood vessels will not. In chronic procedures using carnivores and primates, it is best to suture the dura after lesion, both to protect the remaining cortex and to minimize excessive scar-tissue proliferation.

Lesions in the depths of the brain require stereotaxic technique. Monopolar and bipolar electrodes can be used, but more discrete lesions result with the latter. Details of electrode placement and localization do not differ from those of the acute and chronic recording and stimulation procedures described above. Fairly large insulated steel wires are commonly used. Two general methods of producing lesions are (1) electrolytic and (2) high frequency (RF). A d-c power source capable of delivering several milliamperes is required for electrolytic lesions. For RF lesions, surgical cautery machines or inexpensive RF lesion makers can be used.

Electrolytic methods produce destruction by electrolysis of tissue, and RF methods by the heat generated from the RF current. There is no discrete boundary in both cases; the area of damage is graded from total to negligible, depending upon distance from electrodes. A discrete region of destruction develops in chronic lesions, but intermediate histological changes can be seen bordering this. A common and often erroneous assumption in depth-lesion studies has been that behavioral changes are the result of having destroyed tissue. An alternative possibility is that tissue bordering the lesion comes to function in an abnormal manner, e.g., producing epileptic-like discharge, and this produces the behavioral alteration. A methodological study by Reynolds (1963) compared effects of electrolytic and RF lesions of hypothalamic tissue producing the hyperphagic response in the rat. Electrolytic lesions produced more immediate deaths from edema than did RF lesions. Staining procedures indicated strong concentrations of electrode metal ions in tissue bordering the region of total destruction by electrolysis, but not after RF lesion. It appears that at least part of the behavioral syndrome after electrolysis may have been abnormal tissue function rather than tissue destruction. It would seem advisable to use RF for depth lesions (however, see the recent study by Hoebel, 1965).

Brain lesions have been made by a variety of other techniques, most of which require rather specialized equipment such as focused X rays or ultrasonic sound waves. Cortical lesions can be produced by implanting small pellets of a radioactive isotope (Harlow, 1958). An elegant method for controlled destruction of one or more layers of cortex has been developed by using a cyclotron beam (Rose, Malis, and Baker, 1961).

Histological reconstruction is usually a must because of the uncertainties attendant upon any lesion procedure. A spirited defense for no histology has been presented (Meyer, 1958), and the position would seem to have considerable merit if the hypothesis being tested does not relate structure and function in any detail. Consistent behavioral alterations as a result of a given lesion speak for themselves. If correlations between structure and function are desired, histology is necessary.

The frozen-section method is generally adequate for localization of depth lesions. The procedures do not differ from those described for electrode localization. If cortical lesions of carnivores or primates are to be reconstructed, celloidin embedding and the Nissl method are probably best. The extent of the cortical lesion can usually be determined fairly accurately, but it is difficult to assess the degree to which fibers projecting to other cortical regions have been damaged. For primary sensory areas and certain other regions of cortex, the thalamus can serve as a "mirror" of the cortical lesion. Ablation of either cortex or thalamocortical projection fibers results in retrograde degeneration of thalamic cells projecting to the cortex. Consequently, reconstructions of thalamic degeneration are a useful and sometimes necessary control procedure. The Nissl method is probably best for the study of retrograde thalamic degeneration.

Several methods for producing *reversible lesions* have been developed. One such procedure (Bureš and Buresova, 1963) is to induce *spreading depression*, a process involving temporary inactivation of neural structures, particularly cerebral cortex, as a result of mechanical or chemical trauma. Spreading depression is convenient in that it literally spreads outward from the locus of trauma in a few minutes, lasts for 5 to 30 min, and then disappears. Neural tissue appears to be essentially nonfunctional during the period of depression. A microinjection device or small cannula is implanted in the skull over the appropriate locus, and depression induced by injection of a small amount of 3-molar KCl. The greatest drawback to the method is the impossibility of determining the extent of spread of final boundaries of the depression. Concomitant electrical recording will indicate whether or not a given locus is affected, but boundaries cannot be delimited.

Cortical depression may spread to many subcortical regions.

Another reversible lesion procedure utilizes the *cooling of neural tissue*. For surface cortical lesions, a metal cup may be substituted for skull and a piece of dry ice placed on the cup for brief periods of time. For depth cooling, a U tube is implanted and a compressed gas allowed to expand through it. The rough extent of the cooling effect can be calculated, although the boundaries of such a lesion are difficult to determine.

Conclusions

The many techniques described above are simply variations on the three basic procedures of recording, stimulation, and lesion. The particular methods used in any experiment obviously depend upon the hypotheses to be tested and the kinds of measurement required. It is often unnecessary to use elaborate techniques to obtain a given type of data. If an index of EEG activity is needed and detailed localization of signal is not important, phonograph needles pounded through the skull are perfectly satisfactory. Methods must also be appropriate to the level of analysis. Gross evoked response measures will not tell the experimenter how particular cells are behaving, and extracellular single-cell recording will not provide information about synaptic events or about the overall behavior of cell populations.

RECEPTOR PROCESSES

This section will describe methods used to study receptor activity. Emphasis will be placed on vision and audition, although some attention will be given to the minor senses.

Vision

Only those techniques pertaining to the measurement of electrophysiological activity originating in the retina and optic nerve will be discussed here. For references on the measurement of the image-forming mechanism of the eye, the photoreceptor processes, and the central mechanisms of vision, the reader may consult Bartley (1959), Fry (1959), and Wald (1959).

The *electroretinogram* (ERG) is a recording of the gross electrical response of the retina elicited by the momentary presentation of a light stimulus. The response in its entirety is complex, consisting of four wave components. The first is a brief negative deflection of small amplitude, the *a* wave, which is followed by a relatively large positive deflection of 0.1 to 0.5 sec duration, the *b* wave. The third component consists of a slow positive wave, the *c* wave, and the fourth, the *d* wave, is a small positive deflection superimposed on the *c* wave and occurring when the light goes off. In man, the ERG is used to supplement the information obtained by psychophysical techniques on dark adaptations, spectral sensitivity, brightness discrimination, and flicker (Riggs, 1958).

The response may be detected by placing an active electrode on the cornea, preferably near the external canthus, and an indifferent one on the cheekbone, forehead, or lobe of either ear. Saline-soaked wick electrodes have been used for making contact with the cornea (Adrian, 1945); this type of contact may be painful and often requires the application of a local anesthetic to the cornea. A more convenient attachment is obtained by fitting to the eye a contact lens into which a small silver, or other metal, electrode is embedded (Riggs, Berry, and Wayner, 1941). The electrode is cemented into a small hole drilled into the lens near one edge of the corneal bulge and made flush with the inner surface of the lens. When the contact lens is placed on the eye, the electrode makes contact with a physiological saline solution lying between the lens and cornea. Some investigators have chosen to remove the corneal bulge from the contact lens, leaving only the outer concentric ring that fits over the sclera of the eye (Sverak, Peregrin, Kryspin, and Altman, 1959). This modification eliminates the need for applying physiological saline between the lens and cornea and is said to reduce eye discomfort greatly.

The ERG may be amplified with a direct-coupled d-c amplifier, with a cathode-ray oscilloscope (CRO) and camera, or with various types of oscillograph (Armington, 1955; Boynton, 1953). Most modern EEG amplifier and penwriting oscillographs have a frequency-response range adequate to handle the ERG response, as well as a filter network for eliminating high-frequency phenomena. If a d-c amplifier is used, nonpolarizing electrodes are required. Electrostatic interference may be reduced or eliminated by placing the subject in an electrically shielded room.

The presence of both photopic (cones) and scotopic (rods) receptors in the human eye makes the ERG difficult to analyze and interpret. This is complicated by the fact that the response of the photopic system, the *a* wave, is largely overshadowed by that of the scotopic system, the *b* wave. In animal studies, these difficulties may be overcome by using subjects having only cone or rod vision. In humans, the photopic response may be studied independently by using (1) flickering light of relatively high frequency to which the photopic system will respond but which is too fast for the scotopic system; (2) red light to minimize rod stimulation; (3) flashes with duration of less than 0.04 sec, which is below the critical duration of the rods; or (4) large-area foveal stimulation. (For a discussion of the techniques used in stimulating the retina, see Chap. 7.)

The basic instrumentation and techniques used in recording the ERG in man are also used with animals. When working with animals, the experimenter can choose the type of eye he wishes to work with and also has more freedom in the selection and placement of electrodes. Recordings may be taken from the excised eyes of cold-blooded animals or from intact, as well as opened, eyes of mammals with electrodes placed either on the cornea or in direct contact with the retina.

Methods frequently used for recording the ERG in both cold- and warm-blooded animals

have been described by Granit (1947). To record from a cold-blooded animal such as the frog, the excised eye may be placed upon a pad of cotton wool lying on a silver–silver chloride plate. This consitutes the indifferent electrode. One type of active electrode consists of a U-shaped tube filled with Ringer's solution that has a chlorided silver stem inserted into one end and a cotton wool wick protruding from the other end. The wick, which may be held in the tube with a plug of Ringer clay, makes contact with the cornea; the chlorided silver stem is connected to the input of an amplifier capable of handling frequencies ranging from about 0.5 to 80 cps or more, and the amplified signals recorded.

Responses of single retinal elements or small groups of elements are detectable with microelectrodes. These responses may be recorded from the frog's eye by removing the cornea, lens, and vitreous, and placing the active electrode tip in direct contact with the retina. Good results have been obtained with an electrode constructed of 25-μ-gauge platinum wire inserted into the capillary end of a glass tube. The electrode tip is positioned on the retina with the aid of a micromanipulator. By feeding the amplified signal to a loudspeaker connected in parallel with the recording oscilloscope, one can determine whether the electrode is exerting too much pressure on the retina since this will produce an injury discharge. When the electrode is in contact with the front surface of the retina, signals originating primarily in the ganglion cells and their nerve fibers are recorded.

Wick and platinum wire electrodes have also been used to record ERGs from such warm-blooded animals as the pigeon, owl, rabbit, and cat (Granit, 1959). In each case a special holder is used to immobilize the head and to orient the eye toward the light stimulus. If necessary, the lids and nictitating membrane may be removed to expose the eye. When the cerebrum is removed or decerebration performed, anesthetization is unnecessary while recording. Atropine may be used to dilate and immobilize the pupil so that it will not expand and contract as the amount of light striking the retina is altered. The indifferent electrode may be placed in a cocainized incision made in the skin above the eye; if decerebrated cats are being used, it may be placed in the wound. Attachment of the indifferent electrode to the cornea of the nonstimulated eye is also satisfactory, provided that eye is kept in complete darkness. Elimination of eye movements becomes important when recording with microelectrodes, since the slightest movement will produce artifacts in the records. Such movements may be eliminated by injecting curare into the extraocular muscles.

Detailed procedures for stimulating specific points on the retina and for recording the elicited discharge of single retinal elements of the intact eye of cats and monkeys have been described by Kuffler (1953) and Brown and Wiesel (1961). These investigators utilize a precision multipurpose instrument for holding and positioning the head, eyes, and microelectrodes and for viewing and stimulating the retina. A unique element of this instrument is an ophthalmoscope containing four independent optical systems, one of which is used for viewing the retina, a second for providing continuous background illumination to the retina, and the remaining two for intermittently stimulating specific points on the retina. The eye holder and positioner consists of a metal ring that may be sewn to the rim of the anesthetized cornea. The ring is then connected to the frame of the apparatus to hold the eye completely immobile.

The microelectrodes used in stimulating and recording from single elements may be constructed of platinum-iridium wire, 5 to 15 μ in diameter, which is inserted through a 0.5-mm glass tube having a fine tip; or they may be constructed of an 0.8-mm glass tube with a tip diameter of 0.5 μ filled with a potassium chloride solution. The microscopic-tipped KCl–glass electrode is produced with a mechanical glass puller such as that described by Alexander and Nastuk (1953). The latter electrode enables one to record from single elements located at various depths within the retina, whereas the platinum-iridium wire electrode is more suitable for recording from elements (ganglion cells and nerve fibers) located on or near the surface of the retina.

The platinum-iridium wire electrode is inserted into the eye near the edge of the cornea. Since the electrode is very fragile, the sclera and choroid coat are first punctured with a #19-gauge hypodermic needle, and the electrode is passed through the needle's core. The electrode is positioned on the retina with the aid of the ophthalmoscope viewing system and micromanipulator. It is held in position by applying spring tension to a ball joint through which the electrode passes before entering the eye. The KCl–glass electrode is inserted in a similar manner except that the hypodermic needle merely punctures the outer layers of the eye, leaving the membrane enclosing the vitreous intact. This membrane is easily punctured by the microelectrode as it is inserted into the eye.

The indifferent electrode used in conjunction with either type of microelectrode may be inserted into the skin near the eye. A chlorided silver wire makes contact with the KCl–glass electrode, and a similar wire is used as the indifferent electrode. Since the resistance of the KCl–glass electrode is relatively high, 15 to 30 megohms, a high-impedance push-pull amplifier is required to amplify the signals. A capacitance-coupled amplifier may be used provided its frequency response is flat over a sufficiently wide range to respond to all single-element retinal responses elicitable, approximately 0.5 to 1,000 cps. Since the resistance of the platinum-iridium wire electrode is less than that of the KCl–glass electrode, an amplifier with lower input impedance may be used. The amplified responses may be recorded with a mirror galvanometer on photosensitive paper or with an oscilloscope and camera. Most penwriting devices have an upper frequency response that is too low for recording single-element responses.

Responses of the optic nerve often are recorded simultaneously with records obtained from the retina. Several techniques that have been employed for this purpose deserve consideration.

It is relatively easy to obtain a record of the massed discharge from the whole nerve of cold-blooded animals, since the eye and part of the optic nerve may be excised. After carefully removing the tissue surrounding the nerve trunk, the nerve is laid across two silver–silver chlorided electrode wires whose leads are connected to the input of the amplifier (Granit, 1947, pp. 327–348).

The task is more difficult when warm-blooded animals are used, since the eye and nerve are injured when the blood supply is disrupted. Bartley (1941) has described a technique used in obtaining records from the rabbit that is generally applicable to other mammals. Since it is impractical to try to attach the electrodes to the nerve by passing them along the side of the eye within the bony orbit, it is necessary to remove most of the skull of the anesthetized animal, beginning just above the eyes. The optic chiasma is then exposed by removing the frontal area of the brain and applying backward pressure on the remaining tissue. The chiasma may be severed from the brain without damaging the basal artery by carefully snipping below the chiasma with scissors or by sliding a scoop with an attached scalpel just underneath the nerve. Although bleeding is slight, a pool of blood may form about the nerve and may short out the electrodes attached to it. The nerve should be raised and kept dry so that such a shunting effect cannot occur. If single-element responses are being obtained with insulated microelectrodes embedded in the nerve, the accumulation of blood about the nerve cannot produce a short circuit.

To record from a single optic nerve fiber of cold-blooded animals, one may use the dissection technique developed by Hartline and Graham (1932) or the microelectrode technique of Granit (1947, pp. 92–95, 347–349).

Records may be obtained from the horseshoe crab (*Limulus*) by removing the eye from the animal along with about 1 cm of the attached optic nerve and laying the nerve trunk over two silver–silver chlorided electrodes. The nerve bundle can be carefully split until only a single fiber remains, thereby making it possible to record from a single unit. The dissection procedure is slightly different when recording from the frog. The eye is removed and opened, and the cornea, lens, and vitreous humor removed to expose the retina. Small bundles of nerve fibers lying on the surface of the retina near the point where they enter the optic disk are excised, and the ends of the fibers still attached to receptor elements are gently picked up with a miniature tool and laid across two electrodes. The fibers are then carefully teased apart until only a single one remains in contact with the electrodes. By exploring the retina with a small spot of light, the experimenter is able to determine the area that must be stimulated to elicit a series of impulses in the single fiber (Hartline, 1938). When microelectrodes are used, the tip of the active electrode is simply placed in proximity to the fiber lying on the retinal surface.

Audition

Recording techniques discussed here will be limited to those involving the electrical responses of the inner ear or cochlea. For a discussion of the activity of the tympanic membrane and ossicles of the middle ear and the auditory pathways within the brain, and for a list of references pertaining to their measurement, see Mickle and Ades (1954) and H. Davis (1959).

Several types of potential can be detected in the inner ear, including (1) a d-c potential between the endolymph of the cochlear duct and the perilymph of the vestibular and tympanic canals, (2) microphonic and summating potentials generated by the bending of the hair cells embedded in the basilar membrane, and (3) action potentials that originate in the auditory nerve fibers attached to the hair cells. Each of these is altered when a segment of the basilar membrane is displaced either up or down.

The *gross cochlear response* is recorded in the guinea pig and cat by placing an active electrode on the round window and an indifferent electrode in the skin of the neck and displaying the amplified signals on an oscilloscope. To expose the cochlea one must open the bony cavity (bulla) within which it is housed. This operation can be performed with little or no loss of blood. The bulla is approached by making an incision in the skin of the lower jaw of the anesthetized animal and clearing away the underlying muscle. The clearing process involves severing the masseter muscle and mandible and gently pushing aside the digastric muscle. The surface of the bulla is then cleaned with a scraping tool and forceps, and a dental drill is used to make an opening to expose the cochlea (Tasaki, 1954). Contact with the round window may be made with a Ringer's soaked-wick electrode secured in a loop at the tip of a fine silver wire, shielded except at the tip. The electrode is positioned with a micromanipulator and held by cementing it to the edge of the bulla opening with dental cement (H. Davis, Gernandt, and Riesco-MacClure, 1950).

While the gross cochlear response yields certain information about inner ear mechanisms, it is limited by the facts that (1) microphonic and action potentials are confounded and (2) microphonic potentials from the round window primarily reflect the activity of the basal turn and give very little information about the more distal parts of the membrane. Consequently, techniques have been developed for separating the two types of potential and for recording at different points along the cochlea.

Microphonic and action potentials may be separately recorded by means of an electronic cancellation technique. It is based on the fact that simultaneous recordings of auditory nerve action potentials from the three canals of the cochlea, namely, scala vestibuli, scala media, and scala tympani, appear in phase relative to a reference neck electrode, whereas microphonic potentials do not. When the latter are detected with an electrode located in scala vestibuli or scala media, they are 180° out of phase with those detected in scala tympani. By electronically adding or subtracting the amplified signals simultaneously detected in the two canals, microphonic and action potentials may be canceled respectively, leaving only one type of signal. A detailed account of the electronic cancellation procedure has been given by Tasaki, H. Davis, and Legouix (1952).

A variety of types of electrode may be used for detecting potentials in various parts of the cochlea, e.g., small copper wires insulated except at the tip, small Nichrome steel wires 20 to 100 μ in diameter, #38 enamel-insulated silver wire, and KCl–glass microelectrodes (Eldredge, Bilger, and H. Davis, 1961; Fernandez, Gernandt, H. Davis, and McAuliffe, 1950; Riesco-MacClure, H. Davis, Gernandt, and Covell, 1949; Tasaki, H. Davis, and Eldredge, 1954; Tasaki and Fernandez, 1952). The electrodes are inserted into tiny holes drilled into various turns of the cochlea and sealed in position with dental cement. To avoid distortion of the potentials by polarization at the tips of the copper, steel, or silver electrodes, it is desirable to have a cathode follower in the circuit of the preamplifier. Such a circuit, along with a balancing network for canceling either action potentials or cochlear microphonics, has been described by Tasaki, H. Davis, and Legouix (1952). The amplified signals may be recorded with an oscilloscope and camera or any other recording oscillograph having a sufficiently high frequency response.

The recording of cochlear potentials requires a high degree of specialized skill and knowledge, which can be obtained only through practical laboratory experience. Further details on operative procedures, apparatus, and stimulating and recording techniques may be obtained by consulting articles by H. Davis (1959) and von Békésy (1953a; 1953b).

Gustation

Psychophysiological studies of taste have dealt with such problems as (1) the relationship between taste quality and the molecular structure of chemical stimuli, (2) receptor thresholds to various types of stimuli, and (3) the relationship between receptor sensitivity and food preferences. Descriptions of the anatomical and functional characteristics of taste receptors and their neural connections, as well as the results of studies relating electrophysiological events arising in the gustatory system to various stimulus and behavioral parameters, have been summarized by Pfaffmann (1959).

Although at least one attempt has been made to record receptor activity directly from taste receptors (Kimura and Beidler, 1956), such activity is generally recorded indirectly by placing electrodes in contact with a nerve or nerve fibers attached to the cells. A common technique taps the chorda tympani nerve (Pfaffmann, 1960). This nerve, which connects with taste receptors located on the anterior two-thirds of the tongue, passes through the middle ear cavity close to the eardrum and enters the brain stem as part of the VIIth cranial nerve. Its activity has been recorded from several types of animal, including the rat, cat, rabbit, and hamster. To expose the nerve, the animal is anesthetized, the trachea is cannulated to ensure an adequate oxygen supply, and the head is mounted in a vertical position so that the mouth and tongue are accessible from above. A deep dissection similar to that used in auditory studies is then made at the angle of the jaw. When all the underlying muscular tissue has been severed and pushed aside, the chorda tympani is exposed from the point where it leaves the bulla until it joins the lingual nerve.

Whole nerve potentials may be detected by placing silver–silver chloride wick electrodes a few millimeters apart on the intact nerve (Pfaffmann, 1955) or by laying the peripheral end of the severed nerve over two such electrodes (Hagstrom and Pfaffmann, 1959). Such electrodes are no different from the wick type sometimes used in recording cochlear potentials. They are easily constructed by mounting a small piece of cotton wool thread in a spiral located at the tip of a chlorided silver wire. Single fiber potentials are obtainable by dissecting the chorda tympani with the aid of sharpened needles and a binocular dissecting microscope until only a single fiber remains (Pfaffmann, 1955).

In addition to the bipolar recording technique used by Pfaffmann and his coworkers, monopolar recordings may be obtained by placing a wick electrode in contact with the nerve bundle or single nerve fiber and an indifferent chlorided silver electrode in the subdural tissue of the neck or in the surgical wound. Other types of metal electrode may be used, including Nichrome steel, provided that a cathode follower is included in the preamplifier circuit to counteract polarization effects. The potentials may be recorded with an oscilloscope and camera, mirror galvanometer, or any other oscillograph with a sufficiently high frequency response. Pfaffmann (1957) integrates the amplified potentials and records the integrated signals with a penwriting oscillograph.

Receptor activity is elicited either by electrically stimulating the taste buds or by applying chemical solutions to various parts of the tongue. Such solutions are frequently applied with a medicine eye dropper. When very precise control of the amount is required, the liquid may be fed through a small capillary tube by means of a finely calibrated syringe. Since the sensitivity of the receptors varies as a function of the temperature of the stimulus, temperature must be controlled.

Olfaction

In man and most other mammals, the receptors for smell are embedded in a thick epithelial layer, located in the dorsal part of the nasal cavity, which lies above the main air flow during inspiration. Even though the receptors are located close to the exterior of the body, it is relatively difficult to measure thresholds for various odors and to register receptor activity. Some of the major stimulation problems include (1) maintaining precise control over both the chemical and the physical intensity of the stimulus, (2) avoiding contamination with other stimuli, and (3) establishing appropriate eddy currents in the nasal cavity to bring the odorous material in contact with the receptor organs. A recording problem arises from the inaccessibility of the sensory hair cells and the very short length and diameter of the olfactory nerve fibers that connect the cells to the olfactory lobe.

Numerous devices, called *olfactometers*, have been used to present odorous stimuli to the nasal receptors of man. Such devices are necessarily complex, since they are designed to control for such variables as (1) the molecular concentration of the stimulating substance; (2) the purity of the air containing the substance; (3) the temperature and humidity of the air containing the substance; and (4) the pressure, volume, and duration of the air jet presented to the nostrils.

Olfactometers permitting a high degree of control over the above variables have been described by Wenzel (1948) and Jones and Jones (1953). A relatively simple stimulating technique for obtaining thresholds measures the amount of odorous air that must enter the subject's nostril to elicit an odorous sensation (Elsberg and Levy, 1935). This is accomplished by compressing odorous air a known amount in a hypodermic syringe, releasing it through a stopcock to the nostril, and having the subject report whether he experienced an odor. This technique has been criticized by Jones (1953), who states that thresholds obtained in this manner are unrelated to the molecular concentration of the odorous substance.

Pfaffmann, Goff, and Bare (1958) have described a stimulating technique for studying olfactory discrimination in the rat. The "rat olfactometer" consists of a tunnel, into the mouth of which is mounted a bar-pressing device and a water reinforcement mechanism. The stimulus is presented by adding known concentrations of an odorous substance to deodorized air that flows at a constant velocity through the tunnel. The rat is trained to face the air stream when pressing the bar so that all extraneous odors are blown away from the nostrils.

A device for stimulating smell receptors in acute rabbit preparations has been described by Mozell (1958). An odorous substance, mixed with a stream of deodorized air in various proportions, is passed through a glass tube sewn to the anesthetized rabbit's nostril. The trachea is severed and both ends are cannulated. The cannula attached to the lower end of the trachea is connected to a respiratory pump to provide oxygen to the organism. The nasally oriented cannula has a syringe attached to it, which is used to create an artificial sniff by suddenly pulling out on the plunger. A falling weight is used to exert exactly the same amount of pull on the plunger from one trail to the next.

Recordings of the electrical activity of the receptors are generally obtained indirectly by placing electrodes on the surface of the olfactory lobes or by inserting them into the lobes. This is due to the inaccessibility of the olfactory end organs and their afferent fibers. The methods used by Adrian on hedgehogs (1942) and Mozell on rabbits (1958) are representative of the techniques that are employed. The hedgehog is used because the neocortex does not completely overlap the olfactory bulb; the bulbs are easily accessible by simply removing the frontal part of the skull. Cotton wool wick electrodes are held in a spiral of silver wire coated with silver chloride when recording from within the lobes. Bipolar recordings are obtained by placing the electrodes a few millimeters apart. The signals are amplified and recorded oscillographically. A loudspeaker is connected to the output of the amplifier so that the signals may be monitored and used as an aid in positioning the electrodes (Adrian, 1942).

The olfactory lobes of the rabbit are exposed by opening the frontal part of the skull, but the neopallium covering the lobes has to be removed surgically or with a suction pump. Mozell obtained bipolar recordings with electrodes made of 120-μ Nichrome steel wire, enameled except at the tip. The electrodes were attached to a capacitance-coupled push-pull amplifier whose output was connected to an electronic integrator circuit, and the integrated olfactory potentials were recorded oscillographically.

Although it is difficult to obtain electrical recordings from olfactory cells, it has been done in cold-blooded animals, e.g., Ottoson's work on the frog (1956). The nasal mucosa is exposed by decapitating the frog and removing the dorsal wall of the main cavity of the olfactory organ. The preparation is maintained in a moist chamber of cotton wool irrigated with Ringer's solution. The receptor organs are stimulated by blowing odorous air onto the nasal mucosa through a glass pipette, which is kept at a distance of 5 to 8 mm from the epithelium surface. The volume of air is precisely controlled. The electrical response of the sense cells is recorded by placing a silver–silver chloride electrode on the surface of the olfactory epithelium and an indifferent electrode in contact with the moistened cotton wool on which the preparation is placed.

Vestibular sense

The vestibular organs, which are concerned with the sense of balance, are located in the semicircular canals, the utricle, and the saccule of the inner ear. These structures are contained within the same bony cavity as the cochlea and are centrally located with respect to the latter, making them virtually inaccessible from the outside of the skull. For this reason, most electrophysiological studies of these organs have been limited to the measurement of activity in the vestibular nucleus located in the medulla and the vestibular nerve as it courses from the internal auditory meatus at the base of the skull to the medulla. Procedures for recording from these structures will be treated very briefly here, as the techniques for recording from neural structures have already been described.

One procedure for recording impulses from the vestibular nucleus of the cat has been described by Adrian (1943). The cat is anesthetized, the skull opened posteriorly, and the cerebellum removed to expose the fourth ventricle. Monopolar recordings may be obtained by inserting a fine silver wire, insulated except at the tip, through the floor of the ventricle into the vestibular nucleus with the aid of a stereotaxic instrument; an indifferent chlorided silver electrode may be sewed to the scalp. The electrode leads are attached to the input of a push-pull a-c or d-c amplifier, and the amplified signals are recorded with an oscilloscope and camera. The receptor organs are stimulated by placing the cat on a suspended board that can be either tilted or rotated.

The operative procedures for exposing the vestibular nerve are very similar to those for exposing the nucleus (Gernandt, 1959). The animal is anesthetized and tracheotomized, and part of the occipital bone is removed. The VIIIth cranial nerve is exposed upon removal of the cerebellum. With the aid of a micromanipulator, a fine needle electrode insulated except at the tip may be inserted into the vestibular branch of the nerve, and, with an indifferent electrode in the subdural layer, impulses are detected, amplified, and recorded with an oscilloscope and camera. Single units may be isolated by monitoring the amplified signals with a loudspeaker.

With cold-blooded animals, it is possible to record impulses directly from the vestibular receptor organs (Gernandt, 1959). Detailed instructions for preparing thornback-ray specimens for measuring electrical activity of sense cells in the utricle and saccule have been published by O. Lowenstein and Roberts (1950). After the labyrinth of this animal is isolated, it is prepared and mounted on a torsion swing (O. Lowenstein, 1955). The active electrode consists of a chlorided silver forceps used to pick up the nerve twig, and the neutral electrode is a chlorided silver wire applied to the brain. The impulses are amplified and recorded in the conventional manner.

Mechanoreception

Mechanoreceptors serve the senses of touch and kinesthesis and are located in the skin, muscles, tendons, and joints of the body. To understand completely the operative procedures utilized in obtaining electrophysiological records from these receptors, a thorough knowledge of the anatomy of the blood vessels and nerves supplying the receptors is required.

Because of its relatively easy accessibility, the Pacinian corpuscle has been the most extensively studied pressure receptor (Rose and Mountcastle, 1959). It is most accessible in the mesenteric membrane that surrounds the intestines. After anesthetizing the subject, usually a cat, an incision is made in the abdominal wall and a piece of the mesentery containing one or more Pacinian corpuscles and their attached nerves is excised and pinned to a glass plate for dissection (W. R. Lowenstein and Altamirano-Orrego, 1958). The nerve and/or corpuscle is carefully teased away from the mesentery and is placed across recording electrodes constructed of platinum-iridium metal or of silver wire. Care is maintained to keep the blood vessels intact so that an adequate blood supply exists. The preparation is immersed in special solutions, either Kreb's or Locke's, which approximate the internal environment. The electrodes are connected to a capacitance-coupled push-pull amplifier, and the activity is recorded with an oscilloscope and camera. Mechanical stimulation may be provided with an electrically driven piezoelectric crystal or other vibrating body whose amplitude and frequency can be precisely controlled. Although the task is more difficult, Hunt (1961) has also successfully recorded potentials from Pacinian corpuscles located in the hind limb of the cat.

Investigators have recorded the activity of cutaneous pressure receptors by tapping the dorsal and ventral roots of the spinal cord (Armett, Gray, and Palmer, 1961). In general, the spinal cord is exposed in the sacro-lumbar region from segments S1 to L5, and the potentials generated in the dorsal and ventral roots are recorded with platinum wire electrodes or with glass–KCl microelectrodes connected to a high-impedance capacitance-coupled push-pull amplifier and oscilloscope. Mechanical stimulation may be applied to the skin receptors with a blunt stylus attached to the piston of a syringe (Hunt and McIntyre, 1960) or with an electrically driven crystal (Armett and Hunsperger, 1961). In some instances the receptors are bypassed and their afferent nerves stimulated electrically.

The role that joint receptors play in transmitting kinesthetic information has been ascertained primarily from studies of the knee joint of the cat (Rose and Mountcastle, 1959). Two nerve branches are attached to the joint receptors, one of which lies underneath the sartorius muscle, the medial branch, and the other under the gastrocnemius muscle, the posterior branch. Either nerve branch is exposed by severing the overlying muscle of the anesthetized or decerebrated animal. Recordings of receptor activity are obtained by cutting the nerve and laying the receptor-attached end over platinum or silver wire electrodes. With the aid of a dissection microscope and needle, the nerve may be subdivided until only one or two twigs remain. The action potentials are amplified and recorded in the conventional manner. The receptors are stimulated by rotating the leg through known angles at various angular velocities.

Thermoreception

Measurement of thermal receptor activity may be exemplified by the techniques employed by Hensel, Iggo, and Witt (1960) on temperature receptors of the cat's tongue and leg. With the animal under anesthesia, the lingual nerve is dissected near the point where it joins the chorda tympani nerve; filaments that supply only the upper surface of the tongue are isolated and placed over recording electrodes constructed of platinum or silver wire. The potentials are fed to a capacitance-coupled amplifier and recorded with an oscilloscope and camera. The receptors are stimulated by placing the tongue between two metal chambers through which water is circulated. The conductivity of the two metal surfaces is such that temperature gradients can be generated across the top and bottom of the tongue. Fine thermocouples are used to record the temperature of the upper and lower surfaces.

To record from thermal receptors of the leg, the saphenous nerve is dissected and isolated filaments of the distal end of the nerve are laid on silver electrodes connected to an amplifier and oscilloscope. The receptors are stimulated with a water-circulated thermode, the temperature of which can be precisely varied. Thermal radiation may also be used to heat the skin. The temperature of the receptive field is recorded with a fine thermocouple taped to the skin. For a further discussion of thermal receptor activity and for references pertaining to its measurement, see Zotterman (1959).

Pain

The electrophysiological techniques employed in the assessment of pain receptor activity are similar to those used in the measurement of other somatic receptors. A discussion of the problems encountered in the measurement of pain has been published by Sweet (1959).

EFFECTOR PROCESSES

This section will cover the measurement of those peripheral physiological processes which reflect the activity of the effector organs of the body, the muscles and glands. A wide variety of bodily processes have been measured by psychologists interested in relating such processes to motivation level, emotional states, learning, and other behavioral variables. For convenience, the various physiological events have been grouped into seven categories: (1) skeletal muscle activity, including muscular tension, muscular tremor, and latency of muscular reaction; (2) eye movements, eyelid

and pupillary reflexes; (3) cardiovascular activity, including heart rate, blood pressure, blood volume, and cardiac stroke output; (4) respiration; (5) body temperature; (6) gastrointestinal activity; and (7) glandular activity, particularly that of the salivary and sweat glands.

Skeletal muscle activity

The electrical method for recording muscular tension, known as *electromyography* is based on the fact that cell membrane depolarizes just prior to the contraction of a muscle fiber. A 50- to 100-μv change in potential results, which lasts for a period of about 1 msec (Jasper and Ballem, 1949). A single electric discharge recorded with microelectrodes from within a muscle is a summation of the nearly simultaneous depolarization of 10 to 100 muscle fibers connected to a single motor nerve (motor unit). The electromyograph EMG obtained from a whole muscle with electrodes attached to the surface of the skin is compounded of action potentials generated by many motor units independently discharging at their individual frequencies.

It is important to note that the EMG is not a direct measure of degree of muscular contraction or tension level but rather an indirect one, since the electric discharge of a motor unit and the contraction that follows are two different events. A high correlation exists between the electrical and mechanical events, but the relationship is not perfect, for muscular tension level can vary while EMG level remains constant, and vice versa.

The EMG is more directly an index of motor nerve activity than of physical tension level since the magnitude of the gross electrical response is a direct function of the amount of neural bombardment imposed upon the individual motor units of skeletal muscle (Adrian and Bronk, 1929). The neural mechanisms controlling such activity exist at all levels of the nervous system, the lowest being the reflex gamma afferent and efferent system described by Granit (1955). Such reflex activity is modulated by reticular mechanisms that receive information from all sensory modalities and higher neural stations. Emotional and motivational factors influence skeletal motor nerve discharge through the activation of diencephalic and limbic structures that interact with the motor system at the reticular level. Finally, volitional factors, such as the amount of effort exerted in the performance of some muscular act, elicit discharges in the long pyramidal motor fibers that have their cell bodies in the motor cortex (Paillard, 1960). These mechanisms provide the neural basis for changes in tension level that accompany variations in arousal and alertness, motivation, emotion, and voluntary effort.

The general equipment and procedures used in recording *muscle action potentials* (MAPs) are the same as those used in recording the electrical activity of neural tissue. MAPs may be recorded with needle electrodes inserted into the muscle or with disk electrodes attached to the surface of the skin. Needle electrodes are generally used when the activity of a single motor unit or a few such units is being studied or when information is needed as a clinical aid in diagnosing muscular disorders. When muscular activity is being related to behavioral events, surface leads are generally used to detect the gross activity of the entire muscle.

Lindsley (1935) has described several types of electrode for detecting MAPs *intramuscularly,* any one of which is satisfactory for recording from single motor units during weak contractions or from small groups of units during moderately strong contractions: (1) A concentric needle electrode constructed of fine wire, #36 gauge, cemented with baking varnish into the lumen of a #20-gauge hypodermic needle. The cement serves the dual purpose of holding the wire in place and insulating it from the inner surface of the needle. The lower tip of the wire is free of cement and constitutes the active electrode. The needle serves as the "inactive" electrode. (2) A hypodermic needle containing two fine insulated wires, the bared tips of which are only a fraction of a millimeter apart. (3) A fine insulated #36-gauge wire with a minute portion of the insulation removed, designed for monopolar recording. This active electrode is drawn through a muscle with a surgical needle until the bared part makes contact with an active motor unit. The inactive electrode is composed of a small metal plate covered with saline-soaked cotton flannel attached to a neutral place on the skin surface. (4) Two fine wires with a knife-edge cut in the insulation. They are drawn through a muscle together until an active motor unit is encountered.

Surface MAPs may be recorded either monopolarly or bipolarly. To record monopolarly a silver metal disk 0.5 to 1.0 cm in diameter may be attached to the skin over the active muscle and a relatively large (5 cm sq) saline-soaked felt pad attached to an inactive area such as the elbow. If it is necessary to ground the subject, as is frequently the case, a third metal electrode may be attached to the ear lobe or some other convenient body location and connected to ground (R. C. Davis, 1940). To record bipolarly, both electrodes are placed over the active muscle; a third may be connected to ground if desired.

Electrodes for recording MAPs at the surface of the skin have been constructed of (1) a highly conductive metal, such as silver or stainless steel; (2) bentonite mud mixed with potassium, calcium, or sodium chloride; and (3) natural or cellulose sponge saturated with electrode jelly or saline. Procedures for constructing electrodes of bentonite mud and of sponge have been described by J. F. Davis (1952). Choice of electrodes is largely a matter of convenience, since each is satisfactory when properly attached to the skin. Commercially available silver disk EEG electrodes mounted in plastic adapters are recommended because the plastic mounting process greatly facilitates the process of attaching the electrodes to the skin.

Before attaching the electrodes the skin resistance should be reduced to below 10,000 ohms. This may be done by washing the skin with warm, soapy water, then rubbing briskly with a rough textured cloth or paper towel to remove the outermost layer of epidermis as well as the sebum from the pores of the skin. After drying, electrode jelly containing an abrasive, e.g., Sanborn Reddux jelly, may be applied until the skin reddens. The jelly should then be removed with warm, soapy water, and the skin thoroughly dried. The electrode disks may then be filled with a jelly metabolite and attached to the skin. After the electrodes have been attached, their combined resistance may be ascertained with a sensitive ohmmeter. The combined electrode resistance should not exceed one-tenth the input resistance of the voltage amplifier. Generally, the lower the resistance the lower the probability of picking up 60-cps artifacts, "beat" artifacts in chopper-type amplifiers, or slow-movement artifacts. Should the total resistance exceed 10,000 ohms, it may be wise to remove the electrodes and repeat the procedure for reducing skin resistance.

The electrodes may be attached to the skin with collodion, with elastic bands or belts, or with tape. Black plastic electrical Scotch tape is ideal for attaching plastic-mounted electrodes to muscles of the neck, back, chest, forehead, and limbs. It adheres well to the skin and will not come loose even when the individual perspires. Stretching the tape before adhering it to the skin creates a downward pressure on the adapter that seals the jelly within each electrode cup. This procedure ensures a firm attachment and reduces the possibility of electrode slippage. Gluing the electrodes to the skin with collodion is laborious in comparison with the tape-on procedure and is recommended only when the electrodes cannot be attached with either tape or elastic bands.

The following precautions should be maintained when attaching electrodes to the skin by any of the above techniques: (1) The amount of pressure applied should be sufficient to ensure good contact with the skin. (2) The electrode attachment should not mechanically inhibit the response being measured. (3) The contact should not impede local circulation. (4) The attachment should be free of irritations that might produce a reflex elevation of tension level (Ellson, R. C. Davis, Saltzman, and Burke, 1952). All these requirements may be readily met by proper use of the tape-attachment procedure.

In independent investigations, Nightingale (1957) and Hayes (1960) analyzed the frequency spectrum of surface-recorded MAPs and found virtually all the energy to lie between 10 and 600 cps. Hayes further noted that the energy level is reduced by only 6 decibels (dB) when the spectral band is narrowed by filtering to a bandwidth of 30 to 100 cps. These observations indicate that it is unnecessary to utilize a high-fidelity system to amplify surface-recorded MAPs. A capacitance-coupled push-pull a-c amplifier having a frequency-response range of approximately 30 to 100 cps, an input impedance of $\frac{1}{2}$ to 1 megohm, and a noise level of approximately 2 μv is satisfactory. Most amplifiers used in amplifying the EEG meet these specifications. When recording intramuscularly from single motor units, an amplifier with a much higher frequency response, approximately 1,500 cps, is required, since the MAP duration of single motor units ranges from 0.5 to 1.5 msec.

In surface electromyography, inkwritten oscillograms constitute a convenient means of monitoring for artifacts during the data recording process. Because of their relatively slow response characteristics most penwriting oscillographs reflect only the lower frequency components of the surface EMG spectrum. This is of little consequence, however, for changes in the lower frequency components of the EMG spectrum are almost perfectly correlated with changes in the total spectrum. To record faithfully the short-duration impulses produced by single motor units, a mirror galvanometer or oscilloscope and camera are required.

Quantification of the amount of energy contained in the surface EMG spectrum is facilitated by integrating the gross MAP activity over a given period of time. A commonly used technique consists in holding the time interval constant and measuring, with a volt-meter or d-c recording instrument, the amount of rectified voltage that accumulates on a capacitor (R. C. Davis, 1948). This method is appropriate for measuring mean changes in energy level over very brief periods of time, 0.1 sec and up. A second technique consists in automatically counting the number of times a capacitor builds up to a specified voltage level and discharges within a given time interval. This is a feasible method for integrating over time intervals of 10 sec or more but is less adequate for shorter intervals because of the discrete nature of the measure. Commercial continuous-averaging devices display the mean MAP voltage in analog form. See Rosenfalck (1960) for a detailed description. An inexpensive photoelectric technique for integrating gross MAPs re-corded with an EEG penwriter has been de-scribed by Eason and White (1959).

Certain *artifacts in EMG records* may ap-pear in any type of electrophysiological re-cord. These include (1) large random spikes resulting from an inconspicuous break in an electrode lead, (2) low-frequency oscillations generated by the electrodes swinging to and fro, and (3) 60-cycle oscillations produced by electrostatic interference arising from 110-volt 60-cycle a-c voltage lines or from appliances and instruments connected to the lines. The latter usually may be corrected by placing the subject in a shielded room. If the artifact con-tinues to appear, it may be because the elec-trode resistance at the surface of the skin is too high. The ratio of amplifier input impe-dance to electrode contact resistance should be at least 10:1.

Certain electrophysiological phenomena may appear in EMG records as artifacts, de-pending on the method and position of elec-trode placement. If the attachments are in the vicinity of the eyes, potentials arising from eye movements and blinks may appear in the records. These may be reduced or eliminated by taping up the lid and having the subject fixate some point. If the nature of the task precludes this procedure, these artifacts may be largely removed by a filter network that eliminates input frequencies less than 30 cps.

The electric potential associated with the heartbeat may appear in EMG records when the recording electrodes are placed several inches apart and the amplifier gain is rela-tively high in order to detect low-amplitude MAPs (20 μv or less). When recording MAPs of moderate amplitude (20 μv and up) with a pair of electrodes separated by approxi-mately 2 in., the cardiac potential usually lies within the "noise" tolerance level of the re-cording system. As with eye movements and blinks, the heart-potential artifact may be eliminated, or at least greatly attenuated, by inserting in the input circuit a filter network that passes little energy below 30 cps.

A second artifact related to the heartbeat is sometimes produced by pulsations of an artery located under the electrode. Such pul-sations may cause the electrode to slip periodi-cally over the skin or may cause the leads to swing enough to generate periodic fluctua-tions in the MAP record. This may be cor-rected by moving the electrode slightly and reattaching it firmly to the skin.

Muscular tremor

Most studies of muscular tremor have been concerned with the finger or the eyes. In measuring finger tremor, pneumatic, me-chanical, optical, and electrical principles have been employed.

One of the first pneumatic techniques was that of Luria (1932), who utilized two tambours connected with a rubber tube. Oscil-lations of the finger were detected by the first tambour and transmitted to the second, result-ing in the activation of an attached lever that recorded the deflections on a kymograph drum.

A mechanical device constructed by Edwards (1946), called a *tromometer*, yields a semi-integrated record of involuntary finger movement in three dimensions by means of a system of tracks and riders. The conventional steadiness tester also may be used to integrate finger tremor over a period of time. It consists of a metal plate with holes of varying diameter drilled through it. The subject inserts a metal stylus into each hole and attempts to prevent its touching the plate. Stylus contacts with the plate are registered by a chromoscope or counters. Although the details of finger tremor are lost when an integrative technique is used, the reduction of large amounts of analog data to a few readings facilitates data analysis.

Travis and Hunter (1931) were among the first to record finger tremor electrically. The subject placed his finger on a freely moving coil mounted between the two poles of a magnet. The magnet was of the concentric ring type, consisting of an inner iron part and an outer iron ring. Movements of the coil resulting from finger tremor induced a current, which was amplified and recorded with an oscillograph camera. Lipton (1953) utilized the reciprocal of this principle by attaching a piece of magnetized iron to the subject's finger and having him insert the finger between the two poles of a stationary coil. Current induced by the coil was converted to voltage fluctuations and recorded with either an EEG or an EKG amplifier and penwriter.

Jasper and Andrews (1938) and Lansing (1957) have utilized a mechanical lever and photoelectric-cell arrangement. One end of a fulcrum-mounted lever is attached to the finger and the other end interrupts a beam of light passing through a V-shaped notch and focusing lens onto a photoelectric cell. Oscillations of the finger cause the lever to move up and down, thereby altering the total amount of light striking the cell. The voltage variations of the cell are amplified and recorded oscillographically.

Cooper, Halliday, and Redfearn (1957) measured finger tremor photoelectrically without the use of a mechanical-lever arrangement. The finger partially occludes a beam of light passing through a vertical slit and convex lens onto the cathode of a photoelectric cell. Vertical oscillations of the finger cause varying amounts of light to strike the cell. Its output is amplified and recorded with an oscillo-

scope and camera or with a penwriting oscillograph. A differentiating circuit permits a simultaneous recording of the first and second derivatives of the output, yielding a measure of velocity and acceleration, respectively.

Each of the above techniques yields satisfactory records of finger tremor, provided the necessary precautions are maintained. The electrical techniques are the most sensitive, and the data may be electronically integrated to facilitate quantification.

Latency of muscular reactions

The classical procedure for measuring muscular latency or reaction time (RT) employs a circuit containing two telegraph keys, a power supply, and a timing element called a *chronoscope*. While the subject depresses one of the keys, the experimenter presents a stimulus and activates the chronoscope simultaneously by pressing down on the other key. As soon as the subject is aware of the stimulus he releases his key, removing the stimulus and stopping the chronoscope. The time required for the reaction is recorded in milliseconds.

A *chronograph* is sometimes used in place of a chronoscope. It consists of a continuously moving strip of paper or film upon which is indicated the presentation of the stimulus, the subject's reaction, and a time mark. The time mark may be generated with (1) a tuning fork vibrating at a frequency of 100 to 1,000 cps, (2) an electronic oscillator, or (3) an electronic pulse generator accurate to 1 msec or less.

By recording the ERG, EEG, and EMG of the finger muscles along with the muscular reaction to a visual stimulus, the various components of RT can be ascertained (Monnier, 1952). For a further discussion of the problems involved in RT measurement see Bartlett and Bartlett (1959), Teichner (1954), Woodworth (1938, Chap. 14), and Woodworth and Schlosberg (1954, Chap. 2).

Eye responses

Most eye motor studies have been concerned with the recording of ocular movements, although in recent years some attention has been given to the measurement of the electrical activity of the extrinsic muscles. In addition, a number of classical conditioning experiments have involved the measurement of the eyelid and pupillary reflexes.

Voluntary eye movements are recorded by photographing with a motion-picture camera some mark or fleck placed on the iris or by reflecting a beam of light from the cornea, or a mirror attached to it, through a lens onto a strip of moving film. The commercial *ophthalmograph* (American Optical Company, 1937) utilizes the corneal reflection method for recording movements of the two eyes during reading. It is sufficiently sensitive to resolve movements of approximately one-half of a degree. A camera designed by Brandt (1945) also utilizes this principle in recording both the vertical and the horizontal components of eye movements.

Mackworth (1961) reports an instrument that permits a recording of the visual field as well as the subject's fixation within the field without restriction of head movements. A small movie camera mounted on the head records a 30° field that changes as the head moves. A miniature periscope transmits the vertical and horizontal deflections of a corneally reflected light beam to the motion-picture camera, permitting the recording of the eye fixations on the visual field record. An immediate picture of the visual field and eye fixations may be obtained by substituting a closed-circuit television (TV) camera for the movie camera and viewing the signals on a TV receiver (Thomas, Mackworth, and Howat, 1960). Recordings of eye position are accurate to within 2° of arc, provided the reflected light beam is properly aligned.

A more sensitive system is required to record minute involuntary deflections that occur during fixation. The desired sensitivity may be attained optically by reflecting a beam of light from a plane surface mirror attached to the eye. The reflected light is focused by a lens onto a strip of moving film located several feet from the eye. The mirror may be directly attached to the anesthetized cornea of a human subject (Adler and Fliegelman,

1934), but a better method is to fit the normal eye with a contact lens into which a front surface mirror has been inserted (Ditchburn and Ginsborg, 1953).

Another sensitive technique is to reflect the light beam directly from the cornea past a straight edge so that approximately one-half of the beam falls upon the cathode of a photomultiplier tuber. Changes in current output of the tube, resulting from changes in the amount of light striking the cathode, are amplified and recorded with an oscilloscope and camera (Lord and Wright, 1948).

Either the plane-mirror or corneal-reflection method may be adapted for recording horizontal and/or vertical components of eye movements. Riggs, Armington, and Ratliff (1954) found that the deflections of a beam of light reflected from a plane mirror are approximately eight times greater than those of a beam reflected directly from the cornea when both are recorded on moving film. Even when the corneally reflected beam is imposed upon a photoelectric cell, the method is less sensitive than the plane-mirror technique. The contact-lens–plane-mirror technique is recommended when one is interested in measuring the minute 30 to 70 per sec tremor that occurs during fixation. The greatest degree of sensitivity is attained by using a photoelectric cell in conjunction with the contact lens–plane-mirror reflection method (Krauskopf, Cornsweet, and Riggs, 1960).

Riggs, Ratliff, Cornsweet, and Cornsweet (1953) have devised a system for recording movements during fixation that keeps the viewed image fixed in the same position upon the retina when the eye moves. The image, a vertical black line, is reflected directly onto a screen from a plane mirror mounted in a contact lens worn by the subject. The screen image is projected back to the eye with the contact lens through a series of mirrors and dove prisms which make the optical distance from the screen to the eye twice the mirror-to-screen distance. The distance from the screen back to the eye must be doubled to compensate for the fact that the angular deflection of the contact lens mirror-reflected image is twice that of the angular displacement of the eye.

Electrical eye movement recording devices are based on the fact that a relatively constant d-c potential of several millivolts exists across the longitudinal axis of the eye, the front being positive with respect to the back (Mowrer, Ruch, and Miller, 1936). Early studies utilizing this principle have been described by Carmichael and Dearborn (1947, Chap. 6) and, more recently, by Shackel (1961). When electrodes are placed on the temples behind the external canthi of the eye, the positive pole of the corneoretinal potential approaches one electrode and the negative pole approaches the other as the eyes move along the horizontal plane. This results in a difference in potential between the two electrodes that may be amplified and recorded oscillographically. Similarly, electrodes mounted above and below each eye permit the recording of vertical movements. Records obtained in this manner are referred to as *electrooculograms* (EOG).

A d-c recording system is used for registering the magnitude and duration of eye movements, but an a-c system may be utilized when one merely wishes to know when and how many times the eyes move within a specified time period. A push-pull capacitance-coupled a-c amplifier and penwriting oscillograph are adequate for the latter purpose. The a-c deflections produced by eye movements may be electronically integrated, or, by having the deflections activate a relay circuit, the movements may be automatically counted.

Ford, White, and Lichtenstein (1959) and Shackel (1961) have specified the conditions under which good d-c recordings may be obtained. The problem of amplifier drift has been solved by the development of highly stable d-c amplifiers. Such instruments should be allowed to warm up thoroughly before collecting data.

Nonpolarizing silver–silver chloride electrodes should be used when obtaining d-c recordings. The electrodes may be mounted in plastic adapters and taped to the skin (Ford and White, 1959), or they may be attached with rubber suction cups (Shackel, 1958). The skin resistance should be reduced to 2,000 to 3,000 ohms before the electrodes are attached. One procedure for reducing skin resistance was described earlier. Another procedure is to use a rapidly rotating diamond dental burr to remove the epidermis (Shackel, 1961). A jig device may be used to aid in the precise placement of the electrodes above and below and on either side of the eyes.

Ford *et al.* (1959) have used the electrooculographic technique to obtain two-dimensional records of eye movements. Voltage variations produced at the temples as a result of horizontal movements are amplified and imposed on the horizontal deflection plates of an oscilloscope. The amplified voltage variations detected by electrodes mounted above and below the eyes are fed to the vertical deflection plates of the scope. With this arrangement the oscilloscope beam moves in the same direction as the eyes. The instrument may be calibrated so that a given position on the scope is known to correspond to a given position of the eyes. Permanent records may be obtained by photographing the scope face with stationary film.

Shackel (1961) has demonstrated the feasibility of combining the optical and electrooculographic methods for recording eye movements and fixations within a visual field. A small TV camera mounted to a helmet worn by the subject photographs his visual field while a second camera mounted to the face of an oscilloscope registers eye position. When both TV images are transmitted to the same monitor, one can tell which part of the visual field is being fixated, provided the equipment is calibrated so that the spatial coordinates of the two displays are identical.

Extraocular muscle activity is recorded electrically and therefore employs the same basic instruments and techniques previously described for recording the EMG. Because the eye muscles are not readily accessible, special skills are required to pick up the action potentials. Detailed descriptions of these techniques have been published by Bjork and Kugelberg (1953) and Marg, Jampolsky, and Tamler (1959). The latter investigators inserted concentric needle electrodes into the extrinsic eye muscles to pick up the MAPs, whereas Bjork and Kugelberg recorded monopolarly with one electrode in the muscle, the other in the conjunctiva of the eye. The insertion technique utilized by Marg *et al.* may be summarized as follows: (1) With the subject in a supine position, a speculum is placed against the upper and lower eyelids to hold them away from the eye. (2) The eye is locally anesthetized with drops of tetracaine or proparacaine, and methylcellulose is applied occasionally to prevent corneal drying. (3) The conjunctiva is lifted with forceps and the needle electrode, which has been previously sterilized with Zephiran, is inserted through the conjunctiva into the muscle. The potentials are amplified and recorded in the usual manner.

Although the Dodge pendulum-photochronograph has been used extensively for recording the eyelid response, a more convenient procedure is to record the electrical response of the eyelid when it moves (Ford, 1957). This may be done by attaching electrodes above and below the eye and recording the electrical event with an a-c amplifier and penwriter. This method requires that the eyes remain fixated to avoid EOG contamination of the records. Oscillographic records may also be obtained by using either a photoelectric cell or a ceramic crystal to detect movement of the eyelid. Neither type of transducer requires the attachment of an artificial eyelid. (See Chap. 9 for further discussion of eyelid reflexes.)

Since the eye is insensitive to infrared radiant energy, the pupillary reflex may be recorded by infrared motion-picture photography (Young and Biersdorf, 1952). The eye may be illuminated by a pure infrared radiant-energy source or by a light that contains a substantial amount of infrared and is passed through an infrared transmitting filter. Pupillary diameter is obtained by projecting the film-recorded image through a known distance onto a screen, measuring the pupil width, and converting the measure to actual scale size.

A more senstitive technique (O. Lowenstein and Lowenfeld, 1959) utilizes a photoelectric cell to detect differences in the amount of infrared energy reflected from the eye. This method takes advantage of the fact that the amount of energy reflected from the eye varies inversely with pupillary diameter. The output of the photoelectric cell is amplified and recorded oscillographically. The instrument may be calibrated for each subject so that the recorded deflection can be expressed in terms of pupillary diameter.

Cardiovascular activity

The oldest and simplest way to measure *heart rate* is to place the fingers over the radial artery of the patient and count the number of pulse waves generated by the heart in a specified time period. The classic laboratory technique employs a device called a *sphygmograph,* which yields a picture of arterial pulsations. The method yields a relative measure of pulse amplitude or pressure in addition to that of heart rate (Young, 1943).

Heart rate is easily obtained by counting the large spikes associated with ventricular contraction that appear in the *electrocardiogram* (EKG) a recording of the gross electrical activity of the heart. Electrodes may be attached to the two arms, one arm and one leg, the two legs, and other places; the exact placement is not critical if one is merely interested in determining heart rate. EKG electrodes are generally made of stainless steel plate approximately 2 sq in. in area, although commercial silver disk EEG electrodes are also satisfactory. Small stainless steel, silver, or lead solder disks may be used as the pickup element to record the surface EKG of animals (Ferraro, Silver, and Snapper, 1965). Needle electrodes inserted underneath the skin and fixed in place with adhesive tape, or stainless steel and silver wires sewn into the skin, may also be used.

Amplification of the EKG requires a medium-gain capacitance-coupled differential-input amplifier with a time constant of about 0.2 sec. Since the signal has an intensity of several millivolts, it may be recorded without placing the subject in a shielded room, and the inherent noise level of the amplifier may be as high as 25 or 50 μv. Most commercial EKG amplifiers have noise levels in this vicinity. Such an amplifier is inadequate for recording the EMG or EEG, although the low-noise EEG amplifiers may be used for amplifying the EKG.

The EKG is conventionally recorded with a penwriting oscillograph, but miniaturized preamplifiers and transmitters are available that may be attached to the subject, permitting remote recording. Holter (1961) has described a portable radio-receiver tape-recording unit that allows transmitted EKG signals to be recorded from subjects engaged in strenuous physical exercise. Heart rate may be automatically counted by feeding the output of the EKG amplifier to a relay activated by the ventricular spike component of the EKG. The relay closes a circuit that activates an electric counter, and a printer mechanism prints out the number of heartbeats at specified time periods. Cardiotachometers automatically measure the duration between adjacent spikes and express the information in analog or digital form. A cardiochronograph draws vertical lines with an oscillographic inkwriter, the amplitudes of which are proportional to the interval between adjacent pairs of spikes. The resulting profile presents an immediate picture of change in heart rate on a beat-to-beat basis.

Modernized versions of the sphygmograph utilize either mechanical-electrical or photoelectric transducers for detecting the pulse wave. One type of mechanical-electrical transducer consists of a piezoelectric crystal strapped to the wrist above the radial artery. The electrical output of the element is amplified with a high-input impedance capacitance-coupled preamplifier designed to operate with ceramic transducers. Once amplified, the signal may be recorded and converted to a frequency measure by any one of the EKG techniques discussed above.

One type of photoelectric transducer consists of a miniaturized light source and a photoelectric cell mounted on opposite arms of a clip-on device. When clipped to the subject's ear or finger, the unit is sensitive to the optical density of the tissue lying between the light and photoelectric cell. The change in optical density produced by each pulsation of the blood is converted to electrical energy, amplified, and recorded in terms of heart rate. Unlike the EKG technique, these sphygmographic methods yield a measure of relative pulse amplitude in addition to heart rate. They tend to be more vulnerable to movement artifacts than the EKG.

Blood pressure may be measured either directly or indirectly, but, since the direct-measurement techniques require the insertion of a cannula or needle into the artery, they are used primarily with animals. The classical direct technique consists in measuring the difference in height of mercury in the two columns of a U-shaped tube. The difference is produced by the blood when it is diverted from an artery, usually the carotid, into one side of the mercury tube. This is accomplished by inserting into the exposed artery a glass cannula connected to the mercury manometer with a rubber or plastic lumen. To insert the cannula, a string is tied around the blood vessel to stop blood flow and a clamp is placed 1 to 2 in. above the cut to stop the flow temporarily and reduce the pressure in that part of the artery into which the cannula is to be inserted. The clamp is removed after the cannula has been inserted through a small opening between the string and clamp and firmly tied into position. A kymographic record may be obtained by floating a cork, to which a writing lever is attached, on the open end of the mercury manometer. This technique can be used only with acute preparations. It is frequently employed in the study of the effects of drugs on the nervous system. Modern direct measuring techniques also require the insertion of a cannula or needle into the artery, but the inverted U-shaped manometer is replaced with a mechanical-electrical transducer that converts the pressure waves to electric signals that are amplified and recorded oscillographically.

An indirect method is generally used for recording blood pressure in man. The classical procedure employs a *sphygmomanometer*. This instrument consists of an inflatable cloth-covered rubber cuff or bag connected by a rubber of plastic lumen containing a needle valve to a mercury manometer or to a pneumographic instrument calibrated to read in millimeters of mercury displacement. The cuff is wrapped around the upper arm and inflated until the flow of blood through the brachial artery is completely occluded. A stethoscope is placed over the brachial artery opposite the elbow and the cuff pressure is reduced until a pulse wave begins to pass through the artery, producing a distinct tapping sound. The manometer reading at this point is the systolic pressure, representing the pressure level during ventricular contraction, or systole. The mercury reading obtained when the sound becomes muffled and suddenly reduced in intensity is the diastolic pressure; at this time the ventricles are relaxed, or in diastole. The difference between the diastolic and systolic pressures is the pulse pressure. Some modification of this instrument is generally used when blood pressure is recorded in the laboratory.

An ingenious technique for continuously recording absolute pressure allows for the recording of both types of pressure for long periods of time without producing ischemia or discomfort. An oscillographic technique for recording absolute pressure every 20 sec is reported by R. C. Davis, Siddons, and Stout (1954). A commercial device utilizes a small air compressor to inflate, periodically, a cuff placed around the upper arm, along with a microphone to detect the Korotkow sounds of the brachial artery during diastole and systole (Gilford Instrument Laboratories, Inc.).

A technique developed by Larson (1932) is commonly used to obtain a continuous measure of relative pressure. A cuff is placed about the arm or ankle and is inflated until the pressure reading is about midway between the diastolic and systolic pressures. Oscillographic records are then obtained of the variations in pressure from this intermediate level. The technique is relatively easy to apply and causes little discomfort to the subject. R. C. Davis (1957) developed a technique for measuring relative pressure that requires the application of a minimal amount of external pressure to the artery.

The *measurement of blood volume* constitutes a means of estimating changes in the degree of vasoconstriction or vasodilation of small arteries and veins in relatively specific parts of the body, usually the limbs and digits. It serves more as an index of the redistribution of blood brought about by autonomic reactions than as an index of total blood volume. The classical technique (Ruckmick, 1936, Chap. 10) utilizes a water *plethysmograph*. Since movement artifacts tend to appear in the blood volume records obtained with the water plethysmograph, the subject must remain immobile during the data-collection period. This requirement limits the usefulness of the instrument as an experimental tool, and investigators have sought other techniques. Three techniques have been developed that employ other principles: (1) one involves injection of a dye or radioactive substance into the bloodstream and measurement of the density of the substance in a digit, ear, or some other limited part of the body (Nyboer, 1955); (2) in another method, a photometer or calorimeter measures the opacity or heat dissipation of the blood (Nyboer, 1955); and (3) the third is based on the fact that the impedance of the blood to an imposed a-c signal increases with an increase in blood volume. This relationship is assumed to be linear, although this has not been definitely established. The application of this principle to the measurement of blood volume is known as *impedance plethysmography*. Two pairs of electrodes are generally employed, one for imposing a current through the blood and surrounding tissue and the other for detecting the voltage drop across the blood and tissue generated by their impedance. The impedance-generated a-c voltage is rectified, amplified with either a d-c or an a-c amplifier with high input impedance and recorded oscillographically. A d-c amplifier is used when one wishes to determine relatively long-term changes in blood volume, whereas an a-c amplifier is adequate for determining the momentary volumetric changes associated with the heartbeat. Electrodes have been adapted for recording from vessels of the pectoral and abdominal regions of the torso; frontal, temporal, and nasal areas of the head; and the forearm, legs, feet, and fingers. They may be constructed of a variety of metals, including silver, copper, aluminum, and stainless steel (Day and Lippitt, 1964; Nyboer, 1955).

The optimal frequency of the a-c signal imposed upon the blood and surrounding tissue has not been definitely established. Nyboer (1955) used an RF of 135 kilocycles (kc), while Sheer and Kroeger (1961) describe an instrument using a 5-kc signal. Schwan (1955) has indicated that if the frequency is much in excess of 1 kc, a capacitative reaction occurs in the tissue surrounding the blood, and the volumetric measure is distorted. If the frequency of the imposed signal lies much below 1 kc, electrode polarization occurs. While considerable progress has been made in the development of impedance plethysmographs, no instrument is considered to be entirely adequate at present.

Stroke volume refers to the amount of blood pumped by the heart per beat. It is dependent upon the strength of ventricular contraction, which varies with the quantity of blood contained in the ventricles just prior to contraction (Carlson and Johnson, 1948). Two peripheral physiological events have been used as indices of stroke volume: the magnitude of body reverberations produced

by each heartbeat and the changes in blood velocity.

When the body is in the prone position, reverberations are produced along its longitudinal axis each time the heart beats. The oscillations vary in frequency from 5 to 25 cps, and their amplitude varies as a function of stroke volume. Movements in the footward direction are thought to be generated by the recoil of the heart during ejection, and headward movements result from the impact of the blood as it strikes the aortic arch and reverses direction. Such movements are recorded with an instrument called a *ballistocardiograph*. It consists of a table that is free to move along its longitudinal axis, and the subject is strapped to it so that his bodily reverberations are transmitted to the table. Although the table ballistocardiograph is a standardized technique used by physiologists, it is of limited value to the psychophysiologist since the subject is completely immobilized. An early *reverberatory technique* that permits the subject to be in a sitting position consists in the use of a tambour attached to the chest between the ribs. Chest reverberations produced by each heartbeat are converted into pressure waves and transmitted through a rubber hose to a recording tambour, which reproduces the vibrations kymographically (Woodworth, 1938, p. 268). A modern version of this technique would consist in attaching a mechanical-electrical transducer to the rib cage and recording with an oscillograph the amplified electric signals generated by the chest vibrations. With the use of a miniaturized amplifier and transmitter, chest reverberations could be recorded remotely without placing any marked restriction on the subject.

Since the reverberations associated with the heartbeat are largely due to the acceleration and deceleration of the blood, a measure of the latter would more directly reflect stroke volume. *Blood flow measurement* is accomplished with a flowmeter device that registers arterial velocity changes. Since the sensing element must be attached to the blood vessel, the method is limited to animals. Even though the method is not applicable to man, at the present time, important advances have been made in the measurement of blood flow of which the psychophysiologist should be aware (Herrick and Anderson, 1959). Devices currently receiving most attention employ ultrasonic and electromagnetic waves of energy. For a detailed description of blood-flow instrumentation problems and methods of measurement, see *IRE Transactions on Medical Electronics*, 1959.

Respiration

A variety of methods have been employed in the measurement of the respiratory response. Two techniques are more amenable to psychophysical investigations. The first method measures the degree of expansion and contraction of the intercostal and/or abdominal muscles with each respiration. The classic procedure for doing this utilizes a device called a *pneumograph*. It consists of an accordion-pleated rubber hose about an inch in diameter that is strapped tautly about the chest or abdomen. Changes in internal air pressure produced by each respiration are transmitted through a small lumen to a tambour with a lever attached to it that describes the oscillations of the tambour on a kymograph drum (Woodworth and Schlosberg, 1954, p. 170). A more modern adaptation replaces the lever with a strain gauge and bridge coupler that converts the mechanical oscillations into electric energy. The electrical activity is then amplified with a d-c amplifier and recorded with an inkwriting oscillograph, an oscilloscope camera, or a d-c tape recorder. Another strain-gauge technique dispenses with the pneumatic system altogether. An inflexible strap with a U-shaped metal spring attached to it is placed around the desired area with sufficient tautness to partially flatten the spring. With each inspiration the spring becomes even flatter, and with each expiration it approaches its normal U shape. A strain

gauge attached to the spring changes its resistance as the spring bends, and the resistance changes are converted by a bridge circuit to current fluctuations, which are amplified and recorded (Ford, 1957).

The other technique measures air flow through the mouth during respiration (Degelman, 1956). For a discussion of the problems involved in the interpretation of respiratory records see Woodworth and Schlosberg (1954, pp. 170–173).

Body temperature

Various types of thermometer are available that permit the recording of temperature from almost any part of the body. Detailed descriptions of their structure and principle of operation, as well as the problems involved in their use, have been published by Prouty and Hardy (1950) and Lion and Harries (1955).

Oral or rectal temperature is readily obtained with the mercury-in-glass clinical thermometer. This instrument is adequate for obtaining intermittent readings of the relatively slow and gross changes in temperature occurring in these body cavities but is inadequate for detecting minute, rapid changes occurring in these or other body parts. A more sensitive instrument for recording minute and rapid fluctuations in temperature of the rectum, skin, and other body parts is the thermoelectric thermometer, or *thermocouple*. It is composed of two units of dissimilar metals joined together. These junctions generate an electromotive force that increases parabolically as the difference in temperature between them increases. Sensitivity may be increased by connecting several thermocouples in series to form a *thermopile*. The latter, when used in conjunction with a recording galvanometer, constitutes a very sensitive thermoelectric device capable of detecting changes in temperature as small as one ten-thousandth of one degree. The thermocouple-galvanometer recorder may be calibrated by comparing changes in its output with changes in a mercury thermometer.

To measure rectal temperature, one of the thermocouple junctions is embedded in a small silver tube placed in the rectum, and the other junction is placed in a sealed container and immersed in water with a constant temperature approximately equal to that of the body. Readings may be obtained from a galvanometer scale calibrated to read in degrees, or permanent records may be obtained oscillographically.

Measures of blood temperature may be obtained by inserting a catheter containing one of the junctions of a thermocouple into an artery or vein and placing the other in a water bath of constant temperature (Bazett and McGlone, 1927). Muscle-temperature measurements are obtained by placing a thermocouple junction in a hypodermic needle and inserting the latter into the muscle (Prouty and Hardy, 1950). Benzinger (1961) measured the temperature of the blood and tissue adjacent to the hypothalamus in man by inserting probes with thermocouples attached to their tips into the thymoid sinus, into the nasopharyngeal cavity, and near the eardrum.

Another temperature-assessing device is the resistance thermometer, or *thermistor*. It is composed of a semiconductor, such as an oxide of nickel or copper, whose resistance changes in a nearly linear manner with temperature variations. Thermistors are made in many sizes and shapes and may be used to record temperature from almost any part of the body. Like the thermocouple, the thermistor may be calibrated by comparing changes in its output with variations in a mercury thermometer. Baker and Caspo (1955) used thermistors for detecting skin temperature. See Prouty and Hardy (1950) for further information on resistance thermometers.

Gastrointestinal activity.

An early laboratory technique for observing *stomach contractions* in man employed a pneumatic device (Cannon, 1934). A subject swallowed a rubber bulb or balloon connected by a long tube to a tambour with a lever attached that wrote on a kymograph drum. Wenger, Engel, and Clemens (1957) had the subject swallow a small magnet covered with a plastic material as protection against the gastric and intestinal juices, and used a magnetometer the output of which was fed to a chopper-type d-c amplifier and penwriter to record the movements of the magnet.

A very promising procedure for studying gastric and intestinal motility involves obtaining an *electrogastrogram* (Alvarez, 1948), a recording of the electric potentials generated by the smooth muscles of the stomach and intestines when they contract. Telemetering techniques have also been applied to the study of gastrointestinal activity. Miniaturized packets no larger than a medical capsule, known as *endoradiosones*, are swallowed by the subject. These detect and transmit information pertaining to pressure, temperature, pH, and other internal conditions of the gastrointestinal tract (Jacobson, 1960; von Ardenne, 1960). The transmitting element consists of a single transistor in an FM circuit and is powered with a miniaturized battery. An FM receiver demodulates and amplifies the transmitted signal, which is recorded oscillographically.

Glandular activity

Studies of *sweat gland activity* have involved the measurement of electrical responses or secretions. Darrow (1927) utilized a device called a *hygrometer*, which detects variations in atmospheric moisture, to measure sweating. The sensing element consists of a strand of dried silk hypersaturated with calcium chloride or glycerine and sodium sulfate. The strands are stretched across a slit in the top of a small air chamber, the open lower end of which makes firm contact with the subject's skin. Minute variations in sweat secretion alter the moisture content of dry air being pumped into the chamber. The increased moisture content alters the resistance of the silk fibers to an applied direct current, and this resistance is recorded with a galvanometer. Roy (1960) developed a device based on the hygrometric principle by which dry air is passed through a chamber containing a moisture-sensing element (copper electrodes) at a rate sufficient to maintain an arbitrarily specified humidity level. Variations in sweat secretion alter the moisture content, thereby changing the resistance of the sensing element. A servomechanism nullifies this change by altering the flow of air so as to restore the original moisture level. The air flow across the element per unit time is taken as a measure of secretion magnitude. According to Roy, the system possesses high reliability and is relatively trouble-free.

Silverman and Powell (1944) developed a *colorimetric method* to detect the presence of sweat. After the skin is cleansed and dried, a 25 percent solution of ferric chloride suspended in alcohol is applied to the area and allowed to dry. A piece of porous paper, previously soaked in a 5 percent solution of tannic acid and then dried, is placed in contact with the treated skin area. As sweating occurs, some of the ferric chloride is dissolved and reacts with the tannic acid to form a stain. Depending on the intensity of the reaction, the stain will vary in color from a light blue-gray to a very dark blue. These variations may be measured with a densitometer (Wilcott, 1959) and expressed in terms of amount of sweat activity. Rough estimates of the amount of sweating may be obtained by having judges categorize a number of different stain samples into several density classes (Silverman and Powell, 1944; Wenger and Gilchrist, 1948). For a detailed treatment of the problems involved in the measurement of moisture content, see Beament (1958).

A great deal of research activity has been directed toward measuring the *electrical activity of sweat glands*. In 1888 Féré observed that when a weak constant current is applied through two electrodes attached to the skin, the presentation of visual, auditory, or olfactory stimuli produces deflections on a recording galvanometer. Two years later Tarchanoff demonstrated that the same phenomenon oc-

curs without application of an *exosomatic* current to the electrodes, i.e., an *endosomatic* current exists between the electrodes of sufficient strength to excite a sensitive galvanometer. Since the discovery of this bioelectrical event, a voluminous number of studies involving its measurement have been conducted, most of which have employed the Féré technique (see Wang, 1957). (See also Chap. 9 for a discussion of GSR conditioning.)

Both the latency and duration of this electrical response are relatively long compared with most bioelectrical events, each being in the vicinity of 2 sec. The response has been given various names, including *psychogalvanic reflex* (PGR), *galvanic skin response* (GSR), and *electrodermal response* (EDR). Since it is now fairly certain that the response is actually a manifestation of the electrical activity of the sweat glands, a more accurate name for it would seem to be *electroglandular response* (EGR).

Since the Féré technique has been most frequently used for measuring the electrical response of the sweat glands, procedures based on the exosomatic principle will be emphasized. Tarchanoff's method has certain advantages worth noting. It provides a relatively easy way to measure changes in skin resistance since no possibility exists for contamination of the measures with current changes in an exosomatic circuit. Furthermore, changes in the base skin resistance level upon which the discrete response is superimposed do not affect the magnitude of the latter, provided a high-impedance amplifier is used.

In general, the exosomatic method consists in applying a constant direct or alternating current to two electrodes attached to the skin and in recording the resistance across the skin with a sensitive galvanometer (impedance if an alternating current is used). This procedure requires that the same amount of current be passed through the subject at all times regardless of the magnitude of skin resistance deflections. An alternative procedure is to measure the voltage potential across the two electrodes, which is proportional to the resistance, with an amplifier and recording oscillograph (Ellson *et al.*, 1952).

Problems of electrodermal measurement are concerned with the electrodes, coupling circuitry, amplifier and recording elements, and methods of data quantification. Each is treated briefly below.

A major problem encountered when direct current is applied to a subject's skin is electrode polarization. Many types of electrode have been used in electrodermal measurement, some of which are quite susceptible to polarization while other are not. An electrode sometimes used in d-c circuits consists of a polished silver disk about the size of a quarter, soldered to flexible silver or copper wire leads. An electrode paste of kaolin, glycerin, and Ringer's solution is sometimes applied to its lower surface to provide better skin contact. This type of electrode is subject to considerable polarization when used in a d-c circuit and should be used with caution (Lykken, 1959). It may be used to record relatively slow changes in skin conductance with minimal polarization effects, provided the current is turned on only when measures are taken and provided the average of two readings is taken, one of which precedes and the other of which immediately follows a reversal of circuit polarity (Kling and Schlosberg, 1961).

A relatively nonpolarizing electrode consists of a zinc plate soldered to copper wire leads and covered with a gauze pad soaked in zinc sulfate solution (Woodworth, 1938, p. 279). Ellson *et al.* (1952) used a pad soaked in magnesium oxide to make contact with the zinc plate; a second pad soaked with sodium chloride was used to make immediate contact with the skin.

Lykken (1959) investigated the polarization effects of various types of electrode. His findings indicate that stainless steel placed in contact with NaCl is highly polarizing when an exosomatic direct current is used and is unacceptable for measuring either changes in resistance or the voltage potential between electrodes attached to the skin. Zinc is also unsatisfactory when used with an NaCl electrolyte but becomes highly satisfactory when the electrolyte is separated from the zinc plate by a weak solution of zinc sulfate. Silver coated with a layer of silver chloride is also satisfactory, provided the electrodes are adequately chlorided and properly stored. A two-element lead electrode composed of an inner core and an outer concentric ring is better than any other type for measuring resistance changes with a d-c circuit. Although platinum has frequently been used, it is more highly polarizing than either stainless steel or plain silver. In view of Lykken's findings, it appears that zinc–zinc, sulfate, silver–silver chloride, and two-element lead electrodes are very satisfactory for electrodermal measurement. Since lead is highly poisonous, it should be used with extreme caution. When an a-c exosomatic current is used in recording the EGR, electrode polarization does not constitute a problem. Stainless steel, silver, or other nonchlorided metals may be used.

A jelly or paste containing NaCl as the electrolyte may be used with silver–silver chloride and two-element lead electrodes without producing marked polarization effects. It is easily made by mixing approximately equal parts of bentonite clay and glycerin and thinning the mixture with Ringer's solution until it becomes soft and placid (Woodworth and Schlosberg, 1954, p. 140). A zinc sulfate paste should be used with zinc plate electrodes. One recipe calls for 30 grams (g) of zinc sulfate, 60 g of gum tragacanth, 85 g of glycerin, and 600 cc of water. The ingredients are mixed and then heated in a double boiler for 2 hr, then thoroughly mixed again and heated for 1 hr. One cubic centimeter of carbolic acid is added and the paste is mixed once more until it becomes creamy (Lykken, 1959). Another method is to mix the zinc sulfate with bentonite and glycerin and thin with distilled water until the desired consistency is attained.

When a constant current is applied across two electrodes attached to the skin, the measured resistance varies linearly with the effective electrode area (Lykken, 1959). With any electrode contact the effective area is defined by the total skin area covered with an electrolyte. When measuring electrodermal activity, sweat-gland secretions can alter the effective area. Precautions should be taken to keep the skin around the electrode as dry as possible, and the applied electrolyte should not exceed the electrode boundary. Because of the lack of standardization in electrode size, meaningful comparisons between results obtained by different experimenters frequently cannot be made. This does not invalidate the relative comparisons made in individual studies in which the same type and size of electrode is used throughout the data-collection period.

Electrodes are usually attached to the palms of the hands, volar tips of the fingers, or soles of the feet, since these areas reflect sympathetic activity that is relatively independent of body temperature regulation. Both electrodes may be attached to the "active" area or one of them may be attached to a "neutral" area such as the dorsal side of the hand, elbow, or ear lobe. If the two electrodes are placed quite far apart, as they sometimes are in monopolar recordings, a low-pass filter that passes frequencies from 0 to 3 cps should be placed in the recording circuit to prevent EKG artifacts from appearing in the records.

Various methods have been used for *attaching the electrodes*. The silver-plate type may be held in position by placing a rubber sponge over the electrode and wrapping an elastic band firmly around the skin area (Woodworth and Schlosberg, 1954, pp. 139–140). Precise pressure may be maintained by wrapping an airtight cuff around the skin over the electrode and inflating it to a specified pressure level (Grings, 1954, p. 237). Another procedure is to tape the electrodes to the skin. If the electrodes are mounted in plastic adapters before attaching them to the skin, the electrolyte used for making contact with the skin can be inserted into the hollow chamber formed by the plastic beneath the electrode. When placed against the skin, the plastic forms a seal that prevents the electro-

lyte from drying out and from spreading beyond the bounds of the electrode (Lykken, 1959). Commercially available electrodermal measuring devices employing a-c bridge circuits utilize simple clip-on silver or stainless steel electrodes, which require no electrolyte for establishing contact.

A simple device for *measuring electrodermal activity* consists of a microammeter and a $1\frac{1}{2}$-volt dry cell wired in series with two electrodes. A voltage divider may be included in the circuit to permit adjustments for changes in sensitivity produced by variations in base skin resistance. Such an instrument does not maintain a constant current flow through the subject's skin, nor is it very sensitive to discrete electrodermal responses superimposed upon the base resistance level. It is used primarily for demonstrational purposes and not for experimental work.

A Wheatstone bridge circuit is usually employed to gain sensitivity. The circuit is so arranged that an exosomatic current either flows through the subject's skin or bypasses him via a parallel route. By placing a variable resistor in the bypass channel, its resistance can be made to match that of the subject's skin, and the current flow through the two alternative routes will be equal. A large fixed resistor of approximately 100,000 ohms is also placed in each channel. Under these conditions, no current will flow through a low-resistance microammeter (galvanometer) connected across the two channels at points between the two resistance components of each. When the subject's skin resistance changes, the current flow through the two channels no longer remains equal and the microammeter will register a deflection. Such current fluctuations may be recorded with a string or mirror galvanometer, or they may be converted to voltage fluctuations, which are amplified with a d-c amplifier and recorded with a penwriter, oscilloscope camera, or d-c tape unit. The purpose of the large fixed resistors is to minimize changes in exosomatic current flow through the subject's skin as his resistance changes. The exosomatic current flow must remain essentially constant if accurate resistance measures are to be obtained.

Several modified versions of the Wheatstone bridge circuit have been used in electrodermal measurement. Grings has described several commonly used circuits (1954, pp. 261–266). Lykken and Roth (1961) have utilized an exosomatic circuit that applies a constant voltage rather than a constant current to the skin, permitting a direct recording of skin conductance. Grant (1946) and Tolles and Carberry (1960) have employed an a-c circuit for applying a constant external current to the skin to avoid the problem of electrode polarization. This seems to be the preferred method of bioelectronics engineers currently interested in electrodermal measurement. A number of late-model polygraphic recorders utilize such a circuit. The reader should be aware that such circuits may register impedance, which is a combination of both d-c skin resistance and capacitive resistance or reluctance. With the use of capacitors, it is possible to cancel out the capacitive effects, leaving only the "pure" skin resistance component.

One of the disadvantages of the exosomatic technique is the fact that the magnitude of the electrodermal response, when expressed in ohms, varies as a function of the base skin resistance level. This creates difficulties when the magnitudes of the response are to be compared under various experimental conditions. To overcome the difficulties, various conver-sions and transformations have been applied to such data. One procedure is to express the response magnitudes in terms of percent change from the base skin resistance level. This requires a simultaneous recording of the base level and the superimposed discrete responses.

Darrow (1937) attempted to gain discrete response independence by converting response magnitudes recorded in resistance units to log conductance values. Conductance, which is the reciprocal of resistance, is expressed in microhms. Darrow's procedure appears to be a valid one (Haggard, 1949) and has been used extensively by others. Lacey and Siegel (1949) found that electrodermal fluctuations expressed in terms of either conductance or log conductance units yield approximately normal frequency distributions. Schlosberg and Stanley (1953) found this to be the case when one takes the square root of conductance. The recording technique of Lykken and Roth (1961) directly expresses electrodermal changes in terms of conductance, thereby eliminating the need for making conversions after the data have been recorded. Another method of expressing discrete resistance changes independently of base skin resistance is known as the *Paintal Index* (Paintal, 1951). It simply expresses the magnitude of the response relative to the magnitude of a response elicited by a standard stimulus such as an electric shock of a specified intensity and duration.

REFERENCES

ADLER, F. H., and FLIEGELMAN, M. Influence of fixation on the visual acuity. *Arch. Ophthalmol. N.Y.*, 1934, **12**, 475–483.

ADRIAN, E. D. Olfactory reaction in the brain of the hedgehog. *J. Physiol.*, 1942, **100**, 459–473.

ADRIAN, E. D. Discharges from vestibular receptors in the cat. *J. Physiol.*, 1943, **101**, 389–407.

ADRIAN, E. D. The electric response of the human eye. *J. Physiol.*, 1945, **104**, 84–104.

ADRIAN, E. D., and BRONK, D. W. The discharge of impulses in motor nerve fibers: Part II. The frequency of discharge in reflex and voluntary contractions. *J. Physiol.*, 1929, **67**, 119–151.

AKERT, K., and WELKER, W. I. Problems and methods of anatomical localization. In D. E. Sheer (Ed.), *Electrical stimulation of the brain.* Austin: Univer. of Texas Press, 1961. Pp. 251–260.

ALEXANDER, J. T., and NASTUK, W. L. An instrument for the production of microelectrodes used in electrophysiological studies. *Rev. sci. Instrum.*, 1953, **24**, 528–531.

ALVAREZ, W. C. *An introduction to gastroenterology.* London: Heinemann, 1948.

ARDENNE, M. VON. Some techniques of the swallowable intestinal transmitter. In C. N. Smyth (Ed.), *Medical electronics.* Springfield, Ill.: Charles C Thomas, 1960.

ARMETT, C. J., GRAY, J. A. B., and PALMER, J. F. A group of neurones in the dorsal horn associated with cutaneous mechanoreceptors. *J. Physiol.*, 1961, **156**, 611–622.

ARMETT, C. J., and HUNSPERGER, R. W. Excitation of receptors in the pad of the cat by single and double mechanical pulses. *J. Physiol.*, 1961, **158**, 15–38.

ARMINGTON, J. C. Amplitude of response and relative spectral sensitivity of the human electroretinogram. *J. opt. Soc. Amer.*, 1955, **45**, 1058–1064.

BAKER, L. M., and CASPO, G. A. An improved device for recording changes in skin temperature. *Amer. J. Psychol.*, 1955, **68**, 474–475.

BARD, P., and MACHT, M. B. The behavior of chronically decerebrate cats. In G. E. W. Wolstenholme and C. M. O'Connor (Eds.), *Neurological basis of behavior.* London: CIBA Foundation Symposium, J. and A. Churchill, Ltd., 1958.

BARTLETT, N. R. and BARTLETT, S. C. Synchronization of a motor response with an anticipated sensory event. *Psychol. Rev.*, 1959, **66**, 203–218.

BARTLEY, S. H. *Vision: A study of its basis.* London: Macmillan, New York: St Martin's, 1941.

BARTLEY, S. H. Central mechanisms of vision. In J. Field (Ed.), *Handbook of physiology.* Section I. Vol. I. Washington: American Physiological Society, 1959. Pp. 713–740.

BAZETT, H. C., and MCGLONE, B. Temperature gradients in tissues. *Amer. J. Physiol.*, 1927, **82**, 415.

BEAMENT, J. W. L. Measurement and control of humidity. In P. E. K. Donaldson (Ed.), *Electronic apparatus for biological research.* New York: Academic, 1958.

BECKER, H. C., PEACOCK, S. M., HEATH, R. G., and MICKLE, W. A. Methods of stimulation control and concurrent electrographic recording. In D. E. Sheer (Ed.), *Electrical stimulation of the brain.* Austin: Univer. of Texas, 1961.

BEIDLER, L. M. Properties of chemoreceptors of tongue of rat. *J. Neurophysiol.*, 1953, **16**, 595–607.

BÉKÉSY, G. VON. Description of some mechanical properties of the organ of corti. *J. acoust. Soc. Amer.*, 1953a, **25**, 770–785.

BÉKÉSY, G. VON. Shearing microphonics produced by vibrations near the inner and outer hair cells. *J. acoust. Soc. Amer.*, 1953b, **25**, 786–790.

BENZINGER, T. H. The human thermostat. *Sci. Amer.*, 1961, **204** (1) 134–147.

BJORK, A., and KUGELBERG, E. The electrical activity of the muscles of the eye and eyelids in various positions and during movement. *EEG clin. Neurophysiol.*, 1953, **5**, 595–602.

BOYNTON, R. M. Stray light and the human electroretinogram. *J. opt. Soc. Amer.*, 1953, **43**, 442–449.

BRANDT, H. F. *The psychology of seeing.* New York: Philosophical Library, 1945.

BRAZIER, M. *The electrical activity of the nervous system.* New York: Macmillan, 1960.

BREMER, F. Cerveau isolé et physiologie du sommeil. *C.R. Soc. Biol.*, 1935, **118**, 1235–1241.

BROWN, K. T., and WIESEL, T. N. Analysis of the intraretinal electroretinogram in the intact cat eye. *J. Physiol.*, 1961, **158**, 229–256.

BUREŠ, J., and BURESOVA, O. Cortical spreading depression as a memory disturbing factor. *J. comp. physiol. Psychol.*, 1963, **56**, 268–272.

BUREŠ, J., PETRÁŇ, M., and ZACHAR, J. *Electrophysiological methods in biological research.* New York: Academic, 1962. Pp. 426–468.

CANNON, W. B. Hunger and thirst. In C. Murchinson (Ed.), *Handbook of general experimental psychology.* Worcester, Mass.: Clark Univer. Press, 1934.

CARLSON, A. J., and JOHNSON, V. *The machinery of the body.* Chicago: Univer. of Chicago Press, 1948.

CARMICHAEL, L., and DEARBORN, W. F. *Reading and visual fatigue.* Boston: Houghton Mifflin, 1947.

COOPER, J. D., HALLIDAY, A. M., and REDFEARN, J. W. T. Apparatus for the study of human tremor and stretch reflexes. *EEG clin. Neurophysiol.*, 1957, **9**, 546–550.

DARROW, C. W. Sensory, secretory, and electrical changes in the skin following bodily circulation. *J. exp. Psychol.*, 1927, **10**, 197–226.

DARROW, C. W. Neural mechanisms controlling the palmar galvanic skin reflex and palmar sweating. *Arch. Neurol. Psychiat.*, 1937, **37**, 641–663.

DAVIES, P. W. Chamber for microelectrode studies in the cerebral cortex. *Science*, 1956, **124**, 179–180.

DAVIS, H. Excitation of auditory receptors. In J. Field (Ed.), *Handbook of physiology.* Section I. *Neurophysiology.* Vol. I. Washington: American Physiological Society, 1959.

DAVIS, H., GERNANDT, B. E., and RIESCO-MacCLURE, J. S. Threshold of action potentials in ear of guinea pig. *J. Neurophysiol.*, 1950, **13**, 73–87.

DAVIS, J. F. *Manual of surface electromyography*. Montreal: Laboratory for Psychological Studies, Allan Memorial Institute of Psychiatry, 1952. (Mimeo.)

DAVIS, R. C. *Set and muscular tension*. Indiana University Publications, Science Series No. 10, 1940.

DAVIS, R. C. An integrator and accessory apparatus for recording action potentials. *Amer. J. Psychol.*, 1948, **61**, 100–104.

DAVIS, R. C. Continuous recording of arterial pressure: An analysis of the problem. *J. comp. physiol. Psychol.*, 1957, **50**, 524–529.

DAVIS, R. C., SIDDONS, G. F., and STOUT, G. L. Apparatus for recording autonomic states and changes. *Amer. J. Psychol.*, 1954, **67**, 343–352.

DAY, J. L., and LIPPITT, M. W. A long term electrode system for electrocardiography and impedance pneumography. *Psychophysiol.*, 1964, **1**, 174–183.

DEGELMAN, J. A strain gauge pneumotachograph. *EEG clin. Neurophysiol.*, 1956, **8**, 517–520.

de GROOT, J. *The rat forebrain in stereotaxic coordinates*. Amsterdam: North Holland Publishing Company, 1959.

DITCHBURN, R. W., and GINSBORG, B. L. Involuntary eye movements during fixation. *J. Physiol.*, 1953, **119**, 1–17.

DOWBEN, R. M., and ROSE, J. E. A metal-filled microelectrode. *Science*, 1953, **118**, 22–24.

EASON, R. G., and WHITE, C. T. A photoelectric method for integrating muscle-action potentials. *Amer. J. Psychol.*, 1959, **72**, 125–126.

ECCLES, J. C. *The physiology of synapses*. Berlin: Springer, 1964.

EDWARDS, A. S. The finger tromometer. *Amer. J. Psychol.*, 1946, **59**, 273–283.

ELDREDGE, D. H., BILGER, R. C., and DAVIS, H. Factor analysis of cochlear injuries and changes in electrophysiological potentials following acoustic trauma in the guinea pig. *J. acoust. Soc. Amer.*, 1961, **33**, 152–159.

ELLSON, D. G., DAVIS, R. C., SALTZMAN, I. J., and BURKE, C. J. Report of research on the detection of deception. ONR Contract N60 nr 18011, 1952.

ELSBERG, C. A., and LEVY, I. The sense of smell: I. A new and simple method of quantitative olfactometry. *Bull. neurol. Inst. N.Y.*, 1935, **4**, 5–19.

EMMERS, R., and AKERT, K. A stereotaxic atlas of the brain of the squirrel monkey (*Saimiri sciureus*). Madison, Wis.: Univer. of Wisconsin Press, 1963.

FÉRÉ, C. Note sur les modifications de la resistance électrique sous l'influence des excitations sensorielles et des emotions. *C.R. Soc. Biol.*, 1888, **40**, 217.

FERNANDEZ, C., GERNANDT, B. E., DAVIS, H., and MCAULIFFE, D. R. Electrical injury of the cochlea of the guinea pig. *Soc. exp. Biol. Med.*, 1950, **75**, 452–455.

FERRARO, D. P., SILVER, M. P., and SNAPPER, A. G. A method for cardiac recording from surface electrodes in the rat during free-operant procedures. *J. exp. Anal. Behav.*, 1965, **8**, 17–18.

FISCHER, G., SAYRE, G. P., and BICKFORD, R. G. Histological changes in the cat's brain after introduction of metallic and plastic-coated wire. In D. E. Sheer (Ed.), *Electrical stimulation of the brain*. Austin: Univer. of Texas Press, 1961.

FORD, A. Foundations of bioelectronics for human engineering. U.S. Navy Electronics Laboratory Research Report No. 761, 1957.

FORD, A., and WHITE, C. T. The effectiveness of the eye as a servo-control mechanism. U.S. Navy Electronics Laboratory Research Report No. 934, 1959.

FORD, A., WHITE, C. T., and LICHTENSTEIN, M. Analysis of eye movements during free search. *J. opt. Soc. Amer.*, 1959, **49**, 287–292.

FRANK, K. Identification and analysis of single unit activity in the central nervous system. In J. Field (Ed.), *Handbook of physiology*. Section I. *Neurophysiology*. Vol. II. Washington: American Physiological Society, 1960.

FRY, G. A. The image-forming mechanism of the eye. In J. Field (Ed.), *Handbook of physiology*. Section I. Vol. I. Washington: American Physiological Society, 1959.

GATENBY, J. B., and BEAMS, H. W. (Eds.) *The microtomists' vade-mecum*. New York: McGraw-Hill, 1950.

GERGEN, J. A., and MACLEAN, P. D. *A stereotaxic atlas of the squirrel monkey's brain (Saimiri sciureus)*. Bethesda: Public Health Service Pub. No. 933, 1962.

GERNANDT, B. E. Vestibular mechanisms. In J. Field (Ed.), *Handbook of physiology*. Section I. Vol. I. Washington: American Physiological Society, 1959.

GRANIT, R. *Sensory mechanisms of the retina*. Fair Lawn, N. J.: Oxford, 1947.

GRANIT, R. *Receptors and sensory perception*. New Haven, Conn.: Yale, 1955.

GRANIT, R. Neural activity in the retina. In J. Field (Ed.), *Handbook of physiology*. Section I. Vol. I. Washington: American Physiological Society, 1959.

GRANT, D. A. A convenient alternating current circuit for measuring GSRs. *Amer. J. Psychol.,* 1946, **59**, 149–151.

GRINGS, W. W. *Laboratory instrumentation in psychology.* Palo Alto: National Press, 1954.

GRUNDFEST, H., SENGSTAKEN, R. W., OETTINGER, W. H., and GURRY, R. W. Stainless steel microelectrodes made by electrolytic pointing. *Rev. sci. Instrum.,* 1950, **21**, 360–361.

HAGGARD, E. A. On the application of analysis of variance to GSR data: I. The selection of an appropriate measure. II. Some effects of the use of inappropriate measures. *J. exp. Psychol.,* 1949, **39**, 378–392; 861–867.

HAGSTROM, E. O., and PFAFFMANN, C. The relative taste effectiveness of different sugars for the rat. *J. comp. physiol. Psychol.,* 1959, **52**, 259–262.

HARLOW, H. F. Behavioral contributions to interdisciplinary research. In H. F. Harlow and C. N. Woolsey (Eds.), *The biological and biochemical bases of behavior.* Madison, Wis.: Univer. of Wisconsin Press, 1958.

HARTLINE, H. K. The response of single optic nerve fibers of the vertebrate eye to illumination of the retina. *Amer. J. Physiol.,* 1938, **121**, 400–415.

HARTLINE, H. K., and GRAHAM, C. H. Nerve impulses from single receptors in the eye. *J. cell. comp. Physiol.,* 1932, **1**, 277–295.

HAYES, K. J. Wave analyses of tissue noise and muscle action potentials. *J. appl. Physiol.,* 1960, **15**, 749–752.

HENSEL, H., IGGO, A., and WITT, I. A quantitative study of sensitive cutaneous thermoreceptors with C afferent fibers. *J. Physiol.,* 1960, **153**, 113–126.

HERRICK, J. F., and ANDERSON, J. A. An ultrasonic flowmeter. *IRE Trans. med. Electron.,* 1959, **6**, 195–197.

HILL, D., and PARR, G. *Electroencephalography: A symposium on its various aspects.* London: Macdonald, 1950.

HOAGLAND, H. A simple method for recording electrocorticograms in animals without opening the skull. *Science,* 1940, **92**, 537–538.

HOEBEL, B. G. Hypothalamic lesions by electrocautization: Disinhibition of feeding and self-stimulation. *Science,* 1965, **149**, 452–453.

HOLTER, N. J. New method for heart studies. *Science,* 1961, **134**, 1214–1220.

HUBEL, D. H. Tungsten microelectrodes for recording from single units. *Science,* 1957, **125**, 549–550.

HUBEL, D. H. Single unit activity in striate cortex of unrestrained cats. *J. Physiol.,* 1959, **147**, 226–238.

HUNT, C. C. On the nature of vibration receptors in the hind limb of the cat. *J. Physiol.,* 1961, **155**, 175–186.

HUNT, C. C., and MCINTYRE, A. K. Properties of cutaneous touch receptors in the cat. *J. Physiol.,* 1960, **153**, 88–98.

JACOBSON, B. Endoradiosonde techniques for telemetering physiological data from the alimentary canal. In C. N. Smyth (Ed.), *Medical electronics.* Springfield, Ill.: Charles C Thomas, 1960. Pp. 300–306.

JASPER, H. H. Unspecific thalamocortical relations. In J. Field (Ed.), *Handbook of physiology.* Section I. *Neurophysiology.* Vol. II. Washington: American Physiological Society, 1960.

JASPER, H. H., and AJMONE-MARSON, C. *A stereotaxic atlas of the diencephalon of the cat.* Ottawa: National Research Council of Canada, 1954.

JASPER, H. H., and ANDREWS, H. L. Brain potentials and voluntary muscle activity in man. *J. Neurophysiol.,* 1938, **1**, 87–100.

JASPER, H. H., and BALLEM, G. Unipolar electromyograms of normal and denervated human muscle. *J. Neurophysiol.,* 1949, **12**, 231–244.

JIMENEZ-CASTELLANOS, J. Thalamus of the cat in Horsley-Clarke coordinates. *J. comp. Neurol.,* 1949, **91**, 307–338.

JONES, N. F. A test of the validity of the Elsberg method of olfactometry. *Amer. J. Psychol.,* 1953, **66**, 81–85.

JONES, N. F., and JONES, M. H. Modern theories of olfaction: A critical review. *J. Psychol.,* 1953, **26**, 207–241.

KIMURA, D., and BEIDLER, L. M. Microelectrode study of taste bud of the rat. *Amer. J. Physiol.,* 1956, **187**, 610. (Abstract)

KLING, J. W., and SCHLOSBERG, H. The uniqueness of patterns of skin-conductance. *Amer. J. Psychol.,* 1961, **74**, 74–79.

KRAUSKOPF, J., CORNSWEET, T. N., and RIGGS, L. A. Analysis of eye movements during monocular and binocular fixation. *J. opt. Soc. Amer.* 1960, **50**, 572–578.

KRIEG, W. J. S. Accurate placement of minute lesions in the brain of the albino rat. *Quart. Bull. Northwestern Univer. med. School,* 1946, **20**, 199–208.

KUFFLER, S. W. Discharge patterns and functional organization of mammalian retina. *J. Neurophysiol.,* 1953, **16**, 37–68.

LACEY, O. L., and SIEGEL, P. S. An analysis of the unit of measurement of the galvanic skin response. *J. exp. Psychol.,* 1949, **39**, 122–127.

LANSING, R. W. Relation of brain and tremor rhythms to visual reaction time. *EEG clin. Neurophysiol.,* 1957, **9**, 497–504.

LARSON, J. A. *Lying and its detection.* Chicago: Univer. of Chicago Press, 1932.

LILLY, J. C. Correlations between neurophysiological activity in the cortex and short-term behavior in the monkey. In H. F. Harlow and C. N. Woolsey (Eds.), *Biological and biochemical bases of behavior.* Madison, Wis.: Univer. of Wisconsin Press, 1958.

LILLY, J. C. The balanced pulse-pair waveform. In D. E. Sheer (Ed.), *Electrical stimulation of the brain.* Austin: Univer. of Texas Press, 1961.

LINDSLEY, D. B. Electrical activity of human motor units during voluntary contraction. *Amer. J. Physiol.,* 1935, **114,** 90–99.

LING, G., and GERARD, R. W. The normal membrane potential of frog sartorius fibers. *J. cell. comp. Physiol.,* 1949, **34,** 383–396.

LION, K. S., and HARRIES, W. L. Elements of instrumentation: II. Temperature transducers. Lab. Appl. Biophysics, MIT, ONR Contract N5 ori-07882, Tech. Rep. 3, 1955.

LIPTON, E. L. A simple device for the recording of tremors. *EEG clin. Neurophysiol.,* 1953, **5,** 450.

LORD, M. P., and WRIGHT, W. D. Eye movements during monocular fixation. *Nature,* 1948, **162,** 25–26.

LOWENSTEIN, O. The effect of galvanic polarization on the impulse discharge from sense endings in the isolated labyrinth of the thornback ray. *J. Physiol.,* 1955, **127,** 104–117.

LOWENSTEIN, O., and LOWENFELD, I. E. Scotopic and photopic thresholds of the pupillary light reflex in normal men. *Amer. J. Ophthalmol.* 1959, **48,** 87–98.

LOWENSTEIN, O., and ROBERTS, T. D. The equilibrium function of the otolith organs of the thornback ray. *J. Physiol.,* 1950, **110,** 392–415.

LOWENSTEIN, W. R., and ALTAMIRANO-ORREGO. The refractory state of the generator and .propagated potentials in a Pacinian corpuscle. *J. gen. Physiol.,* 1958, **41,** 805–824.

LURIA, A. R. *The nature of human conflicts.* New York: Liveright, 1932.

LYKKEN, D. T. Properties of electrodes used in electrodermal measurement. *J. comp. physiol. Psychol.,* 1959, **52,** 629–634.

LYKKEN, D. T., and ROTH, N. Continuous direct measurement of apparent skin conductance. *Amer. J. Psychol.,* 1961, **74,** 293–297.

MCCLUNG, C. E. (Ed.) *Handbook of microscopical technique.* New York: Hober, 1929.

MACKWORTH, N. H. Some suggested uses for the optiscan—a head-mounted eye camera. American Society of Mechanical Engineers, Paper No. 60-WA-304, 1961.

MARG, E., JAMPOLSKY, A., and TAMLER, E. Elements of human extraocular electromyography. *A.M.A. Arch. Ophthalmol.,* 1959, **61,** 258–269.

MARSH, J. T., WORDEN, F. G., and HICKS, L. Some effects of room acoustics on evoked auditory potentials. *Science,* 1962, **137,** 281–282.

MARSHALL, W. H. An application of the frozen section technique for cutting serial sections through the brain. *Stain Tech.,* 1940, **15,** 133–138.

MEYER, D. R. Some psychological determinants of sparing and loss following damage to the brain. In H. F. Harlow and C. N. Woolsey (Eds.), *Biological and biochemical bases of behavior.* Madison, Wis.: Univer. of Wisconsin Press, 1958.

MICKLE, W. A., and ADES, H. W. Rostral projection pathway of the vestibular system. *Amer. J. Physiol.,* 1954, **176,** 243–246.

MILLER, N. E., COONS, E. E., LEWIS, M., and JENSEN, D. D. A simple technique for use with the rat. In D. E. Sheer (Ed.), *Electrical stimulation of the brain.* Austin: Univer. of Texas Press, 1961.

MILLER, N. E., JENSEN, D. D., and MYERS, A. K. A comparison of the Lilly waveform and the sixty-cycle sine wave. In D. E. Sheer (Ed.), *Electrical stimulation of the brain.* Austin: Univer. of Texas Press, 1961.

MONNIER, M. Retinal, cortical and motor responses to photic stimulation in man (retino-cortical time and opto-motor integration time). *J. Neurophysiol.,* 1952, **15,** 469–486.

MORGAN, C. T. *Physiological psychology.* (3rd ed.) New York: McGraw-Hill, 1964.

MOUNTCASTLE, V. B., DAVIES, P. W., and BERMAN, A. L. Response properties of neurons of cat's somatic sensory cortex to peripheral stimuli. *J. Neurophysiol.,* 1957, **20,** 374–407.

MOWRER, O. H., RUCH, T. C., and MILLER, N. E. The corneo-retinal potential difference as the basis of the galvanometric method of recording eye movements. *Amer. J. Physiol.,* 1936, **114,** 423–428.

MOZELL, M. M. Electrophysiology of olfactory bulb. *J. Physiol.,* 1958, **21,** 183–196.

NIGHTINGALE, A. The analysis of muscle potentials by means of a Muirhead-Pametrada wave analyzer. *Technique,* 1957, **11,** 27–28.

NYBOER, J. Electronic plethysmography. *IRE Trans. med. Electron.,* 1955, **3,** 5–21.

OLDS, J. Hypothalamic substrates of reward. *Physiol. Rev.,* 1962, **42,** 554–604.

OLDS, J., and MILNER, P. Positive reinforcement produced by electrical stimulation of septal area and other regions of rat brain. *J. comp. physiol. Psychol.,* 1954, **47,** 419–427.

OLSZEWSKI, J. *The thalamus of the Macaca mulatta: An atlas for use with the stereotaxic instrument.* New York: S. Karger, 1952.

OTTOSON, D. Analysis of the electrical activity of the olfactory epithelium. *Acta Physiol. Scand., Suppl.* 122, 1956, **35**, 1.

PAILLARD, J. The patterning of skilled movements. In J. Field (Ed.), *Handbook of physiology.* Section I. *Neurophysiology.* Vol. III. Washington: American Physiological Society, 1960.

PAINTAL, A. S. A comparison of the galvanic skin response of normals and psychotics. *J. exp. Psychol.,* 1951, **41**, 425–428.

PFAFFMANN, C. Gustatory nerve impulses in rat, cat, and rabbit. *J. Neurophysiol.,* 1955, **18**, 429–440.

PFAFFMANN, C. Taste mechanisms in preference behavior. *Amer. J. clin. Nutrition,* 1957, **5**, 142–147.

PFAFFMANN, C. The sense of taste. In J. Field (Ed.), *Handbook of physiology.* Section I. Vol. I. Washington: American Physiological Society, 1959.

PFAFFMANN, C. The pleasures of sensation. *Psychol. Rev.,* 1960, **67**, 253–268.

PFAFFMANN, C., GOFF, W. R., and BARE, J. K. An olfactometer for the rat. *Science,* 1958, **128**, 1007–1008.

POGGIO, G. F., and MOUNTCASTLE, V. B. The functional properties of ventrobasal thalamic neurons studied in unanesthetized monkeys. *J. Neurophysiol.,* 1963, **26**, 775–806.

PROUTY, L. R., and HARDY, J. D. Temperature determinations. In F. M. Uber (Ed.), *Biophysical research methods.* New York: Interscience, 1950.

REYNOLDS, R. W. Radio frequency lesions in the ventrolateral hypothalamic "feeding center." *J. comp. physiol. Psychol.,* 1963, **56**, 965–967.

RIESCO-MacCLURE, J. S., DAVIS, H., GERNANDT, B. E., and COVELL, W. P. Ante-mortem failure of the aural microphonic in the guinea pig. *Soc. exp. Biol. Med.,* 1949, **71**, 158–160.

RIGGS, L. A. Human retinal responses. *Ann. N.Y. Acad. Sci.,* 1958, **74**, 372–376.

RIGGS, L. A., ARMINGTON, J. C., and RATLIFF, F. Motions of the retinal image during fixation. *J. opt. Soc. Amer.,* 1954, **44**, 315–321.

RIGGS, L. A., BERRY, R. N., and WAYNER, M. Continuous and reproducible records of the electrical activity of the human retina. *Proc. Soc. exp. Biol. Med.,* 1941, **48**, 204–207.

RIGGS, L. A., RATLIFF, F., CORNSWEET, J. C., and CORNSWEET, T. N. The disappearance of steadily fixated visual test objects. *J. opt. Soc. Amer.,* 1953, **43**, 495–501.

ROSE, J. E., MALIS, L. I., and BAKER, C. P. Neural growth in the cerebral cortex after lesions produced by monoenergetic deuterons. In W. A. Rosenblith (Ed.), *Sensory communication.* New York: Wiley, 1961.

ROSE, J. E., and MOUNTCASTLE, V. B. Touch and kinesthesis. In J. Field (Ed.), *Handbook of physiology.* Section I. Vol. I. Washington: American Physiological Society, 1959.

ROSENFALCK, A. Evaluation of the electromyogram by mean voltage recording. In C. N. Smyth (Ed.), *Medical electronics.* Springfield, Ill.: Charles C Thomas, 1960.

ROY, O. Z. An electronic device for the measurement of sweat rates. *IRE Trans. med. Electron.,* 1960, **7**, 326–329.

RUCKMICK, C. A. *The psychology of feeling and emotion.* New York: McGraw-Hill, 1936.

SCHLOSBERG, H., and STANLEY, W. C. A simple test of the normality of twenty-four distributions of electrical skin conductance. *Science,* 1953, **117**, 35–37.

SCHWAN, H. P. Electrical properties of body tissues and impedance plethysmography. *IRE Trans. med. Electron.,* 1955, **3**, 32–46.

SHACKEL, B. A rubber suction cup surface electrode with high electrical stability. *J. appl. Physiol.,* 1958, **13**, 153–158.

SHACKEL, B. *Electro-oculography: The electrical recording of eye position.* Proc. Third International Conference on Medical Electronics. London, 1960. Springfield, Ill.: Charles C Thomas, 1961.

SHEATZ, G. C. Multilead techniques for large and small animals. In D. E. Sheer (Ed.), *Electrical stimulation of the brain.* Austin: Univer. of Texas Press, 1961.

SHEER, D. E. (Ed.) *Electrical stimulation of the brain.* Austin: Univer. of Texas Press, 1961.

SHEER, D. E., and KROEGER, D. C. Recording autonomic responses as an index of stimulation effects. In D. E. Sheer (Ed.), *Electrical stimulation of the brain.* Austin: Univer. of Texas Press, 1961.

SILVERMAN, J. J., and POWELL, V. E. Studies on palmar sweating: I. A technique for the study of palmar sweating. *Amer. J. med. Sci.,* 1944, **208**, 297–305.

SNIDER, R. S., and LEE, J. C. *A stereotaxic atlas of the monkey brain (Macaca mulatta).* Chicago: Univer. of Chicago Press, 1961.

SNIDER, R. S., and NIEMER, W. T. *A stereotaxic atlas of the cat brain.* Chicago: Univer. of Chicago Press, 1961.

SVERAK, J., PEREGRIN, J., KRYSPIN, J., and ALTMAN, J. A new contact electrode for electroretinography. *EEG clin. Neurophysiol.,* 1959, **11**, 352–354.

SWEET, W. H. Pain. In J. Field (Ed.), *Handbook of physiology*. Section I. Vol. I. Washington: American Physiological Society, 1959.

TASAKI, I. Nerve impulses in individual auditory nerve fibers of guinea pig. *J. Neurophysiol.*, 1954, **17**, 97–122.

TASAKI, I., DAVIS, H., and ELDREDGE, D. H. Exploration of cochlear potentials in guinea pig with a microelectrode. *J. acoust. Soc. Amer.*, 1954, **26**, 765–773.

TASAKI, I., DAVIS, H., and LEGOUIX, J. P. The space-time pattern of the cochlear microphonics (guinea pig) as recorded by differential electrodes. *J. acoust. Soc. Amer.*, 1952, **24**, 502–519.

TASAKI, I., and FERNANDEZ, C. Modification of cochlear microphonics and action potentials by KCl solution and by direct currents. *J. Neurophysiol.*, 1952, **15**, 497–512.

TEICHNER, W. H. Recent studies in simple reaction time. *Psychol. Bull.*, 1954. **51**, 128–249.

TEITLEBAUM, P. *Fundamental principles of physiological psychology*. New Jersey: Prentice Hall, 1966.

THOMAS, L. E., MACKWORTH, N. H., and HOWAT, M. R. The television eye-marker as a recording and control mechanism. *IRE Trans. med. Electron.*, 1960, ME-7, 196–199.

THOMPSON, R. F. *Foundations of physiological psychology*. New York: Harper & Row, 1966.

TOLLES, W. E., and CARBERRY, W. F. The measurement of tissue resistance in psychophysiological problems. In C. N. Smyth (Ed.), *Proc. Int. Med. Conf. Electr.* Springfield, Ill.: Charles C Thomas, 1960. Pp. 24–27.

TRAVIS, L. E., and HUNTER, T. A. Tremor frequencies. *J. gen. Psychol.*, 1931, 5, 255–260.

WALD, GEORGE. The photoreceptor process in vision. In J. Field (Ed.), *Handbook of physiology*. Section I. Vol. I. Washington: American Physiological Society, 1959.

WANG, G. H. The galvanic skin reflex. A review of old and recent works from a physiologic point of view. *Am. J. physical Med.*, 1957, **36**, 295–320.

WENGER, M. A., ENGEL, B. T., and CLEMENS, T. L. Studies of autonomic response patterns: Relationale and methods. *Behav. Sci.*, 1957, **2**, 216–221.

WENGER, M. A., and GILCHRIST, J. C. A comparison of two indices of palmar sweating. *J. exp. Psychol.*, 1948, **38**, 757–761.

WENZEL, B. M. Techniques in olfactometry: A critical review of the last one hundred years. *Psychol. Bull.*, 1948, **45**, 231–247.

WILCOTT, R. C. Silverman-Powell index of sweating vs. skin conductance and humidity index of surface moisture. *J. comp. physiol. Psychol.*, 1959, **52**, 33–36.

WOODWORTH, R. S. *Experimental psychology*. New York: Holt, 1938.

WOODWORTH, R. S., and SCHLOSBERG, H. *Experimental psychology*. New York: Holt, 1954.

WORDEN, F. G., and MARSH, J. T. Amplitude changes of auditory potentials evoked at cochlear nucleus during acoustic habituation. *EEG clin. Neurophysiol.*, 1963, **15**, 866–881.

YOUNG, F. A., and BIERSDORF, W. R. An apparatus for taking rapid photographs of the pupil in visual darkness. *Amer. J. Psychol.*, 1952, **65**, 617–618.

YOUNG, P. T. *Emotion in man and animal*. New York: Wiley, 1943.

ZOTTERMAN, Y. Thermal sensations. In J. Field (Ed.), *Handbook of physiology*. Section I. Vol. I. Washington: American Physiological Society, 1959.

Chapter 4

PSYCHOCHEMISTRY

V. J. POLIDORA *and* ROBERT E. BOWMAN

Psychochemistry is an amalgam science integrating the contributions of neurochemistry, biological psychiatry, endocrinology, biochemistry, pharmacology, and psychology. This chapter will cover psychopharmacology and biochemical measurements since these areas are most likely to be of immediate interest to psychologists conducting psychochemical research with animals. For a recent authoritative and exhaustive review, the reader is referred to Eiduson, Geller, Yuwiler, and Eiduson (1964).

PSYCHOPHARMACOLOGY

Conditions determining drug effects

The most important single determinant of drug action is the chemical property of the drug itself. Since a discussion of the structural characteristics of drugs and the evidence of relationships between structures and effect are beyond the scope of methodology, however, the reader is referred to Eiduson, *et al.* (1964, pp. 316–399) and Otis, Bosley, and Birzis (1960) for a classification and description of frequently used psychoactive drugs; to drug manuals (such as Jordan, 1958; Stecher, Finel, Siegmund, and Szafranski, 1960; and the March, 1962, *Psychopharmacology Service Center Bulletin*) for drug chemical and trade names, formulas, manufacturers, and

other relevant drug information; and to textbooks of pharmacology (Goodman and Gilman, 1955; Krantz and Carr, 1961; Sollmann, 1957).

Of the many conditions known to determine the effectiveness of a drug, the factors that regulate its presence at the active site are most important. *Active site* refers to the conceptualized single site where the principal pharmacological effect is finally produced.

Drug quantity is generally positively correlated with the resultant effect. Since the administered quantity is usually distributed over the entire body, however, the concentration at any given location is roughly a function of some measure of the total mass of the organism, such as total body weight. A drug *dose* is conventionally expressed as the quantity of drug per unit body weight in units of milligrams per kilogram (mg per kg). It is more advisable to express dose in terms of the molecular weight of the entire drug in *moles*. This can be calculated by dividing the total weight of the drug by its molecular weight, the values of which can be obtained from drug manuals. One gram of a drug with a molecular weight of 200 would be 0.005 moles (M), or 5 millimoles (mM). In this preferred notation, dose is expressed as X mM per kg of the drug, citing the chemical name of the drug rather than the trade name. Dose may also be calculated in terms of milligrams per kilogram of the active base. This calculation permits comparisons across studies that use different salts of the same drug.

Drug actions may be classified as *direct* versus *indirect* and *local* versus *systemic*. Local actions have an effect at the site of application only, while systemic actions have a general effect on the whole body. Indirect or remote actions refer to an effect produced as a result of the drug's effect on an intermediary system. Most psychopharmacological research is concerned with drugs that exert their effects by systemic action. An important exception is the application of drugs directly to the brain. Systemic action is characterized by the absorption of the drug into the general blood circulation, but this does not necessarily imply that all tissues are equally affected.

The rate at which a drug is absorbed into the blood and extracellular fluid that bathes the cells is a function of many parameters. The parameters most relevant to this discussion are (1) the chemical nature and dose of the drug; (2) the drug's solubility in the aqueous fluids of the body; (3) the nature of the vehicle within which it is suspended for administration; (4) the presence of substances competing with the drug for absorption (e.g., passage of the drug into the blood at the intestine is diminished when mixed with food); and (5) the route of administration into the body.

Aside from the primary controls of active site drug concentration, i.e., dose and control of absorption rate by choice of drug form, vehicle, and route, the remaining factors of drug utilization, namely, *distribution, metabolism,* and *excretion,* are less controllable. The drug is usually distributed to cells in a selective, preferential manner called *elective affinity.* When the concentration of the drug in blood is known, concentration at the active site can be stated only when the drug's distribution pattern has been empirically determined, e.g., by studies of the distribution of radioactively labeled drugs. Most drugs display rather specific elective affinity to a particular organ, organ system, or, in some cases, type of cell.

Although absorption and elective affinity tend to increase drug concentration at the active site, metabolic alteration and excretion tend to decrease it. Appreciable chemical alteration and inactivation of some drugs by food occurs within the stomach and intestine. Digestive juices, e.g., pepsin and hydrochloric acid, and intestinal flora are so effective that in some cases routes of administration other than oral are mandatory. Natural *detoxification mechanisms* of the body also alter drugs administered by systemic routes and are primarily responsible for the final elimination of the drug from the body. The principal site of detoxification is the liver, where enzymatic degradation, chemical inactivation, and active storage in "safe" areas are accomplished. To a lesser extent, muscle, blood plasma proteins, and the lymphatic system also detoxify. Drugs are eliminated from the body unchanged or are inactivated by such means as oxidation, reduction, or in combination with body fluids. They are excreted primarily in urine but also in feces, sweat, and expired air. Chemically altered forms of drugs offer experimental control over drug metabolism and excretion, but competent pharmacological assistance will be necessary to choose such compounds.

In general, the onset of a drug's action is correlated with its rate of delivery to the active site in an active form, where a long latency of onset often indicates retarded absorption or intermediary metabolic steps. The duration of action is correlated with the interplay between the rate of buildup and the rate of elimination and with the rate of exhaustion of the active site.

Variability in drug effect may also be attributed to the natural *biological variation* existent even between individuals of the same subspecies. For this reason a drug measure as simple and unambiguous as "lethal dose" is expressed as an LD_{50}, or the dose that kills 50 percent of the animals. Quantitative biological variation is thus accounted for by appropriate statistical expressions of suitably large populations of animals.

Quantitative biological variation in the extreme takes the form of idiosyncratic, or atypical, responsiveness to certain drugs. Strain, species, and family drug idiosyncrasies are known to exist (e.g., hypersensitivity of cats to sulfa compounds or the ineffectiveness of emetic drugs in rodents, which do not have the vomiting reflex).

In some cases seasonal or cyclical variations correlated with sex, e.g., estrus in some species, distort drug effects. These effects may be controlled partly by testing females only at a chosen point of the estrous cycle or by using only male animals.

Psychological stress with its resulting sequence of nonspecific biochemical defense reactions, e.g., ACTH, epinephrine, and steroid hormone release, can alter drug effects, necessitating care during drug injection and subsequent testing to minimize the associated trauma. Many species, particularly rats, adapt to repeated, adroitly administered injections, so that a week or two of saline injections before an experiment begins invariably minimizes this factor. Although drug modifications associated with electric shock stress and its biochemical and physiological consequences have never been established, the possibility of alteration certainly exists.

There are a number of effects due to *temporary states*: (1) the organism is generally more resistant to drugs in the morning, after sleep, than later in the day; (2) older animals are more resistant than younger ones; and (3) the time and route of administration of the drug after feeding and drinking influence the drug effect, especially when the drug is administered orally. These factors may be attributed to drug dilution and chemical alteration in the stomach (oral route), and to related peripheral states such as the degree of dehydration and nutrient depletion in blood and extracellular fluid (all systemic routes). Standardization of the physiochemi-

cal base line of the experimental animal population is especially important in this regard.

The effects of most *pathological* conditions commonly encountered in animal laboratories, such as upper respiratory diseases, diarrhea, and parasitic maladies, have not been determined. It is obvious that the use of animals in transient or chronic pathological states decreases the likelihood that clear-cut drug effects will be obtained.

Tolerance is perhaps the most frequently encountered pharmacologically related biological factor that alters drug effect. *Biological tolerance* refers to an unusual and permanent resistance to an ordinary drug dose by a given organism or species, e.g., the resistance shown by rodents to hallucinogenic drugs. Since biological tolerance is an invariant condition, it cannot be manipulated experimentally, and the researcher must work with whatever doses are effective for a given species. The effective dose range for each species is obtained from an empirically determined dose-response relationship. When species tolerance is present, interspecies comparisons of drug effect in terms of relative effective dose regardless of absolute dose must be made with caution, because dissimilar mechanisms may be involved in the tolerant animals.

Acquired tolerance is induced by repeated, and not necessarily closely spaced, administrations of a drug. It is a state that is irreversible in some cases, such as penicillin, and reversible in others, such as tobacco. It is also a state that is occasionally selective in its action. The tolerance to morphine acquired by the brain but not by the lower bowel (constipation is a continuing symptom in morphine addiction) is an example of selective acquired tolerance. *Tachyphylaxis* is an acute acquired tolerance usually thought of as an exhaustion or depletion of some necessary compound intermediary but crucial to the effect, or as an occupation of receptor sites by the drug or other compounds. The mere passage of time without additional administration generally reverses tachyphylaxis. *Cross tolerance* is an acquired tolerance developed between different but usually similar drugs such that one drug produces a tolerance to the subsequent administration of a second drug.

Acquired tolerance is experimentally controlled by appropriately spaced doses when it is acute, but it is not directly controllable when it is chronic. One effective strategy in detecting and correctly identifying tolerant states is to use experimental designs employing each animal as its own control. In a typical procedure, each subject receives all drug and control doses at least twice, adequately spaced, in a random order. Decreased responsiveness to the second or subsequent administration of the drug may be considered an adequate demonstration of tolerance when decreased responsiveness is not noted to repeated control administrations. When a drug invariably induces chronic tolerance, the data from only the first, and possibly the second, drug administration to a given subject are to be considered as valid. The subject should then be discarded from subsequent use.

Several possible mechanisms are involved in tolerant states: (1) a decreased absorption from the stomach and intestine, as in alcoholism; (2) an increased excretion of the drug before absorption has taken place, as in persistent dysentery or diarrhea; (3) an increased cellular drug catabolism, such as the greatly increased ability to oxidize morphine shown by cells of the morphine addict; and (4) a true tolerance in which the cell no longer responds in the characteristic manner. Processes akin to antigen-antibody reactions have also been implicated as tolerance mechanisms.

Sensitization is the converse of tolerance. Although it is less frequently encountered, procedures identical to those discussed for tolerance may be used to detect and partially control sensitization.

When two drugs are administered in combination, either simultaneously or closely spaced, they seldom give an effect that is a simple summation of their independent effects. *Synergism* refers to a combined effect that is greater than the expected summation, while *antagonism* refers to an attenuated combined effect. Antagonistic actions may occur for several reasons: (1) the drugs may produce opposite and therefore canceling actions; (2) one drug may chemically inactivate a subsystem upon which the second drug must act; or (3) the drugs may compete for the active receptor sites. Antagonistic action is often employed in the use of a second drug to attenuate the unwanted side effects of an otherwise potent and useful one. Synergistic actions are less frequently encountered, but they play an important role in increasing the efficacy of two moderately effective drugs without raising the dose of either to a level that produces undesirable side effects.

The researcher is more likely to encounter a form of synergism when repeated doses of the same drug are administered too rapidly. Under these conditions cumulative effects are noted in which the second administration of the drug results in a larger effect than that observed for the first. This is generally due to incomplete excretion or residual effects of the previous administration. While cumulative effects can usually be avoided by spacing doses according to published data on the drug's metabolic fate, this is not necessarily true for drugs with indirect or long-term action. A reserpine dose, for example, is eliminated from the brain long before its effects are reversed; and unless spaced days apart, repeated doses of reserpine lead to a cumulative effect. These cumulative effects are to be avoided when single dose effects are desired. When the effects of high constant drug levels are to be studied, cumulative effects may be attained by repeated administrations, continuous infusion, or slow-absorbing injections.

Synergistic or antagonistic effects of drug combinations are seldom predictable. Drug spacing is the safest and most convenient procedure to avoid unwanted interactive effects. As a rule, three days between administrations of the drug is sufficient. A week is a conservative interval, which, when compatible with the other aspects of the experiment, provides maximum safety and procedural convenience.

When the purpose is to study the effect of drug interaction, the experimenter must choose carefully (1) the dose of each drug, (2) the interval between them, and (3) the routes and order of administration.

ROUTES OF ADMINISTRATION

Local action of psychoactive drugs is achieved primarily by administration directly to the central nervous system (CNS). Local administration allows the experimenter to keep systemic levels of the drug low enough to preclude the possibility that peripheral effects of the drug mediate its effects on behavior.

When the aim is to drug the brain but to avoid initial systemic detoxification, the drug may be injected into the carotid artery, because this artery transports it directly to the cerebral circulation before distributing it to the detoxification sites of the body. The drug may also be injected by the *intraventricular* route directly into the cerebral-spinal fluid (CSF) of a ventricle of the brain. This procedure is used when the experimenter wishes to achieve somewhat general distribution in the brain but to bypass both systemic detoxification and the blood-brain barrier. The *blood-brain barrier* refers to the tendency for compounds with certain chemical properties to be selectively inhibited from passing from the blood into the brain. If the drug crosses the CSF-brain barrier, it is distributed only to the extracellular fluid and brain cells adjacent to the ventricular walls. When the aim is to study local drug action on a specific group of brain cells, but without systemic detoxification or impediment by the blood-brain or CSF-brain barrier, the drug may be administered by an *intracerebral* route directly to the brain area of interest.

Intracerebral administration may be made by freehand hypodermic injection directly through the skull of young animals or through previously prepared skin-covered holes in the skulls of older or larger animals. Although this technique has been used with some success, it obviously provides inaccurate placement and great possibility of physical damage to the brain from movement of the hand-held syringe. Other routes of direct freehand administration to the CNS are *intrathecal* (within the sheath) injections and *intradural, subarachnoid, intracisternal* (within the cisterna magna at the base of the brain), and *intraspinal* injections. The difficulty and danger of each of these routes contraindicate their use except in experienced hands and where the experiment makes it mandatory.

Better control is achieved by the use of a hollow needle, stereotaxically placed in the brain; the needle is fixed to the skull in a holder that has a rubber-diaphragm-covered entrance into the needle bore. One may then hypodermically inject a solution of the drug directly through the diaphragm and hence to the end of the needle previously positioned at the desired brain site. Several variants of this device, called a *chemode,* have been developed, including multibarreled models and arrays placed in several areas. However, liquid injections leak back along the needle shank and therefore are neither necessarily localized nor exact in quantity. To avoid this, large-bore needles that allow for the administration of drug crystals, or solid needles with crystalline compounds fused to the tip for slow and localized diffusion, may be used (Michaels, in Kety and Elkes, 1961, pp. 465–479).

Caution is necessary to control the volume and chemical state of material injected into the brain.[1] Pressure artifacts are possible when volumes are too large, in most cases larger than 1 microliter. Untoward effects are also likely to be obtained when the drug concentration is made too high in an attempt to reduce the volume but maintain the dose, or when the solution differs from normal brain acidity (pH) or salt concentration (tonicity). Slowly administered or spaced doses of dilute, neutral, and isotonic solutions are mandatory.

Despite the elegant localization obtainable with intracerebral injections, most psycho-

[1] Multi-injection bottles of saline, distilled water, etc., contain bacteriostatic additives which are not mentioned on the label (not required by law) but which should not be used in central injection.

pharmacological studies employ the technically less demanding and more convenient administration of drugs by *parenteral* (within the body) routes to obtain systemic action. Parenteral administration may be contrasted with routes involving absorption across the outer membranes of the body. *Nonparenteral routes* include (1) the *percutaneous* route through the skin; (2) the *oral, rectal, sublingual* routes through the alimentary canal; and (3) the *inhalation* and *intratracheal* routes through the absorbing surfaces of the respiratory apparatus. These routes are rather specialized and are used infrequently (Sollmann, 1957, pp. 23–46).

Since systemic action is predicated upon initial absorption into the general circulation, the *intravenous* (I.V.) and *intra-arterial* (I.A.) routes are the most exact and rapid means of administration available to the researcher. These are accomplished by hypodermic injection directly into a suitable blood vessel. Intravenous injection is more frequently used because (1) veins are more superficial than arteries and hence are more readily available and (2) the use of the I.A. route results in the drug's being transported through, and diluted by, peripheral tissue before arriving at the CNS. Frequently used injection areas and needle sizes are as follows: the tail vein in rodents, #28-gauge needle; the cephalic (in the forearm and the hollow in front of the elbow) and saphenous (on the back side of the large calf muscle) veins in the monkey, #22 gauge; the cephalic vein or saphenous vein (approached best on the side or back of the thigh) in cats, #24 gauge, and in dogs, #22 gauge.

The following procedure should be followed in injection: (1) the area should be shaved and rubbed with 70 percent alcohol (ethanol), (2) the vein occluded on the heart side by finger pressure during intromission of the needle, (3) the occlusion released, (4) the syringe plunger withdrawn slightly until blood is seen to ensure that the needle is in the vein, and (5) the drug injected slowly. After visually checking that the injected material did not escape to form a pocket outside the vein, an alcohol-wetted gauze pad should be placed over the needle at the site of injection and slight pressure maintained while the needle is withdrawn. This prevents seepage and allows the vein to close over the needle hole. Finally, the limb should be flexed to check that no leakage occurs. The use of the extremely sharp disposable needles is suggested to facilitate injection and to avoid undue trauma to the animal.

Intra-arterial injections are used mainly when the locus of administration is important. To ensure that a drug enters the brain before detoxification by the liver, for example, the drug may be injected into the carotid artery. Special surgical preparations that facilitate this procedure include chronic externalization of a loop of the artery in a skin pouch (Verney, 1947) or cannulation of the artery by implanting a plastic tube into the vessel. Drug and saline injections via chronically implanted cannulas, consisting of polyethylene tubing pushed down the jugular vein into the heart, have found recent application in psychopharmacology (Clark, Schuster, and Brady, 1961).

Intravenous and intra-arterial injections are relatively dangerous when improperly administered. Nonsterile syringes or injectants and injections of oils, contaminated compounds, or air all lead to serious blood or systemic pathologies. "Speed shock," a rapid fall in blood pressure and occasionally death, can result from a too-rapid intravenous injection of any drug. "Stormy reactions" may also result from rapid I.V. injections. These are characterized by exaggerated responses to a momentarily high blood-drug concentration. A generally safe procedure is to inject 0.1 cubic centimeter (cc) in 5 seconds (sec) and observe for unusual cardiac, respiratory, or other reactions for 30 sec. If no unusual reactions occur, inject the remainder at a rate of 2 cc per min with large animals (5 cc maximum volume) or 1 cc per min with small animals (1 cc maximum volume).

Intraperitoneal (I.P.) injections refer to

those made within the peritoneum, which is the membrane encasing the viscera. An I.P. injection provides the researcher with one of the most convenient, safe, technically easy, and rapid routes of drug administration. When introduced into the peritoneal cavity, the injectant, which may be as large as 10 cc in large animals and 5 cc in smaller ones, quickly diffuses through the fluids that surround the visceral organs and is quickly absorbed into the blood.

The injection is made into any area of the abdomen below the navel, but well within the pelvic girdle. The area should be swabbed with alcohol, and the needle (rat, #26 gauge; cat and monkey, #22; dog, #20) inserted so as to penetrate the skin and membrane, but not so deep as to puncture the intestine. The plunger should be withdrawn to ensure that the needle does not rest in the urinary bladder or a blood vessel, and the injectant then delivered in about 5 sec.[1] A gauze pad should be placed over the needle, the syringe withdrawn, and the pad held in place for a moment. Opinions differ concerning the need for maintaining aseptic conditions with intraperitoneal injections. Some laboratories never sterilize equipment for injecting rodents and often use the same syringe and needle repeatedly.

An effective technique for administering an I.P. injection with the rat is to (1) hold the rat's tail in the preferred hand; (2) grasp the rat across the back as it attempts to crawl away; (3) cross the forelimbs below the jaw with thumb and forefinger, without squeezing the rib cage with the remaining fingers; (4) hold the rat's hindquarters against the injector's side, thus exposing the abdomen; and (5) inject. Gloves are unnecessary and may act as a hindrance.

Intramuscular (I.M.) injection provides somewhat less rapid entry of the drug into the blood despite the rich vascularization of striated muscle. The general procedure for in-

tramuscular injection is similar to that for intraperitoneal except that the volume of injectant should be smaller, less than 1 cc, or deposited in several locations. The large thigh or upper arm muscles are the most typical injection sites, and the injection is made into the middle of the muscle mass. Care must be taken to ensure that the needle is not in a blood vessel and that the needle hole closes after the injection. Gentle rubbing and limb flexion after withdrawing the needle facilitate drug dispersion within the muscle.

The convenience, safety, and ease of intramuscular and intraperitoneal injections are comparable with smaller animals. With larger animals, such as the dog or monkey, it is probably easier to hold a leg through the bars of a cage to inject intramuscularly than it is to immobilize the whole animal to get at the abdomen.

When slower absorption is desired, *subcutaneous* (sub-Q, s.c.) injection may be employed. The injectant, less than 5 cc, is deposited into the fatty tissue beneath the layers of the skin, where the sparse vascularization of these tissues allows for a slow rate of absorption. To administer a sub-Q injection, any area of loose skin may be chosen, but the back or abdomen are most convenient. The swabbed skin should be pinched between the fingers and lifted to produce a cavity between the inverted V-shaped skin and the underlying tissue adhering to bone. The needle is then inserted into the cavity, keeping the needle parallel to the bone. When the needle is beneath the skin, but not into the tissue attached to the bone, it will be possible to lift the skin by raising the needle parallel to the bone and to depress the needle point without producing a dimple in the skin. The injectant is then delivered and the syringe withdrawn beneath a gauze pad. Light pressure and gentle massage should be applied for a moment to prevent leakage and to spread the injectant into a larger area. Care should be taken not to press the bump formed by the injectant, however, since the needle hole will occasionally open under this pressure.

---

[1] If blood is retracted in the syringe, the material should be discarded because blood in the peritoneum is exceedingly inflammatory.

Prolonged rates of absorption from intramuscular and subcutaneous injections may be obtained by adjusting the vehicle within which the drug is suspended. Drugs for injection are usually mixed with distilled water when the drug already exists as a salt, normal saline [0.9 percent sodium chloride (NaCl)], or buffered saline, which is ionically balanced to resist pH changes. For very slow absorption with intramuscular or subcutaneous injections, the drug may be suspended in various vegetable oils, fats, or waxes. These viscous and non water-soluble vehicles retard the diffusion of the drug in the tissue and hinder its absorption into the blood as well. Extremely long action may be obtained by subcutaneous implantation of solid drug pellets, which produce a depot from which absorption takes place slowly and uniformly. The principal drawback of the retarded absorption techniques is the difficulty of determining the dose actually administered.

Since absorption from intramuscular and subcutaneous injections is slow, inflammation, swelling, and considerable pain can result from contaminated needles or from injectants that are impure, hypertonic or hypotonic, or irritating. An irritating or nonisotonic drug is best administered by slow intravenous injections since the rapidly moving blood quickly dilutes it.

In addition to differences in the rates of absorption among the various routes of administration, there exist also differences in the efficiency with which the drug is absorbed into the general circulation. Decreased efficiency means that some proportion of the drug is not absorbed and distributed in sufficient quantities, or at a sufficient rate, to produce the characteristic effect. Thus proportionally larger doses must be administered by the more inefficient routes to achieve a given effect. The relative efficiencies for most drugs are, in decreasing order, intravenous, intraperitoneal, intramuscular, oral, and subcutaneous. These relationships are not precise, however, and exact dosages for the desired route must be obtained from the experimental literature or

from a drug manual. Differential efficiency occasionally leads to qualitatively different drug effects for different routes. The existence and nature of characteristic differences must be empirically determined in each case that interroute comparisons are to be made.

The choice of a route for drug administration will generally be dictated by an appropriate literature reference or by the specific experimental problem. The route of administration may also be chosen to control the speed of onset and the duration of drug action. In general, the relative rates of absorption given for each route may be taken as indices of the relative rates of onset of drug effect. When a rapid rate of onset is desired, intravenous injection is indicated; for a slow rate, intramuscular or subcutaneous may be used.

Extended duration of action may be obtained by (1) administering large amounts of a drug via a slow absorption route, e.g., by subcutaneous depots or intramuscular injections in oil; (2) administering a large amount of the drug in the molecular form that is converted into its active form at a slow rate; or (3) using continuous, slow intravenous infusion to deliver the exact dose desired continuously, e.g., by "intravenous drip" into a cannulated vein. The study of extended durations of relatively constant levels of drug action is one powerful means of elucidating the "pure" effect of the drug itself since the other potentially interfering variables are allowed to change against the steady background of drug effect (Nash, in Uhr and Miller, 1960, pp. 128–155).

When repeated injections by any route are contemplated, alternate legs or arms and inject at different points since the scar tissue on a vessel and skin (as a result of injection trauma) frequently prohibits subsequent effective injections.

DRUG FORMS AND PREPARATIONS

Most drugs are obtainable in either powder or dissolved liquid forms. If the concentration and vehicle are satisfactory, the liquid form is the most convenient to use. Liquid forms are supplied in sealed glass ampules that may be opened by breaking off the top and withdrawing the drug into a syringe, or in bottles stoppered by a rubber diaphragm. The drug is retrieved from bottles by (1) inverting the bottle, (2) inserting the syringe needle through the diaphragm, (3) injecting air, and (4) withdrawing the desired volume of drug. Since drugs in liquid form are invariably sterile, a sterile needle and syringe should be used.

In the preparation of an injectant from drug powder, two parameters determine how it will be mixed: *concentration* and *total volume*. A third parameter, *dose,* determines the volume of injectant to be delivered to a given animal. In general, the concentration of the drug solution should be kept as low as possible while maintaining a relatively small injectant volume.

Drug powder should be dissolved in the injectant vehicle itself. Normal saline, or a buffered saline such as Ringer's solution, may be used for this purpose. Most commercial drugs will be isotonic, i.e., they will have the same osmotic pressure as body fluids, when mixed in this manner. The injectant should also be neutral (pH, an index of acidity, adjusted to 7.0 ± 0.2, as found in the body). To neutralize an acidic solution: (1) dissolve the drug in one-half to three-fourths of the desired total volume of vehicle, (2) test pH on indicator paper, (3) add a dilute base such as sodium hydroxide dropwise until the pH drops to 7.0 ± 0.2, and (4) bring the solution to the desired volume with the vehicle. A dilute acid such as hydrochloric acid is used to neutralize a basic solution.

One convenient system of drug preparation is to mix the concentration so that the volume to be injected is proportional to the animal's body weight. If a desired rat dose is 1 mM per kg, for example, the drug may be mixed in a concentration of 1 mM per milliliter (ml), and the number of milliliters to be injected into a given animal is given by its body weight

in kilograms. A rat weighing 250 grams (g), or 0.250 kg, would be given 0.25 ml of 1 mM per ml solution, or a total of 0.25 mM distributed in a 0.250-kg body, or 1 mM per kg. These volumes can be measured with a 1-cc (cc $\simeq$ ml) tuberculin syringe graduated in units of 0.01 cc. For the rat, an experimenter may follow the principle of preparing the drug in a concentration (N mM per ml) equal to the dose (N mM per kg) and injecting a volume in cubic centimeters equal to the animal's body weight in kilograms.

With larger animals, the drug concentration may be increased by a factor of 10 so that a 1 mM per kg dose is mixed as a 10 mM per ml solution, and the volume injected in cubic centimeters is 0.1 times the animal's body weight in kilograms. An 8-kg monkey would receive 0.8 cc of a 10 mM per ml solution, or a total of 8 mM per 8 kg, or 1 mM per kg. This system breaks down with large animals and large doses, e.g., 50 mM per kg, since the solution would be prohibitively concentrated, 500 mM per ml, and possibly irritative. As a rule, however, psychoactive drugs are effective in low doses and are amenable to such a system. The system is convenient, avoids the use of cumbersome computations, and provides that the injectant volume is proportional to the animal's mass. If volume effects exist, they are at least standardized.

Drug preparations can be stored in rubber-stoppered injection vials, such as serum bottles, although drug deterioration information from manuals must be noted before storage is attempted. When kept refrigerated, stable drugs can be maintained in such vials for an extended period of time since evaporation is eliminated. Vials also facilitate the injection procedure since the drug is withdrawn and injected with the same syringe.

The researcher who wishes to obtain drugs for investigational use may buy nonprescription drugs through a commercial pharmaceutical company. Moderate quantities may often be obtained from the manufacturer, free of charge, upon receipt of a request (letterhead stationery helps) briefly describing the intended research. It is common practice to acknowledge the gift in resulting publications and to provide the company with at least one reprint. Prescription drugs may be obtained either through a cooperating registered physician or by special arrangement with a pharmaceutical company.

DRUG EFFECTS

Psychoactive drugs frequently have *physiological* effects that can be useful as secondary measures of the drug effect. Many of these effects take the form of autonomic symptoms, such as mydriasis (dilation of the pupil), piloerection (raising of the hair), ptosis (drooping of the eyelids), changes in breathing rate (hyperpnea or hypopnea), heart rate (tachycardia or bradycardia) or blood pressure (hypertension or hypotension), urination, defecation, diarrhea, salivation, lacrimation (tearing), flushing (vasodilatation) or blanching (vasoconstriction), and vomiting. These symptoms usually take one form during sympathetic dominance, as with most energizers, and the opposite during parasympathetic dominance, as with tranquilizers.

The following are the more frequently noted somatic reactions: loss of simple neurological reflexes, convulsion, tremor, fasciculation (appearance of "crawling" of the skin), shivering, hyperactivity, vocalization, and death. Although autonomic symptoms are more common, somatic or autonomic effects may comprise the untoward side effects characteristic of certain drugs and may be used as indices of the degree of drug effect. The exaggerated occurrence of any of these symptoms usually indicates overdosage or injectant contamination.

Little will be said here regarding the behaviors to be studied as dependent variables, for they of course comprise the important subjects that the researcher wishes to elucidate. Several quasi-standard behavioral "tests" are discussed in two reviews (Dews and Morse, 1961; Ross and Cole, 1960) and in several sections of Uhr and Miller (1960), but spe-

cific behavioral procedures, even for the study of a particular drug, are almost totally a function of the experimental question. Conventionally, a researcher may choose a behavior for study and subject it to different drug treatments at several doses. Under some conditions, he may choose a different specific behavior for each drug and for each experiment. Another strategy is to decide upon a battery of behavioral tests that have been independently shown to be differentially sensitive to many types of drug, and to perform all drug experiments on this behavioral test battery. The research of Miller and Barry (1960) typifies this approach.

RESEARCH METHODOLOGY

In the elucidation of the psychopharmacological effects of a given drug, two important parameters should be studied in the initial phase of every research program: the *dose-response* and the *time-response* relationships. Dose–response refers to the relationship between the dose of the drug and the magnitude of the effect on the dependent variable. It is usually graphically expressed with the dependent behavioral variable on the ordinate and the logarithm, base 10, of dose on the abscissa. As a rule this yields a linear function. Although only five or six doses are typically used to determine the function reliably, it should be noted that the function is determined on each of the behavioral measures in the test battery. This is done in order to obtain a picture of the effects of the drug on the spectrum of relevant behaviors.

The "response" to a drug extends over the time during which the drug exerts its action, but in the determination of the dose-response relationship, either the maximal or the total effect is used as a single index of response. To characterize more completely the drug's effect, it is important to determine its time course, i.e., time of onset of effect, rate of rise to maximum, duration of maximum, rate of fall, and total duration. These measures comprise the time-response function, which is expressed as a continuous plot of behavioral effect as a function of time. Since the latter is only a special case of the former, it is convenient to obtain both the time-response and the dose-response relationships from the same series of experiments. Once these functions have been determined, they will serve as the base upon which future research may be built. It is advisable, for example, to work with doses in the linear range so that these relationships need not be redetermined in their entirety until some aspect of the drug, the behavior, or the animal population is changed.

Several variables can produce artifacts that are often indistinguishable from drug effects. The most important of these variables are tolerance, cumulative effects, drug interactions, and the nutritional and somatic state of the animals. The control of many of these artifacts has been discussed, but three important controls should be emphasized: (1) repeated use should be made of injection of the drug vehicle alone to control for those factors associated with the process of administration and the presence of foreign substances in the body; (2) chemically related or "prototype" drugs that produce symptoms similar to the drug of interest should be used to control for effects of a general pharmacological action not necessarily unique to the drug under study—e.g., the use of a sedative drug control group in the study of tranquilizers allows one to partial out the effects of muscle relaxation and depression alone; and (3) important experiments should be replicated under different motivating conditions (drives) to ensure that the results are not an artifact of the particular drive employed. Drug effects peculiar to one drive may arise from drug alteration as a result of deprivation states or electric shock or from the behavioral requirements of the test situation itself, such as differentially drug-sensitive behavioral mechanisms involved in appetitive and aversive drives.

In general, the appropriate standard techniques of experimental methodology, design, and statistical analysis apply to psychopharmacological experimentation. For a more complete discussion of these problems, the reader is referred to Uhr and Miller (1960, pp. 107–224), to Cole and Gerard (1959), and to the publications of the NIH Psychopharmacology Service Center, especially the PSC bulletin of September, 1961, on research methodology and the December, 1960, bulletin on screening techniques.

BIOCHEMICAL MEASUREMENT

In the last few years, biochemical advances have permitted the investigation of endogenous biochemical functions, either as consequent upon independently manipulated psychological treatments or as correlated with various dependent behavioral measures. In these studies, the investigator typically establishes or discovers subjects who differ psychologically, e.g., stressed versus nonstressed or psychotic versus normal, and then takes samples of tissue, blood, urine, or other biological material in which to determine various biochemical compounds. The investigator may then (1) search for new or unspecified compounds for which he must often devise purification, identification, and quantitation procedures or (2) measure only specified compounds for which detailed methods of assay have already been developed.

The second "assay" approach demands less broad biochemical training and therefore merits consideration by psychologists. It requires (1) a general understanding of the biochemical organization of the organism (see introductory biochemistry texts, e.g., Fruton and Simmonds, 1958) and (2) biochemical knowledge concerning the biosynthesis, distribution, metabolism, and excretion of the compounds to be measured. This information, together with the qualitative and temporal nature of the psychological variables, will determine the type of biochemical measure to be made and the choice of biological sample in which to measure it. In addition, the investigator must be able to (3) choose from available assays those which are adequate and practical, (4) use the techniques for obtaining samples, and (5) perform the chosen assay. Practice will be required with the specified laboratory operations by which the chosen assay extracts, purifies, and quantifies the compound.

To aid psychologists in the use of biochemical measurements, the remainder of this section will cover points 1 and 2 above for the areas of (1) psychoendocrinology (measurement of hormones as examples of compounds found in blood and urine) and (2) psychoneurochemistry (measurement of neurohumors and associated enzymes as examples of compounds found in brain tissue). Following this, points 3 to 5 above will be discussed in the section on assay techniques general to psychochemistry (pages 204 to 206).

Psychoendocrinology

The role of hormones has long been of legitimate interest to psychologists who have studied the effects of exogenously administered hormones on behavior. More recently, chemical assays have permitted the psychoendocrinologist to study the endocrinological response to psychological variables such as stress, anxiety, and frustration or to discover the hormonal patterns that correlate with various adaptive, sexual, or parental behaviors.

The initial aim of psychoendocrinological research involving hormone measurements is to determine psychological-hormonal or hormonal-behavioral correlations. Consider a hypothetical psychoendocrinological study which demonstrates that during the stress of an unpleasant interview some subjects exhibit a rise in blood epinephrine levels together with anger directed at the interviewer. Other subjects show a rise in blood norepinephrine levels and anger directed at themselves. This demonstrates a particular hormonal response to an independently manipulated psychological variable and the correlation of specific behavioral patterns with particular hormonal responses. If it is possible to quantitate the

stress content of the interview, e.g., the number of insulting statements, one should hope to determine the quantitative relationship between the magnitude of the independently manipulated stress and the magnitude of the resultant hormonal response. This is analogous to a dose-response relationship in psychopharmacology. The investigator would expect that the magnitude of the hormonal response would vary with time and would investigate onset, duration, and recovery. This type of quantitative time-magnitude information may form the basis for theory and experiment on subsequent somatic or behavioral effects of the induced hormonal response.

In considering the correlation of the dependent behavioral measure, anger, with the dependent biochemical measure, it may be possible to show a quantitative relationship between blood hormone level and magnitude of anger. Time-magnitude relationships also are likely to hold if psychological measures can be found that can be taken as frequently as the biochemical. One should know whether the hormone levels rise before, simultaneously with, or subsequent to the onset of the correlated behavioral change, as well as whether the two measures show similar durations and recoveries. This information may aid in inferring, although not proving, causality between hormonal changes and behavior. It also will provide base-line data for performing or interpreting more definitive psychopharmacological studies on the effects of the hormone levels on behavior.

In this example the measurement of epinephrine and norepinephrine in the blood has been treated as a simple indication of the level of hormonally active compound in the body. The extent to which this is true depends on the hormone measurement made, as will now be shown by a general consideration of the dynamic system of secretion, distribution, and removal of a hormone. Specific details may be found elsewhere (Turner, 1960).

A *hormone* is defined as a chemical secreted by cells at some localized site in the body and carried by the blood to distant target tissues in which it acts. Typically, a hormone is secreted into the blood from some morphologically distinct gland and may be carried either in solution or bound to plasma proteins, in which latter form it may be hormonally inactive. From the blood, the hormone passes into various tissues and subsequently interchanges between the blood and those tissues. Its concentration in the tissues depends on the elective affinity of the hormone for each tissue and on the hormone concentration in the blood. While present in certain tissues, especially liver, some of the hormone is metabolically deactivated. These inactive metabolites, including forms made water-soluble by chemical conjugation to sugar or acid groups, also circulate in the blood. The inactive metabolites and some fraction of the unchanged hormone are eventually excreted from the body, mainly in the urine.

The free hormone, protein-bound forms, metabolites, or conjugated metabolites may be measured. In many assays, mixtures of these forms are measured, and the relationship of these concentrations to the actual hormonal activity may be unknown. Hormonal activity per se can be measured only by bioassay.

Chemical forms of the hormones may be measured in tissue, blood, or excreta, usually urine. The choice of which of these biological materials to sample depends on (1) the experimental problem, (2) the sensitivity of the available assay, (3) the amount of the sample that may be reasonably obtained, and (4) the concentration of hormone in the sample.

A *urinary assay* provides an index of the total output of the secreted hormone. This is an appropriate measure if one is dealing with a behavioral variable that extends over a time period similar to that of the usual 12 to 24 hours of the urine collection period, e.g., sexual receptivity, parental behavior, or chronic stress situations. In addition, measurements in urine are sometimes the only practical choice since (1) hormone concentrations in urine are generally so high that extremely sensitive assays are not required, and (2) urine samples may be obtained repeatedly with minimal physiological disturbance to the subject.

Urine may be collected from animals confined in "metabolism cages" or from monkeys restrained in primate chairs (Mason, 1958). Generally, the urine falls onto a steep-sided collection pan and is funneled through a glass wool plug (to exclude feces) over a central drain hole into a collection jar. Preservation of urine with toluene and acetic acid and storage in brown bottles at $-20°C$ are among recommendations cited by McIlwain and Rodnight (1962, pp. 257–260).

Urine is generally collected in 24-hour pools, the volume measured, and an appropriate, measured volume of this is taken for the biochemical assay. The total amount of hormone or metabolite determined in this fashion to be present in the whole 24-hour pool is frequently assumed to be related by some consistent fraction to the total amount of the hormone secreted by the endocrine gland over the period of the collection, but this fraction or variations from it are seldom quantitatively known. Radioisotopic hormones (see below) are valuable for determining more precise secretion estimates from measurements of the urinary excretion.

Measurements of momentary hormone concentrations in repeated *samples of blood* are appropriate when one is dealing with short experimental periods or rapid changes in behavior, e.g., time periods of minutes up to a few hours. Interpretation of such measurements is complicated, however, by the fact that blood hormone assays often measure a mixture of chemical forms of the hormone, in which the amount of hormonally active forms is unknown. On the assumption of a direct monotonic relationship between such blood hormone measures and hormonal activity, and considering that these are the hormone concentrations that circulate to the target organs, increases or decreases in these concentrations should be closely related to observed hormonal effects. In cases in which the above assumption appears invalid, the investigator may require the use of assays of biological potency (see below) rather than chemical assays to relate behavior to the potency of circulating hormones.

In addition to the ambiguity in hormonal potency, the biochemical meaning of a blood hormone concentration is also ambiguous. It is evident that blood hormone levels may change because of alterations in (1) the rate of glandular secretion, (2) the ratio of amounts of hormone in blood and tissues, (3) the rate of tissue metabolism of the hormone, or (4) the rate of excretion. Therefore, unless rates of secretion or metabolism have been determined, e.g., by the use of radioisotopic techniques, the researcher must be cautious in ascribing measured increases in blood hormone levels to increased glandular secretion. These considerations are important in understanding the nature of psychological-hormonal interactions. Changes in secretion rate imply relatively direct action from the CNS on the endocrine gland, whereas changes in metabolic or removal rates indicate actions via other, often indirect, systems.

A common method for collecting blood from animals is to use a hypodermic syringe and needle. The syringe may be wetted with a minimum measured volume of heparin (500 units per ml) to prevent clotting, or the heparin may be dried in the syringe to avoid correcting the plasma volume for dilution. The earlier section on routes of administration describes surface veins and needle insertion techniques adaptable to blood drawing. Appreciable proportions of total blood may also be drawn from the anesthetized rodent by cardiac puncture, although this results in some mortality. Other techniques may have some application (Antoniades, 1960, pp. 3–11; McIlwain and Rodnight, 1962, pp. 260–263), including chronic catheterization to avoid disturbing the animal (Clark, Schuster, and Brady, 1961; Weeks, 1962) and the sampling of very small volumes of capillary blood from skin cuts (Natelson, 1961, pp. 70–83).

Blood must not be drawn too fast if one is to avoid *hemolysis* (the rupture of red cells)

and the collapse of the vein about the needle point. Venous collapse often results in the clotting of blood in the needle before flow can be restored. To prevent hemolysis, (1) remove the needle from the syringe before ejecting the blood and (2) mix the heparin, if used wet, in isotonic saline.

No exact rule can be given for the maximum amount of blood to be taken from one subject. For most purposes the withdrawal in milliliters of blood of up to 0.5 percent of the animal's weight in grams in one day, repeated monthly, will not be deleterious to the experiment or the animal. For larger withdrawals, or for an animal sampled frequently, hematocrits should be routinely performed to ensure that it is maintaining an adequate ratio of red cells in its blood (Natelson, 1961, pp. 74–79).

To avoid hemolysis, blood should not be frozen, nor should it be stored longer than necessary before performing the assay or discarding the red cells. To remove red cells, the clot formed in nonheparinized blood after one hour should be loosened from the test-tube wall by a glass rod and, after centrifugation, the clear serum taken off by pipette. A *centrifuge* is an instrument used for spinning test tubes or bottles containing the suspension of particles in a fluid. High-speed spinning forces the solid or heavier particles, such as the heavier red cells, to the bottom of the test tube. Heparinized blood may be centrifuged immediately and the clear plasma similarly removed. A reddish color of serum or plasma indicates hemolysis. Serum or plasma should be stored at $-15°C$ and, upon thawing, any protein precipitate present should be removed by centrifugation if the fluid is to be measured by pipetting.

The concentrations of hormones in neural tissue are of interest for locating brain regions having an affinity for the hormone. Since such regions are likely to be those on which the hormone exerts its effects, the concentration in the tissues is likely to be most closely related to any behavioral effects of the hormone. Furthermore, the tissue and blood hormone levels need not correlate, e.g., as a result of blood-brain barrier effects, in which case assay of the tissue level might be the more appropriate measure. Radioisotopically labeled hormones are available for determining hormone levels in tissues.

Psychoneurochemistry

Several theories have suggested that memory is mediated by the information-storing capacity of nucleic acid-protein systems, perhaps through the modification, with learning, of specific nucleic acids or protein enzymes that regulate neuronal function (Briggs and Kitto, 1962; Gaito and Zavala, 1964). Other research has shown that certain enzymes associated with the system of "intermediary metabolism," by which the cell burns sugar for energy, are in differential concentration in different brain regions (Robins, Smith, Eydt, and McCaman, 1956). Since different brain regions also mediate different behaviors, these enzymes and the metabolic pathways they regulate may possibly be correlated selectively with behavior. Learning and conditioning have also been shown to alter the concentration of high-energy phosphate compounds synthesized by the hydrogen transport or oxidative phosphorylating system, which is coupled to the system of intermediary metabolism (Heald, 1960). Changes in the concentration of high-energy compounds may be useful to detect local brain regions involved in specific behaviors.

Much of the work in psychoneurochemistry is related to the hypothesis that biochemical changes affect behavior by affecting neurohumoral systems, which are presumed to mediate synaptic transmission in the CNS (Brodie, Sulser, and Costa, 1961; Wooley, 1962). It is possible that the neurohumors, which include acetylcholine (ACh), epinephrine and norepinephrine, serotonin (5-hydroxytryptamine), and gamma-aminobutyric acid, may represent different functionally organized units in the CNS that employ these compounds as synaptic transmitters or modulators.

Interference with neurohumoral systems seems to explain a number of drug effects, e.g., reserpine and lysergic acid diethylamide (LSD), and has been theorized to mediate mental disease as well (Wooley, 1962).

Psychoneurochemistry is not as simple to characterize as psychoendocrinology, since many different biochemical compounds and systems are involved. Nevertheless, the psychologist will find the assay approach applicable in psychoneurochemistry, provided he has an adequate knowledge of neurochemistry (McIlwain, 1959) to choose appropriate compounds for study. The specification of time-magnitude and magnitude-magnitude relationships between the psychological and the neurochemical variables should be considered an initial goal (McIlwain, 1959, p. 206).

The methodological features differentiating psychoneurochemistry from psychoendocrinology include (1) respective considerations in the judicious choice and interpretation of the biochemical measurement, (2) techniques of sampling that will preserve the compounds unchanged from the instant of sampling to the moment of assay, and (3) sampling procedures to deal with the localization of compounds in the brain and in the cell. Biochemical assays performed on tissue samples are the same in principle as those applied to blood and urine.

Some problems in choosing a biochemical measure relevant to a psychological study are illustrated by considering the following study involving the ACh system. Although based on research reported by Rosenzweig, Krech, and Bennett (1960), this example is not intended to reflect their reasoning and procedure. This example is of value since there is a direct parallel in biochemical reasoning between the acetylcholine and other neurohumoral systems. For other metabolic systems, specific behavioral-biochemical considerations may differ somewhat, but the sampling considerations will still apply.

Suppose that a psychologist sets out to explore biochemical correlates of maze running in the rat after observing that some rats appear to respond to visual cues, while others exhibit spatial tendencies. He might begin by postulating that "visual" behavior correlates with greater synaptic activity in the visual cortex and "spatial" behavior with more activity in the motor cortex. This suggests measuring compounds related to synaptic activity in the selected neocortical areas.

Since acetylcholine appears to be a neurotransmitter in neocortex, the investigator might choose to measure one or more of the three principal compounds comprising the ACh system (Hebb, 1957). In this system, acetylcholine is synthesized when an activated form of acetic acid is joined to choline with the aid of an enzyme, *choline acetylase*. Acetylcholine is then stored by the neuron in axonal vesicles that lie adjacent to the cell body of another neuron. The neurotransmitter is released from these vesicles in response to nerve impulses. After initiating impulses in the next neuron, it is degraded into acetic acid and choline with the aid of another enzyme, *acetylcholinesterase*.

What, then, should one measure to index the amount of synaptic activity? Although synaptic activity is probably determined by the momentary concentration of released acetylcholine at the synapse, this concentration cannot now be measured. However, the momentary concentration of released acetylcholine should be a joint function of the amount of stored acetylcholine available and the rate at which the released acetylcholine is deactivated by acetylcholinesterase, and perhaps also of the rate at which the acetylcholine stores are regenerated by choline acetylase. Ideally, therefore, joint acetylcholine and acetylcholinesterase concentrations should correlate with the maze behavior. Additionally, to prove the relationship of these measures to synaptic activity, a way should be found to compare the biochemical data with electrophysiological measures.

For practical reasons, it may be possible to perform only one of these measures, e.g., acetylcholinesterase. Such a study might still yield significant correlations with behavior, but it should be evident that this correlation with only the single compound will not provide enough data for an unambiguous interpretation.

Samples of neural tissue (McIlwain and Rodnight, 1962, pp. 1–8) must be taken so as to avoid postsampling changes of compounds to be measured. For many compounds, including most enzymes, it is sufficient to remove the brain within a few minutes of death and freeze it in dry ice. When the researcher wishes to obtain a limited number of repeated samples from the living CNS (biopsies), it is possible to remove small cortical samples through skull holes or to take subcortical samples as a core from a hollow needle inserted stereotaxically into the brain (Heath, Leach, Ehrensvard, and Liljekvist, 1961, pp. 210–216).

For more labile compounds, e.g., acetylcholine, brain ammonia, or high-energy phosphate compounds, open-skull surgery may be used and the whole brain frozen *in situ* by pouring on liquid nitrogen. Alternatively, the entire animal, rat or mouse, may be frozen by dropping it into liquid nitrogen. To collect samples at the moment of behavior or to minimize trauma, the subject may be trained to jump through a hole onto a landing of a net, and the landing replaced by a flask of liquid nitrogen on the sampling day. Brains have also been collected by using a scissors or a Harvard guillotine to sever the head, which falls directly into liquid nitrogen, although the freezing is not rapid enough to prevent some biochemical changes induced by the shock of decapitation.

In choosing the tissue sample, the investigator must consider the localization in the brain of the compound to be measured. He may select different brain regions according to electrophysiologically established maps of brain functions relevant to the behavior under study. If this is done, the experimenter must know the compounds that are found in the chosen areas or the compounds that may differentiate various neuronal functions in the area. The acetylcholine system may be investigated because it is an apparent synaptic transmitter known to be present in the neocortex.

Biochemical localization is not limited to morphologically distinct brain areas or to different layers of the cortex. Different cell types, e.g., glia and neurons, also differ biochemically. In the acetylcholine system the neurons contain "true" cholinesterase (acetylcholinesterase), whereas the glia contain "pseudo" cholinesterase. These cholinesterases differ somewhat in their chemical reactions, and only properly designed chemical assays can differentiate between them without separating neural from glial cells (Long, 1961, p. 277).

In general, cell types must be physically separated to differentiate biochemical differences between cells. Some workers have devised elegant but difficult techniques for removing very small neural regions or single neural or glial cells on which to perform microchemical determinations (Eranko, 1955; Hyden, 1960; O. H. Lowry, in Colowick and Kaplan, 1957, pp. 366–381; Robins, Smith, Eydt, and McCaman, 1956; Tower, 1960).

Once the sample has been taken, its preparation for assay should be guided by the known intracellular distribution of biochemical compounds. Different metabolic systems are known to be segregated in different structures within the cell (McIlwain, 1959). These structures, consisting mainly of nuclei, mitochondria, microsomes, and synaptic vesicles, may be separated by differential centrifugation after the cell wall has been broken. In the study of the transmitter systems the ability to separate the synaptic vesicles is an important analytical step in measuring those compounds actually stored and active at the synapse (De Robertis, Salganicoff, Zieher, and Rodriguez de Lores Arnaiz, 1963).

Brain-tissue samples should be kept at −15°C or lower when stored. They may be dissected freehand or sectioned on a freezing microtome (Eranko, 1955, pp. 31–37;

McIlwain and Rodnight, 1962, pp. 109–133; Umbreit, Burris, and Stauffer, 1957, pp. 135–143) to prepare them for assay. Tissue fractionation is then carried out to obtain specific subcellular constituents. Fractionation begins with the grinding or homogenizing of the sample in a suspending fluid, using mortar and pestle, blenders, homogenizer tubes, or ultrasonic dispersion devices (McIlwain and Rodnight, 1962, pp. 189–210; Umbreit et al., 1957, pp. 143–201). The resulting suspension of cell contents may then be centrifuged at a series of increasing speeds. At each speed, particles of a given mass or larger are forced to the bottom of the centrifuge tube, where they form a pellet or layer. The supernatant liquid is then removed from the solid layer and centrifuged at the next higher speed to bring down particles of the next range of mass. If desired, the solid layer may also be resuspended and further fractionated by density-gradient techniques, using a tube containing several layers of sucrose solutions of increasing densities chosen so that particles of different mass collect in each layer. At any stage of centrifugation, the supernatant or the solid layer resuspended in fluid may be subjected to biochemical assay.

Assay techniques

An assay is a set of operations designed to measure the concentration of a compound. Typically, it consists in a number of operations for extracting and purifying the compound from the biological sample, after which the purified compound is subjected to a quantitation operation. Evaluating an assay is most readily done by asking how well these operations perform overall in measuring the compound. The important measurement criteria are those of specificity, precision, accuracy, sensitivity, and practicability (Loraine, 1958, pp. 1–5).

Specificity is achieved if the assay measures only the compound for which it was intended and is jointly determined by the purification of the compound and the specificity of the quantitation procedure. The proof and monitoring of specificity are especially necessary for assays that minimize purification, e.g., many clinical assays. Since assays are often reported without adequate proofs of specificity, this onus is sometimes on the user. Basic proofs include subjecting known contaminating compounds from the biological sample to the assay to determine whether they interfere, and the use of radioisotope dilution methods as standards for specificity. An assay of demonstrated specificity can be used to establish the specificity of other assays by comparison of concurrent determinations on the same biological samples.

Precision, or *replicability,* is expressed as the standard deviation of replicate determinations for assays using a chemical quantitation procedure. This should be computed by the user from his own duplicate determinations on many samples (Bennett and Franklin, 1954, p. 168).

Accuracy refers to the closeness with which the true value for the compound is obtained, and is lessened by a lack of specificity, poor precision, or uncompensated losses of the compound during purification. Losses are revealed by the amount of recovery of known amounts of the compound subjected to the assay. Recoveries of only 70 to 90 percent are common. As a correction for partial recoveries, the sample concentrations are often calculated on the basis of standards taken through the entire assay, on the assumption that the standards and samples will be recovered in the same proportion. To some extent, accuracy may also be measured by including a sample from a control pool of biological material containing a known concentration of the compound to be measured (Knights, McDonald, and Ploompuu, 1957, pp. 2–3).

Practicability includes considerations of whether the money, equipment, skill, or time required for the analysis is available to the investigator. This is an important question only when choosing an assay. Practicability does not excuse the choice of an inexpensive or easy assay that lacks the requisite specificity and accuracy.

Sensitivity refers to the minimum concentration of compound detectable by the assay. When the minimum concentration is more than can be obtained from a single subject, the pooling of samples may provide a measurable concentration. Alternatively, a minute concentration in a single sample may be detected by performing a microchemical assay. Clinical micromethods are often applicable for this purpose in animal research (Caraway, 1960; Knights *et al.,* 1957; Natelson, 1961). Clinical microchemical systems consisting of sets of miniature apparatus and recommended assay procedures are marketed commercially. Besides the gain in sensitivity, micromethods reduce the requirements for laboratory space and equipment. Since their standardization appears to make them more precise than corresponding macromethods in the hands of minimally trained personnel, microprocedures would appear admirably suited to many of the needs of psychologists. The investigator must be alert to possibilities of lessened accuracy and specificity since clinical assays, which do not require research accuracy, often minimize purification steps in the interests of economy. Microprocedures also are particularly liable to error from previously minor sources of contamination such as excess humidity, air-borne dust, and imperfectly cleaned colorimeter cells and therefore must be performed with scrupulous attention to cleanliness.

The psychologist performing a biochemical assay chosen from the literature will find the sequence of assay operations specified. The basic principles by which the most frequently employed of these operations purify or quantify, along with references to descriptions of their performance, will be mentioned here.

Purification procedures are designed to separate compounds physically, and *solvent partition* and *chromatography* are two of the main purification operations. *Quantitation* procedures are based on measuring some feature of the compound that varies as a lawful function of its activity or concentration. The physicochemical procedures of *spectro-*

photometry (colorimetry), *fluorometry,* and *radiography,* as well as *bioassay methods* utilizing a biological response, are quantitation procedures.

The simple, frequently used technique of *solvent partition* is based on the principle that the compound of interest will often dissolve from one solvent into another, whereas many contaminating compounds will not. For example, an aqueous biological sample may be shaken together with an immiscible (non-mixing) organic solvent. The compounds partitioning into the organic solvent may then be partitioned between subsequent pairs of different solvents. This is done until the compound of interest is isolated in sufficient purity in one solvent for quantification. Assays of this type are usually rapid and economical, but specificity must be carefully established. Technical aspects of solvent partitions include basic procedure (Fieser, 1957, pp. 48–55; Hawk, Oser, and Summerson, 1954, pp. 24–28) and the handling of emulsions (failures of the two solvents to separate) (Dorfman, 1962, Vol. I, pp. 210–211).

When solvent partitions do not provide adequate purification, assays often submit a solvent extract containing the compound of interest to more elaborate and exact separations by chromatography. *Chromatography* purifies by the differential tendencies of compounds in the extract to distribute themselves between a liquid or gaseous mobile phase flowed over a stationary phase upon which the sample extract is placed initially. The mobile phase carries each compound to a different spot on the stationary phase or, if flowed long enough, carries each compound off the stationary phase at a different time (Umbreit *et al.,* 1957, pp. 243–267).

Several varieties of chromatography are used. Common techniques are column chromatography, in which the stationary phase is packed in a vertical glass column, and paper chromatography, in which the stationary phase consists of a liquid film coated on strips of filter paper (Smith, 1958). More recently, thin-layer chromatography (Randerath, 1963) has been extensively developed because of its speed, sensitivity, and economy. In this system, the stationary phase consists, for example, of a thin (0.2 mm) layer of adsorbent spread on a 20-cm-sq glass plate. Developing tanks containing the mobile phase are correspondingly small, and the system is quite adaptable to the small laboratory. Another rapidly evolving technique, featuring speed, sensitivity, and resolving power, is *gas chromatography* (Kaiser, 1963), in which the stationary phase, either adsorbent or a liquid coated on inert particles, is packed in a long column, and the mobile phase is a stream of gas. Specific and up-to-date information on these various chromatographic techniques may be found most particularly in the *Journal of Chromatography.*

Other purification procedures sometimes encountered in biochemical assays include precipitation (Hawk *et al.,* 1954, pp. 172–175; Antoniades, 1960, pp. 13–29), electrophoresis (Long, 1961, pp. 161–165), dialysis (Hawk *et al.,* 1954, pp. 1–12; Kabat and Mayer, 1961, pp. 728–732), and distillation and filtration (Fieser, 1957).

Quantitation by *spectrophotometry* or *colorimetry* (Hawk *et al.,* 1954, pp. 497–540; Long, 1961, pp. 75–83; Umbreit *et al.,* 1957, pp. 221–234; and Willard, Merritt, and Dean, 1958) utilizes the fact that certain chemical structures absorb light differentially as a function of wavelength. The intensity of absorbance at any wavelength is often linearly proportional to the concentration of the compound (Beer's law). To obtain suitably absorbing chemical species, the sufficiently purified compound is generally chemically reacted. This is done to obtain an intense absorbance peak in the range of visible light, 400 to 700 millimicrons (mμ), where few compounds normally absorb, thus providing for both sensitivity and specificity.

In practice, the biological samples, standards of known concentrations of the compound to be measured, and blanks, which lack only the compound to be measured, are all similarly purified, dissolved in a suitable reagent, and placed in cuvettes, i.e., glass receptacles of special optical transparency. The absorbances of these solutions are then quantified in a colorimeter or spectrophotometer.

Colorimeters and spectrophotometers are instruments containing a light source emitting a broad spectral band. From this, either a relatively narrow band of wavelengths is selected by a filter, as in a colorimeter, or monochromatic light is obtained through the resolving power of a prism or diffraction grating, as in a spectrophotometer. The selected wavelength is beamed through the solution and the light not absorbed by the solution energizes a photocell. The resultant electric current is measured by an ammeter calibrated to read in either transmission or absorbance units. Absorbance is the negative logarithm of percent transmission.

Quantitation proceeds by placing the blank in the light beam and setting the instrument to read 100 percent transmission, equivalent to zero absorbance, or zero optical density. The absorbance is then recorded for each sample and standard placed in turn in the light path. The concentration of the compound in each sample may be determined from the curve of absorbance versus the known concentrations of the standards.

Assays in which sensitivity and specificity present no problems can be done with colorimeters. More exacting assays, such as those for hormones, require the more expensive spectrophotometers with their greater precision, sensitivity, and ability to provide monochromatic light at any chosen wavelength in their range. Spectrophotometry offers a valuable opportunity to monitor or increase the specificity of an assay by measuring absorbance at several wavelengths. In the absence of contamination, the curve of absorbance versus wavelength must have the same shape and must peak at the same wavelength for both the samples and the standards if they actually represent the same compound. A computational procedure by Allen is widely used for obtaining correct concentrations despite linear distortions from contamination in

the sample absorbance spectrum (Dorfman, 1962, p. 234).

The Beckman model DU spectrophotometer was long the research standard, but improved electronic circuitry and a precision positioning cell compartment for the Beckman monochromator have recently become available. Alternatively, the DU can be conveniently adapted for microwork by substituting a cuvette adapter carriage (Aloe Scientific) or by modifying the Beckman compartment (Glick and Grunbaum, 1957; Umbreit *et al.*, 1957, p. 234), and by using a Bessey-Lowry micro cuvette holder and pinhole mask. The smallest commercial micro cuvette has a Y-shaped chamber, the stem of which holds 0.035 ml of fluid for measurement.

Quantitation by fluorescence depends on the property of some compounds to absorb light and reemit it at a longer wavelength (Udenfriend, 1961). Assays quantifying by fluorescence are similar in detail to those using absorbance measurements, and the shape of the fluorescence peak can similarly be used to monitor the specificity of the assay.

The great advantage of fluorescence measurement over absorbance is its considerably greater sensitivity, which follows from the use of high-energy light sources to induce detectable fluorescence from submicrogram quantities. Because of this, fluorometry is beginning to replace spectrophotometry, especially as its instrumentation, reported assays, and controls for specificity continue to improve.

The simplest, cheapest, and most reliable instruments for measuring fluorescence in assays of established specificity are the fluorometers, which utilize filters. Among these, the Turner instrument has good sensitivity and reliability. Also available are fluorescence spectrometers, which use diffraction gratings to provide continuous spectra of fluorescence versus wavelength and thus permit a check on specificity.

Radioisotopic quantitation is based on the fact that many chemical elements exist in several isotopic (chemically similar) forms, of which some are unstable and spontaneously disintegrate to another form by emitting radioactive particles. Therefore, compounds "labeled" by incorporation of a radioisotope in place of a stable isotope are chemically normal but can be detected by counting their radioactive emissions in special detectors. In a Geiger-Muller counter, for example, each emission momentarily ionizes a gas, which causes an electric pulse to activate a counter. The more efficient and expensive scintillation detector operates by counting light flashes emitted from a phosphor when it is excited by radioactive emissions.

Several radioactive techniques are of value in assays. A radioactive form of a compound of interest, if available, may be added in very small, known amounts to each biological sample so as to determine recovery by the recovery of radioactivity (radioisotope dilution). Alternatively, the compound of interest in the biological sample may be labeled by chemical coupling to a reactant of known amount of radioactivity, purified, and then quantified on the basis of radioactivity counts. Simultaneous use of both techniques, employing two different radioisotopes (double isotope derivative) has been used to assay compounds for which no other assays are sufficiently sensitive, e.g., aldosterone. By permitting repeated, precise quantitations on the same material subjected to repeated purifications, these methods can also be used as primary standards of specificity.

Radioisotopic quantitation methods reign supreme in determining biochemical rates and patterns of distribution and metabolism for both endogenous compounds and injected drugs. When labeled compounds are administered to an organism, they mix with the unlabeled compounds and undergo the same biochemical reactions. Subsequently, the presence of radioactivity in various compounds purified from biological samples discloses the metabolites into which the original compound has been converted and the gross biological sites where they are found. If the biological samples are taken at timed intervals, determi-

nation of the change in radioactivity indicates the rate of synthesis and metabolism of the compound (Dorfman, 1962, Vol. I, pp. 318–323; Robertson, 1957).

When tissue sections containing a labeled compound are laid against a photographic film, the radioactive emissions expose the adjacent area of film wherever the labeled compound is localized (autoradiography). This reveals a literal picture of both anatomical and subcellular distribution and also the concentration of the labeled compound (Danielli, 1958). As a psychochemical example, Michaels (in Kety and Elkes, 1961, pp. 465–479) has autoradiographically determined the estrogen concentration gradient around estrogen pellets implanted stereotaxically in cats to determine those brain areas which induce sexual behavior in response to hormones.

Information on radioisotopic regulations, practices, and licensing is available from the Atomic Energy Commission or from university administrations. Laboratory techniques are briefly described by Umbreit *et al.* (1957, pp. 121–129) and Cowgill and Pardee (1957, pp. 137–172). However, the psychologist will require formal training before working independently with radioisotopes.

A compound in solution is often quantified by *titration* by measuring the amount of reagent needed to react with all the compound. The reagent is measured by adding it from a burette or from an automatic titrator (Phillips, 1959). In biochemistry, a compound is also frequently quantified by *manometry* by measuring the gas it evolves during a reaction (Umbreit *et al.*, 1957, pp. 1–121). These methods are encountered in enzyme assays, e.g., in an acetylcholinesterase assay in which the acid, liberated when the enzyme splits a choline ester, is titrated with a base.

A *bioassay* is based on a monotonic, preferably linear, relationship between the amount of an administered compound and a response of a biological system to it. Two types of bioassay may be distinguished: one which determines the *potency* of the compound in producing the response and the second which determines the *concentration* of the compound by the magnitude of the induced biological response.

The measurement of biological potency in terms of magnitude of response is the heart of every psychopharmacological experiment, and it is often the basic question underlying psychoendocrinological studies. This measurement requires that several dose levels of the compound be tested. If an adequate dose range is explored, the assay will reveal whether (1) there is a threshold dose below which the response is not elicited, (2) the response magnitude varies linearly with the dose over any range, and (3) there is an upper response limit beyond which no further increase in response occurs with increasing dose. The relative potencies of different compounds may be conveniently determined by appropriate comparisons of the dose-response curve of each with that of a previously established standard compound (Beecher, 1959, pp. 72–91; Humphrey, Long, and Perry 1957).

The measured potency of a compound will generally differ as a function of the biological response used for its determination. The implications of this have been of concern to Miller and Barry (1960) in psychopharmacology and to Aronson (1959, pp. 113–116) in psychoendocrinology. The potency will also vary as a function of transient physiological and other conditions within the organism, even for such endogenously produced compounds as hormones. This means that one cannot be certain of the biological effect, or potency, of a chemically determined concentration of a hormone unless a relevant bioassay is performed simultaneously. This situation is further complicated by the fact that many chemical hormone assays indiscriminately measure appreciable fractions of biologically inactive forms of the hormone. Although these are recognized problems, virtually no research has been done on ways to cope with them. Until these problems are resolved, caution should be exercised in regarding potency and chemical concentrations as equivalent.

The second use of bioassays, to estimate the concentration rather than the potency of a compound, has been extensively developed (Loraine, 1958; Dorfman, 1962, Vol. II). This type of quantification is performed by comparing the dose-response curve of the sample with that of the pure compound being measured. Because they are generally more expensive, as well as less sensitive, precise, and specific than chemical methods, bioassays should be used to measure concentration only when chemical methods are not available, e.g., for polypeptide and protein hormones.

Specific assays in psychochemistry

The hormones of the pituitary gland are of interest in psychoendocrinology as being the most direct hormonal indicators of the duration and magnitude of the control signal from the central nervous system. With certain recent exceptions, plasma measurements of the pituitary hormones are inadequate in terms of specificity or sensitivity, although urinary or pituitary tissue measurements are sometimes possible (Dorfman, 1962, Vol. II; Loraine, 1958).

The thyroid hormones regulate the overall rate of metabolism. Psychologically, intellectual deficits and loss of initiative occur in their absence, and thyroid function appears to change under conditions of stress. The main thyroid hormones found in the blood, *thyroxin* and *triiodothyronine,* are weakly bound to plasma proteins. They are approximately determined in sum with the other thyroid hormones by precipitating (separating) all plasma proteins and measuring the protein-bound iodine (PBI). For more exact work, the protein precipitates should be dissolved and chromatographed, and fractions corresponding to the individual thyroid hormones quantified by iodine content (Dorfman, 1962, Vol. I, pp. 351–385). Commercial units for PBI or iodine measurements are available from supply houses.

The circulating catecholamines, *epinephrine* (E) *and norepinephrine* (NE), have long been associated with sympathetic function. Their role in acute stress, and possibly in drive mechanisms through activation of reticular systems neurones, has been suggested in recent research (Krayer, 1959).

Concentrations of circulating E and NE may now be fluorometrically determined in urine or in plasma. Assays in which E and NE are converted to fluorescent trihydroxy-indoles may be somewhat more specific than those in which fluorescent compounds are produced by condensing E and NE with ethylenediamine (Udenfriend, 1961, pp. 139–157). Removal rates of E and NE and quantitative relationships between E, NE, and their metabolites may be determined by using radioisotopic hormones (Gray and Bacharach, 1961, pp. 515–582).

Endocrinological interpretation of catecholamine concentrations in body fluids is somewhat difficult. The relationship between urinary values of E, NE, and their metabolites and the rates of synthesis of these compounds are still being clarified. The arterial plasma concentration of E, released mainly from the adrenal medulla, represents a relatively simple balance between its production and metabolism. On the other hand, the venous concentration of NE, secreted by adrenergic nerves, varies with the vein from which the blood sample is taken and reflects mainly the functional state of those nerves in the region drained by that vein.

The hormones of the adrenal cortex are released under chronic stress situations and are possibly involved in promoting adaptive behavior under stress. Those secreted in major amounts are mainly cortisol (man, monkey, cat, dog, and guinea pig) or mainly corticosterone (rat and rabbit), or both in about equal amounts (ferret). Aldosterone is secreted in such small amounts that its assay is difficult (Dorfman, 1962, Vol. I, pp. 265–336).

Cortisol and corticosterone may be determined in blood plasma as the total of chemically free and protein-bound hormones, of which the latter fraction may be hormonally inactive. Sensitive and apparently specific fluorometric assays have been proposed for corticosterone (Udenfriend, 1961, pp.

361–366). To date, colorimetric methods have been generally used for determining the *17-hydroxycorticosteroids,* which consist mainly of cortisol (Dorfman, 1962, Vol. I, pp. 231–240). Assays are also available for the hormonally inactive conjugates of cortisol in plasma and urine, although the exact quantitative relationships between these conjugates and secreted cortisol are not known. Finally, removal and sometimes secretion rates of cortisol may be determined by injecting the C^{14}-labeled hormone intravenously and measuring cortisol and plasma radioactivity in subsequent samples taken at timed intervals over about four hours (Dorfman, 1962, Vol. I, pp. 254–256).

The gonadal hormones are of obvious interest in psychochemistry for their effects on both sexual and parental behavior. Of these, the estrogens, mainly estrone, estradiol, and estriol, are each measured in plasma as the total of the chemically free, protein-bound and biologically inactive conjugated forms. Plasma methods are sensitive enough to detect estrogens only in late pregnancy and at parturition, but, in most cases, estrogen conjugates may be detected in urine (Dorfman, 1962, Vol. I, pp. 1–50).

The method of Short for plasma progesterone (Dorfman, 1962, Vol. I, pp. 91–138), if quantified with 0.035-ml microcells in the Beckman model DU spectrophotometer, should permit detection of even the low nonpregnant levels. Radioactive progesterone may also be used to determine metabolic rates and conversion to metabolites (Gray and Bacharach, 1961, pp. 379–437).

Although the androgenic hormones, mainly testosterone, androstenedione, dehydroepiandrosterone, androsterone, and etiocholanolone, have often been measured *in toto* with nonandrogenic compounds as *17-ketosteroids,* it is necessary to purify the various androgens chromatographically to obtain adequately specific data. When this is done, the gonadal androgens, mainly testosterone, are too dilute to measure in peripheral plasma, although it now appears that urinary testosterone may be measured (Camacho and

Migeon, 1963). Since the most potent androgen is testosterone, its measurement even in urine is likely to prove of most psychochemical interest. Androgens of adrenocortical origin, mainly dehydroepiandrosterone, may also be determined in both plasma and urine (Dorfman, 1962, Vol. I, pp. 51–90), and radioisotopes may be used to quantify their secretion rates and metabolic relationships (Vande Wiele, MacDonald, Bolte, and Lieberman, 1962).

To *assay enzymes*, use is made of their highly specific ability to catalyze or increase the rate at which some compound, termed the substrate, undergoes a reaction (Fruton and Simmonds, 1958, pp. 244–283; Long, 1961, pp. 205–218). A sample containing the enzyme is incubated together with the appropriate substrate and other substances necessary to the enzyme activity, and the rate of transformation of the substrate is quantitated chemically, e.g., by titrimetry. Usually the amount of substrate converted per minute, during the initial several minutes of incubation, is determined. A unit of enzyme activity is then defined as that which gives some arbitrarily chosen substrate conversion rate. Activity, not quantity, of enzyme is determined; however, under proper conditions, activity is proportional to concentration. Kabat and Mayer (1961, pp. 619–621) present an excellent short discussion of the principles of estimation of enzyme activity, listing three basic methods and the conditions under which each is valid.

In psychochemistry, enzyme assays of most current interest are those associated with apparent neurotransmitter systems. In particular, acetylcholinesterase has been measured as a factor in cholinergic synaptic transmission, and monoamine oxidase as a factor in serotonin action. The measurement of acetylcholinesterase in neural tissue, to the exclusion of other cholinesterases that do not appear to function physiologically in splitting acetylcholine, requires a careful choice of substrate. This and other factors are detailed by Augustinsson (1957). Monoamine oxidase can be assayed in various ways; Udenfriend,

Weissbach, and Brodie (1958) describe colorimetric and fluorometric assays using serotonin as a substrate. Other specific enzyme assays are referenced by Long (1961), Robins *et al.* (1956) and Lowry (in Colowick and Kaplan, 1957, pp. 366–381).

The value of correlating behavior with drug concentrations in nervous tissue, blood, or urine has been discussed by Nash (in Uhr and Miller, 1960, pp. 128–155), who also remarks on the paucity of assays. The dynamics of the distribution and metabolism of drugs in the organism (Goodman and Gilman, 1955; Sollmann, 1957) parallel hormone dynamics and essentially the same problems apply in limiting the assay to a determination of the active drug forms. Drug levels of urine or plasma relative to those of local brain regions are seldom known. Fluorometric assays have been described for lysergic acid diethylamide (LSD), reserpine, barbiturates, and other drugs (McIlwain and Rodnight, 1962, pp. 276–285; Udenfriend, 1961, pp. 400–440) and for many tranquilizers (Forrest, Forrest, and Mason, 1961).

There are more compounds of past and potential interest in psychochemistry than can possibly be detailed here. We can refer *en bloc* to sources listing references to assays for compounds studied with respect to "metabolic errors" accompanied by mental retardation (McIlwain and Rodnight, 1962, pp. 256–276; Stanbury, 1960) or with respect to psychotic behavior (Fessel, 1962; Kety, 1959). For compounds not specified otherwise, assays sometimes specific enough for research can often be found in texts on physiological or clinical chemistry (Hawk *et al.*, 1954; Natelson, 1961). Since assays for many compounds are continually being improved, the current methodology may best be sought through one of the abstracting journals, such as *Index Medicus* or *Chemical Abstracts*, or through appropriate chapters in the *Annual Review of Biochemistry*. Interpretation of assay measurements always requires knowledge of the biochemical dynamics of the compound, for which the *Biochemists' Handbook* (Long, 1961) is an excellent source.

REFERENCES

ANTONIADES, H. N. (ED.) *Hormones in human plasma.* Boston: Little, Brown, 1960.

ARONSON, L. R. Hormones and reproductive behavior: Some phylogenetic considerations. In A. Gorbman (Ed.), *Comparative endocrinology.* New York: Wiley, 1959. Pp. 98–120.

AUGUSTINSSON, K. Assay methods for cholinesterases. In D. Glick (Ed.), *Methods of biochemical analysis.* Vol. V. New York: Interscience, 1957. Pp. 1–64.

BEECHER, H. K. *Experimentation in man.* Springfield, Ill.: Charles C Thomas, 1959.

BENNETT, C. A., and FRANKLIN, N. L. *Statistical analysis in chemistry and the chemical industry.* New York: Wiley, 1954.

BRIGGS, M. H., and KITTO, G. B. The molecular basis of memory and learning. *Psychol. Rev.,* 1962, **69,** 537–541.

BRODIE, B. B., SULSER, F., and COSTA, E. Psychotherapeutic drugs. *Annu. Rev. Med.,* 1961, **12,** 349–368.

CAMACHO, A. M., and MIGEON, C. J. Isolation, identification, and quantitation of testosterone in the urine of normal adults and in patients with endocrine disorders. *J. clin. Endocrinol. Metab.,* 1963, **23,** 301–305.

CARAWAY, W. T. *Microchemical methods for blood analysis.* Springfield, Ill.: Charles C Thomas, 1960.

CLARK, R., SCHUSTER, C. R., and BRADY, J. V. Instrumental conditioning of jugular self-infusion in the rhesus monkey. *Science,* 1961, **133,** 1829–1830.

COLE, J. O., and GERARD, R. W. (EDS.) *Psychopharmacology: Problems in evaluation.* National Research Council–National Acad. of Sciences, Washington, 1959.

COLOWICK, S. P., and KAPLAN, N. O. *Methods in enzymology.* Vol. IV. *Special techniques.* New York: Academic, 1957.

COWGILL, R. W., and PARDEE, A. B. *Experiments in biochemical research techniques.* New York: Wiley, 1957.

DANIELLI, J. F. (ED.) *General cytochemical methods.* Vol. I. New York: Academic, 1958.

De ROBERTIS, E., SALGANICOFF, L., ZIEHER, L. M., and RODRIGUEZ DE LORES ARNAIZ, G. Acetylcholine and cholinacetylase content of synaptic vesicles. *Science,* 1963, **140,** 300–301.

DEWS, P. B., and MORSE, W. H. Behavioral pharmacology. *Annu. Rev. Pharmacol.,* 1961, **1,** 145–174.

DORFMAN, R. I. *Methods in hormone research.* Vol. I. *Chemical determinations.* Vol. II. *Bioassay.* New York: Academic, 1962.

EIDUSON, S., GELLER, E., YUWILER, A., and

EIDUSON, B. T. *Biochemistry and behavior.* Princeton, N.J.: Van Nostrand, 1964.

ERANKO, O. *Quantitative methods in histology and microscopic histochemistry.* Boston: Little, Brown, 1955.

FESSEL, W. J. Blood proteins in functional psychoses. *Arch. gen. Psychiat.,* 1962, **6,** 132–148.

FIESER, L. F. *Experiments in organic chemistry.* (3rd ed., rev.) Boston: Heath, 1957.

FORREST, F. M., FORREST, I. S., and MASON, A. S. Review of rapid urine tests for phenothiazine and related drugs. *Amer. J. Psychiat.,* 1961, **118,** 300–307.

FRUTON, J. S., and SIMMONDS, S. *General biochemistry.* (2nd ed.) New York: Wiley, 1958.

GAITO, J., and ZAVALA, A. Neurochemistry and learning. *Psychol. Bull.,* 1964, **61,** 45–62.

GLICK, D., and GRUNBAUM, B. W. Microliter absorption cell and its adaptation to the Beckman model DU spectrophotometer. *Anal. Chem.,* 1957, **29,** 1243–1244.

GOODMAN, L. S., and GILMAN, A. *The pharmacological basis of therapeutics.* (2nd ed.) New York: Macmillan, 1955.

GRAY, C. H., and BACHARACH, A. L. (EDS.) *Hormones in blood.* New York: Academic, 1961.

HAWK, P. B., OSER, B. L., and SUMMERSON, W. H. *Practical physiological chemistry.* (13th ed.) New York: McGraw-Hill, 1954.

HEALD, P. J. *Phosphorus metabolism of brain.* New York: Pergamon Press, 1960.

HEATH, R. G., LEACH, B. E., EHRENSVARD, G., and LILJEKVIST, J. A stereotaxic method for precision biopsy of brain tissues in animal and man and techniques for their study. In J. Wortis (Ed.), *Recent advances in biological psychiatry.* Vol. III. New York: Grune & Stratton, 1961. Pp. 210–216.

HEBB, C. Biochemical evidence for neural function of acetylcholine. *Physiol. Rev.,* 1957, **37,** 196–220.

HORWITT, M. Fact and artifact in the biology of schizophrenia. *Science,* 1956, **124,** 429–430.

HUMPHREY, J. H., LONG, D. A., and PERRY, W. L. M. Biological standards in biochemical analysis. In D. Glick (Ed.), *Methods of biochemical analysis.* Vol. V. New York: Interscience, 1957. Pp. 65–106.

HYDEN, H. The neuron. In J. Brachet and A. E. Mirsky (Eds.), *The cell; biochemistry, physiology, morphology, IV specialized cells.* New York: Academic, 1960. Pp. 215–323.

JACKSON, D. D. (ED.) *The etiology of schizophrenia (genetics, physiology, psychology, sociology).* New York: Basic Books, 1960.

JORDAN, E. P. *Modern drug encyclopedia and therapeutic index.* (7th ed.) New York: Drug Publications Inc., 1958.

KABAT, E. A., and MAYER, M. M. *Experimental immunochemistry.* (2nd ed.) Springfield, Ill.: Charles C Thomas, 1961.

KAISER, R. (Translated from the German by P. H. Scott.) *Gas phase chromatography.* Vol. I. *Gas chromatography.* Vol. II. *Capillary chromatography.* Vol. III. *Tables for gas chromatography.* London: Butterworth, 1963.

KETY, S. S. Biochemical theories of schizophrenia. Part I. *Science,* 1959, **129**, 1528–1533. Part II, *ibid.*, 1590–1597.

KETY, S. S., and ELKES, J. (EDS.) *Regional neurochemistry.* New York: Pergamon Press, 1961.

KNIGHTS, E. M., MCDONALD, R. P., and PLOOMPUU, J. *Ultramicromethods for clinical laboratories.* New York: Grune & Stratton, 1957.

KRANTZ, J. C., JR., and CARR, C. J. *The pharmacologic principles of medical practice.* (5th ed.) Baltimore: Williams & Wilkins, 1961.

KRAYER, O. (ED.) Catecholamines. *Pharmacol. Rev.,* 1959, **11**, 241–566.

LONG, C. (ED.) *Biochemists' handbook.* Princeton, N.J.: Van Nostrand, 1961.

LORAINE, J. A. *The clinical application of hormone assay.* Edinburgh: Livingstone, 1958.

MASON, J. W. Restraining chair for the experimental study of primates. *J. appl. Physiol.,* 1958, **12**, 130–133.

MCILWAIN, H. *Biochemistry and the central nervous system.* (2nd ed.) London: J. & A. Churchill, Ltd., 1959.

MCILWAIN, H., and RODNIGHT, R. *Practical neurochemistry.* Boston: Little, Brown, 1962.

MILLER, N. E., and BARRY, H. Motivational effects of drugs: Methods which illustrate some general problems in pharmacology. *Psychopharmacologia,* 1960, **1**, 169–199.

NATELSON, S. *Microtechniques of clinical chemistry.* (2nd ed.) Springfield, Ill.: Charles C Thomas, 1961.

OTIS, L. S., BOSLEY, J. J., and BIRZIS, L. (EDS.) *Animal research in psychopharmacology.* Washington: U.S. Government Printing Office, 1960.

PHILLIPS, J. P. *Automatic titrators.* New York: Academic, 1959.

RANDERATH, K. *Thin-layer chromatography.* New York: Academic, 1963.

ROBERTSON, J. S. Theory and use of tracers in determining transfer rates in biological systems. *Physiol. Rev.,* 1957, **37**, 133–154.

ROBINS, E., SMITH, D. E., EYDT, K. M., and MCCAMAN, R. E. The quantitative histochemistry of the cerebral cortex: III. Analyses at 50 μ intervals compared with analyses by archi-tectonic layers in the motor and visual cortices. *J. Neurochem.,* 1956, **1**, 77–83.

ROSENZWEIG, M. R., KRECH, D., and BENNETT, E. L. A search for relations between brain chemistry and behavior. *Psychol. Bull.,* 1960, **57**, 476–492.

ROSS, S., and COLE, J. Psychopharmacology. *Annu. Rev. Psychol.,* 1960, **11**, 415–438.

SMITH, I. (ED.) *Chromatographic techniques: Clinical and biochemical application.* London: Heinemann, 1958.

SOLLMANN, T. *A manual of pharmacology and its applications to therapeutics and toxicology.* Philadelphia: Saunders, 1957.

STANBURY, J. B., WYNGAARDEN, J. B., and FREDRICKSON, D. S. (EDS.) *The metabolic basis of inherited disease.* New York: McGraw-Hill, 1960.

STECHER, P. G., FINEL, M. J., SIEGMUND, O. H., and SZAFRANSKI, B. M. (EDS.) *The Merck index of chemicals and drugs.* (7th ed.) Merck and Co., 1960.

TOWER, D. B. Chemical architecture of the central nervous system. In J. Field, H. W. Magoun, and V. E. Hall (Eds.), *Handbook of physiology.* Section I. Vol. III. Baltimore: Williams & Wilkins, 1960. Pp. 1793–1815.

TURNER, C. D. *General endocrinology.* (3rd ed.) Philadelphia: Saunders, 1960.

UDENFRIEND, S. *Fluorescence assay in biology and medicine.* New York: Academic, 1961.

UDENFRIEND, S., WEISSBACH, H., and BRODIE, B. B. Assay of serotonin and related metabolites, enzymes, and drugs. In D. Glick (Ed.), *Methods of biochemical analysis.* Vol. VI. New York: Interscience, 1958. Pp. 95–130.

UHR, L., and MILLER, J. G. *Drugs and behavior.* New York: Wiley, 1960.

UMBREIT, W. W., BURRIS, R. H., and STAUFFER, J. F. *Manometric techniques.* (3rd ed.) Minneapolis: Burgess, 1957.

VANDE WIELE, R. L., MACDONALD, P. C., BOLTE, E., and LIEBERMAN, S. Precursors of the urinary 11-desoxy-17-ketosteroids: Estimation of the secretory rate of dehydroisoandrosterone. *J. clin. Endocrinol. Metab.,* 1962, **22**, 1207–1221.

VERNEY, E. B. The antidiuretic hormone and the factors which determine its release. *Proc. Roy. Soc., London,* 1947, **135**, 25–106.

WEEKS, J. R. Experimental morphine addiction: Method for automatic intravenous injections in unrestrained rats. *Science,* 1962, **138**, 143–144.

WILLARD, H. H., MERRITT, L. L., JR., and DEAN, J. A. *Instrumental methods of analysis.* (3rd ed.) Princeton, N.J.: Van Nostrand, 1958.

WOOLEY, D. E. *The biochemical bases of psychoses.* New York: Wiley, 1962.

Part Three

SENSATION
AND PERCEPTION

In recent years the theory of signal detectability (TSD) has led a number of psychologists to question the utility of much of the classical psychophysical data and to reject the traditional threshold concept. The first chapter in this part (Chap. 5, Psychophysics and Signal Detection by Egan and Clarke) critically evaluates the notion of thresholds and outlines basic TSD. More detailed applications may be found elsewhere. Swets (1964), for example, presents a collection of 35 articles covering TSD in speech communication, audition, physiology, vision, and vigilance. Norman (1964) describes a method for evaluating signal-detection data that requires very limited theoretical considerations, and Pollack and Norman (1964) present a nonparametric technique. Atkinson (1963) defines a variable sensitivity TSD that postulates separate but interdependent activation and decision processes. This theory differs from basic TSD in assuming a trial-to-trial change in the decision process as information accumulates and in postulating an activation process that defines a subject's level of sensitivity to external stimuli. Luce (1963), on the other hand, presents a simple sensory threshold model that appears to account for some types of response data as well as does the continuous TSD. Another approach is exemplified by the work of McGill (1965, 1967) which appears to have two principal objectives: (1) to analyze the basic data of human auditory and visual intensity discrimination as possible manifestations of the flux of information in sensory channels; and (2) to devise effective ways, via the principles of stochastic processes and detection theory, for linking threshold responses to their latencies. Comprehension of the statistical properties of information flow, as well as the discrimination laws characterizing such phenomena, has been accelerating, and it seems increasingly clear that limitations on discrimination traceable to the flux of events in sensory channels represent an area of potential significance.

Examples of traditional threshold methodology are presented in Chap. 6, Audition. Hirsh discusses the instrumentation and methodology necessary for determining absolute thresholds for pure tones, difference limens for frequency, lateralization of sound in the head, temporary threshold shift following noise exposure, and intelligibility of speech in noise. It is assumed that these basic techniques will provide the novice with sufficient background to advance to the more detailed procedures. Reviews and extensive bibliographies of auditory research may be found in Elliot (1964) and Thurlow (1965). Methods for the study of background masking are reported by Raab (1963); Scharf (1961) covers complex sounds and critical bands. Refer to Coleman (1963) for an analysis of techniques for studying monaural and binaural cues to auditory depth perception and to Yates (1963) for a discussion of methodological problems in delayed auditory feedback. The consistency of auditory detection judgments is analyzed by Green (1964).

Boynton's chapter on vision (Chap. 7) introduces the reader to research methodology by covering the variables and techniques of a simple experiment in dark adaptation. This general introduction is followed by more technical discus-

sions of light, colorimetry, and the principles of ocular stimulation. Subsequent information describes methods of delivering light to the eye, the advantages and disadvantages of various light sources, techniques for controlling and mixing light, the control of wavelength and time variables, measurement of basic variables, and general apparatus considerations such as Maxwellian views and the mounting of optical components.

Chapter 8, the last in this part, considers methodology in perception and recognition. Hake and Rodwan critically evaluate the role of classical psychophysics in perception and point out important implications of TSD for this type of research. General classification procedures are described for metric and nonmetric cases, and illustrative experiments are presented utilizing linear discriminant functions and uncertainty-analysis procedures. A discussion of scaling methods covers subjective space and distance models, Euclidian and non-Euclidian space, "similarity" as a judgment, and factor analysis. Information on the measurement of perceptual recognition precedes a section on procedures for inducing and controlling familiarity with stimuli. The chapter concludes with a discussion of laboratory materials and apparatus.

Consult Chap. 3, Physiological Psychology, for techniques applicable to the measurement of electrophysiological activity in the retina and optic nerve and for the instrumentation required for recording eye movements. The same chapter covers the means for measuring electrical responses in the inner ear and cochlea, as well as the methodology necessary for psychophysiological studies of other senses. Further discussions of the physiological and psychological bases of vision and visual perception may be found in Graham (1965).

Chapter 5

PSYCHOPHYSICS AND SIGNAL DETECTION

JAMES P. EGAN *and* FRANK R. CLARKE

The psychophysical analysis of the properties of sensory systems has rested to a considerable degree upon the measurement of absolute and differential thresholds. In this sense, the topic of signal detection has a long history within psychology, and the classical psychophysical methods deal largely with the estimation of various types of threshold (Guilford, 1954; Postman and Egan, 1949; Woodworth and Schlosberg, 1954). However, it should be realized at the outset that the notion of a threshold is used in two quite distinct ways in the literature on sensory psychology. Within the context of a particular experiment, the threshold is given an operational definition; for example, the threshold may be defined as that intensity of the stimulus to which the observer responds with "Yes, I detect it" on 50 percent of the stimulus presentations. Given such factors as the instructions, the nature of a trial, and the population of observers sampled, such a definition has a clear meaning. It is equally clear that the stimulus inten-

The preparation of this chapter was supported in part by an Air Force Contract, No. AF 19(628)-266, monitored by the Operational Applications Laboratory, Laurence G. Hanscom Field, Bedford, Massachusetts, and submitted as Rep. No. ESD-TDR-62-305.

sity so defined within a particular experiment is a property of the observer. A second meaning of the threshold is usually introduced into the discussion of the results of such psychophysical measurements. The measure of the threshold becomes an inferred property of the sensory system, and most investigators have taken their measures of the threshold as equivalent to the threshold of the afferent channel. The recent developments in the psychophysics of signal detection seriously call into question the justification for the inferences made about sensory function on the basis of the measurement of thresholds, especially when these measurements are secured by certain psychophysical methods. The following introductory remarks elaborate upon this criticism of classical procedures for the measurement of thresholds.

It has been known from the earliest beginnings of psychophysics that a "simple threshold model" is much too simple to account for the most basic phenomena of signal detection. When the method of limits is used, it is always found that the "threshold" varies from trial to trial; when the method of constant stimuli is used, it is always found that a given stimulus does not result in a uniform response of "Yes, I detect it" or "No, I do not detect it." The notion of a variable threshold was introduced early to account for these results. There was the additional fact that a given stimulus was "more detectable" on some trials than on others, and observers would state that they were more confident of some of their positive ("yes") responses than of others. For this reason, it seemed necessary to train the observers, and the trained observer was one who could maintain a constant criterion for a response of "Yes, I detect it." Therefore, it has become rather generally recognized that the numerical value of a threshold, as typically measured by the classical methods, must be interpreted in terms of the criterion that results from the training sessions and from the particular instructions given to the observer. The classical methods for the determination of an absolute threshold provide an estimate that is usually contaminated by nonsensory factors. Although the numerical value of such a threshold is a property of the observer, this numerical value cannot be taken as a property of the sensory system whose threshold it is desired to measure.

The scope of the present chapter is confined to those recently developed methods which make it possible to estimate independently both the sensory capacity for the detection of a signal and the response criterion of the observer. These newer methods grew up under the influence of the theory of signal detectability (TSD), which was developed primarily by engineers and by mathematicians to provide a rational basis for the design of receivers and for making decisions in the face of the uncertainty involved when a weak signal is to be detected in the presence of noise. TSD incorporates the concept of an *ideal observer* in its approach to signal detection. For the present, we may think of an ideal observer as one who utilizes all information available to him in the "best" possible way. Clearly, the ideal observer in TSD is confronted with much the same problem as that faced by the real observer in the psychophysical experiment; and, as will be seen, some of the con-

cepts and methods developed in TSD provide a more satisfactory framework for the psychophysical analysis of detection than the classical procedures (Egan, Schulman, and Greenburg, 1959; Licklider, 1959; Swets, Tanner, and Birdsall, 1961; Tanner, Birdsall, and Clarke, 1960; Tanner and Swets, 1954).

TSD incorporates into a single model many disparate factors that affect the detection and recognition of signals. This theory emphasizes that the decision of an observer may depend upon (1) the informational content of the stimulus, (2) the information available to the observer before the presentation of the stimulus, (3) the properties of the sensory analyzer, and (4) motivational variables as they relate to the consequences of each decision. TSD stipulates procedures by which the data should be obtained in an experiment on signal detection; the theory then provides the process by which the data should be analyzed to obtain a measure of the capacity for discrimination.

Those aspects of TSD which are most relevant to psychophysics will be developed in terms of the *fundamental detection problem*. The concepts will be presented in the concrete experimental setting of auditory detection. Of course, TSD has applicability to other sensory modalities, and we shall discuss this point in a later section.

THE FUNDAMENTAL DETECTION PROBLEM

For each observation by the listener, a single temporal interval is well defined, and this single observation interval constitutes a trial. These observation intervals, or trials, consist of two types: (1) those which contain the signal plus noise (*SN* trial) and (2) those which contain noise alone (*N* trial). After each interval, the listener responds with "yes" or "no." Thus, the *single-interval experiment* is one in which (1) the listener knows that a signal, if presented, will occur in a well-delimited interval of time and (2) a decision is required after each observation as to whether or not the signal was in fact presented.

Because the signal is embedded in noise, the physical stimulus, or *input to the receiver*, fluctuates at random from trial to trial, and this variability in the input occurs for intervals that contain the signal as well as for those which contain noise alone. Therefore, when a listener tries to detect a weak signal in the presence of a continuous noise, he must decide whether his momentary input arose from the signal added to a sample of noise or from a sample of noise alone. Furthermore, in the situations of our present interest, any given stimulus, or input, may arise either from signal plus noise or from noise alone. Consequently, if the listener desires to detect some of the signals, he runs a definite risk that he will falsely respond "yes" to some of the observation intervals containing only noise. Of course, almost all inputs carry some information regarding the presence or absence of the signal, because the probability of receiving a given input is different when it arises from signal plus noise than when it arises from noise alone.

The variations in the input from trial to trial produce corresponding variations in their sensory effects, and as a result the listener is uncertain as to the event that gave rise to a particular sensory effect. To perform well, the listener must classify the various inputs into two categories according to some set of criteria. Those inputs which fall in the category of acceptance lead to the affirmative response "Yes, the signal was present." Such inputs are said to be in the listener's *criterion;* the other inputs are outside his criterion. In the present type of analysis, the classification of a given input into one of two categories by the listener depends upon the following factors: (1) the likelihood that this given input would arise from an *SN* trial relative to the likelihood that it would arise from an *N* trial; (2) the a priori probability of an *SN* trial; and (3) the consequences, such as reward or punishment, of the decision.

Before we proceed to the examination of the basic concepts in TSD, let us define a few more terms. Suppose that a listener has made a binary decision ("yes," *y*, or "no," *n*) after each of a long series of trials. There will be four conjunctions: *SN-y, SN-n, N-y,* and *N-n*. These four conjunctions have the following names. The conjunction *SN-y* is called a *hit*, and its complement *SN-n*, is a *miss*. The conjunction *N-y* is termed a *false alarm*, and its complement *N-n* is a *correct rejection*. Of course, the data may be simply displayed in a 2×2 matrix, as shown in Table 5-1. The entries f_i in the table are the raw data, and they constitute the frequencies with which each conjunction occurs. The data may be cast in more usable form by forming proportions, which are then taken as estimates of probabilities; for convenience in exposition, these proportions will be referred to as probabilities. When the four entries are expressed as conditional probabilities, only two of them are formally independent, and the two that have been selected for descriptive purposes are the *hit rate* (HR) and the *false-alarm rate* (FAR). The hit rate is the probability $p(y|SN)$ that the observer will respond with "yes" given an *SN* trial, and it is estimated by the proportion $f_1/(f_1 + f_2)$. The false-alarm rate is the probability $p(y|N)$ that the observer will respond with "yes" given an *N* trial, and it is estimated by $f_3/(f_3 + f_4)$.

Of course, if the signal is large relative to the noise, the listener can make his hit rate $p(y|SN)$ nearly 1.0 without allowing his false-alarm rate $p(y|N)$ to become very large. On the other hand, for a weak signal, the listener can again make $p(y|SN)$ nearly 1.0,

Table 5-1   The form in which the raw data from the single-interval experiment may be displayed.

	y	n	
SN	f_1	f_2	$p(y|SN) \doteq f_1/(f_1 + f_2)$
N	f_3	f_4	$p(y|N) \doteq f_3/(f_3 + f_4)$

but to do so he must allow $p(y|N)$ to become large. Clearly, the numerical value of $p(y|SN)$, taken by itself, does not specify how easy or how hard it is for the listener to detect the signal. However, if a sufficient number of noise-alone trials are included, the value of $p(y|N)$, as well as $p(y|SN)$, may be estimated. If the numerical value of $p(y|N)$ is the same for both the weak and the strong signal, the respective values of $p(y|SN)$ will indicate the relative degree of detectability of the two signals. It will be our task to develop a measure of detectability along these lines by using both the HR and the FAR. In this analysis, the detection task is treated as a decision process, and a method is developed by which the listener's criterion for the presence of the signal may be dealt with in an effective manner. This method provides an analysis of the listener's responses such that the measure of his ability to detect a signal will be largely independent of the particular criterion he happens to adopt. Unlike classical methods, this analysis avoids confounding variables that affect the observer's ability to detect signals with variables that affect his criterion for responding that he "heard" a signal. Both classes of variable may then be studied independently or in conjunction.[1]

The above description applies to experiments conducted in the "quiet" as well as those in which noise is deliberately added by the experimenter. It is physically impossible to have a noise-free situation. Aside from irreducible noise in the equipment, Brownian movement, etc., an important source of noise is that associated with physiological processes such as breathing and circulation. Thus, no matter how "quiet" an environment may appear to a listener, noise is always present.

Therefore, in a very real sense, an absolute threshold is a masked threshold.

For a better understanding of the fundamental detection problem, we must now examine TSD in more detail. As has been customary, the exposition of TSD will involve the examination of two areas of knowledge: (1) decision theory (with emphasis upon the concepts of likelihood ratio, decision rules, and the criterion) and (2) signal analysis (with emphasis upon the sampling theorem and the statistical characteristics of noise).

DECISION THEORY

The theory of signal detectability uses a few fundamental concepts of decision theory. These concepts are *likelihood ratio, decision rule,* and *criterion.* Let us develop these conceptions in terms of a series of simple examples. (For further discussion, see Bross, 1953.)

For the following three examples, let us retain the same definition of a trial as that used in the single-interval experiment. On each trial, or during each observation interval, there occurs one of two environmental events, A or B. We could think of these two mutually exclusive events A and B as corresponding to SN and N in our discussion above, but for the purposes at hand A and B are simply two physical events easily distinguished by the experimenter. In all examples, only one event occurs on any given trial, and it does so with a fixed a priori probability. The event A or B is not presented directly to the receiver (observer) but is represented to him by a stimulus S_i. The task set for the receiver is to decide on the basis of the stimulus which of the two events, A or B, occurred. Thus, the decision required of the receiver does not concern the

[1] For this introduction to the application of TSD to psychophysics, we have made the simplifying assumption that sequential effects are negligible. The general approach to signal detection adopted in this chapter has applicability regardless of the existence or the nonexistence of sequential effects. Actually, the assumption that the practiced human observer closely resembles a Bernoulli observer is a good approximation for a broad class

of psychophysical experiments. Of course, when sequential effects are marked, the analysis of the data must take account of these effects; the methods presented in this chapter for the analysis of data cannot be applied in cookbook fashion. However, the general principles may be utilized to develop methods appropriate to situations in which sequential effects are considerable.

stimulus but does concern the event that gave rise to it. Furthermore, a judgment by the receiver is not necessary regarding any of the characteristics of the event; the response is simply a decision based upon the evidence provided by the stimulus as to which of the two events happened.

It might be mentioned that the distinction made here between the event, which is the object of the decision, and the stimulus, which carries the evidence about the event, has been made by many psychologists. The consequences of a decision, or act, usually are more closely correlated with environmental objects and events than with the stimuli that arise from these objects and events.

In our first example, let us assume that both events are represented to the receiver by the same stimulus S_1. The stimulus S_1 occurs on every trial irrespective of which event gives rise to it. Therefore, S_1 does not transmit any information regarding which of the two events occurred. In this case, the decision task is called a simple game of chance, or *a priori game*.

If the receiver knows the a priori probabilities $p(A)$ and $p(B)$ in the above simple game of chance, he can maximize his percentage of correct decisions by always guessing that the event which occurred is the one having the larger a priori probability. Such a rule for a decision is called a *decision rule*. In the present example, the decision rule may be stated in terms of the ratio of the two a priori probabilities, $p(A)/p(B)$, and this ratio gives the odds in favor of event A. The rule would be as follows: "If $p(A)/p(B) > 1$, always say event A occurred. If $p(A)/p(B) < 1$, always say event B occurred. If the ratio is equal to 1, then either say event A occurred or say event B occurred." Of course, a rule that leads to the maximization of the percentage of correct decisions is but one of many possible decision rules.

As a second example, let it be assumed that each of the events A and B may give rise to one or the other of two stimuli, S_1 or S_2. Thus, each event may give rise to the same stimulus,

but, in general, the probability that a given stimulus arose from A is different from the probability that it arose from B. Of course, the receiver does not know which event gave rise to a particular stimulus, but for simplicity we shall assume that he has complete information regarding the a priori probabilities $p(A)$ and $p(B)$ and complete information regarding the probabilities $p(S_i|A)$ and $p(S_i|B)$ that associate each stimulus with each of the two events. In this second example, we have an *a posteriori game* of chance, and the reception of S_1 or S_2 by the receiver makes it possible for him to improve his proportion of correct decisions or to increase his expected earnings, as compared with the simple game of chance. For instance, if S_1 is received, he may compute the odds in favor of event A by the following ratio:

$$\frac{p(A|S_1)}{p(B|S_1)} = \frac{p(A)}{p(B)} \cdot \frac{p(S_1|A)}{p(S_1|B)} \tag{5-1}$$

In the above expression, the left-hand term is the ratio of the a posteriori probabilities. This ratio gives the odds in favor of event A, after having received the information carried by S_1. The right-hand term shows explicitly the two types of information that enter into the calculation of these odds. (1) The ratio of the a priori probabilities, $p(A)/p(B)$, which was used in the simple game of chance, summarizes the receiver's knowledge of the situation before the evidence S_1 was received. (2) The other ratio, $p(S_1|A)/p(S_1|B)$, expresses the likelihood of obtaining the evidence S_1 from the event A relative to the likelihood of obtaining the same evidence from the event B. This ratio is called the *likelihood ratio* $l_A(S_1)$. Thus, Eq. (5-1) gives an explicit expression of the manner in which information available before the observation is combined with information carried by the observation in order to arrive at a statement of the information state following the observation.

It may help in the understanding of an a posteriori game to assign some numerical values to the various probabilities. Suppose that the behavior of the receiver is evaluated in terms of his percentage of correct decisions. For optimum behavior, the receiver tries to maximize this quantity. Let $p(A) = 0.25$, so that the odds are $3:1$ in favor of event B before the evidence from the stimulus is received. First, consider the situation when S_1 is received so that Eq. (5-1) applies directly without a change of subscripts. If the ratio of a posteriori probabilities, $p(A|S_1)/p(B|S_1)$, is greater than 1.0, the receiver should respond with "Event A occurred." Otherwise, he should respond with "Event B." Since the ratio of a priori probabilities is $1:3$, we see from Eq. (5-1) that the likelihood ratio $p(S_1|A)/p(S_1|B)$ must be greater than 3.0 in order that the product of these two ratios will be greater than 1.0. Thus, we see that if the a priori probabilities are known for the two events A and B, the decision rule may be stated in terms of a likelihood ratio. Consequently, it is said that the decision rule is based upon a *likelihood-ratio criterion*. Of course, if the likelihood ratio is less than 3.0, the receiver responds with "Event B." The above analysis was based upon the reception of S_1; when S_2 is received, the same decision rule may be used as for S_1, provided Eq. (5-1) is always used to compute the "odds in favor of event A." Thus, the likelihood-ratio criterion is the same for the various stimuli, and in this example only one decision rule is necessary. To complete the numerical example, let $p(S_1|A) = 0.9$ and $p(S_1|B) = 0.2$. Then $p(S_1|A)/p(S_1|B) = l_A(S_1) = 4.5$, and whenever the evidence S_1 is received, the receiver should respond with "Event A occurred." Because $l_A(S_2) = 0.1/0.8 = 0.125$, the receiver should respond with "Event B occurred" whenever the evidence S_2 is received. If the receiver uses the appropriate decision rules, the probability of a correct decision will be

$$p(C) = p(S_1|A)p(A) + p(S_2|B)p(B)$$
$$= 0.825 \qquad (5\text{-}2)$$

It may be noted that the first example (the a priori game) is a special case of the present example (the a posteriori game). In the first example, the likelihood ratio $p(S_1|A)/p(S_1|B)$ is 1.0, so that the a posteriori information is identical to the a priori information.

The decision rule is formulated in terms of a likelihood-ratio criterion and not in terms of the a priori probabilities, simply because in most situations the receiver has freedom of choice among various values of likelihood ratio, whereas he has no direct control over the a priori probabilities.

It was tacitly assumed in the above situation that the conditional probabilities that associate the two stimuli with the two events were independent of the a priori probabilities of those events. This assumption was made because, in the context of signal detection, the experimenter can determine arbitrarily whether or not a signal will be presented on a given trial, but, in doing so, he does not affect the distribution of probabilities that associate the various stimuli with a particular event. This is to say that the relative frequencies of occurrence of the various stimuli are properties of the particular event; therefore these relative frequencies are characteristic of that event. A consequence of this assumption is that the likelihood ratio associated with a given stimulus is independent of the a priori probability of the event that gave rise to that stimulus.

Before we proceed further, we must emphasize that a decision procedure based on the numerical value of likelihood ratio achieves optimum performance for an important class of specific objectives. In the above example, optimum behavior was specified in terms of maximizing the percentage of correct decisions. External considerations might require that some other quantity be maximized. For example, if values and costs are associated, respectively, with the two ways of being correct and the two ways of being incorrect, the decision rule may require that the expected value of decisions be maximized. Other criteria that suggest themselves include the following: the maximization of the number of correct decisions for one of the decision alternatives

Table 5-2   The probability of receiving each of five stimuli, given event A or B.[1]

Stimulus	s_1	s_2	$p(S_i|A)$	$p(S_i|B)$	$l_A(S_i)$
S_1	1	3	0.28	0.04	7.00
S_2	6	7	0.16	0.32	0.50
S_3	5	2	0.20	0.16	1.25
S_4	8	8	0.06	0.33	0.18
S_5	2	3	0.30	0.15	2.00
		Total	1.00	1.00	

[1] Each entry in the last column shows the ratio of the two conditional probabilities in the corresponding row, and each of these numbers represents a likelihood ratio.

when the error rate on the other alternative is held at some constant value (the Neyman-Pearson criterion), the maximization of information transmitted, and the maximization of the probability of survival. We have already seen that when estimates of a posteriori probabilities are required, they may be obtained by an appropriate combination of likelihood ratio and a priori probabilities. In all these cases, as well as others, it can be shown that the appropriate decision rule is based upon the numerical value of likelihood ratio.

Let us note that the degree of discriminability between the two events A and B is determined by the magnitudes of the likelihood ratios and not at all by the a priori probability of the two events. Thus, in the first example, there was only one likelihood ratio, and it was unity; therefore, the two events could not be discriminated by the receiver. In the second example, the stimuli did carry information to the receiver, and the magnitudes of the likelihood ratios could be used to define a measure of how well the receiver could tell event A from event B. When many stimuli arise from each event, a larger set of likelihood ratios is required to characterize the degree of discriminability of the stimuli. It will be our task in the third example to show how the information regarding such a set of likelihood ratios may be summarized. This final example is basically similar to the preceding

one; it is made more complex so that a few additional conceptions may be developed. (This example is adapted from one discussed by Green, 1960*b*.)

Consider again that one of two mutually exclusive events, A or B, occurs on a given trial. This time, however, there are five stimuli, each of which may arise from either A or B. Of course, only one event and only one stimulus occur on a single trial. Thus, event A has a certain probability of giving rise to each of the five stimuli, and these five discrete probabilities sum to 1.0. Similarly, the five possible stimuli have conditional probabilities that associate them with event B.

In this example, we shall consider that the five stimuli vary along two independent dimensions, so that two numbers are required to specify each stimulus. For example, the five stimuli might be sinusoids, which vary in both frequency and amplitude. It may help to be concrete, so, in this example, numerical values will be assigned to the stimuli and to the probabilities.

Table 5-2 displays the hypothetical values for the stimuli and the conditional probabilities. Column 1 shows the stimuli, the next two columns give the two numbers that specify each stimulus, and the next two columns give the probabilities with which each stimulus is associated with each event. The last column is the ratio of the two probabilities in the corresponding row, and each number represents a likelihood ratio.

We have said that the receiver should adopt a likelihood-ratio criterion to achieve best performance with respect to any one of a number of different objectives. The conditional probabilities in Table 5-2 that associate the various stimuli with each event may also be thought of as the probabilities that associate the corresponding values of likelihood ratio with the two events. Table 5-2 may therefore be reconstructed so that the stimuli are ordered with respect to the magnitude of the likelihood ratio associated with them. This has been done in Table 5-3. There it can be seen that the two columns representing the

Table 5-3   The probability, given event A or B, that $l_A(S)$ will have the indicated value.

Stimulus	$l_A(S)$	$p[l_A(S)|A]$	Cumulative	$p[l_A(S)|B]$	Cumulative
S_1	7.00	0.28	0.28	0.04	0.04
S_5	2.00	0.30	0.58	0.15	0.19
S_3	1.25	0.20	0.78	0.16	0.35
S_2	0.50	0.16	0.94	0.32	0.67
S_4	0.18	0.06	1.00	0.33	1.00

conditional probabilities of Table 5-2 have simply been relabeled. Thus, the first entry of column 3, namely, 0.28, is the probability of obtaining the stimulus S_1, given that event A has occurred. However, this entry is also the probability of obtaining the corresponding value of likelihood ratio, 7.00, again conditional upon the occurrence of event A. The first entry in column 5, namely, 0.04, is the probability of obtaining this same likelihood ratio of 7.00, given that event B has occurred. Let us now see why the cumulative columns in Table 5-3 are necessary.

When it is said that the receiver adopts a likelihood-ratio criterion, this means that he responds one way when the likelihood ratio is greater than some critical value and he gives the complementary response when the likelihood ratio is less than that value. Of course, it is a matter of indifference how he responds when the likelihood ratio is equal to the critical value.[1] For example, if the receiver for some reason adopts a likelihood-ratio criterion of 1.2, or greater, for the response "event A," he should give this response whenever S_1, S_5, or S_3 is received. Therefore, the probability that he will respond with "event A" given that event A occurred is the sum $(0.28 + 0.30 + 0.20)$, which is the value 0.78

given in the cumulative column opposite the entry S_3. The corresponding cumulative probability given that event B occurred is 0.35. Each pair of cumulative probabilities in Table 5-3 could be used to construct a separate 2×2 matrix (Table 5-1), and the particular matrix that describes the receiver's performance depends upon the likelihood-ratio criterion he adopts.

The cumulative probabilities shown in Table 5-3 characterize the difficulty of the task as set by the environmental conditions. These two sets of cumulative probabilities are so important that they are usually displayed graphically, and the resulting function is called a *receiver operating characteristic*, or ROC. Figure 5-1 shows the ROC for Table 5-3. The coordinates of the points on the curve come from the cumulative probabilities in the table. The ROC has many interesting and important properties, and several of these deserve explicit discussion.

Note first that the slope of the ROC between two points equals the likelihood ratio associated with the higher point. This is so because the differences in the coordinates of the two points are, respectively, the two conditional probabilities that form the likelihood ratio corresponding to the higher point. Consequently, the slope of the curve for "best" performance must be monotonically decreasing. Otherwise, the receiver would be responding with "event A" when the likelihood ratio equals a particular value but responding with "event B" when the likelihood ratio is some greater value.

If the receiver does not give the response appropriate for the likelihood ratio received, the point that describes his performance will lie below the ROC. If the receiver ignores the stimuli and guesses, the point describing his behavior will fall on the diagonal running

---

[1] For ease of exposition, the word "criterion" is used by some writers to refer to two distinct concepts. Consider that the receiver must make one of two responses, A or B, to each stimulus. Then all stimuli in a particular situation form a set. Those stimuli in the subset which lead to the response A are said to be *in the criterion*.

If the stimuli may be represented by a single number, such as a likelihood ratio, the *criterion* is the subset of numbers each of which *exceeds* a critical value. This critical value is frequently referred to as the *cutoff*. The cutoff is the threshold, or dividing point, between the numbers that are in the criterion and those that are not.

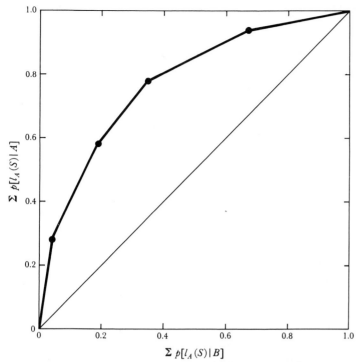

Fig. 5-1   The receiver operating characteristic, or ROC, for the third example. The coordinates of the points on the curve come from the cumulative probabilities in Table 5-3.

from the origin to the upper right-hand corner. This diagonal is called the *chance line*. Of course, his worst possible performance results when he responds with the complement of the response that he should give according to a likelihood-ratio criterion.

Another fundamental property of any particular ROC is the degree to which it differs from the line-of-chance performance. If likelihood ratios that differ markedly from unity are also very likely, the two events *A* and *B* are easily discriminated by the receiver; in such a case, the ROC will leave the origin with a steep slope, and it will deviate considerably from the chance line. On the other hand, if the likelihood ratios that are nearly 1 are very likely, the ROC must lie close to the chance line. Because ROC curves may have many shapes, no single number can satisfactorily characterize this property of the degree of discriminability of the events.

However, as we shall see in a later section, many ROC curves have much the same shape for an important class of situations in signal detection. For these situations, there are good reasons for defining a single measure of how much an ROC deviates from chance performance.

Another point is concerned with the dimensions used in the third example to characterize each stimulus. The numerical values taken by these two dimensions s_1 and s_2 make it possible for the receiver to discriminate among the various stimuli $S_1, \ldots, S_5$. However, after the receiver identifies the stimulus, the numerical values of s_1 and s_2 are no longer relevant in the decision process. Once a stimulus has been identified, the associated likelihood ratio determines the response. Obviously, the stimulus may have many dimensions, and the identification of that stimulus may depend upon that fact. Nevertheless, with only two events *A* and *B*, all the stimuli may be mapped from a multidimensional space down to a single *decision axis,* regardless of the dimensionality of the stimuli. This decision axis represents the dimensionless set of numbers, the ordered set of likelihood ratios. If there are more than two events, and therefore more than two hypotheses, the maximum number of decision axes required is $(m — 1)$, where *m* is the number of alternative hypotheses.

The final point to be made here is related to the use of the actual numerical values of the likelihood ratios in the decision process. The ordinate of a given point on the ROC represents the probability of obtaining a likelihood ratio equal to or greater than some critical value, given that event *A* occurred. The abscissa of the same point represents the corresponding probability given that event *B* occurred. Furthermore, any monotonic transformation of the ordered set of likelihood ratios preserves the order of these likelihood ratios. Consequently, the ROC will not be affected by a monotonic transformation of the set of likelihood ratios. Of course, in order to make equivalent decisions with the transformed decision axis, the monotonic transformation must be applied to the likelihood-ratio cutoff as well as to the original decision axis. For example, if we take the logarithm of the likelihood ratios shown in column 2 of Table 5-3 but leave the corresponding conditional probabilities the same, any decision made on the basis of the value of likelihood ratio may also be made equivalently on the basis of the logarithm of the likelihood ratio. Thus, if the cutoff is 1.2, the same behavior will result if the receiver responds with "event *A*" whenever the logarithm of the obtained likelihood ratio equals or exceeds log 1.2.

It was assumed throughout the above examples that the stimuli were perfectly discriminable by the receiver. The source of uncertainty in the receiver's response was completely assigned to the uncertainty with which

any given stimulus represented one or the other of the two events. The limitation on performance was imposed entirely by the structure of the environment, and the analysis showed how well an ideal observer could perform.[1] Of course, the stimuli will usually not be perfectly discriminable for the real observer. Consequently, the real observer introduces additional uncertainty into the overall process, and his performance will fall short of that of the ideal. The analysis that shows the performance of the ideal observer makes it possible to determine in a quantitative way the efficiency of the real observer. Clearly, less than perfect performance on the part of a real observer may in fact be very good indeed if it approaches that achieved by an ideal observer.

We are now in a position to apply the concepts developed above to the more realistic situations encountered when a signal is to be detected in the presence of noise. We shall continue our discussion in terms of the single-interval experiment, and the two types of trial *SN* and *N* will replace the two events *A* and *B*. The stimuli that represent the two events *SN* and *N* will be continuous waveforms, and we shall be concerned in the next section with the sampling theorem in signal analysis and with the statistical properties of noise.

THEORY OF SIGNAL DETECTABILITY

The theory of signal detectability developed largely around the analysis of the waveforms of signals and of noise. Thus, in the single-interval experiment, the stimulus presented to the receiver is a waveform that occurs during the observation interval. Consequently, the waveform, which is relevant to the decision as to whether or not the signal occurred, extends from the beginning of the observation interval to its end, that is, from zero to *T*. This waveform is a sample of noise to which a signal may or may not be added. The wave-

---

[1] The theory of signal detectability is so called because the emphasis is upon the inherent *detectability* of a signal in noise. When the concepts are applied to the study of a real observer, rather than an ideal observer, we speak of signal *detection*.

form is a function $x(t)$ that shows amplitude against time. The sample of noise is represented by $n(t)$, and the signal is called $s(t)$. Thus, the waveforms in the two types of observation interval may be represented by the following two equations:

$$x(t) = n(t) + s(t) \qquad (5\text{-}3)$$
$$x(t) = n(t) \qquad (5\text{-}4)$$

The a priori probability that the signal will occur is $p(SN)$, and this is the probability that $x(t)$ will be the sum of $n(t)$ and $s(t)$; $p(N) = 1 - p(SN)$ is the probability that $x(t)$ will consist of only $n(t)$.

Figure 5-2 illustrates possible waveforms in a detection experiment. The top line shows the signal $s(t)$, the next line shows a particular sample of noise $n(t)$, and the bottom line

shows the sum $x(t)$. It will be assumed that the signal $s(t)$ is exactly the same each time it is added to the noise $n(t)$. However, the waveform $n(t)$ is only one sample of noise, and $n(t)$ will differ from one observation interval to the next. Therefore, the waveform $x(t)$, upon which the decision must be based, changes from trial to trial. The problem at hand is to associate a probability with the waveform $x(t)$, and this must be done for both SN and N in order to calculate a likelihood ratio.

Waveforms have the appearance of continuity, and it would seem that an infinite set of ordinates would be required to specify each $x(t)$. However, in the practical situations of interest here, each waveform may be considered as the output of a channel with finite

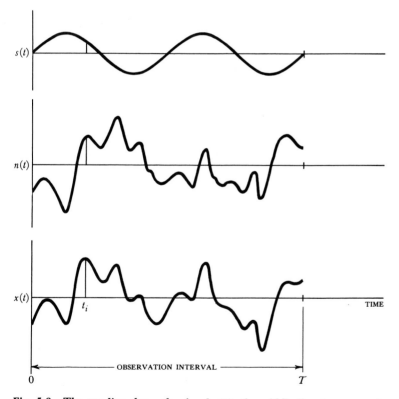

Fig. 5-2   The top line shows the signal $s(t)$, the middle line is one sample of noise $n(t)$, and the bottom line shows the sum $x(t)$. If the observation interval 0.0 to T had been a noise-alone trial, then $x(t)$ would be the same as $n(t)$. The waveform of the noise $n(t)$, and therefore the sum $x(t)$, changes from trial to trial.

bandwidth; thus, it is assumed that each of the infinitude of waveforms $x(t)$ may be analyzed into a finite series of harmonically related sinusoids with an upper frequency limit. These waveforms are considered to be Fourier series band-limited; and each waveform may be specified, except at the end points of the observation interval, by a finite number of Fourier coefficients. This is one way of describing a band-limited waveform by a finite set of numbers. A more useful description for our purposes is based upon the *sampling theorem* (Goldman, 1953). This theorem states that if a function $x(t)$ does not have any frequency components higher than W cycles per second (cps), then the function is determined by its ordinates at a series of points spaced $1/(2W)$ sec apart. Therefore a waveform of duration T sec is specified, over the open interval from 0.0 to T, by stating the amplitude of that waveform at $2WT$ equally spaced points along the time axis.[1]

There is an additional aspect of the sampling theorem that is important in the calculation (by the ideal observer) of the detectability of a signal embedded in noise. If $x(t)$ is the voltage across a 1-ohm resistor, then the mean of the sum of the squares of the $2WT$ amplitudes *is* the time-average power of $x(t)$; of course, the energy E dissipated in the resistor during the observation interval is the product of the time-average power and the duration of the interval T:

$$E = \frac{1}{2W} \sum_{i=1}^{2WT} x(t_i)^2 \qquad (5\text{-}5)$$

This statement about the relation between the power, or energy, of a waveform and the $2WT$ amplitudes which describe the waveform simplifies certain mathematical expressions in TSD.

Let us now see how the sampling theorem may be used in TSD. (For additional details

see Clarke, 1960b; Helstrom, 1960; Kotel' nikov, 1960; Peterson, Birdsall, and Fox, 1954.)

Consider again the waveforms shown in Fig. 5-2. One ordinate has been erected at the value t_i along the time axis. From the point of view of the ideal observer, the input to the receiver for a single observation interval consists of $2WT$ of these amplitudes; but for the moment let us consider only the single amplitude $x(t_i)$.

We have emphasized that the value of $n(t_i)$, and therefore the value of $x(t_i)$, fluctuates at random from trial to trial. As in our third example in the section on decision theory (pages 217 to 220), each of the two events, SN or N, may give rise to the same stimulus, or input, $x(t_i)$. However, in general, the probability that a given $x(t_i)$ will arise from SN will be different from the probability that it will arise from N alone. In this situation, the ideal observer would calculate the likelihood ratio associated with the given input $x(t_i)$.

In order for the ideal observer to calculate the likelihood ratio associated with a given value of $x(t_i)$, it is necessary for him to know something about the signal and something about the noise. We shall consider only the situation in which (1) the signal is exactly the same on each SN trial, (2) the statistical properties of the noise are of a given type, and (3) the ideal observer has the necessary information regarding the previous two items.

As just indicated, the ideal observer must know the statistical properties of the noise. The present analysis will consider a noise widely used in psychoacoustic experiments; this noise is called white, Gaussian noise. The noise is white if it has the same power per unit bandwidth at all frequencies in the band whose width is W cps, and it is Gaussian if the distribution of amplitudes is normal (Gaussian) in form. As previously stated, the waveform

---

[1] The consequences of the assumption that the waveforms $x(t)$ are Fourier series band-limited have been discussed by Tanner (1960) with an emphasis upon the relation between this assumption and the nature of actual experiments. Tanner concludes that the consequences of this assumption are useful in the experimental study of signal detection and of recognition.

$n(t)$ is assumed to be Fourier series band-limited.

With these assumptions, let us examine a large number of observation intervals. Then there will be two distributions of $x(t_i)$, one for SN trials and one for N trials. For the moment the index number i is fixed because only the amplitude at the time t_i is being considered for each observation interval. Consider first the distribution for N trials. This distribution of amplitudes, $n(t_i)$, is a distribution taken over a collection (ensemble) of observation intervals. It is assumed that the parameters of the population distribution, from which $n(t_i)$ is sampled, are independent of the time at which the sampling point t_i is fixed; briefly said, the ensemble averages are assumed to be the same as the time averages. Such a noise is said to be stationary and ergodic (Bendat, 1958).

As we are dealing with a Gaussian noise, the amplitude $x(t_i)$ is a random variable drawn from a normal distribution. The reader may recall that the ordinate (or probability density) of a normal curve is given by an expression of the following form:

$$f(x) = \frac{1}{\sqrt{2\pi\sigma^2}} \exp\left[\frac{-(x - \bar{x})^2}{2\sigma^2}\right] \quad (5\text{-}6)$$

The symbol "exp" means that the expression following it is the exponent of the number e. Thus, $\exp(-x)$ stands for e^{-x}. From Eq. (5-6), we see that only two parameters, the mean and the variance, are required to specify a normal distribution. We shall assume that the noise does not contain a d-c component. Consequently, the mean of $x(t_i)$ for the N trials is zero. Given that the noise is ergodic, it follows from Eq. (5-5) that the variance of $x(t_i)$ is the long-time average noise power N.

In the case of SN trials, the amplitude of $x(t_i)$ will be equal to the amplitude of the noise at the time t_i plus the amplitude of the signal at this same time. That is to say, $x(t_i) = n(t_i) + s(t_i)$. It should be recalled

that for this derivation the signal is specified exactly. Therefore, from trial to trial, the amplitude of the signal at time t_i is a constant. Consequently, the mean of the distribution from which $x(t_i)$ is sampled for the SN trials is $s(t_i)$. Of course, the constant signal amplitude at the time t_i does not contribute to the variance, so the variance for the SN trials is the same as it is for the N trials. The reader should visualize two overlapping normal curves with a separation between the two means of $s(t_i)$ and with a common variance of N.

If the sensory information consisted only of the amplitude $x(t_i)$ at one sampling point t_i, the ideal observer would compute the likelihood ratio associated with this particular input $x(t_i)$. Let us see how this may be done, first for the single amplitude $x(t_i)$ and then for all the $2WT$ amplitudes that constitute the total observation. Because the amplitude at the fixed time t_i is a continuous variable, the likelihood ratio in this case is a ratio of two probability densities, one density for the SN distribution of amplitudes and one density for the N distribution.

In the present application, the expression given by Eq. (5-6) is written separately for N trials and for SN trials. Thus, x becomes the amplitude $x(t_i)$ for both types of trial, $\bar{x}$ becomes 0.0 for N trials and becomes $s(t_i)$ for SN trials, σ^2 becomes the noise power N for both types of trial, and the probability density $f(x)$ becomes $f_N[x(t_i)]$ for N trials and becomes $f_{SN}[x(t_i)]$ for SN trials. The likelihood ratio $l[x(t_i)]$ for a given input $x(t_i)$ is the ratio of the two probability densities:

$$l[x(t_i)] = \frac{f_{SN}[x(t_i)]}{f_N[x(t_i)]}$$

$$= \frac{\dfrac{1}{\sqrt{2\pi N}} \exp\left[\dfrac{-[x(t_i) - s(t_i)]^2}{2N}\right]}{\dfrac{1}{\sqrt{2\pi N}} \exp\left[\dfrac{-[x(t_i)]^2}{2N}\right]} \quad (5\text{-}7)$$

$$l[x(t_i)] = \exp\left\{\frac{1}{2N}[2x(t_i)s(t_i) - s(t_i)^2]\right\}$$

$$(5\text{-}8)$$

Actually, there should be a subscript attached to "l" as a reminder that the ratio gives the likelihood of $x(t_i)$ given event SN relative to the likelihood of $x(t_i)$ given event N. However, the subscript SN on "l" is omitted because, in all instances in this chapter, the likelihood ratio will be written with f_{SN} in the numerator and with f_N in the denominator.

We have pointed out that the decision axis for the ideal observer is likelihood ratio, or any monotonic transformation of likelihood ratio. If we take the natural logarithm of $l[x(t_i)]$, the expression in Eq. (5-8) that follows the symbol "exp" will no longer be an exponent, and the mathematical development will be simplified. So $\log_e l[x(t_i)]$ becomes

$$\log l[x(t_i)] = \frac{1}{2N}[2x(t_i)s(t_i) - s(t_i)^2] \quad (5\text{-}9)$$

Equation (5-9) gives the value of $\log l[x(t_i)]$ for some specific value of the amplitude $x(t_i)$ taken at the ith sampling point. We have already seen that the amplitude at the ith sampling point is a random variable that is normally distributed for each of the two types of interval, SN and N. So, we must now determine the corresponding distributions of $\log l[x(t_i)]$.

Case 1. SN intervals. When the signal occurs, $x(t_i)$ may be replaced by $[n(t_i) + s(t_i)]$ in Eq. (5-9), and, after simplification, we obtain

$$\log l[x(t_i)]_{SN} = \frac{s(t_i)^2}{2N} + \frac{s(t_i)n(t_i)}{N} \quad (5\text{-}10)$$

The left-hand term has the subscript SN written at the end of the expression to indicate that the likelihood ratio is conditional upon an SN interval. The first term on the right is a constant, and the second term will have an expected value of zero because the signal amplitude $s(t_i)$ and the noise amplitude $n(t_i)$ are uncorrelated. Therefore, the mean and variance of the distribution from which $\log l[x(t_i)]_{SN}$ is sampled will be given

by the following equations:

$$\text{Mean of } \log l[x(t_i)]_{SN} = \frac{s(t_i)^2}{2N} \quad (5\text{-}11)$$

$$\text{Variance of } \log l[x(t_i)]_{SN} = \frac{s(t_i)^2}{N} \quad (5\text{-}12)$$

Equation (5-10) shows that the only variable quantity in $\log l[x(t_i)]_{SN}$ is the term $n(t_i)$. Because $n(t_i)$ is normally distributed, $\log l[x(t_i)]_{SN}$ is also a normally distributed variable.

In the above development, we have considered the amplitude at only one sampling point, t_i. Actually, the total observation consists of $2WT$ amplitudes. The ideal observer would calculate a likelihood ratio for each of these $2WT$ values, and, because the amplitudes at successive sampling points are independent, the likelihood ratio for the total observation is the product of the $2WT$ likelihood ratios. The logarithm of a continued product of a series of terms is equal to the sum of their logarithms. Consequently, we can obtain the mean of a distribution of a large number of values of $\log l[x(t)]_{SN}$, with each likelihood ratio based upon the total observation, by simply adding together the $2WT$ means, letting the index number i run from 1 to $2WT$ in Eq. (5-11). Thus,

$$\text{Mean of } \log l[x(t)]_{SN} = \sum_{i=1}^{2WT} \frac{s(t_i)^2}{2N}$$
$$= \frac{WE}{N} = \frac{E}{N_0} \quad (5\text{-}13)$$

In Eq. (5-13), E is the energy of the signal, and $(N/W) = N_0$ is the noise power per unit bandwidth.

The variance of the values of $\log l[x(t)]_{SN}$ is simply the sum of the separate variances, each of which is given by Eq. (5-12). Therefore,

$$\text{Variance of } \log l[x(t)]_{SN} = \sum_{i=1}^{2WT} \frac{s(t_i)^2}{N}$$
$$= \frac{2E}{N_0} \quad (5\text{-}14)$$

Finally, we note that the sum of a set of independent random variables, each of which is normally distributed, is itself a normally distributed variable. Therefore, $\log l[x(t)]_{SN}$ is normally distributed with a mean of E/N_0 and a variance of $2E/N_0$.

Case 2. N intervals. For observation intervals consisting of only a sample of noise, $x(t_i)$ becomes $n(t_i)$ in Eq. (5.9). By a development similar to that for Case 1, it may be shown that

$$\text{Mean of } \log l[x(t)]_N = \frac{-E}{N_0} \quad (5\text{-}15)$$

$$\text{Variance of } \log l[x(t)]_N = \frac{2E}{N_0} \quad (5\text{-}16)$$

We are now in a position to summarize the results of the above derivations. There are two distributions of the likelihood ratio, with each ratio based upon the $2WT$ amplitudes of the total observation. The statistical properties of these distributions are simplified by dealing with the logarithm of the likelihood ratio rather than with the ratio itself. The SN distribution of $\log l[x(t)]$ has a mean of E/N_0, and the N distribution has a mean of $-E/N_0$. Each of these distributions is normal in form with a common standard deviation of $\sqrt{2E/N_0}$. Of course, $\log l[x(t)]$, or *log likelihood ratio*, is the logarithm of the ratio of two probability densities. Let us realize that the primary statistical parameters of both distributions of log likelihood ratio may be expressed entirely

in terms of the signal energy and the noise power density. In particular, note that the parameters of the N distribution depend upon the energy of the signal. This is so because we are dealing with log likelihood ratio, and the reader may infer from Eq. (5-8) that the input waveform is cross-correlated with the stored waveform of the signal.

Figure 5-3 shows two normal distributions of log likelihood ratio. A value of $2E/N_0$ of 1.0 was arbitrarily selected. With a smaller signal energy E, but with the same noise power density N_0, the distributions would overlap to a greater extent. With a larger signal energy, the distributions would overlap less than those shown.

The detectability of the signal for the ideal observer is specified by the *separation between the alternative hypotheses*. This separation, or difference, between the means states the limitation placed upon performance by the environment. The difference between the means of the two normal distributions of Fig. 5-3 may be divided by their common standard deviation σ_N, and this standardized difference between the means then expresses, in a single dimensionless number, the detectability of a signal in noise. This number is called the index of detectability, d':

$$d' = \frac{M_{SN} - M_N}{\sigma_N} = \sqrt{\frac{2E}{N_0}} \quad (5\text{-}17)$$

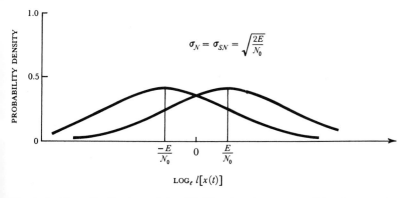

$$\sigma_N = \sigma_{SN} = \sqrt{\frac{2E}{N_0}}$$

PROBABILITY DENSITY

$\dfrac{-E}{N_0}$ 0 $\dfrac{E}{N_0}$

$\text{LOG}_e \; l[x(t)]$

Fig. 5-3 Two distributions of log likelihood ratio, one conditional upon SN and the other upon N alone, for the case of the "signal specified exactly."

The decision axis shown in Fig. 5-3 is the log likelihood ratio. These distributions may be cast into more standardized form by the application of two transformations to the numbers along the decision axis. First, E/N_0 is added to all values of log likelihood ratio so that the origin of the decision axis is shifted to the mean of the N distribution. Second, the resulting values are divided by the common standard deviation $\sqrt{2E/N_0}$, so that the standard deviation of each distribution becomes 1.0. This new decision axis will be called Z:

$$Z = \frac{\log l[x(t)] + E/N_0}{\sqrt{2E/N_0}} \quad (5\text{-}18)$$

Clearly, Z is a monotonic transformation of the likelihood ratio. The values of Z form two normal distributions, one conditional upon SN and the other conditional upon N. The mean of the N distribution is now 0.0, and that of the SN distribution is $\sqrt{2E/N_0}$, or d'. Both distributions have a standard deviation of 1.

It has been said earlier that each waveform $x(t)$ requires $2WT$ dimensions for its specification. However, for the purpose of making a decision between the two alternatives SN and N, all waveforms that may arise in a particular situation can be mapped onto a unidimensional axis, Z. In this case, the boundary between those inputs which lead to an affirmative response and those inputs which do not is a single number; it is some numerical value of Z. This particular value of Z will be referred to as the cutoff C in the remainder of this section.

In the section on decision theory (pages 214 to 220), we saw how the performance of an ideal observer could be summarized in the form of an ROC. For an ideal observer, an operating characteristic summarizes the conditional probabilities associated with a set of likelihood ratios. As the reader may recall, each coordinate of a point on an operating characteristic for an ideal observer is the sum of the appropriate conditional probabilities associated with likelihood ratios that exceed

a critical value called the cutoff. Let us now see how the hit rate $p(y|SN)$ and the false-alarm rate $p(y|N)$ are derived from the two normal curves that show, respectively, the distribution of Z given SN and the distribution of Z given N.

On each trial, the ideal observer transforms the sensory input into a value of Z; if this value of Z exceeds the cutoff C, he responds "yes." Of course, if the transformed input Z is less than the cutoff C, he responds "no." Thus, $p(y|SN) = p[(Z > C)|SN]$, and $p(y|N) = p[(Z > C)|N]$. Figure 5-4 illustrates the construction of an ROC from two overlapping normal curves. Consider first that the observer has adopted the cutoff C_1, as indicated by the arrow under the abscissa for the two normal curves. The conditional probability $p(y|SN)$ is then given by the stippled area under the SN curve and to the right of the cutoff C_1. The corresponding value of $p(y|N)$ is given by the cross-hatched area under the N curve and to the right of the same cutoff C_1. These two probabilities define the coordinates of a point on the operating characteristic, and the resulting point is labeled C_1. If the cutoff is changed to some new value, such as C_2 in Fig. 5-4, two new values for the conditional probabilities are obtained. For each value of the cutoff, there corresponds an HR and an FAR. As the cutoff is changed from one series of trials to the next, these two conditional probabilities change, and the relation between them is the ROC.

In an earlier section, the performance of an observer was presented in the form of a 2×2 matrix (see Table 5-1), and we have seen that such a matrix corresponds to one point on an operating characteristic. If the observer changes his cutoff to some new value in a second series of observation intervals, a different 2×2 matrix and a different point on the operating characteristic will result. Thus, the operating characteristic shown in Fig. 5-4 describes completely in a convenient form the successive matrices obtained as the observer adopts different criteria from one set of trials to the next. However, the detectability

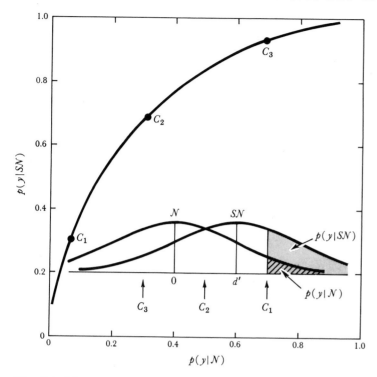

Fig. 5-4 The process by which an ROC is generated by passing the cutoff C through two overlapping curves. The value of d' is 1.0.

of the signal, as measured by d', does not change as different criteria are adopted by the ideal observer. The detectability of the signal is independent of the criterion for an affirmative response of "yes."

Let us examine what happens when successively larger and larger values of the signal energy E are used in an experiment on detection, but with the noise power density N_0 held fixed. We shall assume that the two Gaussian distributions of log likelihood ratio have been normalized according to Eq. (5-18). Then for all values of signal energy, the distribution of Z for noise-alone trails will remain unchanged with its mean at the origin and its standard deviation equal to 1.0. When the signal energy is zero, the distribution for SN trials will coincide with that for noise-alone trials, and the corresponding ROC will lie on the chance line. For a small value of E, the SN distribution will largely overlap with that of the N

distribution, and the corresponding ROC will lie close to the chance line. As E is increased from one series of trials to the next, the mean of the SN distribution, d', will also be increased, but the standard deviation will remain constant at 1.0. Consequently, the overlap of the two distributions will decrease as E becomes larger and larger, and the signal will become more and more detectable. Figure 5-5 shows a family of operating characteristics with d' as the parameter.

The paradigm used thus far in our discussion of signal detection has been that of the single-interval experiment. This experiment involves a response of "yes" or "no" to a single observation interval. When the signal energy E is specified exactly for the ideal observer, the index of detectability d' is equal to $\sqrt{2E/N_0}$. It is instructive to see how the index of detectability d', as defined for the single-interval experiment, is related

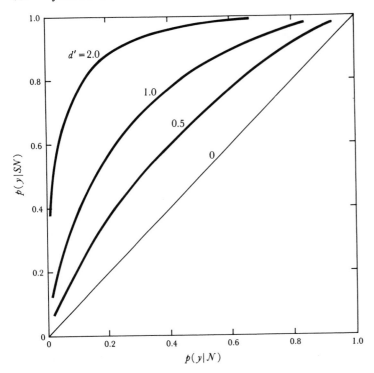

Fig. 5-5 A family of operating characteristics with d' as the parameter. When the signal is specified exactly for the ideal observer, the numerical value of d' is $\sqrt{2E/N_0}$. Each operating characteristic is obtained with the average environmental condition E/N_0, held fixed, and the curve is generated by changing the criterion for an affirmative ("yes") response.

to the numerical value of d' in a *forced-choice procedure*. In a temporal forced-choice procedure, two or more observation intervals are presented in succession to the observer. The signal energy E is added to the noise in just one of the observation intervals, and the task of the observer is to state which one of the intervals contained the signal. We shall consider only the case in which two observation intervals are presented during each trial. We shall label the value of d' for the single-interval experiment, or "yes-no" experiment, by the symbol d'_{yn}. For the forced-choice procedure, the corresponding value of d' will be called d'_{fc}.

There are several ways of deriving the relation between d'_{yn} and d'_{fc}. One way requires the ideal observer to compute the

likelihood ratio for each of the two observation intervals in the forced-choice task. He then selects the interval with the larger likelihood ratio as his response. When this derivation is carried through, it is found that $d'_{fc} = \sqrt{2}\, d'_{yn}$. Another way of obtaining this same result is presented in the next paragraph.

Let us consider Fig. 5-6. Line A of the figure shows the waveform of the signal when it is presented in the first interval, and line B shows this waveform when it is presented in the second interval. Of course, a different sample of noise is added to each of the two intervals on each trial, and the waveforms shown represent only the signal. The ideal observer may convert this forced-choice task to the "yes-no" task of the single-interval experiment by always subtracting the waveform of the signal to be detected from the waveform he receives during the first of the two intervals. Remember, this is a case in which the waveform of the signal to be detected is known to the ideal observer. If he subtracts the waveform of the signal from the waveform of the first interval for every pair of observation intervals, he neither adds nor loses information. He simply transforms the input information into a different form. With this transformation, the waveform of line A in Fig. 5-6 is changed to that represented by line C, and that of line B is changed to the waveform shown in line D. The ideal observer then makes his decision in terms of lines C and D. The two intervals of a single trial of the forced-choice procedure have been converted into a single observation interval of a "yes-no" experiment. If the signal is in fact in the first interval (line A), the transformed input of the observation interval consists of noise alone (line C). If the signal is in the second interval (line B), the transformed input contains a signal (line D). The waveform in line D has twice the energy of the signal that was initially presented in either the first or the second interval of the forced-choice task. Therefore, the separation of the two normal curves (Fig. 5-3) becomes $\sqrt{4E/N_0}$. Now the energy of the signal used in the forced-choice task is E. If this same signal were used in a "yes-no" task, d'_{yn} would equal $\sqrt{2E/N_0}$. Consequently, $d'_{fc} = \sqrt{2}\, d'_{yn}$. The structure of a forced-choice trial provides more information to the observer than does a "yes-no" trial. We shall see in a section below that the performance of the human observer is consistent with this interesting result for the ideal observer.

Let us summarize the salient features of the process of the detection of a signal by an ideal observer. Figure 5-7 is a block diagram illustrating the separate operations performed. On a given trial, an input is transferred to the likelihood ratio computer. This computer must have information concerning the properties, or parameters, of the signal and of the noise. These properties are statistical in nature, and the distribution function computer feeds to the likelihood ratio computer the appropriate information regarding the conditional probabilities of sampling a given input. The likelihood ratio, or a monotonic transformation of it, is computed and passed along to the decision computer, and a simple comparison is made between the value of Z, Eq. (5-18), and a cutoff C. The value of C has come from the criterion computer; this computer utilized information concerning the a priori probabilities of the alternative events SN and N and information concerning the consequences, such as the values and the costs, of the decisions. For the situation we have studied, the value of d' and the associated operating characteristic can be determined solely by the succession of outputs from the likelihood ratio computer. Of course, the particular point at which the observer operates on the operating characteristic is determined by the output of the criterion computer. In the operation of the ideal observer, the decision computer performs the only operation

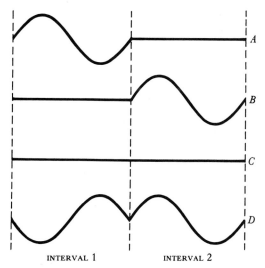

INTERVAL 1   INTERVAL 2

Fig. 5-6 These signal waveforms illustrate how the ideal observer can convert a forced-choice task with two intervals into a "yes-no" task with a single observation interval. Of course, a different sample of noise should be added to each interval to obtain the waveform presented to the observer.

that is based upon a "threshold," and this threshold is readily changed by the criterion computer.

APPLICATIONS OF TSD TO PSYCHOPHYSICS

The theory of signal detectability describes the performance of an ideal observer, an observer who utilizes all relevant information available to him in order to arrive at a "best" decision. Although TSD is a normative theory, it may be used in the study of signal detection and of signal recognition by the human observer in various ways. For one thing, it can be determined experimentally whether the classes of variables known to be effective for the ideal observer are also effective in human performance. The variables in the schematic of Fig. 5-7 may be readily identified as factors that may affect human performance. A decision or judgment made by a human observer clearly depends upon (1) the sensory input on a given trial; (2) his "set" and his "expectancies," as these are established by previous training and instructions; and (3) the rewards and punishments associated with the various outcomes of his decisions. In such an analysis, TSD can serve as a framework or as a descriptive model for the study of detection and of recognition of signals. Let us refer again to

Fig. 5-7 and use this schematic of an ideal observer as an analogy to the operations performed by the real observer. The responses of the real observer in a psychophysical experiment reflect the properties of the overall system. However, the sensory psychologist is usually interested in only a portion, or a subsystem, of this total system. With this interest in the sensory subsystem, it is important that the measure of performance be relatively independent of the effects of the observer's criterion (criterion computer). From the present point of view, we may say that, in a psychophysical experiment, the usual goal is to determine how well the observer can compute a quantity *like* likelihood ratio, and that to do so the procedure must make it possible to evaluate the effects of the observer's criterion upon his performance. TSD shows us how to take the FAR of the human observer into account so that a d' measure of performance may be secured. Furthermore, psychophysical experiments are sometimes designed to secure a measure of performance that will reflect the capacity of the afferent channel to process and to transmit information. In terms of the schematic of Fig. 5-7, the interest of the sensory psychologist may be said to be confined to the sensory subsystem that processes and transmits information from the input space to the likelihood ratio computer. Obviously, it is de-

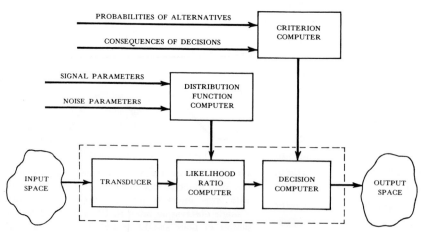

Fig. 5-7   Schematic of an ideal observer. (*After Tanner, 1961b*).

sirable in such experiments to instruct and to train the observer carefully before the collection of data so that the information stored in the distribution function computer will remain relatively constant as the experiment progresses. Another advantage of the use of concepts taken from TSD is that a d' measure of performance is relatively invariant when different psychophysical methods are used. For another thing, the performance of the ideal observer may serve as a standard with which the performance of the real observer may be compared. Thus, a measure of efficiency can be defined. Also, the operating characteristic may be employed as a quantitative description of human performance in situations other than signal detection. One additional application will be mentioned here. For the situation discussed in the section on TSD the signal was specified exactly and the statistical characteristics of the noise were known to the ideal observer. It is possible to introduce additional uncertainties into the stimulus situation, and it can then be determined, both for the ideal and for the real observer, how much these uncertainties affect performance. These uncertainties may be introduced in various amounts and in various combinations to see whether the performance of the ideal observer may be made to match that of the human observer. As a counterpart to this approach, it has been found possible to improve the performance of the human observer by the introduction of aids to memory for the various aspects of the signal. We shall now consider in greater detail a few of these applications of TSD to psychophysics.

The single-interval experiment

The basic procedure in the single-interval experiment requires that the observer make a simple response of "yes" or "no" after each observation interval. According to this binary-decision procedure, the observer adopts one criterion for a series of observation intervals. The coordinates for one point of an operating characteristic are estimated from these data. The observer then adopts a different criterion for the next series of intervals, and this process is continued until the number of points is sufficient to determine the relation between the HR and the FAR.

Operating characteristics for auditory detection by human listeners may be readily secured by the use of simple instructions. Two response keys are provided for the listener, and he is asked to press one of the keys after each observation interval. A fairly wide range of FARs will usually result by an attempt to induce the three criteria of *strict, medium,* and *lax.* For example, the listener may be told: "Be strict. You should press the 'yes' key each time that you are fairly sure that a tone was presented." At the other extreme, he may be instructed: "Be lax. You should press the 'yes' key each time there was any indication that a tone was presented." During the training sessions, the listener may be praised or admonished in order to induce him to press the "yes" key the desired number of times under each criterion. (This procedure appears to be acceptable when the absolute number of "yes" responses is not the primary datum. The question in signal detection usually has to do with how well the observer can *partition* his affirmative responses between the two events *SN* and *N.*)

Of course, the criterion adopted by the human observer may be manipulated in various ways. As just described, the use of simple instructions is usually quite effective. Another way is to assign values and costs to each of the outcomes of a decision. With this procedure, the payoff matrix is usually such that the observer can increase his earnings (somewhat) for participation in the experiment. A third way is to vary the a priori probability of the occurrence of a signal. All these ways have been successfully employed in experiments on signal detection.

Although the details of experimental procedure will depend upon many factors, certain useful procedures will be described. In some laboratories, 200 or more observation intervals are presented under one criterion with a few short rest periods during such a series. Unless the effects of the a priori probability of the signal are being studied, about one-half of the trials are SN trials. Such a block of about 200 trials is used to estimate $p(y|SN)$ and $p(y|N)$. If the block of trials is repeated under the same instructions, during either the same session or a different session, another pair of probabilities is usually estimated. This procedure is especially important when the listener is instructed to adopt a different criterion before the replication of the original criterion. This procedure is followed because the listener may adopt somewhat different criteria from time to time even though the same instructions have been used. Even the practiced listener interprets such words as "strict" and "lax" differently from one occasion to the next; consequently, a fairly wide range of FARs usually results from the use of just three types of instruction. Although the probabilities $p(y|SN)$ and $p(y|N)$ may change from session to session, even with the same instructions, the operating characteristic defined by these probabilities is very stable over many thousands of trials (Egan, Greenberg, and Schulman, 1961a).

The listener may be brought to a near-asymptotic level of performance for auditory detection in a single session of about one hour. The process of learning is greatly facilitated by allowing the listener to hear the signal well above the noise at the beginning of the training session; the use of this mnemonic aid makes trial-by-trial feedback relatively unnecessary in the determination of an operating characteristic for the detection of sinusoids by the human listener (Gundy, 1961).

Operating characteristics for auditory detection of a signal in noise show much smaller differences among individuals than are shown by *masked thresholds* as determined by the method of limits or by Békésy audiometry. Results from the single-interval experiment indicate that a change of about 4 decibels (dB) in signal energy would convert the operating characteristic for the "worst" listener into that for the "best." When a psychophysical method

is employed that does not take into account the various criteria adopted by the different listeners, about 10 dB may be required to achieve the same transformation. (These results are based upon trained listeners with normal hearing.)

The rating method

If the human observer adopts a given criterion for a long series of observation intervals, many of his "yes-no" decisions are well within and many well outside that criterion. Therefore, he should be able to order his "yes-no" decisions and thereby assign ratings to each of his responses. The rating method utilizes the fact that, during a single series of observation intervals, the human observer is capable of adopting multiple criteria. In effect, the rating method requires a statement by the observer about the odds that the signal was presented. Such a statement provides more information concerning the observer's decision than does a simple response of "yes" or "no" made under a fixed criterion (Clarke, 1960a). Consequently, it is possible in some situations to obtain nearly the same index of signal detection in fewer trials with the rating method than with the binary-decision procedure (Egan et al., 1959). Furthermore, experience has shown that nearly all observers find the rating method simple and easy to use.

The relation between the binary-decision procedure and the rating method is as follows. In the rating method, a response of "1" represents a "yes" under a strict criterion. If the observation interval in fact contains the signal, then $p(r_1|SN)$ is equivalent to $p(y|SN)$, where r_1 is the assigned rating "1." Similarly, for the noise-alone intervals, $p(r_1|N) = p(y|N)$. Next, the conditional probability of a response of "2" to an SN interval is computed. The following assumption is then made: observation intervals accepted as containing the signal under a given criterion will also be accepted under a less strict criterion. Therefore, the second value of $p(y|SN)$ is $p(r_1|SN) + p(r_2|SN)$. Thus, the value of $p(y|SN)$ corresponding to the criterion established by the rating c is the cumulative probability

$$p(y|SN) = \sum_{i=1}^{c} p(r_i|SN) \qquad (5\text{-}19)$$

For the same criterion, the corresponding value of $p(y|N)$ is

$$p(y|N) = \sum_{i=1}^{c} p(r_i|N) \qquad (5\text{-}20)$$

Computation of $p(y|SN)$ and $p(y|N)$ over the entire rating scale $i = 1, 2, \ldots, r$ generates the operating characteristic.

Curve fitting and an index of performance

When a single-interval experiment is conducted using a human observer, the resulting operating characteristic is similar in shape to the curves shown in Fig. 5-5. Accordingly, it is reasonable to fit a curve to the data by the process illustrated in Fig. 5-4. Thus, the means and variances of two normal curves may be adjusted until the corresponding operating characteristic gives a good fit to the data. A simple procedure for the estimation of the parameters of the two normal curves that correspond to a particular operating characteristic will be briefly discussed. Fitting a given function to a set of data is easily and quickly accomplished if the coordinate system is rescaled so that the given function becomes a straight line with respect to the new coordinates. To reduce the function of our present concern to a straight line, each probability scale, $p(y|SN)$ and $p(y|N)$, is so transformed that the corresponding normal deviates, or z scores, are linearly spaced along the coordinate axes. The z-score axes are referred to as $z(y|SN)$ and $z(y|N)$. Graph paper so constructed is called *normal-normal paper*. Then all operating characteristics generated by passing the cutoff C through two overlapping normal curves will be linear with respect to the z coordinates. A linear function requires that two parameters be estimated. One of these parameters is the difference between the means of the two overlapping normal curves, expressed as follows: $d' = (M_{SN} - M_N)/\sigma_N$.

This value is equal to the $z(y|N)$ intercept of the straight line. The slope m is taken as the other independent parameter of the straight line, and this slope equals the ratio of the standard deviations, σ_N/σ_{SN}, of the corresponding normal curves. Thus, each of the operating characteristics of Fig. 5-5 becomes a straight line with unit slope when it is plotted on normal-normal paper, and the detectability of the signal, d', determines the distance of this straight line from the chance line.

Figure 5-8 shows an operating characteristic plotted on normal-normal coordinates. The points (closed circles and x's) were obtained in a single-interval experiment in which a listener assigned a rating to each of 960 observation intervals. The computations performed upon the raw data are explained in Table 5-4.

The data secured in a single-interval experiment with the human observer are nearly always satisfactorily fitted by a straight line on normal-normal paper, and this fact has interesting and important consequences for the concept of a threshold. The data controvert the notion of a threshold, both as a performance measure and as an inferred property of the sensory system. For a full discussion of this matter, refer to Clarke and Bilger (1963) and to Swets (1961*b*).

The slope of the operating characteristic for the human observer is typically somewhat less than 1 (see Fig. 5-8), so that the distance of the straight line from the chance line changes to a certain degree over the course of the operating characteristic. Therefore, it is necessary to be somewhat arbitrary in the selection of a single index of signal detection for the real observer. One such index, called d_s, has been found useful in a variety of situations (Clarke, Birdsall, and Tanner, 1959; Egan, 1958; Egan, Schulman, and Greenberg, 1961; Pollack, 1959*b*).[1] This index may be defined with the aid of Fig. 5-8. Distance along the negative diagonal is scaled so that

---

[1] The measure d_s, as here defined, is the same as $\sqrt{d_e}$.

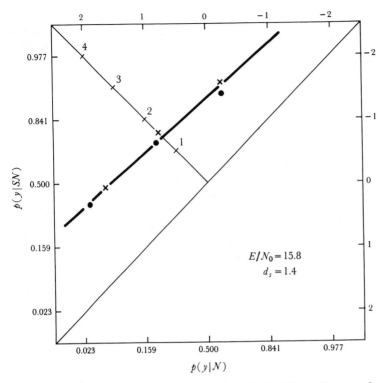

Fig. 5-8   This operating characteristic was obtained with one listener who rated 480 trials on each of two sessions. The signal was a sinusoid (1,000 cps of 0.5 sec duration). The data are plotted on normal-normal co-ordinates, and the index of signal detection, d_s, is scaled along the nega-tive diagonal. Table 5-4 shows the computations for the data plotted as the three closed circles; these data were obtained in the first session. The data for the other session were treated in the same way, and they are shown as the three x's. (*After Egan, Schulman, and Greenberg, 1959*).

each point on it is equal to the abscissa $z(y|N)$ minus the ordinate $z(y|SN)$ of that point. The numerical value of d_s may then be read directly from the *point of intersection* between the operating characteristic and the negative diagonal.

The measure d_s was selected as an index of signal detection for several reasons. For one thing, the coordinates of the point of intersec-tion have certain interesting properties. If $p(SN) = p(N)$, at the point of intersection the probability of a correct acceptance is equal to the probability of a correct rejection; or, alternatively stated, one-half of the inputs are in the criterion. A more important reason for using d_s to characterize an operating charac-

teristic stems from experimental results. It has been found that day-to-day variability in the operating characteristic for signal detection by a listener is manifested primarily by changes in slope, not by changes in d_s. Thus, a large portion of the variability in operating char-acteristics obtained under the "same" condi-tions may be accounted for by the (slight) rotation of a straight line with the point of intersection as the pivot.

Sometimes a numerical value of d' is re-ported in the literature on TSD for an oper-ating characteristic, or as the result of a forced-choice experiment, based upon the real observer. In such a case, the numerical value of d' refers to that value of $\sqrt{2E/N_0}$

Table 5-4   Data for an operating characteristic obtained by the rating method in a single-interval experiment with one listener.[1]

	Rating			
	1	2	3	4
	90	91	44	18
	0.37	0.37	0.18	0.07
SN	0.37	0.74	0.92	0.99
	0.33	−0.64	−1.41	
	7	42	93	95
	0.03	0.18	0.39	0.40
N	0.03	0.21	0.60	1.00
	1.88	0.81	−0.25	

[1] The top half of the table is based on 243 *SN* trials, and the bottom half on 237 *N* trials. Opposite *SN*, the first row gives the frequencies with which each rating was given. The frequencies are converted into estimates of conditional probabilities, $p(r_i|SN)$, for the second row. These probabilities are cumulated in the third row to give the values of $p(y|SN)$ for the various criteria. The *z* scores for the values of $p(y|SN)$ are listed in the fourth row. The four rows in the bottom half of the table for *N* trials have a corresponding interpretation.

which would be required for the ideal observer to achieve the same performance as that of the real observer.

A measure of efficiency

Let us suppose that a single-interval experiment is performed and that a point on an operating characteristic is obtained for the real observer. The energy of the signal used for this real observer will be called E_r. Let the energy of the signal be attenuated to E_i, so that the performance of the mathematically ideal observer matches that of the real observer. Then the efficiency of the real observer may be defined as follows: $\eta = E_i/E_r$.

An alternative but equivalent definition of the efficiency η is the following. Consider that an operating characteristic is secured with a real observer with a value of $\sqrt{2E_r/N_0}$, where E_r is the energy of the signal used for the real observer. The resulting index of signal detection is d_s. If the same energy E_r and the same N_0 are used for the ideal observer, the index of signal detectability d_i' will be $\sqrt{2E_r/N_0}$. Then the efficiency is the square of the ratio of the measures of performance for the two observers. That is,

$$\eta = \left[\frac{d_s}{d_i'} \right]^2 \qquad (5\text{-}21)$$

When the operating characteristic does not have a slope of 1, the value of η depends somewhat upon the particular point on the operating characteristic chosen for the computation of the efficiency. (See Tanner and Birdsall, 1958, for further discussion.) The measure of efficiency has been used to good advantage by Tanner and his associates (Creelman, 1961; Tanner, 1958, 1961a).

The asymmetry of the operating characteristic

The human observer is not capable of cross-correlating the input waveform with the waveform of the stored signal. In the simple detection experiment, the real observer is uncertain about several parameters of the signal, e.g. its frequency, its phase, or its starting time. Under these circumstances, the capacity to detect a signal in noise may be improved by the use of a filter centered near the frequency of the signal. The output of this filter is then used in the operation of detection. Thus, one view of detection by the real observer envisions the following set of operations. The input is first passed through a narrow-band filter centered near the frequency of the signal. The output of this filter is then rectified and integrated, or smoothed, over a short interval of time. This rectified, integrated output of the filter fluctuates from trial to trial; and, according to this view, the operating characteristic for the single-interval experiment will be determined by the distribution of the outputs of the filter for *N* trials and the corresponding distribution for *SN* trials. These distributions are skewed, and the resulting operating characteristics based upon them closely resemble those for the human observer. (For a full discussion of this matter, see Jeffress, 1964.)

Comparison of single-interval and forced-choice procedures

The difference between the "yes-no" task of the single-interval experiment and the forced-choice task of the two-interval experiment has important consequences in the study of detection by real observers. For example, if the focus of interest is the shape of the N distribution and of the SN distribution, then the single-interval experiment is an appropriate procedure; the operating characteristic obtained by this method reflects rather directly the forms of these two underlying distributions. In contrast, the two-alternative forced-choice method is not suitable for this problem. In the forced-choice task, the input is sampled from the SN distribution for one of the intervals and from the N distribution for the other interval, and the detectability of the signal is determined fundamentally by the separation of the SN distribution from the N distribution. However, the observer obtains a sample from each distribution on each trial, and he can use the input from the first interval to set his criterion for a decision about the input from the second interval. Therefore, the two distributions most directly involved in his decision in the forced-choice method are derived from the N and the SN distributions. The variable relevant to the decision in the forced-choice task is the difference between the transformed input for the first interval and the transformed input for the second interval. When the signal is in the first interval, one distribution of differences is obtained; when the signal is in the second interval, another distribution of differences results. For the ideal observer, either of these two distributions of differences will be an exact mirror image of the other, and they will tend to be so for the real observer. The shape of the operating characteristic for the forced-choice task will be determined by these distributions of differences, and for the real observer this operating characteristic will tend to be symmetric about the negative diagonal. The operation of the central limit theorem will also tend to make the two distributions of differences normal in form even though the underlying N and SN distributions are not normal. Thus, an operating characteristic based upon the performance of the human observer in the single-interval experiment is typically asymmetric with respect to the negative diagonal of the ROC plot (see Fig. 5-8), and this fact implies that the SN distribution has a greater variance than that of the N distribution. On the other hand, the corresponding operating characteristic for the forced-choice task not only is linear on a normal-normal plot but also has a slope of nearly *one*.

The symmetry of the operating characteristic for the forced-choice task has its advantages. If the problem under investigation revolves around a comparison of the detectability of a signal under various stimulus conditions, rather than a determination of the shape of the ROC, a forced-choice method is more expeditious than the single-interval procedure. For example, the effect of the duration of a signal upon its detection by an observer may be efficiently determined by a forced-choice method.

Comparison of measures of performance

A measure of sensory capacity should be largely independent of the particular criterion that the observer happens to adopt, and we have seen that a d' measure of performance has this attribute. Furthermore, if an index of capacity is to be useful, different procedures should give substantially the same measure of sensitivity. Again, a d' measure of detection, such as d_s, has this desirable property. For example, when the "yes-no" procedure of the single-interval experiment is compared experimentally with the temporal forced-choice procedure, consistent estimates of sensitivity are obtained, provided an index like d' is derived from the data (Swets, 1959). This agreement in the estimates of sensitivity was found by using as many as eight intervals in the forced-choice procedure. Such results favor the interpretation that, when the effects of the observer's criterion are largely eliminated, various methods give comparable measures of sensory capacity. This finding is in contrast with the fact that measures of the "threshold" differ considerably from one procedure to another. (For a discussion of the particular merits of the two-alternative forced-choice procedure, see Marill, 1956.)

Let us examine other, more familiar, measures of sensory capacity from our present vantage. When necessary, we shall use for convenience the FAR as a "measure" of the observer's criterion. A few comments upon experimental procedure will be included in the discussion.

To evelute the effects of the observer's criterion upon the measure of performance, it is usually necessary to provide in the experimental design an external correlate for each of the responses allowed to the observer. Thus, in the single-interval experiment in which the observer may respond "yes" or "no," it is necessary to include both SN trials and N trials to evelute the observer's criterion. Reconsideration of the 2×2 matrix (Table 5-1) will emphasize the importance of the inclusion of the N trials, or so-called "catch tests," as well as the SN trials. Without the N trials, the hit rate $p(y|SN)$ cannot be separated from the probability of a "yes" response. Note that the probability of a "yes" response is given by the following equation:

$$p(y) = p(y|SN)p(SN) + p(y|N)p(N) \quad (5\text{-}22)$$

Obviously, the value of $p(y)$, sometimes called the *response bias*, becomes equal to the hit rate $p(y|SN)$ when $p(N)$ equals zero. Unfortunately, some studies have reported the relation between $p(y|SN)$ and the intensity of the stimulus without making it clear that the label on the ordinate, $p(y)$, represents only the hit rate $p(y|SN)$. Even if the number of N trials is made substantial, the numerical value of $p(y|SN)$ depends upon the observer's criterion; taken by it-

self, $p(y|SN)$ is a poor index of performance.

Some of the techniques used by investigators do not provide the external correlates necessary for a proper analysis of the data. Let us consider as an example the method of limits for the measurement of visual thresholds for the recognition of words that are tachistoscopically exposed. Assume that only an ascending series is employed, so that the word is first presented "well below the threshold." The same word is presented on each flash, and the duration of exposure is increased until the subject identifies the word correctly. It is obvious that the observer's criterion may have a marked effect upon the threshold as measured by this procedure. In particular, the observer may change his criterion from one series of trials to the next, even depending in part upon the particular word being tested! This technique may have its use in certain areas of behavioral and social research, but very little can be concluded from the results obtained with this technique regarding the "threshold for seeing words." If it is desired to make valid inferences concerning *recognition thresholds* for a set of words, a procedure must be employed that will allow for the estimation of the effects of the observer's criterion, or response bias (Brown and Rubenstein, 1961). For a full discussion of this particular area of research, see Goldiamond (1958).

Let us return to a consideration of other measures of performance based upon data obtained in the single-interval experiment. One such measure involves a *correction for guessing*, which is supposed to give the true value for the conditional probability $p(y|SN)$. This *corrected value* of $p(y|SN)$ will be called p_t, and it is calculated as follows:

$$p_t = \frac{p(y|SN) - p(y|N)}{1 - p(y|N)} \quad (5\text{-}23)$$

If Eq. (5-23) is rearranged, it will be seen that it expresses the observed hit rate $p(y|SN)$ as a linear function of the observed false-alarm rate $p(y|N)$. Thus, Eq. (5-23) represents an operating characteristic that is

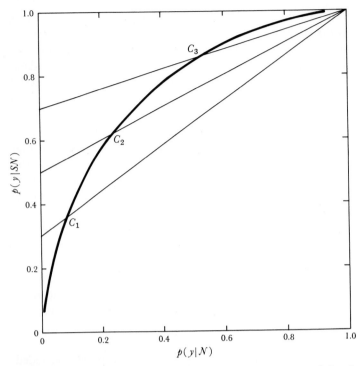

$p(y|N)$

Fig. 5-9 **The curved operating characteristic was generated by the process illustrated in Fig. 5-4, and a curve of this form describes fairly well the data obtained with the human observer. Each of the three straight lines was calculated by Eq. (5-23), using the coordinates of the three points C_1, C_2, and C_3, respectively. Each value of p_t is the $p(y|SN)$ intercept of the corresponding straight line. Thus, p_t is correlated with the criterion.**

a straight line on linear coordinates for $p(y|N)$ and $p(y|SN)$. This straight line begins with a value of p_t at the vertical axis for $p(y|SN)$ and extends to the upper right-hand corner of the ROC plot. (Such an operating characteristic is concave upward with respect to the z coordinates of normal-normal paper.) Figure 5-9 shows why p_t is highly correlated with the observer's criterion, or with $p(y|N)$. The curved operating characteristic shows fairly well how $p(y|SN)$ varies with $p(y|N)$ for the human observer. The three points on this curve represent three possible criteria. If the coordinates of these three points are used to obtain values of p_t by Eq. (5-23), the result is as shown along the ordinate. The correlation of p_t with the observer's criterion is obvious.

In this context, let us rewrite Eq. (5-2), which gives the proportion of correct responses in the single-interval experiment:

$$p(C) = p(y|SN)p(SN) + p(n|N)p(N) \quad (5\text{-}24)$$

If $p(N)$ is nearly zero, as it is in those experiments in which only a few "catch tests" are used, the observer can, at will, make $p(y|SN)$ equal to 1.0 and at the same time have a large value for the proportion of correct responses by simply saying "yes" on each and every trial. Of course, even when the relative number of "catch tests" is increased, the proportion of correct responses, $p(C)$, is still a poor measure of performance because it depends upon the false-alarm rate $p(y|N)$.

We have mentioned four measures that

might be used to characterize the performance of an observer in the single-interval experiment. These are (1) d_s, (2) $p(y|SN)$, (3) p_t, and (4) $p(C)$. Only the first measure, d_s, may be considered as an adequate measure of sensory capacity because the other three depend upon the observer's criterion.

It is instructive to plot measures 2 to 4, mentioned in the previous paragraph, on a single graph. Figure 5-10 shows these three measures of performance, and the ordinate scale is common to the three curves. We note that the measures shown in Fig. 5-10 strongly depend upon the FAR. In fact, two of the measures vary over their total range as the FAR covers its range. Clearly, these three measures are a function of variables not generally considered to be primary determiners of the sensitivity of the sensory mechanism.

On the other hand, the measure called d_s is not plotted in Fig. 5-10. The measure d_s is not a probability. For a particular ROC, d_s is a constant, and its numerical value is largely unaffected by variables that affect the decision process.

We should like to suggest that a psychometric function based upon data from the single-interval experiment should show the relation between a d' measure and signal energy. If either $p(y|SN)$, p_t, or $p(C)$ is used as a measure of performance, the form of the psychometric function and its position relative to the origin depend too much upon the observer's criterion. If a psychometric function depends upon the criterion, it becomes necessary to state in what sense the observer's criterion has remained invariant from one signal energy to another. Psychophysical studies done in the framework of TSD ordinarily em-

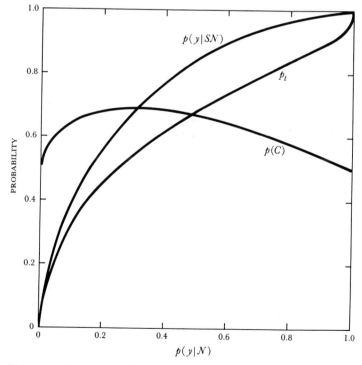

Fig. 5-10 Each curve shows how the indicated measure of performance depends upon the criterion, or false-alarm rate, of the observer. The curve for $p(y|SN)$ defines an operating characteristic with a d' of 1.0. For the calculation of $p(C)$, it was assumed that $p(SN) = p(N)$.

ploy either the single-interval experiment with both N trials and SN trials or a forced-choice procedure with two or more observation intervals. With these methods, a d' measure may be secured, and this measure is relatively independent of both the observer's criterion and the number of observation intervals.

Our criticism of the use of $p(C)$ as a measure of performance was made with reference to the results of a single-interval, or "yes-no," experiment. In such experiments, the observer may have a strong bias, usually against saying "yes," so that $p(C)$ is lower than the value the observer could achieve if he relaxed his criterion for the response "yes." However, it should be pointed out that the percentage of correct decisions is a useful measure of performance, when the data are secured by a forced-choice procedure. When two observation intervals are employed in a forced-choice method, the human observer usually does not show a strong bias toward one of the two intervals. The observer knows that the signal is presented in one of the two intervals on every trial. When he is uncertain, he is not allowed to say "no"; he must select one or the other interval. The human observer can readily be trained to respond about equally often to the two intervals, so that the effect of bias upon the percentage of correct decisions is largely removed. Of course, at very low signal energies, a strong bias may still show up, and in this case the 2×2 matrix can be treated in the same manner as the 2×2 matrix for a single-interval experiment. If desired, the value of d' may then be converted to the percentage of correct decisions the observer would have obtained if he had operated without bias.

One psychophysical procedure that has been used for the measurement of the differential threshold allows the observer the two responses "same" and "different." As ordinarily employed, the thresholds obtained by this technique are influenced to an unknown degree by the observer's criterion for *sameness*. The proper analysis of the data for this procedure is fairly complicated, but it has been worked out in detail in the context of TSD (Sorkin, 1962).

Of course, we cannot recommend the use of certain experimental methods. The choice of a procedure depends upon the particular problem under investigation. Furthermore, demands of expediency may dictate that compromises be made. For instance, the measurement of a person's threshold of audibility for clinical purposes does not ordinarily require a d' measure simply because an error of 5 to 10 dB may be tolerated. On the other hand, it should be realized that there are available powerful methods for the investigation of small differences in the capacity for the detection or for the recognition of a signal. In certain instances, the differences are small among the predictions of alternative hypotheses concerning the mechanisms involved in detection. Thus, a detector that computes only the power of the input wave at the frequency of the signal is not markedly different from the detector that cross-correlates the input with the known waveform of the stored signal. In fact, it has been demonstrated that gross differences in the detection mechanisms among different types of receiver may lead to differences in performance that are the equivalent of about 3 dB. Consequently, if we are to determine the manner in which a sensory system processes information in certain situations, we may need exceedingly precise measures of sensitivity.

Uncertainty with respect to signal parameters

The performance of the real observer is quite inferior to that of the ideal in the type of detection experiment described throughout this chapter. This fact may be shown by a comparison of their psychometric functions, that is, by a graph with d' plotted against $\sqrt{2E/N_0}$ (Tanner, 1959). When the signal is specified exactly to the ideal observer, his psychometric function is a straight line with unit slope and zero intercepts. The psychometric function for the human observer is shifted far to the right of the function for the ideal. The curve for the human observer leaves the origin with a very low slope; as a signal energy increases, the slope of the curve also increases, but the slope remains less than 1.0 throughout the course of the function. Undoubtedly, there are several processes operating in conjunction to reduce the efficiency of the human observer. For one thing, the human observer cannot maintain an exact cutoff for the criterion he adopts. Variation in the cutoff from trial to trial has the effect of an increase in the noise level N_0. For another thing, the sensory processes and the decision processes of the human observer may be noisy. This internal noise will result in a deterioration in performance. Another plausible reason for the relative inferiority of the real observer is that he has a faulty memory for the parameters of the signal. Let us suppose that the signal is a sinusoid. Then, five parameters must be given to the ideal observer in order for him to know the amplitude of this signal "point for point in time." These parameters are (1) frequency, (2) amplitude, (3) phase at onset, (4) starting time, and (5) duration. Of course, it is not possible to specify them exactly for the human observer. Furthermore, his memory for certain of these parameters, such as the frequency of the sinusoid, is imperfect. Now it may be shown that, if the signal is specified statistically rather than exactly to the ideal observer, his psychometric function is shifted to the right so that it resembles more closely the function for the human observer. As the degree of uncertainty with respect to signal parameters is increased for the ideal observer, the degree of similarity between the psychometric functions for the two observers also increases. It may also be noted that, when additional uncertainty is introduced into the typical detection experiment with human observers, the resulting decrement in performance is quite small (Egan *et al.*, 1961*a*; Green, 1961). This fact may be interpreted to mean that there is a large degree of initial uncertainty so that the deliberate introduction of additional uncertainty has a small effect.

These considerations have led to an attempt to provide within the experimental procedure various aids to the human observer's memory for the parameters of the signal (Tanner, 1961*b*). For example, memory for the frequency and the phase of the signal (sinusoid) may be made unnecessary by the introduction of a continuous, audible tone of the same frequency and phase as that of the signal. The signal to be detected is an increment in the carrier wave. Because this carrier is present at all times, it does not carry any information regarding the presence or the absence of the signal. This procedure results in an improvement in the human observer's performance. However, there is still uncertainty with respect to the starting time and the duration of the signal. In auditory experiments, the observation interval is usually marked off by flashing lights, and this procedure cannot delimit exactly the temporal aspects of the auditory signal. To specify further these temporal parameters of the signal, a clearly audible pulsed carrier is introduced into each observation interval. If a forced-choice procedure is employed in these experiments with a pulsed carrier, there is no need for memory for amplitude beyond a single trial. Thus, this experimental design provides information within each trial regarding all five signal parameters. With these aids to memory, the psychometric function for the human observer approaches the psychometric function for the ideal observer who has had the signal specified exactly. In some instances, the difference between the two psychometric functions is as small as 3 dB. These results lend support to the hypothesis that the human observer is capable of approaching the decision processes of the ideal observer.

Applications of TSD to vision

The theory of signal detectability is based upon a very general theory of testing statistical hypotheses. Mathematical derivations based upon this latter theory lead to the result that likelihood ratio is the optimal decision axis for the detection and the recognition of signals. This result may be utilized in the analysis of a broad class of problems in psychophysics, for the derivation does not depend upon the nature of the signals; the signals may be auditory, visual, tactile, etc. Therefore, much of the material presented in the context of auditory psychophysics is equally applicable to other sensory areas. This is particularly true of our discussion of methods by which appropriate measures of performance may be obtained. However, when we attempt to define an ideal observer, the properties of the stimuli must be specified. TSD emphasizes the importance of the analysis and the representation of the stimulus. Consequently, it is necessary to know the relevant stimulus variables in a particular situation and to know how these variables are distributed over trials. Of course, we have a better understanding of the adequate stimulus for some sensory modalities than for others. Auditory waveforms have well-understood modes of representation, and TSD may be readily developed for this area of psychophysics. In audition, it is relatively easy to study an idealized case, the case in which the signal is known by the observer to be exactly the same from trial to trial. Once a specific sensory modality has been selected for study, the equations necessary for the calculation of likelihood ratio are specific to that sensory modality. Let us illustrate this point by a brief discussion of the detection of a visual signal by an ideal observer.

Tanner and Jones (1960) have derived an approximate equation for an ideal observer for the detection of a visual signal presented against a background of light. Light comes in packets of energy called photons, and when the signal source is typical of that used in visual studies, the number of photons at the entrance pupil of the detector fluctuates from trial to trial in a manner described by the Poisson distribution. Consequently, the noise-alone distribution has a mean proportional to the intensity of the background light, whereas the signal-plus-noise distribution has a mean proportional to the intensity of the background plus the signal. In their derivation,

Tanner and Jones assume that the increment in the signal is small relative to the background. In this case, the following equation for the ideal observer is obtained:

$$d' = \sqrt{\frac{F\omega AT}{\pi}} \frac{B_s}{\sqrt{B}} \qquad (5\text{-}25)$$

In this equation, F is the number of photons in a lumen-second of light; ω is the solid angle at the entrance pupil of the detecting device, and this solid angle subtends the area of the target; A is the area of the entrance pupil of the detector; T is the duration of the observation interval; B_s is the increment in luminescence which is to be detected; and B is the luminescence of the background (noise) expressed in lambert-type units.

The importance of the ROC in signal detection by human observers was first established in the area of vision (Tanner and Swets, 1954). In this early work, it was shown that the concept of a high threshold, and the associated process of correction for guessing, led to contradictory results. However, most of the recent applications of the concepts of TSD to psychophysics have been in the field of psychoacoustics.

Two types of ROC

The operating characteristic is a useful tool in the analysis of behavior in various types of situations. Thus far, we have limited our discussion primarily to the single-interval experiment as it relates to the fundamental detection problem. The operating characteristics obtained in this context may be called *stimulus-conditional* ROC curves. They are so called because the estimated probabilities $p(y|SN)$ and $p(y|N)$ are conditional upon the stimuli, or, more properly speaking, upon the events SN and N, respectively, that give rise to these stimuli. A second type of ROC has been defined for certain situations in which the observer is instructed to make a response of identification. This identification is intended to represent the observer's "best guess" as to which event gave rise to the stimulus received. However, if the task is limited to responses of identification, some of the observer's information about the stimulus (event) is discarded. It is well known that the observer is more confident of some of his identifications than of others, and he can assign ratings of confidence to his identifications in a nonchance manner. Such ratings carry additional information about the stimuli (events). This aspect of behavior can be described in terms of a *response-conditional* ROC. For this type of ROC, the question is, how well can the observer partition his ratings of confidence between his correct and his incorrect identifications? Let us assume that the observer adopts a criterion according to which he can accept or reject each of his identifications. Then, for a given criterion of acceptance, the probability that the observer will accept as correct his own response of identification is estimated separately for his correct and for his incorrect responses. The response-conditional ROC is the relation between the probability $p(y|C)$ that the observer will accept his identification as being correct when it is in fact correct and the probability $p(y|I)$ that he will accept his identification as correct when it is actually incorrect. These response-conditional ROC curves are usually linear on normal-normal paper. An index of performance, d_r, may be defined in the same manner as that used to define the index d_s for the stimulus-conditional ROC (Clarke *et al.*, 1959; Egan and Clarke, 1956; and Pollack, 1959a).

Operating characteristics in speech communication

Even a causal examination of the events that occur when two individuals talk to each other over a noisy two-way system shows that both operators make decisions concerning the accuracy of their own responses. For example, if a listener is in doubt about his identification of a message, he usually either (1) asks for a repeat of the message or (2) sends back what he has just heard to the source for a confirmation. Part of the communication process involves the use of criteria by the oper-

ators according to which they can reach a decision as to whether a message has been received correctly. The talker and the listener evaluate their own behavior, and their decisions help govern the accuracy with which communication takes place between them. These evaluative aspects of behavior may be studied experimentally by the determination of operating characteristics. The response-conditional ROC is particularly useful in this type of research (Carterette, 1958; Egan and Clarke, 1956; Pollack and Decker, 1958).

Comment on sequential effects

Several experiments have shown that an observer's response in a detection experiment may depend in part upon the events of previous trials. Such dependencies are troublesome to the sensory psychologist, and it is important that sequential effects be controlled and reduced insofar as it is possible in sensory-perceptual studies. Of course, sequential effects are easy to demonstrate for situations in which there is no correct response and for situations in which $\sqrt{2E/N_0}$ is either zero or very nearly so. The question of interest in the present context is whether intertrial dependencies have a serious effect upon the results of the typical experiment in signal detection. The results of only two studies will be described, and these studies were selected because they employed procedures that provide adequate measures of signal detection. The results of some of the earlier studies are not relevant here, simply because the psychophysical methods employed did not exert sufficient control over the observer's criterion.

Shipley (1961) analyzed separately the data obtained by a two-alternative forced-choice method and those obtained by a single-interval procedure ("yes-no"). She found that the probability of a correct response depended upon whether or not the response on the previous trial was correct. However, this dependency was so small as to be negligible in its effects upon the results of most studies of signal detection. The other study of particular relevance is that of Speeth and

Mathews (1961), who thoroughly analyzed a set of extensive data obtained with four well-practiced observers. These investigators found sequential effects for extremely small values of $\sqrt{2E/N_0}$, but these dependencies practically vanished for their highest, but still very small, value of $\sqrt{2E/N_0}$. Both of these studies provide direct evidence that the *Bernoulli assumption* is a reasonable and useful assumption to make, especially if care is taken in the instructions and in the training given to the observers. Further research is needed to determine efficient techniques and procedures so that, if necessary, the sensory psychologist can control and compensate for the minor sequential effects that have been found.

Other applications of TSD

We have selected for description in the above section only a few experimental studies conducted within the framework of TSD. Here are some other applications of TSD that may be of interest to the reader: (1) a stimulus-oriented approach to detection (Jeffress, 1964); (2) a useful extension of the rating technique (Watson, Rilling, and Bourbon, 1964); (3) detection as a function of signal intensity and duration (Green, Birdsall, and Tanner, 1957); (4) detection of a noise signal (Green, 1960a; Green and Sewall, 1962); (5) extension of detection theory to a theory of recognition (Tanner, 1956); (6) effect of multiple observations and sequential decisions (Smith and Wilson, 1953; Swets and Green, 1961; Swets, Shipley, McKey, and Green, 1959); (7) discrimination of auditory duration (Creelman, 1962); (8) specification to the observer of the response alternatives before and after the stimulus is presented (Swets and Sewall, 1961); (9) the criterion in the task of monitoring a speech channel (Egan, 1957); (10) analysis of detection in a vigilance, or free-responding, situation (Egan, Greenberg, and Schulman, 1961b); (11) application of TSD to neural discharges in the retina of the cat (FitzHugh, 1957); (12) recognition memory and the operating characteristic (Egan, 1958); (13) a further study of sequential effects (Friedman and Carterette, 1964); (14) a brief, excellent review of signal detection (Swets, 1961a); and (15) a collection of papers by various authors on signal detection and recognition by human observers (Swets, 1964).[1]

[1] For this brief introduction to the theory of signal detectability and to its applications, we have chosen not to discuss attempts to derive the ROC from assumptions that stem primarily from theories of learning and judgment (Atkinson, 1963; Luce, 1963; Restle, 1961).

REFERENCES

ATKINSON, R. C. A variable sensitivity theory of signal detection. *Psychol. Rev.*, 1963, **70**, 91–106.

BENDAT, J. S. *Principles and applications of random noise theory.* New York: Wiley, 1958.

BROSS, I. D. J. *Design for decision.* New York: Macmillan, 1953.

BROWN, C. R., and RUBENSTEIN, H. Test of response bias explanation of word-frequency effect. *Science*, 1961, **133**, No. 3448, 280–281.

CARTERETTE, E. C. Message repetition and receiver confirmation of messages in noise. *J. acoust. Soc. Amer.*, 1958, **30**, 846–855.

CLARKE, F. R. Confidence ratings, second-choice responses, and confusion matrices in intelligibility tests. *J. acoust. Soc. Amer.*, 1960a, **31**, 35–46.

CLARKE, F. R. The theory of signal detectability. In *Signal detection and psychophysics.* Prepared for one of the University of Michigan Engineering Summer Conferences, University of Michigan, Ann Arbor, Mich., 1960b.

CLARKE, F. R., and BILGER, R. C. The theory of signal detectability and the measurement of hearing. In J. F. Jerger (Ed.), *Modern developments in audiology.* New York: Academic Press, 1963.

CLARKE, F. R., BIRDSALL, T. G., and TANNER, W. P., JR. Two types of ROC curves and definitions of parameters. *J. acoust. Soc. Amer.*, 1959, **31**, 629–630.

CREELMAN, C. D. Detection of complex signals as a function of signal bandwidth and duration. *J. acoust. Soc. Amer.*, 1961, **33**, 89–94.

CREELMAN, C. D. Human discrimination of auditory duration. *J. acoust. Soc. Amer.*, 1962, **34**, 582–593.

EGAN, J. P. Monitoring task in speech communication. *J. acoust. Soc. Amer.*, 1957, **29**, 482–489.

EGAN, J. P. Recognition memory and the operating characteristic. *Tech. Note No. AFCRC-TN-58-51.* Hearing and Communication Laboratory, Indiana University, Bloomington, Ind., June, 1958.

EGAN, J. P., and CLARKE, F. R. Source and receiver behavior in the use of a criterion. *J. acoust. Soc. Amer.,* 1956, 28, 1267–1269.

EGAN, J. P., GREENBERG, G. Z., and SCHULMAN, A. I. Interval of time uncertainty in auditory detection. *J. acoust. Soc. Amer.,* 1961a, 33, 771–778.

EGAN, J. P., GREENBERG, G. Z., and SCHULMAN, A. I. Operating characteristics, signal detectability, and the method of free response. *J. acoust. Soc. Amer.,* 1961b, 33, 993–1007.

EGAN, J. P., SCHULMAN, A. I., and GREENBERG, G. Z. Operating characteristics determined by binary decisions and by ratings. *J. acoust. Soc. Amer.,* 1959, 31, 768–773.

EGAN, J. P., SCHULMAN, A. I., and GREENBERG, G. Z. Memory for waveform and time uncertainty in auditory detection. *J. acoust. Soc. Amer.,* 1961, 33, 779–781.

FITZHUGH, R. The statistical detection of threshold signals in the retina. *J. gen. Physiol.,* 1957, 40, 925–948.

FRIEDMAN, M. P., and CARTERETTE, E. C. Detection of Markovian sequences of signals. *J. acoust. Soc. Amer.,* 1964, 36, 2334–2339.

GOLDIAMOND, I. Indicators of perception: I. Subliminal perception, subception, unconscious perception: An analysis in terms of psychophysical indicator methodology. *Psychol. Bull.,* 1958, 55, 373–411.

GOLDMAN, S. *Information theory.* Englewood Cliffs, N.J.: Prentice-Hall, 1953. Pp. 67–71.

GREEN, D. M. Auditory detection of a noise signal. *J. acoust. Soc. Amer.,* 1960a, 32, 121–131.

GREEN, D. M. Psychoacoustics and detection theory. *J. acoust. Soc. Amer.,* 1960b, 32, 1189–1203.

GREEN, D. M. Detection of auditory sinusoids of uncertain frequency. *J. acoust. Soc. Amer.,* 1961, 33, 897–903.

GREEN, D. M., BIRDSALL, T. G., and TANNER, W. P., JR. Signal detection as a function of signal intensity and duration. *J. acoust. Soc. Amer.,* 1957, 29, 523–531.

GREEN, D. M., and SEWALL, S. T. Effects of background noise on auditory detection of noise bursts. *J. acoust. Soc. Amer.,* 1962, 34, 1207–1216.

GUILFORD, J. P. *Psychometric methods.* (2nd ed.) New York: McGraw-Hill, 1954.

GUNDY, R. F. Auditory detection of an unspecified signal. *J. acoust. Soc. Amer.,* 1961, 33, 1008–1012.

HELSTROM, C. W. *Statistical theory of signal de-tection.* New York: Pergamon Press, 1960.

JEFFRESS, LLOYD, A. Stimulus-oriented approach to detection. *J. acoust. Soc. Amer.,* 1964, 36, 766–774.

KOTEL 'NIKOV, V. A. *The theory of optimum noise immunity.* New York: McGraw-Hill, 1960.

LICKLIDER, J. C. R. Three auditory theories. In S. Koch (Ed.), *Psychology: A study of a science.* Vol. I. New York: McGraw-Hill, 1959. Pp. 41–144.

LUCE, R. D. A threshold theory for simple detection experiments. *Psychol. Rev.,* 1963, 70, 61–79.

MARILL, T. Detection theory and psychophysics. *Tech. Rep. No. 319,* Research Laboratory of Electronics, Massachusetts Institute of Technology, Cambridge, Mass., October, 1956.

PETERSON, W. W., BIRDSALL, T. G., and FOX, W. C. The theory of signal detectability. *IRE Trans. Profess. Group Inform. Theory,* 1954, PGIT-4, 171–212.

POLLACK, I. On indices of signal and response discriminability. *J. acoust. Soc. Amer.,* 1959a, 31, 1031.

POLLACK, I. Message uncertainty and message reception. *J. acoust. Soc. Amer.,* 1959b, 31, 1500–1508.

POLLACK, I., and DECKER, L. R. Confidence ratings, message reception, and the receiver operating characteristic. *J. acoust. Soc. Amer.,* 1958, 30, 286–292.

POSTMAN, L., and EGAN, J. P. *Experimental psychology: An introduction.* New York: Harper & Row, 1949. Pp. 9–32.

RESTLE, F. *Psychology of judgment and choice: A theoretical essay.* New York: Wiley, 1961.

SHIPLEY, E. F. Dependence of successive judgments in detection tasks: Correctness of the response. *J. acoust. Soc. Amer.,* 1961, 33, 1142–1143.

SMITH, M., and WILSON, E. A. A model of the auditory threshold and its application to the problem of the multiple observer. *Psychol. Monogr.,* 1953, 67, No. 9, 1–35.

SORKIN, R. D. Extension of the theory of signal detectability to matching procedures in psychoacoustics. *J. acoust. Soc. Amer.,* 1962, 34, 1745–1751.

SPEETH, S. D., and MATHEWS, M. V. Sequential effects in the signal-detection situation. *J. acoust. Soc. Amer.,* 1961, 33, 1046–1054.

SWETS, J. A. Indices of signal detectability obtained with various psychophysical procedures. *J. acoust. Soc. Amer.,* 1959, 31, 511–513.

SWETS, J. A. Detection theory and psychophysics: A review. *Psychometrika,* 1961a, 26, 49–63.

SWETS, J. A. Is there a sensory threshold? *Science,* 1961b, 134, 168–177.

SWETS, JOHN A. (Ed.) *Signal detection and recognition by human observers.* New York: Wiley, 1964.

SWETS, J. A., and GREEN, D. M. Sequential observations by human observers of signals in noise. In C. Cherry (Ed.), *Information theory.* London: Butterworth Scientific Publications, 1961.

SWETS, J. A., and SEWALL, S. T. Stimulus vs. response uncertainty in recognition. *J. acoust. Soc. Amer.,* 1961, **33**, 1586–1592.

SWETS, J. A., SHIPLEY, E. F., MCKEY, M. J., and GREEN, D. M. Multiple observations of signals in noise. *J. acoust. Soc. Amer.,* 1959, **31**, 514–521.

SWETS, J. A., TANNER, W. P., JR., and BIRDSALL, T. G. Decision processes in perception. *Psychol. Rev.,* 1961, **68**, 301–340.

TANNER, W. P., JR. Theory of recognition. *J. acoust. Soc. Amer.,* 1956, **28**, 882–888.

TANNER, W. P., JR. What is masking? *J. acoust. Soc. Amer.,* 1958, **30**, 919–921.

TANNER, W. P., JR. Graphical presentation of data in the framework of the theory of signal detectability. *J. acoust. Soc. Amer.,* 1959, **31**, 243–244.

TANNER, W. P., JR. Theory of signal detectability as an interpretive tool for psychophysical data. *J. acoust. Soc. Amer.,* 1960, **32**, 1140–1147.

TANNER, W. P., JR. Application of the theory of signal detectability to amplitude discrimination. *J. acoust. Soc. Amer.,* 1961a, **33**, 1233–1244.

TANNER, W. P., JR. Physiological implications of psychophysical data. *Ann. N.Y. Acad. Sci.,* 1961b, **89**, 752–765.

TANNER, W. P., JR., and BIRDSALL, T. G. Definitions of d′ and η as psychophysical measures. *J. acoust. Soc. Amer.,* 1958, **30**, 922–928.

TANNER, W. P., JR., BIRDSALL, T. G., and CLARKE, F. R. The concept of the ideal observer in psychophysics. *Tech. Rep. No. 98,* Electronic Defense Group, University of Michigan, Ann Arbor, Mich., 1960.

TANNER, W. P., JR., and JONES, R. C. The ideal sensory system as approached through statistical decision theory and the theory of signal detectability. In A. Morris and E. P. Horne (Eds.), *Visual search techniques.* Publ. No. 712, National Academy of Sciences–National Research Council, Washington, D.C., 1960.

TANNER, W. P., JR., and SWETS, J. A. A decision-making theory of visual detection. *Psychol. Rev.,* 1954, **61**, 401–409.

WATSON, C. S., RILLING, M. E., and BOURBON, W. T. Receiver-operating characteristics determined by a mechanical analog to the rating scale. *J. acoust. Soc. Amer.,* 1964, **36**, 283–288.

WOODWORTH, R. S., and SCHLOSBERG, H. *Experimental psychology.* New York: Holt, 1954. Pp. 192–233.

Chapter 6

AUDITION

IRA J. HIRSH

This chapter will be devoted to the ways in which sounds and responses to sounds must be described and controlled in order to obtain quantitative results pertaining to the auditory process.

TYPES OF AUDITORY PROBLEM

Auditory problems can be defined according to a particular kind of auditory phenomenon, an experimental method, a type of response, or a kind of sound. Such criteria for classification are not mutually exclusive, and the following listing uses several of them simultaneously.

Sensitivity

The sensitivity of the auditory system is described by the absolute threshold, or threshold of audibility, i.e., the smallest amount of acoustic energy that will elicit one or another kind of response. This definition, in terms of a phenomenon and a kind of response, may be further restricted by the kind of sound used. Thus we can speak of the sensitivity of the auditory system for pure tones, for complex tones, for noise, or for speech. In the first case, that of sensitivity for pure tones, the absolute threshold is usually measured as a function of the frequency of the pure tone

(Hirsh, 1952, Chap. 4). The result of this measurement, the so-called audibility curve, is the most frequent illustration of auditory sensitivity. The capacity of the auditory system to detect very weak sounds is not restricted to pure tones. Sensitivity for more complex sounds cannot be stated so easily as a function of frequency because the stimuli contain more than one frequency simultaneously. Thus sensitivity for complex tones might be measured as a function of the fundamental frequency, the number and spacing of harmonics, and the relative intensities and phases of the harmonics. A special case would be the sensitivity of the auditory system for the different vowels of speech (Fletcher, 1953, pp. 84–88). Similarly, we might measure sensitivity for noises, but here the relations among the frequencies are not so simple as those in a complex tone; therefore the description of the stimuli would involve such parameters as bandwidth, spectrum envelope, and peak factor.

Some of these physical dimensions of the stimulus will be detailed below. The general point to be made here is that the capacity of the auditory system to detect weak sounds can be measured with a variety of sounds, and in all cases the dependent variable will be some measure of amplitude sufficient to evoke a simple response.

Discrimination

By definition, any sound whose energy level is above the absolute threshold is audible, but the auditory system performs many more complicated tasks than a simple "yes" or "no" response. All auditory experience is built on the capacity of listeners to distinguish among sounds. The experimental problems inherent in measuring discrimination have to do with specifying the physical dimensions within which sounds may be differentiated and then fashioning some kind of procedure wherein a listener can respond differentially to such sounds. Classical psychophysics was almost wholly concerned with the difference limen (DL) or differential threshold (Boring, 1942). In most cases these early measurements concerned the minimal difference in either frequency or intensity that enabled a listener to distinguish between two pure tones.

When the variety of recognizable sounds is considered, we find that there are many other dimensions along which discriminability might be measured. Thus, for example, two sounds that contain the same frequency or spectral composition and the same intensities may be judged different if one has a shorter duration than the other (Woodrow, 1951). Two noises may be judged different if their bandwidths are centered in different parts of the audible frequency range. Two musical instruments playing the same note at the same loudness may be discriminated on the basis of spectral or harmonic composition. When other sounds like the brief sounds of speech are considered, judgments of difference are given by listeners without our knowing, in all cases, the most important physical dimension of difference.

A special case of discrimination is the ability of listeners to judge that two sounds appear to be coming from different places (Licklider, 1951). Here the physical dimensions along which the sound is changed may be the actual position of a sound source in external space (Mills, 1958) or the contrived relations between signals presented separately to the two ears, via earphones, which give rise to auditory localizations within or near the head (Deatherage and Hirsh, 1959).

Interference

Most listening takes place with the signals presented against a background of some kind of noise or interfering sound. One type of interference can be demonstrated when the interfering sound and the signal occur simultaneously; a second, when the interfering sound precedes a signal. The first case includes a variety of situations classified under the term *masking*. There is, however, another subclass of interferences brought about not so much by a sound whose masking may reside within the auditory system itself but rather by one whose interference has to do with attention or distraction. This might be considered an extension of masking, where the masking effectiveness of a sound includes not only its acoustic properties but also its semantic properties.

Auditory masking is most often measured as the change in the absolute threshold for one sound that is brought about by a second, masking sound. Some practical examples include the effects of noise in a subway train on conversation or noise of a jet airplane overhead on an outdoor concert. It is obvious that the sensitivity of the auditory system must be stated in different ways with different physical parameters, depending on the kind of sound used. In the case of masking, we have confounded the number of different ways that the masked threshold must be stated, depending upon the interactions of different kinds of masked and masking sounds. For example, pure tones may be masked by other pure tones (Wegel and Lane, 1924), or tones may be masked by different kinds of noise (Bilger and Hirsh, 1956; Greenwood, 1961). The sounds of speech may be masked by tones, noise, or competing speech (Miller, 1947). The amount of masking will depend upon frequencies, bandwidths, levels, and durations of both signals and masking sounds. Furthermore, in the case of masking of speech, not only are these acoustic variables important, but effects have been demonstrated most clearly with regard to contextual or semantic factors (Broadbent, 1958; Webster and Solomon, 1955).

Not all kinds of auditory *adaptation* are easily classified as interference phenomena. Loudness adaptation, for example, is demonstrated when the continuation of a sound in the ear produces a diminution in the loudness of that sound relative to its initial loudness (Egan and Thwing, 1955; Hood, 1950; Jerger, 1957). This is a strange kind of interference at best but may be regarded as the interfering effect of a sound upon its loudness at some later time. This relationship is more easily seen in those studies which have demonstrated a reduction in the loudness of one sound that is brought about by adaptation to a different sound (Thwing, 1955).

The various kinds of *shift* in the auditory threshold that are brought about by preceding stimuli seem to be closely analogous to adaptation in vision. Exposure to a loud noise or other sound, for example, will render the ear less sensitive to certain sounds. This phenomenon may be observed within minutes after moderate exposures (Hirsh and Bilger, 1955; Hood, 1950) or after more intense exposures by taking successive audiograms (threshold measures for one or more pure tones) over a period of hours (Ward, Glorig, and Sklar, 1958). Such shifts in threshold following exposure to noise are called temporary threshold shifts, or temporary hearing losses, since the sensitivity eventually returns to normal if the noise does not exceed a certain intensity.

Even very weak sounds may produce a change in the threshold for subsequent sounds, but here the threshold shift must be observed within a few milliseconds (msec) or seconds (sec) after the exposure sound (Lüscher and Zwislocki, 1947; Munson and Gardner, 1950). This phenomenon has been called auditory adaptation or residual masking.

After prolonged exposure (years) to intense noise, a person may also develop permanent threshold shifts or hearing loss (Nixon and Glorig, 1961). Such a phenomenon in

human beings is suitable only for field observation, but experimental studies have been carried out with animals (Miller, Watson, and Covell, 1963).

Pattern perception

The phenomena listed under sensitivity, discrimination, and interference may involve relatively simple responses with relatively well-defined sound stimuli. Just as the perception of forms, letters, or scenes in vision cannot be predicted solely on the basis of data on brightness discrimination, color discrimination, or visual acuity, so the perception of the acoustic patterns that comprise environmental or natural sounds or the melodies and harmonies of musical compositions introduces variables other than those associated with more elementary sensory processes.

One general principle seems clear, namely, that whereas a complex pattern for visual perception is composed of changes in such visual dimensions as intensity and spectral composition along various directions in space, the appropriate patterns for auditory perception consist of analogous changes in such dimensions as intensity, frequency, and complexity as a function of time (Hirsh, 1959).

Speech perception

The sounds of speech comprise examples of all kinds of sound (complex tones, clicks, noises, etc.), and the flow of speech in sentences or in conversation contains not only these elemental speech sounds but also continuous change along certain dimensions that require more complicated perceptual laws than those which would govern the identification of speech elements.

From one point of view, speech comprises a class of sounds that may be used in special ways in auditory experiments. Our concern here will be primarily with the hearing of speech. We cannot proceed, however, without giving some attention to the acoustical nature of speech (Fant, 1960; Fletcher, 1953). In general, the voice can be regarded as a complex-tone generator whose output is fed through the vocal tract. The tract has different diameters at different points along the way, depending upon the position of the lips, the tongue, etc., and these different diameters give rise to different resonances or points of reinforcement for certain harmonics of the complex tone generated in the larynx. In addition to the voiced sounds or *vowels,* the consonants may include sources of sound not from the larynx. For example, the sound source for /s/ and /t/ is the air turbulence around the hard surface of the teeth, and the acoustic features of such sounds come from the particular configuration of the vocal tract as well as certain features of the source, for example, its duration. Some of the specific descriptions that result from these purely acoustic analyses and electrical analogs have been tested with human listeners by using machines whose acoustic outputs can be manipulated directly in the terms suggested by speech analysis. One of the most interesting developments along these lines is the pattern playback of the Haskins Laboratories (Liberman, Ingemann, Lisker, Delattre, and Cooper, 1959).

Phonemic discrimination

In its simplest form, the recognition of speech is exemplified by experiments whose results show the bases on which listeners discriminate one speech sound from another. Even though the continuous flow of conversational speech is not well represented as a series of discrete phonetic events, linguistic theory has shown that most of the rules governing the structure of a spoken language can be stated in terms of combinations and sequences of individual speech sounds, called phonemes. In most American dialects of spoken English, there are about 40 such phonemes, divided into approximately 15 vowels and about 25 consonants (Hirsh, 1952). The comprehension of any long speech message will depend at least partly upon the individual recognition of such phonemes.

Experiments in which individual talkers enunciate individual phonemes that listeners are then required to identify have proved un-wieldy. Formal articulation tests present a compromise between the elementary phonemes taken individually and the complex sequences of such phonemes that constitute the words, phrases, or sentences of spoken English. In so-called *articulation tests* (Egan, 1948), a listener is asked to identify short, monosyllabic words made up of a succession of only two or three individual speech sounds. *Confusion tests* utilizing pairs of words like "cap" and "cat" can reveal the ability of listeners to distinguish or discriminate the individual speech sounds as embedded in the ordinary phonemic context provided by a word (Fairbanks, 1958; Miller and Nicely, 1955).

The recognition of words is a complex process in which phonemic discrimination is a necessary but not a sufficient condition. In order for a listener to identify easily an isolated word as being a member of his own language, he must have learned that word on previous occasions; it must be a member of his vocabulary. In addition to past learning, the recognition of words will also depend upon the contextual constraints of the phrase or sentence in which the word is embedded (Miller, Heise, and Lichten, 1951). Furthermore, such factors as frequency of usage and emotional tone, which have been demonstrated to affect the visual recognition of words, may also influence the auditory recognition of such words.

At a still higher level it should be noted that the comprehension of a long speech message, like a paragraph, will be influenced not only by phonemic discrimination and all those factors which determine individual word recognition but also by the syntactic and semantic relations within the message and by many of the same considerations that are known to affect reading comprehension.

In situations where linguistic constraints have been removed, articulation tests have enjoyed a wide use in testing communications systems of various kinds. Here, the talker and the group of listeners serve as a kind of "intelligibility meter" for evaluating a system. By articulation-testing techniques, much information has been uncovered about the effects on speech exerted by such acoustic variables as amplitude distortion, filtering or limiting of the passband, compression of the dynamic range, and different kinds and levels of noise (Miller, 1951).

DESCRIPTION AND CONTROL OF SOUNDS

The physical stimulus for hearing, sound, is a change or series of changes in air pressure in the external ear canal, which brings about displacements of the eardrum and eventual stimulation of the auditory nerve fibers (Davis and Silverman, 1960).

In the following sections we shall introduce several different ways of describing sound and of measuring its dimensions (Hirsh, 1952). This discussion is facilitated by the development of electroacoustic transducers, like earphones and loudspeakers, whose acoustical output represents the electrical input reasonably well. Thus it is possible to describe many of the features of sound in terms of related electrical features, which can be measured by voltmeters and oscilloscopes.

Waveform and the oscilloscope

One convenient way of representing any particular sound is to describe the course of its amplitude or sound pressure as a function of time. This function is the acoustic waveform of the sound. The analogous electrical waveform can be displayed on the cathode-ray oscilloscope (CRO) when the horizontal axis displays time and the vertical axis displays amplitude. Most often, the electrical analog of sound pressure is the voltage used to energize the transducer.

A first and most convenient use of the waveform is to classify different kinds of sound. Continuous or prolonged sounds may be pure tones, complex tones, noises, or combinations of these. In addition to these steady-state sounds, we can also describe certain transient or brief sounds such as clicks, which have correspondingly transient waveforms.

A *pure tone* is a sound whose sound pres-sure as a function of time yields a waveform that looks like the function relating the sine of an angle to the angle. Any realizable pure tone is only an approximation to the mathematically defined sine wave, because it does not last for an infinite time but is turned on and off at some time within an experimental session. Thus the waveform representation in Fig. 6-1a should be taken to represent a sample over a short time (2 cycles) of a 50-cps pure tone during its steady state.

A *complex tone* is a sound whose basic waveform, although repeated periodically, is more complicated than that of a sine wave (Fig. 6-1b). Complex tones may be thought of as containing two or more pure-tone components. The lowest, or fundamental, frequency of a complex tone is the rate at which the basic pattern is repeated (here 50 cps), and the reciprocal of the fundamental frequency is the time for one period of the basic pattern (here 0.02 sec). There is an almost infinite variety of combinations of components that would yield different complex-tone patterns. Examples of the source for a complex tone include musical instruments, the human voice, and certain machines having rhythmic or repetitive mechanisms that give rise to buzz-like or humlike sounds. A complex tone may be physically and mathematically analyzed into its component frequencies, all of which will be integral multiples of the fundamental frequency. Any time the waveform of a complex tone is changed, that change corresponds to a change in the number, amplitude, or phase of one or more of the component frequencies.

Noise has been defined in at least two ways. One definition states that noise is unwanted sound, and another states that noise is an aperiodic, random sound. The difficulties encountered in making the first definition both unique to this particular kind of sound and general over a variety of human beings suggests use of the second, physical definition of noise. Its waveform is irregular, demonstrating no recurrence of a periodic pattern (Fig.

(a) PURE TONE

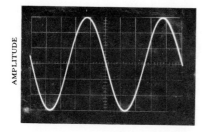

(b) COMPLEX TONE

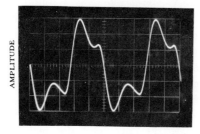

(c) NOISE

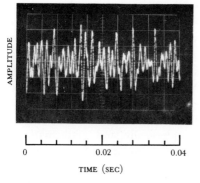

AMPLITUDE

0   0.02   0.04

TIME (SEC)

Fig. 6-1 Waveforms (oscillograms) for three different kinds of continuous sound: a, pure tone; b, complex tone; c, noise. Amplitude is shown on the ordinate and time on the abscissa.

6-1c). Thus we cannot speak of a fundamental frequency in a noise nor can we state, as we did above for complex tones, that all the frequencies are integral multiples of such a fundamental. If a noise is analyzed into component frequencies, they are bound to be crowded together, not easily separable in the ways used for analyzing complex tones, and therefore must be treated quite differently.

The source for such a random noise is often found to be a flow of air across a sharp edge; thus we may recognize that sources of such noise are exemplified by air or steam escaping from a valve or by the exhaust of a jet engine. Certain consonants of speech, produced by air turbulence, are other examples of noise.

The waveforms described above differentiate three kinds of continuous sound. The waveforms shown in Fig. 6-1 have been utilized as samples of this steady-state behavior. The snap of a whip or of the fingers produces a change in pressure in the ear canal and thus also constitutes sound. Clicks or snaps do not have steady states over any examinable duration and must, therefore, be described in ways more suitable to transient phenomena.

A simple rectangular pulse, shown in Fig. 6-2, top, may be defined by its amplitude and duration. When such an electrical waveform is passed through an earphone or a loudspeaker, however, the resonant properties of the transducer will change the waveform so that the acoustic output will look more like the damped oscillation shown below. A highly damped transducer will cause these oscillations to die out quickly, while a less damped transducer will cause them to be sustained over a much longer time, just as the string of a guitar or a piano will vibrate long after it has been struck. Of course there are many other waveforms that describe transients (sawtooth waves, step functions, etc.), and, within certain limits, they will sound qualitatively different. When a series of such transient sounds is generated with a regular repetition rate higher than about 20 per sec, a complex tone is formed that can be described as a series of harmonically related frequencies.

Among the *sounds of speech* one can find examples of the kinds of sound thus far described. The vocal cords produce complex tones whose harmonics are accentuated or subdued by the resonant properties of the oral cavities. Examples are the vowels /æ/ (as in *bat*) and /i/ (as in *beet*). Whenever a voiceless consonant like /ʃ/ (sh) or /s/ is produced by forcing air through a constriction, we have a noise. Combining a friction noise with voice yields a noisy tone like the sound /ʒ/ in *azure*. The plosive sounds, like /p/ and /t/, are described as relatively complicated transients. Indeed, speech, defined acoustically, is a succession of these various kinds of sound.

Frequency spectrum

Although any sound can be completely described by its waveform, or amplitude as a function of time, there are certain features not easily abstracted from such a graphic display.

The specification of the spectrum of a sound is the most general way to describe its frequency content. This concept is borrowed from optics, where the spectrum of light shows the relative strengths of different wavelengths. The method of measuring the spectrum depends upon the kind of sound.

A pure tone has been defined as a sound whose amplitude varies sinusoidally as a function of time. This type of waveform implies the presence of only a single frequency; thus the specification of the spectrum of a pure tone requires the measurement of its single frequency.

Single-frequency measurement is not a simple process. Since pure tones are usually produced, in electrical form, by electronic oscillators in which a variable capacitor in combination with a resistor or an inductance is responsible for the different frequencies, many users of pure tones depend on the manufacturer's calibration of frequency, which is indicated on the tuning dial of the oscillator. Frequency can be measured, however, in several ways. The simplest (and most expensive) method is to use a frequency meter that is essentially a counter of successive waves in a fixed period of time. The results are ordinarily given on numerical indicators in such devices as the Berkeley Eput Meter, the Hewlett-Packard counter, or the General Radio Frequency Meter.

If such frequency meters are not available,

the frequency of a pure tone can be found in the following way. If the voltage of the unknown frequency is applied to the horizontal plates of a CRO and the voltage from a pure-tone source of known and variable frequency is applied to the vertical plates, the known frequency can be changed until a single line or slowly changing circle is displayed. The unknown frequency is equal to the known frequency that will yield such a pattern. A listener can also be used in place of an oscilloscope if the known and unknown frequencies are mixed and then fed to an earphone. The known frequency can then be changed until a null or zero beat is heard. When two frequencies are sounded together with almost equal amplitudes, pitches corresponding to the two frequencies will be heard, as well as certain combination tones. As the difference between the two frequencies is reduced, one hears the pitch of *difference tones* decreasing; when the difference becomes very small, one hears a waxing and waning of the loudness at a rate corresponding to the frequency difference. As this periodic change is further reduced in rate or beat frequency, a frequency or frequency difference can be

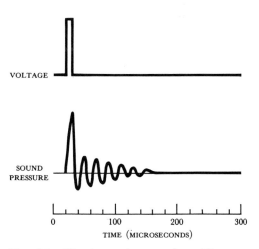

Fig. 6-2 Waveform of a transient. The upper trace (*a*) shows an electrical pulse that is delivered to an earphone, while the lower trace (*b*) shows the acoustic waveform of the output of the earphone.

found where the loudness no longer changes, that is, the beat frequency has reached a value of zero. Some readily available *fixed* known frequencies are broadcast by station WWV in Washington, D.C., and can be used in the laboratory for frequency calibration if one has a short-wave receiver.

A third method for measuring frequency is the use of oscilloscopes with carefully calibrated horizontal time bases. The horizontal sweep rate of the electron beam can be adjusted until exactly one or two or any small number of sinusoids appear on the face of the oscilloscope when the unknown frequency is applied to the vertical plates. The time taken for the particular number of sinusoids can then be read directly from the sweep-rate controls.

One cannot speak of *the* frequency of a complex tone because it contains several or many frequencies. Since the frequencies of such a complex tone are mostly multiples of some common lowest frequency, it is usual for the most general specification of frequency to be that of this fundamental or lowest frequency. It is possible to use a single pure tone of known frequency as a search or probe tone so that when it is combined with a complex tone, single-line or circle patterns can be produced on an oscilloscope as described in the second method above, or an audible zero beat can be sought for each component of the complex. While such a method can be used to describe the particular frequencies present, it is a cumbersome way to find the relative amplitudes of these frequencies. A more convenient instrument for these purposes is the *harmonic wave analyzer*, which selects only a very narrow band of frequencies, or passband, that can be positioned anywhere within the audible frequency range. The analyzer output feeds a voltmeter that reads the amount of energy passing through the instrument within the narrow band about any selected frequency. Two recently developed instruments can provide the spectrum of a complex tone graphically. One is the Panoramic Sound Analyzer, which shows amplitude as a function of frequency and is essentially a harmonic wave analyzer, with an automatically driven passband, whose output is shown vertically on a cathode-ray tube and whose center frequency is displayed along the horizontal axis. Another is the *sound spectrograph,* to be described below; only one of its functions is to display the spectrum of a steady-state sound.

Noise was defined above as an irregular, aperiodic, random sound in which the frequencies are not algebraically related to one another. One cannot easily specify the frequencies of bandwidth of a noise with a search or probe tone, but the harmonic wave analyzer described above could be used to show the relative amplitudes in different frequency regions of a noise. A simpler and more usual method utilizes the same principle but records the spectrum in larger intervals of frequency (Beranek, 1949). Among the most common filters for crude frequency analysis are those that pass one octave, that is, a band of frequencies whose upper limit is twice the lower frequency. If the noise of unknown spectrum is passed through a set of such filters, one can read the voltage output from the various octave bands and provide an octave-band analysis. There are many instances in which a somewhat finer analysis is provided by filters whose passbands equal one-third octave or one-half octave. These octave or fractional-octave filters always pass a constant percentage of the frequency range or include limits that have a constant frequency ratio. The harmonic wave analyzer, which provides very fine detail in frequency, often has a constant frequency passband, for example, an interval of 5 cps instead of a constant percentage or ratio.

Speech contains many kinds of sound that are not usually amenable to the kinds of spectral measurement mentioned above. Such measurements require that a sound remain in a measurable steady state for a long enough time to permit a meter reading. The individual sounds of speech transpire too quickly. If the researcher is interested in the overall distribution of energy as a function of frequency in speech (averaging overall speech sounds that would occur in proportion to their frequency of occurrence), he can make a magnetic tape recording of some speech and then play the tape over and over, cumulating the energy in each of the frequency bands as if it were a steady noise (Benson and Hirsh, 1953). The results of such measurement yield a long-time average spectrum of speech.

Suppose that we wish to know the spectra of individual speech sounds as they occur in a stream of speech. Such information is now available in the recordings of the *sound spectrograph*. This instrument permits the recording of a short sample of speech (2.4 sec) and then analyzes each element in the sample as a function of frequency and as a continuous function of time. The results of the analysis are recorded automatically on a special paper. The record shows frequency on the ordinate and time on the abscissa, with intensity represented by the darkness of the filled areas. The words used in the speech sample are displayed underneath the spectrograph. Phonetic symbols that correspond to the individual phonemes are shown along with the words (Pierce and David, 1958). The advantage of the spectrograph is that it can show not only individual distributions as a function of frequency but also changes in these distributions as a function of time. Its disadvantage is that the measurements of frequency and intensity are not very precise.

Amplitude

How does one specify the amplitude of a pure tone? The waveform of a pure tone as a function of time is always changing. The waveform on the oscilloscope does indeed display amplitude graphically, but it is no single quantity. This particular amplitude that changes with time, the *instantaneous amplitude,* can be specified only for an instant in time. A more general quantity that can be read from the oscilloscope is the *peak amplitude,* or the maximum value that the instantaneous amplitude achieves. A voltmeter, responding to integrated energy over time, reads root-mean-square (rms) amplitude, that is,

the square root of the average value of the squared instantaneous voltages. (Students of statistics will note that this rms voltage is the standard deviation of the distribution of instantaneous amplitudes.) A voltmeter will, in fact, yield an integrated measure of an electrical waveform fed into it, but a simple relation between the typical rms reading and the peak value of the waveform exists only for the pure tone. For complex waveforms the specification of voltage amplitude with an rms meter must be accompanied by a description of the spectrum (Beranek, 1949).

Voltage measurements have been described even though we were to specify sound amplitude or magnitude. The assumption has been made that in most instances where sound is to be generated for experimental study, the particular waveform is generated electrically, and then only after suitable control and measurement is it applied to an electroacoustic transducer like an earphone or loudspeaker. A problem remains in specifying the relation between electrical amplitude and acoustical amplitude. This response characteristic of the transducer (earphone or loudspeaker) is usually given in terms of acoustic output (sound pressure or sound power) as a function of frequency for a fixed-amplitude electric input.

The most frequently used measure of the strength of a sound is sound pressure, that is, the alternating variation in atmospheric pressure that is brought about by the sound source. Sound pressure, measured in dynes per square centimeter (or microbars, since a steady pressure of 1 million dynes per sq cm is, roughly, normal atmospheric pressure, 1 bar), may range from inaudible values of the order of 0.0001 microbar to painful values of the order of 1,000 microbars. Just as the large range of intensities that must be encompassed in vision are often expressed as logarithmic ratios, so this large range of sound pressures of interest in audition is compressed into a logarithmic scale in which the unit of measurement is the *decibel* (dB).

More fundamental measures than pressure or voltage concern power-acoustic or electric power. These terms have not been introduced into our working vocabulary because the common instruments for measurement in hearing laboratories are either electrical voltage (with voltmeters) or acoustical sound pressure (with calibrated microphones or sound-level meters). The decibel, however, is based on power. The number of decibels by which two levels of power differ is ten times the logarithm of the power ratio. Whereas sound power is measured in watts, sound power level is measured in decibels relative to a fixed reference power like 10^{-12} watt. Thus a power of, say, 1 watt (10^0) is 10^{12} times as large as the reference power and thus has a power level of 12 bels, or 120 dB.

While the total sound power or sound power level emitted by a sound source like a jet engine is of interest to design engineers, such a quantity must be integrated over a surface in which point measurements have been made of the power per unit area. Sound intensity is more often used because the actual measurement is made at a point or a small area. The decibel scale is applied in the same way except that the reference intensity is 10^{-16} watt per sq cm. Thus a sound intensity of, say, 1 watt per sq cm has an intensity level of 16 bels, or 160 dB, relative to the standard reference intensity.

If the decibel and its related ratios are so defined in terms of power or intensity (power per unit of area), then it can also be used to express ratios of voltage or of sound pressure, because these quantities squared are proportional to power. Thus the number of decibels can also be defined as ten times the logarithm of the *square* of a voltage ratio or of a sound pressure ratio. One decibel is one-tenth the logarithm of the power ratio 10:1, or one-twentieth of the logarithm of the voltage or pressure ratio 10:1.

In the same way that altitude may be described as so many feet above or below sea level, a sound pressure level (SPL) can be described as so many decibels above or below a standard reference sound pressure. The most frequently used reference is 0.0002 microbar.

The magnitude of a sound at a particular location is most often defined by its SPL relative to this reference. For example, the SPL of a sound whose sound pressure is 0.0002 microbar is 0 dB. The formula for the relation given above

$$dB_{SPL} = 20 \log_{10} \frac{X \text{ microbar}}{0.0002 \text{ microbar}}$$

indicates that the sound pressure of 0.002 microbar would have an SPL of 20 dB; one of 0.02 microbar, an SPL of 40 dB; one of 0.2 microbar, an SPL of 60 dB; etc. A sound pressure of 0.0001 microbar would have an SPL of −6 dB.

The decibel notation is also convenient for describing voltage levels. There is no single standard reference voltage, but a convenient one often used is 1 volt. By the above definitions, in which it is recalled that voltage is also proportional to the square root of power, 20 dB would correspond to a ten fold change in voltage. Thus, a voltage of 0.1 volt can also be expressed as −20 dB relative to 1 volt, and a voltage of 10 volts can also be expressed as 20 dB relative to 1 volt. Indeed, many voltmeters show a double scale, in which one set of markings may range from 0.001 to 0.01 volt or from 0.01 to 0.1 volt, depending upon the setting of a scale switch, and an equivalent set of markings ranges from 0 to 20 dB. An important point to remember is that when a particular voltage is applied to an earphone or loudspeaker whose output increases linearly as the electric input is changed, any change in the input voltage level of X dB will produce a corresponding change in the output sound pressure level of X dB.

There are two quite different situations in which sound pressure or SPL is measured. The first involves measurement of the magnitude of sound waves in free air or in a large space at a particular point at some distance from the sound source. Typically the electroacoustic transducer generating such a sound field is the loudspeaker. The most widely used instrument for making such measurements is the *sound-level meter* (Beranek, 1949), which consists of a microphone, amplifier, and voltmeter. The sound-level meter is an instrument of very general use, particularly when the sounds involved are complex wide-band sounds. It is not usually used to measure pure tones even in free air because the usual sound-level meters include microphones whose response characteristics as a function of frequency are not smooth. Sound pressure level may be read directly from the sound-level meter, when it is in proper calibration.

An earphone does not radiate sound into free air very efficiently because it has been designed to work into the relatively smaller volume of the ear canal. The sound pressure generated by an earphone is ordinarily measured within a small coupler (a cavity linking the earphone with the calibrated microphone) whose shape and volume are intended to simulate the characteristics of a typical human ear. One ordinarily measures this sound pressure in the coupler with a laboratory microphone of the capacitor type especially designed to fit tightly in the end of the coupler opposite to that of the earphone (Beranek, 1949, Chap. 16). This kind of measurement (Fig. 6-3) is

reliable, but it does not represent precisely the sound pressure that the same earphone would produce at any place in the ear canal of a listener, whether at the entrance of the canal or near the eardrum. Intra-aural measurements can be made with a laboratory microphone coupled to a small probe tube inserted into the ear canal. A single set of these measures can be used as a transfer reference for determining intra-aural SPLs when further measurements are restricted to the coupler.

In many laboratories or clinics where hearing is studied, acoustic measurements in a coupler often are not made. They are difficult and time-consuming and involve expensive equipment. In such instances the laboratory must rely on a description of the response of the earphone to a fixed input voltage as a function of frequency (Fig. 6-4) that is supplied either by a reliable manufacturer or by an acoustical laboratory.

We have only touched upon some of the most frequently encountered aspects of frequency measurement and the measurement of amplitude, whether acoustical or electrical. More specific details will be brought out when

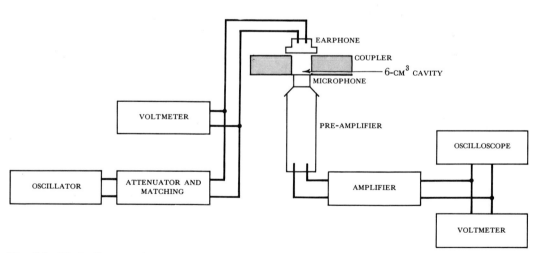

Fig. 6-3 Block diagram of apparatus used to measure the pressure response of an earphone as a function of frequency in a 6-cc coupler. The three blocks at the left comprise the system for supplying and measuring voltage to the earphone. The three blocks at the right comprise the system for amplifying and measuring the voltage output of the microphone in the coupler whose voltage response for a given sound pressure delivered at its face is known. (*From Hirsh, 1952.*)

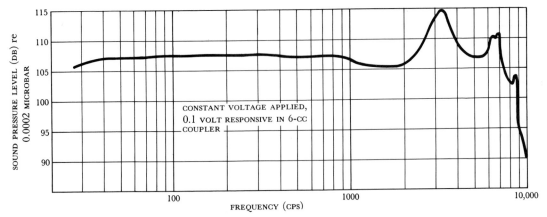

Fig. 6-4 Pressure response of a dynamic-type earphone (impedance = 10 ohms) as a function of frequency for a constant voltage applied of 0.1 volt or a constant power of 1 milliwatt.

these principles are put to work in some specific problems.

TYPICAL EXPERIMENTS

It is hoped that the choice of a few procedures typical of the most thoroughly studied aspects of audition will permit the reader to familiarize himself with such experimentation to the point where he can move relatively easily to others in which he has an interest. The methods outlined here cover the measurement of absolute thresholds for pure tones, difference limens for frequency, lateralization for sound in the head, temporary threshold shifts following noise exposure, and the intelligibility of speech in noise. Block diagrams of apparatus used for measuring responses in the above experiments are also presented. However, the procedures do not utilize some of the experimental methods of signal detection theory, to be found in Chapter 5, [Psychophysics and Signal Detection, by Egan and Clarke (pp. 211–246)]. More technical discussions of general circuitry and apparatus may be found in Chapter 2, [Basic Instrumentation].

Absolute threshold for pure tones

The experimenter wishes to measure the absolute threshold for pure tones in order to know about the sensitivity of the auditory system to weak sounds at different frequencies (Hirsh, 1952). Such an experiment may have as its purpose the description of absolute threshold for a single listener in terms of SPL in a standard coupler. Or, as one aspect of a health survey, the purpose may be the statistical description of such an absolute threshold for a large group of listeners (Glorig, Quiggle, Wheeler, and Grings, 1956).

To avoid a sound field and minimize the influence of the acoustic environment of the listener, pure tones will be produced through earphones. Since the researcher wishes to observe a change in the listener's response as the level of sound is changed, he must provide a means for changing the voltage level at the earphone. The source of the electric sinusoidal voltage will be a beat-frequency oscillator capable of producing frequencies from about 20 to 20,000 cps. Figure 6-5 shows a block diagram of the required apparatus. A typical oscillator is capable of delivering up to 10 volts to a 600-ohm resistive load, and no further amplification will be required for normal listeners.

Variation in the voltage level applied to the earphone will be accomplished by a variable attenuator in which the ratio of output to input voltage may be changed manually.

The advantage of such attenuators is that the voltage at the output can be changed while the voltage and impedance at the input remain constant. Since this attenuator is designed to be loaded with 600 ohms and since the electrical impedance of typical earphones is about 12 ohms, it is necessary to interpose either (1) a transformer that will match these two impedances and make the 12-ohm impedance of the phone at the secondary look like 600 ohms at the primary or (2) a resistive network with an input impedance of 600 ohms and an output impedance of 12 ohms.

For measurements, the beat-frequency oscillator has the considerable advantage of including controls that permit the experimenter to calibrate a frequency of 0 or 60 cps (the latter against line frequency). More complicated frequency measurement is then needed only as a check on the calibration of these controls.

The voltage output of the oscillator should be set at some convenient value, such as 1 volt, at the input to the attenuator. This voltage should be carefully checked at all frequencies to be used, because only the best-designed oscillators maintain a truly constant output for all frequencies.

The operation of the attenuator can be checked, after the circuit is hooked up, by noting that the voltage at the output bears the relation to the input voltage that is indicated on the attenuator dial. For example, when the attenuator is set at 0 dB, its output should still be 1 volt, whereas if it is set at 40 dB, its output should be 0.01 volt. It is not always possible, except with the most sensitive vacuum-tube voltmeters, to be sure that as much as 80 or 100 dB attenuation is actually available, because the voltages involved, namely, 0.0001 and 0.00001 volt, respectively, are too weak to measure.

Next the voltage ratio across the transformer must be measured. A transformer designed to match impedances of 600 to 12 ohms should have a voltage ratio of about $7:1$ (voltage ratio = turns ratio; impedance ratio = turns ratio^2). That is, the voltage across the secondary should be approximately 17 dB below the voltage across the primary $[N = 20 \log_{10} (7 \text{ volts}/1 \text{ volt}) = 20 \times 0.84 = 17 \text{ dB}]$. If this is shown by actual measurement, the experimenter is ready to say that the voltage across the earphone at any time is equal to the 1 volt that was set at the input to the attenuator minus the number of decibels in the attenuator and the 17-dB voltage drop across the transformer.

In lieu of a sound pressure measurement for this experiment, let us assume that we are using a calibrated earphone whose response in a 6-cc standard coupler for an rms electric input of 0.1 volt is the function of frequency shown in Fig. 6-4.

The listener will be instructed that he is to make a response, either raising his finger or pushing a button, whenever he hears a tone. The experimenter can, after placing the earphone over the listener's ear, demonstrate the kinds of sound that he will use.

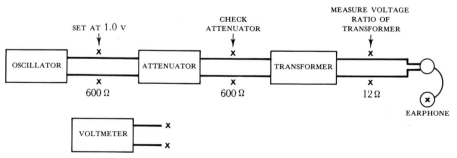

Fig. 6-5   Block diagram of apparatus for measuring absolute threshold for pure tones.

The psychophysical procedure in this particular instance will be a modification of the method of limits, the modification consisting in interrupting the tone between successive levels. The details of this procedure are available in a more complete form in Guilford (1954). In general, the procedure consists in the presentation of a tone at a particular frequency at a clearly audible level. Then the level is decreased in steps until the tone no longer elicits a response. At this point the intensity variation changes direction and the experimenter increases the level of the tone until the listener again responds. The former point is called the *descending threshold*, while the latter is called the *ascending threshold*. The experimenter's task is to record the level of the tone at which these response changes occur. It can be seen that an original fixed voltage setting followed by variation in an attenuator requires only the recording of attenuator settings without the continuous monitoring of a voltmeter. A series of threshold crossings, involving perhaps three or four descents and ascents, will usually be sufficient to define a threshold. The entire set of measurements for a single frequency should be completed before a new frequency is used.

The results of the experiment are accumulated in several stages. For a single frequency (say 250 cps) and for a single listener, one records the attenuator settings and the listener's responses. Assuming that the voltage and frequency had been set as described above, one can work with attenuator readings alone. A piece of paper with vertical and horizontal lines is convenient for recording successive, numbered steps in a column and, alongside of each, a symbol for the presence (+) or absence (−) of a response. If the first series is a descent with numbers at 70, 72, 74, etc., and the listener responds to a tone at each setting down to 82, a new column is used to record an ascent from 90 or so. A new column should be used each time the response changes. In the method of limits, it is usual to find that the listener can follow a descending tone to a point well below the first level to which he will respond again on ascent. The ascending and descending thresholds may be averaged separately and then combined. The mean setting is still an attenuator reading, perhaps 82 dB. This is the listener's threshold for 250 cps in decibels relative to the set values of 1 volt into the attenuator and the constant voltage changes (differences) in the rest of the apparatus. Now one can proceed to measurement at a different frequency.

These thresholds for each frequency, recorded as attenuator settings, may now be converted to SPL. At 250 cps, for example, we found that the listener's threshold was 82 dB below 1 volt (into the attenuator), and we know that the voltage at the phone is 17 dB below that. Thus, the threshold voltage at the phone is 99 dB below 1 volt. Referring to the response characteristic of the earphone shown in Fig. 6-4, the reader can see that at 250 cps an SPL of 107 dB is produced when a voltage of 0.1 volt is applied to the earphone, and therefore 1 volt (20 dB higher) should have produced 127 dB SPL. The threshold voltage is 99 dB below 1 volt; therefore the threshold SPL is 99 dB below 127 dB SPL. The threshold SPL is 28 dB.

Repetition of this procedure will yield threshold SPLs for each frequency tested, and these results may be given either in tabular form or graphically, where SPL (in decibels) is plotted as a function of frequency (in cycles per second). If a study is to average the threshold of several listeners, these averages may be obtained again on attenuator settings alone, and conversion to SPL need not be made until after all averages have been obtained in attenuator settings.

Other psychophysical methods are available for measuring the absolute threshold. When they are used, different arrangements of experimental apparatus are required. In the method of adjustment (Guilford, 1954) the listener should be supplied with an additional attenuator so that he can be instructed to adjust the attenuator until a tone is just audible. An interesting variation is found in the Békésy audiometer (Békésy, 1947), in which the listener is instructed to push a button when he hears the tone and release it when the tone disappears. These responses in turn control a motor that automatically increases or decreases the attenuation in the circuit and at the same time provides a graphic recording of the amount of attenuation.

Although an example of the masking of pure tones by noise is not included in this series of typical experiments, it should be pointed out that the same psychophysical procedures used for measuring the absolute threshold are also used in measuring the threshold for a pure tone in the presence of noise. The primary difference lies in the additional circuitry required to present both noise and signal to the same ear (Bilger and Hirsh, 1956; Hawkins and Stevens, 1950).

Difference limen for frequency

Measurements of the DL for frequency are carried out to obtain information on the resolving power or sensitivity to differences in frequency (Hirsh, 1952). Here again the interest may be in the differential sensitivity of a single listener or in the statistically defined differential sensitivity of a group of listeners.

Since the listener will be asked to judge whether two frequencies are the same or different, two separate oscillators must be used. The experimenter will present the two frequencies alternately to the same ear of the listener and thus will employ a two-channel electronic switch. The purpose of this switch is to provide one of two frequencies at any given time, each of which is turned on gradually so that no starting transient is audible. Figure 6-6 shows connections of the two separate oscillators to the two channels of the electronic switch, with separate attenuators in the outputs of the two channels, after which the controlled voltages are combined in a mixing network for delivery to a single matching transformer and earphone.

The response characteristic of the phone as a function of frequency must be known so that the level for presentation can be adjusted by a combination of voltage measurements at the output of the electronic switch, preceding the attenuator, and by settings of the attenuators themselves. It may be that both frequencies will be set at the same SPL or at the same sensation level, that is, the same number of decibels above the listener's absolute threshold at each frequency.

The most difficult part of calibration in this experiment is the frequency measurement. If a frequency counter is available, it can be used first to adjust the standard frequency, for example, at 1,000 cps. It may also

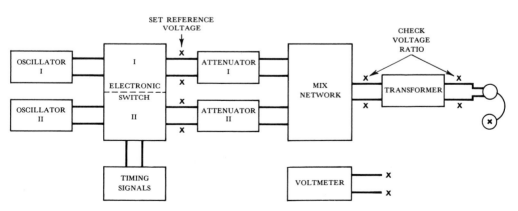

Fig. 6-6 Block diagram of apparatus used for the measurement of the difference limen for frequency. Alternation between two frequencies transmitted through separate channels is required by the method of constant stimuli.

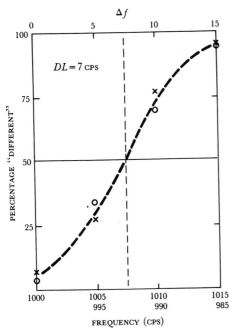

Fig. 6-7 Results of measurement of the frequency difference limen. The ordinate shows the percentage of judgments in which the listener reported that the two frequencies were "different." The abscissa at the bottom shows the variable frequency: variable frequencies lower than 1,000 cps (the standard) should be read for the circles, and variable frequencies higher than the standard should be read for the X's. The abscissa at the top groups the sets of two lower numbers and displays the difference (Δf) between either variable frequency and the standard.

be used to monitor the variable frequency during the course of the experiment. If two beat-frequency oscillators are available, their frequencies may be read directly from the dial after the usual zero-frequency calibration. A difficulty with this method is that listeners are extremely sensitive to small frequency changes, and very small differences can be read accurately only on oscillators having a "cycles increment" dial for vernier control.

An adaptation of the method of constant stimulus differences may be used to determine the DL (Guilford, 1954). Suppose the standard frequency is set at 1,000 cps and the variable frequency is set at 1,020 cps. The listener

is instructed to listen to five alternations and then judge whether the members of the pairs are the same or different with respect to pitch. The experimenter records the subject's judgment and changes the variable frequency to a new value, for example, 1,005 cps. The particular values of the variable frequency should be chosen beforehand, and their order of presentation should be scheduled according to a random series. Without specific statistical considerations, experience suggests that within such a series each value of the variable frequency should appear at least 50 times, although in laboratory exercises it may be satisfactory to cut this number down to about 20.

If the experimenter had no knowledge or expectation of what the frequency DL should be, some preliminary trials under very informal procedures might be used to block out the range of necessary values. Let us suppose that the listener is always able to distinguish 1,020 from 1,000 cps and, similarly, can always distinguish 980 from 1,000 cps. Then the variable values might be 1,015, 1,010, 1,005, 1,000, 995, 990, 985. Each of these values should appear about 20 times alternated with 1,000 cps, the standard frequency. All the measurements described so far employ a single standard frequency. If one is interested in sensitivity to frequency differences around other standard frequencies, he must repeat the whole procedure for each standard.

The results of the experimental session consists of judgments "same" or "different" for the 20 presentations at each variable value. The graphic presentation of such results for a single observer is shown in Fig. 6-7. The circles show results for the variable frequency lower than the standard, while the X's show results for the variable higher than the standard. The single curve, fitted by eye, shows the combined results for frequency difference (Δf). (More accurate techniques for curve fitting are cited in Guilford, 1954). The differential threshold is the Δf that yields "different" judgments 50 percent of the time. This procedure is more like Guilford's application of the constant method to the absolute threshold than to the differential threshold, where we should have asked the listener to judge whether one tone is "higher" or "lower" than the other in pitch.

It is probably not so important to point out here how the experimental procedure might be varied for measurement of the DL for frequency as to suggest how the psychological dimension of pitch may be measured for other than pure-tone stimuli. It is reasonable to suppose that the ability of the human listener to distinguish frequencies is one of those abilities basic to the perception of speech, but frequencies to be discriminated in speech are rarely if ever those of pure tones and are mostly not those of continuous tones. It is of interest to note, therefore, that the frequency DL can be measured for tonal stimuli that are not pure tones. An example is the difference in frequency between two damped oscillations (sounds that might be produced by plucked strings) required for a listener to judge that the pitch of the two brief sounds generated is different (Rosenblith and Stevens, 1953). The quantification of pitch through the measurement of the frequency DL has also been extended to complex tones (Thurlow and Small, 1955). The effect of varying psychophysical procedures on pitch discrimination has also been reported (König, 1957). Similar dependence on psychophysical procedures of intensity discrimination has been reported (Pollack, 1954).

Lateralization of sound in the head

Small differences in the time of arrival of two brief sounds at the ears will produce different apparent locations of a single sound image within the head (Licklider, 1951). The experimenter may wish to know how small a difference in time of arrival is required to move a sound image from the midline.

To utilize a different type of sound, we shall perform this experiment with brief transients. The electrical source may be the discharge of a capacitor or a more elegant source

like a pulse generator that can produce rectangular pulses with known amplitude, duration, and repetition rate. The experimenter chooses such a pulse with a duration of 0.1 millisecond (msec). This electrical pulse is fed to an attenuator for amplitude control and then to a mixing transformer and earphone. Voltage amplitude, measured on an oscilloscope, may show a peak value of approximately 1 volt. Since a pure tone with electrical peak amplitude (measured on the oscilloscope rather than on the voltmeter) of 1 volt should produce an SPL of 127 dB SPL (peak), we might assume that such a pulse would generate a peak of the same SPL. This is almost correct, but most earphones will not transduce a brief rectangular pulse without introducing some distortion due to the resonances of the earphone diaphragm and cavity. For the localization experiment two such pulses are required, one to be delivered to each earphone, as shown in Fig. 6-8. The two pulses should be as nearly identical as possible.

The time difference between two electrical pulses can be manipulated by means of an electric delay line or, most conveniently, by operating both pulse generators from a common driver in which the ON time of the two pulses can be controlled separately. Particularly convenient arrangements for such experimentation are available in the waveform generators and pulse generators of the Tektronix Corporation. Movable contacts engaged by a mechanical device on the periphery of a rotating wheel can also be used for such purposes.

The procedural problem is very similar to that shown in the measurement of frequency DL. In fact, the same psychophysical procedure might be used, but the experimenter would choose particular values of time difference (Δt) instead of variable frequencies. Also here we should not necessarily present the standard in each pair, on the assumption that the center of the listener's head is a sufficiently well-remembered standard location that an outside stimulus is not required. In the measurement of the frequency DL the

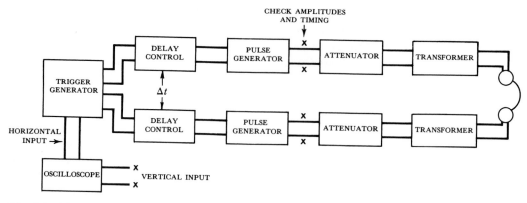

Fig. 6-8   Block diagram of apparatus used to measure judged localization of a click as a function of the time interval between two clicks, one delivered to each of two earphones.

observer was asked to judge whether frequencies were same or different. Now, however, the observer is asked where a particular click appears to be, whether to the right or to the left of the midline. Results of this *forced-choice* technique are more easily interpreted than are "right-center-left" judgments.

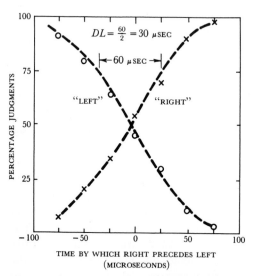

Fig. 6-9   Results of measurement of the difference limen for localization. The ordinate shows percentage of judgments that were "left" (circles) or "right" (X's). The abscissa shows the difference in time of arrival of the clicks at the two earphones.

Preliminary experimentation will show that if one click leads the other by approximately 0.5 msec the click image will almost always be heard at the side where the click leads. Values of time difference, therefore, should be less than this. Let us suppose, on the basis of such preliminary trials, that we set values in microseconds (μsec) of 100L, 75L, 50L, 25L, 0, 25R, 50R, 75R, and 100R, where the letter following the number of microseconds indicates the ear (left or right) that is leading.

The form of the experimental results will be the percentage of trials for each value of time difference that results in a judgment of "right" or "left." A graphic display is shown in Fig. 6-9. Since the curves pertaining to right and left judgments do not cross each other and 50 percent at exactly 0 μsec, there appears to be some bias in the observer, perhaps due to a difference in absolute threshold for the click in the two ears. Here the time DL will be defined as one-half the horizontal distance between the 75 percent points on the two curves (Guilford, 1954). For these particular clicks, at this particular level, this listener can report correctly 75 percent of the time which side leads, if the leading click precedes the lagging click by 30 μsec.

The procedure described above is one of many that might have been used to demonstrate some of the interesting phenomena under the general topic of auditory localization. The use of earphones permits the control of stimuli led separately to the two ears and thus affords the possibility of more analytical experiments on the localizing process. The particular experiment described requires some fairly complicated timing apparatus, which is not always available. If this is the case, one can take a single click and feed its output separately to two channels of amplification and attenuation, so that only the levels at the two ears will be varied. Under these circumstances, changes in spatial judgments within or near the head may be measured as a function of the difference between the stimuli at the two ears with respect to intensity. In the experiment reported by Deatherage and Hirsh (1959), both of these variables were manipulated and, in fact, pitted against each other. Many of the other variables related to auditory localization are summarized in Licklider (1951), and some of the most ingenious methods for studying auditory localization are included in Chap. 8 of Békésy (1960).

Temporary threshold shift
following noise exposure

The experimenter may wish to measure the absolute threshold of a listener at a particular time after the cessation of a noise exposure (Ward *et al.*, 1958) or to trace the time course of the absolute threshold after such an expo-

sure (Hirsh and Bilger, 1955). To introduce further variation in the experimental techniques described so far, we shall set as our purpose the measurement of the absolute threshold for a single ear at a particular frequency, 2,000 cps, as a function of the time following a 3-min exposure to white noise at 100 dB SPL.

The apparatus comprises two parts (Fig. 6-10). A commercially available electric noise generator is used as a source. Since the response of the earphone drops off rather abruptly above about 7,000 cps (see Fig. 6-4), a filter is inserted after the noise generator that will pass only frequencies below 7,000 cps. In this way we make more certain the correlation between the measured electrical noise and the transduced acoustical noise. Since a high noise level is required for the exposure, an amplifier follows whose output will feed an attenuator that will enable precise control of the electrical level reaching the earphone. The output of the attenuator is fed through a switch to the transformer and earphone. The switch permits the noise level to be introduced at a particular time and terminated, say, 3 min later. This switch could be operated by a mechanical or electrical timer, but the experimenter can operate it manually while he is observing a stopwatch for the exposure duration.

As a separate system, the experimenter must arrange for an ordinary pure-tone cir-

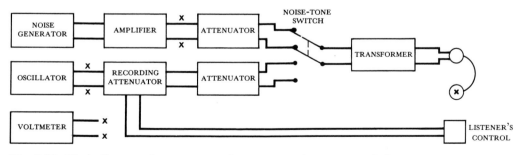

Fig. 6-10 Block diagram of apparatus used to measure the recovery of the threshold of audibility for a pure tone following exposure to a noise. The experimenter must select the appropriate noise voltage for the exposure period and the tone for the preexposure and postexposure periods. The listener monitors his threshold continuously, and his responses are automatically recorded.

cuit, as described in the first experiment on the absolute threshold. The oscillator is set at a frequency of 2,000 cps and its output fed to an attenuator for control. Another attenuator, operated by the listener, will permit the use of the method of adjustment. The experimenter is interested in changes in the threshold with time and will ask the listener to monitor his own threshold continuously after the noise exposure. The output of the second attenuator is connected to the switch and then to the transformer and earphone. The switch should be of the double-pole double-throw type, so that in one position it connects the noise attenuator to the transformer, and in the other it connects the pure-tone attenuator to the transformer.

The observation of threshold as a function of time calls for some kind of graphic recording of attenuator settings. An ordinary attenuator with a rotary shaft can be connected to a rack-and-pinion mechanism so that a certain angle of turn (in degrees or decibels) corresponds to a linear displacement of a pen on a piece of recording paper. This paper can be carried on a drum rotating at a fixed velocity so that time is displayed along the length of the paper while decibels of attenuation are displayed across its width. There are also recording attenuators (Grason-Stadler Company) in which the attenuating mechanism is laid out linearly and a slider contact is moved back and forth by a motor actuated by a switch that the listener operates. If the subject is told, for example, to depress the switch as soon as he hears a tone and to release it when he does not, a back-and-forth tracing of his responses will result. This same principle is utilized in the Békésy audiometer (Békésy, 1947), where the horizontal dimension not only displays time but also displays a slowly changing frequency.

The noise circuit should be calibrated as follows: The voltage output of the amplifier should be adjusted to some convenient level like 10 volts across the 600-ohm input of the noise attenuator, but should be set in such a way that an oscilloscopic display shows that the peaks of the waveform are not clipped or distorted. If the response characteristic of the earphone is that shown in Fig. 6-4 and the desired noise SPL is 100 dB, we know that the voltage supplied to the phone should have an average rms value of about 7 dB below 0.1 volt, because 0.1 volt applied yields an SPL out of the earphone at about 107 dB throughout most of the frequency range involved. Here one has averaged the level as a function of frequency by eye. Since there will also be a voltage drop of 17 dB across the transformer, the voltage out of the attenuator that is introduced to the transformer's primary should be 10 dB above 0.1 volt, and this means that there should be 30 dB of attenuation following the 10-volt attenuator input.

With the switch in the "tone" position, the oscillator frequency should be calibrated and adjusted to 2,000 cps, and the voltage output to 1 volt. Further checks on the attenuator system in the tone circuit should follow the routine described above in the experiment on the absolute threshold. There, it will be remembered, an input voltage of 1 volt to the attenuator (with 0 dB of attenuation) would have resulted in an SPL at the earphone of 110 dB. This should be a sufficiently great SPL to measure any temporary threshold shift from this noise.

The experimenter will ask the listener to adjust his attenuator control until he can barely hear the 2,000-cps tone *before* noise exposure. If a recording attenuator is used, he should bracket his threshold continuously for a period of about 1 min in order to give a reliable estimate.

The listener should be warned that some time after this initial threshold has been recorded a loud noise will be turned on for 3 min during which he should not try to listen for the tone. The listener should be signaled, usually by means of a light, just before the end of the noise exposure so that he can be ready to focus his attention on the tone again. Anticipating an initial temporary threshold shift of some 30 or 40 dB, the experimenter should reduce the amount of attenuation in his tone attenuator about 40 dB so that the listener need not wait for the tone to grow sufficiently in intensity for him to hear it after the noise exposure.

The termination of the noise exposure brought about by the experimenter's changing the switch from "noise" to "tone" initiates the recovery period during which the listener's threshold adjustments in the tone circuit should be made during the noise exposure so that the tone circuit is ready for use immediately upon the termination of the noise. The recovery period should be allowed to continue until the threshold has returned to its preexposure level.

The graphic tracing of the listener's threshold adjustments can be converted to SPL so long as units of displacement on the record can be interpreted in terms of decibels on the listener's attenuator and the initial level and the experimenter's attenuation settings are known. The result of such a conversion gives a graphic measure of threshold SPL for 2,000 cps as a function of time. (The ordinate on this record shows decibels of attenuation. The absolute threshold for the 2,000-cps tone, recorded for about a minute before noise exposure, shows at the left on the graph. Then a short, straight line indicates the period when the noise is on and the listener is not responding, e.g., an exposure noise of 90 dB presented for 3 min. A tracing at the right shows the continuously changing threshold after the noise exposure is terminated. The abscissa, under this tracing, shows time after exposure, in minutes.

The above procedure requires a recording attenuator that can be adjusted by the listener. Other procedures can be used, but the particular procedure will depend upon the level of the stimulating sound and the time interval after stimulation when the threshold shift is to be measured. Even relatively weak sounds will raise the threshold of a subsequent sound if the threshold is measured only a few milliseconds after stimulation. The measurement of this phenomenon, called either *fast*

adaptation or *residual masking,* requires timing apparatus that will generate a sequence of two sounds, one following the other by a short, fixed interval of time (Munson and Gardner, 1950). Suppose one presents a 1,000-cycle tone for 500 msec and then 30 sec later presents a brief pulse of tone at, say, 2,000 cps. The listener may be asked whether he heard one or two tones. Variation in the level of the second tone can be used to specify its threshold, and variation of the time interval between the first and second tone can be used to detail the recovery function.

Longer exposures to stimulating sounds at higher levels will result in sufficient threshold shift to permit relatively slow measurement over seconds or minutes. Indeed, the exposures may be sufficiently severe that one can measure hearing losses at several frequencies at each of several points in time during the recovery period (Ward *et al.,* 1958).

Intelligibility of speech in noise

For a more practical orientation, let us suppose that a particular factory has a continuous background noise whose overall level remains at about 90 dB. This noise makes conversation somewhat difficult, and the management wants to install a public address system so that persons working in the factory will be sure to hear announcements. The experimenter cannot go to the factory, but he has a tape recording of the factory noise and wishes to determine the intelligibility of speech at different speech levels in the presence of this noise (Licklider and Miller, 1951).

The problem has been introduced in this particular way in order to change the electroacoustic transducer to a loudspeaker and change to recorded sources of electric signals.

The electrical source for factory noise in the laboratory is a magnetic tape recording. If the noise is reasonably homogeneous over time, it is possible to cut out a length of tape suitable for a tape loop that can run over and over through the magnetic tape reproducer. The output of a tape reproducer is usually read on a volume-unit (VU) meter, which is essentially a voltmeter with specified response time and damping characteristics and scaled in decibels. Zero VU represents an electric power of 1 milliwatt (mw) in 600 ohms or a voltage of 0.778 volt across 600 ohms. With a relatively high sound level to produce and an inefficient loudspeaker to produce it, the experimenter must feed the output of the tape reproducer through a power amplifier to a mixing network, matching transformer, and loudspeaker (Fig. 6-11).

Intelligibility of speech can be measured conveniently with an adaptation of the method of constant stimuli in which lists of speech items are presented at different levels and the percentage of correct repetitions (in which the listener writes down the word or other speech item that he hears) becomes the dependent variable. Measured intelligibility depends upon the kind of speech material used. For example, in a given acoustic background, sentences or polysyllabic words will be much more intelligible than nonsense syllables or monosyllabic words. Adopting what has become almost a standard procedure in the evaluation of equipment, the experimenter shall use monosyllabic word lists, originally described by Egan (1948).

It would be possible to use as an electrical source of speech a microphone into which the experimenter reads these words for all listening sessions. Greater reliability from test to test will be available if the experimenter or some other talker records in a quiet place a large number of lists on tape; then the various recorded lists can be used throughout the listening experiments. Care should be taken to ensure that a talker can monitor his speech level visually so that, for example, on a particular gain setting in the tape recorder the VU meter reads 0 at those instants corresponding to the acoustic peaks in his words. There are complicated schemes for equating electrically the level from word to word in such recordings, but it will be found that a talker can adjust his level quite well after a little practice. The circuit shown in Fig. 6-11 uses the tape playback as an electrical source of speech. Its output should also be fed to a power amplifier, then to an attenuator, the mixing network, the matching transformer, and the loudspeaker. Notice that the attenuator is inserted in the speech circuit before the mixing network so that the speech level can be controlled independently of the noise level. No attenuator was introduced into the noise circuit, because the experiment calls for measuring the intelligibility of speech in a constant noise background at 90 dB SPL.

In previously described procedures where earphones were used, very little control was required over the acoustic environment. Here, however, the loudspeaker, situated at some

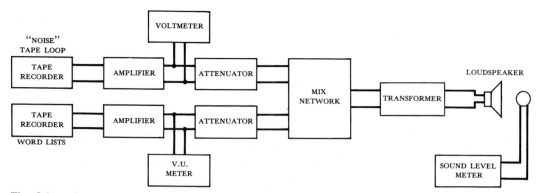

Fig. 6-11 Block diagram of apparatus used to measure the intelligibility of tape-recorded speech in a sound field against a background of tape-recorded noise.

distance from the listener or listeners, is only the beginning of an acoustic transmission system that includes the walls, ceiling, and floor. Where some validity is sought in representing the acoustic environment of the factory, it would be well to use a room with relatively hard walls and floor for a group of listeners. Here there will be multiple echoes and a relatively diffuse sound field.

In carrying out measurements the gain of the noise amplifier should be adjusted so that the loudspeaker produces an SPL of 90 dB somewhere in the center of the room (while the listeners are in their chairs) as read by a standard sound-level meter (weighting network A).

The gain of the speech amplifier should be set so that the carefully monitored peaks (VU-meter readings corresponding to spoken vowels) yield SPLs of approximately 100 dB when there is 0 dB in the attenuator following the speech amplifier. This measurement is sometimes facilitated if one has recorded a pure tone or other steady sound at a constant level corresponding to the speech peaks on the original tape recording. Then the level of this tone can be adjusted in the listening room without the experimenter's having to average by eye over the large fluctuations that occur in speech. Decibels of attenuation in the circuit correspond to decibels below a speech SPL of 100 dB. When, for example, the attenuator is set on 10, the average speech level should be 90 dB, and the speech-to-noise ratio is 0 dB [S/N in decibels $= 10 \log_{10}$ (speech power/noise power)].

In this case, where we wish to make some predictions about the behavior of people in general in response to speech in noise, our interest will be not in a single listener but rather in a group of listeners. A suitably large room can house a crew of about 10 listeners, who should be placed at roughly similar distances from the loudspeaker. The distances and directions are not made more precise because the sound field is made diffuse by hard, reflecting walls and because it is known that the crucial variable for the intelligibility of

speech in noise is the signal-to-noise ratio. Thus, for example, a listener seated far away from the loudspeaker when the speech attenuator is set at 10 dB might be exposed to a noise level of only 84 dB; but since the speech is coming from the same place, its level would also be only 84 dB and the speech-to-noise ratio would be the same as for a listener seated exactly in the center of the room where the sound level measurements were made. Each listener should be supplied with a pencil and blank paper on which there are numbered blank spaces corresponding to the number of items in each list.

Assuming some previous knowledge of speech intelligibility in noise (Licklider, 1951; Miller, 1951), we shall choose speech levels of 95, 89, 83 and 77 dB (or S/N ratios of $+5$, -1, -7, -13 dB). To obtain stable scores, the experimenter should plan to present about four 50-word lists at each of these levels. All the words for each list should be presented at the same level, but the order in which the different lists are used and the order in which different speech levels are used should be randomized. Thus there will be 16 list presentations.

A comparison of the responses of each listener with the recording script will yield the percentage of correct responses. If the resulting percentages are not too near 100 or 0 percent, they may be averaged across listeners. Here we have a group of data amenable to statistical treatment where the main effect is speech level but also where the variability among listeners can be evaluated relative to the variability among the four replications or repetitions of the lists. In a graphical presentation of typical results (Hirsh, Reynolds, and Joseph, 1954), the ordinate would show the average percentage of words correct for a group of listeners; the abscissa would show the signal-to-noise ratio in decibel units (e.g., values from left to right of -13, -7, -1, and $+5$) that describes the different presentation levels of speech against a constant background-noise level.

The procedure outlined above is applicable to a variety of situations where the experimenter is interested in the intelligibility of speech as a dependent variable. In the foregoing case, we have examined the influence of masking noise on the intelligibility of speech. It is possible, however, with essentially the same procedure to examine other variables that may affect speech besides the competing noise. If one has available, for example, filters that cut off different frequency bands, he may insert them after a tape recorder on which speech has been recorded through a wide-band system and may examine the intelligibility of speech as a function of the cutoff frequency (Hirsh et al., 1954). The same tape recorder might be followed by an amplifier producing specifiable degrees of amplitude distortion or peak clipping. In such a situation, the experimenter may relate the intelligibility of speech to different degrees of clipping (Licklider, 1951; Miller, 1951).

There has been considerable interest recently in manipulating the speech material itself. Either in the quiet or in a fixed level of noise, one might wish to study the intelligibility of different kinds of words, whether of one syllable, two syllables, or more than two syllables (Hirsh et al., 1954). One could also study the intelligibility of isolated words and that of the same words embedded in the normal context of an English sentence (Miller et al., 1951). One could also carry out, for hearing, studies similar to those which have already been done in vision on the recognizability of words as a function of their meaningfulness, frequency of usage in the language, or emotional content.

CONCLUSION

Clearly, the problems outlined at the beginning of the chapter and the experiments described at the end do not exhaust all the possible kinds of study in hearing. We have attempted to make the selection sufficiently variegated that the student can proceed from these experiments to others in related areas without too much further instruction. Details concerning particular kinds of procedure will be found in the references given within each experiment described.

REFERENCES

BÉKÉSY, G. V. A new audiometer. *Acta Oto-Laryngol. Stockh.*, 1947, 35, 411–422.

BÉKÉSY, G. V. *Experiments in hearing.* New York: McGraw-Hill, 1960.

BENSON, R. W., and HIRSH, I. J. Some variables in audio spectrometry. *J. acoust. Soc. Amer.*, 1953, 25, 499–506.

BERANEK, L. L. *Acoustic measurements.* New York: Wiley, 1949.

BILGER, R. C., and HIRSH, I. J. Masking of pure tones by bands of noise. *J. acoust. Soc. Amer.*, 1956, 28, 623–630.

BORING, E. G. *Sensation and perception in the history of experimental psychology.* New York: Appleton-Century-Crofts, 1942.

BROADBENT, D. E. *Perception and communication.* New York: Pergamon Press, 1958.

DAVIS, H., and SILVERMAN, S. R. *Hearing and deafness.* New York: Holt, 1960.

DEATHERAGE, B. H., and HIRSH, I. J. Auditory localization of clicks. *J. acoust. Soc. Amer.*, 1959, 31, 486–492.

EGAN, J. P. Articulation testing methods. *Laryngoscope*, 1948, 58, 955–991.

EGAN, J. P., and THWING, E. J. Further studies on per-stimulatory fatigue. *J. acoust. Soc. Amer.*, 1955, 27, 1225–1226.

FAIRBANKS, G. Test of phonemic differentiation: The rhyme test. *J. acoust. Soc. Amer.*, 1958, 30, 596–600.

FANT, G. *Acoustic Theory of Speech Production.* The Hague, Netherlands: Mouton and Co., 1960.

FLETCHER, H. *Speech and hearing in communication.* Princeton, N.J.: Van Nostrand, 1953.

GLORIG, A., QUIGGLE, R., WHEELER, D., and GRINGS, W. Determination of the normal hearing reference zero. *J. acoust. Soc. Amer.*, 1956, 28, 1110–1113.

GREENWOOD, D. C. Auditory masking and the critical band. *J. acoust. Soc. Amer.*, 1961, 33, 484–502.

GUILFORD, J. P. *Psychometric methods.* (2nd. ed.) New York: McGraw-Hill, 1954.

HAWKINS, J. E., JR., and STEVENS, S. S. The masking of pure tones and of speech by white noise. *J. acoust. Soc. Amer.*, 1950, **22**, 6–13.

HIRSH, I. J. *The measurement of hearing.* New York: McGraw-Hill, 1952.

HIRSH, I. J. Auditory perception of temporal order. *J. acoust. Soc. Amer.*, 1959, **31**, 759–767.

HIRSH, I. J., and BILGER, R. C. Auditory threshold recovery after exposures to pure tones. *J. acoust. Soc. Amer.*, 1955, **27**, 1186–1194.

HIRSH, I. J., REYNOLDS, E. G., and JOSEPH, M. Intelligibility of different speech materials. *J. acoust. Soc. Amer.*, 1954, **26**, 530–538.

HOOD, J. D. Studies in auditory fatigue and adaptation. *Acta Oto-Laryngol. Stockh.*, 1950, *Suppl.* 92.

JERGER, J. F. Auditory adaptation. *J. acoust. Soc. Amer.*, 1957, **29**, 357–363.

KÖNIG, E. Effect of time on pitch discrimination thresholds under several psychophysical procedures. *J. acoust. Soc. Amer.*, 1957, **29**, 606–612.

LIBERMAN, A. M., INGEMANN, F., LISKER, L., DELATTRE, P., and COOPER, F. S. Minimum rules for synthesizing speech. *J. acoust. Soc. Amer.*, 1959, **31**, 1490–1499.

LICKLIDER, J. C. R. Basic correlates of the auditory stimulus. In S. S. Stevens (Ed.), *Handbook of experimental psychology.* New York: Wiley, 1951.

LICKLIDER, J. C. R., and MILLER, G. A. The perception of speech. In S. S. Stevens (Ed.), *Handbook of experimental psychology.* New York: Wiley, 1951.

LÜSCHER, E., and ZWISLOCKI, J. The decay of sensation and the remainder of adaptation after short pure-tone impulses on the ear. *Acta Oto-Laryngol. Stockh.*, 1947, **35**, 428–445.

MILLER, G. A. The masking of speech. *Psychol. Bull.*, 1947, **44**, 105–129.

MILLER, G. A. *Language and communication.* New York: McGraw-Hill, 1951.

MILLER, G. A., HEISE, G., and LICHTEN, W. The intelligibility of speech as a function of the context of the test materials. *J. exp. Psychol.*, 1951, **41**, 329–335.

MILLER, G. A., and NICELY, P. E. An analysis of perceptual confusions among some English consonants. *J. acoust. Soc. Amer.*, 1955, **27**, 338–352.

MILLER, J. D., WATSON, C. S., and COVELL, W. P. Deafening effects of noise in the cat. *Acta Oto-Laryngol.*, 1963, *Suppl.* 176.

MILLS, A. W. On the minimum audible angle. *J. acoust. Soc. Amer.*, 1958, **30**, 237–246.

MUNSON, W. A., and GARDNER, M. B. Loudness patterns—a new approach. *J. acoust. Soc. Amer.*, 1950, **22**, 177–190.

NIXON, J. C., and GLORIG, A. Noise-induced permanent threshold shift at 2000 and 4000 cps. *J. acoust. Soc. Amer.*, 1961, **33**, 904–908.

PIERCE, J. R., and DAVID, E. E., JR. *Man's world of sound.* Garden City, N.Y.: Doubleday, 1958.

POLLACK, I. Intensity discrimination thresholds under several psychophysical procedures. *J. acoust. Soc. Amer.*, 1954, **26**, 1056–1059.

ROSENBLITH, W. A., and STEVENS, K. N. On the DL for frequency. *J. acoust. Soc. Amer.*, 1953, **25**, 980–985.

THURLOW, W. R., and SMALL, A. M., JR. Pitch perception for certain periodic auditory stimuli. *J. acoust. Soc. Amer.*, 1955, **27**, 132–137.

THWING, E. J. Spread of perstimulatory fatigue of a pure tone to neighboring frequencies. *J. acoust. Soc. Amer.*, 1955, **27**, 741–748.

WARD, W. D., GLORIG, A., and SKLAR, D. L. Dependence of temporary threshold shift at 4 kc on intensity and time. *J. acoust. Soc. Amer.*, 1958, **30**, 944–954.

WEBSTER, J. C., and SOLOMON, L. N. Effects of response complexity upon listening to competing messages. *J. acoust. Soc. Amer.*, 1955, **27**, 1199–1203.

WEGEL, R. L., and LANE, C. E. The auditory masking of one pure tone by another and its probable relation to the dynamics of the inner ear. *Physical Rev.*, 1924, **23**, 266–285.

WOODROW, H. Time perception. In S. S. Stevens (Ed.), Handbook of experimental psychology. New York: Wiley, 1951.

Chapter 7

VISION

ROBERT M. BOYNTON

This chapter will be restricted to a consideration of concepts and techniques needed to do well-controlled experiments in visual psychophysics. The typical experiment in this area is one wherein combinations of physical variables are manipulated to elicit some criterion response from an observer. Stimulus programming and the recording of responses may be automated, but these do not ordinarily impose any severe problems of instrumentation. Nor are there electrodes buried in the observer, or difficult surgical techniques to be mastered. The fruitfulness of the method depends almost entirely upon precision of physical control.

The techniques of conceptualization, measurement, and instrumentation are by no means simple. The experimenter must understand the properties of light as well as those of the eye, and he must know the methods for presenting, controlling, and measuring the light stimulus. A thorough knowledge of this information enables the researcher to obtain answers to numerous questions that might be raised concerning the manner in which the

Preparation of this chapter was supported by Grant NB-00624 from the Institute of Neurological Diseases and Blindness U.S. Public Health Service. Some of the techniques became familiar to the author during a year spent with Dr. W. S. Stiles, National Physical Laboratory, England.

visual system handles the critical input variables of space, time, wavelength, and intensity.

The application of the concepts and methods included in this chapter has provided answers to the following questions: (1) How does the response of the eye depend upon the wavelength of the stimulating light? [Maximum sensitivity varies from about 430 mμ to nearly 600 mμ depending upon the state of adaptation of the eye and the method of measurement.] (2) To get the most visual response for a given amount of energy input, how should this energy be organized? [It should be presented as a very small and very brief flash. Large and long flashes are much less efficient.] (3) Is there any particular duration of a light flash that will cause it to appear maximally bright? [Yes. For dim flashes, the longer the exposure, the brighter the appearance, up to a limit beyond which further exposure does not increase brightness. For bright flashes, an exposure of 50 to 75 milliseconds (msec) produces maximum brightness. Longer or shorter flashes look dimmer.] (4) How far apart in time must two very brief (e.g., 1-msec) flashes be spaced in order to be perceived as two flashes? [From about 15 to more than 150 msec, depending upon the area, intensity, and spatial position of the flash, as well as the state of adaptation of the eye.] (5) How far apart must two pin-points of light be positioned in order to be just barely perceived as double? [About 0.036 in. at a distance of 10 ft, under optimal conditions, much farther under other conditions.] (6) How fast must a light flicker before it becomes phenomenally steady? [This depends upon so many factors that a general answer is impossible, although flicker beyond 60 cycles per second (cps) is seldom perceived.] (7) What is the effect of prior exposure of the eye to light upon subsequent sensitivity? [Sensitivity will usually be reduced, sometimes very markedly. In the dark, sensitivity will improve rapidly at first and then progressively more slowly, with maximum sensitivity under some conditions being achieved only after 40 to 45 minutes in the dark. This process is called *dark adaptation*.] (8) How much separation must there be between two stimuli of different wavelengths in order for a color difference to be perceptible? [In the "yellow" region of the spectrum, less than 1 millimicron (mμ), or 1 part in 580; more in most other parts of the spectrum.] (9) What relative intensity difference can the eye detect? [Under optimal conditions, about two parts in a thousand.] (10) What is the smallest amount of energy incident upon the eye which, under ideal conditions, can produce a perceptible flash of light? [About 100 quanta at a wavelength of 510 mμ, corresponding to a total energy of about 4×10^{-10} erg.][1]

It is obvious that answers to the above questions are dependent upon various experimental factors, e.g., state of adaptation of the eye, method of measurement, exposure, presentation of long or short flashes of light, distance away from the light stimulus, speed of presentation, prior exposure of the subject to light, color, and the intensity and area of the light flash. Even the determination of an *absolute threshold*, or the minimum energy required to excite, requires the experimenter to consider the response of the eye to four major critical physical variables.

1. *Intensity.* The number of quanta incident upon the eye is the dependent variable, as it is in most visual experiments, and is measured in quantum units.

2. *Spectral sensitivity.* Since the sensitivity of the eye is not the same at all wavelengths, the wavelength of peak sensitivity must be chosen. An inspection of the literature indicates that the maximal sensitivity of the dark-adapted eye is in the neighborhood of 505 mμ.

3. *Geometry.* The two aspects of the geometrical problem are the size of the stimulus flash and the positioning of the stimulus for maximum quantum sensitivity. Experimental data indicate that the eye is maximally efficient in response to small flashes. To take account of the higher density of rod receptors in the area of the retina receiving the image of the flash, the stimulus is presented about 15 to 20° to one side of the fixation point.

4. *Time.* The duration of the stimulus must be determined in order that the stimulus flash be maximally efficient.

Once the desired conditions of the experiment have been created by setting each of the above variables at a value within the range calculated to produce maximum sensitivity, the experimenter chooses a suitable psychophysical method. This, together with his ability to measure the physical aspects of the stimulus, allows the researcher to attack the problem.

REFERENCE EXPERIMENT IN DARK ADAPTATION

One of the parameters that the experimenter has to control in the threshold study, and in other experiments in vision, is the state of adaptation of the eye. This is necessary because the numbers of quanta required for threshold vision are many thousands of times greater if presented to an eye that has just been exposed to light. The decrease in thresh-

---

[1] Evidence supporting the answers to these questions may be found in Brindley (1960), Davson (1962), Judd (1951), Koch (1958, 1962), Le-Grand (1957), and Wright (1958).

old that occurs during time in the dark, following exposure to an adapting light, is called *dark adaptation*.

Many people become familiar with the phenomenon of dark adaptation by studying the effects of entering a darkened room, such as a theater, after outside exposure to daylight. Students in introductory and advanced courses in experimental psychology bring the problem into the laboratory and attempt to determine absolute thresholds or to study dark-adaptation effects under "controlled" conditions. Unfortunately, the conditions are often neither controlled nor adequate enough to subject the student to the requirements of acceptable research in vision. The remainder of this section, therefore, will consider an experiment on dark adaptation in detail. It is assumed that this example will provide the reader with some background in the various aspects of vision methodology before proceeding to the more technical information provided in the remainder of the chapter.

The basic paradigm of the experiment is as follows: (1) a preadapting stimulus is presented that can vary in duration, area, intensity, and spectral composition; (2) the subject spends time in the dark; and (3) the test stimulus is presented—this stimulus may also vary in duration, area, intensity, and spectral composition. Instead of being asked to report on the increasing brightness of a stimulus of constant intensity, a test stimulus is used, which—to avoid adaptation to the test stimulus itself—is flashed to the subject in an effort to find the radiance[1] that will produce some criterion response. The most common criterion is a 0.50 probability of seeing. The radiance that produces it is called the *threshold radiance,* or simply threshold. The threshold of the test flash will decrease with increasing time in the dark—less and less light in the flash will be necessary in order for the subject just barely to see it—thus revealing the increase in sensitivity. Typical results are plotted in Fig. 7-1, where the threshold radiance of the test flash is on the ordinate, expressed in logarithmic units, and time in the dark is on

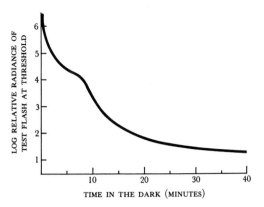

Fig. 7-1 A schematic dark-adaptation curve following exposure of the eye to white light.

the abscissa. It should be noted that both variables are expressed in physical units and that what is actually being done is to find combinations of physical variables that produce the criterion threshold response from the subject.

The subject, who has just come into the laboratory from an uncontrolled visual environment, is seated in a chair that is comfortable and adjustable. If the duration of the preadapting stimulus is not to be a variable, the experimenter will ask the subject to view a preadapting field for about 5 minutes, which (for many conditions) has been found sufficiently long to produce a steady state of visual sensitivity. When there is an attempt to cover the entire visual field, the preadapting field may fill the inside of a sphere or hemisphere into which the subject inserts the front of his head, or it may be more restricted in area. If the radiance of the field is low, it is not too difficult to fill nearly the entire field; but if very high radiances are needed, the experimenter will probably use a Maxwellian view [see the section on methods of delivering light to the eye (pages 301 to 304) for a detailed description]. If the Maxwellian system is used, the subject will find himself biting on a "biting board," which is a rigidly mounted yet adjust-

---

[1] See the section on photometry (pages 280 to 292) for a definition of the term *radiance*. The concept concerns the energy emitted per unit time and area from the flash.

able plate bearing a wax dental impression. He will then look into a lens from which a high-intensity beam of light is projected into the pupil of his eye.

Because of the gross inhomogeneity of receptor distribution and other characteristics of the retina (Pirenne, 1948, pp. 21–34), it is vital to control the region stimulated. This is done by means of a fixation point. With the teeth fixed, the position in space of the eye's center of rotation is reasonably well fixed also. To the extent that a subject can then orient his eye toward the fixation point, the rotary position will be controlled and the eye can be brought back to the same position again and again with little error. For very critical work, a forehead rest is also advisable.

A trained subject is able to keep a fixation point imaged within his central fovea with good enough accuracy for most purposes, although perfect fixation is impossible (Riggs, Armington, and Ratliff, 1954). Fixation points should be arranged geometrically and kept dim enough that they do not interfere with the perception of the test flash. If a background field is used, a cross-hair reticle or black fixation dot can be used instead. A number of *stopped image techniques* are available (Ditchburn and Ginsborg, 1952; Riggs, Ratliff, Cornsweet, and Cornsweet, 1953) where the stimulus, as seen by the subject, moves with the eyes and is thereby rendered motionless with respect to the retina. The techniques provide almost perfectly accurate fixation.

The area of preadapting stimulus is known to have little effect on visual functions within the center of the preadapting area if increased beyond about 6° of visual angle. Therefore, a 10° diameter circular field would be a good, safe choice for presentation to the subject.

The color of the field must be controlled by varying its spectral distribution, perhaps by the use of filters that selectively absorb some wavelengths of incident white light. Spectral distribution, the basic physical specification of color, refers to the radiance of the preadapting light present at each wavelength throughout the visible spectrum. The adapting field may be nearly monochromatic, or it may contain all wavelengths and be white in appearance. If monochromatic, the wavelengths of all radiant energy from the field will be the same, or all quanta will have the same energy. Color is not uniquely related to spectral distribution, since two adapting fields of very different spectral distribution can look the same in color. *Color* consists of those "characteristics of light other than spatial and temporal inhomogeneities" (Judd, 1951). The concept includes *hue, brightness,* and *saturation* and does not exclude white and black. It has been found that three variables are sufficient to specify color, since, disallowing minor complications, three narrow spectral bands, if mixed together and presented to the eye, can reproduce all colors if their relative intensities are adjustable. If the experiment being discussed involves the effect of color upon the course of dark adaptation, it should ideally utilize an optical system capable of providing such color "mixture." A standard system for specifying color in terms of *chromaticity* and *luminance* is widely used and will be described in this chapter.

After the subject views the preadapting field for about 5 minutes, a warning signal will be given and the preadapting field extinguished. The entire visual environment is then dark, except the fixation point, which remains with its intensity adjusted downward, either by the experimenter or by the subject, so that it is just barely visible. A variety of psychophysical methods could be used to measure the radiance threshold of the test flash. There is a special problem here in that the threshold changes continuously with time in the dark and therefore must be measured while the change is taking place. Perhaps the experimenter will choose the "up-and-down" method, so that when the subject responds "yes," the radiance of the test flash will be slightly decreased on the subsequent exposure; and if "no," increased. The subject could be instructed to respond "yes" or "no," by means of a switch, to stimuli presented once every 5 seconds, each associated with an audible click. Some kind of shutter must be used to deliver the test flashes. Apparatus can be built that automatically records responses at each radiance level and adjusts the radiance appropriately for the next presentation, or the experimenter can record data and make radiance changes manually.

Decisions must also be made regarding the color, area, and duration of the test flash. Means for varying and specifying the values of these parameters will be considered in this chapter.

Unless measurements are made during the first 2 seconds after extinction of the pre-adapting light, about half the dark-adaptation curve and much important information may be lost (Baker, 1963). To measure this part of the curve (not represented in Fig. 7-1), only one test flash can be presented, and one judgment made after each preexposure. To do this, the preadapting stimulus can be turned on again after the test flash, but not so soon as to affect the subject's judgment. The original state of adaptation will become re-established very quickly, and the entire stimulus sequence can be repeated many times to determine a threshold.

If the test stimulus is red, small, and presented at the fixation point, the amount of dark adaptation will be relatively slight, and the process complete within 8 to 10 minutes. If the test stimulus is blue, large, and presented to one side of the fixation point, the course of dark adaptation will last for 45 minutes or more (Bartley, 1951).

In vision experiments, almost all parameters have effects that not only are statistically significant but also are very large and replete with complex interactions. There is, for example, no such thing as "a" dark-adaptation curve. Every variable and parameter is important. Unless these are controllable and measurable, the experiment will be useless from the standpoint of its relevance to visual theory.

When variables are properly controlled and measured, it is usually found that the differences between the results of different subjects are among the smallest to be found in psychological research. Deviations from this expectation can often be physiologically understood and related to other anomalies in the same subject. It is customary in such research to use very few subjects by psychological standards: sometimes only two will suffice. A time-honored recommended procedure is for two investigators to alternate in their roles as experimenter and subject. The principal advantages of this arrangement are twofold: (1) The investigator gains insight from the subjective experiences of being subject. While these experiences are not admissible as data in their own right, and their mere description is of doubtful value, hypotheses generated from this source can often be subjected to later experimental test. (2) Apparatus as complex as that required for the experiment just described is subject to occasional failure. An experienced subject can often detect difficulties that the naïve observer could not discern.

The responses recorded in experiments of the sort described in this example are so little affected by variables such as learning and set that, by proceeding with an objective spirit and by taking reasonable precautions, there is little danger of biasing the results by using sophisticated subjects. Furthermore, because learning is not importantly involved, each subject can act as his own control for all conditions. Differences between thresholds can be discerned within a given experimental session with an accuracy of about 0.03 to 0.05 log unit, assuming about 50 judgments per condition taken from an experienced and stable subject. The threshold values are subject to uncontrollable day-to-day variations, which should be no greater than 0.20 log unit if the apparatus is properly calibrated. Because the between-sessions variance is greater than the within-sessions variance, it is desirable to design the experiment so that the most critical comparisons are based upon data obtained within the same session.

The remainder of this chapter will cover

(1) the characteristics and measurement of the visual stimulus; (2) colorimetry; (3) the principles of ocular stimulation; (4) methods of delivering light to the eye; (5) light sources; (6) methods for mixing light; (7) the control of luminance, wavelength, and time; (8) the measurement of basic variables; (9) general apparatus considerations, including the mounting of optical components and the partitioning of experimental areas; and (10) special systems, e.g., eye-movement recording, and clinical techniques.

DEFINITIONS, UNITS, ABBREVIATIONS, AND SYMBOLS

It will be necessary to define many terms in this chapter that may be unfamiliar to the general reader who is seeking advice about how to set up and measure a visual stimulus. Definitions will be based whenever possible upon those given in glossaries already assembled in handbooks, particularly those having some kind of organizational sanction. Since these are not necessarily identical, some choice must be made among definitions. The four sources of definitions for this chapter, along with their identifying symbols, are as follows: (AIP) *American Institute of Physics Handbook* (1957); (CIE) *International Lighting Vocabulary of the International Commission on Illumination* (1957); (DBJ) Glossary by D. B. Judd (1951); (OSA) *Optical Society of America* (1953).

Where units, symbols, and abbreviations in visual research are concerned, there has been an unfortunate degree of chaos. The unit "millilambert" is variously abbreviated "ml," "mL," "mlam," and possibly other ways. The American Institute of Physics published in *Physics Today* (June, 1962, pp. 19–30) a recommended list of symbols and abbreviations prepared by the International Union of Pure and Applied Physics that are "in general in agreement with recommendations of five international organizations." These will be employed in the present chapter.

LIGHT AND OPTICS

Light is defined (CIE) as *radiation capable of stimulating the organ of vision*. *Optics* (OSA) is the *science treating of light and other related phenomena, such as vision*. Although optics is a highly developed and expanding science, it is impossible, at the present time, to understand fully the nature of light. This chapter cannot be the place to discuss optics in detail. The following references are suggested: the *American Institute of Physics Handbook* (1957); Condon and Odishaw (1958); Ratliff (1962); Sears (1949); and Strong (1958). For physiological optics, see Bennett and Francis (1962), Fry (1959), LeGrand (1952), Ogle (1961), and Zoethout (1947).

There are three rather distinct ways of looking at light: *rays, waves,* and *quanta*. This triple perspective has become necessary because a given problem or phenomenon in optics can very often be treated practically or theoretically in terms of only one of the three concepts. Vision is no exception. Therefore the vision psychologist should consider himself free to use whichever concept suits his particular problem.

The ray concept is most likely to be useful for dealing with light outside the observer. For example, in treating the problem of depth perception, it is helpful to show the location of object points in relation to the reference point of the eye. One can roughly calculate the size and position of the retinal image by using ray concepts. It is important to remember, however, that these schemes are not fundamental. Although the ray can be thought of as a line perpendicular to a wave front or as the path of a quantum, it has no physical existence.

In general, the wave properties of light are most important in the consideration of the behavior of light as it passes into and through the ocular media, as well as for certain aspects of the control of light before it enters the eye. The wave properties of light are most important in connection with the following optical phenomena: *refraction* (OSA), the deflection of radiant energy from a straight path in passing from one medium to another; *diffraction* (CIE), the deviation of the direction of propagation of radiation, determined by the undulatory nature of radiation and occurring when the radiation passes the edge of an obstacle; *dispersion* (CIE), the property of an optical device or medium giving rise to the separation of the monochromatic components of a complex radiation; *polarization* (OSA), the process by which vibrations of light are given a definite orientation, also the state produced by that process; and *interference* (CIE), the attenuation or reinforcement of the amplitudes of the vibrations of a radiation, occurring in certain regions of overlap of different parts of the same wave train. Polarization seems to be of no fundamental significance for human vision, although the use of polarizing material outside the eye to control intensity or to produce stereoscopic effects is common. Dispersion produces chromatic aberration in the eye, meaning that the eye cannot focus properly for all wavelengths at the same time. Diffraction and interference phenomena are seldom of visual importance, although the use of unusual conditions, e.g., small pinholes in front of the eye, can make them so. Refraction accounts for the image-forming properties of the eye and is definitely of fundamental importance.

The transformation of radiant energy to a different form of energy by the intervention of matter is called *absorption* (CIE). Wherever absorption is involved, wave concepts fail and quantum concepts must be brought into play. This is true therefore for the first energy transduction in the visual process, the absorption of a quantum of light by a molecule of visual photopigment. It is conceived that light exists in packets of small but fixed energy called *quanta*. The energy value per quantum is not the same for all quanta, but varies as an inverse function of wavelength. Highly abstract thinking is required to comprehend the meaning of the wavelength of a single quantum. This imposes severe problems upon one's attempts to visualize quanta. It would be con-

venient to consider quanta as tiny bullets of light, but unfortunately a quantum cannot be said to have a definite and precise location in space at a given time. The most dramatic evidence for this is derived from experiments involving two slits of the sort that produce diffraction-interference patterns at high levels of illumination. These experiments can be conducted also under conditions of irradiation so low that only one quantum is involved at any given time. Evidence of interference is nevertheless obtained; e.g., there are regions where, over a period of time, very few quanta are detected although a much larger number would have been detected had either of the two slits been employed alone. In some real sense, then, each quantum must have wave properties and somehow must pass through both slits. A quantum is probably best conceived as a wave packet having indefinite boundaries.

The interaction between one quantum and another may be assumed to be negligibly small. Therefore we may visualize that the density of light falling upon a particular area, i.e., the *illuminance,* is simply related to the number of quanta per unit time per unit area and that there is no physical interaction among these quanta. Each quantum may be assumed to have an existence of its own, a precarious life that depends upon a long series of probabilities. For example, a given quantum leaving a distant star, even if starting exactly in the direction of an observer's eye, stands a very low overall probability of contributing to a visual response. To do so, it must traverse vast distances without being absorbed, scattered, or reflected, either outside the eye or within. Even if absorbed by a molecule of visual photopigment, the quantum sometimes may not make a contribution to visual response, since a certain number of other such absorptions must occur within a given time and within a given spatial region in order for a visual sensation to occur. Quanta either exist or do not exist, with no possible in-between state. Such a conceptualization stresses that an individual quantum of light, such as one from a distant star, may exist for many thousands or millions of years without losing any of its capacity to stimulate.

PHOTOMETRY

The measurement of quantities referring to radiation, evaluated according to the visual effect produced, is known as *photometry* (CIE). Photometric units are by convention expressed in terms of energy. The concept most closely associated with what we ordinarily think of as light is *luminous flux*. Luminous flux is proportional at a given wavelength to the number of ergs per second of light energy being transferred under specified conditions. One might cite the amount of luminous flux emitted by a source, or the amount entering the pupil of the eye. Because the sensitivity of the eye to light energy depends upon wavelength, luminous flux values are not the actual energy values, but are weighted according to the *spectral sensitivity* of the eye, as described later in this section. The analogous physical concept is called *radiant flux,* the total number of ergs per second regardless of wavelength. To introduce this subject, we shall talk first of quanta, rather than energy, in the hope that quanta are easier to visualize. In quantum terms, light flux at any given wavelength is simply proportional to the number of quanta per second that are involved.

Point sources

The term *intensity*, when applied to light, actually refers only to a *point source*, a conceptual source of zero volume, meaning that all quanta are emitted from a single point in space. The intensity of a point source is proportional, at any given wavelength of the source, to the number of quanta of light (of energy per quantum corresponding to that wavelength) emitted by the source per unit solid angle. Solid angles are measured in *steradians*, where one steradian is the solid angle subtended by a surface area of r^2 at the center

of a sphere of radius r. Since the area of a sphere is $4\pi r^2$, there are 4π steradians of solid angle around a point. For most sources, this value will be different for different directions (automobile headlights provide an extreme example). Suppose that we have a device, e.g., a calibrated photocell, capable of measuring the number of quanta per second irradiating it. Suppose that we remove this device from the source to such a distance that it subtends a solid angle of $1/1,000$ steradian and that the device then shows that 10^5 quanta per sec are incident upon it. The reading of the instrument, multiplied by 1,000, would give the number of quanta per second per steradian in that direction (10^8 quanta per sec per steradian). This would be a measure of the intensity of the source in that direction. The concept of the intensity of a point source is illustrated at the top in Fig. 7-2, where the rays emerging from this source are shown passing through two areas of the same shape but different size, depending upon their distance from the source. It will be clear from this figure that intensity in a given direction is independent of the distance at which it is measured, since the luminous flux in the solid angle ω is the same at A_2 as at A_1. Intensity is to be regarded as a property of the source.

Extended sources

Suppose that a second source is added somewhere above the one diagrammed in Fig. 7-2. The flux from this source passing through area A_1 will then only partially pass through area A_2; the measurement of flux per unit solid angle will not be the same for the two areas, and the concept of solid angle becomes ambiguous because it cannot refer simultaneously to both sources as the vertex. There are no point sources in real life, since energy cannot be emitted from a source having no volume. If the distance from the source to the surface being irradiated is large relative to the dimensions of the source, little error of the type noted here is introduced by treating it as if it were a point source. As a rule of thumb, opticists treat sources as effective point sources

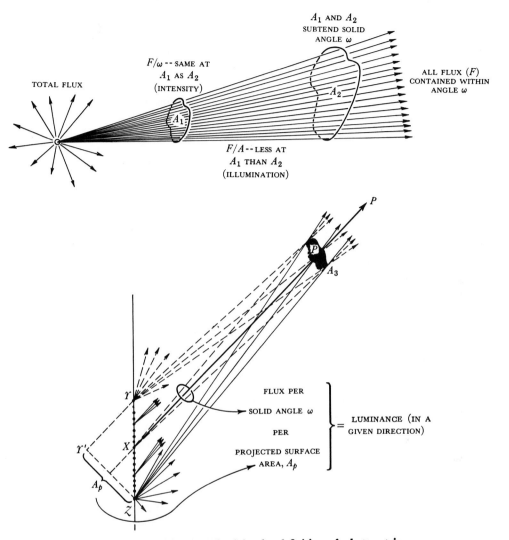

Fig. 7-2 Some geometric relations involved in the definition of photometric concepts. *Top:* Only some of the total flux emitted by a point source will be contained within the areas delimited by similar figures A_1 and A_2, each of which subtends the same solid angle. Diagram shows how intensity and illumination are related. *Bottom:* Consider a surface perpendicular to the plane of the paper. Assume that it is of square shape, with height ZY and an equal width which cannot be shown. It will project as a rectangle of height ZY'. Consider next receiving area A_3, which is receiving light irradiated from the square surface. Light is shown being irradiated from a few points only, with arrows to show that it is irradiated in many directions. In measuring luminance of the surface in the direction XP, only that light from each point which passes through area A_3 will be effective. This total amount of flux (coming from everywhere on the surface, and not just from the points shown from illustration), divided by the solid angle subtended by receiving area A_3, divided by the projected surface area, will specify the luminance of the surface in the direction XP. This diagram shows why luminance becomes exactly specified only as the projected area of the irradiating surface and the solid angle subtended by receiving area A_3 both approach zero.

if their maximum dimension is less than 10 percent of the distance of the surface being irradiated; for the 10 percent condition, the error of measurement is about 1 percent. In the visual case, many sources cannot be discriminated from smaller sources provided the total energy output is the same for each case. Such a source would appear the same as the hypothetical point source if it could emit the same energy. The limit at which an extended source no longer looks like a point source depends upon the state of adaptation of the eye (Blackwell, 1946). When this condition is exceeded and the source no longer appears as a point (always well within the 10 percent condition), a source must be treated as an extended source. Such a source can be conceived as being made up of a very large number of point sources.

Suppose now that the measuring device is placed at a given distance from a diffuse surface, so that it subtends 1/1,000 steradian with respect to a given point upon the surface. Assume that the device reads 10^6 quanta per sec; multiplied by 1,000, this would mean that the "effective intensity" of the surface is 10^9 quanta per sec per steradian. Suppose that the surface is too large actually to be considered as a point source. We measure the area of the surface and define a new concept, luminance. Luminance is proportional to the intensity *per unit projected area* of the surface. Since intensity may vary with direction, luminance may also do so. Furthermore, most surfaces have nonuniform luminances. Consider a semigloss painted wall illuminated by light coming through a window. The luminance of the wall depends upon the angle of view; the *specular* (mirrorlike) reflection where the angle of view equals the angle of incidence will be much higher than any other. For any given angle of view, luminance will vary, being much higher near the window than at the back of the room.

The area value used in the definition of luminance is not the actual area of the surface, but its *projected area*. Imagine that you are looking through a long tube with a hole at the end. If you view the wall through the tube, the more obliquely the wall is viewed, the more actual area will be seen through the hole. For the eye, camera, or other image-forming device, the area of the image of a given surface at a given distance is directly related to the projected area of that surface, becoming smaller in relation to the actual surface area as the surface is photographed or viewed at an increasingly oblique angle.

The luminance of a field is independent of the distance from which it is measured, because as one moves the quantum-counting device further from the surface, two things happen that cancel each other. The number of quanta per second reaching the device per unit of actual area of the surface decrease in proportion to the square of the distance of the device from the surface. This so-called *inverse-square law* is fundamental in photometry and applies here because of the divergence of light from each elemental point making up the surface. The size of the solid angle subtended at the quantum counter by any given point on the surface also decreases as the square of the distance of the quantum counter from the surface. Thus, the calculated luminance value, which is obtained by dividing the reading of the quantum counter by the solid angle that it subtends at a point on the surface, will not change as a function of distance. Just as intensity is a property of a point source, luminance is a property of a surface, having nothing to do with the distance from which it is viewed.

Illumination and illuminance

Illumination (DBJ) is the process of supplying an area with luminous flux. The areal density of the incident luminous flux is called *illuminance* (DBJ). Illumination, being a generic and descriptive term, does not imply a measured quantity, although the term is often used incorrectly to mean illuminance. Illuminance, which concerns the density of light upon a surface, can be measured in quanta per second per square meter by the hypothetical instrument if (1) we know the area of the receiving surface of the instrument and (2) the instrument displays no directional sensitivity, e.g., all incident quanta are equally effective, regardless of the angle of incidence. The inverse-square law applies to illumination; i.e., as the distance between a point source and the receiving instrument is increased, the reading will fall inversely with the square of the distance. This is because the same number of quanta are contained in a unit solid angle at all distances, but they are spreading out, more and more thinly, as the cross section of a cone defining a unit solid angle becomes larger and larger with increasing distance.

The property of real objects that correlates most closely with subjective brightness is their luminance. Most objects are not self-luminous, but merely reflect light from their surfaces, some of which enters the eyes of an observer to render the object potentially visible. The property of the retinal image of real objects that correlates most closely with subjective brightness is *retinal illuminance*, which is directly proportional to the luminance of the object, other things being equal. The interrelations between illuminance and luminance must be understood to comprehend the relations among illumination of objects, object luminance, and retinal illuminance.

The illuminance of a surface can be calculated from the following equation:

$$E = \frac{L_s A_s}{a_s^2 + D^2} \qquad (7\text{-}1)$$

where L_s is the luminance of a circular source, A_s is the area of the source, and their product is the effective intensity of the source. The term a_s^2 represents the square of the radius of the source, and D is the distance between the source and the object. All measures must be in the same length unit. The illuminance E is in lumens per square unit area.

Although the photometric concepts have been introduced using quanta per second as the measure of luminous flux at any given wavelength, the unit actually used is the *lu-*

men. The lumen comes already adjusted to take account of the spectral sensitivity of the eye. Specifically, two stimuli of different color that produce equal numbers of lumens per unit area at the retina should look equally bright [see section on the problem of wavelength (pages 285 to 286)]. The idea of luminous flux outside the eye—flux that may never stimulate an eye—being weighted according to its potential stimulating power is not wholly satisfactory. It is only partially physical and, since the "psycho-" part of the psychophysical relation has not yet been entered into, partially fictitious. The idea is firmly established, however, and one must learn to live with it.

The lumen corresponds at a wavelength (λ) of 555 mμ to 4.12×10^{15} quanta per sec and to more quanta per second than this at most other wavelengths. At 555 mμ, this number of quanta per second, spread uniformly over a square meter, produces an illuminance of 1 lumen per square meter (sq m).

As the illumination upon a surface increases, luminance increases in direct proportion. This is because of the characteristic nature of surfaces that they reflect a certain proportion of incident quanta, whatever the actual number. Black surfaces may reflect about 1 to 5 percent, whereas white surfaces may reflect 80 or 90 percent. The subjective experience of *brightness* is correlated with luminance but is an entirely different concept, referring strictly to the sensation and not measurable except by introspective techniques.

A perfectly diffuse surface with a *reflectance* of 1.0 is one whose luminance is invariant with respect to angle of measurement and from which all incident quanta are assumed to be reflected; the luminous intensity of each elemental point decreases in proportion to the cosine of the angle of regard, with a normal viewing angle taken as 0°. It can be shown that such a perfectly diffuse and totally reflecting surface receiving 1 lumen per square centimeter (sq cm) will produce a reflected luminance of $1/\pi$ lumen per steradian per sq cm in all directions. This quantity is called 1 *lambert* (L). One lumen per steradian is called a *candela* (cd) of intensity, a notion stemming from the older term *candlepower. The millilambert* (mL) is the most commonly used luminance unit for scientific purposes in the United States, while the candela per square meter is widely used in Europe.

The definition of the luminance unit *lambert* simplifies the definition of the reflectance ρ_λ of a perfectly diffuse surface, which becomes

$$L_\lambda = \rho_\lambda E_\lambda \qquad (7\text{-}2)$$

where L_λ is luminance in lamberts and E_λ is illuminance in lumens per square centimeter. The same simple relation also holds when E_λ is in lumens per square foot, often called *foot-candles,* and L_λ is said to be in *foot-lamberts.* Each of these quantities is a function of wavelength λ.

It is a good idea to have the information needed to convert from one system of photometric units to another (Judd, 1951, p. 816; LeGrand, 1957, p. 77) and then learn to "think" in only one of these systems, converting all unfamiliar units to the familiar ones. A summary of the basic photometric concepts and some typical units is given in Table 7–1.

The troland unit and the pupil problem

Illuminance upon the retina of the eye (which helps to determine brightness) depends upon the product of the luminance of the surface being viewed and the area of the pupil. If one wants to ensure that retinal illuminance is proportional to the luminance of an external field, it is necessary to use an *artificial pupil.* Ordinarily, this is a small aperture cut in a thin metal plate and positioned in front of the eye, as close to the cornea as possible. Because it is not in the plane of the real pupil, it will partially reduce the field of view and is not very satisfactory for stimuli that are in the far periphery of the visual field. (It is possible to provide an artificial pupil optically in the plane of the real pupil, as discussed later in connection with the Maxwellian-view optical system.) Since the area of the pupil is normally variable, retinal illuminance is not ordinarily directly proportional to luminance, becoming under normal viewing conditions somewhat less than

Table 7-1   Summary of radiometric and photometric concepts, symbols, and typical units.[1]

Concepts and symbols		Photometric units
Radiometric	*Photometric*	
Radiant intensity (I_e)	Luminous intensity (I)	Lumens/steradian (cd)
Radiance (L_e)	Luminance (B, L)	Lumens/steradian/sq m (cd/sq m)
		Lamberts $\left(\dfrac{1}{\pi}\text{ cd/sq cm}\right) = 3{,}183$ cd/sq m
		Ft-lamberts $\left(\dfrac{1}{\pi}\text{ cd/sq ft}\right)$
Irradiance (E_e)	Illuminance (E)	Lumens/sq m (lux)
		Lumens/sq ft (ft-c)
Radiant flux (ϕ)	Luminous flux (F)	Lumens
	Retinal illuminance	Trolands (1 troland ≈ 0.1 mL) = 1 cd per sq m seen through pupil of 1 sq mm in area ≈ 0.0036 lumen per sq m

[1] Basic conversion factor: 6.8×10^{-5} lumen is equivalent to 1 erg/sec at λ = 555 mμ.

proportional at high luminances, because the pupil gets smaller. For this reason, the *troland* (tr) is used as a unit of retinal illuminance. The troland is defined as the retinal illuminance produced by viewing a surface having a luminance of 1 cd per sq m (1 lumen per steradian per sq m) through a pupil having an area of 1 square millimeter (sq mm). To convert from millilamberts to trolands when the pupillary diameter in millimeters is known, it is necessary merely to square the diameter of the pupil and multiply by 2.5. For a pupillary diameter of 2 mm, 1 mL = 10 tr, so that a 10:1 relation is a good one to keep in mind for making a rough conversion.

One major fact has mitigated against the total acceptance of the troland unit. In 1933, Stiles and Crawford discovered that light from a given part of the visual field entering through the edge of the pupil is considerably less effective in arousing a visual response than that entering through the center: in extreme cases, as much as ten times as much light will be required in the less efficient case, from fields of the same size, in order to produce a brightness match. Retinal illuminance alone therefore will not predict the brightness of a field any more than luminance alone will. Whereas luminance fails because of pupil fluctuations, retinal illuminance fails because the light passing through the margin of the pupil, which is refracted more and strikes the receptors at a greater angle of incidence than that passing through the center, is less efficient.

In specifying the visual stimulating situation, whether luminance or retinal illuminance units are used, it is necessary therefore to state explicitly the diameter of the pupil involved. A satisfactory specification might read either (1) "the luminance of the system was 1 mL seen through a pupil of 2 mm diam" or (2) "the retinal illuminance provided by the system was 10 tr through a pupil of 2 mm diam." The two statements are exactly equivalent, and one is as satisfactory as the other. Note that each specification states the pupil size, so that in careful work an artificial pupil must be used, or the actual visual input will not be specifiable.

The problem of wavelength

Just about everyone knows that hue and wavelength are closely associated. Wavelength has been chosen as the variable against which the spectral sensitivity of the eye is plotted, and many studies have been done on the subject of wavelength discrimination and color appearance as related to wavelength. What everyone does not know is that for vision, wavelength is not a very fundamental variable and that it probably has been a rather bad choice. A wavelength of 550 mμ incident upon the cornea of the eye will be shortened to about 420 mμ upon entering the eye and will be approximately of this shorter wavelength when incident upon the visual receptors. The reason for this is expressed in two simple relations of great physical importance. The first is $v = c/\lambda$, where v is frequency in cycles per second (hertz), c is the speed of light (2.998 $\times$ 10^{17} mμ per sec), and λ is wavelength, usually expressed in millimicrons [1 mμ = 10 angstroms (Å) = 0.001 μ] or thousandths of millionths of a meter. (The term *nanometer*, where nano = 10^{-9}, is widely used in Europe, but is not common in this country.) In words, the frequency of radiation is inversely proportional to wavelength, with the speed of light acting as the constant of proportionality. The reason wavelength changes upon entering the eye is that the speed of light changes, becoming slower as the light passes from air with an index of refraction of 1.0 into the eye media with an index of refraction of about 1.3. Frequency, on the other hand, is independent of the speed of light and does not undergo any such change from one optical medium to another.

Although more fundamental than wavelength, frequency is still not the most fundamental concept. The absorption of quanta is the initial event in photoreception. We now conceive that a given receptor can react in proportion to the number of quanta that it absorbs. The critical physical variable that determines the *probability of quantum absorption* in the visual receptor is probably the energy per quantum, ϵ. There is a good deal of indirect evidence to indicate that when a quantum is absorbed there is no information about energy, frequency, or wavelength available to the receptor. Some quanta are, however, much more likely to be absorbed than others. When large numbers of quanta are incident per unit time upon a receptor, the relative absorption at any given wavelength will vary in direct proportion to the probability of each given quantum's being absorbed, with this probability depending upon the energy that each quantum possesses. This will be true only if the probability of absorption is low at maximum, since photopigment molecules exist at different depths in the receptor with respect to the incident light, and fewer quanta will reach the deeper levels for those quantum energies yielding high absorption probability than for those yielding low. This has been called "self-screening" by Brindley (1960). To summarize: the notion presented here is that when a photopigment molecule receives a quantum, either it absorbs it or it does not, in an all-or-none fashion; this event contributes to subsequent visual events (e.g., retinal potentials and/or transmission of impulses to the brain) in exactly the same way, whatever the energy of the absorbed quantum and the probability of its being absorbed. This very important idea has frequently been misunderstood.

Energy per quantum is related to frequency by the very simple relation $\epsilon = h\nu$, where h is Planck's constant (6.62377×10^{-27} erg-sec), which, along with the speed of light, is one of the fundamental constants of physics. Like frequency, the energy per quantum does not depend upon the optical medium.

Spectral sensitivity

This is usually expressed as the reciprocal of the radiance required to elicit a criterion response, as a function of the wavelength of the light. The criterion response may be a threshold probability of seeing, a brightness match, the elimination or minimization of flicker (flicker photometry), an adaptive effect, or an electrophysiological response. There are three other ways to express spectral sensitivity: reciprocal radiance as a function of energy per quantum, reciprocal number of quanta as a function of wavelength, and reciprocal number of quanta as a function of energy per quantum. It is possible to display the information in all four ways upon the same graph, using a method developed by the author (1963). The use of a logarithmic abscissa allows both wavelength (bottom scale) and energy per quantum (top scale) to be expressed as shown in Fig. 7-3. This plot also permits sensitivity to be expressed in quantum units as well as radiance units, since the energy per quantum decreases as a linear function of log wavelength, permitting the use of oblique axes for quantum sensitivity. Five visual sensitivity functions are shown in Fig. 7-3. The CIE scotopic and photopic luminosity functions V'_λ and V_λ are shown as the heavy curves. The values in parentheses on the right-hand ordinate apply to V'_λ, indicating the logarithm of the approximate number of quanta entering the pupil of the eye that are necessary to elicit a visual sensation (assuming a short, brief flash presented to the most sensitive part of the peripheral retina). To render the V_λ curve comparable to the V'_λ curve on an absolute basis (for a 1° diameter test field), the V_λ curve must be lowered without change of shape until its right side approximately fits the V'_λ curve, a vertical distance of about 1.6 logarithmic units.

Also shown in Fig. 7-3 are three functions derived by Stiles (1959), which are the spectral sensitivities of three photopic mechanisms that are probably related in some way to the blue-, green-, and red-sensitive cone types. The figures not in parentheses on the right-hand ordinate show the intensity per unit area of a steady state adapting field found to raise the increment threshold for the indicated photopic mechanism to ten times its absolute

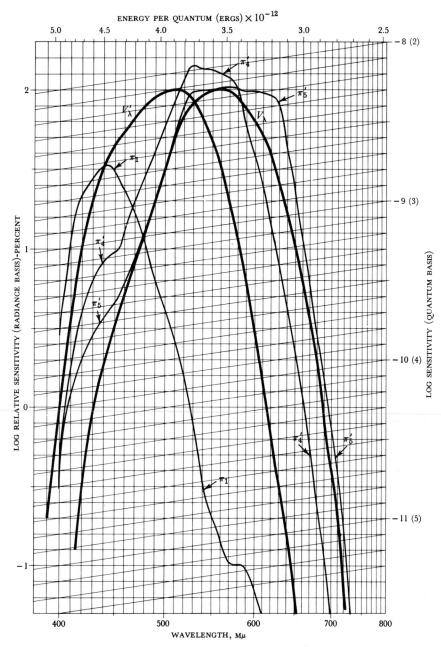

Fig. 7-3 Visual sensitivity curves plotted so that sensitivity can be evaluated on either a reciprocal radiance basis (left-hand ordinate) or a reciprocal quantum basis (right-hand ordinate), as a function either of wavelength (bottom abscissa), or of energy per quantum (upper abscissa). The oblique coordinates refer to the right-hand ordinate. Shown are the photopic (V_λ) and scotopic (V'_λ) luminosity functions for the CIE standard observer, as well as spectral sensitivities for three of Stiles's photopic mechanisms.

threshold, where the intensity of the adapting field is expressed as the number of quanta incident per second upon the cornea of the observing eye, per square degree of the uniform monochromatic adapting field.

It is generally agreed that the variable number of quanta required for a criterion visual effect as a function of wavelength reflects the varying probability of absorption by photopigment molecules of quanta having different energy values. The response to the absorption of light by a given molecule is believed to be nonspecific, carrying with it no information about what wavelength of light activated it. Thus, for scotopic conditions (V'_λ), 10,000 quanta at wavelength $\lambda = 610m\mu$ each stand only one hundredth as much chance of being absorbed as do those at $\lambda = 505$ mμ. If one hundred times as many are delivered, the resulting sensation will be indistinguishable in every way from the much smaller number delivered at the wavelength of peak sensitivity. The total effectiveness of a stimulus of complex spectral distribution may be estimated by integrating it with the scotopic spectral sensitivity curve. Therefore, if V'_λ represents the scotopic relative luminous efficiency curve (see Table 7-2, column 7) and if $L_{e\lambda_1}$ and $L_{e\lambda_2}$ represent the spectral radiance distributions of two stimuli, these stimuli will match for brightness if

$$\int L_{e\lambda_1} V'_\lambda \, d\lambda = \int L_{e\lambda_2} V'_\lambda \, d\lambda \qquad (7\text{-}3)$$

where in this and other cases to follow, the limits of integration will be taken as from $\lambda = 380$ mμ to $\lambda = 750$ mμ.

Photopic versus scotopic vision

Photopic vision is vision mediated by cones, at moderate and high levels of luminance, while *scotopic vision* is vision mediated by rods alone, at very low levels of luminance (OSA). Intermediate levels, where rods and cones are believed to work together, are called *mesopic*. The spectral sensitivity of the eye depends upon the level of stimulation. For truly scotopic conditions, the wavelength of peak sensitivity is about 505 mμ; for truly photopic

conditions, given a neutral state of adaptation of the eye, it is about 555 mμ. The shift from one to the other as one goes from photopic to scotopic conditions is gradual. The usual photometric quantities are defined in terms of photopic vision. Although these units have often been extrapolated to the description of scotopic stimulus conditions, this is a dangerous procedure since two stimuli having the same luminance will not generally match at low levels if their spectral distributions differ.

It is possible to develop a system of photometric units based on scotopic spectral sensitivity. This was done by the CIE in 1948. The blackbody radiator at the melting point of platinum was used as a reference (temperature 2042°K), and it was arbitrarily decided that the luminance of such a stimulus would be 60 cd per sq cm for both the photopic and the scotopic systems. This corresponds to a scotopic luminous flux value of 1,746 lumens per watt at $\lambda = 555$ mμ, for which it will be recalled that the photopic value is 680 lumens per watt. This system has not been widely used, although a few authors have utilized the *scotopic troland*, the retinal luminance produced by viewing a surface having a luminance of 1 scotopic cd per sq m through an artificial pupil having an area of 1 sq mm. If photopic quantities are to be applied to stimuli at scotopic levels, the spectral distribution of the stimulus must be given; otherwise the visual effect of the stimulus is quite unpredictable.

Figure 7-4 illustrates the range of photopic and scotopic vision with two scales of luminance.

Table 7-2 contains the following useful information as a function of wavelength: (1) *frequency* ν; (2) *photopic luminosity factor* V_λ; (3) *relative energy required for equal brightness*, which is simply the reciprocal of V_λ; (4) *energy per quantum*, ϵ; (5) *relative number of quanta for equal brightness*, Q_λ; (6) *quantized spectral sensitivity* Q^*_λ, the normalized reciprocal of the previous value (normalization has been

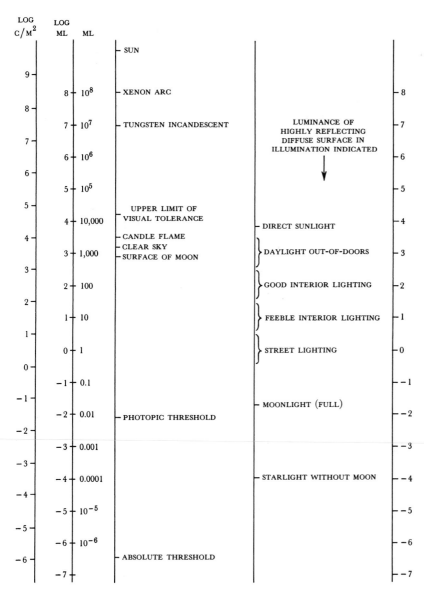

Fig. 7-4   Chart to show the luminances of typical sources and of a highly reflecting diffuse surface illuminated as indicated. Luminances are given in candelas per square meter and in millilamberts. (*After Bartley, 1951, and LeGrand, 1957.*)

taken with $Q_\lambda^* = 1.000$ at 555 mμ, although it should be noted in this case that the peak of the curve has actually shifted to 550 mμ); and (7) values of V_λ' for scotopic vision, based upon the data of Crawford (1949) and Wald (1945) and standardized by the CIE.

The usefulness of these values can perhaps be illustrated by a few simple problems and

their indicated solutions. (1) A field has a measured luminance at 500 mμ of 100 candles per square meter (cd per sq m) (31.8 mL). How many quanta per second per steradian per square meter are irridiated by this surface? *Ans:* 100 cd per sq m = 100 lumen per steradian per sq m by definition. Reading across for $\lambda = 500$ mμ to column 5, note that there are 11.41×10^{15} quanta per sec per lumen at this wavelength. The answer is 1.141×10^{18} quanta per sec per steradian per sq m. (2) How many quanta per second per steradian per square meter would be required at 550 mμ to match this field for brightness? *Ans.:* Quantized sensitivity at $\lambda = 550$ mμ is 1.0043; at $\lambda = 500$ mμ, it is 0.3587. The higher sensitivity at $\lambda = 550$ mμ means that fewer quanta will be required for a match in

proportion to the relative quantized sensitivity $(0.3587/1.0043 = 0.359)$. This multiplied by the answer to question 1 provides the answer to the question, 4.12×10^{12} quanta per sec. (3) What happens to the peak of the photopic spectral sensitivity curve when it is changed from an energy to a quantum basis? *Ans.:* Column 2 indicates that the peak is at $\lambda = 555$ mμ, while column 6 indicates a value of approximately 550 mμ. The peak has

Table 7-2   Values of importance for vision, as indicated, for 10 mμ intervals throughout the visible spectrum.

	(1) Frequency $\times 10^{14}$ $v = c/\lambda$ sec^{-1}	(2) Photopic luminosity factor V_λ	(3) Relative energy (ergs) for equal brightness $1/V_\lambda$	(4) Energy ϵ $\times 10^{-12}$ per quantum, $\epsilon = h\nu$	(5) No. quanta $\times 10^{15}/$ sec/lumen, Q_λ	(6) Quantized photopic luminosity factor Q_λ^*	(7) Scotopic luminosity factor V_λ'
Wavelength λ, mμ							
390	7.687	0.0001	10,000	5.092	28,870	0.0001	0.00221
400	7.495	0.0004	2,500	4.964	7,406	0.0006	0.00929
410	7.312	0.0012	833	4.843	2,529	0.0016	0.03484
420	7.138	0.0040	250	4.728	777.6	0.0053	0.0966
430	6.917	0.0116	86.20	4.618	274.5	0.0150	0.1998
440	6.813	0.023	43.48	4.513	141.6	0.0290	0.3281
450	6.662	0.038	26.32	4.413	87.70	0.0469	0.455
460	6.517	0.060	16.67	4.317	56.75	0.0724	0.567
470	6.378	0.091	10.99	4.225	38.24	0.1074	0.676
480	6.246	0.139	7.194	4.137	25.57	0.1607	0.793
490	6.118	0.208	4.808	4.052	17.43	0.2357	0.904
500	5.496	0.323	3.096	3.972	11.41	0.3587	0.982
510	5.878	0.503	1.988	3.893	7.508	0.5473	0.997
520	5.765	0.710	1.408	3.819	5.421	0.7582	0.935
530	5.656	0.862	1.160	3.746	4.553	0.9025	0.811
540	5.552	0.954	1.048	3.678	4.188	0.9814	0.650
550	5.451	0.995	1.005	3.611	4.092	1.0043	0.481
555	5.402	1.000	1.000	3.578	4.110	1.0000	0.402
560	5.353	0.995	1.005	3.546	4.167	0.9862	0.3288
570	5.259	0.952	1.050	3.483	4.434	0.9268	0.2076
580	5.169	0.870	1.149	3.424	4.936	0.8326	0.1212
590	5.081	0.757	1.321	3.366	5.770	0.7122	0.0655
600	4.996	0.631	1.585	3.309	7.044	0.5834	0.0315
610	4.914	0.503	1.938	3.255	8.980	0.4577	0.01593
620	4.835	0.381	2.624	3.202	12.05	0.3411	0.00737
630	4.758	0.265	3.774	3.152	17.70	0.2335	0.003335
640	4.684	0.175	5.714	3.102	27.08	0.1517	0.001497
650	4.612	0.107	9.346	3.055	44.96	0.0914	0.000677
660	4.542	0.061	16.39	3.008	80.14	0.0513	0.0003129
670	4.474	0.032	31.2	2.963	154.8	0.0265	0.0001480
680	4.409	0.017	58.8	2.920	296.1	0.0139	0.0000715
690	4.345	0.0082	122	2.878	623.4	0.0066	0.00003533
700	4.283	0.041	244	2.837	1,264	0.0032	0.00001780

moved 5 mμ toward the shorter wavelengths. (4) What is the radiance of the field of problem 1? *Ans.:* The field puts out 1.141 × 10^{18} quanta per sec per steradian per sq m. The energy per quantum at 500 mμ is, by column 4, 3.972 × 10^{-12} erg per quantum. Multiplying these two values yields 4.53 × 10^6 ergs per sec per steradian per sq m (= 0.453 watt per steradian per sq m).

Radiance and quanta

The stimulus for vision is commonly measured in energy rather than quantum units. Since the energy per quantum decreases in inverse proportion to increasing wavelength, the two are not the same measures. Let us consider this in terms of a simple example, making reference to the values supplied in Table 7-2. Assume that we have a stimulus, in the form of a diffuse field, which has an intensity per unit projected area of 2 × 10^{20} quanta per sec per ω per sq m, where ω stands for the solid angle in steradians. Assume that half these quanta are of wavelength 390 mμ, and the other half are of wavelength 700 mμ. Now consider the following example:

Case 1

1 × 10^{20} quanta/sec/ω/sq m at λ = 390 mμ
    (= 5.092 × 10^8 ergs/sec/ω/sq m)
        plus
1 × 10^{20} quanta/sec/ω/sq m at λ = 700 mμ
    (= 2.837 × 10^8 ergs/sec/ω/sq m)
        equals
2 × 10^{20} quanta/sec/ω/sq m in the mixture
    (= 7.929 × 10^8 ergs/sec/ω/sq m)
        in the mixture

Case 2

0.1 × 10^{20} quanta/sec/ω/sq m at λ = 390 mμ
    (= 0.509 × 10^8 ergs/sec/ω/sq m)
        plus
1.9 × 10^{20} quanta/sec/ω/sq m at λ = 700 mμ
    (= 5.390 × 10^8 ergs/sec/ω/sq m)
        equals
2 × 10^{20} quanta/sec/ω/sq m in the mixture
    (= 5.899 × 10^8 ergs/sec/ω/sq m)
        in the mixture

In Case 1, equal quantum amounts of light at a wavelength λ of 390 mμ, which would look violet, and at 700 mμ, a deep red, are added. The total of 2 × 10^{20} quanta per sec per ω per sq m in the mixture is shown to be equal to 7.929 × 10^8 ergs per sec per ω per sq m. In Case 2, the same total quantum amount of light is distributed differently, with 95 percent of it in the red, where there is less energy per quantum. For this reason, the result, 5.899 × 10^8 ergs per sec per ω per sq m, is less than in Case 1.

The values given in parentheses in the example, expressed in energy rather than quantum units, are values of radiance. *Radiance* is the energy per unit time, per unit solid angle and per unit projected area, in a particular direction from an extended source. There is no general term for the units quanta/sec/ω/sq m of the example, although they could be called *quantized radiance values*.

The photopic luminous efficiency factor $V\lambda$

When two stimuli at scotopic levels are adjusted to match for brightness, they will be equivalent and indistinguishable no matter how they are used in an experiment. At the higher levels of photopic vision, where color perception enters in, this is no longer true. If one establishes spectral sensitivity by means of threshold measurements in the rod-free area of the fovea, these results will be similar to, but not exactly the same as, those obtained by brightness matching at suprathreshold levels. Two stimuli that have equal brightness may, if different in spectral composition, have radically different adaptive effects and not behave in exactly the same way in a number of other situations. It is impossible, in a general sense, to scale the visual effectiveness of stimuli of different wavelength at photopic levels of stimulation by a single sensitivity function. The problem is too significant to be left unsolved merely because it has no unique solution. Two criteria were adopted by the CIE on which to base photopic spectral sensitivity: brightness matching and flicker photometry.

In the first case, the observer must abstract brightness as a concept from two fields that differ in color, stating in effect when the brightnesses are equal. *Flicker photometry,* which is perhaps less fundamental, involves the slow alternation (e.g., at 10 to 20 cps) of two stimuli whose relative radiances are adjusted until the perception of flicker is minimal. The results of the two methods do not agree exactly (LeGrand, 1957, p. 68), but certain results from each were combined by the CIE and smoothed to provide the *luminous efficiency function* of the so-called "standard observer." This function is given in Table 7-2, where it is labeled "V_λ," and is also shown in Fig. 7-3.

Reference standards

The present reference standard for the system of photometry, whereby the conversion between *radiometric* and *photometric* units (e.g., from ergs per second to lumens) is specified, is the luminance of a blackbody aperture at 2042°K (the temperature of platinum at its melting point), which as previously mentioned is taken to be 60 cd per sq cm. The candela is the photometric intensity unit and was formerly the reference standard of the photometric system, so that the intensity of an ordinary candle flame is actually on the order of 1 cd. A photometric intensity of 1 cd is equal to 1 lumen per steradian, where the lumen is the unit of luminous flux and is defined by this relationship.

The official conversion between radiometric and photometric values is made in terms of flux: 680 lumens of luminous flux are taken as equal to 1 watt (10^7 ergs per sec) of radiant flux at a wavelength of 555 mμ. One watt of radiant flux at this wavelength corresponds to 2.795×10^{18} quanta per sec.

The definition of luminance implies that luminances are additive, despite differences in spectral composition. If this assumption were true, any two surfaces having the same luminance, by calculation, would appear equally bright, in a fashion completely analogous to

that already discussed for scotopic vision, when

$$\int L_{e\lambda_1} V_\lambda \, d\lambda = \int L_{e\lambda_2} V_\lambda \, d\lambda, \qquad (7\text{-}4$$

where $L_{e\lambda_1}$ refers to the radiance of a surface as a function of wavelength. $L_{e\lambda_2}$ is an analogous value for a second surface. Although there have been many studies to show that this relation is not exactly true, any two surfaces yielding equal values by the above equation are nevertheless equal, *by definition and convention,* in luminance. The additivity of luminances is known as Abney's law. It is a relation that one would expect to find in an eye containing only one class of receptor contributing to brightness, since for such an eye a given brightness would be associated with a given rate of quantum absorption and it would make no difference to the eye what the energy per quantum was. This would closely parallel the scotopic case. Since the real eye contains at least four classes of receptor, which differ in spectral sensitivity, it is not surprising that Abney's law is not actually true. The breakdown of Abney's law implies that more than one class of receptor contributes to the sensation of brightness and that the summation of their individual contributions is nonlinear. In addition to the failure of additivity as implied by Abney's law, there are sufficient differences in spectral sensitivity among observers that brightness matches made by one observer may not be accepted by another, even though each would be classified as being within normal limits. Readers wishing to learn more about photometry are referred to LeGrand (1957), Walsh (1953), and Wright (1949, 1958).

COLORIMETRY

Two photopic fields of equal luminance will not generally look exactly the same, since they may differ in color. There are, however, some special cases of photopic fields that match exactly, even though their spectral distributions are not identical. The most dramatic example is a match that can be made between a white light made up of a continuous spectrum and another white containing only monochromatic radiations from the red, green, and blue regions of the spectrum. Such matches of physically different stimuli are termed *metameric* matches. The science, largely applied, that deals with the specification of color and its measurement with particular emphasis on metameric relations is called *colorimetry*.

Consider a split field, divided into left- and right-hand parts, to which energy may be delivered independently to the two halves. A given stimulus C is delivered to the left half of the field, and three other stimuli R, G, and B are available to the experimenter and can be added to either side of the field. The results of color-mixing experiments, in which R, G, and B are called primary stimuli, indicate that

$$c(C) = r(R) + g(G) + b(B) \quad (7\text{-}5)$$

where r, g, and b are the amounts of the three primaries required to equal c units of the color to be matched, C. To translate this mathematical statement into experimental terms, it is necessary to be explicit about the empirical meaning of the operations "$=$" and "$+$." Equality in the mathematical realm translates to "matches with" in the laboratory. The operation of addition implies optical superposition, meaning that the quantities indicated are added together by combining the lights, in one way or another, so that they superpose in the visual field. If one of the quantities should be negative (for example, "b"), this must imply that this quantity must be added to the opposite side of the equation, since negative amounts of light are physically unrealizable. For example,

$$c(C) = r(R) + g(G) - b(B) \quad (7\text{-}6)$$

is experimentally realized only as

$$c(C) + b(B) = r(R) + g(G) \quad (7\text{-}7)$$

An important outcome of experiments in this domain has been to establish that for a given amount c of the color to be matched, exactly three primaries are required for the

normal subject to establish a unique match. Such matches for spectral colors are shown in Fig. 7-5, based on the experiments of Wright (1946). No match will in general be possible if only two primaries are allowed to vary; and with four or more primaries, the values required for a match are not unique. Photopic vision is therefore said to be *trivariant*. An important constellation of rules known as Grassman's laws may be summarized by stating that an isomorphism exists between the formal mathematical statement of Eq. (7-6) and the experimental domain of color matching to which it relates. Therefore, the additive, multiplicative, associative, and transitive operations of algebra can be applied to the quantitative description of color matches. This makes it possible to relate color-matching data obtained with one set of primaries to those obtained with any other set under otherwise similar experimental conditions. One such set in Fig. 7-5 shows the amounts of red, green, and blue primaries ($\bar{x}$, $\bar{y}$, and $\bar{z}$) required to match one energy unit of the monochromatic test stimulus of the wavelength shown on the abscissa. Depending on choice of primaries, many other such sets of curves are possible; each accurately predicts which physically different stimuli will match. To find out, one carries through the following calculations, each analogous to the ones previously discussed for the calculation of equal luminosity. From experimental color-matching studies, it is possible to deduce three visual functions of wavelength, one of which is proportional to V_λ, such that two stimuli will be predicted to match exactly if the following conditions are met:

$$\begin{aligned} X &= X' \\ Y &= Y' \\ Z &= Z' \end{aligned} \quad (7\text{-}8)$$

where

$$\begin{aligned} X &= \int L_{e\lambda} \bar{x}_\lambda \, d\lambda \\ Y &= \int L_{e\lambda} \bar{y}_\lambda \, d\lambda \\ Z &= \int L_{e\lambda} \bar{z}_\lambda \, d\lambda \end{aligned} \quad (7\text{-}9)$$

and X', Y', and Z' are similarly defined. The functions $\bar{x}$, $\bar{y}$, and $\bar{z}$ (the subscript λ is

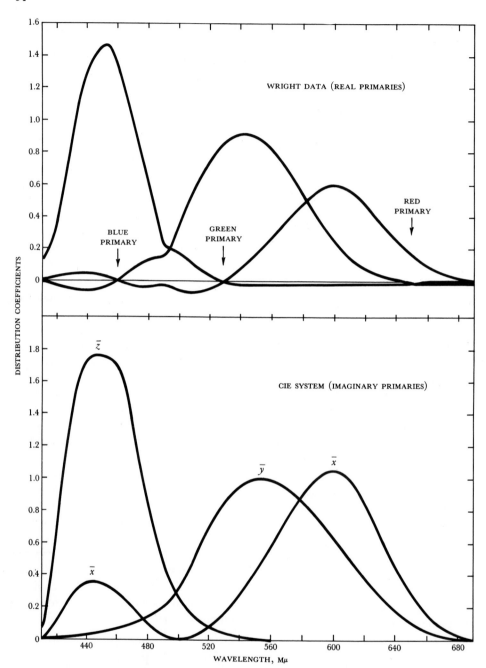

Fig. 7-5 Distribution coefficients describing the results of a real experiment in color mixture for primaries shown (upper curves) and transformed data adopted by the CIE (lower curves).

usually omitted) are known as the *distribution coefficients* of the CIE system of colorimetry. The values X, Y, and Z are known as the tristimulus values.

To a first approximation, color appearance depends upon only the relative tristimulus values, rather than their absolute amounts. This is related to the common experience that color appearance changes relatively little if the intensity of illumination is altered, and this in turn is reflected by the fact that $\bar{y}$ is proportional to V_λ. The *chromaticity coordinates* define such relative values:

$$x = \frac{X}{X + Y + Z}$$
$$y = \frac{Y}{X + Y + Z} \qquad (7\text{-}10)$$
$$z = \frac{Z}{X + Y + Z}$$

The standard chromaticity diagram, upon which the results of such calculations are commonly displayed, is shown in Fig. 7-6. It can be shown that this diagram has the important property that all possible mixtures of two given colors define a straight line connecting the chromaticities of these colors on the diagram (Wright, 1958, Chap. 3). Thus, the curved locus of all real spectral colors, connected by the straight line joining the chromaticities of the spectral extremes, defines a region of real colors. The system of units in terms of which $\bar{x}$, $\bar{y}$, and $\bar{z}$ are defined requires that a stimulus having equal energy at all wavelengths be plotted as $x = y = z = 0.333$. The areas under the $\bar{x}$, $\bar{y}$, and $\bar{z}$ functions are therefore equal. This "equal-energy white" point is shown in Fig. 7-6, together with another "white" point provided by a tungsten source operated at 2854°K, standard source A. The concepts of *dominant wavelength, excitation purity,* and *complementary chromaticities* are illustrated and defined in Fig. 7-6.

Why does the eye behave this way? The most common interpretation, stripped of all superfluous assumptions and details, is simply

this: (1) There are three kinds of visual photopigment in the photopic receptors (cones) of the eye. These differ in their spectral sensitivities, which are proportional either to $\bar{x}$, $\bar{y}$, and $\bar{z}$ or to some other set related to these through a change of primaries. (2) The relative probability of light absorption in a given visual cone pigment is given by these functions, which are unchanged in shape regardless of the actual rate of light absorption. (3) The three types of pigment are unequally distributed in different kinds of photopic receptors (cones), so that the relative responses of these cones differ depending upon wavelength. This information is kept separated in the visual pathways, although it may be recoded. Some difference between the absorption spectrum of the visual photopigments and the appropriate transformation of color-mixture data is to be expected because of the absorption of light by the eye media.

It must be emphasized that the experimental operation underlying the derivation of the chromaticity diagram is color matching. These are *null-method experiments* in which the subjects are at no time asked to comment about the actual appearance of color fields. The resulting diagram is not to be construed as a picture of color space, nor as directly related to a plane through the psychological color solid; e.g., the colors falling on a line defined by a given white point and some point on the spectral locus are not generally of exactly the same hue. Equal excitation purity does not imply equal saturation where different dominant wavelengths are involved. Equally discriminable psychological steps are not represented by equal distances on the chromaticity plane.

Many transformations of the chromaticity diagram are possible, all of which carry the same information about color mixture, some of which are more uniform psychologically than others. Probably the most widely used is the uniform chromaticity diagram of Judd (1935), "formed by plotting in triangular coordinates the ratio $R/(R + G + B)$ called r,

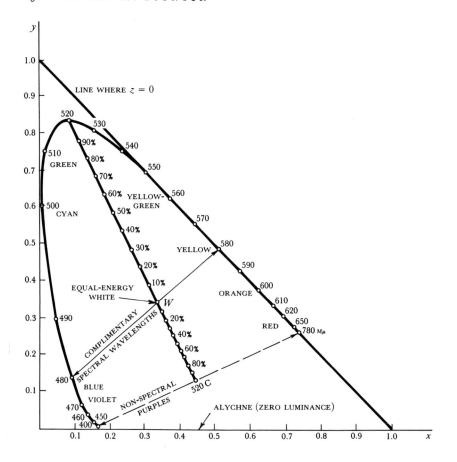

Fig. 7-6 The CIE standard chromaticity diagram. The equal-energy white point, or achromatic point, is located at $x = y = 0.33$. The location of a given stimulus upon the chart can be specified either in terms of the chromaticity coordinates or by *dominant wavelength* and *excitation purity*. For example, the point labeled "30%" is located at approximately $x = 0.26$ and $y = 0.48$. It can also be specified as having a dominant wavelength of 520 mμ and an excitation purity of 30 percent. The dominant wavelength is determined by drawing a straight line from the white point through the point to be specified (sample point) until the line intersects the spectral locus; the spectral wavelength corresponding to the intersection point is the dominant wavelength. Excitation purity (OSA) is the "distance between achromatic and sample points, divided by the distance between achromatic point and the point on the spectrum locus representing the dominant wavelength of the sample." Examples of complementary chromaticities are also shown e.g., 480 and 580 mμ on the spectral locus, or any two points along the line connecting them that fall on opposite sides of the white point. Note that the spectral color 520 mμ has no spectral complementary but intersects the line connecting nonspectral purples. This point is identified with the wavelength of the complementary chromaticity, followed by "C". Excitation purities for non-spectral chromaticities between the white point and 520 C are also shown; in this case 100 percent purity is defined by the intersection of the extension of the 520-white line with the nonspectral purple line.

against the ratio $G/(R + G + B)$ called g, where

$$
\begin{aligned}
R &= 31956X + 2.4478Y - 0.1434Z \\
G &= -2.5455X + 7.0492Y \\
  &\qquad\qquad\qquad + 0.9963Z \\
B &= 0.000X + 0.000Y + 1.000Z."
\end{aligned} \quad (7\text{-}11)
$$

Another set, provisionally recommended by the 1963 convention of the CIE, is "produced by plotting $4X/(X + 15Y + 32)$ as abscissa and $6Y(X + 15Y + 32)$ as ordinate. . ."

Although any two colors that look identical should plot at the same point in the chromaticity diagram, this will be true only if the observer has characteristics nearly identical to those of the so-called standard observer of the CIE system. No real human observer has exactly these characteristics.

PRINCIPLES OF OCULAR STIMULATION

In many psychological experiments, stimuli are defined without much thought to the visual process required for their perception. If one is interested in concept formation, he may draw his stimulus forms on pieces of cardboard and present them to the subject without any particular consideration of conditions of illumination, and with no thought at all concerning how the subject is able, by means of his visual capabilities, to discriminate the forms upon the cards. It is tacitly assumed that variables such as luminance, contrast, chromaticity, visual angle, and time do not make any difference. So long as the subject keeps his eyes open and can clearly "see" the stimuli, this is all that seems to matter.

This kind of tacit assumption is unlikely to be true, even in an experiment on concept formation. In experiments on visual perception, e.g., those involving figural aftereffects, tachistoscopic word recognition, and visual illusions, the assumption is almost certainly false. These basic variables often have been ignored, even in studies of visual perception.

The reason for this may involve, in part, the so-called constancies of visual perception; i.e., an object viewed at various distances, from different vantage points, and under widely differing conditions of illumination and contrast still tends to retain its object properties, although the stimulus, as defined by geometric, spectral, temporal, and intensitive variables, changes radically.

Another reason that such basic variables tend to be ignored is that their control is much more difficult than most beginning students of visual perception can possibly appreciate, since complex optical systems and measuring devices must be used for their control and specification. The term *optical system* will be used here to describe any of a variety of devices used for the control of the geometric, spectral, intensitive, and temporal properties of light fields to be viewed by the eye. Such systems are not easy to design, construct, calibrate, and maintain; but unless these things are done properly, the experiment may be valueless.

To understand the process of visual perception, one must begin with the stimulus as physically defined, then describe how the physical events (light quanta, in the case of vision) interact with the perceiving organism in order to allow behavior based upon adaptive visual perception to occur. Physical specification may be at either of two levels: (1) the object, or field being viewed, or (2) the retinal image. Although the latter involves an additional degree of abstraction and one must make assumptions concerning the optical characteristics of the eye, it is useful. It renders various combinations of stimulus field and eye conditions equivalent for conditions where, for the perceptually impoverished condition, their action upon the eye is equivalent. If a diffuse surface is moved to twice its original distance from the eye but is doubled in linear size, the retinal image is essentially unchanged. For some purposes, a specification of retinal image location and the illuminance of the retinal image may be preferable to a description of fields external to the eye.

IMAGE FORMATION IN THE EYE

If one wishes to stimulate a subject with light, it is necessary to know something about the eye as an image-forming device to be able to understand and control this stimulation. A full discussion of this topic makes up a part of *physiological optics*. An excellent summary chapter on the image-forming mechanism of the eye has been prepared by Fry (1959). Refer also to Bennett and Francis (1962), LeGrand (1952), and Ogle (1961).

Focal length and optical power

The purpose of an image-forming system, such as a lens, is to cause rays of light emanating from a point in object space to be refracted by the lens so as to recombine at a point in image space. If a point in object space is infinitely far away, the rays incident from it upon the lens will be *collimated* or parallel to one another. For a thin lens, *focal length* is easily defined as the distance from the lens to the image for this condition. The focal length of any lens may therefore be estimated by causing it to image a distant object and then measuring the distance from the lens to the image. For thick lenses and/or compound lenses containing many elements, such estimates are inaccurate because one does not know offhand which part of the lens to use as the reference point for measurement. There are two such points, called the *principal points*, depending upon the direction of light travel through the lens. In some systems, most notably in telephoto lenses, one or both of the principal points may be outside the physical lens. In general, a given optical system will have two focal lengths, depending upon the direction of the light.

The *power of an optical system*, in diopters, is defined as the reciprocal of its focal length, where the focal length is expressed in meters. The higher the diopter value, the greater is the degree of refractive power exhibited. Diopter values are convenient in that they are additive for successive stages in an optical system.

Images are formed on the retina primarily because of refraction that takes place as light passes from air into the cornea. This light will not reenter air, which is not the case in most man-made optical systems.

The eyeball is a short-focal-length system, about 17 mm, corresponding to a refractive power of about 60 diopters. Although this means that the retinal image is very small (e.g., the moon, which subtends 0.5° at the eye, provides a geometrical retinal image having a diameter of only about 0.15 mm), the eye shares certain advantages that accrue to short-focal-length systems. The principal advantage is that the eye can be smaller than would otherwise be possible. Also, for a given size of the pupil, the illumination of the retina corresponding to a given external object is higher. For example, if the focal length of the eye were doubled, the area of the moon's image would be increased by a factor of 4, but the flux per unit area would be only one-fourth as great. Finally, for a short-focal-length system, less physical change in the optical system is necessary to adjust its focus for external objects at varying distances. This process, known as *accommodation* in the eye, is accomplished by an indirect action of the ciliary muscle upon the shape of the eye lens. The refractive power of the lens varies from 19 to 33 diopters as the focus of the eye changes from infinity to a very near object. Most of the refractive power of the eye is actually supplied by refraction at the corneal surface, which provides about 43 diopters of refractive power regardless of the accommodative state.

As an object is brought closer to the eye, its image will become out of focus unless accommodation takes place. This action occurs by means of a complex physiological servo system that seeks to sharpen the image by changing the radius of curvature of the lens, particularly its front surface. A part of the same system is involved in the inward turning of the two eyes (convergence), which keeps the two images of the same object on corresponding points of the two retinas. Another such system is involved in the control of the pupil of the eye. The smaller the pupil, the greater the depth of field and the lower the retinal illumination.

It is possible to trace rays through a geometrical representation of the eye and to show how the refraction at each surface is just sufficient to produce an approximation of a point image at the retina. Anyone who has been through this exercise will be impressed with the delicacy of the relations involved and with the fact that a slight error in a radius of curvature (or a distance or an index of refraction) will lead to a badly blurred image.

The nodal-point concept

A simpler method of regarding the image-forming properties of the eye takes advantage of the *nodal-point* concept in optics. In general, all image-forming systems can be regarded as having two nodal points. Given fixed locations of the planes in which the object and image are located, the geometrical dimensions of the image can be calculated by (1) drawing a straight line from a given object point to the first nodal point and (2) drawing a second straight line from the second nodal point parallel to the first until it intersects the image plane (see Fig. 7-7). The path just described is *not* the path taken by a light quantum or a light ray; it is just a convenient fiction that leads quickly to the calculation of the location of the object point.

The eye has two nodal points, like any optical device, but they are so close together that they may be conveniently regarded without serious error as being only one. From average data, the nodal point is about 7.2 mm from the front of the eye and 17.2 mm from the retina, for a distant object. If one accommodates appropriately as an object moves closer to the eye, the nodal point moves toward the retina by about 0.4 mm, an amount small enough to be ignored for practical purposes.

Visual angle can be defined in terms of the nodal-point concept as the angle in minutes, degrees, or radians subtended at the nodal point of the eye by an object in the outside world. It is also the angle subtended at the nodal point of the eye by the retinal image of that object. When calculating the visual angle subtended by an object, it is necessary to add 7.2 mm to the distance between the object and the cornea of the eye. For distant objects, the correction is trivial. It is convenient to remember that a circular object subtending a visual angle of 1° (about twice that of the moon) has an image of about 0.3 mm diameter on the retina.

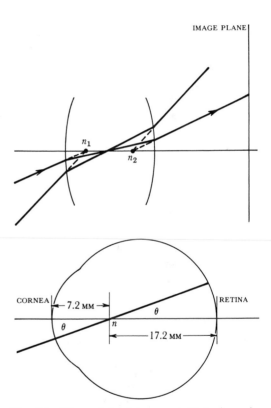

Fig. 7-7 The nodal-point concept. *Top:* A ray is incident upon the thick lens from the lower left. If it is headed exactly in the direction of the first nodal point of the system (n_1), the direction of the emerging ray will be parallel to the incident one but will appear as if coming from n_2. *Bottom:* The eye has two nodal points that are sufficiently close together to be treated as one, located in the position shown. The angle θ defines the *visual angle* subtended by an external object, as well as the angle subtended by the image of the object on the retina with the nodal point taken as the vertex of the angle.

The visual angle, rather than the actual size of the stimulus, is most often used to describe the size of a stimulus in a vision experiment. This is because visual angle is a much more critical variable in the perceptually impoverished viewing situation than is physical size. Computation of visual angle requires little more than a knowledge of simple trigonometry. Suppose, for example, that we had wanted to produce a preadapting field of 10° visual angle for the experiment on dark adaptation. The actual distance of the preadapting field from the eye might depend upon a number of practical considerations such as the size of the room and problems of illuminating very large fields. Suppose that it was decided to place the adapting field 6 ft from the nodal point of the subject's eye. It would then follow that tan $(\theta/2) = 5° = x/10$, where θ is the desired visual angle of 10° and the value 10 on the right-hand side of the equation is the desired viewing distance of 10 ft. Since the tangent of 5° (the half-angle, used so as to provide a right angle between the line of sight and the stimulus field) is 0.0875, $x = 0.875$ ft, or $10\frac{1}{2}$ in. The total field would then be 21 in. in diameter.

The nodal-point concept is so convenient that its highly conceptual nature is easily forgotten: thus introductory textbooks sometimes show an entering beam of light as if it converged at the nodal point and then diverged again to form the retinal image. *This is utterly false.* More importantly, perhaps, the nodal-point concept does not even suggest that the retinal image is always blurred. No optical system can in fact image a point as a point. Diffraction provides the fundamental limitation. All optical systems also have aberrations and stray light. The eye exhibits up to 1.6 diopters of chromatic aberration, which means that blue light is imaged considerably forward of red light to a nonnegligible extent. The accommodation of the eye for distance is not a static affair, but wanders in and out around some optimal value. This, combined with irreducible eye tremor known as physiological nystagmus, means that the image is always wiggling and is variably blurred. Finally, there is a good deal of stray light in the eye, mainly caused by scattering from the cornea and lens, with some light also coming in through the sclera and illuminating the receptors from behind.

METHODS OF DELIVERING LIGHT TO THE EYE

The normal viewing situation of everyday life may be called a "free-viewing" situation, in the sense that the position of the head in space is not very critical for the perception of an illuminated object. This is because most objects are diffuse reflectors. The light reflected from them spreads widely in space, so that some tiny fraction of it will enter the pupil of a viewing eye even though the eye moves with respect to the object. Some limitations on this freedom occur even in the real world. These are associated in part with surfaces that are completely or partially specular (mirror-like).

In visual experimentation, one has a choice whether to use a free-viewing situation or to use one that restricts the position of the subject. Each has its advantages and disadvantages; these will now be described and discussed.

Free viewing

It is characteristic of the light coming from a point source that it is irradiated in straight lines in a variety of directions. Thus the light reaching the eye from a point source is diverging light; i.e., if one were to trace backward from the eye on the paths described by a number of rays, all such paths would intersect at a point. Such a point may therefore be simulated by any means whereby these conditions of divergent light may be produced. One common means is slide projection. In this case, the slide projector causes points on transparencies to be approximately imaged as points at a plane where the screen is located. Light is reflected from these points, and some of it reaches the eye of an observer. Such an image is called a *real image*. A point source may also be simulated by looking at an actual or simulated point source in a mirror. In this case, the diverging rays are reflected and appear to come from a point behind the mirror. Such an image is called a *virtual image*. The reality or virtuality of images depends solely upon whether the point image can be focused upon an intercepting screen. It is not necessary that a real image be focused upon a screen in order to be visible, since any image, whether real or virtual, can act as an object with respect to a second optical component or system, such as the eye. A real image, formed in empty space, can be seen provided that each point in the image actually has light rays diverging from it in the direction of the eye. This is obviously not the case if one retains his normal viewing position and then removes a motion-picture screen and allows the light to enter a black void behind. If one moves behind the former screen position and looks toward the nose of the projector, the full image still is not seen because most points in the image do not radiate light toward the eye. It is quite possible to view such "aerial" images if measures are taken to ensure that light does in fact enter the eye. These concepts are illustrated in Fig. 7-8.

Perhaps the simplest procedure for producing a diffuse light patch is to cut an aperture in the shape of the desired stimulus in an otherwise opaque screen, then place a piece of flashed opal glass against the back of the aperture. Light may then be projected onto the opal glass from behind and the subject sees it transilluminated. Flashed opal glass has good scattering properties, so that the luminance of the field as seen by the subject will be largely independent of the angle of view. If more light is required from a particular system, ground glass may be used, but this has more directional properties, exhibiting mainly forward scatter.

Stimuli may be delivered by reflection from a diffuse or beaded screen using commercially available slide and motion-picture projectors.

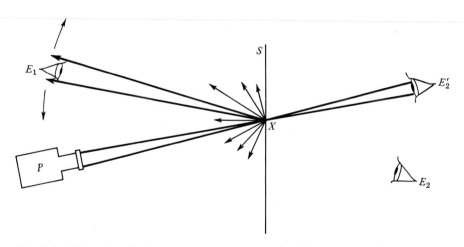

Fig. 7-8 Light from Projector P converges upon the screen at X to form a real image of a point on a transparency within the projector. If a diffusely reflecting screen S is located as shown, the image of the point may be viewed by eye E_1 from a wide variety of positions, including the one shown. If the screen is removed E_1 cannot see X, nor can eye E_2, located on the other side of the screen, because none of the diverging light from X enters the eye in either case. E_2 could see X if a diffusely transmitting screen (e.g., ground glass) were substituted for S or could see X without a screen if the eye were moved to position E_2'.

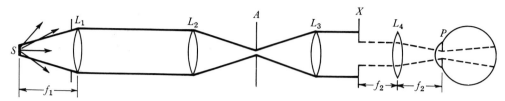

Fig. 7-9   A single-channel Maxwellian-view stimulating system.

It should be noted that any system of reproduction degrades the image, by comparison with the original, by a combination of edge blurring and contrast reduction. This may become a problem in experiments where visual acuity is under assessment, in which case some more direct method of stimulus presentation is preferable.

The principal advantages of free-viewing situations are that they are relatively easy to set up, the alignment of optical components is not too critical, and the subject may be positioned with a simple head rest or, if the distance from subject to stimulus is large, with no head rest at all. The principal disadvantage is that very high luminances are difficult to obtain: 1,000 mL may be taken as a practical upper limit using ordinary projectors at normal distances. Also, artificial pupils are necessary if the natural variation of the pupil is to be controlled.

Viewing of aerial images

Another disadvantage of the free-viewing situation is that only a tiny percentage of the light from the stimulus actually enters the pupil of the eye. The remainder is entirely ineffective for visual purposes. As previously noted, an image formed in space (aerial image) may be viewed by the eye without its first having been intercepted by a screen. An advantage of such a procedure is that the light is not diffusely transmitted or reflected and consequently much more of it can enter the pupil of the eye. The disadvantage of the method is that the eye must be properly positioned to intercept light coming from the aerial image in order for it to be seen.

Maxwellian view

The Maxwellian view is a widely used system in which the subject views the stimulus field through a lens that appears uniformly filled with light. This lens, if the eye pupil is properly located, produces an image entirely within the pupil of the eye and thus causes all the light transmitted by it to enter the eye pupil (neglecting reflection and scatter at the cornea). This is very different from the usual free-viewing situation.

A single-channel Maxwellian-view system is shown in Fig. 7-9. A ribbon-filament source S emits light in various directions. Some of this is directed toward L_1, which has a focal length f_1. Light is approximately collimated between L_1 and L_2 (it would be perfectly collimated only for a point source) and is then brought to a focus at A. An aperture located at A can be smaller than the image of S, helping to exclude stray light and also determining the size of the image P located in the pupil, since S, A, and P are located at conjugate foci. Lens L_3 again approximately collimates the light, which by L_4 produces an image of A at the plane of the pupil, within the actual pupil. The image at the pupil may be regarded as an optical artificial pupil within the natural pupil.

The subject sees whatever configuration is located in the plane X. In order for it to be in focus, for an eye with relaxed accommodation, it must be located at one focal length behind L_4. By bringing it somewhat closer to L_4, some accommodative effort will be required: it is often a good idea deliberately to introduce about 1.5 diopters so that subjects with slight myopia can use the system without correcting lenses. Only in the case of an actual point source, which would result in a pinhole of an optical artificial pupil, could X be located anywhere at all between L_3 and L_4 and still remain in focus. The high efficiency of the system comes from the fact that light coming through an aperture at X, instead of being allowed to scatter in all directions as in the free-viewing system, is constrained to move in a forward direction, nearly parallel to the axis of the system, and then is further constrained by lens L_4 to pass entirely through the pupil of the eye. In other important respects, the situation is just as if a diffuse source were located at X and viewed through L_4. The normal optics of the eye are used, and as the area A decreases, the result is the same that occurs with a reduction of pupil size in the free-viewing situation: the diffraction in the retinal image will become worse, but there will be less chromatic aberration introduced by the eye and its depth of field will increase.

A two-channel Maxwellian-view stimulating system is shown in Fig. 7-10. This would be a suitable system for carrying out the reference experiment on dark adaptation. In this system, light from a single source is reflected from mirrors and then collimated

(rendered parallel) for a short distance. The region between L_1 and L_2 is the best place in the system to interpose neutral filters and/or interference filters for the control of luminance or color of the stimulus. In this system, the image at A and A' acts as a secondary source, with the second collimating lens in each system, L_3 and L_3', rendering the beams parallel. The field as seen by the subject will be delimited by apertures placed in each channel one focal length behind the final eye lens. The visual angle of the field may be computed by treating the physical size of the aperture as the size of the field and taking the focal length of the eye lens as the viewing distance.

It is easy to produce 10^6 mL of effective luminance by using a Maxwellian-view system and a 40-watt source. It is difficult to achieve 10^3 mL of luminance upon a screen by using a projector containing a 750-watt lamp unless the projector is moved unusually close to the screen. Special difficulties are introduced in the Maxwellian view: (1) The efficiency of light entering the eye depends upon the point of entry through the pupil (the Stiles-Crawford effect), and elaborate precautions must be taken to ensure accurate position of the pupil. (2) The optical system must be critically aligned. (3) Dust and imperfections

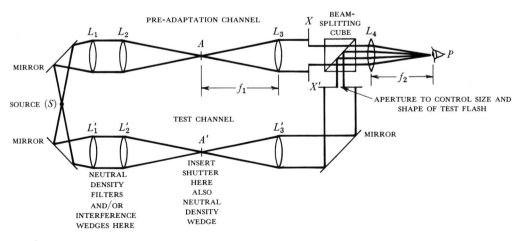

Fig. 7-10   A two-channel Maxwellian-view stimulating system.

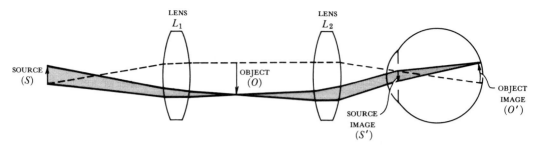

Fig. 7-11   Fundamentals of the Maxwellian-view system. Source S has the shape of an arrow. Many rays of light emanate from the arrow point of source S. Here is shown only a ray which passes through the arrow point object O, an aperture shaped like an arrow in an otherwise opaque screen. Similarly, a ray from the tail of source S is shown passing through the arrow point of object O. Note that these rays are not quite parallel between L_1 and L_2. The shaded area, traced through the system, shows the outer limit of the bundle of rays passing through the arrow point of O which have a physical existence in the system. These rays are parallel between L_2 and the cornea of the un-accommodated emmetropic eye, then converge because of refraction in the eye to form an image at O'. An image S' of the source is formed in the plane of the subject's pupil. Two rays involved in the formation of the tail of the source image are shown—those passing through the head and tail of object arrow at (O). The source image is not directly perceived by the subject. It has a position which is only slightly dependent upon the curvature of the cornea and which is independent of the accommodative state of the eye. If this eye were to accommodate, O' would move forward, meaning that O would be seen as blurred. Its sharpness could be restored by moving O closer to L_2, or vice versa. Actual sources and apertures are of course not usually in the shape of arrows.

near X are painfully evident. Other advantages are: (1) A shutter located at A cuts the beam where it is narrow and provides temporal characteristics superior to those which could otherwise be achieved. (2) A neutral wedge, i.e., one whose density varies along its length, may be located at this point without the need for a balancing wedge to compensate for a luminance gradient across the field. (3) Interference wedges, used to control wavelength, must be located at such a focal point in order to work properly. (4) The train of lenses may be extended to include many points A and to superpose additional fields by means of beam splitters. (5) Very large fields may be provided, by means of a very short focal-length lens at L_4, in a very small space. (6) It provides the best possible artificial pupil. A detailed description of the optical principles of the Maxwellian view is given in Fig. 7-11.

CALCULATION OF RETINAL ILLUMINATION

In the free-viewing situation, retinal illumination (illuminance) is directly proportional to the luminance of a surface being viewed, assuming geometrical optics to be exact. LeGrand (1957, p. 85) has shown that

$$E_r = 0.36LS\tau_\lambda \qquad (7\text{-}12)$$

where E_r is retinal illuminance in lumens per square meter, L is the luminance of the stimulus field surface in candelas per square meter, S is the area of the pupil in square centimeters, and τ_λ is the transmittance of the eye (percentage of incident light transmitted at each wavelength).

One troland is defined as the retinal illuminance produced by viewing a surface having a luminance of 1 cd per sq m through a pupil having an area of 1 sq mm. Substituting these values into Eq. (7-12) (neglecting transmission losses in the eye) shows this to be equivalent to 0.0036 lumen per sq m. This amount of retinal illumination will be less effective if admitted through a large pupil rather than a small one.

For the Maxwellian view, LeGrand has shown, assuming a point source, that

$$E_r = 0.36\tau_\lambda \frac{I}{(f_1/f_2)^2} \qquad (7\text{-}13)$$

where f_1 and f_2 are defined in Fig. 7-9 as the focal lengths of the first and last lenses of the system, respectively, I is the intensity of the source in candelas, and τ_λ is as before. Transmission losses in the Maxwellian-view optics are neglected.

Since real Maxwellian-view systems utilize a source of finite area, the quantity I can be replaced in Eq. (7-13) by $L'A$, where L' is the intrinsic luminance of the source in candelas per square meter and A is the area of the source in square centimeters. This yields

$$E_r = 0.36\tau_\lambda \frac{L'A}{(f_1/f_2)^2} \qquad (7\text{-}14)$$

From these relations, it is possible to compute the luminance of an equivalent freely viewed field that would produce the same retinal illumination and therefore the same subjective brightness as a given Maxwellian-view system. This is done by setting Eqs. (7-12) and (7-14) equal to each other:

$$0.36LS\tau_\lambda = 0.36\tau_\lambda \frac{L'A}{(f_1/f_2)^2} \qquad (7\text{-}15)$$

If we assume that $f_1 = f_2$, as it does in many Maxwellian-view systems, this reduces to

$$L = \frac{L'A}{S} \qquad (7\text{-}16)$$

meaning that the equivalent freely-viewed field luminance is directly proportional to the

luminance of the Maxwellian source and to its area and is inversely proportional to the pupillary area assumed for the equivalent free-viewing situation. This relation holds only over the range where A is small enough to permit all the light flux to enter the pupil of the eye, and it neglects the Stiles-Crawford effect.

LIGHT SOURCES[1]

The ideal light source for visual research, in addition to being as inexpensive as possible, should have the following qualities: (1) complete stability of light output for a given voltage, throughout the life of the source; (2) very rapid rise and decay times when momentarily activated; (3) an equal-energy, or perhaps equal-quantum, output as a function of wavelength; (4) very high and uniform intrinsic luminance and large enough source area for the intended purpose [the intrinsic luminance of a source is the luminance of the source measured directly; from Eq. (7-16) it will be seen that it provides an upper limit to the luminance that can be provided by a Maxwellian-view system]; (5) high efficiency, measured in lumens per watt (this implies a concentration of energy in the visible spectrum); (6) convenience of installation and maintenance.

If such an ideal source could be incorporated into whatever optical device is used for stimulating the eye, the experimenter could (1) determine the luminance of the field as seen by the subject, which would be easily related to voltage; (2) deliver short, uniform flashes of light simply by controlling the voltage supplied to the source; (3) always have enough light for his experimental purposes; and (4) have color work greatly simplified by the availability of an equal-energy white spectrum. Unfortunately, we are still a

[1] The reader is referred to an extremely useful and extensive article on the generation, control, and measurement of visible and near-visible radiant energy (Withrow and Withrow, 1956). This article contains 130 pages of text, plus references, and provides a wealth of detailed information with respect to some of the material covered in this and the next section of this chapter.

very long way from the ideal situation described above. A description of actual sources in common use, along with their advantages and disadvantages relative to the criteria just discussed is presented below.

Tungsten

The most widely used light source for visual experimentation is the gas-filled tungsten-filament lamp. These are available in a wide variety of sizes and types from any of the major electrical manufacturers. The following types are especially useful: (1) 110-watt tungsten helical filament lamp with prefocus base; (2) ribbon-filament lamps, having a large uniform source area; (3) V-filament automobile spotlight bulbs; (4) 150- to 750-watt projection lamps, for use in suitable projectors; (5) "grain-of-wheat" and other miniature sources, good for fixation points and where space limitations are severe; (6) ordinary household lamps, especially the "Q-coated" types, which provide a reasonably uniform luminance over the lamp surface.

Tungsten lamps emit a continuous spectrum whose wavelength dependence is a function of the current through the filament and thus its temperature; at the temperatures that ordinarily must be used, they are somewhat deficient in short-wave energy for use in experiments where high-intensity blue light is needed. As temperature is increased, the ratio of blue to red increases, but lamp life is severely reduced. The resistance of tungsten is related to temperature, increasing as temperature increases.[1]

For many lamps, a reasonably constant light output (± 20 percent) can be maintained throughout the life of the lamp by monitoring current at a constant voltage. The voltage required to maintain this constant current gradually increases, as does the amount of light emitted from the filament. The latter tends to be compensated by tungsten deposits

on the bulb. A relatively sudden voltage increase will occur near the end of the lamp's life. If voltage as well as current is monitored, a prediction may be made that the lamp will shortly burn out, and it may be replaced between experimental sessions. It is better to monitor the output of the light source, which can be done by a method to be described in a later section.

Since alternating-current (a-c) supplies are more readily available than direct-current (d-c) supplies, the former are preferable so long as the needs of the experiment are met. In some experiments, such as the color matching of steady fields or the pre-adapting phase of the illustrative dark-adaptation experiment, continuous or long exposures are used. Although the effect of an a-c source is to cause a slight ripple in the light output of the lamp as a function of time, this ripple is not ordinarily visible at the 120 cps light-flicker caused by a 60 cps voltage fluctuation (the United States standard frequency) and produces no problems for such experiments. When very short flashes are used, the presence of an appreciable ripple means that the total number of quanta per flash will vary depending upon where the onset and extinction of the flash happen to fall in the fluctuating cycle of light output of the lamp. In experiments concerned with the visual perception of flicker, inadvertent fluctuations in the source must be avoided.

A number of methods are available that will reduce or eliminate this source ripple.

1. *High-frequency alternation.* A 60-cps motor can be used to power a 400-cps generator. The higher the frequency of alternation, the less well the lamp filament will follow, in its temperature fluctuations, the current changes within it. The use of a three-phase voltage supply will also materially reduce ripple compared with that produced by a single-phase supply at the same frequency.

---

[1] It is advisable for these reasons to operate tungsten lamps below their rated voltage and to bring them up to temperature gradually by use of a Variac or temporary series resistance. Otherwise, a surge of high current will pass through a cold filament and reduce lamp life.

2. *Rectification with d-c generator.* A 60-cps motor can be used to power a d-c generator.

3. *Electronic rectification.* Diodes, transistors, or selenium rectifiers may be used. The simplest kind of rectification (half-wave) simply cuts off the negative half of each output phase. Such a rectifier will cause an even greater fluctuation in the light output of a lamp than the original a-c source. The ripple can be attenuated to a fraction of 1 percent with the use of bridge rectification with sufficient shunting capacitance. This is found in the better commercially available power supplies.

4. *Batteries.* Although bulky and messy, the storage battery is still the best supply available for supplying a high level of truly steady direct current. A problem with batteries is that the power that they can supply becomes reduced with use; this problem can be solved by "floating" a battery charger (usually an electronic rectifier) across the battery. If the ripple of the battery charger is less than 5 percent, there will be no appreciable fluctuation introduced into the output of the system. The amount of ripple may be measured directly by delivering the output of the lamp to a photocell, such as the Type 929, the output of which is displayed on a cathode-ray oscilloscope (CRO).

The chief advantages of tungsten sources are their availability, stability, variety, low cost, continuous spectral output, high overall output (10^7 cd per sq m at about 3000°K), and the simplicity of the power supply required. The chief disadvantages include relatively low blue-light output, rather low efficiency (a good deal of heat must be dissipated in high-wattage sources), and relatively low intensity.

Xenon

For applications requiring very high intensity, the xenon arc is the best source currently available. The bulb of the lamp is filled with xenon gas at high pressure, which ionizes across the gap between anode and cathode and emits an intense white light. The intensity of such a lamp is about forty times that of tungsten for the shorter wavelengths, with an intrinsic luminance of about 10^8 cd per sq m, at least ten times that of tungsten. The ionization of gas causes a light output that ideally is restricted only to certain lines in the spectrum, with intervening spectral regions being dark. This phenomenon is most pronounced in gas under low pressure. As the pressure of the gas is raised, light is emitted also from the previously dark regions of the spectrum, as the spectral "lines" spread out and also increase in intensity.

The spectral output of the high-pressure xenon lamp thus shows a continuous and rather flat emission upon which smeared spectral lines are superposed; there are several rather prominent ones between 400 and 500 $m\mu$. Elaborate starting equipment is required, and it is best to use the d-c lamp, which requires either that a stable 1,000 watt 110-volt d-c power supply be available or that a heavy-duty rectifier be constructed. If the lamp is being used with a spectrometer to supply monochromatic light [see section on wavelength control (pages 314 to 319)], energy calibrations must be undertaken for each wavelength to be used experimentally. This is done because interpolations can be grossly in error due to the spectral lines. The xenon arc has a tendency to strike in a slightly different position each time it is used, and there is some position instability even over short periods. Its principal advantages are very high intensity and the lack of supporting structures around the arc, which permits light to be taken off horizontally from any direction. Its principal disadvantages are high cost, complex power supply, a major heat-dissipation problem (a ventilating pipe with exhaust fan is mandatory), arc movement, the three-dimensional nature of the arc source (it cannot be imaged in a plane), and some danger of explosion. It is necessary to build the lamp into an enclosed and manipulable housing since it will otherwise be dangerous and/or unadjustable for position once activated. Commercially manufactured lamp housings and power supplies are now available (see Appendix).

Mercury

Another high-intensity source of great potential usefulness is the ultrahigh-pressure mercury arc. The arc can be very small, about 0.3 mm, and an intrinsic luminance of one available type is about ten times higher than that of xenon, although the lamp operates at 20 volts d-c and consumes only 100 watts. Heat dissipation is no problem, since the lamp must be enclosed and unventilated in order to operate properly. This could be an excellent source for use in Maxwellian-view systems, although some magnification of the source image at the eye would probably be required ($f_2 > f_1$ in Fig. 7-9). Its chief disadvantage is that it emits large spectral lines, although these are smeared out because of the extreme pressure, and would need very careful energy and wavelength calibrations where monochromatic light is needed. Its intrinsic luminance never falls below that of a xenon arc anywhere in the visible spectrum, but its effective intensity is not very high because of its very small area.

Glow modulator tubes

These can be easily modulated by electronic circuits and have been used rather often. A continuous monitoring of the outputs of these tubes is essential. Otherwise, there will be unwanted intensity variations or changes in temporal relationships due either to the lamp itself, which is photometrically unstable, or to changes in the electronic circuitry.

The principal disadvantages of the neon glow tube are its poor spectrum and low intensity, although its intrinsic luminance is high. Higher-intensity flashing sources are available: the Strobotac is probably the most convenient, especially if repetitive stimulation is desired, but has an exponential decay and very blue spectrum. It is also possible to pulse the xenon arc to provide flashes of only a few microseconds' duration. Photographic flash devices may also be used. Accurate calibration of intensity versus time for very short flash devices can be achieved with the use of a 929 photocell and oscilloscope.

Fluorescence

In the phenomenon of fluorescence, absorbed light is reradiated, generally at a lower frequency (longer wavelength) than the incident light. This is not what occurs with most surfaces, where the reflected light is of the same wavelength as that which is incident. The use of "black" (ultraviolet) light to excite fluorescent materials is now commonplace and could be used in research in vision. The ordinary household variety of fluorescent tube is not very useful for most visual research because of its flicker, very poor spectral qualities, and inconvenient shape.

LASER

A recent development is the optical MASER (Microwave Amplification by the Stimulated Emission of Radiation). The optical maser, called a laser, involves the amplification of light energy, as it passes through certain solids or gases in artificially induced metastable states, and the multiple reflection of the light from the ends of a chamber or crystal by carefully aligned mirrors. Although the mirrors may transmit only a small percentage of the light, the multiple amplification results in the transmission of large amounts of coherent, collimated light away from the device. Light in the visible region is now available at several wavelengths, is focusable at extraordinarily high intensity levels, can be pulsed in very brief flashes, and has a very high degree of monochromaticity. Collimated laser light, if directly viewed (or seen with a reflecting surface having high specularity) can punch holes in the retina. Extreme caution is therefore urged.

Cadmium-mercury

For wavelength calibrations, the best all-purpose source is the low-pressure cadmium-mercury (Cd-Hg) lamp, which emits a number of strong spectral lines through the visible region. These are listed in Table 7-3. A special power supply is required to operate this lamp.

MIXTURE OF LIGHT

In many experiments it is necessary to superimpose one field of light upon another, so that the radiance of all or part of the total field is the sum of the radiances of the components. Examples of such experiments include (1) color mixture experiments; (2) increment threshold experiments, where the threshold visibility of a small light flash against a larger adapting field is measured; (3) light- and dark-adaptation experiments where the adapting level is shifted suddenly from one level to another.

The two-channel Maxwellian-view optical system of Fig. 7-10 would be suitable for use in either the second or the third experiment cited above. The optical superposition of light may be obtained by five fundamental methods: (1) beam splitters, (2) integrating spheres, (3) projection, (4) dispersion with dispersive recombination, and (5) taking advantage of the limited temporal and spatial resolving power of the eye.

Beam splitters

A beam splitter is a device (Fig. 7-12) that causes some of the incident light to be transmitted, while most of the remainder is reflected. In visual experiments, beam splitters are used mainly in reverse in order to combine beams of light from separate systems. They are used in Maxwellian-view systems, where

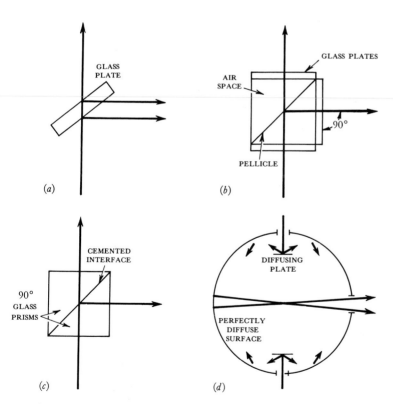

Fig. 7-12 **Four methods of optically superimposing light.** (*a*) **Simple beam splitter.** (*b*) **Pellicle beam splitter.** (*c*) **Double-prism beam splitter.** (*d*) **Integrating sphere.**

they can be very small, but can be used also in free-viewing situations, most conveniently if placed near to the eye. The simplest beam splitter is a glass plate, e.g., a microscope cover slip or a section of plate glass, which will reflect a small percentage of the light and transmit a high percentage. More complex partially silvered mirrors are commercially available, many of which are deliberately *dichroic,* meaning that the percentage of reflectance versus transmittance varies with wavelength. A difficulty with such plates is the problem of double reflection of the reflected beam from the back and front surfaces of the plate (Fig. 7-12a). There are fundamentally two ways to solve this problem. One is to use a reflecting layer so thin that, for all practical purposes, there is only one surface. These thin membranes, called *pellicles,* are commercially available. They should be completely enclosed since they are extremely delicate (see Fig. 7-12b). They are unsuitable for applications where any considerable amount of vibration is likely to occur. Another method of eliminating double reflection is the use of the beam-splitting cube (Fig. 7-12c), where following the evaporation of a partially-transmitting layer of aluminum on the diagonal face of one of two prisms, the interfaces of the two triangular prisms are cemented together to form a single reflecting surface. Reflected light becomes partially polarized. Fortunately, the eye is not an analyzer of polarized light and thus polarization often makes little difference.

Integrating sphere

When a beam of light is allowed to enter a diffusely coated sphere, multiple reflections from the sides of the sphere cause the entire inside of the sphere to "light up." Additive light mixture will take place by bringing in two or more separate beams. Care must be taken not to view light from that part of the sphere upon which the beam is directly incident; in careful work, a diffusing plate should be introduced, as shown in Fig. 7-12d, to intercept the direct light from each beam. The

larger an integrating sphere, the more perfect will be the multiple reflection and mixture, but the less efficient it will become. No polarization is introduced when this method is employed, provided that the sphere coating has no specular component of reflection.

Projection

In superposed projection, the light from two separate projectors is caused to fall upon the same area of a projection screen. Complex images, e.g., photographs of real objects, may be superposed in this way. Special precautions must be taken to ensure that the separate projectors have closely matched lenses and that the two images are precisely registered in space.

Dispersion

It is possible to disperse white light with a prism, focus a sharp image of the spectrum that it produces, and then recombine the spectrum into a uniform field of white light by reversing the processes (dispersive recombination). By placing a template in the image of the spectrum, light of any desired spectral composition may be produced, including nearly monochromatic light if narrow slits are used. This system is used in at least two of the finest colorimeters in the world (Stiles and Burch, 1958; Wright, 1946).

Spatial and temporal resolution of the eye

Because of the inability of the eye to resolve very small distances and very short time intervals, light mixture may be simulated by successive presentation in time or by means of many small dots that form a mosaic. The Guild colorimeter is an example of a device in which sequential mixture is employed. A color TV tube produces its image with many tiny colored dots of light, produced by cathode rays which excite appropriately placed phosphors. These tiny dots are below the spatial resolution threshold of the eye when viewed at an appropriate distance. Neither of these techniques is particularly desirable for visual research unless the spatial or temporal integrative capacity of the eye is itself the subject under investigation.

CONTROL OF LUMINANCE

The luminance of a test field can be altered by (1) changing the intrinsic luminance and thus the intensity of a source that irradiates it; (2) the use of filters, apertures, and/or a rapidly rotating sector disk; or (3) changing the distance between the source and the field.

Changes in source intensity

The intensity of an incandescent source is easily changed by altering the voltage impressed across it. This, however, produces a concomitant change in the color temperature of the source, which is objectionable for many purposes. If a fluorescent tube can be used as a source, dimming circuits are available that allow the luminance of the tube to be reduced without much change in spectral distribution. If a source is used to supply two or more optical channels in a complex visual stimulator, the control of luminance by changing source intensity will change all channels proportionally and will probably be inconvenient for that reason. On the other hand, the use of the same source for powering all optical channels is advisable, since fluctuations of source intensity will tend to be correlated in the various channels. Even with some fluctuation in source intensity, the relative luminance values of the separate fields will not change much. This is often very advantageous, e.g., in a colorimeter, where such correlated fluctuations will not upset a color match.

Interposition techniques

1. *Filters.* The luminance of a field may be altered by the interposition of an optical filter between the source and the field being illuminated by that source. See, for example, Fig. 7-10 and the associated discussion concerning filters in the Maxwellian-view system. Optical filters either absorb or reflect a certain percentage of the incident light, transmitting the remainder. The *transmittance* of an optical filter is defined as ϕ_t/ϕ_i, where ϕ_i is a measure of the flux incident upon the filter and ϕ_t is a measure of that which is transmitted, each in the same units. The *density* of an optical filter is defined as the logarithm of reciprocal transmittance, $\log_{10}(\phi_i/\phi_t)$, and therefore becomes larger as the percentage of transmitted light becomes smaller. Some values of transmittance and density are given in Table 7-4.

A high-quality optical filter should be uniform over its entire surface, scatter as little light as possible, and be neutral or spectrally flat, i.e., have a density independent of wavelength. The scattering of light by filters is particularly objectionable in highly directional systems like the Maxwellian view, since in addition to the light reflected and absorbed, some will be scattered out of the beam, and the quality of images formed by the system will be reduced. Filters may be calibrated either with or without the scattered component included in the measurement of transmitted flux. When the scattered component is included, one speaks of *diffuse transmittance;* when it is not, one speaks of *specular transmittance.* The Q factor, or Callier coefficient, of a filter is the ratio between the logarithms of the two, becoming larger as the

Table 7-3   Prominent lines of Cd-Hg gas lamp used for wavelength calibration.

Wavelength, mμ	Description
404.7	Two violet lines; will appear as overlapping under many conditions of exit and entrance slit widths
407.8	
435.8	Violet
467.8	Blue
480.0	Greenish blue
491.6	Green-blue (dim)
508.6	Bluish green
546.1	Yellowish green
578.0	Yellow
634.8	Red

scatter increases. The basic principles of specular versus diffuse filter calibration are given in Fig. 7-13.

Since all filters scatter some light and since the directionality of the light passing through the filter can never be completely specified, filters ideally should be calibrated in the position that they will occupy in the optical system. Otherwise it is necessary that the supplier specify exactly the conditions under which the filter was calibrated and that these conditions be precisely duplicated in the experimental situation. The nominal values of neutral filters should *not* be used as a standard of luminance control in careful experimental work. In most Maxwellian-view systems, intensity calibrations can be done by placing a photomultiplier tube in the position normally occupied by the eye, provided that the output of the tube is amplified and displayed on a scale that is exactly linear with respect to the irradiance of light incident upon the tube. Commercial photomultiplier units are available for this purpose, some of which include calibrated

scales and instructions for using them to adjust the linearity of the instrument. In the absence of a photomultiplier unit, use may be made of Talbot's law [Eq. (7-18)], provided that the experimental apparatus has two channels (e.g., like that of Fig. 7-10) that can produce juxtaposed photometric fields. The two fields can be matched for brightness by adjusting a neutral wedge in one of them. Then a high-speed sector disk with a known light-to-dark ratio can be placed in the other channel and the neutral wedge adjusted for a new match. If, for example, the sector disk has a 50:50 light-to-dark ratio, the wedge should have moved a distance equal to $\log_{10}$ 2, or 0.301 log unit.

Filter densities are additive. This may be shown in terms of an example, with reference to Table 7-4. If a filter having a density of 2.0 is combined with one having a density of 1.0, the first will have a transmittance of 1 percent, the second of 10 percent. This means that 10 percent of the 1 percent of the original incident light will pass through both filters (0.10 percent). A transmittance of 0.10 percent corresponds to a density of 3.0. The addition of filters having densities of 1.0 and 2.0 produces an equivalent density of 3.0.

Filters are also available whose density is variable along one dimension. These *neutral wedges* are used for a continuous variation in luminance. Such filters may be rectangular (Fig. 7-14c), in which case the density varies along their length but is constant across their width, or they may be annular (Fig. 7-14d), in which case density is constant along a radius but varies circumferentially. Except when used at a focal point of a system, neutral wedges must be used in conjunction with *balancing wedges* whose gradient runs in the opposite direction, as shown in Fig. 7-14c. If the density gradient of each wedge is the same, the transmittance through a pair of wedges so arranged will be constant for any relative position. If, in Fig. 7-14c, the upper wedge were moved one unit to the right, the density of the overlapping region of the wedge pair would be 5.0.

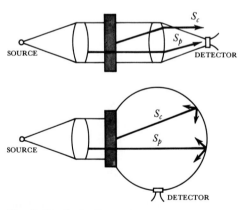

Fig. 7-13 Basic filter calibration technique. *Top:* Calibration for specular transmittance. A reading of the illuminance at the detector is taken first without the filter in the system. The filter is then interposed. Only those rays which pass through a filter without deviation can reach the detector, e.g., ray S_p. Scattered rays, such as S_c, will not be imaged upon the detector. *Bottom:* Calibration of diffuse transmittance. All the light passing through the filter will be integrated in the sphere regardless of its directionality.

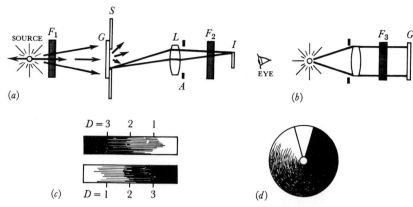

Fig. 7-14 Methods of luminance control. (*a*) **The illuminance upon milk glass *G* is controlled either by varying the intensity of the source or by moving it with respect to *G*. The luminance of the right-hand side of *G* depends upon transillumination, and is thus proportional to the illuminance of the left side. The area of the field seen by the subject is determined by screen *S*. Lens *L* images the field at *I*, where it is seen as an aerial image by the eye (the optical role of the eye is not shown). The luminance of the field at *I* may also be controlled by means of filters at F_1 or F_2; but because of the lack of collimation it would be preferable to use a filter in collimated light, if available, as in (*b*). Control of the luminance at *I* is also given by varying the size of aperture *A*. (*c*) Neutral density wedges, linear in density but running in opposite directions. If the two wedges are placed together, they will have a uniform density throughout their common area, one acting as the balancing wedge for the other. (*d*) Neutral wedge arranged in an annular form.**

A *neutral density filter* is one whose density is independent of the wavelength of incident light. Gelatin filters, e.g., Wratten #96, are inexpensive but not very neutral, showing a higher density at the extremes of the visible spectrum than in the middle. Filters made from exposed and properly developed photographic emulsion are better. Probably the most neutral commercially available filters are the so-called *inconels;* although spectrally flat, this is true only for densities up to 1.0, and their stated densities cannot be trusted.

When filters are not neutral, their *photopic density* is defined as

$$D = \log_{10}\left[\frac{\int \phi_{i\lambda} V_\lambda \, d\lambda}{\int \phi_{t\lambda} V_\lambda \, d\lambda}\right] \quad (7\text{-}17)$$

where $\phi_{i\lambda}$ refers to the amount of incident radiant flux as a function of wavelength, $\phi_{t\lambda}$ is the corresponding amount of trans-

mitted radiant flux, and V_λ is the photopic relative luminous efficiency function. This calculation provides, for the quantity within the brackets, the ratio of incident to transmitted luminous flux.

When absorptive filters are used, care must be taken not to use the filter where it is irradiated at levels sufficiently high to damage the filters. This is most likely to be a serious problem when high-density filters are located at or near a focal point of a system.

2. *Variable apertures.* It is possible to locate a diaphragm in an optical system in such a way that the luminance of the final image is directly proportional to the area of the opening in the diaphragm. A familiar example of this is the diaphragm opening of a photographic camera; another is the pupil of the eye. Caution must be exercised that *vignetting*, i.e., unequal reduction in lumi-

Table 7-4   Percent transmittance as a function of density in 0.10 density steps from 0.00 to 3.00.

Density	Percent trans.	Density	Percent trans.	Density	Percent trans.
0.00	100	1.00	10.00	2.00	1.000
0.10	79.43	1.10	7.943	2.10	0.7943
0.20	63.10	1.20	6.310	2.20	0.6310
0.30	50.12	1.30	5.012	2.30	0.5012
0.40	39.81	1.40	3.981	2.40	0.3981
0.50	31.62	1.50	3.162	2.50	0.3162
0.60	25.12	1.60	2.512	2.60	0.2512
0.70	19.95	1.70	1.995	2.70	0.1995
0.80	15.85	1.80	1.585	2.80	0.1585
0.90	12.59	1.90	1.259	2.90	0.1259
1.00	10.00	2.00	1.000	3.00	0.1000

nance across the field, does not occur. In Fig. 7-14a, the diaphragm A just to the right of lens L controls the luminance of the image of ground glass G formed at I, without changing its area.

3. *Inverse-square law.* The most fundamental way to change luminance is to take advantage of the inverse-square law. Because of the divergence of light from a point source, the illuminance provided by the source decreases as the square of the distance from the source. For extended sources the rule is only approximate. A way to use the inverse-square law is illustrated in Fig. 7-14a.

4. *Sector disks.* Except for special cases, the visual system reacts to rapidly fluctuating light as if it were steady. The brightness produced depends upon the average luminance provided across time (Talbot's law). Thus

$$\frac{1}{t}\int_{t_0}^{t} L_t\,dt = L_c \qquad (7\text{-}18)$$

where L_c is the luminance of a constant, steady field that matches the fluctuating field in brightness and t is the duration of the fluctuating stimulus that is turned on at time t_0. This must not exceed the critical duration of the eye, which is about 15 msec for one cycle of a flickering field and about 25 msec for a single flash, assuming a light-adapted eye and

foveal stimulation. An effective halving of luminance could be achieved by means of a rapidly rotating sector disk having a 50:50 light-to-dark ratio.

5. *Rotatable polarizers.* Transmittance may be varied by varying the angle between two polarizers. Commercially available polarizing materials are not very satisfactory for careful work, especially if high densities are desired, because they are not very neutral. They also transmit less than 50 percent of the incident light even in the position of maximum transmittance. Nicol prisms are far superior optically, do not absorb, are spectrally neutral, and approximate much closer the predicted law. They have the disadvantage of moderate to small aperture.

CONTROL OF WAVELENGTH

Although it is possible to obtain monochromatic light from line sources such as the Cd-Hg source, all such sources contain multiple lines and therefore auxiliary filters must be used to block out the unwanted radiations. The more common procedure is to obtain monochromatic light from white light. This can be done by taking advantage of the fact that the refraction, diffraction, and interference of light all depend upon wavelength. A calibrated device that splits complex radiations according to their spectral components is called a *spectrometer;* a device that contains a source of light and a spectrometer with a fixed exit slit, used to isolate a narrow spectral region, is called a *monochromator.*

Prism monochromator

In a prism monochromator, advantage is taken of the greater refraction of short wavelength radiations compared with long. The spectrum can be obtained with the use of a single triangular prism, but it is inconvenient to have the light of different wavelengths unfocused and traveling in different directions. This is why many more complicated methods have been developed. All involve the use of an entrance slit, lenses or mirrors, prisms, and an exit slit. The entrance slit is illuminated with focused white light and may be considered conceptually as a light source for the system. Light from the entrance slit is collimated, and the narrower the entrance slit, the more perfect will be the collimation. After dispersion by the prism, a second lens or mirror forms an image of the entrance slit. The image will be spread into a spectrum because of the dependence of refraction upon wavelength. By using a narrow exit slit, a given region of the spectrum can be picked out and the exit slit can be imaged as desired by a subsequent optical system. In Maxwellian-view systems such as that of Fig. 7-9, the exit slit or an image of it is treated as a source and is located at the appropriate position S.

There are a variety of monochromators. In some, wavelength is determined by moving a slit; in others, by rotating a prism. In either case, the movement must be done very carefully, and it is the precision of mounting and movement required in monochromators, as well as their optical components, that makes them expensive.

Let us consider, as an example of a monochromator, the one shown in Fig. 7-15, which contains a Broca (constant-deviation) prism, or constant-deviation spectrometer. Diverging light from source S is imaged by L_1 upon an entrance slit EN. Light is next collimated by lens L_2 and delivered to the prism. This constant-deviation prism has the property that, depending upon the angular position of the prism, only radiations of a single wavelength emerge from the prism at exactly a 90° angle with respect to the direction of incident collimation. Light therefore diverges slightly from the prism, with the angle of divergence depending upon wavelength. An imaging lens I_L focuses the light at a plane which contains an exit slit EX. The position of the image of the entrance slit along this plane depends upon wavelength, since the angle of incidence of a narrow, nearly collimated beam upon L_3, corresponding to a single wavelength, depends upon wavelength. It should be noted that all wavelengths are represented in the total di-

verging beam incident upon I_L, even though the entrance slit EN is very narrow. By moving the exit slit EX laterally, different wavelengths may be picked out of the spectrum. In practice, it is better to leave EX fixed and rotate the prism, since this ensures that light will emerge from the instrument along the same axis regardless of the wavelength selected.

The energy level of the emerging light, and its spectral composition, depends upon the relations between exit and entrance slits. Let us consider first the case of a very narrow entrance slit and an exit slit of finite width ΔW_2 which, because of this width, picks out more than just one wavelength in the imaged spectrum of white light at EX. It selects a section of the spectrum having a width of $\Delta\lambda_2$, expressed in terms of wavelength. In this case, the waveband transmitted will depend entirely on ΔW_2. This is illustrated in Fig. 7-16a, where the height of the energy distribution at any given wavelength transmitted by the

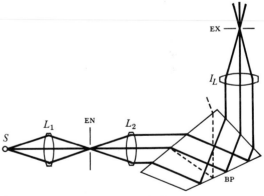

Fig. 7-15 The constant-deviation spectrometer. Diverging light from source S is imaged by L_1 upon entrance slit EN. Light is next collimated by lens L_2 and delivered to a Broca (constant-deviation) prism BP. Depending upon the angular position of the prism, only radiations of a single wavelength emerge from the prism at a 90° angle with respect to the direction of incident collimation. Light therefore diverges slightly from the Broca prism, with the angle of divergence depending upon wavelength. Imaging lens I_L focuses the light at exit slit EX, producing a spectrum in this plane.

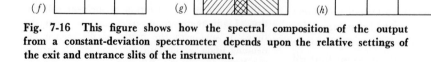

Fig. 7-16 This figure shows how the spectral composition of the output from a constant-deviation spectrometer depends upon the relative settings of the exit and entrance slits of the instrument.

exit slit depends upon ΔW_1 and must approach zero as ΔW_1 also approaches zero.

Consider next the converse case of a very narrow exit slit, which picks out only a point along the spectrum at EX. Assume, however, an entrance slit of finite width ΔW_1. The finite width of the entrance slit means that the light from L_2 to the prism will not be exactly collimated but will travel at various angles, depending upon wavelength. Thus each elemental point along EN will form a spectrum at EX, and the finite slit at EN will form a series of overlapping spectra, with each wavelength being represented not at only one point along EX but along a finite distance, depending upon the width of EN. This is illustrated in Fig. 7-16b, where the height of the energy distribution, which at any given wavelength depends upon W_2, must approach zero as W_2 approaches zero, and has a width dependent upon W_1.

The case of finite entrance and exit slits is somewhat more complicated. Consider a finite entrance slit that produces a spectrum at EX that runs from a to b, as shown in Fig. 7-16c', with the prism in a given position. Suppose that this prism position causes b to be just aligned with c, the left-hand edge of the exit slit. As the prism is rotated, transmittance through the instrument will begin at this point and will become maximal (assuming a constant-energy spectrum) when b becomes aligned with d, the right-hand edge of the exit slit. Maximum transmittance will be maintained until a is aligned with c and then will fall off until a is aligned with d, where transmittance will cease. It should be clear from this illustration that the waveband of maximum transmittance is the difference between the waveband transmitted by the entrance slit, $\Delta\lambda_1$, and that transmitted by the exit slit, $\Delta\lambda_2$. This is also shown in Fig. 7-16c. As $\Delta\lambda_2$ approaches zero, the situation of Fig. 7-16b is approached. The converse situation is shown in Fig. 7-16d and d', where the exit slit is larger. Figure 7-16e' shows a special case where the two slits are of the same width. This triangular distribution of energy shown

in Fig. 7-16e gives the maximum energy transmissible for a given bandwidth.

In doing wavelength calibrations with a gas discharge lamp having spectral lines, one encounters a situation that illustrates the foregoing principles. Consider two spectral lines α and β, imaged at EN upon a very narrow entrance slit. These will appear in the exit slit as shown in Fig. 7-16f. As the entrance slit is widened, the two lines spread out and overlap, as shown in Fig. 7-16g. Figure 7-16h shows how widening the exit slit would allow the transmission of a third spectral line γ for the case of the very narrow entrance slit. For wavelength calibration purposes, it is best to use entrance and exit slits of nearly the same width, with the exit slit just a bit wider, which allows a precise positioning of the spread-out known spectral line just within the exit slit. Then the wavelength transmitted for whatever rotary position of the prism produced this condition is known.

Grating monochromator

In a grating monochromator, a spectrum is formed by transmission through, or reflection from, a diffraction grating, which consists of a series of very closely spaced parallel straight lines. The pattern of interference produced is in the form of a series of overlapping spectra. Throughout most of the visible first-order spectrum, the secondary wavelengths are almost totally unable to stimulate the eye, being of relatively low intensity and also outside the limits of the spectral sensitivity curve of the eye. The exception to this is at the extremes of the visible spectrum. At the red end, the overlapping blue of the adjacent spectrum can easily be removed with a red filter.

In a prism or a grating monochromator, certain common principles apply. In either case, the bandwidth of the transmitted radiations depends upon an interaction between the widths of entrance and exit slits. Perfect spectral purity could be obtained only by having the width of both slits approach zero, which would mean that the percentage of light transmitted would do likewise. In the prism monochromator, the relation between bandwidth and slit width depends upon wavelength, being greater in the red than in the blue end of the spectrum. In the grating monochromator, this ratio is independent of wavelength. Both types of instrument cause partial polarization of the emergent light.

A certain amount of white light is inevitably transmitted by either kind of device, because of stray light in the optical system, caused, for example, by nonselective reflection of light from dusty surfaces. Although this amount may be low when expressed in radiometric units, manufacturers' specifications of stray light are often vague and/or inaccurate, and such phrases as "less than 1 percent" are not to be taken to mean "negligible for visual purposes." One must bear in mind that 1 percent stray light at 555 mμ, where the sensitivity of the eye is at a maximum, would be of equal visual effect when compared with the properly transmitted light at 690 mμ, where the sensitivity of the eye is only one hundredth as great. The amount of stray light can be qualitatively evaluated, with the sensitivity of the eye automatically taken into account, by the use of a *pocket spectroscope* to view the exit-slit image. This device produces a tiny spectrum, which is viewed through a suitable eyepiece. Undesirable stray light can often be eliminated with blocking filters. Otherwise, the only sure method is to use a double monochromator, in which the exit slit of a first spectrometer is imaged upon the entrance slit of a second. Such a device costs more than twice as much as the ordinary single monochromator, but is safest to use for precise research in vision.

Color filters

The classic techniques of dispersion and diffraction have been supplemented in recent years by the development of interference filters. An interference filter consists of at least two precisely separated layers, often with absorptive and dichroic reflecting filters added, that cause most of the light of wavelengths outside the spectral band of interest to be lost by interference—the cancellation of light by light that occurs when coherent radiations are of equal amplitude but opposite phase. These have been available only for discrete wavelengths, so that a battery of filters was required to cover the spectrum. Such a battery of filters, located in turn in the region between L_1 and L_2 in Fig. 7-11, could provide the control of the spectral distribution of the preadapting field desired in the dark-adaptation experiment. More recently, continuous interference filters, which may be called *interference wedges*, have been available. In these, the wavelength dependence of peak transmission depends upon the part of the wedge through which the light is transmitted. They may be used quite conveniently at the focal points of Maxwellian-view optical systems but are quite useless where wide beams are concerned. The discrete interference filters work best in collimated light and should be precisely located accordingly. They should also be used with blocking filters, since all have secondary transmittance in unwanted parts of the spectrum.

A wide variety of gelatin filters are available. These are a poor substitute for monochromatic light because of their relatively broad transmission curves. They may be used to great advantage as blocking filters in conjunction with monochromators of interference filters. A wide variety of filters are available which transmit nearly 100 percent of incident light at long wavelengths but then cut off rather sharply somewhere in the neighborhood from 570 to 650 mμ. These are excellent for blocking filters and can produce a range of highly saturated stimuli suitable for many experimental purposes. Unfortunately, the counterpart of such a "cutoff" filter does not exit for the blue end of the spectrum, where, in order to get a reasonably narrow bandwidth with a combination of gelatin filters, peak transmission may be reduced to 20 percent or less.

At any wavelength, the densities for that wavelength of two or more filters used together are additive. By using suitable combinations of commercially available filters, one can create new, and usually narrower, spectral transmission curves than are otherwise available.

CONTROL OF THE TIME VARIABLE

The proper control of time is important in almost all visual experiments. Variations of luminance in time can be caused by (1) varying the intensity of the source itself or (2) interposing a shutter between the source and subsequent parts of the system. There are many ways in which each of these may be accomplished. In this section, six methods of time control will be discussed, along with three main criteria for judging the performance of each system.

Direct pulsing of source

This method is unsuitable for tungsten sources, because of the length of time required for tungsten to reach its operating temperature and to cool.[1] It can often be used to advantage with single gas tubes, e.g., xenon or argon, and mixed gas tubes, particularly the glow modulator.

Rotary sector disk (Episcotister)

A sector is cut from the outside of a disk that is driven at a known and constant speed. This device will cause a flash of light to be delivered for each revolution of the disk unless an auxiliary shutter is added to block potential flashes as may be desired between actual presentations; the solenoid-operated shutter is excellent for this purpose. Constant speed may be obtained with the use of synchronous motors, although these must be avoided if there is any 60-cps ripple whatever in the light output. In general, other types of a-c or d-c motor are preferable. These can be controlled for

[1] An exception is an ultraminiature lamp called a Pinlight, which has rise and decay characteristics measured in small numbers of milliseconds. Because of its tiny size, it is a very low intensity source despite its high intrinsic luminance.

speed to within 0.1 percent accuracy by means of servo controls or can be calibrated occasionally with a stroboscope if somewhat lesser accuracy can be tolerated.

Solenoid-operated shutters

Use of the rotary solenoid is the most convenient method. A lightweight vane can be attached, which will rotate into or out of the light beam when activated. Rotary solenoids are available with spring return. They may be driven either by electronic timing devices, in which case a special power-amplifier stage will be needed, or by microswitches operated by motor-driven cams.

Photographic shutters

These are generally unsuitable for scientific use where precise time control is needed.

Electromagnetic field control

A variety of complicated devices exist in which the transmittance of liquids or crystals is caused to vary in response to an impressed electromagnetic field. The *Kerr cell* is the most familiar of these.

d-c galvanometer coils with magnetic field and vanes

In this system, conventional timing equipment is used to generate pulses which, through a d-c power amplifier, energize the coil of a d-c galvanometer of the type used in an electroencephalographic polygraph recorder. A lightweight vane is used instead of a recording pen, the movement of which opens and closes the light path. Any of the methods except the first could be used to provide time control in the experiment on dark adaptation. Any of these shutters would be located at plane A in Fig. 7-10.

There are a number of criteria against which the performance of a time-control system should be gauged. Some of these will now be described and related to the six methods just mentioned.

Rise time

In some visual experiments sensitivity changes occur with great speed, e.g., when the masking produced by a sudden conditioning stimulus is evaluated by superposing a test flash. The sensitivity of the eye also depends upon the rate of onset of the stimulus. Furthermore, it is difficult even to specify the duration of a stimulus whose rate of onset (rise time) is slow or whose waveform is variable. For all these reasons, it is often convenient to expose the visual stimulus very suddenly. For some experiments, as when the response of the eye to very brief flashes is being measured, this may mean a few microseconds; in most experiments, it means a few milliseconds. Fortunately, there are no transient responses associated with the harmonics of a square-wave input in vision, as there are in audition.

When a shutter is used, rise time will be determined by two variables: (1) the rate at which the shutter moves out of the way of the beam that it cuts and (2) the cross-sectional area of the beam. An advantage of the Maxwellian-view system is that a large stimulus field can be delivered by a system that contains images of the source, which can be very small. Better rise times will be obtained if the shutter vane is allowed to achieve its maximum velocity before starting to move into or out of the beam.

The electromagnetic field control, e.g., the Kerr cell, can provide rise times as short as 0.1 msec and pulses of light as short as 5 msec total duration. These times are faster than necessary for almost any visual experiment, and the elegance of the Kerr cell is perhaps more than offset by its several disadvantages: (1) it is very expensive; (2) it burns out quickly; (3) it requires a 10,000-volt power supply; (4) it provides no complete extinction (about 0.01 percent transmittance occurs in the "closed" condition); and (5) it causes some color change of the transmitted light if its spectral distribution is broad.

The directly pulsed gas tubes also provide rise times measured in microseconds and also are capable of providing very short flashes. This advantage is perhaps offset because (1)

they require special power supplies for their operation; (2) they are basically photometrically unstable; and (3) a continuous, white spectrum cannot be produced in this way.

The rotary sector disk, solenoid-operated vanes, and photographic shutters all produce rise and fall times from 1 to 5 msec, depending upon conditions.

Accuracy and reliability

The system involving the d-c galvanometer coils is very reliable and will accurately follow the waveform of the input. The rotary sector disk, solenoid-operated vanes, and Kerr cell are also reliable. Directly pulsed sources are less reliable and must be carefully monitored, especially for intensity. The photographic shutter is intolerably bad. Its reliability is no better than ±10 percent, and the time calibration given by the manufacturer may be in error by 100 percent.

Cost and general convenience

The Kerr cell is most expensive and is sufficiently inconvenient that it is almost never used for vision research except for very special applications. The d-c galvanometer coil system costs about $1,000 to set up and is probably the best overall system for very accurate flash stimulation, especially if high-frequency following is required, as in certain flicker experiments. The rise time in such a case is independent of flicker frequency. The rotating sector disk is excellent for many purposes, although it is big, bulky, and noisy and has the disadvantage, for flicker work, that the rise time is a function of frequency, if frequency is varied by changing disk speed, as it usually is. Solenoid-operated vanes are also noisy and cannot be driven to high frequencies, but for short flash work they represent in many respects the best compromise among the many requirements to be considered. They are inexpensive. Directly-pulsed sources and photographic shutters are both convenient and inexpensive, but suffer from serious limitations as discussed above.

Control of timing pulses

Any of the devices mentioned require some sort of impulse to trigger the closing and opening of a circuit that will deliver the voltage needed to rotate the solenoid, operate the vane, turn the source on and off, or whatever the case may be. This can be done electromechanically, by means of a synchronous motor which drives cams which in turn depress microswitches. A variety of such devices are commercially available, and they are not difficult to construct. They are inexpensive and are quite satisfactory for timing relatively long intervals (for example, 0.1 sec and up). Timing pulses can be delivered more accurately by modern solid state electronic timing equipment, the best of which operates with digital clocks whose accuracy can be measured in microseconds or less. Such a device, if it operates at all, will operate accurately. Resistance-capacitance delay circuits are less expensive but suffer from temperature dependence and the more general fact that an alteration in circuit characteristics may cause inaccurate timing without the experimenter's knowing it.

SPATIAL CONFIGURATION OF STIMULI

The simplest yet perhaps the most representative spatial control situation is that of causing a restricted area of a uniform field either to increase or to decrease in luminance for a short period of time. The increment is no problem: a small spot of light is momentarily added to the larger background by any of the superposition techniques earlier described. The decrement is much harder to obtain. There are basically two methods. In the first, a uniform field is replaced, for the desired time, by an annular (doughnut-shaped) field having an equivalent surround with the desired hole in it. If it is not desired to have the hole completely dark, it must be filled by an additional optical system of some sort. The main difficulty with this method is that unless the optical systems are better than those commonly achievable, some detectable flicker of

the surround field will occur and will be undesirable, especially if a detection threshold of the central spot is being measured. In the alternative method, one field provides an annulus, while two separate systems are used to fill the hole. By removing, with a shutter, the light provided by one of these systems, a negative increment of any preset size (to a limit provided by the luminance of the annular surround) may be achieved. This may be preset directly with a Kerr cell.

In systems involving diffuse light, as in the photometer cube of the Macbeth illuminometer, it is possible to cause the ring perceived around the central spot to disappear by suitable luminance adjustment of fields of identical spectral distribution. In systems involving more directional light, including the Maxwellian view, it is not possible to cause this ring to disappear entirely. It can be reduced below the visual threshold by superposing the entire configuration upon a full field of much higher luminance than that of the annulus.

For complex spatial patterns of an arbitrary nature, the slide projector is most conveniently used. Owing to diffraction, aberrations, flare, distortion, and scatter in the optical system of any projector, the contrasts between light and dark areas in the projected image will be reduced in comparison with those of the transparency being projected, and the image will be geometrically somewhat in error.

Television raster

A television (TV) picture is "painted" by an electron gun that causes successive lines of phosphor on the tube face to be irradiated (or alternate lines, in the commercially employed interlace method). The basic sweep speed is fixed, for a given system, as is the number of lines from the top to the bottom of the picture. Although these may be fixed forever at modest values for commercial television, they can be varied for special laboratory use. By modulating the intensity of the electron beam as it sweeps across the picture, more or less excitation of the activated phosphor results, and the familiar TV image is built up. Such images are then presented successively in time, with the spatial variations needed to produce, for example, the illusion of motion. At the present stage of the art, TV pictures are marginally acceptable for visual research of some kinds but not acceptable for experiments where very fine temporal and spatial resolution of the stimulus is requisite. The basic method, however, with more lines per picture, more frames per second, and sharper focus of phosphor excitation, potentially offers a greater degree of flexibility of presentation of visual stimulus (and of its modification, for example, by spatial noise) than that obtained by any of the other methods described in this chapter. This improved basic method has already been used in some experiments, and work is in progress that will undoubtedly lead to future improvements that could make it acceptable for almost any experimental purpose.

Contrast

The contrast between two areas is a fundamental visual variable and has been variously defined. The most acceptable definition for the case of a small spot against a large background is

$$C = \frac{\Delta L}{L} \qquad (7\text{-}19)$$

where C is contrast, ΔL is the luminance of the superposed increment, or decrement, and L is the luminance of the background field. Its acceptability rests mainly upon the nearly identical visual effect, at threshold, that has been shown for positive $(\Delta L + L > L)$ and negative $(\Delta L + L < L)$ contrasts having the same value by this definition (Blackwell, 1946).

Where it is not possible to state clearly which is the background and which is the test area, as in the case of a sinusoidal luminance

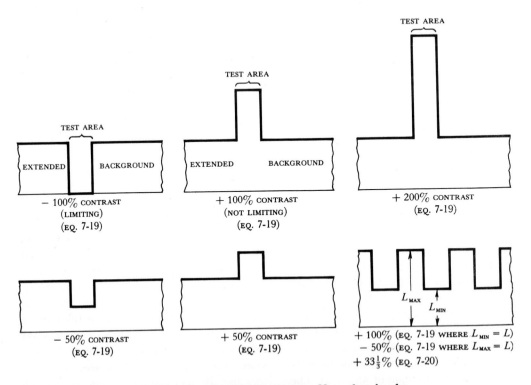

-100% CONTRAST (LIMITING) (EQ. 7-19)

$+100\%$ CONTRAST (NOT LIMITING) (EQ. 7-19)

$+200\%$ CONTRAST (EQ. 7-19)

-50% CONTRAST (EQ. 7-19)

$+50\%$ CONTRAST (EQ. 7-19)

$+100\%$ (EQ. 7-19 WHERE $L_{MIN} = L$)
-50% (EQ. 7-19 WHERE $L_{MAX} = L$)
$+33\frac{1}{3}\%$ (EQ. 7-20)

Fig. 7-17 Fields having test areas of various contrasts. Note that in the lower right-hand example, the specification of contrast by Eq. (7-19) is ambiguous, depending upon whether the light or dark area is taken to be the background. For such a case, the specification of Eq. (7-20) is preferable.

distribution or in alternating light and dark bars of equal width, the more acceptable definition of contrast is

$$C = \frac{L_{max} - L_{min}}{L_{max} + L_{min}} \qquad (7\text{-}20)$$

which is known as *Michelson contrast*.

By the first definition of contrast, the highest negative contrast achievable is 1.0, whereas positive contrasts may increase without limit. By the second definition, 100 percent modulation, where the periodic waveform goes from zero luminance at the minimum to any positive value at the maximum, yields a contrast value of 1.0, which is limiting. See Fig. 7-17 for illustrations of these concepts.

There are two fundamental ways to produce a given contrast between a test area and its background. One is optical superposition; e.g., if a field of 50 mL containing a central hole of 0 mL is superposed upon a uniform field of 50 mL, a negative contrast of 0.50 will be produced. The same result could be achieved by placing a 0.30 density filter of the desired size physically upon a uniform transilluminated field of 100 mL. The easiest way to keep contrast constant while changing luminance is to use reflected light from a surface in which the desired contrast configuration is produced by the variable reflectance of the various areas. This closely approximates the real-life situation, where contrasts never change with a change in the intensity of the illuminating sources unless the geometry of the situation is also altered.

MEASUREMENT OF BASIC VARIABLES[1]

Luminance

The reference standard of luminance is that produced by a blackbody at the melting

[1] The reader is again referred to the article by Withrow and Withrow (1956), which provides extensive detail on some of the material covered in this and the preceding section of this chapter.

point of platinum (2042°K), defined as 60 cd per sq cm. Secondary standards available for laboratory use are usually small sources calibrated for intensity in a particular direction. Calibrated intensity standards are available from the National Bureau of Standards.

Visual photometers allow the user to view a circumscribed part of a diffuse field that illuminates the center of the photometer field, while the annulus surrounding is illuminated by a light source within the instrument. In the Macbeth illuminometer, the internally supplied field is irradiated by an internal lamp whose distance from the reflecting plate can be varied by racking it inside a tube that also forms the handle of the instrument. A calibrated scale is fixed with respect to the lamp, moves with respect to a reference marker, and yields a reading directly in foot-candles or foot-lamberts. The instrument comes with a standard source against which the internal source of the instrument can be calibrated from time to time. Also included is a reflecting test plate of known reflectance, which can be used to measure illuminance. Smaller handheld visual photometers are available but are not generally so well calibrated as the Macbeth illuminometer.

Visual photometers often involve a somewhat heterochromatic brightness match and will therefore yield slightly different results in the hands of different observers. Although much progress has been made in the development of photoelectric photometers, none is yet capable of yielding values for white light as accurately and as easily as can be achieved with the visual instruments. The principle of a photoelectric photometer is simple: a photocell or photomultiplier is irradiated through a filter that renders the spectral sensitivity of the photodetector as nearly as possible the same as that of the standard observer. The output of the photodetector is linearly amplified and causes a meter deflection that can be, in principle, directly calibrated in photometric units. The limitations of such instruments are concerned with the degree of approximation, through filter-photodetector sensitivity combinations, of the luminosity curve of the stand-

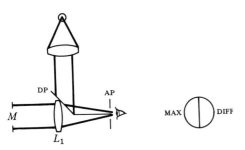

Fig. 7-18 A method of luminance calibration of Maxwellian-view system involving visual match. The eye sees the diffuse plate *DP* through artificial pupil *AP*. The Maxwellian field is seen at *M*. The intensity of illumination upon *DP* is altered until the usual match is achieved; an illuminometer is then used to measure the luminance of *DP*. A statement can then be made that the Maxwellian field matches a diffuse field seen through a certain size of artificial pupil.

ard observer and with the extent to which response linearity can actually be achieved. Despite their limitations, they are very useful for making density calibrations of wedges and filters in the system.

Where monochromatic light is to be used, energy calibrations are most easily carried out by using a calibrated photocell or photomultiplier tube. Such calibrations can be obtained commercially, a procedure recommended for those who are not already equipped to do radiometric measurements. For direct radiometry, of the nonselective radiation detectors available, the thermocouple is the most sensitive and convenient.

Recently, an excellently calibrated standard luminance source has become available. The device provides a 3-in.-diameter diffuse white field of accurately known color temperature and luminance and can be operated for 50 hr before recalibration is needed. This appears to be an excellent basic luminance standard for general laboratory use.

Luminance calibration of the Maxwellian view presents special problems. Because of the small entrance pupil of the Maxwellian view, visual photometers having a large entrance pupil, designed for use with large diffuse surfaces, cannot be used without modification. The SEI portable exposure photometer has a small entrance pupil and can be used directly. Its calibration is not trustworthy. Perhaps the easiest way to do the calibration is to make a visual match between the Maxwellian field and an ordinary diffuse field, using a system like that shown in Fig. 7-18. Another technique is to decrease the field of view of the Macbeth illuminometer by using an auxiliary lens in front of the instrument. Although this procedure negates the absolute calibration of the device, it may be used conveniently for making relative measurements, although a photoelectric photometer is better.

In Maxwellian-view systems, the ideal procedure is to collimate the diverging light behind the eye and allow it to irradiate the full aperture in front of a photodetector (see Fig. 7-19). The resulting measure will be proportional to the illuminance of the phototube given by that part of the field being sampled. The actual size of the sampled area makes no difference, so long as the phototube has a uniform sensitivity and the area being sampled is uniform and larger than the aperture. If the phototube is placed at the source image, the resulting reading will reflect the

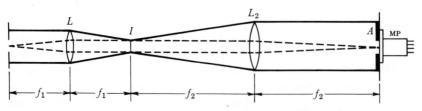

Fig. 7-19 Method of calibration of a Maxwellian-view system using a photoelectric detector.

total flux of the system, which is proportional to the product of area and luminance of the field as seen by the subject.

The effective luminance provided by a Maxwellian-view system can be calculated for any linear photometer reading of any wavelength of monochromatic radiation, if a standard source of known radiometric intensity as a function of wavelength is available. The principle is as follows (method of W. S. Stiles):

Let R_λ = reading of photoelectric photometer at wavelength λ of incident monochromatic light

S_λ = relative spectral sensitivity of photocell or photomultiplier tube

$E_{e\lambda}$ = unknown irradiance of wavelength λ incident upon photocell, ergs per sec per sq cm

$E'_{e\lambda}$ = known irradiance of photocell provided by calibrating lamp at each wavelength, ergs per sec per sq cm

R' = reading of photocell when irradiated by calibrating lamp

Then

$$R' = K\int E'_{e\lambda}S_\lambda \, d\lambda \qquad (7\text{-}21)$$

and

$$R_\lambda = KS_\lambda E_{e\lambda}. \qquad (7\text{-}22)$$

We may then write

$$\frac{R_\lambda}{R'} = \frac{KS_\lambda E_{e\lambda}}{K_\lambda E'_{e\lambda}S_\lambda \, d\lambda}. \qquad (7\text{-}23)$$

Solving for $E_{e\lambda}$,

$$E_{e\lambda} = \frac{R_\lambda}{S_\lambda} \cdot C \qquad (7\text{-}24)$$

where

$$C = \frac{\int E'_{e\lambda}S_\lambda \, d\lambda}{R'}, \qquad (7\text{-}25)$$

which is known.

It is convenient to write Eq. (7-24) in logarithmic form:

$$\log E_{e\lambda} = \log R_\lambda - \log S_\lambda + \log C \qquad (7\text{-}26)$$

When the irradiance $E_{e\lambda}$ is known at the photocell, it is possible to compute the irradiance of the retina of a standard eye, which will be equal to $E_{e\lambda}(f_2/f_e)^2$, where f_2 is shown in Fig. 7-9 and f_e is the focal length of the eye, about 1.7 cm. The luminance of a field outside the eye that would be required to produce the same retinal illuminance E_r may then be calculated by integrating the result with V_λ $[E_r = E_{e\lambda}V_\lambda(f_2/f_e)^2]$ and then, by using Eq. (7-12), solving for L.

Wavelength

The easiest and best method of wavelength calibration is the use of a gas discharge lamp having known spectral lines. Light from the lamp is allowed to illuminate the entrance slit of the spectrometer or the slit adjacent to an interference wedge, with the exit slit adjusted so that a given spectralline just fills it. The scale reading corresponding to the position of prism or slit that produced this setting is then noted. Identification of the spectral lines of a mercury-cadmium lamp is quite easy, on the basis of apparent color and the manufacturer's specification of the spectral locations of the strong lines (see Table 7-3). A calibration curve is finally drawn up relating wavelength to scale reading. This will be a smooth curve if no errors have been made.

A common problem that arises is the specification of the dominant wavelength of filtered light, which cannot properly be said to be monochromatic. Probably the best method is to specify the dominant wavelength of the light in a colorimetric sense. The spectral energy distribution of the source (E_λ) and the spectral transmittance of the filter (τ_λ) must be known. These are integrated with the standard $\bar{x}$, $\bar{y}$, and $\bar{z}$ functions for the standard observer, which are available from many sources. Tristimulus values are then calculated:

$$X = \int E_\lambda \tau_\lambda \bar{x}_\lambda \, d\lambda \qquad Y = \int E_\lambda \tau_\lambda \bar{y}_\lambda \, d\lambda$$
$$Z = \int E_\lambda \tau_\lambda \bar{z}_\lambda \, d\lambda \qquad (7\text{-}27)$$

from which the chromaticity coordinates may be calculated:

$$x = \frac{X}{X + Y + Z} \qquad y = \frac{Y}{X + Y + Z} \qquad (7\text{-}28)$$

A straight line is then drawn from a reference white point on the CIE chromaticity diagram or any transformation of it. The point where this line intersects the spectral locus determines the dominant wavelength (see Fig. 7-6).

Time

Shutter characteristics are best measured by delivering the light output of the system in which the shutter is located to a phototube. The output of the phototube should be delivered, via a cathode-follower circuit, to the vertical deflection plates of a CRO. A photoemissive device, e.g., #929 phototube, never imposes any time limitation; the use of the cathode-follower circuit prevents the amplifier from introducing such an error.

Measuring the shutter in position in this way ensures that the geometry of the light passing through the shutter is exactly as in the actual experiment. Usually two sweep speeds should be used: one fast enough to see the detailed characteristics of the onset and extinction of the stimulus and the other slow enough to measure the flash duration.

A convenient way to specify the duration of a very short flash of complex waveform is in terms of the luminance of a rectangular flash, one of infinitely fast rise and fall times, which contains the same amount of flux (luminance $\times$ time).

GENERAL APPARATUS CONSIDERATIONS

Mounting of optical components

A good general rule is that all optical elements should be rigidly attached to some sort of solid mount, preferably steel or hard aluminum. This includes the dental-impression mount in the case of Maxwellian-view systems. A variety of optical benches are available, consisting of a rail of some sort along which holders can slide in one dimension and to which various optical elements can be mounted. A sampling of equipment, much of which is commercially available, is shown in Fig. 7-20. Such commercially available equip-

ment is expensive. A less expensive substitute, adequate for many purposes, is the steel H beam, ordinarily used for construction purposes, to which homemade supports for lenses, prisms, and other elements can be attached with bolts or clamps.

The alignment of optical systems always involves fine adjustments of components. Provision must be made so that small movements of lenses back and forth along the optical axis and small transverse and rotary adjustments are possible. In the mounting of prisms and beam splitters, it is highly recommended that the elements be placed upon a tiltable platform. This platform is rigidly connected to the optical bench or H beam in such a way that it can be moved forward, backward, laterally, up, down, or tilted. It is impossible to design an optical system in advance so that it will be exactly lined up immediately upon assembly.

Neutral and interference wedges must be mounted so that they are adjustable in position, and the position can be conveniently read by the experimenter. The control of annular wedges can be achieved with selsyns or servomotors, direct chain drive, or stepping switches, and remote readout is possible. The safest and simplest method, where practicable, is to attach a scale directly to the circumference of the wedge. The digital readout of multiturn potentiometer dials is very convenient. Linear wedges must be mounted in some kind of slide. Probably the best is the screw-driven slide. If this can be remotely driven by a rigid rod, or if antibacklash gearing is used, digital-readout dials can be used at a remote position to yield a measure proportional to the position of the wedge.

A completed optical system must be baffled to prevent stray light from leaking from one channel to another. Such baffling is relatively easy in Maxwellian-view systems. In particular, a large screen placed at A (see Fig. 7-9), with an aperture in it only large enough to pass the filament image, will exclude all other stray light except that which passes through A at inappropriate angles by reflec-

Fig. 7-20 A collection of components for use in a Maxwellian-view stimulating system. (*a*) Adjustable mirror mount without mirror. (*b*) General-purpose "saddle," or holder. (*c*) Triangular optical bench. (*d*) A simple type of lens holder. (*e*) Rotary solenoid with vane attached. (*f*) Annular neutral density wedge. (*g*) Bead chain used for remote control of wedge position. (*h*) Interference wedge in frame. (*i*) Screw-drive assembly to vary position of interference wedge. (*j*) Beam splitter in adjustable mount. (*k*) Another type of lens holder. (*l*) Slide assembly for use as biting-board holder. (*m*) Biting board, or dental impression. (*n*) Diffuse test plate of the Macbeth illuminometer.

tion or scatter from other systems. Such light will not enter L_3 and is most unlikely to reach the eye. Baffles on either side of the channel, parallel to the optical axis, are very often useful. Such baffles may be made of cardboard, black cloth, black plastic, or any other convenient material. The baffling of a system is usually the last step in its construction and, although important, is not particularly difficult or time-consuming

Partitioning of experimental areas

It is often convenient to divide an apparatus into three sections: (1) a subject's booth, (2) an enclosure containing the main part of the optical system, and (3) the experimenter's station. In a properly designed apparatus, the last-named can be an open, well-lighted, pleasant room. Attention to a few fundamentals of human engineering principles should make it unnecessary for the experimenter to hunch over his notebook in shrouded light or to run around the apparatus with a flashlight, peering in here and there to take readings. This will be the inevitable outcome if commercially made components are put together without regard for the convenience of the experimenter. The designer should be aware of control engineering, whereby almost any desired remote control or remote readout is possible. The war-surplus market includes many devices and components that are useful for constructing optical systems.

Positioning of the subject

The positioning of the subject is most critical in a Maxwellian-view system. Some of the recommendations made here may be relaxed in the less demanding free-viewing situation. The problem is to position the eye of a subject so that the image of a source filament, or spectrometer exit slit, is properly centered within the pupil of the subject's eye.

An experienced subject can align himself reasonably well in the vertical and horizontal dimensions by noting the following cues: (1) position of the entoptically visible glare spot caused by corneal scatter; (2) moving his eyes to the left, right, up and down, and adjusting so that the field appears to disappear with the same amount of movement in all directions; (3) noting nonuniformities of the fields, reduced brightness, and increased abberrations associated with entry of the incoming light through the outer zones of the pupil. If the convergence of light at the eye is great, as with short-focal-length final lenses and large fields of view, the in-and-out position can be achieved subjectively. When the convergence is small, this position, although then not very critical, should be checked by the experimenter. When the source image is properly located, all light enters the eye and it is difficult for the experimenter to see anything. This can be solved by asking the subject to move his eyes and noting the character of the image upon the iris or sclera.

For very high precision, or when peripheral stimulation is used, excellent alignment may be achieved by remote telescopic examination of the eye using a system in which a reticle is located at a conjugate focus with the source image. The eye may be positioned with very high accuracy with respect to the reticle by introducing the eye into the system and illuminating it from the front. If the telescope has a high numerical aperture (low f-number) and therefore small depth of field, the in-and-out adjustment can also be made with very high precision.

The biting board can be conveniently manufactured from aluminum or stainless steel, to which a layer of dental-impression wax is attached by heating it in water to the softening point and molding it upon the steel or aluminum plate into the desired shape. The subject then sinks his teeth into the wax, which is allowed to harden. Fixation points may be delivered either through a separate Maxwellian-view channel or by reflection from a thin glass plate between the final lens of the system and the eye. It is very helpful to employ a three-dimensional slide mount upon which the biting board is supported, which may also carry a forehead rest and auxiliary lens holder. A forehead rest is necessary to maintain eye position with maximum accuracy. The auxiliary lens holder, just in front of the eye, can carry the subject's normal spectacle correction; alternatively, the final lens of the system can be moved in or out.

The subject should be comfortably seated under circumstances that allow sufficient room for knees and feet, under conditions of ventilation that do not permit a breeze to blow across the eye, and preferably in an adjustable seat. A pneumatic mount, as used in barbers' and dentists' chairs, is good for this purpose. A power-driven automobile bucket seat is ideal and less expensive than a barber's chair. The subject's ability to withstand the constraint of Maxwellian viewing can be increased if occasional shifts in seating position are possible, including height adjustments by the subject.

SPECIAL SYSTEMS

Eye-movement recording

Optical methods involve the reflection of light from the cornea, from a contact lens to which a mirror is attached, as well as direct photography of the eye (Higgins and Stultz, 1953; Riggs, Armington, and Ratliff, 1954). A useful photoelectric method is to record the light reflected from a spot imaged upon the junction between the dark iris and light sclera, whose quantity will vary as the eye moves Stark (1959). The electroculographic method is also useful. An excellent survey of the literature on eye movements is provided by Alpern (1962).

Haploscopic presentation

A *haploscope* is a device that can stimulate the two eyes independently through separate optical systems. It can be used in measuring and controlling the convergence of the eyes or in making brightness matches between the two eyes in different states of adaptation.

Reflection densitometry

The changes in concentration of bleached and unbleached photopigments are measured by comparing the amount of light entering the eye with that which is reflected out after double traversal through the retina and other eye media (Rushton, 1962; Weale, 1960).

Accommodation, convergence, pupillary diameter

Ingenious methods have been devised by means of which continuous measures of these characteristics of the motor aspects of vision can be made (Alpern, 1962; Lowenstein and Loewenfeld, 1962).

Measurement of the quality of the retinal image

A line source external to the eye is imaged upon the fundus in the back of the eye. Reflected light, returning through the pupil, forms an aerial image of the line, which is then scanned by a multiplier phototube arrangement or evaluated by a photographic technique (Krauskopf, 1962; Westheimer and Campbell, 1962).

Clinical techniques

There are many commercially available devices for assessing the refractive state of the eye and its general health. The ophthalmoscope, which allows the examiner to view the fundus of the eye directly, is perhaps the most important. A variety of *refractometers* are used also. The slit lamp illuminates a cross section of the eye media, which may then be examined by using a microscope, by means of the light scattered toward the microscope by the eye media (biomicroscopy). Many other devices are available (see the Bausch and Lomb catalog).

REFERENCES

ABNEY, W. DE W. *Researches in colour vision and trichromatic theory.* London: Longmans, 1913.

ALPERN, M. Accommodation. In H. Davson (Ed.), *The eye.* Vol. 4. New York: Academic, 1962a. Pp. 191–229.

ALPERN, M. Movements of the eyes. In H. Davson (Ed.), *The eye.* Vol. 4. New York: Academic, 1962b. Pp. 3–187.

American Institute of Physics handbook. New York: McGraw-Hill, 1957.

BAKER, H. D. Initial stages of dark and light adaptation. *J. opt. Soc. Amer.,* 1963, **53**, 98–103.

BARTLEY, S. H. The psychophysiology of vision. In S. S. Stevens (Ed.), *Handbook of experimental psychology.* New York: Wiley, 1951.

BENNETT, A. G., and FRANCIS, J. L. Visual optics. In H. Davson (Ed.), *The eye.* Vol. 4. New York: Academic, 1962. Pp. 3–210.

BLACKWELL, H. R. Contrast thresholds of the human eye. *J. opt. Soc. Amer.,* 1946, **36**, 624–643.

BOYNTON, R. M. Quantum and energy-based visual sensitivity on a single plot. *J. opt. Soc. Amer.,* 1963, **53**, 641–642.

BRINDLEY, G. S. *Physiology of the retina and the visual pathway.* London: E. Arnold; Baltimore: Williams & Wilkins, 1960.

CONDON, E. U., and ODISHAW, H. (Eds.) *Handbook of physics.* New York: McGraw-Hill, 1958.

CRAWFORD, B. H. The human scotopic visibility function. *Proc. Roy. Soc.,* B, 1949, **62**, 321.

DAVSON, H. (Ed.) *The eye.* Vol. 2. New York: Academic, 1962.

DITCHBURN, R. W., and GINSBORO, B. L. Vision with a stabilized retinal image. *Nature,* 1952, **170**, 36–37.

FRY, G. A. The image-forming mechanisms of the

eye. In J. Field, H. W. Magoun, and V. E. Hall (Eds.) *Handbook of physiology.* Vol. I. *Neurophysiology.* Washington: American Physiol. Soc., 1959. Pp. 647–670.

HIGGINS, G. C., and STULTZ, K. Frequency and amplitude of ocular tremor. *J. opt. Soc. Amer.,* 1953, **43,** 1136–1140.

International lighting vocabulary of the International Commission on Illumination. Publication CIE-1.1, Bureau Central de Commission Internationale de l'Eclairage, 57 rue Cuvier, Paris 5ᵉ, France, 1957.

JUDD, D. B. A Maxwell triangle yielding uniform chromaticity scales. *J. opt. Soc. Amer.,* 1935, **25,** 24–35.

JUDD, D. B. Basic correlates of the visual stimulus. In S. S. Stevens (Ed.), *Handbook of experimental psychology.* New York: Wiley, 1951.

KOCH, S. (Ed.) *Psychology: A study of a science.* Vol. I. *Sensory, perceptual, and physiological formulations.* New York: McGraw-Hill, 1958.

KOCH, S. (Ed.) *Psychology: A study of a science.* Vol. IV. *Biologically oriented fields: Their place in psychology and in biological sciences.* New York: McGraw-Hill, 1962.

KRAUSKOPF, J. Light distribution in human retinal images. *J. opt. Soc. Amer.,* 1962, **52,** 1046–1050.

LEGRAND, Y. *Optique physiologique.* Tome Premier: La dioptrique de l'œil et sa correction. Editions de la "Revue d'Optique" 165, rue de Sèvres— 3 et 5, Boulevard Pasteur, Paris 15ᵉ, France, 1952.

LEGRAND, Y. *Light, colour, and vision.* Alva, Scotland: Robert Cunningham & Sons, Ltd., 1957.

LOWENSTEIN, O., and LOEWENFELD, I. E. "The pupil." In H. Davson (Ed.), *The eye.* Vol. 4. New York: Academic, 1962. Pp. 231–267.

OGLE, K. N. *Optics: An introduction for ophthalmologists.* Springfield, Ill.: Charles C Thomas, 1961.

PIRENNE, M. H. *Vision and the eye.* London: Chapman & Hall, 1948.

RATLIFF, F. Some interrelations among physics, physiology, and psychology in the study of vision. In S. Koch (Ed.), *Psychology: A study of a science.* Vol. IV. New York: McGraw-Hill, 1962. Pp. 417–482.

RIGGS, L. A., ARMINGTON, J. C., and RATLIFF, F. Motions of the retinal image during fixation. *J. opt. Soc. Amer.,* 1954, **44,** 315–321.

RIGGS, L. A., RATLIFF, F., CORNSWEET, J. C., and CORNSWEET, T. N. The disappearance of steadily fixated visual test objects. *J. opt. Soc. Amer.,* 1953, **49,** 741–745.

RUSHTON, W. A. H. Visual pigments in man. *Sci. Amer.,* 1962, **207,** 120–132.

RUSHTON, W. A. H. Increment threshold and dark adaptation. *J. opt. Soc. Amer.,* 1963, **53,** 104–109.

Science of color. Comm. on Colorimetry, Opt. Soc. of America. New York: Crowell, 1953.

SEARS, F. W. *Optics.* Reading, Mass.: Addison-Wesley, 1949.

STARK, L. Stability, oscillations, and noise in human pupil servomechanism. *Proceedings of the IRE,* 1959, 1925–1939.

STILES, W. S. Color vision: The approach through increment threshold sensitivity. *Proc. Natl. Acad. Sci. U.S.,* 1959, **45,** 100–114.

STILES, W. S., and BURCH, J. M. NPL Colour-matching investigation: Final report. *Optica Acta,* 1958, **6,** 1–26.

STILES, W. S., and CRAWFORD, B. H. The luminous efficiency of rays entering the eye pupil at different points. *Proc. Roy. Soc.,* 1933, 112B, 428–450.

STRONG, J. *Concepts of classical optics.* San Francisco: Freeman, 1958.

WALD, G. Human vision and the spectrum. *Science,* 1945, **101,** 653–658.

WALSH, J. W. T. *Photometry.* London: Constable, 1953.

WEALE, R. A. *The eye and its function.* London: Hatton Press, 1960.

WESTHEIMER, G., and CAMPBELL, F. W. Light distribution in the image formed by the human eye. *J. opt. Soc. Amer.,* 1962, **52,** 1040–1045.

WITHROW, R. B., and WITHROW, C. A. Generation, control, and measurement of visible and near-visible radiant energy. In A. Hollaender (Ed.), *Radiation biology.* Vol. III, Chap. 3. New York: McGraw-Hill, 1956.

WRIGHT, W. D. *Researches on normal and defective colour vision.* London: Henry Kimpton, 1946.

WRIGHT, W. D. *Photometry and the eye.* London: Hatton Press, 1949.

WRIGHT, W. D. *The measurement of color.* New York: MacMillan, 1958.

ZOETHOUT, W. D. *Physiological optics.* (4th ed.) Chicago: Professional Press, 1947.

Chapter 8

PERCEPTION AND RECOGNITION

HAROLD W. HAKE *and* ALBERT S. RODWAN

The number of topics and theories included in the area of perception is tremendous, yet each appears to emphasize a specific laboratory situation and methodology. The purpose of this chapter is to consider perceptual methodology as it is applied to the study of recognition behavior. Perceptual recognition cuts across research topics and across theories, and an adequate coverage of this topic excludes a minimum of crucial methodology in the perceptual area.

Since many methods arise in specific theoretical settings and appear compelling only there, perhaps the single most important step in the study of perceptual methodology is a study of the theories that motivate work in this area and determine the choice of topic and method. The scholarly researcher will find that familiarity with all theories tends to discourage undue enthusiasm for one. At least it seems clear that the two traditional pieces of equipment, a weak tachistoscope and a strong theoretical bias, no longer suffice for adequate perceptual research.

Adequate description of the important theoretical positions may be found in a number of sources. The Koch volumes (1959) describe gestalt theory (pp. 427–455), Brunswik's probabilistic functionalism (pp. 502–564), Hebb's recent position (pp. 622–643), Helson's adaptation-level theory (pp. 565–621), and Gibson's perceptual psy-chophysics (pp. 456–501). The perceptual applications of the sensory-tonic position of Werner and Wapner are described in Beardslee and Wertheimer (1958). Graham (1958) poses questions about perception in the same terms as those posed and answered by psychophysical methodology in the area of sensation. Transactional functionalism is covered by Ames (1953). Wohlwill (1958) provides a review of research on perceptual development, and Bevan (1958) presents an excellent overview of major systems of perceptual thought. Allport's text (1955) is also available.

These positions involve a variety of objectives in the study of perceptual behavior, but all involve a crucial interest in the topic recognition, broadly defined. This topic comprises a wide variety of situations, including the conditions under which the subject (1) recognizes a stimulus seen previously; (2) recognizes that a stimulus is in a standard position, e.g., vertical; (3) recognizes the similarity between two stimuli; or (4) recognizes that a seen pattern of movement represents the rotation of a rigid body. In short, we deal here with just about all situations in which a subject is asked to judge a presented stimulus situation. Much of the language of perception is the language of psychophysics, and much of perceptual methodology is psychophysical. The following section, therefore, will critically evaluate the topic of psychophysics as it has been applied to perceptual problems.

THE ROLE OF PSYCHOPHYSICS IN THE STUDY OF RECOGNITION

Much of the content of perceptual research reflects preoccupation with the measurement of thresholds, an emphasis that represents a natural outgrowth of work on the sensory systems. These sensory absolute thresholds were concerned with the "detection of anything." That is, some kind of stimulus was presented to the subject and he was required to report its presence or absence.

Perceptual thresholds

Many investigators interested in the study of perception have been concerned about perceptual thresholds, as opposed to sensory thresholds. The former term was applied to the ability of the subject to identify what he saw and the latter term applied to his ability to detect its presence. To many, the identification threshold seemed to be measurable in the same way as the detection threshold. The recognition task merely required more light, i.e., enough to illuminate all the details of the visual target. Presence of detail was assumed to be the parameter that set the position of the threshold: the higher the degree of resolution required, the higher the threshold. Given this point of view, all the methods developed and employed in the case of sensory "detection of anything" thresholds appear directly applicable. *Research has shown that this simple approach is not justified.* For example, even in the case of simple acuity targets, the correlation between detection thresholds and recognition thresholds measured in the same subject is surprisingly small (e.g., 0.179 for the subjects of Ives and Shilling, 1941). There is ample other evidence to indicate that recognition thresholds are only partly dependent upon variables determining the detectability of a visual stimulus (Craik and Vernon, 1942; Miles, 1953; and Semeonoff, 1950). In spite of this evidence much perceptual research still

involves the unquestioning use of the methodology of sensory psychophysics for the study of complex and involved perceptual situations. Many examples are provided by the large numbers of studies involving the recognition of complex stimulus patterns presented briefly in the tachistoscope. The crucial variable is the measurement of the recognition threshold, usually a duration determined by simple psychophysical methodology. This apparent emulation of the hard approach of the sensory psychologist is a modern phenomenon. Actually, early psychophysics was developed in an attempt to deal directly with a perceptual problem, namely, the description of experience, rather than the measurement of sensory efficiency. Concern with techniques enabling the subject to indicate the nature of his experience has endured.

The good student of perception must have solid knowledge of psychophysical procedures. The greater complexity of his research often brings to a sharp focus aspects of traditional psychophysics that are only vaguely troubling when applied to simple sensory problems. The following sections make these troubles explicit in the case of some familiar perceptual studies.

Psychophysical methods

No single description of adequate psychophysical methods exists. This lack results from the rather radical revisions that are being strongly indicated. Excellent traditional presentations of the methods can be found in Guilford (1954), Woodworth and Schlosberg (1954), Torgerson (1958), and Postman and Egan (1949). At least some familiarity with these traditional presentations is assumed here.

The three most useful methods in the study of perceptual problems are the *method of limits,* the *method of adjustment,* and the *method of constant stimuli.*

The method of limits requires that the stimulus aspect controlled by the experimenter be ordered on a continuum, e.g., illumination, duration, or length. In its simplest form the method has been used to estimate absolute thresholds for a simple stimulus. In an ascending series, a stimulus value clearly below threshold is presented first. Then a series of stimuli of increasing strength is presented until the subject changes his report from "no" to "yes" or meets some other criterion of response change. In a descending series, stimuli begin above threshold and decrease in steps. This procedure results in two threshold measurements, one for the ascending series and one for the descending series. The response of the subject is limited to two alternatives, "yes" and "no."

In the perceptual area this method has been used in a much more open form because of the greater complexity of the stimuli and the questions being asked about the sensitivity of subjects. One important early use of the method was concerned with the tachistoscope, a laboratory instrument with its own troubles. Several attempts (for a brief review, see Hake, 1957) were made to learn about the course of perceptual development at very brief durations of illumination. Subjects were asked to describe what they saw at brief and, later, at longer durations of illumination. It was assumed that as the stimulus became more and more adequate (duration of view longer and longer) the perception of subjects went through an orderly development involving, for example, a sensory stage, then an exploratory stage, followed by an interpretive stage. This method represents an extreme case of the method of limits—one in which there is no restriction upon the variety of responses available to the subject, who at each duration of exposure can use whatever response he chooses. This variety of responses was considered necessary because of the richness and variety of experience possible in this situation. This has proved to be a methodological trap. The free choice permitted the subject precludes any possibility of our learning about the crucial relation between his response and experience. Unless the experimenter knows something about the subject's use of responses generally, he can not make inferences about the subject's

experience in specific situations on the basis of these responses. Where the subject is permitted wide latitude of choice, the requirement that the experimenter know something about the subject's use of responses generally is an impossible one. This crucial point has been discussed previously (Garner, Hake, and Eriksen, 1956) in terms of a distinction between those phenomena which we want to call perceptual and those which we should call purely response effects. This distinction is easily seen in the case of studies in which the subject was required to draw what he saw when complex stimuli were presented briefly. It was easy to demonstrate that many effects of the brief duration of exposure that were called perceptual were purely artifacts of the drawing method. Subjects "see-to-draw," i.e., try to perceive those aspects of the stimuli which are most easily drawn (Hake, 1957, pp. 42–46). The principle applies equally where the subject describes his experience verbally. The subject's verbal output cannot be interpreted unless we can show that the conditional probability of each response, i.e., the relative frequency of the response given a particular stimulus, departs from the probability of that response's occurring generally in the absence of stimuli or in the presence of all. This requirement dictates sharp restriction of responses in perceptual studies and requires extensive study of the responses used. Students often believe that the choice between a large set of responses, permitting adequate description of the richness of the subject's experience, and a small set, permitting the specification of response probabilities, is a personal choice. The logic of the situation, where the results of an experiment are to be meaningful, denies this belief.

The method of limits has also been used in a more restricted form with the tachistoscope. A stimulus pattern is chosen from a small set and presented first at a brief duration and then at steadily increasing durations. The task of the subject, after each flash, is to choose a response alternative from a small set of alternatives. Again, this is a case where only the ascending series of the method of limits is used. The objective in this case, however, is that of estimating a *recognition threshold*, i.e., the duration at which each stimulus pattern is adequately recognized. This sort of research has been important where a hypothesis about these thresholds is under test, e.g., the gestalt hypothesis that "good" figures should be recognized more easily than others. This methodological application has had great intuitive appeal because it appears to conform to the paradigm of sensory studies in which the method of limits is used to estimate a sensory absolute threshold. Goldiamond (1958) has effectively described the important artifacts created in this situation. Thresholds measured in this way will be more characteristic of the responses used than of the stimulus patterns. Take as an example the case where recognition thresholds are measured for stimuli having various degrees of familiarity for the subject. A common finding is that stimuli with high familiarity are recognized at shorter durations of view than are those with low familiarity. In this situation, where viewing conditions are made deliberately poor, certain responses have high probability of occurrence. The high-frequency responses often are appropriate for the highly familiar stimuli—often the responses are simply the common names for the stimuli. This leads to the measurement of lower thresholds for highly familiar stimuli because the high-frequency responses for these stimuli tend to occur earlier in the ascending series of durations. Hence, highly familiar words will be read at shorter durations, and "dirty" words that are also low-frequency words will be recognized at unusually long durations of view. (See also Pierce, 1963.)

These difficulties with the method of limits arise in the measurement of recognition thresholds where only an ascending series of trials makes sense. In sensory psychophysics both ascending and descending series are typically used with just two response categories, e.g., "yes" and "no." This two-way methodology can be used also for some problems arising

in perception. One example is provided by the measurement of the *subjective vertical*. In this example the investigator is concerned with the *point of subjective equality* (PSE). Traditionally, this refers to the value of one stimulus that is judged equal to another. What distance over an empty meadow is judged equal to 50 yards over a meadow containing several objects? What is the length-to-width ratio of an ellipse judged equivalent to a circle tipped 30° to the line of sight? What is the diameter of a disk adjusted to be equal in size with a silver half-dollar?

It is useful to consider this and the other types of traditional threshold as specific measures deriving from the same general judgmental process. The subject is presented in all situations with a pattern of stimulation. Associated with this particular pattern at that moment is any one of a range of possible experiential states. The subject must then decide whether his experience in some small interval of time is within the range, which permits him to respond one way, or whether his experience is outside that range and indicates the use of other response alternatives. Essential to the process is a subjective standard, or set of standards, and a decision rule to be followed. In the *absolute-threshold* situation the subject responds "yes" if his experience exceeds a subjective standard and "no" if his experience does not. With the *differential threshold* the subject responds "same" if the experienced difference apparently existing between two stimuli falls in the range between two limiting subjective standards and "different" if the experienced difference does not. The determination of PSE is completed when the difference between a stimulus being adjusted and another standard stimulus is as small as or smaller than a subjective standard difference. In the example to be discussed the process is quite explicit. The question asked is: what orientation of a rod in real space is apparently vertical for the subject? The underlying decision process is one in which the subject decides whether his experience for an orientation of the rod corresponds to the small range of experiential states that permit him to say "vertical."

This exposition is presented as an assumption, not because we doubt that the process occurs in subjects but rather because we do not know whether the variable factor in the presence of a stable stimulus is the experience of the subject or his ability to hold and use a precise, stable judgmental standard. Both the *discriminal process* of Thurstone (1927) on which this exposition is based and the assumptions of the *theory of signal detectability* (TSD), described in Chap. 5, attribute variability to experience rather than to the subjective standard. For our purposes it does not matter. We wish here to emphasize the generality of the process underlying all the several types of threshold measurement, especially the role of subjective standards, both in the production of stimulus adjustments by a subject and in the determination of his verbal responses. This emphasis leads to evaluative comments that apply to the following example as well as to all the traditional methods.

In our example the subject is tipped in a chair somewhat from the vertical, and an attempt is made to estimate the orientation of a rod in front of him that he accepts as being vertical. The rod can be rotated propeller fashion in a plane perpendicular to the subject's line of sight. The ascending series is a series beginning with the rod rotated physically counterclockwise from true vertical and rotating in steps clockwise. The descending series begins with the rod rotated clockwise from true vertical and rotated by steps in the counterclockwise direction. For each orientation of the rod the subject responds either "too far clockwise" or "too far counterclockwise." The typical result in this example would be two apparent verticals (points of subjective equality), one for the ascending series and one for the descending series. These would be the orientations in each series at which the subject made a stable change from one response category to the other. The existence of these two measures, rather than a single one, has been taken to be the indication of a series-dependent bias in the judgments of the subject. The approach to the apparent vertical from one direction is not the same as the approach from the other. This bias is evidence of the subject's active role in the process, his ability to adopt arbitrarily a decision rule and subjective standards in evaluating his experience. The subject who determines not to change his response until his experience overwhelmingly indicates that the rod has reached or passed the vertical position commits the traditional *error of habituation*. His ascending series produces a PSE clockwise from that produced by the descending series. The subject who determines to change his response when his experience merely tends to indicate that the rod has reached the vertical position commits the traditional *error of anticipation*. His ascending PSE will be counterclockwise from the descending PSE. Evidently a major part of what is being measured is the result of the subject's arbitrary choices of a decision rule and subjective standards. In this method these choices are unlikely to produce the same PSE in the ascending and descending series.

The experimenter could hope to eliminate some of the contamination due to rigor or laxity of the subject's *subjective criteria of judgment* by averaging his two points of subjective equality. Unfortunately, there is no good rational system dictating the means whereby the true point of subjective equality may be interpolated between the obtained points of subjective equality. The average produces only a rough approximation. A crucial lack is an assurance that the subjective standards applied in the ascending series are the same as, or symmetrical to, those used in the descending series.

The series-dependent bias may be decreased by a variant of the method of limits, the *staircase* or *up-down method*. In this variant the experimenter can begin measurement with the rod rotated counterclockwise from true vertical. If the subject responds "too far counterclockwise," the rod is rotated a predetermined amount clockwise. In this way the adjustment of the rod is controlled indirectly

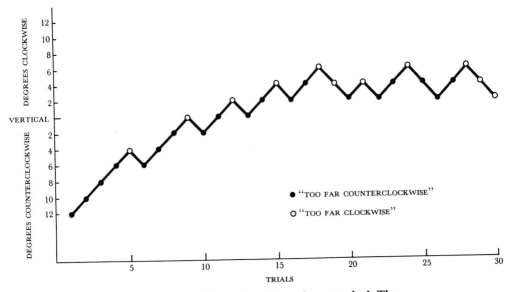

Fig. 8-1   Fictitious data from an ascending series of the staircase method. The subject judged whether a rod was apparently vertical.

on each trial by the subject. The experimenter always makes the adjustment in the direction opposite that indicated by the judgment of the subject. After many trials, a record of the stimulus adjustment should indicate a small range of adjustments within which the apparent vertical lies. This is indicated in Fig. 8-1. The statistical treatment of such data, permitting the computation of the apparent vertical, is discussed by Dixon and Massey (1957). Unfortunately, the treatment assumes that each response of the subject is independent of previous stimulus adjustments and previous responses. These assumptions are unwarranted for the case of human observers.

Cornsweet (1962) has warned that the ordered nature of the series of stimulus adjustments and the dependence of the series upon the subject's responses are obvious to the subject in this situation. Hence, any reasonable subject can discover that he can manipulate the series. He can, if he chooses, manipulate the adjustments of the stimuli to indicate a threshold value at any arbitrary angle of adjustment; e.g., arbitrary alternation of responses would indicate a stable degree of rotation acceptable as being vertical. Cornsweet

suggests that subjects are not likely to malinger voluntarily in this way but, more crucially, are free to change from time to time the subjective standard corresponding to the stimulus adjustment dividing responses of one kind from responses of the other kind. As long as he is permitted this freedom, the measurement of the apparent vertical is contaminated by the subject's arbitrary criterion of judgment.

The staircase method can represent an explicit model for a single trial of the second major psychophysical method, *the method of adjustment*. In this method, typically, the subject would be given remote control of the stimulus figure. Beginning with the rod rotated away from vertical, he would be instructed to rotate it to apparent vertical. The subject would rotate the rod toward apparent vertical, perhaps overshoot it, and, by means of small adjustments back and forth, produce the orientation of the rod he accepts as vertical. A series of such trials would provide a set of measures for which a mean and standard deviation could be computed. This would provide an average apparent vertical and a measure of its reliability. The resemblance between a single trial of this method and the staircase method is striking if the subject is asked to prolong his final adjustment of the rod. In this case, he would provide a series of small adjustments identical to those provided by the staircase method after many trials. This similarity suggests that the method of adjustment should have faults in common with the staircase method. Certainly the subject could malinger or fake a position of the rod, acceptable as apparently vertical, with either method. The adjustment method typically has other faults: (1) Usually no record of stimulus adjustments is kept. This means that there is no record of the stimulus values to which the subject has been exposed. (2) No control of the rate of change of the stimulus is imposed, as in the staircase method, and the subject can experience any rate of change he chooses. This undoubtedly has an effect upon his final choice of adjustment.

The ability of the subject to voluntarily establish a threshold value by means of his control of the stimulus in either the staircase method or the method of adjustment is con-

trolled by Cornsweet in his suggested *double-staircase* methods (1962). In one of these methods two staircases are run concurrently, with the trials of one staircase occurring on odd trials and trials of the other staircase occurring on even trials. One staircase, in the case of the rod, would begin with the rod far counterclockwise (staircase *A*), and the other staircase would begin with the rod far clockwise (staircase *B*). The result of this method could be that of Fig. 8-2. Even in this case a clever subject could willfully produce an arbitrary apparent vertical.

Cornsweet's second method precludes this possibility. Instead of running one staircase on even trials and the other on odd trials, the choice of which staircase will be run on a given trial is made randomly. Figure 8-3 illustrates data that could be obtained by this method. The subject still controls the stimulus adjustments by the nature of his responses, but not in a coherent fashion. The series of discrete stimulus orientations would no longer have an ordered or controlled character-istic.

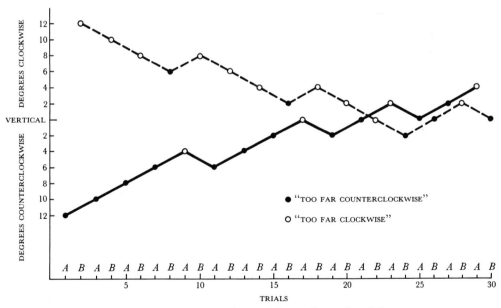

Fig. 8-2 Fictitious data from running ascending and descending series of the staircase method on alternate trials. The subject judged whether a rod was apparently vertical.

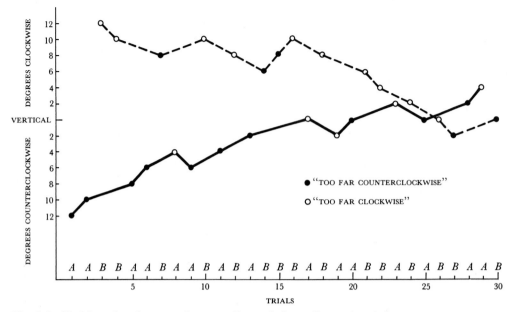

Fig. 8-3   **Fictitious data from running ascending and descending series of the staircase method in random order. The subject judged whether a rod was apparently vertical.**

The random double-staircase method is similar to the method of constant stimuli in that the subject experiences a random series of discrete stimulus values to which he responds with one of a small set of response categories. Compared with the constant method, the double-staircase method has important deficiencies. The chief drawbacks include the following: (1) The rationale for the treatment of data, i.e., the derivation of a single number that provides a best estimate of the apparent vertical, has not been thoroughly considered for the case of the human subjects for whom trials are not likely to be independent. (2) The stimuli experienced by the subject are still under his control; hence, the stimulus set experienced may not represent the most efficient set that could have been used for the purpose. (3) There is no explicit control of response bias reflecting the subject's criterion of judgment. (What is his decision rule dictating choice of response?) Final adjustments are contaminated by this factor.

The typical experimental situations in which the method of limits and the adjustment method have been used extensively include those in which the stimulus characteristic of interest is adjustable continuously, or in steps, while the threshold measures are being made. This is true of many attempts to measure the extent of illusion. In the simple Müller-Lyer illusion (see Woodworth and Schlosberg, 1954, pp. 417–423) the methods can be used to learn the length of line bounded by feathers, which is judged equal to a length bounded by arrowheads. They can be used also to answer a question such as: What is the distance between two lights flashing successively that is judged equal to the distance between two lights that are on continuously? As a third example: Subjects can be asked to adjust the width of a rectangle to appear equal to its height or to create a pleasing proportion of height to width. Subjects can be asked to adjust the size of a disk, located a short distance away, to apparent equality with a disk located at a greater distance. Usually the methods are concerned with fundamental measures of stimulus characteristics, length, weight, or time, or some measure derived from them. It is also characteristically true that the precise time of threshold measurement is not important. The serial nature of the methods and the subject's control over the stimuli partially control the time at which a threshold measurement is attained.

In summary, the method of limits and the method of adjustment have had a great deal of use in the perceptual area because of their high face validity. They appear, at first glance, to be natural ways in which to measure thresholds. On closer examination, they can be defended only as rough, approximate techniques with contaminating artifacts. Very precise statements made on the basis of measures obtained from these methods are questionable.

Perhaps the most useful psychophysical method in perceptual research is the method of constant stimuli. This method now has a good rational underpinning and appears a natural method for all those cases in which the stimulus aspect of interest is not adjustable easily by the experimenter or by the subject. An example is provided by a recognition experiment discussed by Woodworth and Schlosberg (1954, pp. 699–700) and by Egan (1958). One hundred stimulus forms were first shown one at a time to subjects and then mixed with 100 stimulus forms that they had not seen previously. The 200 forms were used in a recognition test. They were shown to the subject one at a time; and after seeing each, he was required to say "Yes, the stimulus shown is an old form" or "No, the stimulus shown is not an old form." "Old" refers to a form that he had seen prior to the recognition trials. An interesting parameter in this situation is the number of times the subject had seen an old form before the recognition trials were begun. This is a variable that must be established before recognition trials and is not adjustable during recognition trials in the way demanded by either the method of limits or the method of adjustment.

The proper objective of this research would be that of determining the extent of the subject's ability to discriminate between old and new stimuli as a function of the number of times he had seen the old stimuli (frequency). Let us concern ourselves with a single value of this frequency variable and suppose that 50 old stimuli, each of which had been seen once, were mixed with 50 new stimuli and presented in the recognition series. The data of this series are presented symbolically in Table 8-1. Columns represent the presentation of old and new stimuli; rows represent the judgment of the subject. The number of correct recognitions of the old stimuli is represented in the upper left-hand cell, and the number of incorrect recognitions, i.e., declaring them to be old, of the new stimuli is represented in the upper right-hand cell.

The usual evaluation of such data involves the computation of a single number measuring the extent of the subject's discriminative acuity (i.e., his ability to discriminate old from new stimuli). This appears at the outset to be an impossible requirement. Where the total number of trials represented in Table 8-1 is fixed, the 2×2 matrix of data is completely determined by just three more independent numbers, degrees of freedom. Where the number of appearances of each of the two classes of stimuli (old and new) is fixed also, two more independent numbers will completely describe the matrix of data. Evidently one number will not suffice in describing the subject's performance. For example, we know of one quantity that will certainly not do the job. This is a number representing the ability of the subject to detect old stimuli when they occur. The measure of this ability is the hit rate (HR):

$$HR = P(o|0) = \frac{N_{oo}}{N_O} \qquad (8\text{-}1)$$

This is an inadequate measure of the subject's performance because it involves just one independent number, N_{oo}. The relative frequency with which the subject emits the response "old" contaminates this measure. A subject

Table 8-1   Symbolic presentation of the results of a simple recognition experiment.

		STIMULI	
		Old	New	Totals
RESPONSES	"Old"	N_{oO}	N_{oN}	N_o
	"New"	N_{nO}	N_{nN}	N_n
	Totals	N_o	N_N	N

Definitions:

$$P(o|O) = \frac{N_{oO}}{N_O}$$
$$= \text{hit rate (HR)}$$

$$P(o|N) = \frac{N_{oN}}{N_N}$$
$$= \text{false alarm rate (FAR)}$$

who says "old" relatively often will always show great discriminative acuity, as measured by the HR alone.

A typical measure that is a composite of two independent numbers is provided by the traditional *correction for chance* formula (Woodworth and Schlosberg, 1954, p. 700). In this case it would be: True score = percent of old stimuli recognized — percent of new stimuli falsely recognized, or

$$P'(o|O) = P(o|O) - P(o|N) \qquad (8\text{-}2)$$

where $P'(o|O)$ represents the "true" HR uncontaminated by the relative tendency of the subject to say "old." The assumptions underlying the use of this measure of discriminative performance are most surely not valid in any perceptual, or sensory, research. These assumptions have been made explicit by Egan (1958):

(A_1) In the experiment there are just two kinds of trials for each type of stimulus. During trials of one kind the stimuli were clearly recognized as being old or new stimuli and the responses were perfectly accurate. The proportion of trials on which this occurred is defined as $P'(o|O)$ for the old stimuli and $P'(n|N)$ for the new stimuli. Stimuli presented on the remaining trials could not be recognized at all as being old or new. The relative occurrence of these trials is given by

$[1 - P'(o|O)]$ for the old stimuli and $[1 - P'(n|N)]$ for the new.

(A_2) The threshold values above which stimuli are clearly recognized as being old or new, and below which they are completely unrecognizable as being old or new, are the same for old and new stimuli.

(A_3) On trials in which stimuli are below recognition threshold, the subject guesses with a constant guess rate, $P(o)$ and $P(n)$:

$$P(o) = 1 - P(n)$$

Given assumptions A_1 and A_3, then

$$P(o|O) = P'(o|O) + P(o|N)\frac{1 - P'(o|O)}{1 - kP'(o|O)} \qquad (8\text{-}3)$$

where $\quad k = \dfrac{P'(n|N)}{P'|(o|O)} \qquad (8\text{-}4)$

Given assumption A_2, then $k = 1$ and

$$P(o|O) = P'(o|O) + P(o|N)$$

or

$$P'(o|O) = P(o|O) - P(o|N)$$

The last equation is (8-2), the traditional correction for chance.

Other simple *corrections for guessing* can be concocted from the use of other pairs of numbers from Table 8-1. For example, another standard equation yielding a "true" HR, given the same assumptions, is

$$P'(o|O) = 1 - P(n|O)\frac{N_{oN} + N_{nO}}{N_{nO}} \qquad (8\text{-}5)$$

which accounts for the two available degrees of freedom by utilizing the two error cells, the upper right-hand cell containing N_{oN} and the lower left-hand cell containing N_{nO}. This equation is often used in the form

$$N'_{nO} = N_O - \frac{N_{nO}}{1 - \dfrac{N_{oN}}{(N_{oN} + N_{nO})}} \qquad (8\text{-}6)$$

which reduces to the equivalent form of (8-2) by simple manipulation, as will any equation that derives from the same set of assumptions.

The validity of all such equations depends crucially upon the linear relation between the HR and the false-alarm rate (FAR) which is specified. That is, Eq. (8-2), restated, is

$$HR' = HR - FAR \quad \text{or}$$
$$HR = FAR + HR' \quad (8\text{-}7)$$

where HR' is the true hit rate. The relation between HR and FAR can be checked empirically by means of a simple experiment. This amounts to several runs through the experiment, using different but equivalent stimuli each time, once while the subject is under instruction to use the response "old" very sparingly, once while he uses the response "old" freely and often, and once while he attempts to use the response "old" with an intermediate frequency. The subject can manage these three frequencies of usage by the use of three different criteria of judgment: one very stringent criterion, i.e., no stimulus is called old unless the subject is very sure it is old; one intermediate criterion, i.e., any stimulus that reasonably could be old is called old; and one lax criterion, i.e., any stimulus that seems even a little old is called old. This method would provide three HR-FAR pairs.

If the assumptions underlying the use of the typical correction for chance formula are valid, then the relationship between HR and FAR should be a straight line with a slope of unity and an intercept on the HR axis of the true hit rate HR'. This relationship and three hypothetical experimental points are depicted in Fig. 8-4. If the true thresholds for old and new stimuli were not identical, the slope would be the quantity $[1 - P'(o|O)]/[1 - kP'(o|O)]$, from Eq. (8-3). The primary finding of research sparked by the TSD is that the relation between HR and FAR is not linear; i.e., the assumption that just two kinds of trial exist in this situation

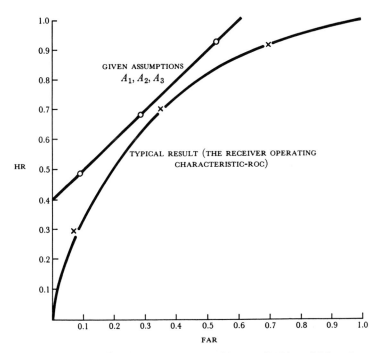

Fig. 8-4 Two possible relations between hit rate (HR) and false alarm rate (FAR). The straight line derives from the assumptions of usual correction for chance methods; the curved line derives from the theory of signal detectability and is described by empirical results.

(A_1) is clearly false. Instead, if a subject increases the rate at which he emits "old" responses from a rather low rate of emission, the increase in the rate at which he says "old" to old stimuli will be greater than the overall increase in the rate at which he says "old" to new stimuli. Some of the errors he had made while using the lower rate of emission of old responses resulted from his unwillingness to say "old" rather than the fact that he saw nothing at all and guessed. A typical relation between HR and FAR, the receiver operating characteristic (ROC), is shown in Fig. 8-4. This has been shown to result for a variety of discrimination tasks, including the discrimination of an auditory signal in noise and the discrimination of a square from a rectangle, as well as discrimination of old from new stimuli.

The usual corrections for chance represent *invalid* procedures. For the proper use of the 2 degrees of freedom in Table 8-1 in the estimation of how well the subject discriminated old from new stimuli, the student is referred to Chap. 5, which describes a defensible treatment of data from two-choice discrimination situations. The TSD has important implications for the kind of perceptual study we have been considering: 1. No single 2 × 2 table of data, of the type shown in Table 8-1, is sufficient to define completely the acuity of the subject in the two-choice discrimination task described. The model states and evidence supports that the relation between HR and FAR (the ROC) is not linear. Each ROC has two parameters, d' and m. The measure d' provides a measure of acuity independent of response bias. The data of a single 2 × 2 table yield but a single point, a pair of HR-FAR values. With a single point, a value for d' cannot be determined unless an assumption is made about m, the slope. Two 2 × 2 tables yielding two different pairs of HR-FAR values can estimate the two parameters of the ROC and define the acuity of the subject.

2. Variation in the pairs of HR-FAR values as shown from one 2 × 2 table to another in the same discrimination situation is due to changes in the criterion of judgment (relative frequency of "old" and "new" responses). The two parameters of the ROC are constant in a given discrimination situation and independent of this criterion. They must be estimated, however, by means of variation in the subject's criterion of judgment. This may be accomplished by asking the subject to hold one criterion of judgment for a series of trials and to hold another criterion for another series. This would yield two pairs of HR-FAR values, sufficient to estimate the two parameters of the ROC.

Another useful methodology is that of asking the subject to hold multiple criteria of judgment during a series of trials. He does this by using a response scale, such as

1. "Very sure the stimulus just seen was old"

2. "Somewhat sure the stimulus just seen was old"

3. "Do not know which it was"

4. "Somewhat sure the stimulus just seen was new"

5. "Very sure the stimulus just seen was new"

A response scale with n categories makes it possible to obtain $n - 1$ points in the HR-FAR plot. Let Y represent the presentation of any old stimulus on a particular trial and X represent the presentation of any new stimulus. If the frequency of responses, in response category i when old stimuli occurred, is denoted by h_i, where $i = 1, 2, \ldots, n$, and N_Y is the total number of presentations of old stimuli, then the estimate of HR for response category c (hr_c) is given by

$$hr_c = \frac{1}{N_Y}\left(\sum_{i=1}^{c} h_i\right) \qquad (8\text{-}8)$$

The estimate of FAR for category c (far_c) is equal to the sum of the frequencies of responses in response categories 1 through c when new stimuli were presented $\left(\sum_{i=1}^{c} fa_i\right)$

divided by N_X, the total number of presentations of new stimuli:

$$far_c = \frac{1}{N_X}\left(\sum_{i=1}^{c} fa_i\right) \qquad (8\text{-}9)$$

The computations indicated for an illustrative set of data are set forth in Table 8-2.

In the case in which there are more than two categories in the response scale the estimates of HR and FAR obtained for category c by the cumulative procedures indicated are assumed to be equivalent to estimates of HR and FAR that would be obtained in a 2-category experiment with a criterion of judgment corresponding to the upper boundary of category c. The estimates for category n are always equal to unity. The cumulative procedure, in effect, involves breaking down the n categories into a series of $n-1$ pairs of categories in order to obtain $n-1$ HR estimates and $n-1$ FAR estimates.

The approximate equivalence of d' values obtained from multiple two-choice experiments and d' values obtained from response scales with more than two categories has been uniformly demonstrated. Egan, Schulman, and Greenberg (1959) found that d' values for the detection of an auditory signal from a noise background obtained from a series of two-choice experiments and from 4-category rating scale experiments were almost identical within subjects. Weintraub and Hake (1962) found that points obtained with 2-, 3-, and 4-category rating scales for the same stimulus conditions were fitted quite well by a single function for each subject. Evidence has been reported indicating that d' is not completely independent of the nature of the rating scale (Swets, Tanner, and Birdsall, 1961).

Table 8-2   Illustrative computation of pairs of hit rate (HR) and false-alarm rate (FAR) values from rating scale data.

	STIMULI	
	Old	New
"1"	20	5
"2"	50	5
"3"	20	20
"4"	5	40
"5"	5	30
Totals	100	100

RATINGS

$$HR_1 = \frac{20}{100} = 0.20 \qquad\qquad FAR_1 = \frac{5}{100} = 0.05$$

$$HR_2 = \frac{20+50}{100} = 0.70 \qquad FAR_2 = \frac{5+5}{100} = 0.10$$

$$HR_3 = \frac{20+50+20}{100} = 0.90 \qquad FAR_3 = \frac{5+5+20}{100} = 0.30$$

$$HR_4 = \frac{20+50+20+5}{100} = 0.95 \qquad FAR_4 = \frac{5+5+20+40}{100} = 0.70$$

$$HR_5 = 1.0 \qquad\qquad FAR_5 = 1.0$$

Rating scales with more than two categories are extremely useful because it takes considerably less time to obtain $n - 1$ points with a single n-category rating scale experiment than it does to obtain $n - 1$ points by repeating a two-choice experiment $n - 1$ times with a different criterion of judgment being attempted by the subject each time.

3. Perhaps the most neglected aspect of psychophysics has been the concept of a criterion of judgment in discrimination situations and the factors controlling the subject's choice of the criterion. This is an important and explicit aspect of the theory of signal detectability which has considerable meaning for perceptual research in which we often confuse the subject's willingness to make a response with his ability to do so.

Schemes by which we have tried to get along with a single 2×2 matrix of data should be mentioned here. One of these is the forced-choice technique (Blackwell, 1953). The experiment could have been run by showing the subject one old and one new stimulus on each trial, one after the other, and asking him to state which stimulus was the old stimulus, the first or the second. In effect, he is required to make one "old" response and one "new" response on each trial, and this means that the two response categories occur with equal frequency. All experiments of this type are comparable because the HR obtained does not reflect variation in relative response frequencies.

Another method uses as a measure of discrimination the sum of the negative diagonal in Table 8-1, $(N_{oo} + N_{nN})$, the total number correct. This is simply another invalid correction for chance because N_{nN} is perfectly related to N_{oN}. The use of the two types of correct response, $N_{oo} + N_{nN}$, does not avoid the basic difficulty. As the subject increases the rate at which he uses the "old" response category, the increase in the number of old stimuli correctly identified as old will not exactly compensate for the decrease in the number of new stimuli identified as new. The relationship between these two quantities can-

not be linear because the relationship between HR and FAR under the same conditions is not linear.

Perhaps the major implications of TSD for perceptual research involve its insistence that the threshold concept itself may have dubious validity. In fact, the empirical shape of the ROC denies the existence of the threshold, i.e., denies the existence of occasions (trials) in the usual perceptual research situations in which the subject purely and simply guesses at the identity of the stimulus. This is denied also by the evidence indicating that second judgments, made following a first incorrect judgment, are nonrandom (Swets, Tanner, and Birdsall, 1961).

Careful psychologists have always taken pains to describe the threshold as a *statistically defined point*, meaning that it is an arbitrary point and that some sensing and recognizing occurs below it. Unfortunately, this has led less careful investigators to use terms like *subthreshold* or *subliminal* in an absolute sense. Much bad research and research interpretation have resulted. Students are warned against the tempting research arising from the use of these unacceptable terms. Further specific warnings and descriptions of other artifacts involved are provided by Eriksen (1960), Goldiamond (1958), and Pierce (1963).

TSD has no concept corresponding to the threshold and argues that the concept may be unnecessary (Swets, 1961*b*). Instead of defining a stimulus value at which all subjects achieve the same thing, e.g., recognize the stimulus on 75 percent of the trials, the theory provides a means for describing the efficiency of the subject, in terms of his acuity and use of the response categories, for any value of the stimulus.

Even where the subject is required only to discriminate between two types of stimuli or between a stimulus and its absence, the methodology that provides a good, defensible measure of discriminative acuity is quite demanding. Typical perceptual psychophysics, usually done to answer even more complex questions, demands more, not less, rigor than typical sensory psychophysics. For example, the very frequent case in perceptual research in which the subject is asked to discriminate among more than two stimuli is much tougher to treat rigorously and clearly. Usually one of two typical situations is involved:

1. *The level of perceiving situation.* Here the subject is asked to recognize a presented stimulus as being a certain one of a set containing *n* members. The measure of performance desired is a single overall measure of his ability to recognize the stimuli in this situation. An example is provided by the intelligibility test in which a subject's overall ability to recognize test words in a communication situation is evaluated (Postman and Egan, 1949, pp. 73–76). The measure of interest might be the proportion of the words spoken by the talker that are received by the listener; or an estimate is made of the average duration of presentation at which one-half of a set of typical geometric figures can be recognized correctly.

2. *The individual threshold situation.* The subject is asked to identify a presented stimulus as being a certain one of a set containing *n* members. Here, however, a threshold value for each member of the set is to be estimated. Is a circle recognized at briefer durations than is a square? Are stimuli that

have been seen frequently recognized at lower levels of illumination than stimuli that have not?

The first of these situations is essentially the one we have discussed for the case of just two kinds of stimuli. There was no interest in comparing thresholds for old versus new stimuli. The traditional procedures for chance correction assume that thresholds for old and new stimuli are identical. The first of the two cases now being described is the same, with the exception that more than two stimuli and more than two responses are involved. In the second situation several stimuli and responses are involved, and the efficiency with which each stimulus is recognized is the measure desired. Both experimental situations typically lead to a table of data such as that presented in Table 8-3.

For the case of the *level of perceiving situation,* attempts to derive a true measure of the ability to recognize a set of stimuli presented one at a time in some random order come mainly from the testing area (Lylerly, 1951). An example is provided by a typical multiple-choice test with *n* questions on each of which the student is asked to choose among four alternative answers. The question ordinarily asked of the result: What is the best estimate of the "true" number correct; i.e., how best correct for chance? One answer is

Table 8-3   Illustrative table of data from a multiple-stimulus recognition experiment.

		STIMULI				
		Circle	Square	Triangle	Diamond	Totals
RESPONSES	"Circle"	70	20	20	60	170
	"Square"	3	40	30	17	90
	"Triangle"	2	40	40	7	89
	"Diamond"	25	0	10	16	51
	Totals	100	100	100	100	400

provided by Abbott's formula (Finney, 1947),

$$p' = \frac{p - c}{1 - c} \qquad (8\text{-}10)$$

where p is the proportion of total correct responses, c is the a priori probability of being correct $(c = 1/n)$, and p' is the estimate of the "true" proportion correct. This is a widely used treatment of data that can be shown to assume (1) perfect knowledge or perfect ignorance of each item; (2) pure random guessing at unknown items; (3) a binomial distribution of success at guessing at unknown items; and (4) the mean of the binomial as a good estimate of its mode. This is the linear model that was rejected in the dichotomous case considered above. It must be rejected here also on the same grounds: Items on which the student makes errors do not represent trials on which he purely guesses. For this reason no linear model will enable us to correct for chance or the response bias of the student. This applies to the common method of analysis involving the use of the total number of correct responses on all stimuli as an indicator of discriminative acuity. This is simply an extension of the testing model and the linear model of the dichotomous case. *It is invalid.*

It is important to recognize that the invalidity of the linear models, in this case, does not rest upon the existence of information in the subject's error choices. That is, when the error responses of Table 8-3 are examined, it can be seen that the subject's errors can be predicted with some accuracy if we know which stimulus had been presented to him on each trial. This does indicate that he is not purely guessing on error trials, but the major reason for discarding the linear model is the nonlinear form of the HR-FAR relationship. This nonlinearity will hold even though the errors of the subject are homogeneous with respect to the incorrect stimuli.

The *individual threshold situation* is still more difficult to handle. Usually the intention here is to measure a recognition threshold for each of several stimuli. The stimuli may be shown to the subject one at a time at constant, brief durations or low intensities of illumination, and he is required to identify each as it occurs by using one of a small set of response categories. After many trials of this procedure, it would be interesting to specify for each stimulus a "true" number of correct responses. Again, linear correction models have been used. For example,

$$N'_c x = N_X - \frac{N_x X}{1 - P_x} \qquad (8\text{-}11)$$

where $N'_c x$ is the corrected number of correct responses to form X, N_X is the total number of appearances of form, X, $N_x X$ is the number of form X appearances that were incorrectly identified, and P_x is the proportion of total errors made on all forms that were called form X. This correction for chance is designed to be sensitive to the subject's response biases. The model can be shown to derive from the assumptions discussed above in connection with the dichotomous stimulus case and from the assumption that the real thresholds for all stimulus alternatives are identical! If this assumption is not made, this linear correction model becomes quite complex.

The threshold approach to an understanding of the data in the matrix of Table 8-3 is inadequate, if not misguided. It is inadequate because the concept of a recognition threshold has never been defined in sufficient detail in this context. It is misguided because of its concern with the *correctness* of the subject's responses rather than with the information contained in them about what he was really doing. Both of these shortcomings can be made explicit when the experimental situation providing the data matrix of Table 8-3 is viewed as a part of the general schema of experimental situations to which it belongs. It is an instance of *general classification procedures*. These include all situations in which stimuli are presented to a subject who is required to classify them by the use of discrete concept names or categories. In all such cases the model for the analysis of the subject's performance is provided by statistical classification procedures (Anderson, 1958).

CLASSIFICATION PROCEDURES

In statistics the classification problem arises in the need to make an inference about an object or event: given the measurements of that object or event along several crucial dimensions, decide from which of several known populations the object was drawn as a sample. For example, given test scores on an individual, does he belong to the class of passing students or to the class of failing students in college?

The study of statistical decision functions permits useful statements to be made about these classification problems. For example, if each object, the measurements of which are known, is considered a point in n-space, we may define regions in this space and some simple decision rules. Such a rule may be: If an object's measurements place it in region A of the n-space, we classify it as coming from population a; if it falls in region B of the n-space, we classify it as coming from population b. Classification theory has been developed sufficiently to permit the specification of regions and decision rules that lead to minimum misclassifications and/or minimum costs. In the following, a classification job is given to the subject, who must classify his experiences in simple situations in order to achieve certain objectives, e.g., minimum errors as defined by the experimenter. This permits a complete look at the laboratory classification procedures that have been, or could be, used. There are two general cases considered. The *metric case* includes all procedures in which the stimuli are at least partly measurable in a quantitative way. The intensity and wavelength of light are obvious examples, but included also are faces varying in nose length, playing cards varying in size and viewing distance, or rectangles varying in height and width. The second of the general cases, the *nonmetric case,* includes those situations of which the stimuli may be classified only in a nominal sense, or in which only a nominal scale of measurement is utilized. Examples are provided by a set of geometric figures composed of a square, a rectangle, a triangle, or a set of nonsense syllables, e.g.,

"BIV," "JUB," "MOV." In the metric and the nonmetric cases, the responses of the subject are discrete classifications or concepts that have no intended metric. Both cases are exceedingly useful in the perceptual area of research where responses often refer to concepts with real boundaries; e.g., stimuli are old or new, square or circular, colored or colorless, clear or unclear, dangerous or safe.

The metric case

The metric cases, for purposes of presentation, are grouped according to dimensionality of the stimuli and the number of responses used. *Case a* includes *multidimensional stimuli with more than two response classes.* There are a number of experimental examples that fall in this category. One example, a_1, involves plane stimuli differing in size and texture that are varied also in distance from the subject. The subject views the stimuli one at a time and makes one of the following three responses (R): "far away" (R_1), "at a medium distance" (R_2), or "close by" (R_3). In a second example, a_2, lights varying in dominant wavelength, luminance, and purity are viewed singly by the subject, who responds by saying "not seen" (R_1), "seen but colorless" (R_2), or "seen and colored" (R_3). Example a_3 refers to rectangular stimuli varying in height and width that appear singly to a subject who responds by saying "tall rectangle" (R_1), "square" (R_2), or "squat rectangle" (R_3).

Case b covers *multidimensional stimuli with two response classes.* Five examples are presented for this case. Example b_1 is the same as a_1 with the exception that only two response categories, "near" (R_1) and "far" (R_2) are used. In b_2 lights differing in area and luminance are presented singly to the dark-adapted subject, who responds "seen" (R_1) or "not seen" (R_2). Example b_3 describes stimuli that differ in the frequency with which they had been seen previously, the degree of rotation from the position in which originally seen, and duration of view. These are presented singly to a subject who responds by saying that the stimulus was seen previously

(R_1) or not seen previously (R_2). In b_4 the schematic faces of Brunswik and Reiter (see Rodwan and Hake, 1964) differing in nose length, distance between the eyes, height of forehead, and size of chin are shown singly to a subject who states that the face is "intelligent" (R_1) or "not intelligent" (R_2). In example b_5 words differing in scaled hostility value and frequency of pairing with shock are presented singly to a subject at short durations of view, and he is required to respond that the stimuli "stand out clearly" (R_1) or "do not stand out" (R_2).

Case c describes *unidimensional stimuli with two or more response classes.* In example c_1 a stimulus is varied in distance from a subject who responds "close" (R_1) or "far" (R_2). In example c_2 complex stimuli seen before or not seen before are shown to the subject, who responds "old" (R_1) or "new" (R_2). In example c_3 a pair of stimulus forms composed of two examples of the same form, or of two different forms, is shown to the subject, who responds "same" (R_1) or "different" (R_2).

We shall first consider case *b* and example b_5. Words differing in the scaled hostility value (h) and frequency of prior pairing of the word with painful shock (f) are each presented just once to the subject at a very brief, constant duration of view. He classifies each as having "stood out clearly" (R_1) as he saw it or as having "not stood out clearly" (R_2).

The set of stimuli (a small set for purposes of illustration) is described in Table 8-4. Although all are shown at the same duration of view, the subject is not told this and accepts the reasonableness of his response classifications.

The data of the illustrative experiment are shown in Table 8-5 in the form of two matrices. The first contains the stimuli assigned to response class R_1; the second contains the stimuli assigned to response class R_2. The analysis of the data provides the decision rules of the subject in terms of a *linear discriminant function* (LDF), which is a linear, weighted combination of the two stimulus variables:

$$Y = v_1 h + v_2 f \qquad (8\text{-}12)$$

In the equation, h and f are values of the stimulus characteristics and v_1 and v_2 are the extents to which the subject weights each in making his judgments. The value Y represents the attribute being judged. Values of Y greater than the subject's subjective standard or cutoff lead to the response R_1; values less than his standard lead to response R_2. A reconstruction of the LDF and the subject's subjective standard for evaluating Y should permit us to reproduce his responses to the stimuli.

The computation of the LDF for a subject in this situation proceeds from the data of Table 8-5. Four basic matrices are involved in the computation. The first of these is T, the variance-covariance of the elements of S (Table 8-4):

$$T = \begin{bmatrix} t_{11} & t_{12} \\ t_{21} & t_{22} \end{bmatrix} \qquad (8\text{-}13)$$

where t_{11} is the sum of squares of column 1 in S, $t_{11} = \sum\limits_{i=1}^{9} X_{i1}^2$; t_{12} is the sum of products of columns 1 and 2 of S, $t_{12} = \sum\limits_{i=1}^{9} X_{i1}X_{i2}$; and t_{22} is the sum of squares of column 2 in S. The matrix T is a symmetric matrix with $t_{21} = t_{12}$.

Table 8-4   The matrix S of the nine stimuli classified in Table 8-5.

	STIMULUS	
	h	f
1	9	9
2	10	10
3	11	11
4	12	12
5	9	10
6	9	11
7	9	12
8	10	11
9	10	12

$= S$ (for rows 1–4)

Table 8-5   Illustrative set of data from a hypothetical experiment.

CLASS R_1		CLASS R_2	
h	f	h	f
9	9	9	10
10	10	9	11
11	11	9	12
12	12	10	11
		10	12
$\bar{X}_{i1}$ 10.5	10.5	$\bar{X}_{i2}$ 9.4	11.2

The subject classified words differing in scaled hostility value (h) and frequency of pairing with shock as "clear" (R_1) or "not clear" (R_2).

The second matrix involved is W, the matrix of "within-classes" variances and covariances:

$$W = \begin{bmatrix} w_{11} & w_{12} \\ w_{21} & w_{22} \end{bmatrix} \qquad (8\text{-}14)$$

where w_{11} is the sum of squares of column 1 in class R_2 (subject responded "not clear") plus the sum of squares of column 1 in class R_1 (subject responded "clear"). The element w_{12} is found by cross-multiplying columns 1 and 2 in class R_2 and adding this to the sum of the cross multiplication of columns 1 and 2 in class R_1. The element w_{22} is the sum of squares of column 2 in class R_1 plus the sum of squares of column 2 in class R_2. Again, $w_{12} = w_{21}$.

The third matrix is D, the vector of differences:

$$D = \{d_1 \quad d_2\} \qquad (8\text{-}15)$$

where the difference $d_1 = \bar{X}_{12} - \bar{X}_{11}$ and $d_2 = \bar{X}_{22} - \bar{X}_{21}$. Here, $\bar{X}_{i1}$ and $\bar{X}_{i2}$ are the means of columns in class R_1 and class R_2.

The fourth matrix is V, the vector of weights:

$$V = \{v_1 \quad v_2\} \qquad (8\text{-}16)$$

where the linear discriminant function is

$$Y = v_1 X_1 + v_2 X_2 \qquad (8\text{-}17)$$

Then

$$V = W^{-1}D \qquad (8\text{-}18)$$

where W^{-1} is the inverse of matrix W. For the illustration,

$$W = \begin{bmatrix} 889 & 973 \\ 973 & 1,076 \end{bmatrix} \qquad (8\text{-}19)$$

$$\det W = w_{11}w_{22} - w_{12}w_{21} = 9,835 \qquad (8\text{-}20)$$

$$W^{-1} = \begin{bmatrix} \dfrac{w_{22}}{\det W} & \dfrac{-w_{12}}{\det W} \\ \dfrac{-w_{21}}{\det W} & \dfrac{w_{11}}{\det W} \end{bmatrix}$$

$$= \begin{bmatrix} 0.1091 & -0.0989 \\ -0.0989 & 0.0904 \end{bmatrix} \qquad (8\text{-}21)$$

$$V = \begin{bmatrix} 0.1091 & -0.0989 \\ -0.0989 & 0.0904 \end{bmatrix} \begin{bmatrix} 1.1 \\ -0.7 \end{bmatrix}$$

$$= \begin{bmatrix} v_1 \\ v_2 \end{bmatrix} = \begin{bmatrix} 0.1992 \\ -0.1720 \end{bmatrix} \qquad (8\text{-}22)$$

The weights are transformed to relative values by requiring that the length of vector V be unity. This is achieved by dividing the square of each element of V by the sum of the squared elements of V. The square roots of these two quantities provide the normalized v's.

$$Y = 0.756X_1 - 0.654X_2 \qquad (8\text{-}23)$$

Considerable ease of computation is possible where the stimulus set S is an orthogonal set with respect to the physical dimensions of variation defining the stimuli. Such a set is shown in Table 8-6. In this case T is a diagonal matrix and determinant (det) W is zero. Then

$$V = KM_2 \qquad (8\text{-}24)$$

where M_2 is the vector of means of class R_2 in deviation scores. Table 8-7 reproduces Table 8-6 in deviation form and shows the stimulus classes as classified by a hypothetical subject. Then

$$K = \cfrac{1}{(M_2'M_2)^{\frac{1}{2}}} \cfrac{1}{\left(\begin{bmatrix} \frac{1}{3} & -\frac{1}{3} \end{bmatrix} \begin{bmatrix} \frac{1}{3} \\ -\frac{1}{3} \end{bmatrix} \right)^{\frac{1}{2}}}$$

$$= \frac{1}{\sqrt{\frac{2}{3}}} = \frac{3}{\sqrt{2}} \qquad (8\text{-}25)$$

$$V = \frac{3}{\sqrt{2}} \begin{bmatrix} \frac{1}{3} & -\frac{1}{3} \end{bmatrix} = \begin{bmatrix} \frac{1}{2} & -\frac{1}{2} \end{bmatrix}$$

$$Y = 0.707X_1 - 0.707X_2 \qquad (8\text{-}26)$$

Table 8-6   An orthogonal set of plane circles differing in diameter (X_1) and texture of surface (X_2).

$$S = \begin{bmatrix} 9 & 9 \\ 9 & 10 \\ 9 & 11 \\ 10 & 9 \\ 10 & 10 \\ 10 & 11 \\ 11 & 9 \\ 11 & 10 \\ 11 & 11 \end{bmatrix}$$

	X_1	X_2
$\bar{X}$	[10	10]

[1] The experiment is the same as b_1. The subject classifies the stimuli as "near" (R_1) or "far" (R_2).

Table 8-7   The stimuli of Table 8-6 in deviation form and the classification of the stimuli by response classes.

	X_1	X_2
$S =$		

$$S = \begin{bmatrix} -1 & -1 \\ -1 & 0 \\ -1 & +1 \\ 0 & -1 \\ 0 & 0 \\ 0 & +1 \\ +1 & -1 \\ +1 & 0 \\ +1 & +1 \end{bmatrix}$$

$\bar{X}'$ [0   0]

CLASS R_1

$$\begin{bmatrix} X_1 & X_2 \\ -1 & 1 \\ 0 & 1 \\ -1 & 0 \end{bmatrix}$$

$\bar{X}'_i \quad -\frac{2}{3} \quad \frac{2}{3}$

CLASS R_2

$$\begin{bmatrix} X_1 & X_2 \\ 1 & -1 \\ 0 & 0 \\ 1 & 0 \\ -1 & -1 \\ 1 & 1 \\ 0 & -1 \end{bmatrix}$$

$\bar{X}'_{i2} \quad \frac{1}{3} \quad -\frac{1}{3}$

The saving in computation where the stimulus variables are orthogonal is greater where the stimuli are defined in terms of more than just two dimensions of physical variation.

The information provided by these procedures is considerable.

1. We may determine whether the two response classes were used for sets of stimuli that were not random assortments; i.e., we can test the significance of the difference between the multidimensional means of the stimuli identified by each response class. If we denote the distance of the multidimensional mean of all stimuli to which the response R_1 was made from the multidimensional mean of all stimuli to which the response R_2 was made by the symbol D^2, then

$$F = \frac{(N_1 + N_2 - n - 1)T^2}{(N_1 + N_2 - 2)n}$$
$$= \frac{N_1 N_2 (N_1 + N_2 - n - 1)D^2}{(N_1 + N_2)(N_1 + N_2 - 2)n} \quad (8\text{-}27)$$

with n and $N_1 + N_2 - n - 1$ degrees of freedom. The quantity T^2 is the generalization of Student's t-test derived by Hotelling (1931). The quantity D^2 is the square of the vector of differences [Eq. (8-15)], N_1 and N_2 refer to the numbers of stimuli classified as R_1 and R_2, and n refers to the number of dimensions of the stimuli considered in the analysis.

The LDF of Eq. (8-23) and (8-26) indicate the relative weighting, as indicated by the subject's classifications of the stimuli, of the two measured stimulus characteristics. They may be used in reproducing the stimulus classifications after determining that critical value of Y, the *cut off value* or *criterion* which best separates stimuli assigned to R_1 from those assigned to R_2. An iterative procedure in reproducing the classifications of Table 8–7 must be followed in determining this critical value. The LDF of Eq. (8-26) works well by following the decision rule: all stimuli for which $Y < 0$ are assigned to R_1.

Where the classifications are made in terms of stimulus characteristics that are unspecified in the analysis, the LDF and associated decision rule will not duplicate well the classifications of the subject.

2. The measure of distance between the means is analogous to the detectability of signal measure (d') of the theory of signal detectability. It is important to note, however, that the distance provided in the LDF methodology is a *directed distance*. The LDF indi-

cates the relative degree to which the subject weighted each of the measurable dimensions of variation in the stimuli. It locates the dimension of variation being judged in a multidimensional space. The d' value of TSD is dimensionless and measures a nondirected distance.

3. Information can be provided about the objectives that the subject was trying to achieve in his judgments. In one of the examples, b_3, a real criterion exists against which to compare the performance of the subject, i.e., either he had seen the stimuli previously or he had not. In this case he could have tried to achieve an *accuracy criterion,* and his performance can be compared with that of an *ideal observer* trying to minimize misclassifications of particular kinds (Swets, 1961*a*).

In the example providing the basis for the computation of the LDFs, Eqs. (8-23) and (8-26), *no accuracy criterion exists* against which to test the accuracy of the subject's classification. The subject classifies the stimuli in terms of a characteristic that does not exist in the stimuli themselves. We know of no physical reason for one stimulus "standing out" more than another. In effect, the subject classifies his experience, and we have no way of knowing whether his classifications represent his experience accurately. This is true also of example b_4, in which subjects are asked to judge the "intelligence" of schematic faces. Hence, we have provided examples of the troubling distinction of Goldiamond (1958) between *accuracy* and *semantic* indicators of perception. It is important to realize that the classification methods described here apply equally well to both types of indicator. The LDF can be highly predictive of the subject's responses (account for what he did) whether an objective accuracy criterion exists or not. In either case the discriminant function describes the way in which the subject combines and evaluates the stimulus dimensions in arriving at his judgments.

4. The classification model underlying the use of the discriminant function has considerable power as a model for perceptual judgment. Rodwan and Hake (1964) showed that in the judgment of schematic faces, judgments of a subject are highly predictable from the appropriate LDF. A particular function is highly stable over time, even in the case where the subject shifts radically the relative proportion of the two types of response. The model assumes that the subject classifies his experiences by doing the equivalent of locating them in multidimensional space so that the distance between the regions corresponding to the two response concepts is maximized. This maximization may be achieved by classifying the stimuli so that between-concept and within-concept correlations among stimulus dimensions are created even where none exist in the stimulus presentations. Even though stimuli represent an orthogonal set in n dimensions, the stimuli, as classified by the subject, will not represent orthogonal subsets. In fact, the maximization can be achieved by creating between-concept and within-concept correlations of opposite sign. This interesting and crucial result can be made explicit by the classification method described.

5. The LDF methodology makes explicit an important distinction between two objectives of the subject in these types of perceptual task. The first of these is the satisfaction of an *accuracy criterion.* The subject acts to achieve the greatest possible number of correct responses. The second possible objective is the satisfaction of a *coherence criterion.* The subject acts to create classes of apparent stimulus states that are as different as possible; i.e., the dispersion of stimuli *within* response classes is as small as possible relative to the variation evident *between* response classes (Rodwan and Hake, 1964). Much research and analysis has been concerned with determining merely how well the subject satisfies the accuracy criterion and has failed to learn the details of how his responses are related to the stimulus values. This is unfortunate. There is good reason to suppose that satisfaction of the coherence criterion is the primary objective of perceiving. Accuracy considerations often only modify behavior determined

by the coherence of the subject's experience and stimulus classifications.

To this point, we have considered stimuli that can be described in terms of variation along more than a single physical dimension. Where a unidimensional stimulus is involved, e.g., case *c*, and two responses categories are used, the methodology of TSD is most useful. The methodology yields the nondirected distance measure d'. This necessarily means that the attribute being judged by the subject is not discoverable. This is a considerable loss because we may compare the performance of the subject with an accuracy criterion only. In most cases the perceptive behavioral scientist is only mildly interested in the accuracy of judgments. He would much rather know in detail what subjects actually are judging. The LDF methodology reveals this in the case where the dimensions along which stimuli vary can be specified.

We have emphasized the single-discriminant-function methodology here because it appears applicable in much perceptual research and because the computations involved are not lengthy. The more powerful methodology is that of *multiple-discriminant analysis*. This is applicable where the subject is asked to use more than two response classes, as in the examples of case *a*. In all such examples analysis may show that more than a single discriminant function is involved. The centroids of the stimuli in each response class would not then be located on a line, and in that case two or more orthogonal discriminant functions would be required to account for the response classes created by the subject. The assumption is that the stimuli, as experienced and classed by the subject, vary significantly along more than a single dimension. Analysis permits the specification of these dimensions as well as the proportion of the judgmental variance accounted for by each. The details of this analysis and useful computer programs are described by Cooley and Lohnes (1962, pp. 116–150).

The task of specifying in detail how the responses of the subject are related to com-

ponent aspects of stimuli has been described also in the framework of multiple correlation by Hursch, Hammond, and Hursch (1964). That analysis permits the specification of the relation between the responses of the subject and components of the stimulus series. The analysis can be quite helpful because it reflects possible real intercorrelations among the components of the stimulus series and their effects upon responses. However, the responses of the subject must be meaningfully quantitative; for that reason, the analysis is more closely related to the analyses described in a later section on perceptual scaling.

The nonmetric case

In these experimental situations the stimuli are discrete and designated in the nominal sense only. They can be classified in terms of the number of ways in which they vary. For example, the subject may be asked to identify a set of six nonsense syllables presented either as positives (black on white) or diapositives and having either three or four letters. These would be considered two-dimensional stimuli.

Analogs of the classification procedures for the metric case exist in terms of the *uncertainty-analysis procedures* described in Garner and McGill (1956), Attneave (1959), and Garner (1962). The important descriptive symbol U has an analogous term in statistics with which students have some familiarity, the variance of a distribution of measures, σ_x^2. A univariate distribution of measures may also be specified in terms of its uncertainty:

$$U = -\sum_{i=1}^{n} p(x_i) \log_2 p(x_i) \quad (8\text{-}28)$$

$$p(x_i) = \frac{N_{x_i}}{N} \quad (8\text{-}29)$$

The quantity U is useful in thinking about our ability to specify in advance the value of an x_i drawn randomly from the distribution. If U is small, the average uncertainty about x_i will be small. If U is large, the uncertainty is large. The maximum value of U is

$-\log_2 (1/n)$, the value of U where all the x_i are equally likely to be chosen.

In the classification situation the responses of the subject form a set of values that we should like to predict. We can compute a U value for these responses and then compute the extent to which this U is reduced if in predicting a response we have certain critical information: some aspect of the stimulus to which the subject is responding, some knowledge concerning the viewing situation, or how far along we are in the trial series. Uncertainty analysis is directly analogous to a description of sources of variance in variance analysis. For example,

$$\sigma_y{}^2 = \sigma_{y\cdot x}{}^2 + r_{y\cdot x}{}^2\sigma_y{}^2 \qquad (8\text{-}30)$$

and $$U(y) = U_x(y) + U(y:x) \qquad (8\text{-}31)$$

are parallel equations. The first shows that the total variance of y, a continuous variable can be partitioned into two parts, $r_{y\cdot x}{}^2\sigma_y{}^2$, that part which represents covariation with x, and $\sigma_{y\cdot x}{}^2$, the average error of estimating y with x constant. Part of the variance of the measure y may be identified with variation in x and part may not. In the second equation the total uncertainty in predicting values is partitioned into a part $U(y:x)$, representing a measure of the contingency or correlation between x and y, and a part $U_x(y)$, the average uncertainty in predicting y with x held constant.

Where a set of stimuli is presented to a subject who is required to respond with one of a set of responses, his performance after many trials can be described in uncertainty-analysis terms. Such analyses differ only in terms of the dimensionality of the stimuli and responses. Table 8-8 presents the analysis in the case of an experiment involving five nonsense syllables to be identified by a subject. Such syllables differ from each other in many ways, but here they are considered to be stimuli differing unidimensionally. Hence, the analysis measures the relationship between this single dimension of variation, the stimuli, and the other single dimension

of variation, the responses. Following the notation of Garner (1962), this relationship is estimated by the contingent uncertainty $U(y:x)$:

$$U(y:x) = U(y) - U_x(y) \qquad (8\text{-}32)$$

This is computed by subtracting the average uncertainty of the response distributions within the columns from the uncertainty of the response distribution (row totals in Table 8-8). The computed value of $U(y:x)$ is 1.1355. This is a value smaller than the maximum possible value 2.322 (possible if all responses were used equally often) and smaller than the maximum possible given the actual use of the responses, 2.2841.

The contingent uncertainty term should be interpreted with some caution. It has, for example, been suggested as a measure of the amount of information about stimulus events that has been transmitted through the subject (Garner and Hake, 1951). This emphasizes the usefulness of the measure when the subject is considered a link in a communication channel. Garner suggests an analogy between contingent uncertainty and a main effect variance in analysis of variance. It is a measure of correlation, but Garner cautions that it measures amount of correlation rather than degree, since it indicates the amount of uncertainty that can be predicted with knowledge of a predictor variable rather than the amount that cannot be predicted.

Two other cautions are in order. One is that $U(y:x)$ is a statistic whose sampling distribution is not completely understood (but see Cronholm, 1963; Miller and Madow, 1954). It is also subject to bias when small numbers of trials are involved, especially when a large number of stimuli and responses are involved. This bias may be corrected statistically (Miller, 1955), but a direct comparison of contingent uncertainties based upon different total numbers of trials and different numbers of stimuli and responses is hazardous.

Secondly, the contingent uncertainty is not a measure of acuity of discrimination, as is d' (detectability of a signal), because it is not

Table 8-8 Illustrative uncertainty analysis.[1]

RESPONSES (y)	SYLLABLES (x) 1	2	3	4	5	Ny_i
1	30	20	10			60
2	10	30	10	N_{yx}		50
3	5		30	25		60
4	5			20	5	30
5				5	45	50
N_x	50	50	50	50	50	250

$$P(y) = \frac{Ny}{N}$$

$$P(y|x) = \frac{Nyx}{Nx}$$

(1) $U(y) = \sum_{i=1}^{5} P(y) \log_2 P(y) = 2.2841$

(2) $U_x(y) = \sum_{x=1}^{5} \sum_{y=1}^{5} P(x)P(y|x) \log_2 P(y|x)$

$= (0.2)(1.5710) + (0.2)(0.9710) + (0.2)(1.3710) + (0.2)(1.3610) + (0.2)(0.4690)$

$= 1.1486$

(3) $U(y:x) = U(y) - U_x(y)$

$= 2.2841 - 1.1486 = 1.1355$

(4) Maximum possible $U(y:x) = \log_2 5 = 2.322$

(5) Maximum possible, given the subject's use of responses $= U(y) = 2.2841$

[1] Five nonsense syllables, symbolized by x, are presented to the subject, who uses five responses in identifying them.

free from the effect of the subject's use of response categories. This is illustrated in Table 8-9. The 2×2 contingency table *i* was constructed by assuming that the subject could discriminate between stimuli *A* and *B* to a degree given by the measure d'. This, plus the assumption that m (the slope) is unity, defines an ROC for the subject. From this ROC a hit-rate value and a false-alarm value were selected. These selections are shown as HR_1 and FAR_1 in Fig. 8-5 and entered as frequencies in subtable i of Table 8-9. We next assume that the subject shifts his criterion of judgment to permit freer use of the response *a*. This shifts his operating point along the ROC and produces the new pair HR_2 and FAR_2. These are entered as frequencies in subtable ii. The computation of $H_a(y:x)$ for subtable i and $H_b(y:x)$ for subtable ii yields two different numerical results. Uncertainty analysis does not correct for response bias to provide a bias-free estimate of the acuity of discrimination. It reflects the *efficiency* as well as the *acuity* of judgments. For example, with equally likely stimuli, responses must be equally likely also to achieve efficient discrimination.

With all these cautions, uncertainty analysis is strongly recommended as a useful tool in the study of perception. It offers a number of advantages.

1. The parallel between the types of analyses possible in uncertainty analysis and those with which we are familiar in variance analysis makes uncertainty analysis extremely valuable as a conceptual tool (Ross, 1962). It permits us to apply the powerful logic used in the metric situations to those involving non-

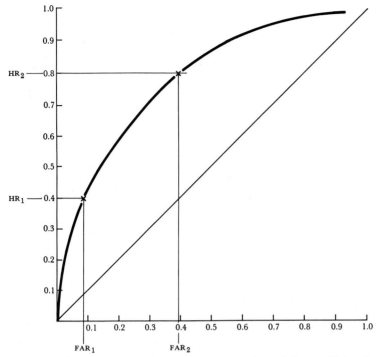

Fig. 8-5   The reviewer operating characteristic (*ROC*) from which values of $HR_1 - FAR_1$ and $HR_2 - FAR_2$ are obtained for Table 8-9.

Table 8-9   Two illustrative uncertainty analyses.

Subtable i

		STIMULI		
		A	B	Σ
RESPONSES	a	HR₁ 20	FAR₁ 4	24
	b	30	46	76
	Σ	50	50	

$$U_a(a:A) = 0.4941 + 0.3009 - (0.5)(0.5288 + 0.4422) - (0.5)(0.2915 + 0.1107)$$
$$= 0.1084$$

Subtable ii

		STIMULI		
		A	B	Σ
RESPONSES	a	HR₂ 40	FAR₂ 19	59
	b	10	31	41
	Σ	50	50	

$$U_b(a:A) = 0.4491 + 0.5274 - (0.5)(0.2575 + 0.4644) - (0.5)(0.5304 + 0.4276)$$
$$= 0.1365$$

Subtable i differs from subtable ii only in the relative use made of the two responses, *a* and *b*.[1]

[1] The cell entries in the two subtables reflect the same acuity of judgment, as measured by *d'*. Uncertainty analysis yields two results.

metric stimuli and responses. Perceptual responses are often nonmetric in that they are bounded concepts, and stimuli often are nonmetric because we do not know the metric involved in their adequate description.

2. The nonmetric characteristics of the analysis permit greater generality. We may directly compare responses to stimuli ordered on a metric with responses to stimuli that are not. Where possible the subject may prefer to order his responses to reflect an ordered relation among the stimuli, or he may assign responses to stimuli according to some private code. The same degree of relationship can be measured in either case. The generality of the analysis results from the fact that the only characteristic of a stimulus reflected in the analysis is its surprise value, the inverse of its probability of occurrence. Hence, all stimuli are equivalent so long as their surprise values are equivalent.

3. Uncertainty analysis has provided new concepts and new ways of describing the performance of the perceiver. One obvious example is the concept of 'channel capacity, which suggests that some upper limit exists to the amount of information that can be processed by the human observer. This capacity has been demonstrated because of the generality of the analysis. It has been possible to measure channel capacities for the various modalities and for the dimensionality of stimulation by use of a single measure. This single measure is the contingent uncertainty. For the case of a situation like that in Table 8-8, for example, the size of $U(y:x)$ is limited by the size of $U(y)$. The latter can be increased by increasing the number of stimuli. Even though the number of permissible response categories is increased along with the stimuli, these increases most probably will not result in an appreciable increase in $U(y:x)$. The fact that $U(y:x)$ already is less than $U(y)$ and $U(x)$ indicates that the subject is operating somewhere near his capacity to perform this discriminative task. This capacity remains unchanged to an impressive degree even when the total range of stimuli (and differences existing among stimuli) is increased (Garner,

1962, pp. 63–75). Thus, channel capacity measures on aspect of the subject different from simple discriminative acuity.

In Table 8-10 the nonsense syllables of Table 8-8 were presented as black letters on a white background or as white letters on a black background, and the subject was again asked to identify each as it was presented. For the sake of simplicity of computation and presentation only, the set of syllables has been reduced from five to two. Following the analogy with analysis of variance, we now have two orthogonal independent variables x and w. The analysis should contain two main effect uncertainties $U(y:x)$ and $U(y:w)$ and an interaction term $U(\overline{wxy})$. This breakdown is shown in line (8) of the table. The contingent uncertainty $U(y:wx)$, our ability to predict y from w and x, is accounted for mainly by our ability to predict y from knowledge of x alone, $U(y:x)$. The amount of uncertainty of y that is predictable from unique combinations of x and w, $U(\overline{wxy})$, or from knowledge of w alone, $U(y:w)$, is quite small.

Negative interaction terms occur at times in these analyses and provide a surprising result for investigators accustomed to viewing negative terms as the result of computational errors. Garner and McGill (1956) show that negative interaction terms are possible in both uncertainty analysis and analysis of variance under certain conditions, namely, in the case where predictor variables (independent variables) are nonorthogonal (correlated). This does not happen often, especially in the case of analysis of variance, because usually great care is taken to provide orthogonal independent variables.

There are many important situations in which we cannot control predictor variables and produce this orthogonality. Table 8-11 illustrates an analysis for a case in which the set of predictor variables is highly likely to be nonorthogonal. The dependent variable y is the subject's dichotomous response. We are wondering here about the relationship between this response and his previous responses; i.e., does knowledge of his response on trial

Table 8-10   Illustrative uncertainty analysis.[1]

(a)							(b)				(c)			
	W_1			W_2										
	X_1	X_2	N_{N1Y}	X_1	X_2	N_{W2Y}	N_Y		X_1	X_2	N_Y		W_1	W_2	N_Y
Y_1	40	20	60	45	10	55	115	Y_1	85	30	115	Y_1	60	55	115
Y_2	10	30	40	5	40	45	85	Y_2	15	70	85	Y_2	40	45	85
N_{WX}	50	50	100	50	50	100	200	N_X	100	100	200	N_W	100	100	200

$$(1) \quad U(y{:}x) = U(y) - U_x(y)$$
$$= 0.9859 - 0.7456 = 0.2403$$
$$(2) \quad U(y{:}w) = U(y) - U_w(y) = 0.9859 - 0.9819$$
$$= 0.0040$$
$$(3) \quad U_{wx}(y) = \sum_{wxy} p(wx)p(y/wx)\,\log_2 p(y/wx) = 0.7210$$
$$(4) \quad U_w(y{:}x) = p(w_1)U_{w1}(y{:}x) + p(w_2)U_{w2}(y{:}x)$$
$$= p(w_1)[U_{w1x}(y) - U_{w1x}(y)] + p(w_2)[U_{w2}(y) - U_{w2x}(y)]$$
$$= (0.5)(0.1245) + (0.5)(0.3973) = 0.2609$$
$$(5) \quad U(\overline{wxy}) = U_w(y{:}x) - U(y{:}x) = 0.2609 - 0.2403 = 0.0206$$
$$(6) \quad U(y{:}wx) = U(y) - U_{wx}(y) = 0.2649$$
$$(7) \qquad\qquad = U(y{:}w) + U_w(y{:}x) = 0.2649$$
$$(8) \qquad\qquad = U(y{:}x) + U(y{:}w) + U(\overline{wxy}) = 0.2649$$

[1] Two nonsense syllables X_1 and X_2 are presented as black on white (W_1) or as white on black (W_2). The subject identifies the syllables using two responses, Y_1 and Y_2.

$n - 2$ and on trial $n - 1$ enable us to predict his response on trial n? The predictor variables are w, his response on trial $n - 2$, and x, his response on trial $n - 1$. Because we cannot control these predictor variables w and x, they are likely not to be orthogonal, and this is the case in Table 8-11, as shown in subtable d^1. As indicated, the analysis includes a sizable interaction term $U(\overline{wxy})$, and this term is negative. This warns that the relatively high relationships between x and y, $U(y{:}x)$, and between y and w, $U(y{:}w)$, are partially due to the intercorrelations between x and w. It warns of duplication of predictive power in $U(y{:}x)$ and $U(y{:}w)$, which total 1.0620, and corrects $U(y{:}wx)$ for this duplication. Our total ability to predict y from knowledge of the preceding two responses is just slightly better than our ability to predict y from knowledge of either x or w alone, $U(y{:}wx) = 0.8647$.

[1] We consider here only nonoverlapping triplets of trials. The response on trial 3 is predicted from responses on trials 1 and 2; the response on trial 6 is predicted from responses on trials 4 and 5,

The usefulness of uncertainty analysis may be judged from the data discussed by two important books dealing with the application of information theory to psychological topics, Attneave (1959) and Garner (1962). Its usefulness is indicated by the contributions made to such traditional areas as sensory action as well as by its new contributions: the consideration of language as a perceptual stimulus, the specification of the uncertainty of the subject about stimulation as a variable related to his response, and the meaningful separation of the effects of stimulus uncertainty and response uncertainty. Important contributions have been made in spite of the drawbacks considered above.

Among these drawbacks, perhaps the student will consider the most important to be the lack of obvious, appropriate statistical tests. Uncertainty analysis provides only a separation of total uncertainty into com-

etc. The analysis presented is questionable in the case of overlapping triplets of trials, where responses are used as both predicting and predicted variables (Binder and Wolin, 1964).

Table 8-11   Illustration of a negative interaction in uncertainty analysis.[1]

(a)

	w_1			w_2	
	x_1	x_2		x_1	x_2
y_1	85	5	y_1	5	5
y_2	5	5	y_2	5	85

(b)

	w_1	w_2
y_1	90	10
y_2	10	90

(c)

	x_1	x_2
y_1	90	10
y_2	10	90

(d)

	w_1	w_2
x_1	90	10
x_2	10	90

Then:

(1) $U(y:wx) = U(y:w) + U(y:x) + U(\overline{wxy})$

(2) $U(y:w) = U(y) - U_w(y) = 1.0000 - (0.3322 + 0.1368) = 0.5310$

(3) $U(y:x) = U(y) - U_x(y) = 1.0000 - (0.3322 + 0.1368) = 0.5310$

(4) $U(\overline{wxy}) = \frac{1}{2}[U_{w1}(y) - U_{w1x}(y)] + \frac{1}{2}[U_{w2}(y) - U_{w2x}(y)] - U(y:x)$

$= \frac{1}{2}[1.0000 - 0.6632] + \frac{1}{2}[1.0000 - 0.6632] - 0.5310$

$= 0.1682 + 0.1682 - 0.5310 = -0.1946$

(5) $U(y:wx) = 0.5310 + 0.5310 - 0.1946 = 0.8674$

[1] $U(y:wx)$ represents our uncertainty in predicting the subject's response y when we know his preceding response x and the response w preceding x.

ponents without accompanying tests analogous to those provided in an automatic, cookbook fashion in analysis of variance. In answer to this complaint we can only point out that this nonmetric analysis has provided researchers with a large amount of useful information. Other important means of testing the stability of a result exist, such as efforts to replicate experiments and the use of care in experimental design to produce clear-cut results uncontaminated by uncontrolled factors. The former provides the most impressive demonstration of the stability of an experimental result; and without the latter, the power of inferential statistical testing is lost anyway.

A shift in approach

This completes the consideration of the general classification procedures. Some of these are suggested to be applicable to the confusion matrix of Table 8-3. Since the data

result from the use of stimuli for which there exists no descriptive metric (the stimuli consist of a square, a circle, a diamond, and a triangle) and the responses are discrete names, the nonmetric procedures are applicable. If the data had resulted from the use of stimuli related by a metric (e.g., a set of ellipses) and the responses were discrete, the metric procedures could be made applicable. But even the data of Table 8-3, as they now exist, imply a more powerful approach than is usually applied. This implication involves the use of the numbers in the cells of the table as indirect measures of the distances separating the stimuli as they could be plotted in a hypothetical space; and this is a crucial shift of emphasis or approach, a shift implied also by the consideration of the classification procedures.

The traditional psychophysical approach consists in attempts to measure thresholds. This approach is usually involved in the *level of perceiving* and *individual threshold* situations described earlier. In the case of the latter situation what is precisely desired for each stimulus is that duration of view at which it can be recognized with some specified degree of accuracy. The contrasting approach, that of classification procedures, suggests that the measurement of thresholds in this situation is an improbable goal. What can be achieved instead is knowledge of the extent to which the stimuli in the set are separable or discriminable under a given set of viewing conditions. In the nonmetric case we can obtain a single number that indicates the ability of the subject to classify the stimuli in unique bins or categories. In the metric case we obtain distance measures. i.e., measures of the separation between means of all the stimuli placed in distinct response categories. These measures of the *separability of the stimuli* under a given set of viewing conditions should be one of the legitimate goals of recognition studies of the type described. The other goal is *the determination of what it is that the subject is judging,* i.e., *the attribute of judgment.* The metric classification procedures can provide this information by showing how the subject weighted the physical dimensions of the stimuli, relatively, in making his classifications.

In brief, the shift in approach advocated here is away from dubious threshold-measuring attempts in the study of recognition behavior and toward the goals and procedures of multidimensional scaling. These are considered in the next section.

THE ROLE OF SCALING IN THE STUDY OF RECOGNITION

Traditional considerations of scaling topics usually involve cases where the responses of the subject have a metric and the relations between values of stimulation and values of response are specified in detail. The relevance of scaling topics to more general problems of recognition may be made more pointed by consideration of some work of Helm and Tucker (1962), who were interested in the study of individual differences in color recog-

nition. A test for color blindness, the Hardy, Rand, and Rittler pseudoisochromatic charts (American Optical Co.), was used to sort a set of subjects into "normals" and "color-weak" individuals. This was a scaling operation that scaled subjects with respect to their ability to detect differences in color plates. Relative ability to detect differences permits color-weak subjects to be sorted into crude classifications; normals all fall in the same class. Helm and Tucker attempted a more precise scaling of the subjects in terms of their judgments of the degrees of dissimilarities existing among ten stimuli, judged three at a time. Subjects actually located three colored chips on a neutral gray background so that the physical distances among the chips represented the dissimilarities apparently existing among them.

The analysis of these distances yielded corresponding scaled distance values for all possible pairings of the 10 chips, and the resulting scaled distances existed in a two-dimensional space. In this space the points representing stimuli were located roughly on a circle, for normal subjects. For color-deficient subjects, the configuration of points in the space departed from circularity.

A most important result was the ability of the procedures to scale all subjects, including the "normals." Figure 8-6 illustrates this scaling for normal (closed circles) and color-deficient (open circles) subjects. Subjects are plotted with respect to two factors that the judgments of all had in common, to some degree at least. The color-deficient individuals varied from minor deficiency (point B-4) to marked deficiency (point B-1) in detecting differences among the chips. The normals also show marked variation. This variation, however, is a different sort than that existing among the color-deficient subjects, whose judgments tended to be more nearly one-dimensional. The normals differed in the degree of over- or underestimation at larger distances relative to small. Thus, a scaling procedure applied to individuals revealed marked variation in the recognition of hue

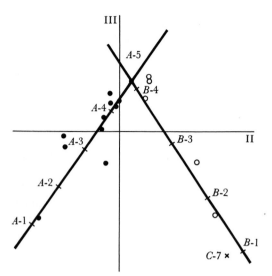

Fig. 8-6 The plotting of normal observers (filled circles) and color-weak observers (open circles) with respect to two factors which the judgments of all observers (open circles) had in common. (*From Helm and Tucker, 1962.*)

differences, this variation being different among normals and color-deficient subjects.

There is much of value to the student of perceptual recognition in the scaling literature (Torgerson, 1958). This chapter can do little more than sketch in this value.

Scaling in perception, as elsewhere, has two concerns: (1) the characteristics of a *sub-jective space model* in which stimuli can be represented by points and (2) the basis upon which apparent differences among the stimuli can be related to distances among the points in the space model. If we think of stimuli as being located perceptually in a subjective space, with the dimensionality of the space and distances among stimuli located in it corresponding to the personal characteristics of stimuli, it is important to be concerned with the characteristics of the space.

Subjective space models

It appears most natural and useful to conceive of a spatial model for the judged relations among stimuli. This has long been a useful conceptual tool in understanding the judged relations among colors. Figure 8-7

gives an example of a subjective space illustrating the relations among colors as they might have been experienced by an observer in a particular situation. The colors of the spectrum, specified by wavelength, have been matched by a mixture of three primary wavelengths. In the figure the spectral colors are located in terms of the *relative* amounts of the three primaries required to produce a match in hue, saturation, and brightness.[1] Since the amount of the primaries required is specified relatively, we plot the spectral colors in a plane. The relative amounts of all three primaries always add to unity. Given the relative amounts of the red and green primaries, we can easily determine the relative amount of blue required for the match.

The spatial model of Fig. 8-7 represents only two characteristics of perceived color, hue, and saturation. It is, however, a powerful and useful model. Location in the plane of the figure represents the hue and purity aspects of color experience. Distances among points in the plane represent apparent differences among stimuli.

The representation of colored stimuli in terms of a spatial model is now quite familiar to us all, and we tend to lose sight of much of the thinking and questioning that led to the particular model derived. In fact, we tend not to question the crucial characteristics of the model. These characteristics include the dimensionality of the space and the type of geometric space involved.

The fact that colors may be located in three-dimensional space must depend upon relations among colored stimuli as experienced by an observer. In the case of Fig. 8-7, the dimensionality of the space is determined by the crucial fact that just three numbers will specify any color in this system. Two numbers will suffice when the *amount* aspect of experience is ruled out, as in Fig. 8-7.

When dealing with many other types of

---

[1] Negative values occur when it is necessary to add an amount of a primary to the spectral color in order to produce a match between that color and the mixture of primaries.

stimulation we lack the ability to match stimuli by mixtures of basic ingredients in the same way. The dimensionality of the space in which the stimuli can be represented is then derived from distance relations among the stimuli evident in the judgments of subjects. These distance relations could be obtained in a rather direct fashion. For example, subjects could be asked to actually locate stimulus objects, taken three at a time, on a surface so that their apparent similarities are represented by their distances apart on the surface. This was the technique described for the work of Helm and Tucker (1962). Their stimuli were designed to differ only in terms of the hue of the colored surfaces of tiles; the reflectances and the saturation of the surfaces were required to be equal. If these requirements were met in the manufacture of the tiles, the distance relations exhibited by the way in which the subjects located the tiles on a surface should reflect this. That is, the distance relations among the stimulus tiles should be consistent with the hypothesis that the stimuli can be represented by points arranged in a rough circle in a plane.

For any one subject the methodology provides $n(n-1)/2$ independently determined distances among the tiles. This number is 45 for the case of the 10 tiles used. If we consider only the distances between a stimulus i and the other nine tiles, we can derive a matrix of numbers arranged in nine columns and nine rows. Each of these numbers, elements of the matrix, is derived from the physical distances existing between a particular tile i and the other two members of a triad as positioned by the subject. Each element is the scalar product of vectors from i to the other stimuli in a triad. A matrix of such numbers, B, can be formed for each tile.

Each matrix will provide the following crucial information about the judgments of the tiles: (1) If the matrix B is positive semidefinite, then the distances among the stimuli are consistent with the hypothesis that the stimuli can be represented by points in a real, Euclidean space. (2) The number of positive characteristic roots of B indicates the number

of dimensions in this space necessary to account for the interpoint distances represented and to specify each point in the space. (3) The positive semidefinite matrix B may be factored to obtain another matrix in which the elements represent the coordinates of the points on orthogonal coordinate axes whose origin corresponds to point i.

This general methodology as applied by Helm and Tucker indicated that two dimensions were required to account for distances among the tiles within the judgments of each subject. The plotting of the stimulus points in the Euclidean plane defined by two orthogonal dimensions is represented in Fig. 8-8 for two "ideal" normal subjects (the points A-1 and A-4 in Fig. 8-6) and two "ideal" color-deficient subjects (points B-1 and B-4 in Fig. 8-6). The points representing stimulus tiles appear to be located with respect to hue (angular location around the origin) and saturation (distance from the origin). The fact that the judgments are adequately accounted for by location of the points in two dimensions indicates that the tiles were equal in lightness (value) and were not judged in terms of that

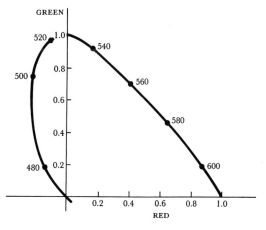

Fig. 8-7 **Plotting of monochromatic wavelengths of light in terms of relative amount of red, green, and blue primaries required to match them. Negative values mean that an amount of a primary was added to the monochromatic wavelength to produce a match. The data are fictitious and approximate matches for a normal observer.**

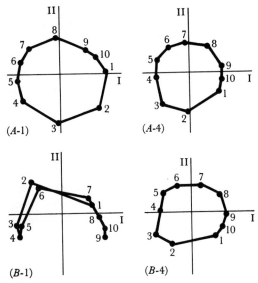

(A-1)   (A-4)   (B-1)   (B-4)

Fig. 8-8   The plotting of the stimulus points in a plane defined by two orthogonal dimensions for two "ideal" normal subjects (the points A-1 and A-4 in Fig. 8-6) and for two "ideal" color-deficient subjects (the points B-1 and B-4 in Fig. 8-6).

experimenter. In much of traditional scaling in the sensory and perceptual areas of research, an underlying unidimensional scale is assumed. The subject's manipulation of a set of stimuli or his responses to them are used to devise a line on which the stimuli are represented by points. Over the years we have developed a number of methods to achieve this result. These methods and their underlying assumptions are presented in Table 8-12. They follow, in part, the classification of Torgerson (1958). All except the comparison methods, in their usual application, involve instructions to the subject that lead him to assume that the stimuli can be ordered or related unidimensionally.

In the comparison methods, because the subject is asked normally to compare each stimulus with every other one or to compare differences existing within all possible pairs, a result can be obtained that rules out a unidimensional scale. This occurs where the scaled distances separating stimuli are not consistent with the hypothesis that the stimuli can be represented by points on a line. This is illustrated in some detail by simple examples in Dember (1960, pp. 78–91).

Many scaling attempts in the perceptual area do not involve complete sets of comparisons of all stimuli, and in many the attribute of judgment is an assumption only. For example, a familiarity scale has been established for nonsense words (Noble, 1954). Subjects were asked to judge the familiarity of stimuli differing in the frequency at which they had been seen previously. A categorical judgment method, Attneave's method of graded dichotomies (1949), was used in which the subject rated the familiarity of each word as he saw it. In this case there was little chance for anything but a unidimensional scale to result, and little chance also to learn about stimulus characteristics other than frequency of prior seeing that might be related to the judgments.

Certainly, at least in the early stages of scaling studies, much can be gained by not restricting responses to particular, arbitrary

third possible color dimension. The result is essentially what the traditional psychophysical approaches to the study of color perception would predict. There are, however, a number of distinct and important advantages to this multidimensional scaling approach.

1. The methodology is generally applicable to cases where stimuli are much less well understood: e.g., the development of appropriate perceptual space models for judgments of pictorial patterns; judgments of the similarity of auditory words and voices; judgments of the familiarity of representative and nonsense forms; judgments of the similarity of forms tilted and rotated in real space; and any of the many topics of interest in the perceptual area of research. In each case the methodology can yield a perceptual space model of value in understanding the perceptual world of the observer.

2. The dimensions of stimulation important in determining the judgments of the subject are yielded by analysis rather than being assumed or imposed arbitrarily by the

names, e.g., pitch, complexity, familiarity, or tilt; by describing as adequately as possible all the physical dimensions along which stimuli vary; and by the use of one of the complete comparative methods. Along with this methodology, the investigator must consider the perceptual space model adequate to account for the results.

3. The methodology includes a detailed study of individual differences, which are often of interest. Generally, experimental results tend to hide such differences. This is due to the fact that data from many subjects are grouped to provide a more clean or stable result, or data are reported for each of a very small set of subjects. We have described how the techniques of Helm and Tucker can provide perceptual space models for individuals in the case of color vision. A powerful advance in methodology was provided by their ability to specify models for "ideal observers;" i.e., persons not actually studied who epitomize a particularly interesting type of observer making judgments within the schema provided by the space model, e.g., the "ideal" stimulus maps of Fig. 8-8.

The inclusion of individual differences in perceptual space models represents the contribution of Tucker and Messick (1963). The general methodology leading to the specification of perceptual space models may be found in Torgerson (1958). Although Helm and Tucker applied the methodology to the case where observers positioned stimuli on a real surface, the methodology applies as well to other judgmental techniques, e.g., judging which of two stimuli is more similar to a third stimulus (Torgerson, 1958, pp. 280–290), rating the similarity between members of pairs of stimuli on a rating scale (Attneave, 1957), or using intrusion errors in identification learning as measures of similarity (Shepard, 1958).

Subjective distance models

A perceptual space model, explicitly described, relates the distances among points representing stimuli in a subjective space to

data measures relating actual stimulus objects. In the Helm and Tucker data, these measures were the physical distances separating the tiles after the subject had adjusted each triad of stimuli to his satisfaction. The distances were analyzed to obtain the appropriate space model in which the stimulus points and their distances apart could be represented.

In many cases the measures relating stimulus objects are not direct distance measures themselves, and a distance model relating these measures to interpoint distances in the space model must be specified. The selection of an appropriate distance model was an arbitrary affair prior to the work of Shepard. A traditional distance model is supplied by the law of comparative judgment, which relates comparative judgments to distance by reference to the normal distribution function.

Torgerson provides an example (1958, pp. 280–290) involving the method of triads in which stimuli are presented to the subject in sets of three. For each set, the subject must state which of two stimuli is more similar to the third. In the complete method each stimulus is compared with every possible pair of stimuli, and these comparisons provide proportions of occasions on which a stimulus i is judged more similar to stimulus j than to stimulus k. These proportions are assumed to be a function of the distances between i and j and between i and k. Specifically, they are assumed to be areas under sections of the normal curve.

In another case (Shepard, 1958) distance measures were derived from intrusion errors in a paired-associate learning experiment. A proximity measure s_{ij} was derived from

$$s_{ij}^2 = \frac{P(j|i)P(i|j)}{P(i|i)P(j|j)} \qquad (8\text{-}33)$$

in which, for example, $P(j|i)$ is the conditional probability that response j will be given to stimulus i. These proximity measures were then assumed to be related to interpoint distances in a spatial model by an exponential decay function.

Table 8-12   The scaling methods.

Method	Description	Assumptions	Procedures
Subjective estimate	The subject assigns response labels to stimuli such that the responses represent subjective scale values for the stimuli.	The response is the scale value for a stimulus on a linear attribute scale.	Absolute judgment method; some means of obtaining the average response for each stimulus.
Fractionation	(a) The subject reports the subjective ratio that two stimuli represent. (b) He adjusts one of two stimuli to produce a given subjective ratio.	The subject is able to perceive directly the magnitude of "sense ratios."	Absolute or adjustment methods and then either (a) the ratio estimates are combined to provide scale values for stimuli, or (b) a psychophysical magnitude function is obtained by curve-fitting methods.
Equisection	(a) The subject adjusts stimuli to space them equally in terms of subjective scale value. (b) He locates stimuli spatially so that physical distances represent differences in subjective scale value.	The subject is able to perceive directly the magnitude of "sense distances."	Method of adjustment followed by curve fitting techniques to relate the perceived "sense distances" to the stimuli as specified physically.
Differential sensitivity	A psychophysical method is applied to obtain differential sensitivity thresholds at many points along the range of stimulus variation.	Any pair of stimulus values that are just noticeably different are separated by a distance D on a sensory subjective scale. This distance D is the same for all JND's measured in the same way.	Differential sensitivity thresholds (DLs) are measured by a psychophysical method and a function relating the DLs to stimulus values is obtained. The integral of this function is the scale relating "subjective distance" between stimulus values to the difference in physical values.

The choice of an appropriate distance model is crucial. The choice can influence the spatial model resulting from the application of the methodology of the previous section. In particular the dimensionality of the model can be determined by this choice.

Computer methodology (Shepard, 1962a, 1962b) is now available to achieve three objectives simultaneously, by using numbers relating stimulus objects, which are an unknown, monotonic function of distance in an unknown space model. The basic requirement is that the rank order of the numbers relating stimuli be the inverse of the rank order of the interpoint distances among points representing the stimuli in the space model. An iterative computer method is followed to produce simultaneously (1) the optimum function relating the original data numbers to distance in a spatial model, (2) the minimum number of dimensions in a Euclidean space model required to permit distances in the model to be monotonically related to the original data numbers, and (3) the set of orthog-

Table 8-12 (continued)

Method	Description	Assumptions	Procedures
Paired comparison	Stimulus values are presented in sets to the subject, who indicates which member of the set exceeds with respect to the attribute being judged.	The law of comparative judgment: the momentary subjective difference x_{jk} separating stimulus j and stimulus k is a normally distributed variate. The first moment of this distribution is the scale distance between j and k measured in standard deviation units.	The number of times each stimulus is judged to exceed every other stimulus is obtained by the paired-comparison method. The tabled unit normal curve and simplifying assumptions are used to derive corresponding scale distances.
Categorical judgment	Stimulus values are presented singly to the subject, who sorts them into categories or identifies each with a categorical response.	The subjective experience associated with each stimulus value is a normally distributed variate. Misclassification of stimuli arise because of the overlap of these distributions. In assigning a stimulus to a category the subject relates his experience to subjective "category boundaries" or "cutoffs" and follows a stable set of decision rules.	Absolute judgment method yields a confusion matrix indicating the number of times each stimulus was assigned to each response category. Normal curve methodology and simplifying assumptions are used to transform misclassifications to scale distances separating stimuli.
Comparative	Stimulus values are presented in sets to the subject, who ranks them with respect to his own preference.	Preferences of subjects can be accounted for by assuming an underlying attribute which exists in Euclidean space. Subjects and stimuli are represented in the space, the distances between a subject and the stimuli are proportional to the extent of his preferences for each stimulus.	Ranking methods and then the "unfolding" procedures.

onal coordinates for the points representing stimuli in this minimum space.

Two examples (Shepard, 1962b) involving perceptual recognition are included here because of the importance of the method. In the first example, subjects were required to respond with appropriate verbal responses to each of a small set of stimuli. One set of stimuli consisted of nine black circles differing in size. Another set consisted of nine circles differing only in lightness and saturation with hue and size held constant. The data for the analysis were provided by the $P(j|i)$, that is, the conditional probabilities that response j is given to stimulus i. Figure 8-9 presents the unidimensional spatial model accounting for responses to the black circles. A typical scale resulted showing the traditional "end-anchoring" effect (Volkmann and Engen, 1961). Figure 8-10 illustrates the two-dimensional space accounting for responses to the colored circles.

Figure 8-11 illustrates the function that related the original conditional probabilities to

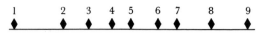

Fig. 8-9 The unidimensional spatial model accounting for responses to the black circles. (*From Shepard*, 1962b.)

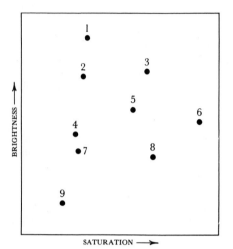

Fig. 8-10 The two-dimensional spatial model accounting for responses to the colored circles. (*From Shepard,* 1962b.)

distance in the space model for both the unidimensional model and the two-dimensional model. Although the black circles and the colored circles are mapped in different perceptual space models, the function relating distance in the models to the conditional response probabilities was identical for the two space models.

In the second example, Shepard (1962b) applied the methodology to judgments of facial expression. The data were from Abelson and Sermat (1962). Subjects saw two photographs at a time (Lightfoot series from Engen, Levy, and Schlosberg, 1957) and were required to judge their dissimilarity in a nine-step response scale. For purposes of analysis the response numbers were reversed so that "one" represented low judged similarity and "nine" high similarity. The Shepard methodology was then applied to these numbers. Figure 8-12 illustrates the resulting location of the points representing photographs in an adequate two-dimensional space (Axis I:

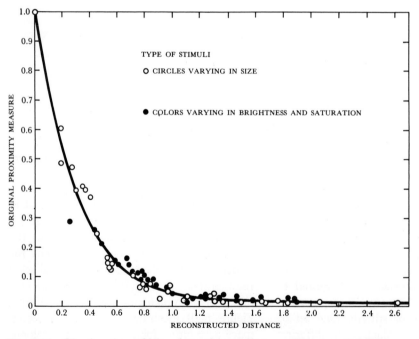

Fig. 8-11 The function which relates the original conditional probabilities to distance in the space model for both the unidimensional model (Fig. 8-9) and the two-dimensional model (Fig. 8-10). (*The figure is taken from Shepard,* 1962b.)

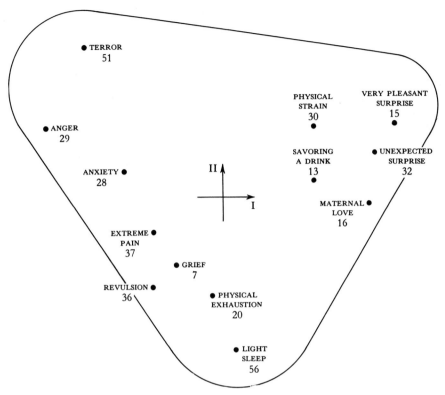

Fig. 8-12 The point locations accounting for judgments of facial expression.
(*From Shepard, 1962b.*)

pleasantness-unpleasantness; Axis II: activity-passivity). This is the current status of a series of attempts to scale facial expression, a series that recapitulates the development of multidimensional scaling methods (Hake, 1967).

Euclidean and non-Euclidean space

The discussion of perceptual space models has assumed that we are dealing in all cases with Euclidean space in which the interpoint distances are related as they are in the geometry with which we are most familiar. A straight line is the shortest distance between points, and the distance d_{ab} between two points in a plane, for example, is given by

$$d_{ab} = [(a_{i.} - b_{i.})^2 + (a_{.j} - b_{.j})^2]^{\frac{1}{2}} \quad (8\text{-}34)$$

where the subscripts refer to the projections of the points a and b on the orthogonal axes;

i.e., the i and j are the x and y coordinates, respectively, of a and b.

Some judgments may not locate stimulus points in such a space. Attneave (1950) reported a city-block model that best fits the perceived similarity of triangles. In this model distances are measured as they might be in the downtown section of a large city. In Chicago, for example, the distance between the Art Institute and the La Salle Street Station is nine blocks; i.e., to go to the station, go two blocks south and seven blocks west. We cannot go along the diagonal distance, $(2^2 + 7^2)^{\frac{1}{2}}$ blocks. Torgerson (1958) suggests the general applicability of this model in all cases where the dimensions of variation in the stimulus objects are obvious, compelling, and judged separately in an additive fashion: "Stimulus A differs from stimulus B by s units of apparent size and c units of saturation in color. Therefore, stimulus A differs from stimulus B by s *plus* c units." This is a different judgmental system from that in which the s units of size and c units of saturation lead to a judgmental difference less than $(c + s)$ in magnitude, as in the Euclidean model. Many types of schemes for combining the c and s units are possible, and the particular scheme applying in a particular case is an important aspect of what we should like to know about perceptual judgments. Fortunately, most judgmental schemes can conform to the Euclidean model. A close examination of Attneave's evidence revealed no real support even there for the city-block model (Hake, 1967). In most cases, dimensions of stimulus variation are not judged and combined separately, as the city-block model requires; instead, they seem to be perceived together and judged on a decision axis oriented in Euclidean space. This permits us to apply powerful methods to the understanding of perceptual recognition and judgment.

Judgments may fail to satisfy other requirements of Euclidean space. The very elegant Luneberg model for perception of location and distance of points in real space is non-Euclidean (Koch, 1959, pp. 395–426). Perhaps many other adequate perceptual space models may be so also. Fortunately, many such models can be considered Euclidean locally, including the Luneberg model, and are adequately treated as such unless very large differences among stimulus values are being considered.

"Similarity" as a judgment

The judgment of the similarity of stimuli is a ubiquitous subject for study in multidimensional scaling and is treated as though it were potentially a more general and less biased case of more specific judgments, such as complexity, loudness, or clearness. The supposition is that in judging the similarity of stimulus objects, the observer judges their substitutibility or equivalence (Shepard, 1962a). This provides a measure of the proximity of stimulus objects analogous to their distance or closeness in the subjective space model.

Earlier we discussed the dangers of biasing the responses of the subject and thereby hiding information about the nature of his judgments. In this section, we are more positive in recommending judgments of similarity or equivalence. Given these judgments, the investigator may learn the dimensions along which stimulus objects appear to vary in being more and less similar, or equivalent, for the observer. Thus, the similarity of stimuli can be used as a general proximity measure of a higher order than that provided by the use of more specific response names. The nature of the ways in which stimuli are judged equivalent (loudness? intelligence? hue? size?) should be determined *by analysis* and should not determine the analysis.

Multidimensional scaling and factor analysis

The scaling methodology discussed has a great deal in common with factor analysis. In the latter, the measures analyzed are correlations indicating relatedness rather than proximity measures. The result, however, is similar, namely, the description of a set of dimensions and spatial coordinates. Factor analysis has provided a useful methodology in the perceptual area, although the results of this work have been largely ignored. Psychologists like to be concerned with perceptual theory. We like our theories to be simple and to treat perception as though it were a unitary function or trait. Factor analyses of perceptual performance have indicated this to be a highly complex affair (Guilford, 1947; Roff, 1952; Thurstone, 1944). Among the perceptual factors listed as important are closure, reaction time, perceptual speed, judgmental speed, directional thinking, length perception, sequential perception, complex reaction time, perception through camouflage, visual memory, paired-associates memory, reproductive memory, and memory for name-object associations. These aspects are relatively important or unimportant, depending upon the nature of the perceptual task involved.

Factor analysis has been important also in more specific applications. For example, in the work of Hochberg and Brooks (1960), three factors accounted for judgments of depth in two-dimensional drawings. These were complexity of stimuli (number of angles), continuity of stimulus elements (number of continuous line segments), and symmetry (number of different angles divided by total number of angles) of the stimuli. In another traditional perceptual area Jenkin and Hyman factor analyzed size-distance judgments made under analytical (perspective size) and under objective (real size) instructions (1959). Analysis indicated that judgments made under the two attitudes were independent of each other. One of these factors appeared to be important in situations in which the subject must use judgments of one dimension of variation to indicate apparent variation in two or more (Hake, 1967). This finding is of great interest and comes late in the history of the problem area. Its tardiness may be attributed to our disinclination to apply really adequate methodology and systems of analysis to deserving problems.

MEASURING PERCEPTUAL RECOGNITION

The discussion of scaling topics has treated perceptual recognition very broadly. This chapter has not limited itself to the restricted meaning of the term: the reexperiencing of a stimulus object or the recognition of the object as something seen previously. The term has no such specific and restricted definition in the perceptual literature. Theories of perceptual recognition (Bartlett, 1932; Woods, 1915) refer to many possible processes, including the following: (1) Recognition occurs when an immediate perceptual pattern is compared with a revived percept or image, and a judgment of likeness is possible. (2) There is no necessary comparison and no explicit judgment, but the revived image fuses with the immediately perceived pattern. This process is called *pair formation*. (3) Neither comparison nor fusion occurs. Instead, a configuration seen again evokes an affective response, a feeling of familarity, and this feeling constitutes recognition. (4) Recognition is not a judgment, fusion, or feeling, but rather an immediate intellectual appreciation or knowledge that a perceived configuration has been seen before or is similar to one seen before. (5) Recognition occurs when the observer is aware of a relation between what he sees and something retained.

It is clear that the term *recognition* has rather broad meaning as a theoretical concept. It is used to describe the case where an observer experiences a stimulus object as an object that has occurred before in his experience. The term also means that a recognized stimulus pattern is accepted as being an example of a class of patterns seen before and perhaps related in particular ways to other examples of the class seen previously. A subject shows recognition behavior when he categorizes colored stimulus objects according to their apparent color characteristics or when he gives a set of proximity estimates for a set of complex plane figures. He locates the stimulus objects in a perceptual space model (experiential space), and this is recognition.

One of the possible characteristics of the stimuli being judged is the number of times the subject had seen each object previously. If he responds to this stimulus characteristic, the analysis will indicate that one of the dimensions of the perceptual space model corresponds to frequency of prior seeing. We should expect the frequency variable to be related to almost any type of judgment, and we should also expect a judgment of frequency of prior seeing, or familiarity, to be related to many other physical characteristics of the stimulus object (Arnoult, 1960).

The definition of recognition behavior followed here reflects the general use of the term in the description of methods used for testing the observer's knowledge concerning stimulus patterns. There are two major methods: (1)

the *recall method,* in which the subject is required to reproduce or explicitly construct a stimulus seen earlier; and (2) the *recognition method,* in which the subject makes a response to a presented stimulus pattern. The recognition method may be broken down into *preference, recognition,* and *identification tasks,* following in part the classification of Wohlwill (1958). With the preference task, the question is: Which stimulus pattern is "preferred," or to which stimulus pattern is a single response most frequently made? With the recognition task, it is: Which of these stimuli have you seen before? How many times? How familiar is this stimulus? In the identification task, the subject demonstrates his ability to discriminate among a set of stimuli or to identify each. Identification tasks are of four types. *Type I* deals with *identity versus differences* and asks the following questions: Are the stimuli in this set identical or different? Is the stimulus just presented in the following sample? *Type II* identification deals with the *judgment of quantitative relations* and asks: Is the difference between these two stimuli larger or smaller than the difference between the other two? Is stimulus *A* more similar to *B* than to *C*? *Type III* covers *ordered magnitude* judgments, i.e., the assignment of ordered responses to ordered stimulus values. *Type IV* deals with *categorization,* i.e., the identification of stimulus patterns with nonmetric response categories.

These tasks parallel the psychophysical and scaling methodologies discussed earlier. They permit several measures to be taken, including measures of accuracy and response time. Learning methods in which the subject is required to learn to respond to each of a set of stimuli with a response item represent a kind of categorization task. In this case trials to criterion performance or total correct responses in a set number of trials provide the measure of interest. The preference task is useful in the sampling of esthetic preference and also in testing in subhuman forms for the attractiveness of stimulus forms or colors. Fantz has made extensive use of the method

in demonstrating discriminative ability in the newborn (1961).

Anyone with a serious interest in the recognition literature finds a bewildering variety of recognition methods and measures in use. Which is best, and do the methods have much in common? Arnoult, Gagne, and Vanderplas (1951) compared the following four methods involving the use of randomly generated nonsense forms. (1) The time taken to respond "same" or "different" to pairs of forms was measured. Forms were exposed to view for 1 sec. (2) A determination was made of the number of successive exposures of pairs of forms for 0.02 sec duration that were required to elicit a correct response of "different." (3) Response time was measured when the subject's reaction terminated the stimulus exposure. (4) The pairs of stimuli were presented in a tachistoscope, and in successive sets of exposures the duration of view ranged from 10 to 200 msec. Correctness of responses was measured at all intervals.

These four methods all represent variations of the Type I task. The results indicated that all methods ranked the forms in the same way in terms of ease of discrimination. The forms were separated best by the last method. However, as we indicated earlier in discussing the threshold methods, this is perhaps the most dubious method. The correctness of response to each of a set of stimulus forms obtained in this way provides an extremely complex set of measures.

Adams, Fitts, Rappaport, and Weinstein (1954) studied 11 different measures of the discriminability of a set of 16 stimulus forms composed of four basic block figures. Each appeared as outline and solid figures and in nondistorted and distorted versions. The 11 measures included (1) two threshold measures; (2) four measures of identification time under constant illumination and one under constantly increasing illumination; (3) two measures of sorting performance; and (4) two learning measures. These measures do not cover a wide variety of the methods and tasks described above. The results showed that the two learning methods agreed closely with identification time under high illumination and less closely with sorting time. Identification time under low illumination correlated moderately with all other measures. The two threshold measures agreed with the identification measures and with the subject's choice of sorting order. The hypothesis of the study, that differences would be found between visibility measures (the subject can take all the time he needs) and legibility tasks (in which the subject needs to minimize the time required) was supported. The factor analytic method was applied to extract three orthogonal factors from the intercorrelations among the methods. The first factor was identified as a contrast factor producing differences between outline and solid figures. This factor was most important in the first three methods. The second factor was associated with differences between symmetrical and asymmetrical shapes. This was most important in the learning method and in the identification task under high illumination. The third factor appeared to be related to identification tasks.

The recognition methods sample a wide variety of abilities. This is to be expected since they represent a variety of tasks and attempt to answer a variety of questions. At present the choice of method is a matter of taste and opinion. Our bias is in favor of Type II and Type III tasks because of the overwhelming importance of specifying the appropriate perceptual space models underlying experience and judgment.

Although we have included, under the term recognition, tasks in which the subject responds to overlearned stimulus patterns, such as sounds, colors, and geometric shapes, recognition tasks often emphasize cases in which the effect of recent learning is of interest. An important part of perceptual experimentation consists in training procedures, especially with stimulus patterns that the subject sees for the first time. These patterns are typically novel either because the experimenter is interested in the course of perceptual learning, starting from as close to

scratch as possible, or because he wants to be able to specify the amount of learning that has occurred.

FAMILIARIZATION PROCEDURES

If we begin with a set of nonrepresentational stimuli (e.g., nonsense words or forms) or representational stimuli (e.g., full-face photographs, map sections, or objects) with which the subject may be assumed unfamiliar, how can we proceed to induce adequate and controlled familiarity with these stimuli? Several methods have been suggested and used.

1. *Passive viewing.* Subjects are asked to view a set of stimuli together or in succession. A common method is that in which the stimuli are presented in a random temporal series in which they occur with different frequencies, e.g., one pattern occurring 24 times, another 12 times, and a third 6 times. This provides a set of stimuli in which the stimuli vary in the characteristic frequency of prior seeing. Usually the subjects are told that they can expect to be tested on the patterns later.

2. *Passive viewing with questioning.* In this method the subjects view a pattern and then are questioned immediately about what they have seen. The hope is that this forces attention to the critical features of the forms. Often the subjects are permitted to see the patterns again after questioning, and, in this case, the method has much in common with recommendations concerning the most efficient methods for studying anything.

3. *Stimulus predifferentiation.* Subjects learn to associate a unique response item with each of a small set of stimuli. Usually the paired-associate learning technique is employed. Responses can be meaningful or nonsense items.

4. *Familiarity with a prototype.* Subjects are familiarized with a particular stimulus pattern representative of a set of pattern constructed by following the same rules or otherwise related to it. Actual familiarization procedure follows one of the other methods.

5. *Incidental learning.* For example, sub-

jects are asked to discriminate the number of patterns presented in each view. Patterns differ also in some other characteristic, such as shape, color, or size. The extent to which these characteristics, irrelevant to the discrimination required, are learned is of primary interest.

6. *Practice in discrimination.* Subjects are given practice in discriminating among a set of stimuli, using one of the identification tasks described above, until proficient at the task.

7. *Task familiarization.* Subjects are given practice in identifying stimuli in a particular viewing situation. Of particular interest is skill in identifying stimuli shown briefly in a tachistoscope. Practice in identifying a particular set of stimuli presented briefly can transfer positively to other sets. In fact, much of the learning that occurs with naive subjects in the use of the tachistoscope is not specific to the set of forms being viewed.

8. *Reproductive method.* Subjects view a stimulus pattern and then immediately try to draw it in some simple, schematic fashion. Often this is done repetitively for a fixed number of attempts.

Unquestionably, these methods can be expected to produce different kinds of familiarization. For example, a good deal of effort has been expended to learn about the effects of stimulus predifferentiation. This technique produces ability to discriminate among the set of stimuli involved in paired-associate learning, but it is difficult to show that the method increases ability to discriminate members of that set from any others. (For a review, see Arnoult, 1957.) This result is probably also true of many of the other methods that focus attention on the aspects of complex stimulus patterns required to successfully complete the training task. These aspects may or may not be critical in a later criterion recognition task.

Few studies compare the effects of these tasks. Arnoult (1956a) reported a study comparing several methods. In the reproductive method, subjects attempted to draw the stimulus patterns. In passive viewing with ques-

tioning, subjects viewed the patterns and then were asked questions about them. In the third method, subjects were instructed to study the stimuli while in view and to "hold an image" (passive viewing). In the criterion recognition task, the subjects were required to select the learned stimulus from a recognition field containing five other patterns similar to it. The reproductive method produced the best results, and passive seeing with questioning produced the worst. This recommendation of the reproductive method must be qualified, however. In this study each stimulus consisted of 16 objects arranged randomly in a circular field, and the subjects were merely locating the 16 objects on paper rather than drawing them. In cases where the subjects are asked to draw complex forms, a serious difficulty arises. Subjects introduce systematic distortions in their drawings that tend to persist through successive attempts and to contaminate memory for what was actually seen (Bridgen, 1933).

Sprague (1959) measured identification duration thresholds by using the ascending method of limits in the tachistoscope for nonsense words learned under three conditions: (1) *pronouncing* (subjects were shown words and required to pronounce them); (2) *reading* (subjects pronounced each when it first appeared and subsequently read it silently); and (3) *repeating* (subjects heard the experimenter pronounce each word and repeated it after him). Only the repeating methods, in which subjects did not see the words prior to the recognition task, failed to affect the duration thresholds. These methods, which are variations of the passive viewing method, are of special interest because of the relation between frequency of seeing and two other variables: *discriminative ability* and *judged familiarity*. These relations have been described by Arnoult (1956b).

The relation between the various familiarization techniques and the various available criterion recognition tasks deserves much more study. We tend to assume that any recognition task will serve to demonstrate the perceptual learning occurring in the particular familiarization method used. This is far from true. Vanderplas (1958) suggested that we are dealing here with a transfer-of-training situation. Current thinking on this subject predicts a variety of results depending upon the stimuli, the familiarization method, and the recognition method used.

LABORATORY MATERIALS

The materials of laboratories devoted to the study of perceptual recognition tend to consist mainly of stimulus patterns. Usually a good deal of care is taken in the preparation of the patterns in order to relate them to some particular theoretical interest.

Many of the stimulus patterns with which we are familiar are of a special sort. This includes the many visual illusions, reversible figures, and embedded or hidden figures that have played a large part in the study of perceptual performance. Many of these illusions and reversible figures were very much concerned in the gestalt beliefs concerning the process of cortical satiation. This also led to concern with very simple visual patterns and the demonstration of the visual figural aftereffect. The very specialized hidden and embedded figures were concerned mainly in notions about perceptual organization—how a visual pattern is organized into figure and ground, (analogous to current thinking about the perceiver's ability to separate signal from noise) (Hake, Rodwan, and Weintraub, 1966). As Woodworth and Schlosberg suggest, *if* we knew all there is to know about how to conceal one figure in another, we should have all the important facts about form perception. We know far less than this. Some of the important principles of construction can be reviewed in Woodworth and Schlosberg (1954).

Another important general class of visual stimuli consists of plane geometric forms. These have been important because of their simplicity and because they can be so easily specified as stimuli in physical terms. A rectangle, an ellipse, a diamond, or a cross can be specified by single numbers within each form class, and these single numbers related to a measure of visibility (e.g., see Casperson, 1950). The geometric shapes have other unique properties which have been of value and which have, at times, led to argument. A circle tipped to the line of sight is an ellipse, as projected to the eye of the viewer. Hence, this figure has been important in studies of shape constancy because two different ways of producing the same projective shape are possible with its use. Where cues to tipping are absent, an ellipse and a circle viewed at an angle from a distance are equivalent stimulus patterns.

There is a major drawback to the geometric figures considered as stimuli. They do not provide a continuous, or even easily related, series of figures. The apparent differences between a square and a circle, for example, tend to wash out apparent differences within any set of variations of the same form (Casperson, 1950).

Until recently, we lacked any general understanding of patterned visual stimuli that could be used in the generation of more general sets of stimulus forms, and each type of stimulus seemed unique and specific. Investigators needed some nonrepresentational stimuli, analogous to the very useful nonsense syllables of the learning area. These have been provided by following a set of probability rules in generating a set of points located randomly in a plane. Either the points are used as generated or they are joined by straight or curved lines to provide an outline figure (Attneave and Arnoult, 1956). Such forms have several distinct advantages. (1) All forms generated by the same process have something in common. This commonality can be specified with a good deal of precision by the set of probability rules followed in generating them. Sets of forms generated by such rules can contain a very large number of forms. These large sets can be used in experimentation; therefore, results can be related to the characteristics of the *set* of forms rather than to the individual characteristics of each of a small num-

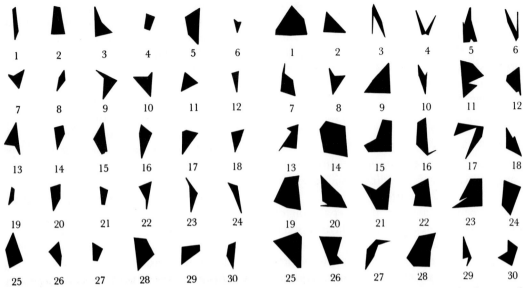

Fig. 8-13 The scaled four-pointed shapes of Vanderplas and Garvin (1959*a*.)

Fig. 8-14 The scaled six-pointed shapes of Vanderplas and Garvin (1959*a*.)

ber of forms. (2) The fact that the forms are generated by a chance process allows us to relate the forms, considered as sets, to probability theory, especially to some of the concepts of information theory. For example, the redundancy of a visual pattern can be specified either as a unique characteristic of a form or as a characteristic of the system that generated the forms (Attneave, 1954; Garner, 1962).

The generation techniques are rather simple and make the task of stimulus preparation not too burdensome. There is good reason, however, not to be too eager to generate a new set. There is much to be gained from the use of a standard set with known characteristics. This permits results to be related much more clearly to experimental manipulation and permits easier comparison of results obtained in different experiments and different laboratories. An extremely useful set has been provided by Vanderplas and Garvin (1959*a*). This set includes 30 forms at each of six levels of complexity, defined by the number of points determining inflections on the perimeter of the form. Forms were con-

structed using 4, 6, 8, 12, 16, or 24 points. Figures 8-13 through 8-18 present the forms classified by complexity. The forms have the important advantage of having been scaled for association value, where this value is defined as the proportion of subjects who make associative responses to the forms. Three measures are provided for each form: (1) the proportion of subjects providing any associative response, including those who admitted the occurrence of an associative response without specifying it; (2) the proportion of subjects giving specific content responses; and (3) a measure of the heterogeneity of responses. This was the *uncertainty* per content response,

$$H = - \sum_i p_i \log p_i \qquad (8\text{-}35)$$

where p_i is the proportion of content response of the *i*th class. These measures are shown for each form in Table 8-13. The forms have been used by Vanderplas and Garvin (1959*b*) in a study of form recognition following paired-associate training and by Goldstein (1961), who studied the effect of orientation of the

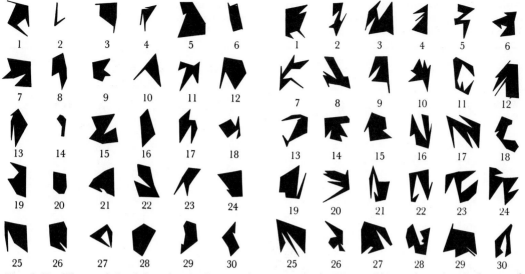

Fig. 8-15 The scaled eight-pointed shapes of Vanderplas and Garvin (1959a.)

Fig. 8-16 The scaled twelve-pointed shapes of Vanderplas and Garvin (1959a.)

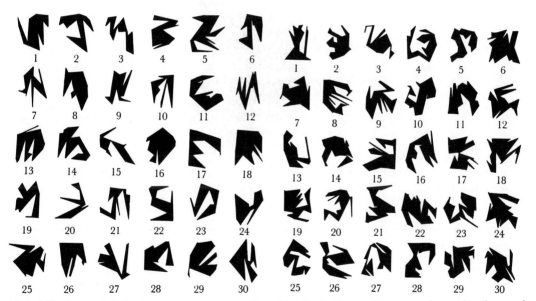

Fig. 8-17 The scaled sixteen-point shapes of Vanderplas and Garvin (1959a.)

Fig. 8-18 The scaled twenty-four-point shapes of Vanderplas and Garvin (1959a.)

forms upon associative responses, using 60 forms of the original set.

These forms add another class to the classification of forms provided by Gibson (1951): real forms, solid and surface forms; representational forms, e.g., outline drawings, pictures, and plans; and symbolic forms, i.e., geometrical and projected forms. With the exception of simple symbolic forms, we have not yet reached the point where we can specify in physical terms a set of stimuli of any of these three classes (Attneave and Arnoult, 1956).

Table 8-13   The association value A, proportion of associations which were content C, and the heterogeneity H of the content responses for each of the shapes of Vanderplas and Garvin (1959a).

Shape no.	4-point shapes			6-point shapes			8-point shapes			12-point shapes			16-point shapes			24-point shapes		
	A	C	H	A	C	H	A	C	H	A	C	H	A	C	H	A	C	H
1	56	32	3.7	62	33	2.7	62	35	2.9	50	32	3.3	52	27	3.6	60	33	3.9
2	54	39	3.0	58	34	2.7	58	33	3.0	48	38	2.9	50	28	3.1	54	31	3.0
3	54	31	4.1	54	33	3.7	46	24	3.0	48	35	3.5	42	33	3.6	48	25	2.7
4	52	33	3.8	54	31	3.5	44	30	3.4	48	27	3.4	42	21	3.2	48	23	2.6
5	50	36	3.7	52	35	3.8	42	31	3.0	46	30	3.6	40	33	3.6	44	25	3.0
6	50	34	2.9	52	29	3.3	42	26	2.8	46	26	3.5	40	30	3.3	42	38	3.5
7	50	36	4.1	50	34	4.1	40	30	3.0	46	26	4.4	40	28	3.1	42	24	2.7
8	48	42	2.3	48	38	4.0	38	34	3.8	42	29	3.0	38	32	2.7	42	21	2.4
9	48	31	2.9	46	39	2.9	38	32	2.9	42	26	2.8	38	32	3.3	40	35	3.4
10	48	29	3.4	44	32	3.5	36	33	2.5	40	33	2.4	38	21	3.1	40	25	3.1
11	46	39	3.1	40	40	3.3	36	28	3.1	40	30	3.5	38	16	2.6	40	28	2.9
12	46	33	3.5	40	33	3.4	36	22	3.0	40	25	3.3	36	30	3.0	38	37	3.4
13	46	28	3.9	40	33	3.4	36	22	2.5	40	25	2.5	36	30	2.6	38	29	2.5
14	46	28	3.8	38	34	2.9	34	29	2.6	38	32	3.3	36	25	2.6	38	26	3.0
15	44	34	3.9	38	29	2.8	34	24	3.0	38	29	2.8	36	22	3.1	38	24	2.3
16	44	23	2.6	38	21	2.8	32	28	2.6	38	29	3.4	36	22	3.1	36	28	2.7
17	42	40	2.6	38	26	3.1	30	23	2.8	38	24	3.1	36	17	2.6	36	19	2.5
18	42	33	2.9	38	26	2.8	28	32	3.1	36	28	3.1	34	35	3.3	34	32	2.8
19	42	29	3.3	38	26	2.9	28	32	2.9	34	38	3.6	34	29	2.6	34	29	2.4
20	42	29	3.0	36	28	2.8	28	29	2.8	34	26	2.9	34	29	2.8	34	29	3.3
21	40	38	3.5	36	25	3.2	28	29	1.5	34	24	2.8	34	18	2.6	34	21	2.2
22	40	30	3.0	34	41	2.8	28	23	3.1	32	31	2.8	32	34	3.0	34	18	2.6
23	40	30	3.5	34	38	2.6	28	29	3.1	30	13	2.0	32	31	3.3	32	34	3.1
24	40	25	2.5	34	35	2.3	28	29	3.1	28	25	2.8	32	28	1.2	30	20	2.3
25	38	26	3.1	34	24	2.4	28	25	2.8	28	25	2.1	30	37	3.1	28	25	2.8
26	36	34	3.8	30	37	2.7	28	25	2.8	28	25	2.8	30	27	2.8	28	25	2.5
27	36	32	3.2	26	31	2.0	26	23	2.2	26	42	3.4	30	27	3.1	28	21	2.6
28	36	32	3.3	26	27	2.1	26	15	1.5	26	23	2.2	26	23	1.8	28	14	2.0
29	36	29	3.0	26	23	2.6	22	32	2.8	26	23	2.6	24	25	1.8	24	25	2.6
30	28	43	2.6	26	23	2.6	20	20	1.5	20	30	2.6	22	21	1.9	22	27	2.6

The intention has been to specify a form or pattern in terms of a quantitative specification from which the form or pattern can be reconstructed. Such specification of patterned visual stimuli, in terms of physical measures, could provide the type of stimulus specification possible in the case of simple auditory and visual stimulation.

Some rather simple characteristics of forms have been explored. For example, the complexity of forms, loosely defined, has been related to the ability of subjects to reproduce forms from memory (Drury, 1933; Fehrer, 1935) to name forms (Attneave, 1955; French, 1954), and to match forms (Fitts, Weinstein, Rappaport, Anderson, and Leonard, 1956). Other physical aspects of forms studied include (1) area, perimeter, and maximum dimensions of geometric forms (Casperson, 1950); (2) number of elements in dot patterns (French, 1953, 1954); (3) number of angles and line segments (Hochberg and McAlister, 1953); (4) number of indefinitely extended straight lines

(Birkhoff, 1933); (5) texture (Gibson, 1950); (6) perimeter-to-area ratio (Bitterman, Krauskopf, and Hochberg, 1954; Krauskopf, Duryea, and Bitterman, 1954); and (7) regular-irregular, simple-complex (Deese, 1956).

Investigators have made progress in specifying stimulus patterns in terms of psychologically relevant dimensions. For example, Attneave (1957) related judgments of the complexity of forms to physical characteristics that appeared intuitively related to shape complexity. These included the number of independent turns or angles in the contour of the forms, symmetry of the forms, and whether they are curved or angular. The first of these accounted for nearly 80 percent of judgmental variance. A rather exhaustive study of judged similarity of triangular shapes was reported by Stilson (1956). Arnoult (1960) found that judgments of meaningfulness of forms were related to physical measures of curvature and symmetry. Judgments of size were a function mainly of the area of the stimulus pattern.

Much more of this multidimensional approach is required before we shall understand visual patterns as stimuli for perception. So far, it appears clear that even for relatively simple shapes or forms, judgments are complex. They tend to be made along multiple dimensions combined in unique ways from judgment to judgment. Judgments are not always confined to characteristics of the forms themselves. Comparative judgments of forms may depend upon other factors, such as the relative orientation of the forms in space (Attneave, 1950; Stilson, 1956). Although it appears that a large number of psychological dimensions may be used in the comparative judgments of forms, this number is certainly far smaller than the number of physical dimensions that we can specify (see, especially, Stilson, 1956).

APPARATUS

A discussion of general apparatus to control the manner in which a subject views stimulus patterns in the laboratory could be quite extensive. We shall restrict ourselves to the most extensively used devices, the tachistoscope T-scope), which permits the subject to look at a stimulus pattern for a controlled duration under a controlled amount of illumination.

There are times when a very simple device will suffice, e.g., when the illumination of the pattern is critical but the duration of view is long enough that slight variation is unimportant. A light can be mounted to illuminate the stimulus, which is placed on an angled board. The subject views the stimulus through a viewing aperture cut into a plywood or masonite board that restricts his view to the evenly illuminated stimulus. The experimenter slips a card bearing the stimulus pattern down to viewing position at the beginning of a trial and withdraws it at the end.

Another simple device, suitable for projecting stimuli before a group, is the projection tachistoscope. This is essentially a good standard projector utilizing slides made from 35-millimeter film. A shutter and iris are mounted in the beam of the projector to permit control of duration and intensity of projection to a screen. Some tachistoscopes of this type also permit control of the light source to produce extremely short exposures. These are useful devices, especially where subjects can be tested in groups, but control of view duration leaves something to be desired. Shutters of the mechanical type have a short useful life and show a good deal of variability in durations produced. Extremely short durations *cannot* be managed by mechanical means alone.

Many other mechanical devices providing a controlled view have been used. Klopfer (1953) described an apparatus providing extremely short exposures, good onset and offset characteristics of the stimulus view (offset complete in 1.9 msec), and multiple view; i.e., stimulus patterns can be presented before and after the controlled view of a critical stimulus pattern.

The present emphasis is on electronic devices. An example is the device of Merryman and Allen (1953) providing two viewing fields that can be used, e.g., for a preexposure and exposure field. Controlled illumination is provided by mercury-argon gas tubes fired by a rectilinear pulse of current. The subject looks through a viewing hood and then either through a small plate of clear lucite at stimulus pattern *A* or at pattern *B* reflected off the face of the lucite plate. The device of Koletsky and Kolers (1959) provides three fields illuminated by cold-cathode gas-discharge tubes.

Devices that use electronic control of gas tubes give good service if the power supply and timing circuitry are maintained and kept in calibration. They have the following disadvantages: (1) It is generally not safe to assume that the light pulses are truly rectilinear. This means that duratión and luminance of stimulation are not truly independent. This is especially true of short-duration flashes. (2) Where the subject views a stimulus pattern through a plate of glass or lucite at an oblique angle to the line of sight he sees two reflections, one off the front surface of the plate and another off the back. This is true of half-silvered mirrors (beam splitters) also. These reflections are slightly displaced with respect to each other, the degree of displacement depending upon the thickness of plate, and provide a double image. (3) The transmission characteristics of a plate of lucite or glass are not the same as the reflectance characteristics. The same pattern viewed in the two channels of the typical T-scope will have different color characteristics in the two positions. The apparatus of Koletsky and Kolers attempts to correct for this factor. In each viewing channel, light from the stimulus pattern is reflected off one plate and transmitted through two. However, transmission through a plate normal to the line of view is not quite the same as transmission through a plate oriented obliquely to the line of view. A good test is: Can the subject discriminate in which channel a stimulus pattern is located?

The elimination of these problems is costly. Devices are available with onset and offset times as small as 0.0025 msec. Reflecting mirrors can be made very thin and coated so that multiple reflected images are greatly diminished. Special filters can be used to match the color characteristics of several channels. These devices are available commercially.

Some of the new devices created as teaching machines are useful where many different patterns are to be presented. One such device is the Auto-Tutor. This will store as many as 10,000 frames of 35-mm film and seek any particular one for presentation. It will also permit any sequence of frames to be presented as a motion-picture sequence.

These devices greatly enlarge our ability to present many different stimulus patterns and often provide for response recording. Many are especially useful where the response determines subsequent stimulus presentations. These advantages are gained usually at the price of some loss in control of stimulus duration and intensity.

REFERENCES

ABELSON, R. P., and SERMAT, V. Multidimensional scaling of facial expressions. *J. exp. Psychol.*, 1962, **63**, 546–554.

ADAMS, O. S., FITTS, P. M., RAPPAPORT, M., and WEINSTEIN, M. Relations among some measures of pattern discriminability. *J. exp. Psychol.*, 1954, **48**, 81–88.

ALLPORT, F. H. *Theories of perception and the concept of structure.* New York: Wiley, 1955.

AMES, A., JR. Reconsideration of the origin and nature of perception in situations involving only inorganic phenomena. In S. Ratner (Ed.), *Vision and action.* New Brunswick, N.J.: Rutgers, 1953. Pp. 251–274.

ANDERSON, T. W. *Introduction to multivariate statistical analysis.* New York: Wiley, 1958.

ARNOULT, M. D. A comparison of training methods in the recognition of spatial patterns. *Tech. Note* No. AFPTRC-TN-56-27, Lackland AFB, 1956a.

ARNOULT, M. D. Familiarity and recognition of nonsense shapes. *J. exp. Psychol.*, 1956b, **51**, 269–276.

ARNOULT, M. D. Stimulus predifferentiation: Some generalizations and hypotheses. *Psychol. Bull.*, 1957, **54**, 339–350.

ARNOULT, M. D. Prediction of perceptual responses from structural characteristics of the stimulus. *Percept. mot. Skills*, 1960, **11**, 261–268.

ARNOULT, M. D., GAGNE, R. M., and VANDERPLAS, J. M. A comparison of four measures of visual discrimination of shapes. *USAF HRRC, Res. Bull.* No. 51–23, 1951.

ATTNEAVE, F. A method of graded dichotomies for the scaling of judgments. *Psychol. Rev.*, 1949, **56**, 334–340.

ATTNEAVE, F. Dimensions of similarity. *Amer. J. Psychol.*, 1950, **63**, 516–556.

ATTNEAVE, F. Some information aspects of visual perception. *Psychol. Rev.*, 1954, **61**, 183–193.

ATTNEAVE, F. Symmetry, information, and memory for patterns. *Amer. J. Psychol.*, 1955, **68**, 209–222.

ATTNEAVE, F. Physical determinants of the judged complexity of shapes. *J. exp. Psychol.*, 1957, **53**, 221–227.

ATTNEAVE, F. *Applications of information theory to psychology.* New York: Holt, 1959.

ATTNEAVE, F., and ARNOULT, M. D. The quantitative study of shape and pattern perception. *Psychol. Bull.*, 1956, **53**, 452–471.

BARTLETT, F. C. *Remembering.* Cambridge: Cambridge Univer. Press, 1932.

BEARDSLEE, D. C., and WERTHEIMER, M. *Readings in perception.* Princeton, N.J.: Van Nostrand, 1958.

BEVAN, W. Perception: Evolution of a concept. *Psychol. Rev.*, 1958, **65**, 34–55.

BINDER, A., and WOLIN, B. R. Informational models and their uses. *Psychometrika*, 1964, **29**, 29–54.

BIRKHOFF, D. B. *Aesthetic measure.* Cambridge, Mass.: Harvard Univer. Press, 1933.

BITTERMAN, M. E., KRAUSKOPF, J., and HOCHBERG, J. E. Threshold for visual form: A diffusion model. *Amer. J. Phychol.*, 1954, **67**, 205–219.

BLACKWELL, H. R. Psychophysical thresholds: Experimental studies of methods of measurement. *Engng. Res. Bull.* No. 36, Univer. of Michigan, 1953.

BRIDGEN, R. S. A tachistoscopic study of the differentiation of perception. *Psychol. Monogr.*, 1933, **44**, No. 197, 153–166.

CASPERSON, R. C. The visual discrimination of geometric forms. *J. exp. Psychol.*, 1950, **40**, 668–681.

COOLEY, W. W., and LOHNES, P. R. *Multivariate procedures for the behavioral sciences.* New York: Wiley, 1962.

CORNSWEET, T. N. The staircase-method in psychophysics. *Amer. J. Psychol.*, 1962, **75**, 485–491.

CRAIK, K. J. W., and VERNON, M. D. Perception during dark adaptation. *Brit. J. Psychol.*, 1942, **32**, 206–230.

CRONHOLM, J. N. A general method of obtaining exact sampling probabilities of the Shannon-Wiener measure of information. *Psychometrika*, 1963, **28**, 405–413.

DEESE, J. Complexity of contour in the recognition of visual form. *Tech. Rep.* No. 56–60, USAF WADC, 1956.

DEMBER, W. N. *Psychology of perception.* New York: Holt, 1960.

DIXON, W. J., and MASSEY, F. J., JR. *Introduction to statistical analysis.* (2nd ed.) New York: McGraw-Hill, 1957. Pp. 318–327.

DRURY, M. B. Progressive changes in nonfoveal perception of line patterns. *Amer. J. Psychol.*, 1933, **45**, 628–646.

EGAN, J. P. Recognition memory and the operating characteristic. *Tech. Note* No. AFCRC-TN-58-51. Hearing and Communication Laboratory, Indiana University, 1958.

EGAN, J. P., SCHULMAN, A. I., and GREENBERG, G. Z. Operating characteristics determined by binary decisions and by ratings. *J. acoust. Soc. Amer.*, 1959, **31**, 768–773.

ENGEN, T., LEVY, N., and SCHLOSBERG, H. A new series of facial expressions. *Amer. Psychologist*, 1957, **12**, 264–266.

ERIKSEN, C. W. Discrimination and learning without awareness: A methodological survey and evaluation. *Psychol. Rev.*, 1960, **67**, 279–300.

FANTZ, R. L. The origin of form perception. *Sci. Amer.*, 1961, **204**, 66–72.

FEHRER, E. V. An investigation of learning of visually perceived forms. *Amer. J. Psychol.*, 1935, **47**, 187–221.

FINNEY, D. J. *Probit analysis.* Cambridge: Cambridge Univer. Press, 1947.

FITTS, P. M., WEINSTEIN, M., RAPPORT, M., ANDERSON, N., and LEONARD, J. A. Stimulus correlates of visual pattern recognition: A probability approach. *J. exp. Psychol.*, 1956, **51**, 1–11.

FRENCH, R. S. The discrimination of dot patterns as a function of number and average separation of dots. *J. exp. Psychol.*, 1953, **46**, 1–9.

FRENCH, R. S. Identification of dot patterns from memory as a function of complexity. *J. exp. Psychol.*, 1954, **47**, 22–26.

GARNER, W. R. *Uncertainty and structure as psychological concepts.* New York: Wiley, 1962.

GARNER, W. R., and HAKE, H. W. The amount of information in absolute judgments. *Psychol. Rev.*, 1951, **58**, 446–459.

GARNER, W. R., HAKE, H. W., and ERIKSEN, C. W. Operationism and the concept of perception. *Psychol. Rev.*, 1956, **63**, 149–159.

GARNER, W. R., and MCGILL, W. J. The relation between information and variance analyses. *Psychometrika*, 1956, **21**, 219–228.

GIBSON, J. J. *Perception of the visual world.* New York: Houghton Mifflin, 1950.

GIBSON, J. J. What is form? *Psychol. Rev.*, 1951, **58**, 403–412.

GOLDIAMOND, I. Indicators of perception: I. Subliminal perception, subception, unconscious perception: An analysis in terms of psychophysical indicator methodology. *Psychol. Bull.*, 1958, **55**, 373–411.

GOLDSTEIN, A. G. Spatial orientation as a factor in eliciting associative responses to random shapes. *Percept. mot. Skills*, 1961, **12**, 15–25.

GRAHAM, C. Sensation and perception in an objective psychology. *Psychol. Rev.*, 1958, **65**, 65–76.

GRAHAM, C., BROWN, R. H., and MOTE, F. A., JR. The relation of size of stimulus and intensity in the human eye. I. Intensity thresholds for white light. *J. exp. Psychol.*, 1939, **24**, 555–573.

GUILFORD, J. P. (Ed.) *Printed classification tests.* Army Air Forces Aviation Psychology Program, *Res. Rep.* No. 5, U.S. Government Printing Office, 1947.

GUILFORD, J. P. *Psychometric methods.* (2nd ed.) New York: McGraw-Hill, 1954.

HAKE, H. W. Contributions of psychology to the study of pattern vision. *Tech. Rep.* No. 57-621, USAF, WADC, 1957.

HAKE, H. W. Multivariate methods in perception. In Cattell, R. B. (Ed.) *Handbook of multivariate experimental psychology.* Chicago: Rand McNally, 1967.

HAKE, H. W., RODWAN, A. S., and WEINTRAUB, D. Noise reduction in perception. In K. R. Hammond (Ed.), *Egon Brunswik's psychology.* New York: Holt, 1966.

HELM, C. E., and TUCKER, L. R. Individual differences in the structure of color perception. *Amer. J. Psychol.*, 1962, **75**, 437–444.

HOCHBERG, J., and BROOKS, V. The psychophysics of form: Reversible-perspective drawings of spatial objects. *Amer. J. Psychol.*, 1960, **73**, 337–354.

HOCHBERG, J., and MCALISTER, E. A quantitative approach to figural "goodness." *J. exp. Psychol.*, 1953, **46**, 361–364.

HOTELLING, H. The generalization of Student's ratio. *Ann math. Stat.*, 1931, **2**, 360–378.

HURSCH, C. J., HAMMOND, K. R., and HURSCH, J. L. Some methodological considerations in multiple-cue probability studies. *Psychol. Rev.*, 1964, **71**, 42–60.

IVES, W. C., and SHILLING, C. W. Object identification with the Hecht-Shlaer adaptometer. S24-1 (102) WCI/fgl/aam., Night Vision Board, U.S. Submarine Base, New London, Conn., December 26, 1941.

JENKIN, N., and HYMAN, R. Attitude and distance-estimation as variables in size-matching. *Amer. J. Psychol.*, 1959, **72**, 68–76.

KLOPFER, F. D. A semi-automatic bright-field tachistoscope. *Amer. J. Psychol.*, 1953, **66**, 105–109.

KOCH, S. (Ed.) *Psychology: A study of a science.* Vol. I. *Sensory, perceptual, and physiological formulations.* New York: McGraw-Hill, 1959.

KOLETSKY, H. S., and KOLERS, P. A. A multi-field electronic tachistoscope. *Amer. J. Psychol.*, 1959, **72**, 456–459.

KRAUSKOPF, J., DURYEA, R. A., and BITTERMAN, M. E. Threshold for visual form: Further experiments. *Amer. J. Psychol.*, 1954, **67**, 427–440.

LYLERLY, S. B. A note on correcting for chance success in objective tests. *Psychometrika*, 1951, **16**, 21–30.

MERRYMAN, J. G., and ALLEN, H. E. An improved electronic tachistoscope. *Amer. J. Psychol.*, 1953, **66**, 110–114.

MILES, W. R. Light sensitivity and form perception in dark adaptation. *J. opt. Soc. Amer.*, 1953, **43**, 560–566.

MILLER, G. Note on the bias of information estimates. In H. Quastler (Ed.), *Information theory in psychology.* Glencoe, Ill.: Free Press, 1955, Pp. 95–100.

MILLER, G. A. and MADOW, W. G. On the maximum likelihood estimate of the Shannon-Wiener measure of information. *Tech. Rep.* 54-57, Air Force Cambridge Res. Center, 1954.

NOBLE, C. E. The familiarity-frequency relationship. *J. exp. Psychol.*, 1954, **47**, 13–16.

PIERCE, J. Determinants of threshold for form. *Psychol. Bull.*, 1963, **60**, 391–407.

POSTMAN, L., and EGAN, J. P. *Experimental psychology: An introduction.* New York: Harper & Row, 1949.

RODWAN, A. S., and HAKE, H. W. The discriminant function as a model for perception. *Amer. J. Psychol.*, 1964, **77**, 380–392.

ROFF, M. A factorial study of tests in the perceptual area. *Psychometric Monogr.*, 1952, No. 8.

ROSS, J. Informational coverage and correlational analysis. *Psychometrika*, 1962, **27**, 297–306.

SEMEONOFF, B. Form perception in dark-adapted vision. *Brit. psychol. Soc. quart. Bull.*, 1950, **7**, 281–282.

SHEPARD, R. N. Stimulus and response generalization: Tests of a model relating generalization to distance in psychological space. *J. exp. Psychol.*, 1958, **55**, 509–523.

SHEPARD, R. N. The analysis of proximities: Multidimensional scaling with an unknown distance function. I. *Psychometrika*, 1962a, **27**, 125–140.

SHEPARD, R. N. The analysis of proximities: Multidimensional scaling with an unknown distance function. II. *Psychometrika*, 1962b, **27**, 219–246.

SPRAGUE, R. L. Effects of differential training on tachistoscopic recognition thresholds. *J. exp. Psychol.*, 1959, **58**, 227–231.

STILSON, D. W. A psychophysical investigation of triangular shape. Unpublished doctoral dissertation, Univer. of Illinois, 1956.

SWETS, J. A. Detection theory and psychophysics: A review. *Psychometrika*, 1961a, **26**, 49–63.

SWETS, J. A. Is there a sensory threshold? *Science*, 1961b, **134**, 168–177.

SWETS, J. A., TANNER, W. P., and BIRDSALL, T. G. Decision processes in perception. *Psychol. Rev.*, 1961, **68**, 301–340.

THURSTONE, L. L. A law of comparative judgment. *Psychol. Rev.*, 1927, **34**, 273–286.

THURSTONE, L. L. *A factorial study of perception.* Chicago: Univer. of Chicago Press, 1944.

TORGERSON, W. S. *Theory and methods of scaling.* New York: Wiley, 1958.

TUCKER, L. R., and MESSICK, S. An individual differences model for multidimensional scaling. *Psychometrika*, 1963, **28**, 333–367.

VANDERPLAS, J. M. Transfer of training and its relation to perceptual learning and recognition. *Psychol. Rev.*, 1958, **65**, 375–385.

VANDERPLAS, J. M., and GARVIN, E. A. The association value of random shapes. *J. exp. Psychol.*, 1959a, **57**, 147–154.

VANDERPLAS, J. M., and GARVIN, E. A. Complexity, association value, and practice as factors in shape recognition following paired-associates training. *J. exp. Psychol.*, 1959b, **57**, 155–163.

VOLKMANN, F. C., and ENGEN, T. Three types of anchoring effects in absolute judgment of hue. *J. exp. Psychol.*, 1961, **61**, 7–17.

WEINTRAUB, D., and HAKE, H. W. Visual discrimination, an interpretation in terms of detectability theory. *J. opt. soc. Amer.*, 1962, **52**, 1179–1184.

WOHLWILL, J. F. The definition and analysis of perceptual learning. *Psychol. Rev.*, 1958, **65**, 283–295.

WOHLWILL, J. F. Developmental studies of perception. *Psychol. Bull.*, 1960, **57**, 249–288.

WOODS, E. L. An experiment analysis of the process of recognizing. *Amer. J. Psychol.*, 1915, **26**, 313–327.

WOODWORTH, R. S., and SCHLOSBERG, H. *Experimental psychology.* (Rev. ed.) New York: Holt, 1954.

Part Four

CONDITIONING
AND LEARNING

Part Four includes three chapters: Classical Con-
ditioning, Operant Conditioning, and Animal
Learning. Chapter 9, Classical Conditioning, pre-
sents some general considerations aimed at prob-
lems of response definition and measurement,
time intervals, instructions, animal restrainers,
data collection, and controls. Specific methodol-
ogical information is provided for human re-
search in salivary, eyelid, and GSR conditioning,
while animal preparations are detailed for sali-
vary conditioning in the dog, eyelid conditioning
in the rabbit (nictitating membrane), and GSR
conditioning with the cat. Refer to Chap. 3 for
further information on the GSR and for descrip-
tions of instrumentation that might be utilized
for other types of classical conditioning research.
Additional information covering this area may be
found in Grant (1964) and Prokasy (1965).

Chapter 10, Operant Conditioning, begins
with a discussion of general operant methodol-
ogy, including the advantages of automation and
immediate monitoring, and presents some experi-
mental problems of control. Dinsmoor then de-
fines the experimental environment commonly
encountered in these studies along with various
conditioned and discriminative stimuli. Sub-
sequent information describes animal chairs and
restrainers, response and reinforcing devices, re-
ward substances, and aversive stimuli. Several
basic relay circuits are presented along with a
discussion of electromechanical and solid state

programming devices. The chapter concludes with methods for recording operant data that stress the use of cumulative recorders and the programmed tallying of responses. Other solid state digital elements for the programming and recording of operant research are reported by Herrick and Denelsbeck (1963), and Weiner (1963); Ellen and Wilson (1964) describe a data recording and retrieval system for use with multiple chamber work. Weiss and Laties (1965) report a technique that warrants the attention of anyone interested in future methodological developments in this area. A digital computer is used to generate an auto regressive schedule of reinforcement, the programming of which would not have been possible with ordinary operant laboratory facilities. Inspecting the data from several points of view, the authors present photographs representing distributions of interresponse times, differences between successive interresponse times, expectation density functions, tabulation of sequences, and serial correlation plots, all of which were obtained directly from the computer oscilloscope.

Chapter 11, Animal Learning, covers a range of techniques under three headings: Thorndikian, Pavlovian, and avoidance. Although these categories normally could include much of the op-

erant and classical conditioning methodology mentioned earlier, the emphasis here is upon those techniques which are not treated in the two preceding chapters. Instrumentation and methodology are presented for the study of drive and reward variables, unitary processes (e.g., runways), discrimination learning (mazes and jump stands), activity conditioning, shuttle boxes and other avoidance techniques. The experimental subjects include fish, rats, turtles, monkeys, and pigeons. Refer to Warren (1965) for a review of the recent literature covering the conditioning of paramecia, learning in planaria, and species differences in classical and operant conditioning. Mason and Riopelle (1964) present an extensive bibliography and brief coverage of research in the social behavior of various primates; Schrier, Harlow, and Stollnitz (1965) cover modern research trends. Research methods in motivation are discussed and referenced by Cofer and Appley (1964). Additional information on areas of operant research may be found in Honig (1966). Methods used in the study of learning and associated phenomena in invertebrates (including protozoa, coelenterates, annelids, crustacea, insects, and octopus) are presented in Animal Behaviour Supplement No. 1, published by Baillière, Tindall, and Cassell Ltd., 7 & 8 Henrietta St., London, W.C. 2, England.

Chapter 9

CLASSICAL CONDITIONING

I. GORMEZANO

The essential feature of classical conditioning is a set of experimental operations involving an *unconditioned stimulus* (UCS) reliably evoking a measurable *unconditioned response* (UCR), along with a *conditioned stimulus* (CS) that has been shown by test not to elicit the UCR. The CS and UCS are then presented repeatedly to the organism in a specified order and temporal spacing, and a response similar to the UCR develops to the CS that is called the *conditioned response* (CR).

The order and temporal spacing of the CS and UCS give rise to a variety of forms of the classical conditioning experiment. Typically, the CS begins a brief time before the onset of the UCS. When the CS remains on at least until UCS onset, the procedure is described as *delay* conditioning; if the CS terminates before UCS onset, the procedure is described as *trace* conditioning. When the CS and UCS are coextensive in time, *simultaneous* conditioning results. If the UCS alone is presented at constant time intervals, the interval between presentations serves as the CS for *temporal conditioning;* the procedure is described as *background conditioning* if the UCS precedes the CS.

Classical conditioning is called *classical reward conditioning* if the UCS is a positive reinforcer and *classical defense conditioning* if it is a negative reinforcer (Spence, 1956). Technically, the notation positive and negative reinforcer depends upon an independent assessment of the UCS in an instrumental conditioning situation. The relative efficacy of positive reinforcers in classical reward conditioning will more likely be related to the current motivational state of the organism than will that of negative reinforcers.

Anticipatory instructed conditioning is another subclassification of classical conditioning (Grant, 1964). The reference experiment for this type of conditioning involves the formation of CRs based upon the instructed voluntary squeezing of a rubber bulb in response to a sound stimulus (Ivanov-Smolensky, 1933). The sound stimulus is preceded regularly by some neutral CS and presents, in effect, a reaction-time experiment with a constant fore-period signaled by CS onset. The occurrence of bulb-squeezing responses to the CS prior to or in the absence of the sound stimulus constitutes the CR. Although it is commonly assumed that the UCS must be some stimulus that elicits its response reflexively without previous learning, as may be true in most cases of classical reward and defense conditioning, the only requirement within the framework of a classical conditioning experiment is that some manipulatable stimulus reliably evoke the desired response.

GENERAL CONSIDERATIONS

Response measurement

Ideally, repeated pairings of the CS and UCS produce a change in some measurable aspect of the CR from some initial base level to some terminal level, and this change constitutes an index of conditioning. The acquisition of CRs has been assessed according to their frequency, latency, and amplitude (or magnitude). Generally, experimenters have settled upon the response measure found to be most sensitive to the course of acquisition. In salivary and galvanic skin response (GSR) conditioning, amplitude or magnitude is most widely employed. In *magnitude measurement* the "extent" of the responses is summed and divided by the number of conditioning trials. This involves averaging zero responses. In *amplitude measurement* the extent of the responses is averaged only for obtained responses. The amplitude measure should be employed, since it is desirable to make frequency and extent measures as independent as possible; furthermore, magnitude, as a measure, would be expected to be more variable. Amplitude and latency will then be descriptive measures of the obtained CR, and frequency will refer to the number of CRs relative to the number of trials. Another descriptive measure of the CR is *recruitment,* which is generally defined as the time elapsing between initiation of the response and the time at which the response reaches maximum amplitude. The recruitment measure would have a high positive correlation with the amplitude measure for most response systems.

The amount of instrumentation required to obtain reliable indices of amplitude and latency is generally greater than that required to determine the occurrence or non-occurrence of the CR. Frequency and latency measures are dependent upon (1) the sensitivity of the recording system and (2) the amplitude criterion employed by the experimenter to determine when a response has occurred. If measurements are taken within a single conditioning session, the reliability of amplitude measures will generally be higher than in multiple sessions since some variability in attaching the recording system to the subject must usually be expected.

Although the selection of the UCS also affects the selection of the CR, the response to the UCS is rarely a single discrete response; usually it is a constellation of UCRs, and the experimenter must decide which of these responses he wishes to observe. The decision will be governed in part by the degree of instrumentation involved, the organism, and whether some response systems are more sensitive to change than others. For these as well as theoretical reasons, some experimenters elect to concentrate upon one response system whereas others take concurrent measurements of several. Whether one or several response systems are under observation, the experimenter must make every effort to ensure that concurrent processes activated by UCS occurrences are not obscuring the influence of the experimental operations on the relevant response systems, e.g., the influence of respiration on heart rate.

Interstimulus interval

Employing an interval between the CS and UCS at least as long as the typical latency of the CR permits one to observe the course of conditioning through the examination of CRs prior to the onset of the UCS, i.e., anticipatory CRs. Current evidence suggests that the "optimum" interstimulus interval for classical defense conditioning, i.e., the interval producing the fastest learning rate and/or highest asymptotic level, is generally under several seconds and perhaps as short as 0.25 to 0.50 second (sec) (Kimble, 1961). This information is not yet available for classical reward conditioning. Although the latency of CRs may vary as a function of the CS-UCS interval and other conditioning parameters, e.g., intensity of the UCS and number of conditioning trials, the commonly observed CR latencies of autonomic responses, e.g., salivary, GSR, and pupillary, can average 2 to 5 sec; and for skeletal response systems e.g., eyelid, leg flexion, and finger withdrawal, 0.20 to 0.50 sec. If the typical CR latency is longer than the selected optimal interval, it is necessary to obtain measures of the CR on trials other than the conditioning trials. Frequently employed procedures consist in measuring CRs on interspersed test trials in which the UCS is omitted or in an extended series of extinction trials. The utilization of test trials can markedly alter the course of conditioning, and the measurement of CRs on extinction trials does not permit an assessment of the growth of conditioning. Whether an experimenter employs the short but optimal interstimulus interval or the longer interval will depend upon strategic interests.

Instructions

Instructions are an important variable in the classical conditioning of skeletal (Gormezano and Moore, 1962; Grant and Norris, 1947; Lindley and Moyer, 1961) and autonomic responses (Cook and Harris, 1937; Grings, 1960; Razran, 1935a). In the absence of formal instructions, subjects often adopt self-instructions that may facilitate or interfere with the acquisition of CRs. The problem is perhaps most acute in the conditioning of response systems where substantial visual and proprioceptive feedback occur, e.g., finger withdrawal and the patellar knee reflex. Experimenters attempt to control the problem by providing the subject with instructions designed to provide a "neutral" set or by the deliberate deception of the subject concerning the purpose of the experiment. The subject who is instructed not to "aid or inhibit your natural reactions to the stimuli" is faced with an essentially ambiguous situation. The experimenter, by the very nature of the classical conditioning paradigm, provides no criteria for the response system under observation that will permit the subject to evaluate the desirability or undesira-

bility of the behavior elicited. In the absence of objective criteria, subjects may provide self-instructions that tend to increase between-subject variability and that may or may not be consistent with the objectives of the experimenter. On the other hand, if the experimenter provides informational feedback concerning the adequacy of the response under observation, the classical conditioning paradigm will become markedly altered. An experimenter must recognize these difficulties and realize that his efforts to control self-instructional factors do not mean that attitudinal and perceptual factors are artifactual. It is possible that subjects undergo attitudinal and perceptual modifications as concomitants of the conditioning process. The investigation of their contributions to the conditioning process remains an experimental program of major importance (Grings, 1960).

After carefully formulating instructions to obtain compliance and reduce between-subject variability, the experimenter is faced with the task of establishing criteria for determining instances where the subject fails to comply. Subjects who block out sensory input by falling asleep, closing their eyes, plugging up their ears, or removing a noxious source of stimulation are readily recognized as demonstrating a failure to comply with the instructions. The experimenter who infers failure of the subject to comply through examination of the course of acquisition or the form of the CRs, i.e., latency, magnitude, duration, and recruitment, is relying in part upon a theoretical preconception of what constitutes the conditioning process. The methodological difficulties confronting the investigator who uses such an approach are considerable. This problem will be discussed more extensively in the section on eyelid conditioning (pages 397 to 410).

Animal restrainers

In conditioning infrahuman organisms consideration must be given to the need for restraining devices. If the stimulating or recording equipment requires attachment to the subject, the experimenter must exercise precautions to prevent the organism from disturbing the preparation. It may be possible to attach the equipment on a portion of the body surface that is inaccessible to the subject. Shapiro (1960) has developed a preparation for recording salivary secretions that emerges from the back of the dog's neck, and Perez-Cruet, Tolliver, Dunn, Marvin, and Brady (1963) have obtained electrocardiographic (EKG) recordings from monkeys through chronically implanted subcutaneous tantalum electrodes placed in the arms and brought out to a fixed pedestal secured to the animal's skull. Such preparations require the use of minimum restraints and can, in some instances, permit free movement of the organism within the experimental enclosure.

If the preparation cannot be made inaccessible or if gross skeletal movements interfere with the recording of the response, restraining devices are necessary to immobilize the subject. This is particularly true in classical defense conditioning. The construction of restraining devices is often the experimenter's most difficult instrumentation problem. If the subject persists in resisting its restraints, one cannot expect to obtain high levels of conditioning. The experimenter must attempt to construct a holder that minimizes competing behavior and must often employ periods of adaptation sufficient to eliminate "struggling" behavior. Considerable species differences may exist in the amount of adaptation required. Rats, cats, and pigs appear to resist restraints vigorously, whereas sheep and rabbits may adapt readily.

Data collection

Automated programming devices are employed for controlling stimulus events and intertrial intervals. A tape reader, e.g., a Western Union tape reader, model 1-A, in which prepunched paper tapes key various relays and timers, can control durations of the CS, UCS, CS-UCS intervals, and intertrial intervals. A cam-microswitch arrangement driven by a synchronous motor can be employed for pulsing the solenoid of the transmitter and advancing the tape. Interest in the form of the unconditioned and the conditioned response has led investigators to obtain analog records. Although the experimenter can often devise simple circuits, e.g., an electronic switch, to record a response, sufficiently sensitive and reliable records of its form characteristics, i.e., latency, recruitment, duration, and amplitude, in automated form generally require expensive analog-to-digital conversion systems. (See Chap. 1 for a discussion of programming and recording devices.)

An experimenter can substantially increase the efficiency of data collection by running squads of subjects. Since the sequence of stimulus events is under the experimenter's control, squads of subjects appropriately isolated from one another can be run concurrently under the same stimulating conditions by the simple expedient of providing multiple channels for data recording (Gormezano, Schneiderman, Deaux, and Fuentes, 1962; J. W. Moore and Gormezano, 1961; Schneiderman and Gormezano, 1964). If only one recording channel is available, a selector switch can permit the successive presentation of conditioning trials to each subject in the squad (Gonzalez, Longo, and Bitterman, 1961; Noble and Adams, 1963). The size of the squad will be limited by the length of the intertrial interval, but the length of the experimental session will not be appreciably greater than that required for a single subject.

Response definition

In many response systems, e.g., GSR, eyelid, and cardiac, a reflex response is elicited to the CS. This is known as an *alpha response*. Generally a careful detailing of the latency, duration, amplitude, and course of adaptation of the alpha response will provide a basis of eliminating them from consideration. Since alpha responses are usually of shorter latency than CRs, both responses can be observed and scored if a sufficiently long

CS-UCS interval is employed. Problems arise when a CS-UCS interval is employed in which CRs would be expected to fall in the latency range of the alpha response. Under such conditions a common procedure is to precede conditioning trials with repeated presentations of the CS until the alpha response adapts out. The difficulty with such a procedure is that a single CS-UCS pairing may often be sufficient to reinstate the alpha response. The reinstatement or augmentation of the alpha response to the CS through the experimental operation of UCS-alone presentations or CS-UCS pairings is referred to as *sensitization*. A classical discrimination procedure is commonly employed to aid in distinguishing reinstated alpha responses from CRs. If the responses to the positive and negative stimuli are similar prior to acquisition training, then conditioning would be demonstrated by a difference in responding to the positive one. Another approach to the problem of sensitization is to employ a control group receiving the same number of presentations of the UCS as the experimental group, but without temporal pairing with the CS. Differences in performance between the experimental and the control group are used to assess conditioning. These procedures do not eliminate the occurrence of augmented or reinstated alpha responses. They simply permit a determination of their contribution to responses scored as CRs.

Controls for conditioning

Once the characteristics of alpha responses have been carefully delineated by the use of a control group given CS-alone presentations and another group employed as a sensitization control, the possible contribution of other sources of nonassociative responses to CR measurement must be assessed. When a noxious UCS is presented one or several times prior to presentation of the CS, the procedure will frequently result in the occurrence of a response that is apparently indistinguishable from a CR. This procedure is called *pseudoconditioning,* and the resulting responses are treated as separate from those acquired by classical conditioning per se because of their occurrence in the absence of previous CS-UCS pairings. Although the one or several mechanisms by which pseudoconditioned responses occur are not presently known, they are clearly a result of UCS presentations and therefore might be expected to contribute to the responses scored as CRs under the classical conditioning procedure. Another possible nonassociative effect of UCS occurrences is that they may alter the spontaneous response rate. To control for pseudoconditioned and spontaneous responses, the single control group procedure may be employed in which CS-alone and UCS-alone presentations are given an equal number of times, as in the experimental group, but in a random fashion. Examination of the responses in the time interval prior to UCS trials corresponding to the CS-UCS interval of the experimental group will give a measure of spontaneous responses. Those occurring to the CS trials, excluding responses in the alpha latency range, will give a summative measure of pseudoconditioned and spontaneous responses. Where pseudoconditioned responses would be expected to fall in the latency range of alpha responses, separate CS-alone and UCS-alone control groups would be employed and comparisons made on CS-alone test trials.

SALIVARY CONDITIONING

To appreciate the instrumentation problems involved in salivary conditioning, it is necessary to understand the complex modes of action of the three symmetrically placed salivary glands—the parotid, submaxillary, and sublingual. The combined secretions of these glands consist of a liquid containing 98.5 to 99.0 percent water. The residue consists of salts and organic substances. The parotid gland, via Stenson's duct, secretes into the mouth cavity from the inner surface of the cheek opposite the second molar of the upper jaw; the submaxillary secretes at the side of the frenum of the tongue in the lower jaw via Wharton's duct; and the sublingual secretes in the floor of the lower jaw via the 8 to 20 small ducts of Rivinus. In dogs a large sublingual duct runs parallel to Wharton's duct and merges to form a common opening (Bykov, 1958).

The receptor surface of the salivary reflex is located in the oral cavity where mechanical and chemical stimulation, particularly of the tongue, will elicit the reflex. Chewing and swallowing movements will cause appreciable quantities of secretion through mechanical stimulation (Lashley, 1916; Winsor and Bayne, 1929). The nature and strength of the stimulus determine the precise composition of the saliva. If a dog is given meat there is a secretion of thick, mucous saliva chiefly from the submaxillary gland; if the meat is dried and pulverized, a very copious and watery saliva is secreted by the parotid gland (Bykov, 1958). Rejectable substances will also elicit saliva, e.g., when the oral cavity is irrigated with acid or alkaline solutions. The composition of saliva also depends upon the rate of secretion; if secreted rapidly, it is richer in dense residue and is more alkaline (Gilchrist and Furchtgott, 1951). Because of the differential sensitivity of the tongue and mucous membrane of the oral cavity the quantity of saliva secreted will vary with the type of stimulus applied (e.g., salts, acids, sugar, and quinine) and the area stimulated.

Conditioning in infrahumans

Because of their structure, the ducts of the sublingual glands are not used for isolated study in investigations of salivary conditioning. To observe secretions from the parotid and submaxillary glands, the salivary flow is directed to a fistula outside the animal's mouth. The fistula for the parotid gland is generally made on the cheek and that of the submaxillary gland under the animal's chin. In the Pavlov preparation the mucous membrane surrounding the opening of the duct

is cut to form a small disk of tissue at the center of which is the duct opening. The duct is freed from the surrounding tissue for a short distance by careful dissection, and the disk, passed through the wound in the cheek or floor of the mouth, is sewn to the surrounding tissue. The piece of mucosa then grows into the surrounding tissue and healing takes place within 7 to 10 days (Barron, 1932). Although conditioning has been carried out with the submaxillary gland (Crisler, 1928; Kleitman, 1927), it generally secretes a more viscous substance that is more difficult to record than secretions from the parotid gland.

In the early Pavlovian preparations a glass bulb was cemented tightly over the fistula to permit measurement of the amount of saliva secreted. Progressive refinements have led to the development of a drop counter for measuring the discrete number of drops of saliva. The secretion of saliva displaces drops of saline solution from a column and short-circuits an electric contact that energizes an electromagnetic marker that graphically records the number of drops (Makarychev, 1951). Sutherland and Katz (1961) have developed a drop-detector circuit that integrates electrical pulses generated by the displacement of the drops of saline and graphically records a rate curve of secretion.

With the use of continuous recording methods, aberrations in salivary flow have been noted with the Pavlov fistula. Some of the factors contributing to these aberrations have been attributed to (1) the constriction of the lumen of the duct of the gland resulting from downward movement of the animal's head (Podkopaiev, 1956) and (2) general movement of the animal in the restraining stock (Soltysik and Zbrozyna, 1957). Soltysik and Zbrozyna deduced that the major difficulties in the Pavlov preparation arose from a removal of structural support of the duct and contractions of the musculature surrounding the orifice. They modified the preparation for the parotid gland by severing Stenson's duct near the gland and externalizing it, thus removing a major portion of unsupported duct and muscles of the orifice.

Although the Soltysik and Zbrozyna preparation appears to ensure a uniform flow of saliva to the external surface, a difficulty with this preparation, as well as the Pavlov preparation, is associated with securing a capsule to the external labial tissue surrounding the fistula. This connection, usually achieved by the use of a wax preparation, presents the following problems: (1) it often takes an hour to accomplish the connection (Kozak, 1950); (2) constant precautions must be maintained to ensure a tight seal of the capsule since any air leakage would result in the saline solution's moving down the tube even in the absence of salivation; and (3) wax may seep into the fistula and impair the flow of saliva. A. V. Moore and Marcuse (1945) have eliminated the major problems of coupling to the fistula by employing a Lashley disk. A suction cup is applied around the external labial surface with an inner cup placed over the fistula and leading to a collection tube. This preparation does not control for variations in the lumen of the duct.

Lauer, Shapiro, and Radell (1961) have reported a parotid fistula preparation for the dog that warrants serious consideration. It incorporates the advantages of previous preparations and eliminates their major disadvantages. The technique involves externalizing, through a wound in the cheek, a section of polyethylene tube implanted and ligated directly into the dog's parotid duct. A polyethylene plug is secured in a wound on the opposite cheek to provide the means for introducing acid into the oral cavity as an unconditioned stimulus. The major advantages of the preparation are the following: (1) the insertion of the semirigid polyethylene tube into the duct eliminates the artifacts of salivary flow due to changes in the volume of the duct and to muscular contractions of the orifice; (2) occasional swabbing of the polyethylene tube, as well as stimulating secre-

tions from the gland by massaging it prior to the experimental session, ensures the removal of any substances that may impede salivary flow; (3) the surgical procedure requires less than one hour and the prepared dog can, if necessary, be used as a subject within 24 hours after surgery; and (4) the animal, once restrained in the apparatus, can be attached to the stimulating and recording system within a few seconds by simple friction plug-in devices. A current limitation of the preparation is that it remains stable for only five to six weeks because of necrosis of the tissue ligated to the tube entering the duct.

In preparing a dog for conditioning, a few sessions of adaptation to the restraining stock are necessary. Following adaptation the animal is anesthetized and surgery is performed for diverting the flow of saliva from the parotid duct to the external surface. In the Lauer et al. (1961) preparation, two incisions are made on the external surface of the cheek, one anterior to the course of the duct and the other over the course of the duct. A PE 160 polyethylene tube is then led under the skin between the two incisions and sutured into place within the anterior incision. By operating within the posterior incision, the duct is pierced and a smaller polyethylene tube (PE 50), with a shoulder on it, is introduced into the duct. After the tubing has been pushed posteriorly into the duct, the duct is ligated around the tubing to secure it and then passed through the larger tube. The shoulder on the tube prevents it from being pulled out all the way. The incisions are then closed and the secretion from the parotid gland flows through the polyethylene tubing to the outside. The tube is generally permitted to extend out from the cheek about 9 to 10 centimeters (cm). A hole is then made in the animal's opposite cheek with a leather punch, and a short piece of PE 260 polyethylene tube is slipped through the hole. Polyethylene flanges are then put on each end of the short piece of tube and the ends

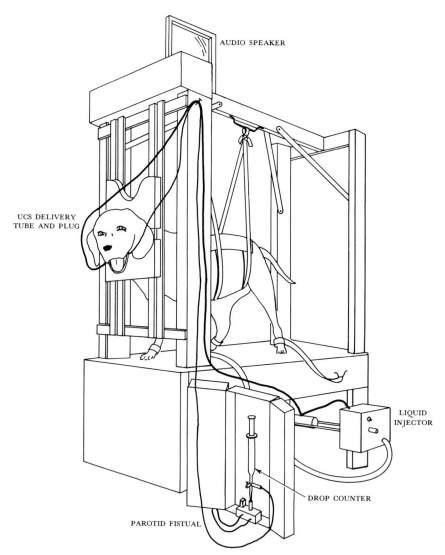

AUDIO SPEAKER

UCS DELIVERY
TUBE AND PLUG

LIQUID
INJECTOR

DROP COUNTER

PAROTID FISTUAL

Fig. 9-1   A view of the dog in the restraining stock prepared for salivary recording from the parotid gland. (*Courtesy of D. W. Lauer and M. M. Shapiro.*)

flared out to secure the flanges. This plug provides a means of introducing liquids into the subject's mouth.

Following recovery from the surgical preparation, the animal is placed in a restraining stock (see Fig. 9-1) by bringing his head through an adjustable head stock, wrapping a denim sling around his body, and securing straps around his legs. The saliva is collected by slipping a polyethylene tube (PE

100) over the protrusion of the polyethylene tube (PE 50) ligated within the dog's parotid duct and emanating from its cheek. The PE 100 tube is filled with a saline solution (a concentration of $2 \times 10^{-5} M$ will provide adequate electrical conductivity) and is led to a valve and hypodermic needle. Secretions by the subject into the tube will displace drops of saline solution through the hypodermic needle. Two pieces of wire, platinum

or some other relatively inert material, separated by an air gap are placed directly below the opening of the needle. When a drop forming on the end of the needle falls on the gap, an electric circuit is completed that activates a pen marker. Event markers should also be employed to record the onset and offset of the CS and UCS. A paper speed of 0.5 to 1.0 cm per sec will generally provide good temporal resolution of the drops of saliva.

A wide range of possible drop sizes can be employed as the response criterion by varying the gauge of the hypodermic tube. In recording the salivary flow, consideration must be given to the pressure differential between the point of hookup to the salivary preparation and the drop counter. The drop counter should be mounted at some distance below the preparation so that the gland can secrete freely without working against a hydrostatic pressure. A PE 100 tube filled with saline, the head of which is 2 ft above a #27 gauge hypodermic needle of the drop counter, will produce free-falling saline drops of about 0.01 cubic centimeter (cc) at the rate of 2 per sec. When the saline tube is hooked up to the preparation, one observes a salivary flow of CRs up to 2 to 3 drops per sec and UCRs up to 8 to 10 drops per sec. An experimenter can obtain resolution of the latency of salivary flow with minimum temporal distortion by using such a closed recording system, i.e., a liquid-filled system, and a relatively rigid polyethylene tube.

A complication in the measurement of salivary responses arises from the effect of rate of flow on the quantitative measurement of amount of saliva secreted. In conventional drop-detector circuits employing a closed system, the size of the drops falling from the gauge may decrease in size as flow rate increases (Ost, 1963). This problem appears to occur during measurement of the amount of unconditioned secretions. An empirical correction must then be applied to the data or a drop-detector system employed incorporating concurrent measurement of the volume of saliva secreted. As the rate of salivary flow increases, a back pressure will develop in the gland which may operate to produce a systematic change in salivary flow rate and volume and which may, in fact, contribute to the decrease in drop size. One can reduce the amount of back pressure by increasing the gauge of the needle in the drop detector. This is done at the cost of reducing the sensitivity of measurement of the rate of salivary flow.

An attractive property of the salivary response is that the experimenter may employ an appetitive or aversive UCS. Although dog biscuits and meat powder have been most frequently employed as the UCS, a liquid reinforcer permits the investigator more precise temporal control over its presentation. In the Lauer, Shapiro, and Radell preparation the UCS is presented by a liquid injector (Davis LR-130) equipped with a 20-cc syringe that delivers 5 cc of an acetic acid solution within a 1-sec interval. A polyethylene tube leading from the syringe is connected to the subject's cheek by a sawed-off #13 hypodermic needle inserted into the polyethylene plug secured in the hole prepared in the cheek. Although the acidity and amount of the UCS have not been systematically investigated, conditioning of the salivary response has been obtained for 0.3, 1.5, and 7.5 percent acetic acid solutions with some indication of better conditioning with the stronger concentrations (Fitzgerald, 1963; Warstler, 1963).

The investigator must recognize that the use of a liquid reinforcer presents some methodological difficulties. Since the amount of the unconditioned secretion will depend upon the area of the oral cavity stimulated, variability in the area of stimulation will produce variability in salivary flow. Furthermore, the animal may impede the flow of the reinforcer by placing his tongue over the plug in his cheek. If the animal were to persist in such behavior, the experimenter would have no choice but to discard him.

Considerable variability exists among dogs in the amount of saliva secreted and in degree of conditioning. Russian experimenters attribute between-animal variability to different "nervous types" (Podkopaiev, 1956). It might be expected that the use of pure strains of dogs would substantially reduce between-animal variability. Considerations of cost, laboratory temperament, and resistance to infection, as well as the size of the duct and gland, would be some of the factors determining the breed of dog to employ.

Although the fundamental principles of salivary conditioning have been derived from the studies of Pavlov and his students, the Russian tradition of utilizing the conditioned reflex as a technique for studying the functions of the higher nervous system (Pavlov, 1927, 1930) has provided little quantitative information on the basic conditioning parameters. An examination of the Russian literature (see *Pavlov Journal of Higher Nervous Activity*) reveals a marked omission of procedural details; selective presentation of data; a relinquishing of experimental control through the selective and differential treatment of subjects; and the utilization of subjects previously or concomitantly conditioned under a diversity of conditions.

On the other hand, investigations of salivary conditioning by United States experimenters have not been extensive. They have focused on the possibility of conditioning the response with drugs (Collins and Tatum, 1925; Crisler, 1928, 1930; Crisler, Booker, Van Liere, and Hall, 1933; Finch, 1938a, 1938c); the effects of food or water deprivation on the CR and UCR (Finch, 1938a; Gantt, 1929, 1938; Kleitman, 1927); and "fatigue" of the CR and UCR (Gantt, 1940; Kleitman, 1930). Some studies have provided data on the conditioning process (Ellison, 1964; Fitzgerald, 1963; Shapiro, 1959, 1960, 1961; Zener, 1937; Zener and McCurdy, 1939), but few generalizations are presently possible.

Response measurement

A substantial amount of salivary flow may be observed between conditioning trials that presents problems for response measurement. There appear to be several possible contributors to these interval secretions: secretions persisting from presentations of the UCS and those that may arise from swallowing or chewing movements to stimuli still present in the oral cavity. In the presence of a base line of salivary flow, a percentage measure of responding to the CS, i.e., the presence or absence of salivary flow, is insensitive to changes in the strength of the salivary response. Hence, amplitude or amount of saliva secreted to the CS is generally employed as a measure of strength of salivary conditioning. To correct for the interval secretions a common procedure is to subtract the number of drops secreted in an interval preceding CS onset (comparable to the CS-UCS interval) from the amount secreted in the CS-UCS interval. If a CS-UCS interval of 15 sec is employed, the amount of saliva secreted 15 sec before CS onset is subtracted from the amount of saliva secreted in the CS-UCS interval.

Since a major contributor of intertrial interval secretions appears to be the time required for a trailing off of the UCR, a substantial increase in the reliability and sensitivity of the amplitude measure can be obtained by using an intertrial interval of sufficient length to permit unconditioned secretions to subside. Gantt (1938, 1940), using food as the UCS, maintains that unconditioned secretions in the dog practically always subside within 20 to 45 sec. The trailing-off time will depend upon the amount and type of UCS as well as the organism. Warstler (1963), using a 1.5 percent acetic acid solution as the UCS, observed unconditioned secretion in the dog that may require over 60 sec to subside. Moore and Marcuse (1945), in conditioning pigs, observed unconditioned secretions to food that generally persisted for about three minutes. A good rule of thumb is to employ intertrial intervals at least two to three times as long as the duration of unconditioned secretions. It should be clear, however, that a liquid reinforcer generally permits the investigator tighter control over the duration of the UCS.

Human conditioning

Three methods are generally employed in measuring salivary flow in man aside from the accidental occurrence of a salivary fistula: (1) insertion of a small cannula into the mouth of the duct; (2) absorption of saliva by a roll of cotton; and (3) application of a suction disk (Lashley disk) over the mouth of the gland. The cannula method is most commonly employed for obtaining samples of salivary secretions but is not very suitable for quantitative measurement. One can never be sure that some of the secretions are not leaking past the walls of the cannula, and frequently the expanding walls of the duct will permit the cannula to slip out.

Razran introduced a technique for inserting small rolls of dental cotton $\frac{1}{2}$ by $1\frac{1}{2}$ in. under the subject's tongue and employed the method in a number of conditioning studies (Razran, 1935a, 1935b, 1939a to e, 1949a to d, 1955a, 1955b). The cotton roll is weighed before placement under the tongue and then weighed again after a specified period, and the increment or amount of saliva secreted is recorded. To avoid changes in weight due to absorption, evaporation, and adhesion, the dry rolls are weighed in small waterproof envelopes before each trial. After a trial has been completed, the wet cotton is returned to the envelope and weighed again. A conditioning trial consists of a 2- to 4-min eating period, e.g., chewing gum, sucking a lollipop, eating pretzels or small cheese sandwiches, in the presence of a CS, e.g., a flashing light. Each conditioning trial is then followed by a 5- to 7-min testing period in which the subject places a dry roll of cotton under his tongue for a 1-min period of absorption. Two control measurements are taken during the testing period. An initial roll of cotton always follows the eating period and serves to eliminate the supernormal accumulation of saliva in the glands and is discarded. A second roll is rotated in the interval and is used to calcu-

late the effect of a roll of cotton in the mouth per se on salivary flow. To assess conditioning, additional rolls of cotton are then presented in the interval paired with a 1-min test presentation of the CS alone.

Although Razran's technique for recording the combined salivary flow from all glands has permitted him to demonstrate the effects of attitudinal factors on conditioning (1935a) as well as semantic conditioning (1949c), considerable trial-to-trial variability must be expected in the amount of saliva secreted. In part, these variations would appear to be associated with the lack of rigorous control over the CS-UCS interval, duration of the UCS, and consistent placement of the roll of cotton. Furthermore, the technique does not permit the determination of response latency, nor has it successfully permitted detailing the acquisition function through the use of anticipatory CRs (Jones, 1939; Razran, 1935a).

Lashley (1916) invented a device for recording secretions from the human parotid gland that does not suffer from some of the limitations of the cotton technique. The device shown in Fig. 9-2 consists of a silver-plated metal disk 12 to 18 millimeters (mm) in diameter, composed of two concentric chambers. The inner chamber B, 8 to 10 mm in diameter and 3 mm deep, is placed against the cheek over the opening of Stenson's duct, and the outer chamber A, in the form of a circular groove about 2 mm wide and 3 mm deep, is used to adhere the disk to the cheek. When negative pressure is applied to tube C with a suction pump, air is exhausted from

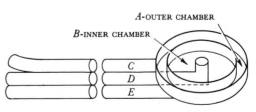

Fig. 9-2 A modified version of the Lashley disk. (*Adapted from Watson, 1924, p. 30.*)

the outer chamber, thus sealing the disk to the cheek. The saliva then collects in the inner chamber and is free to flow out of the mouth through tube D and onto a drop-detector circuit. Progressive refinement of the Lashley disk (Finesinger and Finesinger, 1937; Finesinger, Sutherland, and McGuire, 1942; Sutherland, 1959; Sutherland and Katz, 1961) has led to the introduction of a third tube E to serve as a mechanical point of attachment for a polyethylene tube delivering a liquid UCS, e.g., 2 cc of sweetened lemon juice or orange juice. The UCS is squirted into the subject's mouth by means of a liquid pump through small pinholes in a polyethylene tube close to its point of attachment to tube E. The polyethylene tubes connected to C, D, and E, each about 7 mm long and 2 mm in diameter, pass between the cheek and the upper molars and out through the corner of the subject's mouth.[1]

In the conditioning situation the disk is removed from an antiseptic solution, and the polyethylene tube leading from the drop-detector circuit is filled with a saline solution and connected to the salivary collection chamber. The disk is then inserted into the subject's mouth and the amount of negative pressure to apply to the suction ring (generally 10 to 30 cm of mercury pressure) is empirically determined. If too much pressure is applied, the tissue surrounding the opening of the duct may become irritated and serve as a source of discomfort to the subject. Insufficient pressure may permit the disk to become dislodged. The experimenter can check on the stability of the preparation by asking the subject to open and close his mouth and to swallow vigorously. Another precaution is to record simultaneously from the left and right parotid glands with two Lashley disks. This is done in order that any disruption of salivary flow, such as might result from a dis-

placement of one of the disks, can be readily detected (Finesinger et al., 1942). The drop detector should be positioned several feet below the subject's head to permit the gland to secrete freely.

The base rate of salivary flow from the parotid gland is about 0.02 to 0.15 cc per min (Sutherland, 1959; Winsor, 1929); but yawning, swallowing, and chewing movements can raise the rate to as high as 0.6 cc per min (Lashley, 1916; Winsor, 1929). A marked asymmetry in salivary flow can be detected from each of the parotid glands when chewing objects on the left or right side of the mouth (Winsor, 1929). Thus the subject can produce considerable variability in unconditioned secretions by shifting the position of food in his mouth. The experimenter can control this problem to a considerable extent by employing a liquid UCS.

The characteristics of the unconditioned secretions in humans (as in infrahuman organisms) place certain restrictions on the intertrial interval parameter. The presentation of 2 cc of sweetened lemon juice will produce secretions from the parotid gland in a series of spurts rather than a uniform series of drops. The rate of salivary flow rises to a maximum within 10 to 15 sec and then takes 8 to 10 min to subside to its base level (Sutherland, 1959). In general, approximately six conditioning trials would be employed within an experimental session at intertrial intervals of at least 8 to 10 min. When long intertrial intervals are used, the experimenter must realize that subjects may become bored and fall asleep. One precaution against such a possibility is to present the subject with a task during the intertrial interval, e.g., reciting numbers to himself as they appear in front of him.

A difficult methodological problem in both human and infrahuman salivary condi-

---

[1] Krasnogorski (as reported by Razran, 1933) independently developed parotid disks and kidney-shaped disks for recording from the submaxillary glands. The greater possibility of irritating the surrounding mucosa of the submaxillary ducts through suction disks and of dislodging them through tongue and swallowing movements makes recording from them less satisfactory than recording from the parotid glands.

tioning is the possible contribution of jaw, tongue, and swallowing movements to salivary flow. In dogs considerable variability may be noted in the motor components of behavior to the presentation of acetic acid. Some dogs open their mouths and the acid and saliva bathing the oral cavity flow out. Other dogs keep their mouths closed and swallow the acid. Each of these motor patterns will contribute differentially to unconditioned secretions. If they occur to the CS in anticipation of the UCS, they could differentially affect the recording of conditioned secretions. With humans, the experimenter may attempt to maintain some control over the motor contributors to unconditioned secretions by instructing the subject to hold the liquid UCS in his mouth for several seconds before swallowing and to refrain from other mouth movements. A signal could be employed to indicate when the subject should swallow. The contribution of anticipatory chewing, swallowing, and tongue-licking movements to conditioned secretion appears to present a more difficult methodological problem. Specifically, the possibility can be entertained that what becomes conditioned is not the salivary response per se but motor or skeletal responses that act as unconditioned stimuli (Smith, 1954). Although the frequently observed uniformity of the amount of saliva secreted as anticipatory CRs would argue against such an interpretation, the problem has not been put to an experimental test. In infrahuman organisms conditioning under curare-type drugs, e.g., *d*-tubocurarine, might permit an assessment of the possible contribution of motor responses to conditioned secretions. With humans the problem might be attacked indirectly by assessing the effects of instructing subjects to inhibit or refrain from motor responses in the CS-UCS interval.

Although investigators other than Razran have also reported successful conditioning of the human salivary response (Finesinger and Sutherland, 1939; Finesinger *et al.*, 1942; Krasnogorski, 1926; Naito, 1957, 1958), few

of the parameters of conditioning are presently known.

EYELID CONDITIONING

Conditioning in humans

Cason (1922) reported the first attempt to condition the eyeblink reflex. An auditory CS was paired with a UCS consisting of an electric shock applied to the orbital region of the eye. A mechanical coupling attached to the subject's eyelid permitted a lid closure to break an electric contact that controlled a chronoscope recording response latencies. Switzer (1930) employed an auditory CS and the blow of a padded miniature hammer to the facial tissue below the subject's eye as the UCS. A silk thread cemented to the eyelid and coupled to a writing lever provided a continuous record of eyelid movement. Telford and Anderson (1932) employed essentially the same technique, but the UCS was the fall of a hammer against a piece of plate glass positioned 3 cm in front of the subject's eye.

Although various mechanical lever systems have been devised, it was not until the Dodge pendulum photochronograph (Dodge, 1913) was employed by Hilgard (1931) that sufficiently detailed records of eyelid movement were obtained. The photochronograph simultaneously controls the presentation of the CS and UCS and photographically records eyelid movement. The record is obtained by passing a beam of light through a slit onto a photographic plate attached to the bob of the pendulum, while an artificial eyelash of stiff paper attached to the subject's upper eyelid casts a shadow on the free-falling photographic plate.

The degree of precision obtained by the Dodge pendulum photochronograph has not been exceeded by other techniques, but advances in electronics and the development of inkwriting oscillographs have permitted the development of methods for recording eyelid movement that are more economical and less demanding upon both the subject and the experimenter. An experimenter can obtain a record of eyeblinks by placing electromyograph (EMG) electrodes in the orbital region of the eye and amplifying the signal onto oscillograph paper. This system does not separate sharply those signals arising from lid movements and those arising from rotation of the globe of the eye. Spence and Taylor (1951) reported a technique involving the use of a lightweight rotary potentiometer, amplifier, and inkwriting penmotor that is widely used for obtaining detailed records of eyelid movement. The rotary arm is mounted on an adjustable headband just above the subject's eyelid; and a lever, attached at right angles to the rotating arm of the potentiometer, is coupled to the eyelid by a length of string. A tiny plastic tab attached to the end of the string is fastened to the subject's upper eyelid by a piece of adhesive tape. A small clock spring is wound around the poten-tiometer arm to provide a small restoring force, thus permitting the potentiometer arm to follow the eyelid's movements. The headgear and/or oscillograph system is commercially available from the Hunter Manufacturing Company. The use of standard oscillograph systems (e.g., Brush, Gilson, Grass, Offner, Sanborn) will provide the experimenter with a more versatile recording system for only a modest increase in cost.

A modification of the Iowa eyelid transducer (Grant, Schipper, and Ross, 1952), which is currently employed in several laboratories, appears in Fig. 9-3. The subject wears an adjustable elastic headband that supports an aluminum plate padded with a sheet of foam rubber. A rigid plastic stimulus air jet and a rotary potentiometer (Giannini, model 85153) are mounted on the aluminum plate. The orifice of the air jet is positioned to the subject's eye by adjustment of the angle between the strips of aluminum and

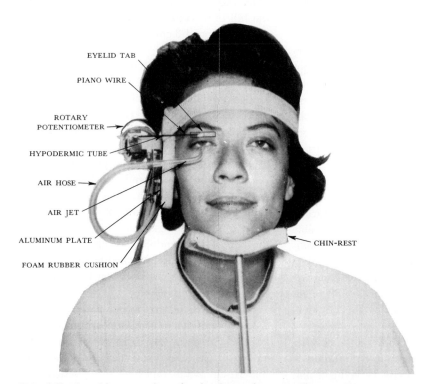

EYELID TAB

PIANO WIRE

ROTARY POTENTIOMETER →

HYPODERMIC TUBE

AIR HOSE →

AIR JET

ALUMINUM PLATE

FOAM RUBBER CUSHION

CHIN-REST

Fig. 9-3 A subject wearing the headgear for recording eyelid movement.

the lateral movement of the plastic air jet through a brass ring. The essential modification of the headgear is the coupling of the potentiometer to the upper eyelid. A hypodermic tube is mechanically coupled at right angles to the shaft of the potentiometer, and a length of piano wire is inserted in the tubing. A swivel-mounted circular piece of thin aluminum is at the other end of the piano wire. The aluminum tab is attached to the subject's eyelid by a piece of adhesive tape, permitting the movement of the lid to be transmitted to the shaft of the potentiometer. This attachment permits the investigator to obtain a continuous record of eyelid movement without the use of a restoring spring and also provides a record that reflects the arcing movement of the eyeblink.

In the conditioning situation the subject is seated comfortably in a straight-backed chair within a sound-treated experimental enclosure or room. The experimenter mounts the headgear on the subject, connects the tab to the eyelid, and adjusts the height of a chin rest. A circular milk-glass window positioned several feet in front of the subject's eyes and slightly above his line of vision can serve as a fixation point as well as the source of a visual CS. Although movements of the subject's head do not interfere with the recording of eyelid responses, the chin rest and fixation point minimize shifts in the subject's visual line of regard and serve to reduce variability in the position of the subject's eyelid. If a visual CS is employed, an increase in the illumination of the milk-glass window by the discharge of an electric bulb can serve as the CS. A neon bulb with a rise time of only several milliseconds is preferred, e.g., a 2-watt General Electric NE 40 neon lamp, because of the relatively slow rise time of an incandescent bulb. An auditory CS may also be presented through a speaker or by the use of earphones. When a visual CS is employed, the experimental enclosure should be well illuminated to minimize the occurrence of nonassociative eyeblinks, i.e., beta responses. A two-way intercommunication system should

also be employed to permit the experimenter to give instructions and to allow other communications.

The frictional torque of the potentiometer is rated at about 0.004 inch-ounce (in.-oz) and, when properly coupled to the subject's eyelid, places a negligible load upon its movement. To translate the movement of the rotary arm of the potentiometer to an electric signal, a d-c voltage is impressed upon the end terminals of the potentiometer and the common center tap is fed to a d-c amplifier. The amplifier then drives a penmotor to provide a graphic record of the subject's eyelid movements. Event markers are employed to indicate the onset and offset of the CS and UCS. Although d-c voltages as high as 150 volts may be applied to the terminals of some Giannini potentiometer models, namely, those with specifications of at least 2.2 watts and 10,000 ohms, the use of a well-regulated 20- to 30-volt d-c supply and medium-gain d-c amplifier will give very satisfactory graphic recordings.

A number of stimuli can reflexively elicit an eyeblink, e.g., electric shock to the skin over the orbital nerve, intense auditory or visual stimuli, and objects moving toward the eye, but the corneal air puff is the most commonly employed UCS. In order to deliver a corneal air puff to the subject, a flexible air hose is connected between the stimulus air jet and the source of the compressed air. The orifice is generally positioned about $\frac{1}{2}$ in. from the cornea. The air hose is interrupted by a d-c voltage air solenoid, and a corneal puff of specified duration is delivered to the subject as a result of the electrical activation of the solenoid. Since the solenoid provides auditory cues, it is generally sound-treated with insulation material and placed at a distance from the subject, usually in the experimenter's control room. The greater the separation of the solenoid from the subject, the longer is the time lag from activation of the solenoid to delivery of the air puff to the subject's cornea. It is necessary, therefore, to calibrate the delay in presentation of the air puff in order to determine the effective CS-UCS interval. A pressure switch coupled to the air jet (commercially available from the Hunter Manufacturing Company) will permit calibration of the delay in the puff when it is connected to a latency clock. A simpler technique is to adjust the orifice of the air jet so that it hits a tab taped to the hypodermic needle mounted to the shaft of the potentiometer that will be graphically recorded by a deflection of the penmotor. If the recording paper is moving at a fixed speed, an accurate determination can be made of the delay in presentation of the air puff by measuring the distance between the deflection of the event marker for UCS onset and the deflection of the penmotor.

Generally, a tank of compressed air or nitrogen is used for presenting the corneal puff. A two-stage pressure regulator, which must be mounted on the tank, permits the investigator to control the air pressure. The gauges on pressure regulators are usually not sufficiently accurate to allow for rigorous control over puff pressure. Control may be obtained by connecting the bottom arm of a Y joint to the pressure regulator and running a rubber hose from one arm of the Y joint to a manometer; the other arm is connected to the air hose leading to the solenoid and subject. When the above connections have been completed, the experimenter can accurately adjust the pressure at the source by reading the height of the manometer. The pressure at the source is not necessarily the pressure of the puff at its point of delivery to the eye. The pressure at the orifice of the air jet will depend upon such factors as the duration of the air puff and the characteristics of the air valve; the size of the orifice of the air jet; and whether there are small leaks in the line. To calibrate the intensity of the air puff at its point of delivery to the eye, connect a rubber hose from a manometer to the air jet, activate the air solenoid, and read the pressure in millimeters of mercury. The practice of specifying the

puff pressure at the orifice of the air jet has not been general enough to permit between-laboratory comparisons. Puff pressures from 20 to 300 mm of mercury have been used at the Indiana Laboratory, but a puff of 80 to 100 mm pressure and a duration of 100 milliseconds (msec) are usually employed.

A common practice in eyelid conditioning laboratories is to record graphic deflections of 1 mm or more from the base line as eyeblinks. The manner of coupling to the eyelid, i.e., whether or not the device tracks the arcing movement of the lid, and the amount of amplification of the signal are factors that determine the sensitivity of the system to eyelid movements. The gain on the amplifier should be set so that the recording of UCRs does not overdrive the penmotors and result in peak clipping of the signal. Since the downward excursion of the upper eyelid is about 15 mm in the average human adult, an arrangement in which a 1-mm movement of the eyelid results in a 1-mm excursion of the penmotor will generally be quite satisfactory.

It is desirable to employ high paper speeds, e.g., 100 to 300 mm per sec, to permit good resolution of the latency and form of the eyelid response. On the other hand, when high paper speeds are employed, it becomes impractical to obtain continuous records throughout the session. Thus, the paper drive is generally started a fraction of a second before the start of a trial and made to terminate shortly after the end of the trial.

To monitor the subject's eyelid position, the experimenter can (1) employ a one-way viewing mirror, (2) read the pointer on a voltmeter in series with the penmotor, or (3) use a multiple-speed paper drive that can be kept running continuously at a low speed and then switched to a high speed during conditioning trials (e.g., Offner oscillographs with a Type 504A or 504B paper drive). When an experimenter monitors continuously, he is better able to detect difficulties that might arise from the headgear's slipping, the tab's falling off, or the subject's falling asleep.

An equipment component frequently employed in eyelid conditioning laboratories is the differential amplifier connected in series or in parallel with the response amplifier. The deflection of a penmotor driven by the differential amplifier occurs at the point of inflection of the eyelid response pen and serves as an aid in the resolution of response latency (see Fig. 9-4). The deflection magnitude of the penmotor also provides an objective measure of the speed of eyelid closure, i.e., recruitment. Normally, a conventional thyratron circuit or supersensitive relay can be activated by the voltage change produced by a shift in the base position of the subject's eyelid. Firing a thyratron or supersensitive relay with the positive output from a differential amplifier gives the experimenter an effective device for activating eyeblink contingent events that are uncontaminated by shifts in the base position of the eyelid. If an experimenter is interested in investigating instrumental avoidance conditioning, the output of the differential amplifier can be used to activate a relay that prevents the occurrence of the UCS whenever an eyeblink occurs in the CR range.

An innovation in classical conditioning involves the use of a *yoked-control procedure*. This procedure is used for comparisons of classical and avoidance conditioning and involves running pairs of subjects concurrently (Gormezano, J. W. Moore, and Deaux, 1962; J. W. Moore and Gormezano, 1961; Runquist, Sidowski, and Gormezano, 1962). When one of the subjects, designated as the avoidance subject, makes a CR, the UCS is omitted for both subjects on that trial. If the avoidance subject fails to make a CR, the UCS is presented to both subjects at the usual CS-UCS interval. The noncontingent-yoked subject is being classically conditioned under a reinforcement schedule determined by the performance of the avoidance subject. The requirements for running two subjects simultaneously include a multiple-channel oscillograph, two headgears, two subject enclosures, and a Y joint with flexible

tubing leading from the air hose to the subjects' air jets. The output of the differential amplifier of the avoidance subject is used to activate an avoidance circuit constructed so that eyeblinks that occur within the CR latency range, i.e., 150 to 200 msec after CS onset to the usual time of UCS onset, can prevent the occurrence of the UCS by gating out the relay that activates the air solenoid. One can control the latency range of eyeblinks defined as CRs, which can activate the avoidance circuit by feeding the output of the differential amplifier through the contacts of an electronic timer.

The yoked-control technique has permitted an experimental test of the relative efficacy of conditioning under classical and avoidance procedures equated for pattern and number of UCS occurrences. However, investigators must recognize the limitations of the technique. Specifically, for the yoked-classical subject the experimenter sacrifices one of the most elegant aspects of the classical conditioning paradigm—the experimenter's control over the pattern and frequency of UCS presentation.

The eyelid response appears to be the most frequently employed response system in American classical conditioning laboratories, with delay conditioning (using either a visual or an auditory CS) being the most commonly employed procedure. The most frequently used values of the conditioning parameters are (1) a CS-UCS interval of 500 msec; (2) UCS duration of 50 to 100 msec; (3) a mean intertrial interval of 15 to 25 sec; (4) 60 to 100 conditioning trials within an experimental session, frequently followed by 20 to 30 extinction trials; and (5) reinforcement schedules of 25, 50, 75, and 100 percent.

Response definition

Figure 9-4 presents a series of records obtained in an eyelid conditioning experiment. The top line in each record represents the onset (upward deflection) of the CS, and the second line represents a record of eyelid

RECORD NO. 1

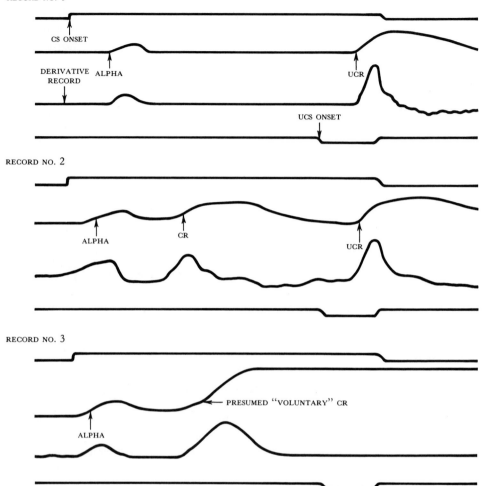

CS ONSET

DERIVATIVE ALPHA
RECORD

UCR

UCS ONSET

RECORD NO. 2

ALPHA

CR

UCR

RECORD NO. 3

PRESUMED "VOLUNTARY" CR

ALPHA

Fig. 9-4 A series of graphic records obtained in the human eyelid condition-ing experiment. The records were obtained at a paper speed of 200 mm per sec, CS-UCS interval of 500 msec, and UCS duration of 100 msec.

movement. The third line shows a record of the first derivative of eyelid movement, and the fourth line indicates the onset (down-ward deflection) and offset of the UCS. Since the recording paper moves at a fixed speed, e.g., 200 mm per sec, the latency of eyelid responses from CS onset can be meas-ured by placing a template with millimeter divisions on the record and converting dis-tance to time.

The response latency of CRs will vary as a function of the CS-UCS interval, UCS in-

tensity, and other conditioning parameters. This makes it difficult to state precisely a standard latency for a conditioned eyelid re-sponse. One can observe CRs with a latency as short as 120 to 150 msec after CS onset. Other types of eyelid closure (not CRs) also occur in the interval between the CS and UCS. The first of these responses is a re-flexive blink to the CS (alpha response) that differs from the CR in latency, magnitude, and duration. The small eyelid deflection pre-sented on the left-hand side of the first record in Fig. 9-4 is the alpha response. The alpha response is generally one-tenth the amplitude of the UCR, has a duration of 30 to 50 msec, and has a latency range of 40 to 120 msec with a mode of about 75 msec (Grant and Adams, 1944; Hilgard, 1931; J. W. Moore and Gormezano, 1961). The alpha response to an auditory CS has not been systematically investigated, but it appears to have essentially the same response characteristics (Runquist, Sidowski, and Gormezano, 1962). The magnitude and frequency of alpha responses decrease over conditioning trials (Hansche and Grant, 1960), and the experimenter can appreciably reduce their frequency of occurrence by employing a visual or auditory CS of low intensity. Alpha responses are not elicited from all subjects, and blinks may occur in the alpha latency range that do not appear to be alpha responses. Nevertheless, laboratory practice is to record as CRs blinks that are initiated at least 150 msec after CS onset.

A secondary reflex response to a light CS (beta response) was isolated by Grant (1943a, 1943b, 1945) while employing the Dodge pendulum photochronograph. Grant noted that a reflexive response occurred to a light CS that was of a longer latency than the alpha response. These increased in frequency as the subject became more dark-adapted under the dimly illuminated conditions required by the photographic procedure. The frequency of beta responses also increased with increasing intensity of the light CS. Grant and Norris (1947) demonstrated that beta responses occurred in a latency range of 120 to 240 msec after CS onset and appeared comparable in magnitude and form to responses generally designated as anticipatory CRs. To avoid the contamination of beta responses in the scoring of CRs, investigators have shifted the latency criterion of CRs from 120 to 150 msec to 240 msec after CS onset. Since the occurrence of beta responses appears to interfere with the acquisition of CRs (Grant and Norris, 1947), the experimenter should make

every effort to eliminate them. This may be done by employing a nonvisual CS or maintaining the subject in a well-illuminated enclosure. Although most eyelid laboratories maintain subjects under light-adapted conditions, many persist in the practice of scoring responses as CRs that are initiated at least 200 or 250 msec after CS onset. A latency criterion of 150 msec appears to be sufficiently conservative.

Another problem in the identification of CRs is whether or not to count any eyeblink occurring 150 msec after CS onset as a CR. This problem exists when comparing groups having the same or different CS-UCS intervals. It arises from (1) the fact that subjects spontaneously blink at fairly regular intervals, about once every 6 sec; and (2) the fact that as the subject's cornea dries from corneal air puffs, or his tension level increases, the spontaneous blink rate may increase. Since spontaneous eyeblinks have not been reliably distinguished from conditioned eyeblinks on the basis of latency or form, experimenters approach the problem by (1) instructing subjects to blink and then fixate at a point upon presentation of a ready signal (a weak buzzer or the verbal statement "ready") 1 to 4 sec prior to CS onset, (2) restricting the intensity or duration of the air puff, and (3) rejecting subjects who prior to conditioning persist in making responses in the CR latency range to repeated presentations of the CS alone. Each of these procedures will reduce the frequency of spontaneous blinks but will not eliminate their occurrence. An alternative approach is a correction procedure. In investigations that varied CS-UCS intervals, McAllister (1953) subtracted the percentage of responses in the first block of trials from the percentage in subsequent trial blocks; Boneau (1958) counted as CRs only those responses in a latency interval which increased over conditioning trials. Hansche and Grant (1960) counted the first response to occur in an interval and then applied a linear correction for increasing CS-UCS intervals. In the former procedure the correction is heavily weighted by the performance of the subject during the early conditioning trials. The Hansche and Grant procedure involves the assumption that the frequency of spontaneous blinks is a simple linear function of the CS-UCS interval. The utilization of pseudo-conditioning control groups, in which subjects are given unpaired presentations of the CS and UCS at the same parametric values as the experimental groups, would appear to be the most statisfactory solution to the problem. An empirical correction could then be applied to the experimental groups from a determination of the frequency of eyeblinks in the CR range given on CS trials by each of the respective control groups. This technique assumes no interaction between the rate of spontaneous blinking and paired or unpaired presentations of the CS and UCS.

The eyeblink as a skeletal response can be brought under the subject's verbal control. Therefore, the experimenter generally employs a set of neutral instructions that request the subject to neither aid nor inhibit his eyelid responses (Gormezano and J. W. Moore, 1962). Aside from the difficulty of ensuring compliance to these instructions, eyeblinks that occur prior to and overlap with the occurrence of a corneal air puff can prevent it from striking the cornea. Spence and his coworkers (Spence and Ross, 1959; Spence and Taylor, 1951) have argued for the elimination of subjects from the data as "voluntary responders" if 50 percent or more of their CRs have a latency between 200 and 300 msec, when a "ready" signal is employed before each conditioning trial. The rejection procedure rests on the theoretical assumption that there is a class of subjects participating in eyelid conditioning studies who (1) "voluntarily" blink to the CS in order to "cooperate" with the experimenter or (2) "voluntarily" blink to the CS to attenuate the noxious effects of a corneal air puff, i.e., have the air puff fall on the eyelid rather than on the cornea. It is maintained that

subjects who "voluntarily" blink to the CS demonstrate eyeblinks of a form characterized by sharp closure, long duration, and short latency (see record 3 in Fig. 9-4) and that ready agreement can be attained between judges in the selection of these "voluntary" and "nonvoluntary" form responses (Spence and Ross, 1959). Furthermore, Spence and Ross (1959) have indicated that one can effectively eliminate the greatest number of *judged voluntary form responses* and the fewest *judged nonvoluntary form responses* by removing the data of subjects classified as "voluntary responders" by the latency criterion.

Although alternative formulations can be made for subjects demonstrating judged voluntary form responses (these are subjects with higher learning-rate parameters; see Gormezano and J. W. Moore, 1962; J. W. Moore and Gormezano, 1963), the basic difficulty with the Iowa rejection procedure is methodological. In contrast to the contention of ready agreement in judging eyelid responses as voluntary or nonvoluntary on the basis of form, complete agreement between sophisticated judges have been obtained for only 71.4 percent of the responses in one instance (Spence and Ross, 1959) and for only 68.8 percent of the responses in the other (Hartman and Ross, 1961). Such relatively mundane considerations as differences in "hardware" among conditioning laboratories also enters into the classification problem. The relative frequency of (as well as the degree of agreement in judging) various recorded forms of the eyelid response will vary, for example, as a function of the amount of peak clipping of the response signal, the paper speed employed in recording, and the type of hookup employed in coupling the eyelid to the transducer. Spence and Ross (1959) assume that they have demonstrated the validity of employing their latency criterion, but its validity necessarily depends upon the amount of agreement in making form judgments. Consequently, the obtained degree of concordance of 71.4 and 68.8 percent places a serious limitation upon the validity of the latency criterion.

Although by improving the fidelity of recording the eyelid response and standardizing apparatus one could reduce between-laboratory differences in the frequency of various recorded forms of the response (and perhaps increase the coefficient of concordance of form judgments), such modification would not mitigate more fundamental within-laboratory problems. As indicated, Spence and Ross (1959) have maintained that in removing the data of subjects classified as "voluntary responders" by the latency criterion, one can effectively eliminate the greatest number of judged voluntary form responses and the fewest judged nonvoluntary form responses. But the validity of the latency criterion (or any other criterion) minimally requires demonstrating that when subjects are rejected as voluntary responders there is an invariant elimination of the greatest number of judged voluntary form responses and the fewest judged nonvoluntary form responses. However, it has been noted that the latency distribution of so-called judged voluntary form responses is affected by air-puff intensity (Spence and Ross, 1959, p. 378) and by the presence or absence of a ready signal (Hartman and Ross, 1961). Similarly, the distribution of response latencies of subjects instructed to blink to the CS (in the absence of a ready signal) has been shown to vary as a function of massed or spaced conditioning trials (Hartman, Grant, and Ross, 1960) and with UCS intensity (Gormezano and Moore, 1962). Consequently, since any variable affecting the latencies of judged voluntary form responses also affects the validity of the latency criterion employed to eliminate them, the failure of the latencies of judged voluntary form responses to remain invariant renders the latency criterion employed to classify subjects as "voluntary responders" methodologically inadequate.

Hartman and Ross (1961) have suggested employing a recruitment criterion (based upon an objective measure of speed of eyelid closure) to classify subjects as voluntary responders. However, the recruitment measure also requires demonstrating that the rejection of subjects as voluntary responders leads to an invariant optimal elimination of the greatest number of judged voluntary form responses and the fewest judged nonvoluntary form responses. Whether or not this condition of invariance can be satisfied by the recruitment criterion remains an empirical question, but from the present vantage point the logical requirements make such an outcome highly unlikely. A study by Goodrich (1964) indicated that even when a ready signal was employed, over 60 percent of the responses classified as "voluntary responses" by the recruitment criterion occurred 300 msec after CS onset. On the other hand, in the Spence and Ross (1959) investigation only 13.5 percent of their judged voluntary form responses occurred after 300 msec. The reported results of these two studies do not permit one to determine whether the disparity arises from the fact that the recruitment measure and/or the latencies of judged voluntary form responses are uniquely affected by possible differences in parameters and procedures, but clearly the Goodrich results provide an empirical basis for questioning the validity of the recruitment criterion. If the investigator is concerned with the theoretical possibility that subjects "voluntarily" blink to modify the sensory consequences of a corneal air puff, the problem may have to be treated by the use of a UCS that does not appear to permit this possibility (e.g., electric shock to the orbital region of the eye).

Conditioning in infrahumans

The eyelid reflex is a prompt, stable response as comparable in direction and extent of excursion from species to species as any moving member of the mammal (Strughold, 1930). Nevertheless, the literature contains only a few references to infrahuman species. Hilgard and Marquis (1935, 1936) conditioned four dogs and four monkeys by employing the Dodge photochronograph with light as the CS and a corneal air puff as the UCS. Hughes and Schlosberg (1938) conditioned four rats to a buzzer with a corneal air puff, and graphic records were obtained by hooking a muscle lever to a surgical loop sutured into the subject's eyelid. Biel and Wickens (1941) conditioned the eyelid response of rats to a visual CS and recorded the frequency and latency of eyelid closures by the breaking of an electric contact with a thread sutured in the eyelid.

More recently, Schneiderman, Fuentes, and Gormezano (1962) have conditioned the eyelid; Gormezano, Schneiderman, Deaux, and Fuentes (1962), the nictitating membrane (third eyelid); and Deaux and Gormezano (1963), eyeball retraction in the albino rabbit employing an auditory CS and a corneal air puff as the UCS. These studies, as well as others from the Indiana laboratory (Bruner, 1965; Papsdorf, Fishbein, and Gormezano, 1964; Schneiderman and Gormezano, 1964; Suboski, Di Lollo, and Gormezano, 1964), reveal that the albino rabbit has certain behavioral characteristics that make it more ideally suited for conditioning studies than other species previously conditioned. The advantageous characteristics are as follows: (1) when properly restrained the animal will remain relatively passive in the conditioning situation for extended periods of time; (2) the eyelid, nictitating membrane, and eyeball retraction responses have extremely low rates of spontaneous occurrence with a range of about 1 to 3 responses per hour; and (3) there is an apparent absence of alpha responses to an auditory CS for the eyelid and nictitating-membrane response systems.

Stimulation of the cornea of the rabbit's eye with a puff of air or shock to the infraorbital region (Brelsford and Theios, 1965; Papsdorf, Longman, and Gormezano, 1965) is accompanied by a closure of the eyelids, retraction of the eyeball into its orbit, and a sweeping of the nictitating membrane across the surface of the cornea. The rabbit's nicti-

tating membrane consists of a fold of conjunctiva structurally supported by a triangular sheet of cartilage that moves from the inner canthus of the eye laterally across the surface of the cornea. Extension of the membrane is reliably elicited by a corneal air puff or orbital shock with a latency of about 25 to 50 msec. The membrane rarely extends past the midline of the pupil when activated. This leaves a portion of the receptor surface exposed and provides the investigator with a high degree of control over the sensory consequences of a corneal air puff. When an air puff is applied to the temporal portion of the cornea, anticipatory membrane extensions, i.e., CRs, do not appear to attenuate its noxious effects.

Some investigators contend that the rabbit's membrane has no connection with any muscle and simply moves passively across the cornea when the eyeball retracts (Gigenbauer, 1898; Last, 1961; Zietschmann, 1904). Other investigators (Lierse, 1960; Parson and McManus, 1962) report the presence of a striated muscle connected to the upper temporal portion of the membrane that appears to pull the membrane forward upon stimulation of the cornea. Although the mechanism of movement and innervation of the nictitating membrane remain subject to controversy, eyeball retraction is a skeletal response accomplished by the retractor bulbus or choanoid muscle, activated by the VIth cranial nerve (Duke-Elder, 1958).

When a rabbit is prepared for eyelid recording, it is placed in a restraining stock, the hair over the upper eyelid is clipped, and the remainder of the hair is removed by a depilatory. If recording is to be done over more than one session, a small piece of velcro, i.e., material used in the making of cloth zippers, is then cut to the shape of the eyelid and its back surface is glued to the lid with Eastman-Kodak 910 adhesive or collodion. If the velcro tab is properly applied, it will remain on the lid for several weeks. In any event, the tab can be reapplied if it should fall off. Use of the velcro tab ensures repeat reliability of amplitude recording over successive sessions.

In preparing the nictitating membrane for recording, the upper and lower eyelids are pulled back while a slight downward pressure is applied concurrently on the eyeball to extend the membrane out from the inner canthus of the eye. A length of 00 Ethicon monofilament nylon is then sutured through the epithelium layer of the membrane, starting in at about $\frac{1}{8}$ in. from its temporal edge and coming out almost at the edge. The length of nylon is tied to form a small loop several millimeters in diameter. This provides the means for recording the membrane movement. A few drops of an ophthalmic solution of Gantrisin are applied to the prepared eye to reduce the possibility of infection. The animal will readily adapt to the nylon loop if it is not larger than several millimeters in diameter, and the preparation

will remain stable for several weeks. A new suture may be applied if the nylon loop is dislodged.

After preparing the rabbit for recording, a few sessions of adaptation to the restraining stock are necessary before starting the conditioning sessions. The animal, shown in Fig. 9-5, is placed in a Plexiglas box 9 in. long, 4 in. wide, and 8 in. high. It is restrained (1) by inserting the head through an adjustable stock that comprises the front of the box and (2) by an adjustable backplate. The headgear contains a rotary potentiometer and a stimulus air jet with a 2-mm orifice. An isolated view of the headgear, which is arranged for recording from the nictitating membrane, is shown in Fig. 9-6. It consists of two parts: (1) a thin metal head plate A on which is mounted the rotary potentiometer a_1, a circular ring of flexible copper tubing a_2, and two strips of velcro a_3; and (2) a circular ring B consisting of flexible

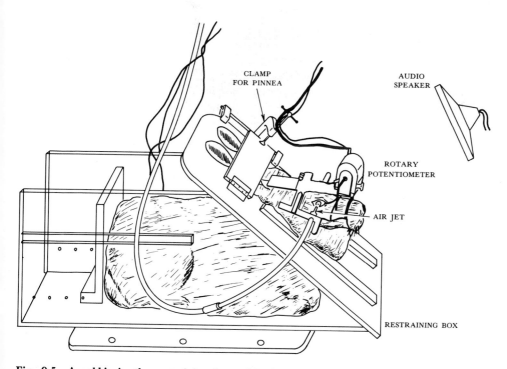

Fig. 9-5 A rabbit in the restraining box with the headgear arranged for recording from the nictitating membrane.

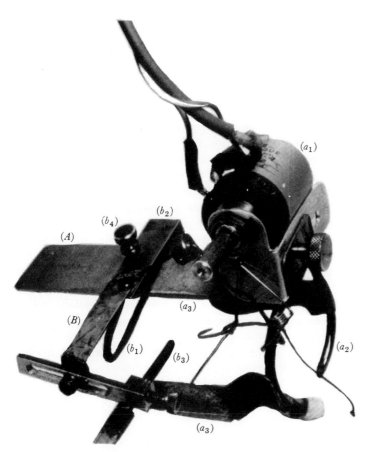

Fig. 9-6 An isolated view of the headgear arranged for recording from the nictitating mebrane of the rabbit.

copper tubing b_1 and a brass guide plate b_2 on which is mounted the stimulus air jet b_3, and a turn screw b_4 that permits fastening the ring to the head plate. The headgear is mounted by fitting the circular ring a_2 firmly around the animal's snout and slipping the circular ring B over the ears and fastening it to the head plate by means of the turn screw b_4. Gross head movements of the animal are reduced by fastening the pinna of the ears to the front of the stock with a foam-rubber coated clamp.

The restraining box is positioned in an experimental enclosure (a refrigeration shell) where a speaker for presenting auditory stimuli is mounted about 5 in. in front of the subject. To record *nictitating-membrane move-ment* and to ensure continuous exposure of the cornea, the subject's upper and lower eyelids are held open by velcro-backed clips. These are fastened to the lids and then anchored to the headgear by meshing them with the velcro strips a_3. A silk thread is attached to a rod mechanically coupled to the shaft of the potentiometer, and a small metal hook connected to the other end of the silk thread is attached to the nylon loop sutured in the rabbit's nictitating membrane. The rod, which is mechanically coupled to the potentiometer shaft, is balanced and weighted to eliminate slack in the thread. The signal from the potentiometer, which is generated by extension of the membrane, is amplified and graphically recorded.

To record eyeball retraction the position of the potentiometer is modified by rotating it 90°. A length of piano wire on one end of which is mounted a 9-mm-diameter loop made of PE 60 polyethylene tubing is attached at right angles to the rod coupled to the shaft of the potentiometer. To permit unimpeded recording of eyeball retractions the upper and lower eyelids of the rabbit's eye are held open by velcro-backed clips, and the nictitating membrane is held back by a metal hook fastened to the nylon loop sutured in the rabbit's nictitating membrane. The polyethylene loop is then placed on the cornea of the prepared eye, and retractions of the eyeball cause the shaft of the potentiometer to rotate.

The coupling to the rotary potentiometer is again modified to *record from the external eyelid*. This modification allows the coupling to operate as it does in human eyelid recording. A hypodermic tube is coupled to the shaft of the potentiometer, and a length of piano wire is inserted in the tubing. A velcro tab fastened to the other end of the piano wire is made to mesh with the velcro tab glued to the animal's lid. The movement of the lid is thus transmitted to the shaft of the potentiometer. The lower lid is held open to ensure continuous exposure of the cornea, and the air jet is positioned at this opening about $\frac{1}{2}$ in. from the cornea. When recording is to be accomplished in only one session, an aluminum tab similar to that used in human eyelid conditioning can be applied to the lid by a piece of adhesive tape.[1]

Additional preparations are required if shock to the infraorbital region of the eye is to be employed as the UCS in conditioning the eyelid, nictitating membrane, or eyeball retraction response. The hair around the orbital region of the rabbit's eye is clipped and the remainder of the hair removed by a depilatory. Two 9-mm stainless steel sutures are secured to the skin approximately 1 in. caudal to the eye socket and approximately $\frac{3}{4}$ in. apart. Alligator clips are then attached to the sutures embedded in the skin to deliver shock from a constant-current shock source.

The experimental data permit a few statements to be made concerning conditioning parameters for these response systems in the rabbit: (1) Conditioning can be obtained in 85- to 100-day-old albino rabbits to an auditory CS of 800 to 5,000 cycles per second (cps) [72 decibels (dB) sound pressure level (SPL)] or to a vibrotactual CS; (2) classically conditioned discriminations can be established to auditory CSs of 800 versus 5,000 cps (72 dB SPL); (3) asymptotic levels of performance of 95 to 98 percent CRs can be observed within three or four experimental sessions when each session consists of 50 to 60 conditioning trials with a CS-UCS interval of 250 msec and an average intertrial interval of 1 min; (4) a 150-mm puff of compressed air of 100 msec duration calibrated at its point of delivery to the eye will produce a faster rate of conditioning than a 75-mm puff; (5) rate of conditioning is a direct function of a 100-msec shock from 1.5 to 4.5 milliamperes (ma); (6) an average intertrial interval of 2 min will produce a faster learning rate than one of 30 sec; and (7) rate and level of conditioning appear to be inverse functions of CS-UCS intervals from 250 to 4,000 msec.

Phyletic comparisons of performance among species are restricted by the few studies available and the variety of conditioning parameters employed. The UCR is unilateral in rats and rabbits, i.e., the response occurs in only the stimulated eye; and is bilateral in primates, i.e., the response occurs in both the stimulated and the nonstimulated eye. The alpha response to a light CS is a closing of the eye in rabbits and man and

[1] The headgear employed at the Indiana Laboratory for recording eyelid movement from human subjects and the headgear and restraining box developed for rabbits can now be purchased commercially from Waltke Instruments. The developmental work and research on the rabbit have been supported by grants to the author from the National Science Foundation.

a slight opening in dogs, whereas to tones there is a closure in man and no observable response in rabbits. In rats, rabbits, dogs, and man the amplitude of CRs appears to be positively correlated with the frequency of CRs, but in the rhesus monkey the amplitude of the CRs appears to be of an all-or-none character (Hilgard and Marquis, 1936).

GSR CONDITIONING

The *galvanic skin response* (GSR) is defined as either a *decrease in resistance* or an *increase in electric potential* between two points on the skin. A great deal of work has been done on electrical skin effects (Landis, 1932; Landis and DeWick, 1929; McCleary, 1950), and it is now generally accepted that the GSR results from the bioelectric changes attendant upon excitation of the eccritic sweat glands and not upon the amount of moisture on the skin (Darrow, 1936; Davis, 1930: Hober, 1945; Jeffress, 1928; Lykken and Roth, 1961; Thouless, 1930). The GSR will be elicited by stimulation of any sense modality, particularly if it is intense. Although the reflex does not appear with ordinary breathing, it does occur to deep respiratory movements as well as to sudden respiratory movements such as coughing, sneezing, yawning, and laughing. Muscular contractions, either local—e.g., contraction of muscles in the arm—or general—e.g., a diffuse skeletal tensing—will also produce the reflex.

Human conditioning

In recording the GSR the investigator has a choice of essentially two techniques: (1) the potential method (i.e., recording the Tarchanoff phenomenon) and (2) the apparent resistance method (i.e., recording the Féré phenomenon). In the potential method, recording electrodes are placed on two points of the skin and measurements taken of the change in potential between the two points. Since potentials of opposite electrical sign may be picked up by the two electrodes, the response is likely to be weak and irregular unless one of the electrodes is placed on an inactive area of the body where there are no sweat glands. The mucous membrane inside the mouth is such an area. Another approach is to place the inactive electrode on a skin area having a low density of sweat glands, e.g., wrist or ear lobe, or bypassing the electrical skin effects under the electrode by making one or two punctures of the skin with a needle. Whether one or two active electrodes are employed, the potential changes are generally small i.e., 0.5 to 10 millivolts (mv), and will frequently produce an electric potential of either positive or negative polarity. This indicates that the current flowing under the active electrode is sometimes in one direction and sometimes in the other. The response is also commonly observed to be diphasic, with a small potential change in one direction quickly followed by a major change in the opposite direction (Forbes and Bolles, 1936; Jeffress, 1928).

Graphic records can be obtained with the potential method by simply connecting the electrode leads into a standard oscillograph system with a high-gain d-c amplifier (e.g., Brush, Grass, or Offner). The occurrence of both monophasic and diphasic responses and shifts in the polarity of the reflex from trial to trial, coupled with spontaneous deflections and shifts in the base potential, presents the investigator with formidable difficulties both in response definition and in ensuring consistency in reading the records (Liberman, 1944). Consequently, current investigators of GSR conditioning employ the resistance method of measurement. An external subthreshold current is passed through the skin between two recording electrodes, and a determination is made of the drop in resistance that accompanies adequate stimulation of the sweat glands.

Measurement is made of resistance or impedance change, depending upon whether the investigator passes a direct or an alternating current through the skin. The use of direct current has some advantages over the use of alternating current. With direct current the distribution form of GSRs is more symmetrical and regular, and the experimenter need not worry about stray capacitance and noise pickup, e.g., 60 cycles a-c, by the subject (Grings, 1953). On the other hand, it is necessary with direct current to be particularly attentive to the polarization of the recording electrodes. When a direct current is passed through metallic electrodes in contact with an electrolytic solution, the ions of the metal will go into solution and hydrogen gas bubbles will form on the cathode electrode to increase markedly its resistance. In principle, nonpolarizable electrodes are made with a metal and one of its salts, e.g., silver–silver chloride, platinum–platinum chloride, zinc–zinc sulfate, to keep the process of polarization constant. Even these electrodes are subject to some degree of polarization. The use of a small direct current, generally 10 to 100 microamperes (μa), and "nonpolarizing" electrodes will provide a satisfactory solution for GSR conditioning. An a-c measure is preferred where the investigator is concerned with obtaining precise measurement of base resistance levels of the skin rather than the GSR.

For d-c base resistance measurement, the base level may vary from less than 5,000 ohms to more than 200,000 ohms with a mode somewhere between 25,000 to 50,000 ohms. The magnitude of most GSRs ranges from 0 to over 20,000 ohms with most decreases being under 5,000 ohms (Grings, 1954).

The base skin resistance and GSR values depend upon numerous physical factors such as (1) the type, placement, size, and pressure of the electrodes on the skin; (2) the magnitude of the direct current—within the 25- to 400-μa range there is an inverse relationship between current and base resistance (Grings, 1953); and (3) the individual skin characteristics of the subject. Therefore, there are certain instrumentation requirements for obtaining d-c GSR measurements if the results are to be subjected to quantitative interpretation. The instrument (1) should indicate the total apparent resistance of the subject as well as the GSR since, over the range generally encountered, the magnitude of the reflex is positively correlated with the base skin resistance, and (2) should pass the same current through the subject regardless of wide fluctuations in his apparent resistance.

Grings (1954) and Woodworth and Schlosberg (1954) discuss various input circuits that have been employed in electrodermal measurement, e.g., simple series circuits, Wheatstone bridge, Wynn-Williams bridge, and constant-current input circuits. In recent years many investigators have settled upon the Fels dermohmmeter and an Esterline-Angus milliammeter recorder to obtain graphic records. One of the procedural difficulties in measuring the GSR is the necessity for having to adjust manually the recording ranges necessitated by broad changes in a subject's base skin resistance. Normally the experimenter must expend a great deal of effort in maintaining the position of the recording pen within the limits of the recording surface, and a critical point in the record is often lost while the change is being made. The amplifier of the Fels dermohmmeter will automatically adjust itself to its proper recording range without changing the sensitivity. This instrument uses a bucking voltage provided by a series of resistors mounted on a stepping switch. The bucking voltage adjusts itself to the size of the slow d-c potentials produced in the circuit by shifts in the subject's base resistance. The Fels dermohmmeter is also a constant-current system and provides a continuous record of skin resistance from 0 to 500,000 ohms, utilizing five sensitivity scales. The sensitivity setting is adjusted to permit the recording of the subject's unconditioned reflex within the range of the recording surface. By reading dial positions, i.e., range setting and sensitivity, and the deflections on the graphic records, the total resistance and the change in resistance are known at all times.

The Fels dermohmmeter receives its input signal from a series circuit containing the subject connected by two nonpolarized electrodes, a variable resistance, and a regulated constant current of 70 μa. The electrodes, available from the manufacturer, consist of 0.75-in.-square zinc set at the base of Plexiglass cups 0.125 in. deep. The cups are filled with paste made from zinc oxide or zinc sulfate and agar-agar. In the conditioning situation, the subject is comfortably seated and the area of application of the recording electrodes cleaned with alcohol or some other solvent to remove oil deposits on the skin. The electrodes are then attached on two points of the skin by means of adjustable straps. A disk of foam rubber or a wad of cotton moistened in a 0.9 percent salt solution may be placed between the skin and the plastic cups to ensure uniform pressure and good contact.

Since the GSR is related to sweat-gland activity, those portions of the skin containing the greatest number of sweat glands, namely, the palms of the hands and the soles of the feet, will give the most clearly defined electrical changes. There is evidence to indicate that the central palm and the tips of the fingers are particularly responsive to emotional stimuli, e.g., electric shock, and therefore appear to be the best places to locate electrodes for GSR recording (Neumann, 1950). Because of the greater ease of attaching the cup electrodes to the palm, this is the technique most commonly employed. The electrodes may be attached to the central palm of each hand, the palm and back of one hand, or both electrodes spaced about 1 in. apart (center to center) on the central palm. The attachment of the electrodes to both palms will give the most sensitive recording. When the electrodes are attached to the subject's hand, the experimenter must be alert to the fact that a pronounced deflection of the recording pen can be produced if the subject clenches his hand. This problem can generally be eliminated by providing instructions requesting the subject to refrain from

such movements. In any case, the deflections produced are more rapid and in the opposite direction from the GSR and can be readily distinguished. These deflections indicate an increase in resistance probably produced by disturbing the electric contact between the skin and electrode.

The most commonly employed conditioned stimuli in GSR conditioning are visual and auditory. Although sufficiently intense stimulation of any sense modality will reflexively elicit the GSR, an electric shock is most commonly employed as the UCS. Shock electrodes are generally constructed of $\frac{1}{2}$-in. disks of silver or of polished copper pennies and are taped or strapped to the subject. If the recording electrodes are attached to both hands, the shock electrodes are usually attached, about 1 in. apart, to the ankle or other portions of the leg. If GSR measurements are being taken from a single hand, the shock electrodes are generally applied to the finger, hand, or upper portions of the opposite arm. Before applying shock electrodes, experimenters usually clean the skin area with alcohol. EKG electrode paste is applied to reduce skin resistance.

Instructions are presented after the stimulating and recording equipment has been attached. The instructions generally request the subject to refrain from body movements and to relax and maintain a natural attitude toward the experimental situation. A 5-min rest period should be permitted before conditioning to allow the base skin resistance level to stabilize. The skin resistance level will generally increase during this rest interval. If the instructions include reference to the fact that shock will be administered, the apprehension of the subject to the impending shock will generally lead to a decrease in the base resistance level. Care should be exercised in ensuring uniformity in introducing the subjects to the experimental situation and in presenting instructions. An excellent technique for reducing potential sources of subject-experimenter interactions is to place the subject in the system, read him instructions through an intercom, and then use a random selection device for assigning him to a treatment combination.

An unfortunate practice is to present a conditioning trial only after the subject's base resistance level has met some predetermined criterion. This practice superimposes an instrumental contingency on the classical conditioning paradigm and can well provide the opportunity for base-line performance to interact with the experimental treatment, particularly since the base line generally changes systematically over conditioning trials. The use of a preprogrammed schedule of trial presentations eliminates the problem.

A wide variety of shock sources producing sine-wave, square-wave, half-wave, or full-wave rectified current have been employed. Shock durations of 100 to 500 msec are frequently used with a modal value of 2 to 2.5 ma of alternating current for assumed skin resistance values of 25,000 to 50,000 ohms (e.g., Kimmel and Pennypacker, 1962; Wickens, Cross, and Morgan, 1959). A common procedure for determining shock intensity is to present a series of shocks prior to the conditioning trials. During this time the intensity is adjusted until a consistent GSR is observed and some behavioral expression of discomfort is indicated by the subject, e.g., verbal complaints or jerking of the arm or leg. Many investigators adjust shock intensity during conditioning trials to maintain the subject's UCR at about the same amplitude. Generally, some uncontrolled variability in the amount of current passing through the subject is common. An improvement in present practices would be (1) the use of a constant-current shock source, i.e., a shock source constructed to pass the same amount of current through the subject despite wide variations in skin resistance; and (2) application of the same shock intensity to all subjects.

An unconditioned GSR (1) has a latency range of 1 to 5 sec with a mode around 2 sec, (2) reaches its maximum amplitude within 4 to 5 sec, and (3) takes as long as 30 to 45 sec before coming back to the base level. The investigator increases the reliability and sensitivity of conditioned GSR measurement by using an intertrial interval of sufficient length to permit the UCR to subside. Since the response has a relatively slow waveform and long duration, it is common practice to obtain a continuous graphic record at slow paper speeds (e.g., 3 in. per min). Faster paper speeds should be employed to obtain good resolution of the latency and form of the response; e.g., Prokasy, Fawcett, and Hall (1962) have employed a paper speed of 24 in. per min to obtain accurate latency and form measurement.

Investigators generally adjust the amplifier sensitivity, i.e., gain, so that the UCRs elicited by the subject during preconditioning shock trials do not exceed the limits of the recording surface. The experimenter can change the sensitivity setting during the course of the conditioning session. When the sensitivity is adjusted for each subject, the investigator must exercise precautions to ensure that the same criterion for the occurrence of a response is applied under all sensitivity settings. If preconditioning shock trials are *not* introduced and the Fels dermohmmeter is employed, a fixed sensitivity setting of 12,000 ohms (a 12,000-ohm decrease in resistance results in a full-scale deflection) will generally be quite satisfactory in minimizing instances where the magnitude of the response exceeds the limits of the recording surface. The automatic range setter on the Fels dermohmmeter will bring the recording pen back within the limits of the recording surface, but the exact form of the response will be obscured. Investigators frequently switch the automatic range-setting knob to a manual override just prior to a conditioning trial and position the recording pen at one end of the writing surface. The knob is then switched back to the automatic setting, and deflections as large as 11,000 ohms (at the 12,000-ohm sensitivity setting) can be recorded without the recorder's shifting to a new subrange. In any event, the investigator indicates the base resistance level at the point of CS onset on the graphic record. This is done on each trial.

Response definition

The latency of a conditioned GSR will vary as a function of the conditioning parameters employed, e.g., the CS-UCS interval. The latency of a CR is commonly reported to be as short as 1 to 5 sec after CS onset, but almost any stimulus used as the CS will reflexively elicit the GSR, i.e., an alpha response, within approximately the same latency range. Although alpha responses are generally smaller in magnitude, particularly if the CS is of low intensity, their presence can serve to obscure CR measurement.

Serious consideration has been given to the possibility of delineating alpha responses from CRs on the basis of response latency (Stewart, Stern, Winokur, and Fredman, 1961). A relatively long CS-UCS interval must be employed (e.g., 7 to 10 sec) to permit both responses to be observed in the interval because of the alpha-response latency. If a latency criterion is used, alpha responses can be observed in the 1- to 5-sec latency range, and CRs can be noted from 5 sec after CS onset to about 1 sec after UCS onset. This procedure would restrict the investigator to the use of relatively long CS-UCS intervals. Alternatively, investigators generally employ short CS-UCS intervals, i.e., under 5 sec, and measure responses in the CR range on test trials or during extinction, where the interval of GSR measurement may be extended to a period of as much as 10 to 15 sec after CS onset. However, the acquisition function is partly determined by the intermittent reinforcement schedule, and at the short CS-UCS intervals a high percentage of CRs would be expected to fall in

the alpha range and thus prevent their measurement.[1]

The most commonly employed approach to the problem of alpha responses is the use of an adaptation procedure. As many as 20 presentations of the CS alone are given to the subject prior to the conditioning trials in order to reduce the frequency and amplitude of alpha responses. A number of CS-UCS pairings are then given on test trials or during extinction, and measurement is taken of the amount of resistance change from the point of CS onset to the point of maximum deflection. Conditioning is then defined as the difference in response magnitude or amplitude between the last few adaptation trials and the test or extinction trials. A simple increase in response magnitude or amplitude cannot be regarded as sufficient evidence of conditioning. Under some conditions the alpha response may be reinstated rapidly after one or several CS-UCS pairings, and the amplitude or magnitude change may simply reflect sensitization. Unfortunately, most studies of GSR conditioning have not employed control-group procedures, e.g., a group receiving unpaired presentations of the CS and UCS at the same parametric values, to assess the contribution of sensitization to the presumed measure of conditioning.

Another problem in the identification of CRs is to determine the amount of resistance change necessary to specify that a response has occurred. Little agreement has been reached among investigators concerning an employable criterion. In some instances (e.g., Stewart et al., 1961) a specific amount of deflection of the recording pen is required (e.g., 2 mm). This criterion will vary with the sensitivity setting of the amplifier. In other instances (e.g., Grings, Lowell, and Honnard, 1961; Prokasy et al., 1962) responses have been defined by resistance decreases from 25 to 500 ohms. Deflections not

[1] Several papers have appeared in the literature on the problem of alpha responses in GSR conditioning (Grings, Lockhart and Dameron, 1962; Kimmel, 1964; Lockhart and Grings, 1963; Prokasy, Hall, and Fawcett, 1962). Of particular interest is the attempt of Grings et al. and of Kimmel to delineate several "types" of conditioned GSRs, including those commonly designated as alpha responses. It is recommended that the interested reader critically read these papers.

meeting this criterion are given zero scores when amplitude or magnitude measurements are used and are recorded as instances of "no response" with frequency measurements. It is not possible to recommend a "best" amplitude criterion, but a resistance decrease of 100 ohms appears to be sufficiently sensitive and reliable.

Event markers on the recorder are used to indicate the onset and offset of the CS and UCS, respectively. The latency of the response may be measured by placing a template marked in millimeter units over the graphic record. A template appropriately marked for each sensitivity setting can also be employed to measure the amplitude of the response in ohms. A complication arises with magnitude and frequency measurement if multiple responses occur in the interval of observation. There are few difficulties if (1) only the first response in the interval is being measured or (2) the concern of the investigator is simply to obtain the point of maximum deflection independent of the number of deflections. If the investigator is interested in obtaining the frequency and amplitude of multiple deflections, an a priori criterion should be established for determining the amount of resistance change necessary to constitute a response. The sensitivity and reliability of the criterion generally determine whether or not the experimenter employs the same amplitude criterion for all responses in the interval. Strategic interests of the investigator may dictate the use of different criteria for each response.

For statistical treatment the resistance measure of amplitude is generally found to be characterized by nonnormality, heterogeneity, and a lack of independence from the subject's base resistance level. Most of the transformations proposed for removing undesirable features of the resistance measure have been empirically derived by subjecting a set of data to one transformation after another until some undesirable characteristics have been removed (Darrow, 1937; Grings and O'Donnell, 1956; Haggard, 1949a,

1949b; Lacey, 1956). These empirical transformations do not provide an assurance of generality. Therefore, it is necessary for the investigator to determine a satisfactory transformation for the particular set of data he has collected. Lacey has employed the technique of reducing each reflex by the regression of the reflexes upon the base resistance level. This approach appears to provide a general method for eliminating the effect of base resistance level on the amplitude of the reflex, but it interferes with the independence of measurement of each response. Other transformations have included (1) conductance change, i.e., the resistance at the point of CS onset and the maximum deflection are converted into conductance units and the difference obtained; (2) the logarithm of conductance change; (3) the logarithm of resistance change; (4) the difference in the logarithms of conductance or resistance; (5) the square root of conductance change; and (6) the difference in the square root of conductance. The square root and logarithm of conductance change appear to be most widely employed.

Conditioning in infrahumans

The GSR can be observed in a variety of animals. The reflex has been found to occur to visual, auditory, or tactile stimuli with rats, cats, dogs, and monkeys (Landis, 1932; Landis and DeWick, 1929; Wang, 1957, 1958). Ischlondsky (1930) reportedly conditioned the GSR in cats and dogs, but adequate evidence for successful GSR conditioning in infrahumans was not provided until recently. Wickens, Meyer, and Sullivan (1961) have reported classical conditioning and conditioned discrimination of the GSR in cats. Because of the possible presence of sensitized alpha responses, their most convincing evidence of conditioning was provided with the discrimination procedure.

Although the Wickens et al. (1961) study must be regarded as preliminary, certain aspects of their procedure warrant serious consideration for investigators interested in conditioning cats. Prior to the conditioning sessions the animal is gradually adapted to the conditioning situation. On successive days the cat (1) is introduced to the experimental room baited with fish or liver, (2) is placed in a sling made of nylon net, (3) has its paws restrained by straps, and (4) has shock and recording electrodes attached. Approximately two weeks are required for the animal to become sufficiently adapted through this procedure to remain quiet and calm in the restraining device. The relative calmness of the animal is particularly important since a general emotional response to the enforced restraint can reduce the base resistance level to such a degree that no GSR may be observed following the administration of shock. Violent struggling reactions can also produce GSR deflections that obscure measurement.

Shock is administered to the rear haunch of the animal, and GSR records are obtained by strapping or clamping the electrodes on the central pad and shaved top of the front paw. Differential responding, i.e., a greater magnitude of responding to the positive CS, appears to be established within 30 days of a training period involving (1) 8 to 10 trials per day at random intertrial intervals of 45 to 120 sec, (2) a CS-UCS interval of 600 msec, (3) a 100-msec shock of 3 ma, and (4) CS tones of 2,000 and 300 cps. As more extensive work is carried out with the cat, other conditioning parameters may prove to be more effective. The possibility of using curare-type drugs with cats would appear to permit one to assess the potential contribution of conditioned respiratory and gross skeletal movement to GSRs. Such a preparation might also permit the conditioning of GSR without extensive adaptation sessions.

REFERENCES

BARRON, L. E. Reflex salivary response in dehydration. *Amer. J. Physiol.,* 1932, **100**, 559–563.

BIEL, W. C., and WICKENS, D. D. The effects of vitamin B₁ deficiency on the conditioning of eyelid responses in the rat. *J. comp. Psychol.,* 1941, **32**, 329–340.

BONEAU, C. A. The interstimulus interval and the latency of the conditioned eyelid response. *J. exp. Psychol.,* 1958, **56**, 464–471.

BRELSFORD, J., and THEIOS, J. Single session conditioning of the nictitating membrane in the rabbit: Effect of intertrial interval. *Psychon. Sci.,* 1965, **2**, 81–88.

BRUNER, F. UCS properties in classical conditioning of the albino rabbit's nictitating membrane response. *J. exp. Psychol.,* 1965, **69**, 186–192.

BYKOV, K. M. *Textbook of physiology.* Moscow: Foreign Language Publishing House, 1958.

CASON, H. The conditioned eyelid reaction. *J. exp. Psychol.,* 1922, **5**, 153–195.

COLLINS, K. H., and TATUM, A. L. A conditioned salivary reflex established by chronic morphine poisoning. *Amer. J. Physiol.,* 1925, **74**, 14–15.

COOK, S. W., and HARRIS, R. E. The verbal conditioning of the galvanic skin reflex. *J. exp. Psychol.,* 1937, **21**, 202–210.

CRISLER, G. The effect of withdrawal of water on the salivary conditioned reflex induced by morphine. *Amer. J. Physiol.,* 1928, **85**, 324–331.

CRISLER, G. Salivation is unnecessary for the establishment of the salivary conditioned reflex induced by morphine. *Amer. J. Physiol.,* 1930, **94**, 553–556.

CRISLER, G., BOOKER, W. T., VAN LIERE, E. J., and HALL, J. C. The effect of feeding thyroid on the salivary conditioned reflex induced by morphine. *Amer. J. Physiol.,* 1933, **103**, 68–72.

DARROW, C. W. The galvanic skin reflex (sweating) and blood pressure as preparatory and facilitative functions. *Psychol. Bull.,* 1936, **33**, 73–94.

DARROW, C. W. The equation of the galvanic skin reflex curve: I. The dynamics of reaction in relation to excitation-background. *J. gen. Psychol.,* 1937, **16**, 285–307.

DAVIS, R. C. Factors affecting the galvanic reflex. *Arch. Psychol.,* 1930, No. 115.

DODGE, R. The refractory phase of the protective reflex wink. *Amer. J. Psychol.,* 1913, **24**, 1–7.

DUKE-ELDER, S. *System of ophthalmology.* London: Kempton, 1958. Vol. 1.

ELLISON, G. D. Differential salivary conditioning to traces. *J. comp. physiol. Psychol.,* 1964, **57**, 373–380.

FINCH, G. Hunger as a determinant of conditional and unconditional salivary responses. *Amer. J. Physiol.,* 1938*a*, **123**, 379–382.

FINCH, G. Pilocarpine conditioning. *Amer. J. Physiol.,* 1938*b*, **124**, 679–682.

FINCH, G. Salivary conditioning in atropinized dogs. *Amer. J. Physiol.*, 1938c, **124**, 136–141.

FINESINGER, J. E., and FINESINGER, G. L. A modification of the Krasnogorski method for stimulating and measuring the secretion from the parotid gland in human beings. *J. lab. clin. Med.*, 1937, **23**, 267–273.

FINESINGER, J. E., and SUTHERLAND, G. F. The salivary conditioned reflex in man. *Trans. Amer. neurol. Ass.*, 1939, p. 50.

FINESINGER, J. E., SUTHERLAND, G. F., and MCGUIRE, F. F. The positive conditional salivary reflex in psychoneurotic patients. *Amer. J. Psychiat.*, 1942, **99**, 61–74.

FITZGERALD, R. D. Effects of partial reinforcement with acid on the classically conditioned salivary response in dogs. *J. comp. physiol. Psychol.*, 1963, **56**, 1056–1060.

FORBES, T. W., and BOLLES, M. M. Correlation of the response potentials of the skin with "exciting" and non-"exciting" stimuli. *J. Psychol.*, 1936, **2**, 273–285.

GANTT, W. H. Salivary secretion and the intake of fluid. *Amer. J. Diseases Children*, 1929, **37**, 1124–1127.

GANTT, W. H. The nervous secretion of saliva: The relation of the conditioned reflex to the intensity of the unconditioned stimulus. *Amer. J. Physiol.*, 1938, **123**, 74–75.

GANTT, W. H. Relation of unconditioned and conditioned reflex: Effect of prolongation of the work period from the usual one hour to a period of ten to twenty hours. *J. gen. Psychol.*, 1940, **23**, 377–385.

GIGENBAUER, C. *Vergleichende Anatomic der Wirbeltiere*, Bd. 1, S. 941–947. Leipzig: Wilk. Engelman, 1898.

GILCHRIST, J. C., and FURCHTGOTT, E. Salivary pH as a psycho-physiological variable. *Psychol. Bull.*, 1951, **48**, 193–210.

GONZALEZ, R. C., LONGO, N., and BITTERMAN, M. E. Classical conditioning in the fish. Exploratory studies of partial reinforcement. *J. comp. physiol. Psychol.*, 1961, **54**, 452–460.

GOODRICH, K. P. Supplementary reports: Effect of a ready signal on the latency of voluntary responses in eyelid conditioning. *J. exp. Psychol.*, 1964, **67**, 496–498.

GORMEZANO, I., and MOORE, J. W. Effects of instructional set and UCS intensity on the latency, percentage, and form of the eyelid response. *J. exp. Psychol.*, 1962, **63**, 487–494.

GORMEZANO, I., MOORE, J. W., and DEAUX, E. Supplementary report: Yoked comparisons of classical and avoidance eyelid conditioning under three UCS intensities. *J. exp. Psychol.*, 1962, **64**, 551–552.

GORMEZANO, I., SCHNEIDERMAN, N., DEAUX, E.,

and FUENTES, I. Nictitating membrane: Classical conditioning and extinction in the albino rabbit. *Science*, 1962, **138**, 33–34.

GRANT, D. A. The pseudo-conditioned eyelid response. *J. exp. Psychol.*, 1943a, **32**, 139–149.

GRANT, D. A. Sensitization and association in eyelid conditioning. *J. exp. Psychol.*, 1943b, **32**, 201–212.

GRANT, D. A. A sensitized eyelid reaction related to the conditioned eyelid response. *J. exp. Psychol.*, 1945, **35**, 393–402.

GRANT, D. A. Classical and instrumental conditioning. In A. W. Melton (Ed.), *Categories of human learning.* New York: Academic Press, 1964. Pp. 1–31.

GRANT, D. A., and ADAMS, J. K. "Alpha" conditioning in the eyelid. *J. exp. Psychol.*, 1944, **34**, 136–141.

GRANT, D. A., and NORRIS, E. B. Eyelid conditioning as influenced by the presence of sensitized beta-responses. *J. exp. Psychol.*, 1947, **37**, 423–433.

GRANT, D. A., SCHIPPER, L. M., and ROSS, B. M. The effect of intertrial interval during acquisition on extinction of the conditioned eyelid response following partial reinforcement. *J. exp. Psychol.*, 1952, **44**, 203–210.

GRINGS, W. W. Methodological considerations underlying electrodermal measurement. *J. Psychol.*, 1953, **35**, 271–282.

GRINGS, W. W. *Laboratory instrumentation in psychology.* Palo Alto: National Press, 1954.

GRINGS, W. W. Preparatory set variables related to classical conditioning of autonomic responses. *Psychol. Rev.*, 1960, **67**, 243–252.

GRINGS, W. W., LOCKHART, R. A. and DAMERON, L. E. Conditioning autonomic responses of mentally subnormal individuals. *Psychol. Monogr.*, 1962, **76**, No. 39 (Whole No. 558).

GRINGS, W. W., LOWELL, E. L., and HONNARD, R. R. GSR conditioning with preschool-age deaf children. *J. comp. physiol. Psychol.*, 1961, **54**, 143–148.

GRINGS, W. W., and O'DONNELL, D. E. Magnitude of response to compounds of discriminated stimuli. *J. exp. Psychol.*, 1956, **52**, 354–359.

HAGGARD, E. A. On the application of analysis of variance to GSR data: I. The selection of an appropriate measure. *J. exp. Psychol.*, 1949a, **39**, 378–392.

HAGGARD, E. A. On the application of analysis of variance to GSR data: II. Some effects of the use of inappropriate measures. *J. exp. Psychol.*, 1949b, **39**, 861–867.

HANSCHE, W. J., and GRANT, D. A. Onset versus termination of a stimulus as the CS in eyelid conditioning. *J. exp. Psychol.*, 1960, **59**, 19–26.

HARTMAN, T. F., GRANT, D. A., and ROSS, L. E. An investigation of the latency of "instructed voluntary" eyelid responses. *Psychol. Rep.*, 1960, **7**, 305–311.

HARTMAN, T. F., and ROSS, L. E. An alternative criterion for the elimination of "voluntary" responses in eyelid conditioning. *J. exp. Psychol.*, 1961, **61**, 334–338.

HILGARD, E. R. Conditioned eyelid reactions to a light stimulus based upon the reflex wink to sound. *Psychol. Monogr.*, 1931, **41**, No. 184.

HILGARD, E. R., and MARQUIS, D. G. Acquisition, extinction, and retention of conditioned lid responses to light in dogs. *J. comp. Psychol.*, 1935, **19**, 29–58.

HILGARD, E. R., and MARQUIS, D. G. Conditioned eyelid responses in monkeys with a comparison of dog, monkey, and man. *Psychol. Monogr.*, 1936, **47**, (212), 186–198.

HOBER, R. *Physical chemistry of cells and tissues.* New York: McGraw-Hill, 1945.

HUGHES, B., and SCHLOSBERG, H. Conditioning in the white rat: IV. The conditioned lid reflex. *J. exp. Psychol.*, 1938, **23**, 641–650.

ISCHLONDSKY, N. E. *Neuropsychose und Hirnrinde.* Berlin u. Wien: Urban u. Schwarzenberg, 1930.

IVANOV-SMOLENSKY, A. G. *Metodika issledovaniya uslovnykh refleksov u cheloveka* (Methods of investigation of conditioned reflexes in man). Moscow: Medgiz (Medical State Press), 1933.

JEFFRESS, L. A. Galvanic phenomena of the skin. *J. exp. Psychol.*, 1928, **11**, 130–144.

JONES, L. F. A study of human salivary conditioning. *J. exp. Psychol.*, 1939, **24**, 305–317.

KIMBLE, G. A. *Hilgard and Marquis' conditioning and learning.* New York: Appleton-Century-Crofts, 1961.

KIMMEL, H. D. Further analysis of GSR conditioning: A reply to Stewart, Stern, Winokur, and Fredman. *Psychol. Rev.*, 1964, **71**, 160–164.

KIMMEL, H. D., and PENNYPACKER, H. S. Conditioned diminution of the unconditioned response as a function of the number of reinforcements. *J. exp. Psychol.*, 1962, **64**, 20–23.

KLEITMAN, N. What causes the psychic secretion of saliva in the dog. *Proc. Soc. exp. Biol. Med.*, 1927, **24**, 585–586.

KLEITMAN, N. The effect of continued stimulation and of sleep upon conditioned salivation. *Amer. J. Physiol.*, 1930, **94**, 215–219.

KOZAK, W. Method of graphic registration of salivary secretion. *Acta Biol. exp.*, 1950, **15**, 185–192.

KRASNOGORSKI, N. Die letzten Fortschritte in der Methodik der Erforschung der bedingten Reflexe in Kindern. *Jb. f. Kinderhk.*, 1926, **114**, 256–269.

LACEY, J. I. The evaluation of autonomic responses: Toward a general solution. *Ann. N.Y. Acad. Sci.* 1956, **67**, 123–164.

LANDIS, C. Electrical phenomena of the skin. *Psychol. Bull.*, 1932, **29**, 693–752.

LANDIS, C., and DEWICK, H. N. The electrical phenomena of the skin (psychogalvanic reflex). *Psychol. Bull.*, 1929, **26**, 64–119.

LASHLEY, K. S. Reflex secretion of the human parotid gland. *J. exp. Psychol.*, 1916, **1**, 461–493.

LAST, R. J. *Wolff's anatomy of the eye and orbit.* Philadelphia: Saunders, 1961.

LAUER, D. W., SHAPIRO, M. M., and RADELL, A. A chronic preparation for salivary conditioning. *Bull. Acad. Polon. Sci.*, 1961, **9**, 121–123.

LIBERMAN, A. M. The effect of interpolated activity on spontaneous recovery from experimental extinction. *J. exp. Psychol.*, 1944, **34**, 282–301.

LIERSE, W. VON. (The mechanism of movement of the nictitating membrane of the rabbit.) Der mechanisms der Nickhanthemegung des Kaminchens. *Anat. Anz. Bd*, 1960, **109**, 1–6.

LINDLEY, R. H., and MOYER, K. E. Effects of instructions on the extinction of a conditioned finger-withdrawal response. *J. exp. Psychol.*, 1961, **61**, 82–88.

LOCKHART, R. A., and GRINGS, W. W. Comments on "An analysis of GSR conditioning." *Psychol. Rev.*, 1963, **70**, 562–564.

LYKKEN, D. T., and ROTH, N. Continuous direct measurement of apparent skin conductance. *Amer. J. Psychol.*, 1961, **74**, 293–297.

MCALLISTER, W. R. Eyelid conditioning as a function of the CS-UCS interval. *J. exp. Psychol.*, 1953, **45**, 417–422.

MCCLEARY, R. A. The nature of the galvanic skin response. *Psychol. Bull.*, 1950, **47**, 97–113.

MAKARYCHEV, A. I. An attempt to improve the method of registration of salivary secretion in conditioned reflex experiments. *Zh. vysshei nervnoi Deyatel'nosti im. I. P. Pavlova*, 1951, **1**, 446–456.

MOORE, A U., and MARCUSE, F. L. Salivary, cardiac, and motor indices of conditioning in two sows. *J. comp. Psychol.*, 1945, **38**, 1–16.

MOORE, J. W., and GORMEZANO, I. Yoked comparisons of instrumental and classical eyelid conditioning. *J. exp. Psychol.*, 1961, **62**, 552–559.

MOORE, J. W., and GORMEZANO, I. Effects of omitted versus delayed UCS on classical eyelid conditioning under partial reinforcement. *J. exp. Psychol.*, 1963, **65**, 248–257.

NAITO, T. The serialization of salivary conditioned reflexes in human subjects. *Jap. J. Psychol.*, 1957, **27**, 411–420.

NAITO, T. Serialization of salivary conditioned reflexes in human subjects. *Jap. psychol. Res.*, 1958, 5, 51–63.

NEUMANN, E. A study of palmar skin resistance. Unpublished doctoral dissertation, Brown University, 1950.

NOBLE, M., and ADAMS, C. K. Conditioning in pigs as a function of the interval between CS and US. *J. comp. physiol. Psychol.*, 1963, 56, 215–219.

NORRIS, E. B., and GRANT, D. A. Eyelid conditioning as affected by verbally induced inhibitory set and counter reinforcement. *Amer. J. Psychol.*, 1948, 61, 37–49.

OST, J. W. P. Personal communication, 1963.

PAPSDORF, J. D., FISHBEIN, H. F., and GORMEZANO, I. A comparison of an intermittent versus continuous CS in classical conditioning of the nictitating membrane response of the rabbit. *Psychon. Sci.*, 1964, 1, 305–306.

PAPSDORF, J. D., LONGMAN, D., and GORMEZANO, I. Spreading depression: Effects of applying potassium chloride to the dura of the rabbit on the conditioned nictitating membrane response. *Psychon. Sci.*, 1965, 2, 125–126.

PARSON, R., and MCMANUS, J. F. A. Personal communication, 1962.

PAVLOV, I. P. *Conditioned reflexes.* (Translated by G. V. Anrep) London: Oxford, 1927.

PAVLOV, I. P. A brief outline of the higher nervous activity. In C. Murchison (Ed.), *Psychologies of 1930.* Worcester, Mass.: Clark Univer. Press, 1930.

PEREZ-CRUET, J., TOLLIVER, G., DUNN, G., MARVIN, S., and BRADY, J. V. Concurrent measurement of heart rate and instrumental avoidance behavior in the rhesus monkey. *J. exp. Anal. Behav.*, 1963, 6, 61–64.

PODKOPAIEV, N. A. *Methodik zum Studium der bedingten Reflexe.* Berlin: Veb Verlag Volk und Gesundheit, 1956.

PROKASY, W. F., FAWCETT, J. T., and HALL, J. F. Recruitment, latency, magnitude, and amplitude of the GSR as a function of interstimulus interval. *J. exp. Psychol.*, 1962, 64, 513–518.

PROKASY, W. F., HALL, J. F., and FAWCETT, J. T. Adaptation, sensitization, forward and backward conditioning, and pseudoconditioning of the GSR. *Psychol. Rep.*, 1962, 10, 103–106.

RAZRAN, G. H. S. Conditioned responses in children. *Arch. Psychol.*, 1933, No. 148.

RAZRAN, G. H. S. Conditioned responses: An experimental study and a theoretical analysis. *Arch. Psychol.*, 1935a, No. 191.

RAZRAN, G. H. S. Salivating and thinking in different languages. *J. Psychol.*, 1935b, 1, 141–151.

RAZRAN, G. H. S. Studies in configural conditioning: I. Historical and preliminary experimentation. *J. gen. Psychol.*, 1939a, 21, 307–330.

RAZRAN, G. H. S. Studies in configural conditioning: II. The effect of subjects' attitudes and of task-sets upon configural conditioning. *J. exp. Psychol.*, 1939b, 24, 95–105.

RAZRAN, G. H. S. Studies in configural conditioning: III. The factors of similarity, proximity, and continuity in configural conditioning. *J. exp. Psychol.*, 1939c, 24, 202–210.

RAZRAN, G. H. S. Studies in configural conditioning: IV. Gestalt organization and configural conditioning. *J. Psychol.*, 1939d, 7, 3–16.

RAZRAN, G. H. S. Studies in configural conditioning: VI. Comparative extinction and forgetting of pattern and of single-stimulus conditioning. *J. exp. Psychol.*, 1939e, 24, 432–438.

RAZRAN, G. H. S. Attitudinal determinants of conditioning and generalization of conditioning. *J. exp. Psychol.*, 1949a, 39, 820–829.

RAZRAN, G. H. S. Semantic and phonetographic generalization of salivary conditioning to verbal stimuli. *J. exp. Psychol.*, 1949b, 39, 642–652.

RAZRAN, G. H. S. Sentential and propositional generalizations of salivary conditioning to verbal stimuli. *Science*, 1949c, 109, 447–448.

RAZRAN, G. H. S. Some psychological factors in the generalization of salivary conditioning to verbal stimuli. *Amer. J. Psychol.*, 1949d, 62, 247–256.

RAZRAN, G. H. S. A direct laboratory comparison of Pavlovian conditioning and traditional associative learning. *J. abnorm. soc. Psychol.*, 1955a, 51, 649–652.

RAZRAN, G. H. S. Partial reinforcement of salivary CRs in adult human subjects: Preliminary study. *Psychol. Rep.*, 1955b, 1, 409–416.

RUNQUIST, W. N., SIDOWSKI, J., and GORMEZANO, I. Yoked comparisons of classical and avoidance conditioning in differential conditioning of the eyelid response. *Psychol. Rep.*, 1962, 11, 43–50.

SCHNEIDERMAN, N., FUENTES, I., and GORMEZANO, I. Acquisition and extinction of the classically conditioned eyelid response in the albino rabbit. *Science*, 1962, 136, 650–652.

SCHNEIDERMAN, N., and GORMEZANO, I. Conditioning of the nictitating membrane of the rabbit as a function of CS-US interval. *J. comp. physiol. Psychol.*, 1964, 57, 188–195.

SHAPIRO, M. M. Classical salivary conditioning in dogs. Unpublished doctoral dissertation, Indiana University, 1959.

SHAPIRO, M. M. Respondent salivary conditioning during operant lever pressing in dogs. *Science*, 1960, 132, 619–620.

SHAPIRO, M. M. Salivary conditioning in dogs during fixed-interval reinforcement contingent upon lever pressing. *J. exp. Anal. Behav.*, 1961, **4**, 361–364.

SMITH, K. Conditioning as an artifact. *Psychol. Rev.*, 1954, **61**, 217–225.

SOLTYSIK, S., and ZBROZYNA, A. The chronic fistula of shortened Stensen's duct in dogs. *Acta Biol. exp.*, 1957, **17**, 339–344.

SPENCE, K. W. *Behavior theory and conditioning.* New Haven, Conn.: Yale, 1956.

SPENCE, K. W., and ROSS, L. E. A methodological study of the form and latency of eyelid responses in conditioning. *J. exp. Psychol.*, 1959, **58**, 376–381.

SPENCE, K. W., and TAYLOR, J. A. Anxiety and strength of the UCS as determiners of the amount of eyelid conditioning. *J. exp. Psychol.*, 1951, **42**, 183–188.

STEWART, M. A., STERN, J. A., WINOKUR, G., and FREDMAN, S. An analysis of GSR conditioning. *Psychol. Rev.*, 1961, **68**, 60–67.

STRUGHOLD, H. The mechanical threshold of the cornea-reflex of the usual laboratory animals. *Amer. J. Physiol.*, 1930, **44**, 235–240.

SUBOSKI, M. D., DI LOLLO, V., and GORMEZANO, I. Effects of unpaired pre-acquisition exposure of CS and UCS on classical conditioning of the nictitating membrane response of the albino rabbit. *Psychol. Rep.*, 1964, **15**, 571–576.

SUTHERLAND, G. F. The salivary curve: A psychiatric thermometer? *Amer. J. Psychiat.*, 1959, **116**, 20–24.

SUTHERLAND, G. F., and KATZ, R, A. Apparatus for study of salivary conditional reflex in man. *J. appl. Physiol.*, 1961, **16**, 740–741.

SWITZER, S. A. Backward conditioning of the lid reflex. *J. exp. Psychol.*, 1930, **13**, 76–97.

TELFORD, C. W., and ANDERSON, B. O. The normal wink reflex; its facilitation and inhibition. *J. exp. Psychol.*, 1932, **15**, 235–266.

THOULESS, R. H. The technique of experimentation on the psycho-galvanic reflex phenomenon and the phenomenon of Tarchanoff. *Brit. J. Psychol.*, 1930, **20**, 219–240.

WANG, G. H. The galvanic skin reflex: A review of old and recent works from a physiologic point of view. *Amer. J. phys. Med.*, 1957, **36**, 295–320.

WANG, G. H. The galvanic skin reflex: A review of old and recent works from a physiologic point of view. *Amer. J. phys. Med.*, 1958, **37**, 35–57.

WARSTLER, H. Effect of UCS intensity on salivary conditioning in dogs. Unpublished B. A. thesis, Indiana University, 1963.

WATSON, J. B. *Psychology from the standpoint of the behaviorist.* (2nd ed.) Philadelphia: Lippincott, 1924.

WICKENS, D. D., CROSS, H. A., and MORGAN, R. M. CS termination and the response strength acquired by elements of a stimulus complex. *J. exp. Psychol.*, 1959, **58**, 363–368.

WICKENS, D. D., MEYER, P. M., and SULLIVAN, S. N. Classical GSR conditioning, conditioned discrimination, and interstimulus intervals in cats. *J. comp. physiol. Psychol.*, 1961, **54**, 572–576.

WINSOR, A. L. Inhibition and learning. *Psychol. Rev.*, 1929, **36**, 389–401.

WINSOR, A. L., and BAYNE, T. L. Unconditioned salivary responses in man. *Amer. J. Psychol.*, 1929, **41**, 271–276.

WOODWORTH, R. S., and SCHLOSBERG, H. *Experimental psychology.* New York: Holt, 1954.

ZENER, K. Significance of behavior accompanying conditioned salivary secretion for theories of the conditioned response. *Amer. J. Psychol.*, 1937, **50**, 384–403.

ZENER, K., and MCCURDY, H. G. Analysis of motivational factors in conditioned behavior: I. Differential effect of changes in hunger upon conditioned, unconditioned, and spontaneous salivary secretion. *J. Psychol.*, 1939, **8**, 321–350.

ZIETSCHMANN, O. Vergleichend histologische untersuchugen uber den Bander Augenlider der Haussaugetiere. *Graefes Arch. Opthalmol.*, 1904, **58**, 61–122.

Chapter 10

OPERANT CONDITIONING

JAMES A. DINSMOOR

The boundaries for a contemporary definition of operant conditioning are difficult to specify except by pointing to a set of experimental practices. Originally, the term *operant* was coined by Skinner to refer to "a kind of response which occurs spontaneously in the absence of any stimulation with which it may be specifically correlated" (1937, p. 274). To strengthen this type of response, it was necessary to correlate the reinforcing stimulus with the response itself (Type R conditioning) rather than with an eliciting stimulus (Type S). In practice, however, the term has been restricted to work making use of the techniques that Skinner developed for investigating this type of behavior. What distinguishes operant conditioning from other areas of investigation, then, is not so much the problems that are considered—which cover an extensive range—but the mode of attack.

Current practices reflect several methodological criteria. (1) Accidental fluctuations should be reduced to the lowest possible level, so that systematic relationships will be easier to recognize and to substantiate. (2) To reduce the number of alternative interpretations, the situation should be simplified by elimination of all but the most necessary components. These components may then be combined in different ways to reproduce a wide variety of functional patterns. (3) The role of incidental properties of the particular organism, response, or environment chosen for study should be restricted as much as possible, in order to permit the derivation of principles potentially applicable to a wide range of behavioral situations. (4) Finally, the stimuli should be suitable for automated delivery and the responses readily recordable by electronic or electromechanical means. These criteria are the source and justification of the apparent abstraction and artificiality that are sometimes deplored by casual critics of the technique.

It should be added that rate (frequency) of response occurrence is the preferred measure of behavior and that considerable stress is laid on examining the performance of the individual subject.

Application of these criteria usually leads the investigator to choose infrahuman subjects, since lower animals can be reared under restricted conditions, where they have less opportunity to acquire learned responses that might distort the basic, biologically determined characteristics of their behavior. Animal subjects have no significant verbalizations, for example, to add to the situation and presumably do not regard the experiment as a type of social interaction to which certain specialized responses are applicable (Orne, 1962). Uniformity of life history also limits the range and variety of individual idiosyncrasies that might complicate or conceal the common pattern. Animal subjects can be kept in the experimental environment for much longer periods than are ordinarily possible with human subjects; more effective reinforcers can be used; and the experimenter is free to present conditions to which the human organism may not be exposed. Cross comparison of rats, pigeons, monkeys, and, on occasion, human subjects, serves to establish the generality of key findings from species to species, at least within the upper reaches of the phylogenetic scale.

The particular response employed as an indicator of behavioral relationships is not chosen for its social significance or for its role in the natural economy of the species; instead it is selected on such technical grounds as its low frequency of occurrence prior to and outside of the experimental situation, the range of frequencies that can be achieved inside the experimental situation, its precision of definition, and its ease of recording. Since these considerations are, in a sense, arbitrary, there is no reason why this response should not be representative of other forms of behavior.

The subject is enclosed in an experimental chamber to insulate him from accidental fluctuations and to restrict the complexity of the natural environment, to prevent contact with unspecified and possibly biased behavior on the part of the experimenter, and to eliminate stimuli that might produce innate or previously learned behavior that would strengthen or disrupt the selected response. Arbitrary stimuli having little prior significance to the organism are substituted for the world of nature. These stimuli can be at least roughly specified in terms of such basic physical dimensions as wavelength and intensity and can easily be presented by electrical or mechanical means.

AUTOMATION

The use of a response that operates a switch makes it possible to conduct the experiment and record the data by means of an electronic or electromechanical system. At a practical level, this frees the experimenter from much of the routine drudgery otherwise involved in collecting and tabulating his data and leaves more time for the creative aspects of his work. This provides the initial reinforcement for automation.

Other benefits are soon recognized. In conducting a repetitive routine of a certain degree of complexity, the human experimenter is liable to errors of detail and often subject to pressures that may bias his results. Programming apparatus, it must be admitted, is also subject to error, but as the reliability of available instrumentation increases and as experimenters become better versed in the subtleties of its use, these errors are being greatly reduced. The electrical circuitry also provides a much faster reaction to the subject's behavior and a much finer temporal analysis of the data. Automatic recording and data analysis have opened the way for collecting and treating more complete and detailed information on the subject's performance.

Automation has also influenced experimental strategy, by reducing the previous dependence of time spent by the subject on time spent by the experimenter. The heaviest work load comes at the beginning of the experiment, when it is necessary to select, purchase, construct, assemble, and troubleshoot the programming and recording circuits. It is also relatively time-consuming to place large numbers of animals on deprivation and to train them in the basic performance before collecting the critical data. Once they are trained, however, it is relatively easy to collect additional data from the same subjects. This has a number of advantages. (1) The experimenter feels free to spend much more experimental time than he would otherwise be able to afford on exploratory work, seeking suitable conditions and techniques for the particular problem and the particular set of subjects. (2) Studies of behavioral change are no longer required to take the haphazard performance of the experimentally naive animal as their point of departure but can begin with a specified base line. (3) Processes requiring many hours for their development are now open to examination. Complex behavior patterns may be built up, step by step, from their constituent elements. (4) The experimenter can afford to wait for the performance to reach its full development and to stabilize to a degree that makes reliable comparisons possible for the same individual under varying conditions. Individual differences can then be removed as a source of experimental error and can be examined in their own right.

Finally, the immediate feedback of data in a form sufficiently clear for at least a preliminary understanding of what the subject is doing from moment to moment provides extremely useful information for monitoring of the experiment as it progresses.

MONITORING

The form of the relationship, if any, that is discovered between some experimental operation and the corresponding alterations in the subject's behavior depends on the total experimental setting and on the level, form, and variability of the resulting base-line performances. For example, we cannot study interactions in complex chains if we cannot establish the chained performance. We cannot study recovery from punishment if the punishment is not sufficiently severe to produce a substantial decrement in the previous performance. Parameters of conditioned reinforcement cannot be evaluated unless the reinforcer has a substantial effect on the subject's behavior. If random variability is large, systematic changes may be obscured. To obtain a satisfactory picture of the process he sets out to investigate, the experimenter must adjust each of a number of variables to appropriate values. Although these values can usually be estimated, within limits, on the basis of previous work in the area, two experimental situations are rarely completely comparable, and pioneering work, in particular, requires the empirical evaluation of a variety of background parameters. Moreover, the subject often requires a period of exposure of unknown duration to the experimental situation to approach the required level or pattern of behavior and to stabilize there. *If the experimenter fails to establish an appropriate base-line performance for each of his subjects, his entire experiment may be vitiated and all his efforts wasted.*

To adjust experimental parameters by delayed calculation of group averages is a very slow and cumbersome process. Brief "pilot work" is usually insufficient. A succession of experiments may be required, in which only the final member makes a substantive contribution. With immediate monitoring of individual performances, preliminary exploration moves much faster and can be carried much further. If the subject's early performance appears too sluggish, his food or water deprivation can be increased until the level of activity rises to a satisfactory value. More frequent or more effective reinforcement can be supplied. If a discrimination is poor, new stimuli may be substituted or added to those already in use. If unexpected complications appear in the behavioral pattern due to adventitious reinforcement, the unintended contingencies can be corrected by imposing additional criteria, such as delays inserted between the occurrence of one response and the scheduling of reinforcement for another. If the subject warms up only gradually to the day's task, the initial portion of each session's data can be discarded; if he slows down toward the end of the session, the duration can be reduced. In some recent work, the monitoring data have been fed directly back to the programming circuit and used for continuous adjustment of procedural requirements to the behavior of the subject. On a ratio schedule, for example, the length of the pause following reinforcement or the time required for the ratio may be used to determine the number of responses that will be required for the next reinforcement.

Continuous, immediate feedback of the subject's performance under a variety of conditions, some of them purely exploratory, also shapes the performance of the experimenter. Through selective reinforcement he learns new skills in behavioral control. Monitoring data also makes the investigator more sensitive to the performance of the individual subject. Individual functions become far more conspicuous, and it is seen that they often differ substantially from the averages for the group. Indeed, individual deviations in the level or pattern of performance may suggest new leads for further investigation that prove more rewarding than the original subject of inquiry.

Furthermore, monitoring the data provides an important method for coping with one problem that may otherwise be accentuated by the use of experimental enclosures and automated programming devices, the problem of apparatus failure. The response device may shift in its sensitivity or become completely inoperative; the reinforcing device may jam or the storage bin become exhausted; the signal stimulator may burn out a filament; electrical connections may be parted, or programming circuitry may prove unreliable; or the recording device itself may fail to operate. Such failures can usually be discovered if a continuous check is maintained on the output from the system as a whole.

It is possible, of course, that the use of a data-recording device to detect failures of the apparatus will bias the experimental observations. When the data develop as expected, the investigator assumes that all is well with his apparatus; but when they take an unexpected turn, he looks for and perhaps then finds difficulties in his instrumentation. This means that unexpected data are more likely to be corrected than expected data. However, the costs of such a bias must be compared with the costs of collecting data that reflect apparatus failures rather than the performance of the subject under the conditions stated. To some extent, the functioning of the experimental equipment can also be monitored more directly. For example, electric eyes or microphones can be used to pick up visual or auditory stimuli inside the subject's chamber; meters and neon lamps can be used to monitor shock; mechanically actuated switches can be used to check the operation of dippers or pellet dispensers. These sensing devices can then be connected to visual or auditory displays on the experimenter's panel.

PROBLEMS OF CONTROL

When the experimenter compares performances for the same individual rather than for different individuals, he faces control problems that may not be familiar to those who in the past have worked exclusively with group designs. Although he has eliminated differences between individuals as a source of error, he must still deal with differences in the time at which the behavior is observed. His data may be influenced by (1) the previous history of the subject, (2) the effects of immediately previous conditions that have not yet had time to dissipate, or (3) processes occurring in time that may be confounded with the changes introduced by the experimenter.

The traditional method for dealing with successive observations in time is to present the experimental conditions either in a balanced order, which permits systematic separation of the variables of sequence and condition, or in a random order. In either case, the duration of each period of observation is specified in advance. This method makes possible an unbiased estimate of the amount of variation that can be attributed to chance factors and hence provides statistical criteria for determining whether the changes with experimental conditions can reasonably be attributed to these factors. If the applicability of conventional statistical tests were, as is sometimes implied, the sole criterion of experimental design, the issue would be settled. Knowing, however, that one's data are not purely a matter of chance is but a small advance. Furthermore, the traditional procedure imposes severe restrictions on the freedom of the investigator in solving other problems of experimental design.

When to shift conditions

Consider first the traditional practice of specifying in advance the length of time, or number of times, for which behavior will be observed under a given experimental condition before going on to the next. This procedure is a safeguard against bias through selection of data and may be particularly important when seeking precise quantitative determination of a function. For example, using the level of performance to determine the cutoff point for a series of observations will bias the data in the direction of the criterion. That is, if the experimenter waits for a high level of performance before changing conditions, the average will be higher than if he terminates his sample at an arbitrary point. If he waits for a low level, the average will be lower. Similarly, if the experimenter permits the stability of the performance to determine the cutoff point, he will bias his data in the direction of lowered variability. If he now applies random-sampling statistics to his data, his error term will be unrepresentative of the true variability of his data, and he will reject the null hypothesis more frequently than he should.

Many discussions of experimental design indicate that the criterion of avoiding bias is decisive. There are, however, other considerations. Serious difficulties may arise from the practice of specifying the length of observation in advance. To be sure that sufficient time has been allowed to complete the change in performance from the previous level or pattern to the new one and to be sure that sufficient observations will have been collected to provide a stable average despite random variation, the experimenter must make each period of observation exceedingly long. A great deal of experimental time is wasted that might better be devoted to se-

curing additional information. The danger of bias must be weighed against paucity of data. Even in terms of his confidence in the findings, statistical considerations must be weighed against the possibility of gaining additional time in which to replicate the data. On the other hand, what all too often happens is that the period of observation is made too short. As the length of the period is reduced, the risk increases that transitions will be incomplete and averages unstable. Although the investigator may know whether his data differ from chance, too short a period may lead to retention of null hypotheses which should be rejected, and he may get a distorted picture of the function being examined.

Another danger is that the particular point at which the change in conditions is made may turn out to be a poor one. If a substantial shift in the level of performance appears just before the change, it may alter the average value to be assigned to the current condition. It may also indicate that the level of performance is for some reason unrepresentative, that it has not reached its final value, or that some unknown change has occurred in experimental conditions, e.g., change in pattern of response or breakdown of apparatus.

All these considerations argue for adjustment of the length of the period of observation to the characteristics of the data. If we are permitted to make use of the incoming data in making our decisions, we can solve these problems much more satisfactorily. If a sudden deviation occurs, we can postpone the shift in conditions until this deviation is evaluated as either an isolated occurrence or a systematic change in performance. If performance quickly rises or falls to a new value and stays there, and if variability is low in comparison with the magnitude of change to be expected from our experimental manipulations, we can move on to a new condition. If, on the other hand, performance continues to shift over a long period of time or shows substantial variability, we may extend our observations before we make this change. This freedom to adjust the length of the period of observation to the characteristics of the data is particularly important when exploring new relations or techniques, when we may have little idea how long the transitions will take or how variable the data will be.

Sequence of observations

As noted previously, when the period of observation has been made too short, each average may be contaminated by a contribution from the immediately preceding condition. To control for such effects, the experimenter often collects his observations in a counterbalanced sequence. On one occasion, for example, he presents successive values of his experimental variable in an ascending order of magnitude; on the next, he uses a descending order. In the ideal case where equal increments are used for successive values of the experimental variable, where the behavior is a linear function of this variable, and where transitions are equally rapid in either direction, the errors produced by an ascending series will be equal and opposite in direction to the errors produced by a descending series. If the ascending and descending series are then averaged, the resulting values will be those which would have been obtained if each set of observations were of sufficient length. (The results for the highest and lowest values of the experimental variable, of course, cannot be corrected by this technique.) In less ideal cases, where the functional relation is curvilinear or the upward and downward transitions are of unequal speed, the correction will in turn be less satisfactory but may still afford some improvement. Furthermore, this technique offers a degree of control for a systematic upward or downward drift of the data with time, to the extent that this trend is linear for the complete set of observations. A value of the experimental variable that is examined early in the ascending series, for example, will be examined at a point that is correspondingly late in the descending series, and again the unwanted sequential effects will cancel out.

If each value of the experimental variable is to be examined a number of times, more sophisticated controls may be used. During successive replications, the sequence may be varied in such a way that each value is preceded once by each of the other values. The same type of balance may be approximated by using a random sequence. Statistical techniques may then be applied to estimate the contribution of random or series effects to differences observed among the experimental conditions. However, once we have obtained a number of replications the evaluation of chance factors becomes less crucial; as we shall see later, it is often better to keep the successive replications independent than to average them and test the averages.

Moreover, determination in advance of the sequence in which successive values of the experimental variable will be presented imposes severe restrictions on the investigator in his attempt to maximize the information he can obtain from a series of observations. (1) Consider, for example, the possibility that the experimenter may wish to cover an extended range during his initial observations, to determine where the largest or most interesting changes occur, before going on to fill in the gaps or to replicate the most important points. In a study by Boren and Sidman (1957), for example, there was virtually no change in performance until the experimental variable was reduced to 20 percent of its initial value. Below this point, a very substantial change was observed. (2) Again, consider the possibility that the subject may die before a complete set of data has been collected or that the time available for the experiment may be exhausted. To deal with such eventualities, the experimenter may wish to collect the data that he considers most important first. He may wish, for example, to complete a set of data under a given set of parameters before altering one of them and proceeding with a replication. (3) Consider the possibility that after the experimenter has collected his original set of data he may decide to extend a function, examine more closely a region of rapid change, check deviant points, or determine whether observations early in the series can be reproduced despite subsequent accretions to the history of the subject.

While using a relatively flexible strategy to pursue such objectives, the experimenter can still try to balance high and low values, for example, of the experimental variable, either by systematic but imperfect counterbalancing or by random selection among a limited set of alternatives. To carry the process further, the experimenter may then replicate his findings, using other sequences, and may evaluate his success in controlling for sequence effects by comparing the results of these replications.

Subject generality

An advantage claimed for the traditional technique of comparing the mean performance of two or more groups of individuals is that it permits the application of statistical tests that indicate whether the findings are representative of subjects in general. The assumption is made, for statistical purposes, that the groups of subjects used in the experiment are random samples drawn from some hypothetical population. If the differences among the means of these groups cannot reasonably be attributed to sampling error, they are assumed to be characteristic of differences that would arise throughout the population under the same experimental treatments.

Unfortunately, the larger the hypothetical population we have in mind, the weaker is the assumption that our experimental groups approximate a random sample from that population. Even a second shipment of animals from the same supply house to the same laboratory, for example, may differ from the first because of seasonal variations in the breeding colony, different parents, differential experience in transit, or the progressive changes that normally occur in the housing

or laboratory environment. Replication of statistically solid findings in another laboratory often proves extremely difficult. Differences in age, sex, or strain of animal, let alone species, may affect the results.

In the final analysis, replication of the original findings with other subjects, in other laboratories, and with variations in procedure and instrumentation is necessary before great confidence can be placed in their generality. The conventional statistical tests add little to our confidence in generality, as distinguished from the likelihood of success in a hypothetical replication with the same group of subjects. And mere replicability of results may be demonstrated with a single subject.

Replication

A simple technique for increasing the confidence we may place in an observed relationship between two variables is to replicate it. In doing this, there are several alternative strategies we may follow. In the simplest type of replication, we may repeat our observations for each value of the experimental variable for the same subject, using a different sequence. If the results are substantially different for successive replications, we may wish to average the data in order to balance out effects arising from random variation or from the sequence in which the observations were collected. This may provide in some cases a more satisfactory description of the relationship under examination, particularly if we can assume that there have been no systematic changes in the function from one replication to the next. However, when successive replications have been averaged the relationship has been determined only once, and even the ability to reject a chance interpretation of the data on the basis of statistical criteria adds little to our confidence that we have obtained a correct description of its form. On the other hand, if the relationship is consistent for each replication, at the level of description we wish to use, the successive independent determinations may yield a high level of confidence in our findings, at least for the individual subject. In this case, the individual replications should be displayed, both to demonstrate the reliability of the relationship and to describe its shape most accurately.

Moreover, if the experimenter believes his first set of points to have been reliably determined, he may wish to extend the generality of his findings by altering one of the parameters of the situation that hitherto has been held constant. Then the same function may be redetermined under different conditions. Sidman (1960) has called this systematic, as distinguished from direct, replication. If the results are consistent, the second determination tends to confirm the results of the first and at the same time to extend the generality of the relationship. If the results vary, however, direct replication of each item becomes desirable in order to distinguish between systematic differences, on the one hand, and chance or sequence effects on the other.

Another way of increasing generality, this time among subjects rather than among conditions, is to replicate a series of observations with a second individual. Again, successful duplication of the functional relation contributes both to our confidence in the validity of the relationship and to our estimate of its generality.

A further step would be to replicate the proceedings with a different species. Since equivalent parametric values cannot be determined for two different species, difficulty may sometimes be encountered in locating appropriate values for the new species. On the other hand, since the parametric values cannot be equated, successful species replication is inherently a systematic replication. Thus, generality is greatly extended.

There are considerable risks involved in averaging data from different subjects or from systematic replications with the same subject. In cases where the individual functions are different, the differences will be obscured; even in cases where the individual functions are the same, the averaged function

may distort them (Estes, 1956; Sidman, 1952). Furthermore, to pursue the same argument in the opposite direction, if the experimenter finds a certain function for a set of means, he cannot conclude that this function holds for each individual in the group or for each level of the second experimental variable in a systematic replication. Thus, averaged data are not very helpful in extending the generality of our findings.

Multiple schedules

Earlier it was indicated that a major design problem in within-subject comparisons is that of controlling differences in the time at which observations are collected under different conditions. Another method for controlling differential time effects is simply to eliminate the time difference or, strictly speaking, to reduce it to a minimal level. Behavior under two or more conditions can be studied in rapid alternation throughout a period of time if the separate conditions are placed under stimulus control. For example, when the key is red, pecking may be reinforced on an interval schedule; when green, on a ratio schedule. Or behavior may be examined under two different mean intervals. Or food-maintained and shock-maintained behavior may be studied simultaneously, and the effects of some pharmacological agent observed. This technique, in which different procedures are applied under differing stimulus conditions, is known as a multiple schedule (Ferster and Skinner, 1957). Much the same arguments apply to concurrent schedules for two or more independent responses.

As might be expected, the advantages gained through the use of a multiple schedule are offset by corresponding difficulties. The main question in making comparisons of this type is whether the component behaviors remain completely independent, each associated only with its corresponding stimulus condition, or whether some interaction takes place (e.g., Dinsmoor, 1951; Herrnstein and Brady, 1958; Reynolds, 1961). The discrimination between the two stimuli may be incomplete. The onset of one stimulus may provide adventitious reinforcement or punishment for behavior under the other stimulus. Or a change in the schedule of reinforcement during one component may produce changes in rate in the opposite direction under the other component (behavioral contrast).

Two general types of precaution seem to be in order: (1) Before a multiple schedule is used to evaluate a given comparison, an attempt can be made to examine directly the degree of interaction between the two components under the general conditions to be employed in the main body of the experiment. (2) It may be possible to compare a given set of conditions in two different ways, once by using a multiple schedule and once by using a sequential comparison. This can be considered an advanced form of systematic replication; and if the results are consistent, they strongly suggest that the technical difficulties of both types of procedure have been circumvented. That is, we now have what might be termed a procedural generality for our data.

Yoked controls

One of the important characteristics of operant research is that what the subject does determines, in part, what happens to him. Various conditions, including the delivery of reinforcement, are made dependent upon the subject's performance. This means that changes in performance may often lead to changes in conditions that will produce further changes in performance. In other words, there is a circular relationship at work. The task of disentangling the relationships between procedure and performance becomes more complicated. In particular, if the experimenter wishes to determine whether a given alteration in procedure is directly responsible for a certain effect on the subject's behavior, he may be faced with a problem of controlling for subsidiary effects. For example, under a ratio schedule of reinforcement, the subject is apt to speed up his rate of responding. In turn, the high rate of response produces more frequent reinforcements. It is not clear what part of the final pattern of behavior is due directly to the ratio contingency per se and what part is due to more frequent reinforcement.

Ferster and Skinner (1957) have suggested a relatively sophisticated technique for dealing with this problem. Two subjects are studied simultaneously, but the conditions for both subjects are determined insofar as possible by the performance of one of them. In the original example, one pigeon was reinforced on a ratio schedule; reinforcement became available for the second pigeon whenever the first had completed his ratio. Thus, assuming a sufficient rate of responding by the second pigeon, the average frequency of reinforcement would be the same. In fact, the entire frequency distribution and sequence of times between reinforcements would be closely matched for the two birds, but the determining contingency would be different for each.

Traditionally, the yoked-control technique has been practiced with two individuals operating at the same time. This tends to restrict it to situations where the systematic differences are so large that individual differences may safely be ignored. However, there is no reason why a single organism should not be yoked to himself. The sequence of shocks or reinforcements could be recorded on tape and played back to the same subject later on. It would not be possible, of course, to counterbalance the order of the two conditions, since the schedule for one would be determined by the performance on the other, but a number of alternations would be possible.

THE EXPERIMENTAL ENVIRONMENT

Integrated systems for confining the subject, insulating him from stray stimulation, and providing him with an experimental *operandum* and environment may be purchased from a number of firms (see Appendix). Component devices may, of course, be purchased from different firms, but they are not always easily fitted together.

Although the prices for such facilities may seem high, building them locally often involves considerable planning, the purchase of a number of specialized components, a substantial amount of machine work, and large expenditures of time. Many laboratories have been held back in their work by the attempt to substitute cheaper devices which do not give satisfactory performance. In planning a new laboratory, it is wise to give careful study to a number of catalog descriptions, to inspect the equipment at convention exhibits, and to solicit evaluations from other investigators who have been using a given model.

Restraining chairs intended primarily for concurrent behavioral and physiological work with primates are available commercially. Their general construction and use have been described by Mason (1958), and a system which is similar but which offers somewhat less restraint has been described by Findley (1959). A restraining system for dogs has been described by Kaplan, Campbell, Martin, Wulp, and Lipinski (1962).

Specialized experimental environments have also been developed for work with human subjects. Laboratory rooms for operant work with children are described in Chap. 14. A laboratory designed for a survey of effective reinforcers for autistic children has been reported by Ferster and DeMyer (1961). Facilities for the study of operant behavior in chronic psychotic patients are described by Lindsley (1956a, 1956b).

Conditioned and discriminative stimuli

Stimuli that are used merely to distinguish experimental environments or to signal oncoming events are usually not specified with great detail or precision in operant experiments, since their relative effectiveness is not usually at issue. They are ordinarily selected on the basis of their neutrality, their distinctiveness, and their convenience. That is, the stimulus should (1) have little or no effect on the subject's behavior prior to training; (2) be readily discriminable by the subject, in order to yield large effects following training; and (3) be easily presented or removed by electrical means. In most cases, these criteria indicate the use of either a visual or an auditory stimulus.

To provide a sufficiently distinctive signal, visual stimulation for rats usually consists simply of the presence or absence of illumination. In some cases, the entire box is illuminated from above; in others, a restricted area surrounding the manipulandum will be lighted. Since lamps operating on the low-voltage d-c supply may dim when excessive current is drained off by other devices, 110-volt lamps may be preferable. If complete darkness is available as one condition, the level of illumination in the other need not be high. Indeed, high levels may depress the animal's activity. When a gradient of stimulation is required, the intensity of the light may be varied by use of a rheostat, although this introduces changes in color as well. If more precise control is needed, (1) neutral density filters or wedges may be interposed; (2) the distance of the lamp may be varied; or (3) the number of lamps may be changed. Sometimes the lamp is flashed on and off by a switch mounted on a rotating cam. The danger of a lamp's burning out may be reduced by using "long-life" bulbs or by placing a resistor in series to limit the flow of current. A more sophisticated system proposed by Herrick (1960) places the coil of a relay in series with the signal lamp. When the original lamp burns out, blocking the flow of current, the normally closed contacts of the relay apply power to a substitute lamp in the animal's chamber.

If large incandescent bulbs are used, the temperature may rise inside a closed chamber. Fluorescent bulbs are cooler, but ordinarily require an appreciable time to light. This is true even of the "instant start" type. The experimenter can place the fluorescent lamp under satisfactory control, however, by providing continuous current to the filaments and a high voltage for the arc (Harrison and Warr, 1959).

Since the pigeon will not ordinarily work well without illumination, darkness cannot be used with complete freedom as a signal for this species. It can, however, be used to interpolate a period of suspended activity between two events, known as a *blackout* or *time out*. For other purposes, the usual visual signal is a change in the color of the key. A red, a green, and a blue light, for example, may be mounted in a position to illuminate the key from behind. The color can then be changed by the simple device of switching the current from one light to another, or the key can be darkened by switching off all the lights. A variable clock or counter stimulus may be produced by placing a rectangular window or slot behind the key and altering its length (Ferster and Skinner, 1957). Wavelength has proved a convenient dimension for studies of the gradient of generalization (e.g., Blough, 1961; Guttman, 1956).

For the monkey, the usual signal is a $\frac{1}{2}$- or 1-in.-diameter pilot lamp of the type used to monitor the presence of power in electrical equipment. An ordinary electric meter may be used as a counter or clock.

For the rat, many experimenters prefer auditory stimuli. An economical device for producing a tone is the code practice oscillator, available from most radio and electronic supply houses. Some of these oscillators are equipped with controls for varying either volume or pitch. A telegraph sounder, or even a relay, may be used to produce a series of clicks, and the number of clicks per second may be varied to produce a gradient. A circuit for a simple electronic click generator has been described by Malis and Curran (1960). A buzzer seems to be particularly effective in avoidance work, but care must be exercised to prevent the confounding of inherent with conditioned effects (Myers, 1962). White noise, an equal-energy spectrum for the range of audible frequencies, may be used as a signal if it is not needed for the masking of sounds from outside the chamber. White noise may be especially useful for procedures in which the stimulus may acquire aversive properties. The broad spectrum of frequencies prevents the formation of standing-wave patterns within the chamber and thus keeps the animal from substantially reducing the stimulus by finding a relatively quiet locus within such a pattern.

Response devices

Since most operant work takes rate of occurrence as its primary datum, the free operant method is sometimes defined in terms of "a response which takes a short time to occur and leaves the animal in the same place ready to respond again" (Ferster, 1953, p. 263). If automated recording is to be used, the subject's activity must be translated into electric signals. This means that some form of switch is usually employed as the response device, sometimes called an *operandum* or *manipulandum*.

It is generally considered desirable to use a form of behavior that has a low frequency of occurrence prior to training or outside the experimental environment. This reduces non-experimental contributions to the performance generated by the experimental operations. Major variations in topography are to be avoided, since they may introduce non-orderly variations in the recorded rate. Gnawing and jumping, for example, were sometimes a problem with early response levers used with rats (Bersh, 1951; Dinsmoor, 1950). The device should be low in its pressure and amplitude requirements and high in its possible frequency of operation, not only to reduce topographical variations but also to expand the range of values which the rate may assume under given conditions. The pigeon's rate of pecking, for example, may reach 15 responses per second (Ferster, 1953; Ferster and Skinner, 1957). Auditory feedback from the operandum or its associated circuitry is generally considered desirable, particularly if the proprioceptive feedback is small.

The standard operant for rats is bar-pressing. A crossbar is mounted parallel to the wall of the box on the projecting arm or lever of a switching device. The crossbar is usually constructed of stainless-steel tubing of sufficient diameter, i.e., at least $\frac{3}{8}$ in., to discourage biting. It is at least 2 in. long and is placed 3 to 4 in. above the floor of the box. Counterbalances are sometimes added to the further end of the arm to adjust the pressure, which can be measured with a pressure gauge such as that used to measure the weight of the tone arm in high-fidelity music systems (e.g., George Scherr Co., model GIBRU). Low pressures in the neighborhood of 10 to 20 grams are preferred by most experimenters. The structure of the lever should be sufficiently rugged to prevent jamming or shifts in sensitivity. To eliminate contact bounce most commercial models make use of a snap-action microswitch; the excursion can be limited by placing a stop near the far end of the lever.

An economical lever that can be constructed with a minimum of shop facilities has been described by Verhave (1958). A crossbar is substituted for the Bakelite knob on a Switchcraft 3002 (normally closed) lever switch, and the entire assembly is mounted on a circular hole in the wall of the box. If an appropriate tap is not available for threading the hole, a standard mounting nut may be used.

For human subjects or for monkeys, a lever switch or a telegraph key is sometimes used. Hanson (1962), however, reports that the telegraph key may yield irregular variations in rate if the subject bounces it repeatedly, in a low-amplitude motion, against the electrical contact at the maximum point of its excursion. Also, transistorized circuits will pick up substantial contact bounce from this device. A special lever for use with fish is described in Chap. 11, a lever for dogs by Waller (1960), and a lever for kittens by Symmes (1963).

Levers that can be retracted from the experimental chamber by the programming system have traditionally proved difficult to construct with local shop facilities; high-quality machine work is ordinarily required to prevent them from jamming. Commercially constructed models are available from several sources. The insertion and retraction times required for various models vary from $\frac{1}{2}$ to 4 seconds.

The standard response device for pigeons consists of a thin plate of translucent Plexiglas suspended behind a circular opening of $\frac{3}{4}$ to 1 in. diameter in the wall of the box. When struck by the beak of the pigeon, the plate pivots on a horizontal axis and separates a pair of normally closed electrical contacts. A standard key has been described in detail by Ferster and Skinner (1957), and a special key for mounting on a projection unit by Ferster, Holtzman, and Leckrone (1962). The height of the key should be adjusted to the height of the pigeon for convenient striking. For the White Carneaux, the key should be about $8\frac{1}{2}$ in. from the floor; for smaller birds, a little lower. A suitable auditory feedback may be provided by mounting a relay behind the stimulus and response panel, in series with the key. The pigeon key can be used without modification for rats, although there is some tendency for topographical variation between nose and paw responses. A height of about $2\frac{1}{2}$ in. is suitable. Larger and more rugged versions of the pigeon key have been used successfully with primates. One virtue of this type of operandum is that discriminative stimuli may be displayed directly on the face of the key itself, a favorable position for effective control of the subject's performance.

In general, data comparable to those obtained in other laboratories may be obtained with a minimum of risk by employing standard devices. For special purposes, such as providing a second operandum for concurrent or chained responding or for monitoring the receipt of reinforcement, other devices are available. Light-beam and photocell systems can be obtained through most radio-electronics dealers. Contact recording devices have been described by Hunter (1952), Otis and Boenning (1959), and Pilgrim (1948). Drinkometers for recording contact of the animal's tongue with a liquid dispenser are marketed commercially.

For humans, a panel or push button with a visual display is offered by Grason-Stadler. A plunger similar to those used on candy-vending machines is available from Gerbrands or from Scientific Prototype. The use of a voice key in operant research has been described by Shearn, Sprague, and Rosenzweig (1961) and by Starkweather (1960).

A number of specialized devices have been suggested for recording variations in some property of the individual response occurrence, i.e., in the way in which the response is made. Antonitis (1951), for example, photographed the position of the rat's nose along a horizontal slot each time it was thrust in. Herrnstein (1961) substituted a 10- by 1-in. rubber strip to be pecked by the pigeon, with automatic recording of location. Dinsmoor (1958a) described a circuit for amplifying the output of a miniature d-c motor used as a generator, in order to record rotary speed for a bar-pressing or wheel-turning response; however, the system has proved somewhat temperamental, and a more sophisticated amplifier is needed. Herrick and Karnow (1962) have provided specifications for a constant-torque displacement-measuring lever. Trotter (1956a, 1956b) has described two simple force-recording devices and has discussed their characteristics. Notterman (1959) has used a pair of strain gauges to measure the force of pressing. Hefferline, Birch, and Gentry (1961) have studied the use of pressure cells and pressure-sensitive paint, which they believe provide a simpler and more economical system.

Reinforcing devices and substances

For rats, the most commonly used reinforcers are pellets of food. They are available in 20-, 37-, 45-, 94-, and 97-milligram (mg) sizes from Noyes Co. or in 150- and 700-mg sizes from Foringer and Co. Although more of the small pellets may be delivered to the animal before satiation sets in, their control of behavior tends to be less satisfactory. The 97- or 150-mg sizes are generally to be preferred. Note, however, that eating may interfere with other activities.

Pellet dispensers or feeders are available from most commercial suppliers of operant equipment. The heart of the standard dispenser is a circular plate bearing a series of holes. The size of the hole must be specified in terms of the size of the pellet that will be used. As the plate is rotated by an a-c motor or a solenoid and ratchet mechanism, successive holes pass beneath the storage hopper, and a pellet falls into each, resting on a stationary plate below. When it reaches the appropriate position, the pellet drops through an opening in the stationary plate and down a length of plastic tubing to a tray in the animal's box. The velocity of descent may need adjustment to make sure that the pellet reaches the tray regularly but does not bounce out. To prevent excessive drain on the d-c power supply, the solenoid may be operated by the discharge of a large capacitor inserted in the programming circuit. Faster delivery results if the pellet drops when the solenoid is actuated rather than when it is released. A "universal feeder" manufactured by Gerbrands operates on a similar principle. It consists of a series of buckets mounted on a loop or belt. A variety of foods or other objects, including small toys, can be loaded into the buckets and delivered in sequence by successive movements of the belt. This feeder is designed primarily for use with primate or human subjects.

For pigeons, the standard reinforcing device is a tray of grain that can be raised to an accessible position for a specified period of time, usually 3 to 4 seconds, by solenoid action and then dropped back into a position where it cannot be reached by the bird. The inclusion of a small lamp inside the magazine housing facilitates stimulus control of the eating behavior.

Devices for delivering liquid reinforcement to rats or monkeys are of two general types. The more common type consists of a cup or dipper on a pivoted arm. The cup is lifted to a drinking position by cam or solenoid action, held there for a brief period, and then allowed to drop back into a reservoir tank below. Commercial versions are available with cup volumes ranging from 0.01 to 0.3 cubic centimeter (cc) for rats and up to 1 cc for primates. The same device may be constructed locally, but care should be exercised to damp the action sufficiently to avoid spilling the liquid when the cup stops at the top of its excursion. If the arm is to be actuated by an a-c motor, the motor can be braked by application of low-voltage direct current. If it is to be actuated by a solenoid, a continuous-duty coil may be needed. Adequate provision should be made for a substantial drain on the power supply.

A cheaper but sometimes less satisfactory system for delivering liquid reinforcement involves a gravity feed from an open storage tank. Opening a solenoid valve (e.g., Skinner model C2DA1031, 24 volts d-c, with GD mounting bracket) permits the liquid to flow through a tube to the underside of a delivery cup in the experimental box. The volume to be delivered can be controlled by adjusting the height of the reservoir and the length of time the valve is held open. Some restriction of the rate of flow may be needed to prevent the liquid from shooting up too forcefully in the cup and spilling over. Furthermore, the length of time for which the liquid remains accessible cannot readily be restricted with this system as it can with the moving dipper. On the other hand, there is no danger of catching the rat's tongue between the dipper and its access hole. Several variants of this system have been described by Polidora and Meyer (1961). A similar system for primates has been described by Grunzke (1961). A liquid pump, using a hypodermic syringe, can be obtained from Davis or Foringer.

Although it is easy to vary the volume and composition of a reinforcing solution, there is little systematic information available on the relative effectiveness of various combinations. This is due in part (1) to the prevalence of theoretically oriented designs in which only two values of the experimental variable have been tested, rather than parametric surveys, and (2) to the complexity of the interrelationships encountered among such variables as concentration, volume, degree and kind of deprivation, interval between reinforcements, and numbers of reinforcements (Collier, 1962; Collier and Myers, 1961; Collier and Willis, 1961). The results of several studies (e.g., Collier and Myers, 1961; Collier and Siskel, 1959; Collier and Willis, 1961; Conrad and Sidman, 1956; Guttman, 1953, 1954; Stebbins, 1959; Stebbins, Mead, and Martin, 1959) indicate that the addition of large quantities of sucrose (granulated cane sugar) to water substantially raises the level of performance of food-deprived rats and monkeys on a variety of procedures. For interval schedules, at least, the optimal concentration by weight must usually lie above 32 percent and sometimes above 64 percent, although care must be taken to avoid satiation effects. For saccharin, maximum effectiveness may be reached with concentrations of the order of 1 to 3 percent (Cockrell, 1952; Collier, 1962; Dinsmoor, 1962). These solutions do not quite match the effectiveness of sugar solutions, but the small quantities of saccharin are easier to store and the resulting solution is not as thick or as sticky as the highly concentrated sugar solution. Saccharin sodium in powdered form is sometimes available at retail drug outlets. With both sugar and saccharin, care should be taken to replace the solution frequently to prevent alterations in the concentration due to evaporation.

Using a progressive-ratio technique, Hodos (1961) found that increasing proportions of sweetened condensed milk to the highest level tested, 50 percent by volume, were increasingly effective. Even with ad-lib feeding and watering the effects appeared to be large, as measured by this technique. There appear to be no data on higher concentrations.

The selection of an appropriate reinforcing substance is sometimes a problem when working with a new species. Valenstein (1959) reports difficulties in using food, milk, or water for guinea pigs. Gundy (1959) notes that carrot juice is effective, even without food or water deprivation; however, there appears to be some variation among different brands. Elliot, Frazier, and Riach (1962) have conducted an informal test of various food substances for cats, and conclude that bonito, salmon, and condensed milk are relatively effective. Hodos, Laursen, and Nissen (1963) recommend a fish and milk paste. Banana pellets, sugar pellets (Noyes), water, sweetened condensed milk, and orange juice have been used with monkeys.

Reinforcers available for use with children are described in Chap. 14. A popular device for reinforcing adult subjects is provided by a dial that is briefly illuminated whenever the subject presses a key. Under appropriate instructions, deflections of the pointer on the dial may be programmed as a reinforcer (Holland, 1957). A variant involving the lighting of a signal lamp has been described by Weiner (1962). Verplanck (1956) reports that recorded "points" provide reliable reinforcers. Reinforcers used in verbal conditioning experiments are discussed in Chap. 12; reinforcers for psychotic patients in Ayllon and Haughton (1962).

Aversive stimuli

Electric shock is the most commonly used aversive stimulus. It is typically delivered to the subject through a set of parallel rods serving as a grid floor to the experimental chamber. There are a number of technical difficulties, however, in using this technique. The simplest way to wire the grid, for example, is to connect half the grid rods to the positive terminal of the shock stimulator and the other half, in alternation, to the negative terminal. Unfortunately, the shock is interrupted whenever the animal moves onto two rods of like polarity. If the duration of the shock is substantial, the animal soon learns to hold fast to his nonshocked position, and other behavior becomes extremely difficult to establish. When only brief pulses of shock are used, the animal is less likely to find a safe position; but even on a random basis, he may receive shock on as few as half the occasions on which it is purportedly delivered. The remedy for this problem is to reverse the polarity of each rod with respect to the others (Skinner and Campbell, 1947). For the most uniform distribution of shock density, each electrode should be set opposite in polarity to the remaining electrodes for an appropriate fraction of the cycle. This means that the shock actually received by the animal will consist of a series of pulses. In escape work these pulses should be kept relatively brief (Dinsmoor, 1958c).

A number of devices have been used with some success to alternate the polarity of the grid elements. A stepping switch, for example, may be wired for continuous operation by bringing power to the coil through the interrupter contacts. To protect the mechanism from excessive wear, the rate of stepping may be slowed down by adding a relay which will be operated by the interrupter contacts and which will in turn control the stepping coil. Other systems use pressure-actuated microswitches around one large cam or along a bank of staggered cams, ganged rotary selector switches, wire brushes, a relay ring, or magnetically operated switches. Most of these devices should be operated only when shock is being delivered; they are not sufficiently rugged to withstand continuous usage.

One hazard involved in the use of a polarity alternator or grid scrambler is that a substantial part of the effectiveness of the stimulus can be dissipated in transit, probably because of capacitive loss, if the several conductors in the cable leading to the grid are not kept well separated. The use of a relatively substantial insulating sheath on each conductor, however, seems to meet this difficulty. Individual conductors may be bundled by hand. Another way of handling this problem is to place the scrambler close to the grid.

The effectiveness of the stimulus will also be reduced if moisture and organic material accumulate on mounting surfaces between the grid rods, permitting leakage of a part of the current through paths in parallel with the subject. Some circulation of air is needed in the chamber to prevent the development of excessive levels of humidity, and the grid mounting should be scrubbed regularly to remove organic deposits. The use of stainless steel is desirable for the grid rods, to prevent corrosion, and frequent sanding is helpful.

Another hazard to both subject and equipment is the arcing that may occur between adjacent surfaces, contact to contact or animal to electrode, when the circuit is open. This difficulty may be substantially reduced by inserting a series of neon lamps in the circuit in parallel with the animal (Dinsmoor, 1960). When the circuit is opened, the voltage across the lamps rises from a value characteristic of the drop across the subject toward a value characteristic of the supply source. When it reaches the threshold value of the string of lamps, however, it arcs through this shunt rather than across the parallel air gap. The lamps should *not* parallel the tube or resistor used to limit the current through the subject.

Under prolonged exposure to shock, particularly if the desired response is not very strong, the animal tends to develop his own techniques for dealing with the situation. Even if all surfaces within the test chamber are electrified, the animal may learn to recline on his back, interposing a coat of hair between his skin and the grid. Clipping and depilatory creams are of considerable help. But given sufficient time, many animals learn to balance on a single grid rod, touching the wall only occasionally, to maintain a shock-free position. Once learned, this pattern is difficult to disrupt.

The obvious remedy for unauthorized escape responses would seem to be the substitution of attached or implanted electrodes for the grid. To date, however, despite a number of attempts known to the author, no one has published a reliable technique for attaching or implanting shock electrodes with the rat. For pigeons, the outlook seems more promising. Hoffman (1960) has described a technique for attaching a temporary electrode harness, and Azrin (1959) an implanting technique (see also Sidley and Schoenfeld, 1963). Monkeys may be placed in a restraining chair and shocked through an electrode attached to the foot (Weiss and Laties, 1962) or to the tail (Hake and Azrin, 1963).

A number of writers have addressed themselves to the problem of specifying a power source suitable for shocking animals, but none of their recommendations has commanded general acceptance. The generality of most of the empirical comparisons has been restricted by other aspects of the particular stimulator employed. The problem that has occasioned most concern is that the resistance of the rat, at least, to the passage of electric current varies over a considerable range. Using threshold currents, Muenzinger and Mize (1933) found an average resistance of 338,000 ohms, with readings ranging from 60,000 to 1,150,000 ohms and successive readings varying on the average by 186,000 ohms. Using a current of 10 milliamperes (ma), Kaplan and Kaplan (1962) obtained resistances ranging from 50,000 to 2 million ohms, with higher momentary resistances as the rat broke contact with the grid. They also noted changes related to the animal's "alertness" and to the general stimulus configuration; in particular, they noted a substantial drop following a 5-sec 5-ma shock. Campbell and Teghtsoonian (1958) found that median resistances dropped roughly from a level of 300,000 to

500,000 ohms at threshold current (0.01 or 0.02 ma) to 5,000 ohms at a high level (6 or 7 ma). If the rat were exposed to a simple fixed-voltage shock, the amount of current passing through him would vary in similar fashion, since it would be directly proportional to the reciprocal of the animal's resistance.

The level of current can be stabilized to a considerable extent merely by placing a substantial resistance (e.g., 100,000 to 1 million ohms) in series with the secondary winding of a high-voltage (e.g., several hundred volts) transformer. In this circuit, variations in the resistance added by the rat have less effect, proportionately, on the total resistance and, therefore, less effect on the level of current. The amount of resistance to be used depends, of course, on the voltage available and on the level of current desired, but the higher the resistance the greater is the stabilization. This is the principle used in most commercial shock stimulators for animal subjects.

More precise stabilization of the current over a wide range of subject resistances may be obtained with any one of a number of published circuits by using the feedback from the voltage drop across a series resistor to regulate tube conductance (e.g., Davidon and Boonin, 1956; Dinsmoor, 1961; Lovibond and Turner, 1956). A commercial stimulator incorporating this form of control is sold by Lehigh Valley Electronics.

Campbell and Teghtsoonian (1958), among others, have suggested that it is better to stabilize the multiplicative product of current and voltage (power) than the current alone. Their animals showed more orderly changes in unconditioned activity (locomotion and jumping) at low shock levels with a matched impedance source than with current-stabilized circuits; however, an expanded mimeographed version of their paper shows that more orderly changes were obtained with a stabilized source than with the matched-impedance source when data were obtained for aversion thresholds. Much may depend on the particular dependent variable employed.

Campbell and Teghtsoonian's matched-impedance source differed from the typical current-stabilized circuit only in having a relatively modest series resistance of 150,000 ohms. The resulting decline in current as the resistance of the rat increases helps to compensate for the increasing voltage drop across the animal, so that the multiplicative product of current and voltage, i.e., power, remains somewhat more stable. In theory, it is possible to construct more precise power-stabilized circuits by using voltage-sensing and current-sensing feedbacks from resistors in parallel and in series with the animal to regulate the conductance of a tube.

White noise (e.g., Harrison and Abelson, 1959) and bright light (e.g., Keller, 1941) have also been used as aversive stimuli for rats. Neither stimulus, however, appears to be as effective as shock. In the case of light, the instrumentation needed to prevent unauthorized escape and avoidance appears to be fully as cumbersome as that needed for shock (Kaplan, 1952, 1956). Low atmospheric temperature with heat reinforcement has also been used (e.g., Weiss and Laties, 1961), but it, too, appears to be relatively cumbersome for general experimental purposes.

PROGRAMMING CIRCUITRY

The timing, counting, and switching elements used to program operant experiments are of two basic types. The older type employs electromechanical devices such as the relay; the newer type depends on transistors. This section will first consider relay systems and the panels and racks used to house such elements. A discussion of their solid state equivalents will follow.

Electromechanical devices

The larger units of electromechanical equipment are built on standard 19-in. steel or aluminum panels obtained from radio-

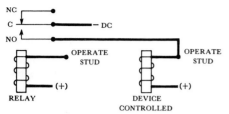

Fig. 10-1　Schematic diagram of a circuit for control of some other device by switching contacts of a relay.

electronics supply houses. These panels are then bolted directly onto telephone-type relay racks. Smaller units are built on panels made of Bakelite or some similar substance, which in turn are mounted by means of Littelfuse No. 101002 clips on pairs of $\frac{1}{4}$-in. diameter steel or brass rods set horizontally across the face of the rack, $6\frac{1}{2}$ in. apart. The rods also serve as bus bars for the d-c power supply.

The experimenter who is planning to build his own laboratory is strongly urged to copy existing equipment. The use of direct current, for example, permits the addition of capacitor circuits to adjust timing relationships and diodes (rectifiers) to block "sneak paths." Limitation of the power supply,[1] to a nominal 24 to 28 volts instead of 110, protects the operator from fire hazards, violations of the building code, and painful or lethal shock. Mounting the individual units on clip-on panels with stud terminals makes it easy to add, subtract, or exchange components, or to make alterations in the circuit. The locally built components will also be compatible with most commercial lines of programming equipment. The experimenter is also urged to use enclosed relays to prevent tampering and the collection of dust on the contacts, small coils for fast action, plug-in mountings for ease of replacement, and large contacts for reliability and durability. Mercury-wetted contacts should also be con-

sidered, although they are a bit more expensive.

In the standard systems, all terminals except those leading to plus d-c power or 110 a-c are brought out to the face of the panel as Nuway studs. The studs are then interconnected as needed to complete the circuit by leads composed of No. 18 stranded wire ending in snap fasteners, which mate with each other and with the studs. Behind the panel, one side of each relay coil or other load device is connected through the upper fuse clip directly to the plus power rod. As the plus side of power does not appear on the panel, it is not possible by normal means to connect it to the minus side of power without passing through a load; that is, it is impossible to create a short circuit. Since no damage can result, the experimenter is free to plan his circuits on the panels themselves, testing the empirical consequences of each step as he proceeds. The provision of a permanent connection to the plus side of power also means that to operate a relay the experimenter need only bring the minus side of power to the panel stud leading to the coil. This is known as the operate or signal stud.

To place a timer, a counter, or some stimulating device under the control of a relay, it is only necessary to make connections (1) from a minus or *ground*[2] stud to a stud representing one of the common switching contacts on the relay and (2) from the stud of the accompanying normally open or normally closed contact to the operate stud of the device in question (see Fig. 10-1). When the contacts are in touch with each other, the circuit is complete, or "closed," and current flows through the load. When the contacts are separated, the circuit is incomplete, or "open," and no current can flow across the gap. (For a general description of relays and their operation, see Chap. 2 or Cornsweet, 1963; for highly sophisticated

---

[1] The current rating of the power supply should be adequate to handle large loads, such as solenoid-actuated feeders and dippers, for brief periods of time without depriving other circuit elements.

[2] Contrary to general electrical practice, it is the minus side of power that is grounded in electromechanical systems for operant programming.

techniques, see Keister, Ritchie, and Washburn, 1951.)

The basic function of an operant programming system is to produce certain changes in stimulation (e.g., signal on, shock off, food delivered) when certain criteria are met involving combinations of response occurrence, time, and number. The system is also used to control graphic or numerical recording devices and sometimes to change its own rules when appropriate criteria are met. Simply and abstractly, this boils down to the occurrence of some event C being made to depend upon the status of events A and B. In an electromechanical system, A, B, and C may each be represented by a corresponding relay, which may be active or inactive at a given moment. The procedural rules or contingencies are expressed by leads running from one relay to another.

To make event C depend for its occurrence on the concurrent presence of both event A and event B, the following circuit may be used (see Fig. 10-2). The coil of relay C is connected to the normally open contact of relay A; and the common contact of relay A is connected to the minus side of the power supply. When both relay A and relay B are activated, the circuit will be completed and current will flow through the coil of relay C. Note that the two sets of contacts are in series; i.e., the circuit passes through them successively, so that both of them must be closed before the circuit is complete. In logic, A and B are known as *necessary* conditions

for C. In solid state circuitry, this type of connection is known as an AND gate, since both A *and* B are necessary for C. (See Chap. 2 for detailed discussion of gating circuitry and logic.)

If we wish the occurrence of C to depend on the presence of A and the *absence* of B, we merely substitute the normally closed contact of B for the normally open. The circuit is then completed when A is activated but B is not. It may be helpful to remember that the normally open and normally closed contacts of a relay work like mirror images as a function of time—when one is open the other is closed, and when the first is closed the second is open.

Another way in which two or more prior conditions can be combined is the OR gate. In relay circuitry, the OR gate is expressed by placing the contacts of A and B in parallel (see Fig. 10-3). Both are connected to power and both are connected to C. If *either* A or B is activated, C operates. In the language of logic, A and B are each said to be *sufficient* conditions for C.

In describing the AND gate, we assumed that both A and B were present at the same time. In many cases, however, we may wish to use an event A that occurs *prior* to event B. For example, we may wish to deliver reinforcement when a certain interval of time has been completed (event A) and the subject has thereafter made a response (event B). The circuitry should reflect the fact that some event A has occurred in the past, even

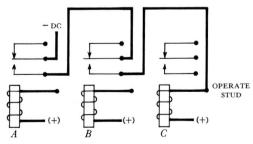

Fig. 10-2 A circuit in which relay C will be activated only when both A and B are active.

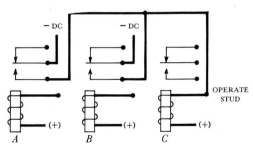

Fig. 10-3 A circuit in which relay C will be activated when either A or B is active.

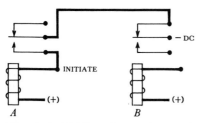

Fig. 10-4 Holding circuit. Once activated, relay *A* maintains itself until released by the activation of relay *B*.

though it is no longer present. In relay programming, this memory is accomplished through the use of a lock-up or holding circuit (see Fig. 10-4). The activation of the relay is initiated in the usual manner by direct connection of the coil to the power supply through the output switch of the timing mechanism. However, to maintain the activation of the relay after the timer switch has opened again, another connection is made to the normally open contact of the same relay and from the common to power. Now relay *A* will hold through its own contacts, and the initial input may be terminated without terminating the action of the relay. Eventually, of course, we shall wish to break this holding action. This means that the lead from the common contact must not be connected *directly* to power but must pass through the contacts (usually normally closed and common) of some other relay, in series, on its way to the power source. When the second relay is activated, the holding circuit is broken and the first relay returns to its resting position.

In some programs there is a change in conditions that depends not on a single occurrence of a given event but on a specified *number* of occurrences. In this case, some form of counting device must be used. In an electromechanical system, the successive pulses of current may be directed to the coil of a stepping switch. This device bears a series of stationary contacts arranged in the form of a circle or an arc and a common contact mounted on a moving arm or wiper.

The wiping arm is mounted on a ratchet wheel, which turns one notch each time current is supplied to the coil. As the wheel turns, the common contact moves successively from one stationary contact to the next. If the common is connected to power and one of the stationary contacts is connected to the device to be controlled, the external device will operate when the proper count is reached (see Chap. 2).

For programs in which the number of events to be counted is beyond the capacity of a stepper, a predetermining counter may be used. The desired number is set by hand on the face of the counter. As successive pulses of current are fed into it, the unit counts backward to zero, at which point an output switch is closed. When current is supplied to a separate reset coil, the count is returned to its original value.

If the count to be required differs on successive occasions, as in a variable-ratio schedule, holes may be punched at irregular intervals in a loop of tape, usually 16-millimeter (mm) motion-picture film. The tape is mounted on a sprocket that is rotated in successive steps by the actuating mechanism of a stepping switch. Normally the arm of a switch rests on the tape. Each time this arm drops into one of the holes, however, the switch is actuated. These units are available from commercial sources (see Appendix).

Another criterion that may be used to change conditions in an operant program is the passage of a specified interval of time. Sometimes this interval is measured from each instance of a repeated event, such as a response, so that something happens (e.g., shock is delivered, reinforcement is made available) only when *x* seconds have passed without a recurrence of the original event. This type of interval is usually timed by a device that includes a constant-speed motor and an arm that trips a switch at the end of its excursion. The arm is reset to its original position by spring action whenever the input is interrupted to an electromagnetic clutch that links it mechanically with the shaft of the motor. The electrical input to the clutch is then brought through the normally closed contacts of a relay representing the response, so that each occurrence of the response releases the clutch and allows the arm to spring back. The length of the time interval can be set by fixing the position of a movable stop to which the arm returns when it is released. The further the stop is set from the switch, the longer the interval required for the arm to travel through the intervening arc. Timers of this type are manufactured commercially. Although the typical clutch is designed for 110 volts a-c, it operates reliably on 24 volts d-c. The same timers can be secured ready-mounted on operant programming panels. For intervals below 30 seconds, electronic timers may be preferable.

If no resetting is required, e.g., in fixed- or variable-interval reinforcement schedules, a simpler type of time input may be used. When the interval is of constant duration, this instrument may consist merely of a motor driving a notched wheel or cam. The cam operates a switch each time it completes a revolution. External circuitry may be arranged to stop and start the wheel, if necessary. When the time interval is to vary on successive occasions, a length of tape may be punched with holes at irregular intervals and conducted over a sprocket to operate the switch. This unit is also available from standard sources of operant equipment.

After a relatively simple circuit has been developed to handle the basic relationships desired, further adjustments often prove necessary in the temporal action of the relays. Sometimes the problem is one of sequence. In a chaining procedure, for example, the programmer may plan not only to tally a response on the appropriate recorder but also to use the same response to produce a change in stimulus conditions and a corresponding transfer of incoming responses from one recorder to another. If all these operations occur simultaneously, the response will be tallied on the second recorder instead of or in addition to the first. To establish the proper sequence, the programmer needs a pulse that

can be used to switch recorders immediately *following* the cessation of the response. Such an end pulse may be obtained from a circuit suggested by Ames (1963).

As may be seen in Fig. 10-5, a capacitor is placed in series with the coil, and a rectifier in parallel. When the initiating switch is thrown, the capacitor charges, but the current flows through the rectifier rather than through the coil. (Because of the low-resistance parallel branch, there is virtually no voltage drop across the coil.) When the switch is opened, however, the capacitor discharges through the coil and the 200-ohm resistor in series, since the rectifier offers a relatively high resistance to the passage of current in the opposite direction.

The same circuit may also be used to limit the duration of a switching action. If the subject responds during the closure of the switch on a cam or tape timer used to schedule reinforcement, one reinforcement might be delivered and another scheduled, illegitimately, before the switch opens again. But in the foregoing circuit, the duration of the final switching action is determined by the discharge time of the capacitor and may be reduced, by choosing the appropriate capacitance, to a length that is just sufficient to operate the next piece of equipment.

When the initiating event is the subject's response, the experimenter may wish to limit not only the maximum duration of the resulting pulse but also its minimum. On the one

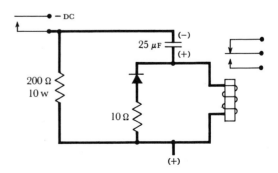

Fig. 10-5 End-pulse circuit. The relay operates briefly when the initiating switch is opened.

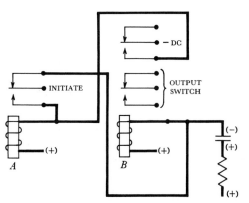

Fig. 10-6   Pulse-forming circuit. Relay B operates for a fixed duration that is independent of the length of the input pulse initiating its action.

hand, he may wish to reinforce the first response after a given point in time but not a response that has been initiated earlier and maintained until the proper moment; or he may wish to protect intermittent-duty equipment from the effects of prolonged activation. On the other hand, he may wish to make sure that the resulting pulse is sufficiently long to operate subsequent programming and recording equipment. Commercial pulse formers are available that respond to any input over a bare minimum of, say, 5 milliseconds (msec), with a pulse of fixed duration, typically 30 to 45 msec. Lacking a commercial unit, the experimenter can build his own pulse former, using a circuit described by Gollub (1958). This is diagrammed in Fig. 10-6. When the common contact on relay *A* is initially connected to the power source to operate the pulse former, relay *B* is activated and the capacitor is charged. (The resistor merely limits the initial surge of current in the capacitive branch of the circuit.) Once activated, relay *B* activates relay *A,* which locks itself for as long as the original connection to power remains unbroken but which also disconnects relay *B* and the associated capacitor. This action is very fast. Relay *B* continues to operate while the capacitor discharges through its coil, then releases. The duration of the action of relay

B is governed by the value of the capacitor, regardless of the duration of the original input. (If a fine adjustment is desired, a variable resistor or potentiometer may be added in parallel with the coil of relay *B*.) But only when the initial connection with power is broken does relay *A* release and open the system for a subsequent pulse. The second set of contacts on relay *B* provides the fixed-duration switching output.

To the novice, the completed programming circuit may seem quite complex, because of the large number of leads running in various directions. But the essential simplicity of such a network may be illustrated by the block diagram for a fixed-interval schedule of reinforcement, shown in Fig. 10-7. Ordinarily, the electrical output from the subject's response does not reach the reinforcing mechanism. When the timing notch on a revolving cam actuates a switch, however, a holding relay is locked up. Through the contacts of this relay, the output from the next response reaches a timer controlling the actual reinforcing device, e.g., dipper, pellet dispenser, or tray of grain. In turn, a switch on the reinforcing device or, alternatively, an end-pulse circuit like that presented in Fig. 10-5, is used to release the holding relay, preventing the reinforcement of further responses until another interval of time has elapsed.

Solid state devices

Complete but mutually incompatible lines of manufactured modules for solid state programming are offered by several companies. The internal design of these modules varies from one manufacturer to another, and their construction is definitely a job for professionals. Fortunately, however, prepackaging of the basic functions makes the overall programming circuit simpler to design with these modules than with corresponding electromechanical units. The solid state modules are inherently faster than electromechanical circuitry, smaller, quieter, and ultimately more reliable. Caution must be exercised, however, to prevent their activation by stray voltage changes (electrical noise) originating outside the system, particularly by inductive spikes arising in nearby electromechanical equipment. If such spurious signals do appear, they may be suppressed by (1) the use of a capacitor-resistor series across the offending coil, (2) physical separation of components and leads belonging to the two systems, or (3) shielding and grounding.

Solid state modules fall into two categories with respect to their response to an input signal. Level-sensing modules respond to the presence of a previously selected voltage, which is standard for a given manufacturer, at the input terminal. Change-sensing modules respond to the onset, or in some cases to the offset, of the same voltage. The output is either a brief pulse or a sustained voltage at the same level.

The AND-gate module, for example, bears two or more level-sensing input terminals (legs). Normally, there is no output signal, but whenever the appropriate voltage is applied simultaneously to both input terminals, a corresponding voltage is concurrently maintained at the output. This can then be connected to the input terminal of the next module in the program. The OR gate is similar in appearance, but provision of the signal

voltage to *either* of the input terminals maintains a corresponding voltage at the output. Actually, the function of this unit corresponds to that of the rectifier (diode) used to block sneak paths in relay circuitry, for it merely avoids the direct linkage of two output terminals that are intended to serve the same input. To activate a gate during the *absence*, rather than the presence, of a given event, various techniques are available. (1) Some modules have a second output that is the complement of the first; that is, it delivers a signal whenever the first output does not. (2) Some gates are equipped with an inhibiting input terminal, so that provision of a signal voltage to that leg of the gate prevents rather than permits the activation of the output. (3) The ON state of the event in question can be reversed to OFF and the OFF state to ON by interposing an inverter module between the original signal source and the input to the second module. These arrangements correspond to the transfer of a lead from a normally open to a normally closed contact in a relay circuit.

Like the ordinary relay, the gating and inverting modules are level-sensing and reflect immediate conditions. They do not maintain an output once the input has terminated. The flip-flop or memory module, however,

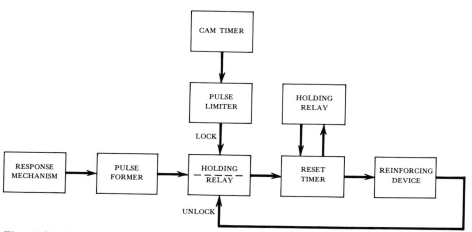

Fig. 10-7 Block diagram of the complete programming circuit for a fixed-interval schedule of reinforcement.

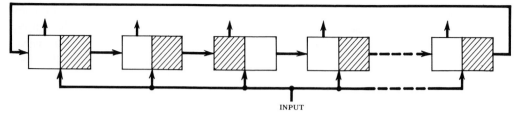

INPUT

Fig. 10-8   Block diagram of a ring counter.

responds to the onset of the signal and thereafter maintains its action in a manner analogous to that of a holding or latching relay. Two input terminals are normally provided. A pulse to one turns the output on; it then remains on until a pulse to the other turns it off. In this way, the flip-flop records the fact that a certain event has occurred in the past, even though it is no longer present. When the information has been utilized, the record can be erased by a signal to the reset input.

The simplest type of solid state counter or stepper uses a cascaded series of flip-flop units, each feeding the next. The first flip-flop switches on each count, the second on alternate counts, the third on every fourth count, and so on. A binary readout, e.g., a set of lamps, may be provided, or the information may be fed directly into the programming network. In another configuration, a series of flip-flops may be wired in such a way that when a common input pulse is provided to all, the state assumed by each will be determined by the previous state of its predecessor in the series (see Fig. 10-8). If one unit in the series is initially set to ON, successive units will turn on in sequence as successive pulses arrive, but each will turn off again at the next pulse. In other words, one and only one flip-flop will provide an output signal at any given time; each flip-flop assumes this role in succession. If the last unit in the series is linked back to the first one, we have a *ring counter*, which is the solid state equivalent to the electromechanical stepping switch (see Chap. 2).

Intervals of time are generated by charging or discharging a capacitor through resistance, as described in Chap. 2. The length of the interval is determined by inserting an appropriate resistance value in the circuit or by counting a given number of equally spaced pulses.

Special modules are also available for suppressing the effects of contact bounce in switching inputs, e.g., bars or keys, to the solid state system and standardizing the length of the pulse. Other modules are available for driving lights, relays, solenoids, counters, and recorders. A wealth of concrete and detailed information on the use of solid state equipment is rapidly being made available by the manufacturers. Chapter 2 of this volume covers a number of solid state circuits in detail.

RECORDING DATA

The cumulative recorder

An investigator with limited experience in operant work and a limited budget for the purchase of equipment may decide that cumulative recorders are a luxury that he can do without. This is an extremely dangerous conclusion. If for no other purpose, a cumulative recorder is needed in almost any experiment as a monitoring device. It provides a permanent and sensitive indicator of changes in the level and pattern of performance from the beginning of the session to the time at which the observation is made. Neither counters, event recorders, nor direct viewing provide satisfactory substitutes.

Even in terms of formal experimental findings, there are certain types of data that are far more readily collected by the cumulative recorder than by any other device. These include (1) the time course of behavior within the session, (2) transitions in performance from one experimental condition to another, and (3) short-term time series data, such as the localized variations in rate that show up as the "grain" in the record and cyclic deviations like those observed with fixed-interval or fixed-ratio schedules of reinforcement. Moreover, the cumulative record is capable of representing hundreds or thousands of responses in a very condensed form, convenient for overall inspection.

The versatility of the cumulative recorder can be greatly increased if the investigator is familiar with a few special techniques. For example, all but the simplest classroom models are equipped with a provision for momentary or sustained displacement of the position of the stepping (response) pen from the cumulative record. The resulting pip or stroke can be used to locate the exact incidence of such key events as reinforcements, shocks, or changes in condition on the record. In this way, cyclic deviations can be related to reinforcements, level of performance can be related to the frequency with which shocks are received, or changes in the character of the record can be related to changes in the experimental procedure or environment. Sometimes the pen is kept in a displaced position for one or several segments of time, to distinguish the record during these periods from the rest of the curve. Common examples are the period during which the warning signal is present for conditioned suppression or one segment of a multiple or chained schedule.

On most types of recorder, a second pen is provided, which rides just below the zero point for the cumulative record. This is known as the event marking pen. It cannot be stepped across the paper like the cumulative pen, but it can be displaced one unit when energized, returning to its original position when de-energized. Momentary displacement of this pen is sometimes used to record

concurrent responses on a second operandum, the delivery of shocks, or similar events Sustained displacement can be used to distinguish segments of the cumulative record obtained under differing conditions. On the one hand it is more difficult to locate accurately corresponding points on the cumulative record with this pen, because it is too distant and may not be correctly aligned. On the other hand, it leaves the cumulative record free of "hash marks" that may obscure the grain. This pen may also be used to provide a horizontal base line for measuring the slope of the cumulative record or as a replacement for the stepping pen if the latter should clog or break.

The recorder can be turned off completely to avoid complicating the record with segments of time when the subject is consuming reinforcement, a time out is in force, or another segment of a multiple or chained schedule is in effect. When the excluded behavior is also important, it can be represented independently on a second recorder. The use of separate recorders for different segments of the subject's performance sometimes makes it difficult to determine which portions of each curve correspond in time. If the two segments of a multiple schedule are equal in length, corresponding times will be represented by corresponding points along the horizontal dimension. But if one segment of the schedule lasts longer than the other or varies substantially in duration, corresponding points may be difficult to locate. This problem can often be solved, however, by marking the end of successive cycles on each record with a stroke of the pen or by resetting both pens to zero.

Resetting the pen can also be used to facilitate comparisons of successive phases or cycles within the session, even when a single recorder is used. Successive ratios, for example, may be laid out in a horizontal row for comparison of their curvatures; or, the height reached by the pen on successive segments specified by time may be compared to monitor the time course of a drug.

Some care should be exercised in choosing appropriate time and response scales for a given experiment. Note that it is the tangent (vertical excursion divided by horizontal progress) that is a linear function of the rate of responding (responses divided by time), not the slope itself in degrees from the horizontal. When the slope is steep, large deviations in rate produce only small deviations in slope and are not readily observed on the record. Too low a slope, on the other hand, may produce another type of difficulty, since deviations that are large in proportion remain small in absolute magnitude. An intermediate slope seems to provide the most sensitive indicator. On the standard Gerbrands recorder, the usual scale for pigeons or primates is $\frac{1}{8}$ mm per response and 30 cm per hour. The usual scale for rats is $\frac{1}{4}$ mm per response, to allow for the lower rates characteristic of the species.

Programmed tallying

At first glance the use of time meters and counters might seem to be restricted to such simple determinations as the length of the session and the total number of responses obtained. More detailed analyses, such as the length of the pause following reinforcement, the acceleration in rate within the cycle, or the distribution of interresponse times, might seem to require a tedious perusal of detailed graphic records such as those provided by event or operations recorders. Indeed, graphic records sometimes provide a useful form of insurance. If, however, the experimenter is in a position either to specify in advance what data he will need or to secure additional data once the need has become apparent, he can save a great deal of clerical labor by automating the process. Generally speaking, analyses of data begin with the measurement of time or the counting of events within certain limits or categories. If these categories can be defined in terms of their initiating and terminating events, the timer or counter can be inserted into or re-

moved from the circuit at the appropriate signal. Any category that can be specified in words should be specifiable electrically, in the same way that procedural rules are. Mean values can readily be calculated by dividing the total count for the session by the number of periods of observation; rates can be evaluated by dividing number by time; and distributions can be determined by dividing the range to be investigated into the desired number of class intervals and collecting separate tallies for each.

Some examples may serve to clarify the techniques required. First, let us consider the problem of analyzing a ratio performance in terms of the mean length of the pause following reinforcement and the mean rate of the "run" once the animal has begun responding. For the pause following reinforcement we shall use periods of time specified by delivery of reinforcement as the initiating event and the first subsequent response as the terminating event. A holding relay or a memory flip-flop can be activated by the reinforcement and reset by the response. Through this gating device a continuous input will be directed to the time meter. Total accumulated time can then be divided by the number of reinforcements to determine the mean duration of each pause. For the rate of response during the completion of the ratio requirement, we shall use periods of time specified by the first response as the initiating event and reinforcement as the terminating event. Since we know how many responses are made during the session, we need only collect time data, as before, and divide total responses by total time for mean rate.

To obtain a distribution of interresponse times, a stepping switch or its solid state equivalent is needed. The common contact is connected to the power source and the stationary contacts to a set of counters. The stepping coil is connected to a device, e.g., a recycling timer or motor-driven cam switch, that passes electrical pulses at regular intervals corresponding to the length of the class interval to be used for the distribution.

Each response resets the wiping arm to its home or zero position. With this arrangement, a given counter is actuated each time a pause equal to or exceeding a specified duration occurs between responses. If desired, the resulting frequency distribution can readily be translated into a noncumulative form by subtracting the sum of counts for all higher intervals from the count for a given interval.

If more detailed minute-by-minute or cycle-by-cycle data are required, rather than overall means for the session, printing counters may be used to record either temporal duration (number of timed pulses) or number of responses. In the extreme case, more complex calculations can be automated by punching data directly into cards used for electronic computers. Data depending on lengthy calculations, however, are not ordinarily available for monitoring purposes or for making day-to-day decisions on the conduct of the experiment.

REFERENCES

AMES, L. L. A pulser circuit for relay programming. *J. exp. Anal. Behav.*, 1963, 6, 422.

ANTONITIS, J. J. Response variability in the white rat during conditioning, extinction, and reconditioning. *J. exp. Psychol.*, 1951, 42, 273–281.

AYLLON, T., and HAUGHTON, E. Control of behavior of schizophrenic patients by food. *J. exp. Anal. Behav.*, 1962, 5, 343–352.

AZRIN, N. H. A technique for delivering shock to pigeons. *J. exp. Anal. Behav.*, 1959, 2, 161–163.

BERSH, P. J. The influence of two variables upon the establishment of a secondary reinforcer for operant responses. *J. exp. Psychol.*, 1951, 41, 62–73.

BLOUGH, D. S. The shape of some wavelength generalization gradients. *J. exp. Anal. Behav.*, 1961, 4, 31–40.

BOREN, J. J., and SIDMAN, M. Maintenance of avoidance behavior with intermittent shocks. *Canad. J. Psychol.*, 1957, 11, 185–192.

CAMPBELL, B. A., and TEGHTSOONIAN, R. Electrical and behavioral effects of different types of shock stimuli on the rat. *J. comp. physiol. Psychol.*, 1958, 51, 185–192.

COCKRELL, J. T. Operant behavior of white rats in relation to the concentration of a nonnutritive sweet substance used as reinforcement. Unpublished doctoral dissertation, Indiana Univer., 1952.

COLLIER, G. Some properties of saccharin as a reinforcer. *J. exp. Psychol.*, 1962, 64, 184–191.

COLLIER, G., and MYERS, L. The loci of reinforcement. *J. exp. Psychol.*, 1961, 61, 57–66.

COLLIER, G., and SISKEL, M. Performance as a joint function of amount of reinforcement and inter-reinforcement interval. *J. exp. Psychol.*, 1959, 57, 115–120.

COLLIER, G., and WILLIS, F. N. Deprivation and reinforcement. *J. exp. Psychol.*, 1961, 62, 377–384.

CONRAD, D. G., and SIDMAN, M. Sucrose concentration as reinforcement for lever pressing by monkeys. *Psychol. Rep.*, 1956, 2, 381–384.

CORNSWEET, T. N. *The design of electric circuits in the behavioral sciences.* New York: Wiley, 1963.

DAVIDON, R., and BOONIN, N. A constant current stimulus-generator. *Amer. J. Psychol.*, 1956, 69, 466–468.

DINSMOOR, J. A. A quantitative comparison of the discriminative and reinforcing functions of a stimulus. *J. exp. Psychol.*, 1950, 40, 458–472.

DINSMOOR, J. A. The effect of periodic reinforcement of bar-pressing in the presence of a discriminative stimulus. *J. comp. physiol. Psychol.*, 1951, 44, 354–361.

DINSMOOR, J. A. A device for measuring and programming the speed of execution of a single response. *J. exp. Anal. Behav.*, 1958a, 1, 57–58.

DINSMOOR, J. A. A new shock grid for rats. *J. exp. Anal. Behav.*, 1958b, 1, 182, 264.

DINSMOOR, J. A. Pulse duration and food deprivation in escape-from-shock training. *Psychol. Rep.*, 1958c, 4, 531–534.

DINSMOOR, J. A. Arc suppression in shock circuits. *J. exp. Anal. Behav.*, 1960, 3, 15–16.

DINSMOOR, J. A. A wide-range, constant-current shock stimulator. *J. exp. Anal. Behav.*, 1961, 4, 273–274.

DINSMOOR, J. A. Rate of pressing as a function of concentration of saccharine. 1962, unpublished paper.

ELLIOT, D. N., FRAZIER, L., and RIACH, W. A tracking procedure for determining the cat's frequency discrimination. *J. exp. Anal. Behav.*, 1962, 5, 323–328.

ESTES, W. K. The problem of inference from curves

based on group data. *Psychol. Bull.,* 1956, **53,** 134–140.

FERSTER, C. B. The use of the free operant in the analysis of behavior. *Psychol. Bull.,* 1953, **50,** 263–274.

FERSTER, C. B., and DEMYER, M. K. The development of performances in autistic children in an automatically controlled environment. *J. chronic Dis.,* 1961, **13,** 312–345.

FERSTER, C. B., HOLTZMAN, E. P., and LECKRONE, W. R. A response key for use with projection-type display units. *J. exp. Anal. Behav.,* 1962, **5,** 322.

FERSTER, C. B., and SKINNER, B. F. *Schedules of reinforcement.* New York: Appleton-Century-Crofts, 1957.

FINDLEY, J. D. An intermediate restraining device for working with monkeys. *J. exp. Anal. Behav.,* 1959, **2,** 121–125.

GOLLUB, L. R. A simple pulse shaper. *J. exp. Anal. Behav.,* 1958, **1,** 122.

GRUNZKE, M. E. A liquid dispenser for primates. *J. exp. Anal. Behav.,* 1961, **4,** 326.

GUNDY, R. F. Some techniques in operant conditioning of the guinea pig. *J. exp. Anal. Behav.,* 1959, **2,** 86.

GUTTMAN, N. Operant conditioning, extinction, and periodic reinforcement in relation to concentration of sucrose used as reinforcing agent. *J. exp. Psychol.,* 1953, **46,** 213–224.

GUTTMAN, N. Equal-reinforcement values for sucrose and glucose solutions compared with equal-sweetness values. *J. comp. physiol. Psychol.,* 1954, **47,** 358–361.

GUTTMAN, N. The pigeon and the spectrum and other perplexities. *Psychol. Rep.,* 1956, **2,** 449–460.

HAKE, D. F., and AZRIN, N. H. An apparatus for delivering painshock to monkeys. *J. exp. Anal. Behav.,* 1963, **6,** 297–298.

HANSON, H. M. Response patterns following manipulandum change. *J. exp. Anal. Behav.,* 1962, **5,** 237–238.

HARRISON, J. M., and ABELSON, R. M. The maintenance of behavior by the termination and onset of intense noise. *J. exp. Anal. Behav.,* 1959, **2,** 23–42.

HARRISON, J. M., and WARR, W. B. An instant-start circuit for fluorescent lamps. *J. exp. Anal. Behav.,* 1959, **2,** 226.

HEFFERLINE, R. F., BIRCH, J. D., and GENTRY, T. Simple transducers to detect or record operant amplitude. *J. exp. Anal. Behav.,* 1961, **4,** 257–261.

HERRICK, R. M. Instantaneous lamp replacement. *J. exp. Anal. Behav.,* 1960, **3,** 244.

HERRICK, R. M., and KARNOW, P. A displacement-sensing, constant-torque response lever. *J. exp. Anal. Behav.,* 1962, **5,** 461–462.

HERRNSTEIN, R. J. Stereotypy and intermittent reinforcement. *Science,* 1961, **133,** 2067–2069.

HERRNSTEIN, R. J., and BRADY, J. V. Interaction among components of a multiple schedule. *J. exp. Anal. Behav.,* 1958, **1,** 293–300.

HODOS, W. Progressive ratio as a measure of reward strength. *Science,* 1961, **134,** 943–944.

HODOS, W., LAURSEN, A. M., and NISSEN, T. A reinforcer for cats. *J. exp. Anal. Behav.,* 1963, **6,** 162.

HOFFMAN, H. S. A flexible connector for delivering shock to pigeons. *J. exp. Anal. Behav.,* 1960, **3,** 330.

HOLLAND, J. G. Technique for behavioral analysis of human observing. *Science,* 1957, **125,** 348–350.

HUNTER, T. A. An electronic contact relay. *Amer. J. Psychol.,* 1952, **65,** 458–459.

KAPLAN, M. The effects of noxious stimulus intensity and duration during intermittent reinforcement of escape behavior. *J. comp. physiol. Psychol.,* 1952, **45,** 538–549.

KAPLAN, M. The maintenance of escape behavior under fixed-ratio reinforcement. *J. comp. physiol. Psychol.,* 1956, **49,** 153–157.

KAPLAN, M., CAMPBELL, S. L., MARTIN, J. M., WULP, D. G., and LIPINSKI, C. E., JR. A restraining device for psychophysiological experimentation with dogs. *J. exp. Anal. Behav.,* 1962, **5,** 209–211.

KAPLAN, S., and KAPLAN, R. Skin resistance recording in the unrestrained rat. *Science,* 1962, **138,** 1403–1404.

KEISTER, W., RITCHIE, A. E., and WASHBURN, S. H. *The design of switching circuits.* Princeton, N.J.: Van Nostrand, 1951.

KELLER, F. S. Light-aversion in the white rat. *Psychol. Rec.,* 1941, **4,** 235–250.

LINDSLEY, O. R. New techniques of analysis of psychotic behavior. *Annual Tech. Rep. 3,* Group Psychology Branch, Office of Naval Research, Sept. 1955–Nov. 1956*a.*

LINDSLEY, O. R. Operant conditioning methods applied to research in chronic schizophrenia. *Psychiat. Res. Rep.,* 1956*b,* **5,** 118–139.

LOVIBOND, S. H., and TURNER, K. G. A constant current electronic stimulator for use in psychological experiments. *Austral. J. Psychol.,* 1956, **8,** 77–83.

MALIS, J. L., and CURRAN, C. S. A reliable, low-cost generator for audio stimuli. *J. exp. Anal. Behav.,* 1960, **3,** 200.

MASON, J. W. Restraining chair for the experimental study of primates. *J. appl. Physiol.,* 1958, **12,** 130–133.

MUENZINGER, K. F., and MIZE, R. H. The sensitivity of the white rat to electric shock: Threshold and skin resistance, *J. comp. Psychol.*, 1933, 15, 139–148.

MYERS, A. K. Effects of CS intensity and quality in avoidance conditioning. *J. comp. physiol. Psychol.*, 1962, 55, 57–61.

NOTTERMAN, J. M. Force emission during bar pressing. *J. exp. Psychol.*, 1959, 58, 341–347.

ORNE, M. T. On the social psychology of the psychological experiment: With particular reference to demand characteristics and their implications. *Amer. Psychologist*, 1962, 17, 774–783.

OTIS, L. S., and BOENNING, R. A. A transistorized circuit for recording contact responses. *J. exp. Anal. Behav.*, 1959, 2, 289–291.

PILGRIM, F. J. A simple electronic relay for counting, timing, or automatic control. *J. Psychol.*, 1948, 26, 537–540.

POLIDORA, V. J., and MEYER, P. M. Simple devices for liquid reward delivery. *J. exp. Anal. Behav.*, 1961, 4, 382.

REYNOLDS, G. S. Behavioral contrast. *J. exp. Anal. Behav.*, 1961, 4, 57–71.

SHEARN, D., SPRAGUE, R., and ROSENZWEIG, S. A method for the analysis and control of speech rate. *J. exp. Anal. Behav.*, 1961, 4, 197–201.

SIDLEY, N. A., and SCHOENFELD, W. N. Induced electric current flow in the pigeon as a function of impressed voltage and pulse frequency. *J. exp. Anal. Behav.*, 1963, 6, 99–100.

SIDMAN, M. A note on functional relations obtained from group data. *Psychol. Bull.*, 1952, 49, 263–269.

SIDMAN, M. *Tactics of scientific research: Evaluating experimental data in psychology.* New York: Basic Books, 1960.

SKINNER, B. F. Two types of conditioned reflex: A reply to Konorski and Miller. *J. gen. Psychol.*, 1937, 16, 272–279.

SKINNER, B. F., and CAMPBELL, S. L. An automatic shocking-grid apparatus for continuous use. *J. comp. physiol. Psychol.*, 1947, 40, 305–307.

STARKWEATHER, J. A. A speech rate meter for vocal behavior analysis. *J. exp. Anal. Behav.*, 1960, 3, 111–114.

STEBBINS, W. C. Relation of amount of primary reinforcement to discrimination and to secondary reinforcement strength. *J. comp. physiol. Psychol.*, 1959, 52, 721–726.

STEBBINS, W. C., MEAD, P. B., and MARTIN, J. M. The relation of amount of reinforcement to performance under a fixed-interval schedule. *J. exp. Anal. Behav.*, 1959, 2, 351–355.

SYMMES, D. Operant manipulandum for kittens. *J. exp. Anal. Behav.*, 1963, 6, 457–458.

TROTTER, J. R. The bar-pressing recorder. *Quart. J. exp. Psychol.*, 1956a, 8, 182–184.

TROTTER, J. R. The physical properties of bar pressing behavior and the problem of reactive inhibition. *Quart. J. exp. Psychol.*, 1956b, 8, 97–106.

VALENSTEIN, E. S. The effect of reserpine on the conditioned emotional response in the guinea pig. *J. exp. Anal. Behav.*, 1959, 2, 219–225.

VERHAVE, T. A sensitive lever for operant-conditioning experiments. *J. exp. Anal. Behav.*, 1958, 1, 220.

VERPLANCK, W. S. The operant conditioning of human motor behavior. *Psychol. Bull.*, 1956, 53, 70–83.

WAGMAN, W. Control of the operate and release time of relays. *J. exp. Anal. Behav.*, 1963, 6, 236.

WALLER, M. B. A manipulandum for use with dogs. *J. exp. Anal. Behav.*, 1960, 3, 311–312.

WEINER, H. Some effects of response cost upon human operant behavior. *J. exp. Anal. Behav.*, 1962, 5, 201–208.

WEISS, B., and LATIES, V. G. Behavioral thermoregulation. *Science*, 1961, 133, 1338–1344.

WEISS, B., and LATIES, V. G. A foot electrode for monkeys. *J. exp. Anal. Behav.*, 1962, 5, 535–536.

Chapter 11

ANIMAL LEARNING

M. E. BITTERMAN

This chapter is designed (1) to describe certain useful techniques for the study of animal learning which are not treated in the two preceding chapters, (2) to illustrate the application both of the new techniques and of those treated in the preceding chapters to the comparative study of learning in a variety of infrahuman species, and (3) to develop a classificational scheme in terms of which the interrelations among the different techniques may be understood.

CLASSIFICATION OF TECHNIQUES[1]

Techniques for the study of learning in animals may be grouped into three categories: *Thorndikian, Pavlovian,* and *avoidance* techniques. Those dealt with in Chap. 10, Operant Conditioning, fall almost entirely into the first category, although there are some operant techniques which fall into the third. Those dealt with in Chap. 9, Classical Conditioning, fall into the second category.

Thorndikian situations

Much of the information on which contemporary conceptions of animal learning are based has been obtained with a set of closely interrelated techniques that date back to the turn of the century (Kinnaman, 1902; Por-

ter, 1904; Small, 1900, 1901; Thorndike, 1898; Yerkes, 1907). It seems appropriate to describe them as Thorndikian both because of Thorndike's pioneering role in their development and because their operation is predicated on an empirical law of effect. Familiar examples are the problem box and the maze. In each of these situations, traditionally, the experimenter sets out to change behavior by *manipulating its consequences,* that is, by arranging a contingency between some motivationally significant state of affairs (reinforcement) and the behavior in question. Thus, pulling a loop in a problem box or turning to the left in a T maze may be encouraged with food or discouraged with shock. Indeed, the motivational significance of any event may be assessed in terms of its effect on the response which produces it in such a situation. An event that facilitates the occurrence of a response upon which it is contingent is called a *reward;* an event that has the opposite effect is called a *punishment;* while an event that produces no measureable change in behavior is motivationally insignificant or neutral. An *aversive* stimulus is one whose onset is punishing. In *escape training* the offset of such a stimulus functions as reward.

An important distinction between two types of Thorndikian situation is illustrated by a comparison of problem box and maze.

---

[1] This section is taken in large part from Bitterman (1962).

In both apparatuses, the animal is afforded numerous possibilities for action, one of which the experimenter chooses to reward. The main difference between them has to do with the treatment of irrelevant responses. In work with the problem box, the experimenter may take some qualitative notice of the variety of fruitless activities which appear, but his interest is centered on the rewarded response and the readiness with which it comes to expression. The basic datum is time. In the maze, by contrast, the unrewarded behavior of the animal is structured more clearly; certain major alternatives to correct response are delineated, and the interest of the experimenter is centered on their decline and disappearance. The basic datum is error. Time may be recorded, but it does not as clearly reflect progress in the choice among alternative courses of action, the aspect of selective learning which the maze is so well suited to display.

The designation *unitary Thorndikian situation* (or T-1 situation) is used for the problem box and for any other Thorndikian situation in which but a single course of action is defined and the readiness with which it comes to expression is measured. The designation *Thorndikian choice situation* (or T-2 situation) is used for the maze and for any other Thorndikian situation in which two or more incompatible courses of action are defined and choice among them is studied. The nature of the responses delineated and the general properties of the environments in which they appear are ignored in this classification. Thus, a problem box which offers a choice of manipulanda is classed with the maze as a choice situation, while the runway is classed as a unitary situation despite its structural resemblance to the maze. The runway may, of course, provide a measure of error, as in the early work of Hicks (1911), who plotted the learning of cul-less maze in terms of retracing; while the potentialities of the maze for the study of choice may be ignored, as in the early work of Thorndike (1898), who, measuring only time, used the maze as though it were just another problem box. In such cases, the classification is based on the use to which the apparatus actually is put in a given experiment. For the most part, contradictions between potentiality and use are rare. An investigator interested in choice among alternative courses of action is not likely to use a runway, nor, unless he is interested specifically in choice among alternative courses of action, is he likely to use a maze.

Thorndikian situations may be *chained*. The most common example of a chained choice situations is the maze of many choice-points, once widely used but rarely encountered today, perhaps because of the conviction early expressed by Lashley (1918) that the single-unit maze is quite as sensitive as the multiple-unit maze to the effects of significant variables and much less costly in time and effort. The two kinds of apparatus are not fully equivalent. Certain problems, e.g., correction *versus* noncorrection, arise only when the number of choice-points is reduced to one, while other problems, e.g., serial order, disappear. Chained unitary situations never have been widely used. An example may be found in a string of problem boxes, each presenting one manipulandum, the first giving access to the second, the second to the third, and continuing until the reward finally is attained (Herbert and Arnold, 1947). For certain purposes, conceivably, mixed chains composed both of unitary and of choice units might be used.

Each of the two main types of Thorndikian situation—unitary and choice—may occur in *discriminative* as well as in *generalized* form. This new distinction is orthogonal to the first, yielding a fourfold classification of Thorndikian situations: generalized unitary (T-1g), discriminative unitary (T-1d), generalized choice (T-2g), and discriminative choice (T-2d). In a discriminative problem, the experimental environment is varied systematically and with it the consequences of response, the capacity of the animal to discriminate the change being inferred from a corresponding change in its behavior. In a generalized problem, there may be some variation in the experimental environment (intentional or unintentional) and there may be some variation in the consequences of response (as in experiments on partial reinforcement), but there is by definition no correlation between the two kinds of change and, hence, no basis for systematic variation in behavior. The Thorndikian situations mentioned thus far—the runway, for example, or the simple T maze—have been considered in their generalized use, but any such situation may be converted to a discriminative one by introducing systematic changes in the stimulating conditions and correlated changes in the consequences of response.

In the simplest T-1d case, a defined response is rewarded under one set of conditions but not rewarded (or punished) under another set of conditions, and the readiness with which the response comes to expression under the two conditions is compared. For example, response in a single-window jumping apparatus is rewarded when the card displayed is white but punished when the card is black (Solomon, 1943). Performance in such a problem may be expressed in terms of error, but a temporal criterion is implied. For example, in an early experiment by Thorndike (1898), cats were fed for climbing to the top of their cage in response to the words "I must feed those cats," but not for making the same response to the words "Tomorrow is Tuesday." An error was recorded whenever they climbed up promptly in response to the second phrase or failed, in a reasonable period of time, to climb up in response to the first. Grice (1949) computed the median response time for a series of trials and counted as an error any response to the positive stimulus slower than the median or any response to the negative stimulus faster than the median. A clear distinction should be made between *error* thus defined and erroneous choice in a T-2d situation.

In a T-2d problem, two or more alternative responses are defined—two in the simplest case. One of the responses is rewarded and the second unrewarded (or punished) under a given set of stimulating conditions, while the consequences of the two courses of action are reversed under another set of conditions, and erroneous choices are counted. For example, in a conventional jumping apparatus (Lashley, 1930), a jump to the right window is rewarded when the card in the right window is white and the card in the left window is black, but a jump to the left window is rewarded when the positions of the two cards are interchanged; or, in the same apparatus, response to the right window may be rewarded when two white cards are displayed, but response to the left window rewarded when two black cards are displayed. Problems of the first description have been termed *simultaneous,* while problems of the second have been termed *successive.* The term *successive* has been used on occasion for discriminative problems of the unitary kind (T-1d), in which the stimuli to be discriminated also are presented successively, and considerable confusion has resulted from the failure to distinguish between the two types of problem.

The simultaneous problem usually is described as offering a choice of stimuli rather than a choice of responses, and under certain conditions the animal does seem to be making a choice between the two members of each pair of stimuli (Nissen, 1950). Under other conditions, however, the animal seems to be responding differentially to certain global properties of each pair of stimuli as a pair (Teas and Bitterman, 1952). Whatever the functional facts, the stimulus-choice language certainly is the more convenient, especially for the description of certain more complex T-2d problems.

Consider, for example, a conditional discrimination which involves four pairings of four different stimuli (Lashley, 1938a): how simple to describe it by saying that the animal must choose the upright triangle when it appears on a black ground and the inverted triangle when it appears on a striated ground. Consider the intermediate-size problem or the oddity problem, each involving three stimuli, presented in six different spatial arrangements, and three responses (Lashley, 1938b). The first may be described as requiring the animal to choose the stimulus of intermediate size, and the second as requiring the animal to choose the stimulus different from the other two. Multiple choice (Yerkes, 1917) may be described as requiring the animal to choose that stimulus which bears a certain relationship to the others that are presented on any trial, the relationship remaining constant from trial to trial as the stimuli themselves vary. The delayed-response problem (Hobhouse, 1901; Hunter, 1913) is another complication of the discriminative choice (T-2d) design. It may be described as requiring the animal to choose a stimulus which has been baited or otherwise designated as correct at some time previous to the moment of choice. Delayed alternation, a variant of delayed response, may be described as requiring the animal to choose on any trial that one of two stimuli which was *not* correct on the immediately preceding trial (Carr, 1917a). Convenient as it may be, however, the stimulus-choice language obscures an essential property of choice situations, namely, that they are structured to detect on each trial the occurrence of one or the other of two distinctively different responses.

Like generalized choice situations, discriminative choice situations have been chained. For example, an animal is required to make a series of choices based on brightness before the reward is attained (Stone, 1928). Discriminative unitary chains also are possible, although an instance of such a chain is hard to find in the literature. For example, response to a manipulandum in one unit gives immediate access to the next unit when the positive stimulus is present; when the negative stimulus is present, access to the next unit is given after a predetermined period of time whether or not the animal responds.

Skinnerian (free-operant) situations. There has been little clarity on the relation of Skinner's technique to other techniques for the study of learning in animals. Woodworth (1938) has asserted that the Skinner box "bridges the gap" between the problem box and the classical conditioning situation, and a similar view is expressed by Spence (1956), who places the Skinner box on a continuum at a point intermediate between the methods of Thorndike and Pavlov. The notion of continuity is difficult, however, to justify. Skinner (1935, 1937) has succeeded very well in drawing a sharp line between his method and that of Pavlov on the basis of criteria which fail to distinguish his method from that of Thorndike.

Skinnerian situations are *Thorndikian* situations as that term is defined here. The original Skinner box differs from the older problem box only in that it delivers food to the response compartment (when the defined response is made) instead of admitting the animal to a separate feeding compartment. This feature eliminates the necessity of handling the animal between trials and sets the stage for automated experiments. Equipped with a retractable lever, which is introduced to begin each trial and withdrawn after response, the Skinner box may be used in exactly the same manner as the older problem box. In fact, a retractable manipulandum which delivered food to the responding animal was developed for the monkey by Thorndike (1901). Skinner preferred to use his apparatus as what he called a "repeating" problem box (1932), now called a *free-operant* situation. Working with an intertrial interval of *zero*, he inverted the traditional measure of performance, substituting for *time per response* (or latency of response) on discrete trials *number of responses per unit time* (or rate of response) to a continuously available lever. Whether free-operant rate is a more reliable or a more sensitive measure than latency of response in discrete trials is an empirical question; certainly, the extravagant claims which have been made for rate are thus far unsupported by data. Whichever measure is used, a Skinner box containing one lever may be classified as a unitary Thorndikian (T-1) situation: a single response is delineated, its consequences are manipulated, and the readiness with which it comes to expression is measured. A Skinner box with two levers in which differential rate is measured may be classified as a Thorndikian choice (T-2) situation.

A general definition of Thorndikian situations. In each of the Thorndikian situations considered thus far, a change in behavior is measured which springs from a contingency between some defined response and some motivationally significant state of affairs. Experiments on latent learning suggest, however, that a Thorndikian situation may be characterized without reference either to the actual occurrence of change in behavior or to the motivational significance of the consequences of response. In the unitary case, an investigator may set out deliberately to minimize the motivational significance of the consequences of response in an effort to minimize the extent of change in behavior. For example, a hungry rat is trained in a runway which leads to an empty end box or to one which contains only water. It is not always easy to arrange a set of end-box conditions which are entirely without motivational significance, but it can be done (Gonzalez and Diamond, 1960). In the choice case, the consequences of alternative responses, whether motivationally significant or not, may be balanced in an effort to forestall the development of a preference for one or the other

response. For example, a hungry rat is run in a simple T maze with both end boxes empty, or one empty and the other containing only water, or one containing food and the other both food and water; or a rat that is both hungry and thirsty is run in a T maze with one end box containing food and the other water. Such situations are intended merely to provide *occasions* for learning, the effects of which are estimated in later tests. The tests always involve a change in the motivational significance of the consequences of response. For example, food is added to a previously empty end box; or the end box is associated with food in direct feedings; or the prevailing condition of deprivation is altered, and with it the relevance of previously encountered incentives. Nevertheless, despite the careful attention which must be paid to motivational significance in evaluating the *outcome* of exposure to a Thorndikian situation, the situation itself may be defined without reference to motivational significance. The essential factor is a *contingency of some specified event on some measurable bit of behavior*—a contingency arranged by an investigator who is interested in studying its effects on the animal.[1]

Pavlovian situations

In the traditional Pavlovian experiment as in the traditional Thorndikian experiment, the behavior of the animal is altered by the introduction of some motivationally significant stimulus such as food or shock (reinforcement), but there are important differences. In a Thorndikian experiment, reinforcement is contingent on response. Doing one thing leads to food or to shock; doing another does not. In a Pavlovian experiment, reinforcement is scheduled without regard to

[1] Not considered here are some situations closely related to the problem box, used by certain of Thorndike's critics, beginning with Hobhouse (1901), in which animals were rewarded for responses such as string pulling, rake wielding, and box stacking. Designed to conceal nothing from the subject and, although simple in principle, to render chance solutions unlikely, these situations present Thorndikian contingencies of a rather loose sort and *may* be used, like Thorndike's problem boxes, to study the way in which the experience of such contingencies affects subsequent behavior. Their principal use, however, has been in inquiries into the ability of animals to discover appropriate modes of behavior in advance of reinforcement, i.e., in quests for evidence of "productive" or "inferential" as contrasted with "reproductive" or learned solutions.

response. The experimenter does not set out to mold behavior in some predetermined fashion, but only to study the way in which the functional properties of one stimulus are altered by virtue of its contiguity with another. Because their introduction is not contingent on the animal's behavior, Pavlovian reinforcements are not equivalent to rewards and punishments, although they may act as such on occasion because of accidental contingencies unforeseen by the experimenter. Nor can rewards and punishments be distinguished in a Pavlovian experiment; pairing a stimulus with another does not tell whether it is rewarding or punishing. Another difference between the two techniques is worth noting. In a Thorndikian experiment, the choice of the behavior which is to serve as the index of learning is independent of the choice of reinforcement. Any of a large variety of responses which the animal is likely to make may be encouraged with food or discouraged with shock. In a Pavlovian experiment, the choice of reinforcement restricts the choice of a behavioral indicator. While conditioned and unconditioned responses are not identical, as Pavlov (1927) thought, the investigator is guided in his search for evidence of learning by his knowledge of the functional properties of the reinforcing stimulus. Sharp as the distinction may be between the traditional Thorndikian and Pavlovian procedures, it has often been ignored by theorists preoccupied with the task of deriving all the data of learning from the operation of a single process.

Coordinate with the unitary Thorndikian situation is the *unitary Pavlovian situation* (or P-1 situation), in which the tendency for a conditioned stimulus (CS) to produce some defined effect is measured in terms of latency or magnitude. The defined effect may be a response which is reflexly elicited by the unconditioned stimulus (UCS) as in the salivary conditioning experiment, or something quite different, as when the rate of fixed-interval responding in a Skinnerian situation is depressed by shock and by a stimulus

paired with shock (Estes and Skinner, 1941). A unitary Pavlovian situation may be *generalized* (P-1g) or *discriminative* (P-1d). In the discriminative case, the CS is varied systematically from trial to trial and with it the likelihood that the UCS will be presented; e.g., a bright light always is followed by food but a dim light is not.

With two unconditioned stimuli, each eliciting a different response, it is possible to set up a *Pavlovian choice situation* (or P-2 situation). The discriminative case perhaps is easier to conceive than the generalized. For example, one CS is paired with acid introduced into the mouth of a dog, while another CS is paired with shock to the forelimb. The generalized case must involve some inconsistency of reinforcement, which is not true of the analogous Thorndikian case. For example, a CS is paired with shock to the right forelimb on a random 75 percent of trials and with shock to the left forelimb on the remaining 25 percent of trials. This is a Pavlovian analog of the probability-learning experiment which has been done with Thorndikian situations. For example, a right turn at a choice-point leads to food on a random 75 percent of trials while a left turn leads to food on the remaining 25 percent of trials (Behrend and Bitterman, 1961; Brunswik, 1939).

A Pavlovian situation, like a Thorndikian situation, may serve merely as an occasion for learning, its effects being measured only in subsequent tests. One such case is that in which the presentation of CS and UCS is strictly simultaneous; only when the training procedure is altered can the effects of pairing be assessed. A second is that of sensory preconditioning, analogous to a Thorndikian experiment with consequences of response which are lacking in motivational significance; neutral stimuli are paired, then one is given some behavioral property, and the effects of the pairing are estimated from response to the other. A third case is that in which attention is centered on the acquisition, not of response-eliciting properties, but of rewarding properties (Williams, 1929); for example, an animal is fed repeatedly in a distinctive box, i.e., box and food are paired, after which access to the empty box is made contingent upon response in a Thorndikian situation. In general, a Pavlovian situation may be defined without reference to the occurrence of any particular kind of behavioral change or to the functional properties of the stimuli which are paired. The essential factor is a *sequence or conjunction of stimuli which is independent of the animal's response.*

Avoidance situations

The only learning situations which cannot be classified unequivocally as Pavlovian or Thorndikian are those which involve the avoidance of aversive stimulation. On the one hand, a neutral stimulus is paired with an aversive stimulus, thereby acquiring certain arousing properties. The pairing is not, on the other hand, entirely independent of the animal's behavior. The aversive stimulus is introduced only if the CS fails to elicit some defined response, whose likelihood of occurrence (low at the outset) the pairing serves to increase. This contingency of reinforcement on response is not displayed on the very first trial, as it is in a pure Thorndikian situation. In avoidance training, the contingency is a negative one which, since the mere *possibility* of avoidance cannot influence the animal, does not become manifest until the Pavlovian procedure has taken effect.

There is another Thorndikian contingency which operates in *some* avoidance situations, a contingency which makes itself felt from the very first trial. Termination of the aversive stimulus may be contingent on some defined response, often, but not always, the same response as that which avoids the aversive stimulus. In flexion conditioning, when shock to the limb is administered through a grid on which the limb of the animal rests, and when the scheduled duration of shock is substantial, flexion both escapes and avoids

shock. In the shuttle box, too, the conditions of training may be such that changing compartments both escapes and avoids shock, although as Warner (1932a) noted, the response which escapes shock may be different from that which avoids it, e.g., leaping over a hurdle as compared with crawling under. It is possible, however, to set up an avoidance situation in which there is no escape at all. In flexion conditioning, shock may be administered through a bracelet attached to the limb, and a control circuit so arranged that the conditioned response (CR) will forestall the shock but the unconditioned response (UCR) will not alter its scheduled duration. In the shuttle box, the shock may be very brief, terminating quite independently of any response the animal may make to it (Hunter, 1935). Yet even without escape, there remains the contingency of aversive stimulation on failure of response to the CS, an essential feature of avoidance training which distinguishes it from Pavlovian training. The paired stimulation which is responsible for the emergence of response to the CS distinguishes avoidance training from Thorndikian training.

In its most common use, the shuttle box may be classified as a *unitary* and *generalized* (or A-1g) situation. A single course of action is defined, and the readiness with which it comes to expression is measured under sensory conditions that are not systematically varied. A *unitary discriminative* (A-1d) situation also may be generated in the shuttle box; e.g., a bright light is followed by shock unless the defined response is made, but a dim light never is followed by shock. In such a situation, discrimination can progress only as the animal *fails* to respond to the dim light, since the consequences of responding to the two lights are identical. In the T-1d case, by contrast, the consequences of responding to the stimuli to be discriminated are different, and discrimination therefore is facilitated by response to the negative stimulus. In P-1d, discrimination may progress quite independently of response.

The shuttle box may be used also for a Skinnerian variant of avoidance training developed by Sidman (1953). There is no exteroceptive warning signal, but shock is scheduled every *x* seconds by a clock which is reset by shuttling, and rate of response is measured (Behrend and Bitterman, 1963). The lack of an exteroceptive signal does not subvert the definition of avoidance training as originating in a quasi-Pavlovian contiguity of stimulation; as Pavlov showed, internal processes correlated with the passage of time since the occurrence of a specified event may play the role of CS. In Sidman discrimination, the clock which schedules shock runs only under one of two sensory conditions.

Choice among alternative courses of action also may be studied in avoidance situations. Suppose, for example, that shock from a grid in the floor of a T maze is scheduled *x* seconds after an animal is placed in the starting box. In the generalized choice case (A-2g), shock is avoided by prompt entrance into the end box on the right, but not by entrance into the end box on the left (Longo, 1964). In the discriminative case (A-2d), a turn to the right avoids shock when the stem of the maze is black, while a turn to the left avoids shock when the stem is white. Two unconditioned stimuli are not required to generate an A-2 situation as they are to generate a P-2 situation, but two unconditioned stimuli may be used. For example, one signal is followed by avoidable shock to the right limb, while a second is followed by avoidable shock to the left limb (James, 1947).

Although the term implies threat of an aversive condition which the animal learns to forestall, avoidance training may be characterized without reference to the nature of the stimuli employed. It would be possible, for example, to use food instead of shock in a standard avoidance design and to look for the *disappearance* of some response to the CS with a high initial probability of occurrence. Nor need avoidance training be characterized in terms of any *change* in behavior at

all. For example, an animal might be trained with some neutral stimulus instead of shock in a shuttle box designed to produce a substantial frequency of spontaneous crossing and tested after the neutral stimulus has been paired with shock. Irrespective of outcome, the mere conception of such an experiment is sufficient to delineate what is here regarded as the essential feature of avoidance training: *A sequence of stimuli is scheduled with the occurrence of the second contingent upon the failure of the animal to make some specified response to the first.* The relation of the avoidance paradigm to the Pavlovian and Thorndikian paradigms now should be quite clear. In Pavlovian training, stimuli are paired independently of the animal's behavior. In Thorndikian training, the second stimulus is presented only after the animal has made a given response to the first. In avoidance training, the second stimulus is presented only if the animal *does not make* a given response to the first.

Terminology

Some comment is in order on the relation between the terminology used here and that which is to be found in the literature. The term *conditioning* usually is used for the kind of training here called Pavlovian, but that term also is used rather widely to designate techniques which are not here classified as Pavlovian, and often as a synonym for learning itself. The term *classical conditioning* is closer to what is here intended by Pavlovian, although in some contexts it has a narrower meaning, suggesting a harnessed animal, and in other contexts a broader one, encompassing avoidance. *Avoidance* remains a useful term, although the broad sense in which it has been used here might better be conveyed by Sheffield's *omission training* (Prokasy, 1965). The term *instrumental conditioning* is ambiguous since it has been applied indiscriminately both to avoidance training and to pure Thorndikian training. The term *operant conditioning* also is ambiguous. It has a narrow, Skinnerian sense which implies the measurement of rate, as well as a more general sense in which it is equivalent to instrumental conditioning. The term *selective learning* has a relatively pure Thorndikian connotation, but it often designates a process of learning rather than a method of studying it. In general, the terminology in the literature leaves much to be desired, and the reader must be alert to the possibility of variation in meaning even greater than has been suggested here.

THORNDIKIAN TECHNIQUES

In this section we shall consider some Thorndikian techniques of the discrete-trials variety, which have been in use since the turn of the century and some newer ones which are more conducive to automation.

Drive and reward

Performance in Thorndikian situations is rather sensitive to variation in drive level and in amount and kind of reward, which must be carefully controlled. Control of drive is more difficult to achieve than control of reward. Most experiments on learning in animals have been done on hungry rats rewarded with food. Until 10 or 15 years ago, the usual procedure was to control degree of hunger by controlling time since feeding to satiation, 23 hours being the favorite interval. Twenty-three hours of deprivation does not, however, produce a substantial level of hunger, and variation in deprivation time involves an objectionable disruption in feeding rhythms. A better method is to vary drive by varying body weight. Rats are maintained on an ad-lib schedule for a week or so, and then gradually reduced to some percentage of the ad-lib weight. A common value is 85 percent. A rat reduced to 75 percent of its ad-lib weight is hungry indeed. The usual procedure is to weigh the rat before the daily feeding and give it enough food to bring it to the specified percentage of the ad-lib weight. Since the experimental session precedes the daily feeding, the experimental weight is less than the specified percentage when this procedure is used. Since the overnight weight loss of an adult animal tends to remain fairly constant, it is easy to determine the amount of food which is necessary to bring the rat to a specified percentage of its ad-lib weight at the *beginning* of the next day's session. For more rapid manipulation of drive level without disruption of the daily feeding rhythm, prefeeding is used, i.e., the animal is fed some portion of its daily ration just before the experimental session begins (the greater the proportion prefed, the lower the drive in training). To maintain a constant level of drive within experimental sessions, it is necessary that the amount of food earned in the session be as small as possible in relation to the daily ration. It takes 8 to 10 grams of food per day to maintain the average rat at 85 percent of its ad-lib weight, which means that 40 reinforcements (Noyes pellets) of 0.098 gram each comprise about half the daily ration, and 40 pellets of 0.045 gram each about one-fifth of the ration.

Hunger in the pigeon is manipulated in the same way as in the rat. In fact, the relation between amount fed and body weight in the pigeon is so stable that daily weighings are not necessary. One weighing per week will give rather good control (Bullock, Roberts, and Bitterman, 1961). It takes about 10 grams of grain per day—a mixture of 50 percent milo, 40 percent vetch, and 10 percent hemp is common—to maintain the average adult cock at 75 percent of ad-lib weight, and about 15 grams to maintain it at 85 percent. The average bird can take about 8 grams of the mixture in forty 2.5-second presentations of a food magazine, although there are wide individual differences. In other animals, manipulation of hunger by manipulation of body weight is impractical or impossible. For the fish, in which the growth process is very different from that of mammals, daily rations have been worked out by trial and error; e.g., a 3-inch African mouthbreeder will do nicely on 60 milligrams per day of the dry food developed by Aronson (1949), or on 30 milligrams of this food to supplement 40 *Tubifex* worms earned in the daily experimental sessions. A 4-inch goldfish is fed 20 milligrams of trout chow to supplement 40 worms earned in each experimental session. The goldfish does not take dry food very rapidly and will not work well for it, but the mouthbreeder will work about as well for Aronson's mixture as for worms. Dry food is easier to dispense automatically, but goldfish are cheaper and more readily available than mouthbreeders. Drive level in the fish has been varied successfully by prefeeding (Eskin and Bitterman, 1960). One should not be afraid to give a fish all the food it will *take* at any time. The superstition about overfeeding of fish probably is based on the fact that the decay of uneaten food permitted to remain in the animal's tank produces illness.

The trial-and-error approach is used also in work with turtles. A 200-gram painted turtle (width of carapace about 4 inches) may be given 2 to 3 grams of *lean* hamburger or fish per day. The food is earned bit by bit in the 10 or 20 trials of each daily experimental session with no apparent diminution of drive during the session. In work with monkeys, the usual practice is to feed a basic daily ration and to reward the animal in the learning situation with specially preferred foods, such as peanuts and raisins. The same technique is appropriate for work with rats, the animals being rewarded with drops of sugar or saccharin solution. The reward need not have nutritive value to be effective (Sheffield and Roby, 1950), nor need the animals be particularly hungry. Information on the nutritive requirements of a variety of animals as well as a wealth of advice on their maintenance in the laboratory may be found in the VFAW handbook (Worden and Lane-Petter, 1957).

Water deprivation and water reward also have been used rather widely in work with the rat and are more convenient for some purposes than food hunger. Degree of thirst may be manipulated by varying time since drinking to satiation, but the preferred method is to give some portion of the estimated intake before the experimental session. In some experiments, rats deprived of both food and water have been studied with the reward, e.g., milk, meeting both needs. From time to time it has been necessary to work with rats which are hungry in some experimental sessions and thirsty in others. Purification of drive is not easy to achieve because water deprivation produces some reduction in food intake, and food deprivation some reduction in water intake. Verplanck and Hayes (1953) offer the following solution to this problem: To make a rat thirsty alone, deprive it of food but give it free access to water; then feed dry food to satiation. The opposite procedure is used to produce a rat which is hungry alone. Water deprivation and water reward have also been used successfully in work with certain submammalian species, such as the turtle (Gonzalez and Bitterman, 1962).

A variety of considerations may lead to the use of escape from noxious stimulation instead of access to food or water as reward in Thorndikian experiments. The investigator may be interested in the relation between the different kinds of incentive, or he may be interested in the learning of a species, such as the Bermuda land crab (Datta, Milstein, and Bitterman, 1960), which has an undependable appetite for food or water. The favorite aversive stimulus is shock, probably because it can be turned on and off so readily, although the use of shock is not without its special problems (Longo, Holland, and Bitterman, 1961). For some species, however, shock cannot be used at all. In the Bermuda land crab, shock intense enough to activate the animal will produce detachment of the limbs. This species has been trained successfully with escape from distilled water, or from distilled water to which acetic acid has been added, as reward. It should be recognized that certain important kinds of experiment cannot be done with escape. For example, a conventional discrete-trials par-

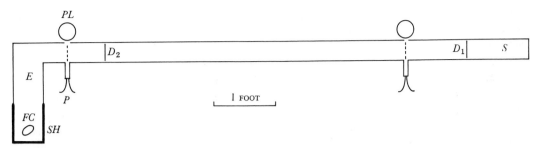

Fig. 11-1 A runway for the rat. *S*, starting compartment; *D₁*, guillotine door; *D₂*, one-way door; *PL*, photocell lamp; *P*, photocell; *E*, end compartment; *SH*, Plexiglas shell; *FC*, food cup.

tial-reinforcement experiment is ruled out because there can be no unreinforced trials in escape training. Reinforcement may be delayed, but it cannot be withheld entirely, since the noxious stimulation must terminate with each trial.

Unitary Thorndikian situations

Of the traditional Thorndikian situations, the one which finds the widest contemporary application is the runway, a maze without blind alleys and usually without turns. The response rewarded in the runway is locomotion from one point to another. A trial begins with the introduction of the animal into a starting box or with the opening of the starting-box door. It ends with the entrance of the animal into the goal box or with the removal of the animal from the apparatus if it has not reached the goal box in some fixed period. The measure of performance is time, often a series of times, one for each of several segments of the runway. Elevated and enclosed runways in a great variety of dimensions have been used, but without systematic study of relative merit.

A satisfactory runway for the rat is diagrammed in Fig. 11-1. It is made of gray-painted wood and has a hinged cover of wire mesh divided into several sections. The main pathway is 3 inches wide by 5 inches high (inside), and the width increases to 6 inches beyond the right-angle turn into the goal area. The goal area is so designed that shells of black or white Plexiglas may be inserted

and removed easily. The shells are convenient for manipulating goal-box color and serve to keep the goal area clean. There are two doors in the apparatus, one a starting-box door of the guillotine type which is raised by the experimenter at the beginning of each trial, and the other a one-way door which prevents retracing from the goal area. Two times are measured. One clock begins to run as the guillotine door is raised by the experimenter. When the animal breaks the first photobeam 1 foot beyond the guillotine door, the first clock is stopped to provide a measure of *starting time,* and a second clock is started. To provide a measure of *running time,* the second clock stops when the second photobeam is broken, at which point the animal is beyond the one-way door. The right-angle turn in the pathway is used to keep the animal from seeing the goal compartment until the second photobeam has been broken. After a fixed time in the goal compartment, or after being permitted to consume a fixed amount of reward, the animal is removed to a waiting cage for the intertrial interval.

The runway has been used successfully with a number of species other than the rat, e.g., the turtle (Gonzalez and Bitterman, 1962) and the pigeon (Roberts, Bullock, and Bitterman, 1963). When performance is motivated by some positive incentive, such as food, the reward value must be great enough to overcome any aversion which the animal may have to being handled. Aversion to handling in the pigeon and in the turtle may be reduced considerably in the course of contact with human beings who provide food. In the fish, aversion to handling usually is so great that runway experiments with food reward are impracticable, even very hungry subjects often refusing to enter the goal compartment. Only when escape from shock instead of food is used as reward do runway experiments with the fish become possible, since intense shock is more aversive than handling. A technique which has been used in work with the rat to eliminate handling, between trials if not between sessions, involves interchangeable starting and goal boxes. When the animal reaches the goal box on a given trial, the box is detached from the runway with the animal still inside and substituted for the starting box, which now becomes the goal box (Finger, 1942). Unfortunately, this procedure tends to blur the distinction between the sensory antecedents and the sensory consequences of response, a distinction which it may be important to preserve (Lawrence and Miller, 1947). Another way to eliminate handling is to substitute a manipu-

lative response for the locomotor response and to deliver the reward to the response compartment (Skinner, 1932). An added advantage of this technique is that it makes fully automated experiments possible.

Diagrammed in Fig. 11-2 is a retractable-lever situation used for automated experiments with the rat. The lever is mounted in a plate of $\frac{1}{8}$-inch aluminum which is slipped into a ventilated picnic chest to divide it lengthwise into two compartments, one for the animal and the second for a pellet dispenser and other equipment. After an intertrial interval in darkness, the light above the lever is turned on, the lever is introduced, and a latency-measuring device is started. Depression of the lever stops the timer (providing a measure of latency), turns off the lever light, and retracts the lever. On reinforced trials, depression of the lever also causes a pellet of food to be discharged by the feeder and a magazine light to come on for a few seconds. The magazine light signals the presence of reward and enables the animal to find it readily. On unreinforced trials, response to the lever initiates the intertrial interval without an intervening magazine cycle.

The programming of experiments with this apparatus is a simple matter. An intertrial-interval timer runs a preset interval and, at its finish, turns on trial power. This is the power for the relays which introduce the lever and turn on the lever light. A stepping switch pulsed at the end of each trial by an end-trial relay may or may not energize a contingency relay which determines whether the response will be reinforced. Whether the contingency relay is energized on any trial is controlled by a toggle switch wired to the corresponding step on the stepping switch. The output of a response relay energized by a lever press is led to the common contact of one switch on the contingency relay, and from there, *via* the normally closed contact, to the end-trial relay, or *via* the normally open contact, to a reinforcement relay. The reinforcement relay locks on with power

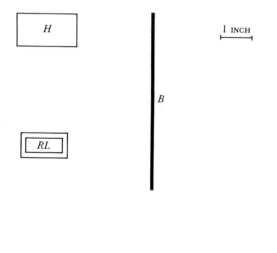

Fig. 11-2 **A retractable-lever apparatus for the rat.** *RL,* **retractable lever;** *H,* **housing for lever lamp;** *B,* **barrier;** *FC,* **food cup.**

from the normally closed contact of a reinforcement timer which times the reinforcement cycle. The reinforcement relay also provides the power to run the reinforcement timer, to turn on the magazine light, to operate the feeder, and to record the reinforcement. At the end of each reinforcement cycle, the end-trial relay is activated. The intertrial interval timer is reset by the end-trial relay. It also is reset by the reinforcement relay, which prevents it from running for the duration of the reinforcement cycle. To limit the amount of time permitted for response on any trial, a limiting timer is used, which is powered as the lever is presented. At the end of a preset interval, e.g., 30 seconds, the limiting timer pulses a trial-limit relay which, in turn, pulses the end-trial relay. If the trial-limit relay also operates a criterion stepper which is reset by the response relay, an extinction session may be terminated automatically after some given number of successive failures to respond within the time limit. At a preset position, the criterion stepper activates an extinction-criterion relay which cuts off power to the intertrial-interval timer.

Latencies may be measured with a printing counter pulsed every half or tenth of a second by a multivibrator which is activated at the start of each trial and stopped by response or by the trial-limit relay. The counter is caused to print and reset by a pair of relays activated by the end-trial relay. Where response is defined, not as a single depression of the lever, but some greater number, e.g., 5 or 10, it is useful to take two time measures: the latency of the first depression and the total time for the entire group. The response relay activates a response stepper which, in its first position, causes the counter to print. At the subsequent position of the stepper which defines the completion of the response, power is sent *via* the contingency relay to the end-trial relay or to the reinforcement relay. The activation of the end-trial relay at the completion of the reinforcement cycle causes the counter to print and

to reset. It also resets the response stepper. Another way to make these time measurements is with a graphic event recorder, a paper speed of 5 millimeters per second yielding a degree of accuracy sufficient for most purposes. The recorder may be off in the intertrial interval to save paper. Since a brief period of time is required for the recorder to reach constant speed after it has been turned on, a delay relay is used to turn on the recorder several seconds before the start of the trial. With trial power led to one of the pens through a set of normally closed contacts on the response relay, the pen rises when the trial begins and falls each time the lever is depressed. The exact temporal distribution of lever depressions thus can be recorded with a single pen. The graphic method is especially economical when several animals are studied concurrently, because a good six-pen recorder costs no more than a single good printing counter.

To anyone who has expended the considerable effort required to do experiments with the runway, the advantages of an automated lever apparatus are striking. It is by no means established, however, that the retractable lever is a satisfactory substitute for the runway. There is some indication, for example, that the minimal expenditure of effort required by lever depression may prolong extinction to the point of obscuring the effects of certain training variables on resistance to extinction. The effort required may be increased by weighting the lever, but then the pretraining procedure is complicated—the animal must first be trained with a light lever and transferred gradually to the more heavily weighted one. Another way to increase the effort required is to define a response on each trial as not one, but several lever depressions. This solution, however, might cause trouble in certain kinds of experiment, such as on partial reinforcement, since, even the 100 percent animals would, in a sense, be partially reinforced. Only systematic, parametric work with the runway and lever will provide the basis for a decision as to their equivalence (Gonzalez, Bainbridge, and Bitterman, 1966).

Less expensive than a retractable lever is a hinged panel bearing against a microswitch, which can be nosed or otherwise displaced by the rat. The panel can be made of diffusing Plexiglas and illuminated by a lamp mounted behind it to signify the start of a trial. One difficulty with this device is that the panel can be pushed during the intertrial interval, and high rates of intertrial activity may be developed by adventitious reinforcement (Skinner, 1948); panel pushing in the intertrial interval is in effect reinforced on a fixed-interval schedule by illumination of the key, which presumably derives its reinforcing properties from the opportunity to earn food which it brings. Interval responding may, however, be suppressed effectively by having each intertrial response reset the intertrial-interval timer and thus postpone the next trial—a Sidman avoidance schedule with a *favorable* consequence of failure to respond which therefore *decreases* the probability of the defined response. An advantage of the panel over the retractable lever is that patterns of light can be projected on it from behind in experiments on visual discrimination.

Since T-2 situations have been used for most of the work on discriminative learning in animals, there are many questions of T-1d methodology which remain to be decided. The simplest discrete-trials procedure is to reward response to (or in the presence of) one stimulus and not to reward response to (or in the presence of) another stimulus. If the response is not very effortful and the discrimination difficult, the animal may not respond differentially under these conditions, especially if prompt response to the nonrewarded stimulus brings on the next trial sooner than does failure to respond. At the very least, the nonrewarded stimulus should be presented for a fixed period which is not reduced by response. Even so, the animal may respond with low latency to both stimuli, and then simply stop responding when no reinforcement is produced; i.e., the animal may

find it easier to discriminate the consequences of response to the two stimuli than the properties of the stimuli themselves.

A better procedure is to reward response to the positive stimulus on a ratio schedule or an interval schedule, e.g., the nth response to the stimulus, or the first response after n seconds have elapsed since the presentation of the positive stimulus, produces a reinforcement and terminates the trial. With this procedure, which combines discrete-trials and free-operant features, the consequences of immediate response to the two stimuli are the same, and further responses are required to discriminate the schedule. Under these conditions, the animal may be led to discriminate the properties of the stimuli themselves, which should produce a difference in latency. If the positive stimulus is reinforced on a variable-interval schedule with some components equal to the time of nonrewarded-stimulus presentation, e.g., 30 seconds, response to the two stimuli may be compared in terms of frequency of response in 30 seconds as well as in terms of the latency of the first response.

Experiments of this kind are not difficult to program automatically. A scrambler calls for one of a series of contingency relays, each relay being set with switches before the start of the experiment for a given stimulus and a given consequence of response. For example, contingency relay 1 may be set to present an upright triangle for 30 seconds without reinforcement, and the scrambler may be set to call for this relay on trials 1, 3, 4, 6, and so forth. The various consequences of response are easy to arrange. When the nonrewarded stimulus is presented, the limiting timer is started, and the response relay serves only a recording function. In reinforcement on an interval schedule, a tape motor is started when the stimulus is presented. After the punched interval has elapsed, the limiting timer is started, and a relay is activated which connects the output of the response relay to the reinforcement relay. In reinforcement on a ratio schedule, the limiting timer begins to run when the stimulus is presented, and the response relay activates the response stepper, which, after the required number of impulses, activates the reinforcement relay. Latency of response may be recorded with a printing counter or on a polygraph. If each contingency relay activates a different pen of the polygraph when it is called for, a record is provided of the experimental conditions in effect on any given trial as well as of the temporal distribution of responses on that trial.

The customary free-operant procedure, which involves an alternating presentation of two stimuli (each for a substantial period of time and on a different schedule of reinforcement) is not as satisfactory as the combined discrete-trials–free-operant procedure. Simple alternation of the two stimuli certainly is to be avoided, since the animal may discriminate the *change* from one stimulus to the other rather than the static stimulus properties. At the very least, a time-out should follow each stimulus presentation, and the two stimuli should be scheduled in quasi-random order. There then remains the question of whether a reinforced stimulus should be presented beyond the time required to earn the first reinforcement, or an unreinforced stimulus beyond the time normally required to earn a reinforcement in the presence of a reinforced stimulus. Longer times are wasteful. They provide no dependable information about discrimination of the stimuli, since the possibility exists that the animal may be discriminating the schedule. Furthermore, the use of longer times is not conducive to precise measurement of the *rate* of learning. With restricted presentation, as in the combined discrete-trials–free-operant method, rate of learning can more meaningfully be specified in terms of the number of presentations necessary to achieve some specified criterion of discrimination.

Automated unitary situations analogous to those developed for the rat are used also for other species. A heavy-duty retractable lever is made for the monkey, response to which may be reinforced with peanuts or raisins dropped into a food cup by a feeder. For discriminative training, the lever may be replaced by a Plexiglas panel on which colored lights and patterns are projected. In work with the pigeon, a panel or pigeon key at which the animal pecks, and on which colored lights and patterns may be projected, is used. The pigeon is rewarded by a brief period of access to a tray of grain which is illuminated upon presentation. The pigeon key and the grain magazine are mounted on an 11- by 11-inch aluminum plate with the key centered 4 inches from the top and the magazine aperture 2 inches from the bottom. The plate is set into a picnic chest in such a way as to provide a cubical compartment for the animal which is about 11 inches on the side.

A T-1 situation for the turtle is diagrammed in Fig. 11-3. The manipulandum con-

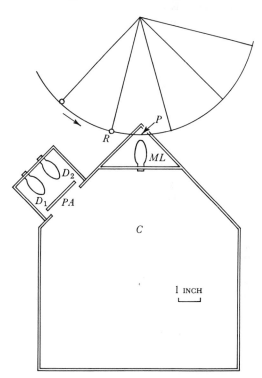

Fig. 11-3 An automated unitary Thorndikian situation for the turtle. *C*, chamber filled with water to the depth of about 1 inch; *PA* panel nosed or pushed by the animal; *D₁*, *D₂*, colored lamps that illuminate the panel; *ML*, magazine light that turns on during the presentation of reward; *R*, pellet of hamburger rotated into the chamber; *P*, position of pellet during reinforcement cycle.

sists of a Plexiglas panel on which colored lights and patterns may be projected. The reward is a pellet of ground beef or a small cube of fish which is rotated into the enclosure on a tray. The animal, standing in an inch or so of water, bites the food from the tray, lowers it into the water, and eats it. A feeding device for the turtle is best operated on the principle of the pigeon's grain magazine rather than the rat's pellet dispenser, i.e., on the principle of limited access. The food is rotated into the chamber for 10 seconds (longer periods are used in pretraining) during which time a magazine light is turned on. Immediately following this period, the tray is rotated once more, and the food becomes unavailable if it has not already been taken. The tray is superior to a device which simply drops a pellet into the water, not only because it permits the necessary prompt food taking, but because the

food is more easily localized and taken by the turtle, a relatively clumsy animal.

An automated T-1 situation for the fish is diagrammed in Fig. 11-4. The animal is brought in its individual 2-gallon living tank to a black Plexiglas enclosure. The manipulandum is a disk of diffusing Plexiglas on which colored lights and patterns may be projected. The target is fixed on a rod which is set into the needle holder of a crystal phonograph cartridge mounted on the cover of the enclosure. When the fish noses the target, a voltage difference is generated at the output of the cartridge, which is amplified and used to operate a response relay (Longo and Bitterman, 1959). Mechanical levers sometimes have been used for the fish (Haralson and Bitterman, 1950; Hogan and Rozin, 1962), but the electronic one is much more sensitive and reliable. The fish is rewarded with *Tubifex* worms discharged into the tank

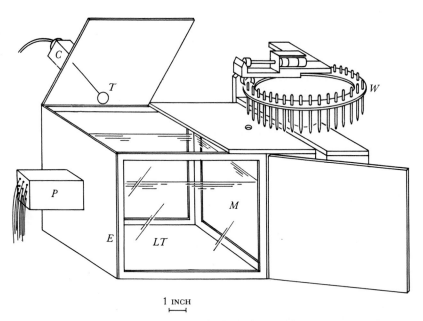

1 INCH

Fig. 11-4 An automated unitary Thorndikian situation for the fish. The animal is brought in *LT*, its individual living tank, to *E*, a black Plexiglas enclosure; *P*, colored-light and pattern projector; *T*, Plexiglas target upon which the discriminanda are projected when the lid of the enclosure is lowered; *C*, phonograph cartridge; *W*, worm dispenser, with solenoid-operated jaws that squeeze the bulb of a dropper and so discharge a worm into the water; *M*, diffusing Plexiglas panel illuminated by a magazine light for several seconds following the discharge worm. (Scale only approximate.)

by droppers which are squeezed by solenoid-operated jaws (Longo and Bitterman, 1963), and a magazine light is turned on for a few seconds when the dispenser is operated to permit the animal to find the worm. Another kind of worm dispenser developed by Hogan and Rozin (1961) is not sufficiently reliable. The Hogan-Rozin technique is to load each worm into a small vial of water which is emptied into the tank. The expectation is that the worm will fall with the water as the vial is tipped over, but too often the worm remains in the vial, adhering to the wall.

It will be noted that the situations for monkey, rat, pigeon, turtle, and fish are all of the same general type and geared to experiments of the same kind. They may, in fact, be wired in such a way that they can be plugged into a programmer of common design, i.e., the same programmer may be used on one occasion for work with monkeys and on another occasion for work with pigeons or turtles. All of the situations are appropriate for free-operant as well as for discrete-trials experiments. Analogous situations geared to the special properties of other species remain to be developed.

Thorndikian choice situations

The systematic analysis of maze learning began with the experiments of Small (1901), whose method soon was adopted to the study of many other animals, e.g., monkey (Kinnaman, 1902), sparrow (Porter, 1904), snail (Thompson, 1917), and worm (Yerkes, 1912), although the rat remained the favorite animal for maze experiments. The Hampton Court pattern was popular in the beginning, but innovations both in pattern and in construction soon appeared. The 14-unit multiple T maze of Tolman and Honzik (1930) was widely used for a time; before each of its choice points but the first, there was a one-way door to prevent retracing, and curtains were hung in the alleys to rule out the possibility of choice based only in the presence or absence of these doors. The feasibility of the elevated maze as distinct from

the alley or tunnel maze was demonstrated by Vincent (1915), who devised a maze set on posts with hinged sides that could be dropped to permit a direct comparison of performance on walled and unwalled paths; the elevation of the maze served to prevent escape. Miles (1930) described an elevated multiple T maze; made up of interchangeable units, each providing a strip of path 36 inches long, 1 inch wide, and 30 inches above the ground, it was recommended for ease of construction and flexibility of pattern.

Although each junction of a multiple T maze has the same form, the relative difficulty of the various blinds, usually measured in terms of order of elimination, may vary considerably (Buel, 1935). Carr (1917b) discovered that the initial attractiveness of blinds, as measured in terms of the probability of entry on the very first trial, is a good predictor of order of elimination. For the Tolman-Honzik maze, correlations between first-trial entries into the various blinds and total entries in subsequent trials range from 0.70 to 0.83 (Ballachey and Buel, 1934). Multiple-unit mazes are used only rarely today, because one-unit T or Y mazes are quite satisfactory for most purposes. A T maze suitable for the rat is diagrammed in Fig. 11-5. Its relation to the runway of Fig. 11-1 is obvious. The one-way doors leading to the

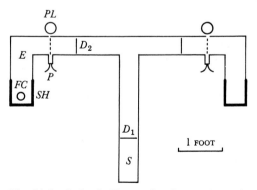

Fig. 11-5   A simple T maze for the rat. *S*, starting compartment; *D₁*, guillotine door; *D₂*, one-way door; *PL*, photocell lamp; *P*, photocell; *E*, end compartment; *SH*, Plexiglas shell; *FC*, food cup.

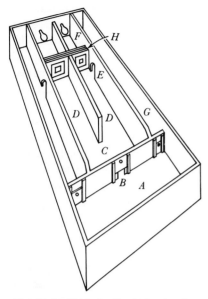

Fig. 11-6 Yerkes's discrimination box. *A*, starting compartment; *B*, guillotine door; *C*, choice compartment; *D*, grid; *E*, door to food compartment; *F*, light-box; *G*, food compartment; *H*, reversible frame containing the translucent forms used as stimuli (*Lashley, 1912*).

end compartments are used for training by the noncorrection method. They are removed when the animal is to be permitted to correct its errors.

The problems of drive and reward are the same for the maze as for the runway, although it is interesting to note that accuracy of choice seems far less sensitive to these variables than running speed (Pubols, 1960). Most of the work on maze learning has been done with food deprivation and food reward, although many other motivating techniques, including shock and escape from shock (Yerkes, 1907) have been employed. In a T maze designed for a study of the earthworm (Datta, 1962), the animal escapes to its dark, cool, and moist home compartment from the bright, warm, and dry stem in which shock may be administered. Shock is used also to punish incorrect choice. It is delivered when the animal makes contact with a metal door used to convert one arm of the maze into a cul. As the shock is delivered from a con-

stant-current supply, a sensitive relay in series with the animal is activated, providing an objective index of error. The problem of resistance to handling and the problem of efficiency (experimenter effort per datum) are much the same for the maze as for the runway. There have been some interesting attempts to automate the maze (Tolman, Tryon, and Jeffress, 1929), but it is a cumbersome device at best.

The number of T-2 situations developed for discrete-trials work on discriminative learning is enormous. In some early experiments with a variety of species, e.g., monkey (Shepherd, 1910), bird (Katz and Révész, 1909), and fish (Reighard, 1908), a rather interesting *ingestive* technique was used. The discriminanda were visually differentiated food objects, e.g., grains of rice dyed different colors, which the animal was invited to ingest. Objects of one kind (such as red grains) were edible, but the alternative objects (white grains) were made inedible by some means, e.g., saturated with quinine or glued to the substrate. For the most part, however, instrumental rather than consummatory indicator-responses have been employed.

An apparatus developed originally by Yerkes (1907) for the dancing mouse and later modified for work with a variety of species is shown in Fig. 11-6. Approach to the positive stimulus is rewarded with food, and approach to the negative stimulus is punished by shock from a grid in the floor. This apparatus, shown only for purposes of contrast, is a poor one; its use leads to marked underestimation of discriminative capacity. For example, early work with the Yerkes apparatus suggested that rats were incapable of visual pattern discrimination. Then Lashley (1930) invented the jumping apparatus and demonstrated that the earlier failures represented deficiencies in the apparatus rather than in the rat. Lashley's apparatus is illustrated in Fig. 11-7. The rat jumps from a platform, sometimes equipped with a grid to break any resistance to jumping that may develop, to one of the two cards placed in the windows. A jump to the correct card, which is unfastened, gives access to a feeding platform in the rear, while a jump to the incorrect card, which is locked in place, precipitates the animal into the net below.

An advantage of Lashley's apparatus lies in the fact that the animal is required to make contact with the stimuli to be discriminated; the discriminanda are also the manipulanda. In Yerkes's apparatus, by contrast, the animal simply runs past the discriminanda. Another advantage of Lashley's apparatus is that the consequences of response follow directly upon the animal's choice and are closely associated with the discriminanda. In Yerkes's apparatus, food is given at a point remote both from the point of choice and from the positive stimulus, while shock for erroneous choice is given at a point remote (although somewhat less so) from the negative stimulus. There is a good deal of evidence from monkey experiments to show that contiguity of cue with response, and of both with reward and nonreward (or punishment), are important factors in discriminative learning (Jarvik, 1956; McClearn and Harlow, 1953; Murphy and Miller, 1958). These essential contiguities may, of course, be incorporated in apparatus quite different from Lashley's. Grice (1949) has developed a technique for the rat which requires that the animal simply walk up to one of two stimulus plaques, each of which has a small door in it. Nosing the door in the correct plaque gives access to a pellet of food. A popular technique for the monkey (Kinnaman, 1902) offers the animal a choice of objects on a tray, one of which contains food or covers a small food well, while the other is empty or covers an empty well. Figure 11-8 shows the Wisconsin General Test Apparatus (WGTA), an object-discrimination apparatus that has been widely used in experiments with the monkey (Harlow, 1949) and, more recently, in work with the cat (Warren, 1960) and the rat (Rollin, Shepp, and Thaller, 1963); see Chap. 1, page 28.

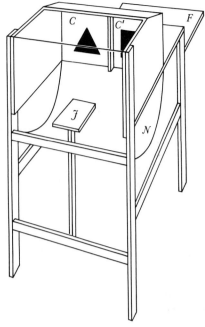

Fig. 11-7 Lashley's jumping apparatus. *J*, jumping platform; *C, C'*, stimulus cards; *N*, net; *F*, feeding platform. The cards are 6 inches on a side (*Lashley, 1938b*).

Another advantage of Lashley's apparatus may lie in the nature of the punishment for error, which seems to be particularly effective for the rat. There is unpublished evidence that modifications of Lashley's apparatus which eliminate punishment for error yield poor estimates of the rat's discriminative capacities. One way to eliminate punishment is to have a ledge in front of each window. The animal is either returned by hand to the starting platform when it jumps to the negative ledge or required to jump back to the starting platform. Another way is to dispense with jumping altogether by interposing a Y-shaped elevated pathway between the starting platform and the windows. Difficult discriminations, i.e., discriminations between closely similar stimuli, which the rat makes reliably when punishment is used, may not be made without punishment. The animal simply takes up a position habit, which brings it reinforcement on half the trials

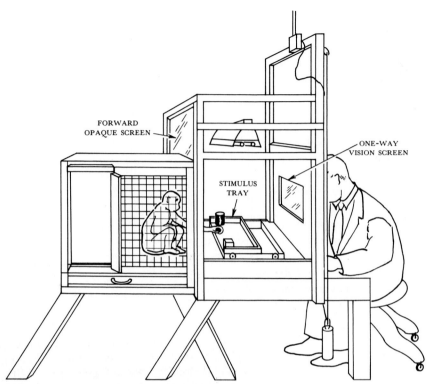

FORWARD
OPAQUE SCREEN

ONE-WAY
VISION SCREEN

STIMULUS
TRAY

Fig. 11-8 The Wisconsin General Test Apparatus. The two stimulus objects cover wells in the food tray. The well covered by the correct object contains food.

since the position of the positive card is shifted from trial to trial in quasi-random order (Gellermann, 1933). Faced with a difficult discrimination, the rat may develop rigid position habits even when punishment is used, but, given the proper technique, punishment will yield lower difference limens than nonpunishment.

Proper training procedures are essential to get the most from the jumping apparatus. The rats first jump through open windows to the feeding platform with the distance between the jumping platform and the windows being increased gradually from 1 to 10 inches. Manual guidance is used from time to time to ensure equal experience with both windows. Then two identical training cards which must contrast sharply with the background are introduced, covering the windows only partially at first, and then gradually

moved into their proper places. Manual guidance is used frequently to discourage the formation of position biases. The best training procedure when the discriminanda are at last introduced is *limited correction*. After each incorrect choice, the animal is placed on the jumping platform and permitted to choose again until some maximal number of repetitive errors, e.g., two or three, has been made, after which the animal is guided toward the correct card. Each trial thus ends with a reinforced response to the positive stimulus. After mastering one or two easy problems in this way, rats become quite expert and are prepared to provide good estimates of their discriminative capacities.

Automated T-2 situations for a variety of species have been patterned after the automated unitary situations. In work with the rat, a pair of retractable levers may be substituted for the T maze; depression of one lever produces a pellet of food, while depression of the other does not. With two Plexiglas panels on which lights of different brightness or pattern are projected, discriminative as well as generalized problems may be studied. Such an apparatus is diagrammed in Fig. 11-9. The chamber is a standard picnic chest. One end contains two panels behind which are mounted In-Line units of 80ooo series that project patterns up to about 3 inches in size on the panels. Between the panels is a recessed food cup, into which a feeder discharges Noyes pellets, and a divider, which gives access to the cup from both sides. The food cup, made from a block of clear Plexiglas, is illuminated by a magazine light for a few seconds when a pellet is discharged. At the other end of the chest is a retractable lever.

After an intertrial interval in darkness, a trial begins with the introduction of the lever and the turning on of a light over the lever. Response to the lever retracts it, turns off the lever light, and turns on the pattern projectors. Pushing the positive-stimulus panel turns off the discriminanda and initiates a reinforcement cycle, after which the next intertrial interval begins. Pushing the negative-stimulus panel may have one of several different consequences at the option of the experimenter. In *noncorrection,* the trial is ended by an incorrect response. In *guidance,* the discriminanda are turned off and after an interval of darkness (time out) the lever is reintroduced. Response to the lever now produces the positive stimulus alone, and the response to it, which is reinforced, ends the trial. In *correction,* presentation of the lever follows the time out as in guidance, but response to the lever produces *both* discriminanda; under these conditions, the animal can make an unlimited number of repetitive errors. In *limited correction,* the correction procedure is in effect on each trial until a preset number of repetitive errors has been made, after which guidance supervenes.

The primary function of the lever is to get the animal away from the discriminanda when they are presented. The shape of the chamber is such that, having turned on the discriminanda, the animal first views them from a fixed central position. If the experimenter wishes, the animal may be required to make 10 or 20 responses to the lever in order to produce the discriminanda. In guidance and correction, this requirement serves as a kind of punishment for errors; after making an error the animal must work for another chance at the discriminanda. A similar function is served by the time out when no lever is used; discriminative performance in the pigeon is far better with a time out of 6 sec-

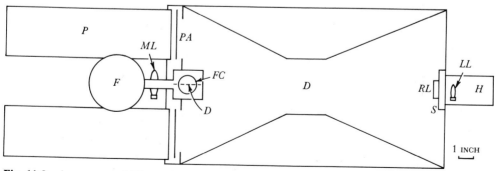

Fig. 11-9   An automated Thorndikian-choice situation for the rat. *P,* projector; *PA,* panel on which patterns of light are projected; *F,* feeder; *ML,* magazine light; *FC,* food cup; *D,* divider; *RL,* retractable lever; *LL,* lever light; *S,* shade for lever light; *H,* lever housing.

onds between error and guidance than with a time out of 0 second (Bullock and Bitterman, 1962). It is possible also to punish errors with shock from the floor of the chamber, which may be a conventional grid or a resistive surface (Longo, Holland, and Bitterman, 1961).

Central to the programming of Thorndikian choice experiments is a set of contingency relays, one of which is called for by a scrambler (stepping switch) on each trial. The setting of a series of switches for each contingency relay determines which stimulus will appear on the left, which stimulus will appear on the right, and what the consequences of the left and right responses will be on trials governed by that relay. A generalized choice (T-2g) problem requires only one contingency relay since the conditions are the same on every trial. For example, this relay may be set for circle on the left, circle on the right, left response reinforced, and right response unreinforced. A simple horizontal-vertical discrimination requires two relays to be called for by the scrambler in quasi-random orders. One relay presents the vertical on the left, the horizontal on the right, and reinforces the left response. Another relay gives horizontal on the left, vertical on the right, and reinforces the right response. For an experiment on probability learning, four or more contingency relays may be required. Consider a 70:30 horizontal-vertical discrimination, i.e., one in which horizontal is positive on a random 70 percent of the trials (as often on the right as on the left) and vertical is positive on the remaining 30 percent of the trials. The scrambler calls on any given trial either for a horizontal-positive vertical-negative, a horizontal-negative–vertical-positive, a vertical-positive–horizontal-negative, or a vertical-negative–horizontal-positive relay.

When so complicated an experiment is considered, the advantages of automatic programming become particularly apparent. An experimenter required to schedule these conditions from trial to trial as the experiment

progressed would have a difficult time indeed, even if it were not necessary for him to keep track of the animal's responses. In the automated case, the experimenter is relieved of the burden of detecting and recording responses. Initial and, where permitted, repetitive errors are registered on a six-pen polygraph which may be used also to record the contingency relay in operation on each trial, response to the lever, and the occurrence of reinforcement.

Each contingency relay is a four-pole affair. One common receives power from the left-response relay, and the second from the right-response relay. The corresponding normally open contacts are connected by a rotary switch either to the reinforcement relay or to the error relays which produce end trial, guidance, or correction. The third and fourth commons of the contingency relay receive lamp power for the left and right projectors. The corresponding normally open contacts are led to rotary switches which select lamps, each pattern being produced by a different lamp. Other features of the programmer, which is a perfectly general one that will control chambers appropriate to a variety of species, may be left to the ingenuity of the reader who wishes to construct one.

An automated T-2 situation for the rhesus monkey may be constructed with three manipulanda consisting of circular Plexiglas panels, 3 inches in diameter, which the animal pushes with its fingers. They are mounted about 2 inches apart in one wall of the animal's chamber, and about 10 inches above the floor. Each trial begins with the illumination of the center panel (center key) by a white light. Response to the center key turns off the center-key light and presents the discriminanda, which consist of colored lights or patterns projected on the side keys. A magazine aperture about 6 inches below the center key is illuminated when a peanut or raisin is delivered. An analogous situation for the pigeon may be constructed by adding side keys to the unitary apparatus described earlier. An automated ingestive technique for the pigeon which produces very rapid discrimination and discrimination reversal (Stearns and Bitterman, 1965) is shown in Fig. 11-10. Response to the center key turns off the center-key light and causes the apertures of the magazines to be illuminated with colored lights, e.g., red versus green. If the animal inserts its head into the correct magazine, the grain tray is presented for a few seconds. An incorrect choice turns off the colored lights and initiates an intertrial interval (in noncorrection) or a time out (in guidance and correction). The choices of the animal are detected by photocells in the lips of the magazines. An automated T-2 situation for the turtles may be patterned after the T-1 situation shown in Fig. 11-3, with a second target and a second set of colored lamps added on the right-hand side. In work with the fish, a situation is used which is similar to Fig. 11-4 in all respects except that there are two targets and two projectors. For the fish, as for the turtle, no center key seems to be required.

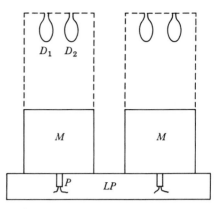

Fig. 11-10 An ingestive Thorndikian choice situation for the pigeon. *CK*, center key; *M*, magazine aperture illuminated from above by colored lamps (D_1, D_2) that serve both as discriminanda and as photocell lamps; *P*, photocell; *LP*, lip that contains the photocells.

PAVLOVIAN TECHNIQUES

In a Pavlovian experiment, one stimulus acquires new functional properties as a result of its contiguity with another stimulus. The new properties may be response-eliciting properties, i.e., the CS comes to elicit responses which it did not before; or they may be motivational properties, i.e., the CS, previously neutral, comes to have some appetitive or aversive significance for the animal. This section supplements Chap. 9, Classical Conditioning, in two respects: (1) It describes a technique of general-activity conditioning which is applicable to a variety of species, and (2) it deals with some techniques for the conditioning of drive and reward properties.

General-activity conditioning

The traditional method of motor conditioning in the dog and other large mammals

(Liddell, James, and Anderson, 1934) is to pair a CS with shock to one of the animal's limbs. The shock elicits generalized struggling at first, which may or may not become restricted to a fairly localized limb flexion, depending on the animal and on the intensity of the shock. The character of the conditioned response also varies widely, although records of limb flexion made with a string running from the shocked limb to a recorder may give a spurious impression of specificity. Another procedure is to use a more general measure of the activation of the animal by shock and by stimuli paired with shock. For example, Warner (1932b) used a tambour-mounted cage in experiments with the rat, and a similar arrangement was used later for the monkey by Harris (1943). In his experiments on classical conditioning in the fish, Bull (1928) used kymographic tracings of movements of the surface of the water in the animal's aquarium as an index of activity. Froloff (1925) simply ran a thread from the

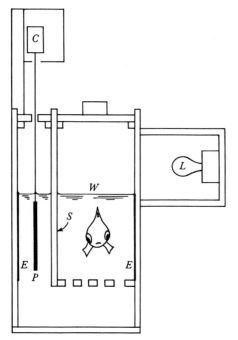

Fig. 11-11 A classical conditioning situation for the fish. *L*, lamp, the onset of which serves as the CS; *E*, electrode; *P*, paddle; *S*, slatted wall; *W*, water level; *C*, phonograph cartridge.

pen of a kymograph to a hook implanted in the fish. These early methods lacked sensitivity, and such records of activity which they provided were difficult to quantify.

A contemporary technique for general-activity conditioning in the fish is illustrated in Fig. 11-11. The fish is transferred by net from its individual living tank to a small, dark Plexiglas compartment in which it can be stimulated by light and shock while its activity is monitored by a paddle inserted into the water a short distance away. The paddle, which is displaced by the fish's movement, is fixed on a rod set into the needle holder of a crystal phonograph cartridge. The output, amplified and integrated, is used to drive a counter or the pen of an event recorder. The basic procedure is to pair light with brief low-voltage a-c shock and to measure the generalized activity which the light comes to evoke in consequence. The graphic

records resemble Pavlov's records of salivary response in the dog except that the pips represent units of activity instead of drops of saliva. The latest model of this apparatus differs in a number of respects from that described in 1960 by Horner, Longo, and Bitterman. The most important change is in the integrator, the revised circuit for which is given in Fig. 11-12. The frequency of pulses put out per unit of activity is now large enough that fractional quantities can be disregarded. (Further applications of this technique for measuring general activity are noted later.) The shocking electrodes also have been changed, the stainless steel plates used earlier being replaced by a low-resistance mixture of carbon and Styrofoam in methyl ethyl ketone which is applied with a brush to the long walls of the compartments containing the animals. (Carbon electrodes are thought to be safer for fish.) There are actually six compartments like that shown in Fig. 11-11, in which six fish are studied concurrently. The six compartments, which are contained in a unitary Plexiglas structure, have a common, continuously filtered and aerated water supply.

Two different approaches have been taken to the programming of experiments in this apparatus. One kind of programmer is so designed that only one of the six fish is given a trial at any given time. A scrambler (stepper) is wired to give the first trial to each of the six fish in one order, the second trial to each of the six in another order, and so forth through the series of trials. As each fish is to have a trial, the integrator is connected to the output of its phonograph cartridge, the source of CS power to its lamps, and the source of UCS power to its electrodes. A printing counter activated by the integrator prints once at the end of the CS-UCS interval to give a measure of the CR. It prints again at the end of a second interval, usually 10 seconds beginning with the onset of the UCS, to give a measure of the UCR. On selected trials, an event recorder provides a graphic record of the distribution

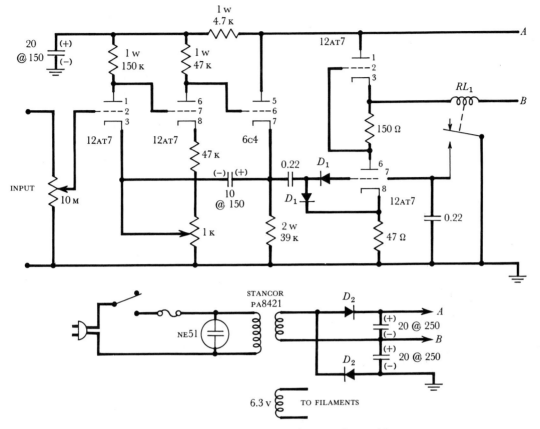

Fig. 11-12 An integrating circuit for the output from a phonograph cartridge used for the measurement of activity in experiments on classical conditioning. D_1, IN459A; D_2, Sarkes Tarzian M500; 0.22-microfarad capacitors should be Electron D-2 or equivalent; RL_1, Potter and Bromfield, 10,000 = ohm plate sensitive relay or equivalent; adjust 1K pot for maximal sensitivity.

of activity over each of the two intervals. A second kind of programmer is so designed that each trial is given to all six fish simultaneously. This system requires six integrators and six recording devices. Instead of a six-channel printing counter, a six-channel event recorder is used which provides a graphic record of the activity of each of the six fish on any trial in which the experimenter is interested.

In both programming systems, the conditions of each trial are determined by a set of contingency relays which are called for by a scrambler. A bank of switches for each relay is used to select CS (lamp color) or no CS (for trials on which shock alone is to be given, or for determinations of interval activity which involve no stimulation at all); UCS or no UCS; and the CS-UCS interval in tenths, units, and tens of seconds. Only a single contingency relay is required for experiments in which the events of each trial are the same. In other cases, more than one relay may be used. Two contingency relays are required, for example, in a sensitization control experiment in which the CS alone is presented on some trials and the UCS alone on others, in a quasi-random order. Where the CS-UCS interval is varied from trial to trial, as many different contingency relays are required as there are different CS-UCS intervals.

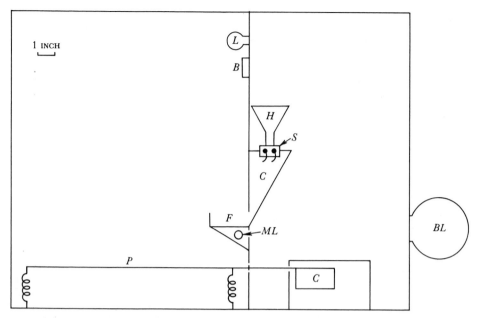

Fig. 11-13 A situation for the study of classical conditioning in the pigeon. *L, B,* light and buzzer, used as CS; *H,* grain-hopper; *S,* solenoid; *C,* chute; *F,* food tray; *ML,* magazine light; *BL,* blower; *C,* phonograph cartridge connected by a light rod to *P,* a spring-mounted platform on which the animal stands and which is coated with resistive paint through which shock may be delivered for experiments on aversive conditioning. The feeding mechanism is used in experiments on classical appetitive conditioning.

The same programmers used with the fish apparatus may be used for analogous experiments with the pigeon (Longo, Milstein, and Bitterman, 1962) in a chamber like that which is diagrammed in Fig. 11-13. The food magazine and grain tray, which are put in for purposes to be considered later, should be ignored. The animal stands on a spring-mounted platform from one edge of which there extends a light rod running to the needle holder of a phonograph cartridge. Shock is delivered through wing clips or through an electrically resistive surface painted on the platform (Longo, Holland, and Bitterman, 1961). The CS is a light or a buzzer mounted on one wall of the chamber which is set into a picnic chest. The pigeon, like the fish, is activated by stimuli paired with shock, and the technique yields orderly conditioning and extinction functions. This technique has not, however, been successful for all animals on which it has been tried. Longo *et al.* (1961) worked with harnessed blowflies standing on a platform which was mounted on a rod set into the needle holder of a phonograph cartridge. The arrangement was sensitive to very slight movements of the fly but no conditioning could be detected, either with light onset or light offset as the CS; the CS did not activate the animal. Negative results have been obtained also in experiments with various species of cockroach, which were not harnessed like the fly, but permitted to move freely about in a plastic enclosure mounted like the fly platform. Work with the rat, too, has given only negative results. The rat, after a brief startle reaction, tends to crouch motionlessly in the presence of the CS or to sit up on its hind limbs with its head turned to the CS source.

Experiments on general-activity conditioning in the pigeon also have been done with an appetitive UCS. A light or a buzzer paired with the presentation of food soon begins to elicit anticipatory activity (Longo, Klempay, and Bitterman, 1964). The apparatus of Fig. 11-13 also is used for appetitive experiments; hence the food cup, and the solenoid-operated hopper which discharges an ounce or so of mixed grain into the cup each time the solenoid is energized. The programmer developed for the shock experiments serves for the food experiments as well, with the UCS power triggering the feeders instead of the shock circuits. Activity is recorded in the same way. It is, in fact, impossible to tell from looking at the record of a conditioned animal on any given trial whether the UCS is shock or food. The appetitive technique for the pigeon was suggested by observations of the behavior of pigeons at feeding time, when the removal of the cover of the grain bucket or the approach of the experimenter to a rack of cages provokes a fury of anticipatory activity. Since the same sort of behavior can be observed in the fish and in a variety of other species, there is every reason to believe that the technique will have wide application (Davis and Ellison, 1964).

Drive and reward conditioning

With the exception of a few largely unsuccessful attempts to condition response-eliciting properties (e.g., Schlosberg, 1934), research on classical conditioning in the rat has been confined to the acquisition of drive and reward properties. The usual experiment is a two-stage affair. First, a neutral stimulus is paired with food or shock in Pavlovian fashion; then the consequences of the pairing are studied in Thorndikian or avoidance situations so structured that the onset or the offset of the CS is contingent on the occurrence or the nonoccurrence of some defined response. For example, food may be paired with shock, after which the animal is tested with a lever which turns on the light briefly each time it is depressed (Bersh, 1951). For

the most part, shock rather than food has been used as the UCS. In one kind of experiment (Miller, 1948), the animal is shocked in a given compartment; i.e., compartment stimuli are paired with shock. The experimenter then measures the readiness with which the animal learns to make some instrumental response that permits it to leave the compartment. It is convenient to do this kind of experiment with a shuttle box (Behrend and Bitterman, 1964). Light and shock are paired while the animal, in this case a fish, is confined in one of the two compartments. Then the barrier is removed and the readiness with which the animal learns to escape from the light by changing compartments is measured.

In a second kind of experiment, response is not rewarded by the termination of a stimulus which has been paired with shock, but punished by its onset. For example, Mowrer and Aiken (1954) trained rats to press a lever for food, and then studied the decline in response rate which resulted when a light paired with shock came on with each depression of the lever. The extent of the decline was taken as a measure of the acquisition of aversive properties by the light. In a third kind of experiment, the acquisition of aversive properties by a neutral stimulus paired with light is measured in terms of the extent to which it disrupts some ongoing instrumental activity, such as lever pressing on a variable-interval schedule (Estes and Skinner, 1941; Libby, 1951). This so-called *conditioned suppression* experiment differs from the first two in that it involves no response contingency; neither the offset nor the onset of the CS has any relation to the occurrence of the instrumental behavior in terms of which its disruptive properties will be assessed.

Although the extensive use of these designs primarily reflects the difficulty which has been encountered in adapting the traditional Pavlovian methods to the rat, they have considerable intrinsic interest and they are applicable to a wide variety of other species, such as the fish, as exemplified by the shuttle-box work of Behrend and Bitterman (1964) and by a study of conditioned suppression reported by Geller (1963). The instrumentation of such experiments poses no special problems. The situations and the programming techniques are much the same as those which have already been considered or which will be considered in the next section.

AVOIDANCE TECHNIQUES

Most of the modern work on avoidance has been done with Warner's shuttling technique (1932a) or some variation of it, although certain other techniques also are of interest.

The shuttle box

In the most general sense of the term, a *shuttle box* is an apparatus of two or more compartments in which response is defined as moving from one compartment to another. The animal is shocked if it remains in the compartment which it occupies when the CS is introduced, but avoids shock if it goes to one of the other compartments. A common procedure in work with the rat is to use an apparatus of two compartments consisting of a starting compartment in which the stimuli are presented, and an end compartment to which the animal may retreat. In the intertrial interval, the animal is replaced by hand in the starting compartment. An alternative procedure is to have each compartment serve a dual function. At the start of the trial, the CS is presented in whichever compartment the animal happens to be, and the animal avoids shock by going to the other compartment. For example, Warner (1932a) used two compartments separated by a hurdle over which the animal could jump, or under which it could crawl. Hunter (1935) used four compartments separated by doorways instead of hurdles, which made it unnecessary for the animal to turn around after each

response. The animal could avoid successfully by moving clockwise or counterclockwise from one compartment to the next. If dual-function compartments are used, performance will be better with a highly localized CS, which helps to differentiate the compartment that the animal occupies at the start of a trial from the other compartments. For example, where light onset is the CS in a two-compartment apparatus, there should be two CS lamps so arranged that the light given by each falls only in one compartment. The dual-function procedure, which eliminates the need for handling the animal between trials, permits automated experiments.

A shuttle box designed for the fish, which is a modification of an apparatus described by Horner, Longo, and Bitterman (1961), is shown in Fig. 11-14. An elongated chamber of black Plexiglas is divided into two smaller compartments by a hurdle. The distance between the top of the hurdle and the ceiling of the chamber is great enough to permit crossing, but small enough to discourage loitering in the region of the hurdle. At any given time, the animal is in one compartment or the other, or in the act of crossing from one to the other. The position of the animal is monitored by two photocells which pulse a rachet relay. Response is defined as breaking the beam *farthest* from the animal at any given time; otherwise the animal could make a response without actually changing compartments. If the animal is on the right, the left photocell is functional. Breaking the left beam activates the rachet relay, which takes the left cell out of the circuit and substitutes the right cell. At the same time, the right CS lamps are taken out and the left lamps put in with the result that, when a trial is scheduled, a CS lamp on the side occupied by the animal will be turned on. The lamps are colored Christmas-tree bulbs set behind diffusing Plexiglas panels in such a way that there is a sharp gradient of illumination from the bright CS compartment to the darkened alternative. Shock is administered through

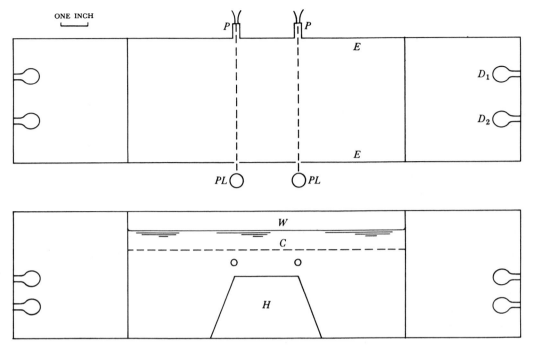

Fig. 11-14 Two views of a shuttle box for the fish. Top, plan; bottom, side view; *P*, photocell; *PL*, photocell lamp; *E*, electrode; D_1, D_2, colored lamps, the onset of which serves as the CS; *W* water level; *C*, ceiling of the animal's chamber; *H*, hurdle.

painted electrodes, a low-resistance mixture of carbon, Styrofoam, and methyl ethyl ketone, applied with a brush to the long walls of the chamber. Continuous shock cannot be used in work with the fish because it tends to immobilize the animal. Where prolonged shock is called for, a train of pulses, e.g., a ¼-second pulse every 2 seconds, generated by a multivibrator is used.

It is convenient for large-scale investigations to have six such shuttle boxes in which six fish are trained concurrently, with all of the events of the experiment being programmed automatically and recorded on tape. The programming is very much like that used for classical conditioning, except that a response which antedates the onset of the UCS must terminate the trial. The conditions of each trial, as in the programming of experiments on classical conditioning, are controlled by contingency relays selected by a scrambler. The conditions which each relay

will put into effect when it is called for are determined by switches which are set before the experiment begins. One switch controls the CS (lamp color) or calls for no CS. The no-CS condition comes into effect on pure escape trials as well as on blank trials which are used to assess the basal probability of crossing during a period of no stimulation. A second switch is used to select UCS or (on unreinforced trials and on basal-probability trials) no UCS. Three switches are used for the CS-UCS interval in tenths, units, and tens of seconds. Master switches set for all trials of the session select trace versus delay, shock intensity, and shock duration. Shock consists of either a single brief pulse (for experiments on avoidance without escape) or a train of pulses (for experiments with an escape contingency). Where a train is called for, a time limit (usually 15 seconds) is put on the duration of the train, the trial terminating automatically if the animal does not respond in that time. Other switches fix the duration of the experimental session, which may be terminated after (1) a given number of trials; (2) a criterion number of avoidances, total or successive; or (3) a criterion number of failures to avoid, total or successive. A six-pen event recorder, one pen for each animal, is used to keep track of responses. Latencies can be measured accurately enough for most purposes with a paper speed of 5 millimeters per second.

Illustrations of shuttle boxes for the rat (Brush and Knaff, 1959) and for the dog (Solomon and Wynne, 1953) may be found in the literature. The chief problem encountered in the design of shuttle boxes is to keep the animal from straddling the two compartments. Straddling destructures the situation for the animal as well as for the programmer, which must decide where the animal is when it is time for a trial to begin. If a simple fence is used for the rat, the animal often will sit on it and so avoid shock altogether. Electrifying the fence keeps the animal off it, but provides a barrier to crossing and otherwise complicates the experiment. A drop gate may be used instead of the fence, or to supplement the fence. It is dropped between trials to keep the animal in one or the other compartment and, if a fence is used, off the fence. The gate is raised at the start of the trial and its elevation becomes a component of the CS. One difficulty with this arrangement, aside from its cumbersomeness, is that it prevents intertrial responding, which the investigator may be interested in studying. Another solution is to have a hinged door through which the animal must push its way from one compartment to the other. A situation which has been used successfully in pilot experiments with the rat consists of two elevated platforms separated by a narrow gap across which the animal jumps. The weight of the animal depresses the platform to which it jumps and operates a sensitive microswitch which pulses the ratchet relay that keeps track of the animal's location.

Other avoidance techniques

One way to solve the straddling problem is to reduce the number of compartments to one. This permits the animal to terminate the CS and avoid the UCS by making some response *within* the compartment. For example, a retractable lever may be introduced and a lever light turned on to start each trial, under conditions in which response retracts the lever, turns off the light, and forestalls shock. With a retractable lever, intertrial responding is ruled out. If the lever is not retractable, the animal tends to hang on it, which gives rise to a problem similar to straddling, at least in discrete-trials experiments. Another difficulty with the use of a lever-pressing response is that it is not readily developed without special shaping, which the experimental design may not permit.

A better technique from this point of view is one which requires simply that the animal be active in order to avoid shock. Running in an activity wheel has been used successfully in several types of experiment with the rat (Brogden, Lipman, Culler, 1938; Mowrer and Keehn, 1958). A technique which restricts still less the nature of activity that avoids shock has been used with the pigeon (Graf and Bitterman, 1963). The situation is like that shown in Fig. 11-13, except that the feeding device is omitted. Brief shock, administered either through wing-clips or through the platform, is scheduled every 20 seconds by a timer which is reset by a defined amount of activity. The technique recommends itself also for discrete-trials work on avoidance. It seems especially well suited to comparative work with a variety of species, since it makes no special motor demands upon the subject beyond an ability to move in a detectable manner.

DIVERSITY OF ANIMALS

One of the emphases in this chapter has been on the appropriateness of the techniques described for experimental work with a wide variety of animals. No such emphasis is to be found in the literature. While many different animals have been brought into the laboratory since the turn of the century, few have been studied systematically. Interest has centered for the most part on a small number of mammalian forms, primarily the rat, selected largely for reasons of convenience and treated as representative of animals in general (Bitterman, 1960, 1965). Almost from the beginning, work in the field has been dominated by the conviction that the processes of learning are the same everywhere in the animal series. All animals, said Thorndike, "are systems of connections subject to change by the law of exercise and effect," differing only in the particular connections formed and in the efficiency of connection (1911, p. 280). Although this view was greeted with considerable skepticism, the skepticism was short-lived, and Thorndike's "working hypothesis" soon became for the growing body of investigators in the field more like an article of faith. There was disagreement only on the *nature* of the laws which generally were presumed to operate alike in all animals.

If the laws of learning were the same everywhere in the animal series, it would be reasonable that the choice of experimental animal should be dictated by practical considerations alone. Why work with a more expensive animal when a cheaper one is available? Why work with an animal which is difficult to maintain in the laboratory when one which is easier to maintain is available? Why devote time and effort to the development of experimental techniques appropriate to animal *B* when techniques appropriate to animal *A* already have been developed? One might be led by practical considerations to work with several different animals where, for example, the properties of one animal were best for one kind of experiment while the properties of another animal were best for another kind of experiment, but diversity of animals for its own sake would be avoided, because the practical advantages of specialization are many. It is only now, however, that Thorndike's bold and attractive hypothesis is beginning to receive the searching sort of empirical examination which its importance warrants (see, for example, Bitterman, Wodinsky, and Candland, 1958). The emphasis in this chapter on diversity of animals reflects the conviction that the phyletic base of research on learning will be broadened considerably in the decades to come.

REFERENCES

ARONSON, L. R. An analysis of reproductive behavior in the mouth-breeding cichlid fish, *Tilapia macrocephala. Zoologica,* 1949, **34,** 133–158.

BALLACHEY, E. L., and BUEL, J. Food orientation as a factor determining the distribution of errors in the maze running of the rat. *J. genet. Psychol.,* 1934, **45,** 358–370.

BEHREND, E. R., and BITTERMAN, M. E. Probability-matching in the fish. *Amer. J. Psychol.,* 1961, **74,** 542–551.

BEHREND, E. R., and BITTERMAN, M. E. Sidman avoidance in the fish. *J. exp. Anal. Behav.,* 1963, **6,** 47–52.

BEHREND, E. R., and BITTERMAN, M. E. Avoidance-conditioning in the fish: Further studies of the *CS-US* interval. *Amer. J. Psychol.,* 1964, **77,** 15-28.

BERSH, P. J. The influence of two variables upon the establishment of a secondary reinforcer for operant responses. *J. exp. Psychol.,* 1951, **41,** 62–73.

BITTERMAN, M. E. Toward a comparative psychology of learning. *Amer. Psychologist,* 1960, **15,** 704–712.

BITTERMAN, M. E. Techniques for the study of learning in animals: Analysis and classification. *Psychol. Bull.,* 1962, **59,** 81–93.

BITTERMAN, M. E. Phyletic differences in learning. *Amer. Psychologist,* 1965, **20,** 396–410.

BITTERMAN, M. E., WODINSKY, J., and CANDLAND, D. K. Some comparative psychology. *Amer. J. Psychol.,* 1958, **71,** 94–110.

BROGDEN, W. J., LIPMAN, E. A., and CULLER, E. The role of incentive in conditioning and extinction. *Amer. J. Psychol.,* 1938, **51,** 109–117.

BRUNSWIK, E. Probability as a determiner of rat behavior. *J. exp. Psychol.,* 1939, **25,** 175–197.

BRUSH, F. R., and KNAFF, P. R. A device for detecting and controlling automatic programming of avoidance-conditioning in a shuttle-box. *Amer. J. Psychol.,* 1959, **72,** 275–278.

BUEL, J. Differential errors in animal mazes. *Psychol. Bull.*, 1935, **32**, 67–99.

BULL, H. O. Studies on conditioned responses in fishes. *J. Marine Biol. Ass., U.K.*, 1928, **15**, 485–533.

BULLOCK, D. H., and BITTERMAN, M. E. Habit reversal in the pigeon. *J. comp. physiol. Psychol.*, 1962, **55**, 958–962.

BULLOCK, D. H., ROBERTS, W. A., and BITTERMAN, M. E. Techniques of housing and maintaining a large pigeon colony. *J. exp. Anal. Behav.*, 1961, **4**, 285–286.

CARR, H. A. The alternation problem. *J. anim. Behav.*, 1917a, **7**, 365–384.

CARR, H. A. The distribution and elimination of errors in the maze. *J. anim. Behav.*, 1917b, **7**, 145–159.

DATTA, L. G. Learning in the earthworm, *Lumbricus terrestris*. *Amer. J. Psychol.*, 1962, **75**, 531–553.

DATTA, L. G., MILSTEIN, S., and BITTERMAN, M. E. Habit reversal in the crab. *J. comp. physiol. Psychol.*, 1960, **53**, 275–278.

DAVIS, J. D., and ELLISON, G. D. A general purpose activity recorder with variable sensitivity. *J. exp. Anal. Behav.*, 1964, **7**, 117–118.

ESKIN, R. M., and BITTERMAN, M. E. Fixed-interval and fixed-ratio performance in the fish as a function of prefeeding. *Amer. J. Psychol.*, 1960, **73**, 417–423.

ESTES, W. K., and SKINNER, B. F. Some quantitative properties of anxiety. *J. comp. Psychol.*, 1941, **29**, 290–400.

FINGER, F. W. The effect of varying conditions of reinforcement upon a simple running response. *J. exp. Psychol.*, 1942, **30**, 53–68.

FROLOFF, J. P. Bedingte reflexe bei Fischen. *Arch. ges. Physiol.*, 1925, **208**, 261–271.

GELLER, I. Conditioned "anxiety" and punishment effects on operant behavior of goldfish. *Science*, 1963, **141**, 351–353.

GELLERMANN, L. W. Chance orders of alternating stimuli in visual discrimination experiments. *J. genet. Psychol.*, 1933, **42**, 206–208.

GONZALEZ, R. C., BAINBRIDGE, P., and BITTERMAN, M. E. Discrete-trials lever-pressing in the rat as a function of pattern of reinforcement, effortfulness of response, and amount of reward. *J. comp. physiol. Psychol.*, 1966, **61**, 110–122.

GONZALEZ, R. C., and BITTERMAN, M. E. A further study of partial reinforcement in the turtle. *Q. J. exp. Psychol.*, 1962, **14**, 109–112.

GONZALEZ, R. C., and DIAMOND, L. A test of Spence's theory of incentive motivation. *Amer. J. Psychol.*, 1960, **73**, 396–403.

GRAF, V., and BITTERMAN, M. E. General activity as instrumental: Application to avoidance training. *J. exp. Anal. Behav.*, 1963, **6**, 301–305.

GRICE, G. R. Visual discrimination learning with simultaneous and successive presentation of stimuli. *J. comp. physiol. Psychol.*, 1949, **42**, 365–373.

HARALSON, J., and BITTERMAN, M. E. A lever-depression apparatus for the study of learning in fish. *Amer. J. Psychol.*, 1950, **63**, 250–256.

HARLOW, H. F. The formation of learning sets. *Psychol. Rev.*, 1949, **56**, 51–65.

HARRIS, J. D. The auditory acuity of pre-adolescent monkeys. *J. comp. Psychol.*, 1943, **35**, 255–265.

HERBERT, M. J., and ARNOLD, W. J. A reaction chaining apparatus. *J. comp. physiol. Psychol.*, 1947, **40**, 227–229.

HICKS, V. C. The relative values of different curves of learning. *J. anim. Behav.*, 1911, **1**, 138–156.

HOBHOUSE, L. T. *Mind in evolution*. New York: St. Martin's, 1901.

HOGAN, J., and ROZIN, P. An automatic device for dispensing food kept in a liquid medium. *J. exp. Anal. Behav.*, 1961, **4**, 81–83.

HOGAN, J., and ROZIN, P. An improved mechanical fish-lever. *Amer. J. Psychol.*, 1962, **75**, 307–308.

HORNER, J. L., LONGO, N., and BITTERMAN, M. E. A classical conditioning technique for small aquatic animals. *Amer. J. Psychol.*, 1960, **73**, 623–626.

HORNER, J. L., LONGO, N., and BITTERMAN, M. E. A shuttle box for the fish and a control circuit of general applicability. *Amer. J. Psychol.*, 1961, **74**, 114–120.

HUNTER, W. S. The delayed reaction in animals and children. *Behav. Monogr.*, 1913, **2**, 1–86.

HUNTER, W. S. Conditioning and extinction in the rat. *Brit. J. Psychol.*, 1935, **26**, 135–148.

JAMES, W. T. The use of work in developing a differential conditioned reaction of antagonistic reflex systems. *J. comp. physiol. Psychol.*, 1947, **26**, 135–148.

JARVIK, M. E. Simple color discrimination in chimpanzees: Effect of varying contiguity between cue and incentive. *J. comp. physiol. Psychol.*, 1956, **49**, 492–495.

KATZ, D., and RÉVÉSZ, G. Experimentellpsychologische Untersuchungen mit Hühnern. *Z. Psychol.*, 1909, **50**, 93–116.

KINNAMAN, A. J. Mental life of two *Macacus rhesus* monkeys in captivity. *Amer. J. Psychol.*, 1902, **13**, 98–148, 173–218.

LASHLEY, K. S. Visual discrimination of size and form in the white rat. *J. anim. Behav.*, 1912, **2**, 310–331.

LASHLEY, K. S. A simple maze: With data on the relation of the distribution of practice to the rate of learning. *Psychobiol.*, 1918, **1**, 352–367.

LASHLEY, K. S. The mechanism of vision: I. A

method for rapid analysis of pattern-vision in the rat. *J. genet. Psychol.*, 1930, **37**, 453–560.

LASHLEY, K. S. Conditional reactions in the rat. *J. Psychol.*, 1938a, **6**, 311–324.

LASHLEY, K. S. The mechanism of vision: XV. Preliminary studies of the rat's capacity for detail vision. *J. gen. Psychol.*, 1938b, **18**, 123–193.

LAWRENCE, D. H., and MILLER, N. E. A positive relationship between reinforcement and resistance to extinction produced by removing a source of confusion from a technique that had produced opposite results. *J. exp. Psychol.*, 1947, **37**, 494–509.

LIBBY, A. Two variables in the acquisition of depressant properties by a stimulus. *J. exp. Psychol.*, 1951, **42**, 100–107.

LIDDELL, H. S., JAMES, W. T., and ANDERSON, O. D. The comparative physiology of the conditioned motor reflex. *Comp. Psychol. Monogr.*, 1934, **11**, 1–89.

LONGO, N. Probability-learning and habit-reversal in the cockroach. *Amer. J. Psychol.*, 1964, **77**, 29–41.

LONGO, N., and BITTERMAN, M. E. Improved apparatus for the study of learning in fish. *Amer. J. Psychol.*, 1959, **72**, 616–620.

LONGO, N., and BITTERMAN, M. E. An improved live-worm dispenser. *J. exp. Anal. Behav.*, 1963, **6**, 279–280.

LONGO, N., HOLLAND, L. R., and BITTERMAN, M. E. The resistive sheet: A gridless and wireless shocking technique. *Amer. J. Psychol.*, 1961, **74**, 612–618.

LONGO, N., KLEMPAY, S., and BITTERMAN, M. E. Classical appetitive conditioning in the pigeon. *Psychon. Sci.*, 1964, **1**, 19–20.

LONGO, N., MILSTEIN, S., and BITTERMAN, M. E. Classical conditioning in the pigeon: Exploratory studies of partial reinforcement. *J. comp. physiol. Psychol.*, 1962, **55**, 983–986.

MCCLEARN, G. E., and HARLOW, H. F. The effect of spatial contiguity on discrimination learning by rhesus monkeys. *J. comp. physiol. Psychol.*, 1953, **47**, 391–394.

MILES, W. R. The comparative learning of rats on elevated and alley mazes of the same pattern. *J. comp. Psychol.*, 1930, **10**, 237–261.

MILLER, N. E. Studies of fear as an acquirable drive: I. Fear as motivation and fear-reduction as reinforcement in the learning of new responses. *J. exp. Psychol.*, 1948, **38**, 89–101.

MOWRER, O. H., and AIKEN, E. G. Contiguity vs. drive-reduction in conditioned fear: Temporal variations in conditioned and unconditioned stimulus. *Amer. J. Psychol.*, 1954, **67**, 26–38.

MOWRER, O. H., and KEEHN, J. D. How are intertrial "avoidance" responses reinforced? *Psychol. Rev.*, 1958, **65**, 209–221.

MURPHY, J. V., and MILLER, R. E. Effect of the spatial relationship between cue, reward, and response in simple discrimination learning. *J. exp. Psychol.*, 1958, **56**, 26–31.

NISSEN, H. W. Description of the learned response in discriminative behavior. *Psychol. Rev.*, 1950, **57**, 121–131.

PAVLOV, I. P. *Conditioned reflexes: An investigation of the physiological activity of the cerebral cortex.* London: Oxford, 1927.

PORTER, J. P. A preliminary study of the psychology of the English sparrow. *Amer. J. Psychol.*, 1904, **15**, 313–346.

PROKASY, W. F. (Ed.) *Classical conditioning: A symposium.* New York: Appleton-Century-Crofts, 1965.

PUBOLS, B. H., JR. Incentive magnitude, learning, and performance in animals. *Psychol. Bull.*, 1960, **57**, 89–115.

REIGHARD, J. An experimental field study of warning coloration in coral reef fishes. *Publ. Carnegie Inst., Washington*, 1908, **103**, 257–325.

ROBERTS, W. A., BULLOCK, D. H., and BITTERMAN, M. E. Resistance to extinction in the pigeon after partially reinforced instrumental training under discrete-trials conditions. *Amer. J. Psychol.*, 1963, **76**, 353–365.

ROLLIN, A. R., SHEPP, B. E., and THALLER, K. E. A modified Wisconsin general test apparatus for the rat. *Amer. J. Psychol.*, 1963, **76**, 500–502.

SCHLOSBERG, H. Conditioned responses in the white rat. *J. genet. Psychol.*, 1934, **45**, 303–335.

SHEFFIELD, F. D., and ROBY, T. B. Reward value of a nonnutritive sweet taste. *J. comp. physiol. Psychol.*, 1950, **43**, 471–481.

SHEPHERD, W. T. Some mental processes of the rhesus monkey. *Psychol. Monogr.*, 1910, **12**, 1–61.

SIDMAN, M. Avoidance conditioning with brief shock and no exteroceptive warning signal. *Science*, 1953, **118**, 157–158.

SKINNER, B. F. On the rate of formation of a conditioned reflex. *J. gen. Psychol.*, 1932, **7**, 274–285.

SKINNER, B. F. Two types of conditioned reflex and a pseudo type. *J. gen. Psychol.*, 1935, **12**, 66–76.

SKINNER, B. F. Two types of conditioned reflex: A reply to Konorski and Miller. *J. gen. Psychol.*, 1937, **16**, 272–282.

SKINNER, B. F. "Superstition" in the pigeon. *J. exp. Psychol.*, 1948, **38**, 168–172.

SMALL, W. S. An experimental study of the mental processes of the rat. *Amer. J. Psychol.*, 1900, **11**, 135–165.

SMALL, W. S. Experimental study of the mental processes of the rat: II. *Amer. J. Psychol.*, 1901, **12**, 206–239.

SOLOMON, R. L. Latency of response as a measure of learning in a "single-door" discrimination. *Amer. J. Psychol.*, 1943, **56**, 422–432.

SOLOMON, R. L., and WYNNE, L. C. Traumatic avoidance learning: Acquisition in normal dogs. *Psychol. Monogr.*, 1953, **67**, 1–119.

SPENCE, K. W. *Behavior theory and conditioning.* New Haven, Conn.: Yale Univer. Press, 1956.

STEARNS, E. M., and BITTERMAN, M. E. A comparison of key-pecking with an ingestive technique for the study of discriminative learning in pigeon. *Amer. J. Psychol.*, 1965, **78**, 48–56.

STONE, C. P. A multiple discrimination box and its use in studying the learning ability of rats: I. Reliability of scores. *J. genet. Psychol.*, 1928, **35**, 557–573.

TEAS, D. C., and BITTERMAN, M. E. Perceptual organization in the rat. *Psychol. Rev.*, 1952, **59**, 130–140.

THOMPSON, E. L. An analysis of the learning process in the snail, *Physa gyrina Say. Behav. Monogr.*, 1917, **3**, 1–89.

THORNDIKE, E. L. Animal intelligence: An experimental study of the associative processes in animals. *Psychol. Rev. Monogr. Suppl.*, 1898, **2**, 1–109.

THORNDIKE, E. L. The mental life of monkeys. *Psychol. Rev. Monogr. Suppl.*, 1901, **3**, 1–57.

THORNDIKE, E. L. *Animal intelligence.* New York: Macmillan, 1911.

TOLMAN, E. C., and HONZIK, C. H. Degrees of hunger, reward and nonreward, and maze learning in rats. *Univ. Calif. Publ. Psychol.*, 1930, **4**, 241–256.

TOLMAN, E. C., TRYON, R. C., and JEFFRESS, L. A. A self-recording maze with an automatic delivery table. *Univ. Calif. Publ. Psychol.*, 1929, **4**, 99–112.

VERPLANCK, W. S., and HAYES, J. R. Eating and drinking as a function of maintenance schedule. *J. comp. physiol. Psychol.*, 1953, **46**, 327–333.

VINCENT, S. B. The white rat and the maze problem: III. Introduction of a tactual control. *J. anim. Behav.*, 1915, **5**, 175–184.

WARNER, L. H. The association span of the white rat. *J. gen. Psychol.*, 1932a, **41**, 57–89.

WARNER, L. H. An experimental search for the "conditioned response." *J. genet. Psychol.*, 1932b, **41**, 91–115.

WARREN, J. M. Oddity learning set in a cat. *J. comp. physiol. Psychol.*, 1960, **53**, 433–434.

WILLIAMS, K. A. The reward value of a conditioned stimulus. *Univ. Calif. Publ. Psychol.*, 1929, **4**, 31–55.

WOODWORTH, R. S. *Experimental psychology.* New York: Holt, 1938.

WORDEN, A. N., and LANE-PETTER, W. (Eds.) *The VFAW handbook on the care and management of laboratory animals.* (2nd ed.) London: The University Federation for Animal Welfare, 1957.

YERKES, R. M. *The dancing mouse.* New York: Macmillan, 1907.

YERKES, R. M. The intelligence of earthworms. *J. anim. Behav.*, 1912, **2**, 332–352.

YERKES, R. M. Methods of exhibiting reactive tendencies characteristic of ontogenetic and phylogenetic stages. *J. anim. Behav.*, 1917, **7**, 11–28.

HUMAN BEHAVIOR

To this point, methods for the study of human behavior have included some basic research considerations, detailed descriptions of classical conditioning methodology, sensation and perception, and techniques for measuring physiological responses. Part Five will encompass experimental methodology and instrumentation in five areas: verbal behavior; complex processes; child and social psychology; and the study of motor skills.

Laboratory investigations of verbal behavior have utilized a number of techniques ranging from the classical rote serial methods of Ebbinghaus to the current modes for studying psycholinguistics. In this volume Runquist (Chap. 12, Verbal Behavior) has chosen to cover those methods that deal with word association and related techniques, the scaling of verbal materials, traditional verbal learning (i.e., serial and paired-associate learning, transfer, forgetting, and retention), multiple language units, and verbal conditioning. Within these general categories information is presented for the selection and presentation of stimuli, research designs, instructions, problems of control, and response analyses. Refer to Keppel (1965) for additional information covering design and control problems in the study of short-term memory and to Bilodeau and Levy (1964) for information on long-term memory. A critical evaluation of conventional techniques for representing the retention process is presented by

Bahrick (1964, 1965). The contributors to Melton's volume (1964) discuss research problems and methods in various categories of human learning; Diebold (1965) references the research in psycholinguistics from 1954 to 1964. Chap. 12 lists a number of sources containing word ratings and associations; additional word association norms from grade school through college may be found in Palermo and Jenkins (1964). Bilodeau and Howell (1965) present an extensive list of free association nouns obtained by both the continuous (subject responds three times to stimulus word which is administered three times) and discrete (subject responds only once to stimulus word) methods.

It is obvious that the typical subject in a verbal-learning experiment enters the situation with some experience in the use of language, and that even in the simplest laboratory condition (e.g., the study of rote serial learning or simple verbal conditioning), subjects utilize modes of mediation and thought that are very complex. These higher processes encompass behaviors that also have been subjected to experimental analyses. In Chap. 13, Complex Processes, Bourne and Battig conceptualize thinking as consisting of three stages corresponding to three methodological distinctions: conceptual behavior, problem solving, and decision making. Criteria for useful experimental methods are defined and procedures are cited for concept-formation studies, one-shot verbal and nonverbal problem series, multistage problems, modified parlor games, decision making, and productive thinking. The chapter concludes with a discussion of dependent-variable measurement and analysis, along with suggestions for research programs.

Of course methods and instruments developed for studies of human behavior in the various areas covered in this volume are not mutually exclusive. The basic investigatory methods of sensation and perception, conditioning, verbal behavior, motor skills, and complex processes, for example, are made use of in child psychology, as well as in studies of social processes. Working

with children or groups, however, often produces experimental problems unlike those encountered in studies utilizing normal adult subjects, serving singly.

In Chap. 14, Child Psychology, Stevenson and Wright are concerned with the selection of subjects, experimental settings and general apparatus, stimulus and response variables (e.g., displays and the selection of stimuli), instructions, withdrawal of reward, failure, and stress effects. A section covering research with exceptional children concludes the chapter. Consult Keppel (1964) for a review of the techniques used to study verbal learning in children and Maccoby (1964) for references covering cognitive processes. A cross-indexed bibliography on research in infant behavior may be found in Brackbill (1964); Ellis (1963) reports on several methods for studying the mentally deficient child.

The methods of social psychology are represented by a wide range of categories. Research techniques are provided and referenced for the study of person-perception, attitude research, social reinforcement, conformity behavior, leadership, interactional processes, and group variables such as group structures and composition. In Chap. 15, Shaw discusses the limitations of some of these methods and suggests modifications wherever possible. Detailed information on experimental and quasi-experimental designs applicable to group research is reported by Campbell and Stanley (1963).

Two chapters in this volume cover methods pertinent to the study of motor skills. Bahrick and Noble's discussion of motor behavior (Chap. 16) emphasizes the variables, tasks, and procedures involved in the study of motor learning and covers quantitative indicants of performance, specification of stimuli, independent variables (e.g., displays and input signals), response characteristics, and procedural variables. An analog-computer application of a motor skills problem is presented in Part Six, Chap. 17. Consult Smith (1962) for a method that utilizes a closed-circuit television system and delayed sensory feedback.

Chapter 12

VERBAL BEHAVIOR

WILLARD N. RUNQUIST

The study of verbal behavior has no fixed boundaries. Any experiment in which a verbal response is used to indicate some state of the subject, or a verbal stimulus or cue provides the occasion for some other kind of response, could be construed as a study of verbal behavior. If, in addition, we include studies in which the experimenter's or the subject's overt verbalizations influence the subject's behavior, the study of verbal behavior encompasses virtually all studies performed on the human organism older than two years.

Only investigations directly concerned with verbal processes will be considered in this chapter. Even with this restriction, the methods used to study verbal processes are limited only by the ingenuity of experimenters. A tremendous variety of specific procedures has been devised to meet special purposes of a single or small set of investigations. Many of these special techniques have not been used extensively enough for experimenters to learn their advantages and limitations. However, some techniques have been used to such an extent that they might be considered standard. This extensive use serves as an empirical justification for their general usefulness in studying verbal processes.

This chapter will consider four classes of techniques: (1) word-association and related techniques, (2) scaling of verbal materials, (3) traditional verbal-learning procedures, and (4) verbal conditioning. The first two represent attempts to assess existing language habits or the structure of verbal processes. The last two procedures usually are concerned with the dynamics of these processes.

ASSOCIATION TECHNIQUES

Word-association techniques long have been part of the clinical psychologists and psychiatrists' battery of diagnostic procedures, although in recent years the association test has been one of the primary research tools for the study of verbal processes in general. Earlier studies (Kent and Rosanoff, 1910) were concerned primarily with establishing norms. Recent applications of the method have suggested its usefulness for discovering relationships between variables involved in the structure of verbal processes and testing specific hypotheses concerning their nature (e.g., Deese, 1962b; Palermo and Jenkins, 1963).

In this section, procedures involved in collecting data by the association techniques will be described, followed by discussion of some of the more generally useful methods of analyzing association data.

The basic procedure involves presenting

the subject with some kind of stimulus and asking for a verbal response. There is virtually no limit to the variations on this procedure, so that such diverse kinds of task as scaling association value (Glaze, 1928) and the Rorschach or Thematic Apperception Test (TAT) projective techniques could be considered variations on the association technique. Most of the methodological problems are common regardless of the variations in either stimuli or kinds of response demanded.

Selection of stimuli

Stimuli can consist of virtually anything that the experimenter desires to fit the purposes of the investigation, although, for the purposes of investigating verbal behavior, the stimuli have generally been words or word-like items such as combinations of two or three letters (bigrams and trigrams). The first consideration is to select the class of stimuli to be used. The experimenter usually desires to generalize his findings to classes of stimuli not used in the specific study as well as to subjects not used in the specific study. Thus, the class of stimuli selected should be representative of a broader class of stimuli in which an experimenter is interested (Attneave and Arnoult, 1956; Brunswik, 1947). Random selection provides a statistical basis for generalizability, but this procedure is seldom used except, perhaps, in exploratory studies where there is little rational basis for using particular stimuli. There are some advantages to be obtained by using classes of stimuli that have been used previously. The main advantage is comparability of findings, but it is also helpful to have some knowledge concerning the kinds of data that are likely to be obtained from a given set of stimuli. Regardless of the reasons for selecting a given class of stimuli, the population from which the specific items are selected should be clearly specified.

The same principles are involved in selecting specific items. The number of items depends upon the purposes of the experiment, as well as certain practical considerations

such as amount of available time. If a study is to produce norms, it is desirable to use as many stimuli as possible, preferably the entire population of a given class. If the study is to test some specific hypothesis, it is necessary to use enough stimuli to contain a representative sample of stimuli of the desired type and to produce stable data. A larger number of stimuli allows uncontrolled variables and idiosyncratic characteristics of particular items to exert less effect on the overall results. Generally speaking, the sample should be as large as possible within the practical limitations of the procedure.

Procedures

Word-association tasks can be classified in terms of two variables: continuous versus discrete associations and restricted versus unrestricted responses (Woodworth and Schlosberg, 1954). The combinations of these variables provide four different methods of collecting association data. The continuous procedure requires the subject to give a series of associations to each stimulus in a fixed length of time (Noble, 1952). Subjects may be instructed to respond only to the stimulus word or they may be allowed to respond to their own responses, although it is doubtful that careful instructions and cooperative subjects can produce responses entirely independent of previous responses. The discrete-association method simply allows a single response to each stimulus, with the subject instructed to give the "first word he thinks of" (Russell and Jenkins, 1954). This method has two advantages: (1) More stimuli can be used in a given time period since the time necessary for one association can be quite short (5 to 10 seconds), and (2) the single response usually occurs directly to the presented stimulus. The restricted-unrestricted dimension refers to the class of responses from which the subject is allowed to draw. "Free" association puts no restrictions upon his responses, but for some purposes it may be desirable to restrict associations to some general class. For example, Underwood and Richardson (1956b) allowed their subjects to give only words referring to a sensory description of the stimulus. When restricted associations are desired, the subjects must be carefully instructed to ensure that they understand the restrictions involved. Extended examples should be given during the instruction period and the subjects allowed to give associations to "practice" stimuli.

The simplest procedure for presenting verbal stimuli is the use of booklets. The subjects are required to work through the booklet, writing their responses to each word. The fact that subjects work at their own pace may be either an advantage or a disadvantage. The disadvantages arise largely from the possibility of subjects thinking about their responses rather than simply writing down the first response that occurs. This difficulty may be avoided, and the advantages of group data collection maintained, by presenting stimuli on slides or filmstrips and/or auditorily. When a visual method of presentation is used, an auditory signal (e.g., a buzzer) may be useful to indicate that a new stimulus is being presented. The ordinal number of the stimulus also should be announced so that the subject's responses are recorded in the appropriate place on the data sheet. Allowing subjects to see previous responses may not be an ideal procedure, but most investigators have not been concerned with this problem. Specific order effects may be minimized by using different random orders of presentation with different subgroups, so that having several items on a single page probably does not seriously influence results.

The only apparent drawback to group methods of data collection is the restriction placed on useful response measures. Latency and other physical characteristics of the response cannot be obtained from large groups of subjects. When subjects are run individually, oral responses may be recorded on a tape recorder and scored later for latency or qualitative characteristics. Latency may also be recorded by a voice-key arrangement in which the sound of the verbal response closes a relay, thus stopping a clock or making a mark on a moving paper strip. This method does have drawbacks in that extraneous sounds also may cause the switch to operate.

Group methods are less suitable for the continuous-association technique since the process of writing each associate slows the subject considerably (a subject can generally think of associates faster than he can write) If individual words are not necessary, the subject may be required to make tally marks as he thinks of a word. Most of the specific words can be recalled later (Woodworth and Schlosberg, 1954). There are few data comparing the results obtained by these various procedures.

Amount of material

When material is presented in booklets, subjects can handle up to 300 items per hour, depending upon the material. It is wise to run a small pilot group to ascertain the exact amount of material that can be handled in a given session. The length of the instruction period is also an important determiner of amount of material to be given in the first session. The best estimate is about 10 seconds for each stimulus.

Studies of word associations require relatively large numbers of subjects by usual experimental standards. For normative studies 500 to 1,000 subjects usually are used; whereas for studies in which specific hypotheses are being tested, approximately 50 subjects seem to give relatively stable data (Deese, 1962a). Sample size depends to some extent upon the kind of data that must be collected. If common responses are of concern, fewer subjects are needed to obtain stable results. If an analysis of relatively idiosyncratic responses is intended, more subjects may be necessary to obtain enough of these responses to analyze.

Experimental design

The main problem in design is the sequence in which the stimuli are presented to the subjects. Experimenters are often advised to balance out specific order effects by presenting different orders of stimuli to different subgroups of subjects. In most studies, the number of stimuli is so large that complete counterbalancing is impractical. The simplest way to handle systematic progressive changes or context effects is to arrange the stimuli in relatively large blocks of 20 to 50 items. The blocks then may be presented in different random orders for different subgroups, or a Latin-square counterbalancing procedure may be used. The latter has some advantage in that analysis of variance techniques may be used to assess the contribution of overall progressive effects and interactions.

One convenient procedure for the booklet-type task is to randomize or partially counterbalance the pages. Different subjects can be given different orders in the same sessions.

If the number of stimuli is extremely large or the amount of time that a subject can serve is limited, it is often desirable to reduce the amount of work required of the subject. Compromise designs are possible in which large groups of subjects are tested on different sets of stimuli (Krueger, 1934). If normative data are desired, it is necessary to test large groups to obtain scores that have a small standard error. It is also useful to overlap the sets of stimuli to compare results from the same stimuli in the two or more samples.

Instructions

A typical set of *discrete-association instructions* (Russell and Jenkins, 1954) for presentation to a group of subjects reads as follows:

"This particular experiment is on free association. Please write your name on the outside of the paper passed to you. When you open these sheets, you will see a list of 100 stimulus words. After each word write the first word that it makes you think of. Start with the first word; write the word it makes you think of; then go on to the next word. Use only a single word for each response. Do not skip any

words. Work rapidly until you have finished all 100 words. Are there any questions? Ready. Go."

Special instructions suitable for use with elementary school children are given by Goodenough (1942); and instructions used with Navajos, which might be adapted for use with equivalent populations of other language and culture groups, are given by Ervin (1961b). Typical instructions for *continuous associations* contain the following information (Noble, 1952):

"This is a test to see how many words you can think of and write in a short time. You will be given a key word and you are to write as many other words as the key word brings to mind. The words which you write may describe things, places, ideas, events, or whatever you happen to think of when you see the key word. For example, think of the word KING. Some of the words or phrases which KING might bring to mind are: queen, kingdom, King Cole, ruler, Sky-King, England, imperial, kingfish.

"No one is expected to fill in all the spaces on a page, but write as many word associations as you can. Be sure to think back to the key word after each written response since the test is to determine the number of other words that you associate with the key word. A good way to do this is to repeat the key word over and over to yourself as you write."

Response analyses

In most association studies, particularly those where data are collected by the group method, a number of unacceptable responses are obtained. When the discrete-association technique is used, these are largely limited to illegible responses, although if restrictions are placed on the kinds of response allowed there may also be failures to comply with the restrictions. A common problem with the continuous procedure is perseverative responses or chaining, i.e., responding to the previous response. The usual way of handling these unacceptable responses is to eliminate from the data the subjects who make these responses. To avoid bias, however, objective criteria for unacceptability should be established prior to investigation of the data.

Two basic measures usually are obtained from word-association experiments; both are simply frequency counts. The first measure is restricted to procedures in which a fixed time interval is given for an association to occur (Glaze, 1928) or in which the continuous-association method is used (Noble, 1952). The measure is either the percent of subjects who can give some response to that stimulus (association value) or the mean number of associations occurring to a stimulus in the fixed time interval (meaningfulness). The second measure consists of a frequency count of each specific response to each stimulus. These are the results typically presented in free-association norms (Russell and Jenkins, 1954). Idiosyncratic responses, i.e., those occurring in a very small segment of about 0.5 percent of the sample, are a problem with this measure. Unless they are the special focus of a study or exact norms are desired, these responses may be tabulated together. Measures also may be presented in terms of percent of the total number of responses to each stimulus. This has the advantage of direct comparability across samples of different sizes.

Great care should be exercised in the interpretation of the percent of each particular response occurring to a given stimulus. It is quite tempting to interpret these norms in terms of verbal hierarchies for single subjects. For example, assume that the word "needle" has been presented as a stimulus and 16 percent of the subjects respond "thread," while 4 percent respond "point." Generally the results are interpreted to represent a hierarchy for a single subject in which the response "thread" would occur 16 percent of the time and "point" 4 percent. Theoretically, it should be possible to test this assumption by repeating the association test several times. Unfortunately, successive retests are not likely to be independent; hence, it would be difficult to interpret consistencies from test to test even if they were to be found.

Complex response measures

It is often useful to categorize associations in some way. Many such categorization schemes are possible (Woodworth and Schlosberg, 1954), but no scheme has had general acceptance. In most of the classification schemes, there is a great deal of subjectivity in assigning responses to classes. The safest way to deal with this problem is to use several independent judges, who preferably, do not know the purpose of the study. Although this does not guarantee a reliable classification system, it does provide data from which the reliability may be assessed in terms of interjudge agreement. About 80 percent agreement has been obtained with the classification described by Woodworth and Schlosberg (1954) and Karwoski and Berthold (1945). The following measures are among those more commonly used:

1. *Commonality* is a measure taken on individuals rather than on stimuli, and usually is computed by counting the number of times the subject responds with the most frequent response given by a norm group; e.g., "thread" is the common response in the above example. These scores are objective, thus avoiding classification reliability problems.

2. A *superordinate* response is one in which the response names the class of objects to which the stimulus word belongs; e.g., a superordinate response to "dog" would be "animal." Jenkins and Russell (1960) have devised a procedure for determining superordinate responses using an objective procedure. A standardization group is given a set of sentences of the form "_____is a member of the class_____." Each sentence begins with one of the stimulus words to be used in the association test, and each subject fills in the second blank with a single word response. A superordinate response can be defined as any response given by more than 50 per cent of the subjects. Scoring the association data is completely objective.

This empirical definition of various response classes would appear to be adaptable to many different kinds of classification although it has not been used frequently except with superordinates.

3. The *grammatical (syntactical) analysis* is a method originated by Fries (1952, pp. 65–109) that has been found useful in classifying words in terms of grammatical usage (parts of speech). Contexts are established in test frames; a word then is assigned to a class if it can fit into the frames altered by substitutions from the same grammatical class as the words in the frame. Fries lists several grammatical categories obtained by this method. At its simplest, the procedure involves a test frame consisting of a "minimal free utterance," which is a simple short, direct sentence such as "The concert was good." All words that can occupy the same set of positions are taken as belonging to the same part of speech. For example, "food," "taste," "family," and "container" all can be substituted for the term "concert" and still make sense. Adjustments in word forms in the test frame are allowed; e.g., "the" may or may not occur, and plurals may demand a different ending. A given word may occur in more than one category. Fries (1952) presents extended examples and suggests test frames for obtaining the classes. Sets of judges may be used to sort words given as responses into the various classes. Ervin (1961a) has obtained reliabilities of near .90 for most classes, which suggests that more than one judge may not be necessary.

This sentence-transformation method has possible uses with other classification schemes (Deese, 1962b). With the increasing recognition of the importance of grammar and syntax (Glanzer, 1962; Miller, 1962), the procedure may be of considerable value.

4. *Associative overlap* or partial response identity, is a measure of the relationship of two or more words to one another. A simple procedure for computing a quantity called associative overlap from word-association data has been presented by Bousfield, Cohen, and Whitmarsh (1958) and P. M. Jenkins and Cofer (1957). Overlap is defined as the relative frequency of common associations to two words. Consider the two words "needle"

and "scissors." Ignoring the idiosyncratic responses made by less than 0.5 percent of the population, we find that of 1,008 subjects tested on the word "needle," 464 responded with "thread," 55 with "sharp," 64 with "sew," and 18 with "sewing," a total of 601. For "scissors," the responses were "sharp," 90; "thread," 13; "needle," 9; "sew," 8; and "sewing," 8; a total of 128. The remaining 407 responses to "needle" and 880 responses to "scissors" were not shared by these two stimuli. The indices of overlap are computed separately for the two stimuli. When "needle" is the stimulus, it overlaps 601/1,008, or .60, with "scissors." When scissors is the stimulus, the overlap is 128/1,008, or .12, with "needle."

Several different measures of associative relationship have been proposed, each of which may have some advantages for specific research purposes. Marshall and Cofer (1963) review 10 of these measures, including their computation and potential uses, and give relevant references.

When continued association is used, the sequence of responses may be of interest. One measure based on sequences is *clustering*, defined as repetition of words in the same class. This measure is discussed more completely in relation to free-recall studies, where it has had its most extensive use.

SCALING VERBAL MATERIALS

Psychological scaling techniques also may be of great value in assessing the verbal responses to many kinds of stimuli. In general, the use of these techniques for studying verbal behavior follows their use in other areas of psychology in that they represent ways of assigning numbers to stimuli along certain dimensions or attributes. In studying verbal behavior, either the stimuli are words or wordlike (nonsense syllables) or the dimensions or attributes are presumed to represent verbal processes, e.g., meaningfulness.

The use of psychological scaling techniques for verbal materials or verbal attributes is in no way different from their use in measuring attitudes, preferences, or worker ratings. Once an experimenter has decided upon the particular stimuli he is going to scale and the dimension along which he is going to scale these stimuli, several standard scaling procedures are available. Refer to Edwards (1957) for a description of the methods of paired comparisons, equal intervals, and successive intervals. The Coombs methods are described in general terms by Dember (1960) and in greater detail by Coombs (1950, 1953). When collecting data with these techniques, it is not necessary to use the complex card-sorting techniques often used in attitude scaling when single unitary stimuli are being scaled. Often the subjects can record their ratings directly on standard IBM sheets, which can then be machine-scored. A booklet method of presentation is often the most satisfactory from a practical point of view. Many of the advantages of this method have been discussed above in relation to presenting stimuli for association tests. In general, the same procedures apply to the presentation of material for scaling. Typically, however, samples have been somewhat smaller (50 to 350) and the presentation time per item somewhat shorter. Presentation time will depend, to some extent, upon the complexity of the materials and the attribute being rated. Archer (1960) used 2 seconds, but 8 to 10 seconds per stimulus seems to be adequate (Noble, 1961).

Some criticism has been leveled at the booklet method of presentation when rated meaningfulness or association value, i.e., percent of subjects who can think of an association, is being scaled (Archer, 1961). The problem involves the possibility that subjects spend more time on items that are of low association value and hence can think of more associations. This difficulty should be considered when differential rating time is liable to provide interpretive problems.

Semantic differential

The semantic differential is one general scaling method that is used almost exclusively with verbal material. A complete description of the technique and analyses of the data is presented by Osgood, Suci, and Tannenbaum (1958). The subject's task is to rate a series of words or concepts on a series of subjective polar opposite scales; e.g., the word "needle" may be rated on a series of scales such as "BAD-GOOD," "BLACK-WHITE," "SHARP-DULL," or "LOUD-SOFT." A seven-point scale is usually used, with the anchor words representing the extremes and four being neutral. A complete description of a word, such as "needle," consists of the profile of the word on all the scales. Other measures of a word, such as its polarity, or tendency toward extreme scores, may be obtained with each word. The semantic-differential techniques show considerable promise, but there are some difficulties involved, primarily in statistical analysis of data when comparing different sets of words or the same sets of words from different groups of subjects. Since the scores are in terms of a profile on the various scales for each word being rated, multiple comparisons are necessary, and this presents the usual problem of interpreting specific significant differences. Analysis of variance may be used wherever assumptions can be met, but usually this is not sufficiently focalized to point out significant variables. Although the problem is not insurmountable, it is a limitation on the differential technique.

One solution is to derive a single measure, e.g., polarity, for each word or set of words. Factor analysis also can be used to combine some of the scales. For example, Osgood *et al.* (1958) have found three factors labeled evaluative ("GOOD-BAD"), potency ("HARD-SOFT"), and activity ("FAST-SLOW"). Following a factor analysis, scales can be selected for subsequent studies that load high on a desired factor; then the results can be combined for this factor, thus reducing the number of variables to be dealt with. A given word then might be described in terms of four scores: one on each factor and polarity. This solution is not without its difficulties. Carroll (1959), in a general critique of the semantic differential, points out that the factors obtained are most likely a function of the particular scales used in combination with particular concepts.

Reliability

The procedures for obtaining measures of reliability for specific scales usually are given in the general sources (e.g., Edwards, 1957). Generally these are measures of the consistency of mean scale values in successive samples, and for most scales of verbal materials are quite high. Another check on reliability is provided by having the subjects rate some of the material more than once (Archer, 1960). This may be done by mixing the repeated material with the regular material or by repeating an entire sequence at the end of the experiment. The problem is largely the same as that with association tests, namely, ensuring that the successive scalings are independent. When the number of stimuli is large, such independence is likely.

Scaled materials

An extensive list of scaled materials is shown in Table 12-1. Tables 12-2 through

Table 12-1   Selected scaled verbal materials.

Reference	Materials	Attribute	Method	N
Noble (1961)	2,100 trigrams	Association value	Rating	200
Noble (1961)	2,100 trigrams	Rated associations	Rating	200
Noble (1961)	2,100 trigrams	Meaningfulness	Rating	200
Archer (1960)	2,480 trigrams	Meaningfulness	Rating	216
Witmer (1935)	4,524 consonant trigrams	Association value	Association	25
Battig (1959)	High-meaningfulness trigram pairs	Difficulty of learning	Rating	82
Richardson and Erlebacher (1958)	Word pairs and trigram pairs	Associative connection	Rating	25–56
Noble (1958)	Paralogs	Emotionality	Rating	200
Noble (1952, 1958)	Paralogs, words	Meaningfulness	Association	131 (119)
Noble (1953)	Paralogs, words	Familiarity	Rating	200
Russell and Jenkins (1954)	Kent-Rosanoff words	Association norms	Association	1,008
Woodrow and Lowell (1916)	Kent-Rosanoff words	Association norms (children)	Association	
Underwood and Richardson (1956)	Common nouns	Restricted associations (physical description)	Association	153
Battig and Spera (1962)	Numbers 1–100	Association value	Rating	95
Vanderplas and Garvin (1959)	180 random shapes	Association value	Association	50
Jenkins, Russell, and Suci (1958)	360 words	Semantic profiles on 20 scales	Semantic differential	30
Jenkins, Russell, and Suci (1958)	360 words	Semantic distances	Semantic differential	30
Jenkins (1960)	360 words	Polarity, factor scores	Semantic differential	30
Haagen (1949)	400 adjectives in pairs	Vividness	Rating	80
		Association value	Rating	80
		Similarity	Rating	80
		Familiarity	Rating	40
Melton and Safier (1951)	Adjective pairs	Similarity	Rating	96
Thorndike and Lorge (1944)	10,000 words	Frequency	Frequency count	
Underwood and Schulz (1960)	Single letter, bigrams, trigrams	Frequency	Frequency count	
Underwood and Schulz (1960)	239 trigrams	Pronounceability	Rating	181

Table 12-2   Trigrams scaled for association value (Noble, 1961), and meaningfulness (Archer, 1960).

Low	Assoc. value	Meaning	Medium	Assoc. value	Meaning	High	Assoc. value	Meaning
CIJ	25	8	BEH	53	44	BIM	98	100
FOJ	24	11	BOH	60	53	CAT	100	100
GAQ	22	11	BEQ	50	42	DON	100	100
JIH	23	13	CIY	57	40	FOR	100	100
HUJ	24	7	LUQ	49	42	GEM	100	100
KUQ	17	11	JAT	56	41	HUT	98	100
QAH	22	14	FIP	58	42	JOY	98	100
QAZ	21	10	FOH	47	43	LAG	98	100
QEF	22	8	DEH	52	44	MAT	100	100
QIY	20	8	MOY	60	45	PIN	100	100
QUE	24	19	TOH	58	46	WIG	100	100
WIJ	22	13	SIQ	56	47	PUB	97	100
WUQ	22	8	JIR	58	41	GIL	98	95
XAB	17	8	NEF	54	49	JOG	92	95
XAK	22	17	RAJ	60	44	LAM	99	95
XAW	15	8	YOM	48	51	NAT	100	96
XIN	16	10	YUH	43	45	DOL	98	94
XIQ	17	5	ZIN	50	47	CAL	100	96
XEP	22	13	WIY	52	42	WAG	98	99
XEV	16	6	NEQ	56	42	BOR	97	92
XOC	16	9	VEM	59	46	LOB	94	92
YIX	22	9	GEZ	58	42	DIK	92	90
ZEH	24	14	PIF	59	57	SEL	98	90
ZIH	16	6	SOQ	48	49	BUR	98	91
ZUF	22	8	WEH	56	41	RIN	93	92

12-5 show samples of representative items and their scaled values. Low, medium, and high scaled values are presented for trigrams (Tables 12-2 and 12-3), paralogs (Table 12-4), and numbers (Table 12-5). In describing the attribute scaled, the author's terminology has been used for the most part even though the operations defining attributes given the same name are not identical. An experimenter using these materials for further studies should check the original procedures to ensure that the appropriate measure is being used. Noble (1963) has provided an excellent discussion of some of the different procedures used to scale meaningfulness. The correlations between mean scaled values on different attributes are extremely high, .75 to .96, for most measures of trigrams, although not all the relationships are linear. Diverse attributes such as fa-

miliarity, meaningfulness, pronounceability, association values, emotionality, and frequency of occurrence in written discourse, as determined by letter counts, are highly correlated (Noble, 1958, 1963; Underwood and Schulz, 1960). Although these high intercorrelations have provided a fascinating theoretical problem (Staats and Staats, 1959; Underwood and Schulz, 1960), they also indicate that different scaling procedures are not likely to produce very great differences in obtained scale values.

MULTIPLE LANGUAGE UNITS

Although the psychologist's analytical approach to the study of verbal behavior typically has been through the study of single verbal units (words and simple letter combinations), there is a growing interest in the

Table 12-3   Trigrams scaled for pronounceability (Underwood and Schulz, 1960).

Low		Medium		High	
CFL	—7.38	CYR	—5.44	CUB	—1.80
CKB	—8.39	ABL	—5.57	CAT	—1.60
DFL	—7.66	EIG	—5.86	ART	—1.97
EQR	—7.80	GOI	—4.60	FEM	—1.95
FJQ	—8.73	GUD	—4.36	HAT	—1.77
GHT	—7.63	IFO	—4.34	HUM	—1.80
GVS	—8.04	JOK	—4.89	LED	—1.91
LTY	—7.03	LIR	—4.03	MAN	—1.66
MBE	—7.80	NIQ	—5.33	MEL	—1.99
MBK	—8.18	NUW	—5.56	PAR	—1.74
QZP	—8.28	PEH	—5.04	RAT	—1.81
TJU	—7.74	QAD	—4.89	SAY	—1.82
UNH	—7.10	SOU	—4.15	SUD	—1.99
VGF	—8.73	WUX	—4.15	BAD	—1.50
VXK	—8.64	WIH	—5.93	BUT	—1.91
XFH	—8.72	XOL	—5.91	FIB	—1.92
XOQ	—7.71	VIR	—4.69	KIT	—2.15
ZJM	—8.34	YOX	—4.57	BAL	—2.33
YLV	—8.37	KNO	—4.40	LAR	—2.23
WFI	—7.93	BUV	—4.37	VAD	—2.06

study of connected discourse. Indeed, Miller (1962) makes the case that the most important aspect of verbal behavior is the way in which the symbols (words) are arranged in useful combinations. Although studies of connected discourse are not new, particularly in the area of learning (Henderson, 1903), few procedures have appeared that have achieved standard use.

Two general approaches have been used to study multiple language units: (1) analysis of verbal discourse and (2) analytical experimentation in which subjects are required to respond to connected discourse in some way.

Analysis of verbal discourse

One method for obtaining discursive material for analysis is the "eavesdropping" technique. "Eavesdropping" simply involves recording free speech. Since the technical and ethical aspects of this procedure are difficult to surmount, a restricted eavesdropping

Table 12-4   Paralogs scaled for meaningfulness (m), familiarity (f), and emotionality (e) (Noble, 1952, 1958).

Low	m	f	e	Medium	m	f	e	High	m	f	e
GOJEY	0.99	0.21	2.16	NIMBUS	2.26	1.34	2.13	HUNGER	6.02	3.98	2.98
NEGLAN	1.04	0.69	1.99	LEMUR	2.28	1.01	2.06	ZERO	6.15	3.85	2.84
MEARDON	1.05	0.73	2.03	CAPSTAN	2.41	1.31	1.85	INCOME	6.24	4.06	2.27
BYSSUS	1.13	0.39	2.20	PERCEPT	2.43	2.30	2.13	UNCLE	6.57	4.34	2.15
BALAP	1.22	0.74	2.10	LICHENS	2.48	1.67	2.29	YOUNGSTER	6.75	3.85	2.24
VOLVAP	1.22	0.17	2.12	JETSAM	2.54	0.67	2.16	TYPHOON	6.83	2.81	2.87
TAROP	1.24	0.62	2.05	ENDIVE	2.59	1.59	2.16	CAPTAIN	6.88	4.27	2.41
XYLEM	1.24	0.40	2.07	TARTAN	2.63	1.85	2.20	ZEBRA	7.12	2.74	2.19
LATUK	1.26	0.17	2.23	OVUM	2.69	1.31	2.35	GARMENT	7.17	3.69	2.37
QUIPSON	1.26	0.64	2.04	ROSTRUM	2.73	1.93	2.20	VILLAGE	7.28	3.67	2.26
GOKEM	1.27	0.16	2.13	VERTEX	2.76	2.17	2.17	INSECT	7.39	3.97	2.87
NARES	1.28	0.96	2.10	BODICE	2.80	1.58	2.21	JEWEL	7.58	3.71	2.12
ZUMAP	1.28	0.19	2.12	TANKARD	2.89	1.71	2.47	JELLY	7.70	4.11	2.10
POLEF	1.30	0.00	2.14	PALLOR	3.06	2.33	2.27	HEAVEN	7.91	4.19	1.99
SAGROLE	1.33	0.42	2.12	SEQUENCE	3.21	2.54	2.16	OFFICE	7.95	4.44	2.55
NOSTAW	1.34	0.10	2.20	ARGON	3.34	2.00	2.08	WAGON	8.12	3.93	2.35
BODKIN	1.39	0.90	2.07	RAMPART	3.36	2.21	2.27	DINNER	8.33	5.22	2.06
ULNA	1.50	0.81	2.09	JITNEY	3.51	2.17	2.20	MONEY	8.98	5.66	2.28
WELKIN	1.53	1.49	1.99	ENTRANT	3.55	2.60	2.11	ARMY	9.43	4.79	3.00
ICON	1.54	0.91	2.07	PALLET	3.62	2.52	2.26	KITCHEN	9.61	4.71	2.34

procedure is often more suitable. The subject may be given some kind of interview that is recorded either by the experimenter or, preferably, on a tape recorder. The trick is to keep the subject talking while directing his discussion as little as possible. This procedure is similar to the "nondirective" interview in that it takes much skill and practice to be used most effectively. Brown and Fraser (1963), reporting a technique for recording the verbal discourse of children, point out that direct questions are seldom effective at eliciting conversation since they often are answerable by one or two words and hence have the effect of ending discussion. To increase the operant level of speech, they purposely "brought up" topics of interest to the subject. The same procedure may be effective with adults.

More structure can be imposed by the use of specific stimuli such as TAT cards. The use of such standardized stimuli has some advantage in that the topic of discussion is the same for each subject, making linguistic analysis somewhat easier. The sentence-completion test is a method that may be useful in obtaining sentences for analysis.

There are several schemes for the analysis of connected discourse, none of which have achieved standard use with the exception of the clinical analyses used on projective tests. The problem in analysis is to reduce the mass of data to some easily comprehensible and reliably scorable set of numbers or categories. Reliability is a primary concern since some schemes do not exhibit this property (Cronbach, 1960, p. 569). Two classes of analysis can be made: *structural analysis* and *content analysis*. Structural analysis consists in its simplest form of tabulating the frequency of occurrence of particular words or analyzing the grammatical structure of the material presented. Content analysis consists of an analysis of the "meaning" of the material. Although a kindling interest in grammar and its function in verbal behavior has led to several recent studies (Brown and Fraser, 1963; Miller, 1962), no good sum-

Table 12-5   Numbers scaled for association value (Battig and Spera, 1962).

Low	Medium	High
31—0.72	56—1.55	100—3.56
53—0.79	81—1.61	1—3.38
83—0.79	97—1.61	0—3.31
71—0.83	70—1.65	2—3.11
57—0.84	28—1.69	13—3.06
46—0.85	32—1.69	21—3.03
73—0.86	76—1.69	10—2.96
59—0.88	44—1.73	25—2.85
74—0.90	80—1.74	99—2.80
37—0.93	58—1.78	16—2.72
47—0.95	17—1.85	4—2.71
87—0.95	48—1.86	50—2.69
58—0.98	96—1.91	18—2.67
41—1.00	30—1.96	7—2.62
51—1.02	27—1.98	5—2.57

mary techniques have been achieved for grammatical analysis. Most summaries of data simply represent frequency counts of various kinds of grammatical usage, with the particular categories varying as a function of the purpose of the investigation. For example, Brown and Fraser (1963) categorized children's utterances in terms of the mean number of morphemes, whether "be" was in progressive form and whether the modal auxiliaries "will" and "can" were used appropriately.

The analysis of content of verbal discourse is similarly complicated. Useful scoring schemes may be found among methods designed for clinical use (Klopfer, 1942) or for the study of individual differences (McClelland, Atkinson, Clark, and Lowell, 1953). One of the oldest methods of analyzing verbal discourse is the use of idea units (e.g., Henderson, 1903). With any discursive passage, the number of possible ways of dividing the passage into units of ideas is tremendous, so that reliability of scoring is a primary problem. Unfortunately, the problem is not easy to solve. Levitt (1956) had 31 presumably competent subjects attempt to divide four prose passages into idea units and found significant variations in his judges. He suggests that division into grammatical entities or grammatical idea groups may be more suitable. An example of such a division is, "He/went/for days/ with very little sleep/ and is/so tired/that he/can barely move/a muscle."

A second method of reducing discourse for content analysis has been devised by Laffal (1961). A "dictionary" of verbal categories was devised by analyzing the free speech of a standardization group of subjects. These are conceptual categories selected so that any major concepts, whether noun, modifier, or verb, can be placed in one of the categories. Passages then can be compared in terms of their profile frequencies on each category. Although Laffal's particular categories may not be of general use, his method of deriving them and scoring samples of discourse is promising, provided that suitable reliability in defining categories and sorting words into them can be obtained.

Responses to discourse

A second class of connected discourse procedures involves the presentation of passages to which the subject makes a response. The two procedures that have been used most often are *speech-intelligibility tests* (recognition) and *sentence or prose-passage recall.*

The usual method for conducting speech-intelligibility studies is to read sentences, or words, over a background of random noise and demand that the subject repeat the sentence immediately. Percent words correct is the common measure, although a measure of complete recognition of the sentence may also be used (Miller, Heise, and Lichten, 1951). Since there are a number of variables that determine the absolute level of accuracy, a type of recognition threshold may also be obtained. Various signal-to-noise intensity ratios are used and the number of correct recognitions determined at each point. Although several standard psychophysical methods may be used to collect the data, there are some problems peculiar to the use of verbal materials. A decision must be made concerning the advisability of repeating the same sentence at the same or different noise levels. If not, complex counterbalancing schemes are necessary to handle effects of differential sentence difficulty. Standardization of presentation can be achieved by tape recording both material and noise. Careful calibration of the intensity of stimuli is essential. Sentences should be short enough to be repeated accurately under no-noise conditions, or the results will be confounded with memory.

Immediate or delayed recall procedures are similar to the intelligibility test except that no physical masking of the material is used. The procedures are much the same as those used for short-term memory or free-recall studies. Sentences may be presented auditorily or visually. With the visual method, old reading habits may allow some subjects to skip part of the material. This problem is alleviated somewhat by forcing the subject to read aloud. Slamecka (1960) has used a standard serial anticipation learning procedure for presenting connected discourse visually. The material is presented one word at a time, the subject being required to anticipate the next word in the sequence. The one drawback to this procedure is that the initial stages may involve a large component of rote learning until the subject is able to "make sense" of the material. A variation on the Slamecka technique is to use the recall rather than the anticipation method (Battig and Brackett, 1961).

The main problem in all recall procedures is scoring. It is possible to score correct responses in terms of complete recall of a given sentence or in terms of the percent or number of words recalled. When the material consists of a whole passage, however, there are some defects in these procedures. Complete recall even of single sentences is unnecessarily restrictive and may not be sensitive enough to actual differences in performance. The usual method involves some kind of idea groups (Henderson, 1903).

Problems involved in scoring idea groups have already been discussed in relation to measures of free verbal discourse.

A relatively simple procedure has been devised by Taylor (1953). The method, called the Cloze procedure, is a variation of the sentence-completion method. A written statement is presented to the subject in which certain words or phrases are deleted, and the subject must fill in the blanks. His score is the number of words correctly filled in. The method may be used as a retention test, as a way of generating norms, or as a way of testing sentence recognition, depending upon how it is administered.

At least one study (King, 1960; King and Schultz, 1960) has shown that several measures of recall of connected discourse are highly correlated. These measures are the following: number of idea groups recalled; number of sentences present in recall; number of content words present; total number of words present; number of identical words; rank ordering by a set of judges; and modification of the Cloze procedure, which consists in deleting every tenth word from the original passage and then determining whether it can be filled in from the recall protocol. Factor analysis revealed two factors, one related to content, the other to length (total number of words). King suggests that measures of recall of various kinds of material under various conditions may be reflected in changed factor loadings.

When the exact recall of sentences is demanded, it may be useful to score the different types of error made. Several schemes may be used, depending on the purposes of the study. One classification that appears promising involves syntactical errors (transformation of the sentence to a new grammatical form), omissions, and other errors (Miller, 1962). "Other" errors may be broken down into such categories as word substitutions and omitted modifiers.

Two additional procedures show promise for studying the grammatical aspects of verbal behavior. The first of these is a simple sentence-completion task devised by Berko (1958). The ubiquitous nonsense syllable was used in a relatively new way. A child was shown a picture of a small animal and told, "This is a 'WUG.' Now there are two of them. There are two _____." The child was to complete the sentence. The procedure was used to determine the child's rules for grammar. It readily can be adapted to verb forms and other parts of speech. In a modification of the technique, Brown and Berko (1960) showed children pictures of a little girl and told them, "This is a girl thinking about a 'WUG.' Can you make up what that may mean?" The children then made up sentences using "WUG." Its grammatical meaning, in this case a singular noun, was given by its use in the sentence. The response measured was the number of sentences in which "WUG" was used correctly. Other sentences can be given using nonsense words as other parts of speech, e.g., "She wants to 'WUG' something." This procedure may need some modification if it is to be used with adults; otherwise it is too simple. One such modification is to use a multiple-choice procedure in which a key sentence is given, e.g., "She is thinking about a 'WUG,'" followed by a series of sentences in which "WUG" is used in different contexts and as different parts of speech. The subject is required to select those which reflect the original meaning of "WUG."

A technique quite similar to this has been presented by Miller (1962) and is called the sentence-transformation test. The purpose of this test is to investigate the transformation of sentences from one grammatical form to another. The test consists in presenting a set of simple "kernel" sentences and measuring the number of these sentences that can be transformed in a given time. The sentences may have the affirmative-passive form ("Joe was liked by the small boy"), and the instructions may be to transform this to the negative-passive form ("Joe was not liked by the small boy"). Miller has used 18 kernel sentences, and measures transformation time by having the subjects match each "kernel" with its appropriate transformation, which occurs in another list of 18 sentences. One minute is allowed for the subject to proceed as far as possible. Under a variety of conditions reported by Miller (1962, pp. 758–759), the mean number of sentences matched ranged from approximately five to eleven with college student subjects.

VERBAL LEARNING

Although some investigations of the learning of verbal materials have presented prose passages or connected discourse, most of the work has been concerned with the learning of single verbal units, words or nonsense syllables, arranged in lists.

Verbal-learning techniques can be classified on the basis of how the materials are arranged for learning and what is required of the subject. Four basic procedures may be identified, with a number of variations within each procedure. The basic procedures are paired-associate learning, serial learning, verbal-discrimination learning, and free recall. The arrangement of material for the first three methods is shown in Table 12-6. The paired-associate procedure is the more commonly used and may be likened to the learning of a foreign-language vocabularly. The words are arranged in pairs, the first member of the pair being called the *stimulus* or *stimulus term,* and the second member of the pair called the *response* or *response term.* The subject is required to associate the two

Table 12-6   Three arrangements for presenting verbal materials for learning.

Paired-associate learning	Serial learning	Verbal-discrimination learning	
LOVELY-RESTING	RANCID	NIMBLE VAGRANT	VAGRANT
UPHILL-FILMY	BARBED	HUMAN WAXEN	HUMAN
OLDISH-INSTANT	ADRIFT	FILTHY ICY	ICY
DRASTIC-LATENT	EQUAL		
PIOUS-MATURE	JELLIED	VACANT DUAL	VACANT
ROBUST-HEATHEN	UPHILL	LOVELY RESTING	RESTING
EXACT-WAXEN	FILMY	UPHILL FILMY	UPHILL
VACANT-DUAL	OLDISH		
NIMBLE-ADRIFT	INSTANT	OLDISH INSTANT	OLDISH
ADRIFT-EQUAL	DRASTIC	DRASTIC LATENT	LATENT
	BIZARRE	PIOUS MATURE	PIOUS
	WARLIKE	ROBUST HEATHEN	HEATHEN
		EXACT ADRIFT	ADRIFT
		JELLIED RANDOM	RANDOM

words in the pair so that he can recall the response term when presented with the stimulus term. In the serial-learning technique, a series of words is presented, the subject being required to learn the items in order. The verbal-discrimination procedure has not been extensively employed. In this method, the words are presented in pairs, one of the words being arbitrarily selected by the experimenter as being "correct." The subject is required to learn which of the words is the correct one in each pair. The fourth method, free recall, is similar to serial learning in method of stimulus presentation. The subject, however, is not required to learn the order of the words, but may recall them in any order. This procedure also may be used with the paired-associate method of presentation if the subject is asked simply to recall the response terms without concern about the particular stimuli with which they are paired (Underwood, Runquist, and Schulz, 1959).

Paired-associate learning

Line drawings of common objects, nonsense shapes, English words in various grammatical categories, nonsense combinations of English letters, foreign words, and single letters and numerals have been used to make up lists for paired-associate learning. With such a wide variety of materials it is virtually impossible to make specific recommendations about choice of particular stimuli for a given experiment. Since it is generally to an experimenter's advantage to know the kinds of verbal associations that are elicited by the items in his lists, as well as their other attributes, the most useful sources of materials are the scaled materials listed in Tables 12-1 to 12-5. The use of these materials also provides comparability to many other studies in which they have been used.

The criterion of representativeness is also of concern. Ideally, a class of stimuli should be selected that is representative of the class of stimuli to which the experimenter wishes

to generalize his results. Random sampling of specific instances from this class should provide the materials for a given experiment. If an experimenter were concerned with learning lists of English adjectives, he might sample randomly from a group of adjectives that had been scaled for various attributes such as Haagen's lists (1949). Such random selection often can lead to difficulties of interpretation, particularly in studies where characteristics of the materials rather than procedural variables are being investigated. Many of the attributes of verbal materials produce large effects on rate of learning, e.g., meaningfulness, association value, pronounceability, and similarity. Even if these attributes were completely independent (uncorrelated), which they are not, random sampling with respect to any one or all of them might produce lists differing widely in average value on other attributes. For example, an experimenter might be interested in comparing lists of three-letter combinations (trigrams) of differing meaningfulness. A source for such materials is Archer's list (1960) of all consonant-vowel-consonant (CVC) trigrams scaled for meaningfulness. Drawing two random samples from the Archer lists, one from the 0 to 20 percent range and one from the 80 to 100 percent range could easily result in lists differing in similarity. Since similarity is defined in terms of the number of repeated letters among the syllables within the samples, fewer letters appear in the trigrams of 0 to 20 percent than in those of 80 to 100 percent. Differences in learning rate could be seriously influenced by small variations in similarity and either enhance or inhibit the effects of meaningfulness.

A more sound procedure than the vagaries of random sampling is to sacrifice some generality and select only from populations of items with restricted characteristics, e.g., items of low similarity. Restrictions may be added indefinitely, thus gaining in precision at the expense of generality. Since not all the attributes of the materials that affect the rate of learning are known, it is inevitable that selection of items will have to be essentially random for some attributes. It is recommended that attributes known to have a very large effect on learning rate be held constant. To obtain generality, factorially designed studies may be used in which the effects of one attribute are investigated over several values of another.

A procedure used to minimize the confounding effects of accidental sampling errors with respect to items utilizes several sets of lists for a given study rather than a single list or a single set of lists. It would be unlikely, in the example cited above, that four sets of lists would contain the same bias with respect to similarity. Averaging the learning results across sets of lists usually minimizes the effects of such variables. This method does well in handling the effects of attributes that are unknown, although controlling these effects would appear to be a superior procedure when it is desirable to eliminate the effects of attributes that are known to have a particularly powerful effect.

When the experimenter is interested in a procedural variable, the sampling problem is not so acute. The major effect of sampling from material that has a wide variety of values on one or several attributes is to increase the variability. No bias will occur unless there is an interaction involving the attribute and the procedural variables being investigated. A choice must be made between generality and precision. The methodological and analytical predilections of the experimenter are often the only guides. Generality may be increased by constructing several equivalent lists to be used in a given experiment (Underwood and Schulz, 1960). Two or more sets of items may be selected, and several different pairings of these items used to reduce the likelihood that a single item can influence the overall results to any great extent.

In paired-associate learning, both stimulus and response items must be selected. Most of the earlier studies used lists in which the stimulus terms and response terms came from the same class, e.g., paired adjectives or paired trigrams. In recent studies different classes have been used for stimulus and response terms, e.g., trigram-adjective pairs. Although the choice of material will depend upon the purpose of the investigation, the use of different classes for stimulus and response terms has some advantages when it is possible to use lists of this type. The main advantage is to minimize the interference between stimulus and response terms. If the stimulus terms are all trigrams and the response terms two-syllable adjectives, the subject should be less likely to confuse them during learning.

Certain classes of material may be more appropriate for use as stimulus terms or response terms, depending upon the purpose of the study. When selecting stimuli, two factors are important in addition to the problem of representativeness: (1) the associations elicited by these stimuli and (2) whether or not the subject treats the stimulus as an integrated unit or tends to analyze the stimulus into separate dimensions or components (Shepard, 1963; Underwood, 1963). Most stimulus materials of general use have been scaled for the number of associations elicited, but it is not possible to compare the association value across different classes. Intuitively, when one desires stimulus items that are high in association value, English words of high frequency of occurrence probably represent the extreme (Thorndike and Lorge, 1944). For materials of low association value, trigrams of low meaningfulness (Archer, 1960) or nonsense shapes of low association value represent the extremes. Since there has been little systematic work on the problem of analyzability, recommendations are more difficult to justify. Materials that clearly seem to be treated as units are common words and simple geometrical figures that vary only in a single attribute, e.g., colored circles (Shepard and Chang, 1963). Examples of stimuli that appear to be analyzed are low-meaningfulness trigrams (Underwood, Rehula, and Keppel, 1962) and geometrical figures differing in more than one clearly defined attribute (Shepard, Hovland, and Jenkins, 1961).

Similar problems arise in selecting materials to be used for response terms. Three main candidates for use as response terms are common words, various letter combinations not forming words (trigrams, bigrams, or single letters), and numerals. When it is desirable to use response terms that already are treated as single units, common words and single numerals or letters are probably most suitable. Letter combinations that do not form words usually must be integrated into a single unit during learning before the subject can repeat the response term correctly (Underwood and Schulz, 1960). Although some integration may be necessary with common words, this factor would appear to be minimized. Numerals consisting of more than a single digit also must be integrated in most cases.

Numerals or single letters are particularly useful when the experimenter desires to specify either the stimulus-term or response term population to the subject before learning begins (Bower, 1961; Marshall and Runquist, 1963). The subject may be told, for example, that the response terms consist of numbers from 1 to 10 or the letters from A to E.

Once the class of materials for both stimulus and response terms has been selected, the experimenter must select the particular members of these classes and arrange them into pairs. Although it may be possible to select items at random, care must be taken that "bad items" do not result from this procedure. Unless the specific purposes of the experiment demand otherwise, the usual procedure in both selection and pairing is to avoid items that can somehow be associated with one another. If the items within the set of stimuli or within the set of responses are related, usually the result is interference. If the stimulus and response terms are easily associated, facilitation of the learning of this pair is likely to result. The relation may be in terms of direct similarity of meaning ("UNCLEAN-DIRTY"), similarity of sound ("STUFF-ROUGH"), similarity in identical elements ("XUC-XUH"), commonality of association ("SNOW-WHITE"), or

a common mediating association ("ARMY-OCEAN," mediated by "NAVY"). The final list should be checked carefully to make sure that material related in these ways is not included unless specifically desired. Several people should search the material independently for poor items. It is particularly difficult to discover mediated relationships. Many of these are so idiosyncratic to individuals that it may be impossible to select items that are unrelated for all subjects. Most of the items likely to influence data from several subjects can be discovered with a careful search. Such mediated relationships may be discovered by using the overlap measure obtained from word-association data. Although evidence concerning the effect of complex mediating associations on learning is not great, such effects do appear to occur with some regularity (McGehee and Schulz, 1961). The safest procedure is to avoid them if they present an interpretive problem. It is also advisable to guard against effects produced when a stimulus for one item is related to the response term of another item. Published scale values or word-association norms may often be used to check the items for powerful mediation phenomena.

All items in the lists may begin with a different letter and contain as few common syllable sounds, prefixes, and suffixes as possible in order to further reduce the possiblity of word-item interaction. When relatively low meaningful material is used, the interactive effects usually are due to the use of identical letters in different stimulus or response terms. Similarity may be reduced by using as many different letters as possible and by not repeating a given letter in the same position in two separate items. It is impossible to avoid some duplication of letters and other formal characteristics if the lists consist of many items. As the number of items increases, the formal similarity between items increases.

The degree of relationship between items used in lists is relative, and formal similarity (identity in sounds and spelling) could be reduced even further by using one item from various classes of material such as one trigram, one bigram, one number, one picture, one nonsense shape, or one two-syllable word.

Detailed specifications of each list should be given in reporting the results of studies. A description of how the list was constructed should also be included. One procedure for selecting materials is to take lists that have been used in previous investigations. Many experimenters present their materials in reports, and others supply their lists upon request. Lists selected in this way should be checked as carefully as newly constructed lists since they often contain defects.

The number of pairs making up a list depends upon the available time, difficulty of material, and ability of the population. Lists have commonly averaged about ten pairs, the range being from four pairs of consonant trigrams of extremely high similarity (Underwood and Richardson, 1957) to twenty pairs of common words. For most materials, eight to twelve pairs can be learned easily to one perfect recitation within a 50-minute period when college students are used as subjects.

Care must be taken not to make lists too short, or learning time will be so rapid that the effects of many variables will not be measurable. If too many items are used, learning time is often increased to the extent that the subject loses his motivation or cannot complete the learning within an experimental session. Differential loss of subjects from various experimental conditions may result if lists are too difficult to be learned by all subjects in the time allotted (Underwood and Archer, 1955). A short pilot study is often the only way to determine whether or not the number of items is suitable. Some representatives learning times to one perfect trial by college students are shown in Table 12-7. These values are only approximate and are intended to give some idea of expected learning times for low-similarity material. If a constant number of trials is given rather than carrying the subject to a performance criterion, learning times can be estimated exactly. About five minutes should be allowed for the reading of instructions and other details when estimating time.

There is no requirement that a different response term be used for each stimulus term,

Table 12-7   Estimated learning time in several paired-associate experiments.

Reference	Subjects	Method	Materials	Approx. mean[1] learning time, min	Approx. SD,[2] min
Underwood (1951)	College, practiced	Antic.	Adjectives (10)	7	3
Schulz and Runquist (1960)	College, naive	Antic.	Adjectives (10)	17	9
Battig and Brackett (1961)	College, practiced	Antic.	Shape-No. (12)	20	4
Battig and Brackett (1961)	College, practiced	Recall	Shape-No. (12)	14	4
Underwood (1953a)	College, practiced	Antic.	Trigrams (10); meaning = 46%	18	5
Runquist (1957)	College, naive	Antic.	Adjectives (8)	11	
Underwood, Rehula, and Keppel (1962)	College	Recall	No.-Bigrams (12)	9	
Battig (1962)	College	Recall	Letter-No. (12)	5	2
Battig (1962)	College	Recall	Word-No. (12)	8	2
Lockhead (1962)	College	Recall	Shape-No. (12)	11	2
Lockhead (1962)	College, naive	Antic.	Trigrams (9)	15	8
Lockhead (1962)	College, naive	Recall	Trigrams (9)	18	4

[1] These values were obtained by multiplying the number of trials to one perfect recitation by the time per trial. Intertrial or interitem interval was not taken into account.
[2] Standard deviation.

Table 12-8   Special arrangements of pairs in paired-associate learning.

Standard paired associates	Classification variation	Probability-learning variation
BIH-VERBAL	BIH-VERBAL	BIH-VERBAL
SUJ-TWOFOLD	SUJ-VERBAL	BIH-TWOFOLD
VOM-DIRTY	VOM-DIRTY	VOM-DIRTY
NAC-FLUID	NAC-DIRTY	VOM-FLUID
ZET-PLAYFUL	ZET-PLAYFUL	NAC-PLAYFUL
RUK-URGENT	RUK-PLAYFUL	NAC-URGENT
TAH-WARLIKE	TAH-WARLIKE	TAH-WARLIKE
WEP-SILENT	WEP-WARLIKE	TAH-SILENT
LOZ-EXACT	LOZ-SILENT	WEP-EXACT
DUY-RANDOM	DUY-SILENT	WEP-CUNNING
		LOZ-RANDOM
		LOZ-NOONDAY
		DUY-GLEAMING
		DUY-STEADY

nor that a different stimulus term be used for each response term. Many of these variations have been used to study different aspects of the verbal-learning process. Examples of short lists using the classification and probability-learning variations are given in Table 12-8, along with the standard paired-associate list.

The classification techniques (Bower, 1961; Shepard, 1963) involve the use of more stimulus terms than response terms and may be particularly helpful when the experimenter desires to control for guessing. The data may be corrected for responses that are correct guesses and do not represent learning by using the limiting case of two response terms, such as the numbers 1 to 2 or the letters A and B, and forcing the subject to give one of the two responses when he is tested for learning. A second and more important use of this procedure is the study of concept formation, whereby the various stimulus terms associated with the same response have something in common (identical elements, similarity in meaning, common associates).

The second variation is somewhat similar to the probability-learning techniques (Estes, 1959). The same stimulus is sometimes paired with one response term and sometimes with another. There are no special principles involved in constructing lists for these special purposes, except perhaps in the probability-learning procedure when different frequencies of occurrence of the two response terms are used (Voss, Thompson, and Keegan, 1959). Two lists should be constructed in which each response term serves as the more frequently occurring one. One list might have "VOM-DIRTY" occurring twice for every single occurrence of "VOM-FLUID," while the second list would have two occurrences of "VOM-FLUID" and one occurrence of "VOM-DIRTY."

Experimental designs in verbal learning

Principles involved in good experimental design in any area are also applicable to studies in verbal learning. It is useful, however, to discuss some of these general principles in the special context of verbal-learning experiments, where specific problems often arise.

Verbal-learning experiments can be classified into two main types: those in which the main concern is variations in some characteristic of the material to be learned and those in which the concern is variations in conditions under which learning takes place. There are also experiments involving factorial designs manipulating both procedures and materials, but these do not involve any special problems. Furthermore, there are three general design methods that have been used in these studies: (1) separate groups for different conditions; (2) counterbalanced designs, including Latin squares and variants, in which the same subjects serve in all or some of the conditions; and (3) mixed-list designs in which variations in material are incorporated in the same list, which is learned by all subjects.

The use of separate groups for each condition of the experiment is always appropriate, although other designs are often more efficient under specific circumstances. If this method is used, 20 to 30 subjects per group are usually necessary to obtain adequate sensitivity, although for some conditions as many as 100 subjects per group have been used. If it is desirable to form matched groups, subjects are often given a practice list of the same type of material and matched on trials to criterion or total correct responses. Underwood reports correlations of .57 to .60 between trials to learn a practice list and trials to learn similar lists under various experimental conditions with trigrams and adjectives, respectively (1953a, 1953b). If the learning of practice lists is not appropriate, some paper and pencil tests might be suitable. Kjeldegaard (1962) has had some success with Part IV of the Modern Language Aptitude Test, which correlates approximately .40 to .50 with verbal paired-associate learning, although this is actually a miniature group paired-associate task. There is also the possibility that ability or personality variables differentially predict paired-associate performance with different kinds of material or conditions of learning (Spence, 1956, Chap. 7).

One other recommendation may be made when using the separate-groups design in which the variable under investigation is different lists. If it is possible, one or more pairs should be made common to all lists. Data from these pairs may be analyzed separately to determine whether specific findings are a result of the effect of uncontrolled attributes of the different items used in the different lists.

The extensive use of counterbalanced designs in which the subjects serve in all conditions of the experiment is probably unique to verbal-learning research, although these designs appear to be waning in popularity. Principles involved in using these designs in verbal-learning research have been thoroughly discussed by Underwood (1949a, Chap. 10), who shows applications to experiments where the nature of the material and/or the procedures are varied. The essential characteristics of these methods may be described by a simple experiment involving two conditions: lists of high versus low similarity. Each subject learns both lists, with the counterbalancing accomplished by having half of the subjects learn the high-similarity list first, and half learn the low-similarity list first. This may be conceived of as a simple factorial design with similarity and order of learning as the two variables. The major problem with counterbalanced designs of this type stems from a similarity $\times$ order interaction. If such an interaction is obtained, it is difficult to interpret significant main effects of similarity unless the interaction is of such a nature that differences in the same direction are obtained under both orders. The overall effect of order, usually interpreted as general practice effects, must be the same for both conditions of learning. Failure to meet this condition is usually referred to as *differential transfer* (Underwood, 1949a, p. 107). The problem of order $\times$ conditions interactions is not peculiar to verbal-learning research, but the popularity of these designs makes it particularly important in this area.

Designs of this type are often highly efficient. In many practical situations, e.g., mental hospitals and small colleges, subjects are in short supply. When differential order effects are unlikely and the other assumptions necessary for repeated-measurements designs can be met (Winer, 1962), these designs are suitable.

It is necessary to use different lists for each condition when conditions of learning are manipulated as the independent variables; e.g., if the experiment is concerned with massed versus distributed practice, the subject must learn two lists, one under massed and one under distributed conditions. Since two lists are necessary, half the subjects might learn list 1 and half learn list 2 under massed practice, with each group learning the other list under distributed practice. This procedure would control for the effects of list difficulty, barring, of course, a list × conditions interaction, but would not control for practice effects. Thus, one might split the groups in half again, with each half learning a particular list and conditions of practice combination either first or second. This complication may be avoided if the experimenter does not wish to assess practice effects separate from effects of list difficulty. In the previous example, if list 1 is always given first and list 2 second, the overall order effect is confounded with list difficulty, as are some of the interactions. If the interaction is not significant, and the order effect is not of particular interest, which it usually is not, this partially confounded design is often suitable.

Counterbalanced and partially counterbalanced designs can be quite complex, although the design problems are the same regardless of the number of variables involved.

Refer to Underwood (1949a), Archer (1952), and general texts on design (Edwards, 1960; Winer, 1962) for general considerations involving the use of these designs and their applicability.

There is one other general recommendation that can be made concerning the use of counterbalanced designs. In many cases, an experimenter wishes to avoid interference in either learning or recall from other material learned in the laboratory. When this is the case, counterbalanced designs are not appropriate.

The mixed-list designs are used only when characteristics of the material being learned are the main independent variable. Items from two or more types of material are included in the same list, performance on the different kinds of items being analyzed separately. An example of this procedure is a ten-pair list of trigrams in which five pairs have meaningfulness ratings of 0 to 15 percent and five pairs have ratings of 100 percent. The same principles are involved in constructing mixed or unmixed lists.

These designs have had considerable use in verbal-learning research and will be discussed more fully in relation to transfer studies, where they seem to be of particular value. They have the same advantages as counterbalanced designs in that comparisons of the effects of independent variables are made with correlated means, thus reducing the size of the error variance. The problem of differential transfer is eliminated. There are several minor disadvantages: (1) The generality of the findings may be limited since in a mixed list there are generally fewer pairs of each kind of item than there would be if separate lists were used; and (2) with fewer items, there is a proportionally greater chance that a poor item will bias the results. Both of these objections can be met by using different lists, each consisting of several different items of each type. Underwood and Schulz (1960, p. 244) used six lists of eight number-trigram pairs. Each list contained four sets of two pairs of items in which the sets of trigrams differed in frequency of occurrence. Analysis for frequency of occurrence took advantage of the sensitivity of the mixed-list design, while generality was achieved by having 12 different items at each level, two items in each of six lists. Care should be taken in directly comparing findings from these designs with those using separate groups. This is due to the fact that interactions of various kinds are possible between the different types of item in the mixed-list design. There has been little systematic study of this issue, but it is possible that the two designs could provide different results.

Since list length is usually restricted by practical considerations, there may be some problem in mixed-list designs when there is a larger number of conditions than items. It is possible to construct mixed lists that are not completely mixed, i.e., the lists do not contain the same conditions. In a study concerned with 10 levels of meaningfulness, one list may contain two items from each level from 1 to 5, and another list may contain items from levels 6 to 10. The difficulty with this procedure is the possibility of differential interaction between the various levels. Counterbalancing or a Latin-square-type design might be used, but complete counterbalancing of the above would involve all combinations of the ten levels taken five at a time, or 252 different lists. Although selected orders might be used, it is simpler to use the separate-lists design. There are problems of statistical analysis since any comparison of means involves some subjects contributing to both means and some subjects to only one. Usually other designs can be used that give the same information without these problems.

An experimenter must also consider the effects of using a practice list. One use of practice lists was mentioned above in connection with selecting matched groups of subjects. The major beneficial effect of practice lists is to reduce variability; the major detrimental effect is to produce interference with the material to be learned later. The less similar the learning material is to the material on the practice list, the less likely are interference effects. A compromise often is made by using completely different kinds of material for practice lists and experimental lists, e.g., relatively meaningless trigrams in practice and two-syllable adjectives in learning. Interference effects during learning are probably reduced by using the practice list and the experimental list on different days, although there is no empirical evidence on this matter. Even though practice lists appear to be of some advantage when interference is not of concern, practical considerations such as time and availability of subjects often make it difficult to use this procedure. Not too much appears to be lost when such practice is not given.

The simplest method of presenting materials for learning consists in presenting the subject with the entire list and allowing him to study it for some fixed length of time. Tests are given following the study period. Occasionally a series of shorter study periods, each followed by a test, can be given. This method has shortcomings and is seldom used in analytical studies of the learning process. It may have some uses in applied settings such as educational research, particularly in the learning of connected discourse. The main objection to this method is a failure to control the study time spent on each item. To control this problem, several methods have been devised in which each item gets an equal exposure time on each presentation of this list. The assumption usually is made that this procedure, along with proper instructions, does an adequate job of ensuring equal study time.

Generally three procedures have been used: the *anticipation method*, the *recall method*, and the *prompting method*. The most commonly used measure is the *anticipation method*. The stimulus term for a given pair is presented alone for a brief period of time (anticipation interval) followed by the occurrence of stimulus and response terms together for a brief period (study interval). The subject attempts to repeat the correct response term during the time that the stimulus alone is present. Each presentation consists of a learning trial, when the two terms are both present, and a test trial for previous learning, when only the stimulus is present.

The presentation may be either subject-paced or automatically paced. With subject pacing, the stimulus term is presented alone until the subject makes an overt response. The anticipation interval is of fixed duration for all stimuli with automatic pacing. The duration of the study interval is the same for all pairs in both procedures. The automatically paced procedure usually is considered somewhat better for most purposes since it controls presentation rate. The subject-paced procedure is particularly useful if the population of response terms is specified to the subject before learning and the experimenter wishes to correct the data for guessing. It may not be necessary to use a subject-paced procedure to obtain a response to each item. With some practice and appropriate instructions, it is often possible to get subjects to respond to each item within quite short fixed periods of time such as two to four seconds. The disadvantage to this procedure is that the time between the overt response and the appearance of the paired items may be considerably variable if the anticipation interval is very long, and there is little control over the subject's behavior during this time.

A variation of the subject-paced method allows for "no response" on the part of the subject (Deese and Hardman, 1954). The stimulus term is exposed until the subject either makes a response or indicates that he cannot respond. This procedure appears to be extremely useful when the experimenter desires to analyze overt errors, as it more nearly brings out all potential responses in the subject.

When the procedure is automatically paced, the time intervals of stimulus alone

and stimulus and response term are quite crucial. The "standard" rate is 2 seconds for the stimulus and 2 seconds for stimulus and response (the 2:2 rate). Despite the fact that it is somewhat arbitrary, there appear to be some advantages to the 2:2 rate. If the anticipation interval is much shorter, it may put undue stress upon the subject and hinder his performance (Castaneda, 1956). Time intervals much longer than two seconds introduce variability between the overt response and study interval. In addition, many phenomena, particularly those involving interference or negative transfer, do not appear as clearly with longer intervals (Underwood, 1950). The length of the study interval is governed by similar considerations. To some extent, the choice of a time interval is also dependent upon what is required of the subject. Some experimenters have preferred to have the subject pronounce or spell the stimulus term aloud before attempting to anticipate the correct response term. This takes up some of the time of the anticipation interval and should be allowed for (Schulz and Tucker, 1961). It is also possible to have the subject overtly pronounce or spell the response term when it is shown. There is some advantage to this procedure in that it makes certain that the subject is paying attention to the item being exposed and is not attempting to rehearse the other pairs.

The *recall method* has several variations, but the essential characteristic is a study trial in which all pairs are presented followed by a test trial in which only the stimulus terms are presented. (The main difference from the anticipation method is the temporal separation of learning and test.) Presentation rate is controlled by presenting each pair for a fixed length of time during the study trial. The test trial can be given by exposing each stimulus term in order, the subject being instructed to give the appropriate response term. The recall phase may be paced or unpaced. Problems in pacing are the same as those encountered in the anticipation method. If a subject-paced procedure is used,

8 to 10 seconds is sufficient for the recall interval for each item since few correct responses are likely to occur after this time. Another procedure for presenting the test trial involves a written recall test in which all the stimulus terms are listed on a sheet of paper followed by a blank space in which the subject attempts to write the correct response term. About three minutes is sufficient for the recall of 12 or fewer items. This method may be inferior for analytic studies since (1) it allows more interaction between items than a technique that presents each stimulus term separately and (2) it allows uncontrolled rehearsal.

The *prompting technique* can be categorized as a variation of the recall method. The stimulus term is presented alone for a fixed interval followed by the response term either together with the stimulus term or alone. There is then a short period during which the subject reproduces the response term he has just seen (Cook and Kendler, 1956). Since there is no adequate performance measure on each trial, test trials are given after every trial or at selected points in acquisition. Some data show more rapid acquisition with this method than with the anticipation procedures, and about the same rate as that for the recall method (Sidowski, Kopstein, and Shillestad, 1961). An experimenter can expect the estimated learning times in Table 12-7 to be somewhat less if equivalent materials are used with the prompting technique.

Some studies have used a blank interval between presentations of each item. Often the apparatus or the specific experimental purpose makes this necessary; however, such intervals allow for covert rehearsal and represent a source of uncontrolled variation.

A *trial* usually is defined as one complete presentation of the list. With the recall method a trial consists of both study and recall presentations. A single complete trial is presented before an item is repeated in order to avoid complex interpretative problems.

The pairs are presented in a different order on successive trials to minimize serial learning. Usually three different orders are sufficient with lists consisting of 10 or more items, and four or five orders with shorter lists. Orders may be arranged at random, but usually some restrictions are placed on complete randomness so that the same items do not precede or follow each other more than once and occur in different parts of the list on different orders. Different subjects are usually started on different orders. This procedure smooths out the acquisition curves by balancing out the effects of one order's being easier or harder than the others. There may be a blank interval between successive trials which, for convenience, is of length equal to one presentation interval. Experimenters should not use a blank interval or any other cue separating trials when the number of pairs is small. The subject might increase his performance by "elimination," i.e., by recalling which response terms have not yet appeared. This would seem to be particularly important in short lists run to a criterion. Elimination of the cues marking off a trial may avoid the problem to some extent.

When the intervals between trials are longer than a few seconds, special activities are used to prevent rehearsal. Any activity can be used with the restrictions that it not interfere with learning and that it absorb the subject's attention sufficiently that rehearsal is unlikely. A symbol-cancellation task has many advantages, one being that it does not involve special equipment. It is a paper-and-pencil task in which rows of symbols from the top keys of the typewriter (for example, %, *, $, #) are typed across the page in a random sequence. Three symbols are listed at the side of the page, a different three for each row. The subject is required to go along the row canceling out any instances of the three symbols that appear. Instructions and some practice are given before learning begins, and subjects are told to stop canceling and get ready approximately five seconds before the beginning of a learning trial. Although some interference is liable to occur in the early trials, particularly with naive subjects, this task seems admirably suited for filling these intervals (Underwood and Richardson, 1958).

Another task that can be used is color naming (Hovland, 1940). Small patches of familiar colors are attached to a piece of cardboard, making a randomly arranged grid. The subject is required to go across or down the board, naming each color. Rate may be timed with a metronome, or the subject may simply be told to use about a one-second rate. This activity appears to inhibit rehearsal, but the subject may develop a set for making overt responses (Underwood, 1952). If the task is one where increased overt responses can affect crucial performance measures, either overt errors or correct responses, color naming is not a suitable task. Such a task might be one in which a specified group of numbers is used as response terms.

A third rest-interval activity suitable for shorter intervals up to one minute was devised by Peterson and Peterson (1959) for use with studies of short term-memory. The subject is presented with a three-digit number and then counts backward by 3's or 4's until a signal is given to stop. A different number is given each time.

In studies where an interitem interval is used, controls for rehearsal usually are not used since the rapid changes in set from learning to interval task might interfere seriously with performance. A variation of the color-naming procedure could be used when it is possible to present materials between items. Small patches of colors can be presented at the same rate as paired items, the subject being required simply to name each color as it appears (Thune, 1950). The disadvantage of this procedure is that the subject develops a warm-up set, which facilitates overt responding.

Two procedures are available for determining the number of trials to be given: learning to a fixed performance criterion, or presentation of a fixed number of trials. In the criterion method, the subject is required to obtain a specified number of correct responses, learning being terminated immediately when the criterion is reached. The criterion method, despite its frequent use, has several disadvantages: (1) One cannot determine exactly how long a learning session will be since subjects reach the criterion in different numbers of trials (in the first study cited in Table 12-7, the range might run from 1 to 15 minutes); (2) the variability is often great enough to lead to differential loss of slower subjects who are unable to complete the learning within the allotted time (if the list is not overly difficult or the criterion is low enough, this will not be a problem); and (3) there is an element of chance involved in reaching the criterion. Nearly all subjects show a performance drop, fewer correct, on the trial immediately following the criterion. Furthermore, this drop may be differential for different experimental conditions (Underwood, 1957a). This means that the main purpose of the criterion method, getting subjects to the same degree of learning, is not realized. This problem will be discussed more fully in the section on measuring, forgetting, and transfer since it is of primary importance there. More stringent criteria, such as two or three consecutive perfect trials, may be set because of the variability of the criterion. Despite these inadequacies, the criterion method is useful in retention and transfer studies in that it does produce approximately equal stages of learning, clearly more so than alternative methods.

The procedure of giving all subjects a constant number of trials has the main practical advantage that duration of the learning session is fixed. Two problems, neither of them serious, arise from the use of this method. The first problem is to give enough trials that most subjects show an adequate amount of learning. Twenty trials are sufficient with most verbal materials and college-student subjects. More trials may be necessary if the materials involve much interference. Often combinations of the fixed trials and criterion measure are used in which subjects are run a fixed number of trials unless they reach a performance criterion first. Usually this criterion is a high one, such as three consecutive perfect trials, since in analyzing data from this procedure, the experimenter assumes that no more errors would be forthcoming. A fixed number of trials can be given, but the subjects who do not attain the criterion in the fixed number of trials continue until the criterion is reached.

Instructions are crucial since they formulate the subject's learning strategy to a great extent. Typical instructions for paired number-word learning read as follows:[1]

"This is a learning experiment in which you will learn to associate words and numbers. It is very important that you follow the instructions to the best of your ability. Should you fail to follow any instruction, be sure to tell me since the interpretation of the results may be affected.

"The list will consist of 8 pairs of items like the pair on this card. (The experimenter gives the subject the example card.) These pairs will be presented in the window in front of you. When we begin, the number will always appear in the window alone, while the word is covered by a piece of metal called a shutter. (The experimenter demonstrates by covering the right-hand item of the card.) After a short time, the shutter will lift and reveal the word. Your task is to associate or connect the word with the number, so that you will be able to say the word while the number is in the window alone, that is, before the shutter goes up. Since the order in which the pairs follow each other will not always be the same, you must learn these pairs *as pairs* and not in the particular order in which the pairs follow each other.

"When I start this drum we will go through the list once so that you can study the list and try to make associations between the members of the pairs. After we have gone

through the 8 pairs once, another tape, like the one now in the window, will appear. The appearance of the tape means that we are starting another trial, in this case, the second trial. It is on the second trial that, when the number appears, you must begin trying to say the word that goes with it *before* it appears in the window. We will then continue to go through the list while you attempt to anticipate the second members of the pairs before they appear in the window. You will continue through the list, trial after trial, until I stop you.

"Always try to anticipate the word just after the number has appeared. If you are able to say the word before the shutter goes up, I will count it as correct; on the other hand, if you say nothing or say the word *after* the shutter goes up, I will count it as incorrect.

"Always try to get as many of the pairs correct as you can on each trial. You should try to do the best that you can on each trial, even though you may have them all correct on some of the preceding trials. If you are having trouble anticipating some of the words or are giving some incorrectly, try not to let this discourage you or prevent you from doing the best that you can. We have found that most students find this type of learning a little more difficult than they first thought it would be."

Note that a number of restrictions are placed upon the way in which the subject is to learn the list. The subject is told to give as many correct responses as possible each time, i.e., he is to respond when he thinks he knows it, and to check the response term each time even if he thinks he is correct. In addition, certain "therapeutic" statements are made in order to reduce the subject's anxiety both over what might happen to him and over poor performance. Although there is little systematic data on the effect of instructions on performance, experience in many laboratories suggests two generalities: (1) If you want the subject to do something in a particular way, tell him in the instructions and repeat it several times in different ways; and (2) special motivational techniques are of

[1] Instructions for paired-associate, serial, and verbal-discrimination learning were supplied by B. J. Underwood and G. Keppel.

dubious value unless extreme procedures, e.g., shock, are used. Subjects often are told that the learning task is a test of intelligence. It is doubtful that this makes motivation more uniform. It is highly probable that most subjects already perceive the verbal-learning task in this way. Of course the example instructions are not meant to be "standard." They merely serve to point out what a subject should be told if you want him to perform in a certain way. Unless subjects are told specifically what to do, one can be certain that they will devise their own procedures. It may be advisable for some studies that subjects devise their own procedures (Runquist and Farley, 1964; Underwood and Keppel, 1962b), but the interpretation of results may be difficult because the experimenter did not attempt to fix the subject's strategy with his instructions.

Subjects usually are required to spell out their anticipations with relatively short and meaningless verbal units, trigrams or bigrams, and to pronounce words. The reason for the spelling procedure is that it allows the use of comparable materials which are unpronounceable or for which the pronounciation is questionable.

The main equipment need for verbal-learning studies is automatically timed stimulus-presentation devices. Several types of equipment are available for this purpose. Among the least expensive devices are manually operated card changers, the most expensive being a filmstrip projector that automatically selects any given frame from the strip according to a prearranged program.

For visual presentation, three classes of equipment are useful: card changers, memory drums, and projectors. The simplest and generally least expensive equipment is a card changer. Although commercial models are available (Hunter Cardmaster), most card changers can be built inexpensively. The simplest arrangement is an easel-like stand in which the cards are bound together by loose-leaf binder rings. The materials are typed on standard 3- by 5-inch cards and ar-

ranged so that the experimenter exposes each item by manually flipping over a card. The main limitation of all card display equipment is its limited capacity. This limitation often forces the experimenter to collect the cards after each trial and shuffle them before replacing them in the display unit, particularly with longer lists. One use to which card display devices are admirably suited, however, is pilot work where an experimenter wishes to try out various kinds of material. The fact that the cards can be prepared quite rapidly and new combinations arranged easily may compensate for the greater difficulty in collecting data.

The most universally used apparatus for verbal-learning experiments has been the memory drum. Many different models are available, some of which are not suitable for laboratory work. The characteristics one should look for in a good memory drum are (1) variable exposure times, (2) an automatic shutter that covers the response term during the anticipation interval when the anticipation method is being used for paired associates, and (3) arrangements for handling lists of quite different lengths. The best drums have pegs, on one or both sides of the drum, that hold the lists in position. Lists are typed with a standard typewriter on specially prepared paper or cloth strips. Strips should be cut and punched, if a pegged drum is used, before typing the lists. Most drums come with instructions for preparing lists. Memory drums in which shutters are operated mechanically rather than electronically tend to be more reliable.

Various projection devices also have wide usage in presenting verbal materials. Any good, reliable automatic 35-millimeter slide projector can be used. A simple method for preparing verbal materials on slides is to type the words on an ordinary mimeograph stencil. Squares containing the words can be cut out and mounted between glass in standard slide mount frames. The projected words will appear white on a bright blue background.

Special carbon paper can be obtained for typing words onto cellophane. Slide projectors generally have the same restrictions as card displayers with respect to their limited capacity, although more expensive models (Kodak Carousel) have a larger capacity. Some models can be programmed to select any one of a large number of slides for viewing (e.g., Selectroslide).

The major disadvantage of slides can be overcome by using filmstrips. Both 16- and 35-millimeter filmstrip projectors are available. Strips of any length can be prepared. Usually only one or two repetitions of the three or more orders are prepared and the strip is spliced end to end, making a continuous loop. The continuous loop can be run as many repetitions as necessary. The 16-millimeter strips are probably most satisfactory since 35-millimeter film is quite bulky in long strips (see Chap. 2).

Words can be printed in black ink on 5- by 7-inch cards by using a standard lettering kit or can be arranged from preprinted letters, such as Fototype. The letters should be about $\frac{1}{2}$ inch high. Nonsense shapes may be cut out of black paper and mounted on white cards. This avoids streaks and shadows that would appear if they were drawn in ink. Any 16-millimeter movie camera that takes single frame exposures can be used to photograph the materials. Alternate frames contain the stimulus term and the stimulus and response terms together. Strips should be at least 100 frames long to run smoothly. One caution with respect to the use of filmstrips: Very few photographic services have facilities for processing short pieces of 16-millimeter film. An experimenter should check local processing facilities before using this method. For individual data collection, words can be projected from behind a frosted glass or Plexiglas screen (the subject does not see the projector). It is also possible to utilize projectors for group data collection when the procedure is suitable.

Although most studies have used visual presentation of learning materials, the audi-

tory method may also be used. Any tape recorder is suitable for presenting the learning materials. The words may be read onto the tape by reading them from a simple memory drum (Martin and Schulz, 1963). The timing can be checked later with a voice key and recorder.

Data collection procedures for verbal learning are accomplished most efficiently by having the experimenter score each item as it is presented. In constructing data sheets, the items are listed in only one order on the left, with a blank space for each trial on the right. This means that the experimenter must be somewhat familiar with the data sheet since he must skip around a bit in scoring. Despite this complexity, it is more efficient in the long run since it greatly facilitates the analysis of the data. Each item can be scored as correct, incorrect, or no response. All incorrect responses are recorded verbatim. Some system must be devised for multiple responses, i.e., more than one response given by the subject during the anticipation interval. Any system is largely arbitrary, but should remain constant for all subjects. One system is to always score the last response that occurs. Another is to give the subject credit if any of the responses are correct, except on the criterion trial, when it must be the last one.

The morphemic bounds defining a correct response may produce a scoring problem. A subject may respond with the word "exactly" when the correct response is "exact." Since there is no uniform answer to the problem, the best solution is to record any deviation from the correct response verbatim. Various responses may be combined and counted correct at a later time, depending upon the particular interests of the investigator. Similar confusions may arise over words of similar sound (Deese, 1961).

Personal scoring may be obviated by using a tape recorder to record all responses. This method is particularly useful when materials are being displayed manually and the experimenter is too busy to record responses. A signal may be input onto the tape to indicate the limits of the anticipation interval. It is helpful to have the subject articulate the stimulus, although this may be undesirable for theoretical reasons. The experimenter can review the tapes at leisure and record all data on data sheets or punched cards. One disadvantage is that the experimental time is almost doubled.

Another measure of learning is response latency, but the technical problems of recording latencies are considerable. The usual arrangement is a voice key connected to an event recorder or clock. Unfortunately, the voice key does not choose between correct responses, incorrect responses, and miscellaneous noises such as coughs, stutters, and feet shuffling. Furthermore, the anticipation method may produce a kind of paced responding that makes latencies difficult to interpret. For these reasons, latency has not been a commonly used measure in verbal learning.

The standard performance measures are trials to criterion and total correct responses over a constant number of trials. Often, however, measures of performance at various stages of acquisition are desired. When a constant number of trials has been given, the measure is usually total, mean, or percent correct on each trial. When trial-to-trial variability is large, the acquisition curve may be smoothed by blocking trials. Trial-by-trial analysis is particularly valuable in that it may show an interaction between conditions and trials. Overall performance measures do not reflect this interaction.

The procedure is somewhat more complex when the criterion method is used. If the criterion is high enough that it is almost certain that further trials would produce perfect performance, a regular learning curve may be drawn, assuming that all subjects performed perfectly past the criterion. If this assumption cannot be made, various methods are applicable. The successive criterion curve is the simplest technique and is described completely in Underwood (1949a). The number

of trials to reach one, two, three, four, etc., correct responses up to one perfect trial is noted for each subject. The mean number of trials to reach each successive criterion is then plotted. Curves plotted in this way are necessarily monotonic; hence differential rate of acquisition is indicated by divergence. A second technique is the Vincent method. The total number of learning trials to criterion is divided into an equal number for each subject, e.g., into tenths. Performance is plotted in terms of mean percent correct in each unit. Discussions of the interpretative difficulties involved in Vincent methods are given by Hilgard (1938).

A second set of useful performance measures is the overt incorrect response made by the subject during learning. When the subject is not required to respond each time, the total errors or errors per trial may be of interest. Total errors may be used when subjects are given an equal number of trials; errors per trial (error rate) are used when a criterion method is selected. There may be some difficulty in interpreting total-error data when a criterion method is used. The more trials it takes the subject to reach criterion, the more opportunities exist for errors to occur. On the other hand, the error-rate measure may show equal mean errors per trial, when the increase in trials to criterion could be produced largely by an increase in total errors. It is a sound procedure to look at total errors, even when a criterion method is used.

The particular overt errors may be of concern, especially in mixed-list, transfer, and forgetting studies. Words may be categorized as incorrect responses that actually are correct response terms for some other items (intralist intrusions), words from another list being learned (interlist intrusions), or extralist errors that are not involved in the learning materials at all. The last-mentioned errors are usually quite rare. Interpretation of specific errors when nonsense trigrams are used as response terms is more difficult since many errors consist of partial responses that cannot be identified as to source.

Several methods of analyzing data have been devised for special purposes, but may have some general use. Paired-associate data on a single item consist of a sequence of correct and incorrect responses over trials. There are many measures used that reflect the characteristics of this sequence. Bower (1961) has presented an analysis in which he reports such measures as mean errors before first correct response, mean errors between first and second success, trial of the last error, and runs of correct responses or errors of various lengths. The main characteristic that appears to be reflected by most of these measures is oscillation, i.e., the tendency of the subject to make errors following correct responses. Another measure of oscillation is the correct-opportunity ratio devised by Schulz and Runquist (1960). The percent of correct responses on all trials following the first correct response is used in this analysis. Certain conditional-probability measures also have been used, such as the probability of a correct response following the nth error (Bower, 1961) or following the nth correct response (Underwood, 1954). These measures often can be of use in comparing different conditions; however, the experimenter must be quite cautious in their use since many of the phenomena reportedly shown by these analyses can be attributed to the particular way in which items from different subjects are grouped for analysis (Anderson, 1960; Suppes and Ginsberg, 1963).

A final special response measure has been used by Underwood and Postman (1960) in an attempt to obtain measures of different aspects of the learning of lists. Trigrams were the response terms. This measure simply analyzes acquisition into two parts: (1) integration of the trigram into a single response unit as measured by the trial on which the trigram is first given correctly, regardless of whether it is paired with the correct stimulus term or not; and (2) the associative phase

in which the response term is "connected" to its appropriate stimulus term as measured by the trial on which the response term is first given correctly to its appropriate stimulus term minus the duration of the integration phase. The adequacy of this measure for this purpose depends upon the assumption that the subject will give a response term as soon as he has it integrated. This assumption is of dubious value since many subjects seem to inhibit responses unless they have them associated. This measure would appear to overestimate the integration stage and underestimate the associative phase.

Serial learning

Most of the general procedures for serial learning are the same as those for paired-associate learning. Selection of materials for serial lists should be guided by the same principles as for paired-associate learning. It is particularly advisable to use several different lists, especially when investigating the effects of different kinds of material. Idiosyncratic items seem to have a much more serious effect on serial learning.

Lists designed to be learned in a single session range from eight to sixteen items. With unpracticed subjects, a few more trials appear to be necessary for learning lists of serial items than for comparable paired-associate lists, but the learning time is actually reduced under the anticipation method since a single repetition of the serial list takes only half as long. The general practice effect is much greater in serial learning than in paired-associate learning, with investigators reporting improvement through as many as 16 successive serial lists. With the anticipation method, trials to one perfect recitation typically have means of 25 to 30 trials with lists of 10 to 14 items. This means a learning time of about 15 minutes. The variability from subject to subject also appears to be higher than in paired-associate learning. Underwood and Richardson (1956a) report a mean of 29.15 trials, 12 minutes, and a standard deviation of 15 trials, 7 to 8 minutes, for a 10-item nonsense trigram list based on 100 subjects. This is probably a reasonable standard to use for estimating learning time of serial lists.

When items are to be analyzed by serial position, it is necessary to counterbalance items over all positions; otherwise the score for a single serial position can result from specific item difficulty as well as serial position. Usually complete counterbalancing is unnecessary as long as each item appears equally often at each serial position and does not precede nor follow another item more than once. Making up these orders may be a problem with long lists. Tables of Latin squares can be used for this purpose (Fisher and Yates, 1957). Lists should be checked carefully to ensure that there are no peculiarly associated items in any of the orders.

Mixed-list designs are not optimal for studies using the serial-learning method unless the experimental purpose specifically requires it. The main difficulty is the possibility that serial position will interact with the independent variables. Although this interaction may be of theoretical interest, it makes interpretation of other findings difficult unless it is the specific focus of an investigation.

Serial learning also may occur by anticipation, recall, prompting or whole presentation. The prompting method is not particularly suited to serial learning and has not been used. The other methods generally have the same advantages and disadvantages discussed in relation to paired-associate learning.

The anticipation method, as adapted for serial learning, consists in presenting each item in order and instructing the subject to try to reproduce the succeeding item each time; i.e., when the first item is shown, the subject responds with the second item. The items usually are presented at a fixed rate, the common rate being two seconds per item. The subject-paced procedure is not appropriate for serial learning since the study phase is confounded with the anticipation phase, so that subject pacing would destroy one of the main advantages of the anticipation procedure, i.e., equal exposure time to all items.

The first item in the list serves only as a stimulus term used to start the subject. Many investigators have used a completely different class of item to start the list. A typical first stimulus term is an asterisk or some other typewriter symbol. The advantage of this procedure is that it more clearly defines the beginning of the list and differentiates it from the other items.

Each presentation of the list is marked by a blank time interval or some other signal indicating the end of the list. This cue for list end and list beginning appears to be a necessity if the phenomena of serial learning are to be obtained fully. Intertrial intervals longer than a few seconds should be filled with some appropriate activity if it is desirable to prevent rehearsal. The serial-learning process appears to be affected more by the set effects of the color-naming task than does the paired-associate procedure, possibly because serial learning involves a response to every item whereas paired-associate learning does not.

In presenting instructions, the experimenter must take special care to ensure that the subject understands the task. The serial-anticipation procedure is a somewhat unnatural one, and it is easy to misunderstand the procedure. A set of typical instructions for serial learning by the anticipation method might be as follows:

"This is a learning experiment in which you will learn a list of English words. It is very important that you follow the instructions carefully. We would like to request that you do not discuss this experiment with other students who might serve in the study.

"The list will be presented with this machine. The words will appear one at a time every 2 sec in the window—here. Immediately after the tape disappears, the first thing that you will see is an asterisk. Following the asterisk each of the words will appear one by one in the window. It is essential that you pay strict attention to each word while it is in the window. Your job will be to learn the list so that you can say each word just *before* it comes into the window.

"We will go through the list once, so that during this first trial you will simply study the letters and try to remember the order in which they appeared. After we have been through the list once, the tape will appear again and the list will start over again in the same order. The appearance of the tape means that we are starting another trial. It is on the second time through the list that you begin trying to say each word *out loud* just before it appears in the window. When you have seen the first word, try to anticipate the second word and so on. Do not try to anticipate the appearance of the *tape,* but wait for it to appear in the window and then try to anticipate the first word. Always try to anticipate as many words as possible, each and every time we go through the list.

"It is extremely important for the purposes of this experiment that you exert maximum effort at all times in trying to anticipate as many letters as possible on each and every trial, regardless of whether you have anticipated all of the words or only a few of them on the preceding trials. Your task is to learn the list as well as you can during the time allotted. If you think you know what a word will be, but are not sure, guess. It is all right to guess and guessing will not count against your score."

Subjects should be checked periodically to make sure that they are following instructions to respond to each item as it is presented. Some subjects, when they think they know the list, will not look at the items as they appear; instead, they respond to the sound of the apparatus as it exposes successive items. Occasionally the subject will get out of synchrony with the list. This is especially true when he thinks he knows the list.

The recall method can be used for serial learning by using the complete reproduction method for the recall trials. Items are pre-

sented to the subject in order under instructions to study, pronounce, or spell each item. On the recall trial, the subject attempts to reproduce the items *in order,* either by writing them down or verbally. Two or three minutes is sufficient time for the recall trial.

Data are recorded and scored the same as paired-associate data. Standard measures, such as total correct responses over a fixed number of trials, or trials to a criterion as well as the acquisition curve measures, are obtained in the same way. Some of the more exotic response analyses may be used with serial learning, although they seldom have been.

The rigid structure of the serial list makes other measures possible; in particular, measures can be made of performance at each serial position. When the total correct or total errors, including omissions, are plotted as a function of serial position, the result is the usual bowed function with the point of maximum difficulty near the center of the list. The serial-position curve may also be plotted by taking the percent of the total errors occurring at each position.

Overt errors may be plotted as a function of their distance from the correct position, in addition to usual classifications, although such plots tend to be somewhat unstable unless large numbers of subjects are run. Nevertheless, this measure does serve as an indication of position errors. Another measure of position errors was proposed by Schulz (1955), who had subjects attempt to recall only the serial position of each of a set of syllables that were verbally presented in a random order following serial learning. Schulz gives complete instructions for this procedure as well as characteristic data in his article.

Verbal-discrimination learning

The verbal-discrimination procedure may be likened to the choice maze situation in animal learning. A set of words is presented to the subject, and he must select the one that has been designated arbitrarily as correct by the experimenter (see Table 12-6). Although most verbal-discrimination experiments have been restricted to choosing one of two items, this is not a necessary requirement, and the number of alternatives may be as large as can be handled by the subject within the time restrictions of the experiment.

The same general suggestions for the construction of lists apply to verbal-discrimination lists as to other verbal lists. Verbal-discrimination learning is comparable in difficulty to paired-associate learning, although it may be somewhat easier. Using an anticipation technique, Underwood and Archer (1955) report a mean of 12 trials to learn 14 pairs of consonant trigrams, while Runquist and Freeman (1960) report that all subjects reached one perfect trial within 20 repetitions on 16 pairs of trigrams. Verbal-discrimination lists should be somewhat longer than comparable paired-associate lists to produce equal learning time. Short lists suffer from two inadequacies: (1) There is a large element of chance involved since the subject has a limited number of responses to choose from each time (with short lists a criterion may be reached by chance before the subject has learned many items), and (2) learning may be so rapid with short lists that many independent variables have little measurable effect.

The most effective way of presenting materials for verbal discrimination is to use an anticipation learning procedure. Recall procedures are possible but have not been explored. By using the anticipation technique, the two alternatives are presented for a fixed length of time during which the subject is required to select the one of the two stimuli that he thinks is correct. The correct alternative then is shown either together with the alternatives or alone. With two alternatives, the procedure can be automatically paced at rates down to about 1.5 seconds without producing failures to respond. Subjects readily establish a pace and with careful instructions

will respond to each item. This is a necessity in the verbal-discrimination procedure so that correction for guessing can be made. If more than two alternatives are used, the anticipation interval must be lengthened.

In presenting items, the alternatives usually are presented one above the other. This means that some randomization of position is necessary to prevent the subject from using position cues. It is not necessary to have each alternative appear equally often in each position, although it is desirable. Different orders of presenting the pairs should be used on each trial to minimize serial learning. Three orders are sufficient, although four orders may be used to balance out completely the position of the alternatives within each pair.

A variation is provided by using more than two alternatives and requiring the subject to discover which of the alternatives is correct. This is done by having the subject choose one of the alternatives and then telling him whether he is correct or not. Any kind of informative feedback is appropriate, e.g., verbal statements of "right" or "wrong," lights, or buzzers. Position of alternatives and order of presentation must be varied from trial to trial.

Items are presented in trials with a blank period usually following each trial. Long intertrial intervals should be filled with some standard activity.

A complete set of typical instructions for verbal-discrimination learning is as follows:

"This is a learning experiment. Today you will memorize a list of nonsense syllables. This is the procedure to be used in learning. A pair of syllables will appear in the window, one above the other. You will see this pair for 2 sec. Then, one member of the pair will appear on the right. During the time that the two are present, you must choose one or the other of the syllables as the correct answer and spell it out loud before the correct answer appears to the right. If you can spell the syllable which we have chosen as correct before it appears on the right, you will be credited with a correct response. You will see the correct response for 2 sec also. During that time try to make some association to enable you to remember it the next time. After the pair and its correct answer have been seen for 2 sec, another pair of syllables will appear. Altogether there are 16 different pairs of syllables. In every case one of the two syllables in a pair has been chosen as being correct. Your problem is to discover which of these is correct and to spell it during the 2 sec the syllables appear together. We shall go through the list twenty times.

"Each time we go through the list the pairs will be in a different order and the position of the syllables will also vary. Sometimes the correct syllable will be the upper member of the pair; at other times it will be the lower member. Consequently, do not try to remember the correct syllables by their position in a list or in a pair.

"Do not let your attention stray from the screen. If you are inattentive or do not learn the list as quickly as possible, your data will not be useful to us.

"Since one of the two syllables in a pair is always correct, you are to spell one or the other when a pair is presented. Even on the very first trial you are to guess which is correct and to spell it aloud before the shutter rises. On the second trial you will be able to make better guesses but, in any case, YOU MUST SPELL OUT ONE OF THE TWO SYLLABLES EVERY TIME A PAIR APPEARS.

"At first you will not be able to spell very many of the correct syllables. However, when you fail to get one correct, be sure to check to see what the correct syllable is.

"There are certain special rules about studying and reciting the lists which must be clearly understood and carefully followed if your work is to be of value: (1) Never spell a syllable except one of the two appearing in the window; (2) you must spell one of the two syllables before the correct syllable is revealed; (3) if you are unable to get many correct after only a few trials, do not permit this to discourage you or to prevent you from trying to learn as many as possible on that and on succeeding trials.

"Most students have found that learning a list of nonsense syllables is somewhat more difficult than it appears it should be. Under no circumstances should you ever give up trying to learn the correct members of the pairs.

"Do you have any questions?"

It is very important that the subject understand that he is to respond to each item, even on the first trial. The spelling procedure typically is used with trigrams and a pronouncing procedure with meaningful words.

The mixed-list design can be put to excellent use in verbal-discrimination learning studies in which characteristics of the learning material are being manipulated. For example, the alternatives may consist of one high-association-value trigram and one low-association-value trigram. Rather than have two separate conditions where the high trigrams are correct in one and the low trigrams are correct in the other, the mixed-list design can be used so that for half of the items the high alternative is correct and for the other half the low alternative is correct. This prevents the subject from learning the list by discovering a principle; e.g., all wordlike ones are correct. Whenever the alternatives are such that a principle can be used, and it is undesirable to have subjects solve the task in this way, the mixed-list design is most effective.

Verbal-discrimination data are limited by the fact that a response is made each time. With only two alternatives correct, responses and errors are reciprocal measures. Trials-to-criterion measures and correct responses can be used. The criterion measures tend to be somewhat unreliable because of the large element of chance involved in the two-choice problem. When more than two alternatives are used, error data may be meaningful, and the experimenter should score which alternative was chosen on each trial.

Free recall

The free-recall procedure can be thought of as a variation on the recall method for serial and for paired-associate learning in which the subject simply is required to re-produce the response terms or items without pairing them with the stimulus term or without concern for serial order.

The principles for constructing and presenting lists are no different from the standard procedures. The information demanded of the subject is much less than in the paired-associate and serial tasks, and performance is much better. After one trial of anticipation learning of 10 trigram-adjective pairs, subjects are able to recall an average of four of the adjectives, whereas comparable performance on the paired-associate task is less than one correct. When the subjects are given only a list of 10 adjectives to learn, recall is approximately 5.5 after one trial (Underwood et al., 1959). With meaningless material, e.g., low-association-value trigrams, performance would be considerably less. Performance on relatively long lists is quite good after one repetition. Bousfield and his associates have used lists of 40 words and have achieved performance levels after one repetition ranging from 17 to 26 items recalled, depending upon the structure of the list (Bousfield et al., 1958). The words were exposed for 2.5 seconds each in their studies.

The free-recall procedure is suited admirably to group data collection. The materials may be projected on a screen or read aloud at a constant rate, the subjects being given time to write down as many words as they remember. Recall is terminated after 5 minutes since very few responses appear after that time. Generally, subjects learn only a single list since interlist confusion is high with long lists.

Data obtained by free-recall techniques can be analyzed much the same as data from standard learning situations. If repeated learning trials are given, correct responses over trials or trials to some performance criterion can be plotted, as well as measures such as overt errors or conditional probabilities. This procedure has been useful for studying the factors determining organization of memorized material since it does not struc-ture the order of emission of recalled items. The most common measures denoting response sequences are items recalled according to serial position during presentation and a measure of clustering called the *ratio of repetition*. The ratio of repetition is obtained by grouping the words in the list in one of a variety of ways, e.g., taxonomic categories (animals or plants), frequencies of occurrence, or associative overlap as determined by association tests. The ratio of repetition is computed as the frequency of repetition belonging to the same category or group divided by the total number of words recalled minus one. A repetition is defined as a word following another word in the same category. Consider the recall sequence: *dog, bear, lion, lettuce, carrot, deer, fox, bean, rabbit, kangaroo, corn*. The number of repetitions is 5 and the total recall is 11. The repetition ratio is then 5:10 or 0.50. The complete rationale and a discussion of some of the statistical properties of the repetition ratio are given by Cohen, Sakoda, and Bousfield (1954). If the experimenter wishes to study clustering effects, it is necessary (1) to present the words in random order, a different order being used on different trials, and (2) to use different orders with different subjects or groups of subjects in order to balance out serial-position effects (Murdock, 1962).

There is one free-recall procedure which utilizes material that is neither discourse nor lists of words. This material is known as approximations to English. Zero approximation is defined as a sequence of words selected at random. First-order approximation is a sequence in which the words occur with the same frequency as in written English. Second-order approximation is a sequence arranged so that each word depends only upon the preceding word for its selection, having a probability of occurrence equal to that in written English. In third-order approximation each word depends upon the preceding two words. Word sequences for these studies are usually constructed by a sentence-completion procedure. Second-order lists can be obtained by giving a subject a word and asking him to make a sentence of it. The word that the subject used, after the initial word, is added and the first word dropped. This new word is given to another subject who repeats the process. Higher-order sequences are constructed in a similar way. Third-order lists use completions to groups of two words (Miller and Selfridge, 1950). There are problems in this procedure when the order of approximation becomes very high since a subject faced with a long sequence often has a difficult time making a good English sentence. After about sixth order, the passages stray farther away from English since they contain a great deal of grammatical awkwardness. Coleman (1963) suggests that this difficulty may be partially absolved by equating passages on "word-complexity." This may be accomplished by matching passages for frequency of occurrence of words and for syllabic length.

The most straightforward way to score approximated English is to simply count the number of words recalled correctly. Other measures may be used to reflect the sequential characteristics of recall. Coleman (1963) scored correct two-word sequences up through correct seventeen-word sequences.

RETENTION AND FORGETTING

Certain experimental problems arise when a time interval exists between learning and the test for learning. This section will cover design, procedural, and measurement problems involved in studies of retention defined by time intervals longer than the usual intertrial interval used in acquisition.

Experimental design

The use of counterbalanced-type designs where the subject serves in several conditions or learns several different lists is not recommended in studies of "pure" retention, since large amounts of interference from the specific lists learned in the laboratory usually are present (Underwood, 1957b). Unless an investigator is specifically interested in such interference, separate groups should be run under each condition, or possibly the mixed-list type of design utilized. Data on proactive inhibition, however, suggest that the effect of previous laboratory learning increases with the passage of time (Underwood, 1948, 1949b). The interference produced by the use of counterbalanced-type designs can be expected to be less when retention intervals of a few minutes are used.

The choice of retention intervals apparently has been guided more by convenience than by theoretical considerations. The advantage of the 24-hour interval in scheduling subjects is obvious. Nevertheless, retention after this time has been found to be quite high when only a single list is learned (Underwood, 1957b), so that it may be necessary to use either longer intervals or lower criteria of learning than the usual one perfect trial in order to produce substantial amounts of forgetting. Underwood and Postman (1960) used a one-week interval and found it satisfactory with serial lists of 12 trigrams. They obtained recall of approximately 30 to 50 percent in lists of various kinds after learning to one perfect trial.

Another consideration in the design of retention experiments is the inclusion of a control group tested as soon as possible after learning in order to provide a performance base line from which to measure retention. Whether or not one uses a control group depends on several factors. This problem will be discussed in some detail in relation to measuring forgetting.

Procedures

The basic procedures for obtaining retention data are *recall, recognition,* and *relearning.* The *recall technique* usually can be combined effectively with relearning so that both measures are obtained. If the anticipation method is being used, relearning consists of trials given just as they were in acquisition, with the exception that the subject is carefully instructed to begin trying to anticipate correct words on the first presentation. It is extremely important that the subject understand this. Performance on the first relearning trial can be used as a recall measure. Often it is advisable not to give the subject any of the response terms on the first recall trial. In some studies, the number of response alternatives is small, and the subject may increase his recall score by simply devising an effective guessing strategy. With long lists and many alternatives, this does not appear to be a problem; however, an experimenter who desires to eliminate this factor from his recall data may present only the stimulus terms on the first trial of paired associates or may demand complete reproduction of the list, if serial learning is involved. This special recall trial may be followed by relearning given by any of the usual methods.

Recognition methods of studying retention have not been used frequently, although there is general feeling that the recognition procedure involves different processes than the recall procedure (Murdock, 1963). Two different methods may be used: the subject may be required to select the correct response term from a "pool" of completely unfamiliar items, or he may be given all the response terms in a particular list and asked to select the one that goes with a particular stimulus term. The first procedure is probably most useful when a measure of sheer familiarity is desired. The second procedure appears to involve particular associations. In presenting alternatives for selection in recognition situations, it may be advisable to present them in different orders. There is some evidence, at least in multiple-choice situations, of position preferences in the choice of alternatives (McNamara and Weitzman, 1945).

A variation of the recognition procedure is a matching technique whereby all the stimulus terms are listed along with a list of all the response terms in random order. The subject is required to pair them appropriately.

These procedures have some application in separating the effects of response learning from the effects of associative learning. The requirement for measuring associative learning independent of response learning is that the response terms be available to the subject; hence, either the multiple-choice recognition task or the matching task appears to best meet this requirement.

It is not necessary that these procedures be used only after lengthy time intervals. If they are used to separate response learning from associative learning, they will probably be used as immediate recall trials.

Instructions are extremely important in obtaining good retention data. It must be made clear to the subject exactly what is expected of him from the start of the recall session. If this is not done, performance obtained on recall may underestimate the amount of "true" retention (Irion, 1949). A case might be made for including some kind of warm-up task prior to recall, but the data on this are conflicting (Adams, 1961; Dinner and Duncan, 1959; Irion and Wham, 1951; Rockway and Duncan, 1952).

A final problem related to instructions pertains to rehearsal during the retention interval. There is no doubt that subjects rehearse during the retention interval even though attempts often are made to prevent the subject from discovering why he is returning to the laboratory. The effects of this rehearsal on retention scores are not clear either after short intervals (Shaklee and Jones, 1959) or after long intervals (Underwood and Keppel, 1962a). Specific instructions not to rehearse often appear to result in more rehearsal than no specific instructions at all. A thorough discussion of the rehearsal problem is presented by Underwood and Keppel (1962a).

Measuring forgetting

A distinction may be made between measures of recall and measures of forgetting. Recall refers simply to performance following some specified retention interval; forgetting refers to performance losses occurring during the retention interval.

Recall, or recognition, measures may take the form of any of the standard measures discussed under acquisition, i.e., number or percent of correct responses, error, or trials to relearn. Forgetting, since it is measured in terms of a loss, implies a performance level at the end of acquisition that can be used as a base line. Forgetting can be measured in two ways: absolute loss in terms of difference scores (number or percent correct at the base-line level of performance minus number or percent correct at recall) or relative loss, which is obtained by taking the absolute loss and dividing it by the number or percent correct at base-line performance. The absolute measure has one defect in that a base line of less than 100 percent results in maximum loss scores less than 100 percent; i.e., a loss of 50 percent when the base-line performance is 50 percent is represented by zero recall, hence maximum forgetting. The use of the relative-recall measure simply allows measurements on a scale from 0 to 100 percent loss regardless of base line. Where the base-line measure is very high (90 to 100 percent), the two methods generally produce nearly equivalent results.

Savings scores obtained from relearning data usually are expressed as a percentage of the original learning scores. When the criterion method is used, percent savings is equal to the trials to criterion in relearning divided by the trials to criterion in acquisition. If a constant number of trials is given, the measure may be total or percent correct responses in acquisition divided by total or percent correct responses in relearning over an equivalent number of trials.

The primary problem in measurement of forgetting is the establishment of the base line. This problem has been most extensively discussed by Underwood (1954, 1964), Underwood and Keppel (1962a), and tangentially by Anderson (1963). The simplest solution would be to train all subjects to the same performance criterion, such as one perfect recitation, then use this performance criterion as a base line for all comparisons. If equal base line for all subjects or conditions is established, the raw recall scores can be used to compare forgetting without any ne-

cessity of transforming to loss scores. It can be shown empirically that subjects who learn at different rates to the same criterion are not at the same performance level, as indicated by an immediate retention test. The one-perfect-trial criterion (100 percent) is an inadequate estimate since the trial succeeding one perfect trial invariably results in some loss (Underwood, 1957a). The problem becomes particularly acute when retention of different lists is compared and the learning rate differs for those lists. Not only is there a loss on an immediately given postcriterion trial, but the loss is differential for the different lists, being greatest for the most slowly learned list. If absolute loss scores are used, they may reflect these initial differences and not differences in rate of forgetting.

There are three kinds of solution that may be used when the problem of estimating a base line arises: (1) control groups, (2) projected immediate recall scores, and (3) different criteria for different subjects or groups. If the recall method is used there is no need to estimate a base line, as the final recall trial provides this estimate.

The most direct solution to the criterion problem is to run a control group that is given immediate recall under each condition of the experiment. These groups are taken to the established criterion of learning and then given a retention test immediately. The mean immediate recall score then can be used as an estimate of the base-line performance level. A variation on this procedure is to carry the control subjects to one trial past the criterion and use this as a base-line measure. If the recall method of learning is used, this additional trial should be recall only. Approximately the same base-line estimates are obtained with immediate recall and an additional trial (Underwood and Keppel, 1962a).

Procedure 2 has some advantages in that a base-line estimate is obtained for each subject by projecting his learning score for an additional trial. Several procedures are available and have been described in detail by

Underwood (1954, 1964) and Underwood and Richardson (1957). Estimates of the probability of each item being correct on immediate recall are obtained by one of several procedures. When learning is carried a constant number of trials, the *single-entry* technique is most appropriate. Items are first classified in terms of how many times they were correctly anticipated during the first $N - 1$ trials: The percent of items in each category that are correct on the last trial (N) is then computed. A smooth curve is then drawn on a plot of percent correct on trial N as a function of number of correct responses on the first $N - 1$ trials. A predicted probability for the projected trial $N + 1$ is then read directly off the graph; i.e., if an item was correct five times in the N trials, its projected probability is the value of the function at five correct. It is assumed, of course, that the proportion of items correct on the seventh trial for each category will be the same as on the sixth trial. The forgetting score for an individual subject is obtained by summing the predicted proportions for all items and subtracting the obtained numbers correct on the retention test. When subjects are run to a criterion, a *multiple-entry technique* is more appropriate. Estimates of the probability of each item's being correct on immediate recall are obtained by determining the probability of a correct response on the trial following the first, second, third, . . . *n*th correct response pooled over all subjects and items and taking the number of correct responses on a given item and assigning it the probability associated with that number of correct responses. Forgetting is then determined in the same way as with the single-entry technique. A comparison of the predicted recall scores with those actually obtained in immediate recall show that projected recall scores consistently overestimate actual performance unless the subjects are carried to relatively high degree of learning. To some extent, this error is due to pooling of items of divergent learning rates in obtaining the probability estimates. If sufficiently large

samples are used, only items and subjects with relatively homogeneous learning rates may be used for estimation, thus reducing these sources of bias (Runquist, 1957; Underwood and Keppel, 1962a). Both control-group technique and projected-score technique assume no correlation between relative forgetting and end performance level, whenever direct comparisons of forgetting scores are used to assess the amount of forgetting produced by variables that also affect final level of performance in acquisition.

The third method, running different subjects or groups to different criteria, seldom has been exploited, although Young (1955) used it in a transfer experiment. The object of this method is to obtain groups that would perform equally on an immediately succeeding recall trial if it were given. To determine this, it is necessary to run a pilot group to some fixed criterion for each condition of the experiment. The groups are run up to but not including the predicted criterial trial for their condition; i.e., if a pilot group learned in 15 trials to one perfect trial, they would be given 14 trials in the experiment. Another group might be given 10 trials in the experiment. For both groups, predicted performances on the next trial, corresponding to immediate recall, would be 100 percent; thus raw recall scores could be used without transformation. The main disadvantage of the procedure is the extensive pilot work necessary, particularly since the pilot groups must be large in order that the predicted mean trials to learn have some stability. This method assumes that relative forgetting and the rate of learning are uncorrelated, at least to the extent of the differences obtained in particular experiments.

Item-analysis techniques

Often it is useful to compare retention of various specific items. An experimenter might wish to compare items differing in number of correct responses during learning (Underwood, 1953a) or to compare recall of items correct on a terminal learning trial with items incorrect on this trial (Estes, 1960). Great care must be exercised in drawing conclusions from these analyses since a consistent source of bias is present whenever items are selected from different subjects. In an analysis that determines percent correct at recall as a function of number of correct responses during learning, different subjects contribute different numbers and kinds of items to each point. This results in a sampling bias both with respect to subjects and with respect to particular items. Bizarre relationships, sometimes obtained in these analyses, may be a function of this sampling procedure.

TRANSFER

Experimental design

There are a few special problems that arise when verbal materials are used to study transfer of training. The basic procedure in transfer studies is to have subjects learn two consecutive different lists, the primary purpose being the assessment of the effects of the learning of the first list on the learning of the second. These effects may be classified into two categories: (1) specific transfer effects, i.e., those dealing with specific relationships between the material in the two lists, and (2) nonspecific transfer effects, i.e., those due simply either to learning experience per se or to experience in the experiment in general.

Since most experimenters have found it desirable to separate these processes, many of the specific design and measurement problems represent procedures used to effect this separation. The other problems in designing transfer studies stem from the necessity of ensuring that second task performance results from differences in the nature of the first task and not from characteristics of the second task itself. A complete summary of experimental designs for transfer studies and methods of measuring transfer is presented

by Murdock (1957). Essential design principles will be discussed here.

The classical transfer design involves two groups of subjects: one group learns list A, then list B; the second group learns only list B. This design assesses the effects of list A, including its nonspecific effects, relative to the uncontrolled activity that takes place before list B is learned in the control group. The usefulness of this design generally is restricted to studies in which nonspecific transfer is the focus of attention. In such studies it is necessary to minimize specific transfer effects by making list B unrelated to list A in terms of the specific material being learned.

In studying specific transfer effects, the base line from which transfer usually is measured is the learning of a list of unrelated material. Rather than learning only list B, the control group learns another list prior to this in which the material is unrelated to list B. The experimental group's performance then is compared with the control group's performance, both groups being influenced by nonspecific effects, while the experimental group's performance is influenced also by specific relationships between lists A and B. Barring the appearance of interaction effects between nonspecific and specific transfer, interpretation is straightforward.

A second method of accounting for nonspecific transfer effects is to use a mixed-list procedure whereby some of the items in list B have a specific relationship to the items in list A and others do not. This is a highly efficient design statistically and seems to produce results almost identical to those of the separate-groups design (Twedt and Underwood, 1959).

Counterbalancing procedures are necessary with both designs in order to control for possible differential-item difficulty. The success of these procedures depends upon the nonoccurrence of certain confounding interaction effects (Edwards, 1960). When separate groups are used, the assumption is made that the nonspecific transfer effects resulting from the two different first lists are equal in the experimental and control groups. If this assumption can be made, the experiment is usually designed so that both groups learn the same second list while different first lists are learned. Since transfer is measured by comparing performance on the second list for the control and experimental groups, the comparison is made on the same list. Ex-

amples of transfer lists and designs are given in Table 12-9, in which the specific relationship between first- and second-list items is one of synonymity. For example, in Table 12-9 groups E-I and C-I or groups E-II and C-II would be the appropriate groups. If there are gross discrepancies in the learning rates of the two different first lists, the assumption of equal nonspecific transfer effects

Table 12-9   Examples of separate-groups and mixed-list designs with appropriate counterbalancing.

SEPARATE GROUPS

E Group I		E Group II		C Group I		C Group II	
List 1	List 2	List 1	List 2	List 1	List 2	List 1	List 2
A	A'	B	B'	B	A'	A	B'
DOUBLE	TWOFOLD	HAPPY	CHEERFUL	HAPPY	TWOFOLD	DOUBLE	CHEERFUL
FATAL	DEADLY	AWARE	CONSCIOUS	AWARE	DEADLY	FATAL	CONSCIOUS
ORAL	VERBAL	CUNNING	CRAFTY	CUNNING	VERBAL	ORAL	CRAFTY
PERFECT	FAULTLESS	URGENT	PRESSING	URGENT	FAULTLESS	PERFECT	PRESSING
UNCLEAN	DIRTY	EMPTY	VACANT	EMPTY	DIRTY	UNCLEAN	VACANT
GLOOMY	DISMAL	EVIL	WICKED	EVIL	DISMAL	GLOOMY	WICKED
SILENT	QUIET	AWKWARD	CLUMSY	AWKWARD	QUIET	SILENT	CLUMSY
CONSTANT	STEADY	INSANE	CRAZY	INSANE	STEADY	CONSTANT	CRAZY

MIXED LIST

Group I—List 1	Group II—List 1	List 2
E1 HAPPY*	C2 DOUBLE	A CHEERFUL
AWARE*	FATAL	CONSCIOUS
CUNNING*	ORAL	CRAFTY
URGENT*	PERFECT	PRESSING
C1 UNCLEAN	E2 EMPTY*	B VACANT
GLOOMY	EVIL*	WICKED
SILENT	AWKWARD*	CLUMSY
CONSTANT	INSANE*	CRAZY

Group III—List 1	Group IV—List 1	List 2
C3 HAPPY	E4 DOUBLE*	C TWOFOLD
AWARE	FATAL*	DEADLY
CUNNING	ORAL*	VERBAL
URGENT	PERFECT*	FAULTLESS
E3 UNCLEAN*	C4 EMPTY	D DIRTY
GLOOMY*	EVIL	DISMAL
SILENT*	AWKWARD	QUIET
CONSTANT*	INSANE	STEADY

* Synonym pairs.

is difficult to justify regardless of whether a criterion method or a constant-trials method is used. Although careful selection of the two lists usually will produce lists of nearly equivalent difficulty, the problem can also be handled by using a four-group design in which the subjects in the experimental group learn list A followed by list A', which is specifically related to A, and a control group learns list B followed by list A', where B is unrelated to A'. A second experimental group learns B followed by B', while a comparable control group is learning A followed by B'. Barring an unusual interaction effect, the results on the second list are confounded neither by differences in list A nor by differences in list B. In terms of Table 12-9, all four groups (E-I, E-II, C-I, C-II) are used.

A similar scheme is necessary to handle problems of differential-item difficulty in mixed-list designs. If the experimental and control items do not differ greatly in difficulty in list 1, a simple counterbalancing scheme using two groups may suffice. Both groups would learn a common second list consisting of A and B items mixed. One group would then learn a first list made up of items related to the A items and items unrelated to the B items. The second group learns a first list made up of items related to the B items and unrelated to the A items. Thus, if A and B items differ in difficulty, performance in experimental and control conditions is not biased. Referring to Table 12-9, this design would involve either groups I and II or groups III and IV. In these lists the pairs synonymous with items in List 2 are marked with asterisks and are labelled as the E items.

If the two first lists differ greatly in difficulty, all four groups illustrated in Table 12-9 are necessary, with two groups learning a second list constructed of A and B items and two groups learning a second list of C and D items. One of the two groups learns a first list of A' and D' items; the other learns C' and B' items. Although this scheme is quite complicated when more than two conditions are used in a mixed-list design, it does control adequately for the possibility that both first- and second-list items will differ in difficulty for the different conditions of the experiment.

Another solution is to utilize A and B materials that are of equivalent difficulty. Since this may involve considerable pretesting or familiarity with materials, counterbalancing procedures are probably more efficient.

Transfer studies often are conducted in more than two stages, e.g., studies of mediated transfer where three or more lists are learned or studies of retroactive or proactive inhibition in which the third stage consists of retention of one of the first two tasks. The only problem introduced here is one of controlling for differential learning of the tasks prior to the final test task. In a mediated transfer study, the lists A, B, C in that order are compared with A, D, C. If the transfer from A to B is different from A to D, there is some difficulty in interpretation involved since differences on test C could be attributed either to the relationships between it and the prior tasks or to differential rate or degree of learning. It does not seem possible to isolate these effects at the present time. The safest procedure is to run lists B and D to the same performance criterion, letting rate vary since differences in rate of learning are unlikely to produce differences in performance on list C if degree of learning is equated. The same problem arises in retroactive and proactive inhibition studies and usually is handled in the same way. When retention rather than transfer data is the main interest, the list to be recalled should be the same for all conditions, regardless of whether it is learned first or second.

Measures of transfer

Transfer usually is measured by comparing any of the standard response measures with the control, e.g., number or percent correct on all or a selected portion of trials or trials to criterion. The early trials on the second list are usually of special interest. Although the comparisons may be made directly, transfer often is transformed to percentage measures by various means. Several authors discuss the different percent transfer measures and their relative advantages (Andreas, 1960, pp. 483–487; Gagne, Foster, and Crowley, 1948; Murdock, 1957). The same transfer measures may be used in determining the amount of retroactive and proactive inhibition by comparing recall or relearning score.

Interlist intrusions may be used in addition to usual overt error measures. An interlist intrusion is a response term from list 1 given during the learning of list 2. Although these responses occur relatively infrequently, they usually are tabulated and serve as an index of relative interlist interference.

Modified free recall is a measure of transfer that involves a special procedure for collecting data (Underwood, 1948). Its use is restricted to transfer situations where the stimulus terms of lists 1 and 2 are identical but the response terms are different. After some or all learning of the second list has taken place, the subject is presented the stimulus term and asked to recall the first response term that occurs to him. Responses may be classified as being list 1, list 2, or "other," and serve as an index of the relative strength of the responses. A further modification of this procedure is to ask the subject for the other response term after he has recalled one of them (Barnes and Underwood, 1959). The item-analysis techniques described in the retention section (pages 525 to 526) may be used also, but the problems of interpretation are still present.

*Familiarization or
predifferentiation training*

A special form of transfer is involved in the familiarization of the subject with part of the list he is going to learn later. The object of such procedures is to have the subject become familiar with or learn various parts of the material that is later to be learned in serial or paired-associate fashion. The simplest procedure for familiarization training is to present the single words or units at a fixed rate and to require the subject to read them as they appear (Noble, 1954). Overt reading or spelling of the items often is required to ensure that the subject follows directions. Repeated presentation of the series of items is given in a different order so that serial-position learning does not take place. Special procedures, other than simple overt reading, have been used for familiarization training, the main purpose being to force the subject to make some kind of differential response to each item. Some of these procedures have been to require the subject to select the familiar items from a set of alternatives and make some kind of unique response to each item, e.g., circle it with a red pencil (Sheffield, 1946), copy the items in alphabetical order (Waters, 1939), or supply the missing letter of a trigram (Underwood and Schulz, 1960). These procedures usually are given in addition to the general familiarization training described above.

There are three minor points to be made concerning familiarization training: (1) with low-meaningful material considerable familiarization appears to be necessary to produce much effect, e.g., 20 to 40 "trials" (Underwood and Schulz, 1960); (2) some of the complex familiarization procedures may produce interference by using irrelevant materials; and (3) control for nonspecific transfer effects may be accomplished by familiarizing the subject with an irrelevant set of materials. This may produce interference also. A sounder procedure would be to use a mixed-list design in which the subject learns both familiarized and unfamiliarized material (Schulz, 1958).

SHORT-TERM RETENTION

Short-term retention studies have been concerned with the retention of verbal materials over short periods of time. With the exception of the classic memory span (Woodworth and Schlosberg, 1954), the amount of work on short-term memory has not been extensive. Recent interest in this topic has resulted in several techniques that show considerable promise.

Memory span

The classic memory-span task is exemplified best by the digit-span test of the Wechsler Adult Intelligence Scale (WAIS). A series of one-digit numbers is repeated to the subject at a fixed rate of one per second. He then is required to recall them in order, either forward or backward. A time interval may or may not be given between "learning" and recall. This does not differ in principle from serial learning conducted by the recall method except that familiar material from a restricted pool of items is used and the items usually are presented aurally rather than visually. In the classic memory-span experiment, rather than learn a single series to a performance criterion through repeated presentation, several series are given for one trial, each with performance measured in terms of the mean number of items correctly recalled. A measure called the subject's *memory span* is determined with a method-of-limits procedure whereby each succeeding series is lengthened by one item until the subject cannot exhibit perfect recall. The procedure used in the WAIS provides two chances for the subject at each series length, with one correct recall causing him to "pass" at that length. This is in keeping with the usual 50 percent threshold definition in psychophysics. The series start with three numbers and run up to nine. It may be necessary to extend the series somewhat to determine memory span for all subjects, but Wechsler reports that 90 percent of the population tested have spans between five and eight items forward and four and seven items backward (Wechsler, 1958).

Peterson and Peterson (1959) have used units made up of letter sequences. The main modification in their procedure was an arrangement whereby the time could be varied between the presentation of the letter sequence and the recall of that sequence. The subject was presented a sequence of letters aurally; then, after varying lengths of time, a signal was given to repeat the series. The technique also has been adapted to a visual presentation in which the letter sequence is presented *in toto* on a memory drum. Series of words may be used, but the procedure then represents the first trial in a standard serial-learning situation using the recall method.

Running memory span is a modification of this technique (Pollack, Johnson, and Knaff, 1959). Long series of digits, i.e., 25 to 40, are presented aurally and the subject is asked to recall as many of the *last* numbers in the series as possible. The subjects are allowed to recall the digits in any order that they occur to them, but have to place each digit correctly. The score for a given trial is the number of digits correctly identified and correctly positioned from the end of the sequence. Scoring the results in terms of successively correct digits from the end of the series does not reduce span significantly. Pollack *et al.* report "spans" of approximately four to seven items, depending upon such variables as rate of presentation and length of series.

Complex tasks

Several more complicated procedures have been devised for studying retention of verbal materials over short periods. Lloyd, Reid, and Feallock (1960) have utilized a procedure in which the subject is presented with a series of words belonging to several conceptual classes. He is required to recall the most recent word belonging to a particular class. For example, a list might be as follows: pine, tin, pole, copper, baseball. Following the word "baseball," the subject is presented the word "metal." The correct response would be "copper." The words and the recall cues are presented aurally at a constant rate of one item every three seconds. A signal of some kind (tone, bell, or light) appears to be useful in aiding the subject to detect the occurrence of a recall point. Following a recall "trial" the series is resumed. Common and readily identifiable instances of each class should be used since the use of the procedure to study memory processes assumes that the subject readily recognizes the concepts. In the Lloyd *et al.* studies, 144 items were presented in a given sequence, including the recall points. Two or three such sequences can be given in a one-hour experimental session. Careful instructions appear to be necessary to ensure that the subject completely understands his task. A brief practice task involving recall of grouped words may also be used.

Mackworth (1959) reports the use of a task in which a stimulus of a single letter is presented and the subject responds by pressing a switch marked with that letter. The procedure is to present a sequence of letters, the subject being required to press the switch of the letter that appeared a fixed number of steps back. This task appears to have some advantages in that it can be adapted relatively easily to automatic data collection. It also has some disadvantages: it is quite complex, so that a long instructional period would appear to be necessary, and the subject may respond to the switches in terms of position while ignoring the labeling letters completely.

Experimental design and procedural problems

In contrast to other verbal-learning studies, aural rather than visual presentation has been the norm in short-term retention studies. Many investigators simply have read the stimuli to the subject. Although this procedure is probably adequate in most cases, a better standardization of the rate, loudness, and inflection from subject to subject can be obtained if the material is presented by means of a tape recorder. However, acoustic similarity of words can be a problem whenever the auditory method is used (Wickelgren, 1965). The aural method is naturally limited to serial presentation, whereas visual presen-

tation may occur either serially or *in toto*. Memory drums, slide or filmstrip projectors, or card-changers are all adequate for this purpose.

Tests for recall of the material are given immediately following presentation of stimuli. Therefore, complete instructions including instructions for recall must be given prior to the experiment. The time allowed for recall is usually quite brief, on the order of 3 to 10 seconds, since little recall is likely to occur after that time. Correct responses generally are defined as correct recall of all items in a sequence, although schemes for scoring partial responses can be devised (L. R. Peterson, 1963). Occasionally latencies are measured as well.

In most short-term memory studies, particularly those involving the continuous presentation of material (Lloyd *et al.*, 1960; Pollack *et al.*, 1959), some signal for recall must be given. A brief tone or buzzer is adequate, although anything can be used that helps the subject determine that he is now to attempt a recall. If latencies are being recorded, this signal also provides a convenient reference point for their measurement.

A problem of utmost importance in short-term memory studies arises when some time interval is used between presentation of the material and attempted recall. If the experimenter wants to prevent rehearsal during this interval, a task must be provided to keep the subject occupied but not produce any specific interference.

Two tasks have been used that might be suitable. Peterson and Peterson (1959) followed the presentation of a given letter sequence with a three-digit number. The subject was required to repeat the number, then count backward by 3s or 4s until the signal for recall was given. Groups of dots or asterisks may be presented, and the subject is asked to estimate their number (Underwood and Keppel, 1963).

The fact that short-term memory studies take such a short time for presentation and recall of a single sequence has led to the extensive use of designs whereby the subject is presented with and recalls several sequences, either under the same conditions or under different conditions in counterbalanced order. Counterbalanced designs offer the usual interpretative problems of order interactions. Two other sources of difficulty arise in short-term memory studies: nonspecific transfer effects and proactive interference. Nonspecific transfer effects can be avoided to some extent by careful instruction and examples using material grossly different from the experimental materials. Nevertheless, Melton (1962) has found some evidence on general practice effects in a simple memory-span task, and such effects are not unusual (P. R. Martin and Fernberger, 1929). With regard to interference from previous presentations, Keppel and Underwood (1962), Murdock (1961), and Melton (1962) all report finding such interference, whereas L. R. Peterson (1963) does not. With many procedures (Lloyd et al., 1960; Mackworth, 1959; Pollack et al., 1959), the role of interference has not been assessed, although these studies also used repeated-measurements designs. The ubiquity of interference in most tasks involving human performance would suggest careful consideration of the particular design procedure to be used in studies of this type.

Problems of measuring short-term forgetting after different conditions of acquisition or for different types of material are the same as those of measuring long-term forgetting: it is necessary to equate degree of learning, as measured by immediate recall, if meaningful comparisons are to be made following longer time intervals. The issues and proposed solutions are basically the same as those involved in studying forgetting in general. In many immediate memory studies, performance on immediate recall (i.e., zero seconds) is used as an index of degree of learning. If performance is nearly perfect on such tests, it may be dangerous to assume that two items both having equal perfect immediate recall are equally well learned, since 100 percent performance is a performance

ceiling that cannot reflect differences in degree of learning above this point (Underwood, 1964). See Keppel (1965) for a discussion covering problems of method in short-term memory studies.

VERBAL CONDITIONING

Verbal conditioning refers to three distinct types of experimental arrangement: (1) the operant conditioning of verbal behavior, (2) the use of verbal reinforcements in concept-formation and discrimination learning studies, and (3) the probabilistic discrimination task devised by Humphreys (1939). Only the first of these arrangements will be described here since the second situation only involves using a verbal reinforcer with any kind of task and the third is related only tangentially to verbal behavior.

The use of Skinnerian operant conditioning procedures in the study of verbal behavior began with Greenspoon's study in 1950. The fundamental procedure is to produce a series of verbalizations by the subject and to reinforce some class of these responses while not reinforcing others.

Several variations on this basic procedure can be used. Krasner (1958) classifies these procedures into four categories: *saying words, sentence construction, story telling,* and *testing.* The last two procedures have been used most often in clinical or social settings. The main problems of design, however, are similar regardless of the specific technique or setting. In each of these situations the main problems are the response to be reinforced, the reinforcing stimulus, the instructions to the subject, necessary controls, and analyses of the data. The problem of awareness will be discussed following a description of the procedures.

Saying words

This technique is patterned after the non-directive interview. The subject simply is told to say words. The experimenter picks out a certain class of words such as plural nouns or animals and, following the emission of one of these words, provides a potential reinforcing stimulus of some kind, e.g., "good" or a light blink.

There are two considerations in choosing a response class. First, it should have a low enough operant level to enable an increase to take place but should occur frequently enough that some reinforcement can be given and "learning" may take place within the time limits of the experiment. Secondly, the response class must be easily identifiable. This is important both from the subject's point of view and from the experimenter's point of view. Since the experimenter must make a rapid judgment as to when an instance of the required response class has occurred, the more easily and consistently this judgment is made, the less variability will appear in learning records. Plural nouns commonly have been used with some success (Greenspoon, 1955; Sidowski, 1954) and with some failure (Spielberger, 1962). There is some suggestion (Matarazzo, Saslow, and Pareis, 1960) that the difficulty is due, at least in part, to failure to discriminate the response class.

Subjects have also been required to emit unsystematically varied three-digit numbers (Tatz, 1960). There are some advantages to this technique in that the population from which the subject draws his responses appears to be high. So far, there does not appear to be a completely successful response class, i.e., one which results in "learning" for all subjects; however, besides plural nouns and numbers, adverbs, "travel" verbs (Wilson and Verplanck, 1956), verbs (Kanfer, 1958), and "human" responses (Matarazzo et al., 1960) apparently are learnable under appropriate conditions in the "say words" situation.

Matarazzo et al. (1960) provide a method for determining the reliability of different experimenters in delivering reinforcing stimuli and scoring responses. Two independent observers simultaneously score the subjects' responses along with the experimenter. Reliability coefficients of .96 to .99 were obtained, plural and human responses being reinforced

categories in two separate studies. Not all experimenters are likely to show this agreement even when carefully trained (Kanfer, 1958).

Sentence construction

A more structured version of the verbal-conditioning technique has the subject make up sentences (Taffel, 1955). A series of 3- by 5-inch index cards are used, each card containing a single verb and the pronouns "I," "we," "you," "he," "she," "they." Instructions are for the subject to make up a sentence using the verb along with one of the pronouns. Subjects are reinforced for using either a single pronoun, e.g., "you," or a class of pronouns, e.g., "I," "we." The pronouns usually are typed in different orders on different cards to avoid bias. It is also wise to vary the order of presentation of the particular cards from subject to subject. This may be done either by shuffling the deck of cards before each subject is run or by arranging the sentences in blocks of 25 or fewer cards and using a counterbalanced or partially counterbalanced sequence.

Sentence construction is more popular than the word-saying technique and has several advantages: objectivity of scoring and ease in determining a reinforced response. This eliminates the problem of experimenter reliability and appears more likely to result in "learning."

Reinforcing stimuli

The most common reinforcing stimulus during early studies was the "um-hmm" sound verbalized aloud in as natural a tone as possible. The stimulus is given immediately following a word of the correct class being emitted by the subject. Other verbal responses that have served as reinforcers are the words "good," "fine," "all right." Other "physical" stimuli such as lights and buzzers also have been successful; however, it has been suggested that unless such stimuli have some meaning to the subject, i.e., convey some kind of information in terms of confirming a hypothesis, learning will not occur

(Taffel, 1955; Tatz, 1960). The most common complaint is that a supposedly reinforcing stimulus serves to distract the subject from his task (Farber, 1963; Spielberger and DeNike, 1962). One thing is clear: just as there are no response classes that always result in learning, there are no potential reinforcers that always result in learning.

Instructions

The data clearly indicate that the subject's attitudes are of primary importance (Dulany, 1961; Spielberger, Levin, and Shepard, 1962). It would appear that the more the subject is told concerning the nature of the experiment, the more likely it is that conditioning will occur. If simple concept discovery, rather than problems of conscious control, is the main purpose of a study, an experimenter might be wise to utilize "directed" instructions in order to produce concept-seeking behavior (Sidowski, 1954; Sidowski and Naumoff, 1964; Tatz, 1960). Basic noninformational instructions for both word-saying and sentence-construction methods are as follows:

> *Word saying.* "When I tell you to begin, I want you to start saying words. Any words will do, but you are not to count or to say sentences or phrases. Remember that you are to keep saying words until you are told to stop.
> "All right, go ahead."[1]
> *Sentence construction.* "This is an experiment in verbal behavior which uses a sentence construction task. I will show you some cards like this one. Each card will have a word above and six words on a line underneath. What I want you to do is to make up a sentence containing the word above and beginning with any one of the words on the line below. For example, you might make up this sentence: They built a house, or this one: I built a boat. In every case use the word above in a sentence which begins with any one of the words in the line below. Do you have any questions?"[2]

[1] Sidowski, 1954.
[2] Spielberger and Levin, 1962.

Experimenters may add appropriate extra information when it is desired.

Experimenters

Experimenters should be trained carefully since the highly interpersonal nature of the verbal-conditioning situation makes experimenter differences quite likely (Kanfer, 1958). There is some suggestion that the physical characteristics of the experimenter (Binder, McConnell, and Sjoholm, 1957), as well as his social status, are important (Verplanck, 1955). Many investigations have matched the sex of the experimenter with that of the subject to attenuate possible complex interactions.

The proficiency of the experimenter is most important in the "say words" situation where immediate decisions concerning the relevance of a word and presentation of reinforcement are necessary. Some subjects say words at such a rapid rate that a naive experimenter will find it impossible to keep up.

Experimental Design

The primary consideration in designing experiments is the use of proper control groups. It is desirable to attribute the changes in frequency of a particular response class to the effects of a reinforcing stimulus. Two kinds of control have been used to assess this effect. One method is to use a preexperimental control session to assess the operant rate. Performance following reinforced trials then is compared with performance during the operant-rate pretest in which no reinforcement is given. The length of the pretest session varies but must be long enough to allow an accurate assessment of operant rate. About 5 to 10 minutes (Babladelis, 1961) or 100 responses (Matarazzo *et al.*, 1960) seem to be adequate. Two problems occur with this control. A long nonreinforced pretesting period often results in a startle response or a response such as "Am I finished?" when the first reinforced trial is given. These effects may be removed by giving one or two reinforcements at random during the pretesting period (Matarazzo *et al.*, 1960).

The second problem is that an overly long pretesting period may produce an "extinction" effect on the class that is later to be reinforced.

A second method of control is the nonreinforced control group, which is given the same session as the reinforced group but with reinforcement eliminated. But the complete omission of reinforcement may not always be considered a suitable control. Since it is often desirable to attribute differences between experimental and control groups to reinforcement of specific responses, a group that receives reinforcing stimuli at random intervals uncorrelated with specific responses should be considered also. The frequency of this random reinforcement may be "matched" with the obtained average frequency of reinforcement in either a pilot group or the experimental group (Sidowski, 1954). The inclusion of such a group in verbal-conditioning designs would allow assessment of any general effects of the potentially reinforcing stimulus during the experiment.

An experimental session usually is arranged so that it lasts 30 to 50 minutes. Either constant time or a constant number of words may be given. The later procedure has some advantages, particularly in the analysis of the data. When the sentence-construction technique is used, about 80 to 120 sentences seem adequate (Farber, 1963). With the "say words" technique about 250 responses can be given in a 50-minute period (Dulany, 1961). Often a signal to say a word is given in order to pace the subject (Sidowski and Naumoff, 1964; Tatz, 1960). This has some advantages in that it prevents the subject from going too fast and keeps rate of emission constant, but may act to confuse him about the nature of the reinforcement, especially if some other physical stimulus is used as a reinforcer. With unpaced subjects, the variability in rate is quite large.

Analysis of data

The most common measure of performance is frequency of responses in the reinforced class. If constant time is used, e.g.,

a 40-minute session, the data may be blocked in successive five-minute periods and tabulated in terms of percent correct. Cumulative response frequency curves also may be used to present data collected over a constant time interval. Conditioning effects are indicated by a change in slope from the pretest period or by a difference in slope from that of a control group. The main advantage of the constant number of "trials" technique is the ease with which data are handled. The trials may be grouped into blocks of 20 to 50 responses and results plotted in terms of number or percent "correct." Results appear to meet assumption of trend analysis of variance and can be compared with this technique.

Another measure of performance is provided by using an extinction procedure whereby the reinforcing stimulus is omitted for a fixed length of time or fixed number of words. This procedure also acts as a control, since failure to obtain extinction when reinforcement is withdrawn may cast some doubt upon the validity of the conditioning data. Either criterion or response rate may be used as a measure.

In the sentence-construction procedure, latency is a possible but seldom used measure.

Awareness

A theoretical issue of some importance has been the role of conscious awareness of the reinforcement contingencies in the verbal-conditioning situation (Farber, 1963). The typical procedure is to question the subjects following the experimental session to determine whether they can verbalize the correct relationship between response class and reinforcement. [Dixon and Oakes (1965) report that intertrial activity interferes with the "awareness"-conditioning relationship but not with the conditioning per se.]

Questionnaires are presented in Spielberger and Levin (1962) and Farber (1963). The means for handling the data from these questionnaires or interviews are presented in Farber (1963), Dulany (1961), Spielberger and Levin (1962), and Tatz (1960).

REFERENCES

ADAMS, J. A. The second facet of forgetting: A review of warm-up decrement. *Psychol. Bull.*, 1961, **58**, 257–273.

ANDERSON, N. H. Effect of first order conditional probability in a two choice learning situation. *J. exp. Psychol.*, 1960, **59**, 73–93.

ANDERSON, N. H. Comparison of different populations: Resistance to extinction and transfer. *Psychol. Rev.*, 1963, **70**, 162–179.

ANDREAS, B. G. *Experimental psychology.* New York: Wiley, 1960.

ARCHER, E. J. Some greco-latin analysis of variance designs for learning studies. *Psychol. Bull.*, 1952, **49**, 521–537.

ARCHER, E. J. Re-evaluation of the meaningfulness of all possible CVC trigrams. *Psychol. Monogr.*, 1960, **74**, No. 10 (Whole No. 497).

ARCHER, E. J. Some comments on Noble's "Measurement of association values (a), etc." *Psychol. Rep.*, 1961, **9**, 679–680.

ATTNEAVE, F., and ARNOULT, M. D. The quantitative study of shape and pattern perception. *Psychol. Bull.*, 1956, **53**, 452–471.

BABLADELIS, G. Personality and verbal conditioning effects. *J. abnorm. soc. Psychol.*, 1961, **62**, 41–43.

BARNES, J. M., and UNDERWOOD, B. J. Fate of first list associations in transfer theory. *J. exp. Psychol.*, 1959, **58**, 97–105.

BATTIG, W. F. Scaled difficulty of nonsense-syllable pairs consisting of syllables of equal association value. *Psychol. Rep.*, 1959, **5**, 126.

BATTIG, W. F. Paired associate learning under simultaneous repetition and nonrepetition conditions. *J. exp. Psychol.*, 1962, **64**, 87–93.

BATTIG, W. F., and BRACKETT, H. R. Comparison of anticipation and recall methods in paired associate learning. *Psychol. Rep.*, 1961, **9**, 59–65.

BATTIG, W. F., and SPERA, A. J. Rated association values of numbers from 0–100. *J. verb. Learn. verb. Behav.*, 1962, **1**, 200–202.

BERKO, J. The child's learning of English morphology. *Word*, 1958, **14**, 150–177.

BINDER, A., MCCONNELL, D., and SJOHOLM, N. A. Verbal conditioning as a function of experimenter characteristics. *J. abnorm. soc. Psychol.*, 1957, **55**, 309–314.

BOUSFIELD, W. A., COHEN, B. H., and WHITMARSH, G. A. Associative clustering in the recall of words of different taxonomic frequencies of occurrence. *Psychol. Rep.*, 1958, **4**, 39–44.

BOWER, G. Application of a model to paired associate learning. *Psychometrika*, 1961, **26**, 255–280.

BROWN, R., and BERKO, J. Word association and the acquisition of grammar. *Child Develpm.*, 1960, **31**, 1–14.

BROWN, R., and FRASER, C. The acquisition of syntax. In C. N. Cofer and B. S. Musgrave (Eds.), *Verbal behavior and learning.* New York: McGraw-Hill, 1963.

BRUNSWIK, E. *Systematic and representative design of psychological experiments: With results in physical and social perception.* Berkeley, Calif.: Univer. of California Press, 1947.

CARROLL, J. B. Review of "The measurement of meaning," *Language*, 1959, **35**, 58–77.

CASTANEDA, A. Effects of stress on complex learning and performance. *J. exp. Psychol.*, 1956, **52**, 9–12.

COHEN, B. H., SAKODA, J. M., and BOUSFIELD, W. A. The statistical analysis of the incidence of clustering in the recall of randomly arranged associates. *Tech. Rep. 10, Contract Nonr 631(00)*, Univer. of Connecticut, 1954.

COLEMAN, E. B. Approximations to English: Some comments on the method. *Amer. J. Psychol.*, 1963, **76**, 239–247.

COOK, J. O., and KENDLER, T. S. A theoretical model to explain some paired associate learning data. In G. Finch and F. Cameron (Eds.), *Symposium on Air Force human engineering, personnel, and training research.* Washington, D.C.: National Academy of Sciences–National Research Council Publ. 455, 1956. pp. 90–98.

COOMBS, C. H. Psychological scaling without a unit of measurement. *Psychol. Rev.*, 1950, **57**, 145–158.

COOMBS, C. H. Theory and methods of social measurement. In L. Festinger and D. Katz (Eds.), *Research methods in the behavioral sciences.* New York: Holt, 1953.

CRONBACH, L. J. *Essentials of psychological testing.* New York: Harper & Row, 1960.

DEESE, J. From the isolated verbal unit to connected discourse. In C. N. Cofer (Ed.), *Verbal learning and verbal behavior.* New York: McGraw-Hill, 1961.

DEESE, J. Form class and the determinants of association. *J. verb. Learn. verb. Behav.*, 1962*a*, **1**, 79–84.

DEESE, J. On the structure of associative meaning. *Psychol. Rev.*, 1962*b*, **69**, 161–175.

DEESE, J., and HARDMAN, G. W. An analysis of errors in retroactive inhibition of rote verbal learning. *Amer. J. Psychol.*, 1954, **67**, 299–307.

DEMBER, W. N. *The psychology of perception.* New York: Holt, 1960.

DINNER, J. E., and DUNCAN, C. P. Warm up in retention as a function of degree of verbal learning. *J. exp. Psychol.*, 1959, **57**, 257–261.

DIXON, P. W., and OAKES, W. F. Effect of intertrial activity on the relationship between awareness and verbal operant conditioning. *J. exp. Psychol.*, 1965, **69**, 152–157.

DULANY, D. Hypotheses and habits in verbal "operant conditioning." *J. abnorm. soc. Psychol.*, 1961, **63**, 251–263.

EDWARDS, A. L. *Techniques of attitude scale construction.* New York: Appleton-Century-Crofts, 1957.

EDWARDS, A. L. *Experimental design in psychological research.* (Rev. ed.) New York: Holt, 1960.

ERVIN, S. M. Changes with age in the verbal determinants of word association. *Amer. J. Psychol.*, 1961a, **74**, 361–372.

ERVIN, S. M. Semantic shift in bilingualism. *Amer. J. Psychol.*, 1961b, **74**, 233–241.

ESTES, W. K. The statistical approach to learning theory. In S. Koch (Ed.), *Psychology: A study of a science.* Vol. II. New York: McGraw-Hill, 1958.

ESTES, W. K. Learning theory and the new mental chemistry. *Psychol. Rev.*, 1960, **67**, 207–223.

FARBER, I. E. The things people say to themselves. *Amer. Psychol.*, 1963, **18**, 185–197.

FISHER, R. A., and YATES, F. *Statistical tables for biological, agricultural, and medical research.* London: Oliver & Boyd, 1957.

FRIES, C. C. *The structure of English.* New York: Harcourt, Brace & World, 1952.

GAGNE, R. M., FOSTER, H., and CROWLEY, M. E. The measurement of transfer of training. *Psychol. Bull.*, 1948, **45**, 97–130.

GLANZER, M. Grammatical category: A rote learning and word association analysis. *J. verb. Learn. verb. Behav.*, 1962, **1**, 31–41.

GLAZE, J. A. The association value of nonsense syllables. *J. genet. Psychol.*, 1928, **35**, 255–267.

GOODENOUGH, F. L. The use of free association in the objective measurement of personality. In Q. McNemar and M. A. Merrill (Eds.), *Studies in personality.* New York. McGraw-Hill, 1942.

GREENSPOON, J. The reinforcing effect of two spoken sounds on the frequency of two responses. *Amer. J. Psychol.*, 1955, **68**, 409–416.

HAAGEN, C. H. Synonymity, vividness, familiarity, and association value ratings of 400 pairs of common adjectives. *J. Psychol.*, 1949, **27**, 453–463.

HENDERSON, E. N. Memory for connected trains of thought. *Psychol. Monogr.*, 1903, No. 23.

HILGARD, E. R. A summary and evaluation of alternative procedures for the construction of Vincent curves. *Psychol. Bull.*, 1938, **35**, 282–297.

HOVLAND, C. I. Experimental studies in rote learning theory. VII. Distribution of practice with varying lengths of lists. *J. exp. Psychol.*, 1940, **27**, 271–284.

HUMPHREYS, L. G. Acquisition and extinction of verbal expectation in a situation analogous to conditioning. *J. exp. Psychol.*, 1939, **25**, 294–301.

IRION, A. L. Retention and warming up effects in paired associate learning. *J. exp. Psychol.*, 1949, **39**, 669–675.

IRION, A. L., and WHAM, D. S. Recovery from retention loss as a function of amount of pre-recall warming up. *J. exp. Psychol.*, 1951, **41**, 242–246.

JENKINS, J. J. Degree of polarization and scores on the principal factors for concepts in the semantic atlas study. *Amer. J. Psychol.*, 1960, **73**, 274–279.

JENKINS, J. J., and RUSSELL, W. A. Systematic changes in word association norms. *J. abnorm. soc. Psychol.*, 1960, **60**, 293–304.

JENKINS, J. J., RUSSELL, W. A., and SUCI, G. J. An atlas of semantic profile for 360 words. *Amer. J. Psychol.*, 1958, **71**, 688–699.

JENKINS, P. M., and COFER, C. N. An exploratory study of discrete free association to compound verbal stimuli. *Psychol. Rep.*, 1957, **3**, 599–602.

KANFER, F. H. Verbal conditioning: Reinforcement schedules and experimenter influence. *Psychol. Rep.*, 1958, **4**, 443–452.

KARWOSKI, T. F., and BERTHOLD, F. Psychological studies in semantics. II. Reliability of the free association tests. *J. soc. Psychol.*, 1945, **22**, 87–102.

KENT, G. H., and ROSANOFF, A. J. A study of association in sanity. *Amer. J. Insanity*, 1910, **67**, 37–96, 317–390.

KEPPEL, G. Problems of method in the study of short-term memory. *Psychol. Bull.*, 1965, **63**, 1–13.

KEPPEL, G., and UNDERWOOD, B. J. Proactive inhibition in the short term retention of single items. *J. verb. Learn. verb. Behav.*, 1962, **1**, 153–161.

KING, D. J. On the accuracy of written recall: A scaling and factor analytic study. *Psychol. Rec.*, 1960, **10**, 113–122.

KING, D. J., and SCHULTZ, D. P. Additional observations on scoring the accuracy of written recall. *Psychol. Rec.*, 1960, **10**, 203–209.

KJELDEGAARD, P. M. Predicting paired associate learning speed. *Psychol. Rep.*, 1962, **11**, 353–354.

KLOPFER, B. *The Rorschach technique.* New York: Harcourt, Brace & World, 1942.

KRASNER, L. Studies of the conditioning of verbal behavior. *Psychol. Bull.*, 1958, **55**, 148–170.

KRUEGER, W. C. F. The relative difficulty of nonsense syllables. *J. exp. Psychol,* 1934, **17**, 145–153.

LAFFAL, J. Changes in the language of the schizophrenic patient during psychotherapy. *J. abnorm. soc. Psychol.,* 1961, **63**, 422–427.

LEVITT, E. E. A methodological study of the preparation of connected verbal stimuli for quantitative memory experiments. *J. exp. Psychol.,* 1956, **52**, 33–38.

LLOYD, K. E., REID, L. S., and FEALLOCK, J. B. Short-term retention as a function of the average number of items presented. *J. exp. Psychol.,* 1960, **60**, 201–207.

LOCKHEAD, G. R. Methods of presenting paired associates. *J. verb. Learn. verb. Behav.,* 1962, **1**, 62–65.

MACKWORTH, J. F. Paced memorizing in a continuous task. *J. exp. Psychol.,* 1959, **58**, 206–211.

MARSHALL, G. R., and COFER, C. N. Associative indices as measures of word relatedness: A summary and comparison of ten methods. *J. verb. Learn. verb. Behav.,* 1963, **1**, 408–421.

MARSHALL, M. A., and RUNQUIST, W. N. Facilitation of performance in paired-associate learning by distributed practice. *J. verb. Learn. verb. Behav.,* 1963, **1**, 258–263.

MARTIN, E., and SCHULZ, R. W. Aural paired associate learning: Pronounceability and the interval between stimulus and response. *J. verb. Learn. verb. Behav.,* 1963, **1**, 389–391.

MARTIN, P. R., and FERNBERGER, S. W. Improvement in memory span. *Amer. J. Psychol.,* 1929, **41**, 91–94.

MATARAZZO, J. D., SASLOW, G., and PAREIS, E. N. Verbal conditioning of two response classes: Some methodological considerations. *J. abnorm. soc. Psychol.,* 1960, **61**, 190–206.

MCCLELLAND, D. C., ATKINSON, J. W., CLARK, R. A., and LOWELL, E. L. *The achievement motive.* New York: Appleton-Century-Crofts, 1953.

MCGEHEE, N. E., and SCHULTZ, R. W. Mediation in paired associate learning. *J. exp. Psychol.,* 1961, **62**, 565–570.

MCNAMARA, W. J., and WEITZMAN, E. The effect of choice placement on the difficulty of multiple choice questions. *J. educ. Psychol.,* 1945, **36**, 103–113.

MELTON, A. W. Implications of short term memory for a general theory of memory. Vice Presidential Address, Section I, A.A.A.S., Philadelphia, December, 1962.

MELTON, A. W., and SAFIER, D. E. Pairs of two syllable adjectives arranged in order of rated similarity. Unpublished study listed in E. R. Hilgard, Methods and procedures in the study of learning. In S. S. Stevens (Ed.), *Handbook of experimental psychology.* New York: Wiley, 1951.

MILLER, G. A. Some psychological studies of grammar. *Amer. Psychologist,* 1962, **17**, 748–762.

MILLER, G. A., HEISE, G. A., and LICHTEN, W. The intelligibility of speech as a function of the context of the test materials. *J. exp. Psychol.,* 1951, **41**, 329–335.

MILLER, G. A., and SELFRIDGE, J. A. Verbal context and the recall of meaningful material. *Amer. J. Psychol.,* 1950, **63**, 176–185.

MURDOCK, B. B. Transfer designs and formulas. *Psychol. Bull.,* 1957, **54**, 313–326.

MURDOCK, B. B. The retention of individual items. *J. exp. Psychol.,* 1961, **62**, 618–625.

MURDOCK, B. B. The serial position effect in free recall. *J. exp. Psychol.,* 1962, **64**, 482–488.

MURDOCK, B. B. An analysis of the recognition process. In C. N. Cofer and B. S. Musgrave (Eds.), *Verbal behavior and learning.* New York: McGraw-Hill, 1963.

NOBLE, C. E. An analysis of meaning. *Psychol. Rev.,* 1952, **59**, 421–430.

NOBLE, C. E. The meaning-familiarity relationship. *Psychol. Rev.,* 1953, **60**, 89–98.

NOBLE, C. E. The familiarity-frequency relationship. *J. exp. Psychol.,* 1954, **47**, 13–16.

NOBLE, C. E. Tables of the *e* and *m* scales. *Psychol. Rep.,* 1958, **4**, 590.

NOBLE, C. E. Measurement of association value (a), rated associations (a'), and scaled meaningfulness (m') for the 2100 CVC combinations of the English language. *Psychol. Rep.,* 1961, **8**, 487–521.

NOBLE, C. E. Meaningfulness and familiarity. In C. N. Cofer and B. S. Musgrave (Eds.), *Verbal behavior and learning.* New York: McGraw-Hill, 1963.

OSGOOD, C. E., SUCI, G. J., and TANNENBAUM, P. H. *The measurement of meaning.* Urbana, Ill.: Univer. of Illinois Press, 1958.

PALERMO, D. S., and JENKINS, J. J. Frequency of superordinate responses to word association test as a function of age. *J. verb. Learn. verb. Behav.,* 1963, **1**, 378–383.

PETERSON, L. R. Immediate memory: Data and theory. In C. N. Cofer and B. S. Musgrave (Eds.), *Verbal behavior and learning.* New York: McGraw-Hill, 1963.

PETERSON, L. R., and PETERSON, M. J. Short term retention of individual verbal items. *J. exp. Psychol.,* 1959, **58**, 193–198.

POLLACK, I., JOHNSON, L. B., and KNAFF, P. R. Running memory span. *J. exp. Psychol.,* 1959, **57**, 137–146.

RICHARDSON, J., and ERLEBACHER, A. Associative connection between paired verbal items. *J. exp. Psychol.,* 1958, **56**, 62–69.

RICHARDSON, J., and UNDERWOOD, B. J. Comparing retention of verbal lists after different rates of acquisition. *J. gen. Psychol.*, 1957, **56**, 187–192.

ROCKWAY, M. R., and DUNCAN, C. P. Pre-recall warm-up in verbal retention. *J. exp. Psychol.*, 1952, **43**, 305–312.

RUNQUIST, W. N. Retention of verbal associates as a function of strength. *J. exp. Psychol.*, 1957, **54**, 369–375.

RUNQUIST, W. N., and FARLEY, F. H. The use of mediators in the learning of verbal paired associates. *J. verb. Learn. verb. Behav.*, 1964, **3**, 280–285.

RUNQUIST, W. N., and FREEMAN, M. Roles of association value and syllable familiarization in verbal discrimination learning. *J. exp. Psychol.*, 1960, **59**, 396–401.

RUSSELL, W. A., and JENKINS, J. J. The complete Minnesota norms for responses to 100 words from the Kent-Rosanoff word association tests. *Tech. Rep. 11, Contract N8 onr 66216*, Univer. of Minnesota, 1954.

SCHULZ, R. W. Generalization of serial position in rote learning. *J. exp. Psychol.*, 1955, **49**, 267–272.

SCHULZ, R. W. Paired associate learning as a function of amount of prior experience with stimulus and response. Doctoral dissertation, Northwestern Univer., 1958.

SCHULZ, R. W., and RUNQUIST, W. N. Learning and retention of paired adjectives as a function of percentage occurrence of response members, *J. exp. Psychol.*, 1960, **59**, 409–413.

SCHULZ, R. W., and TUCKER, I. F. Stimulus familiarization in paired associate learning. Paper read at Psychonomic Soc. New York, September, 1961.

SHAKLEE, A. B., and JONES, B. E. Problems in method and theory in controlling rest activity. *J. gen. Psychol.*, 1959, **60**, 11–16.

SHEFFIELD, F. D. The role of meaningfulness of stimulus and response in verbal learning. Doctoral dissertation, Yale Univer., 1946.

SHEPARD, R. N. Comments on Professor Underwood's paper. In C. N. Cofer and B. S. Musgrave (Eds.), *Verbal behavior and learning*. New York: McGraw-Hill, 1963.

SHEPARD, R. N., and CHANG, J. J. Stimulus generalization in the learning of classifications. *J. exp. Psychol.*, 1963, **65**, 94–102.

SHEPARD, R. N., HOVLAND, C. I., and JENKINS, H. M. Learning and memorization of classifications. *Psychol. Monogr.*, 1961, **75**, (Whole No. 517).

SIDOWSKI, J. B. Influence of awareness of reinforcement on verbal conditioning. *J. exp. Psychol.*, 1954, **48**, 355–360.

SIDOWSKI, J. B., KOPSTEIN, F. F., and SHILLESTAD, I. J. Prompting and confirmation variables in verbal learning. *Psychol. Rep.*, 1961, **8**, 401–406.

SIDOWSKI, J. B., and NAUMOFF, H. Pacing and problem solving instructions in verbal conditioning. *Psychol. Rep.*, 1964, **15**, 351–354.

SLAMECKA, N. J. Retroactive inhibition of connected discourse as a function of practice level. *J. exp. Psychol.*, 1960, **59**, 104–108.

SPENCE, K. W. *Behavior theory and conditioning*. New Haven, Conn.: Yale Univer. Press, 1956.

SPIELBERGER, C. D. The role of awareness in verbal conditioning. *J. Pers.*, 1962, **30**, 73–101.

SPIELBERGER, C. D., and DeNIKE, L. D. The operant conditioning of plural nouns: A failure to replicate the Greenspoon effect. *Psychol. Rep.*, 1962, **11**, 355–366.

SPIELBERGER, C. D., and LEVIN, S. M. What is learned in verbal conditioning. *J. verb. Learn. verb. Behav.*, 1962, **1**, 125–132.

SPIELBERGER, C. D., LEVIN, S. M., and SHEPARD, M. C. The effects of awareness and attitude toward the reinforcement on the operant conditioning of verbal behavior. *J. Pers.*, 1962, **30**, 106–121.

STAATS, A. W., and STAATS, C. K. Meaning and *m*: Correlated but separate. *Psychol. Rev.*, 1959, **66**, 136–144.

SUPPES, P., and GINSBERG, R. A fundamental property of all-or-none models, binominal distribution of responses prior to conditioning with application to concept formation in children. *Psychol. Rev.*, 1963, **70**, 139–161.

TAFFEL, C. Anxiety and the conditioning of verbal behavior. *J. abnorm. soc. Psychol.*, 1955, **51**, 496–501.

TATZ, S. J. Symbolic activity in learning without awareness. *Amer. J. Psychol.*, 1960, **73**, 239–247.

TAYLOR, W. L. "Cloze procedure": A new tool for measuring readability. *Journ. Quart.*, 1953, **30**, 415–433.

THORNDIKE, E. L., and LORGE, I. *The teacher's word book of 30,000 words*. New York: Teachers Coll., 1944.

THUNE, L. E. The effects of different types of preliminary activities on subsequent learning of paired-associate material. *J. exp. Psychol.*, 1950. **40**, 423–438.

TWEDT, H. M., and UNDERWOOD, B. J. Mixed vs. unmixed lists in transfer studies. *J. exp. Psychol.*, 1959, **58**, 111–116.

UNDERWOOD, B. J. Spontaneous recovery of verbal associations. *J. exp. Psychol.*, 1948, **38**, 429–439.

UNDERWOOD, B. J. *Experimental psychology*. New York: Appleton-Century-Crofts, 1949a.

UNDERWOOD, B. J. Proactive inhibition as a function of time and degree of prior learning. *J. exp. Psychol.,* 1949*b*, **39**, 24–34.

UNDERWOOD, B. J. Retroactive inhibition with increased recall time. *Amer. J. Psychol.,* 1950, **63**, 67–77.

UNDERWOOD, B. J. Studies of distributed practice. II. Learning and retention of paired adjective lists with two levels of similarity. *J. exp. Psychol.,* 1951, **42**, 153–161.

UNDERWOOD, B. J. The influence of rest interval activity in serial learning. *J. exp. Psychol.,* 1952, **43**, 329–340.

UNDERWOOD, B. J. Studies of distributed practice. VIII. Learning and retention of paired nonsense syllables as a function of intralist similarity. *J. exp. Psychol.,* 1953*a*, **45**, 133–142.

UNDERWOOD, B. J. Studies of distributed practice. IX. Learning and retention of paired adjectives as a function of intralist similarity. *J. exp. Psychol.,* 1953*b*, 143–149.

UNDERWOOD, B. J. Speed of learning and amount retained: A consideration of methodology. *Psychol. Bull.,* 1954, **51**, 276–282.

UNDERWOOD, B. J. A graphical description of rote learning. *Psychol. Rev.,* 1957*a*, **64**, 119–122.

UNDERWOOD, B. J. Interference and forgetting. *Psychol. Rev.,* 1957*b*, **64**, 49–60.

UNDERWOOD, B. J. Stimulus selection in verbal learning. In C. N. Cofer and B. S. Musgrave (Eds.), *Verbal behavior and learning.* New York: McGraw-Hill, 1963.

UNDERWOOD, B. J. Degree of learning and the measurement of forgetting. *J. verb. Learn. verb. Behav.,* 1964, **3**, 112–129.

UNDERWOOD, B. J., and ARCHER, E. J. Studies of distributed practice. XIV. Intralist similarity and presentation rate in verbal discrimination of consonant syllables. *J. exp. Psychol.,* 1955, **50**, 120–124.

UNDERWOOD, B. J., HAM, M., and ECKSTRAND, B. Cue selection in paired associate learning. *J. exp. Psychol.,* 1962, **64**, 405–409.

UNDERWOOD, B. J., and KEPPEL, G. An evaluation of two problems of method in the study of retention. *Amer. J. Psychol.,* 1962*a*, **75**, 1–17.

UNDERWOOD, B. J., and KEPPEL, G. One trial learning? *J. verb. Learn. verb. Behav.,* 1962*b*, **1**, 1–13.

UNDERWOOD, B. J., and KEPPEL, G. Personal communication. 1963.

UNDERWOOD, B. J., and POSTMAN, L. Extra-experimental sources of interference in forgetting. *Psychol. Rev.,* 1960, **67**, 73–95.

UNDERWOOD, B. J., REHULA, R., and KEPPEL, G. Item selection in paired associate learning. *Amer. J. Psychol.,* 1962, **75**, 353–371.

UNDERWOOD, B. J., and RICHARDSON, J. The influence of meaningfulness, intralist similarity, and serial position on retention. *J. exp. Psychol.,* 1956*a*, **52**, 119–126.

UNDERWOOD, B. J., and RICHARDSON, J. Some verbal materials for the study of concept formation. *Psychol. Bull.,* 1956*b*, **53**, 84–95.

UNDERWOOD, B. J., and RICHARDSON, J. Studies of distributed practice. XVII. Interlist interference and the retention of paired consonant syllables, *J. exp. Psychol.,* 1957, **54**, 274–279.

UNDERWOOD, B. J., and RICHARDSON, J. Studies of distributed practice. XVIII. The influence of meaningfulness and intralist similarity of serial nonsense lists. *J. exp. Psychol.,* 1958, **56**, 213–219.

UNDERWOOD, B. J., RUNQUIST, W. N., and SCHULZ, R. W. Response learning in paired associate lists as a function of intralist similarity. *J. exp. Psychol.,* 1959, **58**, 70–78.

UNDERWOOD, B. J., and SCHULZ R. W. *Meaningfulness and verbal learning.* Chicago: Lippincott, 1960.

VANDERPLAS, J. M., and GARVIN, E. A. The association value of random shapes. *J. exp. Psychol.,* 1959, **57**, 147–154.

VERPLANCK, W. S. The control of the content of conversation: Reinforcement of statements of opinion. *J. abnorm. soc. Psychol.,* 1955, **51**, 668–676.

VOSS, J. F., THOMPSON, C. P., and KEEGAN, J. H. Acquisition of probabilistic paired associates as a function of $S-R_1$, $S-R_2$ probability. *J. exp. Psychol.,* 1959, **58**, 390–399.

WATERS, R. H. The law of acquaintance. *J. exp. Psychol.,* 1939, **24**, 180–191.

WECHSLER, D. *The measurement and appraisal of adult intelligence.* (4th ed.) Baltimore: Williams & Wilkins, 1958.

WICKELGREN, W. A. Acoustic similarity and retroactive interference in short-term memory. *J. verb. Learn. verb. Behav.,* 1965, **4**, 53–61.

WILSON, W. C., and VERPLANCK, W. S. Some observations on the reinforcement of verbal operants. *Amer. J. Psychol.,* 1956, **69**, 448–451.

WINER, B. J. *Statistical principles in experimental design.* New York: McGraw-Hill, 1962.

WITMER, L. R. The association value of three-place consonant syllables. *J. genet. Psychol.,* 1935, **47**, 337–359.

WOODROW, H., and LOWELL, F. Children's association frequency tables. *Psychol. Monogr.,* 1916, **22**, No. 97.

WOODWORTH, R. S., and SCHLOSBERG, H. *Experimental psychology.* New York: Holt, 1954.

YOUNG, R. K. Retroactive and proactive effects under varying conditions of response similarity. *J. exp. Psychol.,* 1955, **50**, 113–119.

Chapter 13

COMPLEX PROCESSES

LYLE E. BOURNE, JR., *and* WILLIAM F. BATTIG

The purpose of this chapter is to describe some methods and techniques uniquely applicable to the experimental investigation of human behavior, which is characterized by a high order of complexity and the involvement of a considerable degree of internal representational, mediational, or symbolic activity.

GENERAL DESCRIPTION

The study of complex processes has been unnecessarily complicated by a plethora of confusing terminology, often employed in sufficiently ambiguous or inconsistent fashion to present serious semantic difficulties. Thus, it will be necessary at the outset to make certain procedural distinctions between basic types or aspects of complex processes and to indicate those terms which we have chosen (often arbitrarily) for use in the present discussion.

Thinking

In the vocabulary of the layman, the term *thinking* probably comes closest to representing the critical features of the complex processes we shall be principally concerned with, since this connotes activity that is complex, takes place largely at an internal or symbolic level, and is to a certain degree organized or structured rather than entirely random or

unsystematic in nature. Consequently, we are dealing with some unobservable intervening variables or processes, about which we can make only inferences. The inferences are generally based on observable behavior that presumably reflects or is related to the underlying symbolic thought processes. Although the necessity for inference from observable behavior to unobservables is not unique to the study of thinking, the problems created thereby are unquestionably magnified by the fact that the intervening variables are probably larger in number and, for the most part, farther removed from observable behavior than in other areas. This is largely responsible for the present primitive state of methodological development in this field as compared with other topical areas in psychology.

Although thinking is generally considered to be a multistage process, there has been far less than complete agreement as to either the number or the descriptive labels to be applied to the various stages. Principally because of its close correspondence with methodological distinctions, we have chosen to conceptualize thinking as a three-stage process, consisting in (1) a preparatory reception and categorization or organization of information, from either internal or external sources, or *conceptual behavior;* (2) largely on the basis of this information, the development and formulation of various alternative

541

response sequences or courses of action that might be attempted, corresponding to what is generally termed *problem solving;* and (3) the choice or decision as to which of these courses of action is to be followed, to be referred to as *decision making.* (Similar classifications have been offered by Edwards, 1960, and Gagne, 1959.)

Conceptual behavior

The term *concept* is a ubiquitous one, both within and outside psychology, and represents for our purposes a general descriptive label applied to any situation where two or more distinguishable objects or events have been grouped or classified together on the basis of some common feature or property characteristic of each. For the experimenter a concept is typically defined in terms of similarity or communality along one or more stimulus dimensions, so that all instances of a particular concept are alike or similar in terms of the defining dimension(s) (e.g., all large red objects), and all stimuli that do not represent the concept are characterized by different values along the dimension(s) involved. Alternatively, and perhaps more realistically insofar as the understanding of actual conceptual behavior is concerned, a concept may be identified on the basis of the subject's response to a variety of stimuli, which may differ considerably from the experimenter's definition. Viewed in this way, all stimuli that elicit the same response represent a single concept, whereas any stimulus that leads to some different response is, thus, not an instance of that concept and may represent instead some other concept. In either case, there is likely to be a further connotation of some implicit "mediating" response on the part of the subject that intervenes between stimulus presentation and the occurrence of an overt response and constitutes the essence of the categorization process reflected in conceptual behavior. It is because of this latter feature that conceptual behavior is generally classified under the subject matter of complex thought processes.

Although the distinction is not always made clear, there are at least two quite different aspects of conceptual behavior, consisting of the initial process of formation or development of a concept and the appropriate utilization of concepts in situations where other concepts may also be involved. The first of these, usually termed *concept formation,* represents a necessary prerequisite to the utilization of the concept but has received somewhat less attention. Instead, the vast majority of research on conceptual behavior has been more directly concerned with situations requiring the identification, recognition, or appropriate utilization of one or more concepts that presumably have been learned or formed previously or with the selection of one from among several possible already learned conceptual bases for the classification of several different stimuli in conformance with some preestablished criterion. To the degree that the emphasis is on the identification or utilization of concepts, rather than their initial development, attention is being directed toward the second aspect of conceptual behavior.

Problem solving

The term *problem solving* has ranged in reference from a specific restricted class of complex thought processes to synonymity with behavior itself, although its most common usage is consistent with the way we shall employ the term here, i.e., as a second stage of thinking involving the discovery and formulation of possible responses or courses of action. More specifically, a "problem" can be said to exist, and problem-solving activity to take place, whenever (1) an individual is trying to attain some goal or to change the present situation into some specified new and different situation; (2) his initial responses or attempts to accomplish this are unsuccessful; and (3) a large number of alternative possible responses or courses of action are available, the strength or probability of occurrence of the behavior that will successfully attain the goal or solve the problem being low relative to that of other inappropriate or unsuccessful responses. When problem solving is defined in this manner, its principal distinguishing characteristics are its emphasis on the *discovery* of the correct response or solution to the problem and the paucity of instructions or information given to the subject concerning what constitutes a successful way of solving the problem or how he is to proceed in finding a solution. The actual responses typically, although not always, have been learned previously, so that the problem is in effect solved upon the subject's discovery of which of the variety of available responses or sequences of responses is correct. Not infrequently the subject may be misinformed concerning some crucial aspect of the situation necessary to problem solution, in order to further increase the amount of discovery required of him. It is largely this lack of information that distinguishes problem-solving procedures from those used in the study of conceptual behavior and various types of multiple-response learning, wherein the subject is characteristically given complete information about the requirements of the task and the responses he is to make, so that his principal task is to learn to make these responses appropriately rather than discover them for himself.

To exclude instances of unsystematic trial-and-error behavior, we must add the further defining criteria for problem solving that (1) the formulation and consideration of alternative courses of action be to some extent organized and systematic and (2) a substantial amount of this activity, particularly the formulation and initial testing of alternatives, take place at a covert or symbolic rather than an overt behavioral level. This latter condition is in a sense inconsistent with one of the basic criteria listed below for useful methods of investigation, which is that observable behavior be maximized. However, the behavior to be maximized is that which indirectly reflects or represents, rather than constitutes, the problem-solving activity itself. Such a restriction is necessary by virtue of the general defining properties of complex thought processes, as well as being characteristic of the experimental methods for the study of problem solving to be discussed in the present chapter.

Decision making

In its broadest sense, a decision is required in any situation where two or more alternative responses are possible and it becomes necessary to select from among these. Since there is little if any human behavior that fails to conform to this description, it is obvious that the present treatment of decision making must be highly selective and incomplete. We shall limit it to a description of certain methods of investigation, initially developed in a decision-making context, which directly involve the process as it takes place in connection with conceptual or problem-solving behavior and which have the further distinguishing feature that the outcome of each decision is uncertain. More detailed descriptions of methods and results of decision-making research are available elsewhere (Edwards, 1954*b*, 1961).

Reproductive and productive thinking

In most instances involving complex thought processes, there is considerable overlap among the conceptual, problem-solving, and decision-making phases, so the present classification of experimental methods is in reality based on which of the three phases receives primary emphasis or is most directly observable and measurable. One additional dimension in which various methods differ is newness or originality of the product of the thinking process, representing what commonly has been referred to as the distinction between *reproductive* and *productive* thinking. The two extremes of this dimension, consisting in the mere repetition of previous thought processes (reproductive), and the development of completely new and original processes (productive), have typically received little attention in experimentation concerned with complex processes; the former because of its almost complete overlap with basic learning or retention phenomena and the latter because of the virtual impossibility of devising experimental procedures adequate for the production and measurement of thinking activity completely different from anything that has gone before. Most of the methods to be discussed herein can best be described as reproductive from the experimenter's point of view, in that the correct responses and solution are already known to him, but are likely to be more or less productive to the subject, depending on the extent to which his behavior involves the repetition of what he had done previously. It is important to distinguish, however, between methods for the study of complex processes that require the repeated use of certain general principles or types of behavior, and therefore emphasize reproductive thinking, and those wherein only a single task or problem is used or each task requires a relatively new and unique type of activity, which are principally concerned with productive thinking.

DESCRIPTION OF EXPERIMENTAL METHODS

Research directed toward the study of complex processes unfortunately has been characterized, and probably significantly retarded, by the use of a tremendous number and variety of different methods and techniques, of which relatively few have been employed on more than one or two occasions. As a result, it is unrealistic to attempt a comprehensive listing and evaluation. The selection of methods to be covered herein has been based principally on their frequency of usage in past experimental investigations, although several relatively new and promising techniques have

also been included. Several methods principally designed for the study of complex processes in animals, children, or social situations have been omitted, but are discussed in other chapters.[1]

Before proceeding to the description of individual methods, it would be well to consider some general criteria for the evaluation of the usefulness of various methods and techniques in experimentation concerned with complex processes. A number of such criteria have been suggested, some of which are presented below.

Maximization of observable behavior

This criterion is probably the most fundamental of all, inasmuch as the scientific study of complex thought processes, by definition implicit and not directly observable, is possible only to the extent that such processes are manifested in overt and observable behavior. Of particular significance in this respect is behavior that occurs *during* each of the various phases of the overall process, as well as behavior that takes place only *at* or *after* its completion. This criterion does not refer indiscriminately to behavior in general, but only the aspects of behavior which directly reflect or are related to the underlying thought processes.

Isolation and control of basic variables

For experimental purposes, it is equally necessary that an acceptable method permit the identification, precise specification, manipulation, and control of basic factors involved in the overall process as independent or controlled variables. To the extent that such variables are unknown or uncontrolled, the general usefulness of the method for experimental investigation and analysis will be correspondingly impaired.

[1] Conspicuous by their absence are discussions of the procedures and data of developmentally oriented researchers (e.g., Piaget, 1953) and of various psychological phenomena peculiar or closely tied to the study of complex processes (e.g., functional fixedness or reversal-nonreversal shifts). No matter how desirable the inclusion of such material might be, neither is pertinent to the purpose of this chapter, the first because of its largely nonexperimental nature and the second because methods and measures involved in exploring such problems are basically no different from those outlined on a more general level later in this chapter.

Adequate specification and measurement of behavior

A similar criterion is also applicable to the response dependent variables, which not only must be clearly specified but also must provide sensitive, reliable, and valid measures that reflect the complex processes of interest. Measures that provide for the evaluation of performance along some meaningful quantitative dimension or continuum are thus generally to be preferred over qualitative (e.g., right-wrong, pass-fail) or purely descriptive (e.g., type of process, elegance of solution) measures. Of particular value are the all-too-rare methods that permit more than one independent behavioral measure to be obtained simultaneously. This not only serves to increase the amount of information available but also permits the ready assessment of the consistency and reliability of various alternative measures.

Objectivity and freedom from observer bias

The controlled and reliable presentation and measurement of basic variables, in a way that is minimally dependent on the characteristics of the experimenter, is at least as important a feature for a method useful in the study of complex processes as in any type of experimentation, and probably far more difficult to achieve. While this often can be best accomplished only through automatization of basic presentation and recording procedures, it does not necessarily follow that the most effective methods are those which involve the most elaborate and expensive apparatus. On the contrary, many of the most useful methods require little special equipment and have the further advantage of being maximally flexible and adaptable to a wide range of research conditions.

Validity in relation to typical thought processes

Especially in applied situations, the relevance and similarity of a method to an actual situation which in practice involves some type of thought process may be a desirable feature. Although some of the methods to be described, originally developed in connection with a particular applied problem, have turned out to be generally useful for the study of complex processes at levels extending far beyond the initial application, this factor in most instances should be a minor consideration governing the choice of a method. Since the study of complex processes is still in its preliminary exploratory stages, any tendency to limit methods of study to those with a direct applied interest may well serve primarily to retard the overall progress of such research.

Intrinsic interest to the subject

The typically high level of difficulty inherent in methods used for the study of complex processes makes it paramount that the subject maintain a sufficient level of interest and motivation to perform the task for a sustained period of time.

Criteria such as these are obviously much more easily listed than they are fulfilled by available experimental methods. They do, however, provide a useful basis for the evaluation and comparison of the variety of methods to be described in the following sections. Because these criteria partially conflict with one another in practice and because there exists no simple way of satisfying them that is generally applicable across all methods, material relevant to this matter has been incorporated in the descriptions of individual methods.

CONCEPT-FORMATION AND CONCEPT-IDENTIFICATION PROCEDURES

Concept formation and concept identification can be conceived most simply as the association of a common response with a set of discriminably different stimuli based on some identical or similar element(s) or relation(s) that exists within the set. The experimental paradigm for the study of conceptual behavior entails the presentation of a group of stimuli to the subject with the requirement that he make or choose one of a fixed and usually small number of distinct classificatory responses for each. Because the total number of available responses is always less than the number of stimuli, the subject must respond to different stimuli in the same way. Following each response, some sort of information is characteristically provided as to its correctness. The task is to discover the basis or principle according to which responses are assigned to stimuli. The principle, which is usually simple but not obvious, is that all stimuli characterized by certain relevant attributes are associated with the same response. In the vast majority of experiments, instructions do not hide the purpose or goal of the task but explicitly suggest the existence of a principle for categorizing (for an excep-

tion, see Hull, 1920) and even include sample solutions illustrating the principle when interest is concentrated on the subject's ability to delineate the relevant attributes rather than to form a general rule.

Stimulus materials

Probably the most commonly used stimulus materials in the study of conceptual behavior are geometric designs or objects. These are typically printed or drawn on cards or are photographed. Ordinarily, the designs vary in a finite number of characteristics or dimensions, and each design may be described in terms of its levels on each of these dimensions. Preliminary instructions to the subject often specify the dimensions and levels involved (Hovland, 1952). This permits the subject to determine the number of possible concepts and the number of different stimuli that would be required to delineate each. However, a careful experimental comparison between conditions varying in completeness of instructions is yet to be made.

To demonstrate some unusual and difficult concepts, stimulus dimensions with three or more levels are required (Hunt, 1962). However, very commonly in experimental practice, dimensions are listed to two levels, as illustrated in the set of designs shown in Table 13-1. This stimulus population consists of eight designs formed by the combinations of two levels within each of the three dimensions color, size, and form. A large number of types of concept can be illustrated with this population. Probably the most frequently studied type is the conjunctive concept, which is defined by using the conjunction "and" to combine one (or more) level(s) on two (or more) dimensions. Within this stimulus population, *red* and *square* or, more idiomatically, *red square,* is an example of a conjunctive concept. Any design of the population that is a red square, regardless of its size, is a *positive instance* of the concept, for it includes both (all) the required characteristics of the concept. Conversely, any stimulus that is not a red square is a *negative*

Table 13-1   Set of geometric stimulus designs reflecting variation in each of three binary dimensions, color, size, and form.*

STIMULUS DESIGNS

CONCEPTS

Unidimensional (color)†:

| 1 | 2 | 1 | 2 | 1 | 2 | 1 | 2 |

Multiple conjunctive, 4 categories (color-form):

| 1 | 2 | 1 | 2 | 3 | 4 | 3 | 4 |

Inclusive disjunctive (color-form):

| 1 | 1 | 1 | 1 | 1 | 2 | 1 | 2 |

Redundant (color-form):

| 1 | ‡ | 1 | ‡ | ‡ | 2 | ‡ | 2 |

Biconditional (color-form):

| 1 | 2 | 1 | 2 | 2 | 1 | 2 | 1 |

---

* Various classifications of these stimuli illustrate types of concepts referred to in the text. Numbers designate the classificatory response which would be correct for each stimulus when the concept to be learned is of the type indicated.

† Dimensions in parentheses are relevant.

‡ Designs of this type do not appear in the stimulus set shown to the subject.

instance, for one or more of the required characteristics is missing. It is conventional to refer to the characteristics that define the concept as *relevant;* thus color and form are relevant dimensions in the example, or, more specifically, red and square are relevant attributes. Other stimulus variations, being unimportant in defining the concept, are termed *irrelevant.* The number of relevant dimensions of a concept is not fixed; simpler concepts, such as *square,* or more complex, such as *large red square,* may be constructed from the above-described population.

With considerably less frequency, verbal materials have been used in studies of conceptual behavior. Word meaning is usually used as the basis of categorization, although such dimensions as word length, frequency of usage, letter composition, or grammatical part of speech may also be employed for this purpose. In most cases, these materials are less desirable than geometric designs primarily because the various dimensions along which words differ are not known, are not easy to manipulate, and may differ for various subjects. However, insofar as the implicit activity

that accompanies overt conceptual behavior may be described as the manipulation of symbols, these materials have an advantage. Words are obviously the most commonly used symbols in everyday behavior.

A useful source of verbal-concept materials has been provided by Underwood and Richardson (1956a), who scaled the associative strength of a number of noun-adjective pairs, where the adjectives are descriptive of sensory impressions aroused by the nouns. The *dominance* of a given adjectival response was calibrated in terms of its frequency, in a large subject population, as an associate to a particular stimulus noun. Table 13-2 contains concept classes of various levels of dominance constructed from these materials by Underwood and Richardson (1956b). Nouns that elicit a common response can be considered positive instances of the class of words to which that adjective is properly applied. For experimental purposes, lists can be constructed containing two or more classes, each requiring a different response. Since most of these 213 nouns were associated with more than one adjective, *limited* information as to

Table 13-2 Examples of verbal-concept classes from Underwood-Richardson materials (1956a, 1956b).

Adjective concept	High-dominance stimulus nouns		Medium-dominance stimulus nouns		Low-dominance stimulus nouns	
SMALL	VILLAGE MINNOW CRUMB GERM	(75%)[1]	BUNGALOW CAPSULE MOUSE POLLEN	(45%)	EARTHWORM CLOSET FRECKLE TACK	(16%)
SOFT	BED CHAMOIS FUR PILLOW	(76.5%)	BREAD FLANNEL JELLYFISH MOCCASIN	(42%)	CUSTARD LIPS MOSS SHEEP	(21.5%)
WHITE	MILK CHALK SNOW TEETH	(76.5%)	BONE COLLAR FROST LINT	(37.5%)	BASEBALL FANG PASTE SUGAR	(12%)

[1] Numbers in parentheses represent mean dominance level in terms of percentage of subjects giving concept adjectives as their first sense-impression response to the four stimulus nouns (Underwood and Richardson, 1956a).

irrelevant dimensions is also provided, although only with respect to those sense-impression responses which were permitted. As an alternative to the scaling technique and materials of Underwood and Richardson, items from the word atlas of Jenkins, Russell, Suci (1958), constructed with the semantic differential in an attempt to identify basic dimensions of verbal materials, may be used. The incomplete specification of irrelevant dimensions constitutes a serious shortcoming of these materials as compared with geometric forms.

Other materials have been successfully employed in concept experiments, such as those based on numerical (Suppes and Ginsberg, 1962) or thematic (Bruner, Goodnow, and Austin, 1956) relationships.

Stimulus-presentation methods

Stimuli can be presented to the subject either *successively*, i.e., one at a time, or *simultaneously*, i.e., all at once (Hovland and Weiss, 1953). There is, of course, the possibility of presenting stimuli in pairs, in triples, etc., but such procedures have not been used often. Sorting tasks, such as the Wisconsin Card Sorting Test (WCST) (Grant, 1951), in which each stimulus design is presented on a separate card, sometimes permit access to a few previously sorted instances, even with successive presentation, since the card last placed in each category may be available for inspection. However, this information is not necessarily beneficial since the top card in some categories may have been placed there incorrectly. In these cases, we recommend either the immediate removal (Kendler and D'Amato, 1955) of each stimulus after the subject's response or the simultaneous presentation of all stimuli as a control on the amount of incorrect information available to the subject.

In any case, the subject is required ordinarily to respond to the particular stimulus designated by the experimenter on each trial. The order in which stimuli are presented, which, incidentally, should be recorded for

use in later data analysis, is usually random or only mildly constrained, e.g., allowing no stimulus to follow itself in the sequence and/or requiring that all possible stimuli be presented once before any one is repeated. Since the stimulus sequence is an important variable (Newman, 1956), orders should be predetermined and held constant or varied systematically across experimental conditions. In one series of experiments (Bruner et al., 1956), however, the subject was free to select the stimuli (on cards) in any desired order within a problem. Such a technique permits the use of stimulus-sequence characteristics as dependent variables and reveals some valuable information on the strategies employed by subjects in such tasks.

Automatic display apparatus, such as a memory drum, card display unit, filmstrip or slide projector, may be used for the presentation of drawn, printed, or photographed stimuli, although it is not unusual simply to hand the subject a deck of cards on which the materials appear. In some cases, response categories are labeled with an illustration (positive instance) of the type of stimulus to be placed there (Grant, 1951); in other cases, response categories are unlabeled (Brown and Archer, 1956). The subject may be required to respond during some fixed (experimenter-determined) stimulus interval or at a self-determined rate. The experimental details of stimulus presentation often have been neglected or left uncontrolled in past research, and there is little evidence on which expectations of effect or recommendations about their use can be made. There is considerable advantage to more thoroughly controlled techniques (to be discussed later), and we suggest that more attention be given to such details in future investigations.

Concepts

Experiments may differ in the type and the number of concepts the subject is required to identify. Some common concept types are illustrated in Table 13-1. In an earlier section, examples were given of the two-response single-concept case of the unidimensional and conjunctive types. For these two concept types, it is possible to construct problems with more than two response categories, the limit depending on the number of discriminable levels within the relevant dimension(s). The unidimensional arrangement shown in Table 13-1 is fixed at two categories because all dimensions of the stimulus population are binary. Here, one might think of the concept as *red* figures, all of which are to be responded to as positive instances or with response category 1. Within the four-category unidimensional problems provided by the WCST (Grant, 1951), however, the subject is required to respond differently to each of four levels within a single relevant dimension (e.g., form, which yields the categories *circle, triangle, square,* and *cross*). Of course, a unidimensional system may consist of any number of categories between two and the number of discriminable levels within the relevant dimension.

Multiple-concept problems can also be constructed by combining levels within two or more relevant dimensions conjunctively. For example, with color (red-green) and form (triangle-square) as relevant binary dimensions, the four concepts to be identified become *red triangle, red square, green triangle,* and *green square* (see Table 13-1). It may be noted that the single-concept problem with the same relevant dimensions, e.g., *red triangle,* lumps the remaining three concepts under the class of negative instances. This procedure for constructing multiple-concept problems generalizes in a straightforward way to combinations on three or more relevant dimensions, although the task rapidly becomes difficult for the subject (Walker and Bourne, 1961). Note that the use of several mutually exclusive concept categories may be logically equivalent to the single-concept case, except that each positive instance of one concept is a negative instance of all others.

As contrasted with the nominal nature of the classification systems described thus far,

some experiments have been based on response scales of the interval variety (Uhl, 1963). Each stimulus pattern presented to the subject consists of a group of illuminated elements, for example, one on each of three linear arrays of lights, *A, B,* and *C*. Each pattern must be responded to according to a weighted sum (or more complicated relationship) of values represented by the single lights within each array or dimension. Typical preliminary instructions are given in this task with the exception that the subject is told to respond with numerical estimates or by selecting one from a large number of linearly positioned response buttons. With this stimulus situation, it is possible to explore a number of unique factors, including the degree of relevancy of each dimension. Consider, for example, the relationship $R = 0.7A_i + 0.3B_j$, where R is the correct numerical response and A_i, B_j, and C_k are the numerical values of the elements in the A, B, and C rows or arrays of lights respectively. Here the A dimension is clearly a more important determiner and, therefore, more highly relevant than either the B or the C dimension. Indeed, C, because it has zero weight, fits our previously formulated definition of an irrelevant dimension.

Concepts other than the conjunctive and unidimensional variety have been explored infrequently. We shall mention some of these briefly, with the suggestion that they need further extensive experimental investigation. Bruner *et al.* (1956) divide concepts into three types, *conjunctive, disjunctive,* and *relational* (see also Hunt and Hovland, 1960). Disjunctives or, more accurately, inclusive disjunctives may be described as "any or all" concepts, since positive instances need have only one of all the relevant attributes. As an example, consider the disjunctive class illustrated in Table 13-1, which includes all *red* and *square* figures. There are two relevant attributes, but a positive instance (category 1) may have only one or both of these. Note that with binary stimulus dimensions, any disjunctive is the complement of a single conjunctive concept. Relational concepts contain instances that need not share a common attribute, in the sense discussed above. Groupings are based rather on some common relationship among stimulus elements or dimensions; and positive instances may differ quite markedly as, for example, in the class of all *obtuse triangles*.

Shepard, Hovland, and Jenkins (1961) were perhaps the first to use concept problems based on the biconditional rule. Consider the biconditional concept formed by the relevant binary dimensions color and form illustrated in Table 13-1. All four possible combinations of levels occur in the stimulus sequence presented to the subject and are assigned to two categories, ignoring irrelevant dimensions, in the following way: (1) positive—*red square* and *green triangle;* (2) negative—*green square* and *red triangle.* (Note that with binary dimensions, the negative category also defines a biconditional concept.) Thus, whether a square belongs in the positive or negative class depends upon its color; the principle for grouping is a conditional arrangement within relevant dimensions. As with other concept types, any number of relevant dimensions may be combined in biconditional problems. These concepts are particularly difficult to learn because each level within dimensions is assigned equally often (here 50 percent) to each concept category (Shepard *et al.,* 1961). The subject must attend to the interaction of dimensions in order to discover the correct conceptual scheme.

One final type, *redundant* concepts, that has been used for certain research purposes will be described. A redundant concept is essentially a subvariety of the unidimensional with several defining attributes all of which provide the same information with respect to categorizing. In a typical two-category unidimensional problem, all red figures are placed is category 1 and all green in category 2 when color is the relevant dimension. If all red designs happen to be squares and all green designs triangles, the stimuli can be sorted on the basis of either color or form; both are relevant but redundant. It is possible to construct concepts that might be described in terms of any number of experimentally defined redundant relevant dimensions (Bourne and Haygood, 1959). Parenthetically, it may be noted that there has been more than one instance where what was intended to be a single dimension actually consisted of two or more redundant dimensions (e.g., colors that differ also in brightness or saturation).

As Hunt (1962) has shown, it is possible to describe the concept types discussed here as examples of the application of the basic operators from symbolic logic to any definable set of objects. Indeed, one fundamental inferential process of concept learning may be conceived of as inherently identical to the inductive discovery of the operators, rules, or principles of this system (Haygood and Bourne, 1965). Although many types of concepts may be generated by such operators, we have chosen to present only those which have been used with some frequency in research reported in the literature. Extensive comparisons of the behavior involved in learning a wide variety of conceptual schemes patterned, for example, after the recent experiment of Neisser and Weene (1962) would be of obvious interest and importance to an understanding of complex human processes.

Any of the above types of concept problem may entail an independent manipulable number of irrelevant dimensions and/or amount of irrelevant intradimensional variability, both of which will increase the complexity of stimuli, and the difficulty of the task. The latter variable is defined and quantified in terms of the number of discriminably different levels within a relevant dimension that are assigned to the same concept category (Battig and Bourne, 1961; Kendler and Vineberg, 1954). It may be mentioned here that except for a few studies (e.g., Newman, 1956), there has been little concern in the past for scaling the similarity or discriminability of levels along stimulus dimensions used in concept studies. There is real need for systematic investigations of the effects of these variables.

Responses

Probably the simplest and most efficient classificatory response procedure used in concept experiments requires the subject to designate each stimulus as a positive or as a negative instance of the concept, verbally or manually (e.g., pressing one of two buttons or sorting into one of two bins). Some experiments have required the subject to learn a nonsense syllable (or unrelated meaningful word) as a label for members of each concept to be identified. Although this procedure does not appear to differ markedly from learning to press a particular button in response to each stimulus, it does impose the added task of learning an artificial language to be applied to the stimuli in question (Richardson and Bergum, 1954), which *may* be critical in multiple-concept problems. The subject is required to invest some of his time in learning labels, which is more a case of verbal response learning than concept identification. The additional factor of response learning becomes less important in tasks that employ related meaningful responses (Underwood and Richardson, 1956*b*). A further advantage of button pressing is that each button can be hooked up to activate one of the pens of an automatic recorder (e.g., Esterline-Angus), thereby providing a permanent record of performance.

Attempts to apply operant conditioning techniques to the study of concept learning have differed markedly from the procedures described above. For example, Green (1955) instructed his subjects to make key-tapping responses in the presence of positive instances (discriminative stimuli) with "points" serving as reinforcement. Although the expressed purpose of such attempts (i.e., demonstrating the adequacy of operant conditioning principles to account for more complex forms of behavior) is creditable, the scientifically in-

valid procedure of modifying conceptual phenomena to fit the method and paradigm of operant conditioning has unfortunately typified this approach. This can be accomplished only by disturbing the essential structure of concept tasks with special response requirements and informative feedback characteristics and by drastically reducing, if not eliminating, information normally provided by instructions, making it difficult or impossible to investigate systematically the fundamental variables of conceptual behavior.

Each of the above procedures requires classificatory or category responses. In certain experiments, the subject has been instructed instead to respond with *hypotheses*, i.e., verbalized or written statements of his "best guess" of the concept, the experimenter designating each new stimulus as a positive or negative instance. Hypotheses may be requested after each stimulus (Bruner *et al.,* 1956) or after a sequence or group of stimuli that contain enough information to delineate the concept (Kurtz and Hovland, 1956). Although trial-by-trial hypotheses may provide considerably more information on the subject's performance, it is impossible to be certain that this requirement does not interfere with the fundamental concept-learning process of immediate interest. Unfortunately, there have been no rigorous investigations of the degree to which these periodic verbalizations may interfere with performance and no comparisons of overall performance with and without the requirement of trial-by-trial statements of hypotheses.

Hypotheses alone rarely provide much useful quantitative information about conceptual behavior. A promising methodological possibility is to require the subject to respond to each stimulus with both a category and a hypothesis. Such a procedure allows for scoring in terms of conventional quantitative measures such as errors, time, or trials to solution and also in terms of the more qualitative characteristics of the subject's hypotheses and hypothesis changes (Bourne, 1965; Wickelgren and Cohen, 1962). One obvious advantage of this method is that it permits the use of conventional indices as criteria for evaluating the adequacy, consistency, or efficiency of hypothesis behavior. Furthermore, it is consistent with the requirement that procedures maximize the amount of observable behavior in concept tasks.

Informative feedback

No matter what type of concept, stimulus material, or response procedure is used, the subject's task is essentially that of determining or discovering the relevant attributes and the rule by which stimuli can be assigned consistently and correctly to available categories. The task can be accomplished only if the subject is regularly provided with some kind of informative feedback regarding the correctness of his responses. When the subject is responding with hypotheses, feedback may consist in nothing more than the presentation of the next stimulus to indicate an incorrect response. When category responses are required, he may be allowed to respond to each stimulus until correct (Archer, Bourne, and Brown, 1955). More typically, he may be presented with a signal, verbal or otherwise, indicating "right" or "wrong" (*noncorrected* when three or more concepts are to be identified simultaneously) or explicitly indicating the correct response (*corrected*). Because experimental investigations support the conclusion that characteristics of informative feedback, such as its completeness, its probability, and its delay, have important effects on performance, automatic timing and programming devices, such as that described in detail by Bourne (1957) and by Byers, Collins and Loughborough (1964), are often used to provide precisely controlled signals.

Critical trial events

It is obvious that a variety of potentially important procedural factors must be considered in the design of any concept-identification experiment. The temporal relationships that exist among intratrial events—stimulus, response, and informative feedback—may be particularly critical, yet have been virtually ignored in most studies. There is a definite need for greater methodological precision in the control and manipulation of temporal factors and additional systematic investigations of their effects.

Some of the critical time characteristics of a trial in a concept experiment may be described as follows:

1. *The duration of stimulus presentation.* The effect of stimulus duration on performance has received little attention. As mentioned earlier, many previous experiments have permitted the subject unlimited access to the stimuli.

2. *The stimulus-response interval.* Consistent with the methods of verbal learning, the subject has typically been allowed to respond at any time during stimulus presentation. Systematic investigations of the effect of controllable delays between the stimulus and the response (delayed reaction) have not been made.

3. *The delay of informative feedback.* In most cases experimenters have attempted to present informative feedback to the subject immediately or soon after his response. There is evidence to suggest that short feedback delays interfere with concept identification (Bourne, 1957), although the problem needs further study.

4. *The postfeedback interval.* The time between informative feedback and the presentation of the next stimulus is a commonly ignored yet potentially important interval, since it probably provides the opportunity for most intratrial learning to take place (Bourne and Bunderson, 1963).

5. *The interstimulus interval.* This is essentially the sum of the delay and postfeedback intervals but may be important in its own right in a way analogous to distribution of practice in verbal and motor learning.

These are some of the most obvious time relationships within a trial; we suggest that they are important, they should be controlled more effectively, and they are in need of further systematic exploration. Precise control may be accomplished only by greater attention than has been given in the past to the methodological requirements of a rigorous concept-identification procedure. This is not to say that strict standardization of concept-identification experiments is desirable, for there is considerable virtue that attaches to procedural flexibility and diversification in relatively unexplored research areas such as this. However, methodological factors have been ignored far too frequently. When their effects are better understood and can be more rigidly controlled, a good deal of the variance that presently obfuscates (or in some cases precludes the determination of) many functional relationships will be eliminated.

PROBLEM-SOLVING PROCEDURES

Perhaps the outstanding characteristic of problem-solving research has been the wide variety of methods and techniques that have been devised and in many instances used only by a single experimenter. As a result, Duncan (1959) concluded that excessive heterogeneity with respect to methods represents a major reason for the presently chaotic and unsystematic state of this area of research. Besides being large in number, problem-solving methods in many instances have been designed or are appropriate only for highly restricted purposes and differ sufficiently from one another that the basis for classifying them together under the common rubric of "problem-solving" may be far from obvious, even to the experienced researcher. We happen to be less convinced of the necessity for standardization of problem-solving research in terms of a few basic procedures than are some others (e.g., Duncan, 1959; Ray, 1955), principally because the relative newness and wide diversity of the area itself would make premature standardization of methods unduly restrictive and therefore decidedly harmful to progress in its present preliminary and exploratory stages. Nevertheless, the plethora of existing methods and procedures for the study of problem solving leads to serious complications for purposes of the present chapter. This section, therefore, will attempt to describe a representative sample of the methods or techniques which have been most frequently employed in past experiments or which offer especial advantages for the study of certain aspects of problem-solving behavior. It should be noted that many of these methods also necessitate the development or usage by the subject of certain basic concepts or principles and, therefore, are closely related to some of the methods discussed in the preceding section. Reviews of problem-solving research may be found in Duncan (1959), Gagne (1959), Ray (1955), and Taylor and McNemar (1955b).

"One-shot" problems

In the earliest stages of problem-solving research, the problems employed were typically the "one-shot" variety in that they involved only a single unique problem and solution, so that the experiment was necessarily terminated for a given subject as soon as the problem was solved. The most frequently used problem of this type has been some version of the *two-string* problem, originally described by Maier (1931), wherein the subject is presented with two strings attached to the ceiling, which are sufficiently short and far enough apart that it is not possible to reach both of them at the same time, and asked to tie them together. To solve the problem the subject must find some way of bringing one of the strings to a position where he can reach it while holding on to the other string (e.g., by tying it to a chair or other stationary object or by attaching a weight to one string and setting it in motion as a pendulum). This method has been particularly popular in studies of the effects of various types of "set" on problem solving.

Duncker (1945), Katona (1927), and Maier (1930, 1931) have introduced other problems requiring the direct manipulation or assemblage of various items of physical equipment to accomplish some specified and often unusual function or purpose. Since complete descriptions of these and other one-shot problems are readily available elsewhere (Ray, 1955), this section will be limited to a brief description of the few methods that have been used on more than one or two occasions.

1. *Pendulum problem.* Given a variety of poles, clamps, wires, weights, etc., the subject is asked to construct two pendulums that will mark a cross at a specified location on the floor.

2. *Hatrack problem.* Given two poles and a C clamp, the subject is asked to construct a device on which he can hang his hat and coat.

3. *Candle problem.* Given several poles, clamps, pieces of glass, and assorted rubber tubing, the subject is asked to devise a means for blowing out candles that are located at a considerable distance.

4. *"Box" problem.* Given several tacks, small boxes of varying shapes, and candles, the subject is asked to put the candles side by side on the door at eye level.

5. *Gimlet problem.* Given a gimlet, screw hooks, and three cards, the subject is asked to hang the cards from a board on the wall.

6. *Paper-clip problem.* Given several pieces of cardboard, paper clips, thumb tacks, and glue, the subject is asked to construct a cardboard container and to hang it from the ceiling.

7. *Cut-pyramid problem.* The subject attempts to fit together two pieces to form a pyramid or orthogonal tetrahedron.

Much of the variety present in problems of the one-shot type is accounted for by the virtually unlimited number of problems presented at a strictly *verbal level* and/or requiring *verbally* stated solutions. Various aptitude and intelligence tests or commercially available puzzle books have been rich sources of problems of this type, particularly those of a mathematical nature. While many problem-solving experiments have employed such tasks, relatively few have been used more than once, and their number and variety clearly preclude their detailed coverage here. A representative example of problems of this type is Szekely's (1950) two-spheres problem, wherein the subject is asked to describe a method by which he could determine, without using apparatus of any kind, which of the two spheres is hollow, when both are identical in size, weight, and external appearance and differ only in the density of the metal composing them. Another, one of a series described by Sweeney (1953) and subsequently employed in several studies under an extended research program directed by D. W. Taylor, is the following:

> "Suppose a simple organism, like an amoeba, divides into two once every three minutes. Every new organism divides into two every three minutes. A single amoeba is placed in a jar and in one hour the jar is filled with amoebae. How long will it take to fill the jar if we start with two amoebae instead of one?"

By changing the content of such problems (e.g., girls spreading rumors to other girls instead of amoebae multiplying), separate but comparable sets have been constructed that are differentially appropriate for men and women and have been particularly useful in the study of sex differences in problem solving (Milton, 1958).

Spatial problems have represented another rich and varied source of one-shot problems, in which the stimuli are presented in *pictorial* or *diagrammatic form*, and the subject's task is to describe or to draw out his solution. Most of these are of the paper-and-pencil variety (e.g., Lindley, 1897), and few have been used often enough to justify detailed description here. Examples of such problems can be readily obtained from aptitude tests or from puzzle books, and several that have been used for research purposes are described by Sweeney (1953). One of the best-known examples is the nine-dot problem, consisting of a square 3×3 array of dots, the subject being required to pass through each dot by drawing four straight lines without retracing or lifting his pencil.

Problem series

Although they may repeatedly involve some particular concept or principle, the problems discussed thus far have generally been treated as isolated individual problems. Particularly because of their distinct advantages for the study of learning and transfer effects as related to problem solving, several experimenters have developed a kind of *problem series,* wherein a large number of different forms or variations of a single general type or class of problems can be presented in succession to a given subject. Such problem series may be particularly useful as a means of testing the generality of the subject's solution to a single problem, as reflected by his ability subsequently to solve other problems of the series that require a similar type or form of solution but may differ considerably in the specific stimulus and response elements involved. Except for the fact that several variations exist so that the solution to one problem does not necessarily imply the direct or immediate solution of the entire class of problems, there is little difference between the problems to be discussed in the present section and those described previously as one-shot problems.

Verbal problem series. Perhaps the best-known example of a problem series is the *water-jar problem* described by Terman (1906) and adapted for the study of the role of set and rigidity in problem solving by Luchins (1942). Measured in terms of absolute frequency of usage, this procedure undoubtedly represents the closest approximation to a "standard" problem-solving method. It has, however, been used far more often as a test of rigidity than for the experimental study of problem-solving behavior, despite the fact that it has been subjected to severe criticism (e.g., Levitt, 1956). In its usual form, the water-jar test consists of a series of problems in which the subject is to imagine that he has

been given two or three jars with a specified capacity and asked how he would measure out a given amount of water by using only the jars available to him, which is possible only by some indirect means. The following problem from the Luchins (1942) series is illustrative: "Given: an empty 18-quart jar, an empty 43-quart jar, and an empty 10-quart jar; measure 5 quarts of water." Used as an "Einstellung" test of set or rigidity, the series typically consists of several such problems soluble only by a given indirect method, followed by problems which can be solved either by the same indirect method or by a simpler more direct method, and in some cases by extinction problems that can be solved *only* by the direct method. Bugelski and Huff (1962) suggest some of the shortcomings of Luchins' technique to reflect the arithmetic complexity of his problems, and offer a simpler revised problem series purported to establish the set after a single problem.

Rivaling the water-jar problems in frequency of usage but somewhat less specifically tied to the study of effects of set are *verbal anagram problems,* wherein the subject attempts to rearrange a scrambled sequence of letters (e.g., "BMEPORL") to form an English word or phrase (e.g., "PROBLEM"). Although the use of such anagram materials dates back to the infancy of problem-solving research, little attention has been directed toward their systematic construction and calibration, or to the specification and standardization of administrative and scoring procedures. As a result, there has been little consistency from study to study with respect to procedural details, leading Ammons and Ammons (1959) to describe a "standard" anagram task. Unfortunately, this task is decidedly nonstandard in that it requires the subject to make as many words as he can out of the letters he is given, using any number or combination of these letters. This contrasts sharply with the limitation to a single solution containing all letters in the anagram that has characterized the majority of problem-solving studies employing anagram materials.

While the literature abounds in number and variety of anagram materials available for research purposes, most of these have been constructed for some particular experiment. Little currently exists in the way of a comprehensive compilation of anagrams of general usefulness for problem-solving experiments. Rees and Israel (1935) have presented perhaps the single most influential source of anagram materials. These include a large number of five-letter single-solution anagrams, and several with two or more solutions that have proved to be generally useful for the study of set. Several of the latter, for which measures of difficulty and relative frequency of the two solutions have been provided by Spera (1962), are presented in Table 13-3. Other investigators have also

presented sets of anagram materials along with limited information as to their relative difficulty (e.g., Maltzman and Morrisett, 1952; Mayzner and Tresselt, 1959, 1962; Rhine, 1955; Ronning, 1965; Taylor and McNemar, 1955a). Most of these, however, were constructed explicitly for the investigation of some particular variable or phenomenon and are therefore severely restricted in their range of application. In view of recent demonstrations of the sizable effects on anagram difficulty of such variables as anagram letter order and frequency of occurrence in the English language of either the word solution itself or letter sequences contained in the anagram or in its solution (Mayzner and Tresselt, 1958, 1959, 1962; Ronning, 1965), there can be little question as to the need for more careful and systematic construction and calibration of anagrams as a prerequisite

Table 13-3   Examples of double-solution anagrams from Rees and Israel (1935).

Anagram	Solutions*		Frequency of no solution
ATRTS	START (90)	TARTS (83)	5
LABET	TABLE (167)	BLEAT (4)	7
LIKSL	SKILL (122)	KILLS (47)	9
RWECS	SCREW (85)	CREWS (70)	23
EOSRS	ROSES (95)	SORES (58)	25
ESWVI	WIVES (86)	VIEWS (64)	28
RTBHO	THROB (78)	BROTH (71)	29
RCAMH	CHARM (71)	MARCH (71)	36
VRACE	CRAVE (119)	CARVE (21)	38
HAICN	CHAIN (136)	CHINA (2)	40
PRELE	LEPER (103)	REPEL (29)	46
ARTCE	TRACE (108)	CRATE (24)	46
TEVSO	STOVE (94)	VOTES (32)	52
ORTEW	WROTE (89)	TOWER (37)	52
RIDFE	FRIED (71)	FIRED (54)	53
MSPAC	CAMPS (81)	SCAMP (44)	53
OTTUR	TUTOR (64)	TROUT (59)	55
AEPHC	CHEAP (74)	PEACH (45)	59
ANGOR	GROAN (83)	ORGAN (29)	66
ACETH	TEACH (61)	CHEAT (50)	67
PIESC	SPICE (93)	EPICS (12)	73
GIRED	DIRGE (73)	RIDGE (21)	84

* Numbers in parentheses represent the frequency of each solution in 1 min. by 178 undergraduate psychology students given neutral instructions (Spera, 1962).

to future research employing these materials.

Another similar but less common problem of the verbal type is the *alphabet maze* wherein several individual letters are presented in matrix form (Cowen, Wiener, and Hess, 1953). Beginning with the letter at a specified start point, the subject is asked to find a path to a particular goal point such that the sequence of letters along the path spells out a complete word or phrase.

In *verbal-oddity problems,* the subject is presented with a series of letter sequences or words (e.g., add, subtract, multiply, increase) and is asked to select the one that is different from the others (e.g., Burack, 1950). As used by Cofer (1957) in the study of factors related to set or direction in problem solving, each problem in the series has two possible solutions (in the above example, either "subtract" or "increase" could be excluded on the basis of failure to describe growing magnitude or arithmetic operations, respectively).

Verbal problem series may well have little in common beyond their largely verbal content and would appear to vary considerably in the extent to which perceptual, spatial, and abstract conceptual relationships are involved. The verbal content of these problems allows them the distinct advantage of representing the realm of behavior in which the bulk of human problem-solving activity takes place. However, it also subjects them to all the complications introduced due to the highly complex, undimensionalized, and individualistic nature of processes at the verbal level. Further complications are created by the extensive and largely uncontrollable effects of differential previous experience of subjects with such verbal materials.

Nonverbal problem series. Few problem series have been devised that are primarily physical or nonverbal in nature, and fewer still have seen sufficient experimental use to merit discussion here. Katona (1940) describes a series of card-trick problems, wherein the subject's task is to arrange a certain number of playing cards in such an order that when "played" face up on the table in a prescribed fashion, the cards will match some specified pattern (e.g., alternate red and black cards, alternate odd- and even-numbered cards). Also introduced by Katona (1940) was a series of matchstick problems that can be presented in paper-and-pencil form as well as with actual matchsticks. Finally, several investigators have used some form of Peterson's disk-transfer problem (Peterson and Lanier, 1929), wherein the subject is presented with a fixed triangular array of three circles, one of which initially contains a stack of disks. The disks, each of a different diameter, are arranged in order with the smallest at the top and the largest at the bottom of the stack. The problem is to transfer, one by one, the entire stack of disks to a specified one of the other circles in as few moves as possible, using the third circle as a way station and without ever putting a larger disk on top of a smaller one. When presented as a series, successive problems may involve the addition of one more disk to the initial stack. Since the difficulty of the problem increases exponentially as the number of disks increases (i.e., minimum number of moves = 2^{n-1}, where n represents the number of disks), problems with more than five or six disks are impractical, although the use of as many as eight has been reported (Ewert and Lambert, 1932).

Multistage problems

One major defect common to most of the methods described thus far is their failure to meet adequately the criterion of maximizing observable behavior, inasmuch as overt behavior (at least that which can be systematically observed and measured) is limited to activity occurring at the time that the problem is finally solved. Efforts to correct this undesirable state of affairs by requiring subjects to verbalize or to write down what they are doing during the presolution process have not been particularly effective under most of these methods, largely because attempts to standardize or to control the kinds of presolution behavior to be observed, an essential prerequisite to their systematic measurement, may seriously interfere with the problem-solving behavior itself.

The most promising way out of this impasse has been provided by the development of problem-solving methods in which several different phases or stages are involved, each of which can be readily reflected in terms of observable behavior. Many of the multistage problems, particularly those most widely used for experimental purposes, also involve a continual modification in the nature or structure of the problem at each successive stage. Although all but a few of these multistage problems have been developed within the past few years, their impact on problem-solving research has already been a significant one. There is every reason to expect that such methods will dominate the future course of experimental work in this area. Consequently, we shall describe several multistage problem-solving methods in some detail, with emphasis on those which are most generally applicable and are not restricted to a particular mode of content or topical area. Each method can also be presented as a series of related problems, although this is not a necessary characteristic of multistage problems. Many of the problems have evolved from military investigations of troubleshooting, i.e., the diagnosis of the causes of malfunctioning in complex mechanical or electronic equipment.

Troubleshooting problems. A representative method derived from troubleshooting investigations is the tab-item technique (Glaser, Damrin, and Gardner, 1954), which consists of three basic units: (1) a description of the problem or symptom; (2) a series of statements of diagnostic procedures or courses of action that can be taken to obtain further information relevant to the solution of the problem, which the subject accomplishes by removing tabs under which are given the results of each particular diagnostic procedure; (3) a list of possible solutions to the problem, each adjacent to another tab covering statements indicating whether that particular solution is correct or incorrect for the stated problem. The subject's task is to find the correct solution by pulling as few tabs as possible, his problem-solving behavior being measurable in terms of the number and content of the tabs pulled, as well as the sequence or order in which they were pulled. A technique of this sort is potentially applicable to problems of a wide range of content and complexity within which a large number of independent variables can be manipulated and their effects determined.

The diagnostic-information-gathering (DIG) problem described by Neimark (1961) differs from tab-item techniques primarily in its greater emphasis on the description and control of task variables and its amenability to the direct observation and description of the characteristics of the subject's sequence of responses. The DIG procedure includes a problem board containing several movable shutters set in a circular pattern. Each shutter or mask covers a single binary (black or white) element. The subject, provided with an answer sheet containing a series of *possible* patterns of black and white elements, attempts to determine which of these patterns is in the problem board by opening as few shutters as possible. Neimark has been able to vary such characteristics as the number of solution patterns and informational uncertainty distribution among elements and to provide detailed descriptions of the response sequences or strategies adopted by subjects in attempting to solve a variety of problems under these conditions. This procedure is relatively simple and inexpensive, although more appropriate for problems with perceptual content than for those with verbal content.

Primarily as a result of the applied origins of the troubleshooting technique, a number of strictly mechanical procedures have also been developed. Several of these, designed explicitly to simulate some particular type of complex mechanical equipment for testing and training purposes, are therefore highly limited in their application for experimental purposes. Their general nature, however, is well illustrated by a device consisting of a complex pattern of lights and switches, originally designed to simulate the troubleshooting process in the APQ-24 radar set, which has been described in detail by Marx, Goldbeck, and Bernstein (1956). The basic components of this apparatus are essentially the same as those of the tab-item procedure, except that a pattern of lights is used to present the nature of the problem or symptom as well as the results of the various checking or information-gathering responses, which consist of the manipulation of switches interconnected with one another in a complex but previously specified fashion. A separate replacement panel of switches is used to represent possible solutions to the problem, and the subject's task is to solve the problem by throwing the correct switch on the replacement panel with as few "checking" responses as possible.

Another such device is the problem solving and information (PSI) apparatus, which consists of an interconnected set of lights and pushbutton switches presented in a circular pattern. The subject's task is to turn on a center light (indicating solution) by operating two or more of the switches in a specified sequence or order. Originally developed by John, Rimoldi, and Miller and described by John (1957), the PSI device is available commercially (Standard Electronics Co., 6728 S. Halstead Ave., Chicago, Ill.). E. G. French and Thomas (1958) describe a similar device consisting of parallel rows of seven lights and switches that are multiply interconnected. The subject is instructed to produce a specified light pattern by operating the appropriate switches. This task, however, also involves the additional complication that when any given switch is thrown, its on-off relationship to each of the lights to which it is connected is reversed. R. S. French

(1954) and Laughery and Gregg (1962) describe similar devices differing mainly in the nature of the sequential relationships involved. Another variation of this technique is a mechanical version of the familiar game of *Battleship* described by Donahoe (1960). In *Battleship,* the subject attempts to locate and sink ships by operating switches corresponding to various possible locations of the ships. After each attempted "shot," information is presented to the subject by lights located on the panel, indicating the amount and direction of error. Other troubleshooting devices of some potential research value include the Gear Train apparatus (Fattu, Mech, and Kapas, 1954) and the AUTO-MASTS test (Bryan, Bond, Laporte, and Summers, 1954).

While such mechanical devices possess the distinct advantage of being fully automatic and, therefore, should provide more objective, reliable, and presumably more sensitive measures of the subject's performance, the investigator must seriously consider their greater expense and lesser adaptability to problems varying in content and mode of presentation. Until the various troubleshooting procedures have received considerably more usage in problem-solving experiments, so that a reasonable basis for comparison between them is provided, any attempt to evaluate their relative merits and demerits would be decidedly premature.

Calculus of propositions. Similar in many respects to the various troubleshooting methods, but developing from an entirely different background of interest, is a procedure described by Moore and Anderson (1954). The distinct feature of this task is its almost complete independence of problem content and therefore its reduction of differential transfer effects based on previous experience. This is accomplished through the use of problems described in terms of symbols of a highly meaningless and abstract nature. The subject is given certain premises from which he is to reach a specified conclusion through the application of given transformation rules, which in stepwise fashion eventually convert the premises and the expressions derived therefrom into the form of the conclusion.

As used by Moore and Anderson (1954), the problem content has consisted of the propositional variables and constants of the calculus of propositions from symbolic logic (also describable as an interpretation of Boolean algebra). Before attempting to solve the problem, subjects are first taught 12 rules of formation and transformation which can be applied to the premises or derived expressions. The abstract content form of the calculus of propositions can be readily translated into highly meaningful variables and relationships between them, thereby demonstrating the wide range of problem content (a primary advantage of this method).

Modified parlor games. One parlor game adapted for research purposes is the "Twenty Questions" procedure described by Taylor and Faust (1952) and Bendig (1953), wherein the subject is told that an object is animal, vegetable, or mineral and attempts to identify the object by asking as few questions as possible, being limited to questions that can be answered by "yes," "no," or "partly." The high proportion of failures to solve the problems in 20 questions or less has caused researchers typically to allow a larger number (e.g., 30).

Similar to several parlor games is the word-formation problem described by Battig (1957), in which the subject attempts to identify a specified word by guessing letters of the alphabet, being told for each letter only whether or not it is in the word at all and, if so, what position(s) it holds in the word. Initially the subject is told only the word length and is asked to identify the word by guessing as few total letters as possible. Another problem with similar origins is the familiar jigsaw puzzle in which the subject attempts to fit several irregularly cut pieces together to form a specified pattern or picture (Solley and Snyder, 1958).

Each of the parlor-game methods is subject to considerable influence from previous experience, both with the problem itself and with the particular content areas employed. Therefore, serious difficulties may evolve with respect to the specification and control of relevant variables. Because of their popularity, however, parlor games may have strong compensating advantages with regard to motivation and interest of subjects in continuing sustained performance. Adequate motivation to persevere in working on the problem is not always inherent in the various troubleshooting devices and would seem to be particularly lacking in such abstract problems as the Moore and Anderson calculus-of-propositions technique.

It is both surprising and highly regrettable that with few exceptions the researchers directly responsible for the initial development of most of the multistage problems described in this section appear to be no longer active in problem-solving research. While it is too early to determine the ultimate significance of this apparent mass defection, it will undoubtedly retard the future development and evaluation of procedures of this type, unless embryo researchers in problem solving are sufficiently attracted to the use of presently existing multistage methods. Rather than reflecting negatively on the potential research value of multistage methods, it is our hypothesis that this phenomenon more directly represents the unfortunate but prevalent tendency among experimental psychologists to be repelled by problems, procedures, or designs characterized by increasing complexity in favor of those which are maximally simple. The obvious inappropriateness of this type of research strategy in the study of "complex processes" requires no further comment.

DECISION-MAKING PROCEDURES

The essential features of decision making are (1) the presentation of some situation wherein either of two or more distinguishable events may occur, (2) less than complete a priori certainty as to which of these in actuality will occur, and (3) the requirement that the subject make some sort of prediction or decision related to these uncertain conditions. Thus, the majority of studies of decision making have adopted a procedure closely related to some typical gambling situation. Unfortunately, and probably because of the unusually heavy emphasis on theoretical and mathematical model-building activities, there has been relatively little research activity directed toward the systematic development and evaluation of experimental procedures for the study of decision making. A further consequence of this theoretical emphasis has been a predominance of experiments designed to test or check particular assumptions or parameters underlying various alternative decision-making models. This not only has led to a concentration on very simple decision-making methods, hardly worthy of the name "complex process," but also has made much of the work carried on by researchers purportedly interested in decision making virtually indistinguishable from that generally classified under the areas of psychophysics, scaling, or perceptual discrimination processes. Moreover, the study of various kinds of small-group interactions has been found to be particularly fruitful in a decision-making context, so that there is a significant overlap between decision-making and experimental approaches to social behavior. Since much of this material has been referred to in other chapters of this book, our coverage will be very limited, consisting of a few methods found to be uniquely useful for the experimental study of individual decision making.

Most experimental studies of decision making have made use of some form of multiple-alternative (usually only two) choice or "bet" whereby, depending on the outcome, the subject receives differential monetary gains, losses, or both. Edwards (1953, 1954a) and others have consistently shown marked differences in decision making as a function of the probability of winning or losing, the extent to which real money is involved, and the type of bet outcomes. There is little indication, however, that these considerations have systematically influenced the development of experimental methods for this type of research. Detailed descriptions are available of experimental procedures using gambling devices that simulate a pinball machine (Edwards, 1953, 1954a), various dice games (Mosteller and Nogee, 1951; Scodel, Ratoosh, and Minas, 1959), or simple verbal bets with no content beyond statements of odds and amount to be won or lost (Coombs and Pruitt, 1960). As an example of the last-named type of procedure, the subject may be presented with the two alternative bets given below and asked to choose which of the bets he would prefer:

1. Win 50 cents with a probability of 1:3, lose 25 cents with a probability of 2:3
2. Win 35 cents with a probability of 1:2, lose 35 cents with a probability of 1:2

Pairs of bets can readily be constructed which vary systematically with respect to the probability of either winning or losing, the amount won or lost, or the expected long-range monetary outcome of each bet. More automatized versions of such procedures, which greatly increase the efficiency of information presentation and significantly reduce the often prohibitive amount of time required in these experiments, are likely to bear little resemblance to any actual gambling or decision-making task, such as those making use of counters (Becker, 1958) or lights (Pruitt, 1961). Particularly valuable for studies concerned with statistical decision making is a method described by Irwin, Smith, and Mayfield (1956), wherein subjects are presented with a long series of cards, each containing one of a specified set of numbers, and asked to make estimates and/or confidence judgments concerning various characteristics (e.g., averages, differences) of these numbers. Similar advantages accrue to Lee's (1963) statistical decision-making procedure, wherein differently positioned individual dots are each to be assigned to one of two or more previously designated spatially overlapping distributions.

Procedures such as the above, characterized by relatively simple types of stimulus situations, have dominated decision-making experimentation to date. However, the development of more complex procedures appears likely to have an impact on future experimentation. Schipper (1961) describes a procedure wherein the stimulus patterns consist of various patterns of the binary (ON-OFF) states of each of five lights, each light being independently manipulable both in overall frequency of occurrence in a long series of patterns and in the relative frequency with which it is followed by each of two outcomes (represented by another set of two lights). The subject's task is to predict which of these two outcomes will occur for each of a long series of patterns. A similar method, which was described earlier in the section on conceptual behavior (page 549), is that of Uhl (1963), which differs primarily in (1) the use of a larger number of possible states of each stimulus alternative (consisting of the lighting of one in each of several rows of lights); (2) the corresponding presence of a larger number of response alternatives; and (3) the existence of a rule or principle permitting errorless performance, defined in terms of a relationship between the various stimulus elements, which are given differential weighting expressible in the form of an algebraic equation. This last-mentioned feature also characterizes a method devised by Cronbach and Azuma (1961), which in most other respects is identical to a typical concept-formation procedure employing geometric forms. Such methods serve to point up the tremendous overlap between procedures for the study of conceptual behavior and decision making, along with the inevitable involvement of each in procedures explicitly designed to study the other.

A similar overlap is evident between decision-making and problem-solving methods, particularly those discussed herein as multi-stage problems, which Edwards (1962) has recently referred to as procedures for the study of dynamic decision making. All this demonstrates that studies of conceptual behavior, problem solving, and decision making represent primarily differences in interest or emphasis, rather than a fundamental distinction in the nature of the subject matter, which suggests that future experimentation will become increasingly characterized by the simultaneous study of more than one of these thought processes.

METHODS FOR THE STUDY OF PRODUCTIVE THINKING

Thinking at the productive extreme of the reproductive-productive continuum is by its very nature highly resistant to laboratory investigation, so that it should come as no surprise to find that relatively little presently exists in the way of methods adequate for its experimental study. Moreover, thinking that is new or original as far as the subject is concerned but is largely reproductive from the experimenter's point of view probably characterizes most of the conceptual, problem-solving, and decision-making methods discussed thus far. Consequently, the present section will be limited to a few methods that for one reason or another appear to be most appropriately included under the heading of "productive" or "creative" thinking.

First of all, it should be pointed out that "reasoning" as a separate thought process, sometimes distinguished on the basis of the characteristic of combining old elements to produce something new, is on at least as shaky ground with respect to methodological distinctions as it is at a semantic level. The overlap is particularly great with problem solving, and several of the procedures included in the section on problem-solving (pages 553 to 560) have been or could be described as methods for the study of reasoning, most notably the Moore-Anderson calculus-of-propositions task, the PSI apparatus of

John *et al.* as employed by Blatt and Stein (1959), and Cofer's version of the verbal-oddity problem. To these we need add only the classical logical "syllogism," obtainable in quantity from any introductory textbook in logic and widely used throughout the history of the study of thought processes, and perhaps the various "incomplete series" methods common to most intelligence or verbal aptitude tests (e.g., what numbers come next in the numerical series 1, 4, 9, 16, —), as adapted specifically for research purposes by Hunter (1957) and Westcott (1961; see also Bartlett, 1958).

Although there is a vast literature concerned with "creativity" in thinking, much of this has been exclusively in the realm of discussion and speculation, and attempts to approach these problems empirically have extended little beyond the development of various tests or diagnostic measures of individual differences in "creativity." Since this work is still in its exploratory stages, little of it has been applied for experimental purposes. One notable exception is an extensive experimental program by Maltzman (1960), who has adopted as his principal tool Guilford's Unusual Uses Test (Wilson, Guilford, and Christensen, 1953). The subject is presented with the names of individual objects (e.g., automobile tire, key, button) and attempts to think of as many uses or functions of these objects as he can. A simple variant of the common word-association test is also used. In this test the subject attempts to give unique or unusual associations to the stimulus words, although the efficacy of this procedure is currently a matter of considerable controversy (Caron, Unger, and Parloff, 1963; Gallup, 1963; Maltzman and Gallup, 1964). Another procedure has been adapted directly from a "brainstorming" context by Taylor, Berry, and Block (1957). It consists in verbally described problem situations capable of eliciting many and varied answers or solutions; e.g., "What steps can you suggest that would get more European tourists to come to this country? What practical benefits or difficulties would result if everyone had an extra thumb, just like the present one but on the other side of the hand?"[1]

The principal distinguishing characteristic of such procedures is their emphasis on the frequency and variability of different responses, with relatively less concern for the adequacy of these as "solutions" to the problem. While variability would appear to be a necessary condition for original or creative thinking, it is clearly not a sufficient condition. Recognition of this fact has led Maltzman (1960) to make a distinction between originality, defined as behavior that is infrequent and uncommon but relevant to the conditions under which it occurs, and creativity, which additionally implies that the results of the original thinking have some important effect on the physical or social environment (see also Mednick, 1962). In terms of this distinction, the methods listed here are concerned solely with originality. Methods designed for the experimental study of creativity have yet to be devised, and there is little in the current situation to make us very optimistic that they ever will be.

DEPENDENT-VARIABLE MEASUREMENT AND ANALYSIS

There is sufficient uniformity among dependent variables in conceptual behavior, problem solving, and decision making to obviate the necessity of a separate description for each, despite previously discussed differences in experimental procedures. Following a few necessary general remarks about performance criteria, a brief discussion of *overall performance measures* (i.e., the ultimate product of the subject's behavior or his terminal or asymptotic performance level) will be presented, to be followed by a section on *detailed* (trial by trial or stage by stage) *performance measures,* which are more closely re-

[1] The methodological problems involved in comparing problem-solving efficiency of individuals working alone and in groups are discussed in Lorge, Fox, Davitz, and Brenner (1958) and Taylor and McNemar (1955b).

lated to the process by which terminal performance is attained.

Performance criteria

In most concept and problem-solving tasks, the subject performs until he solves the problem that confronts him. Some experimenters place a limit on the time allowed for this purpose and assign an arbitrary minimal score to (or ignore) the performance record of any subject who fails to attain solution. Time limits, when they are necessary, should obviously be set so that only a small and equal proportion of subjects fail to meet criterion in all conditions of the experiment, to avoid results vitiated by severe sampling biases.

The subject's attainment of a correct solution is, in some tasks, difficult for the experimenter to identify. For this reason, there is a widespread preference for tasks with only one *ultimate* solution, which also permit more meaningful use of detailed performance measures (Ray, 1955; however, see Saugstad, 1957, for one argument in favor of tasks with multiple solutions). Generally the experimenter will take as evidence of solution some act of behavior on the part of the subject that is extremely improbable if he has not attained solution. A criterion employed in concept experiments, for example, is a series of some preestablished number of consecutively correct category responses, e.g., 16, which has chance probability of approximately 0.000015 in a two-concept problem. In other instances, a single correct motor or verbal response, the *chance* probability of which is infinitesimal, may be sufficient to demonstrate the solution. Less stringent criteria may be employed in those experiments in which perfect performance on the part of all subjects is unlikely or no complete solution exists, as in the typical decision-making task. In such instances, it is not uncommon to allow each subject a fixed number of trials or "plays." This procedure may be desirable when it is necessary that all subjects have equal exposure to problem elements but

should probably be avoided if it is not possible to obtain a trial-by-trial evaluation of performance. If, as is generally the case, the number of trials is fixed so that some subjects can be expected to reach solution before the trial series is complete, the experimenter may release subjects from the experiment upon the attainment of some predetermined criterion of solution. In addition to its obvious motivational advantages, such a procedure avoids the problems created by discarding the data of "nonsolvers" and prevents the contamination of obtained performance measures by behavior occurring after solution, which often reflects something quite different (e.g., resistance to boredom) from what the experimenter is directly interested in studying.

Overall performance measures

Some of the more common overall quantitative measures of performance in studies of complex processes are presented below. This list and the accompanying references to the literature are by no means meant to be complete: (1) the number of subjects attaining the correct solution (Marks, 1951); (2) time to solution (Battig, 1957); (3) in problem series, the number of problems solved (Fattu et al., 1954); (4) the number of subgoals attained (S. B. Anderson, 1957); (5) the total number of responses or number of incorrect or irrelevant responses in problem-solving tasks (S. B. Anderson, 1957; Solley, 1957; Taylor and Faust, 1952), the number of stimuli correctly (or incorrectly) categorized or the total number of stimuli displayed before solution in concept problems (Brown and Archer, 1956), or the proportion of times each alternative event is predicted in decision-making situations (Goodnow, 1955); (6) measures of response stereotypy or redundancy within a single problem (S. B. Anderson, 1957; Fattu et al., 1954); (7) amount of information presented, e.g., number of hints (Gagne and Brown, 1961), number of clues (Neimark, 1961), or size of stimulus sample (Becker, 1958), before a solution is offered or a decision is made. Ray (1955) has provided a more detailed account and exhaustive listing of such measures for problem-solving tasks.

It should be mentioned (in part for theoretical reasons) that many performance measures taken in the context of decision making are aimed at the determination of the *subjective probability* and/or of the subjective value or *utility* of alternative events. As has been elaborated by Edwards (1961), both subjective probability and utility may be measured by direct methods, based on psychophysical estimates by the subject of the probability, proportion, or value of a given event; or by indirect methods, based on the proportion of times a given event is selected or predicted in a gamelike or gambling situation. For a discussion of the assumptions and difficulties entailed in the use of such procedures as tests of static decision models, see Edwards (1961).

The usefulness and implications of overall performance indices are fairly obvious and need no elaboration. Each is readily measurable, is easy to analyze, and has been shown to be lawfully related to a variety of independent variables. But they are at best a superficial description of the effects of these variables and tell nothing about the process or series of steps that contribute to the ultimate form of the subject's behavior. When so little is known of the factors involved in the attainment of solution in these tasks, it is disturbing to find a large number of experiments content with the analysis of overall measures.

Detailed performance measures

For most experimental problems it seems reasonable to assume that an independent variable which affects the characteristics of ultimate performance also influences the sequence of behaviors leading to it. Tasks that permit access not only to the overall product of the subject's activity but also to the detailed structure of performance, such as those

in which there are several clearly identifiable subgoals, would seem to be considerably more useful and informative. The researcher is limited to gross measures only when the task is of the one-shot variety. Whenever there are several clearly definable subgoals to be attained prior to ultimate solution, a series of trials on the same problem, or a series of independent problems of the same type, the absolute amount of overt behavior is increased and more intensive analyses of the subject's performance are possible. The net gain from the use of such tasks should be greater precision in the system of behavioral quantification and an increase in information about otherwise implicit or covert intervening processes contributing to eventual success or failure. Note, however, that many problem series are also restricted to measures in terms of number of solutions attained or time per solution, and yield no more information concerning intermediate stages of performance than do such problems used singly.

Since detailed performance measures are heavily dependent on the characteristics of the experimenter's procedure, those which are appropriate for discussion vary markedly. A representative sample of available techniques important for the evaluation and understanding of various complex processes follows:

1. *Overt errors.* Many tasks permit a variety of finer analyses on the overall performance measure, total number of overt errors to solution. Particularly in multistage and multiple-concept problems, the distribution of errors across task elements or available response alternatives is often a useful indicator of the relative availability, obviousness, or hierarchical structure of various possible solutions, subgoals, or stimulus characteristics. For example, Underwood and Richardson (1956b) have shown that in a multiple-verbal-concept task the number of errors specific to each concept is a direct function of its previously defined dominance. Brown and Archer (1956) have found certain "positional" stimulus dimensions, such as the hori-

zontal location of a geometric design on its background, particularly difficult to use singly or in combination with other dimensions as a basis for categorizing. These findings are reminiscent of Heidbreder's (1946) order of dominance among concepts. Similarly, French (1954) has quantified the relative difficulty of various subgoals (component responses) in a multistage problem in terms of the number of errors made in attaining each.

Grant (1951) and his collaborators, working with the WCST, have shown that perseverative errors (incorrect responses that would have been correct in a preceding sorting stage with a different relevant dimension) and nonperseverative errors may be differentially related to important variables (see Erlebacher and Archer, 1961). In support of Heidbreder (1946), these results indicate that certain concepts tend to perseverate into later sorting stages more than others. In another concept learning task, Cahill and Hovland (1960) isolated two types of incorrect responses, those attributable to the subject's failure to perceive correctly or to make appropriate inferences about the concept from the instance presented (perceptual-inference errors) and those which reflect an incompatibility between the subject's response and information present in previously seen instances (memory errors). A similar index of memory is reflected in Donahoe's (1960) definition of the "goodness" of a response in terms of whether it tested a possible problem solution that had not been eliminated on any earlier trial.

In most tasks of the concept or problem-solving variety, each of the responses is either correct or incorrect, relevant or irrelevant to solution. In concept problems, this arises from the nature of category relationships, which are defined by mutual exclusion. There are concept (Uhl, 1963) and problem-solving (Fattu et al., 1954) tasks, however, in which responses are made on one or more multivalued dimensions and can be scored in terms of extent or magnitude of error. Such a measure may show change even after the subject has delineated the relevant task elements, which affords additional precision in a complete analysis of behavior.

2. *Response sequences.* Nearly always, the experimenter may consider the subject's overt responses to be systematically related to and indicative of his use of some hypothesis about the problem's solution or of a certain overall strategy or method of attack on the problem. Multistage problems such as those produced with the tab-item technique (Glaser et al., 1954) and other troubleshooting tasks are designed so that each hypothesis tested by the subject is expressed in a distinct overt manipulation of task elements. Each response may be evaluated in terms of its correctness or relevancy with respect to solution and in terms of the particular hypothesis of which its selection represents a test. The content of responses and the series of hypotheses tested are straightforward reflections of the subject's method of attack on the problem.

Typically, the subject's task in experiments utilizing the tab-item technique, the DIG apparatus, and similar procedures is to produce a solution in as few response moves or with as few clues as possible. Neimark (1961) has shown that the number of solutions attained in a problem series and the time to solution may be insensitive to the effects of several important task variables (see also Fattu et al., 1954) and that much more precise and complete information is provided by analyses of an overall measure of the absolute amount of information-gathering activity on each problem (see Item 7, overall measures) and the mean informational content of each response. Problems on the DIG apparatus are constructed so that the maximum amount of information provided by any response is one bit; i.e., the best moves reduce the still possible solutions by one-half. Thus, the adequacy of the subject's strategy or sequence of moves may be quantified according to how closely he maximizes the informational content of moves. One other promising measure is the ratio of information transmitted by each move, as reflected by the subject's subsequent responses, to the actual or potential amount of information provided by the move. This index is a quantification of the degree to which the subject effectively uses the available information in exposed clues. Similar measures of information-gathering activity or information demand have been used in other problem-solving tasks (Detambel and Stolurow, 1957; Glaser *et al.*, 1954) and, in a modified fashion, in concept-formation problems that permit the subject to select the successive stimuli to be categorized (Bruner *et al.*, 1956).

In most studies of decision making and concept identification, single response choices cannot be used as indicators of the subject's current hypothesis, since any particular category response or prediction may represent the test of several hypotheses. There are some useful response-sequence analyses, however, that provide a basis for strong inferences about the subject's method of attack. For example, conditional-probability measures of relationships or dependencies of responses on preceding trial events or responses have been used effectively on several occasions to determine the nature of the subject's sequential response tendencies, hypotheses, or strategies (e.g., Anderson, 1960; Goodnow, 1955; Jarvik, 1951).

As an illustration of response-sequence analyses in concept studies, consider the case in which the subject is testing the hypothesis that variation in color is relevant to categorizing geometric stimuli correctly. Until the hypothesis is infirmed, his category responses should change whenever the color of the stimulus design changes but be unrelated to other stimulus variations. A particularly promising technique for the analysis of response sequences was developed by Cronbach and Azuma (1961), but may be adequate only in those cases in which stimuli vary ordinally within each stimulus dimension. Stimulus dimensions used by Cronbach and Azuma were the horizontal and vertical locations of objects in a 16×16 matrix of cells.

The method entails the computation of correlations, within successive blocks of, say, 32 trials, between each subject's category responses (numerical estimates of the stimulus value) and the levels assumed by the stimuli on their various dimensions. If a stimulus dimension (or combination of dimensions) correlates highly with a particular category response sequence, that dimension is said to have *criteriality* for the subject at that time; i.e., the subject is testing the relevancy of that dimension. Correlations for individual subjects may be inspected to determine the various hypotheses tested before criterion is attained, and correlations between responses and the relevant dimension(s) may also be averaged over subjects to show the group trend toward solution.

The task of evaluating hypotheses on the basis of response sequence is often difficult and subject to sizable error, especially when hypotheses are complex and multidimensional in form or when the subject shifts rapidly from one hypothesis to another. When appropriately used, however, the Cronbach-Azuma procedure, and possibly variations thereof for nominal categories based on information-theory measures, offer promising means of delineating some implicit behaviors without recourse to the subject's often invalid verbalizations. Such procedures, however, encounter the serious difficulty that the number of potentially testable hypotheses may be extremely large; and, of course, the larger the number, the greater the amount of computational labor invested in a complete analysis. Nevertheless, this represents perhaps the most objective approach presently available to the study of intervening processes in concept problems. It promises to be increasingly useful in view of the increasing availability of computer techniques to lessen computational burden.

The measures and analyses described above are evaluations of performance characteristics *within* response sequences. Battig (1957) has described an index of flexibility for performance on word-formation problems that is generally useful, in a problem series of comparable problems with a known and fixed number of alternative responses, for comparisons *between* two or more response sequences of the same subject. The measure is essentially the proportion of the total variance attributable to differences between the orders in which response alternatives occur across the subject's response sequences on the various problems, attaining a maximum value of 1 when the same sequence of responses is employed on each of two or more problems, and a minimum of zero when all response alternatives are equally likely to occur at each point in the sequence. Measures of response repetitiousness (Fattu *et al.,* 1954) or redundancy (Anderson, 1957) may be useful for quantifying the same sort of information in other tasks. Because the details of these procedures are lengthy, the reader should consult the primary sources for a complete description.

3. *Time characteristics.* Whenever there are clearly defined boundaries between the trials of a subject-paced experimental task, intratrial time measures are recordable and may provide some useful information about behavioral processes. In studies of conceptual behavior, for example, there are at least two critical intratrial time intervals: *response latency* and the *subject-determined postfeedback interval.* Response latency refers to the time between the onset of a stimulus and the subject's response. On the average it can be expected that the length of this interval will gradually decrease as the subject eliminates the irrelevant information and approaches solution. It may also reflect the amount of implicit activity that goes into the formulation of any particular response. Assuming that intratrial learning is not immediate and complete as an automatic function of the presentation of feedback (knowledge of results), it may be that the subject uses the subject-determined postfeedback interval to process the information retained from the stimulus and feedback signal given on that trial.

The lengths of these intervals have rarely been recorded and used as dependent variables, though it is reasonable to suspect that each of them is a function of various conditions, particularly the amount of information in the stimulus materials (Bourne and Bunderson, 1963). A separate trial-by-trial recording and analysis of these measures would probably yield considerably more precise information than the frequently used analyses of overall time to solution (e.g., Archer *et al.,* 1955). There are only a few problem-solving studies in which response latencies have been analyzed (e.g., Solley and Snyder, 1958).

A measure similar to response latency has been employed in some studies of decision making under the label "decision time," which has shown strong relationships to certain experimental variables, such as uncertainty of response outcome, and tends to be correlated highly with subjective estimates of confidence in the correctness of responses (Festinger, 1943).

4. *Verbalized hypotheses.* We have noted that it is often possible to infer the existence and the nature of underlying processes from detailed considerations of the structure of the subject's overt category, predictive, or manipulative responses. Some experimenters have further attempted to externalize the subject's implicit behavior by eliciting verbalized hypotheses in the form of answers to a standard question or set of questions, e.g., "On what stimulus dimension(s) was your last response based?" or "What do you think the solution is now?" In fact, in certain instances the subject's category response directly represents his hypothesis about the correct means of categorization (Underwood and Richardson, 1956b). It would be a mistake to assume that all verbal accompaniments of thinking are valid measures of underlying processes (Kendler and Kendler, 1962). If, however, the subject's verbalizations are responses to standard questions and are analyzed as such or if they are systematically related to manipulatory responses, they

may reveal additional information not obtainable in any other way.

In the studies of Bruner *et al.* (1956), several systematic approaches to single-concept problems of the conjunctive type, which were a function in part of whether the experimenter or the subject determined the order of stimuli within a problem, were identifiable on the basis of the sequence of verbalized hypotheses given by subjects. The classification of the subject's strategy depended upon the scope of his initial hypothesis, the changes in composition of successive hypotheses, and the nature and order of stimuli selected within subject-determined sequences. A modification of this analysis, concerned more with hypothesis shifts and their relationship to overall performance measures in multiconcept problems, was reported by Bourne (1965). Detambel and Stolurow (1957) and Cohen and Hansel (1956), respectively, have described similar analyses of the subject's verbal behavior during performance on troubleshooting tasks and tasks with uncertain outcomes.

Any particular stimulus in a single-concept problem is either a positive or a negative instance that confirms or infirms the hypothesis verbalized by the subject on the preceding trial. Bruner *et al.* (1956) scored each subject according to the correctness of his hypothesis modifications based on the information available in each of the four stimulus contingencies and, in this way, evaluated the difficulty of handling each.

5. *Individual differences.* Detailed performance measures of the types illustrated above have been shown in several recent studies to be particularly useful in the study of quantitative aspects of individual differences among subjects working on the same problem (e.g., Battig, 1957; Fattu *et al.*, 1954; Westcott, 1961). Analyses of this sort are closely tied to the task and measures of an experiment and cannot be outlined completely here. As an illustration, however, Battig classified subjects as "good" and "poor" problem solvers on the basis of the total number of guesses made prior to solution on each of a series of word-formation problems and then investigated the characteristics of strategies used by these subgroups. As compared with "poor" subjects, "good" solvers tended to guess initial letters on the basis of frequency of letter usage in English text, were more consistent across problems, based guesses on the letter context in which they were to be made, took more time per guess, and made fewer incorrect guesses. In view of the importance of this type of analysis to any complete understanding, description, or account of the processes involved in the attainment of solutions to complex problems, it is reasonable to expect it to encompass investigations of conceptual behavior and decision making. Research of this type has achieved sufficient success to point up the advantages to be gained from a coordination of the analysis of individual differences with experimentation (Cronbach, 1957).

6. *Miscellaneous.* There are several aspects of behavior which have been recorded and analyzed in studies of complex processes and may be useful in particular problems but which, for reasons of restricted implication or lack of frequent usage, will not be outlined in detail. Examples of these include the subject's confidence in his responses (Festinger, 1943; Westcott, 1961); certain measures of verbalizations, such as the number of possible solutions mentioned (Marks and Raymond, 1951), a variation of which is used in creativity-originality research wherein the emphasis is on amount and variability in responses (Christensen *et al.*, 1957; however, see Taylor *et al.*, 1957, for information on the rated feasibility, effectiveness, and generality of such responses); the type and content of responses on particular tasks, such as the PSI (Blatt and Stein, 1959); and special performance measures, the use of which is dictated by the particular theory being tested, such as Becker's (1958) assessment of the applicability of Wald's theory of statistical decision making to human behavior (see also Wiesen and Shuford,

1961). (Obviously, the reader will have to consult the primary reports for detailed information about the use and interpretations of these measures.)

Comments

The tasks and measures employed in studies of complex processes, as in any other research area, must be reliable and replicable. To avoid unwarranted conclusions and generalizations and to delineate the functional relationships that exist between independent and dependent variables, it is necessary that performance be primarily a function of the experimentally manipulated conditions and that measures be maximally sensitive to the influence of such variables relative to the effects of chance or uncontrolled factors. Although the need for reliability is apparent, its determination either for tasks or for measures has rarely been a part of reported studies (for exceptions, see Goldbeck, Bernstein, Hillix, and Marx, 1957; Westcott, 1961), in many cases because the subject performs on the task only once and because only one behavioral measure is used.

In studying complex processes, where little is known of the tasks themselves, to say nothing of the basic phenomena, there is much to be gained from the recording and analysis of a maximum number of performance measures. If several measures correlate highly, confidence in the reliability of these measures and in the task itself may be increased. Equally useful for analytic purposes, however, may be a lack of correlation between two (or more) dependent variables, particularly for identifying and distinguishing between separable component processes in multidimensional tasks, an aim that would appear to be deserving of primary attention in the present exploratory stages of research on complex processes. Several approaches may be effectively employed in the pursuit of this goal. These include the concentrated systematic use of tasks which involve single processes or which have only one solution or one means by which solution may be at-

tained, as well as the development of multidimensional tasks in which the dimensions are known and are differentiated by various overt responses.

Another worthwhile methodological refinement involves the reduction of unnecessary intersubject variability by equating the subjects on special abilities or training that might affect performance (e.g., equating for logical or mathematical skills prior to performance on problems in the calculus of propositions) and by ensuring that all subjects are aware of the form that the correct solution must take (e.g., delimiting the set of permissible responses). Effective use of such procedures is difficult on the basis of present knowledge, and will probably require a good deal of preliminary work devoted to the study of individual differences and to the identification of those variables which account for the high degree of intersubject variability in the typical task used in the study of complex processes.

CONCLUSIONS

Problems of instrumentation, i.e., the important apparatus and equipment used in the methods discussed here, have entered only infrequently into our presentation. This is at least in part a reflection of the facts that (1) in most cases, elaborate and complex equipment has not been necessary to instrument these methods; and (2) the apparatus used is either obvious (e.g., in the pendulum problem) or identical to that discussed elsewhere in this volume (e.g., memory drums).

Some tasks have been automated to the extent that stimulus materials may be presented, responses made and recorded, and informative feedback displayed without the experimenter's assistance (e.g., Bourne, 1957). Although automated equipment offers numerous advantages, there is real doubt that the concern for automated procedures ought to be taken so seriously that the less easily controlled techniques (e.g., card sorting, paper-and-pencil tasks) are discarded. Such procedures have the compensating feature of being maximally flexible, whereas completely automated techniques tend to become highly standardized and resistant to modification, leading to results of limited generality. While the area is still in an exploratory stage there is good reason for procedural diversification and flexibility. However, such diversification can be effective only to the degree that it is orderly and systematic. Completely uncontrolled diversification, i.e., a lack of real concern among experimenters for what others purportedly studying the same phenomena are doing, can only result in complete chaos in an area as complex as this. Excessive past adherence to such a principle undoubtedly represents a major reason why this research area failed to progress significantly for many years.

Although it would seem obvious that research concerned with complex processes must be characterized by a high order of complexity thoughout all its phases, such research has been for the most part at an inappropriately simple level. This seems to be a direct and possibly inevitable result of the thorough prior grounding of most experimenters in research concerned with simpler types of behavior. In any event, the typical investigation of complex processes has been characterized by very close relationships with, if not indistinguishability from, experimentation in other areas with respect to theory, research design, selection of independent and dependent variables, and analytic and interpretative procedures. We are not arguing against legitimate efforts to relate complex processes to simpler learning and perceptual phenomena. We also recognize that limitations in the resources of the typical researcher have represented strong forces leading toward minimal complexity in the study of complex processes. However, this cannot justify the presently predominant limitation of researchers to concepts or variables directly derived from experimental approaches to operant conditioning (Skinner, 1957), trial-and-error learning (Maltzman, 1955),

or discrimination learning (Bourne and Restle, 1959). Thanks largely to the development of the digital computer, high orders of complexity of theoretical structures, research designs, and analytic procedures have now become practically feasible, and preliminary attempts to develop computer programs for the simulation of conceptual behavior (Hovland, 1960) or problem solving (e.g., Newell and Simon, 1961) clearly demonstrate that the vast number (and interrelationships) of variables and processes necessary to an adequate simulation of even the most rudimentary types of complex process is in sharp contrast to that emanating from any alternative research approach.

In summary, a platform for research on complex processes should include the following:

1. *Controlled methodological diversification,* involving a variety of systematically interrelated techniques, each given a fair and objective test.

2. *Systematic investigation of procedural and task variables,* the only satisfactory procedure for determining the nature and extent of the effects of such variables. Far too many procedures described in the literature have been used only once, and information on the effects of procedural modifications within the task, not to mention differences between it and other tasks, has been almost completely lacking.

3. *Avoidance of capricious methodological variations.* Procedural variations are justifiable only when the effect of the change on the phenomenon in question is an object of systematic investigation or has already been empirically determined. No variable, whether procedural or any other type, can be ruled out as insignificantly related to the phenomenon of interest except through its systematic manipulation; and until this has been done, the possible existence of such effects can never be overlooked. As far as initial decisions about the nature of any new method to be adopted are concerned, we suggest that this should depend heavily upon the particu-

lar experimental problem, inasmuch as differences are inevitable between the methods and analyses of studies designed merely to provide a description of overt behavior and those directed toward the analysis of underlying processes or the determination of functional relationships between dimensionalized independent and dependent variables.

4. *More complex experimental tasks and procedures,* wherein the procedure is designed so as to permit the operation of the complex processes under study to their fullest extent, as distinguished from attempts to simplify the experimental task so that the processes involved can be more readily conceptualized, observed, or measured by the experimenter. However desirable this may be on other grounds, it is clearly illegitimate to the extent that it results also in the modification or elimination of essential properties of the complex processes purportedly under study, as has not infrequently been the case in the past.

5. *Higher-order multiple-factor experimental designs,* which simultaneously investigate the effects of a large number of independent variables, both of the task-environmental and subjective (individual difference) variety, and are adequate for the determination and evaluation of complex interactions involving combinations of such variables.

6. *More performance measures,* with particular emphasis on those described as *detailed performance measures,* which concentrate on the description and analysis of behavior occurring at various stages during performance, as distinguished from those overall measures which assess only the final product. Such measures have already seen sufficient use to indicate their greater appropriateness as indices of the covert symbolic processes that are typically of primary interest, as well as being more sensitive to the effects of various independent variables. In addition, the simultaneous use and comparison of several different performance measures in a single experiment represents a highly worthwhile practice, both for purposes of evaluating relative reliability and sensitivity of various measures and also as a means of identifying and operationally distinguishing between individual variables or dimensions in multidimensional situations.

7. *More complex theoretical frameworks,* probably an inevitable by-product of the previous recommendations, adherence to which can only lead to the recognition of inadequacies of those simpler theoretical approaches currently in vogue, and their expansion or revision to keep pace with the increasing number and interdependence of variables emerging from more complete experimental analyses (see Miller, Galanter, and Pribram, 1960, for a further discussion of this point).

REFERENCES

AMMONS, R. B., and AMMONS, C. H. A standard anagram task. *Psychol. Rep.,* 1959, 5, 654–656.

ANDERSON, N. H. Effect of first-order conditional probability in a two-choice learning situation. *J. exp. Psychol.,* 1960, 59, 73–93.

ANDERSON, N. H., and WHELAN, R. E. Likelihood judgments and sequential effects in a two-choice probability learning situation. *J. exp. Psychol.,* 1960, 60, 111–120.

ANDERSON, S. B. Problem solving in multiple goal situations. *J. exp. Psychol.,* 1957, 54, 297–303.

ARCHER, E. J., BOURNE, L. E., JR., and BROWN, F. G. Concept identification as a function of irrelevant information and instructions. *J. exp. Psychol.,* 1955, 49, 153–164.

BARTLETT, F. *Thinking.* New York: Basic Books, 1958.

BATTIG, W. F. Some factors affecting performance on a word-formation problem. *J. exp. Psychol.,* 1957, 54, 96–104.

BATTIG, W. F., and BOURNE, L. E., JR. Concept identification as a function of intra- and interdimensional variability. *J. exp. Psychol.,* 1961, 61, 329–333.

BECKER, G. M. Sequential decision making: Wald's model and estimates of parameters. *J. exp. Psychol.,* 1958, 55, 628–636.

BENDIG, A. W. Twenty questions: An information analysis. *J. exp. Psychol.,* 1953, 46, 345–348.

BLATT, S. J., and STEIN, M. I. Efficiency in problem solving. *J. Psychol.*, 1959, **48**, 193–213.

BOURNE, L. E., JR. Effects of delay of information feedback and task complexity on the identification of concepts. *J. exp. Psychol.*, 1957, **54**, 201–207.

BOURNE, L. E., JR. Hypotheses and hypothesis shifts in classification learning. *J. gen. Psychol.*, 1965, **72**, 251–261.

BOURNE, L. E., JR., and BUNDERSON, C. V. Effects of delay of informative feedback and length of postfeedback interval on concept identification. *J. exp. Psychol.*, 1963, **65**, 1–5.

BOURNE, L. E., JR., and HAYGOOD, R. C. The role of stimulus redundancy in concept identification. *J. exp. Psychol.*, 1959, **58**, 232–238.

BOURNE, L. E., JR., and RESTLE, F. Mathematical theory of concept identification. *Psychol. Rev.*, 1959, **66**, 278–296.

BROWN, F. G., and ARCHER, E. J. Concept identification as a function of task complexity and distribution of practice. *J. exp. Psychol.*, 1956, **52**, 316–321.

BRUNER, J. S., GOODNOW, J. J., and AUSTIN, G. A. *A study of thinking.* New York: Wiley, 1956.

BRYAN, G. L., BOND, N. A., JR., LAPORTE, H. R., JR., and SUMMERS, S. A. The AUTOMASTS: An automatically-recording test of electronics trouble-shooting. *ONR Contract 153-093, Tech. Rep. 11*, 1954.

BUGELSKI, B. R., and HUFF, E. M. A note on increasing the efficiency of Luchins' mental sets. *Amer. J. Psychol.*, 1962, **75**, 655–667.

BURACK, B. The nature and efficacy of methods of attack on reasoning problems. *Psychol. Monogr.*, 1950, **64**, No. 7 (Whole No. 313).

BYERS, J. L., COLLINS, C. C., and LOUGHBOROUGH, W. B. An apparatus for concept attainment research. *Psychol. Rep.*, 1964, **14**, 759–773.

CAHILL, H. E., and HOVLAND, C. I. The role of memory in the acquisition of concepts. *J. exp. Psychol.*, 1960, **59**, 137–144.

CARON, A. J., UNGER, S. M., and PARLOFF, M. B. A test of Maltzman's theory of orginality training. *J. verb. Learn. verb. Behav.*, 1963, **1**, 436–442.

CHRISTENSEN, P. R., GUILFORD, J. P., and WILSON, R. C. Relations of creative responses to working time and instructions. *J. exp. Psychol.*, 1957, **53**, 82–88.

COFER, C. N. Reasoning as an associative process. III. The role of verbal responses in problem solving. *J. gen. Psychol.*, 1957, **57**, 55–58.

COHEN, J., and HANSEL, M. *Risk and gambling.* New York: Philosophical Library, 1956.

COOMBS, C. H., and KAMORITA, S. S. Measuring utility of money through decisions. *Amer. J. Psychol.*, 1958, **71**, 383–389.

COOMBS, C. H., and PRUITT, D. G. Components of risk in decision-making: Probability and variance preferences, *J. exp. Psychol.*, 1960, **60**, 265–277.

COWEN, E. L., WIENER, M., and HESS, I. Generalization of problem-solving rigidity. *J. consult. Psychol.*, 1953, **17**, 100–103.

CRONBACH, L. J. The two disciplines of scientific psychology. *Amer. Psychologist*, 1957, **12**, 671–684.

CRONBACH, L. J., and AZUMA, H. Can we tell what the learner is thinking from his behavior? Univer. of Illinois, dittoed, 1961.

DAVIDSON, D., SUPPES, P., and SIEGEL, S. *Decision-making: An experimental approach.* Stanford, Calif.: Stanford Univer. Press, 1957.

DETAMBEL, M. H. Probabilities of success and amounts of work in a multichoice situation. *J. exp. Psychol.*, 1956, **51**, 41–44.

DETAMBEL, M. H., and STOLUROW, L. M. Probability and work as determiners of multichoice behavior. *J. exp. Psychol.*, 1957, **53**, 73–81.

DONAHOE, J. W. The effect of variations in the form of feedback on the efficiency of problem-solving. *J. exp. Psychol.*, 1960, **60**, 193–198.

DUNCAN, C. P. Recent research on human problem-solving. *Psychol. Bull.*, 1959, **56**, 397–429.

DUNCKER, K. On problem-solving. *Psychol. Monogr.*, 1945, **58**, No. 5 (Whole No. 270).

EDWARDS, W. Probability preferences in gambling. *Amer. J. Psychol.*, 1953, **66**, 349–364.

EDWARDS, W. Probability preferences among bets with differing expected values. *Amer. J. Psychol.*, 1954a, **67**, 56–67.

EDWARDS, W. The theory of decision making. *Psychol. Bull.*, 1954b, **51**, 201–214.

EDWARDS, W. A perspective on automation and decision making. In D. Willner (Ed.), *Decisions, values, and groups.* New York: Pergamon Press, 1960.

EDWARDS, W. Behavioral decision theory. *Annu. Rev. Psychol.*, 1961, **12**, 473–498.

EDWARDS, W. Dynamic decision theory and probabilistic information processing. *Human Factors*, 1962, **4**, 59–74.

ERLEBACHER, A., and ARCHER, E. J. Perseveration as a function of degree of learning and percentage of reinforcement in card sorting. *J. exp. Psychol.*, 1961, **62**, 510–517.

EWERT, P. H., and LAMBERT, J. F. Part II. The effect of verbal instructions upon the formation of a concept. *J. gen. Psychol.*, 1932, **6**, 400–413.

FATTU, N. A., MECH, E. V., and KAPOS, E. Some statistical relationships between selected response dimensions and problem-solving proficiency. *Psychol. Monogr.*, 1954, **68**, No. 6 (Whole No. 37).

FESTINGER, L. Studies in decision: I. Decision time, relative frequency of judgment and subjective confidence as related to physical stimulus difference, *J. exp. Psychol.*, 1943, **32**, 291–306.

FRENCH, E. G., and THOMAS, F. H. The relation of achievement motivation to problem-solving effectiveness. *J. abnorm. soc. Psychol.*, 1958, **56**, 45–48.

FRENCH, R. S. The effect of instruction on the length-difficulty relationship for a task involving sequential dependencies. *J. exp. Psychol.*, 1954, **48**, 89–97.

GAGNE, R. M. Problem solving and thinking. *Annu. Rev. Psychol.*, 1959, **10**, 147–152.

GAGNE, R. M., and BROWN, L. T. Some factors in the programming of conceptual learning. *J. exp. Psychol.*, 1961, **62**, 313–321.

GALLUP, H. F. Originality in free and controlled association responses. *Psychol. Rep.*, 1963, **13**, 923–929.

GLASER, R., DAMRIN, D. E., and GARDNER, F. M. The tab item: A technique for the measurement of proficiency in diagnostic problem-solving tasks. *Educ. psychol. Measmt.*, 1954, **14**, 283–293.

GOLDBECK, R. A., BERNSTEIN, B. B., HILLIX, W. A., and MARX, M. H. Application of the half-split technique to problem solving tasks. *J. exp. Psychol.*, 1957, **53**, 330–338.

GOODNOW, J. J. Determinants of choice distributions in two-choice probability situations. *Amer. J. Psychol.*, 1955, **68**, 106–116.

GRANT, D. A. Perceptual versus analytic responses to the number concept of a Weigl-type card sorting test. *J. exp. Psychol.*, 1951, **41**, 23–29.

GREEN, E. J. Concept formation: A problem in human operant conditioning. *J. exp. Psychol.*, 1955, **49**, 175–180.

HAYGOOD, R. G., and BOURNE, L. E., JR. Attribute and rule learning aspects of conceptual behavior. *Psychol. Rev.*, 1965, **72**, 175–195.

HEIDBREDER, E. The attainment of concepts: II. The problem. *J. gen. Psychol.*, 1946, **35**, 191–223.

HOVLAND, C. I. A "communication analysis" of concept learning. *Psychol. Rev.*, 1952, **59**, 461–472.

HOVLAND, C. I. Computer simulation of thinking. *Amer. Psychologist*, 1960, **15**, 687–693.

HOVLAND, C. I., and WEISS, W. Transmission of information concerning concepts through positive and negative instances. *J. exp. Psychol.*, 1953, **45**, 175–182.

HULL, C. L. Quantitative aspects of the evolution of concepts. *Psychol. Monogr.*, 1920, **28**, No. 1 (Whole No. 123).

HUNT, E. B. *Concept learning: An information processing problem*. New York: Wiley, 1962.

HUNT, E. B., and HOVLAND, C. I. Order of consideration of different types of concepts. *J. exp. Psychol.*, 1960, **59**, 220–225.

HUNTER, I. M. L. The solving of three-term series problems. *Brit. J. Psychol.*, 1957, **48**, 286–298.

IRWIN, F. W., SMITH, W. A. S., and MAYFIELD, J. F. Tests of two theories of decision in an "expanded judgment" situation. *J. exp. Psychol.*, 1956, **51**, 261–268.

JARVIK, M. E. Probability learning and a negative recency effect in the serial anticipation of alternative symbols. *J. exp. Psychol.*, 1951, **41**, 291–297.

JENKINS, J. J., RUSSELL, W. A., and SUCI, G. J. An atlas of semantic profiles for 360 words. *Amer. J. Psychol.*, 1958, **71**, 688–699.

JOHN, E. R. Contributions to the study of the problem-solving process. *Psychol. Monogr.*, 1957, **71**, No. 18 (Whole No. 447).

KATONA, G. Eine kleine Anschauungsaufgabe. *Psychol. Forsch.*, 1927, **9**, 159–162.

KATONA, G. *Organizing and memorizing*. New York: Columbia Univer. Press, 1940.

KENDLER, H. H., and D'AMATO, M. F. A comparison of reversal shifts and nonreversal shifts in human concept formation behavior. *J. exp. Psychol.*, 1955, **49**, 165–174.

KENDLER, H. H., and KENDLER, T. S. Vertical and horizontal processes in problem solving. *Psychol. Rev.*, 1962, **69**, 1–16.

KENDLER, H. H., and VINEBERG, R. The acquisition of compound concepts as a function of previous training. *J. exp. Psychol.*, 1954, **58**, 252–258.

KURTZ, K. H., and HOVLAND, C. I. Concept learning with differing sequences of instances. *J. exp. Psychol.*, 1956, **51**, 239–243.

LAUGHERY, K. R., and GREGG, L. W. Simulation of human problem-solving behavior. *Psychometrika*, 1962, **27**, 265–282.

LEE, W. Choosing among confusably distributed stimuli with specified likelihood ratios. *Percept. mot. Skills.*, 1963, **16**, 445–467.

LEVITT, E. E. The water-jar Einstellung test as a measure of rigidity. *Psychol. Bull.*, 1956, **53**, 347–370.

LINDLEY, E. H. A study of puzzles with special reference to the psychology of mental adaptation. *Amer. J. Psychol.*, 1897, **8**, 431–493.

LORGE, I., TUCKMAN, J., AIKMAN, L., SPIEGEL, J., and MOSS, G. Problem solving by teams and individuals in a field setting. *J. educ. Psychol.*, 1955, **46**, 160–166.

LORGE, I., FOX, D., DAVITZ, J., and BRENNER, M. A survey of studies contrasting the quality of group performance and individual performance, 1920–1957. *Psychol. Bull.*, 1958, **55**, 337–372.

LUCHINS, A. S. Mechanization in problem-solving: The effect of Einstellung. *Psychol. Monogr.*, 1942, **54**, No. 6 (Whole No. 248).

MAIER, N. R. F. Reasoning in humans: I. On direction. *J. comp. Psychol.*, 1930, **10**, 115–143.

MAIER, N. R. F. Reasoning in humans: II. The solution of a problem and its appearance in consciousness. *J. comp. Psychol.*, 1931, **12**, 181–194.

MALTZMAN, I. Thinking: From a behavioristic point of view. *Psychol. Rev.*, 1955, **62**, 275–286.

MALTZMAN, I. On the training of originality. *Psychol. Rev.*, 1960, **67**, 229–242.

MALTZMAN, I., and GALLUP, H. F. Comments on "originality" in free and controlled association responses. *Psychol. Rep.*, 1964, **14**, 573–574.

MALTZMAN, I., and MORRISETT, L., JR. Different strengths of set in the solution of anagrams. *J. exp. Psychol.*, 1952, **44**, 242–246.

MARKS, M. R. Problem solving as a function of the situation. *J. exp. Psychol.*, 1951, **41**, 74–80.

MARKS, M. R., and RAYMOND, C. K. A new technique for observing concept evocation. *J. exp. Psychol.*, 1951, **42**, 424–429.

MARX, M. H., GOLDBECK, R. A., and BERNSTEIN, B. B. An apparatus for investigating the methods humans use in solving complex problems. *Amer. J. Psychol.*, 1956, **69**, 462–465.

MAYZNER, M. S., and TRESSELT, M. E. Anagram solution times: A function of letter order and word frequency. *J. exp. Psychol.*, 1958, **56**, 376–379.

MAYZNER, M. S., and TRESSELT, M. E. Anagram solution times: A function of transition probabilities. *J. Psychol.*, 1959, **47**, 117–125.

MAYZNER, M. S., and TRESSELT, M. E. Anagram solution times: A function of word transition probabilities. *J. exp. Psychol.*, 1962, **63**, 510–513.

MEDNICK, S. A. The associative basis of the creative process. *Psychol. Rev.*, 1962, **69**, 220–232.

MILLER, G. A., GALANTER, E., and PRIBRAM, K. H. *Plans and the structure of behavior.* New York: Holt, 1960.

MILTON, G. A. Five studies of the relation between sex-role identification and achievement in problem solving. *ONR Contract 150-166, Tech. Rep. 3,* 1958.

MOORE, O. K., and ANDERSON, S. B. Modern logic and tasks for experiments on problem-solving behavior. *J. Psychol.*, 1954, **38**, 151–160.

MOSTELLER, F., and NOGEE, P. An experimental measurement of utility. *J. polit. Econ.*, 1951, **59**, 371–404.

NEIMARK, E. D. Information-gathering in diagnostic problem-solving: A preliminary report. *Psychol. Rec.*, 1961, **11**, 243–248.

NEISSER, U., and WEENE, P. Hierarchies in concept attainment. *J. exp. Psychol.*, 1962, **64**, 640–645.

NEWELL, A., and SIMON, H. A. Computer simulation of human thinking. *Science*, 1961, **134**, 2011–2017.

NEWMAN, S. E. Effects of contiguity and similarity on the learning of concepts. *J. exp. Psychol.*, 1956, **52**, 349–353.

PETERSON, J., and LANIER, I. H. Studies in the comparative abilities of whites and negroes. *Ment. Measmt. Monogr.*, 1929 (Serial No. 5).

PIAGET, J. *Logic and psychology.* Manchester Univer. Press, 1953.

PRUITT, D. G. Informational requirements in making decisions. *Amer. J. Psychol.*, 1961, **74**, 433–439.

RAY, W. S. Complex tasks for use in human problem-solving research. *Psychol. Bull.*, 1955, **52**, 134–149.

REES, H. J., and ISRAEL, H. E. An investigation of the establishment and operation of mental sets. *Psychol. Monogr.*, 1935, **46**, No. 210.

RHINE, R. J. The effect on problem solving of success or failure as a function of cue specificity. *ONR Contract 150-149, Tech. Rep. 8,* 1955.

RICHARDSON, J., and BERGUM, B. O. Distributed practice and rote learning in concept formation. *J. exp. Psychol.*, 1954, **47**, 442–446.

RONNING, R. R. Anagram solution times: A function of the "ruleout" factor. *J. exp. Psychol.*, 1965, **69**, 35–39.

SAUGSTAD, P. An analysis of Maier's pendulum problem. *J. exp. Psychol.*, 1957, **54**, 168–179.

SCHIPPER, L. M. Decision-making with unreliable information. *Tech. Rep.*, Boeing Airplane Co., 1961.

SCODEL, A., RATOOSH, P., and MINAS, J. S. Some personality correlates of decision making under conditions of risk. *Behav. Sci.*, 1959, **4**, 19–28.

SHEPARD, R. N., HOVLAND, C. I., and JENKINS, H. M. Learning and memorization of classifications. *Psychol. Monogr.*, 1961, **75**, No. 13 (Whole No. 517)

SIMMEL, M. L. The coin problem: A study in thinking. *Amer. J. Psychol.*, 1953, **66**, 229–241.

SKINNER, B. F. *Verbal behavior.* New York: Appleton-Century-Crofts, 1957.

SOLLEY, C. M. Problem solving difficulty as a function of deviation of "meaning" of physical cues from expected "meaning." *J. gen. Psychol.*, 1957, **57**, 165–171.

SOLLEY, C. M., and SNYDER, F. W. Information processing and problem-solving. *J. exp. Psychol.*, 1958, **55**, 384–387.

SPERA, A. J. Conditioned anxiety and thinking behavior. Unpublished honors thesis, Connecticut College, 1962.

SUPPES, P., and GINSBERG, R. Applications of a stimulus sampling model to childrens' concept formation with and without an overt correction response. *J. exp. Psychol.*, 1962, **63**, 330–336.

SWEENEY, E. J. Sex differences in problem solving. *ONR Contract 153-149, Tech. Rep. 1*, 1953.

SZEKELY, L. Productive processes in learning and thinking. *Acta Psychol.*, 1950, **7**, 388–407.

TAUB, H. A., and MYERS, J. L. Differential monetary gains in a two-choice situation. *J. exp. Psychol.*, 1961, **61**, 157–162.

TAYLOR, D. W., BERRY, P. C., and BLOCK, C. H. Does group participation when using brainstorming facilitate or inhibit creative thinking? *ONR Contract 150-166, Tech. Rep. 1*, 1957.

TAYLOR, D. W., and FAUST, W. L. Twenty questions: Efficiency in problem-solving as a function of size of group. *J. exp. Psychol.*, 1952, **44**, 360–368.

TAYLOR, D. W., and MCNEMAR, O. W. Experimental studies of problem-solving. *ONR Contract 150-149, Tech. Rep. 10*, 1955a.

TAYLOR, D. W., and MCNEMAR, O. W. Problem solving and thinking. *Annu. Rev. Psychol.*, 1955b, **6**, 455–482.

TERMAN, L. M. Genius and stupidity. *Ped. Sem.*, 1906, **13**, 307–373.

UHL, C. N. Learning of interval concepts: I.

Effects of differences in stimulus weights. *J. exp. Psychol.*, 1963, **66**, 264–273.

UNDERWOOD, B. J. An orientation for research on thinking. *Psychol. Rev.*, 1952, **59**, 209–220.

UNDERWOOD, B. J., and RICHARDSON, J. Some verbal materials for the study of concept formation. *Psychol. Bull.*, 1956a, **53**, 84–95.

UNDERWOOD, B. J., and RICHARDSON, J. Verbal concept learning as a function of instructions and dominance level. *J. exp. Psychol.*, 1956b, **51**, 229–238.

WALKER, C. M., and BOURNE, L. E., JR. The identification of concepts as a function of amounts of relevant and irrelevant information. *Amer. J. Psychol.*, 1961, **74**, 410–417.

WESTCOTT, M. R. On the measurement of intuitive leaps. *Psychol. Rep.*, 1961, **9**, 267–274.

WICKELGREN, W. A., and COHEN, D. H. An artificial language and memory approach to concept attainment. *Psychol. Rep.*, 1962, **10**, 815–827.

WIESEN, R. A., and SHUFORD, E. H. Bayes strategies as adaptive behavior. *Psychometr. Lab. Rep. 30*, Chapel Hill, N. C., 1961.

WILSON, R. C., GUILFORD, J. P., and CHRISTENSEN, P. R. The measurement of individual differences in originality. *Psychol. Bull.*, 1953, **50**, 362–370.

Chapter 14

CHILD
PSYCHOLOGY

HAROLD W. STEVENSON *and* JOHN C. WRIGHT

The experimental method is not new to child psychology. A volume devoted to the experimental approach to child study was published as early as 1931 (Goodenough and Anderson, 1931). The early experimental studies, however, were relatively crude, and once the occurrence of a particular phenomenon had been demonstrated, only replication and refinement tended to be undertaken. Many studies attempted literal translation of earlier work with lower animals; and although certain parallels were found, contrasting the behavior of children and animals tested under similar conditions often led to awkward comparisons and insignificant conclusions. There was little experimental manipulation of variables. An experiment was conceived of as a controlled situation yielding quantitative data, and investigations typically led to conclusions concerning behavioral and developmental norms. Psychological theories had not been developed to the point where establishing relationships among variables could command equal attention with normative studies. The rise of theoretical issues and the acquisition of tools for their investigation have led the experimental child psychologist beyond the phases of demonstration and translation. Delineating the behavioral repertoire of the

child and comparing it with that of other animals is no longer of central interest.

The experimental child psychologist makes his unique contribution to behavioral science by selecting those aspects of behavior which can be investigated most productively by utilizing children as subjects and the experiment as his method. General experimental psychologists are gradually recognizing that hypotheses derived from studies with human adults may often best be tested by investigating the variables that affect the emergence and development of the behavior in children, rather than by relying upon the study of less appropriate lower organisms. McCandless and Spiker (1956) have pointed out that current theories in general psychology are replete with hypotheses that can be tested not only satisfactorily but ideally with children.

This chapter considers some of the major problems in experimental work with children: selecting subjects, designing apparatus, presenting stimuli, measuring response, and motivating and reinforcing behavior. More detailed discussions of methodology in research with children may be found in Mussen (1960), Wohlwill (1960), and Bijou and Baer (1963). The present chapter will rely heavily on research in learning and motivation for examples of the application of the experimental method to the study of children. It may be expected that experimental techniques will be applied increasingly to the study of other processes, but it is in the areas of learning and motivation that attention has been concentrated and the most extensive examples of methods and instrumentation appear.

SELECTION OF SUBJECTS

The choice of children as subjects for experimental research is dictated by the research problem. The child is especially appropriate for some types of studies and is inappropriate or inefficient for others. Although the child has a short attention span and is easily satiated and although certain experimental manipulations are impossible, these disadvantages may be compensated for by the child's extreme flexibility and suggestibility and by the high degree of motivation that may be easily aroused.

The most obvious characteristic of children is that their behavior and structure are rapidly and continuously changing. Consequently, the use of children makes it possible to study the complex interaction between experimental variables and maturational changes accompanying development. Some changes, such as the acquisition of language and the process of socialization, are of major importance, and the experimental study of processes related to or dependent upon these changes will undoubtedly increase our understanding of the antecedents and genesis of adult behavior.

Criteria for selection

One of the first problems is the selection of individual subjects. In eliminating unwanted differences between various experimental and control groups, either matching or randomizing of subjects may be appropriate. Because of the large differences among children and the frequent lack of knowledge of the relevance of these differences for the behavior being studied, it is seldom efficient during the early stages of experimental research to use matching techniques. Individual matching on more than a few variables requires an immense amount of information about many more children than will be used, and the procedure quickly becomes unwieldy. It is often the best strategy to randomize such possibly relevant variables as socioeconomic class, IQ, sex, and age. Unless the design of the study requires analysis by a particular variable, subjects need not be selected on the basis of that variable. Random assignment of a sufficient number of subjects will usually control for the variables not explicitly incorporated in the experimental design. Even with the small number of subjects often used in experimental research with children, the general strategy of random assignment for each subgroup may prove to be desirable, although, of course, the use of small numbers of subjects may restrict the generalizations made from the study. (See Chap. 1 for discussions of random selection and assignment that are pertinent to research with children as well as adults.) If the design requires the experimenter to analyze for more variables than are critical to the main hypotheses, then either the number of cases in each group is unnecessarily restricted or the total number of subjects must be increased.

Problems may arise when different experimental groups are not assigned randomly from different schools or from groups differing in degree of experience with experimental tasks. White (1961) found significantly different learning rates between experimentally naive subjects and subjects who had previously participated in a learning study. The experimental treatment turned out to have comparable effects in the two groups, but the results would have been difficult to interpret if group membership and assignment to treatment conditions had been confounded. The experimental sophistication of subjects may have different effects on different response processes. Spiker and

White (1959) present evidence that the superior learning of sophisticated subjects may be due to the greater facility with which they learn not to respond to the negative stimulus.

A variety of standard tests for sampling different types of subjects is available. Scales have been developed for assessing personality variables in children, such as anxiety (Castaneda, Palermo, and McCandless, 1956; Sarason, Davidson, Lighthall, and Waite, 1958), self-concept (Lipsitt, 1958; P. S. Sears, 1957), need for achievement (Atkinson, 1958), sex-role identification (Brown, 1956), and guilt for aggression (Jergard and Walters, 1960). Children may also be selected on the basis of child-rearing practices of parents as assessed by parents' responses to questionnaires or interviews (Schaefer and Bell, 1957; Sears, Maccoby, and Levin, 1957). It is often desirable to consult normative and developmental studies before selecting subjects for a particular task. Developmental studies of number concepts (Martin, 1951), language usage (Templin, 1957), and cognitive style (Bruner and Olver, 1963; Kagan, *et al.*, 1964) provide a basis for selecting age levels from which children may be sampled appropriately for relevant tasks.

Subject variables may be studied by sampling from separate populations, such as institutions, broken homes, and clinics. Although the possibility of utilizing such populations is initially attractive because of the large differences that often exist among them and because of the possibly important implications of the research findings, their use is limited because of the profusion of variables simultaneously differentiating the groups. Institutionalized children, for example, are often found to be of lower intelligence, to come from more deprived backgrounds, and to have had a greater incidence of traumatic experience. The nature of the variables producing differences in performance between institutionalized and noninstitutionalized children is thus unclear. Only by studying each of the characteristics of the special population can the contribution of each characteristic to the obtained differences in behavior be identified and isolated.

Chronological age reflects a cluster of parallel and interrelated variables that should be studied separately. Because of the difficulty of interpreting the results of studies in which chronological age is the sole criterion for assigning subjects to groups, it is preferable to select subjects differentiated by a measure for the presence or absence of the capacity, experience, or characteristic under investigation. Still more satisfactory is the experimental manipulation of the situation to produce experiences otherwise occurring erratically in the normal course of development and, when possible, confirmation of the effectiveness of the manipulation through other measures of performance. Although none of these techniques ensures that the child will utilize his experience when confronted with the experimental task, the last-mentioned techniques permit the most unequivocal interpretation of results.

Certain practical problems are encountered in securing children as subjects. Procedures for setting up experimental research programs in schools have been discussed by Mullen (1959) and by Castaneda and Fahel (1961). The experimenter should not rely on teachers or principals to select the subjects or to determine the order in which subjects are to be tested. The characteristics of the sample may be distorted by this participation to include the brighter, the more willing, or the problem child to the exclusion of the less interesting or more typical child. Samples may be similarly distorted by the self-selection of subjects when parents or children are asked to volunteer the child's participation.

Without adequate preparation, sampling of whole groups of children is often impossible. If the children are familiar with the experimenter or if their suspiciousness and distrust of a stranger are dispelled through contact, subjects' refusal to participate in the experiment can be virtually eliminated. Unless the experimenter is familiar with techniques for handling children, he may have difficulty not only in getting the children to come to the experimental room but also in keeping them there, especially if the experiment requires the children to be left alone. The major responsibility for the preparation of subjects for participation in a study should be undertaken by the experimenter and should not be left to the teacher or parent.

EXPERIMENTAL SETTINGS AND GENERAL APPARATUS

Experimental studies with children have typically been conducted wherever there was a free room. The uncontrolled and inconstant nature of such settings reduces the effectiveness of the manipulations and the reliability of the results. There have been recent attempts to overcome these difficulties by the construction of both mobile and permanent experimental laboratories. Mobile laboratories are especially convenient, for they enable the experimenter to transport elaborate equipment and a standard setting to any location where subjects are available. Plans for modifying a trailer for laboratory use have been described by Bijou (1958a) and Bergman (1964). The increase in research at institutions for children has resulted in the development of specialized permanent laboratories. Orlando, Bijou, Tyler, and Marshall (1960) have described the plans for such a laboratory containing equipment for free-operant and for single- and multiple-response tasks. When an observer is required for studies in classrooms or in temporary experimental rooms, a portable one-way observational booth may be useful. The design of such a booth has been described by Gewirtz (1952), and an economical means of preparing one-way mirrors has been described by Pinneau (1951). The availability of low-cost television cameras, e.g., the SHIBA (see Appendix), has made possible surveillance of children without the use of one-way mirrors. A concealed camera in the room with the subject can be directly connected by coaxial cable to a monitor receiver in the observer's room.

Laboratory design

Many of the requirements of a laboratory for children are the same as those of any good experimental laboratory. The main modification of special value for use with children is the installation of adequate observational facilities. The laboratory should be planned so that the most centrally located rooms are used for control and observation. A series of L-shaped observation rooms has the advantage of conserving space and of allowing observation from two adjacent sides of any experimental room. The experimental rooms can be quite small, but there should be provision for controlled illumination and sound levels, adequate ventilation, one-way observation, and sound recording. It is desirable to have at least one room with direct electrical and mechanical access to a control room when complex or cumbersome apparatus is used to control the presentation of stimuli and the delivery of reinforcements. A playroom may be a useful addition to any laboratory. It provides a place for the children to wait before the experimental session and for the observation of children in a free-play situation. It is especially important in work with children that the experimental rooms be free of distracting stimuli and of stimuli associated with other experiences of the child, such as physical examinations and mental testing. Children are not unduly suspicious (although they may be curious) when mirrors, microphones, or trailing wires are visible, and elaborate concealment of apparatus is ordinarily unnecessary.

There should be separate entrances to the observation and experimental rooms. The same observation room may serve two or more experimental rooms, if light and sound from the experimental rooms do not interfere with their simultaneous operation. The use of earphones and the offsetting of opposing one-way mirrors reduces such interference.

Mirrors should be low in height and should be made of double glass to help reduce sound transmission. The possible distraction resulting from the child's seeing himself in a one-way mirror may be reduced by placing a corrugated plastic shield in front of the mirror.

General apparatus

The most valuable electric components are event-scheduling, decision-making, and recording circuits. Other apparatus for events directly perceived or controlled by the subject will depend upon the nature of the task and the subjects to be used. Standard displays and manipulanda are frequently less appropriate than homemade units wired directly to the standard switching apparatus. General apparatus should be constructed for versatility and interchangeability.

STIMULUS VARIABLES

Although children have been tested with practically every device made for animals or adults, it is now apparent that the special characteristics of children need to be considered in the design of laboratory apparatus. Apparatus designed especially for use with infants has been described in several articles (Crowell, Peterson, and Safely, 1960; Lipsitt, 1963; Lipsitt et al., 1966; Rheingold and Cooley, 1962; Simmons and Lipsitt, 1961).

Children are naive, curious, and sociable subjects. Children's naiveté enables the experimenter to use a wide variety of stimuli that cannot be used with adults because of their familiarity, simplicity, or past associations. At the same time, the child often lacks the associational context in which to respond to stimuli in the intended manner. Children's curiosity about the general situation results in their attending not only to relevant but also to minimal, incidental, and irrelevant aspects of the situation. The child's attention is often diverted from the experimental task by his exploration of the apparatus and the experimental room, and it appears that al-most any stimulus change may serve further to reinforce such activity. The child's sociability may make him eager to follow instructions but also may make it difficult for him to avoid continuing to respond to the experimenter as a social stimulus. Some of these difficulties may be reduced by introducing a period of interaction and habituation prior to the experimental task. If children are allowed to become acquainted with the experimenter and to explore the room visually, their curiosity may be lessened. Extraneous stimuli found in most multipurpose rooms may be reduced by shielding the experimental area from the rest of the room by portable screens.

Stimulus displays

One of the early developments was the Hunter Cardmaster, a device that permits the controlled display of stimuli mounted on cards, such as drawings, photographs, or words. This type of apparatus is rapidly being displaced by more versatile units activated by standard switching equipment. Images may be projected from the rear of a ground-glass screen mounted in a vertical panel by devices such as the Dunning Animatic filmstrip projector, the Davis slide projector, or a modified motion-picture projector, all of which are controlled electrically.

Moving pictures have been used successfully to produce models for identification (Bandura, Ross, and Ross, 1963), to arouse motivational states such as aggression (Albert, 1957; Mussen and Rutherford, 1961), and to provide continuous reinforcement whose interruption may serve as punishment (Baer, 1961). Movies may be projected satisfactorily through ground glass or by means of a portable device such as the Kodak Cinesalesman, as well as on ordinary screens.

Objects may be presented by equipping a vertical panel with an electrically controlled shutter. A shutter can be released by an ordinary solenoid or rotated by a Ledex rotary solenoid (G. H. Leland, Inc.). The former would have to be returned manually, engaging a pawl that would be released by the solenoid. A light spring attached to the shutter provides the force to move the shutter. In the latter case, the shutter is rotated for a specified period of time, exposing the stimulus material, by a timed pulse to the solenoid. The latter procedure is preferable if a predetermined period of exposure and intertrial interval of the stimuli are desired, and the former in most free-response types of task. The use of objects still requires their manual arrangement so that many of the advantages of electrically controlled presentation are lost.

Fluorescent paint and ultraviolet illumination make possible the controlled appearance of forms and objects and rapid variation in the color of stimuli (Rieber, 1961). The stimuli may be painted with fluorescent paint and made visible only while illuminated by the ultraviolet light. Auditory stimuli may be programmed and presented automatically from tape recordings (Jeffrey, 1958; Lockard and Sidowski, 1961).

Selection of stimuli

The selection of stimuli and of dimensions on which to vary stimuli in a particular task is determined in part by the characteristics of the subject, by the type of task, and by the level of difficulty desired. A number of variables not necessarily related to the specific experimental problem may play a significant role in determining the child's response.

Striking differences have been found in the rate with which children discriminate among stimuli, depending upon the number of dimensions the stimuli encompass. In studies of the discrimination of relative size, for example, the average number of trials to criterion has varied from 335.7 (Kuenne, 1946) to 54.8 (Alberts and Ehrenfreund, 1951) to 13.6 (Stevenson and Langford, 1957). Stimuli of the same shape and relative size and subjects of the same chronological age (three years) were used in these studies. In the first study the stimulus squares were mounted on

the doors of boxes containing reinforcers, while in the second the reward boxes were equipped with square doors of different sizes. In the last study, the stimuli were blocks which the child had to lift to obtain the rewards. It appears that the degree to which the child must manipulate the stimuli may pay a significant role in discrimination learning. The dimensionality of stimuli has a more significant effect with four-year-olds than with six-year-olds (Stevenson and McBee, 1958).

Certain stimulus dimensions such as area, color, form, and pattern appear to have greater salience for some groups of children than for others. When stimuli differing in the amount of colored area are used in a discrimination task, no relationship between mental age and interproblem transfer is found if the stimuli are completely colored; as smaller and smaller proportions of the stimulus cards are colored, the correlation increases (Koch and Meyer, 1959). Children respond initially to form, then to color, and rarely to size when they are asked to group stimuli (Kagan and Lemkin, 1961). Furthermore, girls prefer form to color as a basis for conceptualization to a greater degree than do boys (Honkavaara, 1958; Kagan and Lemkin, 1961). Learning to discriminate between different hues may be more difficult than learning to discriminate on the basis of brightness or pattern differences (Calvin and Clifford, 1956). Children cannot disregard extraneous cues so readily as adults (Gollin, 1960); tactual recognition of form is decreased for children when irrelevant cues (large tacks) are placed around the contour of a form outlined with small tacks.

As meaningful stimuli are varied from concrete objects to representations of actual objects, behavior changes systematically. For example, children imitate the behavior depicted in filmed aggression by a cartoonlike character less readily than that depicted in films of a real person (Bandura *et al.*, 1963). Quite different results may therefore be obtained in the same task with comparable subjects, depending upon the number and types of dimensions differentiating the stimuli.

One of the difficulties children have in performing in experimental situations is that of orienting toward the relevant cues. House and Zeaman (1963), for example, have proposed that the poor performance in learning by children with low IQs is related to their difficulty in attending to relevant cues. Backward plots of learning curves indicate a period of minimal improvement followed by rapid increases in the frequency of correct response. A more direct approach to the study of attention may be obtained by the use of eye-movement photography, recently discussed by White and Plum (1964).

There are many ways in which children's attention to relevant cues may be increased. The most common method has been to give children experience with the stimuli (or similar stimuli) prior to the experimental task. For example, the discrimination of classes of objects may be increased by allowing the children during pretraining to test the functional properties of weights and levers (Ervin, 1960). Another common means of increasing the discriminability of stimuli has been to teach children distinctive names for the stimuli during a pretraining period. The degree to which the discriminability is increased may be varied according to the distinctiveness of the names. The stimulus properties of implicit verbal responses have significant effects on increasing the discriminability of stimuli in discrimination learning (Norcross, 1958), motor learning (Smith and Goss, 1955), and concept formation (Goss and Moylan, 1958). Spiker (1963) has summarized the results of a number of experiments dealing with this problem in discrimination learning. Pretraining may be unnecessary with older children, for by the age of seven or eight they appear to utilize verbal labels spontaneously and effectively in their responses to common stimuli. The tendency for children to use implicit labels

spontaneously may provide a partial basis for the superior learning and performance evidenced by older children, but in some simple problems older children often complicate the task unnecessarily because of their strong tendency to label the stimuli and to initiate self-instructions (Weir and Stevenson, 1959).

Reinforcement of relevant observing responses may also increase later attention to relevant cues. If children are presented an easy task during which attention to relevant stimulus dimensions leads readily to reinforcement, subsequent performance is facilitated on a new and otherwise more difficult task (House and Zeaman, 1960b). The school-age child appears to learn the dimensions of stimuli that are relevant to the problem and to transfer such learning with relative ease to different dimensions of the same stimuli or to different values of the same dimension (House and Zeaman, 1960a; Kendler and Kendler, 1959).

The child's familiarity with a stimulus appears to play a significant role in determining the degree to which he will respond to it. For example, children spend significantly longer amounts of time looking at novel than at familiar pictures (Cantor and Cantor, 1964). Novel or unexpected events may function as effective reinforcers of children's behavior (Charlesworth, 1964).

Children respond differentially to stimuli, depending upon their meaningfulness and complexity. Infants less than one month of age show differential visual fixation to black and white stimuli, looking longest at drawn faces, less at random arrangements of features, and least at homogeneous shapes (Fantz, 1961). Preference for randomly generated polygons is an inverted U-shaped function of their complexity, defined as number of turns (Munsinger, Kessen, and Kessen, 1964).

Research on verbal stimuli has revealed limitations in children's use and comprehension of words, but at the same time it has indicated that even very young children respond to linguistic cues with surprising precision and regularity. Children can use nonsense words in a manner conforming to the context in which they have been inserted and with meaning appropriate to the sentence in which they occur (R. W. Brown, 1957). For example, if children are shown pictures depicting an action, a mass substance, or a particular object, they are able to assign the appropriate part-of-speech membership to nonsense syllables which, they are told, describe the content of the picture.

Studies of children's vocabularies and the frequency of occurrence of words in children's literature have made possible the approximate scaling of words in terms of their familiarity to children at various ages (Thorndike and Lorge, 1944). One of the defects of many experiments and many personality tests for children has been the failure to use words explicitly selected for their comprehensibility by children at the age levels studied. Furthermore, little attention has been paid to differences in meaning and association value of words for children at different ages. Two recent projects provide age norms for children's word associations (Castaneda, Fahel, and Odom, 1961; Palermo and Jenkins, 1964). Not only do such factors as the number and complexity of associations increase with age, but also the form-class and syntactical structure change systematically over time. Palermo (1963) has reviewed the background and current experimental use of the data derived from studies of children's word associations.

There are several additional specific considerations concerning the design of stimulus situations for children, in addition to the obvious considerations of designing apparatus of the appropriate size and complexity.

A common tendency in designing stimuli and apparatus for children has been the attempt to make them interesting. It is not difficult to elicit the child's interest in practically any type of device. When the apparatus is made exceptionally appealing through the use of color, decoration, or moving parts, the child is often more interested in exploring the mechanism than he is in performing the appropriate responses. This does not mean that all apparatus must be plain and colorless; in fact, children can often be induced to overcome their hesitancy about operating novel apparatus if the color, size, and function suggest that it was designed for children's use.

Different degrees of difficulty may be easily produced for a problem by the spatial, temporal, or figural relationships of stimulus and response. For example, if the child is forced in a simultaneous discrimination problem to direct his response to the stimulus itself by pushing a lighted stimulus panel, learning is more rapid than if the response is made to a locus some distance removed from the stimulus source (Lipsitt, 1961). Simultaneous presentation of two stimuli results in better visual-discrimination learning than successive presentation when the response is to the source of stimulation. If the response is to a locus removed from the stimulus source, no differences or an inversion in results is produced (Lipsitt, 1961). Similar differences have been reported in rate of learning a simultaneous discrimination when the subjects responded directly to the stimuli rather than to a locus separated from the stimulus source (Jeffrey and Cohen, 1964; Murphy and Miller, 1959).

With a multiple light-button apparatus children initially tend to respond to the button immediately below the light illuminated on a particular trial, and the difficulty of the problem can be varied by changing the spatial correspondence of stimulus and correct response (Castaneda and Lipsitt, 1959).

There is relatively little information about the effects of different rates and durations for presenting stimuli to children. Parametric studies are badly needed, but it seems safe to assume that optimal functioning in children occurs at somewhat lower rates of presentation and longer durations of stimulation than those used with adults. When the presentation of stimuli is too rapid, stress may be produced in the subject, with the consequence that rate of learning is decreased. For example, when the intertrial interval for presenting stimuli is varied from four to two seconds, differences in rate of learning have been found apparently due to the greater stress resulting from the faster rates of presentation (Palermo, 1957). Because of the lack of reliable information on the timing of stimulus presentation and on its probable interaction with stimulus materials and types of subjects, pretesting is ordinarily required.

Various attributes of stimuli are utilized spontaneously by children in grouping objects and events. The experimenter should be aware of such tendencies in designing studies and in interpreting the results. Children may assign attributes of goodness, fairness, or aesthetic value to stimuli on the basis of such dimensions as size, number, and relative frequency of occurrence so that uncommon events are predicted with greater frequency than their incidence warrants (Brackbill, Kappy, and Starr, 1962; Cohen and Hansel, 1956). Children spontaneously classify objects on the basis of perceptible physical attributes, functional attributes, or associational similarities (Bruner and Olver, 1963; Kagan et al., 1963). Such spontaneous, idiosyncratic classifications may or may not correspond to those intended by the experimenter. Children's perceptions of objects may also be influenced by whether or not they own the object (Blum, 1957), so that children judge objects they own to be larger than similar objects they do not own. Children's perception of ambiguous stimuli is influenced by prior reinforcement of particular perceptual organizations of the stimuli (Solley and Engel, 1960).

Apparatus for children should be constructed with attention to the elimination of distracting cues. The child's tendency to respond to irrelevant aspects of the experimental situation requires that small cues such as those resulting from noisy relays, differential ease of operation of the apparatus, or

nonuniformity of stimulus presentation be avoided.

RESPONSE VARIABLES

The most critical decision facing the investigator in any experiment is the selection of the appropriate measures of behavior. Since there are relatively few standard measures of children's responses, the experimenter must utilize his ingenuity in devising such measures. Because of the complexity of children's behavior, it is often difficult to know which of several response measures may most adequately reflect the effect of experimental manipulations. In most experimental designs, there is a particular class of responses to which attention must be directed, such as lever pressing in an operant task or choice of reward in a preference task. It is often possible, however, that the particular measure selected will be less influenced than will other measures such as vigor of lever pressing or delay of decision. Since one is never so certain with a child as with an adult that he understands the instructions, is attending to the intended stimuli, is aware of the alternative responses available, and comprehends the significance of the reinforcing objects and events, the use of supplementary measures of response may be of value in interpreting the primary response measure. As a consequence, it is often desirable to employ many different response measures in the initial phases of experimental studies with children. As the experimental technique becomes more refined, the utility of the alternative response measures is clarified and it is possible that some may be eliminated.

Response devices

There is often a temptation to design complex and interesting response devices that simulate lifelike situations. Many of the most successful response devices for children, however, are simple and artificial and would appear to provide superficial measures of behavior. For example, a simple two-hole board into which marbles are inserted by the subject has been found to yield a sensitive and reliable measure of a variety of motivational and reinforcement variables (Gewirtz and Baer, 1958a, 1958b).

A number of concessions must be made to the physical capacities of children in designing response devices. The response should not require the expenditure of a great deal of energy and should be such that children can complete the experimental session before becoming fatigued. Knobs, buttons, and levers should be large enough to be grasped easily and should involve enough displacement to indicate to the subject that a response has been made. If a variety of responses are available, the number should be small enough that the child remains familiar with the arbitrary meanings assigned to them by the experimenter. Children can be induced to respond to practically any type of apparatus; indeed, often the problem is not to reduce children's hesitancy to respond, but to have the apparatus constructed sturdily enough that it will withstand children's rough treatment.

Response measures

Individual differences among children result in great variability in practically all measures of response. Statistical treatment of the results by the use of transformed scores, partial correlations, analysis of covariance, or nonparametric statistics is often helpful. An alternative experimental technique is to use each child as his own control by testing each child, in a balanced design, under all the experimental conditions. Base-line measures, obtained under neutral conditions or prior to the experimental manipulation, yield change scores that tend to be less variable. The use of base-line measures in operant tasks has been discussed by Bijou (1961).

Strong biases have been found in children's responses, and certain developmental changes in such biases have been noted. In a three-choice discrimination task, five- to

seven-year-old children have a strong tendency to respond in a left-middle-right or a right-middle-left sequence, while nine- to thirteen-year-old children show less stereotyped patterning of responses (Weir, 1964). Responses of children at different ages differ significantly following initial reinforcement. Three-year-old children tend to repeat a reinforced response, but with increasing age children tend to switch their response following initial reinforcement (Stevenson and Weir, 1961). If the subject expects a logical or causal relationship between stimuli and correct responses, the introduction of arbitrary stimulus-response correspondence, however reliable, is resisted by the child (Ausubel and Schiff, 1954). Unless the subjects are explicitly instructed not to make certain types of response, biases are difficult to control and the experimenter can only alert himself to the likelihood of their occurrence.

Situational structure of response

The degree of structure that the experimenter places upon the child's response may vary widely. Most experimental studies employ structured situations in which a particular class of responses is studied. The responses may vary from the subject's choosing from an array of stimuli on the basis of correctness or preference to his choosing whether to respond to serially presented alternatives. In such situations the stimuli toward which the subject's attention is directed are limited, and he is either encouraged or required to respond to them or to make choices among them.

In free situations the child may or may not respond, and the response, if made, may include a wide range of behavior. For example, the child may be left free to express aggression in a variety of ways that are recorded or categorized by an observer. The frequency with which aggressive responses (i.e., hitting, throwing, breaking, or verbal expressions of hostility) are made in a free setting depends upon many factors. Aggression will be more frequent if the child has had previous experience in the laboratory (P. S. Sears, 1951); aggression will be less frequent if the child is left alone than if the child is performing in the presence of an observer (Siegel and Kohn, 1959); aggression will increase if the child's mother accompanies him to the experimental situation and will decrease if a strange woman enters the experimental situation (Levin and Turgeon, 1957). The frequency of aggression the child displays in a free situation is significantly correlated with the child's general activity level (Sears, Whiting, Nowlis, and Sears, 1953). Behavior in free situations is, therefore, highly dependent upon the characteristics of the situation and the types of prior experience children have had in the same or similar situations.

Structured situations have often been arranged to measure such variables as guilt (R. R. Sears, Alpert, and Rau, 1965; Wurtz, 1959) or resistance to temptation (Grinder, 1961) by tempting or inducing children to violate some rule of instruction stressed by the experimenter. These situations must be validated. Although they have been used only for arousal and assessment of motivational predispositions, they are potentially useful in experimental studies of motivation with children. Structured situations designed to elicit rather specific behavior must be carefully standardized to ensure uniformity of interpretation by the child. For example, in a temptation situation designed to measure the child's resistance, all children must be convinced that the risk of detection is low so that self-generated inhibition rather than environmentally produced deterrents control their behavior (Hoffman, 1963). If a manipulation is designed to convince a child that he has made an error of fact, judgment, or propriety, the experimenter must be careful that the child cannot easily blame the task, the apparatus, or the experimenter for the observed outcome.

In addition to observation, free responses

may be measured in a number of other ways. Stabilimeters have frequently been used to measure general activity level in infants (Irwin, 1943), and activity level in older children may be measured in a room equipped with a series of photoelectric beams. Neither of these methods provides information concerning specific types of movement; each yields only measures of gross activity. Motion-picture films have been used in recording and analyzing responses when data concerning specific categories or sequences of movement are desired. Gesell first utilized the method with children; and recently Kessen, Williams, and Williams (1961) have described a new means of analyzing films to obtain measures of infants' behavior. The method, although laborious, provides a sensitive measure of discrete responses made by the infants. Random samples of short sequences of frames are viewed, and the type and degree of movement are scored.

Some degree of structure is imposed on free response in operant situations. Although the child is still free to make many responses, the experimenter is primarily concerned with the class of responses designated as relevant for the production of reinforcement. Responses that have been used in operant tasks include pressing levers or panels (Lipsitt *et al.*, 1966; Siegel and Foshee, 1953; Simmons, 1962), dropping marbles in holes (Gewirtz and Baer, 1958*b*), turning cranks (Lambert, Lambert, and Watson, 1953; Olds, 1953; Screven, 1954; Screven and Nunis, 1954), smiling (Brackbill, 1958), and vocalizing (Rheingold, Gewirtz, and Ross, 1959).

Verbal responses

Before the age of seven or eight there is little positive relationship between children's performance in experimental tasks and their ability to describe their behavior or to give reasons for their particular responses. Preschool children, for example, may solve complex problems yet be unable to explain how they made the response or what aspects of the stimuli formed the basis of responding. Children may learn to discriminate between or among objects but be unable to verbalize the basis of their response (Johnson and Zara, 1960). The inability to verbalize the relevant cue spontaneously even after it has been successfully discriminated has been found in children as old as nine (Miller and Estes, 1961). There are many examples of the strong effects of manipulating the relationship between verbal and motor responses (Spiker, 1956b). The use of easily named familiar forms and primary colors makes it possible to obtain reliable phenomenological reports from children as young as six. Pouliot and Misiak (1959) have successfully studied negative afterimages in first graders by providing the children with animal shapes that could easily be labeled and by using primary colors whose names were familiar to the subjects. After the middle elementary grades children appear to be able to give adequate reports of their basis of response and an accurate description of their behavior.

New modes of analyzing children's verbalizations have recently been introduced, with the aim of studying more general variables than the verbal capacities of the subjects. Rather than being classified according to parts of speech or frequency of use, children's language has been analyzed for affective and stylistic variables. Barnard, Zimbardo, and Sarason (1961) asked children such affective questions as "Tell me about the time that you had a fight or argument with one of your good friends" and general, neutral questions, such as "Tell me about the things that you did last summer." The responses of the children were tabulated or rated on such variables as number and types of affective statements, source or origin of affect mentioned, degree of vocal animation, and concreteness or abstractness of descriptions of people. Differences were found between children differing in anxiety level and between children interviewed in a permissive or evaluative manner. Other measures of

verbal response have been used by Levin and Baldwin (1959), such as length of verbal response, rate of speaking, and mistakes.

Measures of autonomic skin response

Indices of autonomic response have not been used frequently with children. There is an increasing tendency, however, to use such measures as cardiac acceleration, changes in respiration, and vasomotor activity in studies of infants and young children (Bartoshuk, 1962; Bridger and Reiser, 1959; Elkonin, 1957). With older children the galvanic skin response (GSR) has been used most frequently as a measure of autonomic response. To obtain measures of GSR a 20-minute period of inactivity is necessary to allow the palms to dry sufficiently to establish a basal level. It is difficult to keep children quiet and immobile and to allay the apprehensiveness produced by inactivity. Since most children can be kept in an experimental situation for a limited amount of time, the length of the experimental session is reduced. The GSR has yielded useful measures of response in investigations of such diverse problems as the effects of immediate and delayed reward (Terrell and Ware, 1963), verbal conditioning (Patterson, Helper, and Wilcott, 1960), and ability in discrimination learning (Brackbill and O'Hara, 1958).

Additional response measures

Experimental and observational measures may be usefully combined when studying children. Since children's behavior in experimental situations is variable and often unpredictable, observation of children during the experimental task can yield valuable auxiliary response measures. Otherwise obscure results may be clarified by observational data on tension patterns, shifts in degree and locus of attention, irrelevant verbalizations and vocalizations, use of motor mediators, and incidental responses to relevant stimuli and reinforcers.

Current developments in general child psychology are yielding a wide variety of response measures that could be utilized more frequently in experimental studies. Laboratory situations have been devised to arouse and to measure such personal-social variables as resistance to temptation (Burton, Maccoby, and Allinsmith, 1961; Grinder, 1961), dependency (Hartup and Himeno, 1959), aggression (Jergard and Walters, 1960; Lovaas, 1961), sex-typing (Hartup and Moore, 1963; Mussen, 1961), and imitation (Rosenblith, 1959; Stein and Wright, 1964). Other controlled assessment situations include doll play (Levin and Wardwell, 1962), level of aspiration (P. S. Sears, 1940), co-operative and competitive groups (Sherif and Sherif, 1953), public versus private performance (Levin and Baldwin, 1959), and susceptibility to social influence, both in artificial situations (Aronson and Carlsmith, 1963) and in actual social situations (McDavid, 1959).

Although the design of experimental studies requires that certain response measures be utilized, many significant features of performance are lost when additional and less obvious aspects of response are not analyzed. Such measures not only aid in the interpretation of results but also provide the source for many ideas that can later be investigated in studies designed explicitly to determine their relationship to performance. An index of cautiousness, for example, may be obtained by determining the number of times the subject asks to see a comparison stimulus in a perceptual task (Ruebush, 1960). Variability of response may be a more sensitive index of the effects of certain variables than consistency of response (Hanlon, 1960; Hodgden, 1961). Errors are not frequently analyzed in American research with children (as an exception, see Spiker, 1956a), although such analysis has proved to be of great value in studies of problem solving in animals and adults, and in European studies of children. Finally, analysis of response sequences in terms of patterning (such as alternations or repetitions of responses) can yield important information on how the subjects structure a

problem and set about solving it (Weir, 1964).

MOTIVATING CHILDREN

Motivating young children to perform in experiments poses certain special problems not frequently encountered with animals and adults. For example, children may be so interested in the experimenter as a social stimulus that task-relevant motivation cannot be achieved; they may be so negativistic that all requests for cooperation are rejected; or they may be so highly motivated for achievement that experimental manipulation of motivation is impossible. Some of these problems can be reduced if the transitions into and within the conditions of the experimental task are made slowly, allowing the subject to adjust to each phase of the experiment. The requirements of rapport are often in conflict with the standardized procedure, but the experimenter must respond to the particular needs of the child while remaining sensitive to the possible confounding effects of such deviations. The experiment can usually be structured as a game, so as to arouse task-relevant attention in young children and to reduce older children's anxiety about being tested and evaluated. Children become fatigued relatively easily when prolonged attention is required. Sessions for preschool children are usually most successful if they are not longer than 20 minutes and for elementary school children if they are not longer than 40 minutes.

It is often desirable for the child to have experience with each of the stimuli, responses, and reinforcements before beginning the experiment proper. It is useful to intermix practice trials and demonstrations with the instructions. The experimenter may demonstrate the entire sequence of operation and then permit the child to go through the sequence on a practice basis. Since children find it more difficult to follow instructions than to imitate behavior, demonstrations should accompany each phase of the instructions. Further demonstrations not only emphasize relevant aspects of the situation but may enhance the value of the reinforcement. Warm-up effects have been found in a variety of problems, even following instruction and demonstration. These effects may be separated by the use of appropriate control groups. The experimenter must be alert to the possibility that the warm-up period may also induce an inappropriate or erroneous set concerning the task.

Children are generally motivated to please the experimenter, and they can readily perceive the experiment as a game. It is more difficult, however, to convey to them the importance of their behavior in determining the course of the experiment and in controlling the reinforcements obtained. Older subjects also enter the experimental task with a desire to please, but are sensitive to the fact that their performance is being evaluated and can discriminate between the formal and social aspects of the interaction.

Instructions

Instructions must be simple and brief. Repetition of the instructions, followed by questioning and practice trials, provides an opportunity to test the child's comprehension of what is to be done. With younger children instructions should be minimized, for the younger the child the more difficult it is to manipulate behavior by instructions alone. Luria (1961) has discussed the development of children's ability to respond to conditional as opposed to general instructions.

Instructions may reduce irrelevant responses and increase the subject's attention to the relevant features of the task. For example, if children are told that the reward will always be found under the same stimulus, learning rate is more rapid than if they are given no instructions concerning the location of the reward or consistency of the relationship among stimulus, response, and reward (Schaeffer and Gerjuoy, 1955).

Children may have such strong hypotheses about how to respond appropriately that instructions concerning the basis of responses are ineffective. In a study by Weir (1962), half the subjects were instructed that there was no way to obtain a reward on every trial. A probability learning task was employed in which only partial reinforcement was provided. Even with such strongly opposing instructions, no differences were obtained with preschool and elementary school children, and it was concluded that the orientation of the subject to seek a means of predicting the occurrence of reinforcement played a more significance role than instructions in determining his performance.

Osler and Weiss (1962) have investigated the effects of instructions on concept formation with children from six through fourteen years. General instructions were given to half the subjects, indicating that the correct choice would be reinforced but making no mention of the fact that subjects could, by attending to certain aspects of the stimuli, make correct choices on every trial. The remaining subjects were instructed, "There is something in the pictures like an idea that will tell you which one to choose to get a marble every time." The main effect of instructions was not significant; however, there was a significant interaction of instructions with age, with explicit instructions aiding the younger subjects and not affecting the performance of the older subjects. Children with superior IQ's surpassed the average subjects in performance under general instructions, but the difference disappeared under the explicit instructions.

Attempts to increase ego involvement in the task by means of instructions have not been consistently successful. For example, Waite, Sarason, Lighthall, and Davidson (1958) told children after an initial series of paired-associate learning trials, "You can be very proud," and attempted to create a feeling of success. Another group of children was told, "You should have done much better." No significant differences in performance resulted as a function of these instructions. Similiar negative results were obtained by Rosenblum (1956), who attempted to obtain ego involvement in a partial reinforcement situation by instructing elementary school children that he wanted them to do the very best job that they could and to try to make their class the very best. The effect of instructions on the reaction times of elementary school children has been studied by Owen (1959). Following practice on a simple reaction-time task, either the procedure was repeated, or the subjects were urged to press the key faster, or they were told to relax and not to worry about how they were doing. The retest under standard instructions resulted in a significant increase of average reaction time. Urging subjects to accelerate response produced shorter reaction times, and no change was found following instructions to relax.

Withdrawal of rewards

Motivation may be increased by the presentation of rewards, followed by their withdrawal upon incorrect response. Children rewarded with candy for correct responses require significantly more trials to learn a three-choice discrimination than subjects rewarded with candy for correct response but required to relinquish candy on incorrect responses (Brackbill and O'Hara, 1958). The withdrawal of rewards does not simply have opposite effects from the delivery of rewards. Most subjects under reward-withdrawal conditions appear to translate the situation so that withdrawal of rewards becomes the occasion for social interaction with the experimenter and so that positive social reinforcement is potentially introduced (Solley and Engel, 1960).

Deprivation

It is not feasible to increase children's motivation by subjecting them to extensive deprivation. Short-term deprivation can, however, be undertaken. Gewirtz and Baer (1958a, 1958b) have shown that the effectiveness of social reinforcement is significantly increased by isolating the child from social stimuli for 20 minutes prior to the experiment. Even though the simple request that

the child remain alone may be unsuccessful, no great difficulty is encountered when such pretexts are employed as "I have to set up a game," "I have to get the prizes," or "The game is broken and I have to fix it." Having induced the child to remain in isolation, the experimenter still must be concerned about additional effects produced by isolation. Anxiety (Walters and Ray, 1960), frustration (Hartup and Himeno, 1959), and general stimulus deprivation (Stevenson and Odom, 1961) may be produced as well. Interesting and entertaining materials of a nonsocial variety available to the subject during isolation may minimize such reactions; and, with older subjects, instructions may help to reduce anxiety about being left alone.

Frustration

Frustration has been used in many studies to increase motivation. Among the earliest are the studies of Barker, Dembo, and Lewin (1943), in which children were frustrated by the interruption of play with interesting toys, and of Keister (1943), in which children were frustrated by the presentation of very difficult puzzles. A different approach to investigating frustration is to study the effects of eliminating reward following a period of rewarded trials (Holton, 1961; Longstreth, 1960). One of the difficulties in studying children's reactions to frustration is the large amount of variable and uncontrolled behavior that occurs. In extreme cases the experimenter may have difficulty in controlling emotional reactions of the children; and even in less severely frustrating situations, the amount of irrelevant behavior makes it difficult to assess the child's performance.

Failure

Failure must be defined relative to performance itself and has widely variable effects on behavior. The effect of failure on performance is influenced by personality variables, by past history of failure experiences, and by previous reactions to stress; thus failure tends to have different effects on different subjects. It is not surprising, therefore, that the primary consequence of failure has been to increase the variability of response (R. R. Sears, 1942). Failure has been induced by the use of difficult problems and by comparing the subject's performance with some arbitrary or exaggerated norms, with his own past performance, or with the performance of other individual subjects. When the dependent variable is subsequent performance on the same task, the effects of induced failure appear to be more orderly than when the dependent variable is subsequent performance in a new task or setting (Crandall and Rabson, 1960). Alessi (1957) has found that high motivation is retained longer under failure than under success in repetitive tasks. Further, early failure impairs learning, and late failure facilitates performance during the course of solving arithmetic problems. One of the consequences of failure may be to produce a strong avoidance reaction to the task, the setting, and the experimenter; therefore failure is not usually a satisfactory technique for inducing general stress.

Stress

Stress may be created by instructions (Lipsitt and Spears, 1965) or by shortening the time allowed for responses. Instructions such as "I expect you to do very well in this game; please don't disappoint me" may be used to induce temporary stress or anxiety. When the trials are controlled by a ready signal or by the onset of a stimulus, the trial duration or the intertrial interval may be reduced somewhat below the time found in pretesting to be optimal for response. Stress induced by time pressure (Castaneda and Lipsitt, 1959) yields results comparable to those obtained when children are selected on the basis of anxiety test scores (Castaneda, 1961). Stress produced by decreasing the length of the intertrial interval is also reflected in the increase in the number of errors made (Palermo, 1957).

Children's general reactions to stress vary from their leaving the situation, becoming restless, ceasing to follow instructions, and

developing irrelevant response patterns, to crying and urinating. When it is apparent that overly strong reactions have been produced, the session should be terminated or changed to one that permits the child to experience success. Because of the strong reactions that may be produced both during and following the experimental session, it is important that great care be exercised when stress or failure are used with children.

Characteristics of the experimenter

Recent studies have indicated that characteristics of different experimenters influence performance in a wide variety of situations. Even in studies where the experimenter's interaction with the subject is minimized, such as studies of stimulus generalization (Jeffrey and Skager, 1962) and of discrimination learning (Cantor and Hottel, 1955), significant experimenter effects have been obtained. Analysis of preschool children's attention seeking and responsiveness to social reinforcement has indicated that women are more effective as reinforcing agents for boys and men are more effective as reinforcing agents for girls (Gewirtz, Baer, and Roth, 1958). With somewhat younger preschool children, women are consistently more reinforcing than men for children of both sexes, and with children in the later primary grades the sex of the experimenter no longer produces significant effects (Stevenson, 1961). Some evidence indicates that the masculinity or femininity of the experimenter and the degree of sex identification of the subject interact to produce significant differences in performance (Epstein and Liverant, 1961). Sex of the experimenter has been found to have less effect when the experimenter administers standard tests or controlled, semistructured situations (Borstelmann, 1961).

REWARD VARIABLES

A great variety of objects and events can serve as rewards for children. Because of children's curiosity and lack of experience, practically any nonnoxious stimulus can have direct or symbolic reward value when its occurrence or delivery is or appears to be contingent upon the child's behavior. In addition to the types of reward used, differential reinforcement may be produced by varying the amount of reward and the frequency or probability with which it occurs. Bijou and Sturges (1959) have catalogued a wide variety of objects that have been used as rewards in studies which children.

Selection of rewards

There have been several studies of the differential reward value of various objects and events. One approach has been to scale rewards by means of psychophysical methods. A series of paired-comparison choices yields a consistent hierarchy of preferences for common objects (Witryol and Fischer, 1960). This order can be changed, however, by the experimenter's reporting the preferences of other children prior to testing each child (Witryol and Alonzo, 1962). The order is also influenced by the age of the child (Witryol and Ormsby, 1961). For example, kindergarten children prefer objects in the order charm, nickel, bubble gum, and candy, while third and sixth graders prefer social rewards (supportive statements) to any of these objects. With increasing age, the scale differences between adjacent items in the hierarchy increases, indicating a steeper preference gradient for older children. The rank order for preference of incentives obtained by the method of paired comparisons correlates significantly with that obtained in a multiple-choice discrimination task in which the child can demonstrate his preference by choosing the stimulus consistently associated with a particular incentive (Witryol, Tyrrell, and Lowden, 1964).

Significant differences in discrimination learning occur when different types of reward are delivered in addition to a light signaling a correct response (Terrell and Kennedy, 1957). The rewards, in declining order of effectiveness as measured by learning

rates, were candy, praise, token reward, reproof for incorrect response, and the signal light alone. The difficulties of generalizing such results across all groups of children have been demonstrated in another study (Terrell, Durkin, and Weisley, 1959). Middle-class children learn faster when only a light is used as reward for correct response, but lower-class children learn faster when candy is delivered as well. A further demonstration of the interaction between the socioeconomic background of the child and the type of reward used is evident in the relatively better performance of middle-class than lower-class children when "correct" as compared with "good" is used as a verbal reward in a simple task (Zigler and Kanzer, 1962).

Cultural factors also interact with the type of object that children prefer as a reward for performance. Mischel (1958), in a study of West Indian children, offered as a reward for cooperation either a small incentive that could be obtained immediately or a larger incentive that would be delivered a week later. Immediate reward was preferred to a greater degree by Negro than by Indian children; by children whose fathers were absent from the home than by those whose fathers were present; and by seven-year-olds than by eight- or nine-year-olds.

Children of different ages may respond quite differently to the presentation of rewards. Older preschool children appear to develop a relevant goal orientation rather readily; they work to obtain the reward. Younger preschool children appear not to gain reinforcement solely from the rewards offered. Rather, the reward appears to be only one interesting aspect of the total situation, and the subjects appear to derive reinforcement from manipulation, exploration, and the opportunity to interact with the experimenter (Bijou and Sturges, 1959). The younger the child, the less effective a particular reward object may be. Since it is impossible, practically speaking, to modify these differences in developmental characteristics, the only feasible control is to observe the children's task-irrelevant behavior during the experimental session. The effects on performance of differences in the amount of exploration, interaction with the experimenter, and the like may then be determined in the analysis of the data.

Children show strong and individualized preferences among both relevant and irrelevant aspects of rewards. Preferences on the basis of color and taste, for example, are both individualized and resistant to change. Esthetic preferences, such as concern for symmetry and completeness, may produce differential value for otherwise equivalent rewards. There is some evidence indicating that the reinforcement value of successfully predicting an event increases as the relative frequency of the event decreases (Brackbill *et al.*, 1962). Unfortunately, rewards, like other stimuli, may easily distract the child's attention from the task. When interesting stimuli are used to convey correctness of response, attention may be diverted from their intended meaning; the rewards may be interesting in themselves rather than functioning merely as indicators of correct response. The delivery of manipulatable and consumable rewards often results in irrelevant responses.

These problems may often be avoided by the delivery of tokens or activation of a visible counter. Such techniques indicate correct responses and inform the subject how far he has progressed and how far he must go to obtain a reward. At the end of the experiment these tokens or credits may be exchanged for a more desirable object. The reward objects may be displayed prior to the task and the subject may select the one for which he is going to work. Such a technique reduces the satiation often produced by the delivery of a reward object on every trial, helps to maintain the child's task orientation, and helps to equate and increase initial motivation for individual subjects.

In general, pretesting may indicate what preferences are operating in a particular experiment. The pretest data may then be used as a basis for selecting stimuli and rewards and for determining the type of response to be used. For example, it might be found that preferences occurring when stimuli differ in hue disappear when brightness is substituted as the relevant dimension. Similarly, it might be found that left-right preferences are reduced by substituting a single plunger that can be deflected to the left or right.

Secondary reinforcement

The use of primary forms of reinforcement, except in certain studies of infants, is limited by the impracticality of depriving children in order to produce relevant drive states and by the early acquisition of a variety of forms of secondary motivation. The reinforcing value of various stimuli may differ widely among even very young children, depending on the varieties of experience they have had and the kinds of cues that have been provided as indices of adequate or successful performance. The experimenter usually has little knowledge or control of these types of experience. The uncontrolled variability among subjects may be reduced by manipulating the acquisition of reinforcing value for selected cues in the experimental setting (Lambert *et al.*, 1953; Myers and Myers, 1963; Olds, 1953) or by allowing each subject to choose for himself the object that will subsequently function as a reinforcer (Brackbill and Jack, 1958).

Negative reinforcement

Producing reinforcement effects by manipulating motivation to avoid noxious stimuli presents severe problems in studies with children, since stimuli producing fear cannot be used for practical and ethical reasons. Negative reinforcement effects can be obtained, however, by the interruption, withdrawal, or cessation of positive reinforcement (Jeffrey, 1955). The rate of response in an operant-conditioning situation can be manipulated by an arrangement in which each response postpones for a constant interval the interruption of an interesting series of events (Baer, 1960). A technique for avoidance conditioning has been described by Robinson and Robinson (1961), involving the interruption of children's records by a high-pitched, intense tone (50 decibels, 2,000 cycles per second). Differences in the avoidance and escape conditioning of anxious and nonanxious subjects as a function of intensity of the noxious auditory stimulus (98 decibels 2,000 cycles per second) have been reported (Penney and Croskery, 1962; Penney and McCann, 1962). The use of an intense tone may also operate as an effective form of punishment for incorrect response in discrimination learning (Penney and Lupton, 1961). Punishment is a more effective negative reinforcer if it occurs at the inception of a response than on the completion of the response (Aronfreed and Reber, 1965; Walters and Demkow, 1963). Withdrawal of reward by interruption of a motion-picture cartoon may act as a negative reinforcer to reduce rate of response in a bar-pressing task (Baer, 1961). Social withdrawal has been used in a number of studies to increase the effectiveness of positive social reinforcement (Gewirtz and Baer, 1958a, 1958b; Hartup, 1958; Rosenblith, 1961).

Verbal and social reinforcement

The process of socialization results in increased effectiveness of verbal and social reinforcement in modifying the behavior of children. The increase with age of children's relative preference of social to physical reinforcers reflects the increasing degree to which their behavior is controlled by social means. Unfortunately, studies of verbal reinforcement have confounded the verbal reinforcer with the general social reinforcement derived from the presence of an attentive and responsive adult. The mere presence of an adult may have a facilitating effect on performance, and the effect of verbal reinforcement alone should be studied separately from the interpersonal context in which it is ordinarily provided. This can be done by presenting verbal reinforcers in the absence of the adult by tape recordings or by having the

adult play the role of an attentive but non-verbally reinforcing observer of the subject's performance. An interesting alternative has been employed by Baer and Sherman (1964). A mechanized talking puppet is used to provide social reinforcement. The behavior of the puppet can be carefully standardized, and the puppet is possibly less threatening to the child than a strange adult. Line drawings of smiling and frowning faces have reinforcing effects similar to those of approving and critical adults, the direction of the effect depending in part upon the sex of the child (Loeb, 1964).

Verbal reinforcers that imply a general evaluation of the child often draw the child's attention to a wide range of social and interpersonal aspects of the situation, instead of to relevant aspects of his performance. Standardized verbal comments that reinforce specific aspects of response serve to focus attention on appropriate performance rather than on social interaction. Early studies employed praise and criticism to modify the behavior of subjects in experimental situations (Hurlock, 1931). More recently, comments such as "um-hmm," "right," and "good" have been used to reinforce a particular class of response. There are many examples of the systematic modification of behavior by the use of standardized types of verbal reinforcer. The frequency with which children respond with particular parts of speech increases following selective verbal reinforcement (Patterson *et al.*, 1960; Rowley and Keller, 1962); rate of response in a free-operant task increases with the introduction of standardized verbal reinforcement (Stevenson, 1961); the persistence of the subjects in a simple performance task increases under fixed-ratio verbal reinforcement (Zigler, 1961); and the frequency of initially non-preferred response in a two-choice situation increases with varying ratios of verbal reinforcement (Gewirtz and Baer, 1958b).

Satiation effects in the repetitive use of verbal reinforcement have been observed (Abel, 1936; Garmezy and Harris, 1953).

Thus, except in the case of children who are highly responsive to verbal and social support, such as institutionalized or socially deprived children, extended use of verbal reinforcement may result in relatively rapid reduction of its effectiveness. Several alternatives are available to the experimenter; he may either reduce the length of the session, use a lower density of verbal reinforcement, or choose to reinforce a class of responses that occurs infrequently.

Various combinations of positive and negative verbal reinforcement have been studied in discrimination learning problems (Curry, 1960; Meyer and Seidman, 1961). The introduction of negative reinforcement ("wrong"), either alone or in combination with positive reinforcement ("right"), results in more rapid learning than does positive reinforcement alone. Verbal negative reinforcement in the form of threat, scolding, or prohibition of certain responses has been used in a number of studies of the deterrent value of adult interference. Both the timing (Walters and Demkow, 1963) and the intensity (Aronson and Carlsmith, 1963) of verbal negative reinforcement are important determinants of its effectiveness.

Manipulations of reinforcement

There are many ways to manipulate reinforcement regardless of the type of reward being used. They include magnitude, delay, and probability of reward.

Children's high motivation to perform successfully makes it difficult to modify their performance by using different *magnitudes of reward*. For example, no differences in rate of discrimination learning are found when elementary school children are given 1 cent or 50 cents for each correct response (Miller and Estes, 1961). Fewer children in the groups receiving money actually learned the discrimination than in the group reinforced only with a red signal light. In a free-operant situation with four-year-olds, small but significant differences in number of responses made during extinction were found as a function of whether one, three, five, or seven trinkets were delivered per reinforcement during an extended series of acquisition trials (Pumroy and Pumroy, 1961).

Stimuli associated with *delay of reward* are less frequently chosen than stimuli associated with immediate reward (Lipsitt and Castaneda, 1958). When the difficulty of a discrimination problem is increased, delay has an increasingly deleterious effect on performance (Hochman and Lipsitt, 1961). One means of investigating the basis of poorer learning under delayed reward is to study latency of response. In a discrimination problem the interval between presentation of the stimulus and the initiation of response is shorter with delayed reward (Ware and Terrell, 1961), although the response is less frequently correct. Delayed reward has been interpreted as producing impulsive, incorrect response, inattention to relevant features of the task, and inability to use previous experiences in the task effectively. In an operant situation where the illumination of a panel serves as the conditioned stimulus (CS) for a simple movement, delayed reward results in slower starting speed than does immediate reward (Rieber, 1961). If the CS remains on during the delay period, starting speed is still slower. The interpretation is offered that delayed reward results in the conditioning of competing responses during the delay period, especially when the CS persists during the delay. The competing responses in an operant task are reflected in longer latencies, while in a discrimination task the competing responses may appear as incorrect responses occurring with short latencies. Retention of verbal material is better with delayed than with immediate reinforcement if, during the delay period, the child engages in covert rehearsal of response (Brackbill, 1964).

Experimental manipulation of the *probability of reward* may be accomplished either by providing partial reinforcement of correct responses in operant and discrimination learning tasks or by manipulating probabilities of events in a probability learning task.

Partial reinforcement of correct responses results in increased resistance to extinction (Bijou, 1957; Lewis, 1952). Children's performance is significantly affected by their expectation of reward, acquired prior to or during the experiment. For example, rate of learning a discrimination is significantly higher when it is preceded by a task in which, regardless of response, the subject is given a high rather than a low frequency of reinforcement (Steigman and Stevenson, 1960). The degree to which children risk loss in a gambling situation may also serve as an index of expectation of reward. Children rapidly increase the size of their bets when their responses are consistently reinforced, while children receiving 50 percent or no reinforcement are less likely to increase the size of their bets (Rosenblum, 1956).

Studies of probability learning in children have focused on the ages at which they are capable of forming probabilistic discriminations and probabilistic concepts and on the effects of motivation upon rate of change and asymptotic level of responding (S. Siegel and Andrews, 1962; Yost, A. E. Siegel, and Andrews, 1962). When children have been used to test a general mathematical model for discrimination learning, adjustment of learning-rate parameters has sufficed to match the predictions of the model to their performance (Atkinson, 1963). Many of the relationships between behavior and schedules of intermittent reinforcement may be investigated in traditional operant conditioning experiments (Bijou, 1958b).

There are many ways in which probabilities of reward may be varied. The most common is to reinforce only some percentage of the correct responses. In this case the selection of the sequence of reward and nonreward for correct responses is determined according to a table of random numbers. If the subject makes a correct response, the experimenter's sequence determines whether the subject is rewarded or not; if the subject makes an incorrect response (or no response), there is no reward. To eliminate possible interaction effects between pattern of reinforcement and response, different reinforcement schedules employing the same ratio of rewarded to total correct responses should be devised for each subject. Studies of probability learning have typically employed two types of reinforcement schedule. In one the experimenter decides in advance which response or responses will be reinforced on each trial, regardless of the response the subject makes (noncontingent schedule); in the other the trials that will be reinforced are dependent upon the sequence of responses that the subject has made (contingent schedule). For example, in the noncontingent case, reinforcement may be available for a particular response on the first, third, and seventh trials, while in the contingent case reinforcement is delivered on the first, third, and seventh times the particular response is made. The selection of the type of schedule and probability of reinforcement to be used is dependent upon the theoretical model being tested.

Studies of extinction following partial reinforcement are difficult to conduct if the experimenter is present in the experimental situation. When responses cease to be reinforced, children are likely to run to the experimenter for an explanation. Responses to the experimenter can be extinguished if he remains attentive but responds with a standard noncommittal comment, such as "You decide" or "Do the best you can." If the experimenter is not available, children may cease responding, leave the task, or, as is most often the case, perform in a fashion similar to that observed in experiments with adult subjects.

RESEARCH WITH EXCEPTIONAL CHILDREN

There has been a remarkable increase in the number of experimental studies conducted with groups of exceptional children. In most cases this research has involved retarded children (e.g., see House and Zeaman [1965] for citations of miniature experiments in the discrimination learning of retardates). Although the previous discussion is relevant for such research, there are some special conditions that should be pointed out.

The most frequent error is to consider such children more nearly normal than they are. Although their social behavior on first encounter may be misleadingly normal, the high degree of practice that often results in initially easy social interaction has not occurred in more abstract domains of behavior. As a consequence, their behavior in the experimental setting is often surprisingly inadequate. Instructions should be simple, transitions should be slow, and the consequences of a response should be clear. Since oral activity is often increased with retarded or disturbed children, care should be taken to provide reward objects that cannot be swallowed. There is usually no difficulty in motivating the retarded child; in fact, institutionalized retarded children are extremely responsive to a friendly, interested adult, and attempts by the child to initiate social interaction may disturb the experimental session. On the other hand, the severely disturbed child may often be tested only with the most extreme patience. Since many types of deviant children are easily distracted, it is necessary to monitor their performance to be assured that they are continuing to perform. A preliminary period for gaining rapport will ensure more attentive response, for a strange adult and a strange situation may be perceived by the child as potentially threatening as well as potentially rewarding.

The selection of subjects is difficult when deviant groups of children are used. Typically, the data concerning the child that are available in institutions are sparse or poorly organized. Mental test data tend to be old and derived from a variety of tests, and diagnostic categories for any deviant group of children tend to vary across settings. There is little to remedy these difficulties other than retesting all the subjects and attempting to achieve some standard categories by reading case records. When comparisons are made with normal children, the additional problem is faced of deciding whether to select children on the basis of chronological or mental age. Unless the problem dictates the choice of one, the most satisfactory solution is to use separate groups of children, each selected on the basis of one of the variables. The frequent use of drugs has made it difficult to obtain uncontaminated samples of children; and to make appropriate generalizations, information about the use of drugs should be obtained. Further, subject variables are often confounded with the variable of institutionalization. Since institutionalization has significant effects on children, it is frequently necessary to use an additional group of non-institutionalized children of the same type or a group of institutionalized normal children for adequate comparisons.

CONCLUDING REMARKS

Two major bodies of literature devoted to the experimental study of child behavior have been omitted from the present chapter. In the Soviet Union there has been a long history of experimental work with children. Experimental psychology in Russia, as distinct from experimental physiology and pedagogy, has to a large extent been limited to the study of children. Soviet investigators have developed a variety of ingenious experimental techniques. Unfortunately, the available reports by Soviet scientists fail to describe procedures in detail, and the designs and analyses of experiments employed make it difficult to interpret and evaluate the procedures used. Some of the methods of Soviet research with children have been reviewed by Brackbill (1962), Berlyne (1963), Elkonin (1957), and Pick (1963).

The omission of reference of Piaget and the Geneva group is due primarily to the informal nature of many of their procedures. Intriguing demonstrations of children's concepts of causality, quantity, group, reversibility, and the like have been presented through the use of standard materials and the method of the clinical interview. In addition to the better-known cognitive studies, there has been a consistent application of experimental methods to the study of children's perception. The extensive contributions of Lambercier, Inhelder, and Piaget to the study of constancies, illusions, and other perceptual phenomena have been reviewed by Wohlwill (1960).

Certain trends in the experimental study of children's behavior may be anticipated. Much significant behavior has escaped notice in experiments with children, either because it was not measured or because exhaustive analyses of the data were not performed. The introduction of computers makes it possible to perform complex analyses of vast numbers of measures derived from a single experiment and to apply psychometric techniques to data obtained in experimental settings. There are, for example, few studies of the interrelation-

ship of various response measures; factor analysis, scaling techniques, and multiple-regression analysis have not been utilized in the treatment of data derived from experimental studies. The experimental method will undoubtedly be extended to problems arising in the manipulation and control of behavior in educational, remedial, and therapeutic settings. There is a need for a new type of investigator, trained in experimental methods and working in applied settings, who will communicate to practitioners the knowledge gained from experimental studies and who will approach the investigation of practical problems with the experimental method. The controlled study of behavior possible in experimental settings not only will further increase our knowledge about children but also will increase the likelihood of understanding the genesis of adult behavior.

REFERENCES

ABEL, L. B. The effects of shift in motivation upon the learning of a sensori-motor task. *Arch. Psychol.*, N.Y., 1936, 29, No. 205.

ALBERT, R. S. The role of mass media and the effect of aggressive film content upon children's aggressive responses and identification choices. *Genet. Psychol. Monogr.*, 1957, 55, 221–285.

ALBERTS, E., and EHRENFREUND, D. Transposition in children as a function of age. *J. exp. Psychol.*, 1951, 41, 30–38.

ALESSI, S. L. The effects of different social incentive sequences upon the performance of young children. Unpublished doctoral dissertation, Univer. of Connecticut, 1957.

ARONFREED, J., and REBER, A. Internalized behavioral suppression and the timing of social punishment. *J. Pers. soc. Psychol.*, 1965, 1, 3–16.

ARONSON, E., and CARLSMITH, J. M. The effect of severity of threat on the devaluation of forbidden behavior. *J. abnorm. soc. Psychol.*, 1963, 66, 584–588.

ATKINSON, J. W. *Motives in fantasy, action, and society*. Princeton, N.J.: Van Nostrand, 1958.

ATKINSON, R. C. Mathematical models in research with children. J. C. Wright and J. Kagan (Eds.), Basic cognitive processes in children. *Monogr. Soc. Res. Child Develpm.*, 1963, 28, No. 2 (Serial No. 86).

AUSUBEL, D. P., and SCHIFF, H. M. The effect of incidental and experimentally induced experi-

ence in the learning of relevant and irrelevant causal relationships by children. *J. genet. Psychol.*, 1954, 84, 109–123.

BAER, D. M. Escape and avoidance responses of preschool children to two schedules of reinforcement withdrawal. *J. exp. Anal. Behav.*, 1960, 3, 155–159.

BAER, D. M. Effect of withdrawal of positive reinforcement on an extinguishing response in children. *Child Develpm.*, 1961, 32, 67–74.

BAER, D. M., and SHERMAN, J. A. Reinforcement control of generalized imitation in young children. *J. exp. child. Psychol.*, 1964, 1, 37–49.

BANDURA, A., ROSS, D., and ROSS, S. A. Imitation of film-mediated aggressive models. *J. abnorm. soc. Psychol.*, 1963, 66, 3–11.

BARKER, R. G., DEMBO, T., and LEWIN, K. Frustration and regression. In R. G. Barker, J. S. Kounin, and H. F. Wright (Eds.), *Child behavior and development*. New York: McGraw-Hill, 1943.

BARNARD, J. W., ZIMBARDO, P. G., and SARASON, S.B. Anxiety and verbal behavior in children. *Child Develop.*, 1961, 32, 379–392.

BARTOSHUK, A. K. Response decrement with repeated elicitation of human neonatal cardiac acceleration to sound. *J. comp. physiol. Psychol.*, 1962, 55, 9–13.

BERGMAN, M. A mobile laboratory for research in child psychology. Unpublished M. A. thesis, Univer. of Minnesota, 1964.

BERLYNE, D. Soviet research on intellective processes in children. In J. C. Wright and J. Kagan (Eds.), Basic cognitive processes in children. *Monogr. Soc. Res. Child Develpm.*, 1963, 28, No. 2 (Serial No. 86).

BIJOU, S. W. Patterns of reinforcement and resistance to extinction in young children. *Child Develpm.*, 1957, 28, 47–54.

BIJOU, S. W. A child study laboratory on wheels. *Child Develpm.*, 1958a, 29, 425–427.

BIJOU, S. W. Operant extinction after fixed-interval schedules with young children. *J. exp. Anal. Behav.*, 1958b, 1, 25–29.

BIJOU, S. W. Discrimination performance as a baseline for individual analysis of young children. *Child Develpm.*, 1961, 32, 163–170.

BIJOU, S. W., and BAER, D. W. Some methodological contributions from a functional analysis of child development. In L. P. Lipsitt and C. C. Spiker (Eds.), *Advances in child development and behavior.* New York: Academic, 1963.

BIJOU, S. W., and STURGES, P. T. Positive reinforcers for experimental study with children—consumables and manipulatables. *Child Develpm.*, 1959, 30, 151–170.

BLUM, A. The value factor in children's size perception. *Child Develpm.*, 1957, 28, 3–14.

BORSTELMANN, L. J. Sex of experimenter and sex-typed behavior of young children. *Child Develpm.*, 1961, 32, 519–524.

BRACKBILL, Y. Extinction of the smiling response in infants as a function of reinforcement schedule. *Child Develpm.*, 1958, 29, 115–124.

BRACKBILL, Y. Research and clinical work with children. In R. Bauer (Ed.), *Some views on Soviet psychology.* Washington, D.C.: American Psychological Association, 1962.

BRACKBILL, Y. The impairment of learning under immediate reinforcement. *J. exp. child Psychol.*, 1964, 1, 199–207.

BRACKBILL, Y., and JACK, D. Discrimination learning in children as a function of reinforcement value. *Child Develpm.*, 1958, 29, 185–190.

BRACKBILL, Y., KAPPY, M. S., and STARR, R. H. Magnitude of reward and probability learning. *J. exp. Psychol.*, 1962, 63, 32–35.

BRACKBILL, Y., and O'HARA, J. The relative effectiveness of reward and punishment for discrimination learning in children. *J. comp. physiol. Psychol.*, 1958, 51, 747–751.

BRIDGER, W. H., and REISER, M. F. Psychophysiologic studies of the neonate: An approach toward the methodological and theoretical problems involved. *Psychosom. Med.*, 1959, 21, 265–276.

BROWN, D. G. Sex-role preference in young children. *Psychol. Monogr.*, 1956, 70, No. 421.

BROWN, R. W. Linguistic determinism and the part of speech. *J. abnorm. soc. Psychol.*, 1957, 55, 1–5.

BRUNER, J. S., and OLVER, R. R. The development of equivalence transformations in children. In J. C. Wright and J. Kagan (Eds.), Basic cognitive processes in children. *Monogr. Soc. Res. Child Develpm.*, 1963, 28, No. 2 (Serial No. 86).

BURTON, R. V., MACCOBY, E. E., and ALLINSMITH, W. Antecedents of resistance to temptation in four-year-old children. *Child Develpm.*, 1961, 32, 689–710.

CALVIN, A. D., and CLIFFORD, L. T. The relative efficacy of various types of stimulus-objects in discriminative learning by children. *Amer. J. Psychol.*, 1956, 69, 103–106.

CANTOR, G. N., and HOTTEL, J. V. Discrimination learning in mental defectives as a function of magnitude of food reward and intelligence level. *Amer. J. ment. Defic.*, 1955, 60, 380–384.

CANTOR, J. H., and CANTOR, G. N. Children's observing behavior as related to amount and recency of stimulus familiarization. *J. exp. child Psychol.*, 1964, 1, 241–247.

CASTANEDA, A. Differential position habits and anxiety in children as determinants of performance in learning. *J. exp. Psychol.*, 1961, 61, 257–258.

CASTANEDA, A., and FAHEL, L. S. The relationship between the psychological investigator and the public schools. *Amer. Psychologist*, 1961, 16, 201–203.

CASTANEDA, A., FAHEL, L. S., and ODOM, R. Associative characteristics of sixty-three adjectives and their relation to verbal paired associate learning in children. *Child Develpm.*, 1961, 62, 297–304.

CASTANEDA, A., and LIPSITT, L. P. Relation of stress and differential position habits to performance in motor learning. *J. exp. Psychol.*, 1959, 57, 25–30.

CASTANEDA, A., PALERMO, D. S., and MCCANDLESS, B. R. The children's form of the manifest anxiety scale. *Child Develpm.*, 1956, 27, 317–326.

CHARLESWORTH, W. The instigation and maintenance of curiosity behavior as a function of surprise versus novel and familiar stimuli. *Child Develpm.*, 1964, 35, 1169–1187.

COHEN, J., and HANSEL, C. E. M. *Risk and gambling.* London: Longmans, 1956.

CRANDALL, V. J., and RABSON, A. Children's repetition choices in an intellectual achievement situation following success and failure. *J. genet. Psychol.*, 1960, 97, 161–168.

CROWELL, D. H., PETERSON, J., and SAFELY, M. A. An apparatus for infant conditioning research. *Child Develpm.* 1960, 31, 47–52.

CURRY, C. The effect of verbal reinforcement combinations on learning in children, *J. exp. Psychol.*, 1960, **59**, 434.

ELKONIN, O. B. The physiology of higher nervous activity and child psychology. In B. Simon (Ed.), *Psychology in the Soviet Union*. London: Routledge, 1957. Pp. 47–68.

EPSTEIN, R., and LIVERANT, S. Sex-role identification and verbal conditioning in children. *Amer. Psychologist*, 1961, **16**, 355.

ERVIN, S. M. Experimental procedures of children. *Child Develpm.*, 1960, **31**, 703–719.

FANTZ, R. L. The origin of form perception. *Sci. Amer.*, 1961, **204**, 66–72.

GARMEZY, N., and HARRIS, J. G. Motor performance of cerebral palsied children as a function of their success and failure in achieving material rewards. *Child. Develpm.*, 1953, **24**, 287–300.

GEWIRTZ, J. L. Plans for the construction of a portable one-way observation booth. *Child Develpm.*, 1952, **23**, 307–314.

GEWIRTZ, J. L., and BAER, D. M. Deprivation and satiation of social reinforcers as drive conditions. *J. abnorm. soc. Psychol.*, 1958a, **57**, 165–172.

GEWIRTZ, J. L., and BAER, D. M. The effect of brief social deprivation on behaviors for a social reinforcer. *J. abnorm. soc. Psychol.*, 1958b, **56**, 49–56.

GEWIRTZ, J. L., BAER, D. M., and ROTH, C. A note on the similar effects of low social availability of an adult and brief social deprivation of young children's behavior. *Child Develpm.*, 1958, **29**, 149–152.

GOLLIN, E. S. Tactual form discrimination: A developmental comparison under conditions of spatial interference. *J. exp. Psychol.*, 1960, **60**, 126–129.

GOODENOUGH, F. L., and ANDERSON, J. E. *Experimental child study*. New York: Appleton-Century-Crofts, 1931.

GOSS, A. E., and MOYLAN, M. C. Conceptual block sorting as a function of type and degree of mastery of discriminative verbal responses. *J. genet. Psychol.*, 1958, **93**, 191–198.

GRINDER, R. E. New techniques for research in children's temptation behavior. *Child Develpm.*, 1961, **32**, 679–688.

HANLON, C. Response variability in children as a function of age, pretraining, and incentive conditions. *J. comp. physiol. Psychol.*, 1960, **53**, 267–269.

HARTUP, W. W. Nurturance and nurturance-withdrawal in relation to the dependency behavior of preschool children. *Child Develpm.*, 1958, **29**, 191–201.

HARTUP, W. W., and HIMENO, Y. Social isolation versus interaction with adults in relation to aggression in preschool children. *J. abnorm. soc. Psychol.*, 1959, **59**, 17–22.

HARTUP, W. W., and MOORE, S. G. Avoidance of feminine behavior in young boys. Unpublished manuscript, Univer. of Iowa, 1963.

HOCHMAN, C. H., and LIPSITT, L. P. Delay-of-reward gradients for two levels of difficulty. *J. comp. physiol. Psychol.*, 1961, **54**, 24–27.

HODGDEN, L. Variability of behavior as a function of intelligence and incentive. *J. Pers.*, 1961, **29**, 183–195.

HOFFMAN, M. L. Child rearing practices and moral development: Generalizations from empirical research. *Child Develpm.*, 1963, **34**, 295–318.

HOLTON, R. B. Amplitude of an instrumental response following the cessation of reward. *Child Develpm.*, 1961, **32**, 107–116.

HONKAVAARA, S. A critical reevaluation of the color and form reaction, and disproving the hypotheses connected with it. *J. Psychol.*, 1958, **45**, 25–36.

HOUSE, B. J., and ZEAMAN, D. Learning and transfer in mental defectives. *Progr. Rep. NIMH Grant M-1099*, 1960a.

HOUSE, B. J., and ZEAMAN, D. Transfer of a discrimination from objects to patterns. *J. exp. Psychol.*, 1960b, **59**, 298–302.

HOUSE, B. J., and ZEAMAN, D. Miniature experiments in the discrimination learning of retardates. In L. P. Lipsitt and C. C. Spiker (Eds.), *Advances in child development and behavior*. New York: Academic Press, 1965, 313–374.

HURLOCK, E. The psychology of incentives. *J. soc. Psychol.*, 1931, **2**, 261–390.

IRWIN, O. C. The activities of newborn infants. In R. G. Barker, J. S. Kounin, and H. F. Wright (Eds.), *Child behavior and development*. New York: McGraw-Hill, 1943.

JEFFREY, W. E. New techniques for motivating and reinforcing children. *Science*, 1955, **121**, 371.

JEFFREY, W. E. Variables in early discrimination learning. II. Mode of response and stimulus difference in the discrimination of tonal frequencies. *Child. Develpm.*, 1958, **29**, 531–538.

JEFFREY, W. E., and COHEN, L. B. Effect of spatial separation of stimulus, response, and reinforcement in selective learning in children. *J. exp. Psychol.*, 1964, **67**, 577–580.

JEFFREY, W. E., and SKAGER, R. W. Effect of incentive conditions on stimulus generalization in children. *Child. Develpm.*, 1962, **33**, 865–870.

JERGARD, S., and WALTERS, R. H. A study of some determinants of aggression in children. *Child Develpm.*, 1960, **31**, 739–747.

JOHNSON, R. C., and ZARA, R. C. Relational learning in young children. *J. comp. physiol. Psychol.*, 1960, 53, 594–597.

KAGAN, J., and LEMKIN, J. Form, color, and size in children's conceptual behavior. *Child Develpm.*, 1961, 32, 25–28.

KAGAN, J., MOSS, H. A., and SIGEL, I. The psychological significance of styles of conceptualization. In J. C. Wright and J. Kagan (Eds.), Basic cognitive processes in children. *Monogr. Soc. Res. Child Develpm.*, 1963, 28, No. 2 (Serial No. 86).

KAGAN, J., ROSMAN, B. L., DAY, D., ALBERT, J., and PHILLIPS, W. Information processing in the child: Significance of analytic and reflective attitudes. *Psychol. Monogr.*, 1964, 78, No. 1, (Whole No. 578).

KEISTER, M. E. The behavior of young children in failure. In R. G. Barker, J. S. Kounin, and H. F. Wright (Eds.), *Child behavior and development*. New York: McGraw-Hill, 1943.

KENDLER, T. S., and KENDLER, H. H. Reversal and nonreversal shifts in kindergarten children. *J. exp. Psychol.*, 1959, 58, 56–60.

KESSEN, W., WILLIAMS, E. J., and WILLIAMS, J. P. Measurement of movement in the human newborn: A new technique. *Child Develpm.*, 1961, 32, 95–105.

KOCH, M. B., and MEYER, D. R. A relationship of mental age to learning set formation in the preschool child. *J. comp. physiol. Psychol.*, 1959, 52, 387–389.

KUENNE, M. R. Experimental investigation of transposition behavior in young children. *J. exp. Psychol.*, 1946, 36, 471–490.

LAMBERT, W. W., LAMBERT, E. G., and WATSON, P. D. Acquisition and extinction of an instrumental response sequence in the token-reward situation. *J. exp. Psychol.*, 1953, 45, 321–326.

LEVIN, H., and BALDWIN, A. L. Pride and shame in children. In M. R. Jones (Ed.), *Nebraska symposium on motivation*. Lincoln, Nebr.: Univer. of Nebr. Press, 1959.

LEVIN, H., and TURGEON, V. F. The influence of mother's presence on children's doll play aggression. *J. abnorm. soc. Psychol.*, 1957, 55, 304–308.

LEVIN, H., and WARDWELL, E. The research uses of doll play. *Psychol. Bull.*, 1962, 59, 27–56.

LEWIS, D. Partial reinforcement in a gambling situation. *J. exp. Psychol.*, 1952, 43, 447–450.

LIPSITT, L. P. A self-concept scale for children and its relationship to the children's form of the manifest anxiety scale. *Child Develpm.*, 1958, 29, 463–472.

LIPSITT, L. P. Simultaneous and successive discrimination learning in children. *Child Develpm.*, 1961b, 32, 337–347.

LIPSITT, L. P. Learning in the first year of life. In L. P. Lipsitt and C. C. Spiker (Eds.), *Advances in child development and behavior*. New York: Academic, 1963. Pp. 147–196.

LIPSITT, L. P., and CASTANEDA, A. Effects of delayed reward on choice behavior and response speeds in children. *J. comp. physiol. Psychol.*, 1958, 51, 65–67.

LIPSITT, L. P., PEDERSON, L. J., and DeLUCIA, C. A. Conjugate reinforcement of operant responding in infants. *Psychon. Sci.*, 1966, 4, 67–68.

LIPSITT, L. P., and SPEARS, W. C. Effects of anxiety and stress on children's paired-associate learning. *Psychon. Sci.*, 1965, 3, 553–554.

LOCKARD, J., and SIDOWSKI, J. B. Learning in fourth and sixth graders as a function of sensory mode of stimulus presentation and overt and covert practice. *J. educ. Psychol.*, 1961, 52, 262–265.

LOEB, J. The incentive value of cartoon faces to children. *J. exp. child Psychol.*, 1964, 1, 99–107.

LONGSTRETH, L. E. The relationship between expectations and frustration in children. *Child Develpm.*, 1960. 31, 667–672.

LOVAAS, O. I. Effect of exposure to symbolic aggression on aggressive behavior. *Child. Develpm.*, 1961, 32, 37–44.

LURIA, A. R. *The role of speech in the regulation of normal and abnormal behaviour*. London: Pergamon Press, 1961.

MCCANDLESS, B. R., and SPIKER, C. C. Experimental research in child psychology. *Child Develpm.*, 1956, 27, 75–80.

MCDAVID, J. Imitative behavior in preschool children. *Psychol. Monogr.*, 1959, 73 (Whole No. 486).

MARTIN, W. E. Quantitative expression in young children. *Genet. Psychol., Monogr.*, 1951, 44, 147–219.

MEYER, W. J., and SEIDMAN, S. B. Relative effectiveness of different reinforcement combinations on concept learning of children at two developmental levels. *Child Develpm.*, 1961, 32, 117–127.

MILLER, L. B., and ESTES, B. W. Monetary reward and motivation in discrimination learning. *J. exp. Psychol.*, 1961, 61, 501–504.

MISCHEL, W. Preference for delayed reinforcement: An experimental study of a cultural observation. *J. abnorm. soc. Psychol.*, 1958, 56, 57–61.

MULLEN, F. A. The school as a psychological laboratory. *Amer. Psychologist*, 1959, 14, 53–56.

MUNSINGER, H., KESSEN, W., and KESSEN, M. L. Age and uncertainty: Developmental variations in preference for variability. *J. exp. child Psychol.*, 1964, **1**, 1–15.

MURPHY, J. V., and MILLER, R. E. Spatial discrimination of cue, reward, and response in discrimination learning by children. *J. exp. Psychol.*, 1959, **58**, 485–489.

MUSSEN, P. H. (Ed.) *Handbook of research methods in child development.* New York: Wiley, 1960.

MUSSEN, P. Some antecedents and consequents of masculine sex typing in adolescent boys. *Psychol. Monogr.*, 1961, **75** (Whole No. 506).

MUSSEN, P., and RUTHERFORD, E. Effects of aggressive cartoons on children's aggressive play. *J. abnorm. soc. Psychol.*, 1961, **62**, 461–464.

MYERS, J. L., and MYERS, N. A. Secondary reinforcement in children as a function of conditioning associations, extinction, percentages, and stimulus types. *J. exp. Psychol.*, 1963, **65**, 455–459.

NORCROSS, K. J. Effects on discrimination performance of similarity of previously acquired stimulus names. *J. exp. Psychol.*, 1958, **56**, 305–309.

OLDS, J. The influence of practice on the strength of secondary approach drives. *J. exp. Psychol.*, 1953, **46**, 232–236.

ORLANDO, R., BIJOU, S. W., TYLER, R. M., and MARSHALL, D. A. A laboratory for the experimental analysis of developmentally retarded children. *Psychol. Rep.*, 1960, **7**, 261–267.

OSLER, S. F., and WEISS, S. R. Studies in concept attainment. III. Effect of instructions upon concept attainment at two levels of intelligence. *J. exp. Psychol.*, 1962, **63**, 528–533.

OWEN, W. A. Effects of motivating instructions on reaction time in grade school children. *Child Develpm.*, 1959, **30**, 261–267.

PALERMO, D. S. Proactive interference and facilitation as a function of amount of training and stress. *J. exp. Psychol.*, 1957, **53**, 293–296.

PALERMO, D. S. Word associations and children's verbal behavior. In L. P. Lipsitt and C .C. Spiker (Eds.), *Advances in child development and behavior.* New York: Academic, 1963. Pp. 31–68.

PALERMO, D. S., and JENKINS, J. J. *Word association norms: Grade school through college.* Minneapolis: Univer. Minnesota Press, 1964.

PATTERSON, G. R., HELPER, M. E., and WILCOTT, R. C. Anxiety and verbal conditioning in children. *Child Develpm.*, 1960, **31**, 101–108.

PENNEY, R. K., and CROSKERY, J. Instrumental avoidance conditioning of anxious and non-anxious children. *J. comp. physiol. Psychol.*, 1962, **55**, 847–850.

PENNEY, R. K., and LUPTON, A. A. Children's discrimination learning as a function of reward and punishment. *J. comp. physiol. Psychol.*, 1961, **54**, 449–451.

PENNEY, R. K., and MCCANN, B. The instrumental escape conditioning of anxious and nonanxious children. *J. abnorm. soc. Psychol.*, 1962, **65**, 351–354.

PICK, H. Some Soviet research on learning and perception in children. In J. C. Wright and J. Kagan (Eds.), Basic cognitive processes in children. *Monogr. Soc. Res. Child Develpm.*, 1963, **28**, No. 2 (Serial No. 86).

PINNEAU, S. R. A technique for making one-way mirrors. *Child Develpm.*, 1951, **22**, 235–241.

POULIOT, S., and MISIAK, H. The measurement of negative after images in first-grade boys and girls. *J. genet. Psychol.*, 1959, **95**, 13–17.

PUMROY, D. K., and PUMROY, S. S. Effect of amount and percentage of reinforcement on resistance to extinction in preschool children. *J. genet. Psychol.*, 1961, **98**, 55–62.

RHEINGOLD, H. L., GEWIRTZ, J. L., and ROSS, H. W. Social conditioning of vocalization in the infant. *J. comp. physiol. Psychol.*, 1959, **52**, 68–73.

RHEINGOLD, H. L., STANLEY, W. C., and COOLEY, J. A. Method for studying exploratory behavior in infants. *Science*, 1962, **136**, 1054–1055.

RIEBER, M. The effect of CS presence during delay of reward on the speed of an instrumental response. *J. exp. Psychol.*, 1961, **61**, 290–294.

ROBINSON, N. M., and ROBINSON, H. B. A method for the study of instrumental avoidance conditioning with young children. *J. comp. physiol. Psychol.*, 1961, **54**, 20–23.

ROSENBLITH, J. Learning by imitation in kindergarten children. *Child Develpm.*, 1959, **30**, 69–80.

ROSENBLITH, J. F. Imitative color choices in kindergarten children. *Child Develpm.*, 1961, **32**, 211–223.

ROSENBLUM, S. The effect of differential reinforcement and motivation on prediction responses of children. *Child Develpm.*, 1956, **27**, 99–108.

ROWLEY, V., and KELLER, E. D. Changes in children's verbal behavior as a function of social approval and manifest anxiety. *J. abnorm. soc. Psychol.*, 1962, **65**, 53–57.

RUEBUSH, B. K. Interfering and facilitating effects of test anxiety. *J. abnorm. soc. Psychol.*, 1960, **60**, 205–212.

SARASON, S. B., DAVIDSON, K., LIGHTHALL, F., and WAITE, R. A test anxiety scale for children. *Child Develpm.*, 1958, **29**, 105–113.

SCHAEFER, R. S., and BELL, R. Q. Patterns of attitudes toward child-rearing and the family. *J. abnorm. soc. Psychol.*, 1957, **54**, 391–395.

SCHAEFFER, M. S., and GERJUOY, I. R. The effect of stimulus naming on the discrimination learning of kindergarten children. *Child Develpm.*, 1955, **26**, 231–240.

SCREVEN, C. G. The effects of interference on response strength. *J. comp. physiol. Psychol.*, 1954, **47**, 140–144.

SCREVEN, C. G., and NUNIS, T. E. Response strength as a function of reduction in rate of subgoal reinforcement. *J. comp. physiol. Psychol.*, 1954, **47**, 323–325.

SEARS, P. S. Levels of aspiration in academically successful and unsuccessful children. *J. abnorm. soc. Psychol.*, 1940, **35**, 498–536.

SEARS, P. S. Doll play aggression in normal young children. *Psychol. Monogr.*, 1951, **65** (Whole No. 323).

SEARS, P. S. Problems in the investigation of achievement and self-esteem motivation. In M. R. Jones (Ed.), *Nebraska symposium on motivation.* Lincoln, Nebr.: Univer. of Nebraska Press, 1957.

SEARS, R. R. Success and failure: A study of motility. In Q. McNemar and M. A. Merrill (Eds.), *Studies in personality.* New York: McGraw-Hill, 1942.

SEARS, R. R., RAU, L., and ALPERT, R. *Identification and child rearing.* Stanford, Calif.: Stanford Univer. Press, 1965.

SEARS, R. R., MACCOBY, E. E., and LEVIN, H. *Patterns of child rearing.* New York: Harper & Row, 1957.

SEARS, R. R., WHITING, J. W. M., NOWLIS, V., and SEARS, P. S. Some child-rearing antecedents of aggression and dependency in children. *Genet. Psychol. Monogr.*, 1953, **47**, 135–234.

SHERIF, M., and SHERIF, C. *Groups in harmony and tension.* New York: Harper & Row, 1953.

SIEGEL, A., and KOHN, L. Permissiveness, permission, and aggression: The effect of adult presence or absence on aggression in children's play. *Child Develpm.*, 1959, **30**, 131–141.

SIEGEL, P. S., and FOSHEE, J. G. The law of primary reinforcement in children. *J. exp. Psychol.*, 1953, **45**, 12–14.

SIEGEL, S., and ANDREWS, J. M. Magnitude of reinforcement and choice behavior in children. *J. exp. Psychol.*, 1962, **63**, 337–341.

SIMMONS, M. W. Operant discrimination learning in the human infant. Unpublished doctoral dissertation. Brown Univer., 1962.

SIMMONS, M. W., and LIPSITT, L. P. An operant-discrimination apparatus for infants. *J. exp. Anal. Behav.*, 1961, **4**, 233–235.

SMITH, S. L., and GOSS, A. E. The role of acquired distinctiveness of cues in the acquisition of a motor skill in children. *J. genet. Psychol.*, 1955, **87**, 11–24.

SOLLEY, C. M., and ENGEL, M. Perceptual autism in children: The effects of reward, punishment, and neutral conditions upon perceptual learning. *J. genet. Psychol.*, 1960, **97**, 77–91.

SPIKER, C. C. Effects of stimulus similarity on discrimination learning. *J. exp. Psychol.*, 1956a, **51**, 393–395.

SPIKER, C. C. Experiments with children on the hypothesis of acquired distinctiveness and equivalence of cues. *Child Develpm.*, 1956b, **27**, 253–263.

SPIKER, C. C. Verbal factors in the discrimination learning of children. In J. C. Wright and J. Kagan (Eds.), Basic cogmtive processes in children. *Monogr. Soc. Res. Child Develpm.*, 1963, **28**, No. 2 (Serial No. 86).

SPIKER, C. C., and WHITE, S. H. Differential conditioning by children as a function of effort required in the task. *Child Develpm.*, 1959, **30**, 1–7.

STEIGMAN, M. J., and STEVENSON, H. W. The effect of pretraining reinforcement schedules on children's learning. *Child Develpm.*, 1960, **31**, 53–58.

STEIN, A. H., and WRIGHT, J. C. Imitative learning under conditions of nurturance and nurturance withdrawal. *Child Develpm.*, 1964, **35**, 927–938.

STEVENSON, H. W. Social reinforcement with children as a function of CA, sex of E, and sex of S. *J. abnorm. soc. Psychol.*, 1961, **63**, 147–154.

STEVENSON, H. W., and LANGFORD, T. Time as a variable in transposition by children. *Child Develpm.*, 1957, **28**, 365–370.

STEVENSON, H. W., and MCBEE, G. The learning of object and pattern discriminations by children. *J. comp. physiol. Psychol.*, 1958, **51**, 752–754.

STEVENSON, H. W., and ODOM, R. D. Effects of pretraining on the reinforcing value of visual stimuli. *Child Develpm.*, 1961, **32**, 739–744.

STEVENSON, H. W., and WEIR, M. W. Variables affecting children's performance on a probability learning task. *J. exp. Psychol.*, 1959, **57**, 403–412.

STEVENSON, H. W., and WEIR, M. W. Developmental changes in the effects of reinforcement and nonreinforcement of a single response. *Child Develpm.*, 1961, **32**, 1–6.

TEMPLIN, M. C. *Certain language skills in children.* Minneapolis: Univer. of Minnesota Press, 1957.

TERRELL, G. The need for simplicity in research in child psychology. *Child Develpm.*, 1958, **29**, 303–310.

TERRELL, G., DURKIN, K., and WEISLEY, M. Social class and the nature of incentive in discrimination learning. *J. abnorm. soc. Psychol.*, 1959, **59**, 270–272.

TERRELL, G., and KENNEDY, W. A. Discrimination learning and transposition in children as a function of the nature of the reward. *J. exp. Psychol.*, 1957, **53**, 257–260.

TERRELL, G., and WARE, R. Emotionality as a function of delay of reward. *Child Develpm.*, 1963, **34**, 495–501.

THORNDIKE, E. L., and LORGE, I. *The teacher's word book of 30,000 words.* New York: Teachers Coll., 1944.

WAITE, R. R., SARASON, S. B., LIGHTHALL, F. F., and DAVIDSON, K. A. A study of anxiety and learning in children. *J. abnorm. soc. Psychol.*, 1958, **57**, 267–270.

WALTERS, R. H., and DEMKOW, L. Timing of punishment as a determinant of response inhibition. *Child Develpm.*, 1963, **34**, 207–214.

WALTERS, R. H., and RAY, F. Anxiety, social isolation, and reinforcer effectiveness. *J. Pers.*, 1960, **28**, 358–367.

WARE, R., and TERRELL, G. Effects of delayed reinforcement on associative and incentive factors. *Child Develpm.*, 1961, **32**, 789–793.

WEIR, M. W. The effects of age and instruction on children's probability learning. *Child Develpm.*, 1962, **33**, 729–735.

WEIR, M. W. Developmental changes in problem solving strategies. *Psychol. Rev.*, 1964, **71**, 473–490.

WEIR, M. W., and STEVENSON, H. W. The effect of verbalization in children's learning as a function of chronological age. *Child Develpm.*, 1959, **30**, 143–149.

WHITE, S. H. Effects of pretraining with varied stimuli on children's discrimination learning. *Child Develpm.*, 1961, **32**, 745–753.

WHITE, S. H., and PLUM, G. E. Eye movement photography during children's discrimination learning. *J. exp. child Psychol.*, 1964, **1**, 327–338.

WITRYOL, S. L., and ALONZO, A. A. Social manipulation of preschool children's paired comparison incentive preferences. *Psychol. Rep.*, 1962, **10**, 615–618.

WITRYOL, S. L., and FISCHER, W. F. Scaling children's incentives by the method of paired comparisons. *Psychol. Rep.*, 1960, **7**, 471–474.

WITRYOL, S. L., and ORMSBY, E. L. Age trends in children's incentives scaled by paired comparisons. Paper read at East. Psychol. Ass., Philadelphia, April, 1961.

WITRYOL, S. L., TYRRELL, D. J., and LOWDEN, L. M. Five-choice discrimination learning by children under simultaneous incentive conditions. *Child Develpm.*, 1964, **35**, 233–243.

WOHLWILL, J. F. Developmental studies of perception. *Psychol. Bull.*, 1960, **57**, 249–288.

WURTZ, K. R. The expression of guilt in fantasy and reality. *J. genet. Psychol.*, 1959, **95**, 227–238.

YOST, P. A., SIEGEL, A. E., and ANDREWS, J. M. Nonverbal probability judgments of children. *Child Develpm.*, 1962, **33**, 769–780.

ZIGLER, E. Social deprivation and rigidity in the performance of feeble-minded children. *J. abnorm. soc. Psychol.*, 1961, **62**, 413–421.

ZIGLER, E., and KANZER, P. The effectiveness of two classes of verbal reinforcers on the performance of middle and lower class children. *J. Pers.*, 1962, **30**, 157–163.

Chapter 15

SOCIAL PSYCHOLOGY
AND GROUP PROCESSES

MARVIN E. SHAW

Social psychology may be defined as the scientific study of the behavior of individuals as influenced by the actual, imagined, or implied presence of other human beings (Allport, 1954). As such, it may be considered one branch of general experimental psychology, differing from other areas primarily with regard to the criterion of content. Whereas area disciplines such as learning and perception are delimited by the kind of process or phenomenon being studied, social psychology is delimited by the kinds of variables that are considered. Any behavior that involves social variables, either stimulus or response, falls within the domain of social psychology.

In the early part of this century, social psychology was largely speculative in nature. Investigations were limited to casual observations and occasional field studies. In the late 1930s social behavior was brought into the laboratory, and today laboratory experimentation is at least as widely used as the field study. Formerly, social psychology was concerned largely with imitation, prestige suggestion, morale, fads and fashions, crowd and mob behavior, propaganda, public opinion, and similar phenomena. Discussions of these topics still appear in some social psychology textbooks. This chapter is devoted to a consideration of methods and techniques involved in the experimental study of person perception, attitudes, social reinforcement, conformity behavior, leadership, interaction process, group structure, group composition, and task analysis. Most experimenters will be interested in procedures applicable to particular content areas, although certain methodological problems arise regardless of the area of investigation. The more general problems in social psychological research are discussed at length by Festinger and Katz (1953) and by Selltiz, Jahoda, Deutsch, and Cook (1961) and so will not be elaborated further in this chapter. Requirements of the experimental situation are considered, commonly used methods and techniques are described, limitations of such methods are discussed, and, wherever possible, modifications are suggested.

PERSON PERCEPTION

Interpersonal behavior begins with the perception of others. In order to respond to another person it is necessary to perceive, in some way, the relevant characteristics of that person. That we do so more or less accu-

rately is attested to by our day-to-day interactions with others. Our expectations regarding the reactions of others are either
confirmed, permitting coordination of effort
for joint action, or disconfirmed, resulting in
conflicts, and/or in learning and consequent
improvement of future perceptions.

Person perception involves many of the
same principles as perception in general, but
the question of how one person perceives another cannot be answered completely by traditional studies of object perception. The important aspects of the person as an object of
perception are precisely those not found in in-
animate objects: attitudes, emotions, desires,
intentions, and feelings. The way in which
one perceives the intention underlying the
behavior of another, for example, often determines the reaction to that behavior. The
student of social behavior, therefore, is interested in questions of the following type:
What is the nature of interpersonal perceptions? How are they organized? How accurate is the average person in his perceptions
of others? What factors determine the organization and accuracy of these perceptions?
What are the consequences of various perceptions for other kinds of behavior? Let us
examine some of the methods employed in
attempting to answer these questions.

Accuracy of perception

If accuracy-of-perception scores are to be
related to other forms of behavior, one must
have adequate measures of that behavior.
When response agreement is the operational
definition of accuracy, care must be taken
that the accuracy score does not include statistical artifacts, that it corresponds as closely
as possible with the conceptual definition of
accuracy, and, most importantly, that the
perceiver is given adequate response categories for reporting his perception of the
other person.

Accuracy of perception has been studied
under a variety of rubrics such as "social sensitivity," "social insight," "empathy," and

"diagnostic competency." Regardless of the
label, the minimum requirements for the
measurement of perceptual accuracy are the
same: valid and reliable measures of the
"real" characteristics of the stimulus person
and of the perception of these characteristics
by the perceiver. The methods that have
been used are deceptively simple, and often
have failed to meet these requirements. The
measuring instruments include rating scales
(Exline, 1957), questionnaires (Chowdry
and Newcomb, 1952), and Q sorts (Baker
and Block, 1957; Hilden, 1954). Typically,
the investigator gives the subject a measuring
instrument and asks that he respond as he
thinks a particular other person would respond. The other person responds to the
same instrument according to usual instructions. The degree of correspondence between
the two sets of responses is taken as a measure of the accuracy of the subject's perception of the other person. The D score (Osgood and Suci, 1952) is probably the most
common estimate of the degree of correspondence between the two sets of responses, although correlation coefficients also have been
used. The D score is actually a measure of
lack of correspondence, since a high D score
indicates low agreement. It is computed by
finding the discrepancy between the subject's
and the other person's response to each item,
squaring this discrepancy, summing the
squares, and extracting the square root of the
sum. In the simplest application of correlation procedures, the measure is simply the
correlation (r) between the two sets of responses. Both D and r fail to reflect precisely
that which is implied by the conceptual definition of accuracy of perception. The D score
estimates the subject's ability to approximate
the other person's responses to the set of
items. In general the D score is increased by
any systematic error in magnitude of response. Correlation estimates the subject's
ability to vary his responses to items as the
perceived person varies his responses to the
same items. The perceiver's accuracy score is
lowered if his predictions do not vary con-

comitantly with the other person's actual responses, although he may have approximated the responses very well.

Cronbach (1955) has shown that the D score, as a measure of accuracy of perception, is made up of several components, which he labeled elevation, differential elevation, stereotype accuracy, and differential accuracy. A consideration of these components clarifies the difficulties inherent in such composite scores and suggests refinements that produce accuracy measures more nearly congruent with conceptual definitions of accuracy.

The *elevation* component is the consequence of the way the perceiver uses the response scale. It is computed as the average of the subject's estimates (predictions) over all items and all perceived persons. That is, some subjects may use only the upper half of the response scale, whereas others may use only the middle portion, etc. These central tendencies result in decreased accuracy of perception to the degree that the subject's central tendency differs from the central tendency of the other person in his own self-description.

Differential elevation reflects the ability of the subject to estimate deviations of the observed individual's elevation from the average. It contains two components: assumed dispersion in elevation, which expresses the subject's estimate of how much the perceived individuals will differ in elevation, and elevation correlation, which reflects the perceiver's ability to judge which individuals rate highest on the elevation scale.

Stereotype accuracy reflects the subject's ability to predict the relative frequency or "commonness" of possible responses. Thus, the perceiver might have a high accuracy score simply because he accurately predicted the norms for the group rather than because of an ability to correctly perceive personal characteristics in others. In this case, the subject could "perceive" persons he had never met as accurately as close associates.

Differential accuracy indicates the perceiver's ability to estimate differences between individuals on any item. It combines the assumed dispersion on any item, holding elevation constant, with a correlation term (differential-accuracy correlation) that measures the ability to judge which individuals have the highest scores on the item when the score is taken as a deviation from the observed individual's mean.

This analysis implies that two rather different aspects of person perception are involved in the D score, constant processes and reactive processes. Constant processes have to do with systematic errors in the way the subject uses the rating scale, how sensitive he is to norms, and how he organizes the field of personality. These aspects are reflected by the elevation component and the stereotype-accuracy component. Reactive processes are reflected by the differential elevation correlation (DEr) and the differential accuracy correlation (DAr), which are the only components of the D score that reflect the subject's sensitivity to individual differences.

Although the study of constant processes may be important in its own right, social psychologists are generally more interested in reactive processes (Baker and Block, 1957; Chowdry and Newcomb, 1952; Exline, 1957; Tagiuri, Bruner, and Blake, 1958). To study reactive processes, the measure(s) should be DEr and/or DAr. DEr is the correlation between the average of the other person's self-descriptions over all items and the average of the perceiver's descriptions of the other person over all items (DE$r = r_{\bar{x}_o, \bar{y}_{o.s}}$). DE$r$ should be used when the investigator is interested in the subject's ability to judge which individuals are highest on the elevation scale or in the subject's ability to interpret expressive behavior. It is not, however, sensitive to overall differences in elevation.

DAr is the correlation between the subject's and the other person's responses when the score is transformed as a deviation from both item mean and other mean. Thus, DA$r = r_{y'_{ois} x'_{oi}}$, where $y'_{ois} = y_{ois} - \bar{y}_{o.s} - \bar{y}_{.is} + \bar{y}_{..}$, in which y_{ois} is the subject's description of the other person (response) on item i,

$\bar{y}_{o.s}$ is the mean of y_{ois} over all others, $\bar{y}_{.is}$ is the mean over all items, and $\bar{y}_{..}$ is the grand mean over items and others; and, similarly, $x'_{oi} = x_{oi} - \bar{x}_{o.} - \bar{x}_{.i} + \bar{x}_{..}$, in which x_{oi} is the other person's self-description (response) on item i, $\bar{x}_{o.}$ is the mean of x_{oi} over others, $\bar{x}_{.i}$ is the mean over all items, and $\bar{x}_{..}$ is the grand mean over items and others. DAr may be used as the measure of accuracy when the investigator is interested in the subject's ability to diagnose individual differences.

To this point we have been concerned with mathematical characteristics of the usual accuracy score. There are other logical objections to the usual accuracy score that are due to the kind of measuring instruments used rather than to the treatment of responses to the instrument. First, the investigator usually has rather definite conceptual definitions of "social sensitivity," "empathy," "social insight," or "diagnostic competency." In practice, however, the relevant process is defined operationally in terms of response agreement. The operational definition may not, and usually does not, agree with the conceptual definition. The statistical artifacts identified by Cronbach are evidence for some lack of agreement, but there often are other forms of disagreement as well. Secondly, personality test constructors (and others) frequently try to disguise the intent of the test so that the respondent does not know what personality characteristics are revealed by his responses. If the test constructor is successful, there is no reason to assume that the subject will be able to correctly identify the responses that will reveal his perceptions of the other person even if the subject correctly perceives the individual's characteristics. If the test constructor is not successful, the other person may be unable or unwilling to reveal his true personality by his responses. Finally, it is quite possible that the response categories provided to the subject do not correspond to the categories that he typically uses to evalute others. This problem is more closely related to the question of the organi-zation of person perceptions and will be discussed in more detail in a later section.

Measures of similarity

In addition to accuracy, several investigators have been interested in the degree to which the subject perceives himself to be similar to the other person (Fiedler, 1958; Fiedler, Hutchins, and Dodge, 1959). Assumed similarity (AS) is obtained by asking the perceiver to describe himself and also describe the other person by using the same instrument for describing both. Assumed similarity is computed as the degree of correspondence between the two descriptions, with the D score as the usual measure. A related but operationally different score is assumed similarity between opposites (ASo). To obtain this score, the subject is asked to describe his most preferred coworker (present or past) and least preferred coworker (present or past). A comparison of these descriptions via the D score gives a measure of ASo. This score is interpreted (Fiedler, 1958) along a continuum of psychological distance. A high-ASo (small D score) person assumes much similarity and tends to be uncritical and approachable to others. A low-ASo person (large D score) tends to be reserved, critical, and analytical in his relations with others. The evidence for the correctness of the interpretation is still meager.

Although both AS and ASo scores have demonstrable usefulness, they suffer from many of the shortcomings discussed in connection with accuracy scores. Fiedler (1958) recognizes the complex nature of similarity scores but has argued that these scores are less complicated than the usual accuracy score. For example, he feels that stereotype effects are minimized, since the specific content plays little part in the ASo score; however, he has used items similar to those in personality tests. Bass and Fiedler (1961) have followed Cronbach's (1958) suggestion that breaking the D score into its component parts leads to simpler and more meaningful interpretations and have found that in one instance, at least, this expectation is verified. The investigator of perceptual similarity must be certain that his measure of similarity agrees with his conceptual definition of the term and permits unambiguous interpretation. As an aid to the latter, complex scores should be broken into their component parts, and their relation to the criterion examined separately, even though the complex score may be a more powerful predictor than its components.

Organization of perceptions

Logically, it would appear that a study of the nature of person perception should precede studies of accuracy, similarity, etc., and their relation to other aspects of behavior. This has not been the case, however, and it is abundantly clear that we must learn more about the nature of person perceptions if we are to make further progress in this area. To perceive another person as a single entity, we must organize the various data of observation (actions, tendencies, capacities, interests) into a relatively unified whole. The way this is accomplished, the categories into which the data of observation are sorted, and the like are pressing problems. (Compare Cronbach, 1958; Hastorf, Richardson, and Dornbusch, 1958.) Two approaches to the problem of organization have been suggested, the first by Asch (1946, 1952) as an alternative to controlled observation of an actual person. Instead of an actual person, the stimulus was a list of discrete qualities said to belong to a person. Subjects described their impressions of this person in written sketches. The content of the sketches was then analyzed, and comparisons made among various experimental procedures. Examples included comparisons between impressions formed in relation to (1) two lists differing only in regard to one quality (e.g., warm versus cold), (2) lists having only one characteristic in common, (3) two lists differing only in order of presentation, and (4) several lists varying

in number of common elements. A variation of item 3 involved presenting the two halves of a single list separately and then asking the subject to combine the two separate sketches into a composite impression of a single person. Although this technique has revealed many important aspects of perceptual organization, it has several limitations. It is a rather artificial situation and may not be truly representative of day-to-day person perception. This is both a limitation and an advantage. The advantage is that it permits the experimenter to control the kinds of characteristics contained in the stimulus pattern in a way that is impossible with an actual person. The limitation is that the experimenter may not select the qualities that a person typically uses in forming an impression of another person. If the written sketch is taken as the sole unit of response, the value of the results will hinge upon the investigator's skill in content analysis. This procedure would probably be considerably more effective if a more adequate response system were established. Some variation of Asch's adjective checklist suggests itself, or perhaps the use of certain standardized personality measures might be in order. The latter, however, are inappropriate to the degree that the meaning of item responses is hidden from the subject.

A second approach, suggested by Hastorf *et al.* (1958), may be called a *free-response* approach. The free-response approach is designed to meet the objection that low accuracy of perception may be due, in part, to the fact that subjects do not have an adequate response system. In the free-response method, subjects are asked to describe others in their own words, and these free descriptions are analyzed to determine categories and frequency of usage, with the ultimate aim of determining categories that are relevant to the perceiver. The feasibility of this approach has been demonstrated by Beach and Wertheimer (1961). With a similar purpose in view, Cronbach (1958) suggested that a multidimensional rating scale, an adjective checklist, or a set of items for Q sorting could be given to a single subject who describes a number of representative others. Factor analysis could then be employed to isolate the categories or dimensions used by the subject.

A recent approach introduced by Anderson (1965) also merits consideration.

Factors influencing perception

Closely related to the problem of organization is the question of the determinants of person perceptions. The Asch approach permits the examination of the effects of certain characteristics upon the perception of other characteristics, but its usefulness is limited. An approach of more general applicability involves the systematic variation of the attributes and behavior of the stimulus person. This technique is exemplified by the work of Thibaut and Riecken (1955), Jones and deCharms (1957), and Jones, Davis, and Gergen (1961). Variations of the characteristics of the stimulus person can be introduced in several ways, perhaps the most direct method being the use of role-playing confederates. The confederate is "exposed" to subjects under standardized conditions. In each experimental group, the confederate plays a role designed to represent selected attributes of the stimulus person. The subjects' perceptions of the confederate are measured following exposure and related to the particular attributes represented by the confederate's role. When this method is used, it is essential that the confederate understand his role and be capable of playing it with at least moderately high consistency. It is also important to use several confederates to ensure that the observed relationships are not unique to the particular person playing the role.

The use of confederates is relatively costly in terms of personnel payment, a shortcoming that may be alleviated by the use of "canned" confederates. The roles of the confederate may be tape-recorded or recorded on film and presented to subjects in this form

rather than in person. This approach has the advantage of ensuring consistency from group to group, although it may suffer from a certain amount of artificiality. It also has the advantage of permitting more precise control over the content of the role, since the recording can be repeated until just the desired content is obtained.

ATTITUDES

Conceptually, an attitude may be defined as " . . . an enduring organization of motivational, emotional, perceptual, and cognitive processes with respect to some aspect of the individual's world" (Krech and Crutchfield, 1948, p. 152). Campbell defined attitude operationally as " . . . a syndrome of response consistency with regard to social objects" (Campbell, 1950, p. 31). For experimental purposes, the operational definition is usually adopted; it is assumed that the syndrome of response consistency reflects the latent variable identified by the conceptual definition.

The investigator interested in attitude formation or structure must find some way of measuring the attitude in question. The literature may be searched for an existing scale, but this procedure is likely to be time-consuming and has a high probability of ending in failure. The alternative is to develop a scale before proceeding to the main part of the investigation.[1]

Attitude measurement

Basically, the requirements for attitude measurement are the same as those for any other type of measurement; however, the requirements are not as easily met as in some other types of measurement, and compromises are generally necessary. Minimally, a measuring instrument must be reliable (yield consistent results) and valid (measure what

[1] This stituation should be relieved to some extent by a forthcoming source book of attitude scales, *Scales for the measurement of attitudes,* being prepared by M. E. Shaw and J. M. Wright, to be published by McGraw-Hill Book Company.

it purports to measure). A general discussion of the various methods of estimating reliability and validity may be found in *Technical recommendations for psychological tests and diagnostic techniques* (American Psychological Association, 1954).

In attitude measurement, the question of validity is most troublesome. In general, an attitude scale may be said to be valid if the syndrome of responses yielded by it corresponds to our conceptual definition of the attitude purportedly measured, i.e., if it can be demonstrated that certain explanatory constructs account to some degree for the scores yielded by the attitude scale. Campbell and Fiske (1959) have suggested a method of estimating test validity by means of a multitrait-multimethod matrix. The basic assumptions are that different methods of measuring the same "trait" should yield similar results, whereas measures of different traits should be significantly different. These notions of convergence between independent measures of the same trait (or attitude) and discrimination between measures of different traits are implicit in the formulation of construct validity (American Psychological Association, 1954). Construct validity is perhaps more appropriate for attitude measurement than other types of validation, although this is a controversial issue (Bechtoldt, 1959; Campbell, 1960; Ebel, 1961).

If only the minimal requirements of reliability and validity are met, we have a nominal scale: persons can be grouped into mutually exclusive categories, with respect to the attitude, but there is no necessary relation among the categories. If the requirement of unidimensionality (measurement of a single variable) is also met, then we have an ordinal scale: persons can be arranged in rank order with respect to the attitude being measured. Satisfying the additional requirement of equality of units yields an interval scale: a statement can be made concerning how much stronger one person's attitude is than another's. If our scale meets all the above requirements and also the requirement

of having a zero point, we have a ratio scale. Most attitude scales developed thus far are no better than ordinal scales.

The most commonly used methods of developing attitude scales are Thurstone's (1929, 1931) method of equal appearing intervals, Likert's (1932) method of summated ratings, and Guttman's (1941, 1944, 1947) method of scale analysis. Lazarsfeld's (1950, 1954) latent structure analysis represents a departure from the more traditional methods and has not been widely used.

The essential steps in the Thurstone technique are (1) the formulation of a large number of simple statements about the attitude object; (2) the sorting of these items into 11 piles by judges (100 or more) according to their estimate as to whether (and to what degree) assent would reflect favorable, neutral, or unfavorable attitudes toward the object; (3) computation of the median scale position of each item based upon judges' sorting; (4) rejection of items for which there is insufficient agreement among judges; and (5) selection from the remaining items of about 20 items whose median scores represent points more or less evenly spaced along all parts of the continuum. The median scale position of each item is taken as the scale value of that item. The respondent takes the resulting scale by checking all items with which he agrees or by checking two or three items nearest his own position. Experimental findings concerning the effects of various procedures upon obtained scale values are summarized by Webb (1955).

Likert's procedure also begins with the formulation of items related to the attitude to be measured. Instead of being sorted by judges, however, the items are administered to a group of respondents drawn from the target group who respond to each statement by either "strongly approve," "approve," "undecided" "disapprove," or "strongly disapprove." Scores of 5, 4, 3, 2, and 1 are assigned for each of the above categories, respectively. The total score for an individual is the sum of his item scores. Item scores are then correlated with the total, and items that show substantial correlation with the total score are retained for the final scale.

Guttman's scale analysis method approaches the problem somewhat differently. The basic idea is that items can be arranged in an order such that an individual who responds positively to any particular item also responds positively to all other items having a lower rank. In developing a scale, statements related to the attitude are formulated, administered to a group of subjects, and the response patterns analyzed to determine whether or not they form a scale, i.e., can be arranged in the order described above. With N items requiring only agreement or disagreement, there are $2N$ response patterns that might occur; if the items are scalable, only $N + 1$ of these patterns will be obtained. The relative nonoccurrence of deviant patterns allows Guttman to compute a coefficient of reproducibility.

$$\text{Rep} = 1 - \frac{\text{total number of errors}}{\text{total number of responses}}$$

where an error is any deviation of an obtained pattern from an ideal pattern. Theoretically, Rep is equal to the proportion of responses to the item that can be correctly reproduced. A Rep of .90 is usually taken as the standard for acceptance.

There are a number of difficulties with Rep that must be considered. (1) Rep is equal to the average of the individual item reproducibilities. (2) The reproducibility of an item cannot be smaller than the proportion of subjects in its largest category. (3) The expected value of Rep is often high, especially when the total number of categories is small (Festinger, 1947; Green, 1954). Therefore, in evaluating Rep, one must take into account the number of items, the number of categories per item, and the proportion of subjects in the largest category for each item. Torgerson (1958) lists a number of auxiliary criteria for evaluating Rep to ensure that the obtained value is not spuriously high. Edwards (1957) also discusses

problems with Guttman's Rep and suggests an alternative method of computation which he believes yields a more accurate estimate of reproducibility.

Each of the above methods yields reasonably satisfactory scales, although none achieves equality of intervals or a zero point. Attitude scales developed by these procedures should be regarded as ordinal scales. Table 15-1 gives a comparison of the relative advantages and disadvantages of the Thurstone, Likert, and Guttman methods.

Lazarsfeld's latent structure analysis is more theoretical in nature than the methods discussed thus far. In fact, Lazarsfeld (1950, 1954, 1959) is concerned with attitude structure and measurement only as part of the broader issue of relations between concept formation and empirical research in the behavioral sciences. The method assumes a unidimensional continuum of the attitude along which subjects are distributed according to some unknown probability distribution. Statements about the object of the attitude are formulated and administered to a group of subjects with the idea of using the obtained information to say something about the underlying attitude continuum. It is assumed that items are intercorrelated only because of their common correlation with the underlying attitude variable. Following these assumptions, Lazarsfeld develops a general latent structure model that is applicable to any manifest variable. Latent class analysis and the latent distance scale are derived from the general latent structure model. Latent class analysis is based upon the untested assumption that items will be intercorrelated only because of their mutual correlation with the underlying attitude. Individuals concentrated at a given point on the underlying continuum form a latent class. Items are independent within each latent class. Therefore, this analysis is actually a method of dividing a population of subjects into a number of classes or types. As Green (1954) points out, the latent class model implies a nominal attitude scale; if data fit the model, we know

Table 15-1   Comparison of Thurstone, Likert, and Guttman attitude scales.

Characteristics	Thurstone	Likert	Guttman
Ease of construction	Moderately easy	Easy	Difficult
Item content	Must refer directly to attitude object	Need not refer directly to attitude object	Usually must refer directly to attitude object
Ease of scoring	Moderately easy	Moderately easy	Very easy
Score interpretation	Independent of total distribution of scores	Dependent on total distribution of scores	Relatively independent of total distribution of scores
Respondent's reaction	Neutral to moderately negative	Neutral to moderately negative	Negative
Reliability:[1]			
Two-forms	.60–.85	.72–.94	
Split-half	.52–.89	.78–.92	
Test-retest	.82–.88	.79–.90	.85–.95
Reproducibility			
Validity	Not clearly established	Not clearly established	Not clearly established
Unidimensionality	No	Approximate	Yes
Equality of units	No	No	No
Neutral point	Yes	No	No

[1] Representative reliabilities as cited in Edwards (1957).

that they behave as if there were a number of latent classes with stated properties, but we do not know whether the population of respondents can be partitioned into groups having these properties. (For computational procedures, see Anderson, 1954; Green, 1951.) The latent distance scale represents a technique for scalogram analysis based on a probability model. This method has been described by Hays and Borgatta (1954) and by Torgerson (1958). Its advantage over the Guttman procedure is that perfect and imperfect scales can be represented equally well and, since it is based upon a probability model, most of the criteria for the Guttman scale become unnecessary.

This brief survey of methods of developing attitude scales is not intended to be exhaustive. Several other approaches include the unfolding technique (Coombs, 1950, 1953), the semantic differential (Osgood, Suci, and Tannenbaum, 1957), and the several variations and multidimensional extensions discussed by Edwards (1957) and by Torgerson (1958).

Structure of attitudes

There are two aspects to the problem of attitude structure: (1) What are the components of a single attitude and how are they interrelated? (2) How are attitudes related to other attitudes? There are no well-developed procedures for investigating these questions, but several approaches may be suggested for preliminary study. First, the free-response techniques designed to investigate the organization of person perceptions may be adapted to the study of attitude structure. Subjects could be asked to report their feelings and beliefs about the attitude object. These reports could then be analyzed to determine attitudinal components and their interrelations. This procedure is highly subjective, and its efficiency would be expected to depend upon the skill of the person who analyzes the reports.

Another approach makes use of correlations and/or factor analysis. Responses to an attitude scale may be analyzed to discover the factor structure of the attitude. Similarly, responses to scales designed to measure several different attitudes may be analyzed to provide information about the interrelations among attitudes. The effectiveness of this procedure depends heavily upon the quality of the attitude scales. If the scales are not reliable, low correlations may result even if the attitudes are interrelated; on the other hand, too high correlations may serve to invalidate at least some of the scales being used (Campbell and Fiske, 1959). The studies by Smith, Bruner, and White (1956) and by Nunnally (1961) represent complex applications of this general approach.

Finally, certain aspects of latent structure analysis may be applicable to these problems, especially that of single attitude structure. A detailed discussion of these procedures is beyond the scope of this chapter; the interested reader is referred to Lazarsfeld (1950, 1954, 1959).

Attitude change

In the investigation of variables influencing attitude change, there are several factors to consider: (1) If an experimenter attempts to change an attitude, he must have some reason to believe that his subjects have room to change. This is the familiar "ceiling effect." A person near the extreme end of the attitude continuum has very little room to change his attitude in the extreme direction, whereas a person near the middle has relatively much room to move. This ceiling effect is especially bothersome when the initial position is treated as an independent variable. Hovland, Lumsdaine, and Sheffield (1949) discuss ceiling effect and some suggestions for handling this problem. (2) During the course of any experiment, variables other than the one of interest to the experimenter are present. In attitude-change studies, extraneous variables such as contemporaneous events and maturational processes often produce change in attitudes quite independent of the experimental treatment. (3) When two or more groups are compared after experimental treatment, the interpretation of differences between groups is based

upon the underlying assumption that the groups were equivalent prior to the experimental treatment. (4) If an experimental design involves prior measurement of the attitude, it is possible that this measurement alone will have an effect upon the attitude. Such effects are often confounded with the effects of the experimental treatment. (5) When the measure of attitude change is taken as the difference between initial and final attitude scores, regression effects are troublesome. Since both experimental and control groups regress on the mean, the obtained difference between means is expected to be smaller than the true difference.

Some of the many designs that have been suggested for the study of attitude change are outlined in Table 15-2. The table shows what happens to each group of subjects during the course of the experiment, at least from the experimenter's point of view. In these diagrams, a series of dots indicates passage of time only; the series of question marks in Design II implies that the control group may or may not be exposed to the experimental treatment. In all these designs, subjects are assigned to groups randomly. Let us now consider how each of these designs handles the problems listed above.

In Design I, the experimental group is exposed to the experimental treatment, the attitude is measured in both groups, and differences between the two groups are taken as evidence of the effect of the experimental treatment on attitude change. It is assumed that at least some of the subjects in each group have room to change, that both experimental and control groups were exposed to the same extraneous influences, and that randomization produced initially equivalent groups. No initial measurement or change scores are involved. Because of the relative lack of control of variables, this design is not recommended when other designs are possible. However, in order to study the effects of certain unanticipated "natural" events on attitudes, this design is often the only feasible one.

Table 15-2   Paradigms for the experimental investigation of attitude change.

Design I	Experimental group :		Experimental treatment →	Attitude measurement
	Control group :		.... →	Attitude measurement
Design II	Experimental group :	.... →	Experimental treatment →	Attitude measurement
	Control group :	Attitude measurement →	??????????????? →	....
Design III	Experimental group :	Attitude measurement →	Experimental treatment →	Attitude remeasurement
	Control group :	Attitude measurement →	.... →	Attitude remeasurement
Design IV	Experimental group :	Attitude measurement →	Experimental treatment →	Attitude remeasurement
	Control group A :	Attitude measurement →	.... →	Attitude remeasurement
	Control group B :	.... →	Experimental treatment →	Attitude measurement
Design V	Experimental group :	Attitude measurement →	Experimental treatment →	Attitude remeasurement
	Control group A :	Attitude measurement →	.... →	Attitude remeasurement
	Control group B :	.... →	Experimental treatment →	Attitude measurement
	Control group C :	.... →	.... →	Attitude measurement

Design II differs from Design I; only the initial attitude of the control group is assessed. It provides some information about initial position (experimental and control assumed to be equivalent via randomization), and an estimate of room to change is provided by the initial position of the controls. It provides no protection against the effects of extraneous variables. This design is weak, and is recommended only when both groups must be exposed to the experimental treatment.

Design III provides a check on room to move and initial equivalence of groups and provides some safeguards against the possibility that differences between experimental and control groups are due to prior measurement and/or extraneous variables. There is no safeguard against the possibility that these variables interact with the experimental treatment so that its effect is changed. If attitude change is assessed by comparing the experimental and control groups after the experimental treatment, regression effects are not involved; however, if change from initial to final position on the attitude continuum is taken as the estimate of change, regression effects contaminate results.

Design IV is like Design III except that an additional control group is added, which permits an estimate of possible interaction effects between initial measurement and the experimental treatment. It is assumed that control group B is initially equivalent to the other two groups via random selection of subjects. The results obtained by using this design are most easily interpretable when there is some reason to believe that extraneous influences are minimal.

Design V has all the advantages of Design IV and also provides additional information regarding the effects of extraneous variables. The above statements concerning equivalence of groups, room to change, and regression effects in change scores also apply to this design.

It should be evident that more than one experimental group may be used in connection with any of these designs. For example, one may be interested in the relative effects of the experimental treatment upon persons at different points along the attitude continuum. One might select high, medium, and low subjects for three experimental groups, each of which is subjected to the experimental treatment, and compare the amount of change in each group with a corresponding control group, i.e., control groups composed of high, medium, and low subjects that are not subjected to the experimental treatment. Results obtained with this type of design are contaminated by the ceiling effect (room to move) and should be interpreted cautiously. It is possible to use additional experimental groups to study independent variables that are not correlated with subjects' position on the attitude continuum; in such cases, the ceiling effect is less critical but still must be taken into account. More detailed accounts of these and other designs may be found in discussions by Solomon (1949) and by Selltiz et al. (1961).

It is important to include a control group that is not exposed to the experimental treatment, although it may appear unnecessary in some cases. For example, Hovland and Mandell (1952) were interested in comparing amount of attitude change when the communicator did and did not draw the desired conclusion. They found that the net percent of subjects changing in the desired direction was 19.3 when the desired conclusion was not drawn versus 47.9 when it was drawn, a highly significant difference. They concluded that it is generally more effective to state the desired conclusion explicitly than to permit the audience to draw its own conclusion. Consider the interpretation of these results if a control group had been included that was not exposed to the communication and the net percent changing in the desired direction turned out to be 30.1. We might still say that explicit conclusion drawing is more effective than the treatment in which no conclusion is drawn, but we could say further than the change produced by explicit conclusion drawing is in the desired direction, whereas that produced by the no-conclusion treatment is in the undesired direction.

SOCIAL REINFORCEMENT

Social motives and social reinforcement have long been of interest to social psychologists, but methods of study have developed slowly. The problems in this area center around the questions of the nature and effects of social reinforcers in relation to social motivation, and the way that social reinforcers are used or operate in social situations. Correspondingly, there are two general approaches to the study of social reinforcement: (1) social deprivation and reinforcement studies, in which the reinforcement is administered directly by the experimenter, and (2) social interdependency studies, in which the experimenter arranges conditions so that the reinforcement received by each subject depends upon the behavior of another subject. There may be a number of variations within each of these methods.

Social deprivation and reinforcement

The forerunner of this approach probably was the early studies of the effects of praise and blame upon learning in the classroom. The modern version is represented by verbal-conditioning studies (Greenspoon, 1955; Taffel, 1955) and by the social-deprivation studies (Gewirtz and Baer, 1958a, 1958b). In these studies, social motives (e.g., need for approval by others) are assumed to be operative, and the effects of various kinds of social reinforcers upon overt behavior are studied. Typical social reinforcers are spoken sounds such as "um-hmm," "good," or "right" administered by the experimenter each time the subject enacts the behavior selected for investigation (e.g., the emission of plural nouns, self-referent pronouns such as "I," "my," and "me," or stroking the ear lobes). The dependent variable is the change in frequency of occurrence of the reinforced behavior. (See Chap. 10 for a discussion of verbal-conditioning methodology.)

The greatest problem in the use of social reinforcers is control. The human experimenter is far less dependable as a consistent reinforcer than an automatic programmer. He must be able to identify the behavior selected for reinforcement quickly and accurately enough to administer the reinforcement at the appropriate time and in a way that does not contaminate the outcome. This problem can be minimized by selection of a response that is easily identifiable and by extensive training of the human reinforcer, but it probably cannot be entirely eliminated. In addition, some subjects interpret a supposed reinforcer as positive and some as negative (Mandler and Kaplan, 1956), the effect of the reinforcer may be influenced by prior experimenter-subject interaction (Kanfer and Karas, 1959), different experimenters may have different reinforcing effects (Binder, McConnell, and Sjoholm, 1957; Kanfer, 1958), and there is the possibility that the experimenter may influence the behavior of subjects by some method other than verbal reinforcement (Bachrach, Candland, and Gibson, 1961).

If these difficulties can be reasonably handled, the operant-conditioning paradigm may permit the examination of many aspects of the social-reinforcement problem. For example, the effects of social deprivation may be investigated by examining the effects of social reinforcement after the individual has been isolated (Gewirtz and Baer, 1958a, 1958b). This kind of investigation may help answer many questions about the nature of social motivation, particularly with reference to the similarity of physiological drives and social motivation. In this kind of investigation it is necessary to consider length of deprivation and age of subjects; both Gewirtz and Baer (1958b) and Walters and Ray (1960) found social reinforcement more effective after 20 minutes' isolation than under conditions of no isolation with six- to ten-year-olds. Walters and Karal (1960) found no such effect when subjects were college undergraduates. Among others, these variables need to be varied systematically in order to determine more precisely the consequence of social deprivation.

Social interdependency

Methods of studying social reinforcement in the social interdependency situation are derived largely from game theory (von Neumann and Morgenstern, 1947). In this procedure, the reinforcements are controlled by the experimenter indirectly, via the conditions that he establishes. Within these conditions, the particular outcome for a given subject may depend solely upon his own behavior, solely upon the behavior of another subject, or upon both his own behavior and the behavior of another subject. The subject may or may not know the source and/or range of possible reinforcements.

A method of investigating the role of reinforcement in social-interdependency situations has been developed by Sidowski, Wyckoff, and Tabory (1956). Each member of a pair of subjects in this "minimal social situation" is provided with two pushbuttons by means of which he can provide reward (positive points) or punishment (shock and/or negative points) to the *other* member of the pair. Each subject's control panel contains an add-subtract counter, a small signal lamp to indicate trials or beginning and end of the session, a set of finger electrodes, and two pushbuttons. The finger electrodes are detachable and are used when the experiment calls for a physically aversive stimulus. Negative points (a point being subtracted from the counter) are used when a more abstract aversive stimulus is required. Both subjects are generally instructed to make as many positive points as possible on their own counters. Each subject can be placed in a separate room, or the pair may be seated in the same room and separated by a dividing screen or panel. In either case, when subject *A* presses one button, a positive point is registered on *B*'s counter; and when *A* presses the other button, a point is subtracted from *B*'s counter. Similarly, the outcome of *B*'s response is registered on *A*'s counter. Thus, each subject of a pair is rewarded or punished for a response by the response of the other subject, and each subject can influence his own score only indirectly by influencing the response of the other subject. The experimenter may, dependent upon the experimental conditions, make the reward or punishment circuits inoperative for one or both subjects (Sidowski, 1957).

The method described above provides an adequate procedure for isolating the effects of reward and punishment upon social interaction. It is quite likely, however, that the effects of reinforcement parameters will vary with other relevant aspects of typical social situations. Similar techniques may be used to investigate these effects. Several variables appear to be significant:

1. *Instructions* may be manipulated to control or study awareness of social interdependency. The experimenter may inform the subject that another subject controls his rewards and punishments (Sidowski, 1957) or may merely tell him to make points, leaving him unaware of the presence of a second subject (Sidowski *et al.*, 1956). The subject may

also be told the sex of the partner (Sidowski *et al.*, 1960) or that he is playing against a machine or experimenter (Sidowski and Smith, 1961). Results of these studies indicate that few subjects believe that a second subject is involved in the experiment, regardless of instructions and in spite of the fact that they learn to give each other points.

2. *Sex* requires counterbalancing since several studies have shown significant differences in performance between sex pairs, male-male, female-female, and male-female (Sidowski, Kostanzer, Naumoff, and Smith, 1960; Sidowski and Smith, 1961). It also appears that males and females react differently to punishing stimuli (Sidowski, 1961; Sidowski, Stevens, and Greene, 1961), and that the sex of the experimenter has some influence on the interaction (Sidowski, *et al.*, 1960; Sidowski, 1967).

3. *Types of reinforcement,* in addition to shock and points, include money (Crawford and Sidowski, 1964; Willis and Joseph, 1959), credit in course work, and social reinforcers such as "good" or "fine." The relative value of reinforcers also may be manipulated; e.g., earning 20 points versus earning 10 points.

4. *Proximity* of interacting subjects to each other is a variable of interest. The experimenter may control certain instructional or awareness-of-interaction variables when the interconnected subjects are separated from each other and seated in separate rooms or on different floors of a building (Sidowski, 1957). Face-to-face contact and separation of subjects by a masking screen or panel allows for other social considerations.

5. *Orientation* of subjects to the situation varies in an uncontrolled manner unless the experimenter provides the orientation. Because of the gamelike quality of the situation, a competitive orientation may be adopted (Shaw, 1962), resulting in a very different pattern of interaction from that existing when a cooperative orientation is created (Willis and Joseph, 1959). Male and female pairs appear to react differently to coopera-

tive or competitive instructions (Crawford and Sidowski, 1964).

6. *Status relationships* may be manipulated either by instructions or by the selection of subjects of known status differences. Unless status differences are of primary interest, it is probably best to equate the status of subjects. This statement holds for subject characteristics, generally.

7. *Experience* of individual subjects may be manipulated through pretraining. During pretraining, each subject of a pair may be subjected to the same individual experiences, e.g., identical reinforcement schedules (Sidowski, Stevens, and Greene, 1961), or to different experiences, e.g., each subject of a pair pretrained on a different reinforcement schedule (Sidowski and Gregovich, 1963), and then interconnected to the other subject in an interdependent social situation.

8. *Response restrictions* are inherent in any controlled experiment, but it is not necessary to limit each subject to two possible responses. By adding more buttons and circuits, the number of alternatives may be increased to any desired number. The equipment, procedure, and analysis become more complicated as the number of alternatives is increased, but obtained information also increases.

Responses may also be restricted in terms of frequency and order of responding: subjects may be permitted to respond freely (Sidowski, 1957), only on signal from the experimenter (Sidowski and Smith, 1961) simultaneously, or alternately (Kelley, Thibaut, Radloff, and Mundy, 1962). If two subjects are in a paced-trial procedure in which they are expected to respond simultaneously, one will generally react slightly sooner than the other. A relay circuit should be designed to "hold" the earliest response and to release the rewards or punishments simultaneously upon response of the second subject (Sidowski and Smith, 1961).

Responses of both subjects may be fed directly to counters or an event recorder. A continuous event recorder, such as the Ester-line-Angus, allows the responses to be recorded through different pens marking a moving tape. Sequences of interacting responses (e.g., shock followed by score followed by score) may be recorded by passing the subject responses through appropriate relay circuitry before transmitting them to pens on the recorder. The optimal solution is to have the responses fed into card punch or tape equipment, which allows for immediate print-out of data in a form usable in a digital computer.

Social interaction is highly complex, and the variables discussed above are only the more obvious ones influencing the process. These variables may be studied separately or in various combinations. The methods sugested provide the basic experimental setup, but each investigator must make appropriate modifications to meet the requirements of his particular problem or game.

CONFORMITY BEHAVIOR

Conformity and deviation with respect to group norms constitute important aspects of group behavior. Since these processes can be considered either from the standpoint of the subject (the conformer or deviant) or from the standpoint of others, there is often disagreement about the meaning of these terms. For some writers, a person can be said to conform only if his behavior is determined by his perception or awareness of the norms of the group; for others, conformity is merely agreement between the individual's behavior and the norms of the group. If the first definition is adopted, the investigator is faced with the problem of determining whether or not the individual perceives the norms of the group—a difficult undertaking, to say the least. If the latter definition is adopted, the question of the individual's knowledge of norms does not arise, but there is danger that a given behavior will be labeled conformity when the agreement between the behavior and the group norm is fortuitous. Fortunately, it is possible to arrange experimental conditions so that the behavior of the majority, more than 50 percent of the group members, from which norms are inferred is obvious to the subject and it is safe to assume that he is aware of the norm. In this case, the two definitions produce the same results, and agreement between behavior and norms can be taken as an index of conformity.

It is usually easy to measure the dependent variable, amount of conformity. The amount of conformity occurring when the norm has been established experimentally is compared with the amount occurring when the norm has not been established. The difference between these two measures defines true conformity. Manipulation of independent variables poses greater problems. Variables influencing conformity may be classed under four general headings:

1. *Personality variables* include all the unique characteristics of the individual; hence investigation involves all the difficulties associated with the measurement of these characteristics. Manipulation is possible only by selection; i.e., experimental conditions are established by selecting subjects whose personality characteristics represent different points on the independent-variable continuum.

2. *Stimulus variables* refer to aspects of the stimuli that elicit the behavior being studied, and include stimulus ambiguity and task difficulty, among others.

3. *Situational variables* are the aspects of the situation other than the stimulus that affect conformity. Examples are size of the majority, unanimity of group response, and structure of the group.

4. *Relational variables* refer to the relations between the individual group member and the group and include such factors as amount and kind of pressure and degree of identification with the group.

With the exception of personality variables, manipulation of variables is accomplished by way of the assigned task, instructions, and/or the experimental apparatus. In any case, the techniques for presenting the stimulus and the norm are crucial. The technique chosen depends on the nature of the stimulus and the purpose of the investigation. The stimulus may be presented by means of tape recorders, projectors, tachistoscopes, or printed cards or by special equipment such as that required for the autokinetic situation. Norms of the group may be presented and manipulated either by presenting the same stimulus to all subjects but leading each naive subject to believe that others have reacted to it in specified ways (Asch, 1952) or by presenting different stimuli to different subjects but leading them to believe that all have been subjected to the same stimulus (Shaw, Rothschild, and Strickland, 1957). Examples of techniques for presenting stimuli and norms are discussed below.

Stimulus presentation

Stimuli used to study conformity behavior vary in a number of respects, but stimulus ambiguity seems to be one of the most critical. In general, the more ambiguous the stimulus the greater the conformity. Three types of stimuli (autokinetic, auditory, and visual comparison), representing three degrees of ambiguity, are described here.

The autokinetic phenomenon (perceived movement of a stationary light) provides a stimulus situation characterized by near-maximum ambiguity (Sherif, 1935). Basically, all that is required for stimulus presentation is a device for exposing a pinpoint light in a light-tight room. The critical subject then judges the amount of movement of the stationary light during any given exposure, after he has been made aware of the judgments of others. For some purposes it is desirable to provide a timing device such that the light remains on a specified length of time after the subject indicates that he has seen the light begin to move. This permits control of time of perceived movement, thus making it possible to equate time of perceived movement for all subjects. A standard interval timer is easily adapted for this purpose.

The most common form of auditory stimulus is a series of clicks. Subjects are asked to estimate the number of clicks in each series. Ambiguity varies with number, duration, rate, and intensity of the clicks. Moderate ambiguity exists when clicks have the following characteristics: number, 4 to 9; duration, 5 milliseconds (msec); rate, 4 per sec; and intensity, approximately 55 decibels sound pressure level (dB SPL). Stimuli having these characteristics can be judged quite accurately, better than 95 percent correct, but subjects are uncertain about the accuracy of their judgments. Clicks may be presented directly by means of a metronome. It is probably easier to control stimulus characteristics if the stimuli are recorded and presented to subjects through earphones.

Visual comparison stimuli are the least ambiguous stimuli that have been used. Typically, subjects are required to match the length of a given line, the standard, with that of one of three unequal lines (Asch, 1952). One of the three unequal lines is the same length as the standard, whereas the other two differ from the standard $\frac{3}{4}$ to $1\frac{3}{4}$ in. Under normal conditions subjects can make the required judgment accurately and confidently. The stimulus may be projected on a screen or may be presented by exposure of stimulus cards. Matching the areas of geometrical forms or the number of dots on cards may also be used as comparison stimuli, but these are usually more ambiguous than the Asch-type lines.

Norm manipulation

Variations in perceived norms may be accomplished by face-to-face pressures or by mechanical apparatus. Face-to-face pressures involve the use of confederates who have been instructed to respond according to a predetermined plan. This enables the experimenter to vary the amount and kind of pressure exerted upon the critical subject. This technique has several disadvantages. It requires the assistance of several persons other than the experimenter and also requires additional time for training confederates. Face-to-face pressure also may be created and varied by presenting different stimuli to different subjects, while leading them to believe that all are being exposed to the same stimulus. This can be done easily with taped auditory stimuli presented through earphones. This procedure is wasteful of subjects and requires moderately elaborate preparations.

The disadvantages of the face-to-face methods may be avoided by the use of mechanical apparatus (Crutchfield, 1955). It is easy to construct a device for studying the reactions of several subjects simultaneously without the aid of confederates. The apparatus consists of a control panel for the experimenter and a signal-response panel for each subject. Subjects are seated side by side with the signal-response panel in front of them. Each panel has a row of mercury switches and several rows of signal lights, one row for each subject in the group. The subjects are presented with a stimulus pattern calling for a judgment among two or more response alternatives. Crutchfield used a variety of stimuli, e.g., a slide calling for a simple judgment of which of two geometrical figures was larger in area. Each subject reports his judgment by throwing the appropriate switch when it is his turn to respond. The experimenter tells the subjects that each person's response will be signaled to others by way of the signal light on each subject's panel. Order of responding is varied so that each subject at some time responds last, thus being exposed to social pressure to conform.

Actually the subjects are misled. The apparatus is really wired so that the experimenter controls all information appearing on the panels. There is no connection between subject panels; whatever signals are sent by the experimenter appear identically on all panels. The experimenter has signal lights on his panel so that the subject's responses are known. In this way, several naive subjects can be run at one time, the number being limited only by the number of signal-response panels provided.

This apparatus is very useful as a technique for manipulating amount and kind of social pressure, although there is some question regarding its comparability to face–to-face situations. However, Blake and his associates (Blake and McConnell, 1953; Olmstead and Blake, 1955) found no differences between face-to-face pressure and pressure created by subjects listening to tape-recorded judgments by persons represented as other group members.

LEADERSHIP

A major difficulty in the study of leadership has been the problem of definition. Carter (1958) pointed out that there are at least five ideas used in trying to specify the meaning of the concept of leadership. Accordingly, the leader is the person who (1) is able to focus the behavior of the other members, (2) is able to lead the group toward its goals, (3) is selected by the members of the group as being the leader, (4) has demonstrable influence upon group syntality (dimensions along which groups vary), or (5) engages in leadership behaviors, depending upon the underlying idea. The particular definition adopted will affect materially the method of investigation.

To investigate leadership phenomena, it is necessary to identify persons who exemplify the adopted definition and, if leadership is presumed to vary in degree, to measure the leadership characteristics possessed by identified leaders.

Identification and measurement of leadership

Techniques of identification and measurement fall into two general classes: nominations and observational techniques. When nominations are used, the usual procedure is to ask the members of the group to name the leader(s) of the group. A person so iden-

tified most clearly exemplifies definition 3 but might also be made to exemplify other definitions by asking appropriate questions, e.g., asking who is best able to lead the group toward its goals (definition 2). Nominations may be made either by peer members or by superiors, and either by naming one or more persons or by rating all members of the group. Ratings have the advantage of indicating relative standings of group members. Wherry and Fryer (1949) have shown that peer evaluations are more reliable (.75 to .76) than are superior evaluations (.42 to .58) and also appear to have greater predictive validity. Hollander and Webb (1955) present evidence against the common criticism that peer nominations merely reflect friendship relations.

If peers are asked to name more than one person, number of choices accorded an individual may be taken as an index of his leadership potential. If ratings are used, degree of attributed leadership is reflected directly in the ratings.

Observational techniques are designed to identify leaders by observing their behavior in groups under controlled conditions. The basic requirements are a set of criteria for determining when an individual's behavior reflects leadership, and a standardized situation in which the individual is given an opportunity to demonstrate his leadership potential while being observed by a trained observer. This technique most nearly exemplifies leadership defined in terms of leadership behaviors, but may also be used when other definitions are adopted by using different criteria of leadership.

Following the extensive application of this general technique by the United States Army O.S.S., several specific procedures have been developed. The *leaderless group discussion* (LGD) procedure introduced by B. M. Bass (1954) has been more fully developed than others. The basic procedure is to ask a group of examinees to carry on a discussion for a given period of time, either on an assigned topic or on one of their own choosing. Observers rate each examinee for leadership potential. Ratings may be made subjectively after the discussion has ended or may be made by means of a checklist during the discussion. In most cases, Bass had raters indicate the degree to which each examinee "(a) showed initiative, (b) was effective in saying what he wanted to say, (c) clearly defined or outlined the problem, (d) motivated others to participate, (e) influenced the other participants, (f) offered good solutions to the problem, (g) led the discussion" (Bass, 1954, p. 468). Ratings ranged from 4 for "a great deal" to 0 for "not at all." The leadership score is the sum of the ratings assigned. Using this procedure, he reported interrater reliabilities between .82 and .84, and test-retest reliabilities between .75 and .90. Validity estimates vary widely, depending upon the criterion, but are reasonably satisfactory in view of the questionable validity and reliability of the criteria themselves. As Bass has pointed out, there is little standardization with regard to kinds of behavior observed, kind of discussion problem, length of testing time, instructions to examinees, and size of group. Control of these variables should contribute greatly to validity. Validity also could be improved by requiring observers to tabulate the frequency of leadership behaviors by each examinee rather than rely upon the more subjective ratings.

Leadership process

Leadership process refers to the interaction of the leader with other group members and the consequences of this interaction for member behavior and satisfaction. Studies of the leadership process fall into two general types. (1) Leaders are compared with nonleaders in regard to characteristics, behavior, and effect upon the group. This kind of study is represented by the typical trait approach, and has been largely unsuccessful. Occasionally, the leader-nonleader classification serves as the dependent variable, and leader emergence is examined as a consequence of experimental variations.

This application is as good (or as bad) as the criteria used for identifying leaders and nonleaders. It is quite limited in terms of amount of information obtainable. (2) Leadership is varied and its effects upon group process evaluated. This procedure has yielded much more knowledge about the effects and nature of leadership. In this type of study, the leadership variable may be manipulated either by selection or by role playing.

Manipulation by selection requires identification of persons who manifest leadership behavior or leadership potential of varying kinds or to varying degrees. Their behavior in a controlled group situation and/or their effects upon the group's behavior are examined. A typical experiment of this type might include the selection of persons believed to possess either high, medium, or low leadership potential; assignment of these persons to the leadership position in groups faced with an assigned task; and evaluation and comparison of the performance of groups under each level of leadership potential. It is necessary to have more than one person at each level of leadership potential in order to control for the effects of other characteristics of the individuals selected. In theory, this is an acceptable method of manipulating leadership variables, but its effectiveness depends upon the adequacy of selection and measurement procedures.

Role playing appears to be the most effective method available for the laboratory study of leadership behaviors. It enables the experimenter to effectively control those aspects of leadership behavior of interest and at the same time to avoid the difficulties inherent in measurement of leadership potential. It has been objected that results obtained in the role-playing situation are unreal and hence tell us nothing about "real-life" situations. However, those who have worked with role playing agree that it does realistically capture real-life situations; moreover, whenever laboratory-type experiments have been duplicated in a field setting, comparable results have been obtained (see, e.g., Morse and Reimer, 1956).

Role playing as a means of manipulating the leadership variable in laboratory experiments was probably first used in the study of autocratic, democratic, and laissez-faire leadership (Lewin, Lippitt, and White, 1939). In principle, the method can be applied to the study of any dimension of leadership behavior or any combination of behaviors (leadership types). Several considerations are involved:

1. The critical aspects of the role to be played by the assigned leader must be spelled out carefully and in detail, and the experimenter must be certain that the role player understands them and is thoroughly familiar with them prior to the experimental session. Some check should be made to determine whether the leader has carried out his role assignment.

2. Care must be taken to ensure that the leadership variable is not confounded with individual differences. This can be accomplished either by having several individuals play each role or by having the same individuals play all the roles investigated.

3. The role assigned to a given person must be one that he is capable of playing; i.e., he must have the abilities required and the role must not be too foreign to his usual behavior patterns. On the other hand, a socially unacceptable role that "fits" an individual too closely can be threatening and should be avoided.

4. Unless demanded by the hypothesis being tested, it is usually important that other members of the group be unaware that the leader has been assigned any specific role other than that of leader.

In many investigations, the interest is only in the effects of certain leader behaviors upon an unselected group; however, one may be interested in these effects when the behavior of other members is also specified in certain ways. Maier and Zerfoss (1952) outlined a multiple role-playing technique for evaluating various kinds of leadership approaches and simultaneously measuring the effects of different kinds of participants on the group process. In essence, other group members, as well as the leader, are assigned roles. The advantages of this procedure for control of variables are obvious, but it greatly complicates the administration of the experiment. (For a discussion of other advantages and disadvantages of role playing, see Liveright, 1951.)

INTERACTION PROCESS

Interaction refers to the fact that some activity or behavior of one person is stimulated by the behavior of another person. Perhaps the most common form is verbal interaction, but interaction can involve many other forms of behavior, e.g., motor acts such as two persons smiling at each other, or "communion through the eyes" (Heider, 1958). The experimental social psychologist is often interested in studying such interactions under standardized conditions. The content of the interaction process is the datum to be analyzed. In such cases the data may consist of written protocols, tape recordings, movies, or observations by trained observers. Whatever the nature of the data, they must be reduced to quantitative form if adequate analytical procedures are to be carried out. Some form of content analysis is essential. The general technique of content analysis has been described in detail by Berelson (1952).

Applications of content analysis to data obtained in laboratory research are not infrequent, although many are incomplete or inadequately worked-out forms of analysis. Examples of specific applications to specific problems include use of the We/I ratio (the number of times "we" is used in a given interpersonal interaction divided by the number of times "I" is used) as an indicator of group cohesiveness (White and Lippitt, 1953), the analysis of the content of laboratory-created rumors (Allport and Postman, 1947), and the analysis of the content of

Table 15-3   Record sheet for scoring the interaction of a three-person group using Bales's categories.

Categories	Subject 1	Subject 2	Subject 3
Shows solidarity, raise other's status, gives help, reward:			
Shows tension release, jokes, laughs, shows satisfaction:			
Agrees, shows passive acceptance, understands, concurs, complies:			
Gives suggestion, direction, implying autonomy for others:			
Gives opinion, evaluation, analysis, expresses feeling, wish:			
Gives orientation, information, repeats, clarifies, confirms:			
Asks for orientation, information, repetition, confirmation:			
Asks for opinion, evaluation, analysis, expression of feeling:			
Asks for suggestion, direction, possible ways of action:			
Disagrees, shows passive rejection, formality, withholds help:			
Shows tension, asks for help, withdraws out of field:			
Shows antagonism, deflates other's status, defends or asserts self:			

SOURCE: Bales, R. F. *Interaction process analysis. A method for the study of small groups.* Cambridge, Mass.: Addison-Wesley, 1950, p. 59.

communications designed to produce attitude change (Hovland, Janis, and Kelley, 1953). Several more generalized techniques have been developed for the purpose of recording and analyzing the content of interaction as it occurs. In addition to the techniques described below, a recent application of Coombs's nonmetric multi-dimensional unfolding procedures to this problem (Rinn, 1963) merits consideration.

The Bales system

Bales's system, "interaction process analysis" (Bales, 1950), is a technique for analyzing and recording interaction in small, face-to-face groups as it occurs. Basically, it consists of a set of 12 categories used by observers to classify the behavior of individuals in groups. The unit of analysis is the smallest discriminable segment of verbal or nonverbal behavior to which a trained observer can assign a classification under conditions of continuous serial scoring. Examples are simple sentences, components of compound or complex sentences, and words or phrases that express a complete simple thought. The categories are shown in Table 15-3. These were formulated to provide evidence about problems of communication, evaluation, control, decision, tension reduction, and reintegration. These may be indicated by a wide range of behaviors spelled out in detail by Bales. Examples for category 1 (shows solidarity, raises other's status, gives help, reward) include greeting another by saying "hello," waving, shaking hands, expressing sympathy, expressing satisfaction with another's work, and similar forms of behavior.

This system can be applied in a variety of ways. Minimally, an adequately trained observer who has memorized the categories requires only paper and pencil. Ideally, several trained observers using a mechanical recorder make simultaneous observations of the interaction, at the same time making tape recordings for future analysis and comparison with the concurrent analysis. Table 15-3 shows a simple form that can be used quite easily by a trained observer. It does not allow for a time-sequence analysis (unitizing), but for many purposes this is unnecessary. The initiation and direction of the interaction (attributing) can be indicated by recording 1-2 to indicate interaction initiated by subject 1 directed toward subject 2 or by using different columns for each initiator and simply recording the identity of the target person.

The Interaction Recorder (Bales and Gerbrands, 1948) facilitates recording and provides unitizing as well as categorizing and attributing information. It consists of a case containing a drive mechanism for a wide paper tape upon which observations are recorded. The list of categories is placed on the top of the case by means of a detachable glass plate in such a way that the moving tape is exposed in proper position for tabulating scores. As each score is put down, it moves with the tape under the checklist and disappears. A marker inside the case puts a mark on the tape at the end of each minute, and a counter records the number of minutes that have passed. A red light flashes once each minute to remind the observer to canvass the group for expressive tension behavior. The basic elements of this equipment are simple; a device to accomplish the same purposes can be easily constructed by anyone having minimal mechanical ability. The Bales-Gerbrands device is available commercially.

The Bales system has many advantages. It provides a method of analyzing complex situations, it is reasonably easy to use, and interobserver reliability is satisfactory (.75 to .95). It also has several disadvantages. It requires at least one trained observer and preferably two or more (training can be time-consuming), its validity is difficult to establish, and interpretation of results is not always obvious. Agreement between observers about the label to assign to a given bit of behavior does not guarantee accurate interpretation of the meaning of that behavior. Also, there is some question that these 12

categories adequately reflect the group interaction. In spite of these difficulties, it is a useful technique.

Carter's stenograph recorder

Carter and his associates (Carter, Haythorn, Meirowitz, and Lanzetta, 1951b) suggested that the 12 categories used by Bales are inadequate to record the variety of behaviors observed when groups work on tasks requiring manipulation of materials. Alternatively, they provided a list of 59 categories, including such items as "shows a personal feeling of aggressiveness or anger," "calls for attention," "imitates others," and "gives information." Neither the theoretical basis for these categories nor a description of specific indicators is given in detail. Categories are reported to have reliabilities ranging from .24 to .90 (Carter et al., 1951b).

A stenograph recorder is used for recording the observations. The basic unit of this device is a stenograph or stenotype machine, a small manual printing device used by stenographers for taking dictation. It prints numbers from 0 to 9 and several letters of the alphabet, either singly or in combination. For present purposes, it must be modified by attaching a small synchronous motor to the paper-drive mechanism so that the recording paper is moved at a constant rate. A microswitch and relay are added so that one key depresses automatically each half minute to print a time line on the recording tape. Finally, the shift bar is extended to fit under the number keys so that the recorder prints numbers directly when any number key is depressed rather than requiring depression of the shift bar.

To use this device the observer must memorize the categories and their associated numbers, as well as learn how to operate the machine. He then records each interaction by typing a letter to identify the originator of the interaction, a number or numbers to identify the category, and lastly a letter to identify the target of the interaction. This system of analysis has most of the advantages and disadvantages of the Bales system. The larger number of categories provides more information than does the Bales system, but at the same time requires more extensive training procedures for observers.

The interaction chronograph

A device to record individual participation in group interaction was developed by Chapple and Arensberg (1940). It consists of a moving tape driven at a speed of 5 inches per minute, on which lines are drawn by continuously moving, self-inking wheels. A lever is attached to each wheel so that the wheel is lifted from the paper when the observer presses the appropriate key. Each group member is assigned a key. When a given member acts, the observer presses the assigned key, holding it down until the action ceases. The blank space on the tape indicates the length of the action. Each key works independently of the others, and the observer is able to record when two or more individuals are talking at the same time. The original model had six keys, so that the interactions of six persons could be recorded at one time.

In the interview situation, test-retest reliabilities (r) ranged from .464 to .890 for nine variables when the test-retest interval was one week (Saslow, Matarazzo, Phillips, and Matarazzo, 1957) and from .726 to .956 when the test-retest interval was only a few minutes (Saslow, Matarazzo, and Guze, 1955). (Compare with Matarazzo, Saslow, and Guze, 1956.)

The Interaction Chronograph allows discovery of interruptions and alternations, as well as duration of the interactions. It does not give any indication of the content of the interaction, and in this respect is not as useful as the Interaction Recorder or the Stenograph Recorder. It is easy to operate, observers require relatively little training, and the stability of obtained scores is acceptably high.

GROUP STRUCTURE

When individuals are brought together for the first time and interact with each other, the careful observer will soon notice differentiations developing within the group. Some persons exert more influence than others, some have more prestige, some are liked better. Group structure is the term applied to the pattern of relations among these differentiated parts of a group. There are as many group structures as there are dimensions along which the group becomes differentiated. Among the many group structures that might be studied, perhaps the most significant ones for group functioning are status structure, power structure, role structure, and communication structure.

Before detailed consideration is given to techniques, it is necessary to point out that structures may be studied in different ways and for different reasons. First, the experimenter may wish to consider the individual position within the group structure, i.e., differences among positions within a single group, or he may wish to consider the entire group structure, i.e., differences between groups having different structures. Second, group structure may serve as either an independent of a dependent variable; i.e., the experimenter may be interested in creating or identifying different structures and studying their effects upon members or groups, or he may be interested in the formation or change of structure as a function of other experimental variables. In any case, the problem of identification and measurement of group structures is of critical importance and is emphasized in the following discussions.

Status structure

Although the term *status* has been used to refer to a number of different aspects of group structure (see Benoit-Smullyan, 1944), it is used here to refer to the evaluation or prestige associated with a position within a group or a part of the group. It is that aspect of a group position which renders it desirable to others in the group. There are at least three ways by which differing status structures may be identified and/or created for experimental study (see Bales, 1958).

1. *Instructions.* In experimentally created groups the situation and the positions of each group member are described in such a way that varying degrees of status are attributed to the various positions. For example, Kelley (1951) created high- and low-status group members by telling some subjects that their job was very important and required much skill and telling other subjects that their job was the poorer, more menial one, requiring only routine activity. The effectiveness of this technique obviously hinges upon the adequacy of the instructions.

2. *Organizational position.* Status structures are said to exist in extant groups if the members occupy positions presumed to differ in status level. Thus the commander of an aircrew (the pilot) has higher status than other officers in the crew, who in turn have higher status than the airmen; the president of a company has higher status than vice-presidents. With proper controls, differences in behavior between the various positions within groups may be determined and evaluated (Harvey and Consalvi, 1960). In like manner, groups having different status structures may be identified and studied. An aircrew composed of a major and five captains presumably would have a different status structure from one composed of six captains or one of four captains and two airmen.

Harary (1959) developed a formula for computing a status index in such groups, taking into account the number of subordinates each person has and the number of links between them. A given person P is said to be a subordinate of another person A if A is above P in the organization chart and there exists at least one link (path) from A to P. The status of A is given by $s(A) = d(A,P)$, where d is the number of links between A and P. (If one assumes that having high-status subordinates reflects more

status than having low-status ones, appropriate weights may be used.) The gross status of the organization is given by

$$s(H) = s(A_1) + s(A_2) + \cdots \cdot s(A_n)$$

The obvious practical difficulty in applying these formulas is that the organizational hierarchy must be known beforehand. At the conceptual level, it should be noted that this measure of status is dependent on the number of links between positions and, if weights are used, the relative importance of these links. Differences in the meaning of links in different organizations also could be adjusted for by using weights; however, a method of determining appropriate weights has not been developed.

The technique of identifying status structures through organizational positions is effective to the extent that the presumed status does in fact inhere in the positions and that the groups chosen for study are representative of the class of groups from which they were drawn. The major objection to this procedure is the fact that power (control of means by which others satisfy their needs) and status frequently are confounded in extant groups, in which case it is impossible to know whether observed effects are due to status structure or to power structure.

3. *Nominations (sociometric choice).* In this procedure status structure is derived from the responses of group members to questions about others in the group, a technique introduced by Moreno (1934). The meaning of the structure identified or established by this procedure resides in the question(s) asked; therefore, it may be possible to use this technique to measure not only status structure but also other kinds of structure, such as power structure, leadership structure, communication structure, and the like, simply by asking appropriate questions. What questions are appropriate (valid), however, has not been established.

For experimental purposes, it is often desirable to construct sociometric indices. Many formulas have been suggested for this purpose (Glanzer and Glaser, 1959; Proctor and Loomis, 1951), but only a few will be presented here. It seems evident that the more choices a person receives, the higher his status in the group; therefore, when only choices are considered, choice status is given by

$$CS_i = \frac{Nc}{N-1}$$

where Nc is the number of persons choosing the individual i, and N is the number of persons in the group. Similarly, negative choices yield a rejection status index

$$RS_i = \frac{Nr}{N-1}$$

where Nr is number of persons rejecting i, and N is the number of persons in the group. Since both choice and rejection may be taken as indicators of status, the two may be combined by subtracting RS_i from CS_i.

A more sophisticated measure of status structure based on matrix analysis of sociometric data has been developed by Katz (1953). He suggested that the number of persons choosing an individual may be less important than who does the choosing, and his index takes this factor into account. Suppose that the members of a four-person group are asked to name the persons who have prestige in the group, each person omitting himself. The results may be shown in matrix form as follows:

		Chosen			
		A	B	C	D
Chooser	A	0	1	1	0
	B	1	0	0	0
	C	1	1	0	0
	D	0	1	0	0
		2	3	1	0

Thus, person A named B and C, person B named A, etc., and a link is said to exist between A and B, A and C, and so on. Since a person is not permitted to choose himself, zeros are entered in the diagonals. If we assume that members answer the questions correctly and that each link independently has the same probability of being effective,

then the status of a person can be computed as

$$T = aC + a^2C^2 + \cdots + a^kC^k$$
$$= (I - aC)^{-1} - I$$

where T is the status index having elements t_{ij} and column sums $t_j = \Sigma_i t_{ij}$, a is a constant indicating the probability that a link is effective and having values from 0 to 1, C is the matrix, and I is the identity matrix. The major difficulty with application of this particular formula in its final form is the fact that there are matrices, not the zero matrix, which have no inverse. Katz derived an equivalent formula that finds the solution through a set of linear equations rather than by explicitly determining the inverse of a matrix:

$$\left(\frac{1}{a}I - C'\right)t = s$$

where a is a constant reflecting the probability that each link is effective, I is the identity matrix, C' is the transpose of the original matrix C, t is the sum of the columns of T, and s is a column vector whose components are the column sums of C. The linear equations generated by this formula are then solved for t. As Katz points out, this process breaks down in case $1/a$ is not greater than the largest characteristic root of C. The status index is computed as

$$\text{Status} = \frac{1}{m}t$$

where $m =$
$$a(n-1) + a^2(n-1)^{(2)} + \cdots$$
$$+ a^k(n-1)^{(k)}$$

in which a is a constant as in preceding formulas and n is the number of persons in the group; m is the maximum index possible, and is analogous to the $N-1$ in the simpler status indices cited above.

The investigator may justly inquire about the relative merits of the simple status index based upon number of choices and/or rejections and the Katz formula, which takes into account indirect as well as direct indicators of status. Although the latter has the advantage of including more criteria of status than the simpler formulas, there appears to have been no empirical investigations comparing the two approaches. Validation studies are badly needed in this area.

All the sociometric indices described above are designed for studying status positions within a single group; however, the experimenter may wish to compare the functioning of groups having differing status structures or to study the formation of structures in groups under varying experimental conditions. What is needed here is a method of measuring the structure of a group as a unit. There is no easy way to combine the individual indices to form a group index of status structure, since the appropriate mathematical model for such a combination is unknown. There are, however, some indices based upon sociometric data that have been developed to study group structural characteristics. Although these have not been labeled as status indicators, they appear to be very close to our definition of group status structure.

Perhaps the best known of these approaches is represented by the many studies of group cohesion, which is defined as the resultant of all the forces acting on the individual to cause him to want to remain in or to leave the group (Proctor and Loomis, 1951). The most common index is

$$Co = \frac{\Sigma M_p}{[N(N-1)]/2}$$

where N is the number of persons in the group, and M_p is the number of mutual choices, i.e., pairs of individuals who chose each other. Festinger, Schachter, and Back (1960) suggested an index based on ingroup and choices:

$$Co = \frac{\text{choices in own group}}{\text{total choices}}$$

Group integration, a similar concept, may be computed by

$$GI = \frac{1}{\Sigma i}$$

where i is the number of individuals receiving no choices (isolates).

Katz and Powell (1953) have given a method for comparing matrices based upon agreements and disagreements of binary entries. Their index of conformity is given by

$$C = \frac{n(n-1)n_{AB} - n_A n_B}{\sqrt{n_A n_{\bar{B}} n_B n_{\bar{A}}}}$$

where $n(n-1)$ is number of off-diagonal cells, n_A is number of positive entries in matrix A, n_B is number of positive entries in matrix B, $n_{\bar{A}}$ is number of zero entries in A, $n_{\bar{B}}$ is number of zero entries in B, and n_{AB} is number of positive entries in both A and B.

Power structure

Like status, power has been used to mean different things by different writers. For present purposes, person A is said to have power over person B if A controls means for satisfying some of the needs of B; the more means controlled by A, the greater his power over B (Adams and Romney, 1959). By power structure, we refer to the pattern of power distribution in the group. In general, the same techniques are used to study power structure as to study status structure: the experimenter may arrange experimental conditions so that power differences exist (or are presumed to exist) among members of an experimental group (Shaw, 1959), he may select persons who occupy different power positions in an extant group (Torrance, 1955), or he may seek to determine existing power differences by appropriate sociometric questions and applying a formula similar to those given in the preceding section (cf. Lippitt, Polansky, and Rosen, 1952). The criteria are different, but the techniques are the same and have all the advantages and disadvantages discussed in connection with status structure.

Role structure

A social role is a set of behaviors associated with a particular position in a group, and role structure refers to the distribution of roles in a group. Role and status are inter-related but can be separated conceptually and experimentally. It is possible to specify various kinds of role, based upon the criteria used for identifying the set of behaviors (Thibaut and Kelley, 1959). A *prescribed* role is the set of behaviors expected by others in the group; a *subjective* role is the set of behaviors perceived by the individual to be associated with his position; an *enacted* role is the set of behaviors actually exhibited by the individual in any given position.

Roles and role structures may serve as either independent or dependent variables, but, as in the study of status, the major problem in either case is that of identification and measurement. Unfortunately, the techniques so far developed are somewhat less than satisfactory, but repesent steps in the right direction. Bates and Cloyd (1956) developed a 51-item questionnaire for identifying roles in groups. Items are such things as "interprets the discussion question," "brings the group back to the subject," and "is not sure of himself." The questionnaire is given to group members, who are asked to list in rank order the names of others in the group who might be expected to act or feel as each item states. Data are tabulated and role descriptions developed in terms of concentrations of actions in a single person. Reliability was estimated by comparing roles identified in this way with those identified by means of Bales's interaction categories. Reported reliabilities range from .88 to .94. It is unclear whether this procedure yields prescribed or enacted roles, but it could easily be modified, by instructions, to overcome this ambiguity. In principle, any kind of role could be identified by this means.

Thibaut and Kelley (1959) defined role as the class of one or more norms that applies to an individual's behavior. They then suggested that roles can be identified by means of a matrix with norms as rows and group members as columns. When a given norm applies to a particular member, a check is placed in the appropriate cell. Roles are then easily identified by inspection of the resulting clusters. A major shortcoming is that the norms of the group must be known.

Both of these techniques are useful, but neither provides an adequate method of quantifying roles and role structures. Several of the techniques for handling status positions and structures are potentially adaptable for this purpose.

Communication structure

Communication structure refers to the pattern or distribution of communication channels among the members of a group. In addition to distribution, channels may vary in regard to number, directionality, capacity, operational effectiveness, susceptibility to distortion and noise, and ease of usage. All of these affect group functioning and must be controlled if one is interested in isolating the effects of communication structure. The most common procedure is to hold other characteristics of communication channels constant while varying the pattern, or structure. It probably would be more rewarding to vary both structure and other aspects simultaneously in order to determine interaction effects. Standard factorial designs are indicated for this kind of investigation.

The usual procedure in studying the effects of communication structure involves imposing various communication structures upon groups and requiring them to solve problems. The group problem-solving process under these conditions may be separated into organizational operations and task-specific procedures. Task-specific procedures, in turn, may be broken down into information-collection operations and solution operations. Information-collection operations are required when task-relevant information is distributed among the group members and must be assembled in one place (or person) before the problem can be solved. "Solution operations" refers to further procedures required for task completion after the information has been assembled. Some tasks appear to be almost devoid of such further operations in that the solution is evident once all the information is collected in one place, e.g., Leavitt's (1951) symbol-identification task. Others require more extensive manipulation of the information; e.g., arithmetic problems may require addition, subtraction, multiplication, and/or division operations (Shaw, 1954b).

In general, the effects of communication structure upon group process may be considered in terms of either information distribution, organizational development or problem-solving effectiveness. The experimental design and procedure will necessarily be different for each of these approaches. Information distribution is best studied by using a task devoid of solution operations (e.g., Leavitt, 1951). Organizational development studies require the separation of the organizational process from the task solution process. This may be accomplished by dividing the interaction into periods explicitly designated as either organizational or task periods (Guetzkow and Dill, 1957). If the interest is in problem-solving effectiveness, it is necessary to include in the design all elements of problem solving: organizational or procedural requirements, information distribution requirements, and data operations requirement. This is accomplished most easily by assigning a relatively complex task and permitting the group to attack it without interruption (Shaw, 1954a, 1954b).

In designing an experiment to study the effects of communication structure, the experimenter must make several decisions about the communication set up. First, he may permit "free" communication such that each subject can send as many messages as he desires or is able to during any given period, or he may control message interchange in a stepwise fashion such that the subject is permitted to send a message only on signal from the experimenter. Second, message content may be controlled by way of prewritten messages or may be uncontrolled. Third, communication may be accomplished by means of intercom or telephonic systems or by means of written messages. Finally, if written messages are used, transmission may be either indirect via messengers or direct by means of a communication-net apparatus.

In general, these decisions will depend upon the purposes of the investigation. However, it is worth noting that intercom or telephonic systems involve technical problems as well as human ones; e.g., several subjects often try to "get the line" at the same time and jamming occurs. Also, indirect communication by messenger requires the use of an assistant and may be cumbersome for some purposes. The communication-net apparatus is most versatile and so is described in some detail.

The simplest way to construct a communication-net apparatus, hereafter called *net*, is to use a circular table about 5 feet in diameter upon which partitions are mounted so as to divide the table surface into work spaces or cubicles, one for each subject in the group. The net is practical for any size group up to a maximum of about six persons. Partitions may be made of plywood or pressed wood, each measuring about 4 by 4 feet. A column in the center, a pentagon having 2-inch sides, is necessary in order to provide channels (slots) between subjects that are not adjacent to each other. This column may be either solid or hollow; but if it is hollow, enclosed channels must be provided to prevent messages from dropping into the column. Slots are cut through the walls between cubicles and through the center column so that each subject has a channel to every other subject in the net. Channels are color-coded so that the destinations of messages are easily identified. The communication structure is manipulated by closing the appropriate slots, either by providing small doors for this purpose or by simply hanging covers over them.

Each cubicle is fitted with a mercury switch that controls a light and timer located at the experimenter's position. The experimenter has a master switch that controls all circuits; each cubicle switch controls only the light and timer associated with that particular position. Thus, the experimenter can turn on the signal light and start the timers at the beginning of a trial by throwing his master switch. As each subject completes the assigned task, e.g., identification of common symbol (Leavitt, 1951) and arithmetic problems (Shaw, 1954b), he can so indicate by throwing the switch in his cubicle that turns off his signal light on the experimenter's panel and simultaneously stops the timer to record the amount of time required by each position.

To this point, we have considered communication structure as an independent variable. The problem is quite different when communication structure is considered as a dependent variable. Much more needs to be known about variables determining specific kinds of communication structures. The variables that may be expected to influence communication structure include group member characteristics, group goals, size of the group, other aspects of group structure, situational factors such as physical proximity of members, availability of equipments such as tools and machines, and types of communication channels available. Methods of manipulating these variables either are self-evident, e.g., size of group, or are discussed in other sections of this chapter.

Methods of identifying and measuring communication structure as a dependent variable are not so clearly specified, although several procedures may be suggested. (1) Group members may be asked (interview, questionnaries) about their communication habits and structure inferred from their responses. Modified sociometric-type questions may be used (e.g., "With whom do you communicate directly in carrying out your role in the group?") and one or another of the formulas for measuring status structure adapted to communication structure. (2) Records of intragroup communication may be obtained (written messages, tape recordings, etc.) and analyzed to determine communication structure. (3) The channels

of communication available both physically and psychologically to each member may be identified and used as an indicator of communication structure. The assumption here is that available channels are used by group members.

GROUP COMPOSITION

The problem of group composition and its effects upon the behavior of groups and group members is important theoretically, since any comprehensive theory of behavior ultimately must predict outcomes when particular individuals interact. To study group composition, it is necessary to measure relevant characteristics of group members. Although it is possible to select group members at random, make the necessary measurement, i.e., determine the composition of the random group, and relate these composition measures to the dependent variable, it is better to manipulate composition by assigning members to groups systematically so that given degrees of composition are created.

The latter procedure requires that a large population of subjects be available for pretest on the composition variables of interest. Recruiting subjects having particular characteristics is always difficult because the number of subjects possessing the right combination of attributes may be quite small; failure to obtain the cooperation of a very few subjects may prevent completion of the experiment. In general, the more composition variables that the experimenter attempts to manipulate simultaneously, the greater the recruitment problem.

The composition of groups varies in many respects; hence, the investigator must make decisions about which member attributes are relevant to the group process. Having made these decisions, the experimenter must find some technique for measuring these attributes and for combining these measures into a meaningful index of group composition. Unfortunately, there are no procedures that are free of untested assumptions; the appropriate combinatorial model, additive or multiplicative, has not yet been determined. However, attempts have been made to deal with these problems in connection with two aspects of group composition: (1) homogeneity and (2) compatibility.

Group homogeneity

Groups may be composed of individuals who are either similar (homogeneous) or dissimilar (heteogeneous) with regard to individual characteristics, and the behavior of such groups compared. Such composition may be based upon either single traits or profiles. When degree of similarity is based upon a single characteristic, such as intelligence or dominance, we shall refer to this aspect of group composition as *trait homogeneity*. Degree of similarity based upon several characteristics will be defined as *profile homogeneity*. Trait homogeneity may be computed for any given collection of individuals in terms of any standard measure of variability, e.g., standard deviation, average deviation, or in terms of an average discrepancy score (the average of the discrepancies between each pair of individuals in the group). The latter estimate is slightly preferable, although it is positively correlated with other measures (Shaw, 1960).

Profile homogeneity may be determined by computing correlations between profiles of each pair of group members (Hoffman, 1959) and taking the average of these correlations as the measure of homogeneity; or the D score, discussed in connection with interpersonal perception, may be used for this purpose. The D score involves less work, but the significance of differences among D scores is not clear. Profile homogeneity has a marked advantage over trait homogeneity in that it deals with more of the variables in the situation. On the other hand, it assumes that all characteristics behave in the same way; i.e., it assumes that homogeneity in one trait is related to group behavior in the same direction as any other trait. Since this as-

sumption is of doubtful tenability, it is recommended that both profile and trait homogeneity be examined in any given experiment.

Group compatibility

Group compatibility as an independent variable has been approached empirically, in terms of member preferences, and theoretically, in terms of predicted compatibility based on member characteristics. In studying preference compatibility, members are asked to name the persons with whom they most prefer to work in a group (sociometric choice); compatible groups are assembled by putting together persons who choose each other, incompatible ones by putting together persons who either did not choose or rejected each other. Preference compatibility of various degrees may be established by varying the number of ingroup choices. Studies of cohesiveness are typical of this approach.

Predicted compatibility has been considered most extensively by Schutz (1958), who formulated a psychoanalytically oriented theory based upon the needs of inclusion, affection, and control. Guttman-type scales were developed to measure the degree to which an individual characteristically expresses behavior in each area and how much of each kind of behavior they want from others. All together, there are six scales measuring expressed (e) and wanted (w) behavior in each of the three need areas. These scales have Guttman reproducibility coefficients averaging .94, and coefficients of stability, test-retest, ranging from .71 to .83. Validity has been tested in several ways. Concurrent validity was estimated by showing that scores differentiated in the expected direction among subjects having different political orientations, among persons in different occupations, and between yielders and nonyielders in experimental conformity situations (Schutz, 1958). Predictive validity has been evaluated by showing that groups composed on the basis of member's scores performed on problem-solving tasks as expected by theoretical considerations (Schutz, 1955, 1958).

By using scores on these scales, three kinds of compatibility are derived from the theory; these are (Schutz, 1958, pp. 192–194):

Reciprocal compatibility = rK
$$= |e_i - w_j| + |e_j - w_i|$$
Originator compatibility = oK
$$= (e_i - w_i) + (e_j - w_j)$$
Interchange compatibility + xK
$$= |(e_i + w_i) - (e_j + w_j)|$$

where i and j are members of a dyad, and e and w are their scores on the expressed and wanted scales in any given need area. Thus each kind of compatibility can be computed in each of the three need areas, resulting in nine indices of compatibility for each dyad. For groups larger than two, indices are computed for each pair of subjects and indices summed to obtain the compatibility index for the entire group.

The total compatibility index in each need area may be obtained by summing the indices for r^k, o^k, and x^k. For example, affection compatibility is given by

$$K^A = rK^A + oK^A + xK^A$$

Likewise, type compatibilities may be obtained by combining need areas:

$$rK = rK^I + rK^C + rK^A$$

$$oK = oK^I + oK^C + oK^A$$

$$xK = xK^I + xK^C + xK^A$$

Total group compatibility is given by

$$K = rK + oK + xK$$

Variable weights may be assigned to need areas or to types if deemed necessary.

The Schutz scales are easy to administer and score, and have acceptable reliability and validity. It is probably inaccurate to assume that the three need areas specified by Schutz are sufficient to predict all interpersonal behavior, but Schutz's scales and formulas are useful and represent an important contribution to the study of composition effects.

GROUP TASKS

The task variable is one of the most neglected in social science research, and this is particularly true with regard to the group task variable. Its importance, however, is attested to by the difference in functional relationships between other variables when the task is permitted to vary. Part of the neglect is obviously due to the lack of adequate techniques for task analysis.

Roby and Lanzetta (1958) made a highly significant contribution to this problem by developing a rational framework for task descriptions. They proposed that task performance involves a chain of events that can be described in terms of (1) task input variables, events that occur in the environment of the group; (2) group input activities, a correlative set of events that occur within the group; (3) group output activities, resulting from the group input activities; and (4) task output variables, events which occur in the group surroundings following the group output activities and which form the basis for evaluation of group performance. For describing each of these classes of task events, three types of property are suggested: (1) descriptive aspects, which include their qualitative as well as quantitative properties; (2) distribution; and (3) functional behavior of the events, their occurrence over time or as a result of preceding events. Any given task can thus by analyzed by filling in the cells of a 4 × 3 matrix obtained by setting classes of task events against the three types of property used to describe them. The task elements listed in the matrix cells are those distinctive features of tasks which require certain behaviors for adequate performance (called *critical demands*). This system permits at least qualitative variation of task properties and so is superior to the haphazard selection of tasks that has characterized most of the research up to the present.

A somewhat similar approach has been taken by Thibaut and Kelley (1959), who also attempted to classify tasks in matrix form. Certain properties of tasks were described, e.g., steady versus variable states of the task, conjuctive versus disjunctive task requirements, correspondence versus non-correspondence of outcomes, and presented in matrix form. However, no method for assigning dimensional values to specific tasks was provided. Like the Roby and Lanzetta analysis, it is a qualitative or descriptive classification of tasks.

Although both the Roby and Lanzetta analysis and that of Thibaut and Kelley are useful first steps, what is sorely needed is a method for quantifying task dimensions. Of course, before task dimensions can be quantified, they must be identified and described, and rational (theoretical) analysis appears to be the only feasible approach. But let us suppose that a given task dimension has been identified, and we wish to assign a quantitative value to each of a set of tasks that will correctly represent its position on the task dimension in question. If we should do this, the task dimension could be varied systematically and its relation to dependent variables assessed.

Recently, Shaw (1963) suggested an approach to the scaling of task dimensions based upon Thurstone's (1929, 1931) judgment scaling model. Basically the suggested procedure is the same as that described in the section dealing with attitude measurement, except that in this instance the sorting is done with the task dimension as a referent rather than an attitude. To recapitulate, judges are asked to sort a set of items (tasks) into a number of piles so that the first pile contains tasks having the highest value on the task dimension, and the next pile tasks having the next highest value. Scale values are computed as the median scale position given by the judges; and Q values, the interquartile range, provide an estimate of the interjudge consistency.

Using this procedure, 49 judges sorted 104 tasks on each of 10 dimensions. Q values

ranged from 0.54 to 5.30, approximately 71 percent being less than 3.00. According to this criterion, interjudge reliability is acceptable, although far from perfect. A factor analysis of scale values and certain theoretical considerations led to the formulation of six task dimensions. The method was at least minimally adequate for scaling group tasks. The usefulness of dimensional analysis in organizing and understanding group process data has been demonstrated by Fiedler (1964) and by Shaw and Blum (1964). See Zajonc (1965) for requirements and design of a standard task.

CONCLUDING REMARKS

In the preceding sections, we have considered some of the common methods used in experimental investigations in specific problem areas. In general, the methods provide basic procedures for the general problem, but each investigator must make modifications appropriate to his particular problem. Many general methodological considerations, such as standard techniques for controlling extraneous variables and problems associated with experimental subjects and experimenter-subject relations, have significance for social psychological research, but detailed discussion of these problems is beyond the scope of this chapter. It is important that the reader keep in mind the essential interrelatedness of the several problem areas that we have discussed. Conformity behavior, for example, plays an important role in attitude formation and change. We have discussed them separately only for ease and clarity of explication. Eventually, we must devote attention to the more complex interactions among the various aspects of social psychological behavior.

An increasing concern of social psychologists is the question of generalizability of results obtained in the laboratory. For many years we have been aware of the problem of generalizing across populations. We insist that our experimental subjects be representative of the population to which we wish to generalize our findings, and we have devised various sampling procedures to aid in the selection of representative samples, e.g., random sampling, stratified random sampling, and cluster sampling. Brunswik (1955) pointed out that experimental situations also should be representative of the population of situations to which we wish to generalize, and suggested that we need to study stimulus-response relationships in the context of naturally occurring concomitant variations of other stimulus variables. This approach, called representative design, is similar to experiments in field settings (e.g., Coch and French, 1948; Morse and Reimer, 1956) in which primary stimulus variables are manipulated in an ongoing, real-life situation and other variables are allowed to vary "naturally." In applying representative design, however, the investigator is as concerned with the representativeness of the situations as he is with the representativeness of his experimental subjects.

Representative design has both advantages and disadvantages. If the purpose is to understand or predict the effects of the primary stimulus variable in "real" situations, representative design has unparalleled value. However, if the purpose is to understand the role of the primary stimulus per se in the determination of behavior, it is doubtful that this procedure will suffice. Extraneous variables occurring in uncontrolled and perhaps undetermined strengths often obscure the effects of the primary stimulus variable and always obscure its interactions with other extraneous stimulus variables. To ensure greater generalizability, the investigator using representative design must sacrifice the measurement of the interaction of variables in specific situations. Furthermore, representative design requires a knowledge of the universe of situations to be sampled and identification of the dimensions with respect to which the sample is to be representative (Postman, 1955). Thus, the purpose of a given investigation determines whether representative design should or should not be used.

Major deficiencies in social experimentation today are in the area of measurement. Adequate measuring techniques are essential for the meaningful investigation of social-psychological problems. But before adequate measuring devices can be developed, it is necessary to conceptualize clearly what it is we wish to measure. In many areas this conceptualization is lacking. We are hampered, too, by the criterion problem. It is difficult to evaluate a device for measuring something that is intangible and has not been measured before, or only by instruments of unknown validity. Consequently, our measuring instruments are usually no better than ordinal scales, and often only nominal scales. Progress is being made in the improvement of measurement procedures, however, and with more adequate measurement we may expect corresponding improvement in methodological procedures.

REFERENCES

ADAMS, J. S., and ROMNEY, A. K. A functional analysis of authority. *Psychol. Rev.*, 1959, **66**, 234–251.

ALLPORT, G. W. The historical background of modern social psychology. In G. Lindzey (Ed.), *Handbook of social psychology*. Reading, Mass.: Addison-Wesley, 1954.

ALLPORT, G. W., and POSTMAN, L. *The psychology of rumor*. New York: Holt, 1947.

ANDERSON, T. W. On estimation of parameters in latent structure analysis. *Psychometrika*, 1954, **19**, 1–11.

ANDERSON, N. H. Primacy effects in personality formation using a generalized order effect paradigm. *J. abnorm. soc. Psychol.*, 1965, **2**, 1–9.

ASCH, S. E. Forming impressions of personality. *J. abnorm. soc. Psychol.*, 1946, **41**, 258–290.

ASCH, S. E. *Social psychology*. Englewood Cliffs, N.J.: Prentice-Hall, 1952.

ASCH, S. E. A perspective on social psychology. In S. Koch (Ed.), *Psychology: A study of a science*. Vol. III. New York: McGraw-Hill, 1959.

BACHRACH, A. J., CANDLAND, D. K., and GIBSON, J. T. Group reinforcement of individual response experiments in verbal behavior. In I. A. Berg and B. M. Bass (Eds.), *Conformity and deviation*. New York: Harper & Row, 1961.

BAKER, B. O., and BLOCK, J. Accuracy of interpersonal prediction as a function of judge and object characteristics. *J. abnorm. soc. Psychol.*, 1957, **54**, 37–43.

BALES, R. F. *Interaction process analysis: A method for the study of small groups*. Reading, Mass.: Addison-Wesley, 1950.

BALES, R. F. Task roles and social roles in problem-solving groups. In E. E. Maccoby, T. M. Newcomb, and E. L. Hartley (Eds.), *Readings in social psychology*. (3rd ed.) New York: Holt, 1958.

BALES, R. F., and GERBRANDS, H. The "interaction-recorder." *Human Relat.*, 1948, **1**, 456–463.

BASS, A. R., and FIEDLER, F. E. Interpersonal perception scores and their components as predictors of personal adjustment. *J. abnorm. soc. Psychol.*, 1961, **62**, 442–445.

BASS, B. M. The leaderless group discussion. *Psychol. Bull.*, 1954, **51**, 465–492.

BATES, A. P., and CLOYD, J. S. Toward the development of operations for defining group norms and member roles. *Sociometry*, 1956, **19**, 26–39.

BEACH, L., and WERTHEIMER, M. A free response approach to the study of person cognition. *J. abnorm. soc. Psychol.*, 1961, **62**, 367–374.

BECHTOLDT, H. P. Construct validity: A critique. *Amer. Psychologist*, 1959, **14**, 619–629.

BENOIT-SMULLYAN, E. Status, status types and status inter-relations. *Amer. sociol. Rev.*, 1944, **9**, 151–161.

BERELSON, B. *Content analysis in communication research*. New York: Macmillan, 1952.

BINDER, A., MCCONNELL, D., and SJOHOLM, N. A. Verbal conditioning as a function of experimenter characteristics. *J. abnorm. soc. Psychol.*, 1957, **55**, 309–314.

BLAKE, R. R., and MCCONNELL, J. V. A methodological study of tape-recorded synthetic group atmospheres. *Amer. Psychologist*, 1953, **8**, 395. (Abstract.)

BRUNSWIK, E. Representative design and probabilistic theory in functional psychology. *Psychol. Rev.*, 1955, **62**, 193–217.

CAMPBELL, D. T. The indirect assessment of social attitudes. *Psychol. Bull.*, 1950, **47**, 15–38.

CAMPBELL, D. T. Recommendations for APA test standards regarding construct, trait, or discriminant validity. *Amer. Psychologist*, 1960, **15**, 546–553.

CAMPBELL, D. T., and FISKE, D. W. Convergent and discriminant validation by the multitrait-multimethod matrix. *Psychol. Bull.*, 1959, **56**, 81–105.

CARTER, L. F. On defining leadership. In C. G. Browne and T. S. Cohn (Eds.), *The study of leadership*. Danville, Ill.: Interstate Printers and Publishers, 1958.

CARTER, L., HAYTHORN, W., MIEROWITZ, B., and LANZETTA, J. A note on a new technique of interaction recording. *J. abnorm. soc. Psychol.*, 1951a, **46**, 258–260.

CARTER, L., HAYTHORN, W., MEIROWITZ, B., and LANZETTA, J. The relation of categorization and ratings in the observation of group behavior. *Human Relat.*, 1951b, **4**, 239–254.

CHAPPLE, E. D., and ARENSBERG, C. M. Measuring human relations: An introduction to the study of the interactions of individuals. *Genet. Psychol. Monogr.*, 1940, **22**, 3–147.

CHOWDRY, K., and NEWCOMB, T. M. The relative abilities of leaders and nonleaders to estimate opinions of their own groups. *J. abnorm. soc. Psychol.*, 1952, **47**, 51–57.

COCH, L., and FRENCH, J. R. P., JR. Overcoming resistance to change. *Human Relat.*, 1948, **1**, 512–532.

COOMBS, C. H. Psychological scaling without a unit of measurement. *Psychol. Rev.*, 1950, **57**, 145–158.

COOMBS, C. H. The theory and methods of social measurement. In L. Festinger and D. Katz (Eds.), *Research methods in the behavioral sciences*. New York: Holt, 1953.

CRAWFORD, T., and SIDOWSKI, J. B. Monetary incentive and cooperation-competition instructions in a minimal social situation. *Psychol. Rep.*, 1964, **15**, 233–234.

CRONBACH, L. J. Processes affecting scores on "understanding of others" and "assumed similarity." *Psychol. Bull.*, 1955, **52**, 177–193.

CRONBACH, L. J. Proposals leading to analytic treatment of social perception scores. In R. Tagiuri and L. Petrullo (Eds.), *Person perception and interpersonal behavior*. Stanford, Calif.: Stanford Univer. Press, 1958.

CRUTCHFIELD, R. S. Conformity and character. *Amer. Psychologist*, 1955, **10**, 191–198.

DUDYCHA, G. J. A critical examination of the measurement of attitude toward war. *J. soc. Psychol.*, 1943, **18**, 383–392.

EBEL, R. L. Must all tests be valid? *Amer. Psychologists*, 1961, **16**, 640–647.

EDWARDS, A. L. *Techniques of attitudes scale construction*. New York: Appleton-Century-Crofts, 1957.

EXLINE, R. V. Group climate as a factor in the relevance and accuracy of social perception. *J. abnorm. soc. Psychol.*, 1957, **55**, 382–388.

FERGUSON, L. W. An item analysis of Peterson's "war" scale. *Psychol. Bull.*, 1938, **35**, 521.

FESTINGER, L. The treatment of qualitative data by "scale analysis." *Psychol. Bull.*, 1947, **44**, 149–161.

FESTINGER, L., and KATZ, D. (Eds.) *Research methods in the behavioral sciences.* New York: Holt, 1953.

FESTINGER, L., SCHACHTER, S., and BACK, K. *Social pressures in informal groups.* New York: Harper & Row, 1950.

FIEDLER, F. E. *Leader attitudes and group effectiveness.* Urbana, Ill.: Univer. of Illinois Press, 1958.

FIEDLER, F. E. A contingency model of leadership effectiveness. In L. Berkowitz (Ed.), *Advances in experimental social psychology.* Vol. 1. New York: Academic, 1964 pp. 149–190.

FIEDLER, F. E., HUTCHINS, E. B., and DODGE, J. S. Quasi-therapeutic relations in small college and military groups. *Psychol. Monogr.,* 1959, **73**, No. 3 (Whole No. 473).

GEWIRTZ, J. L., and BAER, D. M. Deprivation and satiation of social reinforcers as drive conditions. *J. abnorm. soc. Psychol.,* 1958a, **57**, 165–172.

GEWIRTZ, J. L., and BAER, D. M. The effect of brief social deprivation on behaviors for a social reinforcer. *J. abnorm. soc. Psychol.,* 1958b, **56**, 49–56.

GLANZER, M., and GLASER, R. Techniques for the study of group structure and behavior. I. Analysis of structure. *Psychol. Bull.,* 1959, **56**, 317–332.

GREEN, B. F. A general solution for the latent class model of structure analysis. *Psychometrika,* 1951, **16**, 151–166.

GREEN, B. F. Attitude measurement. In G. Lindzey (Ed.), *Handbook of social psychology.* Reading, Mass.: Addison-Wesley, 1954.

GREENSPOON, J. The reinforcing effect of two spoken sounds on the frequency of two responses. *Amer. J. Psychol.,* 1955, **68**, 409–416.

GUETZKOW, H., and DILL, W. R. Factors in the organizational development of task-oriented groups. *Sociometry,* 1957, **20**, 175–204.

GUTTMAN, L. The quantification of a class of attributes: A theory and method of scale construction. In P. Horst *et al.* (Eds.), *The prediction of personal adjustment.* New York: Bull. No. 48, Social Science Research Council, 1941.

GUTTMAN, L. A basis for scaling qualitative data. *Amer. sociol. Rev.,* 1944, **9**, 139–150.

GUTTMAN, L. The Cornell technique for scale and intensity analysis. *Educ. psychol. Measmt,* 1947, **7**, 247–280.

HARARY, F. Status and contrastatus. *Sociometry,* 1959, **22**, 23–43.

HARVEY, O. J., and CONSALVI, C. Status and conformity to pressures in informal groups. *J. abnorm. soc. Psychol.,* 1960, **60**, 182–187.

HASTORF, A. H., RICHARDSON, S. A., and DORNBUSCH, S. M. The problem of relevance in the study of person perception. In R. Tagiuri and L. Petrullo (Eds.), *Person perception and interpersonal behavior.* Stanford, Calif.: Stanford Univer. Press, 1958.

HAYS, D. G., and BORGATTA, E. F. An empirical comparison of restricted and general latent distance analysis. *Psychometrika,* 1954, **19**, 271–279.

HEIDER, F. *The psychology of interpersonal relations.* New York: Wiley, 1958.

HILDEN, A. H. *Manual for Q-sort and random sets of personal concepts.* St. Louis: Washington Univer. Press, 1954.

HOFFMAN, L. T. Homogeneity of member personality and its effect on group problem-solving. *J. abnorm. soc. Psychol.,* 1959, **58**, 27–32.

HOLLANDER, E. P., and WEBB, W. B. Leadership, followership, and friendship: An analysis of peer nominations. *J. abnorm. soc. Psychol.,* 1955, **50**, 163–167.

HOVLAND, C. I., JANIS, I. L., and KELLEY, H. H. *Communication and persuasion.* New Haven, Conn.: Yale Univer. Press, 1953.

HOVLAND, C. I., LUMSDAINE, A. A., and SHEFFIELD, F. D. *Experiments on mass communication.* Princeton, N.J.: Princeton Univer. Press, 1949.

HOVLAND, C. I., and MANDELL, W. An experimental comparison of conclusion-drawing by the communicator and by the audience. *J. abnorm. soc. Psychol.,* 1952, **47**, 581–588.

JONES, E. E., DAVIS, K. E., and GERGEN, K. J. Role playing variations and their informational value for person perception. *J. abnorm. soc. Psychol.,* 1961, **63**, 302–310.

JONES, E. E., and deCHARMS, R. Changes in social perception as a function of the personal relevance of behavior. *Sociometry,* 1957, **20**, 75–85.

KANFER, F. H. Verbal conditioning: Reinforcement schedules and experimenter influence. *Psychol. Rep.,* 1958, **4**, 443–452.

KANFER, F. H., and KARAS, S. Prior experimenter-subject interaction and verbal conditioning. *Psychol. Rep.,* 1959, **5**, 345–353.

KATZ, L. A new status index derived from sociometric analysis. *Psychometrika,* 1953, **18**, 39–43.

KATZ, L., and POWELL, J. H. A proposed index of the conformity of one sociometric measurement to another. *Psychometrika,* 1953, **18**, 249–256.

KELLEY, H. H. Communication in experimentally created hierarchies. *Human Relat.,* 1951, **4**, 39–56.

KELLEY, H. H., THIBAUT, J. W., RADLOFF, R., and MUNDY, D. The development of cooperation in the "minimal social situation." *Psychol. Monogr.,* 1962, **76**, No. 19 (Whole No. 538).

KRECH, D., and CRUTCHFIELD, R. S. *Theory and*

problems of social psychology. New York: McGraw-Hill, 1948.

LAZARSFELD, P. F. The logic and mathematical foundation of latent structure analysis. In S. A. Stouffer *et al.* (Eds.), *Measurement and prediction.* Princeton, N.J.: Princeton Univer. Press, 1950.

LAZARSFELD, P. F. A conceptual introduction to latent structure analysis. In P. F. Lazarsfeld (Ed.), *Mathematical thinking in the social sciences.* Glencoe, Illinois: Free Press, 1954.

LAZARSFELD, P. F. Latent structure analysis. In S. Koch (Ed.), *Psychology: A study of a science.* Vol. III. New York: McGraw-Hill, 1959.

LEAVITT, H. J. Some effects of certain communication patterns on group performance. *J. abnorm. soc. Psychol.,* 1951, **46**, 38–50.

LEWIN, K., LIPPITT, R., and WHITE, R. K. Patterns of aggressive behavior in experimentally created "social climates." *J. soc. Psychol.,* 1939, **10**, 271–299.

LIKERT, R. A technique for the measurement of attitudes. *Arch. Psychol.,* 1932, No. 140, 1–55.

LIPPITT, R., POLANSKY, N., and ROSEN, S. The dynamics of power. *Human Relat.,* 1952, **5**, 37–64.

LIVERIGHT, A. A. Role-playing in leadership training. *Personnel Journal,* 1951, **29**, 412–416.

MAIER, N. R. F., and ZERFOSS, L. F. MRP: A technique for training large groups of supervisors and its potential use in social research. *Human Relat.,* 1952, **5**, 177–186.

MANDLER, G., and KAPLAN, W. K. Subjective evaluation and reinforcing effect of a verbal stimulus. *Science,* 1956, **124**, 582–583.

MATARAZZO, J. D., SASLOW, G., and GUZE, S. B. Stability of interaction patterns during interviews: A replication. *J. consult. Psychol.,* 1956, **20**, 267–274.

MORENO, J. L. *Who shall survive.* Series No. 58, New York: Nervous and Mental Disease Publishing Co., 1934.

MORSE, N. C., and REIMER, E. The experimental change of a major organizational variable. *J. abnorm. soc. Psychol.,* 1956, **52**, 120–129.

NEUMANN, J. VON, and MORGENSTERN, O. *Theory of games and economic behavior.* (2nd ed.) Princeton, N.J.: Princeton Univer. Press, 1947.

NUNNALLY, J. C., JR. *Popular conceptions of mental health: Their development and change.* New York: Holt, 1961.

OLMSTEAD, J. A., and BLAKE, R. R. The use of simulated groups to produce modification in judgment. *J. Pers.,* 1955, **23**, 335–345.

OSGOOD, C. E., and SUCI, G. J. A measure of relation determined by both mean difference and profile information. *Psychol. Bull.,* 1952, **49**, 251–262.

OSGOOD, C. E., SUCI, G. J., and TANNENBAUM, P. H. *The measurement of meaning.* Urbana, Ill.: Univer. of Illinois Press, 1957.

POSTMAN, L. The probability approach and nomothetic theory. *Psychol. Rev.,* 1955, **62**, 218–225.

PROCTOR, C. H., and LOOMIS, C. P. Analysis of sociometric data. In M. Jahoda, M. Deutsch, and S. W. Cook (Eds.), *Research methods in social relations.* New York: Holt, 1951.

RINN, J. L. Group behavior descriptions: A nonmetric-multidimensional analysis. *J. abnorm. soc. Psychol.,* 1963, **67**, 173–176.

ROBY, T. B., and LANZETTA, J. T. Considerations in the analysis of group tasks. *Psychol. Bull.,* 1958, **55**, 88–101.

SASLOW, G., MATARAZZO, J. D., and GUZE, S. B. The stability of interaction chronograph patterns in psychiatric interviews. *J. consult. Psychol.,* 1955, **19**, 417–430.

SASLOW, G., MATARAZZO, J. D., PHILLIPS, J. S., and MATARAZZO, R. G. Test-retest stability of interaction patterns during interviews conducted one week apart. *J. abnorm. soc. Psychol.,* 1957, **54**, 295–302.

SCHUTZ, W. C. What makes groups productive? *Human Relat.,* 1955, **8**, 429–465.

SCHUTZ, W. C. *FIRO: A three-dimensional theory of interpersonal behavior.* New York: Holt, 1958.

SELLTIZ, C., JAHODA, M., DEUTSCH, M., and COOK, S. W. *Research methods in social relations.* (rev. ed.) New York: Holt, 1961.

SHAW, M. E. Some effects of problem complexity upon problem solution efficiency in different communication nets. *J. exp. Psychol.,* 1954a, **48**, 211–217.

SHAW, M. E. Some effects of unequal distribution of information upon group performance in various communication nets. *J. abnorm. soc. Psychol.,* 1954b, **49**, 547–553.

SHAW, M. E. Some effects of individually prominent behavior upon group effectiveness and member satisfaction. *J. abnorm. soc. Psychol.,* 1959, **59**, 382–386.

SHAW, M. E. A note concerning homogeneity of membership and group problem solving. *J. abnorm. soc. Psychol.,* 1960, **60**, 448–450.

SHAW, M. E. Implicit conversion of fate control in dyadic interaction. *Psychol. Rep.,* 1962, **10**, 758.

SHAW, M. E. *Scaling group tasks: A method for dimensional analysis.* Gainesville, Fla.: Department of Psychology, Univer. of Florida, 1963. [*Tech. Rep. 1, ONR Contract NR 170-266, Nonr-580 (11)*, July, 1963.]

SHAW, M. E., and BLUM, J. M. Effects of the group's knowledge of member satisfaction upon group performance. *Psychon. Sci.,* 1964, **1**, 15–16.

SHAW, M. E., ROTHSCHILD, G. H., and STRICKLAND, J. F. Decision processes in communication nets. *J. abnorm. soc. Psychol.*, 1957, **54**, 323–330.

SHERIF, M. A study of some social factors in perception. *Arch. Psychol.*, 1935, No. 187.

SIDOWSKI, J. B. Reward and punishment in a minimal social situation. *J. exp. Psychol.*, 1957, **54**, 318–326.

SIDOWSKI, J. B. Male and female sensitivity to electric current. *Percept. mot. Skills*, 1961, **13**, 201–202.

SIDOWSKI, J. B. Sex of *E* and amount of social information as variables in a minimal social situation. *Psychon. Sci.*, 1967, in press.

SIDOWSKI, J. B., and GREGOVICH, R. Influence of reinforcement history upon learning in a minimal social situation. *Amer. Psychologist*, 1963, **18**, 467 (Abstract)

SIDOWSKI, J. B., and SMITH, M. Sex and game instruction variables in a minimal social situation. *Psychol. Rep.*, 1961, **8**, 393–397.

SIDOWSKI, J. B., KOSTANZER, A., NAUMOFF, H., and SMITH, M. Variables influencing performance in a minimal social situation. *Amer. Psychologist*, 1960, **15**, 490 (Abstract)

SIDOWSKI, J. B., STEVENS, W. R., and GREENE, W. Pretraining reinforcement schedules and learning in a two-person interaction. Paper read at Amer. Psychol. Assoc., New York, 1961.

SIDOWSKI, J. B., WYCKOFF, L. B., and TABORY, L. The influence of reinforcement and punishment in a minimal social situation. *J. abnorm. soc. Psychol.*, 1956, **52**, 115–119.

SMITH, M. B., BRUNER, J. S., and WHITE, R. W. *Opinion and personality*. New York: Wiley, 1956.

SOLOMON, R. L. Extension of control group design. *Psychol. Bull.*, 1949, **46**, 137–150.

STEVENS, S. S. Mathematics, measurement, and psychophysics. In S. S. Stevens (Ed.), *Handbook of experimental psychology*. New York: Wiley, 1951.

TAFFEL, C. Anxiety and the conditioning of verbal behavior. *J. abnorm. soc. Psychol.*, 1955, **51**, 496–501.

TAGIURI, R., BRUNER, J. S., and BLAKE, R. R. On the relation between feelings and perception of feelings among members of small groups. In E. E. Maccoby, T. M. Newcomb, and E. L. Hartley (Eds.), *Readings in social psychology*. New York: Holt, 1958.

THIBAUT, J. W., and KELLEY, H. H. *The social psychology of groups*. New York: Wiley, 1959.

THIBAUT, J. W., and RIECKEN, H. W. Some determinants and consequences of the perception of social causality. *J. Pers.*, 1955, **24**, 113–133.

THOMAS, E. J. Role conceptions and organizational size. *Amer. sociol. Rev.*, 1959, **23**, 30–37.

THURSTONE, L. L. Theory of attitude measurement. *Psychol. Bull.*, 1929, **36**, 222–241.

THURSTONE, L. L. The measurement of social attitudes. *J. abnorm. soc. Psychol.*, 1931, **26**, 249–269.

TORGERSON, W. S. Theory and methods of scaling. New York: Wiley, 1958.

TORRANCE, E. P. Some consequences of power differences on decision making in permanent and temporary groups. In A. P. Hare, E. F. Borgatta, and R. F. Bales (Eds.), *Small groups: Studies in social interaction*. New York: Alfred A. Knopf, 1955.

WALTERS, R. H., and KARAL, P. Social deprivation and verbal behavior. *J. Pers.*, 1960, **28**, 89–107.

WALTERS, R. H., and RAY, E. Anxiety, social isolation, and reinforcer effectiveness. *J. Pers.*, 1960, **28**, 358–367.

WEBB, S. C. Scaling of attitudes by the method of equal-appearing intervals: A review. *J. soc. Psychol.*, 1955, **42**, 215–239.

WHERRY, R. J., and FRYER, D. H. Buddy ratings: Popularity contests or leadership criteria? *Personnel Psychol.*, 1949, **2**, 147–159.

WHITE, R., and LIPPITT, R. Leader behavior and member reaction in three "social climates." In D. Cartwright and A. Zander (Eds.), *Group dynamics: Research and theory*. New York: Harper & Row, 1953.

WILLIS, R. H., and JOSEPH, M. L. Bargaining behavior. I. "Prominence" as a predictor of the outcome of games of agreement. *Conflict Resolution*, 1959, **3**, 102–113.

ZAJONC, R. B. The requirements and design of a standard group task. *J. exp. Soc. Psychol.*, 1965, **1**, 71–88.

Chapter 16

MOTOR BEHAVIOR

HARRY P. BAHRICK *and* MERRILL E. NOBLE

Definitions of motor learning are either arbitrarily restrictive or so broad as to include most behavioral phenomena. This is so because the motor system is involved in most observable activity and because learning affects most behavior. Neither the criterion of motor involvement nor the criteria of learning provide a sufficient basis for delimiting this area of research. The present arbitrary restriction is based upon the characteristics of motor responses. In this chapter motor learning will refer to patterned responses, i.e., responses that involve relatively high degrees of spatial precision as well as timing or anticipation (Fitts, Bahrick, Noble, and Briggs, 1959). No absolute differentiation of motor skill is possible on this basis, but such diverse tasks as dancing, driving a car, or playing the piano would clearly be included. The response of pushing one of several buttons to indicate one's choice among several stimuli would probably not be included, unless the button had to be pressed in a precise way or at a precise time.

The authors wish to acknowledge permission to use extensive quotes as well as figures and tables from chapter VI of: *Final Report* by the *Ohio State Research Foundation* to Wright Air Development Center Contract AF 41(657)-70 Project 7707 and 686 *Skilled Performance*, Prepared by P. M. Fitts, H. P. Bahrick, M. E. Noble, and G. E. Briggs, March, 1959.

The stimulus conditions in motor learning are complex variables that define the tasks and the procedures. This chapter will discuss the methodology suitable for the dimensional analysis of these task variables. Included are the immediate stimuli presented to the subject, the manner in which the task relates input and output processes, and the constraints placed upon the responses by the apparatus, procedures, and task. Methods for analyzing responses form the first portion of the chapter. These methods help to establish the interrelations among response variables and thus form the basis of our understanding of the nature of motor learning.

METHODS OF ANALYSIS OF MOTOR BEHAVIOR

One of the important jobs of the experimenter is to describe and analyze the spatial-temporal patterning of the subject's motor responses and to relate this to the requirements of the task. To do this, it often is useful to obtain a relatively complete record of the subject's responses in conjunction with records of the input signal that defines the task of the subject. An experimenter can derive any quantitative measure of performance from these continuous records, which contain all the information necessary to reconstruct the movements of the subject's control and the input signal or target. If a particular quantitative score will suffice for his purposes, the investigator usually can devise a means of obtaining this score more directly and will not go to the expense of obtaining more complete data. For reasons described more fully later in this chapter, a given set of quantitative indices may not permit satisfactory answers to some important questions, and it may be necessary to derive new quantitative indices. Moreover, careful examination of graphic plots of these continuous records may provide important insights into various aspects of motor skill that are difficult to obtain in any other way. They may provide a source of hypotheses and hence be the basis for meaningful development of other quantitative indices.

There are several ways of obtaining continuous records of the spatial-temporal aspects of the movement of a limb or control in conjunction with the spatial-temporal aspects of the target movement. Motion pictures, derivatives provided by the cyclograph, and time-lapse photography are sometimes used (Barnes, 1958). A simple means of obtaining complete records for two-dimensional pursuit tasks is to draw the input pattern on a paper tape. This tape is then moved, usually at a constant speed by means of a paper pull, past a narrow slit in a surface that keeps the remainder of the target pattern hidden from view. The subject's task is to keep a pen or pencil on the drawn target line as it passes.

With electronic tracking apparatus, the electric signal that provides the input or target on the oscilloscope or other display can simultaneously be fed into one channel of an oscillograph. Movements of the subject's control provide, through the use of a potentiometer or similar device attached to the control, another electric signal that may be fed into another channel of the oscillograph and recorded simultaneously with the input signal. These graphic plots of position of control and target against time provide all the information needed to reconstruct the movement

patterns and to derive quantitative measures of performance.

Figure 16-1 shows oscillographic records of pursuit tracking as the subject attempts to track a repeating sequence of step inputs presented as a narrow vertical line (the target) on an oscilloscope. The line jumps from one position to another in the horizontal plane. The subject attempts to maintain a second narrow vertical line (the cursor) that is displaced slightly below the target in alignment with the target by movements of a horizontal arm control (Trumbo, Eslinger, Noble, and Cross, 1963). Early in practice the subject consistently lags behind the target, i.e., he waits until after the target has moved before he moves his control. Lag time is approximately 0.2 second, or about the normal reaction time in a choice situation. Late in practice, this subject consistently leads the target by about 0.15 or 0.20 second. It is logical that he should be able to anticipate, since he was tracking a fixed pattern. There is a tendency for good subjects with this task to have many more overshoots than undershoots early in practice. The number of undershoots does not decrease markedly with practice, but the number of overshoots is reduced to about the same level as undershoots by the end of training. With practice the subject begins more and more to move his control at almost the same time as the target moves and to effectively reduce his reaction time to almost zero. The amount of force used to generate the arm movements also increases from the early to later stages of training. This is shown by the changes in acceleration from trial 1 to trial 99 in Fig. 16-1. With the same amount of practice a poor subject tends to continue to lag, although by the end of training he will lead the target perhaps a third of the time. Similarly, the poor subject will not do nearly as well as the good subject in timing his movements so as to eliminate his reaction time.

Figure 16-2 shows a different subject attempting to track a random-step-function

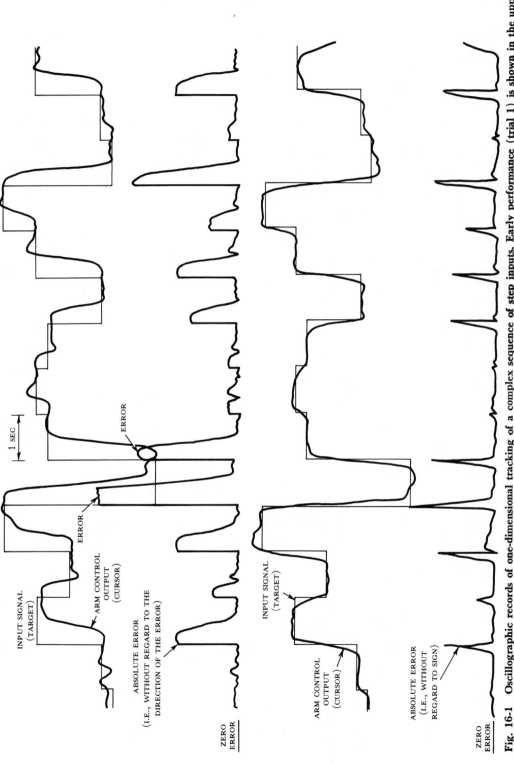

Fig. 16-1 Oscillographic records of one-dimensional tracking of a complex sequence of step inputs. Early performance (trial 1) is shown in the upper portion of the figure, and later performance (trial 100) in the lower portion.

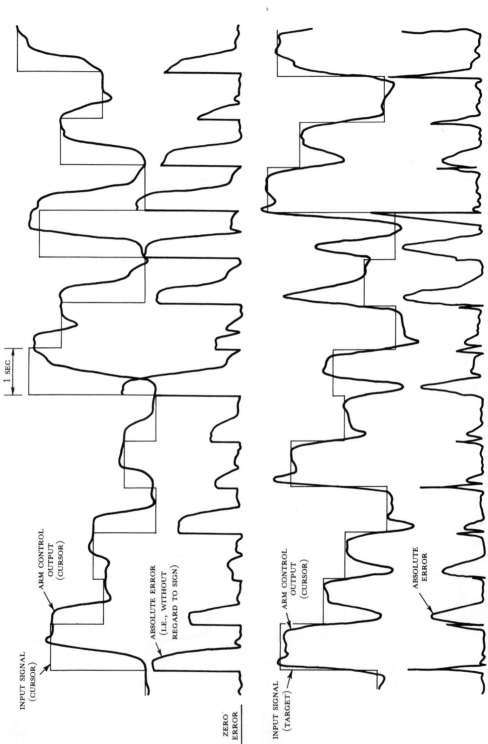

Fig. 16-2 Oscillographic records of one-dimensional pursuit tracking of a random sequence of step inputs. Early performance (trial 1) is shown in the upper portion of the figure, and later performance (trial 100) in the lower portion.

target signal; i.e., the target occurs equally often at each of 15 different positions, but a different random sequence of positions is used on each 60-second trial. The duration of any step is fixed at 1 second throughout all trials. Early in practice the subject consistently lags behind the target, but late in practice the relative frequencies of leads and lags are approximately the same. Poorer subjects tend to lag almost all the time. Of even greater interest is the fact that the subject learns to anticipate the exact moment at which the target moves from one position to another. The subject does just as well in eliminating his reaction time by the end of training as did the subject in Fig. 16-1, who tracked a target that could be predicted with respect to duration, extent of movement, and the time at which the target movement occurred.

When sinusoidal inputs of relatively low frequency are being tracked instead of a step-function input, the cursor movements become smoother as practice continues and come close to matching the input in frequency, amplitude, and phase. Peak accelerations become smaller also as training progresses.

It is possible to derive any quantitative index of performance from oscillographic records such as those shown in Figs. 16-1 and 16-2. In practice, this is seldom done because it requires tedious and time-consuming hand measurements in order to go from the curves on the oscillographic record to quantitative statements that summarize different aspects of performance. If, for example, the experimenter wishes to determine mean error, he might have to measure the difference between the target and cursor positions ten times each second in order to have reliable values. A single 60-second trial would require 600 separate measurements. For this reason, investigators usually utilize equipment that will supply direct summary scores such as time-on-target, time-continuously-on-target (Archer, Kent, and Mote, 1956), and mean error, mean square error, root mean square

(rms) error, or integrated error. When an experimenter utilizes these methods of summarizing continuous functions, he must (1) decide at the start which scores he will use and (2) obtain a different unit of recording equipment for each summary measure derived. The former requires foreknowledge that may not be available and does not permit examination of relationships with other measures; the latter may result in a cumbersome and elaborate set of recording units. A fruitful alternative is to use digital and analog computers. An analog-digital system can frequently sample the analog voltages of the target and cursor and put that information in digital form on punched cards, paper tape, or magnetic tape, in a form suitable for input to a digital computer (Webber and Adams, 1960). Signals can be stored in analog form on magnetic tape as they are generated; then at any convenient time, these signals may be fed into analog computers (Trumbo *et al.*, 1963) or into analog-to-digital converters preparatory to feeding them into digital computers for analysis. Computer methods supply all the quantitative summary scores mentioned above in addition to such analytic information as power-density spectra and autocorrelations and crosscorrelations.

QUANTITATIVE INDICANTS OF PERFORMANCE

Quantitative indicants of motor performance are statistics that refer to response distributions. Sometimes the distributions are actually obtained and the indicants are formally abstracted from the distribution, but more often the indicants are obtained directly, and the distributions to which they refer are ignored. A distribution of responses is obtained in a psychophysical task by using the method of average error; and when using the standard deviation (SD) or other indicants of the subject's performance, the experimenter is likely to remain aware of the fact that he is dealing with a statistic that reflects some, but not all, of the information the subject has generated. A more common situation, however, would be illustrated by the experimenter who records the number of contacts a subject's stylus makes with the edges of a metal slit, as in a steadiness task. Here the experimenter is much more likely to lose sight of the fact that the subject has generated a whole distribution of responses and that the recorded contact score is a statistic that reflects simply the portion of the distribution exceeding a given amplitude value.

The principal danger in using response indicants is not the loss of information illustrated in the above instance. Frequently investigators are interested in certain aspects of performance that are adequately reflected by a given indicant, and the neglect of other potentially available information is justified by the purpose. The danger lies in the arbitrary choice among indicants reflecting somewhat different characteristics of the underlying distribution without detailed knowledge of the nature of these differences. Such arbitrary choice, coupled with the failure to recognize the consequent selectiveness of the obtained information, may lead to apparent conflicts of results from studies using different indicants, as well as to significant misinterpretations of data.

The best methodological assurance against such errors lies in systematic clarification of the interrelations among various types of indicant. This should facilitate more purposive selection among the indicants for a particular experiment and also provide a basis for interpreting the results obtained in several experiments using different indicants.

Criteria for choosing an indicant

The conventional bases for the choice of behavioral measures have been considerations of validity and reliability. While these are still the crucial requirements, their meaning needs to be specified in the present context. Reliability and validity have been discussed most frequently in connection with tests of individual differences and with problems of placement or selection. In these areas, reliability is defined in terms of stability of measurement, and validity in terms of the relation of the measure to some criterion score. The sources of unreliability are usually not specified or investigated in problems of applied psychology. It may not matter whether a test score fluctuates because the behavior of the testee changes or because the testing procedure or the behavior of the test administrator is somewhat variable. Separation of the various sources of unreliability is a critical problem to the experimental psychologist. Unreliability limits the usefulness of a measure to the extent that it is a function of experimental procedure, apparatus fluctuation, or experimenter behavior. To the extent that it reflects changes in the behavior under investigation, however, it may reveal significant facts that may increase, rather than reduce, the validity of the indicant. A measure that is sensitive to particular fluctuations of performance and yields a less reliable score may be more valuable than a measure that is insensitive to these same fluctuations of behavior and is more stable. Procedurally it is often possible to separate these sources of unreliability by substituting a mechanical or electrical source of a constant and known output for the human subject. The remaining fluctuations of the indicant are then due to unreliability of the measuring process.

If our objective is to gain better understanding of motor performance, indicants are valid to the extent that they contribute to the realization of this objective. The problem of validity for the experimental psychologist is basically the question of the extent to which he understands his measures and the extent to which measures and theory are consistent (Melton, 1936). A measure is valid if it permits a definitive test of the variables specified in our theories, and this, in turn, must be judged by the known relations of the measure to other variables. The circularity of this process of validation reflects a limit of all scientific methodology.

Types of measures available

Movements occur in time and space, and two kinds of distribution are needed to specify the spatial and temporal characteristics completely: (1) amplitude distributions and (2) power-density spectra. Particular indicants of performance may reflect characteristics of one, the other, or both of these kinds of distribution. We shall first discuss performance measures derived from the amplitude distribution alone, since these are the ones most commonly used and psychologists are most familiar with the type of distribution involved.

Method of obtaining amplitude distribution of responses in discrete tasks

In discrete or serial tasks where the subject must contact a given target area, the amplitude distribution of his responses may be obtained by recording on separate counters his contacts with each of a number of equally sized zones of the target area. The size of the various zones is somewhat arbitrary within the limits of the distribution formed by the subject's responses, and the decision corresponds roughly to the choice of class intervals in a frequency distribution. One-two-, or even three-dimensional distributions can be obtained in this manner.

Indicators of performance derived from such amplitude distributions are easily interpreted, particularly when the distributions involved are normal or near normal. This is so because the indicants bear a simple, direct relation to conventional statistics, and the interrelations among these statistics for normal distributions are well established. A mean and variance can be computed from the frequencies recorded on the counters. The variance may be computed with reference to the mean of the distribution or with reference to some arbitrary point, such as the center of the target area. The latter variance is larger since it includes also the square of any constant error. The constant error is computed directly by subtracting the mean of the distribution from the target center. Usually the counters are numbered consecutively from 1 to N so that the obtained statistics are in units of intervals subtended by a single counter. If the investigator wishes to obtain measures that reflect actual spatial precision, these statistics must be multiplied by the size of the interval subtended by a single counter, much as the SD computed from a frequency distribution must be multiplied by the size of the class interval. A correlational analysis of the response distributions may be desired if two-dimensional distributions are obtained. Learning is usually evident in such distributions by a reduction of the variance and a reduction of the size of the average absolute error. If only one or two target zones are used, the percent of responses falling outside a given zone is often used as an index of learning, instead of the variance or average absolute error. Such an arbitrary dichotomy of the distribution results in artifacts of slope of the obtained learning curves. The nature of these artifacts will be discussed in detail in connection with the analysis of performance in continuous tasks.

The above types of score are applicable with minor variations in a wide variety of tasks ranging from dart throwing, to steadiness tasks, to psychophysical tasks in which the subject is instructed to maintain or produce a given pressure, a given response amplitude, or a discrete sequence of such responses. In general, the meaning of the scores is best understood with reference to the entire distribution, even though a particular score may reflect only responses that exceed or fall short of certain limits, such as a contact score in a steadiness task. Figure 16-3 shows a response distribution generated by a subject's repeated attempts to produce a given pressure on a pressure stick (Noble and Bahrick, 1956). This distribution has a mean of approximately 10 pounds and an SD of approximately 1.5 pounds. The desired pressure in this particular instance was also 10 pounds; thus there was no appreciable constant error. The amount and direction of con-

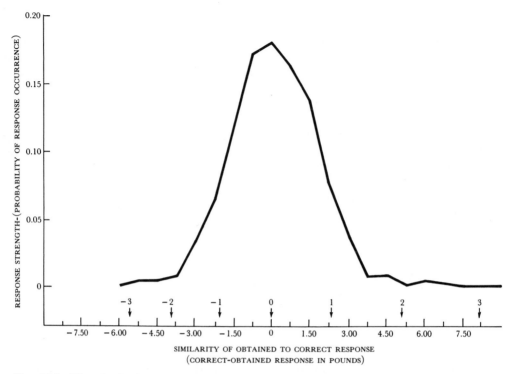

SIMILARITY OF OBTAINED TO CORRECT RESPONSE
(CORRECT-OBTAINED RESPONSE IN POUNDS)

Fig. 16-3 The distribution of responses generated by a subject's repeated attempts to reproduce a pressure of 10 pounds. Knowledge of results was given after each response. (*From Noble and Bahrick,* 1956).

stant error will be a function of a number of factors (Bahrick and Noble, 1961; Helson, 1949; Noble and Bahrick, 1956). Bilodeau and his associates (Bilodeau and Levy, 1964; Bilodeau, Sulzer, and Levy, 1962) have re-

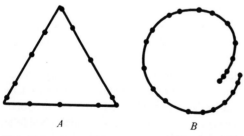

Fig. 16-4 Typical record of attempts to reproduce a triangular and a circular motion with a joystick control. The subject could not see the joystick. In both records the continuous line indicates the path of the tip of the joy stick; the distance between dots is the distance traveled in 0.18 second. (*From Bahrick, Fitts, and Schneider,* 1955).

cently proposed correlational and modified variance measures for the retention of a discrete motor skill. These measures may be equally applicable as indicants of acquisition. The variance measure is based upon the response distribution of many subjects, each attempting to reproduce an earlier response. It is shown that the variance of such a distribution increases as a function of the time interval separating the original response and the attempt at reproduction. The correlational measure relates the original response distribution in a lever-positioning task to a later response distribution of the same subjects, and this correlation is shown to decline as a function of the retention interval.

For complex or two-dimensional movements many other kinds of indicants of temporal and spatial precision may be abstracted. Most of these also bear simple relations to conventional statistics. The records shown in Fig. 16-4 illustrate a subject's attempt to reproduce a circular and a triangular motion with a joy-stick control (Bahrick, Fitts, and Schneider, 1955). The records were obtained by mounting a 16-millimeter camera above the center position of the control. Two small lights were mounted on top of the control column. One light remained on, continuously tracing a spatial representation of the motion, while the other light flashed intermittently at a rate of 5.6 times per second. The photographic records were then projected individually on a screen and compared with a simultaneously projected tracing of the correct pattern of the movements. Twenty-three measures of temporal and spatial accuracy, including measures of mean and median error and variability, were computed. These measures are listed in Table 16-1. The study was concerned with the effect of various types of

control loading upon the accuracy of execution of movements. Perhaps the most significant finding in the present context was that independent variables generally did not affect all performance indicants equally. Rather, a given control loading condition might adversely affect certain measures, produce no significant effect on other measures, and improve performance, as reflected by still other indicants. A systematic study of the interrelations among such indicants is necessary to interpret the effect of the independent variables and to produce some basis for comparison among investigations using different indicants. Without such information opposite conclusions might be reached regarding the effects of an independent variable on the part of investigators who used different indicants.

Many traditional techniques of recording

Table 16-1   Scores derived from analyses of photographic records of movement.

Score	Measures taken from each motion	Scores for the individual
	TRIANGULAR MOTIONS	
1a, 1b, 1c	Maximum speed on sides a, b, and c, respectively	Variability of measures a, b, and c, respectively, over seven trials
2	Same as for scores 1a, 1b, 1c	Variability among a, b, and c within a single trial averaged for seven trials
3	Total movement time for a trial	Mean of seven successive trials
4	Same as for score 3	Variability among seven successive trials
5a, 5b, 5c	Spatial position of sides a, b, and c, respectively	Median position error for seven successive trials for a, b, and c, respectively
6a, 6b, 6c	Same as for scores 5a, 5b, 5c	Variability among seven successive trials for a, b, and c, respectively
	CIRCULAR MOTIONS	
7	Maximum and minimum speed exclusive of initial and final acceleration	Difference between maximum and minimum speed within a given trial averaged for seven trials
8	Same as for score (7)	Difference between maximum and minimum speed at any time over seven successive trials
9	Total movement time for a trial	Mean of seven successive trials
10	Same as for score 9	Variability among seven successive trials
11a, 11b, 11c	Radius at 90°, 180°, and 270° (movement starts at 0°), respectively	Median radial error for seven successive reproductions for a, b, and c, respectively
12a, 12b, 12c, 12d	Radius at 45°, 135°, 225°, and 315°, respectively	Radial error variability over seven successive trials for a, b, c, and d

SOURCE: Bahrick, Fitts, and Schneider (1955).

the temporal and spatial characteristics of discrete movements were summarized some years ago by Meisterling (1931). More recent summaries for discrete and/or continuous movements include those by Helson (1949) and Poulton (1962). Webber and Adams (1960) and Trumbo, Noble, and Baganoff (in press) have described analog and digital systems for measurement of tracking behavior; and Crossman (1960), Fitts (1954), and Garner (1962) are among those who have discussed analyses of motor behavior from the point of view of information theory. McRuer and Krendel (1959) have summarized the mathematical analyses employed by engineers interested in a quantitative description of the human subject in a closed-loop system.

Continuous tasks

Response distributions can also be obtained in continuous tasks such as tracking. The procedure requires more complex instrumentation; and usually the error record, rather than the response record, serves as the basis for abstracting various types of score. In tracking tasks, for instance, the target may be a signal on a cathode-ray tube (CRT) display produced by a corresponding input voltage. The subject's response usually produces variation of a second voltage by means of a potentiometer of similar equipment, the output of which may be represented independently as a cursor signal on the display. Performance indicants in such continuous tasks cannot be directly abstracted from the response characteristics. They must be based upon an analysis of the relation of the response signal to the stimulus signal, i.e., the momentary error. This is necessary because the adequacy of the response cannot be defined independently of the momentary position of the target. To obtain an error signal, the cursor voltage is subtracted from the target voltage. The difference is proportional to the spatial magnitude of the error, and most indicants of tracking performance are

obtained by subjecting this signal to various kinds of transformation.

Time-on-target scores

These scores are usually obtained from the error signal by means of clocks or counters and voltage-sensitive relays. The error voltage will trigger the counter or activate the clock as long as the error is smaller than a limiting value representing the arbitrary target size. When the error exceeds this value, the relay breaks the circuit and this stops the clock. The circuit is reestablished as soon as the error is reduced below the limiting value, and the subject is on target again. At the end of a trial, the reading on the clock or counter corresponds to the amount of time that the error was smaller than the critical value, i.e., the amount of time the subject was on target. The conventional percent time-on-target score is obtained by expressing the score as a fraction of the total trial time. Since the limiting error value defining the target size is arbitrary, it is possible to set this value for so large a target area that a subject would be on target during most of the trial, or it can be set for so small a value that the same performance would result in being on target for only a very small percent of the trial time.

Target band scores

If several time-on-target scores are obtained simultaneously from the same error signal for different-sized target areas, it is possible to subtract the scores obtained on smaller-sized targets from those obtained on larger-sized targets. The difference reflects the time spent in a given target band. By several successive subtractions, series of band scores are obtained analogous to the number of hits obtained in the various concentric rings of a bull's-eye.

Average error scores

A value proportional to the average absolute error is obtained by integrating the rectified error voltage on a capacitor over the length of a trial and dividing the total by the trial time. This value is not directly comparable to the average deviation (AD), since it is computed with reference to the target center and not with reference to the actual mean of the error distribution. Thus, it also contains constant error. The constant error can be computed directly by integrating the unrectified error voltage and dividing the integral sum by the length of the trial.

Root mean square (rms) error

Squaring the error voltage and integrating the output of the squaring circuit on a capacitor yields a score which, when divided by the trial time, is proportional to variance. An rms error value can be obtained by a square-root transformation. This value will not be directly related to the SD of the error distribution because it is computed with respect to the target center, or zero error voltage, rather than with respect to the mean of the actual error distribution. It is necessary to subtract the squared constant error from the integrated squared error score prior to carrying out the square-root transformation, in order to obtain a value proportional to the SD of the error distribution. The values obtained are proportional to, rather than identical to, the desired error magnitudes, and a constant transformation is needed to obtain spatial error values. The value of the constant is determined by the circuit constants. It is usually possible to calibrate and check the reliability of the obtained transformation by creating a known spatial error for the duration of a trial and checking this error against the values obtained from the scoring circuits.

Average error and rms error scores will appear as voltages and ordinarily are shown on a meter or oscillographic record. These scores are a function of the time-varying amplitude of the original error signal and the relative sizes of the resistor and capacitor elements associated with the integrating amplifier. This means that the same input (error signal) fed into the analog squaring and/or integrating devices of different experimenters

is unlikely to yield identical numerical scores. If the gain terms are known, it is possible to transform the scores in order to make a direct comparison of the average error or rms error scores. This is cumbersome. It is suggested that all such scores be converted from units of volts to units of the visual display (see Chap. 17 for procedure).

Interrelations among indicants derived from the amplitude distribution

If the amplitude distribution is normal and ergodic, i.e., remains stable from trial to trial, then the interrelations among the scores described above can be predicted precisely (Fitts et al., 1959, pp. 6–9). This is so since the SD and the AD bear a constant relation to each other for large samples of normal distributions (AD = 0.7979 SD). The percent of the area of a normal distribution located between any two designated z scores can be obtained from a table of the integral values of the normal curve. The rms value of the distribution needs only to be divided into the limiting value defining a given time-on-target score in order to express this value as a z score. The percent of a normal distribution found between the mean and the z score is determined from the normal-probability integral, and that value is multiplied by 2 to include errors on both sides of the target center. Suppose, for example, that examination of tracking data shows a normal amplitude distribution of tracking error with a standard deviation (rms) of 1.2 volts. Assuming that time-on-target limits of 0.4 volt were employed, the investigator can predict the time-on-target scores as $z = \dfrac{\text{target limits}}{\text{rms}} = \dfrac{0.4}{1.2} = 0.33$. The normal-probability integral tables indicate that 12.93 percent of the area falls between the mean and a z value of 0.33. The percent is doubled since the target area extends in both directions from the target center, and we therefore predict a time-on-target score of 25.86 percent. It should be noted that the above provides a statistical estimate of one score given another. Since each score is affected slightly differently by sampling variations from exact normality, the transformations will always be subject to some amount of error in any particular instance.

The portion of the error amplitude distribution falling within the fixed amplitude limits of any given target will increase monotonically as the SD of the distribution diminishes with improved performance, in accordance with a fairly complex function. The relation between the rms value of a normal distribution and the percentage of time-on-target for various sizes of target is shown in Fig. 16-5. Successive values for these curves are found by the procedure described above of transforming target sizes into z scores, i.e., by dividing the target size into the rms value.

It can be seen that each of the curves in Fig. 16-5 shows a maximal slope at a different range of variation of the rms value and becomes insensitive to variations outside that range. The ranges of maximal sensitivity shift toward smaller rms values as we move from larger to smaller target sizes. The sensitivity

of a given time-on-target score is maximum when the target is of a size that includes $+1$ SD of the error distribution, so that the subject is on target about 67 percent of the time. When the SD of the distribution becomes smaller or larger so that the subject is on target considerably more or less than 67 percent of the time, the sensitivity of the time-on-target score diminishes progressively.

Functions similar to those shown in Fig. 16-5 can be plotted for targets of any desired size, and it is apparent that curves for very small target zones would show their maximum sensitivity in an rms range in which the curves of larger target zones have already approached an asymptote. It is obvious that a score cannot reveal improvements once performance is approaching an asymptote of 100 percent on target. The relative lack of sensitivity of each time-on-target score at low performance levels is not generally recognized and has frequently led to misinterpretations of data.

Figure 16-6 presents some empirical learning curves together with theoretically pre-

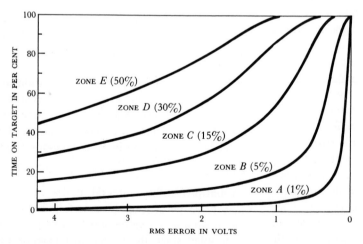

Fig. 16-5 Percentage of time-on-target for various target zones as a function of rms of a normal distribution of error amplitudes. In zone A, time accumulates when the error is within 15 percent of the maximum problem voltage of 5 volts; in zone B, time accumulates when the error is within 5 percent of the maximum problem voltage of 5 volts. (*From Bahrick, Fitts, and Briggs, 1957*).

dicted curves. The predicted curves are based upon the rms values shown in the upper portion of the figure by the procedure outlined above. It can be seen that (1) the predicted and empirical values correspond fairly closely to each other and (2) the curves based upon target sizes *A*, *B*, and *C* give widely different accounts of the relative amounts of improvement at different stages of practice.

It is apparent that the predicted scores are somewhat higher than the obtained scores for target sizes *C* and *A,* but the opposite is true for target size *B*. This is primarily the result of departures from normality in the obtained error amplitude distribution. The curve for target size *C* is negatively accelerated and shows most of the improvement during the early trials, with less improvement during the last few trials. The curve for target size *A* shows the largest gain during the last two trials and relatively less gain during the early trials. It should be remembered that all the scores are derived from the same error voltage. The widely divergent slopes of these curves demonstrate convincingly that time-on-target scores are differentially sensitive to improvement at different stages of practice. They do not approximate an equal-interval scale, and this makes it impossible to draw inferences regarding relative amounts of learning at different stages of practice on the basis of such curves.

To emphasize the danger of disregarding these nonlinear characteristics of time-on-target scores, data are presented in Fig. 16-7 (Howland and Noble, 1953) evaluating the effects of control loading[1] upon tracking performance. The curves show increasing separation as practice progresses, and this led the

[1] Control loading refers to the spring stiffness, viscous damping, and moment of inertia characteristics of the control.

Fig. 16-6 Empirical and predicted learning curves of 25 subjects on a simple tracking task. The predicted curves are based upon the rms values shown in the upper portion of the figure. The zones are the same as in Fig. 16-5. (*From Bahrick, Fitts, and Briggs,* **1957**).

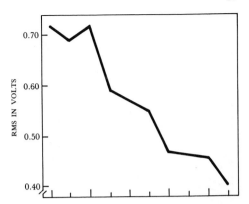

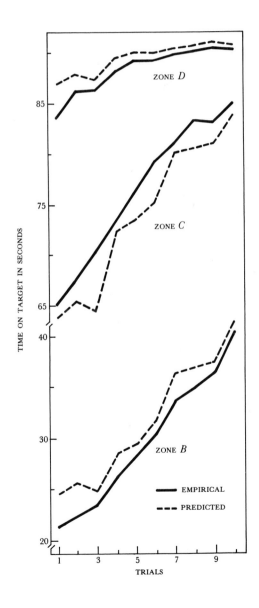

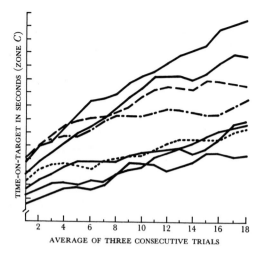

Fig. 16-7 Mean time-on-target scores for eight different control loadings when a simple sinusoidal input is being tracked. The different curves are for different combinations of spring stiffness, viscous damping, and moment of inertia of the arm control, using a 15 percent scoring tolerance (zone C). (*From Howland and Noble,* 1953).

authors to the conclusion that the differential effects of control loading upon performance increase during practice. The curves have been replotted in Fig. 16-8, for a larger scoring area, to illustrate that this increasing separation among learning curves is an artifact of

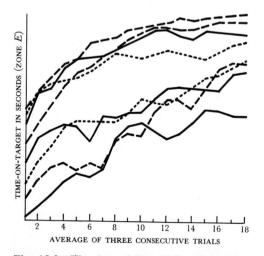

Fig. 16-8 The data of Fig. 16-7 replotted for a 50 percent scoring tolerance (zone E). (*From Bahrick, Fitts, and Briggs,* 1957).

the gradually increasing sensitivity of the scoring area. The conversion of scores is based upon the functions shown in Fig. 16-5. It can be seen that the increasing separation among curves is no longer present in Fig. 16-8. The arbitrary selection of a target size has produced *scoring artifacts* that have been attributed to the effects of the independent variable. The opposite effect might have been attributed to the independent variable if a different target size had been chosen.

The above nonlinear characteristics of time-on-target scores do not invalidate the scores for all purposes. They do make it clear that a single time-on-target score is of limited value, particularly if performance on different task versions at different stages of practice varies over a wide range, and the score is either very low or very high for some of the conditions to be evaluated. Under these circumstances an rms score or average-absolute-error score can best reflect the amplitude characteristics of the error.

Measures reflecting the frequency and time characteristics of performance

Indicants revealing the frequency characteristics of performance are best discussed in relation to the power-density spectrum and its transform, the autocorrelation function. One area of frequency analysis generally familiar to behavioral scientists is the analysis of sounds into component frequencies. A note produced by a musical instrument has several component frequencies, and the perceived pitch is usually determined by the fundamental frequency. This is so because more intensity is associated with it than with the harmonics. Other sounds differ from those produced by musical instruments in that (1) they lack stability and (2) the simultaneously produced frequencies are not simple multiples or harmonics. Rather, the frequencies vary over a range, and the best specification for such sounds is in terms of the power-density spectrum, i.e., a specification of relative power (intensity) associated with the various frequencies within the range involved. A comparable analysis of response and error patterns for motor performance can provide the basis for better understanding of this kind of behavior. Such signals are made up of continuous distributions of frequencies, rather than of a small number of relatively pure frequencies. Whereas most of the power of human speech is contained in the frequency range from 100 to 4,000 cycles per second (cps), almost all the power in a tracking-error record is concentrated in the frequency band below 10 cps (Fitts *et al.*, 1959).

Two graphic records are shown in Fig. 16-9. These have similar amplitude distributions but differ with respect to the frequency with which the signal fluctuates. Power-density spectra for the two signals are shown in Fig. 16-10. It can be seen that the power-density spectrum for the first signal has most of the power associated with frequencies below 5 cps, while the second signal is peaked at 30 cps. The second record shows evidence of many quick corrective movements, while the first record shows comparatively slow, smooth motions. These characteristics of motor performance must be studied in order to gain a better understanding of the nature of skill. The measures discussed thus far fail to reveal them. In particular, an analysis of the frequency characteristics of motor performance allows us to detect the extent to which periodicities appearing in the stimulus are reflected in the response and error patterns and the extent to which other periodicities, which are independent of the stimulus, characterize performance. Such information is valuable in testing various types of hypotheses regarding the manner in which perceptual motor skills are centrally controlled.

The autocorrelation function

The autocorrelation function identifies periodicities in a time-varying series by indicating the correlation of the series with itself at later times. To illustrate how an autocorrelation function can be derived from a tracking-error signal, examine a series of 600

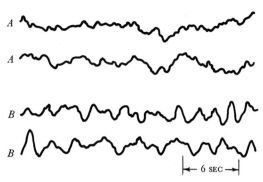

Fig. 16-9   Two graphic tracking records *A* and *B*, showing similar amplitude distributions but differing with respect to the frequency with which the signal fluctuates.

amplitude readings abstracted from the error at successive intervals of 0.1 second by scoring a graphic record of the error amplitude. Assume that 20 counters were used so that the total range of amplitude values has been divided into 20 equal intervals, 10 each for positive and for negative errors, i.e., for errors in which the cursor was lagging the signal by various amplitudes. It is apparent in looking over the series of 600 successive values that every value does not follow every other value equally often. An amplitude of −10 adjacent to one of +10 may never be found in the series. This cannot happen because the

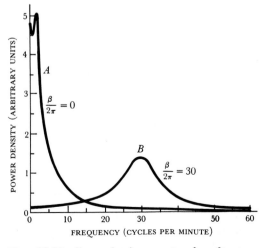

Fig. 16-10   Power-density spectra for the two signals shown in Fig. 16-9.

error signal is bandlimited in frequency so that it is impossible for the amplitude to change from +10 to −10 in 0.1 second.

To compute the first value of the autocorrelation function, it will be necessary to duplicate the series of 600 values and to displace it with respect to itself by one value, or by 0.1 second. Now 600 paired scores have been formed so that value 1 is paired with value 2, value 2 with value 3, and continuing through the series. If the correlation between these paired scores is established, we know how much the series correlates with itself after a time interval of 0.1 second. Similar correlations must be computed for larger time displacements such as 0.2, 0.3, and 0.4 second. The obtained correlations can be plotted opposite the corresponding value of tau, representing the displacement time. When tau is zero and the series is correlated with itself for no time displacement, the correlation is unity. Figure 16-11 shows the autocorrelation functions of the two signals shown in Fig. 16-10. Several properties of the autocorrelation functions may be noted. A function with a power-density spectrum peaked at 30 cpm has a periodicity of 30 cpm. Note that the autocorrelation function of this signal reaches zero at about 0.5 second, indicating that points in the record separated by a time interval of less than 0.5 second are positively

correlated. The autocorrelation function of the second signal, which has its peak energy in a much lower frequency range, does not fall to zero until tau reaches 6 seconds.

The crosscorrelation function

This function differs from the autocorrelation function in that the two sets of values being correlated for different amounts of displacement in time are derived from two different series, rather than from the same series.

In the analysis of tracking behavior, crosscorrelation of the input and output functions can give important information regarding the nature of skill. If a tracker were predicting the stimulus with zero lag or lead, the crosscorrelation function between stimulus and response series would be positive and maximal at tau = 0. If the tracker were lagging the stimulus, the crosscorrelation should reach a maximum at some value of tau corresponding to his average lag time. Indicants derived from the crosscorrelation function enable us to obtain something analogous to a reaction-time score in a continuous task. This type of score is not easily obtainable without such an analysis, since it is not usually possible to identify specific stimuli and their responses in the continuous time series constituting signal and response.

Indicants abstracted from autocorrelation and crosscorrelation functions

Among the significant inferences drawn from autocorrelation functions of error records in tracking is the ability of the subject to eliminate the frequency characteristics of the input from his own error records. Ability to cope with the periodicity of the problem results in the elimination of the target periodicity from the error record. One index of this ability is the height of the autocorrelation function at tau = the period of the target signal as a fraction of the height at tau = zero. This score is illustrated in Fig. 16-12 from a 10-cycle-per-minute (10-cpm) target signal, where W is the height of the

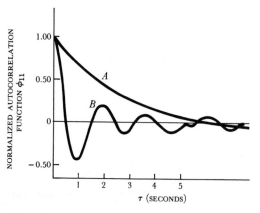

Fig. 16-11 Autocorrelation functions of the two signals shown in Fig. 16-10.

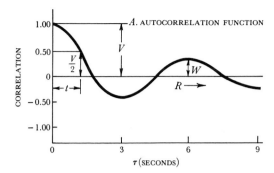

Fig. 16-12 **Autocorrelation function from 10-cpm target signal.** W **is the height of function at a value of tau = 6 seconds (period of input).** t **is the value of tau at which the function has dropped to** $V/2$, **and** V **is the initial value of the function.**

function at a value of tau = 6 seconds, the period of this particular input.

Another aspect of the autocorrelation function that appears significant is the presence of high frequencies in the random component of the error signal. Such high frequencies affect the slope of the initial part of the autocorrelation function, since high-frequency inputs will cause a rapid decline in predictability of the error and, therefore, a rapid drop of the autocorrelation function. As one arbitrary index of this slope, the value of tau may be found at which the function has fallen to 0.5 of its initial value. This may be called an index of random-error frequency and is illustrated in Fig. 16-12, where t is the value of tau at which the function has dropped to $V/2$, and V is the initial value of the function.

Perhaps the most important index that may be derived from the crosscorrelation function between input and response series is the value of tau at which the maximum crosscorrelation between input and output is achieved. This tells us the most typical lag-time characterizing the subject's responses. This score is of interest in many continuous skill situations, since it should be indicative of the subject's ability to deal with the predictable aspects of a stimulus pattern by eliminating or reducing his lags

through anticipation. The score should be particularly revealing in tasks that impose some lag times between the subject's responses and their effect upon the system he is operating. Steering a boat or an airplane are good examples of such tasks. High degrees of skill require that the subject take into account the lags inherent in the system by anticipating stimulus changes, i.e., leading the stimulus series in his responses. Such systems require an optimum lead time. The difference between this lead time and the actual lead time determined from the crosscorrelation function may become an important index of the subject's skill. Other indices are described by Trumbo, Noble, and Baganoff (in press).

Analog computers especially constructed to obtain crosscorrelation functions are commercially available.

Short-cut indicants reflecting both frequency characteristics and amplitudes

In addition to the scores derived from autocorrelations and crosscorrelation functions a number of other indicants more readily obtainable with simple apparatus reflect frequency characteristics of a signal. *Transition scores* give the number of times the subject's error enters a given target zone during a trial. Transition scores may be obtained from the error voltage by means of a voltage-sensitive relay pulsing a counter. Amplitude characteristics are involved because the error must be of a certain amplitude for the subject to make a transition into a given target zone. Frequency characteristics are involved since the number of transitions in and out of the zone depends upon the frequency aspects of the subject's response. Such scores can conveniently be obtained simultaneously for several desired target zones. A transition score can also be obtained for the target center, i.e, the place where the error voltage changes its sign. This score is most likely to be independent of the amplitude distribution.

*Interrelations among amplitude
and frequency indicants*

Interrelations among 13 of the previously discussed measures will now be examined. The measures were obtained simultaneously in a compensatory tracking task where error is the algebraic difference between fixed target position and cursor position on the target display. The input was a 10-cpm sine wave. A filter with a time constant of 0.4 second introduced an exponential lag between the subject's arm control output and the movement of a cursor marked on the CRT oscilloscope. The several scores derived

from the error signal are summarized in Table 16-2. Two scores were also obtained from each of two additional tasks. In a rotary-pursuit task, time-on-target scores were summed for 15 trials to yield one score, and the number of entries into the target disk gave another score. On a positioning task, average absolute error (PAE) in positioning a rotary arm control over 20 trials was one score, and constant error (PCE) was another. The interrelations among all 17 measures are listed in Table 16-3.

The intercorrelation measures based upon the 13 scores derived from the tracking per-

Table 16-2   Measures of tracking performance derived from a single continuous error voltage.

Performance measure	Derived from	Description
1. rms_1	A meter activated by squaring and integrating circuits	The square root of the integral, from 0 to 90 sec, of the squared error voltage
2. rms_2	The OSU amplitude analyzer	$\Sigma d^2/n$, deviations taken from each subject's own mean
3. Constant error	The OSU amplitude analyzer	Zero error minus subject's own algebraic mean error
4. 0–5% target zone	A time-on-target counter pulsed at 10 cps by an electronic time-on-target circuit	Total time accumulated in 0.1-sec increments, during which error voltage is less than 5% of the maximum ± problem voltage
5. 15–5% target zone	The 15% and the 5% time-on-target circuits	Total time during which the error is greater than 5% but less than 15% of the maximum ± problem voltage
6. 30–15% target zone	The 30% and the 15% time-on-target circuits	Total time during which the error is greater than 15% but less than 30% of the maximum ± problem voltage
7. 100–30% target zone	The 30% time-on-target circuit	Total time during which the error is greater than 30% of the maximum ± problem voltage
8. 5% transition	The 5% time-on-target circuit	Number of times subject's error changes from less than to more than 5% of the maximum ± problem voltage
9. 15% transition	The 15% time-on-target circuit	Number of times subject's error changes from less than to more than 15% of the maximum ± problem voltage
10. 30% transition	The 30% time-on-target circuit	Number of times subject's error changes from less than to more than 30% of the maximum ± problem voltage
11. ϕ_{11} frequency	The autocorrelation function of the error	Time required for the correlation to drop from 1.00 to .50
12. ϕ_{11} periodicity	The autocorrelation function of the error	Value of autocorrelation at the point where $\tau = 6$ sec (6 sec = period of the 10-cps problem)
13. ϕ_{12} lag compensation	The crosscorrelation of response with problem input	Absolute value of the difference between 0.38 sec and the value of τ, in seconds, where ϕ_{12} is max

Table 16-3   Intercorrelations of measures of tracking error ($N = 100$ subjects[1]; 90 sec per trial).

	1	2	3	4	5	6	7	8	9	10	11	12	13	14	15	16	17
1. rms₁		.82	.48	−.70	−.74	.00	.78	−.62	−.16	.58	.26	.22	.42	−.25	−.14	.19	.37
2. rms₂			.50	−.81	−.89	−.02	.92	−.67	−.17	.71	.28	.42	.49	−.39	−.22	.17	.35
3. Constant error				−.34	−.47	−.14	.52	−.42	−.36	.18	.14	.41	.30	−.15	−.01	.38	.51
4. 0–5% target zone					.85	−.39	−.78	.78	−.13	−.74	−.38	−.38	−.40	.33	.24	−.09	−.26
5. 15–5% target zone						−.22	−.89	.72	.10	−.80	−.37	−.44	−.48	.40	.27	−.10	−.27
6. 30–15% target zone							−.19	−.32	.35	.18	.21	−.13	−.25	.00	−.13	−.20	−.09
7. 100–30% target zone								−.64	−.17	.74	.24	.41	.53	−.40	−.21	.20	.33
8. 5% transition									.34	−.41	−.48	−.42	−.21	.28	.22	−.14	−.28
9. 15% transition										.34	−.38	−.33	−.18	.13	.04	−.12	−.12
10. 30% transition											.05	.16	.45	−.30	−.24	.02	.15
11. ϕ_{11} frequency												.01	.09	−.35	−.21	−.07	.03
12. ϕ_{11} periodicity													.36	−.35	−.25	.15	.29
13. ϕ_{12} lag-compensation														−.29	−.30	−.06	.22
14. Rotary-pursuit time on target															.51	−.11	−.26
15. Rotary-pursuit transitions																−.11	−.23
16. Positioning-task constant error																	.72
17. Positioning-task average error																	

[1] $N = 57$ for measures 11, 12, and 13.

formance were subjected to a factor analysis by the centroid method. It is recognized that experimental dependence existed among some of the measures, e.g., 4 to 7 and 1 to 2. Fleishman and Fruchter (1960) showed that such dependence among some of the variables in a matrix did not materially affect the outcome of the analysis.

The Dwyer extension method (Fruchter, 1954, p. 209) was used to project scores from the rotary-pursuit and positioning tasks (14 to 17) upon the existing factor structure, and two additional factors had to be extracted to accommodate the variance of these scores (Peters and Van Voorhis, 1940). The factors were then rotated to achieve simple structure, and the final factor loadings are presented in Table 16-4.

Inspection of the factor structure shows that skill as reflected by the overall rms error criterion is principally determined by orthogonal factors I, II, and IV. Further examination of the loadings of these factors gives some insight into the various independent aspects of behavior they represent. Factor I comes close to being a G factor. It has the greatest loadings on the rms score and on the very wide target band (100% to 30%). This suggests that tracking success or failure as reflected by this factor depends upon avoidance of very big errors, and to a much lesser extent upon skill in maintaining close pursuit of the target as reflected by the time spent in the very narrow target band. This avoidance of very large errors seems to depend largely upon adequate detection and compensation for the periodicities of the stimulus. The periodicity score has its heaviest loading on this factor. It is reasonable that inadequate compensation for the target periodicity would result in errors that would frequently become very large. The loading on the periodicity score probably identifies best the specific nature of error accumulation represented on this factor. Other heavy loadings are those covering lag compensation, constant error, and average error in the positioning task. Loadings on these three scores suggest that general muscular control, possibly based upon proprioceptive discrimina-

Table 16-4   **Rotated factor loadings on measures of tracking error.**

	I	II	III	IV	V	VI	VII	VIII	h^2
1. rms$_1$	711	386	000	−390	−123	054	−024	−043	0.827
2. rms$_2$	811	436	001	−288	012	−045	−108	081	0.951
3. Constant error	549	011	249	−013	−269	042	117	372	0.590
4. 0–5% target zone	−512	−822	029	019	102	047	−044	−162	0.980
5. 15–5% target zone	−592	−668	005	058	−030	−042	−014	−439	0.996
6. 30–15% target zone	−246	652	075	249	−093	−056	080	−320	0.674
7. 100–30% target zone	804	339	−112	−334	043	−118	−143	243	0.981
8. 5% transition	−406	−646	−511	169	140	204	−019	−161	0.959
9. 15% transition	−127	263	−628	333	−075	106	110	−378	0.762
10. 30% transition	484	595	−514	−025	044	−070	−079	190	0.902
11. ϕ_{11} frequency	022	403	449	−321	082	333	−204	065	0.631
12. ϕ_{11} periodicity	560	041	310	279	100	−279	−228	073	0.634
13. ϕ_{12} lag-compensation	607	040	−058	−010	291	091	−220	164	0.542
14. Rotary-pursuit time on target	−278	−258	−141	−006	−116	−096	757	−001	0.759
15. Rotary-pursuit transitions	−061	−266	−015	−133	011	−051	605	−252	0.525
16. Positioning-task constant error	197	−171	−019	−042	−885	−096	−225	295	1.000
17. Positioning-task average error	543	−072	145	135	−584	172	−256	−012	0.776

tion, is involved in tracking success and related to the subject's ability to time his movements in accordance with observed periodicities of the target. All other scores, with the exception of the frequency score and success on the rotary-pursuit task, are related to this aspect of skill; therefore, the factor approaches a *G* factor in meaning.

Factor II, the second factor reflecting success or failure by the rms criterion, differs from factor I in several ways. The heaviest loading is not the score in the very wide target band, as in the case of factor I, but rather the score in the very narrow target band. This involves the subject's ability to stay within a very small distance of the target for a considerable portion of the time. Success or failure in this respect seems to depend heavily upon the presence of high-frequency components in the error autocorrelation as reflected by the frequency loading on this factor. This interpretation is supported by loadings on transition scores, which are larger than for factor I despite the fact that the rms loading itself is smaller than for factor I. We may call this a "fine tuning" factor. Success and failure on the rotary-pursuit task

are to some extent related, but lag compensation skill, constant error avoidance, and positioning skill, as well as the ability to detect and compensate for target periodicities, are not involved.

Factor IV is the third factor that reflects behavior significantly related to the rms criterion. This factor has the largest loadings on (1) the rms score itself, (2) time in the very widest band, (3) transitions through the intermediate target band, and (4) the frequency and periodicity indicants. The underlying behavior differs from the pattern suggested by factor I, in that inability to compensate for target periodicity is associated here with smaller rather than larger error scores. This is apparently accomplished by high-frequency corrections that minimize the amount of time in the large error zone once the target has been lost. This is a correction speed factor.

Factor III can clearly be identified as a frequency factor. The highest loadings are observed on the three transition scores and on the frequency score itself. It is very important to note that transitions into every one of the target zones seem to be nearly equally involved, while on the other factors in which transition scores are heavily loaded (factors I, II, VIII), the loadings change in direction, as does the relative time in the various target areas. The behavior abstracted by this factor is quite independent of the amount of time spent in any of the target zones, and yet transitions into these zones are heavily and nearly equally represented. This, together with the presence of high-frequency components in the error-autocorrelation record, clearly sustains the interpretation of this factor as a frequency factor. It seems to abstract those aspects of tracking skill which involve frequency characteristics of responses and which are essentially unrelated to success or failure relative to the amplitude characteristics of error.

Factor V is equally identified as a positioning skill factor, with heaviest loadings in the constant and average errors on the positioning task. The behavior reflected here seems to be relatively unrelated to other aspects of tracking performance. Constant error on the tracking task and the ability to compensate for lags are most involved, and these are the aspects of tracking skill which on an intuitive basis would be expected to relate most to positioning skill.

Factor VII mostly reflects success or failure on the rotary-pursuit task, and the relation to the rms criterion is surprisingly small. Only success on the positioning task, the presence of high-frequency components in the autocorrelation record, and ability to compensate for the target periodicity are involved in the behavior abstracted by this factor.

Factors VI and VII are the most difficult to interpret, because of the small loadings exhibited by both. Neither factor abstracts characteristics of skill highly related to the rms criterion. The highest loading in factor VIII involves performance on the intermediate target zone. Poor performance there seems to relate to a fairly large constant error and large constant errors on the positioning task.

The analysis gives several important insights into the nature of tracking behavior, as well as to the meaning of individual indicants of tracking skill. It is apparent that success or failure as measured by an overall amplitude-of-error criterion, such as the rms score, is attributable to several relatively independent aspects of behavior that are best identified by more analytic indicants. The ability to detect and compensate for target periodicities is one such aspect, and the periodicity score abstracted from the error-autocorrelation records reflects this aspect of skill. High-frequency corrections are a second aspect of skill, chiefly important in the ability to remain in close pursuit of a small target but also important in minimizing the damage due to loss of the target. These corrections are adequately reflected by the frequency score abstracted from the error-autocorrelation records, coupled with large amounts of time spent in the very narrow target zone. A similar but independent aspect of behavior is identified as correction speed. This is manifested by high-frequency components in the autocorrelation function of error, coupled with small amounts of time spent in areas removed from the target, despite inability to compensate for target periodicities.

The following difference should be noted in relating the present findings to earlier factor analyses of motor performance. Earlier studies (Fleishman and Hempel, 1954; Seashore, Dudek, and Holtzman, 1949) have been concerned primarily with the analysis of intercorrelations among various types of motor task, with a single score obtained in each task. The present analysis is based primarily upon a variety of scores abstracted from performance on a single (tracking) task. The principal purpose of previous studies is to identify human abilities common to a variety of motor tasks; the main purpose of the present analysis is to develop better understanding of performance measurement in a particular task. Yet the present findings show an important relation to earlier findings. Seashore, in summarizing results of earlier studies (Stevens, 1951, p. 1345), concludes that changes of musculature or sense modality are only moderately important variables underlying individual differences, but changes in the pattern of movement are very important variables. Although the present analysis is concerned primarily with performance of a single task, differentiation among the factors becomes possible through the identification of individual differences of movement patterns by means of analytic scores. Such scores are capable of differentiating patterns of motion that remain undifferentiated on the basis of the rms criterion or any other indicant of tracking skill derived from the amplitude distribution alone. Additional factor-analysis studies will be needed to cross-validate the meanings of factors established here, as well as the significance of individual indicants.

SPECIFICATION OF STIMULI

There are excellent reasons why it is necessary to identify the parameters of the stimulus in any task. An elementary axiom in experimental research is that adequate control of the variables cannot be accomplished without adequate specification of the variables. Yet, the literature contains reports in which the nature of the stimulus is inadequately specified. In part, this is due to the fact that adequate specification often is difficult, particularly if apparatus was used that did not permit specification of important variables.

The undesirability of leaving some important aspects of the stimulus unspecified can be illustrated by several examples. (1) Assume that the stimulus or target in a continuous tracking task is generated by means of an irregularly shaped cam. Even if the limits of target excursion and rate of movement are specified, the results cannot be compared adequately with those of another study using some other target course unless the statistical properties of the irregular target course are stated. (2) Assume that an experimenter is interested in performance as affected by the amount of organization in a discrete-stimulus sequence, or in the degree of meaningfulness of the stimulus, or in the difficulty in discriminating a particular stimulus from another stimulus or noise. It is quite easy in each of the instances to generate stimuli that obviously differ in the desired respect but not to specify the stimuli in a way that will permit direct comparison with other data. Much more time and effort should be devoted to problems of scaling such variables. Lack of this information has precluded much in the way of quantification and has retarded the development of theory. In the remainder of this section, it is possible to do little more than mention some of the stimulus and task dimensions that affect skilled performance. No attempt will be made to catalog those dimensions exhaustively. The topics of stimulus complexity and task difficulty will not be covered because these terms seem to have different meanings for different writers, and different meanings for a given writer at various times. Task difficulty has been used to refer to the length of a sequence, the number of different alternative stimuli, and the number of trials required to reach some performance criterion. Stimulus complexity has been used to refer to the number of different frequencies in a periodic continuous stimulus, the number and pattern of alternative stimuli in a discrete sequence, and the pattern and number of different interstimulus intervals.

Stimulus classification

Stimuli may be classified as (1) *discrete,* (2) *serial,* or (3) *continuous* (Brown and Jenkins, 1947). The stimuli occur discretely in both discrete and serial sequences. The difference between them is an arbitrary one expressed in terms of the amount of time between successive stimuli. In a serial sequence the stimuli follow one another in rather rapid succession with sufficient time between them that they are perceived as distinct events. In the discrete sequence there is a relatively long time, e.g., several seconds, between successive stimuli. A continuous stimulus is one in which the stimulus exhibits no intermittency.

Discrete, serial, and continuous stimulus sequences are on a continuum for the subject asked to perform the task. It is a discrete sequence if the time interval between stimuli is long enough that the subject can rest or turn his attention to another task for an appreciable length of time before the next stimulus occurs. The sequence is serial when the interval between stimuli is shorter, so that it is difficult or impossible to rest or turn to another task, and yet the successive stimuli are clearly perceived as distinct. As the interval between successive stimuli becomes shorter and shorter, the stimulus begins to appear to the subject to be changing continuously, and he may respond as he would to a continuous signal.

The classification into discrete, serial, and continuous stimuli is made because different methods of analysis may be appropriate. Transient analysis is appropriate with discrete-stimulus sequences, but such analysis would not be appropriate to serial or continuous tasks if the response to these were also considered to be serial or continuous. Although the same general methods of analysis usually are appropriate for both serial and continuous tasks, often it is desirable to distinguish between them for other reasons.

Often it is desirable to consider the following classification if serial or continuous signals are concerned (Clark, Fontaine, and Warren, 1953). (1) *Periodic signals* are signals generated by a source whose characteristics can be specified exactly as a mathematical process and exhibit periodicity, e.g., simple or complex sinusoidal waves, square waves, sawtooth waves, and repetitive numerical sequences. (2) *Aperiodic signals* are signals generated by a source whose characteristics can be specified exactly as a mathematical process but do not exhibit periodicity, e.g., constant-velocity signals, constant-acceleration signals, and progressive

nonperiodic numerical sequences. (3) *Random signals* are signals generated by sources having characteristics that can be specified as stationary statistical functions (Feller, 1950), e.g., electrical noise, atmospheric turbulence, and long sequences from tables of random numbers. (4) *Quasi-random signals* are signals generated by sources which cannot be specified as stationary statistical processes and which do not have a structure that is easily specified in mathematical form. Signals generated by arbitrary irregular cam contours, microphonics due to mechanical vibration of vacuum-tube elements, and most short sequences from tables of random numbers are examples.

Periodic and aperiodic signals permit the precise specification of the values of the signals at any given moment in time. The values of a random signal cannot be specified precisely at future moments in time, but they can be specified on a probability basis. All three of these classes of signals are amenable to general mathematical treatment and are capable of systematic variation. Quasi-random signals ordinarily are not susceptible to systematic variation and are not as amenable to general mathematical treatment. Their use is not recommended. If an experimenter uses a random signal source and specifies its statistical characteristics, e.g., its amplitude distribution and its power spectrum, it is possible (1) for another experimenter to duplicate its essential properties and (2) to specify something about the similarity between any two signals that can themselves be specified. If a quasi-random signal is used, it is necessary to give a complete description of all its time values in order that it may be duplicated, and it may be impossible to specify mathematically its relation to other such signals.

Although a great deal of research has involved serial and continuous tasks, a number of interesting questions can be studied as well or better by methods that involve discrete stimulation and response. For one thing, all types of motor response involve biphasic movements, not just simple responses to discrete stimuli. Complex polyphasic responses to discrete stimuli are composed of sequences of biphasic movements (Woodworth, 1958); similarly, responses to serial stimulation involve a rapid succession of biphasic movements. Even smooth continuous responses normally involve a succession of biphasic responses that follow smoothly one upon the other, e.g., an experienced subject moving a joy stick in response to simple low-frequency sinusoidal inputs or in maintaining a constant rate in handwheel-cranking tasks.

One advantage of a task with discretely presented stimuli is that it may permit better control of some classes of variables than that permitted by serial or continuous tasks. A number of variables have been found to affect responses to discrete stimuli. These include (1) rate and amplitude of movement; (2) the accuracy required in rate of movement or in point of termination of movement; (3) direction of movement; (4) number of alternative stimuli that might occur; (5) knowledge of results; (6) such physical constants in a control as its mass, spring stiffness, and viscous damping; (7) whether or not a "ready" signal is given; (8) the time between a ready signal and the stimulation; (9) the amount of practice; and (10) the compatibility of the stimuli and the responses. The following studies have employed discrete tasks: Davis, (1957), Marill, (1957), Vince, (1948), Welford, (1952).

INDEPENDENT VARIABLES

There are a large number of task, procedural, and intrasubject variables that affect performance. A few of these will be described here.

The subject's display

Most studies in the area of motor skills have employed visual displays, and our discussion will be limited to these. In tracking tasks it is important to specify the display in terms of *pursuit* versus *compensatory tracking*. In pursuit tracking both the target and the cursor move back and forth, and the operator must keep the cursor "on target." In compensatory tracking only the cursor moves; the target remains in a fixed position (e.g., in auto driving the 60-mph mark is the target, while the speed-indicator needle is the cursor that the driver wishes to maintain on the target). The difference between the target and the cursor reflects the amount of tracking error in both types of display. In pursuit tracking, the subject obtains information about tracking error and direct information about the target course by observation of the movements of the target. In compensatory tracking, the subject does not receive direct information about the target course as he attempts to track the target, nor does he receive direct information concerning his response output in pursuit tracking, because the movements of the cursor about the target reflect error as well as the output of the subject's control. Generally, a pursuit display results in better performance than a compensatory display (Chernikoff, Birmingham, and Taylor, 1955; Conklin, 1957; Hartman and Fitts, 1955; Notterman and Page, 1962). The exception to this rule seems to come from *aided tracking* or *rate tracking,* and then only when the target course has a very low frequency (Chernikoff and Taylor, 1957).

An important consideration in any display is *compatibility.* Stimuli are always coded in some form, e.g., written or spoken language, mathematical symbols, musical notation, movements of a line on an oscilloscope, or lights turning on and off. Similarly, the choice of a particular mode of responding may also be thought of as a code. An individual writes, speaks, or makes certain types of motion such as steering an automobile, dancing, or moving a joy stick back and forth in a tracking task. These response codes are, strictly speaking, never identical to the stimulus code, and this raises the question of whether different combinations of codes play a role in determining performance. When the task involves reactions to two or more types of stimulus code, the question is one of stimulus-stimulus (S-S) compatibility, e.g., listening to spoken language and simultaneously observing the same words displayed as changes of a signal on an oscilloscope, or comparing new terrain with a map. Similarly, when more than one response code is used in tasks, e.g., manipulating a steering wheel with the hands while simultaneously depressing the brake or moving one control with the left hand to effect vertical movement of a cursor while simultaneously manipulating another control with the right hand to effect horizontal movement, the question is one of response-response (R-R) compatibility. Stimulus-response (S-R) compatibility involves a particular combination of a stimulus and a response code; e.g., in the United States a light switch ordinarily is off when in the down position and on when in the up position. The reverse is true in England. Apparently through learning, a combination of S-R codes that is compatible for us is incompatible for people living in England, and vice versa. Most experimental work has dealt with S-R compatibility and has indicated that performance is primarily a function of the *combined* S-R code rather than a particular stimulus or response code. A stimulus code that works well with one response code may be highly inefficient when used with another response (Fitts and Deininger, 1954; Kay, 1954; Morin and Grant, 1955). The effects of differences of S-R compatibility may persist for some time (Garvey and Knowles, 1954).

Input signal

In continuous tracking tasks, it is highly important to specify the frequency characteristics of the input signal. Performance in response to continuous signals becomes progressively poorer as signal frequency is increased (Chernikoff and Taylor, 1957; Ellson and Gray, 1948; Hartman, 1957; Noble, Fitts, and Warren, 1955). This is an important consideration in comparing tasks in which the input signals do not have identical frequency characteristics. Other things being equal, one would not expect performance to be as good when responding to a complex sinusoidal signal composed of a 2-cpm plus a 4-cpm sine wave as when responding to a complex sinusoidal signal composed of a 1-cpm plus a 2-cpm sine wave. Similarly, the frequency characteristics of different random signal inputs are important determiners of performance.

The coherence of the input is another important consideration. Signal coherence determines the probability with which the value of a signal at some future moment in time can be specified. Simple or complex sinusoidal inputs (or other periodic signals) and constant-velocity signals (or other aperiodic signals) are completely coherent; i.e., it is possible to specify exactly what the value of such a signal will be at any moment of time. When a periodic or an aperiodic signal has a certain amount of noise associated with it, the amount of coherence is somewhere between zero and maximum. Experimenters frequently find a considerable amount of noise associated with input signals in tasks of all kinds. In many cases in which supposedly random signal inputs are employed, the coherence of the signal is somewhat greater than zero. For example, in continuous tracking tasks when random signals are employed, it is customary to filter out higher frequencies. Since the higher frequencies have been filtered out, the continuous signal goes from one position or amplitude to another rather slowly. This in turn means that certain amplitude values can be excluded from consideration in attempts to specify the value of the signal at a slightly later moment. Thus, it is possible, if the value of a signal at some given moment of time is known, to specify on a probability basis the value of a signal for some short time into the future. It is customary, when continuous random signal inputs are used, to generate signals that have a normal

(Gaussian) distribution of amplitudes. These distributions are truncated so that values greater than a given distance from the mean amplitude cannot occur. These constraints also lead to a signal coherence greater than zero.

Relatively little work has been done regarding the effects of degree of signal coherence in the kinds of motor task being considered here. Adams and his associates (Adams and Chambers, 1962; Adams and Creamer, 1962a, 1962b; Adams and Xhignesse, 1960) have found that anticipatory timing is an important factor in some tasks, as have Bartlett (1958), Conrad (1951), and Leonard (1953). Thus, one should expect that in a task having an intermediate degree of signal coherence with respect to spatial position but completely coherent with respect to temporal aspects, the timing of one's responses would be quite important. This expectation was borne out in a study by Trumbo, Noble, Cross, and Ulrich (1965) that involved tracking an irregular step-function input.

In studies in which the input signal is degraded by the addition of random noise to a coherent signal, marked impairment of performance was found (Briggs and Fitts, 1956; Briggs, Fitts, and Bahrick, 1957). The data strongly suggest that it is important to specify signal coherence as well as other properties of the input (Hyman, 1953; Poulton, 1957). Studies of speed and load stress (Conrad, 1951, 1954, 1955; Wagner, Fitts, and Noble, 1954) and those on advance information (Leonard, 1953) indicate that the number of separate signal channels in a display, the rate at which the signals are arriving, and the amount of time available for the subject to prepare for the required response should be specified along with such variables as coherence and compatibility.

Response characteristics

There are a number of factors related to the nature of the response made by the subject in a motor task that are important determiners of performance and hence should be specified. Consideration of qualitative and quantitative indicants of performance makes it clear that the specification of the subject's response may be a limiting factor in some situations. In addition, the fact that feedback from proprioceptive stimulation arises from the movements of the subject means that factors which determine proprioceptive feedback should be specified. One class of variables that affects proprioceptive feedback comes from the loadings of the subject's control. The forces required to move any control, and the control forces acting upon the subject's limb, can be specified as a function of four physical properties, or control loadings: (1) mass, (2) viscosity, (3) elasticity, and (4) coulomb friction. It has been shown several times that variation in control loadings has an effect upon performance, probably because of (1) an interaction among resulting changes in kinesthetic discriminability, (2) amount of work involved in making the movement, and (3) the mechanical effects upon the pattern of movement in time and space (Adams and Creamer, 1962b; Bahrick, 1957; Bahrick, Bennett, and Fitts, 1955; Bahrick, Fitts, and Schneider, 1955; Howland and Noble, 1953; Weiss, 1954).

Procedural variables

The *intertrial interval* is an important determiner of performance and must be specified carefully, but no simple statement of the relationship between intertrial interval and motor task performance is possible. Many investigators employ intertrial intervals of 20 to 60 seconds, unless they desire to mass practice, in which case intertrial intervals of less than 15 seconds are ordinarily used.

The effects of *work loading* and *trial duration* have not been studied as much as intertrial interval, and it is even more difficult to provide any rules concerning these variables. With continuous tasks, and many serial tasks, performance suffers if trial duration is longer than approximately 60 seconds, although sometimes it is possible to use somewhat longer trial durations. It is sometimes wise not to score the first seconds of a trial. Because of the nature of the task, the subject's initial performance may be poor. For example, in a tracking task, the subject might be instructed to center his control during the intertrial interval and if, at the beginning of the trial, the target suddenly appears some distance away from the center, there will necessarily be large error, initially. In some instances there are also several temporary decremental and incremental factors in the early portion of a trial (see Bilodeau and Bilodeau, 1961, and Adams, 1964, for a summary of this literature).

Some investigators have found very little effect in variation of instructions. In the absence of more definitive information, it may be assumed that instructions are most important in situations where the manner in which the subject structures the task plays an important role in determining his performance. For example, if the task is to track a coherent signal that has noise superimposed upon it, it may be important to tell the subject that he is to attempt to track only the coherent portion of the signal or the noisy portion of the signal as well as the coherent portion. Similarly, in tracking a complex step-function input signal, unless specific instructions are given, some subjects will consistently lag behind the target in order that they may be more sure of not moving in the wrong direction or may have gross errors in the amplitude of their initial movements. In the same situation, other subjects will attempt to time their responses so that their movements coincide in time with the movement of the target and will pay less attention to the accuracy of the initial portion of their response in direction and extent. This difference in strategy can have a very important effect upon performance.

It is important to specify whether serial tasks are *self-paced* or *forced-paced*, e.g., whether the subject determines the rate of responding or whether this is set by a predetermined program. In most instances performance will be superior when the task is self-paced (Alluisi and Muller, 1956; Knowles, Garvey, and Newlin, 1953). If the task is forced-paced, it is important to specify whether there is a single, constant time interval between successive responses or a more complex, but repetitive, sequence of time intervals. If a complex, repetitive sequence of time intervals is employed, performance appears to deteriorate rapidly as other aspects of the task become more uncertain.

Finally, there is a considerable amount of evidence indicating that the immediate stimulus, the background stimuli, and the effects of previous experience combine to determine an adaptation level (Helson, 1964). The range effect (Ellson and Coppock, 1951; Ellson and Wheeler, 1949; Slack, 1953; Weiss, 1955) is one illustration of this in motor tasks.

APPARATUS

A wide variety of apparatuses are used, ranging from mirror drawing equipment to complex electronic tracking apparatus. There is no standard list of such apparatuses to recommend. The kind of apparatus to obtain when setting up a laboratory depends upon (1) specific research interests, (2) the amount of money available, and (3) the availability of good electronics specialists for the design and maintenance of the apparatus. An electronic tracking system, including programming devices, displays and controls, scoring devices, and data storage units, can easily cost thousands of dollars, although it is possible to construct a highly simplified tracking apparatus for a few hundred dollars. For the main part, assembled apparatus to study motor skill is not readily available as a stock item of commercial sources. In most cases the apparatus is designed and the components assembled in the shop of the laboratory employing it. Exceptions include the rotary pursuit and paper pulls. Various types of continuous tracking apparatus have been described in the literature (Adams and Xhignesse, 1960; Chernikoff and Taylor, 1957; Hartman and Wetherbee, 1956; Helson, 1949; Lincoln and Smith, 1952; Poulton, 1952; Trumbo et al., 1963; Warren, Fontaine, and Clark, 1952). A simplified and relatively inexpensive tracking apparatus is described by Gain and Fitts (1959). Melton (1947) describes several apparatus tests, including the two-hand coordinator. Other important devices include the star discrimeter (Duncan, 1955). The dial trainer (Bilodeau and Rosenquist, 1963), the manual lever (Sulzer, 1963), the multiple-serial discrimeter (Morin and Grant, 1959), the mathometer (C. E. Noble and Farese, 1959), the serial discrimeter (Alluisi, Muller, and Fitts, 1957), and closed-circuit television (Smith and Smith, 1962).

Some of the problems associated with qualitative and quantitative analyses of motor performance suggest the limitations of several of these apparatuses. The rotary pursuit, for example, consists essentially of a turntable (like the turntable of a phonograph) with a relatively small circular target located near the periphery. The task of the subject is to maintain a hinged stylus on the target as the turntable moves around. Performance is customarily determined in terms of the amount of time during the trial that the stylus is in contact with the target. Our earlier discussion covering quantitative analyses indicates some important limitations associated with time-on-target scores. In addition, a consideration of the independent variables affecting motor skill performance make it obvious that there are severe limitations with respect to the input variables that can be studied with this apparatus. The only task variables that are easily varied are rate of target movement and target size. It is possible to vary the pattern of the target course, but this is difficult to do quickly and easily in any systematic fashion. It is this lack of flexibility with scoring and with the kinds of

independent variables that can be studied that has led to a decline in the use of the rotary pursuit as a research instrument. Similar limitations occur with several of the other devices listed above.

Considerations such as those just discussed, together with the fact that different groups of investigators have been interested in quite different problems, have led to the proliferation of apparatuses. If one is interested in discrete responses and also wishes to study the time course of the responses, perhaps the simplest device is a paper pull (Poulton, 1952). The target course is put onto a roll of paper and pulled past a slot that permits the subject to see the target. The task of the subject is to attempt to keep a pencil or other simple control on the target. Usually the paper is pulled at a constant rate, and the width of the viewing slot is held at some predetermined distance. The target course, when discrete responses are being studied, consists of a series of abrupt changes in position of the target. A paper pull can be used also to study serial and continuous responses. Such a device permits detailed observation of the subject's responses and is relatively inexpensive and easy to maintain. Its chief disadvantages stem from the large amount of time that must be spent in preparing the tapes and in scoring the records. For this reason other devices are usually employed.

If great flexibility is important, the best solution is to construct an electronic system. An experimenter should recognize, however, that they are expensive to build and require maintenance by skilled electronics technicians. Electronic equipment of this sort is not readily available as a complete system from commercial sources. The required components (oscilloscopes, operational amplifiers, data recording and storage devices, meters, relays, transistors, resistors, and capacitors) must be purchased and put together to provide a complete system. Since new electronic products come on the market constantly, it is well to consult with electronics engineers before obtaining components specified in one of the electronic systems referred to above, in order that obsolete components can be replaced by better ones (see Appendix).

REFERENCES

ADAMS, J. A. Motor skills. *Ann. Rev. Psychol.,* 1964, **15**, 181–202.

ADAMS, J. A., and CHAMBERS, R. W. Response to simultaneous stimulation of two sense modalities. *J. exp. Psychol.,* 1962, **63**, 198–206.

ADAMS, J. A., and CREAMER, L. R. Data processing capabilities of the human operator. *J. Eng. Psychol.,* 1962a, **1**, 150–153.

ADAMS, J. A., and CREAMER, L. R. Proprioception variables as determiners of anticipatory timing behavior. *Human Factors,* 1962b, **4**, 217–222.

ADAMS, J. A., and XHIGNESSE, L. V. Some determinants of two-dimensional visual tracking behavior. *J. exp. Psychol.,* 1960, **60**, 391–403.

ALLUISI, E. A., and MULLER, P. F. Rate of information transmission with seven symbolic codes: Motor and verbal responses. *USAF WADC Tech. Rep. 56-226,* 1956.

ALLUISI, E. A., MULLER, P. F., and FITTS, P. M. An information analysis of verbal and motor responses in a forced-paced serial task. *J. exp. Psychol.,* 1957, **53**, 153–158.

ARCHER, E. J., KENT, G. W., and MOTE, F. A. Effect of long-term practice and time-on-target information feedback on a complex tracking task. *J. exp. Psychol.,* 1956, **51**, 103–112.

BAHRICK, H. P. An analysis of stimulus variables influencing the proprioceptive control of movements. *Psychol. Rev.,* 1957, **64**, 324–328.

BAHRICK, H. P., BENNETT, W. F., and FITTS, P. M. Accuracy of positioning responses as a function of spring loading in a control. *J. exp. Psychol.,* 1955, **49**, 437–444.

BAHRICK, H. P., FITTS, P. M., and BRIGGS, G. E. Learning curves—facts or artifacts? *Psychol. Bull.,* 1957, **54**, 256–268.

BAHRICK, H. P., FITTS, P. M., and SCHNEIDER, R. Reproduction of simple movements as a function of factors influencing proprioceptive feedback. *J. exp. Psychol.,* 1955, **59**, 445–454.

BAHRICK, H. P., and NOBLE, M. E. On stimulus and response discriminability. *J. exp. Psychol.,* 1961, **61**, 449–454.

BARNES, R. M. *Motion and time study.* (4th ed.). New York: Wiley, 1958.

BARTLETT, F. *Thinking: An experimental and social study.* London: G. Allen, 1958.

BILODEAU, E. A., and BILODEAU, I. M. Motor-skills learning. *Ann. Rev. Psychol.,* 1961, **12**, 243–280.

BILODEAU, E. A., and LEVY, C. M. Long-term memory as a function of retention time and other conditions of training and recall. *Psychol. Rev.,* 1964, **71**, 27–41.

BILODEAU, E. A., and ROSENQUIST, H. R. A simple skills device for research on learning and memory. *Percept. mot. Skills,* 1963, **16**, 521–524.

BILODEAU, E. A., SULZER, J. L., and LEVY, C. M. Theory and data on the interrelationships of three factors of memory. *Psychol. Monogr.,* 1962, **76**, No. 20 (Whole No. 539).

BRIGGS, G. E., and FITTS, P. M. Tracking proficiency as a function of visual noise in the feedback loop of a simulated radar fire control system. *USAF Personnel Train. Res. Center TN-56-134,* 1956.

BRIGGS, G. E., FITTS, P. M., and BAHRICK, H. P. Learning and performance in a complex tracking task as a function of visual noise. *J. exp. Psychol.,* 1957, **53**, 379–487.

BROWN, J. S., and JENKINS, W. O. An analysis of human motor abilities related to the design of equipment and a suggested program of research. In P. M. Fitts (Ed.), *Psychological research on equipment design.* Washington, D.C.: U.S. Government Printing Office, 1947.

CHERNIKOFF, R., BIRMINGHAM, H. P., and TAYLOR, F. V. A comparison of pursuit and compensatory tracking under conditions of aiding and no aiding. *J. exp. Psychol.,* 1955, **49**, 55–59.

CHERNIKOFF, R., and TAYLOR, F. V. Effects of course frequency and aided time constant on pursuit and compensatory tracking. *J. exp. Psychol.,* 1957, **53**, 285–292.

CLARK, J. R., FONTAINE, A. B., and WARREN, C. E. The generation of continuous random signals for use in human tracking studies. *USAF HRRC Res. Bull. 53-40,* 1953.

CONKLIN, J. E. Effect of control lag on performance in a tracking task. *J. exp. Psychol.,* 1957, **53**, 261–268.

CONRAD, R. Speed and load stress in a sensorimotor skill. *Brit. J. industr. Med.,* 1951, **8**, 1–7.

CONRAD, R. Speed stress. In W. F. Floyd and A. T. Welford (Eds.), *Human factors in equipment design.* London: Lewis, 1954. Pp. 95–102.

CONRAD, R. Some effects on performance of changes in perceptual load. *J. exp. Psychol.,* 1955, **49**, 313–322.

CROSSMAN, E. R. W. The information capacity of

the human motor system in pursuit tracking. *Quart. J. exp. Psychol.*, 1960, **12**, 1–16.

DAVIS, R. The human operator as a single-channel information system. *Quart. J. exp. Psychol.*, 1957, **9**, 119–120.

DUNCAN, C. P. Development of response generalization gradients. *J. exp. Psychol.*, 1955, **50**, 26–30.

ELLSON, D. G., and COPPOCK, H. Further analysis of the psychological range effect. *USAF WADC Tech. Rep. 6012*, 1951.

ELLSON, D. G., and GRAY, F. E. Frequency responses of human operators following a sine wave input. *USAF Memo, Rep. MCREXD-694-2N*, 1948.

ELLSON, D. G., and WHEELER, L. The range effect. *USAF Tech. Rep. 5813*, 1949.

FELLER, W. *Probability theory and its applications.* New York: Wiley, 1950.

FITTS, P. M. The information capacity of the human motor system in controlling the amplitude of movement. *J. exp. Psychol.*, 1954, **47**, 381–391.

FITTS, P. M., BAHRICK, H. P., NOBLE, M. E., and BRIGGS, G. E. Skilled performance. *USAF WADC Final Rep., Contract AF 41(657)-70 Project 7707*, 1959.

FITTS, P. M., and DEININGER, R. L. S-R compatibility: Correspondence among paired elements within stimulus and response codes. *J. exp. Psychol.*, 1954, **48**, 483–492.

FLEISHMAN, E. A., and FRUCHTER, B. Factor structure and predictability of successive stages of learning Morse Code. *J. appl. Psychol.*, 1960, **44**, 97–101.

FLEISHMAN, E. A., and HEMPEL, W. E., JR. Factorial analyses of complex psychomotor performance. *USAF Personnel Train. Res. Center TR-54-12*, 1954.

FRUCHTER, B. *Introduction to factor analysis.* Princeton, N.J.: Van Nostrand, 1954.

GAIN, P., and FITTS, P. M. A simplified electronic tracking apparatus (SETA). *USAF WADC Tech. Rep. 59-44*, 1959.

GARNER, R. G. *Uncertainty and structure as psychological concepts.* New York. Wiley, 1962.

GARVEY, W. D., and KNOWLES, W. B. Response time patterns associated with various display-control relationships. *J. exp. Psychol.*, 1954, **47**, 315–322.

HARTMAN, B. O. The effect of target frequency on pursuit tracking. *USA Med. Res. Lab. Rep. 263*, 1957.

HARTMAN, B. O., and FITTS, P. M. Relation of stimulus and response amplitude to tracking performance. *J. exp. Psychol.*, 1955, **49**, 82–92.

HARTMAN, B. O., and WETHERBEE, J. E. "Beta"— a special purpose computer for studies in the human control of complex equipment. *USA Med. Res. Lab. Rep. 236*, 1956.

HELSON, H. Design of equipment and optimal human operation. *Amer. J. Psychol.*, 1949, **62**, 473–479.

HELSON, H. *Adaptation-level theory: An experimental and systematic approach to behavior.* New York: Harper & Row, 1964.

HOWLAND, D., and NOBLE, M. E. The effect of physical constants of a control on tracking performance. *J. exp. Psychol.*, 1953, **46**, 353–360.

HYMAN, R. Stimulus information as a determinant of reaction time. *J. exp. Psychol.*, 1953, **45**, 188–196.

KAY, H. The effects of position in a display upon problem solving. *Quart. J. exp. Psychol.*, 1954, **6**, 155–169.

KNOWLES, W. B., GARVEY, W. D., and NEWLIN, E. P. The effect of speed and load on display-control relationships. *J. exp. Psychol.*, 1953, **46**, 65–75.

LEONARD, J. A. Advance information in sensorimotor skills. *Quart. J. exp. Psychol.*, 1953, **5**, 141–149.

LINCOLN, R. W. Rate accuracy in handwheel tracking. *J. appl. Psychol.*, 1954, **38**, 195–201.

LINCOLN, R. S., and SMITH, K. U. Systematic analysis of factors determining accuracy in visual tracking. *Science*, 1952, **116**, 183–187.

MCRUER, D. T., and KRENDEL, E. S. The human operator as a servo system element. *J. Franklin Inst.*, 1959, **267**, 1–49.

MARILL, T. The psychological refractory phase. *Brit. J. Psychol.*, 1957, **48**, 93–97.

MEISTERLING, W. Geschichte der Untersuchung der Koordination. *Arch. ges. Psychol.*, 1931, **80**, 517–554.

MELTON, A. W. The methodology of experimental studies of human learning and retention. I. The functions of a methodology and the available criteria for evaluating different experimental methods. *Psychol. Bull.*, 1936, **33**, 305–394.

MELTON, A. W. (Ed.) *Apparatus tests.* Washington, D.C.: Government Printing Office, 1947.

MORIN, R. E., and GRANT, D. A. Learning and performance of a keypressing task as a function of the degree of spatial stimulus-response correspondence. *J. exp. Psychol.*, 1955, **49**, 39–47.

NOBLE, C. E., and FARESE, F. J. An apparatus for research in human selective learning. *J. Psychol.*, 1955, **39**, 475–484.

NOBLE, M. E., and BAHRICK, H. P. Response generalization as a function of intratask response similarity. *J. exp. Psychol.*, 1956, **51**, 405–412.

NOBLE, M. E., FITTS, P. M., and WARREN, C. E.

The frequency response of skilled subjects in a pursuit tracking task. *J. exp. Psychol.*, 1955, **49**, 248–256.

NOTTERMAN, J. M., and PAGE, D. E. Evaluation of mathematically equivalent tracking systems. *Percept. mot. Skills, Monogr. Suppl.* 8–V15, 1962, 683–716.

PETERS, C. C., and VAN VOORHIS, W. R. *Statistical procedures and their mathematical bases.* New York: McGraw-Hill, 1940.

POULTON, E. C. Perceptual anticipation in tracking with two-pointer and one-pointer displays. *Brit. J. Psychol.*, 1952, **43**, 222–229.

POULTON, E. C. Learning the statistical properties of the input in pursuit tracking. *J. exp. Psychol.*, 1957, **54**, 28–32.

POULTON, E. C. On simple methods of scoring tracking error. *Psychol. Bull.*, 1962, **59**, 320–328.

SEASHORE, R. H., DUDEK, F. J., and HOLTZMAN, W. A factorial analysis of arm-hand precision tests. *J. appl. Psychol.*, 1949, **33**, 579–584.

SLACK, C. W. Some characteristics of the range effect, *J. exp. Psychol.*, 1953, **46**, 76–80.

SMITH, K. U., and SMITH, W. M. *Perception and motion.* Philadelphia: Saunders, 1962.

STEVENS, S. S. (Ed.) *Handbook of experimental psychology.* New York: Wiley, 1951.

SULZER, J. L. Manual level D: A basic psychomotor apparatus for the study of feedback. *Percept. mot. Skills*, 1963, **16**, 859–862.

TRUMBO, D. A., ESLINGER, R. C., NOBLE, M. E., and CROSS, K. E. A versatile electronic tracking apparatus (veta). *Percept. mot. Skills*, 1963, **16**, 649–656.

TRUMBO, D., NOBLE, M., and BAGANOFF, F. Analog computer methods for scoring continuous performance records, *Percept. mot. Skills*, in press.

TRUMBO, D., NOBLE, M., CROSS, K., and ULRICH, L. Task predictability in the organization, acquisition, and retention of tracking skill. *J. exp. Psychol.*, 1965, **70**, 252–263.

VINCE, M. A. Corrective movement in a pursuit task. *Quart. J. exp. Psychol.*, 1948, **1**, 85–103.

WAGNER, R. C., FITTS, P. M., and NOBLE, M. E. Preliminary investigations of speed and load as dimensions of psychomotor tasks. *USAF Personnel Train. Res. Center Tech. Rep. 54-45*, 1954.

WARREN, C. E., FONTAINE, A. B., and CLARK, J. R. A two-dimensional electronic pursuit apparatus. *USAF HRRC RB 52-26*, 1952.

WEBBER, C. E., and ADAMS, J. A. Issues in the use of an analog-digital data system for the measurement of tracking behavior. *USAF Office of Scientific Res. TN-59-528*, 1960.

WEISS, B. The role of proprioceptive feedback in positioning responses. *J. exp. Psychol.*, 1954, **47**, 215–224.

WEISS, B. Movement error, pressure variation, and the range effect. *J. exp. Psychol.*, 1955, **50**, 191–196.

WELFORD, A. T. The "psychological refractory period" and the timing of high-speed performance: A review and a theory. *Brit. J. Psychol.*, 1952, **43**, 2–19.

WOODWORTH, R. S. *Dynamics of behavior.* New York: Holt, 1958.

Part Six

COMPUTERS

Psychologists have used the high-speed and high-capacity characteristics of modern computers for a number of research purposes including data analysis, simulation, and problem solving. The first chapter in this section, therefore, presents a detailed example of analog-computer utilization in the study of tracking skills, along with methods of analog quantification; the last chapter covers applications of digital computers in behavioral research and provides specific information on the use of computer facilities.

Although both machines are capable of accepting information, processing it, and then delivering it in a useful form, their physical characteristics are very different. The general-purpose analog computer is a combination simulator and calculator consisting of a number of computing elements that enable the machine to perform mathematical operations instantaneously and in a continuous manner. These operations are executed by mechanically interconnecting the inputs and outputs of amplifiers, potentiometers, function generators, capacitors, and multipliers in various ways on a problem board or patch panel. Interconnecting a resistor to a feedback-amplifier circuit, for example, results in a summing operation under certain functional conditions; if a capacitor is connected to the amplifier, an integrating operation takes place. Arbitrary scale factors relate the computer voltages to the problem variables so that a machine with components designed to operate within an output voltage range of 100 volts has all computer variables scaled to fall within this range; e.g., a tracking study utilizing a control stick displacement range of 0 to 10 inches would have the displacement variable represented in the computer by a voltage range of 0 to $+100$

V, a scale factor of 10 volts per inch. Thus, continuous voltages represent various input variables, the continuous outputs being led to an oscilloscope, a plotter, or an analog-to-digital converter. Although the classical analog computer can solve various problems and simulate any number of systems, it generally cannot be programmed to make logical decisions.

The digital computer makes logical decisions and performs arithmetic operations on the basis of instructions entered into the machine in the form of a coded program. Proceeding in discrete rather than continuous steps (it deals with pulsed data), the computer utilizes instructions stored in memory to control its own operations, e.g., to act upon data entered into the machine for computation. The result of a computation is not presented instantaneously, as it is with the analog computer, since it takes time for the machine to count electrical pulses representing binary digits. This time lag, however, may be in millionths of a second or faster, enabling the machine to perform logical operations and process data with exceptional speed.

A hybrid computer system combines the accuracy of the digital machine with the speed of the analog. The operations of a hybrid can be controlled by a stored program, a patch panel program, or both; the values represented can be either or both; and the organization may be sequential or parallel. This allows for effective simulation of physiological systems or the high-speed real-time reduction of physiological signals, and can be applied to studies of pattern recognition, complex motor skills, or training problems. In each application, an analog input or output is generally necessary, data sampling rates are high, data storage is required, and a flexible stored program operation may be desirable. Although the hybrid category includes the analog computer with digital logic added, the digital computer with analog elements added, and the digital computer linked to an analog computer, the "true hybrid" consists of an analog/digital system in which neither computer is intended for independent use (Hagan, 1965).

Further discussions of computer operations and a description of various types of computer installations are presented in Chap. 18, Digital Computers. Fliege also provides information on general programming, program libraries, and methods for formulating problems in a way that technical computer personnel will understand. Sections on computer utilization economics and the advantages and disadvantages of computers in research conclude a chapter that provides general coverage of a rapidly changing area. Many computers in current use are being replaced by newer systems. Also, manufacturers are emphasizing the development of software (e.g., basic and expanded assemblers, efficient compilers, and monitor or executive systems which oversee the operation of both software and hardware), an area which in the past has been heavily dependent upon the contributions of users.

Refer to Green (1963) for additional information on digital-computer technology in the behavioral sciences and to Feigenbaum and Feldman (1963) for a collection of readings on artificial intelligence and the computer simulation of human thought. Tomkins and Messick (1963) present a number of articles covering the simulation of personality; Coe (1964) and McWhinney (1964) report the computer simulation of conflict interference and aggression, and social communication networks, respectively. Programs for data analysis may be found in Dixon (1964) and in various journal articles; e.g., see the IBM 7090 FORTRAN program for one-through four-way analysis of variance presented by Sorkin, Enenstein, Grannitrapani, and Darrow (1964), or the three-variable Chi-Square Analysis by Stanners (1965). Useful programs are also available from computer installations. But a survey of programmed instruction materials for computer programming may interest those seeking a relatively simple introduction to FORTRAN or COBOL (Silvern, 1965). Note that Computers and Automation annually publishes a directory and buyer's guide that lists college and university computer centers, descriptions of their facilities, various consulting services, the addresses of most commercial firms in the computer field, and updated sale and rental prices of products. Medical Electronic News (1964) reports numerous biomedical applications of analog and digital computers and references the installation making each application. Refer to the Appendix for an abridged list of computer and accessory equipment suppliers of use in the behavioral sciences.

Chapter 17

ANALOG COMPUTERS

GEORGE E. BRIGGS

Laboratory instrumentation represents an evolutionary process in any field of science: there are relatively few dramatic changes or "breakthroughs" in the tools of the scientist. In the area of perceptual-motor skill research, the rotary-pursuit apparatus has been a stock item for over forty years since Koerth first described the device as a tool for the study of eye-hand coordination (1922). In skill measurement, we see the conservative evolution of techniques employed to quantify performance: time-on-target scores originated with the rotary-pursuit device and remained the "standard" metric for tracking performance until only recently when Bahrick, Fitts, and Briggs (1957) demonstrated the presence of measurement artifacts in such scores. This use of traditional research equipment and standard performance metrics provides for comparability of current research with the background of previously generated information. There are times when a break with past techniques is necessary, and it is such a breakthrough in instrumentation that is described in this chapter.

The direct-coupled (d-c) amplifier, or, as it is sometimes called, the operational amplifier, is the key to this accelerated phase in equipment development. This device has risen from its early development in the 1920s to become the critical component in modern analog computers. Essentially, the analog computer consists of a set of d-c amplifiers with a regulated power supply, resistors, capacitors, diodes, and a problem board. The last-named provides for the interconnections of the several amplifiers so that a number of operations can be performed on input signals. Some of the operations most commonly performed with an analog computer are shown in Fig. 17-1. These operations are all approximations. In amplification, the output voltage e_o is approximately equal to Ke_i, where K is determined by the ratio of the feedback resistor R_F to the input resistor R_i and e_i is an input voltage. Actually, this approximation can be made very close, as now will be shown.

The fundamental characteristic that permits us to write the equations in Fig. 17-1 is that the input (grid) of the d-c amplifier draws no current, and the current flowing through the *input resistor* equals that in the *feedback resistor* from Kirchhoff's law. From Fig. 17-2, then,

$$i_1 = i_2 \qquad (17\text{-}1)$$

Applying Ohm's law, we note that

$$i_1 = \frac{e_i - e_g}{R_i} \qquad (17\text{-}2)$$

and

$$i_2 = \frac{e_g - e_o}{R_F} \qquad (17\text{-}3)$$

679

OPERATION	SCHEMATIC	TRANSFER FUNCTION
AMPLIFICATION	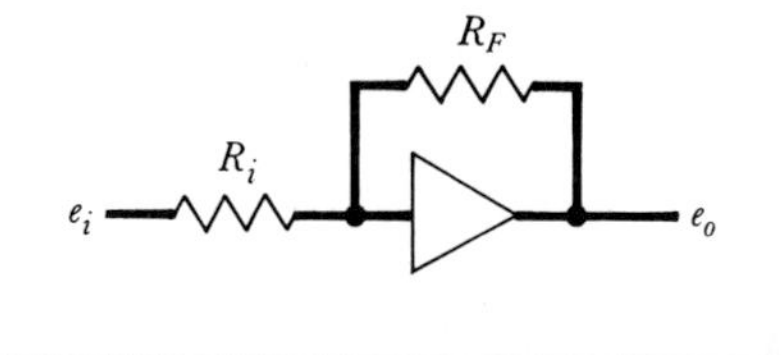 R_F / R_i / e_i — e_o	$e_o \doteq - \dfrac{R_F}{R_i} e_i$
SUMMATION	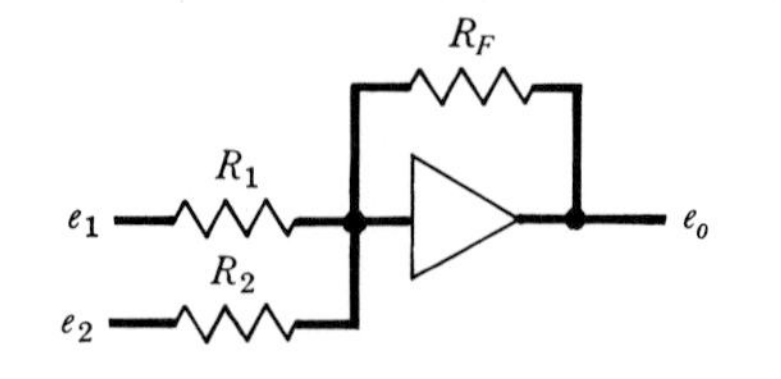 R_F / R_1 / e_1 / R_2 / e_2 — e_o	$e_o \doteq - \left[\dfrac{R_F}{R_1} e_1 + \dfrac{R_F}{R_2} e_2 \right]$
INTEGRATION	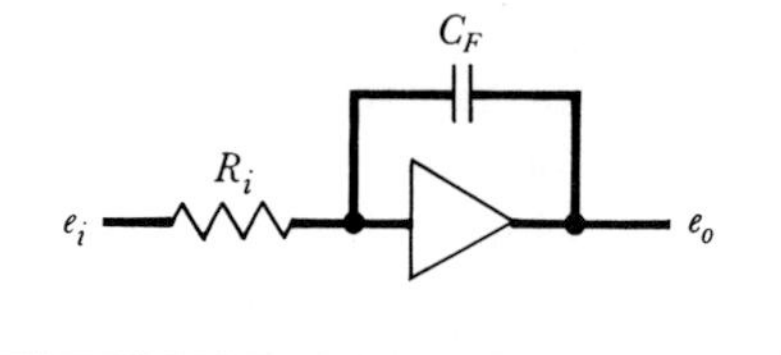 C_F / R_i / e_i — e_o	$e_o \doteq - \dfrac{1}{R_i C_F} \int e_i \, dt$
DIFFERENTIATION	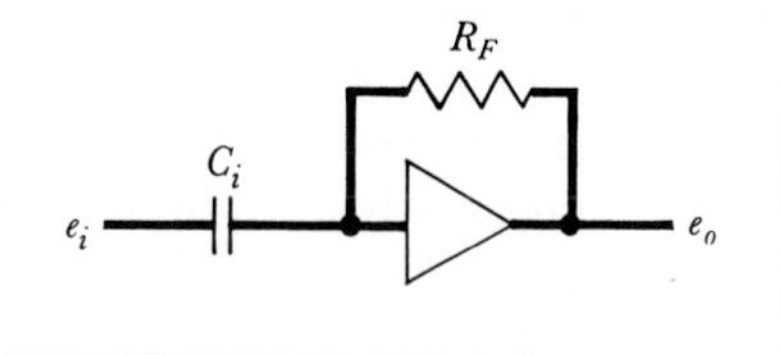 R_F / C_i / e_i — e_o	$e_o \doteq - R_F C_i \dfrac{de_i}{dt}$

—/\/\/— RESISTOR   —||— CAPACITOR   ▷ D-C AMPLIFIER

e_i INPUT e_o OUTPUT

Fig. 17-1   Some common operations performed by the d-c amplifier.

Since the open-loop gain (the gain when there is no feedback resistor) is some quantity A,[1] we further note that

$$e_o = Ae_g \qquad (17\text{-}4)$$

Substituting the identities specified by Eqs. (17-2), and (17-3) into Eq. (17-1),

$$\frac{e_i - e_g}{R_i} = \frac{e_g - e_o}{R_F} \qquad (17\text{-}5)$$

[1] A is built into a d-c amplifier by the manufacturer. This value is always available from the technical specifications of an analog computer.

and from Eq. (17-4) we may further modify Eq. (17-5):

$$\frac{e_i}{R_i} - \frac{e_o}{AR_i} = \frac{e_o}{AR_F} - \frac{e_o}{R_F} \qquad (17\text{-}6)$$

A collection and rearrangement of terms yields

$$e_i = e_o \left(\frac{1}{A} + \frac{R_i}{AR_F} - \frac{R_i}{R_F} \right) \qquad (17\text{-}7)$$

or $\quad e_o = \dfrac{e_i}{1/A(1 + R_i/R_F) - R_i/R_F} \qquad (17\text{-}8)$

If we assume that A is rather large, for example, $A > 30{,}000$, then the quantity

$1/A(1 + R_i/R_F)$ becomes quite small relative to the other terms in Eqs. (17-7) and (17-8) and thus

$$e_o \doteq - \frac{R_F}{R_i} e_i \qquad (17\text{-}9)$$

It is shown, then, that the output voltage e_o can be a close approximation to the input voltage e_i attenuated or amplified by the factor K, where

$$K = \frac{R_F}{R_i}$$

Thus, if R_F is 1 megohm and R_i is 100,000 ohms, then e_o is ten times greater than e_i:

$$e_o = -10e_i$$

It should be noted that a polarity change is indicated for all operations involving the d-c amplifier; i.e., the output is a quantity opposite in sign to the input. For this reason an even number of operational amplifiers usually exists in any circuits in which the polarity of the original signal is to be preserved.

GENERATION OF TRACKING-SYSTEM DYNAMICS

Much of the work on tracking skill has utilized simple positional control or direct linkage between the operator's control device and the controlled element. The rotary-pursuit apparatus is an obvious example. Recently, more complex relations have been inserted between the control device and the controlled element. The operational amplifier provides the critical component in these control dynamics, and Fig. 17-3 illustrates some of the commonly used dynamics. If the input in each case is a step function, as shown, the output voltage as a function of time will vary as indicated.

Exponential lags

Figure 17-4 illustrates how a tracking task may be developed that requires the subject to control through an exponential lag. The flow of information is from left to right starting with a signal generator that provides the system input or forcing function θ_i. Electronic sine-wave generators are quite popular for this purpose. The input, once generated, is displayed to the human operator, a cathode-ray tube (CRT) oscilloscope being a preferred device for the display equipment because of its flexibility and minimal inertia. (The abbreviation CRT is used in this chapter instead of CRO. However, in all instances we are referring to the cathode ray oscilloscope.) One has to make a choice not only of display equipment but also of display mode: pursuit or compensatory or some combination of the pursuit and compensatory modes. In a pursuit display the forcing function affects the position of a target on the CRT, and the operator attempts to keep a cursor on the CRT in coincidence with the moving target; i.e., he pursues the target with the cursor. If a compensatory display is used, there is only one, not two, movable elements on the display, the target appearing as a fixed reference point, and the operator attempts to keep the cursor in coincidence with this fixed reference as the system input forces it away from the target; i.e., the operator attempts to compensate for input-induced movements of the cursor by introducing counteracting signals. A compensatory display is shown in Fig. 17-4. The position of the cursor relative to the fixed target element is determined by system error, which is defined as $\epsilon = \theta_i - \theta_o$. Both the forcing function and the operator's

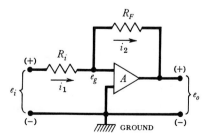

Fig. 17-2 The current and voltage aspects of an operational amplifier.

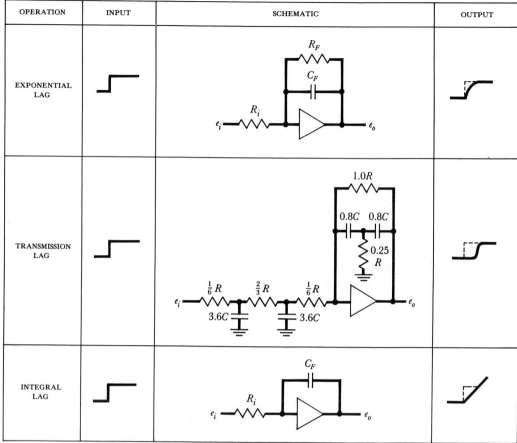

NOTE: POLARITY HAS BEEN IGNORED HERE.

Fig. 17-3   Computer circuits for the three common types of system dynamics.

control actions influence the position of the cursor, but not directly. Their difference, system error, defines the location of the cursor at each point in time.

Once the information appears on the display the operator may observe a discrepancy between target and cursor; i.e., he observes some amount of system error. The operator therefore deflects his control device in an attempt to generate a signal θ_c, which, when acted upon by the exponential lag, will result in a system output θ_o that, hopefully, matches

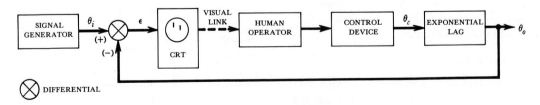

Fig. 17-4   The essential elements of a tracking task including system dynamics (here an exponential lag).

the forcing function θ_i and reduces system error to zero, thereby bringing the cursor on the display into coincidence with the target. The "differential" operation indicated in Fig. 17-4 is nothing more than a summation, as indicated in Fig. 17-2, with the polarities adjusted so that the difference between θ_i and θ_o is obtained.

The circuitry necessary to provide this relatively simple tracking task is shown in Fig. 17-5. The control device is a center-tapped potentiometer with the center tap at ground. The human operator in attempting to stay on target manipulates the arm of the potentiometer, shown as the arrow in Fig. 17-5, thereby generating increasing amounts of voltage (positive or negative, depending upon the direction of arm movement) as the arm is moved away from the null position, ground. This voltage signal is acted upon by the exponential lag, and this in turn is subtracted from the input signal to produce an error signal, which is then displayed via the CRT. Since system error is the basic criterion of performance in most tracking tasks, the same signal going to the display may be picked off and sent to scoring circuits. These operations are described in a later section of this chapter.

During a tracking trial the relays indicated in Fig. 17-5 are closed. They are included in the circuit primarily to permit the experimenter to balance the amplifiers prior to a tracking session. Unless one's analog computer has automatic stabilizing capabilities (this increases the cost), it is necessary to balance the operational amplifiers fairly frequently. The balancing requirement is particularly frequent when temperature changes occur, as during equipment "warm-up." During this operation the experimenter merely adjusts the output to zero volts when the input is grounded through a resistor. This operation removes any constant voltage bias from the system.

The exponential lag in Fig. 17-3 is described as providing an output e_o, which bears the relationship

$$\epsilon_o(s) = \left(\frac{R_F}{R_i} \frac{1}{1 + R_F C_F s} \right) \epsilon_i$$

to the input voltage e_i. In this equation s is a Laplace operator, and the entire formulation is in the Laplace domain. The basic reason for this is convenience. In the time domain one must use calculus and trigonometry to describe and determine various computer arrangements, while in the Laplace

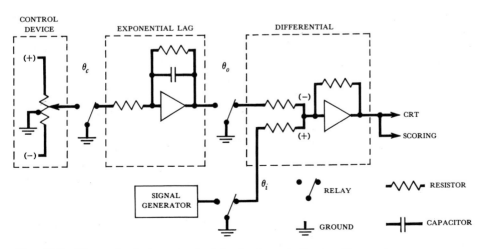

Fig. 17-5 Electronic devices required to implement the tracking system of Fig. 17-4.

domain the rules of algebra are sufficient. The above operation expressed in the notion of the time domain is

$$\epsilon_o(t) = \left[\frac{R_F}{R_i} \left(1 - e^{-t/R_F C_F} \right) \right] \epsilon_i$$

where t is time, and it is obvious that one does indeed have an exponential function of the form e^{-t}. The term R_F/R_i represents d-c gain, and it determines the amount of output voltage that will exist at asymptote. The term $R_F C_F$ is called the time constant of the lag and determines how quickly the output voltage will approach asymptote, for a step function e_i. When inserted between θ_c and θ_o, as in Fig. 17-4, the exponential lag appears or "feels" to the human operator like a sluggish control system, and the degree of sluggishness is a function of the size of the time constant.

It is interesting to note that an ogive or sigmoid lag results when two exponential lags are placed in series. Conklin's dissertation (1957) describes the results of a study in which exponential-lag dynamics were compared with sigmoid lags of various time constants.

Transmission lags

While not commonly used as a system dynamic, transmission lags can be inserted between a control device and the tracking display by utilizing the computer network indicated in Fig. 17-3; i.e., the exponential lag of Fig. 17-5 could be replaced with the appropriate network from Fig. 17-3 to obtain a simple delay lag. Actually, the network for the transmission lag shown in Fig. 17-3 is only an approximation to a pure delay. It is a combination of a pure transmission lag and a sigmoid lag, as indicated in column 4 of Fig. 17-3. The time delay T for the transmission lag is $T = RC$ (sec) following the beginning of the sigmoid. (Engineering convention defines delay time as amount of time for ϵ_o to reach 50 percent of its asymptotic value for a step function ϵ_i, and rise time is defined as the amount of time required for ϵ_o to reach 95 percent of its final value for a step ϵ_i.) A similar dynamic could be obtained by setting up three exponential lags in series; but this is inefficient, as fewer operational amplifiers are used in the network listed in Fig. 17-3.

Integral lags

The most common type of tracking-system dynamic employed in the laboratory involves one or more integral lags. The reason for this is that most real-life systems such as the automobile, the airplane, and the submarine have the equivalent of integral lags between the control device and the system output. Real-life systems are described in part with reference to the number of integral lags between θ_c and θ_o. The system shown in Fig. 17-5 is a zero-order control system since it has no integral lags, while that in Fig. 17-6a is called a second-order system because of the presence of two integral lags between θ_c and θ_o.

Figure 17-6b provides a set of dynamics comparable to that shown in Fig. 17-6a. The second-order system expressed in the Laplace notation is

$$\theta_o = \frac{1}{T_1 T_2 s^2} \theta_c$$

In Fig. 17-6a, T_1 is the time constant for the first integral lag, while T_2 is that for the second integral lag. T_1 determines the rate of change of the ϵ_o voltage for a step function (constant voltage) ϵ_i at operational amplifier 1, while T_2 sets the rate of change of the ϵ_o for amplifier 2. Together, they determine the time constant of the combined double-integral lag operation. Note that $T_1 = R_1 C_1$ and $T_2 = R_2 C_2$, and if $R_1 = R_2$ and $C_1 = C_2$, then

$$\theta_o = \frac{1}{(Ts)^2} \theta_c$$

Expressed in the time domain, the above operation is

$$\theta_o = \frac{1}{T^2} \int\int_0^{t_n} \theta_c \, dt \, dt$$

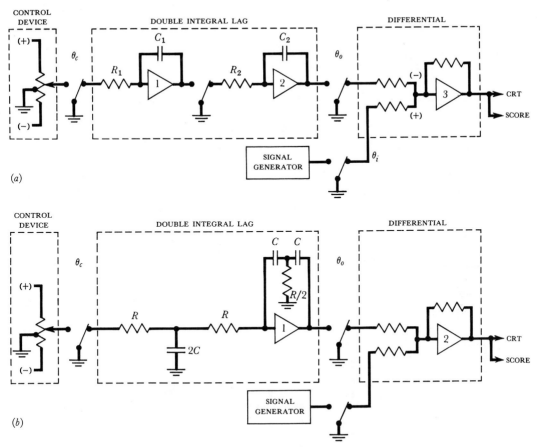

Fig. 17-6 Two ways to provide a double-integral or second-order tracking system.

where t_n is the amount of time over which the double-integral operation was performed (the length of the tracking trial) and T^2, as before, is equal to $R_1 R_2 C_1 C_2$.

It might be desirable to employ the circuitry indicated in Fig. 17-6b since it requires only one amplifier to obtain the same dynamics as those generated in Fig. 17-6a with two amplifiers.

A complex example

A particular system, such as an aircraft, can be simulated by the appropriate combination of these and other computer elements. Briggs and Waters (1958) had occasion to employ the dynamics illustrated in Fig. 17-7.

This arrangement is a first approximation to the dynamics of flight control for the azimuth (X) and elevation (Y) dimensions. The information display, a CRT, is shown in Fig. 17-8. It is seen from Figs. 17-7 and 17-8 that the operator controlled lateral movements of the own-position indicator, the error cursor, through second-order dynamics: amplifiers 1 and 2 both performed integral transformations of the signals generated by left (L) or right (R) movements of the control device; vertical movement of the cursor was achieved through one integral transformation (amplifier 5) and an exponential transformation (amplifier 4) of the control signal generated by forward (F) or backward (B) deflection

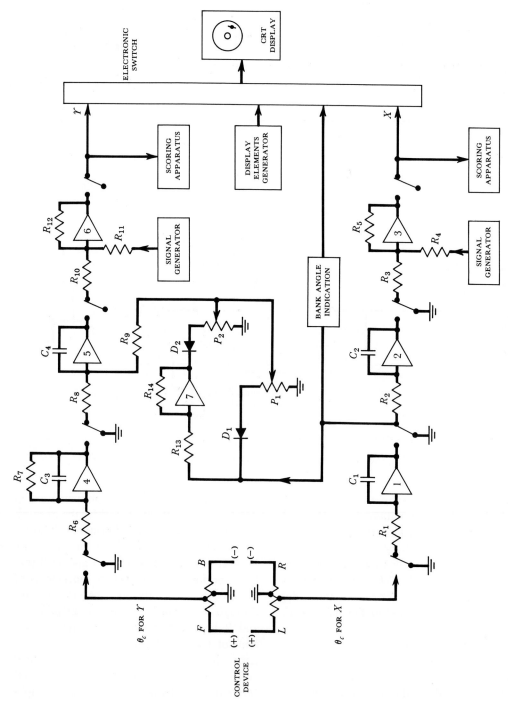

Fig. 17-7 The computer diagram of aircraft control dynamics as employed by Briggs and Waters (1958).

of the control device. The X component of the system is a pure acceleration system, and the Y component approaches this order for small-amplitude high-frequency θ_c corrections for Y. This latter follows in that these small-amplitude short-duration control movements tend to restrict the output of amplifier 4 to the initial near-linear portion of the exponential (see Fig. 17-3).

The linkage of the X to the Y component, which is achieved through amplifier 7 and its circuitry, permits an approximation to a major interaction between system components: loss of lift in bank maneuvers. In the operational system, rolling the aircraft from a horizontal to a banked attitude results in loss of lift; thus a loss of altitude can occur unless the pilot deflects his control column *back* from its trim position concomitant with the right or left deflection needed to introduce the bank angle. Potentiometers P_1 and P_2 permit the experimenter to vary the amount of loss in lift for a given bank angle.

The simulator functioned in the following manner: the operator viewed a 5-in. CRT on which appeared a fixed target circle and a movable cursor. The position of the cursor represented the difference between the input θ_i and the output θ_o; therefore this was a two-dimensional compensatory display of information. Signal generators provided the input θ_i for X and θ_i for Y. If the operator perceived a movement of the cursor to the left, he deflected his control to the right. So long as the control was held in this deflected position, the aircraft would roll in a clockwise direction, the rate of roll being dependent on the amplitude of the deflection and the sensitivity of the system. The latter is a function of overall gain G_x, where

$$G_x = \frac{R_5}{R_1 C_1 R_2 C_2 R_3} \quad \text{volts/sec}^2$$

for steady-state post-transient conditions. Bank angle was indicated to the operator by the angle of incidence of the "wings" of the own-position (error) cursor. To achieve this,

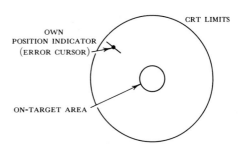

Fig. 17-8 The information display employed with the system defined in Fig. 17-7.

the output of amplifier 1, bank angle, was fed to a special-purpose unit that rotates the wings of the cursor on the CRT (see Fig. 17-8). After achieving the desired bank angle, the operator returns his control to the neutral position and the cursor continues to move to the right at a rate dependent on the degree of bank. If potentiometers P_1 and P_2 are set at zero, the movement will be lateral only; setting P_1 and P_2 at any other position results in a movement with vector to the right and down. As the cursor approaches zero error in the X dimension, the operator must deflect the control column to the left, thereby generating a signal θ_c opposite in sign to that of the original movement. This signal causes the cursor to roll back toward level flight, and, when the wings are level, further movement to the right ceases. If this level attitude is reached at the point of zero lateral error, the operator has achieved his goal; if he "rolls out" too soon or too late, further corrections are necessary.

The control of elevation was achieved through amplifiers 4 to 6. A backward or forward deflection of the control column generates a voltage θ_c for Y that is subjected to the exponential lag at amplifier 4 and then integrated by amplifier 5. Again, the amplitudes of the outputs for a given θ_c are a function of the system sensitivity G_y and

$$G_y = \frac{R_7 R_{12}}{R_6 R_8 C_4 R_{10}} \quad \text{volts/sec}$$

The linkage via amplifier 7 between the X and Y components of Fig. 17-7 ensured that both a right and a left bank angle would generate a loss in elevation. This was achieved by arranging diodes D_1 and D_2 as shown. The diode is a circuit element that permits electron flow only from cathode to plate, and in this sense it is analogous to a one-way value. Thus, if the operator deflected his control to the right, he generated a negative-polarity voltage at the input to amplifier 1; the output of amplifier 1 would be positive polarity and the aircraft would roll into a right bank. This positive signal cannot pass through diode 1 but will become negative at the output of amplifier 7, and diode 2 will permit the signal to pass and appear at the input of amplifier 5 as a negative signal. This will cause a loss in altitude unless the operator deflects the control backward, thereby generating a signal of negative polarity at the input to amplifier 4 and of positive polarity at the input to amplifier 5. Further, if the operator originally generated a bank θ_c of positive polarity, the output of amplifier 1 was of negative polarity, thus causing a left bank, and the signal passed through diode 1. In this way it was ensured that aircraft movement would follow a downward vector course for either a right or a left bank unless, of course, the operator generated a signal at the output of amplifier 4 which was of positive polarity and which matched in amplitude and phase the signal appearing across R_9.

In Fig. 17-9 are indicated several of the vector paths that were generated by a particular right or left bank angle. The settings of potentiometers P_1 and P_2 determined the slopes of these paths. By increasing the P_1 and P_2 settings a larger signal appeared at R_9 and a greater loss of lift was simulated. It should be noted that lift is a function of the cosine of bank angle and therefore the use of a linear relationship was only an approximation.

The other items indicated in Fig. 17-7 include the input signal generator, the scoring apparatus, an apparatus to provide the display elements shown in Fig. 17-8, and an electronic switch. A prototype of the electronic switch and the display-elements generator is described by Harter and Fitts (1956). Essentially, the electronic switch permits a time sharing of the single electron beam of the CRT among the several signals appearing on the display. It is a high-speed, extremely low-inertia switching device. Certain of the scoring apparatuses will be discussed in the following section.

It should be emphasized that the simulation defined by Fig. 17-7 is only a first approximation to aircraft dynamics. A greater degree of fidelity can be achieved by inserting additional lag terms. Bamford and Ritchie (1957) describe a system that more closely simulates the dynamics of azimuth control in an aircraft simulator, while Diamantides and Cacioppo (1957) describe a somewhat more complex simulator for pitch

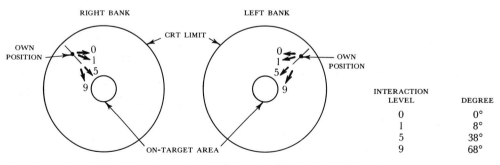

Fig. 17-9 Loss-of-lift effects for a given bank angle as they appeared on the tracking display associated with Fig. 17-7.

control. The present system should be viewed, therefore, as an illustration of how the operational amplifier can be used to build up a simulation of complex dynamics. It is but one of many skill devices that can be formed with the versatile analog computer (e.g., see Chap. 16).

QUANTIFICATION OF HUMAN TRACKING PERFORMANCE

A voltage is available at the output of amplifier 3 in Fig. 17-7 that represents the instantaneous amplitude of error in the X component of the control system. Similarly, the output of amplifier 6 is the error in the Y component. These signals may be operated upon in various ways to provide metrics of operator proficiency in control of the system. This section will describe several such operations as performed by circuits employing the operational amplifier as a basic unit. First, however, let us consider the nature of the tracking error over a period of time. It is apparent that descriptions of a time-varying signal fall into two categories: the amplitude and the frequency domains. The amplitude distribution of tracking error contains all the information from the first domain, while the autocorrelation function and its Fourier transform, the power-density spectrum, contain all information on the frequency characteristics of the error signal. Our primary concern in this section will be the derivation

of summary metrics from the amplitude domain.

It has been found that the amplitude distribution of tracking error, if accumulated over a sufficiently long period, is normal or Gaussian in form (Bahrick et al., 1957). It is meaningful to describe tracking error with metrics analogous to the standard deviation (SD, the root mean square of error, rms), the average deviation (AD, the integrated absolute error or average error), and the constant error (CE, the integrated algebraic error). In two-dimensional skill tasks such as shown in Fig. 17-7, it is possible to obtain the above metrics for both dimensions separately and also to determine a metric analogous to covariance, integrated cross product of X error and Y error.

Analog AD

The circuitry shown in Fig. 17-10 can provide the average-error metric. The diode elements D_1 and D_2 ensure that all signals appearing at the input to the integrator (amplifier 2) are of the same polarity and thus amplifier 2 can accumulate only the absolute value of the error signal. A voltmeter is shown in Fig. 17-10 that permits the experimenter to read the value of integrated absolute error at any time. This signal remains stored in the integrator until the experimenter resets the system by grounding the input of amplifier 2 through the switch S_1, thereby discharging the integrating capacitor

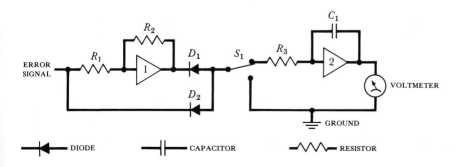

Fig. 17-10   A circuit to provide integrated absolute error.

C_1. The values of R_1, R_2, R_3, and C_1 may be set at the experimenter's convenience with the restriction that $R_1 = R_2$. C_1 is usually greater than 1 microfarad.

This metric is analogous to the **AD** one sees described in elementary descriptive statistics: dispersion of a distribution of discrete scores can be defined by

$$AD = \frac{\Sigma|x|}{N}$$

where x represents deviations of scores from the mean or any point in the distribution, and the summation is taken over all scores. In cases where one has continuous data, as in the tracking-error signal, the equation is

$$\text{Analog AD} = \frac{1}{T} \int_0^T |\epsilon|\, dt$$

where ϵ is the error signal integrated (summed) over the entire signal length for trial duration T. Thus the analog AD, or average error as it is called, is the average deviation of the subject's tracking-error amplitude distribution—it describes the extent of inaccuracy in his tracking performance. In practice, division of the integrated absolute error signal by T is not necessary and is omitted.

Analog CE

Integrated algebraic error can be achieved by removing the diodes around amplifier 1 and connecting that output directly to switch S_1, as in Fig. 17-11. Indeed, with appropriate switching the absolute-integrator circuit can be modified to serve for determinations of either AD (average error) or CE. It is usually wise to include an integrated algebraic error circuit as a separate score, as the tracking operators can generate constant errors in tracking, and the experimenter should use the estimate of this bias to correct the rms metric that he may employ as his major criterion of proficiency. Usually, the latter score is calculated by the analog circuits on the assumption that the mean of the error amplitude distribution is zero, at ground. Thus, the available CE metric permits the experimenter to make standard corrections for "guessed means" (Guilford, 1936). This will be illustrated in the following section.

Analog SD

The circuitry required to perform an analog squaring operation on the error signal is somewhat more complex than that which yields either an AD or a CE metric. The principle of analog squaring, however, is quite simple. The smooth curve shown in Fig. 17-12 is the square function $e_o = e_i^2$. This can be approximated by a series of straight lines, also shown in Fig. 17-12. These straight-line segments can be generated by the diode squaring circuitry, as shown in Fig. 17-13. The number of straight-line segments is directly proportional to the number of diode elements at the input to the operational amplifier. Precision in squaring increases as the number of diodes increases. The author has employed a seven-diode circuit and finds it acceptable. Commercial squarers and function generators may employ larger numbers of diodes.

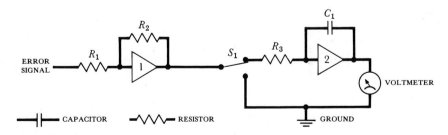

Fig. 17-11 A circuit to provide integrated algebraic error.

The principle of operation is as follows: referring to Fig. 17-13, when e_i is less than E_1, current flows only through D_i and R_i; thus

$$e_o = \frac{R_f}{R_{D_i} + R_i} e_i$$

where R_{D_i} is the resistance of the first diode D_i for current flow with $e_i < E_1$. The gain of the circuit is $R_f/(R_{D_i} + R_i)$. As e_i approaches and exceeds E_1, current begins to flow through D_1 and R_1, and this reduces the total input resistance as the D_i, R_i and D_1, R_1 elements are placed in parallel. Since R_f is fixed and since the gain of an operational amplifier is equal to feedback resistance divided by input resistance, the gain of the squaring circuit is increased. As e_i approaches and exceeds E_2 current flows through D_2 and R_2, thereby increasing the gain, and so on. In this way, straight-line segments relating e_o to e_i are generated, and by a judicial choice of the several E_i voltages and resistor elements one can ensure a reasonable approximation to the square function.

Since the squarer will accept only positive voltages, the error signal is first passed through a rectifying circuit, as shown in Fig. 17-14. The squarer output is connected to an integrator, and the meter reading is, then, integrated error squared. The rms value is determined by first dividing the meter reading by time T and then extracting the square root:

$$\text{rms} = \left(\frac{1}{T} \int_0^T e^2 \, dt\right)^{1/2} \quad \text{volts}$$

Like the analog AD, the rms metric is analogous to the SD, as discussed in elementary statistics:

$$\text{SD} = \left(\frac{\Sigma x^2}{N}\right)^{1/2}$$

where x represents the deviation of scores in a distribution from the mean of the distribution. The rms error metric is the SD of the tracking-error amplitude distribution with an assumed mean of zero, ground. If, in fact,

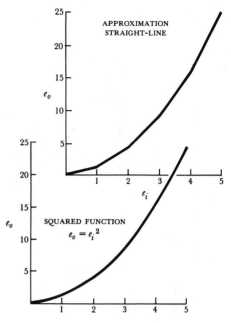

Fig. 17-12 A graphic plot of e_i and e_o for $e_o = (e_i)^2$ and a straight-line approximation to this function.

the tracker generated a constant error, one corrects the above rms errors score as follows:

$$\text{rms}_{\text{corrected}} = \left[\frac{1}{T} \int_0^T \epsilon^2 \, dt - \left(\int_0^T \epsilon \, dt\right)^2\right]^{1/2}$$
$$\text{volts}$$

The circuit shown in Fig. 17-10 is obviously less complex than that shown in Fig.

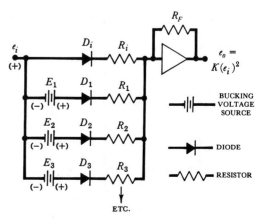

Fig. 17-13 Diode squaring circuit.

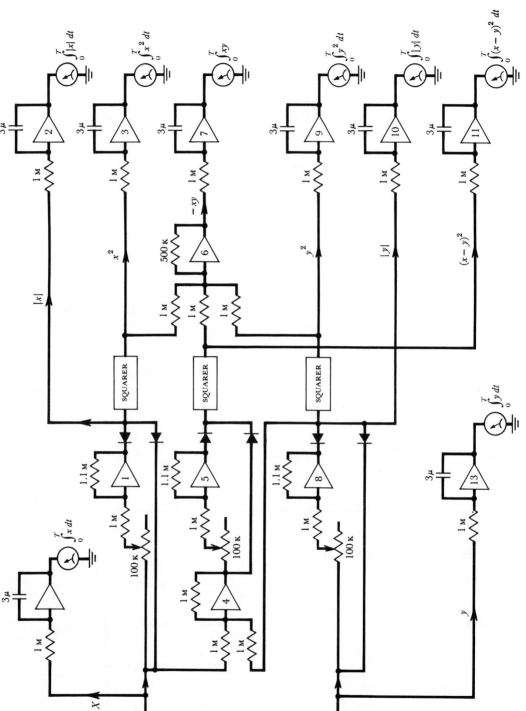

Fig. 17-14   An analog squarer-multiplier circuit. See Figs. 17-12 and 17-13 for details of the squarer components.

17-13. Further, there usually is less accuracy in determinations of rms error as compared with the determination of average error. This inaccuracy arises from the line-segment approximation generated by the diode squarer and from drift in the levels of the several bucking voltages E_i. It is possible to determine reasonably good estimates of rms from the AD metric. If we assume a normal error amplitude distribution, we note (Guilford, 1936) that

$$\text{rms} = 1.2532 \ \text{AD}$$

and thus an rms metric can be obtained with the less expensive and more accurate circuit shown in Fig. 17-10.

Analog covariance

If one has a two-dimensional tracking task, he can measure performance by scoring the X and Y errors separately. With two squaring circuits or with two absolute integrators, it is possible to determine rms_x and rms_y or AD_x and AD_y. It may be preferable to determine proficiency by a single metric, and one such score is the standard error of difference

$$\sigma_d = \frac{1}{\sqrt{n}} \left(\Sigma x^2 + \Sigma y^2 - 2\Sigma xy \right)^{\frac{1}{2}}$$

It is apparent that the squaring circuitry, described above, can provide analogs for two of the three terms on the right of the above equation and that one needs only an analog for the sum-of-the-cross-products term. Assuming the latter, we have an analog standard error metric rms_d as follows:

$$\text{rms}_d = \sqrt{\frac{1}{T}} \left(\int_0^T e_x^2 \, dt + \int_0^T e_y^2 \, dt \right.$$

$$\left. - 2 \int_0^T e_x e_y \right)^{\frac{1}{2}}$$

The integrated cross-products score is also necessary in cases for which it is desired to determine the correlation between two signals X and Y. The familiar Pearson product-moment r,

$$r_{xy} = \frac{\Sigma xy}{(\Sigma x^2 \Sigma y^2)^{\frac{1}{2}}}$$

may be determined for tracking-error signals by

$$r_{xy} = \frac{\int_0^T e_x e_y}{\left(\int_0^T e^2 \cdot \int_0^T e_y^2 \right)^{\frac{1}{2}}}$$

where T is the time in seconds of the integration operation.

Figure 17-14 shows the analog circuitry necessary to provide an integrated cross-products score as well as the other metrics described above. The principle of operation for cross products is quite straight forward; From elementary algebra we note that

$$(x - y)^2 = x^2 - 2xy + y^2$$

To derive xy, the cross product, sum the x and y signals at amplifier 4 to give $(x - y)$, then take the absolute value[1] of this term at amplifier 5 and subject this rectified signal to the analog squaring operation. The output of the squarer, $(x - y)^2$, is then summed with the signals $(x)^2$ and $(y)^2$ at amplifier 6 to yield $x^2 + y^2 - xy - x^2 - y^2 = -xy$. Note that the gain of amplifier 6 is 0.5, thereby canceling the constant 2 that would appear with the cross-products term. This term is then integrated by amplifier 7 to yield $\int_0^T e_x e_y \, dt$. The circuit shown in Fig. 17-14 is intended to provide the metrics when the input signals vary over a ± 5-volt range. The gains of the squarers are all unity.

ARBITRARY UNITS IN QUANTIFYING ACTION

In each of the above scoring operations the final output, as it appears on the meter, is

[1] It is necessary to provide signals of positive polarity to the squarer. Amplifier 5 serves to rectify both the x input signal and the y input signal.

expressed in units of voltage; e.g., integrated absolute error, as read at the end of a tracking trial, may be 24 volts. This score is then divided by the number of seconds of trial duration, e.g., 30 sec, and the resultant analog AD as recorded by the experimenter is 0.8 volt. This score is a function of the time-varying amplitudes of the original error signal. It is also a function of the relative sizes of the resistor and capacitor elements associated with the integrating amplifier. In Fig. 17-10 a change in value for either R_3 or C_1 will yield a different final score for the same input signal. This follows from a consideration of Fig. 17-1, where, for analog integration,

$$e_o \doteq \frac{1}{R_3 C_f} \int_0^T e_i \, dt$$

Since e_o is to be the analog average deviation, in this case,

$$AD \doteq \frac{1}{T} \left(\frac{1}{R_3 C_1} \int_0^T |\epsilon| \, dt \right)$$

and it follows that the particular score read on the meter is arbitrary in that the selection of particular values of R_3 and C_1 is arbitrary.

Assume that an experimenter has purchased two analog squaring devices from different sources. It is likely that the same input when applied to the two devices will not yield the same numerical score. The difference will be due to the particular values chosen for the several elements of the circuits. Does this mean that data gathered with one of the scoring circuits cannot be compared with those from the other device? Such a comparison can be made. The reader may recall other instances in which it is possible to transform data from the units of one scale to those of another; e.g., it is possible to go from Fahrenheit to centigrade readings of temperature by the linear equation

$$C = \tfrac{5}{9}(F - 32)$$

A simple linear transformation also exists in the above case of the squarers. To illustrate this we note that for squarer A

$$(e_o)_A \doteq K_1(e_i)^2$$

and for squarer B

$$(e_o)_B \doteq K_2(e_i)^2$$

Since e_i has been assumed to be the same for both squarers, in this illustration, the only source of the difference between $(e_o)_A$ and $(e_o)_B$ is in the two gain terms K_1 and K_2. The experimenter may easily determine K_1 and K_2 by noting the amplification or attenuation of e_o for several values of e_i. If for squarer A a constant e_i of 5 volts yields an output of 50 volts, then $K_1 = 2$; and if for the same input $(e_o)_B$ is 25 volts, then $K_2 = 1$. All data collected with squarer A may be transformed to the scale of squarer B by dividing the former set of scores by 2:

$$\tfrac{1}{2} \int_0^T e_A{}^2 dt = \int_0^T e_B{}^2 \, dt$$

or

$$\frac{1}{\sqrt{2}} \, \mathrm{rms}_A = \mathrm{rms}_B$$

Thus, the data from any two squarers, analog integrators, or other scoring devices can be compared provided the relative gains of the devices are known. This can prove to be a bothersome chore for the experimenter who wishes to compare his data with those of other laboratories, for the data must be converted to the scale units of each set of data to which comparison is desired, an obviously cumbersome task.

It is clear that some form of standardization is needed. One obvious choice is to agree on a "standard squarer" or a "standard absolute integrator," for example. This is the usual procedure for the several physical scales, and is a most commendable practice. However, until such time as psychologists care to agree on standard units for the several possible scales employed in the measurement of skill, the following is suggested as a means to take such measures out of the realm of arbitrary units and provide a meaningful scale of performance. It is proposed to convert the analog metrics from units of volts to units of the visual display. This is a very simple procedure, and the necessary steps are outlined below.

Let us assume that an experimenter has completed his tracking experiment and taken analog integrated absolute error scores. He sums these across subjects for each of a number of time periods (trials) and plots the group averages in a manner shown by Fig. 17-15. These plots of analog AD are expressed in the arbitrary voltage units. The first step in determining a scale in units of visual extent involves introducing a sinusoidal input into the tracking system and measuring the amplitude of movement of the target indicator on the information display. Assume that the peak-to-peak amplitude, as measured, is 2 in.

The second step involves scoring this input over the same time interval as that employed in the tracking experiment. Let us assume that the integrated absolute value of the sine input as scored was 10.5 volts and that the scoring period was 30 sec. The analog AD of the sinusoid is 10.5 volts for the 30-sec trial.[1] From physics, it is known that the rms value of a sinusoid is expressed by

$$rms = 0.707 I_m$$

where I_m is the maximum amplitude of the sine function. In our illustration we observed that the peak-to-peak amplitude was set at 2 in., and thus, I_m is 1 in. Therefore,

$$rms = (0.707)(1.0) = 0.707 \text{ in.}$$

and since $AD = 0.7979$ rms (Guilford, 1936), the average deviation of the test sinusoid is

$$AD = (0.7979)(0.707) = 0.564 \text{ in.}$$

We now have two values for the AD of the amplitude distribution of the test sinusoid.

[1] It is not necessary to divide 10.5 volts by 30 sec, since this would be reversed by the subsequent steps back to 10.5 volts.

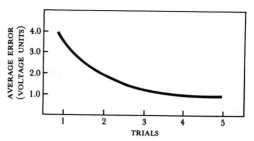

Fig. 17-15   A hypothetical learning curve.

One was determined directly by the same scoring circuit employed for the data collection (10.5 volts), and the other was calculated from the I_m measurement on the tracking display (0.564 in.). Dividing the latter by the former, we note that the relationship between the voltage and the visual display scales is 0.054 in. per volt. Therefore, by multiplying the scale units in Fig. 17-15 by 0.054, we achieve analog AD scores in units of linear extent, or inches (see Fig. 17-16).

The major advantage of this transformation is replacing an arbitrary voltage scale with one expressed in units which are readily interpretable and which permit direct comparison of data for several independent experiments. In the above example, the data plotted in Fig. 17-16 are the AD metrics of the subject's error amplitude distribution generated at each trial if those distributions were plotted to the same scale as that of displayed error information. It is true that the scale, average error in inches, is still arbitrary in the sense that the selection of display sensi-

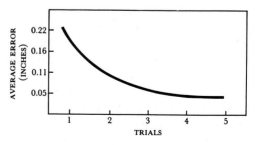

Fig. 17-16   The data of Fig. 17-15 expressed in linear scale units.

tivity is arbitrary, but at least the transformation places the performance of subjects on a meaningful and familiar scale of linear extent which has behavioral implications that are more direct and understandable than would be the case with a voltage scale. If each experimenter selects display sensitivities that provide for optimum performance, a secondary form of standardization exists.

FREQUENCY DOMAIN

The frequency characteristics of a continuous signal provide the second major domain for the description of a time-varying process such as the tracking-error signal. Analog computers are somewhat less useful in describing behavior in this domain than in the case for the amplitude domain, digital-computer techniques being more accurate and efficient in deriving metrics from or related to the power-density spectrum.

The power-density spectrum of a signal is the relation between the power (amplitude squared) of a signal and its frequency characteristics. To determine the power-density-spectrum it is necessary to measure power for successive narrow bands of frequency. A bandpass filter can be set up on an analog computer that attenuates power above and below the upper and lower cutoff frequencies of the filter. The voltage signal passed by the filter may be squared and its value read out via a voltmeter or other recording device. The power of that signal can be plotted by peaking the filter at various points up and down the range of frequencies present in the original signal.

In theory, the filter should have an extremely narrow band and the attenuation at the band limits should be quite sharp; in practice, the bandwidths for a filter is rather broad and the attenuation is gradual at 12 to 24 decibels (dB) per octave. One may wonder why commercially available frequency analyzers are not used for the analysis of behavioral data. The answer is that the power in continuous recordings of behavior is almost entirely in the ultralow-frequency range, direct current to 5 or 6 cycles per second (cps), and the available equipment is useful only above 100 cps. If an experimenter wants to perform power-density-spectrum analyses on behavioral data by analog techniques, he must be content with some rather gross approximations or with some rather inefficient techniques. It is preferable, in terms of both accuracy and efficiency, to convert a continuous behavioral signal to discrete data so that the power-density spectrum can be determined by digital-computer techniques. Analog-to-digital conversion equipment and high-speed paper tape punch or print-out equipment are available for such work (see Appendix).

Information on phase relationships is useful also in describing tracking performance in the frequency domain. Given an input to the human being, it is of interest to know not only whether his output matches the input in amplitude and frequency but also whether the two signals match in phase, the novice being notorious in lagging behind the input, while the skilled operator matches his output to that of the input or even develops some lead if this will improve system stability and rms error.

The crosscorrelation plot provides most direct evidence of phase lag or lead. This methodology has been described by Merrill and Bennett (1956). Essentially, one derives a series of integrated cross products of two signals (the input and the subject's output, in this case), one cross product $\int_0^T x \cdot y \, dt$ for each of several lag times, tau. When tau equals zero, the value will be the same as that obtained from the cross-products circuitry of Fig. 17-14; at tau equals 1, one of the two original signals has been *shifted* one unit while the other signal remains fixed; at tau equals 2, the shifted signal has been displaced two units relative to the fixed signal A plot like that in Fig. 17-17 results. If the input was fixed and the output signal was successively displaced, it is apparent that a maximum correlation occurred at tau equals +0.5 sec. The subject's output led the input by $\frac{1}{2}$ sec in this illustration.

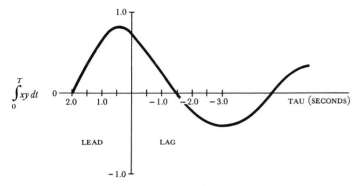

Fig. 17-17 A hypothetical crosscorrelation function.

Clark and Warren (1953) have described an analog technique to derive the crosscorrelation function that utilizes a photometric device, but most derivations rely on digital-computer analyses. Either the analog or the digital techniques are of general applicability to all kinds of signal; Garvey and Mitnick (1957) describe a simple technique to determine leads or lags for ramp (constant rate) and constant acceleration inputs, a special application.

Analog derivatives

It is possible to set up an operational amplifier whose output will be a close approximation to the first derivative of the input signal. The circuitry to do this appears in Fig. 17-18a, where one merely interchanges the

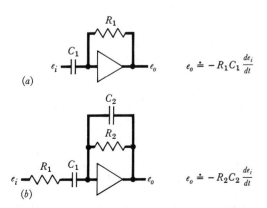

(a)

$$e_o \doteq -R_1 C_1 \frac{de_i}{dt}$$

(b)

$$e_o \doteq -R_2 C_2 \frac{de_i}{dt}$$

Fig. 17-18 Analog-computer circuitry to provide the first derivative of a voltage signal.

capacitor and resistor for analog integration operations. In theory the relationship is

$$e_o \doteq -RC \frac{de_i}{dt}$$

In practice, e_i contains some finite amount of noise; i.e., information uncorrelated with the true values of e_i over time, and the derivative operation amplifies these noise components (since they usually are of higher frequency than true e_i) relatively more than the true e_i so that the true derivative is masked by the derivative of the noise. In practice the circuit shown in Fig. 17-18b is desirable. It filters out the noise at 12 dB per octave if R_1 and C_2 are chosen appropriately. Note that

$$e_o \doteq -R_2 C_1 \frac{de_i}{dt}$$

and that $2\pi f_{co} = 1/R_1 C_1 = 1/R_2 C_2$, where f_{co} is the cutoff frequency beyond which the derivative signal is attenuated at 12 dB per octave.

One can place two operational amplifiers in series, each wired as in Fig. 17-18b, and obtain the second derivative from the output of the second amplifier. This signal would most likely be so noisy, even with extra filtering, as to be almost useless. Derivative information is best taken from digital-computer analysis if accuracy is required.

There is a way to "beat the noise" and still get derivative information for tracking error if one uses a simple sine-wave input sig-

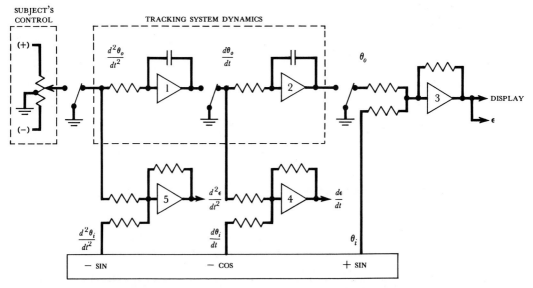

Fig. 17-19 A tracking device using an analog computer to provide error derivatives.

nal and requires the subject to track through integral lags. This technique is shown in Fig. 17-19.

It may be seen from Fig. 17-19 that the subject tracks through two integral lags, a second-order system, and that he attempts to match the sinusoidal input θ_i with a signal θ_o at the output of amplifier 2. By using a sine-cosine potentiometer driven at any selected speed as an input frequency, he can pick off the —cosine signal, the first deriva-

tive of θ_i, to be summed with the first derivative of θ_o at amplifier 4 to yield error rate $d\epsilon/dt$. A similar operation at amplifier 5 yields error acceleration $d^2\epsilon/dt^2$. By integrating the absolute values of the output of amplifiers 3 to 5, the average error, average rate error, and average acceleration error, respectively, are obtained. These outputs could be squared prior to integration to yield rms error, rms error rate, and rms error acceleration, respectively.

REFERENCES

BAHRICK, H. P., FITTS, P. M., and BRIGGS, G. E. Learning curves—facts or artifacts? *Psychol. Bull.*, 1957, **54**, 256–268.

BAMFORD, H. E., and RITCHIE, M. L. Integrated instruments: A roll and turn indicator. *USAF WADC Tech. Rep. 57-205*, 1957.

BRIGGS, G. E., and WATERS, L. K. Training and transfer as a function of component interaction. *J. exp. Psychol.*, 1958, **56**, 492–500.

CLARK, J. R., and WARREN, C. E. A photometric correlator. *USAF HRRC Res. Bull. 53-42*, 1953.

CONKLIN, J. E. Effect of control lag on performance in a tracking task. *J. exp. Psychol.*, 1957, **53**, 261–268.

DIAMANTIDES, N. D., and CACIOPPO, A. J. Human response dynamics: GEDA computer applica-

tion. *Goodyear Aircraft Corp. GER-8033*, 1957.

GARVEY, W. D., and MITNICK, L. L. An analysis of tracking behavior in terms of lead-lag errors. *J. exp. Psychol.*, 1957, **53**, 372–378.

GUILFORD, J. P. *Psychometric methods.* New York: McGraw-Hill, 1936.

HARTER, G. A., and FITTS, P. M. The functional simulation of complex systems by means of an analog computer, with the F-86D, E-4 system as a specific example, Part II. (Confidential) *USAF Pers. Train. Res. Center Res. Rep. 56-133, Part II*, 1956.

KOERTH, W. A pursuit apparatus: eye-hand coordination. *Psychol. Monogr.*, 1922, **31**, 288–292.

MERRILL, W. J., JR., and BENNETT, C. A. The application of temporal correlation techniques in psychology. *J. appl. Psychol.*, 1956, **40**, 272–280.

Chapter 18

DIGITAL COMPUTERS

STEWART FLIEGE

The purpose of this chapter is to present an overview of the computer as a research tool and to provide some detailed information and procedures one should follow to successfully use this tool. It is of the utmost importance that the psychologist realize that, for all the computer's awesome capability, it is nothing more than a tool. A computer will not generate a research idea, it will not replace good experimental design, it will not compensate for poor data. In short, the computer is an aid to help the psychologist achieve a research goal. This chapter will cover an overview of computer applications to psychological research in order to acquaint the reader with the general-purpose characteristics of digital computers; a summary of computer operations and the major components of a computer system; a description of the types of computer facilities available to psychologists; a discussion of computer programs (how to borrow them and how to prepare to write a program); and finally, a discussion of the economics of using computers (most psychologists will find that a few minutes of computer time will buy a very complex T maze). A final section summarizes the advantages and problems of computer uti-

This chapter was completed while the author was employed by the System Development Corp., Santa Monica, Calif.

lization with special attention to pitfalls that can be avoided by careful planning.

USES OF COMPUTERS IN PSYCHOLOGICAL RESEARCH

The purpose of this section is to acquaint the potential computer user with the range of problems to which computers can be applied. For this discussion the writer has chosen an arbitrary classification scheme for the sake of expository convenience. One or two examples are presented where available. These are examples only and do not represent a complete compilation of computer usage in psychological research. It is questionable whether such a compilation could even be produced, because using a computer in a research study is often of minor interest in comparison with the basic aims of the research. In the area of data analysis, for example, few research reports indicate whether the statistics were prepared on a hand calculator, prepared on a computer, or done on paper. A major source of computer-usage information readily available to most psychologists appears in *Behavioral Science,* which allocates a portion of each issue to computer applications. *Computing Reviews* includes sections on artificial intelligence, computer applications in psychology and other disciplines, and statistics and probability.

Data analysis

At the present time data analysis represents the most popular use of computers in psychological research. Indeed, to some psychologists computer utilization and data analysis are synonymous. One area of data analysis on which computers have had a major impact is factor analysis. Factor-analysis calculations are at best a tedious and time-consuming process. But the use of a computer can shorten the elapsed time for such calculations from months to minutes and reduce the probability of calculation errors almost to zero. In addition, it is now possible to consider factor analyses with dozens of variables, problems that could not be physically handled before the advent of computers. An excellent discussion of computer techniques in factor analysis and a bibliography can be found in Harman (1960).

All the commonly used statistical analyses can be performed on computers; the only limitation is the availability of computer programs. But computers can also be used for the analyses necessary in test construction. The writer participated in the analysis of an employee rating checklist where the validity of 90 rating-scale items was required from ratings of 518 supervisory and nonsupervisory personnel. An interitem correlation matrix of 90 entries was computed as well as means, variances, and covariances in approximately 20 minutes of IBM 709 time.

It must be granted that the use of digital computers in data analysis represents a technology that removes a time-consuming and tedious job from the shoulders of the researcher. However, other computer uses have a far greater probability of contributing to the development of scientific psychology in both theory and experimental techniques. Nevertheless, the first contact that most psychologists have with computers concerns data analysis. Because of this there is a large reservoir of application knowledge and a ready-made set of computer programs available for immediate use. For the psychologist who wishes to venture into the world of computers, running some standard data analysis problems is the surest way of obtaining a relatively painless initiation; as his knowledge and understanding increase by experience he will be better able to explore the applications discussed below. Furthermore, he will be able to discuss his computer requirements intelligently with the professional computer applications experts, whose assistance often is needed.

Vicarious behavers

This approach makes use of a computer to model a psychological theory in order to predict behavior. The predicted behavior can then be compared with actual behavior obtained in a controlled experiment. This particular use of computers requires a rigorously explicit statement of theory; but to justify the use of a computer, the theory must be mathematically complex or have many variables. Under these conditions, it is often difficult to predict the behavior expected under a variety of experimental conditions. The computer can assist in such predictions and in some cases may be the only practical tool for so doing. Also, the parameters and variables used in the computer program define the conditions under which live experimentation must be conducted. Remember, however, that the use of computers as vicarious behavers does not alleviate the problem of null results for one cannot be sure whether such results are due to incorrect theory, faulty experimental controls, or incorrect sampling. An additional problem is that the theory might not have been correctly represented in the computer program. If one is willing to assume the correctness of a given theory, it is possible to use the computer to extrapolate backward from observed behavior to possible sets of initial conditions. This is essentially a determination of behavioral parameters. However, this use of computers as vicarious behavers is much less straightforward than the one above in that the theory may be satisfied by a very large set of initial conditions. The difference in these approaches is analogous to the difference between differentiating and integrating in calculus.

Unfortunately, little work of the type mentioned in this section has been performed in psychological research. This is in contrast with the engineering and physical sciences. In fact, computer manufacturers use computers to generate new computer designs based on the vicarious "behavior" of theoretical computer models and components. In psychology, most of this kind of computer usage to date has been with stochastic learning models, thinking, and decision theory.

A good example of this use of computers is given in Gyr, Thatcher, and Allen (1962). This study was an outgrowth of a laboratory experiment using human subjects in a complex problem-solving task. The experiment was such that the inputs and outputs could be objectively measured and a set of mathematical-logical theories specified to relate the inputs and outputs. A computer program that represented one of the theories was written for the IBM 704. The steps followed in generating the model in preparation for computer runs are representative of the general process required for such computer applications.

1. Statement of the hypothesized psychological processes relating the input to the output in objective terms; e.g., possible paths are randomly scanned, and the results of a particular trial change the probability of the next selection in a specified manner.

2. Rigorous definition of the processes, where actual probabilities are defined and the function that specifies changes to the probabilities based on a set of contingencies is clearly stated.

3. Parameter values are established for a particular experimental computer run. This sets the initial probability conditions.

In this particular example, five experimental runs were conducted involving different parameter values; and the results indicated, among other things, that changes in information-retention capabilities in this particular model produced drastic changes in results. In this use of computers it is then necessary to apply the data obtained from the computer runs to observed behavior to ascertain whether the model is a reasonable one to describe the input-output relation. This in turn may require further data analysis and statistical tests, although it is often possible to reject a theory because of a large and obvious discrepancy.

Artificial intelligence

The use of computers as vicarious behavers is directed toward improving theory and experimentation by simulation methods (Feigenbaum and Feldman, 1963) and its successful prosecution involves an interaction of experimentation, theorizing, and computer simulation. However, the goal of studies in artificial intelligence represents the opposite approach: results of psychological experimentation and theory are applied to improving the capability of machines. Therefore, the title "artificial intelligence" might better appear in a chapter entitled "The Application of Psychological Knowledge to Research on Computers." The basic aim of such studies is to develop computer programs that perform as do intelligent organisms. However, it is possible to learn a great deal about human behavior from working on artificial intelligence. Indeed, some interesting hypotheses concerning perception, learning, and even neural networks have grown out of this research. Nevertheless, one basic motivation behind this research effort has been to achieve better understanding of the capabilities inherent in machines in general and digital computers in particular. A bibliography by Minsky (1961) lists some 585 papers, proceedings, symposia, books, and articles related to the subject. A short review of representative studies can be found in Green (1961). For a more detailed discussion see Pfieffer (1962).

Studies in artificial intelligence traditionally deal with learning and heuristics, pattern recognition, and biological processes. Studies in *learning and heuristics* are concerned with the development of computer programs that perform in a manner that meets some definition of learning. This, of course, has led to the inevitable arguments of whether "machines" can really learn. Undoubtedly machines can learn if certain definitions of learning are applied. An example of simple machine learning is that of Marzocco and Bartram (1962), where a two-choice statistical learning model was used as the basis for a computer program. More complex applications are in the area of problem solving (Newell, Shaw, and Simon, 1958; Newell and Simon, 1963). But the difficult computer programming problem involves having the program learn, or develop, appropriate steps for solving a problem without being told the explicit details of the solution. A computer can always be programmed to solve a specific mathematical equation. It is another question to ask the computer to derive the equation from a given set of axioms without exactly representing the derivation in the program instructions. Newell *et al.* (1958) have tried to develop such a program to prove theorems in mathematical logic. The computer is supplied with a basic set of axioms and theorems from which it tries to construct a proof for a particular proposition. It works backward from the conclusion through provable intermediate propositions. A major problem encountered was the large amount of computer time required to examine all possible intermediate propositions. Noting that human beings utilize certain rules of thumb in proving theorems, the researchers included such rules in the program logic. These rules were called heuristics, and the effectiveness and efficiency of machine problem solving depends to a major extent on the choice of good heuristics. The next step in this process would be to program the computer to develop its own heuristics, based on learning from successful and unsuccessful problem-solving attempts. An interesting study of possible heuristics, derived from analysis of human problem solving, was suggested by Hovland (1960). Hovland differentiated three concepts for organizing material for efficient problem solving: conjunctive, disjunctive, and relational. Observation of human learners showed that for the stimulus materials being studied, conjunctive and relational concepts were used more commonly than disjunctive. The computer program first attempted to classify inputs on a conjunctive scheme, then relational, then disjunctive. This was essentially a response hierarchy for the computer that was based on the highly successful way in which human beings use concepts in classifying information.

In its simplest sense, *pattern recognition* in a computer is an attempt to equal, and perhaps surpass, the capability of human beings to categorize stimuli. In most experimental programs to date, the usual stimuli are letters or phonemes that are translated into bit patterns interpretable by a computer. Yet the job of getting the stimuli into a form for inputting to the computer is often a difficult task. In the case of letters, this requires a two-dimensional representation where each letter is represented by a series of X, Y coordinates. These coordinates may be punched on cards or tapes and input in the regular fashion, or a special scanner may be used. Scanners work in much the same way as television cameras and essentially digitalize the letters scanned. The resultant information may be directly input to the computer tapes, or cards are prepared that are subsequently input. An extreme amount of effort is required to put the information on cards manually; therefore, a scanner would be required if a large number of letters were needed or, especially, if different samples of handwriting or printing represented the input. Digitalizing auditory inputs such as human speech is even more difficult because of the number of possible dimensions along which speech can be categorized. Here again the research is dependent on psychological knowledge of what dimensions are used in selective responses to the auditory stimuli of speech.

Once the inputs have been digitalized the computer tries to match the stimuli with pre-specified alternatives according to specific rules. Programs have been written that are successful in recognizing letters in Morse code and less successful in recognizing handwritten letters. (Doyle, 1960; Selfridge and Neisser, 1960). A major problem here is the specification of the rules to be fol-lowed by the computer in effecting suc-cessful recognition. This is due in large part to a lack of understanding concerning the de-tailed manner in which human beings per-form such recognition. With a better devel-opment of these rules it is reasonable to be-lieve that computers could do a better job of simple pattern recognition than human be-ings, because the machine could quickly ap-ply a vast number of these rules in a rigor-ously logical manner.

A more immediately useful type of pattern recognition is represented by language trans-lation programs. Usually, the computer is supplied with a dictionary of words that it matches with input words; the simplest out-put is a literal translation. As any student of language will readily admit, such a transla-tion may be little easier to understand than the original. What is required is the incorpo-ration of rules of grammar plus the capability for recognizing what rules apply where. In addition, for a truly effective translation to occur, a pattern-recognition capability must be provided in that the program must re-spond to the context of the material in order to select the appropriate definition of multi-valued words, idioms, and phrases. Once again, efforts here are limited by psycho-logical knowledge of how people perform such recognition.

A much more sophisticated application of computer pattern recognition is in the area of medical diagnosis (Ledley and Lusted, 1960; Graetz, 1965). It is suggested that symptoms input to a computer be related to the symptom pattern of a partic-ular disease or set of diseases. Additional diagnostic tests would then be suggested to further narrow the range of possi-bilities. A similar approach could be used in clinical research in psychology or even in mental measurements. For example, results of psychological diagnostic tests could be in-tegrated with other measures so that re-sponses symptomatic of various types of or-ganic brain damage could be recognized by the computer, which would in turn output additional physiological and psychological di-agnostic procedures. One can view mental measurements in a similar fashion where a given score on a so-called mathematical diag-nostic test may be achieved by different pat-terns of right and wrong answers. The par-ticular pattern may well be symptomatic of certain deficiencies in training or funda-mentals. The computer can be used not only to score the test but also to point out areas of probable weaknesses and what additional testing might be required to achieve verifica-tion. Once again, however, lack of knowledge about how a human being performs the task of a medical diagnosis hampers development in this area. The situation is even more diffi-cult in psychology because of problems of de-termining and measuring symptoms and of relating these symptom patterns to an agreed-upon psychological condition.

The majority of studies on *biological processes* have been concerned with *neural networks.* Neurons and their interconnections are simulated on the computer along with re-inforcers designed to inhibit some connec-tions and strengthen others. One of the best known neural-net models is the Perceptron (Rosenblatt, 1958). For psychologists, these models serve as validating devices for the hy-pothetical constructs used in describing more molar behavior. But Green (1961) points out that the random net used in the Perceptron model produced very little learning and concludes that the human nervous system cannot be characterized by random neural interconnections. (See McCulloch [1965] for recent discussions of neural networks.)

The field of artificial intelligence covers a wide variety of studies, from neural nets to complex pattern recognition. The basic theme, however, is to maximize the utility of computers in the service of man. This can be accomplished by developing the computer to be sensitive to its environment, to learn from experience, and to abstract and synthesize. The work of Vossler and Uhr (1962) represents such an approach in that it embodies learning, pattern recognition, and biological processes. The work done in artificial intelligence to date indicates that a major stumbling block is lack of knowledge about human behavior. This must be overcome before we can realize the latent capabilities that lie untapped in our current uses of computers.

Stimulus presentation

This use of computers ranges from a complex analogy of the memory drum to the preparation of material for large-scale training and evaluation projects. There are two main ways in which computers have been used for stimulus presentation: environmental simulation and material preparation.

When used in *environmental simulation,* the computer is treated like any other instrument such as a puzzle box or tachistoscope. But the computer system must have a direct output capability such as a cathode-ray tube (CRT), on-line printer, or typewriter. It is also possible to connect the computer to an auditory output device to study perception of complex tonal patterns or to use the computer to control a random-access slide projector. In general, the computer represents a valuable tool when the aim of the research is to study responses to complex environmental stimuli. The important variables in the environment are selected for representation in the computer program, as well as the pattern in which these elements are to be displayed. In this context, the computer can even play a role in the experimental design. If, for example, a research project calls for a number of stimuli to be presented many times in random order or if a number of controlled orders of presentation are required, the computer can be so programmed. Smith (1961) points out the value of such stimulus programming when one wishes to concentrate stimuli presentations at the parts of a function most critical for discriminating between alternative hypotheses. The relatively simple Markov designs suggested by Smith represent only the beginning of what could be done. An additional advantage can be gained if the subjects' responses can be keyed directly into the computer. This enables the researcher to have a complete recording and a data analysis available at the end of a given run. When such analyses of results are made available to the subject on an ongoing basis, we have essentially a teaching machine.

A study by Julesz (1960) illustrates computer-based environmental simulation in the area of perception. Julesz studied depth perception by using a computer to generate pictures that looked like random presentations when viewed monocularly. However, when viewed with binocular vision, correlated point domains could be seen in depth. The power of a computer in this context lies in the almost infinite steps that can be gone through in arriving at a set of patterns which begin to appear as having depth. It is then possible to extract those characteristics which represent the important variable or variables and arrive at a better understanding of basic perceptual principles. Such applications also have the advantage of providing new stimulus patterns that are unlike common objects of everyday perceptual experience, thereby controlling the influence of learning.

When a computer is used in environmental simulation it is essentially a part of the experimental situation. It is also possible to use the computer to prepare experimental material that can be used at locations remote from the computer.

The most extensive computer usage in this respect is the System Development Corporation's System Training Program (STP) for the United States Air Force. STP is a large-scale, man-machine training program used to train Air Defense Command and other military personnel under simulated wartime and emergency conditions. The training takes place in the system operational environment, utilizing the same equipment and procedures that would be required under real emergency conditions. To achieve this training an extensive simulation effort is required. Simulation materials are prepared on a computer at Santa Monica, California, and the materials are shipped to various air defense centers throughout the world. The materials are designed for each location and represent salient operational problems specific to the location. To prepare these simulation materials a complex system of computer programs is used. A typical problem involves aircraft for which radar returns must be calculated as well as flight plans prepared, maps made, computer magnetic tapes generated, and scripts produced. For each such problem millions of calculations are required. It would be impossible to conduct such a large-scale training program without the aid of a computer because of the sheer magnitude of the calculations involved. Needless to say, the cost of such a training program is great, but much less so than equivalent live exercises. In addition, the control and knowledge of system inputs could never be achieved with a live exercise; therefore the feedback required in a training program would be lacking.

A computer would also be helpful in generating stimuli to be used in probability learning studies, especially where dependent probabilities are required in the stimulus sequence. The task is relatively simple where the probabilities required can be specified by a mathematical statement. An additional benefit is the possibility of generating different equivalent stimulus sets when required by the experimental design.

Process control

There has been little application of computers for process control in psychological research. Pioneering work in this field has taken place in the petroleum and chemical industries and in military control systems. Traditionally, such process-control applications have required an extensive use of analog-digital-analog equipment. In industrial applications, temperature, pressure, rate of flow, and other analog metering devices are digitalized for input into a computer. The computer uses this information in arriving at control decisions, which are used in turn to set valves or other devices in a manner to control the process according to specified criteria. Criteria may involve keeping the process within some defined band around a theoretical line or may be used to prevent its exceeding some particular level. It is in the area of process control that computers have some of their greatest potential in experimental control and instrumentation. An ideal place to apply this technology would be in the area of animal learning and its physiological concomitants. A computer-based laboratory could supply control and recording capabilities previously impossible to realize. All external stimuli could be maintained under close control from birth onward, and selected responses could be recorded and used to control subsequent stimulus presentations. With advanced physiological instrumentation, the animal could be tied closely to the computer with appropriate analog-digital-analog conversion devices. Needless to say, the cost of such an experimental laboratory would be very great. The possibilities such as installation would provide for making great gains in basic understanding of psychological concepts and principles are tremendous.

A less ambitious use of computer-based process control is the development of teaching machines (Maher, 1964). The value of a computer-based teaching machine is its capability to vary dynamically the presentation of material as a function of student performance; i.e., it performs a true process-control function. This dynamic material presentation is referred to as *branching*. When a student begins instruction on such a machine, he is presented with a number of moderately difficult items on the subject to be learned. If he does well, he is branched to more difficult material; if he does poorly, i.e., does not meet the programmed criterion of performance, he is branched to a set of easier items. This enables students to proceed at their individual rates. The computer can be programmed to branch on the basis of single questions, cumulative performance scores, student request, or response latencies. In addition it can provide a record of sequence of presentation, student responses, and response latency. (Refer to Swets, Harris, McElroy, and Rudloe [1964], and Weisz and McElroy [1964] for experiments on computer-aided learning of nonverbal sounds and visual tasks.)

There are several problems involved in computer-based process-control experiments. The foremost problem is specifying control variables and their interaction. In teaching machines, the biggest job is preparing the teaching materials. This requires an intimate knowledge of the subject matter as well as a theory about what concepts are easiest to learn and which concept precedes another. The required analysis often exceeds the effort required in writing the controlling computer program, a reversal from the other computer applications discussed above. Even in the chemical and petroleum processing fields, about which much is known, a minimum of 12 months of intensive analysis is usually required prior to establishing a prototype system.

A second problem is that process control represents a *real-time application* of the computer. A real-time application means that the internal data processing of the computer must be keyed to and be responsive to events in the external environment on a continuous basis. This increases the difficulty of the computer programming task and also means the computer time required for an experimental run is likely to be considerable. For example, using a medium to large computer to teach 20 students simultaneously could represent an hourly cost of $7 to $14 per student, significantly more than most school systems can reasonably afford on a continuing basis.

Another problem is associated with the reliability requirements that often exist in process control. If one had the good fortune to have an automated animal behavior laboratory and was making a longitudinal study of learning on a particular generation of monkeys or rats, the failure of the computer after two months of a projected four months' run would be most disheartening. The probability of such an occurrence can be significantly reduced by special designs and manufacturing controls or by *duplexing* (one machine breaks down, another takes over).

The important thing to note is that real-time process-control applications may prove to be extremely expensive. The expense is caused by analysis requirements, costs of programming, and machine reliability requirements. The only reasonable alternative to the machine expense may be to use an existing scientific or business data processing computer. This, in turn, may require the acquisition or even development of the appropriate analog converting devices necessary for process-control work. A common mistake is to complete special equipment design prior to system analysis and program design. These tasks should be well under way before equipment design is frozen.

Information retrieval

Steps are currently under way to automate literature searching. There is no doubt that such computer usage can be viewed as a tool to support researchers. The general goal of information retrieval is to find all the information available on a given subject. The first problem is the definition of subject. Unfortunately, psychological taxonomy is not consistent nor well defined. Much work remains to be done on this problem. A more tedious problem is the encoding of information into the agreed-upon taxonomy. Then the procedure for sorting and selection of the required information from the stored files completes the cycle. The latter problem is trivial from a data processing point of view; techniques for this function have long been known and are used daily in business applications. Recent computer program work has concentrated on the problem of encoding information. Edmundson and Wyllys (1961) discuss recent developments in automatic abstracting and indexing; DuBois (1965) tells how documents from two sources are reconciled with a digital computer. Automated information retrieval is still in the developmental stage and will require some time before it will be of practical value to the research psychologist. Fortunately this problem area is significant to all areas of scientific endeavor and is therefore being attacked from many angles. As with artificial intelligence, psychology can make significant contributions by providing insights into the ways in which human beings do such an excellent job of retrieving information.

System analysis and research

In recent years, particularly with the advent of military command and control systems, a new system technology has risen. Basic to this technology is the tying together of computers, sensors, effectors, communications, and people into an information processing, decision-making system. The fact that such systems exist has presented the research psychologist, along with researchers from other fields, an opportunity to study the manner in which these systems operate. With system research, the problems of interest are no longer bounded by the manner in which an individual learns or perceives but are expanded to include the ways in which people interact with one another, the relative capability of people to perform tasks versus a machine, and the manner in which such systems represent unique or general social orders. It is the area of system research and analysis that shows the most promise for new approaches to study man functioning in a controlled social environment. Computers have played a significant role in most of the studies reported.

COMPUTER OPERATION

This section describes the fundamental concepts of digital-computer operation. The logical nature of the process will be covered rather than the physical and electronic principles. Of necessity, this description will be brief; for a more complete description, see Murphy (1958) or Irwin (1960).

There are five basic elements in any digital computer. These are an input element, a memory, a processor, an output element, and a control unit. Different types of computer vary in the capability and complexity of these elements, which in turn affect the suitability and ease of use of the computer for a given task in psychological research.

The input element enables the user to place in the computer two classes of information: the data to be processed and the instructions that the computer is to follow in processing the data. The latter is called the *computer program*. Both the data and the instructions are stored in the memory unit of the machine until called forth by the control unit. During the operating cycle of a computer program, the instructions in the program operate through the control unit and tell the control unit which data are to be processed in what manner by the processor. Once the processing is complete, the program may instruct the control unit to output the results via the output element. Thus, the program plays a crucial role in the successful employment of a digital computer.

A computer program is a series of instructions that tell the computer exactly how to process a given set of data. The versatility of digital computers lies in their capability to operate with a wide variety of such computer programs. By changing the order of execution of the computer's basic set of instructions, the user can have the computer perform an almost endless variety of tasks.

It is vitally important that the user understand the fundamental manner in which computer programs operate. There are several basic pieces of information that make up a computer program instruction unit. These include the locations of the data to be processed, a description of the processing, what is to be done with the results, and where the next instruction is located. Different computers use different instruction unit formats. The four-address format is the one most closely paralleling the manner in which a human being would perform a calculation. To show how a computer with a four-address system would operate, let us take a simple example. In a four-address system an instruction could logically be represented as follows: Add (102), (103), (104), (2). The control unit would be instructed by the program to place this instruction in the processor. The processor would then take the datum out of box 102, add this to the datum in box 103, store the sum in box 104, and instruct the control unit to get the next instruction out of box 2. The four addresses in this case are the address of the first piece of datum, the address of the second piece, the address where the results are to be stored, and the address of the next instruction. In this respect the memory of the computer can be likened to a set of numbered boxes. Data are stored in some of the boxes and instructions in others. The computer itself does not know which are data and which are instructions—all are numbers. Only the person writing the program need be cognizant of which is which so that he can properly instruct the control unit.

The four-address type of instruction unit is not always economical, because often all four addresses are not required for each operation. Another instruction format utilizes a single-address system with sequential control. With sequential control, instructions are automatically taken in sequential order unless there is a command to take the next instruction from another location. The same addition task would be represented in a single-address system as follows:

(1)	Load	(102)
(2)	Add	(103)
(3)	Store	(104)
(4)	...	

This would be interpreted as load the datum from box 102 into the processor, add the contents of box 103, store the sum in box 104. Note that the first instruction is stored in box 1 and that the control unit automatically takes the next instruction from box 2, etc. These boxes are usually referred to as registers, and the numbered location of each register is its address. A sequence of instructions such as the above could be used in summing test scores for computing a mean.

Two- and three-address systems involve different combinations of data, storage, and next-instruction addresses. While it is not always necessary for the computer user to be concerned with the address system of the computer he is using, there are cases where he may have to do programming for a particular address system. The user must realize that computers do differ in this basic manner and the program he writes may not be usable on any other type of machine. It is obvious that the computer must be given detailed instructions on how to perform. It will do no more than what it is told to do in the program. This, in essence, is nothing more than the codification of what is already in the mind of the researcher, but broken down into tinier steps than are usually represented in daily discourse. Fortunately, it is not always necessary for the psychologist to specify every step that the computer must follow. The availability of programming tools has already reduced the tedious job of preparing minute

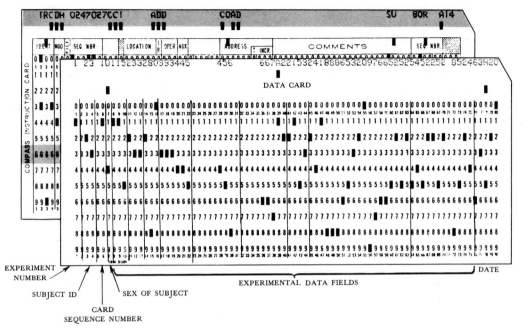

Fig. 18-1 Examples of computer input cards. The upper card is a program card used for program instructions and has a fixed format. The lower card is a data card where the researcher has defined the card fields to suit the needs of the experiment.

instruction units and hence has greatly extended the utility of the computer.

Computer elements and ancillary equipment.

Although digital computers operate on the principles enunciated in the last section, there is a tremendous variation in types of digital computers and their ancillary gear. Digital computers vary in terms of the *input, memory, processor, control,* and *output* components mentioned above. These differences influence the effectiveness of a given computer for handling particular research problems and therefore require discussion.

At the present time the most common types of *internal memory units* are *core* and *drum.* Computers with core memory units can be several thousand times faster in operating speeds than drum machines. For example, the Bendix G-15, a drum machine, has an average memory access time of 14.5

milliseconds (msec) whereas the Bendix G-20, which has a core memory, has an access time of 6 microseconds (μsec, millionths of a second). *Access time* is usually defined as the time required to get information out of any given register and add it to whatever is in the processor. Thus, for addition, the G-20 is over two thousand times faster than the G-15. But the average monthly rental of the G-20 is approximately thirteen times higher than that of the G-15. For simple tasks of data processing, the G-15 may be completely satisfactory and the additional rental costs for the G-20 would not make economic sense. However, when a psychologist is in the fortunate position of having more than one machine at his disposal, he should attempt to have a costing done for performing the processing on each machine, because generally, the faster the machine, the less the cost of a computation unit. For example, the experience of several computing installations has shown that the IBM 7090 is about three times as fast as the IBM 709 in identical data processing tasks, while the rental of the 7090 installation for the same task is less than twice that of the 709. Therefore, substantial savings could be realized by performing the work on the 7090. (Please note that we are here discussing the time/cost relationships for a specific job, and not monthly rental costs of installations per se.) Unfortunately, the cost of computer rental cannot be taken alone as a decision criterion; programming costs for a particular data processing job may significantly exceed costs of machine operation.

There are three other types of memory unit that may be encountered occasionally: disk, electrostatic, and magnetostrictive. Disk and magnetostrictive computers usually are found in business data processing applications. While they may be used in psychological research, there is less likelihood that there would be programs available for immediate use. Computers with electrostatic memories are generally older machines. Past experience has shown that electrostatic memories tend to be less reliable than core or drum machines.

Most computers also use magnetic tape as an intermediate storage device. Tapes provide a permanent record, if desired, and are therefore more accurately described as input-output elements. Data stored on drums or in core are lost should there be a power or machine failure and are never readily accessible to the researcher in a permanent state.

The primary *input* that most psychologists will use is *punched cards*. Such cards are used for both program and data. But most psychologists need not be concerned with the format and processing of program cards for these are usually handled by procedures unique to a given computer installation. Greater flexibility in card format is possible with data cards. In fact, one of the useful features of a computer is the flexibility afforded in input format. Typical input cards

are shown in Fig. 18-1. All digits, letters, and even special characters can be represented by appropriate punches. The columns on a data card can be divided into units called card fields, and the data in each field can represent whatever set of data is required by the research. The data card in Fig. 18-1 is divided into a number of such fields. The fields between columns 8 and 75 are used to encode data collected during the experimental run. The other fields can be prepared before, during, or after the experiment. For example, let us define a set of possible measures that could go into these data fields:

Columns	Data
8–10	Wechsler-Bellevue IQ score
11–13	TAT N-achievement score
14–16	Light source intensity matching score
17–22	Observer ratings on six variables
23–31	Pretest score on mathematical achievement test
32–40	Post-test score on mathematical achievement test
41–44	Test form code
45–63	Individual item scores, post test, task *A* items
64–75	Individual item scores, post test, task *B* items

If more data must be input, a second card can be prepared with a card sequence of two in columns 5 and 6. It is not necessary to define the same data fields on the second card. For example, columns 8 to 13 may be the needle-deflection reading for psychogalvanic skin response on the second card. On the sample card in Fig. 18-1 allowance has been made for up to 99 data cards for a given subject. The computer can be programmed to accept any particular format, using the card sequence number as the key to what is represented in a given data field. If the experiment involves more than one subject, there must be a correspondence of sequence numbers and data fields across subjects so that card number one contains the information in column 8 through 75 as defined above for all subjects, and so on. A procedural checklist for assisting the researcher in setting up cards and other inputs and for guaranteeing compatibility with the program is shown in Table 18-3.

The process of reading cards into digital computers is quite slow in comparison with internal processing speeds. Hundreds of calculations can often be performed in the time it takes to move a card across the reading brushes and deposit its data in the memory of the machine. If a large number of data is involved, e.g., several thousand cards, some savings in the time and money can be achieved by using a separate card-to-magnetic-tape machine. This is simply a one-to-one transformation of the data from the card onto the tape; the data content is not changed. The purpose of performing this operation is to take advantage of the faster input capability of magnetic tape.

A problem encountered with cards is the amount of labor required to enter the data on cards (via keypunch machines) and the possibility that errors will enter during the card punching process. A one-, two-, or three-step process may be required. If response data from the subject can be directly entered onto cards, we have a one-step process, which is usually most desirable. The two-step process would involve the subject's recording his response on a keypunch manuscript form divided into appropriate rows and columns so that a keypunch operator can punch the data onto cards. A three-step process would consist in a subject's responses being recorded on some other device, then being transcribed onto a keypunch manuscript form, and finally being punched onto cards. As can be seen there are three places for errors to enter when this latter procedure is used. However, it is sometimes possible to set up card formats in such a manner that the computer program can recognize and reject cards containing certain types of punching errors. For example, let us assume that the data field defined by columns 14 to 16 in Fig. 18-1 represents the number of degrees through which a knob is turned in adjusting a light source by using the psychophysical method of average error. If the knob has

stops at 0 and 360°, the maximum number that could appear in this field is 360. A check can be built into the program that would reject any card containing a number greater than 360 in this field. Similar checks can often be specified for other fields. Whenever a large number of cards is involved, error checks in the computer program can be very useful. In terms of experimental instrumentation, cards would seldom be used as an *online* (directly connected to the computer) *input* in an experimental configuration. Computer processing time can be many thousands of times faster than card punching and reading time so that inefficient use of the computer would result from on-line card inputs. A much better experimental procedure would involve the collection of a number of data cards that would then be input as a batch. This approach has the additional advantage that preprocessing on inexpensive punched card machines is possible, such as ordering the cards on the basis of age, sex, or other experimental variables. Furthermore, it may be possible to "pack" the data from several cards onto one input card or load the data onto magnetic tape for faster input. Whether such preprocessing would result in any extensive monetary savings should be checked with a system analyst associated with the particular computer installation.

Card punch equipment is so inexpensive to purchase or rent that it should be considered for direct collection of data from subjects. Punches may be either mechanical or electrical. In electrical punches the circuitry is usually simple enough that it can be wired to an experimental apparatus such as a response bar in an operant conditioning experiment. Small inexpensive mechanical punches can be supplied to a number of subjects responding to a questionnaire. Most computer manufacturers supply manuals or other materials giving more detail on punched card processing. Persons interested in taking a course in punched card data processing should contact their local IBM sales representative. For information on the type of experimental instrumentation possible for incorporating card punching equipment, see McConnell, Polidora, Friedman, and Meyer (1959).

A second major input device is tape. Both paper and magnetic tape are commonly used. *Paper tape* is prepared in much the same way as punched cards. Its major advantages over cards are its higher input speeds and easier and safer storage, although it does not have the preprocessing possibilities that are so often useful with cards. For example, it is difficult to insert additional or overlooked data from a given subject on a paper tape. Another advantage of the paper tape is that on many computers it is compatible with teletype output. Even when there is no compatibility, machines are available that will translate teletype tape into the proper computer input tape format. The widespread availability and relative cheapness of teletype equipment make it worthwhile to investigate the feasibility of encoding subjects' responses directly on teletype tape and thereby having the computer input automatically prepared.

The choice between punched cards or paper tape as an input is largely a matter of convenience and availability. A checklist to help decide which device to use considers data collection and data processing. In *data collection* one would check the following factors: "Can it be collected on computer input devices?" This is the most convenient and direct way. "Can it be recorded on keypunch input forms?" This saves one transcription and hence reduces possible errors. "Must the computer respond to the subject's responses during the experimental run?" This usually implies an on-line input-output such as a typewriter, although paper tape or punched cards may sometimes be used. For *data preprocessing*, check the following: "Must the data be sorted, collated etc.?" Punched cards are more convenient than paper tape. "Is it likely that data will be deleted or added at a later date?" Punched cards are more convenient than paper tape. If neither of the above obtains, the choice between punched cards and paper

tape is a matter of equipment availability or ease of experimental instrumentation.

Magnetic tape differs from paper tape and cards in input speed and space required for physical storage. The RCA 301 magnetic tape can store 333 characters per inch and can read-write at 10,000 characters per second. The paper tape can store 10 characters per inch and can read at 100 or 1,000 and can punch at 100 or 300 characters per second. Data from several thousand cards can be stored on a single magnetic reel, and this removes the problems arising if a box of cards are dropped. This is even more critical where program cards are involved. It is good practice to store often-used checked-out programs on tape.

Another standard input device is the *on-line* (i.e., connected directly to the computer) *typewriter*. This device is most often used by the computer operator in answer to machine interrogation during a program run or by the programmer during program testing. *Machine interrogation procedures* are often included in the computer program to enable the operator to make decisions on what the appropriate next step should be. If an error has been detected in an input card, the program may output the error on the typewriter and ask the operator whether the processing should proceed. If the operator feels that the error is not significant, he may type out the appropriate code and the program will then resume operation. Similar man-machine interactions often are included in the program to help the programmer detect and isolate errors while he is writing and testing the computer program. The typewriter may be a convenient input device when small quantities of data are needed midway in a data processing run. However, this input device is the slowest of those discussed and is not an economical way of data entry with large, fast computers. With small machines, the on-line typewriter may prove to be an important device for recording subjects' responses and entering the information directly into the machine. This is necessary whenever the computer is used to generate stimuli as a function of the subject's response or if process control is required, as in a teaching machine. The most salient advantage of the on-line typewriter from an instrumentation point of view is that most computers are wired for the device or already have it attached, and no additional engineering is required. The only requirement for using it is an appropriate computer program. With large computers, it is often possible to connect a number of these typewriters, but it is not likely that the inputs will be sufficiently numerous to warrant the cost of computer time needed to run the experiment. Usually the computer can process an hour's worth of such inputs in a few seconds. This situation can be remedied if the computer can be used concurrently to perform other data processing tasks during the times it is waiting for inputs. This approach requires an elaborate program control system, which may not be available. The potential, however, for improved experimental capabilities with little additional instrumentation is so great that psychologists should seriously discuss the feasibility of such a program system with the professional data processors responsible for their particular computer installation.

One aspect of *processors* that deserves some discussion is the instruction repertoire. The *instruction repertoire* consists of the number and types of instructions available to the programmer. The number of instructions may vary from as few as 30 to more than 200. The greater the number of instructions, the more difficult the job of efficient programming but the greater the potential for performing a variety of complex operations economically. A machine with a large number of instructions requires an experienced programmer to write the program. For example, let us look at the English translation of the logic used by a computer in response to two different instructions:

Add magnitude. The magnitude of the contents of register X is algebraically added to the contents of the accumulator, and the contents of the accumulator are replaced with this sum. The contents of X remain unchanged.

Low-order bit test. If the lowest-order binary digit in the accumulator is a 1, the computer skips the next instruction; if the lowest-order binary digit is a 0, the computer takes the next instruction in sequence.

It is easy to see that the logic and applicability of the first instruction is simple and straightforward. It is not so clear to the nonprofessional programmer when or why one would use the second instruction. The reason for such instructions requires a few words of explanation. It is usually true that the logic of instructions represented by the second example can be achieved by a series of simpler instructions. In fact, programmers have found that certain operations are convenient in solving problems, and the instructions to perform the operation can be broken out as a logical unit. The computer manufacturer receives feedback on these useful logical units and may decide to include them in the wiring of a new machine. Thus it is possible to achieve in the electronic design of the computer one instruction that may replace a dozen or more required to perform that operation in a simpler machine. This, in turn, results in a decrease in operating time to perform one of these useful functions, provided, of course, that the programmer is aware of the capability and how and where to use it. By increasing the number of instructions and the complexity of what these instructions can do, the manufacturer is also increasing the complexity of the machine; hence it is more expensive to produce. The user of the machine must be prepared to take advantage of this new capability, or it will cost him more to do the same job of data processing on the new computer than it did on the old. Therefore, a general principle evolves: the more complex the instruction repertoire, the more expensive the machine and the less the likelihood that it will be economically feasible for the using psychologist to write his own computer program. The psychologist wishing to use such a machine may therefore have to obtain the services of a programmer. However, great strides are being made in the development of user and procedure-oriented languages that should significantly lessen the requirement for the psychologist to work directly with a programmer.

In addition to number of instructions, types of instructions must also be considered. Some computers have only arithmetic and control instructions, while others include logical instructions. The latter are particularly convenient when the problem being solved involves expressions in Boolean algebra. Also, the experimental utility of nonmetric measurement models (Coombs, 1952) may be greatly enhanced by utilizing computers with logical-instruction repertoires.

The *control unit* need be of little concern to the psychologist. The programming aids for a given machine are designed to operate with that machine's control unit, and programs written for a machine with an n address control unit will not necessarily work on a machine with an x address control unit. This may even be so when $n = x$.

All the inputs already described can also be used as *output devices*. Punched cards represent the slowest type of output, even slower than punched card input. If punched cards are desired, it is usually more economical to output on magnetic tape and use a separate tape-to-card machine. This would be especially true if something like animal responses in a T maze were being recorded. These responses would usually occur so slowly in relation to machine operating capability that they would probably be output on tape to keep the memory clear for other processing. If formatted properly, it would be a simple procedure to run this magnetic tape through a tape-to-card machine to end up with a deck of cards. This would be far less expensive than reading in the tape and having the computer output the data on its on-line punch. A very important output device is the on-line printer, which can be used to produce a readable, hard-copy output that can be immediately used and will be a per-

manent record. Printers have been developed that are very fast. For example, the printer of the Control Data Corporation 1604 computer can print up to 1,000 lines per minute. Such printers are very useful where a large quantity of data must be output in a readable form, as is often required when the computer is being used to prepare material for experimental or training purposes. The most common problem that a novice user of computers faces with output is an underestimation of the data generating powers of a computer. The researcher is sometimes tempted to inspect the data partway through the processing cycle or to stop the processing short of a small set of summary statistics. This type of output often results in many pages of data; in one extreme case of this sort it was estimated that the requested intermediate outputs would total over 8,000 pages. Any attempt to peruse this or even much smaller amounts of data for unsuspected relationships or for decisions on what should be done next in the processing is almost certain to be unsuccessful.

In addition to the gear discussed above, different manufacturers offer additional *ancillary equipment,* including such items as automatic plotters, CRTs (sometimes with computer-activated cameras), and analog read-in and readout devices. Plotters are convenient whenever a graphical display of data is required. With large amounts of computer-generated data, not only is it difficult to see relationships within a large set of numbers, but the manual plotting of these numbers in graphic form may prove prohibitive; a direct computer-generated plot may be the only reasonable solution. The CRT is useful if a pictorial display is required during the computer run or if computer-produced data are used during an experimental session. The camera can be used to permanently record data displayed on the tube either for subsequent analysis or to be presented to subjects in the course of an experiment. Digital-analog devices are useful whenever continuous data such as temperature, time, blood pres-

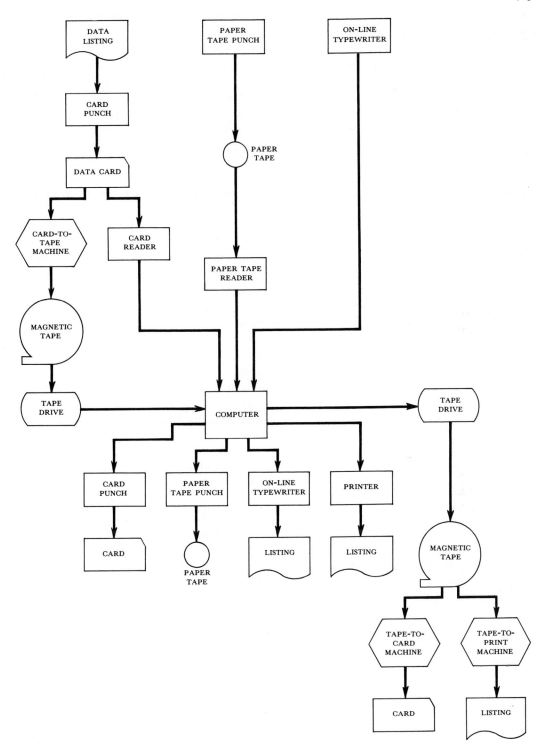

Fig. 18-2 A schematic diagram of typical input and output components of a computer installation.

sure, or tracking performance must be prepared for computer entry or for feedback and process-control purposes. The psychologist using a computer as a research tool should carefully review with knowledgeable facility personnel all equipment available in the computer facility. Often there is equipment that can be used in unexpected ways to provide needed support.

An operating computer-based system consisting of the major input and output devices discussed in this section is schematically represented in Fig. 18-2.

COMPUTER INSTALLATIONS

The purpose of this section is to describe the various types of computer installation that are available to psychologists who may require data processing support. These computer installations include the *in-house computer facility,* the *data processing center,* the *satellite computer complex,* the *service bureau, local industry,* and the *computer rental broker.* Each type of installation poses unique problems to the user, and these problems may in turn limit the types of application possible. It is extremely unlikely that any researcher could not find some type of computer installation available to him for data reduction; but it would be very difficult, short of purchase or rental of one's own in-house machine, to find many installations usable for experiments requiring process control.

A computer installation consists of more than just a computer. Elements of an installation are often differentiated on the basis of their being *on-line equipment, off-line equipment,* and *electronic accounting machines* (EAM). On-line equipment consists of the electronic gear directly connected to the computer. This includes input and output components, tape units, disk files, and other auxiliary computers. Off-line equipment is used to support the computer but is not directly tied into it. Typical off-line gear consists of card-to-tape and tape-to-card units, tape-to-printers, data-link-to-tape units, and

tape record selectors. The purpose of off-line gear is to perform routine pre- or post-processing of data without tying up the computer. The availability of such off-line gear can considerably reduce the cost of data processing and allow the installation to process more data in a given time span. It may also reduce programming time and costs. One unit that may prove of considerable value is a *data translator.* This device can convert data, usually recorded on tape, from one machine format to another. Thus, a central data reduction job can be done at a single facility even though the data to be reduced was produced elsewhere on a variety of machines. This represents a significant step toward intercomputer compatibility. It should be noted, however, that this compatibility is only in the handling of data. True compatibility of programs has yet to be completely realized. Electronic accounting machines consist of the familiar card punching, sorting, collating, and similar electromechanical devices. For many psychological research applications, the EAM devices are the instruments through which data are prepared for computer entry.

The most usual and by far the most convenient installation is the *in-house computer facility* where the computer installation belongs to or is rented by the researcher's own institution. Many such installations have a dual function, the computer being used for administrative as well as scientific data processing. Unfortunately, the administrative uses tend to be preemptive of computer time, and the type of on-line and off-line gear may not be suitable for most of the applications discussed above. At the very least, however, the dual-use installations can be employed for data reduction and statistical analyses. Most of the major universities operate a computer installation exclusively for research work, thus significantly reducing competition for computer time. Many industrial firms, nonprofit corporations, and government agencies also maintain in-house facilities. The major advantage of an in-house installation is the ready availability of analysis, procedures, and programming support that can be obtained on a person-to-person basis.

Next to an in-house installation, the most convenient option available to the academic researcher is the *data processing center*. The pioneer of this type of facility is the Western Data Processing Center, established with the joint support of IBM and UCLA, which provides computing support to numerous universities and colleges in the western states. The major drawbacks to the researcher's using a distant center are restriction in types of projects that can be undertaken, e.g., process control and environmental simulation; the time required for transmitting data and receiving output (usually by mail, although in many situations direct phone links are used); and lack of on-the-spot contact with the installation support staff. There are several techniques by which these disadvantages can be overcome. One such technique is the *satellite computer complex*. Such a complex utilizes small computers, several of which may be connected to a large machine. Small data processing tasks may be performed on these satellites, or the satellites can be used to preprocess data to be input to the large computer. The satellites can also be placed in remote locations, allowing several users easy access to a major computing capability. Both business and research problems can be handled simultaneously, and the researcher can monitor the processing of his own data and obtain rapid feedback. Such systems may be widely dispersed if communication lines or microwave facilities are provided. The satellite concept offers the unique advantages of providing a large, powerful computer capability at the desk of the researcher and at a reasonable cost. For example, the satellite could be connected to analog devices to effect process control, having the large, central computer available on an interrupt basis for processing major blocks of data. Another source of computer support is the service bureau. *Service bureaus* have been provided by most of the larger computer manufacturers in major cities, and provide data processing support on a rental basis to anyone needing it. This support includes programming for in-house installations as well as renting computer time to the occasional user. The bureaus are well staffed with high-caliber personnel and have the latest equipment. However, they will generally prove more expensive for the researcher than an in-house facility, are not available in many locations, and are limited in their research application to nonreal time projects such as data reduction and analysis and projects not requiring special equipment.

Before the researcher rushes out to rent time on a service-bureau machine, he should thoroughly canvass *local industrial* and *research firms*. Many firms own one or more small computers and may be amenable to making these machines available during slack times for research purposes. Some firms may also make their large computer installations available at cost to researchers in order to fully utilize their large computer during slack periods or to completely fill up a shift. Another option only recently available is the *computer rental broker*. Such brokers sell computer time to anyone, any time, on the machine of his choice.

In-house installations, data processing centers, satellite computers, service bureaus, and industrial and research firms represent the major sources of computer support for the psychological researcher. Unfortunately, however, the availability of computer time represents only one of the considerations of successful computer utilization. Other items that must be considered are computer programming and computer economics.

COMPUTER PROGRAMMING

Computer programming represents the most critical element in effective computer utilization and is the biggest hurdle for the occasional user. This section will describe the various sources for computer programs and the approach and techniques the psychologist should use to obtain a satisfactory program.

The open versus the closed shop

Most computer installations operate under one of two modes of programming support, usually characterized as open or closed shops. Each has advantages and disadvantages to the potential user. In the *closed shop,* all programming is performed by a group of professional programmers. The user does not have access to either the program or the computer. He works closely with a programmer in order to clearly and unambiguously define the problem to be programmed. The success of the endeavor depends on the clarity of the problem in the researcher's mind and his ability to communicate the problem to the programmer. Any ambiguity in the problem formulation must be resolved, either by the researcher or by the programmer. If it is left to the programmer to resolve, the solution may not be in concert with the requirements of the research. The researcher should avoid esoteric language because it can produce a major stumbling block in communication and significantly increase the time required to develop the program. In addition, the lack of clearly understood requirements will increase the difficulty of checking out the program, i.e., determining that the program does what it is supposed to do. Because program checkout involves both computer time and professional programmer time, the cost of poor formulation will be intolerable, and all this with the risk that the final product may never be truly satisfactory. One task of the closed-shop programmer is that of maximizing the efficient use of the facility. To do this effectively he must know such things as the amount of data to be handled, the frequency of program operation, and time constraints, if any. The amount of data to be handled determines the allocation of computer memory and any in-out transfers of data that may be required. If more data must be processed than specified, the program may require re-

design; if less data, the computer may not be efficiently used. If the program is to be used once or a very few times, the program should be as direct as possible, minimizing programmer time. If, however, the program will be a general routine likely to be used over and over, the programmer may want to develop a more polished and sophisticated program that will minimize operating time but require a longer period for development. Time constraints are particularly important whenever process control is being programmed.

The simplest tasks to program are those involving the solution of mathematical equations. These equations can be supplied to the programmer by the user and readily translated into program code. Once the program has been written, test cases can be run on the computer to determine whether any errors exist within the equations or their coded representations. It is relatively simple to check test cases by hand calculations. It follows that one of the easiest programming tasks would be a statistical analysis. Programs used as vicarious behavers, or in system research, are at the other extreme in complexity. The former pose problems because the reason they are developed is that the outcomes are too difficult to arrive at by analytical means. It may be extremely difficult to generate unambiguous test cases. The situation with system research and analysis can be even more complicated. Systems are designed to cope with a variety of environmental conditions. The number of permutations of environmental events can reach astronomical proportions so that there is no practical way by which the program system can be completely tested. It is absolutely imperative, therefore, that the problem formulation and program design be of the highest quality. In such program systems the user must accept the possibility that a finite number of errors will remain, even after extensive testing and shakedown have been completed.

Advantages of a closed-shop programming installation can be summarized as follows:

1. All programming and testing are done by data processing specialists, ensuring a high-quality program.

2. Computer-facility utilization is improved because the program is tailored to the facility requirements as well as the user requirements.

3. The problem to be programmed must be well defined and communicable before programming can begin, thus eliminating many potential false starts.

4. The program is usually well documented, which provides a basis for continuity should the project be interrupted and makes the program available to other users.

Disadvantages include the following:

1. The researcher can lose familiarity with his project unless the programmer is willing to interact extensively with the researcher.

2. Regardless of the clarity of specifications, ambiguities arise during programming. The programmer may not know which ambiguities are research-relevant and require resolution by the researcher. Under time pressure he may make decisions on his own that should really come from the researcher.

3. Work priority may pose problems, particularly if the programmer is working on several projects simultaneously. The researcher and the programmer should have an understanding, prior to beginning the project, on such things as schedule, priority, documentation, and maintenance support.

4. Flexibility to make changes in the program as dictated by new ideas or intermediate program outputs may be reduced because the researcher has no access to the program or the computer.

It is only fair to point out that these disadvantages largely disappear if the researcher carefully follows the effective computer-utilization procedures suggested later in the chapter. Most of the disadvantages inherent in a closed-shop operation are reduced in an open-shop installation. In an *open shop,* programming may be done by the user. This, however, introduces a host of

other problems, centered around the difficulty of writing programs.

Programming tools

Before one can completely understand some of the difficulties of programming, it is necessary to return to a discussion of the basic operating characteristics of computers. Most digital computers operate by using a binary number system rather than the decimal system, with which we are all familiar. A comparison between decimal and binary notations is given below for the numbers zero through nine:

0	0000	5	0101
1	0001	6	0110
2	0010	7	0111
3	0011	8	1000
4	0100	9	1001

It takes a minimum of four binary digits (bits) to represent the numbers 0 through 9. While there is nothing intrinsically difficult in representing numbers or quantity in binary notation, it is awkward for us to do so; we find it relatively easy to recognize 111 as 7, but it is not easy to see that 100110110 represents 310. Therefore, if one wished to prepare data directly for input to the computer, he would find it necessary to translate each number from decimal to binary, which can be a tedious and time-consuming process. Furthermore, the computer must respond to a set of instructions on how it is to process these data. Once again these instructions are represented by a binary notation. For example, let us specify the following equivalences:

The binary notation	Means	The operation of
110		Addition
100		Subtraction
010		Multiplication
111		Division

Now you may ask how the computer knows that 110 means "add" rather than the number 6. The answer is that the computer "knows" this distinction only by means of a correctly written program. The notation 110 is treated as an instruction to add only when it is in the instruction processor. When it is not in the instruction processor, it is treated as the number 6. It is therefore possible that given numbers may sometimes be treated as data, sometimes as instructions. It is up to the programmer to see that the program is written so that these numbers are treated correctly. This is usually accomplished by means of addressing; that is, a particular program may reside in the memory at addresses of 1 through 96 while the data may be stored in addresses 97 through 900. But once again these addresses must be represented in binary form so that the computer can find them. Thus a typical computer operation represented in binary might look like this:

$$\underset{A}{\underline{110}} \quad \underset{B}{\underline{110}} \quad \underset{C}{\underline{100110110}}$$

$$\underset{D}{\underline{100110110}} \quad \underset{E}{\underline{011101111}}$$

A is the address of the given instruction that is located in the sixth register in the memory. The instruction consists of two parts: B, which represents the instruction "add" (not the number six), and C, which indicates the address of the number to be added, in this case register 310. D is the address of the number to be added, i.e., register 310, and E is the actual number to be added, 239. This type of notation is called a *machine-language representation*. A simple program for solving the equation

$$Y = \frac{(f_o - f_e)^2}{f_e}$$

is written out in machine language at the top of Table 18-1. The psychologist will recognize the above equation as equivalent to the expression for χ^2 (chi square) where f_o represents the obtained and f_e the expected frequencies. This example illustrates the three classes of information that are represented in binary form: data, instructions, and addresses. Few readers can glance at the machine-language program in Table 18-1

Table 18-1   Program written in machine, programming, and compiler languages.

MACHINE-LANGUAGE SOLUTION TO $(f_o - f_e)^2/f_e$			
1	11011000	11000	011101111
10	10011001	11001	100110110
11	10111011	11011	000000000
100	01011011		
101	11111001		
110	10111111		

PROGRAM-LANGUAGE SOLUTION TO $(f_o - f_e)^2/f_e$

Program = A = 15	B 239	A CLA	B
Data = B = 200	310	SUB	B + 1
Storage = C = 300 + 10		STR	C
	C 0	MULT	C
		DIV	B + 1
		STR	C + 3

PROCEDURE-ORIENTED-LANGUAGE SOLUTION TO $(f_o - f_e)^2/f_e$

FØ = 239

FE = 310

$$Y = ([FØ - FE]**2.0)/FE$$

and immediately tell which is which. If the program consists of 90 instructions and 804 pieces of data, the task is formidable if not impossible. Fortunately, it is seldom, if ever, necessary to write programs in machine language. Quite early in the history of modern computers, techniques were developed for using the computer as a translator from a symbolic or programming language to machine language. It was then possible to write programs in a notation more closely representing the symbols of ordinary English. Using a *programming language,* addresses could be specified by a symbolic location, for example, A, A + 1, . . . , A + n would represent the locations of instructions; B, B + 1, . . . , B + n the locations of data, etc. Furthermore, it was possible to use mnemonic abbreviations to stand for the instructions; e.g., the add operation could be represented by the code ADD rather than 110, and subtract by SUB rather than 100. Finally, data to be processed could be represented in decimal rather than binary notation. The relatively greater ease with which a program written in a programming language can be interpreted is illustrated by the example in the middle of Table 18-1. In the example, the left-hand column defines the addresses where the instructions (A), the data (B), and storage (C) begin and, in the case of storage, end. The middle column identifies the numbers f_o (239) and f_e (310) as data and states that the storage registers C should be set to zero. The right-hand column is identified as the program (A), and lists the instructions the machine is to perform. For purposes of illustration, assume that the machine's processing unit has an accumulator similar to that found in a desk calculator. The instructions are interpreted as:

CLA	B	Set the accumulator to zero and add the contents of address B, that is, 239.
SUB	B + 1	Subtract the contents of address B + 1, that is, 310, from the contents of the accumulator. (This is the expression $f_o - f_e$.)
STR	C	Store the results in address C (while still retaining the results in the accumulator).
MULT	C	Multiply the accumulator by the contents of address C. [This is the expression $(f_o - f_e)^2$.]
DIV	B + 1	Divide the contents of the accumulator by the contents of B + 1. (This is the solution sought.)
STR	C + 3	Store the contents of the accumulator at address C + 3. (The results can then be used in further calculations by addressing it at C + 3.)

Note that this example is for a single-address type of computer.

Once the program has been written in this notation (programming language), it is punched onto program cards and input to the computer along with a computer program known as an assembler, which is also on cards. The *assembler* translates the instructions and data into machine language and assigns the proper addresses (called absolute machine addresses) to instructions and data. The output of this process is an "assembled" computer program ready to operate on the computer. The assembled machine-language program cards are input to the computer along with the researcher's punched data cards and acted upon. From the standpoint of the psychological researcher planning to write a computer program, the use of a programming language and its associated assembler leaves much to be desired. The main problem is that the program must still be written in a form that specifies every single detailed step needed to process the data. In this respect there is no real difference in the number and type of instructions written between a machine-language and programming-language notation. The programming language also cannot take advantage of the symbology found so useful in mathematics. When specifying a simple addition, for example, it is much more convenient to write $Z + Y$ rather than ADD A (location of Z is A), ADD B (location of Y is B).

Fortunately for computer users, the last few years have seen the development of a number of procedure-oriented languages with which it is possible to write programs as general procedures or algorithms rather than as individual program steps. *Procedure-oriented languages* use a computer program called a *compiler,* which takes the procedure notation and expands it into either a programming-language or a machine-language notation. Thus the written program in procedure-oriented language is entered onto program cards. The program cards are input to the computer along with the compiler program cards. The computer acts upon these inputs, and the result is a stack of assembled machine-language program cards or programming-language cards. If the result is the former, a separate set of cards containing the data is entered into the computer along with the machine-language cards. If the output is a programming language, this in turn must be assembled according to the routine described in the section covering programming language.

The advantage of a compiler over an assembler is that the compiler usually enables one to write a program in a procedure- or problem-oriented language rather than the step-by-step programmer language required by an assembler. This advantage can be seen by referring to Table 18-1. A procedure-language program for the same problem can be written in the form

$$Y = \frac{([F\emptyset - FE]**2.0)}{FE}$$

which is a very direct translation of the algebraic representation into a notation that a computer can handle. A compiler program would take the equation as written in procedure language and compile it into a set of programming or machine-language representations. Therefore, as far as the user is concerned all three representations of the simple program illustrated in Table 18-1 are functionally equivalent, but they are ordered from top to bottom in decreasing difficulty of actually writing the program.

Procedure-oriented languages may also make use of a computer program called an interpreter. An *interpreter* differs from a compiler in that it translates the procedure-language instructions into the appropriate machine instructions and immediately executes the instructions rather than requiring an intermediate output. Thus the written program in procedure-oriented language is punched onto program cards and input to the computer along with interpreter program cards and data.

Assemblers, compilers, and interpreters are computer programs that serve as tools for the program writer. They enable the programmer to write instructions for the computer in an understandable language or code, use decimal digits to represent data, and assist in the allocation of memory. These special programs are sometimes referred to as *utility* or *support programs,* and each major computer is equipped with one or more of them. For a more complete description of the evolution of assemblers and compilers plus a discussion of newer utility concepts and their applications to behavior and biological modeling, see Elbourne and Ware (1962). The purpose of this discussion on programming tools is to make the user aware of some of the things he has at his disposal if faced with the task of programming in an open shop. Each computer facility maintains a set of utility programs, thus enabling the user to take advantage of programming or procedure languages when writing his own program. Unfortunately, there are very few such languages that are completely independent of the particular computer or even variations of ancillary equipment on the same basic machine. It is, therefore, seldom practical to teach a potential computer user to program independently of the installation he would actually use. For more detailed information on programming see Leeds and Weinberg (1961), Sherman (1963), or Golden (1965). IBM also includes courses on programming with specific examples for various IBM computers in its Personal Study Program. Although "general machine" independent programming is not practical for the psychologist at this time, developments in this area will be rapid.

One of the best known procedure-oriented languages is FORTRAN (FORmula TRANslator), the compiler for which was originally developed for the IBM 700 series of computers. For most data reduction and analysis tasks, FORTRAN is a satisfactory system for writing programs. A reasonable proficiency can be achieved with several hours of instruction. For a detailed discussion on FORTRAN programming, see McCracken (1961; 1965). There are FORTRAN compilers available for a large variety of computers, so a program written in FORTRAN may represent a high degree of machine independence, i.e., the program is written in a language acceptable to all computers for which that language's compiler is available. From the user's standpoint, machine independence is desirable in that a program once written can be used on any computer (given the necessary compiler) without requiring any reprogramming. Such independence has been the exception, not the rule, and remains an exception to a degree even with FORTRAN.

A list of some of the procedure-oriented languages and computers for which compilers or interpreters have been written is presented in Table 18-2. One or more compilers are available for each of the more commonly used computers. This does not necessarily mean that you can freely use a given compiler. The compiler is usually designed to go with a particular machine configuration (e.g., a compiler written for a Philco 2000 with 32,000 core registers will not necessarily work on a Philco 2000 with 16,000 core registers). Furthermore, a particular computer installation may not be able to incorporate a compiler because of limitations of its *executive system* (i.e., those programs which control the operation of the computer, its utility programs, and its operational programs). Nevertheless, the user who contemplates employing a computer for more than data reduction and analysis should examine, preferably with a data processing expert, appropriate compilers (such as we have cited as examples) in Table 18-2 to see whether he can find one to fit the selected computer. It will usually be easier to learn the grammar and notation of that compiler's language and then write the program in that language than to write the program in a programming language. There is usually a manual available explaining how to use a given language, but this is not enough to gain proficiency. Individual or class instruction plus some time on a machine are necessary before mastery is achieved.

In summary, the researcher who desires to do his own programming in an open-shop installation will probably do it in a programming, compiler, or interpreter language, depending on what types of utility program are available for the particular computer. In any case he must master the language he will use. On small computers an operating proficiency with a programming language can be attained with one to two weeks of instruction plus the same amount of time spent in working on the machine with one's own program. With the larger computers the time required may be several months, particularly if the program skills are commensurate with the types of complex problem for which these large machines were designed. Even with this amount of training the user cannot expect to achieve anything close to the competence of the full-time professional programmers. With simple compilers or interpreters, two or three days of instruction may suffice. Some of the more complex compilers such as JOVIAL may require many weeks of instruction and actual experience before satisfactory proficiency can be achieved. It can readily be seen that there is no easy way to learn programming, particularly for the more complex computer applications. Fortunately, however, much data processing research and development is being directed toward achieving more easily mastered programming tools.

Program libraries

A far less demanding option for programming support can often be found in program libraries developed by computer users. In many cases organizations using the same computer join to form user groups that share the cost of general-purpose program development. SHARE is a nationwide cooperative composed of IBM computer users. Included in the SHARE library are many programs applicable to psychological research problems. The June issues of the periodical *Computers and Automation* list user groups for some of the most common computers. Computer manufacturers also list library programs available for different machines and installation configurations. (For example, see the IBM reference manual, *Catalog of programs for IBM data processing systems,*

Table 18-2   Representative procedure-oriented languages, areas of possible use in psychology, computers for which compilers are available, and organization which constructed compiler.

Language and use	Computer	Constructor of compiler
IPL-V		
Artificial intelligence, process control, real time simulation, vicarious behavers, system research and analysis, stimulus generation	IBM 704/7090	Rand Corp./Carnegie Tech.
	IBM 709	Lincoln Labs.
	Philco 2000	System Development Corp.
	CDC 1604	Univ. of Texas
	UNIVAC 1103	Univ. of North Carolina
	Bendix G-20	Carnegie Tech.
LISP 1		
Same as IPL-V	IBM 704/709/7090	MIT
COMIT		
Same as IPL-V plus information retrieval	IBM 709/7090	MIT
FORTRAN I	IBM 704, 705,	IBM
Algebraic compiler for data reduction and analysis, stimulus generation	7070, 7080, 1401, 1620	
FORTRAN II	IBM 704, 7070/7074,	IBM
Same as FORTRAN	709/7090, 1410, 1620, 7030	
	UNIVAC LARC	Computer Sciences
	RCA 601	Computer Sciences
	Bendix G-20	Bendix
	CDC 1604	Control Data
	MH 400	Minneapolis-Honeywell
ALTAC	Philco 2000	Philco
(Augmented FORTRAN II for Philco 200 series.) Same as FORTRAN		
Algebraic Compiler	MH 800	Minneapolis-Honeywell
(Accepts FORTRAN II.) Same as FORTRAN		
FORTRANSIT		IBM
Same as FORTRAN		
ALGOL 60	IBM 709/7090	IBM
Same as FORTRAN	CDC 1604	Princeton Univ.
	B 5000	Burroughs
	UNIVAC 1105	Armour Research
	IBM 7070	Duke Univ.
Algebraic Compiler	B 220; B 205	Burroughs
Same as FORTRAN		
ALCOM	G-20	Bendix
Same as FORTRAN		
ALGO	G-15	Bendix
Same as FORTRAN		
JOVIAL	IBM 7090	System Development Corp.
Data reduction and analysis, process control, real time simulation, vicarious behavers, stimulus generation, system research and analysis	Philco 2000	System Development Corp.
	CDC 1604	System Development Corp.
MAD	IBM 704, 709/7090	Univ. of Michigan
Same as JOVIAL		
NELIAC	CDC 1604	Naval Elect. Lab.
Same as JOVIAL	IBM 704	Univ. of California
	IBM 709	Ramo-Wooldridge
EXTRAN	IBM 709/7090, 1410	IBM

Forms # C20-1600 to C20-1604, 1964. The psychologist planning to use a particular computer should determine whether a user group exists for that machine; and if so, he should examine the library to see whether it contains any programs potentially applicable to his problem. In addition to formal user groups, each computer installation usually retains its own library of generally useful programs. The following represents a typical library program description for a data reduction and analysis program:

Multiple Correlation and Regression Analysis

This program computes the means, standard deviations, "*b*" weight, as well as the multiple correlation coefficient. The matrix of squares and products, the correlation matrix, the inverse of the correlation matrix, and a test of the accuracy of the inverse computation are displayed. The maximum number of variables that can be processed is 30, the upper limit on the number of observations is 5,000. There must be at least two more observations than there are variables in the problem. At the option of the user, the predicted value of Y can be computed for each of the original cases, and the difference between this theoretical Y and the actual Y displayed. An analysis of the extreme residuals can also be computed.

Any variable in the set of original variables can be named the dependent variable on several analyses performed on a single run through the computer. There is no limit on the number of replacements. The maximum number of independent variables which can be deleted at one time is 28. However, there is no limit to the number of deletions of different sets of independent variables. A number of different problems can be "stacked" to be run at the same time. The program can make a log, square root, square, or cubic transformation on any or all of the variables, as desired.

Running times for typical problems were as follows:

1. Eleven variables, 988 cases, no replacements or deletions, but with theoretical Y's and residuals computed for each case, took 4 min of 709 time.

2. Four problems were run at the same time (stacked); 11 variables, 988 cases; 12 variables, 79 cases (with replacement-deletion to yield 20 different regression analyses); 9 variables, 151 cases; and 9 variables, 72 cases; using a total of 3 min, 7090 time.

This program was developed by the Division of Biostatistics at the UCLA Medical Center and adapted by System Development Corporation programmers. It is interesting to note the greater computing power of the 7090 over the 709 when one compares the running times for typical problems.

The user who locates a library routine within his own computer installation to perform the desired data processing task is fortunate. He needs only to follow the directions supplied with the program for data preparation and operating procedures and he is ready to start. If the program is obtained from some other library, some program modifications are usually required because of different machine configurations, operating procedures, or executive systems. Unfortunately, this is true even of programs written in a language such as FORTRAN. Before a request is made to another installation for a program, it should be discussed with a data processing specialist from the installation where the program is to be run. The specialist can advise on the problems likely to be encountered in getting the library program to operate in his installation, as well as additional information that should be requested. The following information should be requested when ordering a library routine from another installation:

1. *A functional description of the program.* This will indicate what the program does and what its capabilities and limitations are.

2. *The configuration required to operate the program.* This should also include any special equipment needed to take advantage of special input or output options.

3. *A program listing.* This may be either in programmer or in procedure language and consists of all instructions plus notations re-

quired by the assembler or compiler. Such a listing is necessary if any modifications are required and is valuable in locating and correcting errors.

4. *A deck of program cards.* The deck is useful, particularly if no modifications are needed, but is not required. A new deck can always be punched from the program listing.

5. *Instructions.* These will tell the user how to set up his data and how to select output options, if any, and will provide the necessary sequence of steps that must be taken by the computer operator to run the program successfully.

6. *Checking procedures.* It is always a good idea to test any library program on one's own computer even if the machine configuration is supposedly the same as that at the installation from which the library program was obtained. Knowledge of special test and checking capabilities included in the program can prove useful in debugging a recalcitrant program.

Procedures for achieving effective computer utilization

So far we have discussed the open and closed programming shop, programming tools, and program libraries. It is now necessary to discuss the manner in which the researcher should prepare to use a computer. A set of procedures is presented below that apply whether or not the facility features an open or closed programming shop, regardless of the utility programs available, and independent of the use of library or specially designed programs. These are presented in an idealized chronological order.

1. *Determine the possible need for computer support* before any data are collected and preferably prior to freezing the experimental design, methodology, and instrumentation. This will allow you to take maximal advantage of the computer installation.

2. *Decide on the particular computer installation to be used.* Hopefully, this choice can be decided on the basis of convenience. In most cases, the most convenient choice is

your own in-house installation. Unless there is some overriding determinant such as an available program for another machine or free computer time, you are better off doing the work where advice and support are close at hand.

3. *Establish contact with the installation.* Find out the following:

   a. Is it a closed or an open shop?
   b. What kind of programming and procedures support is available?
   c. How is such support obtained?
   d. What kind of program library is maintained by the installation?
   e. What off-line and on-line equipment is in the installation?
   f. Is engineering support available for special equipment modifications?
   g. How are costs determined and who is expected to pay the bill?
   h. Are there written procedures for using the facility?
   i. How is computer time scheduled and what is the lead time required to obtain computer time?

With this information you should be able to determine whether it is reasonable for you to consider using the installation and how you should proceed. It is of particular importance to obtain the name of the person with whom you will work.

4. *Formulate the problem to enable you to communicate it to your support person.* This is the most important job to be done in that a good problem formulation will enable you to communicate effectively with the installation's personnel and will also help you in determining exactly what you want to do. A valuable tool for the purpose of problem formulation is the flow diagram. A flow diagram is essentially a sequence of events that describes what you propose to do in a time-ordered fashion. A flow diagram (flow chart) for the process of deciding on input devices is shown in Fig. 18-3. One should start with the major blocks of the study and then proceed to break each block down into

smaller pieces until every step has been included. The most important blocks are those which indicate a choice point, and you should specify the conditions that dictate the choice and what is to be done when the choice is made. The level of detail of the flow diagram will vary, depending on who does the programming. If you are writing the program, the flow diagram should include the steps required in solving a mathematical equation. You need not go to this minute detail if a programmer is writing the program for you or if a library program is to be used. Examples of flow diagrams at various levels of detail can be found in Borko (1962). For more detail and actual instructions on effective flow diagramming see Wrubel (1959).

In formulating the problem, avoid psychological idioms whenever possible. Instead, use operational definitions or simple examples of the major concept. For instance, a statement such as "Each trial which results in a positive reinforcement is recorded" would be unsatisfactory. Instead, say something like the following: "A trial is defined as the pushing of the lever in the Skinner box, which results in the release of a food pellet. Pushing this lever must activate a recording mechanism which will insert the datum in field X of the card format shown in Figure N." The use of mathematical expressions when appropriate is desirable. In any event, do not trust your memory for specifying the important steps and concepts of your experiment; write these down. This not only ensures against forgetting but may call attention to overlooked items. A detailed written description and a flow diagram of your study will usually save time and money in the long run.

5. *Become familiar with some of the basic concepts and terminology of computers and data processing.* The material in this chapter should be considered as a bare minimum. If possible, review the material in Green (1963), Murphy (1958), and in Irwin (1960), the general concepts in Borko (1962), or any other recommended book on computers. Furthermore, try to obtain a copy of the

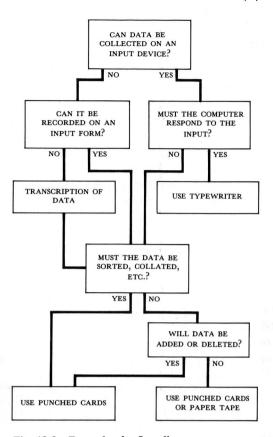

Fig. 18-3 **Example of a flow diagram.**

manufacturer's manual for the computer in your installation and read the descriptive material. If a course on computers and programming is given by your department or organization, take it. This homework will be valuable in establishing a common communication base with the computer installation's personnel.

6. *Contact your support person.* It is at this moment when your preparatory work has its first major payoff. You will be able to clearly and objectively describe and discuss your research project with your support person and also have a common language of discourse concerning computers and data processing. Hopefully, you can thus avoid an all-too-common problem: indifference or even hostility on the part of the installation's

personnel. At the very least you have avoided the risk of being viewed as an inarticulate fool.

In some cases you may be fortunate enough to have a computer specialist in your own department or organization who can serve as a buffer between you and the computer people. This is a useful expedient for the more pedestrian uses of computers such as statistical analysis but will prove unsatisfactory for most other purposes. Such a person cannot spend the necessary time on your project and do much other work. You must face the fact that, to be effective, you must become acquainted with the technology yourself. If the installation works on an open-shop basis, you may even have to learn to do the necessary programming. During the first meeting with your support person, try to cover the following items:

 a. Discuss your project in detail.

 b. Determine where and how the equipment in the installation can be used.

 c. Find out possible library routines and the steps necessary to integrate such routines in your experimental plan.

 d. Note the kinds of question raised so that you can think them out and generate reasonable answers later.

 e. Ask about the type and quantity of support you can expect.

 f. Ask what additional information is required.

 g. Arrive at an understanding on such things as schedule, priority, documentation, working arrangements, instruction, and support.

 h. Establish the next meeting time and what each of you is to do in the interim.

 i. Leave a copy of the flow diagrams and research planning documents that you have generated.

7. *Preparation of the program.* The specific thing you do at this point depends on the type of installation and the kinds of question raised during the meeting with your support person. Certainly you must answer questions raised and clear up any ambiguities in your problem formulation. It may be necessary for you to learn to program or locate library routines. Whether you do the programming or not, there are several kinds of information that must be delineated. These are outlined in the computer program checklist in Table 18-3. Go through this checklist prior to writing any code and provide the necessary data on every relevant item.

8. *Debugging.* There are two kinds of problem that occur in testing computer programs: the program does not meet the specifications, or the specifications may be wrong. The first defines a *program error,* the second a *design error.* To detect a program error, it is necessary to have documentation specifying what the program is to do. This information will be available if you have done the flow diagramming and project description discussed above and have documented the program as it is being written. Some program errors will be obvious—the machine fails to operate or gets into a loop, i.e., a series of instructions that are repeated over and over because the conditions for leaving the series are never realized. Detection of design errors is more difficult and usually requires a test problem, which can be developed concurrently with the programming phase. This test program should exercise all the major options of the program and should include extreme and average values for all program parameters and variables. Once again, the program checklist can be used as a source for test design values. These debugging procedures should also be used on library routines obtained from your own installation's library. When debugging has been completed and you are sure that the program satisfies your design requirements, you are ready to use the program.

9. *Using the program.* How you will use the program will depend to a large extent on what kind of project you have programmed and whether it is an open or a closed shop. In any event, you should follow the procedures called for at the installation.

Table 18-3   Checklist of factors to be considered in preparing to write computer program.

Item	Descriptors
	INPUTS
Source	Describe source of data for processing, i.e., manuscripts, punched cards, typewriter, etc.
Method of collection	Describe special collection methods that may involve computer or special gear.
Preprocessing	Indicate requirements for collating, sorting, listing, etc., of input data.
Quantity	Specify how many data are to be handled on a given run. Give lower and upper bounds.
Frequency	Estimate how often sets of data will be collected and processed. Give minimum and maximum frequency.
Magnitude	Give smallest and largest number to be encountered in any datum unit, e.g., IQ scores from 76 to 147.
Classes of data	Indicate number of classes of data, e.g., IQ scores, error frequencies, etc., to be included in processing. Be sure quantity, frequency, and magnitude are given for each class of data.
Parameters	Define characteristics that may require change at a later date, e.g., input must take 10 scores/subject. It may be necessary to increase up to 15 following preliminary runs.
Error checks	Specify inputs where errors would be most damaging and give meaningful range of values.
Other characteristics	Give any additional information such as number of characters/card, card field definitions, number of cards/subject, etc., wherever possible.
	OUTPUTS
Categories	Describe each category of output data required, e.g., sums of squares, means, frequency counts/subject, etc.
Form	For each category, define form of output, e.g., sums of squares on printed listing, means on cards, frequency counts on paper tapes, etc.
Format	Diagram format of output, including definition of card fields, columns of print-out, etc. Also, note number of decimal places or rounding required.
Post processing	Indicate likely requirements for post processing such as sorting and collating.
Uses	Describe what each output is to be used for and how this use is to be accomplished.
	PROCESSING
State of goal	Give a general statement of what the program is to do.
Relation to inputs	Relate each input to program goal.
Parameters	Indicate the program features that may require modification; e.g., accuracy to three decimal places for first run may have to increase to four.
Frequency of use	Estimate how often program is likely to be run.
Generality	Indicate how generally useful the program is likely to be and hence whether it should be considered as a library program or at least maintained for temporary heavy use.
Conditionalities	Indicate special conditions that may occur and what should be done; e.g., if input error is detected, should program be stopped until error has been corrected or should it skip and proceed?

Furthermore, you should have written instructions on what to do if the program hangs up or the computer fails. Also, note what actions are to be taken if there are intermediate stops or check points included in the program design. These written instructions are particularly important in the closed shop, where the actual running of the program is performed by someone other than yourself.

Methods and procedures support

Before leaving the discussion of computer programming, there is one other facet of support to be discussed. A well-run computer facility usually has a set of operating procedures. New types of computer application must be fitted into these procedures, or new methods and procedures must be developed. These methods and procedures define the way that programs are written, how data are formatted, and how the user prepares and schedules the material for going on the computer. Methods and procedure analysts are usually a part of the computer facility staff and are often available to help the psychologist on tasks such as:

1. Preparation of forms for submission of programs and data to keypunch
2. Flow diagramming of problems to assist in coding and check-out
3. Preparation of instructions for the computer operator
4. Definition of outputs required and output formats
5. Wiring of electronic accounting machine (EAM) control panels for off-line processing

The purpose of this section has been to point out some of the problems of obtaining a satisfactory computer program and the procedures that should be followed to maximize the probability of obtaining such program. The topic of programming has been stressed because the computer program is the critical element in using computers and is the element that most often gives the potential computer user the greatest number of problems. Quite often it is necessary for the user to find or write his own programs. The development of programming tools, particularly procedure-oriented languages and their associated compilers, has done much to simplify the programming required for the more sophisticated computer uses described above. However, there is no "easy" way to solve the programming problem. The user must be prepared to invest heavily of his time and talent in order to achieve the long-term gains that can be his from a mastery of this tool.

COMPUTER ECONOMICS

The final consideration germane to computer usage can be referred to as computer economics. A computer is an expensive piece of equipment to own and operate. Even though the individual researcher may not have to pay rental for time used on his own project, often he must compete with other projects for running time. His research may then be subjected to some type of cost-effectiveness analysis in order to establish a priority.

Another major economic factor is the cost of computer programming. This cost often exceeds computer operating costs; however, once a program has been written it may be used over and over. Thus the cost can be prorated over a number of projects. Programming costs, however, will continue to be a major economic factor for the researcher developing new techniques and theories until significant new advances in compiler technology have been achieved. With a compiler, a large proportion of new program costs on new projects also can be prorated.

Computer costs vary. Small machines such as the Clary DE60 can be rented for as little as $600 per month, while the IBM 7030 (STRETCH) computer may run as high as $200,000 per month for an average installation. These figures represent average monthly rentals. It is theoretically possible for a complete computing system to rent for more than 1 million dollars per month. Monthly computer rental contracts are usually based upon 176 hours (hr) of usable computer time, regardless of the time of day or day of the month. This is equivalent to 8 hr per day on a 5-day week. Overtime rental is usually 40 to 50 percent of the standard rate, although some manufacturers have special provisions. Therefore, it is most economical to operate the installation on a round-the-clock basis. With most computers, however, a certain number of hours must be allocated to maintenance each day. This may run from 8 hr for older vacuum-tube machines to an hour or even less for solid state, or transistorized, machines. Maintenance time is not usable computer time, so no rental is charged. The recent prime-shift monthly rental for the LGP 30 computer averaged $1,300. The prime-shift hourly rate for the same machine was approximately $6.25 while the two-shift hourly rate was $4.38. Representative rental rates for several other computers over the three time periods were as follows: Bendix G-15 (also IBM 1620) $1,600 monthly, $9.09 prime-shift hourly, and $6.36 two-shift hourly rate; Burroughs 205, $8,000, $45.45, and $31.82; IBM 709, $40,000, $227.27, and $159.09; IBM 7090, $65,000, $369.32, and $258.52. The cost differences for one- and two-shift hourly rates are based on a second-shift rental of 40 percent of prime-shift rates. These rental rates also will be close to costs of operation and depreciation on machines that are purchased. While costs for machines are readily attainable, it is quite difficult to estimate programming costs. There is a trade-off between programming and machine costs, depending on the use of the program. A program that will be used frequently should have more programmer time invested in it than a one-shot program, from a strict economics standpoint. Estimates of the amount of work that

can be expected from a programmer also vary with the type and size of the problem to be programmed. These estimates vary from 6 to 15 instructions per programmer per day when a programming language is used. While this may seem like a relatively small number of instructions, the numbers prorate formulation, program writing, testing, error correction, procedures for use, and documentation. These estimates, therefore, provide a convenient abstraction for costing purposes provided that there is also an estimate of program size available. This type of costing requires a skilled and knowledgeable programmer, not only to estimate number of instructions likely but also to estimate what number of instructions, per man day, should be used. In general, the lower range of figures refers to large process-control systems requiring a significant analysis and formulation effort or to the development of assemblers and compilers. The higher figures represent the effort to program relatively straightforward problems such as mathematical equations. Cost of programmer time may run from $40 to $100 and more per day including salary, fringe benefits, administration, and supervision. A relatively simple product-moment correlation program might require approximately 150 instructions. Assuming 15 instructions per day, this program would require 10 days to write. Only a reasonably proficient programmer can write 15 instructions per day, so we can assume a programmer cost of $60 per day, bringing the total programming cost to $600, exclusive of computer time. A multiple-regression program would cost on the order of $3,000. A large military command and control system program may run more than a million dollars in programmer costs alone. The same programs may be written in a procedure-oriented language for 50 to 75 percent of these costs, exclusive of compiler costs. As can be seen, programs are not cheap. The expense of programming makes a diligent search for already existing programs an important part of research planning.

In the economic planning of any research project, computer rental and programming costs should be carefully estimated. For data reduction and analysis these costs should then be compared with costs of electronic accounting machinery or even hand calculation. Competent clerical personnel are less expensive than programmers, and there are undoubtedly many graduate students who feel that they perform such data reduction tasks at the lowest cost of all. Other ways to reduce costs are to do your own manuscripting and keypunching. For other than the data reduction job the range of alternatives to the computer is not so great. While it is true that some research of the type to which computers are now being applied has been done without computers in the past, full exploitation in these areas requires automation. Whether special-purpose devices can reasonably be used in place of a digital computer is a technical and economic problem that must be examined in each case.

PROBLEMS OF COMPUTER UTILIZATION

Throughout this chapter we have pointed out some of the pitfalls and problems of using digital computers. These problems are summarized here with the hope that their recognition will assist the researcher in doing a better job.

1. *Status of psychological theory.* It must always be recognized that a computer is an inexorably logical machine. It will not tolerate ambiguous formulation. Unfortunately, much psychological theory is not stated rigorously enough to be represented by a computer program. Whether this is a good or bad thing can be argued by the various schools of theoreticians. Nevertheless, the researcher must recognize this fact and exercise reasonable caution when applying computer techniques to his problem.

2. *Programming support.* Most research problems utilizing a computer will require some interaction between the researcher and a computer programmer. This interaction will be facilitated if the researcher has a well-thought-out project and has developed a language of discourse for communicating with the programmer. An ambiguous theory or a poorly articulated research plan will work against the attainment of adequate programming, even if the researcher plans on doing the programming himself.

3. *Testing the program.* Each program must be tested to see that it operates correctly. Many errors are uncovered because the program may refuse to work. There are other errors, however, that are not easy to detect, and these can be characterized by the question of whether or not the program does what it is supposed to do. Test cases should be run as a matter of course where the program output is compared with an expected output. With complex programs, there is always the possibility that an error will remain undetected for a long period of time. In these cases the user should try to specify performance criteria for the program.

4. *Quantity of output.* Great care must be taken that the user is not overwhelmed by data. The speed and power of modern computers for data production should not be underestimated. As much data reduction and analysis as possible should be done within the computer, both to cut down output costs and to avoid an unwieldy stack of data.

5. *Losing the feel of the data.* The more data reduction and analysis that is carried on within the computer, the less opportunity the researcher has for insight and intuitive judgment about what may be happening with his experiment. There is no easy solution to the dilemma of restricting quantity of output versus losing the feel of the data. The best that can be said is that experience in handling data via computer programs will help the researcher develop new skills in interpretation and restore confidence that he is not losing vital information in the process. Furthermore, the researcher will soon recognize the extension to his capabilities that is uniquely supplied by the computer.

6. *Input preparation.* Preparation of data for entry into the computer is often a tedious and lengthy operation, prone to human error. Wherever possible, data should be collected in a form that can be directly input to the computer.

7. *High cost.* The cost of computer usage, both from a machine-rental and a programming standpoint, should not be overlooked. Whether this is an important consideration for an individual research project depends on the availability of funds and a computer facility and on whether the project would be feasible if a computer were not used.

REFERENCES

BORKO, H. (Ed.) *Computer applications in the behavioral sciences.* Englewood Cliffs, N.J.: Prentice-Hall, 1962.

COOMBS, C. H. Psychological scaling without a unit of measurement. *Eng. Res. Bull. 34,* Univer. of Michigan Press, 1952.

DOYLE, W. Recognition of sloppy hand-printed characters. *Proc. Western Joint Computer Conf.,* 1960, **17,** 133–143.

DUBOIS, N. S. D'ANDREA. Documents from two sources are reconciled with a digital computer. *Behav. Sci.,* 1965, **10,** 312–319.

EDMUNDSON, H. P., and WYLLYS, R. E. Automatic abstracting and indexing-survey and recommendations. *Communications of the ACM,* **4, 5,** May, 1961, 226–234.

ELBOURNE, R. D., and WARE, W. H. The evolution of concept and languages of computing. *Proc. IRE,* 50, **5,** May, 1962, 1059–1066.

FEIGENBAUM, E., and FELDMAN, J. (Eds.) *Computers and thought,* New York: McGraw-Hill, 1963.

GOLDEN, J. T. FORTRAN *IV: Programming and computing.* Englewood Cliffs, N.J.: Prentice-Hall, 1965.

GRAETZ, R. E. Research utilization of patient data computer files in clinical drug studies. *Behav. Sci.,* 1965, **10,** 320–323.

GREEN, B. F., JR. Computer models of cognitive processes. *Psychometrika,* 1961, **26,** 85–91.

GREEN, B. F. JR. *Digital computers in research: An introduction for behavioral and social scientists.* New York: McGraw-Hill, 1963.

GYR, J., THATCHER, J., and ALLEN, G. Computer simulation of a model of cognitive organization. *Behav. Sci.,* 1962, **7,** 111–116.

HARMAN, H. H. *Modern factor analysis.* Chicago: Univer. of Chicago Press, 1960.

HOVLAND, C. I. Computer simulation of thinking. *Amer. Psychologist,* 1960, **15,** 687–693.

IRWIN, W. C. *Digital computer principles.* Princeton, N.J., Van Nostrand, 1960.

JULESZ, B. Binocular depth perception of computer-generated patterns. *Bell Syst. tech. J.,* 1960, **39,** 1125–1162.

LEDLEY, R. S., and LUSTED, J. B. Computers in medical data processing. *Operat. Res.,* 1960, **8,** 299–310.

LEEDS, H. D., and WEINBERG, G. M. *Computer programming fundamentals.* New York: McGraw-Hill, 1961.

MCCONNELL, D., POLIDORA, V. J., FRIEDMAN, M. P., and MEYER, D. R. Automatic reading and recording of digital data in the analysis of primate behavior. *IRE Trans. Med. Electron.* **ME-6,** September, 1959, 121–125.

MCCRACKEN, D. D. *A guide to FORTRAN programming.* New York: Wiley, 1961.

MCCRACKEN, D. D. *A guide to* FORTRAN *IV programming.* New York: Wiley, 1965.

MCCULLOCH, W. S. Implications of information storage and retrieval in the human brain: A panel discussion. Fall Joint Computer Conference, Las Vegas, 1965.

MAHER, A. Computer-based instruction (CBI): Introduction to the IBM research project. *IBM Res. Rep. RC-1114,* 1964.

MARZOCCO, F. N., and BARTRAM, P. R. Statistical learning models for behavior of an artificial organism. In E. E. Bernard and M. R. Kare (Eds.), *Biological prototypes and synthetic systems.* New York: Plenum, 1962.

MINSKY, M. A selected descripter-indexed bibliography to the literature on artificial intelligence. *IRE Trans. human Factors Electronics,* **HFE-2,** March, 1961, 39–55.

MURPHY, J. S. *Basics of digital computers.* Vols. 1, 2, and 3. New York: Rider, 1958.

NEWELL, A., SHAW, J. C., and SIMON, H. A. Elements of a theory of human problem solving. *Psychol. Rev.,* 1958, **65,** 151–166.

NEWELL, A., and SIMON, H. A. Computers in psychology. In R. D. Luce, R. R. Bush, and E. Galanter (Eds.), *Handbook of mathematical psychology,* I. New York: Wiley, 1963.

PFEIFFER, J. *The thinking machine.* Philadelphia: Lippincott, 1962.

PRESSEY, S. L. A simple apparatus which gives tests and scores—and teaches. *Sch. Soc.,* 1962, **23,** 373.

ROSENBLATT, F. The perceptron: A probabilistic

model for information storage and organization in the brain. *Psychol. Rev.,* 1958, **65,** 386–408.

SELFRIDGE, O. G., and NEISSER, U. Pattern recognition by machine. *Sci. Amer.,* 1960, **203,** 2, 60–68.

SHERMAN, P. M. *Programming and coding digital computers.* New York: Wiley, 1963.

SMITH, J. E. K. Stimulus programming psychophysics. *Psychometrika,* 1961, **26,** 27–33.

SWETS, J. A., HARRIS, J. R., MCELROY, L. S., and RUDLOE, H. Further experiments on computer-aided learning of sound identification. NAVTRADEVCEN Tech. Rep., No. 789–2, U.S. Naval Training Devices Center. April, 1964.

VOSSLER, C., and UHR, L. A computer simulation of pattern perception and concept formation. In E. E. Bernard and M. R. Kare (Eds.), *Biological prototypes and synthetic systems.* New York: Plenum, 1962.

WEISZ, A. Z., and MCELROY, L. S. Response and feedback techniques for automated training of visual identification skills. NAVTRADEVCEN Tech. Rep. No. 789–3, U.S. Naval Training Devices Center, July, 1964.

WRUBEL, M. H. *A primer of programming for digital computers.* New York: McGraw-Hill, 1959.

PART BIBLIOGRAPHY

*References for Introduction to
Psychobiology (Part Two)*

BARNES, C. D., and ELTHERINGTON, L. G. *Drug dosage in laboratory animals.* Berkeley, Calif.: Univer. of California Press, 1964.

DAVENPORT, H. A. *Histological and histochemical techniques.* Philadelphia: Saunders, 1960.

ELLSWORTH, O. T. A manual of stereotaxic technique for the polar stereotaxic system. Los Angeles: BRI, School of Medicine, Univer. of Calif., 1963. (Also available from Davis Scientific Instruments.)

FUDIM, B. Medical applications of display storage oscilloscopes. *Med. Electronic News,* 1965, 5, 14–15.

GEDDES, L. A. A bibliography of biological telemetry. *Amer. J. Med. Electronics,* 1962, 1, 294–298.

MARKO, A. R., MCLENNAN, M. A., CORRELL, E. G., POTOR, G., and GIBSON, J. M. Research and development on pulse-modulated, personal-telemetry systems. *Tech. Rep. AMRL-TDR-63-96,* Wright Patterson AFB, Ohio, 1963.

MILLER, N. E. Chemical coding of behavior in the brain. *Science,* 1965, **148,** 328–338.

MORRIS, C. J. O. R., and MORRIS, P. *Separation methods in biochemistry.* New York: Interscience, 1964.

Psychopharmacology Serv. Center Bull. Vol. 2, No. 7, May, 1963. (Available from Psychopharmacology Service Center, National Institute of Mental Health, Bethesda 14, Md.)

SIMONS, D. G., and PRATHER, W. A personalized radio telemetry system for monitoring central nervous system arousal in aerospace flight. *IEEE Trans. bio-med. Engng.,* **BME-11,** Nos. 1 and 2, 1964.

*References for Introduction to Sensation
and Perception (Part Three)*

ATKINSON, R. C. A variable sensitivity theory of signal detection. *Psychol. Rev.,* 1963, 70, 91–106.

COLEMAN, P. D. An analysis of cues to auditory depth perception in free space. *Psychol. Bull.,* 1963, **60,** 302–315.

ELLIOT, D. N. Review of auditory research. In *Annual review of psychology.* Palo Alto: Annual Reviews, Inc., 1964. Pp. 57–86.

GRAHAM, C. H. (Ed.) *Vision and visual perception.* New York: Wiley, 1965.

GREEN, D. M. Consistency of auditory detection judgments. *Psychol. Rev.,* 1964, **71,** 392–407.

LUCE, R. D. A threshold theory for simple detection experiments. *Psychol. Rev.,* 1963, **70,** 61–79.

MCGILL, W. J. The General Gamma distribution and reaction times. *J. math. Psychol.,* 1965, **2,** 1–18.

MCGILL, W. J. Poisson counting and detection in sensory systems. In E. F. Beckenbach (Ed.), *Conceptual bases and applications of the communication sciences.* New York: Wiley, 1967, in press.

NORMAN, D. A. A comparison of data obtained with different false-alarm rates. *Psychol. Rev.,* 1964, **71,** 243–246.

POLLACK, I., and NORMAN, D. A. A nonparametric analysis of recognition experiments. *Psychon. Sci.,* 1964, **5,** 125–126.

RAAB, D. H. Backward masking. *Psychol. Bull.,* 1963, **60,** 118–129.

SCHARF, B. Complex sounds and critical bands. *Psychol. Bull.,* 1961, **58,** 205–217.

SWETS, J. A. (Ed.) *Signal detection and recognition by human observers.* New York: Wiley, 1964.

THURLOW, W. R. Audition. In *Annual review of psychology.* Palo Alto: Annual Reviews, Inc., 1965, 325–358.

YATES, A. J. Delayed auditory feedback. *Psychol. Bull.,* 1963, **60,** 213–232.

*References for Introduction to Conditioning
and Learning (Part Four)*

COFER, C. N., and APPLEY, M. H. *Motivation: Theory and research.* New York: Wiley, 1964.

ELLEN, P., and WILSON, A. S. Digital recording of simultaneous events in multiple operant chambers. *J. exp. Anal. Behav.*, 1964, **7**, 425–429.

GRANT, D. A. Classical and operant conditioning. In A. W. Melton (Ed.), *Categories of human learning.* New York: Academic, 1964.

HERRICK, R. M., and DENELSBECK, J. S. A system for programming experiments and for recording and analyzing data automatically. *J. exp. Anal. Behav.*, 1963, **6**, 631–635.

HONIG, W. K. *Operant behavior: Areas of research and application.* New York: Appleton-Century-Crofts, 1966.

MASON, W. A., and RIOPELLE, A. J. Comparative psychology. In *Annual review of psychology.* Palo Alto: Annual Reviews, Inc., 1964.

PROKASY, W. F. *Classical conditioning: A symposium.* New York: Appleton-Century-Crofts, 1965.

SCHRIER, A. M., HARLOW, H. F., and STOLLNITZ, F. (Eds.) *Behavior of nonhuman primates. Modern research trends.* Vols. 1 and II. New York: Academic, 1965.

WARREN, J. M. The comparative psychology of learning. In *Annual review of psychology.* Palo Alto: Annual Reviews, Inc., 1965.

WEINER, H. Operant programming with transistorized digital elements. *J. exp. Anal. Behav.*, 1963, **6**, 193–195.

WEISS, B., and LATIES, V. G. Reinforcement schedule generated by an on-line digital computer. *Science*, 1965, **148**, 658–661.

References for Introduction to Human Behavior (Part Five)

BAHRICK, H. P. Retention curves: Facts or artifacts? *Psychol. Bull.*, 1964, **61**, 188–194.

BAHRICK, H. P. The ebb of retention. *Psychol. Rev.*, 1965, **72**, 60–73.

BILODEAU, E. A., and HOWELL, D. Free association norms: By discrete and continued methods. *Tech. Rep. No. 1*, 1965, Nonr-475(10), Tulane Univer. and the Office of Naval Research.

BILODEAU, E. A., and LEVY, C. M. Long-term memory as a function of retention time and other conditions of training and recall. *Psychol. Rev.*, 1964, **71**, 27–41.

BRACKBILL, Y. *Research in infant behavior: A cross-indexed bibliography.* Baltimore: Williams & Wilkins, 1964.

CAMPBELL, D. T., and STANLEY, J. C. Experimental designs for research on teaching. In N. L. Gage (Ed.), *Handbook on research on teaching.* Chicago: Rand McNally, 1963.

DIEBOLD, A. R. *A survey of psycholinguistic research.* In C. E. Osgood and T. A. Sebeok (Eds.) *Psycholinguistics* (A Survey of Theory and Research Problems) with *A survey of psycholinguistic research, 1954–1964,* by A. R. Diebold. Bloomington, Ind.: Indiana Univ. Press, 1965.

ELLIS, N. R. (Ed.) *Handbook of mental deficiency: Psychological theory and research.* New York: McGraw-Hill, 1963.

KEPPEL, G. Verbal learning in children. *Psychol. Bull.*, 1964, **61**, 63–80.

KEPPEL, G. Problems of method in the study of short-term memory. *Psychol. Bull.*, 1965, **63**, 1–13.

MACCOBY, E. E. Developmental psychology. In *Annual review of psychology.* Palo Alto: Annual Reviews, Inc., 1964.

MELTON, A. W. (Ed.) *Categories of human learning.* New York: Academic, 1964.

PALERMO, D. S., and JENKINS, J. J. *Word association norms: Grade school through college.* Minneapolis: Univ. of Minnesota Press, 1964.

SMITH, K. U. *Delayed sensory feedback and behavior.* Philadelphia: Saunders, 1962.

References for Introduction to Computers (Part Six)

COE, R. M. Conflict, interference, and aggression: Computer simulation of a social process. *Behav. Sci.*, 1964, **9**, 186–197.

DIXON, W. J. (Ed.) *BMD: Biomedical computer programs.* Los Angeles: Health Sciences Computer Facility, School of Medicine, Univer. of Calif., 1964.

FEIGENBAUM, E., and FELDMAN, J. (Eds.) *Computers and thought.* New York: McGraw-Hill, 1963.

GREEN, B. F., JR. *Digital computers in research.* New York: McGraw-Hill, 1963.

HAGAN, T. G. Hybrid Computation. *Datamation,* 1965, **11**, 24–28.

MCWHINNEY, W. H. Simulating the social communication network experiments. *Behav. Sci.,* 1964, **9**, 80–84.

SILVERN, G. M. Programmed instruction materials for computer programming: A survey. *Computers and Automation,* 1965, **14**, 26–32.

SORKIN, A., ENENSTEIN, J., GRANNITRAPANI, D., and DARROW, C. W. An IBM 7090 FORTRAN program for one-through-four way analysis of variance. *Behav. Sci.,* 1964, **9**, 377–378.

STANNERS, R. F. A three-variable Chi-Square Analysis program. *Behav. Sci.,* 1965, **10**, 327–328.

Survey of biomedical computer applications. Part VII. *Med. electronic News,* 1964, **4**, 17–18.

TOMKINS, S. S., and MESSICK, S. (Eds.) *Computer simulation of personality: Frontier of psychological theory.* New York: Wiley, 1963.

APPENDIX

BASIC METHODOLOGY (CH. 1)

ANIMALS

Amazon Animal Imports
919 N.W. 13th St.
Fort Lauderdale, Fla.
Monkeys

Animal Import Company
1000 Poydras St.
New Orleans, La.
Rhesus monkeys

ANSCO Labs
1735 Los Carneros Ave.
Napa, Calif.
Albino and mixed color guinea pigs; albino, cream, and golden Syrian hamsters; albino Swiss mice of Webster strain descent; albino or hooded rats of Sprague-Dawley or Long-Evans descent; New Zealand white or California rabbits. All animals cited as being raised in closed colony with random breeding. Animals grouped for ordering according to age and/or weight. Also supply pregnant females, and litter with mother. Complete supply of animal feeds, diets, and bedding material

Asiatic Animal Imports, Inc.
P.O. Box 8125
International Airport

* = **Mailing address referenced under** *Basic Instrumentation* **or** *Basic Methodology* **sources.**
† = **Mailing address referenced elsewhere in this chapter section**

San Francisco 28, Calif.
Primates, all types

Bailey Industrial Supply Co.
P.O. Box 74335
Oakland Station
Los Angeles, Calif.
Monkeys

Bio-Research Consultants
9 Commercial Ave.
Cambridge, Mass.
Hamsters

California Caviary
10824 S. Prairie Ave.
Inglewood, Calif.
Dogs, cats

Carolina Biological Supply Co.
Burlington, N.C.
Planaria

Charles River Breeding Labs., Inc.
251 Ballardvale St.
North Wilmington, Mass.
N.I.H., Sprague-Dawley, Wistar and other rats

Chase Wild Animal Farm
Halifax, Mass.
Monkeys and other animals

C. P. Chase
136 N. W. 57th Ave.
Miami, Fla. 33126
Monkeys

George Clauss
Fairlawn, N.J.
Cats and dogs

Clovelly Farms
5539 Beaver Crest Dr.
Lorain, Ohio
Rabbits

Connecticut Valley Biological Supply Co.
Valley Road
Southampton, Mass.
Planaria, pigeons, frogs, turtles

Cox, Aspden & Fletcher
39 Cortlandt St.
New York, N.Y.

Dogs for Research
4996 S. Redwood Rd.
Murray, Utah
Dogs

Ferndale Pet Supply
2236 Woodward Ave.
Ferndale, Mich.
Monkeys and other animals

G. van den Brink, N.V.
P.O. Box 15
Soest, Holland
Monkeys

Gators of Miami, Inc.
Box 7241
Miami, Fla.
Primates, all types

General Biological Supply House, Inc.
8200 S. Hoyne St.
Chicago 20, Ill.
Protozoa

Harlan Industries
P.O. Box 29176
Cumberland, Ind.
Rats

Hartelust-Thornsen & Co.
Animal Supplies, Inc.
P.O. Box 488
Belmar, N.J.
Primates

Heath Research, Inc.
666 Elm Street
Buffalo, N.Y.
Monkeys

Holtzman Co.
421 Holtzman Rd.
Madison 5, Wis.
Albino rats, descendants of Sprague-Dawley; breeders, pregnant females, etc., of various age categories

International Animal Exchange, Inc.
22041 Woodward Ave.
Ferndale 20, Mich.
Rhesus, squirrel, spider, cynomolgus, baboons, and other subhuman primates

JEJA, Inc.
Freetown Rd.
Simpsonville, Md.
Primates

The Lemberger Co.
1222 W. South Park Ave.
Oshkosh, Wis.
Insecta, arachnida, fish, amphibia, turtles, cats, pigeons

Meems Bros. & Ward
P.O. Box C
Sparkhill, N.Y.
African monkeys

Miami Rare Bird Farm
Box 100
Kendall, Fla.
South American monkeys

Midway Animal Farm
Pritchardville, S.C.
Monkeys

Morris Research Labs., Inc.
4000 Meriden Rd.
Topeka, Kansas
Cats

Nuclear Supply & Service
422 Washington Blvd.
Washington 5, D.C.
Rats, guinea pigs, and other small animals

Okatie Farms
Pritchardville, S.C.
Monkeys

Palmetto Pigeon Plant
P.O. Box 1550
Sumpter, S.C.
Pigeons

The Pet Farm
3310 N.W. South River Dr.
Miami, Fla.
Monkeys

Pratt Labs.
1739 S. 54th St.
Philadelphia, Pa.
Cats

Primate Imports Corp.
P.O. Box 186
Malverne, Long Island, N.Y.
Monkeys

E. Prinz
1415 N. Jackson St.
Waukegan, Ill.
Rhesus monkeys

Redwood Game Farm
2400 So. Redwood Rd.
Salt Lake City, Utah
Tryon strain rats, doves, pigeons

Reptile Aquatic Supply Co., Inc.
75 Route 208
Wyckoff, N.J.
Turtles, lizards, and other reptiles

Research Animals, Inc.
3401 Fifth Ave.
Pittsburgh, Pa.
*Holtzman, Long-Evans, Sprague-Dawley, and
Wistar rats*

Research Animals, Inc.
Box 57
Miami, Fla.

Rider Animal Co.
501 Winchester
Warrenton, Va.
Primates

Shamrock Farms, Inc.
R.R. 2
Middletown, N.Y.
Monkeys

Simonsen Labs., Inc.
Rt. 1, Box 129, Day Road
Gilroy, Calif.
Wistar and Long-Evans rats

Sprague-Dawley, Inc.
P.O. Box 4220
Seminole Hwy. Rt. 2
Madison, Wisc.
Rats

Tarpon Zoo
P.O. Box 847
Tarpon Springs, Fla.
Squirrel monkeys and reptiles, including turtles

Trefflich Bird and Animal Co.
228 Fulton St.
Trefflich Bldg.
New York, N.Y.
Gibbons, chimps, and other primates

Lewis Warren
Reservoir Rd., Box 45
Pana, Ill.
Monkeys

White Animal Farm
R.F.D. 4
West Scarboro, Maine
*Squirrel, marmoset, spider monkeys; doves,
owls, pigeons, parrots, and parakeets*

F. J. Zeehandelaar, Inc.
405 North Ave.
New Rochelle, N.Y.
Monkeys

ANIMAL CAGES AND RACKS

Acme Metal Products
7757 S. Chicago Ave.
Chicago 19, Ill.

Aloe Scientific Div. of Brunswick
1831 Olive St.
St. Louis 3, Mo.

Alvey-Ferguson Co.
3131 Disney St.
Cincinnati, Ohio

Asiatic Animal Imports, Inc.*

Atlantic Metal Products, Inc.
21 Fadem Rd.
Springfield, N.J.

Bussey Products Co.
2750 W. 35th St.
Chicago, Ill. 60632

Crest Ultrasonics Corp.
Scotch Rd., Mercer Co. Airport
Trenton 8, N.J.
   Cage-cleaning equipment

Disposable Lab Cages Inc.
15th and Bloomingdale Aves.
Melrose Park, Ill.

Econo-Lab Div.
Maryland Plastics Inc.
9 East 37th St.
New York, N.Y.

Fenco Cage Products
213 Camden St.
Boston, Mass. 02118

Fischer Scientific
2850 S. Jefferson Ave.
St. Louis 18, Mo.

GF Supply Division
Standard Safety Equipment Co.
431 N. Quentin Rd.
Palatine, Ill.
   Air hoses

Girton Mfg. Co.
Millville, Pa. 17846

Hartford Metal Products Inc.
Box R
Aberdeen, Md.

Hawley Training Devices, Inc.
9616 Roosevelt Way, N.E.
Seattle, Wash. 98115
   Automated small animal colony, including cages

Hoeltge Inc.
5242 Crookshank Rd.
Cincinnati, Ohio
   Transport cages, carts

Industrial Acoustics Co., Inc.
380 Southern Blvd.
Bronx, N.Y. 10454
   Animal acoustical chambers

Industrial Washing Mach. Corp.
32 Main St.
Matawan, N.J.

International Animal Exchange, Inc.†

Kirschner Mfg. Co.
Rt. 2, Box 160
Vashon, Wash.

Lab-Care Division
Research Equipment Co., Inc.
810 S. Main
Bryan, Texas
   Cages with moveable squeeze to force primates out

Labco Div.
Partsco Inc.
2977 Lamb Ave.
Columbus, Ohio

Lab-Crafts Inc.
11 DeHart St.
Morristown, N.J.
   Transport cages

Lenderking Metal Products, Inc.
1000 S. Linwood Ave.
Baltimore, Md. 21224
   Laboratory animal care equipment

M. & J. Associates, Inc.
P.O. Box 24
Timonium, Md. 21093
   Automatic primate watering system

Norwich Wire Works, Inc.
Norwich, N.Y. 13815

Perkins, Samuel, Co.
P.O. Box 302
Brookline, Mass.

Porter-Mathews Co., Inc.
U.S. Route 1
Princeton, N.J.

Ramco Equipment Corp.
40 Montgomery St.
Hillside, N.J.

Ransohoff Co.
5th St. at Ford Blvd.
Hamilton, Ohio

Ryerson Steel Co.
Box 8000 A
Chicago, Ill. 60680

Specialty Equipment Co.
P.O. Box 4182, N. Sta.
Winston-Salem, N.C.
Group monkey cages

Stanford Glassblowing Labs., Inc.
970 San Antonio Rd.
Palo Alto, Calif.
Animal metabolic cages

Ultrasonic Industries, Inc.
6 Ames Ct.
Engineers Hill
Plainview, Long Island, N.Y.
Water bottle and cage-cleaning equipment

Wahmann Mfg. Co.
1123 E. Baltimore St.
Baltimore, Md. 21202

R. G. Wright Co.
2280 Niagara St.
Buffalo, N.Y.
Cage and rack washer

NOTE: Most of the above companies also list bottles.

ANIMAL FOOD

Agway Inc.
Broad St. Ext., Box 148
Waverly, N.Y. 14892
Lab animal feed for dogs, cats, primates, rabbits, and hamsters

Allied Mills Inc.
Lab. Animal Diets Div.
110 N. Wacker Dr.
Chicago, Ill. 60606
Lab animal feed for birds, dogs, cats, rats, rabbits, and monkeys

Animal Feeds Inc.
3255 Park Ave.
Bronx 51, N.Y.
Lab feed for all animals

ANSCO Labs†
Lab feed for small animals

Borden's Feed Supplements Div.
350 Madison Ave.
New York, N.Y.
Lab feed for all animals

CIBA Pharmaceutical Prod. Inc.
Summit, N.J.
Banana pellets

Kennel Food Supply Co.
Fairfield, Conn.
KFS chim crackers for monkeys

P. J. Noyes
Main St.
Lancaster, N.H.
Rat pellets, pigeon pellets, peanut pellets, dextrose pellets, sucrose pellets

Okatie Farms†
Monkey diet in meal form

Old Mother Hubbard Dog Food Co., Inc.
44 Prospect St.
Gloucester, Mass.
High protein primate biscuits

Purina Laboratory Chow
Checkerboard Square
St. Louis, Mo. 63199
Animal feed for all animals

Rockwell-Bellows
(Div. Animal Feeds, Inc.)
3255 Park Ave.
Bronx 51, N.Y.
Lab feed for cats, dogs, rats, rabbits

Teklad Inc.
Room 102–4
Monmouth Trust & Sav. Bank Bldg.
Monmouth, Ill.
  Rockland Laboratory primate diet

NOTE: Some animal food, (feeder machine size pellets excepted), may be purchased through local feed and grain dealers.

ANIMAL ODOR CONTROL

Airkem
241 E. 44th St.
New York, N.Y.
  Airkem Blue Label deodorizes by evaporation and air movement; Airkem A-3 is deodorizer and detergent.

Alconox, Inc.
853 Broadway
New York, N.Y. 10003
  Detergents

Britt Tech. Corp.
Britt, Iowa
  Kleen King, a portable cage cleaner

Diversey Corp.
212 W. Monroe St.
Chicago, Ill. 60606
  Soap and acid disinfectant for portable cage cleaner

Economics Lab, Inc.
250 Park Ave.
New York, N.Y. 10017
  Deodorants, solvents for scale and urine

Fuller, D. William, Co.
2320 E. 75th St.
Chicago, Ill. 60649
  Germicidal equipment

LeFevre
Oklahoma City, Okla.
  Big D deodorant

West Chemical Products, Inc.
Disinfectant Div.
42-16 Wirt St.
Long Island, N.Y.
  Wescodyne disinfectant

Winthrop Labs. Inc.
2020 Greenwood St.
Chicago, Ill.
  Roccol disinfectant

Wyandotte Chemical Corp.
J. B. Ford Div.
Wyandotte, Mich. 48193
  Deodorizer

ANIMAL CHAIRS, RESTRAINERS, TEST CHAMBERS

Atomic Accessories, Inc.
811 W. Merrick Rd.
Valley Stream, N.Y.
  Rat restrainer cages

F & H Machine Co., Inc.
492 Grand Blvd.
Westbury, Long Island, N.Y.
  Monkey chairs, anesthesia boxes

Foringer Co.
Rockville, Md.
  Monkey chairs

Hawley Training Devices, Inc.†
  Monkey chairs

Kirschner†
  Monkey chairs

The Muel Co.
Merrimac, Wis.
  Monkey restraining chairs

Nuclear Supply & Service†
  Restraining cages for implants and monitoring studies

Porter-Mathews Co., Inc.†
  Restrainers

Woodard Research Corp.
34 Station St.
Herndon, Va.
  Activity measuring cages

NOTE: Test chambers for monkeys, rats, cats, and pigeons are listed in the catalogs of firms with psychological apparatus (pages 744 to 745).

BASIC INSTRUMENTATION (CH. 2)

GENERAL SUPPLIES AND
EQUIPMENT

Allied Electronics
100 N. Western Ave.
Chicago 80, Ill.
General electronic supplies

B & B Motor and Control
206 Lafayette
New York, N.Y.
Motors

Bendix
Red Bank
201 Westwood Ave.
Long Branch, N.J.
Solid state supplies

Bodine Electric Co.
2504 W. Bradley Place
Chicago, Ill.
Motors

Bradley Semiconductor Corp.
275 Welton St.
New Haven, Conn. 06511
Solid state supplies, photoelectric cells

Burstein-Applebee Co.
1012-10-14 McGee St.
Kansas City 7, Mo.
General electronic supplies

Cal State Electronics
5222 W. Venice Blvd.
Los Angeles, Calif.
*Terminated inventories of general components;
all new items at discount*

Concord Radio
81 White St.
New York 13, N.Y.

Detroit Controls Corp.
5900 Trumbull Ave.
Detroit 8, Mich.
Switches

Dimco-Gray Corp.
207 E. 6th St.
Dayton, Ohio 45402
Timers

Eico Electric Instrument Co., Inc.
131-01 39th Ave.
Flushing, N.Y.
Electrical equipment and test instruments

Electric Motor Corp.
Racine, Wis.
Motors

Federated Purchasers
11820 W. Olympic Blvd.
Los Angeles, Calif.

General Radio Co.
Concord, Mass.
Variac, strobs, sound measuring equipment

Haydon/Div. Gen. Time Corp.
245 E. Elm St.
Torrington, Conn.
Motors, timers

Heath Company
Benton Harbor, Mich.
Heathkits

Herbach & Rademan, Inc.
1204 Arch St.
Philadelphia, Pa.
General electronic supplies, motors

IBM
General Products Div.
Commercial Sales, Relays
Box A
Essex Junction, Vt.
Relays

Keltner Electronics, Inc.
1045 W. Hampden Ave.
Englewood, Colo.

KRS Electronics, Inc.
4035 Transport St.
Palo Alto, Calif.

Lafayette Electronics
P.O. Box 10
Syosset, Long Island, N.Y. 11791
Electronic supplies and equipment

Lectronic Research Lab., Inc.
715 Arch St.
Philadelphia, Pa.
Surplus material at reduced prices

Newark Electronics
223 W. Madison St.
Chicago 6, Ill.
Electronic supplies and equipment

Philco Corp.
Church Rd.
Landsdale, Pa.
Solid state supplies, implanted receivers

Pomona Electronics
1500 E. 9th St.
Pomona, Calif.
Cables: patch, banana

Sanei Instrument Co. Ltd.
1-95 Kashiwagi, Shinjuku-Ku
Tokyo, Japan

Sigma Instruments, Inc.
180 Pearl St.
S. Braintree, Mass.
Canned photorelays for counting and switching

Tokyo Shibaura Electric Co. Ltd.
Hibiya Mitsui Bldg.
Yuraku-Cho,
Tokyo, Japan

Toyo Electronics Industry Corp.
21 Sain-Misosaki-Cho
Ukyo-Ku, Kyoto, Japan

Transistor Electronics
West Rd.
Bennington, Vt.
Solid state supplies

Vidar Corp.
73 Ortega Ave.
Mt. View, Calif.

Video Instruments
2340 Sawtelle Blvd.
Los Angeles, Calif.
Solid state equipment

GENERAL PSYCHOLOGICAL EQUIPMENT

Avionics Research Prod.
6901 W. Imperial Blvd.
Los Angeles, Calif.

Davis Scientific Instruments
12137 Cantura St.
Studio City, Calif.

Farrall Instrument Co.
P.O. Box 658
Grand Island, Nebr.

Foringer & Co., Inc.
Rockville, Md.

Ralph Gerbrands Scientific Apparatus
8 Beck Rd.
Arlington, Mass.

Grason-Stadler Co., Inc.
West Concord, Mass.

Harvard Apparatus Co.
Dover, Mass.

Hawley Training Devices, Inc.
9616 Roosevelt Way, N.E.
Seattle, Wash. 98115

Hunter Mfg. Co.
P.O. Box 153
Cor. Branch
Iowa City, Iowa

Lafayette Instrument Co.
North 26th and 52 By-Pass
Lafayette, Ind.

Lehigh Valley Electronics
215 S. 3rd St.
Allentown, Pa.

Marietta Apparatus Co.
Marietta, Ohio

Phipps & Bird Inc.
303 S. 6th St.
Richmond 5, Va.

Physiological Electronics, Inc.
P.O. Box 9831
Chevy Chase, Md.

Porter-Mathews
U.S. Rt. 1
Princeton, N.J.

Psychological Instruments
Box 6113
Richmond, Va.

Research Instrument Labs
51-06 216 St.
Oakland Gardens
New York, N.Y.

Scientific Prototype Mfg. Co.
623 W. 129th St.
New York, N.Y.

C. H. Stoelting Co.
424 N. Homan Ave.
Chicago, Ill.

Wichita Apparatus Supply
3026 Stadium Dr.
Wichita, Kans.

NOTE: Refer to the section on *Experimental control systems (solid state and relay units)* for the names and addresses of several other companies dealing in psychological equipment (e.g., Digital Equipment, Massey Dickinson Co., Inc., Tech Serv. Corp., BRS Electronics) that specialize in solid state apparatus (see below).

EXPERIMENTAL CONTROL SYSTEMS (SOLID STATE AND RELAY UNITS)

Beckman Instruments†

BRS Electronics
5451 Holland Dr.
Beltsville, Md.
Solid state equipment and modules

Control Logic
3 Strathmore Rd.
Natick, Mass.

Davis Scientific Instruments†
Relay modules with snap lead coupling and face-to-face modules; also solid state equipment

Digital Equipment Corp.
146 Main St.
Maynard, Mass.
Transistor module cards with banana jack coupling. Patch panel on rear through card carriage receptacles, or face to face. Also taper pin coupling, card receptacle to card receptacle. Uses the preferred matrix "patch" board system.

Foringer & Co., Inc.†
Relay modules with snap lead coupling; also solid state equipment.

Grason-Stadler Co., Inc.†
Relay modules with snap lead coupling

Iconix, Inc.
1175 O'Brien Dr.
Menlo Park, Calif.
Solid state modules for behavioral and biomedical research

Massey Dickinson Co., Inc.
9-11 Elm St.
Saxonville, Mass.
Transistor modules with banana jack coupling, module face to module face

Physiological Electronics, Inc.†

Scientific Prototype Mfg. Co.†

Spacelabs Inc.
15521 Lanark St.
Van Nuys, Calif.

System Engineering Labs, Inc.
P.O. Box 9148
Fort Lauderdale, Fla.
Solid state data acquisition systems, computers

Tech. Serv. Corp.
Beltsville, Md.
Transistor modules with taper pin, card receptacle to card receptacle, or banana jack coupling and module face to module face

NOTE: Many of the computer manufacturers list solid state control systems. Also, refer to *Solid state modules* listed below.

SOLID STATE MODULES

Allegri-Tech Inc.
141 River Rd.
Nutley 10, N.J.
  Active modules

Allied Electronics†

Ansley Mfg. Co.
New Hope, Pa.

Applied Development
1131 Monterey Pass Rd.
Monterey Park, Calif.
  Prefabricated printed circuits, transistor card enclosure carriages, blank transistor cards

Computer Control Co., Inc.
983 Concord St.
Framingham, Mass.
  Digital logic modules

Digital Equipment Corp.†
  Blank transistor cards, prefabricated printed circuits, transistor card enclosure carriages

Electronics Products Corp.
2315 Cecil Ave.
Baltimore 18, Md.

Federated Purchasers†

Mutual Electronics
87 Main St.
Johnson City, N.Y.
  Blank transistor cards, custom printed circuits

Newark Electronics†

Ortho Industries, Inc.
7 Paterson St.
Paterson, N.J.

Tech. Serv. Corp.†
  Prefabricated printed circuits, transistor card enclosure carriages

OSCILLOSCOPES

Analab Instrument Corp.
30 Canfield Rd.
Essex County
Cedar Grove, N.J.
  Display storage oscilloscopes

Associated Research, Inc.
2748 W. Belmont Ave.
Chicago 18, Ill.

Beattie Coleman Inc.
1136 N. Olive St.
Anaheim, Calif.
  Scope camera

Brush Instruments
Div. of Clevite Corp.
37th and Perkins
Cleveland 14, Ohio
  Display storage oscilloscopes

Allen B. Dumont Labs, Inc.
Clayton, N.J.

Electronic Instrument Co., Inc.
3300 Northern Blvd.
Long Island City 1, N.Y.

Grass Instrument Co.
101 Old Colony Ave.
Quincy, Mass.
  Scope camera

Heath Co.†

Hewlett-Packard Co.
1501 Page Mill Rd.
Palo Alto, Calif.

Northern Scientific Inc.
P.O. Box 5247
Madison, Wis. 53705
  Digital memory oscilloscope—reduces noise in recurrent signals

Nuclear-Chicago Corp.
333 E. Howard Ave.
Des Plaines, Ill. 60016
  Digital storage oscilloscopes

Nuclear Data Inc.
100 W. Golf Rd.
P.O. Box 451
Palatine, Ill.
  Enhancetron—a digital storage oscilloscope

Scopes Co., Inc.
P.O. Box 56
Monsey, New York

Tektronix, Inc.
P.O. Box 500
Beaverton, Ore.

OSCILLOGRAPHS

American Optical Co.
Instrument Div.
Eggert Rd.
Buffalo 15, N.Y.

Brush Instruments†

Consolidated Electrodynamics Corp.
360 Sierra Madre Villa
Pasadena, Calif. 91109

Geotechnical Corp.
3401 Shiloh Rd.
Garland, Texas

Gilson Medical Electronics
3000 W. Beltline
Middletown, Wis.

Grass Instrument Co.†

Minneapolis-Honeywell Regulator Co.
Heiland Division
5200 E. Evans Ave.
Denver 22, Colo.

Offner Div.
Beckman Instruments, Inc.
3900 N. River Rd.
Schiller Park, Ill.

Sanborn Company
Industrial Div.
175 Wyman St.
Waltham 54, Mass.

Texas Instruments Inc.
Geosciences and Instrumentation Div.
3609 Buffalo Speedway
Houston 6, Tex.

NOISE GENERATORS

Canadian Marconi Co.
2444 Trenton Ave.
Montreal, Quebec, Canada

Elgenco, Inc.
1231 Colorado Blvd.
Santa Monica, Calif.

General Microwave Corp.
155 Marine St.
Farmingdale, N.Y.

General Radio Co.†

GPS Instrument Co.
180 Needham St.
Newton, Mass.

Kay Electric Co.
Maple Ave.
Pine Brook, N.J.

Varian Associates
611 Hansen Way
Palo Alto, Calif.

FUNCTION GENERATORS

Argonaut Associates, Inc.
P.O. Box 273
Beaverton, Ore.

Allen B. Dumont Labs, Inc.†

Electronic Instrument Co., Inc.†

Electro-Pulse, Inc.
11861 Teale St.
Culver City, Calif.

General Radio Co.†

Hewlett-Packard Co.†

Tektronix, Inc.†

PAPER PULLS

Gorrell & Gorrell
Westwood, N.J.

Harvard Apparatus Co.†

Hunter Mfg. Co.†

Techni Rite Electronics, Inc.
Techni Rite Industrial Park
Warrick, R.I.

RECORDERS

Anadex Instruments
7833 Haskell Ave.
Van Nuys, Calif.
Digital readout

B & F Instruments, Inc.
3644 N. Lawrence St.
Philadelphia, Pa.
Multichannel

Bausch & Lomb Inc.
61463 Bausch St.
Rochester, N.Y.

E & M Instrument Co., Inc.
Box 14013
6030 England St.
Houston, Tex.
Physiological recording systems

Esterline-Angus Instrument Co., Inc.
Box 596
Indianapolis, Ind.
Galvanometers, event recorders

Heath Co.†
Servo chart recorder

Houston Instrument Corp.
4950 Terminal Ave.
Belaire, Tex. 77401
X/Y recorder, readouts, analyzers

F. L. Moseley Co.
409 N. Fair Oaks Ave.
Pasadena, Calif.
Converters, recorders, X/Y plotters

Performance Measurements
15120 3rd Ave.
Detroit 3, Mich.
Digital readout

Photron Instr. Co.
6516 Detroit Ave.
Cleveland 2, Ohio
Miniature, multichannel, strip-chart

Presin Co., Inc.
226 Cherry St.
Bridgeport, Conn.
Digital printout, Elmeg representative

Rustrak Instruments
130 Silver St.
Manchester, N.H.
Miniature event recorder, strip-chart, inexpensive

C. H. Stoelting Co.†

Techni-Rite
65 Centerville Rd.
Warwick, R.I.
Miniature, multichannel, self-balancing potentiometer types, strip-chart, X-Y

Varian Associates
611 Hansen Way
Palo Alto, California

Wright Line Data Processing
Accessories
170 Gold Star Blvd.
Worcester, Mass. 01606
Wright Punch Model 2600, portable precision 80-column card punch

NOTE: See oscillograph section and general psychological equipment for additional references.

PUNCHED PAPER TAPE RECORDERS AND READERS

Digital Equipment Corp.
Maynard, Mass.

Digitronics Corp.
55 West 42 St.
New York, N.Y.

Frieden Corp.
1720 Beverly Blvd.
Los Angeles, Calif.

L. P. Harmond Company
5248 Alhambra Ave.
Los Angeles, Calif.
New and used units of various types

INVAC Corp.
26 Fox Rd.
Bear Hill Industrial Park
Waltham, Mass.
Tape punches, readers, photoelectric keyboards, typewriter and transmitter-receiver subsystems

Ohr-Tronics, Inc.
305 W. Grand Ave.
Montvale, N.J. 07645
Flexi-bit portable paper tape punch

Rheem Electronics
5200 W. 104th St.
Los Angeles 45, Calif.

Soroban Engineering Co.
P.O. Box 1717
Melbourne, Fla.

Tally Register Corp.
1310 Mercer St.
Seattle, Wash.

Tech. Serv. Corp.
Beltsville, Md.

Teletype Corp.
5555 W. Touhy Ave.
Skokie, Ill.

Trak Electronics Co., Inc.
59 Danbury Rd.
Wilton, Conn.

Western Union Telegraph Co.
Plant & Engineering Dept.
60 Hudson St.
New York 13, N.Y.

MAGNETIC TAPE UNITS

Ampex Corp.
934 Charter St.
Redwood City, Calif.

Consolidated Electrodynamics Corp.†

Electro-Medi-Dyne Inc.
60 Baiting Place Rd.
Farmingdale, N.Y.

KRS Electronics
4035 Transport St.
Palo Alto, Calif.

Lockheed Electronics Co.
Rt. 1
Metuchen, N.J.

Minneapolis-Honeywell Regulator Co.
4800 E. Dry Creek Rd.
P.O. Box 8776
Denver 10, Colo.

Sanborn Co.†

Telemedic
Southampton, Pa.

ANALOG COMPUTERS AND ACCESSORY EQUIPMENT (RECORDERS, PLOTTERS, ETC.)

Beckman Instruments, Inc.
Systems Div.
2400 Harbor Blvd.
Fullerton, Calif.
EASE

Computer Systems Inc.
Richmond, Va.
DYSTAC

Electronic Associates Inc.
185 Monmouth Pkwy.
Long Branch, N.J.

Heath Co.
Benton Harbor, Mich.
Heathkit, self-assembly

Mnemotron Div.
Technical Measurements Corp.
202 Mamaroneck Ave.
White Plains, N.Y.

Philbrick Research, Inc.
127 Clandendon St.
Boston 16, Mass.

Syber Corp.
13 Mercer Rd.
Natick, Mass.
Neurac average response computer

Systron Donner Corp.
888 Galindo St.
Concord, Calif.

DIGITAL COMPUTERS AND ACCESSORY EQUIPMENT (READOUT DEVICES, CONVERTERS, MAGNETIC AND PAPER TAPE EQUIPMENT, CONTROL DEVICES, ETC.)

Bendix Computer Div.
5630 Arbor Vitae St.
Los Angeles 45, Calif.

Burroughs Corp.
Electronic Tube Div.
Plainfield, N.J.

Control Data Corp.
8100 3rd Ave.
South Minneapolis, Minn.

Cutler-Hammer Inc.
Airborne Instruments Lab
Deer Park, Long Island, N.Y.
   Analog-digital converters

Data Technology Corp.
238 Main St.
Cambridge, Mass.

Digital Equipment Corp.
146 Main St.
Maynard, Mass.

Dymec Div.
Hewlett-Packard Co.
395 Page Mill Rd.
Palo Alto, Calif.

General Electric Co.
Process Computer Section
2250 W. Peoria Ave.
Phoenix, Ariz.

General Intellitronics Inc.
900 Nepperhan Ave.
Yonkers, N.Y.

Honeywell
Electronic Data Processing Div.
60 Walnut St.
Wellesley Hills, Mass.

International Business Mach. Corp.
Dept. of Information
IBM Data Processing Div.
112 E. Post Rd.
White Plains, N.Y.

Nuclear Data Inc.
P.O. Box 451
Palatine, Ill.
   Enhancetron—signal averaging digital computer

Packard-Bell Computer Corp.
1905 Armacost Ave.
Los Angeles 24, Calif.

Radio Corp. of America
Electronic Data Processing Div.
Cherry Hill, N.J.

Sperry Rand Corp.
Univac Div.
315 Park Ave.
New York 10, N.Y.

Research Specialties Co.
200 S. Garrard Blvd.
Richmond, Calif.
   Analog-digital converter readout

Sanborn Co.†
   Analog-digital converters

TELEMETRY (BIOLOGICAL INSTRUMENTATION)

American Electronic Lab., Inc.
Medical Products Inc.
1303 Richardson Rd.
Colmar, Pa.

Budelman Electronics Corp.
375 Fairfield Ave.
Stamford, Conn.

Collins Radio Co.
Dallas, Texas

Dallons Lab Inc.
5066 Santa Monica Blvd.
Los Angeles 29, Calif.

Electro-med Inc.
4748 France Ave.
North Minneapolis, Minn.

EPSCO Medical
275 Massachusetts Ave.
Cambridge, Mass.

Giannini Scientific Instr.
185 Dixon Ave.
Amityville, N.Y.

Litton Industries, Inc.
5000 Canoga Ave.
Woodland Hills, Calif.

Metronic Inc.
3035 Hwy. 8
Minneapolis, Minn.

Spacelabs Inc.
15521 Lanark St.
Van Nuys, Calif.

Telemedics Inc.
Southampton, Pa.

Texas Instruments, Inc.
Box 6015
Dallas 22, Texas

Varo Inc.
Research Div.
2201 Walnut St.
Garland, Texas

Vector Mfg. Co., Inc.
Keystone Rd.
Southampton, Pa.

COUNTERS AND TIMERS

Accurate Instrument Co.
P.O. Box 66373
Houston 6, Texas
   Solid state counter/timer

Alderson Research Lab
48-14 33rd St.
Long Island City, New York
   Printing counters

Automatic Timing & Controls Inc.
King of Prussia, Pa.

Beckman Instruments, Inc.†
   Electronic counter and digital readout

Bowmar Instrument Corp.
8000 Bluffton Rd.
Fort Wayne, Ind.
   Direct reading counters; print-out

Durant
600 N. Cass St.
Milwaukee, Wis.
   Printing counters

Electronic Counters, Inc.
E. Bethpage Rd.
Plainview, N.Y.
   Photoelectric and electronic counters; binary, decade, battery operated

Foringer & Co., Inc.*

Ralph Gerbrands Scientific Apparatus†

Grason-Stadler Co., Inc.†

Hewlett-Packard Co.†
   Electronic counter and digital readout

Hunter Mfg. Co.
P.O. Box 153
Corolville Branch
Iowa City, Iowa
   Timers and counters

Iconix, Inc.†
   Frequency and pulse counters

Industrial Timer Corp.
1407 McCarter Hwy.
Newark, N.J.
   Timers of all types

Landis & Gyr Inc.
45 W. 45th St.
New York 36, N.Y.
   Sodeco

Larr Optics and Electronics Co.
4901 Ward Rd.
Wheatridge, Colo.
   Photoelectric counters

Matrix Res. & Develop. Co.
11 Mulberry St.
Nashua, N.H.
   Direct-reading and print-out electromagnetic counters

Photocon Research Products
421 N. Alteneda Dr.
Pasadena, Calif.

Presin Co.†
Print-out counters

Radson Engineering Corp.
Box B
Macon, Ill.
Electromagnetic counters; direct-reading and print-out

Robotomics Enterprises
4504 N. 16th St.
Phoenix, Ariz.
Transistorized decade counters

Royco Instruments, Inc.
141 Jefferson
Menlo Park, Calif.
Printing counters

Simplex Time Recorder Co.
26 S. Lincoln
Gardner, Mass.
Circuit controlling motor operated timers; interval timing

Standard Electric Co.
Springfield 2, Mass.
Clock timers

Transistor Specialties, Inc.
120 Terminal Dr.
Plainview, N.Y.
Printing counters

Veeder-Root Inc.
Hartford 2, Conn.
Electromagnetic, mechanical, add-subtract, tally, photoelectric

Woodard Research Corp.
P.O. Box 405
Herndon, Va.
Printing counters

MECHANICAL TIMERS AND STOPWATCHES

Dimco-Gray Co.
213 E. 6th St.
Dayton, Ohio

Meylan Stopwatch Corp.
264 W. 40th St.
New York, N.Y.

Jules Racine & Co., Inc.
20 W. 47th St.
New York, N.Y.

EQUIPMENT BUILT TO SPECIFICATIONS (FROM DESIGN THROUGH PRODUCTION)

Electro-Sonic Control
1625 N. Main St.
Manteca, Calif.

Mutual Electronics†
Custom printed solid circuits

Wisconsin Instrument Co., Inc.
817 Stewart St.
Madison, Wis.
Portable and semi-automatic WGTA, as well as various other types of custom-built psychological equipment

NOTE: Many of the commercial suppliers of psychological equipment will build equipment to specification upon request. Also, see Bio-Soc Sciences Instruments below.

MISCELLANEOUS EQUIPMENT AND SUPPLIES

Advanced Electronics, Inc.
1765 Silas Deane Hwy.
Rocky Hill, Conn.
Sound actuated controls

Allied Control Co., Inc.
2 East End Ave.
New York 21, N.Y.
Relays, subminiature and other types

American Electronic Labs
Box 552 MO
Lansdale, Pa.
Sphygmomanometers, stimulators, and biological research instrumentation

Amphenol Connector Div.
Amphenol-Borg Electronics
1830 S. 54th Ave.
Chicago 50, Ill.
Subminiature and micro-miniature connectors

Bourns, Inc.
Trimpot Div.
1200 Columbia Ave.
Riverside, Calif.
Solid state relays, precision potentiometers

Bio-Soc Sciences Instruments
1450 Pepper Dr.
El Cajon, Calif.
Inexpensive solid state rectifiers, power supplies, noise generators, and animal or human shock units. Custom built solid state equipment as requested.

Carolina Biological Supply
Burlington, N.C.
General biological supplies

Century Electronics & Instr.
6540 E. Apache St.
Tulsa, Okla.
Oscillographs, oscillators, galvanometers, pressure switches, high speed printers

Chicago Dynamic Industries, Inc.
1725 Diversey Blvd.
Chicago 14, Ill.
Mechanical counters, rotary switches

Circon Component Corp.
Santa Barbara Municipal Airport
Goleta, Calif.
Micro-tools, indicator lamps, instrument screws, miniature hardware

Clark Electronics Lab.
Box 165
Palm Springs, Ohio
Pressure-sensitive paints

Dallons Labs. Div.
International Rectifier Corp.
120 Kansas St.
El Segundo, Calif.
Modulized monitor of physiological reactions

E & M Instruments
6030 England St.
Houston, Tex.
Physiological monitoring and electronic instruments

Electronic Associates Inc.
Long Branch, N.J.
Slotted angle iron

Flexprint Products Div.
Sanders Associates
Nashua, N.H.
Flexible printed circuitry and interconnect cable for physiological or computer work

Garlock Electronic Products
8 Fellowship Rd.
Cherry Hill, N.J.
Electronic hardware: transistor sockets, plastics, micro-logic sockets, connectors, etc.

General Electric Co.
1 River Rd.
Schenectady 5, N.Y.
Relays, all types

Globe Industries, Inc.
1900 Stanley Ave.
Dayton 4, Ohio
Motors, motor-operated timers

Gulton Industries, Inc.
212 Durham Ave.
Metuchen, N.J.
Controls of various types: sound actuated, temperature, electronic torque, etc.

Industrial Electronics Engineers
5528 Vineland Ave.
N. Hollywood, Calif.
Single-phase digital displays

International Applied Science Lab.
50 S. Franklin St.
Hempstead, Long Island, N.Y.
Critical flicker frequency units

Kenelco Inc.
1753 Cloverfield Blvd.
Santa Monica, Calif.
Photoelectric transducer for pulse pressure

Kepco Inc.
131-38 Sanford Ave.
Flushing 52, N.Y.
Regulated d-c power supplies

Lapine
6001 S. Knox
Chicago, Ill.
General supplies

Lipshaw Mfg.
7446 Central
Detroit, Mich.
Microtomes

MF Electronics Corp.
118 E. 25th St.
New York 10, N.Y.
Transistorized assemblies

Mar-Kit Electronics Corp.
250 W. 57th St.
New York, N.Y. 10019
Verti-crawl automatic rotating drum for programming visual stimuli

Medical Merchandise Mart
7355 Lincoln Ave.
Lincoln Wood, Ill.
General supplies

Mediquipment Co.
13036A Los Nietos Rd.
Santa Fe Springs, Calif.
Remote five-digit display

Micro Sensor
1809 Ealen Rd.
Philadelphia, Pa.
Transducers

North Atlantic Ind., Inc.
Terminal Drive
Plainview, Long Island, N.Y.
Digital in-line readouts, sealed switches

Pacific Transducer
2301 Federal Ave.
Los Angeles, Calif.
Transducers

Potter & Brumfield
1200 E. Broadway
Princeton, Ind.
Relays, all types

Scientific Products
1210 Leon Place
Evanston, Ill.
General supplies

Signalite, Inc.
Neptune, N.J.
Miniature glow lamps

Sony Corp. of America
580 5th Ave.
New York 36, N.Y.
Electronic equipment, closed-circuit TV

Space Mechanics Inc.
639 Massachusetts Ave.
Cambridge, Mass.
Programming equipment

Synthane Corp.
Oaks, Pa.
Plastic rods, sheets, tubes, and molded parts

Universal Relay Corp.
42 White St.
New York 13, N.Y.
Relays, all types including solid state

U. S. Components, Inc.
1320 Zerega Ave.
Bronx 62, N.Y.
Printed circuit cards, printed circuit connectors, subminiature and miniature connectors

NOTE: See page 768 for stepping switches.

CLOSED-CIRCUIT TV CAMERAS AND ACCESSORIES

Cohu Electronics Inc.
Kin-Tel Div.
5725 Kearny Villa Rd.
San Diego, Calif.
Kin-Tel

K-T Electronics
1885 Atlantic
Long Beach, Calif.
Ling

Packard-Bell Corp.
12333 W. Olympic Blvd.
Los Angeles 64, Calif.

Sarkes-Tarzian Inc.
E. Hillside Dr.
Bloomington, Ind.

Scientific Prototype Mfg. Co.†
Shiba

Shintron Co.
1 Main St.
Cambridge, Mass.

Sony Corp. of America†

Sylvania Elec. Prod., Inc.
700 Elicott St.
Batavia, N.Y.

ELECTRONIC TEST INSTRUMENTS (SCOPES, FUNCTION GENERATORS, METERS, CALIBRATORS, DIGITAL READOUTS, ETC.)

Ballantine Labs Inc.
Boonton, N.J.

Barker & Williamson, Inc.
Bristol, Pa.
Distortion meter, audio oscillator

Beckman Instruments†
Digital voltmeters

Weston Instruments Inc.
614 Frelinghuysen Ave.
Newark, N.J.

Allen B. Dumont Labs, Inc.†
Oscilloscopes, voltage calibrator

General Radio Co.†

Heath Co.†

Hewlett-Packard Co.†

Hickok Electronic Instruments Co.
10514 Dupont Ave.
Cleveland 8, Ohio

Kintel
5725 Kearny Villa Rd.
San Diego, Calif.
Digital d-c voltmeter

Precision Apparatus Co., Inc.
Glendale, Long Island, N.Y.
Transistor tester

Sierra Electronic Corp.
Div. of Philco Corp.
Menlo Park, Calif.
In-circuit transistor tester

Sonex Inc.
20 E. Herman St.
Philadelphia, Pa.
Transistor tester

Tektronix Inc.†
Inductance-capacitance meter, oscilloscopes, etc.

Triplett Electrical Instrument Co.
Bluffton, Ohio
VOM, sweep signal generator, tube tester, etc.

GENERAL-PURPOSE PHYSIOLOGICAL LABORATORY EQUIPMENT

Brookline Surgical Specialties
50 Harris St.
Brookline, Mass.

The Chemical Rubber Co.
2310 Superior Ave.
Cleveland, Ohio

Cole-Parmer Instrument Co.
7330 N. Clark St.
Chicago, Ill.

Daigger and Co.
159 W. Kinzie St.
Chicago, Ill.

Fisher Scientific Co.
1458 N. Lamon Ave.
Chicago 51, Ill.

Harshaw Scientific
1945 E. 97th St.
Cleveland 6, Ohio

Process and Instruments Corp.
15 Stone Ave.
Brooklyn, N.Y.

Schwarz Bioresearch, Inc.
Mt. View Ave.
Orangeburg, N.Y.

RECORDING AND STIMULATING EQUIPMENT

Ampex Corp.*
  Recording equipment

Argonaut Assoc., Inc.
Box 273
Beaverton, Ore.
  Preamplifiers, amplifiers, function generators, power supplies

Beckman Instruments, Inc.*
Offner Div.
  Dynagraphs, EEGs, amplifiers, couplers

Biocom Inc.
5883 Blackwelder St.
Culver City, Calif.
  Miniaturized amplifiers, scopes, recorders, telemetry systems

Bioelectric Instruments, Inc.
P.O. Box 204
Hastings-on-the-Hudson
New York
  Cathode-follower preamplifiers, isolation transformers

Biotronix
10304 Farnham Dr.
Bethesda, Md.
  Cathode-follower preamplifiers

Brush Instruments*
  Recorder, inkwriting oscillographs

CES Electronic Products Inc.
5026 Newport Ave.
San Diego, Calif.
  Peaked amplifiers, filters

Cooke Engineering
4814 Arbutus Ave.
Rockville, Md.
  Cathode-follower preamplifier

Dallons Lab Inc.*
  Amplifiers, telemetry

E & M Instrument Co.*
  Bioelectric recording units, transducers

Electro-med Inc.*
  Amplifiers, telemetry

Electro Medical Engr. Co.
703 Main St.
Burbank, Calif.
  Scopes, recorders, plug-in modules

Electro-Medi-Dyne Inc.*
  Amplifiers, telemetry

Electronics for Life Sciences
P.O. Box 697
Twinbrook Station
Rockville, Md.
Cathode-follower amplifiers

Gilson Medical Electronics
West Beltline Hwy.
Middleton, Wis.
EEG, EKG, bioelectric polygraphs

Grass Instrument Co.*
Polygraph, amplifiers, transducers, scope camera, stimulators

Gritton Industries, Inc.
Metuchen, N.J.
Transducers, recorders

Hewlett-Packard Co.*
Stimulation and recording equipment, counters

Minneapolis-Honeywell Co.*
Amplifiers and recorders

Medical Electronics Dev. Co.
400 Northern Blvd.
Great Neck, N.Y.
Integrators and recorders

Medicraft Electronic Corp.
426 Great East Neck Rd.
Babylon, Long Island, N.Y.
EMG, EEG, and other bioelectric recorders

The Meditron Co.
5440 N. Peck Rd.
El Monte, Calif.
EMG recorders

Mnemotron Div.*
Technical Measurements Corp.
Computer of average transients GSR equipment

Puget Sound Development Lab.
1949-26th East
Seattle 2, Wash.

Sanborn Co.*
Transducers, polygraphs, amplifiers

Schwartzer Co.
46 Salmi Rd.
Framington, Mass.
Bioelectric recording systems

Spacelabs Inc.*
Telemetry, miniaturized amplifiers

Statham Instruments, Inc.
12401 W. Olympic Blvd.
Los Angeles 64, Calif.
Transducers

Tektronix Inc.*
Oscilloscopes, amplifiers, scope camera, signal generators

Texas Instrument, Inc.*
Recorders, counters

Victory Engineering Corp.
118 Springfield Ave.
Springfield, N.J.
Thermistors

The Waters Corp.
P.O. Box 529
18-14th St.
Rochester, Minn.
Heart rate recorder

White Instrument Lab., Inc.
P.O. Box 9006
Austin 17, Tex.
Transistor active filters

ELECTRODES, ELECTRODE MATERIALS, AND RELATED INSTRUMENTS

Amphenol-Borg Electronics*
(Also local electronics distributor)
Electrode plugs

Cleveland Tungsten Inc.
10200 Meech Ave.
Cleveland 5, Ohio
Electrode wire

Driver-Harris Co.
202 Middlesex St.
Harrison, N.J.
Enameled stainless steel wire

Formvar
(Available locally)
Baking enamel

Insl-X Co.
Ossining, N.Y.
Enamel for room-temperature curing

Lehigh Valley Electronics*
Microelectrodes, electrode assemblies, micro-syringes

Magnetic Shield Div.
Perfection Mica Co.
1322 Elston Ave.
Chicago 22, Ill.
Shielding

Malin Co.
2514 Vestry Rd.
Cleveland 13, Ohio
Electrode wire

Microdot Inc.
220 Pasadena Ave.
S. Pasadena, Calif.
Connecting wire

Process and Instruments Corp.†

Rodolfo P. Walther Co.
5321 Hollywood Blvd.
Los Angeles, Calif.
Acrylite dental cement

Winchester Electronics
19 Willard Rd.
Norwalk, Conn.
Electrode plugs

STEREOTAXIC INSTRUMENTS

Baltimore Instrument, Inc.
716 W. Redwood St.
Baltimore, Md.

Burklund Scient.
6 W. Ontario
Chicago, Ill.

Davis Scientific Instruments*
Ellsworth polar system with printed-circuit terminal board

David Kopf Instruments
Box 636
Tujunga, Calif.

Invengineering
Box 360
Belmar, N.J.

H. Neuman & Co.
8136 N. Lawndale Ave.
Skokie, Ill.
For dogs, cats, monkeys, rabbits, and rats

Schwarzer Corp.
46 Salmi Rd.
Framingham, Mass.

C. H. Stoelting Co.*

MISCELLANEOUS PHYSIOLOGICAL EQUIPMENT

All American Engineering Co.
Box 1247
Wilmington 99, Del.
Impedance plethysmograph

Baltimore Instrument, Inc.†
Microdrives

Brinkman
115 Cutter Mill Rd.
Great Neck, Long Island, N.Y.
Microdrives

Burdick Corp.
Milton, Wis.
RF lesions

Carr Corp.
1101 Colorado Ave.
Santa Monica, Calif.
Operating tables and accessories

Clay-Adams, Inc.
141 E. 25th St.
New York 10, N.Y.
Micro surgery and micro dissection instruments

Eberbach Corp.
P.O. Box 1024
505 S. Maple Rd.
Ann Arbor, Mich.
Operating tables and accessories

Gaertner Scientific Corp.
1201 Wrightwood Ave.
Chicago 14, Ill.
Thermopiles, optical instruments, timers

Gilford Instrument Labs., Inc.
132 Artino St.
Oberlin, Ohio
Automatic blood pressure recorder, digital cardiotachometer

Grass Instrument Co.*
Microdrives, RF lesions

David Kopf Instruments*
Pipette puller

Jewelers' Screws
(Local jewelers or suppliers)

La Precision Cinemotographique
19, Rue des Parisiens
Asnieres (Seine), France
Microdrives

Micro-Fine Instruments
Box 11
Campbell, Calif.
Respirators

HRB-Singer Inc.
Science Park
P.O. Box 60
State College, Pa.
Psychogalvanometer, visual testing apparatus

Somanetics, Inc.
2055 Kurtz
San Diego, Calif.
Respiration modulator

Spectrum Instruments Inc.
Box 61
Steinway Station
Long Island 3, N.Y.
Analog filters

Sperry Products
Shelter Rock
Danbury, Conn.
Ultrasonic reflectoscope for echo EEG

C. H. Stoelting Co.*
Vision, perception, sensory equipment

Westgate Lab. Inc.
Box 63
506 S. High St.
Yellow Springs, Ohio
Eye movement camera

BIOCHEMICALS

Nutritional Biochemicals Corp.
21010 Miles Ave.
Cleveland 28, Ohio

Sigma Chemical Co.
3500 De Kalb St.
St. Louis, Mo.

CHEMICAL APPARATUS

Chicago Apparatus
1735 N. Ashland Ave.
Chicago 22, Ill.

Eberbach Corp.
P.O. Box 1024
505 S. Maple Rd.
Ann Arbor, Mich.

Fisher Scientific
1458 N. Lamon Ave.
Chicago 51, Ill.

Hellige Inc.
877 Stewart Ave.
Garden City, N.Y.

Scientific Products
1210 Leon Place
Evanston, Ill.

Arthur H. Thomas Co.
P.O. Box 779
3rd & Vine St.
Philadelphia 5, Pa.

CHROMATOGRAPHY

Applied Research Labs.
3717 Park Place
Glendale, Calif.

Bio-Rad Labs.
32 & Griffin
Richmond, Calif.

Schaar and Co.
7300 W. Montrose Ave.
Chicago 34, Ill.

CUVETTES

Pyrocell Mfg. Co.
207–11 E. 84th St.
New York 28, N.Y.

FLUOROMETERS

G. K. Turner Associates
2524 Pulgas Ave.
Palo Alto, Calif. 94303

HARVARD GUILLOTINE

Harvard Apparatus Co.*

METABOLISM CAGES

George H. Wahmann Mfg. Co.
1123 E. Baltimore St.
Baltimore 2, Md.

MICROCHEMICAL SYSTEMS

Beckman Instruments, Inc.*

Coleman Instruments Co.
42 Madison St.
Maywood, Ill.

SERUM BOTTLES

Will Scientific Instr.
39 Russell St.
Rochester, N.Y.

SPECTROPHOTOMETERS

Beckman Instruments, Inc.*

Allison Labs
11301 Ocean Ave.
Dept. 166
La Habra, Calif.

Ambco
1222 W. Washington Blvd.
Los Angeles 7, Calif.
Audiometers

Belltone Electronics Corp.
4201 W. Victoria St.
Chicago, Ill.
Audiometers, hearing aids

Bethlehem Corp.
225 W. 2nd St.
Bethlehem, Pa.
Soundproof rooms, acoustical barriers

Clevite Corp.
232 Forbes Rd.
Bedford, Ohio
Crystal headphones

Electro Voice Inc.
Cecil & Carroll Sts.
Buchanan, Mich.
Microphones

General Acoustics
12248 Santa Monica Blvd.
Los Angeles, Calif.
Soundproof rooms, acoustical barriers

General Radio Co.*
Sound analyzers, microphones

Grason-Stadler Co., Inc.*
Audiology and psychoacoustics

Hollywood Radio & Electronics Inc.
5250 Hollywood Blvd.
Hollywood, Calif.
Earphones of various types: Brush, Clevite, Electro-Voice, Telex, and Trimm

Industrial Acoustics Co.
341 Jackson Ave.
New York 54, N.Y.
Soundproof rooms, acoustical barriers, sound measuring equipment

Melpar Inc.
3000 Arlington Blvd.
Falls Church, Va.
EVA electronic vocal analog, speech synthesis

Milo Electronics Corp.
530 Canal St.
New York 13, N.Y.
Ultrasonic physiology

E. J. Sharp Instruments Inc.
965 Maryville Dr.
Buffalo 25, N.Y.
Earphones

Shure Bros.
222 Hartrey Ave.
Evanston, Ill.
Microphones

Sonomedic Corp.
245 Old Hook Rd.
Westwood, N.J.
Sound diagnosis, ultrasonic bioinstrumentation

Sonotone Corp.
Elmsford, N.Y.
Audiometers

Oscillators, sound generators, etc., are referenced elsewhere in Appendix. General electronic suppliers (pages 743–744) also reference pertinent items.

GENERAL

Edmund Scientific Co.
101 E. Gloucester Pike
Barrington, N.J.
Probably largest supplier of inexpensive optics for visual research in the United States

Optical Industry Directory
Pub. by Optical Pub. Co.
Lennox, Mass.
A gold mine of information, giving virtually all United States suppliers of the following: beam splitters, benches (optical), cameras, color perception test equipment, color standards and samples, color temperature meters, counters (photoelectric), densitometers, electronic flash units, eye charts, eye models, filters (all kinds), ground glass, illuminometers, lasers, lenses (all kinds), light sources (medical, mercury arc, microscope illumination, monochromatic, pilot, high-intensity point, projection, radio-frequency excited, self-luminous), mirrors, optical laboratory suppliers, photoelectric equipment, photometers, prisms, projectors, reticles, screens, shutters (high-speed, including Kerr cells), stereoscopes, telescopes, thermocouples and thermopiles for radiation measurement, visual test and training equipment, wedges (optical)

LIGHT SOURCES AND POWER SUPPLIES

Edmund Scientific Co.†
Cadmium-mercury lamp: Osram spectral lamp available with power supply

General Radio Co.*
Variable transformers: Variac

Local distributors of General
Electric, Westinghouse, and Sylvania
products
Tungsten lamps

Macbeth Corp.
Box 950
Newburgh, N.Y.
Xenon

Superior Electric Co.
383 Middle St.
Bristol, Conn.
Variable transformers: Powerstat

SUPPLIES FOR MIXING LIGHT

Diffusing materials may be purchased at the local representative for Celanese Corp. of America (Lumerith Sheeting), Pittsburgh Plate Glass Co., Plexiglas, and Lucite distributors.

Denoyer-Geppert Co.
5235 Ravenwood Ave.
Chicago, Ill.
Integrating spheres, unfinished globes

Edmund Scientific Co.†
Beam splitters, cemented prisms

Evaporated Metal Films Corp.
Box 606
Ithaca, N.Y.
Beam splitters

National Photocolor Corp.
225 E. 44th St.
New York 17, N.Y.
Beam splitters, pellicles

SUPPLIES FOR CONTROLLING LUMINANCE

Bausch & Lomb, Inc.
635 St. Paul Blvd.
Rochester, N.Y.
Inconel filters

Eastman Kodak Co.
343 State St.
Rochester, N.Y.
Filters and wedges, neutral density

Polaroid Corp.
Cambridge, Mass.
Linear and circular polarizers

SUPPLIES FOR MEASUREMENT OF LUMINANCE AND RADIANCE

General Electric Co.
Nela Park
East Cleveland, Ohio
Lukiesh-Moss visibility meter

Leeds & Northrup Co.
4901 Stenton Ave.
Philadelphia, Pa.
  Thermocouples, thermopiles, and Macbeth illuminometer

Macbeth Corp.†
  Electronic photomultiplier units

National Bureau of Standards
Washington 25, D.C.
  Standard lamps

Photo Research Corp.
837 N. Cahuenga Blvd.
Hollywood 38, Calif.
  Pritchard photoelectric photometer, spectra spot meter, visual task evaluator

Photovolt Corp.
95 Madison Ave.
New York 16, N.Y.
  Electronic photomultplier units

U.S. Radium Corp.
535 Pearl St.
New York 7, N.Y.
  Phosphor light standards

Zoomar Inc.
55 Sea Cliff Ave.
Glen Cove, N.Y.
  SEI portable exposure photometer

**ITEMS FOR CONTROL
OF WAVELENGTH**

Baird Associates Inc.
33 University Rd.
Cambridge 38, Mass.
  Interference color filters

Barr & Stroud Ltd.
Anniesland, Glasgow, W3
Scotland
  Circular interference wedges

Bausch and Lomb Inc.†
  Grating monochromators, interference color filters, interference wedges

Carl Zeiss, Inc.
444 Fifth Ave.
New York 17, N.Y.
  Prism monochromators

Ealing Corp.
33 University Rd.
Cambridge 38, Mass.
  Hand spectroscope

Eastman Kodak Co.†
  Kodak wratten filter handbook, gelatin color filters

Engis Equipment Co.
431 S. Dearborn St.
Chicago 5, Ill.
  Grating monochromator

Eppley Laboratory Inc.
12 Sheffield Ave.
Newport, R.I.
  Wavelength calibration of phototubes, thermocouples and thermopiles

Farrand Optical Co., Inc.
Bronx Blvd. & E. 238th St.
New York 70, N.Y.
  Prism and grating monochromators, thermocouples, and thermopiles

Fish-Schurman Corp.
70 Portman Rd.
New Rochelle, N.Y.
  Interference wedges and interference color filters

Gaertner Scientific Co.
1201 Wrightwood Ave.
Chicago 11, Illinois
  Prism monochromators

Munsell Color Corp.
10 E. Franklin St.
Baltimore 2, Md.
  Color samples

EQUIPMENT FOR CONTROL OF TIME

General Radio Co.*
  Strobotac

Hewlett Packard Co.*
  Electronic counters

Isomet Corp.
433 Commercial Ave.
Palisades Park, N.J.
Kerr cells and other electro-optical modulators

G. H. Leland Inc.
Dayton, Ohio
Rotary solenoids

Optics Technology Inc.
248 Harbor Blvd.
Belmont, Calif.
Kerr cells, electro-optical modulators

Presin Co.*
Counters

Quantatron, Inc.
2520 Colorado Ave.
Santa Monica, Calif.
Kerr cells, electro-optical modulators

System Research & Development Co.
1557 Seventh St.
Santa Monica, Calif.
Electro-optical modulators

Texas Instruments, Inc.
Electro-Optics Dept.
6000 Lemon Ave.
Dallas, Texas
Electro-optical modulators, thermocouples, and thermopiles

Veedor Root Inc.*
Counters

NOTE: Electronic timing control equipment is referenced in the equipment section for Basic Instrumentation pages 744 to 745 and 751 to 752.

MATERIAL USED IN POSITIONING THE SUBJECT

Local dental suppliers
Kerr perfection impression compound

Louis Levin & Son, Inc.
3573 Hayden Ave.
Culver City, Calif.
Slide rest and milling attachment

MATERIALS FOR MOUNTING OF OPTICAL COMPONENTS

Aeroflex Laboratories, Inc.
48-25 36th St.
Long Island City 1, N.Y.
Shock and vibration isolation

Bead Chain Mfg. Co.
64 Mountain Grove St.
Bridgeport, Conn.
Bead chain for mechanical remote controls

Borg Equipment Div.
George W. Borg Corp.
120 S. Main St.
Janesville, Wis.
Mechanical remote readout equipment

Central Scientific Co.
Irving Park Rd.
Chicago, Ill.
Tacky-wax

Ealing Corp.†
Optical benches and accessories

Eastman Chem. Products
Kingsport, Tenn.
Eastman 910 adhesive glue

Edmund Scientific Corp.†
Slide assemblies, etc.

Gaertner Scientific Corp.†
Slide assemblies, etc.

J. Klinger Scientific
83-44 Parsons Blvd.
Jamaica 32, N.Y.
Optical benches and accessories

Local distributor
Epoxy adhesives

Louis Levin & Son, Inc.†
Slide assemblies

Tropel, Inc.
52 West Ave.
Fairport, N.Y.
Slide assemblies

Voland Corp.
27 Centre Ave.
New Rochelle, N.Y.
   Mechanical remote controls

SPECIAL SYSTEMS

American Optical Co.
32 Mechanic St.
Southbridge, Mass.
   Optometric and ophthalmic instruments

Bausch & Lomb Inc.†
   Optometric and ophthalmic instruments

Fish-Schurman Corp.†
   Nagel anamaloscope

E. Leitz, Inc.
468 Fourth Ave.
New York 16, N.Y.
   Nagel anamaloscope

O. C. Rudolph & Sons, Inc.
Box 446
Caldwell, N.J.
   Hecht-Schlaer adaptometer, optometric and ophthalmic instruments

AUTO-TUTOR

Western Design
Goleta, Calif.

COLOR BLINDNESS TESTS

American Optical Co.
32 Mechanic St.
Southridge, Mass.

PERCEPTION APPARATUS

International Applied Science Lab.
510 S. Franklin St.
Hempstead, N.Y.
   Flicker perception

Lafayette Instrument Co.*

O. C. Rudolph & Sons
Box 446
Caldwell, N.J.

Polymetric Co.
234 S. 8th St.
Reading, Pa.

Research Instrument Labs
51-06 216th St.
Bayside 64, N.Y.

Scientific Prototype Mfg. Co.*

NOTE: See Basic Instrumentation (pages 743–755) and Vision (pages 762–765) sections for additional references.

CLASSICAL CONDITIONING (CH. 9)

GENERAL EQUIPMENT (AMPLIFIERS, RECORDERS, TIMERS, ETC.)

Brush Instruments*

Davis Scientific Instruments*

Esterline-Angus Instrument Co., Inc.*

Gilson Medical Electronics
Middleton, Wis.

Grass Instrument Co.*

Hunter Mfg. Co.*

Offner Div.*
Beckman Instruments, Inc.

Sanborn Company*

AIR REGULATOR

Hoke Inc.
Cresskill, N.J.
Two-stage air pressure regulator

FELS DERMOHMMETER

Yellow Springs Instrument Co.
Yellow Springs, Ohio

GASTRISIN

Roche Laboratories
Div. of Hoffman-LaRoche Inc.
Nutley, N.J.

HEADGEAR FOR HUMAN BEINGS

Waltke Instruments
Bloomington, Ind.
Also manufacture restraining boxes for rabbits

MONOFILAMENT NYLON (Ethilon)

Ethicon, Inc.
Sommerville, N.Y.

POTENTIOMETERS (rotary)

Giannini Control Corp.
918 E. Green St.
Pasadena, Calif.

VALVES

Alco Valve Co.
865 Kingsland Ave.
St. Louis 5, Mo.
Solenoid valves

Skinner Electric Valve Div.
Skinner Precision Industries, Inc.
New Britain, Conn.

VELCRO

American Thread Co.
231 S. Green St.
Chicago, Ill.

WESTERN UNION TAPE READER AND TRANSMITTER

Western Union Telegraph Co.*

GENERAL EQUIPMENT

Behaviour Apparatus, Ltd.
9 Provost Rd.
Hampstead, London, N.W. 3, England

Davis Scientific Instruments*
Skinner boxes, automatically presented levers, M & M dispensers, magnetically operated switch shock unit, etc.

Farrall Instrument Co.*
Operant equipment

Foringer & Co., Inc.*
Pigeon keys, boxes, automatically presented levers, relay ring or pressure activated microswitch shock units, etc.

Ralph Gerbrands Scientific Apparatus*
Recorders, pigeon key, etc.

Grason-Stadler Co., Inc.*
Shock unit, voice keys, drinkometer, reset timers below 30 seconds for intervals, etc.

Hawley Training Devices, Inc.*

Lehigh Valley Electronics*
Drinkometer, automatically presented levers, pigeon key, gauged rotary selector switch shock unit, etc.

Marietta Apparatus Co.*

Merle Ridgley & Co.
1102 Mayfair Rd.
Champaign, Ill.

SOLID STATE OPERANT EQUIPMENT

BRS Electronics*

Lehigh Valley Electronics*

Massey Dickinson Co., Inc.*

Physiological Electronics, Inc.*

Scientific Prototype Mfg. Co.*

SWITCHES

Automatic Electric Sales
2801 Far Hills Ave.
Dayton, Ohio
Stepping switches

IMTRA Corp.
11 University Rd.
Cambridge 38, Mass.
Stepping switches

Kellog Switchboard & Supply Co.
79 West Monroe St.
Chicago 3, Ill.
Stepping switches

Micro Switch Div. Honeywell
11 W. Spring St.
Freeport, Ill.
Microswitches

TIMERS AND COUNTERS

Automatic Timing & Control Inc.*
Reset timers

Cramer Controls Corp.
Centerbrook, Conn.
Time totalizers, meters

Industrial Timer Corp.*
Reset Timers

Landis & Gyr Inc.*
Counters, predetermined counters

Presin Co.*
Printing counters, arc suppressors

RECORDING PENS AND PAPER

Leeds and Northrup Co.
4901 Stenton Ave.
Philadelphia, Pa.
Glass reservoir pens for recorders

C. E. Perry Co., Inc.
77 Washington St.
Boston, Mass.
  Cumulative recorder paper

Texas Instrument, Inc.*
  Recorder ink

MISCELLANEOUS

C. J. Applegate & Co., Inc.
7840 24th St.
Boulder, Colorado
  Shock stimulators

Holtzman-Leckrone
6247 Park Avenue
Indianapolis, Ind.
  Pigeon keys

Industrial Electronics Engineers*
  Visual stimulus units

NOTE: Refer to Basic Methodology supply section (pages 737 to 742) for information on animals and food.

ANIMAL LEARNING (CH. 11)

GENERAL EQUIPMENT

Ralph Gerbrands Scientific Apparatus*
Event recorders, rat pellet feeders, pigeon grain magazines

Herbach & Rademan, Inc.*
Miscellaneous electronic components

Industrial Electronics Engineers*
In-line digital display units

Landis & Gyr Inc.*
Counters

Lehigh Valley Electronics*
Pigeon keys, retractable levers for rats and monkeys, pellets feeders, liquid dippers, animal chambers

Llanerch Instr. Co.
715 Woodland Drive
Llanerch, Pa.
Amplifier-integrators for output of phonograph pickups used for classical conditioning in fish and for other activity-measuring purposes, photocell amplifiers, shocking circuitry for gridless shocker, discrete trial programmers, and any special projects

NOTE: See Basic Instrumentation (743–755) and Operant Conditioning sections (pages 768 to 769) for additional references.

ANIMALS

Amazon Animal Imports*
Monkeys

Asiatic Animal Imports, Inc.*
Monkeys

John R. Humphries
71 Humphries Avenue
Pennsville, N.Y.
Turtles, adult painted and other varieties

Local pet stores
Fish, Tubifex worms, dry fish foods, aquarium supplies

Palmetto Pigeon Plant*
Pigeons

NOTE: See Basic Methodology section (pages 737 to 739) for a more complete list of animal suppliers.

MATERIALS FOR AQUATIC ELECTRODES AND RESISTIVE SHOCKING SURFACES

Fisher Scientific Company
Gulph Road
King of Prussia, Pa.
Carbon-powdered graphite No. G-64, methyl ethyl ketone No. M-209

VERBAL BEHAVIOR (CH. 12)

MEMORY DRUMS

Ralph Gerbrands Scientific Apparatus*

Lafayette Instrument Co.*

Phipps & Bird Inc.*

Psychological Instruments*

C. H. Stoelting Co.*

Gordon Stowe
1728 Chapel Court
Northbrook, Ill.
Variable control

FILMSTRIP PROJECTORS

Anson Research Co.
Box 36487
Wilshire-LaBrea Station
Los Angeles, Calif.

DuRane Corp.
St. Charles, Ill.

SLIDE PROJECTORS

Davis Scientific Instruments*

Sarkes-Tarzian Inc.*
*Random access projector
(Various types of projectors are available
locally)*

CARD DISPLAYER

Hunter Mfg. Co.*
Hunter cardmaster

NOTE: See catalogs of general suppliers of psychological apparatus for additional references (pages 744 to 745).

CHILD PSYCHOLOGY (CH. 14)

CANDIES FOR CHILDREN

M&M's—available at local stores

Kirkman Pharmacal Co.
Seattle, Wash.

**DISPENSERS FOR TOYS
AND/OR CANDY**

Davis Scientific Instruments*

Ralph Gerbrands Scientific Apparatus*

ROTARY SOLENOID

G. H. Leland Inc.
Dayton 2, Ohio

TRINKETS

Merry Mfg. Co.
531 N. Wayne Ave.
Cincinnati, Ohio

Paul A. Price Co.
55 Leonard St.
New York, N.Y.

Penny King Co.
2538 Mission St.
Pittsburgh, Pa.

Plastic Processes, Inc.
83 House Avenue
Freeport, N.Y.

Local distributors of party supplies stock all types of small trinkets and toys.

NOTE: Refer to the Basic Instrumentation (pages 743–755) and Operant Conditioning sections (pages 768 to 769) for other distributors of equipment useful in child research.

ACCELEROMETERS

B & K Instruments, Inc.
3044 W 106th St.
Cleveland 11, Ohio

Boumes, Inc.
6135 Magnolia Ave.
Riverside, Calif.

Columbia Research Lab., Inc.
Woodlyn, Pa.

Systron Donner Corp.
888 Galindo St.
Concord, Calif.

Electra Scientific Corp.
Electra Way
Fullerton, Calif.

Gulton Industries, Inc.
212 Durham Ave.
Metuchen, N.J.

Pace Engineering Co.
13035 Saticoy St.
North Hollywood, Calif.

Statham Instruments, Inc.
12401 W. Olympic Blvd.
Los Angeles 64, Calif.

ROTARY-PURSUIT APPARATUS

Ralph Gerbrands Scientific Apparatus*

Lafayette Instrument Co.*

Marietta Apparatus Co.*

TRACKING SYSTEMS

Measurement Systems, Inc.[1]
140 Water St.
South Norwalk, Conn.
Hand controls, aided tracking networks, servo power amplifiers

[1] (They also publish a free bibliography of 273 references on tracking. Request: *Bibliography on tracking controls,* M. H. Mehr, 1965.)

NOTE: Refer to the apparatus sections of Basic Instrumentation (pages 743 to 755) and Physiological Psychology (pages 756 to 759) for listings of oscillographs, function generators, random noise generators, oscilloscopes, paper pulls, analog computers, and other equipment that may be used in motor behavior research.

AUTHOR INDEX

SUBJECT INDEX